PERFORMANCE EVALUATION REVIEW
Special Issue
Volume 39, No.1
JUNE 2011

**Association for
Computing Machinery**

Advancing Computing as a Science & Profession

SIGMETRICS'11

Proceedings of the 2011 ACM SIGMETRICS International Conference on

Measurement and Modeling of Computer Systems

June 7–11, 2011, San Jose, California, USA

Sponsored by:
ACM SIGMETRICS

Association for Computing Machinery

Advancing Computing as a Science & Profession

The Association for Computing Machinery
2 Penn Plaza, Suite 701
New York, New York 10121-0701

ISBN: 978-1-4503-0814-4

Additional copies may be ordered prepaid from:

ACM Order Department
PO Box 30777
New York, NY 10087-0777, USA

Phone: 1-800-342-6626 (USA and Canada)
+1-212-626-0500 (Global)
Fax: +1-212-944-1318
E-mail: acmhelp@acm.org
Hours of Operation: 8:30 am – 4:30 pm ET

ACM Order Number: 81901101

Printed in the USA

Foreword

Welcome to SIGMETRICS 2011! Performance modeling and measurement continue to be central to every part of computer and communications systems, and we are proud to bring you the best research in performance analysis techniques and their application to current problems. This year, SIGMETRICS is being held jointly with several other conferences at the ACM Federated Computing Research Conference (FCRC), and we hope that you will enjoy the benefit of interacting with researchers from many related areas.

We have a technical program of 26 research papers and 20 posters. We also have two workshops: GreenMetrics and MAMA (MAthematical performance Modeling and Analysis), now in its thirteenth year. Complementing these is a strong program of tutorials and student activities.

I would like to thank all the people who worked hard to make this conference successful. First and foremost, I would like to thank all the authors who submitted their work because, without their work, there is no conference. Kim Keeton and Dan Rubenstein, the TPC chairs, were tireless, and put together a top-notch program. Bianca Schroeder, the Workshops and Tutorials chair, assembled an excellent set of tutorials and workshops. Giuliano Casale brought boundless energy to organizing the student activities, including an industrial visit and talks by potential employers for student attendees. Xiaozhou Li, the finance chair, meticulously kept our conference finances on track and helped with fund-raising. Abhishek Chandra managed the conference proceedings, smoothly keeping everything on schedule. Jun Xu took care of the publicity for the conference, making sure all announcements went out in a timely fashion. I am indebted to Kyung-Wook Hwang for his responsiveness in setting up and maintaining the conference web site. I thank Mark Squillante for organizing the popular MAMA workshop and Martin Arlitt for the GreenMetrics workshop.

Since SIGMETRICS is a part of FCRC this year, the ACM staff took care of all the local logistics and much of the financial planning, easing my task enormously. I would like to thank all of them, particularly Donna Cappo, April Mosqus, Maritza Nichols, and Adrienne Griscti. I would also like to thank Lisa Tolles at Sheridan Printing Company for her help with the proceedings.

I thank our corporate sponsors — which, at the time of this writing, include Google, HP Labs, Intel, IBM Research, Microsoft Research, NetApp, and VMware — for their generous support. This support allowed us to keep the student registration fees low and to offer travel grants to many students.

Finally, I would like to thank all the attendees for participating and making our conference so vibrant. I hope you enjoy the conference and your stay in the beautiful Bay Area.

Arif Merchant
General Chair
Google, USA

Program Chairs' Welcome

Welcome to San Jose, to ACM's Federated Computing Research Conference (FCRC), and to SIGMETRICS 2011! We are proud to carry on the SIGMETRICS tradition of presenting high-quality, innovative research on the measurement and modeling of computer systems. The program includes papers on a wide variety of topics, including resource allocation, multicore processing, network protocols, failure analysis, power management and network characterization, using a wide variety of techniques, including mathematical analysis, simulation, emulation, prototype experimentation, observation of real systems, and combinations thereof.

SIGMETRICS 2011 received 177 submissions, from which 26 papers were accepted, for an acceptance rate of 15%. Additionally, 20 submissions were selected to appear as posters, leading to a combined paper and poster acceptance rate of 26%. Each paper received at least three reviews from PC members. Over 90% of papers received four or more reviews. Overall, program committee and external reviewers provided a total of 756 reviews.

The review process was conducted online using the HotCRP conference management software over a period of two months. The program committee meeting, held at Columbia University in New York, NY, in January 2011, was attended in person by 36 of the 57 PC members, and "virtually" by another four members. During the review, deliberation, and decision process, we emphasized novelty and excitement: papers that took risks and were controversial were viewed more favorably than solid papers that provided limited new insights and took limited risks. As a result, we expect the program to generate active discussion.

It was an absolute pleasure to assemble this program, and we would like to thank everyone who contributed. First and foremost, we are indebted to all of the authors who submitted papers to SIGMETRICS 2011. We had a large body of high-quality work from which to select our program.

We would also like to thank past program chairs Arif Merchant, Mark Squillante, Paul Barford, and Vishal Misra for their advice. Kyung-Wook Hwang served as webmaster for both the paper submission site and the conference website. Lisa Tolles at Sheridan Printing Company coordinated the authors in the preparation of the final versions of papers for the proceedings.

Finally, we would like to express our deep gratitude to our reviewers. The members of the program committee contributed their expertise and time from their busy schedules before, during, and after the PC meeting to ensure the quality of the reviewing and shepherding processes. We also greatly appreciate the efforts and expertise of the external reviewers. Thank you for your assistance in creating this program!

We wish all participants a very interesting, thought-provoking, and enjoyable conference!

Kimberly Keeton　　　　　　　**Dan Rubenstein**

SIGMETRICS '11 Program Co-Chair　　*SIGMETRICS '11 Program Co-Chair*

Hewlett-Packard Labs　　　　　　*Columbia University*

Table of Contents

Session 5: Potpourri

Session Chair: Jun Xu *(Georgia Institute of Technology)*

FCRC Plenary

Maja Mataric *(University of Southern California)*

Keynote Address

Session 6: Power Management

Session Chair: Martin Arlitt *(Hewlett-Packard Laboratories)*

Session 7: Routing

Session Chair: Y. Charlie Hu *(Purdue University)*

Keynote Address

Session 8: Graphs

Session Chair: Augustin Chaintreau *(Columbia University)*

Session 9: Network Characterization and Modeling

Session Chair: Y.C. Tay *(National University of Singapore)*

Posters

Tutorials

Author Index

ACM SIGMETRICS 2011 Conference Organization

General Chair: Arif Merchant *(Google, USA)*

Program Chairs: Kimberly Keeton *(HP Labs, USA)*
Dan Rubenstein *(Columbia University, USA)*

Workshops/Tutorials Chair: Bianca Schroeder *(University of Toronto, Canada)*

Publications Chair: Abhishek Chandra *(University of Minnesota, USA)*

Finance Chair: Xiaozhou Li *(HP Labs, USA)*

Publicity Chair: Jun Xu *(Georgia Tech, USA)*

Student Activities Chair: Giuliano Casale *(Imperial College, UK)*

Webmaster: Kyung-Wook Hwang *(Columbia University, USA)*

Program Committee: Tarek Abdelzaher *(UIUC, USA)*
Martin Arlitt *(University of Calgary/HP Labs, Canada/USA)*
Yuliy Baryshnikov *(Bell Labs Alcatel-Lucent, USA)*
Thomas Bonald *(Telecom ParisTech, France)*
Sem Borst *(Eindhoven University of Technology/Bell Labs
Alcatel-Lucent, The Netherlands/USA)*
Giuliano Casale *(Imperial College London, UK)*
Augustin Chaintreau *(Columbia University, USA)*
Edith Cohen *(AT&T Research, USA)*
Mark Crovella *(Boston University, USA)*
Amol Deshpande *(University of Maryland, USA)*
Derek Eager *(University of Saskatchewan, Canada)*
Daniel Figueiredo *(UFRJ, Brazil)*
Phil Gibbons *(Intel Research Pittsburgh, USA)*
Peter Glynn *(Stanford University, USA)*
Brighten Godfrey *(UIUC, USA)*
Moises Goldszmidt *(Microsoft Research, USA)*
Timothy Griffin *(University of Cambridge, UK)*
Y. Charlie Hu *(Purdue University, USA)*
Canturk Isci *(IBM Research, USA)*
Koushik Kar *(RPI, USA)*
Dejan Kostic *(EPFL, Switzerland)*
Patrick Lee *(CUHK, Hong Kong)*
David Lie *(University of Toronto, Canada)*

Program Committee (continued):

Yong Liu *(Polytechnic Inst of NYU, USA)*
Yi Lu *(UIUC, USA)*
John C.S. Lui *(CUHK, Hong Kong)*
Qin (Christine) Lv *(University of Colorado, USA)*
Laurent Massoulie *(Technicolor, France)*
Sue Moon *(KAIST, Korea)*
Erich Nahum *(IBM Research, USA)*
David Nicol *(UIUC, USA)*
Brian Noble *(University of Michigan, USA)*
Mark Oskin *(University of Washington, USA)*
Alexandre Proutiere *(Microsoft Research, UK)*
Ram Ramjee *(Microsoft Research, India)*
Philippe Robert *(INRIA, France)*
Jim Roberts *(INRIA, France)*
Matthew Roughan *(University of Adelaide, Australia)*
Jiri Schindler *(NetApp, USA)*
Bianca Schroeder *(University of Toronto, Canada)*
Devavrat Shah *(MIT, USA)*
Michael Schapira *(Yale University and UC Berkeley, USA)*
Prashant Shenoy *(UMass Amherst, USA)*
Anand Sivasubramaniam *(Penn State, USA)*
Mark S. Squillante *(IBM Research, USA)*
R. Srikant *(UIUC, USA)*
Y.C. Tay *(Natl University of Singapore, Singapore)*
Alberto Lopez Toledo *(Telefonica Research, Spain)*
Don Towsley *(UMass Amherst, USA)*
Mustafa Uysal *(VMWare, USA)*
Milan Vojnovic *(Microsoft Research, UK)*
Adam Wierman *(CalTech, USA)*
Cathy Xia *(Ohio State, USA)*
Jun Xu *(Georgia Tech, USA)*
Haifeng Yu *(Natl University of Singapore, Singapore)*
Alice Zheng *(Microsoft Research, USA)*
Gil Zussman *(Columbia University, USA)*

Additional reviewers:

Danilo Ardagna
Christopher Batten
Andrey Bernstein
Berk Birand
Claris Castillo
Michele Catasta
Guner Celik
Shimin Chen
John Davis
Xiaoning Ding
Eiman Ebrahimi
Hanhua Feng
Mathieu Feuillet
Dave K. George
Phillipa Gill
Sriram Govindan
Aayush Gupta
Chi-Yao Hong
Yin Huai
Krishna Jagannathan
Evangelia Kalyvianaki
Franck Le

Jon Lenchner
Rubao Li
Yingdong Lu
Frank McSherry
Xiaoqiao Meng
Eytan Modiano
Fabricio Murai
Sebastian Neumayer
Ioannis Papapanagiotouu
Abhinav Pathak
Dzung Phan
James S. Plank
Ramya Raghavendra
Simon Schubert
Larissa Spinelli
Mudhakar Srivatsa
Byung-chul Tak
Mirco Tribastone
Bhuvan Urgaonkar
Nedeljko Vasic
Di Wang
Di Xie

Sponsor:

Modeling Program Resource Demand Using Inherent Program Characteristics

Jian Chen, Lizy K. John, and Dimitris Kaseridis
Department of Electrical and Computer Engineering
The University of Texas at Austin, Austin, Texas, USA
chenjian@mail.utexas.edu, {ljohn,kaseridi}@ece.utexas.edu

ABSTRACT

The workloads in modern Chip-multiprocessors (CMP) are becoming increasingly diversified, creating different resource demands on hardware substrate. It is necessary to allocate hardware resources based on the needs of the workloads in order to improve system efficiency and/or ensure Quality-of-Service (QoS) at certain performance levels. Therefore, it is extremely important to identify the resource demand of the workload in terms of the performance and power efficiency. Existing models are inappropriate for estimating resource demands as they require either partial simulations or time-consuming training. This paper presents an integrated framework that is able to identify the single-resource or multi-resource demands on an array of hardware resources ranging from the issue width of the processor to the memory bandwidth. With an analytical model based on program inherent characteristics, this framework does not require any detailed simulation or training yet is still able to capture the performance trend of the program accurately. Our experiment shows that the proposed framework on average provides no larger than 8.6% error to any given performance target for multi-resource demand estimation. By using the proposed performance model, the framework identifies the multi-resource demands up to 40X faster compared to the state-of-the-art analytical model. The proposed framework can be applied in workload capacity planning, hardware resource adaptation as well as coordinated resource management for QoS in CMP systems.

Categories and Subject Descriptors

C.4 [**Performance of Systems**]: Modeling techniques

General Terms

Measurement, Performance

Keywords

Microprocessor, Resource Demands, Program Characteristics, Performance Modeling

1. INTRODUCTION

The workloads on modern general purpose or embedded computing systems are becoming increasingly abundant and diversified, imposing various demands on hardware resources, such as cache sizes and memory bandwidth. Efficiently modeling and identifying these resource demands is fundamental for many applications, including efficient single-ISA heterogeneous computing [17], resource management for throughput, power efficiency and/or Quality-of-Service (QoS) in Chip Multiprocessors (CMP) [8], and resource consolidation for balancing computation fidelity and response latency in embedded systems [21]. For example, when executing an application in a single-ISA heterogeneous multi-core processor, the application's resource demand needs to be carefully explored and classified so that the application can be properly scheduled to the core that matches its demand for energy efficient execution. Similarly, when managing resources in CMP systems, the resource demands of an application has to be efficiently identified before allocating appropriate hardware resources to meet the power and performance constraints.

While there are some methods proposed to identify the resource demands of the workloads [3][5][14], these methods suffer from either inefficiency or high implementation costs. Existing methods typically leverages analytical models [14][15], regression models [12][18], or neural network models [11] to estimate the performance and/or power of the application-processor pairs, and identify the resource demand of a workload by searching through the design space off-line for the optimum configurations. However, these models require either partial simulations or iterative training for each application, which is expensive and inefficient for resource demand estimation. Moreover, the requirement of partial simulations also implies that when using these models on-line, resource demands can be only identified by using tentative runs in a trial-and-error way [5], which may require many trial iterations and cause significant overhead in performance and energy. To avoid trial runs for resource demand estimation, some predictive schemes have recently been proposed, which include the marginal utility monitoring for last-level cache partitioning [23] and system-level bandwidth management [16], and the on-line machine learning for coordinated management of multiple resources [3]. However, these schemes are either limited to manage only single resource, or impractical to implement and validate.

Therefore, there is a need for a model that does not require any partial simulations or training, is easy to implement, yet still able to identify the demands on single and multiple resources accurately. This paper attempts to develop such model by leveraging the recent advances in analytical modeling and workload characterization. It exploits the fact that resource demand is estimated based on performance trend rather than absolute performance, and hence is insensitive to the second-order effects of the performance. In particular, the contributions of this paper are as follows:

- **Analytical Model Based on Program Characteristics:** We develop an analytical model based on the program character-

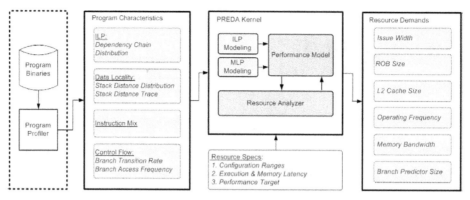

Figure 1: The PREDA framework

istics, such as Instruction Level Parallelism (ILP), Memory Level Parallelism (MLP) and branch predictability. Unlike existing analytical models [14][7], which require simulations on caches and branch predictors, our model avoids any partial detailed simulation; yet is still able to accurately model the performance trend for different hardware configurations. The experimental results show that the modeled performance trend is on average less than 10.7% off the simulated one.

- **Efficient Estimation of Multi-Resource Demands:** We propose a set of algorithms and heuristics that can efficiently estimate the demands on both single resource and the multiple resources under any given performance target. The algorithm for identifying the multi-resource demand is based on marginal utility [23] and the gradient performance gain, which leads to a fast convergence with only a few iterations. We show that the estimated multi-resource demands on average achieves no larger than 8.6% error to any given performance target.

- **Integrated Framework for Resource Demand Estimation:** We encapsulate the analytical model and the resource demand estimation algorithms into an integrated framework called *Program REsource Demand Analyzer* (PREDA), which automatically estimates a broad set of resource demands for a workload. Compared with the framework using state-of-the-art analytical model [7], our framework achieves up to 40X speedup in estimating multi-resource demands.

The rest of the paper is organized as follows. Section 2 gives the overview of the proposed PREDA framework. Section 3 presents the working mechanism of the PREDA kernel. Section 4 describes the experiment and evaluation methodology. Section 5 reports our experimental results. Section 6 compares our work with other related works, and section 7 concludes the paper.

2. OVERVIEW OF PREDA

2.1 Resource Demand Definition

Before we continue, it is important to make a clear definition of resource demand. The meaning of resource demand contains two elements: the performance target and the energy efficiency. On one hand, different levels of performance target may lead to different resource requirements. Specifically, as the performance target increases, the amount of resources required also increase. On the other hand, for a given performance target, there may be a set of different amounts of resources being able to meet that target. Among them, we are only interested in the one that is energy

efficient. Therefore, we introduce the following resource demand definition:

***Definition**: Resource Demand $D(p)$ is the amount of resource a thread requires to efficiently achieve no less than p% of the maximum performance achieved with the entire resources allocated to the thread.*

Note that this definition uses a relative term for the performance target because the absolute performance target, such as the Instruction-Per-Cycle (IPC) rate, may lead to *ill-defined* cases where the target cannot be satisfied no matter how many resources are allocated. The relative performance target avoids this problem, and more importantly it is inline with the satisfiability of the QoS target proposed by Guo et al. [8]. In fact, with this definition, our framework can be treated as a conversion layer that converts the performance targets into the resource demands, which could be used as the *Resource Usage Metrics* for QoS enforcement [8]. Note also that this definition assumes performance monotonicity, which means the performance of a thread increases monotonically as the amount of resource allocated to the thread increases [22].

2.2 PREDA Framework

The proposed PREDA framework consists of two parts: the program characteristics profiler and the PREDA kernel. As shown in Figure 1, the program profiler walks through the dynamic instruction stream and extracts a set of program characteristics, which contain instruction dependency chain distribution, stack distance distribution, instruction mix, and branch transition rate and its access frequency. These characteristics are then fed to the PREDA kernel, which consists of an ILP model, an MLP model, a performance model and a resource analyzer. The models for ILP and MLP are responsible to translate the program characteristics into the ILP and MLP information that can be directly used by the performance model. Hence, these models serve as the key layer to decouple the performance evaluation from detailed simulations. The performance model takes the ILP and MLP information along with the branch predictability characteristics and estimates the program execution time on an out-of-order processor. The resource analyzer converts the estimated performance into the relative performance, and searches the configuration space for the amount of resources required to meet the performance targets. The estimated resource demands include processor issue width, processor reorder buffer (ROB) size, L2 (or last level) cache sizes, operating frequency, memory bandwidth and branch predictor size. These resource demands are estimated either in single-resource mode (other resources are fixed) or in multi-resource mode (combinations of changing resources).

This framework is designed for off-line resource demand estimation, which can be applied in areas such as early-stage design space exploration in microprocessor design and admission control to balance the workloads in computing systems [13]. However, since the proposed performance model in this framework is decoupled from detailed simulation, it could also be applied online for dynamic resource management by using on-line profilers. Nevertheless, this paper focuses on evaluating the accuracy and the complexity of off-line resource demand estimation.

For the rest of the paper, we use 22 SPEC CPU2006 programs [1] to evaluate the proposed framework (*gamess*, *dealII*, *calculix*, *povray*, *tonto*, *lbm*,*wrf* are not included in the workload as we did not manage to compile them to Alpha ISA). Each of the 22 programs is compiled to Alpha-ISA with peak configurations, and we use the single Simpoint interval with 100 million instructions [9] for each program.

3. PREDA KERNEL

This section introduces the working mechanism of the PREDA kernel, which consists of ILP modeling, MLP modeling, performance modeling and resource analyzing.

3.1 ILP Modeling

The goal of ILP modeling is to accurately estimate the background execution rate, i.e., the IPC rate the program can achieve when it is free of any miss events [14]. To do so, we employ the *critical dependency chain length* as the metric to measure the ILP of the program as it determines the number of instructions that have to be executed in serial, and hence sets the limit of the program's ILP. The same metric is also used by Eyerman et al. in their mechanistic model [7], but the difference lies in the profiling method to obtain the critical dependency chain. Eyerman et al. obtain the statistics of the critical dependency chain on a per-instruction basis. Although accurate, it requires time-consuming update in all dependency chains each time an instruction moves out of the instruction window. Our profiling scheme, however, chops the dynamic instruction stream into slices, each with the size of the *maximum* interested instruction window W_{max}. The statistics of critical dependency chain are collected on a per-slice basis, and the dependencies between adjacent slices are ignored. This profiling scheme has the complexity of $O(\frac{N}{W_{max}} \cdot W_{max}) = O(N)$ (N is the number of dynamic instructions), as compared with the complexity of $O(N \cdot W_{max})$ in Eyerman's scheme [7]. Yet, the observed difference between these two schemes is within 1.5% in terms of the profiled critical path statistics, as shown in Figure 2(a). Note that the profiler considers both register dependence and memory dependence when searching for the critical dependency chain because memory dependence could also serialize the instruction execution.

Once the statistics of the *critical dependency chain length* are obtained, the ILP model calculates the average critical dependency chain length L_W for the interested instruction window W. On an idealized machine with unit execution latency, this value is equivalent to the average number of cycles it takes to execute the instructions in the instruction window. Hence, the average throughput could be modeled by W/L_W. However, for a realistic non-unit latency machine, this number should be further divided by the average execution latency Lat_{avg} according to Little's law [14]. Therefore, the average instruction throughput is:

$$\alpha_{avg}(W) = \frac{W}{Lat_{avg} \cdot L_W} \quad (1)$$

The average latency Lat_{avg} can be derived by weight-averaging the percentage of each instruction type (from instruction mix) with

the corresponding execution latency. Note that when calculating the average latency, the latency of the L1 load miss is modeled as the latency of regular functional unit assuming the load never misses L2 cache. The long latency L2 misses will be captured in the MLP model, and treated as the interrupting events that insert intervals in the smooth execution flow. The numbers of L1 and L2 misses are estimated with the stack distance model [20].

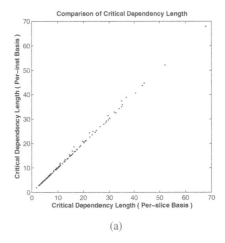

(a)

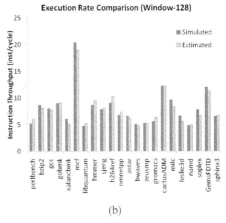

(b)

Figure 2: (a) Comparison of two different profiling schemes for critical paths. The results are based on the profiling of the 22 benchmark programs. (b) The accuracy of execution rate estimation. The simulated machine has perfect branch prediction, perfect memory disambiguation, 32KB L1 data/instruction cache with 10 cycle L1 miss penalty, and infinite L2 cache size.

Figure 2(b) shows the accuracy of using equation 1 to estimate the execution rate. The average error between the estimated execution rate and the simulated one is 8.3% when the instruction window size is 128. The error is mainly caused by imperfect representation of program's ILP in the presence of non-unit execution latency. Specifically, when the execution has non-unit latency, the critical dependency chain in terms of the instruction number may be different with the longest dependence chain in terms of the execution cycle, resulting in mismatch between the estimated execution rate and the simulated one.

3.2 MLP Modeling

The modeling of memory level parallelism is based on Mattson's stack distance model [20]. This model exploits the inclusion property of Least Recently Used (LRU) replacement policy (i.e., the content of an N sized cache is a subset of the content of any cache larger than N) and allows us to accurately estimate the number of misses in any fully associative cache. Specifically, when a load/store accesses a data block with stack distance larger than the given cache size, that load/store triggers a cache miss event in a fully associative cache. When it comes to set-associative caches, however, the accuracy of this model slightly decreases mainly because it is unable to capture the conflict misses.

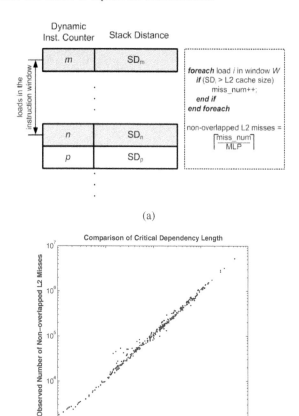

(a)

(b)

Figure 3: (a) The estimation of non-overlapped L2 misses in the presence of MLP. (b) The accuracy of the estimated non-overlapped L2 misses. The results are based on the simulation of the 22 benchmark programs.

While the stack distance model is able to estimate the number of misses for a given cache size, it is unaware of MLP, i.e., multiple independent L2 load misses overlapping with each other. These outstanding L2 load misses could drastically change the average load miss penalty and significantly affect the performance, and hence need to be carefully modeled. Prior research obtains the program's MLP information by simulating caches in detail [14][7]. In this paper, we attempt to decouple MLP modeling from detailed cache simulation. To do so, we augment the proposed ILP profiler to generate the maximum number of loads LD_{max} in a dependency chain and the total number of loads LD_{total} in an instruction window. Then, LD_{total}/LD_{max} indicates the average number of loads that could be overlapped with each other in the instruction window. Assuming that the loads in a dependency chain have the same probability of missing L2 cache with other loads, LD_{total}/LD_{max} becomes the average number of the overlapped L2 load misses, or

the MLP of the program. Meanwhile, the profiler also generates a load trace that contains the stack distance of a load and the dynamic instruction ID of the corresponding load, as shown in Figure 3(a). The MLP analyzer then walks through the trace, counts the number of L2 load misses that could happen in the instruction window for the given L2 cache size, and calculates the number of non-overlapped L2 misses by dividing the miss number with MLP. The total number of the non-overlapped L2 misses of the program is the sum of the non-overlapped misses in each instruction window:

$$N_{L2}(W,C) = \sum_i \left\lceil \frac{miss\_num(W,C)}{MLP} \right\rceil_i \qquad (2)$$

where "$\lceil \ \rceil$" is the ceiling function, $miss\_num(W,C)$ is the number of L2 misses for the instruction window W and L2 cache size C. Figure 3(b) shows the accuracy of this model in estimating the number of non-overlapped L2 misses. The average error between the modeled number of non-overlapped misses and the simulated one is 9.3%, which is reasonably accurate for performance trend modeling.

3.3 Performance Model

The performance model is based on the previously proposed interval analysis [14][6], which treats the exhibited IPC rate as a sustained background execution rate intermittently disrupted by long time miss events, namely, L2 cache misses, branch misprediction, and instruction cache misses. The target of this model is not to accurately predict the absolute performance, but rather to faithfully capture the performance trend as one or multiple resource allocations change.

With ILP and MLP modeling, we are able to obtain the background execution rate, and the number of non-overlapped L2 misses. We can also easily estimate the number of instruction cache misses for any cache size with the stack distance model. However, the instruction cache miss is rare for a reasonable cache size, and its miss penalty is much smaller than that of L2 cache misses. Therefore, in this paper, we do not consider instruction cache misses in our performance model. The remaining part is the number of branch misprediction, which is difficult to accurately estimate purely based on program characteristics. However, the branch transition rate proposed by Haungs et al. [10] contains a clue as to how many branches are hard to predict, and allows us to roughly estimate the number of mispredicted branches. Branch transition rate measures the frequency at which a branch changes direction between taken and not taken. It has been demonstrated that the branches with very low or very high transition rate are easy to predict, and branches with transition rate around 50% are hard to predict. Based on this property, we estimate the number of mispredicted branches by using half the number of branches with transition rate between 0.3 and 0.7. This heuristic essentially assumes that branches with transition rate between 0.3 and 0.7 have 50% prediction rate and all other branches are predicted perfectly. It captures the general trend that the more branches with transition rate near 50%, the more mispredicted branches a program would have. Although this number is only a first-order estimation, it is still reasonable for resource demand estimation as the resource demand estimation is based on performance trend, which is relatively insensitive to the second-order errors.

Hence, our performance model can be built by combining the three major components extracted from the program characteristics, that is, the cycles spent on executing instructions C_{exe}, the cycles spent on accessing the memory C_{mem}, and the cycles spent on serving branch mispredictions C_{br}. Hence, the overall program

Pseudocode 1 Demand on Multiple Resources

```
#define N /*the number of resources that could change simultaneously*/
#define max_resource_array[N] /*the array of maximum available resources*/
#define eval_perf(resource_array) /*Evaluate the execution time with the resource configuration array resource_array*/
#define est_demand(resource_array, i, target_perf)
/*Estimate the demand of resource i under the performance target target_perf*/

for ( i=0; i < N; i++)
    base_demand[i] = est_demand(max_resource_array,i,target_perf);
    /* estimate the demand for resource i when other resources are set to maximum*/
end for
while( TRUE )
    perf = eval_perf(base_demand);
    if( perf > target_perf )
        set the final demands as the base demand estimates;
        break;
    else
        for ( i=0; i < N; i++)
            temp_demand[0..N] = base_demand[0..N]; /* copy the base resource demand to temp_demand array */
            new_demand[i] = est_demand(base_demand,i,target_perf);
            temp_demand[i] = new_demand[i];
            perf_gain[i] = perf - eval_perf(temp_demand);
            /* calculate the performance gain with the newly estimated resource demand */
        end for
        find the index max_index of the maximum value in array perf_gain[N];
        base_demand[max_index] = new_demand[max_index];
end while
```

---

execution time is:

$$Delay = (C_{exe} + C_{mem} + C_{br})/f$$
$$= \frac{N_{inst}}{min(\alpha_{avg}(W), IW) \cdot f} + N_{L2}(W, C) \cdot T_{mem}$$
$$+ N_{br} \cdot T_{br} \tag{3}$$

where N_{inst} is the total number of instructions, N_{br} is the estimated number of mispredicted branches, IW is the instruction issue width, and f is the operating frequency. T_{mem} and T_{br} represent the absolute memory access latency and the absolute time of branch misprediction penalty respectively.

3.4 Resource Demand Analysis

While the performance model allows us to quickly evaluate the performance for a specific resource allocation, it is the resource analyzer that translates the given performance target to a set of resource demands. This subsection presents the details of the resource demand estimation for each type of resources.

3.4.1 Demand on Multiple Resources

In this paper, the estimation of multi-resource demands is built on top of the single-resource demand estimation, which uses the marginal utility to determine the demand on the corresponding resource. The marginal utility originates from economic theory, and is defined as the ratio between the incremental utility over the amount of incremental resource. It has been successfully used as the metric for last-level cache partitioning [23][16]. In this paper, we further extend the application of marginal utility to different hardware resources, and define the marginal utility as follows:

$$MarginalUtility(D_\beta) = \frac{Perf(R_\beta + D_\beta) - Perf(R_\beta)}{D_\beta} \tag{4}$$

where R_β is the amount of resource β, and D_β is the amount of increment in resource β. Note that the maximum marginal utility represents the best (or most efficient) use of a resource increment. Therefore, with marginal utility, we could transform the problem of resource demand estimation to the problem of finding the amount of resource that meets the performance target meanwhile has the

maximum marginal utility. Thus, the estimation of the single resource demand becomes straightforward: sweeping the interested resource from its minimum to its maximum while keeping other resources fixed, and searching for the amount of resource that satisfies the performance target and has the largest marginal utility. However, there is an exception: when the performance with the minimum resource allocation is larger than the target performance, the resource demand is set to the minimum value.

While the single-resource demand estimation is straightforward, the estimation of multi-resource demands is non-trivial because the marginal utility is only comparable among the resources with the same type. To address this problem, we propose an algorithm that uses the gradient performance gain to search for the multi-resource demands, as shown in Pseudocode 1. The first step of this algorithm is to estimate the demand on each resource individually when other resources are configured to be the maximum. The estimated single-resource demands are then combined together as the initial multi-resource configuration, which serves as the starting point of an iterative searching process. In each iteration, the algorithm identifies the single-resource demand that has the largest performance gain over the performance of the multi-resource configuration estimated in the previous iteration. This single resource demand is selected to update the multi-resource configuration, and the process continues until the performance meets the target. The complexity of this algorithm is $O(n \cdot k)$, where k is the number of iterations, and n is the number of the changing resources. This algorithm can estimate the multi-resource demands on four types of resources, including ROB size, issue width, L2 cache size, and frequency.

3.4.2 Demand on Memory Bandwidth

The program's demand on memory bandwidth is important for CMP systems, where multiple programs share the limited memory bandwidth resource. It consists of the bandwidth demand on memory read and memory write. Assuming a write-back L2 cache, a read request to the main memory can be triggered by a load/store miss, and a write request can only occur when a dirty cache block is evicted (i.e., cache write-back). While the conventional stack distance model can capture the read traffic to the memory, it is unable to estimate the write-back traffic. To solve this problem, we augment the conventional stack distance model to capture both reads and write-backs to the main memory.

To do so, during stack distance profiling, we associate each cache block with a dirty bit and mark the dirty bit whenever the block has been written to. We then use a *Dirty Stack Histogram* to record the largest stack distance of a dirty cache block. The reason for only considering the largest stack distance is to avoid multiple write-back counts for one store. The details of updating the dirty stack histogram are described in Pseudocode 2. Note that once the dirty bit is set, it will never be reset during profiling. Therefore, the dirty bit is unaware of multiple writes to the same block at different stack distances, hence is unable to capture the situation where one block may miss cache multiple times and generate multiple write-backs. To handle this situation, we also differentiate the dirty block according to whether the block was most recently accessed by a read or a write. Specifically, if the dirty block was most recently accessed by a write, the corresponding counter in the dirty histogram will be incremented regardless of the stack distance. With the dirty histogram, we are able to estimate the number of dirty evictions by using the property of the conventional stack distance model. Specifically, a dirty eviction happens whenever the dirty stack distance of a block is larger than the given cache size.

Pseudocode 2 Update of the Dirty Stack Histogram

---

if($dirty == 1$)
   if(the block was most recently accessed by a read
   && $stack\_distance > dirty\_stack\_distance$)
      $dirty\_histogram[dirty\_stack\_distance]--;$
      $dirty\_histogram[stack\_distance]++;$
      $dirty\_stack\_distance = stack\_distance;$
   else if(the block was most recently accessed by a write)
      $dirty\_histogram[stack\_distance]++;$
      $dirty\_stack\_distance = stack\_distance;$ **end if**
end if
if(the current access is a write)
   $dirty = 1;$
   $dirty\_stack\_distance = 0;$
end if

3.4.3 Demand on Branch Predictor Size

Branch predictor uses branch history to predict the outcome of a branch instruction before its execution, and usually takes a large fraction of the processor area. Therefore, the program's demand on branch predictor size needs to be identified to prevent unnecessary resource over-provisioning. However, due to the lack of analytical models that can translate predictor size to prediction accuracy, the demand of branch predictor size may have to be estimated by *directly* using the program's branch characteristics. Moreover, since different types of predictors may yield different prediction accuracy levels, the demand on predictor size also needs to be estimated in an *ad hoc* way. Current implementation of PREDA only supports estimating the demand on the size of a two-level PAg predictor [25]. The demand estimation for other branch predictors is in our future work.

PREDA estimates the demand on predictor size based on two branch characteristics: the branch transition rate, and the branch access frequency. As mentioned previously, branch transition rate has its implication on branch history length, which in turn affects the branch predictor size. Branches with very high or very low transition rate are easy to predict and only require short history registers; whereas branches with near 50% transition rate is hard to predict and require long history registers. However, branch transition alone could not tell how often a branch is executed in the dynamic instruction stream. For those branch instructions with very few ac-

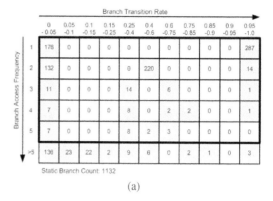

Static Branch Count: 1132

(a)

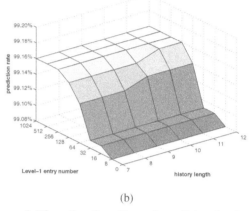

(b)

Figure 4: The estimation of branch predictor size demand

cesses, they have negligible effect on the overall IPC whether they are predicted correctly or incorrectly, hence should be filtered when determining the demand of branch predictor size. Note that these two branch characteristics are in correspondence with the two-level PAg branch predictor, where the first level table (Per-Address History Table) is essentially a cache holding the frequently accessed branches, and the second level is indexed with history register reflecting the predictability of the branches. As an example, Figure 4(a) shows the branch transition rate distribution as well as branch access frequency distribution of the SPEC CPU program *leslie3d*. The total static branch count is 1132, which seems to indicate that the first-level table should contain 1K entries. However, if we filter out the branch instructions with small access frequencies (less than 5 in this case), the static branch count becomes 204, indicating that 256 entries in the first-level table would be sufficient. This is proved by Figure 4(b), which shows that the prediction accuracy does not degrade until the first-level entry is smaller than 256.

Based on this observation, we use the heuristics shown in Pseudocode 3 to estimate the demand on the first level table size and the branch history length. Note that in order to prevent branch filtering from aggressively impacting the prediction accuracy, we ensure that the total number of filtered dynamic branches is less than 0.1% of the total dynamic branches. Note also that the transition rate buckets used in determining the history length are consistent with those used in branch classification by Haungs et al. [10].

4. EXPERIMENT METHODOLOGY

We extensively modified the SimProfile from Simplescalar tool set [2] to profile programs and collect the statistics of the aforementioned program characteristics. We also implemented the PREDA

Pseudocode 3 Demand on Branch Predictor Size

```
#define access_threshold   16
while( TRUE )
    foreach static branches
        if ( branch_access_frequency < access_threshold )
            filtered_static_branch ++;
            filtered_dynamic_branch = filtered_dynamic_branch
            + branch_access_frequency; end if
    end foreach
    if (filtered_dynamic_branch < 0.001 * total_dynamic_branch)
        break;
    else access_threshold - -; end if
end while
first_level_entry = total_static_branch - filtered_static_branch;
foreach remaining branches
    if ∃transition_rate∈ [0.4, 0.6]
        history_length= max_history;
        /* max_history is the maximum history length
        specified in the design space */
    else if ∃transition_rate∈ [0.25, 0.4) ⋃ (0.6, 0.75]
        history_length= (max_history-1) > min_history ?
                max_history-1 : min_history;
        /* min_history is the minimum history length
        specified in the design space */
    else if ∃transition_rate∈ [0.15, 0.25) ⋃ (0.75, 0.85]
        history_length= (max_history-2) > min_history ?
                max_history-2 : min_history;
    else if ∃transition_rate∈ [0.1, 0.15) ⋃ (0.85, 0.9]
        history_length= (max_history-3) > min_history ?
                max_history-3 : min_history;
    else if ∃transition_rate∈ [0.05, 0.1) ⋃ (0.9, 0.95]
        history_length= (max_history-4) > min_history ?
                max_history-4 : min_history;
    else if ∃transition_rate∈ [0, 0.05) ⋃ (0.95, 1.0]
        history_length= (max_history-5) > min_history ?
                max_history-5 : min_history;
    end if
end foreach
```

kernel with C++ and encapsulate it with the profiler into an integrated framework.

The framework is evaluated on an out-of-order superscalar processor with two-level cache subsystem. The configuration ranges of relevant resources are listed in Table 1. Note that the cache associativity and the block size are constant across all possible L2 cache sizes as we do not explore these aspects in this paper. The number of execution units is chosen such that the overall configuration is balanced. In total, the listed configurations cover over 100K design nodes. When evaluating the estimation of single-resource demand, it is required that other resource configuration are fixed. However, due to the large design space, it is impossible for us to evaluate our framework exhaustively over all configurations. Therefore, we use three representative configuration sets: config-S(mall), config-M(edium), and config-L(arge), as the base configurations to evaluate our resource estimation model. The details of these configuration sets are also shown in Table 1.

Table 1: Configuration Options

Items	Configuration Options	config-S	config-M	config-L
Issue Width	1 :: 2x :: 8	1	4	8
ROB size	16 :: 2x :: 512	16	128	512
L2 D-Cache	64KB::2x::2048KB	64KB	512KB	2048KB
	8-way associative	8-way	8-way	8-way
	64B	64B	64B	64B
L1 I-cache	32KB	32KB	32KB	32KB
	2-way	2-way	2-way	2-way
	64B	64B	64B	64B
L1 D-cache	32KB	32KB	32KB	32KB
	4-way	4-way	4-way	4-way
	64B	64B	64B	64B
Branch Predictor(PAg)	1st-level: 8::2x::1K	1024	1024	1024
	2nd-level: 128::2x::4K	4096	4096	4096
Clock Freq.	0.5::0.1::2 (GHz)	0.5 GHz	1 GHz	2 GHz

In this paper, we assume the memory access latency to be 200ns, or 200 cycles at the clock frequency of 1 GHz. This latency number in terms of cycles scales proportionally with the operating frequency. The hit latencies of L1 and L2 caches are calibrated against Cacti 5.0 [24] under 90nm technology. The latencies of other execution units are also scaled to 90nm technology. The branch misprediction penalty is set to 20 cycles at 1 GHz. We employ Wattch [4] to collect the performance and power data of the interested processor configurations.

5. EVALUATION

The evaluation of the proposed framework covers three major aspects: the accuracy of the models, the accuracy of resource demand estimation and the computation complexity of the framework.

5.1 Model Accuracy

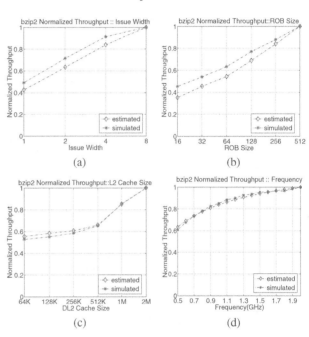

(a)　　　　　　　　(b)

(c)　　　　　　　　(d)

Figure 5: The comparison of normalized throughput for *bzip2* as one of the resources changes. The configurations of other unchanged resources follow config-M.

Since the resource demand estimation is based on the relative performance as opposed to the absolute one, we need to validate whether the performance model could accurately capture the performance trend as the resource allocation changes. To do so, we sweep the resource allocation and calculate the corresponding throughput with the performance model, and then normalized them with respect to the largest throughput. The normalized throughput curve is compared against the one obtained from detailed simulation. Figure 5 shows an example of such comparison for *bzip2*. Ideally, these two curves should be overlapped with each other. However, due to the imperfection of the performance model, the estimated performance curve deviates from the simulated one. To measure the difference between these two curves, we calculate the absolute difference of the normalized throughput on each node of the curves, and then calculate the average difference for each curve to evaluate the accuracy of this model. Figure 6 summarizes these differences for each program. Note that most of the programs have a relatively large error in Config-L. This is mainly because some of the second-order effects, such as the branch misprediction caused by specula-

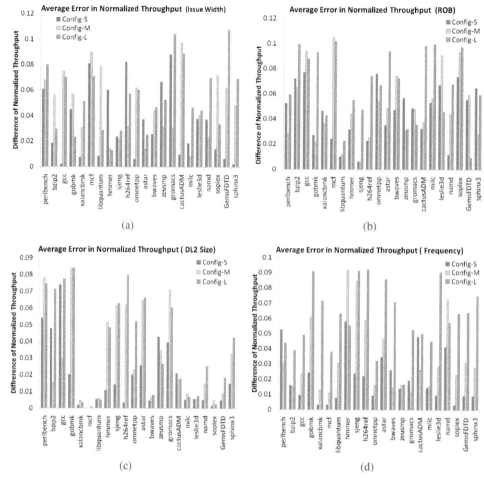

Figure 6: Average error of the normalized throughput for issue width, ROB size, L2 cache size, and frequency. Each resource estimation was evaluated on three configurations: config-S, config-M, and config-L

tive path information, becomes more outstanding in extremely wide machines; whereas our model only capture the first-order effects. However, even in the worst case, the modeled performance trend on average is only 0.107 or 10.7% off the simulated one, which is still reasonable for resource demand estimation.

The error of the performance model consist of two parts: the intrinsic error, which is the inherent modeling error caused by some simplifying assumptions of the model, and the parameter error, which is the error introduced by the estimation of model parameters using program characteristics. Figure 7 shows the comparison between these two errors. As expected, most programs have much smaller intrinsic error than the combined one, especially for *gcc* and *namd*. However, some programs see a slightly higher intrinsic error than the combined error. This is because the parameter error and the intrinsic error may be canceling each other, leading to a smaller combined error. In worst case, the average intrinsic error is 0.076 or 7.6% in terms of the normalized throughput (*mcf* in Figure 7(a)).

5.2 Accuracy of Resource Demand Estimation

5.2.1 Single-Resource Demand Estimation

We evaluate the estimation of single-resource demand on issue width, ROB size, L2 cache size, and frequency at 20 different performance target levels, ranging from 0 to 95% with a step of 5%. Figure 8 shows the comparison between the demand estimated with

our performance model and the one obtained from detailed simulation for program *bzip2*. Because of the imperfection in performance modeling, there are differences between the estimated and the simulated demands at certain performance targets. The average amount of these differences across the entire 20 performance target levels reflects the accuracy of the demand estimation, as shown in Figure 9. We observe that the demand difference at any performance target level is no larger than 4 configuration units. The largest demand difference happens in estimating the frequency demand, and this difference is still reasonable considering there are 16 different configuration options for frequency demand.

To evaluate the estimation of memory bandwidth demand, we compare estimated memory bandwidth with the simulated one at each 100K instruction interval, and accumulate the absolute difference between these two to obtain the overall memory bandwidth estimation error. Figure 10 shows the error rates of bandwidth demand estimation for both memory read and memory write traffics at three different configurations. On average, the total memory bandwidth estimation error increases from 4.76% to 6.26% as the L2 cache size changes from 64KB to 2MB. This is mainly because as the cache size increases, memory traffics become smaller and hence the bandwidth caused by conflict L2 misses, which are not captured in our stack distance model, becomes more significant.

To evaluate the estimation for the demand of branch predictor size, we compare the size and the prediction accuracy of the estimated branch predictor configuration with that of the largest pre-

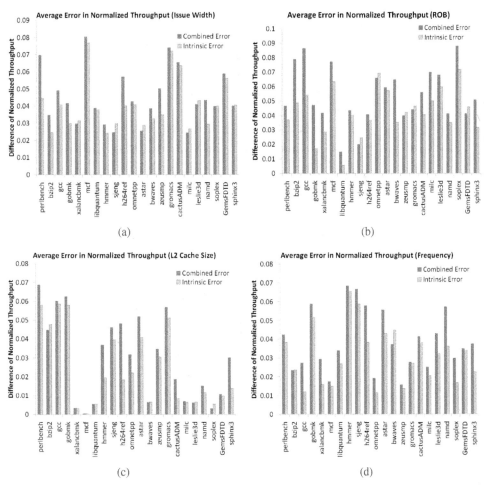

(a)

(b)

(c)

(d)

Figure 7: Comparison of the combined error and the intrinsic error in normalized throughput. The intrinsic error is obtained by using the simulated values of the non-overlapped L2 misses and the branch mispredictions in the performance model. The errors are averaged across three configurations: config-S, config-M, config-L.

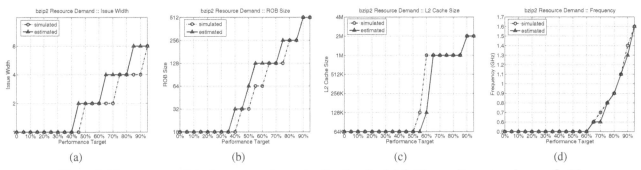

(a)   (b)   (c)   (d)

Figure 8: The accuracy of single-resource demand estimation for *bzip2*. The results are based on config-M.

dictor in the configuration range. The results are listed in the table 2. On average, by using the estimated predictor size, we could achieve 40.3% reduction in area with only 0.12% accuracy loss over the largest branch predictor. Overall, the proposed heuristic captures the demand on branch predictor size very well.

5.2.2   Multi-Resource Demand Estimation

The quality of multi-resource demand estimation includes two aspects: the accuracy in satisfying the performance target and the energy efficiency of the estimated resources.

To evaluate the accuracy, we used the proposed framework to

estimate the resource demands at each performance target ranging from 50% to 95% with the step of 5%, and then performed detailed simulations with the estimated resource configurations for each performance target. The obtained relative performance (normalized to the largest performance in the design space) is compared against the corresponding performance target. The differences are summarized in Figure 11(a). The observed error is up to 12.7% (on *soplex*), and the maximum average error is 8.6% (on *xlanacbmk*). Note that we only report the results with performance target larger than 50% to avoid the *ill-suited* cases that some programs may have a small per-

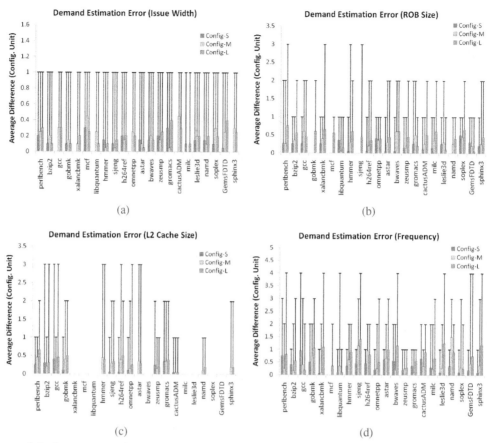

Figure 9: The error of single-resource estimation. Config unit refers to the quantization of each resource shown in Table 1. The error bar represents the largest error in demand estimation for the corresponding program.

Table 2: The Demand Estimation for Branch Predictor Size

Benchmarks	Size Demand		Size Reduction	Accuracy Loss
	L1 entry	History bit		
perlbench	1024	12	0	0
bzip2	128	12	52.5%	0.26%
gcc	1024	12	0	0
gobmk	1024	12	0	0
xalancbmk	1024	12	0	0
mcf	512	12	30%	0.06%
libquantum	8	12	59.5%	0.03%
hmmer	128	12	52.5%	0.09%
sjeng	1024	12	0	0
h264ref	1024	12	0	0
omnetpp	1024	12	0	0
astar	64	12	56.3%	0
bwaves	32	12	58.1%	2.1%
zeusmp	64	9	92.2%	0.05%
gromacs	8	7	98.5%	0
cactusADM	16	7	98.2%	0
milc	32	11	78.3%	0
leslie3d	256	12	45.0%	0
namd	128	12	52.5%	0.1%
soplex	256	12	45.0%	0.01%
GemsFDTD	16	7	98.2%	0.01%
sphinx3	1024	12	0	0
avg	-		40.3%	0.12%

formance variation range and its smallest relative performance may be much larger than the performance target.

To evaluate the energy efficiency, we compare the energy consumption of the estimated multi-resource demand with the energy consumption of other resource combinations that satisfy the given performance target. Due to the large design space, it is prohibitively expensive to exhaustively compare the estimated resource configurations with every eligible design node. Therefore, we use Monte Carlo simulations to simulate 300 random samples in the design space, and group them into the buckets of (0,0.05],(0.05,0.1],...,(0.95,1] according to their performance relative to the highest one in the design space. Within each bucket, we divide the energy of the estimated multi-resource configuration with the maximum energy of the design nodes in that bucket. These ratios indicate the energy efficiency of the estimated resource demands, and are summarized in Figure 11(b). On average, the ratio is no larger than 86.5%, and can be as low as 44.4%, which means the estimated multi-resources reasonably satisfy the energy efficiency requirement in the definition of resource demand.

5.3 Complexity Analysis

The complexity of the PREDA framework involves the complexity of multi-resource demand searching algorithm and the time cost in evaluating the performance model. As explained previously, the complexity of the algorithm depends on the number of iterations required to reach the target performance. To reduce the number of iterations, the algorithm hoists the starting point of the searching process as the target performance increases. This feature allows the algorithm to avoid unnecessary search iterations and significantly speeds up the searching process. In our experiment, the algorithm converges in no larger than 12 iterations. We also compare the CPU time required to finish *one searching iteration* by using our performance model with the time required by using the state-of-the-art analytical model developed by Eyerman et al. [7], and we observe up to 40X speedup with our proposed model. This is mainly be-

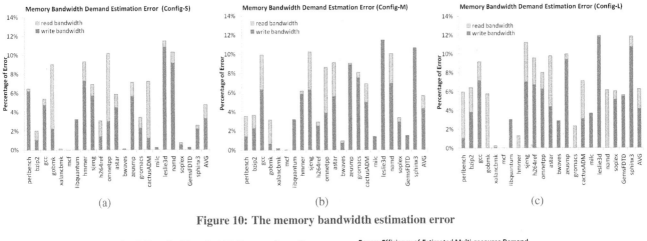

Figure 10: The memory bandwidth estimation error

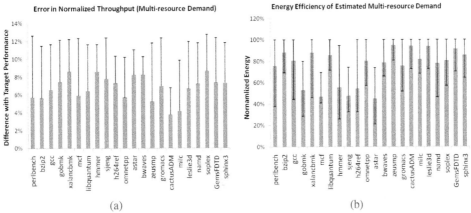

Figure 11: Evaluation of multi-resource demand estimation. The results are based on estimating 4 different resource demands.

cause every time cache size changes, Eyerman's model requires detailed cache simulation to collect cache miss and MLP information for different window sizes, whereas our model only needs to walk through the stack distance trace. Depending on the data footprint of the programs, the profiling time cost of PREDA may be larger than Eyerman's model because of the stack distance profiling. However, this is one-time profiling cost, and could be easily amortized by the speedup in the demand estimation process.

6. RELATED WORK

Our work is most relevant to the predictive resource management framework proposed by Narayanan and Satyanarayanan [21]. However, their framework can only estimate the coarse-grain resource demands, such as CPU cycles and memory sizes; whereas our work estimates resource demands at much finer granularity, and can be applied in the areas that require fine-grain resource tuning. PUNCH proposed by Kapadia et al. [13] also shares some common grounds with our framework as both attempt to predict the resource demands by using application-specific parameters. But again, in their work, the resource demands are limited to CPU time only.

Our work is also closely related with performance modeling, which usually employs analytical models, regression models, or predictive models. The analytical model is typically based on *interval analysis*, which was used by Karkhanis and Smith for their first-order superscalar processor model [14]. They further leveraged this model to automatically explore the design space for the Pareto-optimal design parameters [15]. Recently, this model was improved by Eyerman et al. for a higher accuracy in performance

modeling [7]. However, all of these models rely on detailed simulation of some components, such as caches and branch predictors, to obtain key statistics of the program-microarchitecture interactions. The requirement for partial simulation not only costs time in off-line performance modeling, but also implies that it has to follow the trial-and-error scheme when applying this model for on-line resource management. However, our approach focuses on modeling the performance trend rather than the absolute performance value, and avoids any detailed simulation of any resource component. The decoupling from detailed simulations not only ensures fast off-line resource demand estimation, but also allows this model to be applied in on-line resource management without trial runs.

Both regression models and predictive models are essentially empirical models, which hide the details of program-hardware interactions by fitting high-level equations with the simulated results. The regression model has been applied in estimating the significance of the design parameters and their interactions [12], exploring the design space [18] as well as analyzing the microarchitectural adaptivity [19]. An artificial neural network (ANN) based predictive model was also proposed by Ipek et al. for performance prediction [11]. While the empirical models are relatively simple, they require time consuming training on a per-application basis before they can reasonably model performance. The requirement for training fundamentally limits these models from being applied online. In contrast, our model is based on the analysis of program inherent characteristics and does not require any training.

Besides off-line performance modeling, some on-line resource management techniques have been proposed recently. Qureshi et al. proposed the cache utility monitor (UMON) to estimate the utility of assigning additional cache ways to an application [23]. Kaseridis et al. extended this on-line cache monitor for system-level memory bandwidth management [16]. While these works address single resource management, Bitirgen et al. attempted to manage multiple resources by using on-line machine learning techniques [3]. However, the on-line machine learning model requires periodic training and is expensive to implement and hard to validate. In contrast, our model does not require any training and could be applied on-line for both single or multiple resource management with some hardware support for on-line profiling .

7. CONCLUSIONS

As the applications in computer systems become increasingly diversified, it is important to efficiently identify the hardware resource demands of the applications so that the hardware substrate could be tailored to the needs of the applications for power efficient computing. Existing models are inappropriate for estimating resource demands as they require either partial simulations or time-consuming training. In this paper, we present an integrated framework for program resource demand analysis (PREDA), which leverages the synergy between the performance trend modeling and marginal utility to identify the resource demand of a workload without any detailed simulation. The proposed framework is able to estimate both single-resource and multi-resource demand on an array of processor resources, ranging from the issue width, the operating frequency to the memory bandwidth. Experimental results show that the proposed framework on average provides no larger than 8.6% error to any given performance target for multi-resource demand estimation. By using the proposed performance model, the framework achieves up to 40X speedup in multi-resource demand estimation compared with that by using state-of-the-art analytical model. The proposed framework is useful for workload capacity planning in computing systems, early stage design space exploration, as well as coordinated multiple resource management for Quality-of-Service in CMP systems.

8. ACKNOWLEDGMENTS

The authors would like to thank Giuliano Casale and other anonymous reviewers for their valuable feedback. This work is supported in part through the NSF Award number 0702694. Any opinions, findings, and conclusions or recommendations expressed herein are those of the authors and do not necessarily reflect the views of NSF.

9. REFERENCES

[1] SPEC cpu2006 benchmark suite. In *http://www.spec.org*.

[2] T. Austin, E. Larson, and D. Ernst. Simplescalar: An infrastructure for computer system modeling. *Computer*, 35:59–67, February 2002.

[3] R. Bitirgen, E. Ipek, and J. F. Martinez. Coordinated management of multiple interacting resources in chip multiprocessors: A machine learning approach. In *MICRO'41*, pages 318–329, 2008.

[4] D. Brooks, V. Tiwari, and M. Martonosi. Wattch: a framework for architectural-level power analysis and optimizations. In *ISCA '00*, pages 83–94, 2000.

[5] A. S. Dhodapkar and J. E. Smith. Managing multi-configuration hardware via dynamic working set analysis. In *ISCA '02*, pages 233–244, 2002.

[6] S. Eyerman, L. Eeckhout, T. Karkhanis, and J. E. Smith. A performance counter architecture for computing accurate cpi components. In *ASPLOS-XII*, pages 175–184, 2006.

[7] S. Eyerman, L. Eeckhout, T. Karkhanis, and J. E. Smith. A mechanistic performance model for superscalar out-of-order processors. *ACM Trans. Comput. Syst.*, 27(2):1–37, 2009.

[8] F. Guo, Y. Solihin, L. Zhao, and R. Iyer. A framework for providing quality of service in chip multi-processors. In *MICRO'40*, pages 343–355, 2007.

[9] G. Hamerly, E. Perelman, J. Lau, and B. Calder. Simpoint 3.0: Faster and more flexible program analysis. In *Journal of Instruction Level Parallelism*, volume 7, pages 1–28, 2005.

[10] M. Haungs, P. Sallee, and M. Farrens. Branch transition rate: a new metric for improved branch classification analysis. In *HPCA'00*, pages 241 –250, 2000.

[11] E. Ïpek, S. A. McKee, R. Caruana, B. R. de Supinski, and M. Schulz. Efficiently exploring architectural design spaces via predictive modeling. In *ASPLOS-XII*, pages 195–206, 2006.

[12] P. Joseph, K. Vaswani, and M. Thazhuthaveetil. Construction and use of linear regression models for processor performance analysis. In *HPCA'06*, pages 99 – 108, 2006.

[13] N. Kapadia, J. Fortes, and C. Brodley. Predictive application-performance modeling in a computational grid environment. In *Proceedings of The Eighth International Symposium on High Performance Distributed Computing*, pages 47 –54, 1999.

[14] T. S. Karkhanis and J. E. Smith. A first-order superscalar processor model. In *ISCA'04*, pages 338–349, 2004.

[15] T. S. Karkhanis and J. E. Smith. Automated design of application specific superscalar processors: an analytical approach. In *ISCA'07*, pages 402–411, 2007.

[16] D. Kaseridis, J. Stuecheli, J. Chen, and L. John. A bandwidth-aware memory-subsystem resource management using non-invasive resource profilers for large cmp systems. In *HPCA'10*, pages 1–11, 2010.

[17] R. Kumar, D. M. Tullsen, and N. P. Jouppi. Core architecture optimization for heterogeneous chip multiprocessors. In *PACT '06*, pages 23–32, 2006.

[18] B. Lee and D. Brooks. Illustrative design space studies with microarchitectural regression models. In *HPCA'07*, pages 340 –351, 2007.

[19] B. C. Lee and D. Brooks. Efficiency trends and limits from comprehensive microarchitectural adaptivity. In *ASPLOS XIII*, pages 36–47, 2008.

[20] R. L. Mattson, D. R. Slutz, and I. L. Traiger. Evaluation techniques for storage hierarchies. *IBM Syst. J.*, 9(2):78–117, 1970.

[21] D. Narayanan and M. Satyanarayanan. Predictive resource management for wearable computing. In *Proceedings of the 1st international conference on Mobile systems, applications and services*, MobiSys '03, pages 113–128. ACM, 2003.

[22] K. J. Nesbit, J. Laudon, and J. E. Smith. Virtual private caches. In *ISCA '07*, pages 57–68, 2007.

[23] M. K. Qureshi and Y. N. Patt. Utility-based cache partitioning: A low-overhead, high-performance, runtime mechanism to partition shared caches. In *MICRO'06*, pages 423–432, 2006.

[24] S. Thoziyoor, N. Muralimanohar, J. H. Ahn, and N. P. Jouppi. Cacti 5.1. *HP Technical Reports*, 2008.

[25] T.-Y. Yeh and Y. N. Patt. A comparison of dynamic branch predictors that use two levels of branch history. In *ISCA '93*, pages 257–266, 1993.

METE: Meeting End-to-End QoS in Multicores through System-Wide Resource Management[*]

Akbar Sharifi, Shekhar Srikantaiah, Asit K. Mishra, Mahmut Kandemir and Chita R. Das
Department of CSE
The Pennsylvania State University
University Park, PA 16802, USA
{akbar, srikanta, amishra, kandemir, das}@cse.psu.edu

ABSTRACT

Management of shared resources in emerging multicores for achieving predictable performance has received considerable attention in recent times. In general, almost all these approaches attempt to guarantee a certain level of performance QoS (weighted IPC, harmonic speedup, etc) by managing a single shared resource or at most a couple of interacting resources. A fundamental shortcoming of these approaches is the lack of coordination between these shared resources to satisfy a system level QoS. This is undesirable because providing end-to-end QoS in future multicores is essential for supporting wide-spread adoption of these architectures in virtualized servers and cloud computing systems. An initial step towards such an end-to-end QoS support in multicores is to ensure that at least the major computational and memory resources on-chip are managed efficiently in a coordinated fashion.

In this paper, we propose METE, a platform for end-to-end on-chip resource management in multicore processors. Assuming that each application specifies a performance target/SLA, the main objective of METE is to dynamically provision sufficient on-chip resources to applications for achieving the specified targets. METE employs a feedback based system, designed as a Single-Input, Multiple-Output (SIMO) controller with an Auto-Regressive-Moving-Average (ARMA) model, to capture the behaviors of different applications. We evaluate a specific implementation of METE that manages cores, shared caches and off-chip bandwidth in an integrated manner on 8 and 16 core systems using a detailed full system simulator and workloads derived from the SPECOMP and SPECJBB multithreaded benchmarks. The collected results indicate that our proposed scheme is able to provision shared resources among co-runner applications dynamically over the course of execution, to provide end-to-end QoS and satisfy specified performance targets. Furthermore, the elegance of the control theory based multi-layer resource provisioning is in assuring QoS guarantees.

[*]This research is supported in part by NSF grants #1017882, #0963839, CNS #0720645, CCF #0811687, and CCF #0702519, and a grant from Microsoft Corporation.

Categories and Subject Descriptors

B.3.2 [**Memory Structures**]: Design Styles; C.4 [**Performance of Systems**]: Design Studies

General Terms

Design, Experimentation, Management, Performance

Keywords

Resource Management, Control Theory, End-to-End QoS

1. INTRODUCTION

Multicores are now ubiquitous [1, 2, 3, 4], owing to the benefits they bring over single core architectures including improved performance, lower power consumption and reduced design complexity. Several resources ranging from the cores themselves to multiple levels of on-chip caches and off-chip memory bandwidth are typically shared in a multicore processor. Prudent management of these shared resources for achieving predictable performance and optimizing energy efficiency is critical and thus, has received considerable attention in recent times. Most of this research has focussed around managing either the shared cache [5, 6, 7, 8, 9, 10, 11] or off-chip memory bandwidth [12, 13, 14, 15, 16] in isolation.

In general, almost all these approaches attempt to guarantee a certain level of *quality-of-service* (QoS) like weighted IPC, harmonic speedup, etc by managing a single shared resource or at most a couple of interacting resources. There are at least three fundamental shortcomings with such approaches: (i) Considering that system performance is heavily influenced by complex interactions among multiple resources [17, 18], attempting to optimize performance/guarantee QoS by managing a single resource is not only less effective, but may also be impossible; (ii) In most existing schemes, there is no feedback among mechanisms, trying to provide QoS by managing different resources, and this leads to an anarchy in resource management; and (iii) Working with low-level resources like cache or memory-bandwidth restricts the system-performance metrics that can be controlled to only low-level metrics like IPC, which are not easily comprehended by system administrators or application programmers.

On the other hand, providing *end-to-end* QoS in future multicores is essential for supporting wide-spread adoption of these new architectures in virtualized servers and cloud computing systems. An initial step towards such an end-to-end QoS support in multicores is to ensure that at least the major computational and memory resources on-chip are managed efficiently in a coordinated fashion. In this paper, we propose METE, a platform for end-to-end on-chip resource management in multicore processors. The proposed resource management scheme attempts to address all the three major constraints of existing techniques by (i) providing a multi-level resource provisioning mechanism for end-to-end QoS, (ii) developing

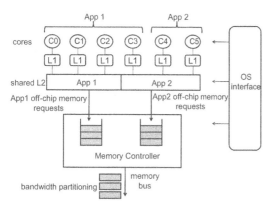

Figure 1: Three types of shared resources provisioned to two co-runner applications.

a control theoretic model for accurately tracking the system state, and (iii) by demonstrating the applicability of the model to system level parameters. While a few recent works [19, 20] have studied the advantages of using feedback control theory for resource management in multicore processors, to our knowledge, no prior study has taken a holistic multi-level control theory approach as proposed here.

Figure 1 shows the high-level view of the three resources managed by a specific implementation of METE (cores, on-chip shared caches and off-chip bandwidth) in an *integrated* manner among two applications. The main goal behind this management is to ensure that any performance target is tracked by provisioning resources in an end-to-end manner. Assuming that each application specifies a (potentially different) performance target, the main objective of METE is to dynamically provision sufficient on-chip resources to applications in order to achieve the specified targets, if it is possible to do so. Apart from low-level metrics like IPC (instructions per cycle) that have been used in the past, METE also accepts high-level (e.g., application specific) performance metrics like transactions per second for database applications. More importantly, the proposed system is flexible enough to handle different metrics for different applications at the same time.

METE employs a feedback based system designed as a Single-Input, Multiple-Output (SIMO) controller with an Auto-Regressive-Moving-Average (ARMA) model to capture the dynamic behaviors of different applications. Control theory [21, 22] is a powerful tool that offers several unique advantages over alternate schemes:

• Feedback control theory provides a robust strategy to track specified objectives over time. It can achieve this by modulating resource allocations in a coordinated fashion.

• A system equipped with a feedback controller can respond quickly to variations in the dynamic behaviors of running applications.

• A feedback controller can be designed to control multiple high-level metrics of interest at the same time under various constraints.

• Using control theory enables rejecting unexpected disturbances in the controlled system. For instance, in the context of multicores, a sudden change in the demands for a shared resource can be interpreted as an external disturbance in the system.

We evaluate METE on 8 and 16 core systems using a detailed full system simulator and workloads formed from the SPECOMP and SPECJBB multithreaded applications. The collected results indicate that our proposed scheme is able to provision shared resources among co-runner applications dynamically over the course of execution, to provide end-to-end QoS and satisfy specified high-level performance targets.

The remainder of this paper is structured as follows. The next section discusses background on feedback control theory, and motivates our solution. Section 3 gives the mechanisms employed to partition each type of resource we target in this work across applications. Section 4 presents our proposed METE platform that enables QoS-aware multi-resource management. Our experimental evaluation is presented in Section 5. Section 6 discusses the related studies and finally, we conclude the paper in Section 7.

2. MOTIVATION AND BACKGROUND

2.1 Motivation

The allocated number of cores, amount of on-chip shared cache space and off-chip memory bandwidth are three major parameters that affect the performance of an application running on a multicore machine. However, the *degrees* to which each of these parameters influences the performance are not the same, both within an application's execution (i.e., across its different phases) as well as across different applications. To illustrate this point, we performed a set of experiments that evaluates the impact of different shared resources on the performance of applications. Two applications, applu and swim from the SPECOMP benchmark suite [23], are used in these experiments. Unless otherwise mentioned, each of these applications is assigned 4 cores, 4 MB, 16 way associative shared on-chip cache space, and 6.4 Gb/s bandwidth. Then, each of the resource allocations, one at a time, is changed to study the impact the resource has on each application's performance. Figures 2(a), (b) and (c) plot the performance (measured in IPC) as the amount of resources (cache ways, percentage bandwidth, and cores) allocated to the applications varies. In all experiments, each application has 8 threads. The detailed simulation parameters and system configuration used in this work are given later in Section 5.1.

Several observations can be made from these plots. First, the overall impact of varying the amount of each type of resource is significantly different from the others. For example, the number of allocated processing cores has much larger impact on the performance as compared to the amount of off-chip bandwidth allocated to the running applications.[1] Therefore, while it is important to consider all resources in the system to provide end-to-end QoS, it is also crucial to consider the differences in their impacts on application performance. Second, for a given change in a resource, different applications react differently, based on the operating point. For example, for a bandwidth allocation change from 5% to 10%, swim receives a bigger boost in performance than applu. That is, the slope of the performance vs. bandwidth allocation curve for swim is greater than that for applu in the 5-10% operating region. However, the corresponding slopes are similar in the 50-100% operating range. Therefore, it is important to consider the operating point of each resource for each application. Third, it is possible to track the same target performance for the same application by allocating different combinations of resources. For example, applu is able to achieve an IPC of 1.2 by using either 4 cache ways and 50% of peak bandwidth (Figure 2(a)), or 10% of the peak bandwidth and 16 cache ways (Figure 2(b)). On the other hand, when some of the resources are constrained, we may not have flexibility in resource allocations to track a specified target performance. For example, once swim is constrained to an allocation of 4 cores and an allocation of 50% bandwidth, it cannot achieve an IPC of 1.7 even with an allocation of 32 cache ways, while the same can be achieved by allocating 4 cores, 16 cache ways and 100% bandwidth. Therefore,

---

[1]Note that, in a more bandwidth constrained system the significance of bandwidth may be reversed.

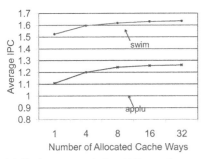
(a) Cache ways variation (Allocated number of cores is 4, Allocated bandwidth is 50%).

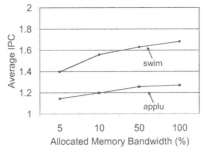
(b) Memory bandwidth variation (Allocated number of cores is 4, Allocated cache ways is 16).

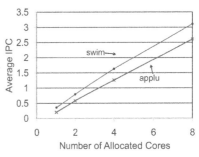
(c) Number of cores variation (Allocated cache ways is 16, Allocated bandwidth is 50%).

Figure 2: The impacts of resource allocation on the performance of two running applications.

it is important to consider the allocations across all resources in unison (end-to-end), such that all performance targets can be met.

A recent work [19] elaborated on the advantages of using formal feedback control and modeling application performance to achieve performance QoS by partitioning only the shared cache (assuming that the other resource allocations do not change). The customized oscillation resistant controller proposed in that work is essentially a Single-Input, Single-Output feedback controller that can track the performance of an application by performing shared cache partitioning. As a preliminary study, we extended this design based on the same principles to design three controllers, one for each type of resource (core, cache and bandwidth). Each of the three controllers takes the same performance QoS target as input (corresponding to an IPC of 1.25) and seeks to satisfy this goal in *isolation*. The observed performance of one of our applications (applu) with such a system is shown in Figure 3. We can see that, the specified QoS target is often violated by this system. One of the major reasons for this behavior is the lack of coordination between the three controllers. Specifically, each of the three controllers decides the resource allocations in their layer without considering the impact that the other may have on the performance. This can often lead to conflicting decisions in different resource allocations [17, 18]. For example, at time $t = 5$, 5 cores, 16 cache ways and 80% of the off-chip memory bandwidth are allocated to the running application. Since the measured performance is higher than the target, the amount of allocated cache space and memory bandwidth are reduced to 7 and 60%, respectively. As a result, the measured IPC decreases to 1.2, which is lower than the performance goal. This simple experiment clearly motivates the need to have a *coordinated* end-to-end feedback controller that takes the specified QoS target as input, but simultaneously controls all the resources based on modeling application behavior.

2.2 Background

In this work, we employ Single-Input, Multiple-Output (SIMO) controller. Figure 4 illustrates a canonical feedback control loop with a SIMO controller. As an example for SIMO controller, consider a water pool (plant) that has to be maintained at a constant temperature by letting in both hot and cold water flows run into it (and correspondingly let equal volume of water out of the pool). Suppose that the rates of the flows can be controlled by a *controller* and the controller's role is to adjust these rates in an automated fashion to keep the pool temperature at the desired value. The desired temperature is called *Reference Input* in the control theory terminology. Since in this case, the controller takes a desired pool temperature as a *single input* and controls it using *multiple* outputs (specifically two: hot and cold water), the controller is a SIMO controller. The

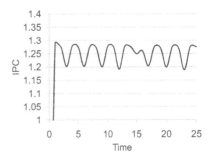

Figure 3: Behavior of applu (one of our applications) in a system consisting of three controllers (one for each resource). Oscillation occurs, since at time t the cache layer controller increases/decreases the allocated cache space to meet the performance target unaware of the changes made by the off-chip bandwidth controller to the memory bandwidth allocation.

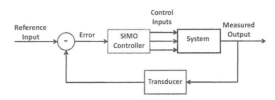

Figure 4: High level view of a feedback control system with a SIMO controller.

controller functions by comparing the reference input to the current water temperature (*System Output*) and based on the obtained *Error* value, the rates of the hot and cold flows are modulated. The *Transducer* converts the *System Output* (pool temperature) to the same type as the *Reference Input* if they have different types and cannot be compared. This component aids in implementing a flexible system with different high-level target specifications by converting the system output into a comparable metric to the target specification. We will discuss the implementation of our transducer component in Section 5.5.

In METE, a separate SIMO controller is assigned for each application. At the end of each time interval (*sampling period*, the controller increases/decreses the control inputs (resource allocation), taking into account the variation observed in the measured IPC value (*Observable System Output*) over the last time interval. Note that the controller requires knowledge on the reaction of the application to the modulations in the resource allocations. A system model in control theory tries to capture this knowledge. Table 1 summarizes

Term	Description in Our Context
Reference Input	Desired IPC value for an application
Control Input	Resource allocation
System	multicore with running applications
System Output	Measured IPC value of an application
Controller	Application Controller
System Model	the employed ARMA model

Table 1: Basic terms used in control theory and their descriptions in our problem domain.

the basic terms used in formal control theory and the corresponding descriptions in our problem domain. We want to emphasize that our scheme can work with any performance QoS. In most of our discussion however, we use IPC as our target metric.

If the values of the model parameters do not change over time, we refer to this type of model as *static*. In *adaptive* feedback control systems on the other hand, the system model is updated dynamically. In this work, we employ the latter type since behaviors of applications do *not* remain constant during the course of execution and each usually has multiple execution phases. Specifically, in METE, we employ an *Auto-Regressive Moving Average (ARMA)* [22] model. The *ARMA* model can approximate the behavior of a system with multiple inputs/outputs in a linear form and also can be updated dynamically, suitable for adaptive control system designs. We also employ a global controller (manager), called the *Resource Broker*, to handle cases where (i) resources requested by applications exceed available capacities, and (ii) after satisfying all requests, there are still idle resources. In the following sub-sections, we study our proposed control design for end-to-end QoS management in multicores.

3. IMPLEMENTATION ISSUES

Figure 1 gives the high-level view of how the shared resources are partitioned between two applications. We envision implementing METE in the operating system (OS), with dynamic feedback from hardware based counters about the different resource usages. The cores need to be partitioned in the OS-level since the OS can manipulate the set of cores used to run an application dynamically over the course of execution. The cache and bandwidth partitioning can also be handled by the OS with hardware support from the shared resources. In the following discussion, we explain the mechanisms METE employs to partition each type of resource across applications.

Core Partitioning: METE uses the *psrset* utility in *Solaris* to create a processor set containing one or more cores and run a particular application on it. Cores can be added or removed from that processor set over execution. Consequently, the OS provides a mechanism to adjust the number of cores allocated to each running application dynamically.

Cache Partitioning: In METE, we adopted the OS-level mechanism proposed in [24] to partition the shared cache space across co-runner applications or threads. In [24], the hardware part of the proposed scheme guarantees that the quotas specified by the OS are enforced in shared caches. In this scheme, an m-bit tag is associated with each cache block indicating which core that block belongs to. Also, each memory request contains an identifier indicating its cache block access domain.

Off-Chip Bandwidth Partitioning: In METE, the available memory bandwidth is partitioned across co-runner applications based on the priority of each sharer. This is similar to the fair queuing systems proposed in [25, 26]. For example, as can be seen in Figure 1, the memory controller serves the requests from the two applications in such a way that each of them receives its quota of the off-chip memory bandwidth based on its relative weight specified by the OS.

A	set of applications running on the multicore
a_i	application number i
ref_i	the desired IPC of a_i
$IPC_i(k)$	the actual IPC of a_i at the k-th time interval
$I\hat{P}C_i(k)$	the predicted IPC by the employed model of a_i at the k-th time interval
c_{ik}	the number of cores requested by the controller associated with a_i at the k-th time interval
w_{ik}	the number of cache-ways from the shared L2 cache requested by the controller associated with a_i at the k-th time interval
b_{ik}	the memory access bandwidth requested by the controller associated with a_i at the k-th time interval
$\mathbf{u_i}(k)$	vector of $\begin{pmatrix} c_{ik} \\ w_{ik} \\ b_{ik} \end{pmatrix}$
$\hat{c_{ik}}$	the number of cores allocated to a_i by the Resource Broker at the k-th time interval
$\hat{w_{ik}}$	the number of cache-ways from the shared L2 cache allocated to a_i by the Resource Broker at the k-th time interval
$\hat{b_{ik}}$	the memory access bandwidth reserved for a_i by the Resource Broker at the k-th time interval
$\hat{\mathbf{u_i}}(k)$	vector of $\begin{pmatrix} \hat{c_{ik}} \\ \hat{w_{ik}} \\ \hat{b_{ik}} \end{pmatrix}$
$\Delta\hat{\mathbf{u_i}}(k)$	$\hat{\mathbf{u_i}}(k) - \hat{\mathbf{u_i}}(k-1)$
C	the number of cores of the multicore
W	the total number of cache ways (associativity) of the shared L2 cache
B	the maximum available off chip memory access bandwidth

Table 2: Notation used in this paper.

To implement this scheme, a service time (which is inversely related to its weight) is computed for each application request flow. The application with smaller service time (as compared to the memory controller's virtual clock) is served at each time.

After explaining these actuators (control knobs), we next discuss the details of our control architecture.

4. CONTROL ARCHITECTURE

4.1 High Level View

Figure 5 illustrates the high level view of METE. Each *Application Controller* shown in Figure 5 is implemented in software. Assuming that each running application is assigned a specified IPC target (desired performance goal, ref_i), the application controller of application a_i determines the amount of resources, u_{ik}, that need to be allocated for that application in order to satisfy the specified performance goal (IPC_{ik}) at the k-th execution epoch (Table 2 gives the notation we use in this paper).

As mentioned earlier, in our current implementation of METE, three types of resources are targeted and can be partitioned among co-runner applications. These resources include processing cores, shared L2 cache space, and off-chip memory bandwidth. The amount of resources in each type is limited, and consequently, at each epoch, if the total amount of resources requested by applications is less than or equal to available total, a successful resource allocation can be performed. Otherwise (if the three resource constraints shown below are not satisfied), a higher level module (called Resource Broker in this work) intervenes to modify the amount of requested resources determined by the application controllers u_{ik} and make the final resource partitioning decision $\hat{u}_{ik}$. Our resource constraints can be expressed as follows:

$$\sum_{a_i \in \mathbf{A}} \hat{c_{ik}} \leqslant C, \qquad \sum_{a_i \in \mathbf{A}} \hat{w_{ik}} \leqslant W, \qquad \text{and} \qquad \sum_{a_i \in \mathbf{A}} \hat{m_{ik}} \leqslant M.$$
(1)

The above constraints ensure that the sum of the allocated cores,

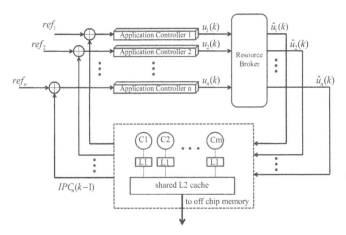

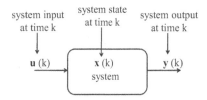

Figure 6: Input, output and state in a state space model.

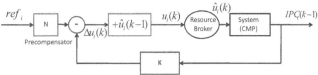

Figure 7: Detailed view of an application controller.

Figure 5: High level view of our control architecture for *n* number of applications.

cache ways and memory bandwidth cannot exceed the total available resources. Below, we first study our employed model and the feedback controller associated with it, and then present the details of the resource broker module.

4.2 System Model

As mentioned earlier, a feedback controller needs to know the impact of variations in control parameters on the measured system outputs. In other words, a system model is a mathematical function f that gives the system output for every feasible control parameters (i.e., $y(k) = f[u(k)]$, where y and u are the output and input of the system, respectively). One way of obtaining the system model is to determine function f directly by mathematical analysis of how the system works. Unfortunately, this approach cannot be applied to most actual computing systems due to the complexity of the desired modeling function. Instead, a more practical approach would be estimating the system behavior through analysis of the sample measured data. In this method, the model is expressed as a parametric function of independent variables with a finite number of parameters. In this case, system model identification is the process of determining these parameters. Inputs with different values are fed to the system and the corresponding measured outputs are collected. Algorithms such as *least square* [22] can be employed in this step to determine the values of the model parameters.

Even though the behavior of most real systems is not linear, linear approximation can be used (and has been successfully used in prior works and actual control based systems) as a method to estimate non-linear characteristics of actual systems. In METE, we employ the ARMA model [27] to capture the effect of the control parameters (u_{ik}) on our system output (IPC_{ik}). The ARMA model is a linear recursive equation that can be updated dynamically and is very suitable for adaptive control system designs. The equation below gives the mathematical representation of our employed model for each application:

$$\hat{IPC_i}(k+1) = a_{ik} \times IPC_i(k) + \mathbf{b_{ik}^T} \times \Delta\hat{\mathbf{u}}_\mathbf{i}(k), \quad (2)$$

where a_{ik} and $\mathbf{b_{ik}^T}$ are the parameters of the model that are dynamically determined for each application. Note that $IPC_i(k)$ and $\Delta\hat{\mathbf{u}}_\mathbf{i}(k)$ correspond to the actual IPC of application a_i and the variations in the resource allocations at the k-th time interval, respectively. In this equation, $\mathbf{b_{ik}^T}$ is $\begin{pmatrix} c & w & m \end{pmatrix}$, where the values of c, w and m capture the influence of the variations in the number of allocated cores, the number of cache ways and the reserved memory bandwidth on the application IPC value. As we later show

in the experimental results section, the value of c for different applications is significantly larger than the value of w, meaning that, if one core is added to the set of cores allocated to an application, the application's IPC will improve much better as compared to the case in which one extra cache way is added to the previously reserved cache ways for that application. The values of our model parameters are determined in this work dynamically using the *recursive least square* algorithm [22]. In this algorithm, at each time interval, the model is updated based on the new operating point that has been obtained (i.e., by considering the performance impact of the last resource allocation). To evaluate the obtained model, the IPCs predicted by the model can be compared against the actual ones, while the inputs are taking different values. We present the results from our model evaluation in Section 5.

4.3 Application Controller

The *State Space* approach is a compact and convenient method to model, analyze and design a wide range of systems [21], especially systems with time-varying characteristics and multiple inputs/outputs. To use this approach, first, the system behavior has to be represented using a *State Space Model*. The following equations characterize the general form of a state space model (as illustrated in Figure 6):

$$\mathbf{x}(k+1) = \mathbf{A}\mathbf{x}(k) + \mathbf{B}\mathbf{u}(k) \quad (3)$$
$$\mathbf{y}(k) = \mathbf{C}\mathbf{x}(k), \quad (4)$$

where $\mathbf{x}$ is the state vector, $\mathbf{u}$ and $\mathbf{y}$ are, respectively, the input and the output vectors of the system, and $\mathbf{A}$, $\mathbf{B}$ and $\mathbf{C}$ are the model parameters. The state vector $\mathbf{x}$ contains the state variables that reflect the current state of the system. Equation (3) is solved to predict the next state of the system based on the current state and input vector $\mathbf{u}$. The input vector contains the *control input* parameters. Equation (4) is called the *output equation* and is used to determine the system outputs.

It should be observed that our system model in Equation (2) can be expressed as a state-space model, described by Equations (3) and (4), where we have:

$$\mathbf{A} = (a_{ik}), \qquad \mathbf{B} = \mathbf{b_{ik}^T}, \qquad \mathbf{C} = (1), \qquad \mathbf{y} = IPC_i. \quad (5)$$

The next step in the state space approach is to design an appropriate controller based on the obtained system model. Figure 7 illustrates the internal structure of an application controller to achieve this goal. The feedback control is composed of two main components: *controller gains* ($\mathbf{K}$) and *pre-compensator* ($\mathbf{N}$), as shown in Figure 7. Our goal is to determine the values of $\mathbf{K}$ and $\mathbf{N}$ in such a way that the stability of the applications around the targets is ensured. Note that, $\mathbf{K}$ and $\mathbf{N}$ are two vectors with three elements. *pole placement* and *linear quadric regulation* [28] are two algorithms that can be employed to determine the values of $\mathbf{K}$ and $\mathbf{N}$. In the pole placement strategy, which is the method employed in this work, first, the values of $\mathbf{K}$ are determined in such a way that the poles of the system ensure the stability of the system. After that, the contents of $\mathbf{N}$ are obtained using the method outlined in [27].

The final resource demands ($\mathbf{u_i}(k)$) of application i (a_i) are determined by adding the amount of decreasing/increasing values of the control parameters ($\mathbf{\Delta u_i}(k)$) and the application resource allocation at the (k-1)th time interval ($\mathbf{\hat{u}_i}(k-1)$), as given in Equation (6):

$$\mathbf{u_i}(k) = N \times ref_i - \mathbf{k} \times IPC_i(k-1) + \mathbf{\hat{u}_i}(k-1). \quad (6)$$

4.4 Stability Guarantees

Stability is one of the most important properties of a feedback control based system [27]. If a system equipped with a feedback controller is stable, the measured output of the system converges to the desired target over time. For instance, the system with the output shown in Figure 3 is not stable, since the controller is not able to adjust the values of the system inputs in such a way that the system output converges to the desired target over time.

Different properties of a control system can be analyzed easily when the system is described in frequency domain (z-domain). Considering Figure 6 and assuming $U(z)$ and $Y(z)$ are the z-domain representations of $u(k)$ and $y(k)$ respectively, the value of $u(k)$ at time $k = k_0$ is the coefficient of z^{-k_0} in $U(z)$. In other words, the values of $u(k)$ for different ks are encoded as the coefficients of z terms in $U(z)$. Further, the *transfer function* of the system is defined as $G(z) = \frac{Y(z)}{U(z)}$ and indicates how an input $U(z)$ is transformed into the output $Y(z)$. In our multicore system, the transfer function can be determined by taking z-transform of all terms in Equation 2 which describes the behavior of our system.

The *Stability Theorem* in the formal control theory states that a system represented by a transfer function $G(z)$ is stable if and only if the poles (roots of the dominator polynomial) of $G(z)$ are within the unit circle in the complex coordinate plane [27]. Therefore, in METE, to ensure the stability of the system, we first need to find the poles of each application controller and then determine the parameters of the controller in such a way that the poles are placed within the unit circle. As shown in [27], if a system is described by a state space model as in Equation (3), the poles of the system can be obtained solving the following equation in terms of z:

$$det[zI - (\mathbf{A} - \mathbf{BK})] = 0, \quad (7)$$

where $\mathbf{A}$ and $\mathbf{B}$ are the model parameters in Equation (3), and $\mathbf{K}$ is the coefficient vector in the feedback path (see Figure 7). By replacing the parameters in Equation (7) with the values given in Equation (5), the pole of each application controller's transfer function would be:

$$z = a_{ik} - c \times k_1 - w \times k_2 - m \times k_3, \quad (8)$$

assuming that, in Equation (7), $\mathbf{B}$ is $(c \quad w \quad m)$ and $\mathbf{K}$ is a vector with three elements, k_1, k_2 and k_3. Consequently, to ensure stability of our system, the $\mathbf{K}$ values are determined such that $|z| < 1$ in Equation (8).

4.5 The Resource Broker

So far, we have discussed how an application controller determines the amount of different types of resources (processing cores,

L2 cache ways, and off chip memory bandwidth) an application needs to satisfy its specified performance QoS (ref_i). However, since each of our application controllers operates independently, there can be cases where (i) the available resources are not sufficient to meet the requirements of all of the running applications or (ii) the available resources exceed the requirements of the entire workload. In METE, these cases are handled by the resource broker component.

Lack of Resources: Note that, resource contention may occur in any of the resource types (i.e, when one or more than one of the constraints in Expression (1) given earlier are not satisfied). In this case, the resource broker is responsible for performing a *best effort* allocation by considering the relative resource demands of the co-runner applications. As an example, suppose that $Q1$ and $Q2$ are the performance targets of two co-runner applications (a_1 and a_2), and the available resources are not sufficient to satisfy both of the specified targets. Assume further that the amount of resources required to satisfy $Q1$ (determined by the application controller) is much larger than the resource demands of the other application to achieve $Q2$. In this situation, it would not be a fair policy to penalize both applications evenly in an attempt to compensate for the lack of resources, since such policy may degrade the performance of the application with lower resource requirement significantly.

Without loss of generality, let us focus now on core allocation. Assuming that the total demands of applications is greater than the total available number of cores, one can observe that δ cores have to be spilled, where $\delta = \sum_{a_i \epsilon \mathbf{A}} c_{ik} - C$. The approach that we adopt in this work (i.e. our default policy) is to distribute δ among the applications in proportion to their demands. The goal here is to distribute the penalty across applications in a fair manner. Consequently, in this case, the core demands (c_{ik}) are modified as:

$$\hat{c_{ik}} = floor \left(c_{ik} \left(1 - \frac{\delta}{\sum_{a_i \epsilon \mathbf{A}} c_{ik}} \right) \right). \quad (9)$$

A similar strategy can be adopted when the contention occurs in other types of resources as well (shared L2 cache ways and off chip memory bandwidth).

Excess resources: If sum of the resources required by co-runner applications is less than the available amount, one has different options. An energy-aware option would be turning off the excess resources (or placing them into a low-power operating mode) if the underlying hardware supports that. A performance-centric option (our default policy) on the other hand would proceed as follows. To extract additional performance from the available resources, we may be able to use the application priorities assigned to applications by system administrators. Assuming that each application in a workload has been assigned a priority/weight, (w_i) indicating its relative importance, δ excess resources can then be distributed across applications based on Expression (10) given below:

$$\hat{c_{ik}} = \lfloor c_{ik} + \frac{\delta \times w_i}{\sum_{a_i \epsilon \mathbf{A}} w_i} \rfloor, \quad if \; \hat{c_{ik}} < 1 \rightarrow \hat{c_{ik}} = 1. \quad (10)$$

Note that, these priorities can be determined based on the values of vector b_{ik} in Equation (2). As mentioned earlier, these values capture the influence of the variations in the number of allocated cores, the number of cache ways and the reserved memory bandwidth on the IPC value of application i. Consequently, if a change in the allocation of the contented resource has a larger impact on the performance of application i, this application would receive more (excess) resources than the other applications to maximize performance benefits.

Processors	8 cores with private L1 data and instruction caches
Processor Model	4–way issue superscalar
Private L1 D–Caches	Direct mapped, 32KB, 64 bytes block size, 3 cycle access latency
Private L1 I–Caches	Direct mapped, 32KB, 64 bytes block size, 3 cycle access latency
Shared L2 Cache (the second layer)	64–way set associative, 8MB, 64 bytes block size, 10 cycle access latency
Memory	4GB, 200 cycle off–chip access latency
Control Enforcement Interval	20 Million cycles

Table 3: Baseline configuration.

Workloads	Applications
Mix 1	*applu, apsi*
Mix 2	*art, gafort*
Mix 3	*galgel, mgrid*
Mix 4	*swim, wupwise*
Mix 5	*mgrid, applu*
Mix 6	*wupwise, galgel*

Table 4: Various mixes (workloads) composed using the SPECOMP applications.

5. EXPERIMENTS

In this section, we present a detailed experimental evaluation of METE.

5.1 Benchmarks and Setup

We used the SPECOMP benchmark suite [23] to evaluate our control scheme. In addition, we also performed experiments with the SPECJBB benchmark [29] in order to evaluate the use of high-level QoS with METE.[2] Our implementation and evaluations are carried out using SIMICS [30], which is a full system simulator that allows simulation of multi-processor systems [30]. Table 3 gives the baseline configuration used in our experimental evaluation.

Our default configuration contains 8 cores. Each core has a private L1 cache and the on-chip L2 cache is shared by all cores. In most of our experiments, we formed our workloads using applications from the SPECOMP benchmark suite. Each workload is composed of two SPECOMP applications. Table 4 shows different mixes (workloads) we consider in most of our experimental evaluation. The SPECOMP benchmark applications are multithreaded programs and the number of running threads can be specified before the execution starts. In our experiments, each of these programs is executed using 8 threads and, therefore, one to eight cores can be allocated to each application by our proposed control centric scheme ($1 \leq \hat{c}_i(k) \leq 8$), since it is not beneficial from the performance and utilization perspectives to allocate more than eight cores to an application with eight running threads (note that, the number of threads does not change during execution when using METE). In other words, the number of threads of a running application indicates the maximum number of cores that can be allocated to it.

To run a workload that consists of two applications in our 8-core multicore machine, first, two processor sets (one core in each) are created using the *psrset* utility provided by the *Solaris* OS, and the minimum number of L2 cache ways (one way) and the minimum amount of memory bandwidth (5% of maximum available bandwidth) are allocated to each set. Each application in the workload is executed on one of the processor sets. At the end of each epoch, METE determines the resource allocations for the next time interval, and all three types of resources are partitioned among the co-runner applications based on that. If, for example, the new parti-

tioning of the cores suggests an increase in the number of allocated cores to the first application by two, two cores are added to the processor set the first application belongs to. The default sampling period (epoch) to enforce our control decisions is set to 20 million cycles. In our sensitivity experiments, we study the impact of varying this default value.

Further, there are three other parameters that need to be specified in our evaluation: (i) *Reference IPC*: As in [19], the reference performance for each application can be specified as a percentage performance degradation with respect to the case when the application is executed independently on the multicore. Note that, this specification can be part of service-level agreement (SLA) between the system administrator and OS. We experimented with 10% to 40% degradations in our simulations for different applications. We also demonstrate the working of METE with a high-level metric (transactions per second) later in the paper. (ii) *Model Parameters*: The model parameters are determined initially by using regression analysis (for each application separately); they are updated during execution to track the variations in the execution phases of the co-runner applications. (iii) *Enforcement Interval*: This is one of the important parameters in control design that affect the transient response and overall stability of the system. In our simulations, its default value is selected to be large enough to capture the effects of phase changes. Although increasing the duration of the intervals can reduce the performance overheads incurred by METE, it may also result in system instability and slow reaction to the environmental variations. In any case, the results presented below include all performance overheads incurred by METE.

5.2 Model Validation

As discussed earlier, the model that we employ (as given in Equation (2)) captures the influence of the variations in control parameters ($\hat{u}_i(k)$) on the measured IPC values ($IPC_i(k+1)$). We determine the values of the model parameters using the *least square* algorithm for each application and these values (**A** and **B**) are shown in Table 5. To evaluate the accuracy of the obtained model, we compare the IPC values predicted by the model ($I\hat{P}C_i(k+1)$) and the actual (measured) IPCs ($IPC_i(k+1)$), as the resource allocation varies. Figure 8 plots the *predicted* and *actual* IPC values for different applications as the layout of the available resource partitioning changes. It can be observed from these plots that the employed model tracks the actual system output with small errors.

The coefficient of determination (R^2) and the *Mean Absolute Percentage Error* (MAPE) are two widely-used metrics to assess the accuracy of a model. MAPE indicates the average error of the model, and an R^2 value which is close to 1 indicates high accuracy. These metrics are calculated as follows:

$$R^2 = 1 - \frac{\sum (I\hat{P}C_i(k) - IPC_i(k))^2}{\sum (I\hat{P}C_i(k) - IPC_i(avg))^2}, \quad (11)$$

$$MAPE = \frac{1}{K} \sum_{k=1}^{K} \mid \frac{I\hat{P}C_i(k) - IPC_i(k)}{IPC_i(k)} \mid . \quad (12)$$

Table 5 lists the obtained values of the above metrics and also the values of the model parameters for the SPECOMP applications. We can see from the values presented in Table 5 that our employed ARMA model is a good approximation of applications' behaviors.

5.3 Dynamics of METE

In this set of experimental results, we first show how different static partitioning schemes fail to satisfy the QoS targets of different applications when they execute on a multicore together. We then

---

[2]SPECJBB is multi-threaded Java program emulating a 3-tier system. In this program, each thread represents a user that initiates transactions within a warehouse [29].

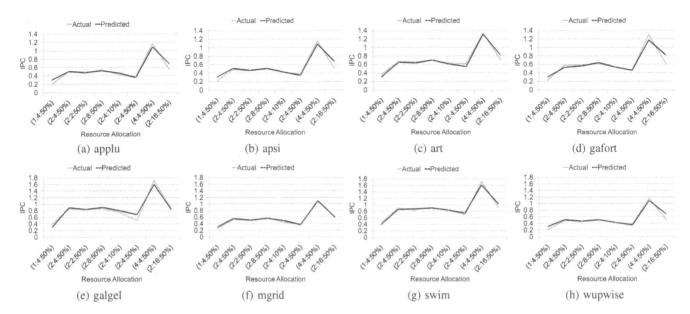

Figure 8: Measured IPC values vs. predicted IPC values by our model. The horizontal axis shows different resource assignments considered for our model evaluation. In (c : w : m), "c" is number of allocated cores, "w" is the number of allocated ways from the shared L2 cache and "m" (%) is the off-chip bandwidth allocation.

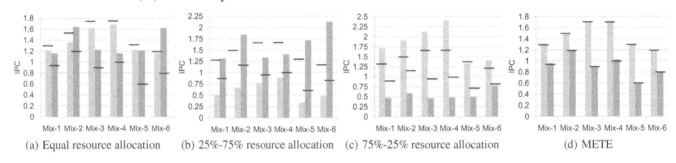

Figure 9: Average IPC values achieved by different mixes (workloads).

Table 5: Model parameters and assessment.

Applications	A	B	MAPE	R^2
applu	1.02	$(\ 0.31, 0.015, 0.077 \ )^T$	0.08	0.91
apsi	1.02	$(\ 0.28, 0.013, 0.067 \ )^T$	0.09	0.89
art	0.98	$(\ 0.33, 0.011, 0.083 \ )^T$	0.06	0.96
gafort	1.01	$(\ 0.32, 0.018, 0.094 \ )^T$	0.11	0.86
galgel	1.06	$(\ 0.34, 0.019, 0.074 \ )^T$	0.1	0.93
mgrid	1.02	$(\ 0.29, 0.014, 0.072 \ )^T$	0.05	0.98
swim	1.01	$(\ 0.33, 0.017, 0.083 \ )^T$	0.06	0.96
wupwise	1.04	$(\ 0.32, 0.016, 0.073 \ )^T$	0.12	0.9

demonstrate that the same targets (QoS values) can be achieved by employing METE, which is able to dynamically track the specified performance targets (desired IPC targets) by partitioning the available resources (cores, L2 cache and off-chip bandwidth) dynamically during the course of execution. In addition, the performance of the running applications can be further enhanced beyond the specified targets by allocating the excess resources, as will be shown later in Section 5.6. We also study a case in which the QoS targets cannot be satisfied by partitioning the available resources due to the lack of resources.

Figures 9(a)-(c) plot the IPCs achieved by the applications in the mixes given in Table 4, when the multicore resources are statically partitioned between the co-runner applications in each mix (for each mix, the two bars denote the two applications, given in Table 4). In

Figure 9(a), each application receives an equal share of each type of resource, whereas in Figures 9(b) and (c), 75% of each type of resource is allocated to one of the applications in each mix; the remaining 25% is given to the other application. The IPC targets set for the applications in these mixes are shown as (horizontal) solid lines in Figure 9. Our main observation from Figures 9(a), (b) and (c) is that these static resource partitioning schemes fail to satisfy some of the specified QoS targets. In comparison, METE takes the specified IPC targets as the reference inputs and decides how the resources we target need to be partitioned in each time interval. Figure 9(d) plots the achieved IPC values when METE is employed. In obtaining these results with METE, when not all the resources are used, we did not distribute them (the use of excess resources will be later discussed). As one can observe from these results, the target QoS values are satisfied successfully in this case for all workloads tested.

Figure 10 illustrates the dynamics of how METE tracks the IPC targets (shown in Figure 9) of different applications during execution. This tracking is achieved by varying the amount of resources allocated to each application dynamically. We observe from Figure 10 that the average maximum overshoot and settling time[3] of different applications are 0.12 and 5 time epochs, respectively. Note

---

[3]The maximum overshoot is the largest difference between the system output and its steady state divided by the steady state value [27].

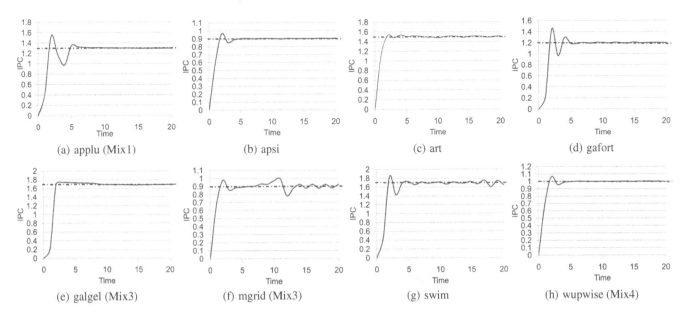

| (a) applu (Mix1) | (b) apsi | (c) art | (d) gafort |

| (e) galgel (Mix3) | (f) mgrid (Mix3) | (g) swim | (h) wupwise (Mix4) |

Figure 10: Tracking the IPC targets for eight applications from Mix1-Mix6. The IPC targets are shown in dash lines in the charts.

that the *maximum overshoot* and *settling time* are two important metrics for the evaluation of feedback control based systems. Based on these results, we can conclude that METE can track specified QoS targets reasonably well. It is important to mention that all types of resources allocated to the applications are dynamically modulated to achieve the results shown in Figure 10. The dynamic variations of these resource allocations are shown in Figures 11, 12 and 13 for caches, bandwidth and cores, respectively. Further, METE is also able to compensate for the changes in the applications' behaviors over time. For instance, in Figure 10(f) the measured IPC of mgrid unexpectedly increases at time 11 due to the variation in the application's behavior (i.e., a phase change). METE compensates for this variation and achieves the target QoS by changing the allocations of the available resources. Note that, in these tracking experiments, the goal is to meet minimum resource requirement of each running application to achieve the specified targets. Consequently, there exist excess resources that have not been allocated, as can be seen in Figures 11, 12, and 13.

As mentioned earlier, typically, the behaviors of the applications are not the same in different epochs and, as a result, we can observe that the controllers try to compensate for this by varying the resource allocations. Note also that the number of allocated cores has a significant impact on the measured IPC. Therefore, as can be observed from Figure 13, partitioning of the cores does not vary much once the IPC values get close enough to the specified targets.

5.4 QoS Sensitivity

The results presented so far were for specific QoS values highlighted in Figure 9. It is also important to study how METE behaves under different QoS values. Figure 14 plots the achieved IPC values by employing METE when different performance targets are specified for applu in mix1. In this experiment, we fixed the target IPC value of the other application (apsi) at 0.5. Our main observation is that, METE is successful in satisfying the QoS targets, even when the specified value is high. Only when the QoS target (IPC) is 1.8, METE fails to satisfy.

5.5 Using High-Level Performance Targets

The settling time is the time in which the system output get close enough to the targets (for instance, 5% of their values)

So far we have assumed that the performance target accommodated by METE are in terms of IPCs. However, depending on the application domain, higher level performance metrics (like the number of transactions per second) may be specified to METE in a flexible manner. The only change necessary to incorporate any high-level metric is the inclusion of a *transducer* component that transforms an observable low-level metric like IPC to high-level metric like the number of transactions per second. Note that, such a conversion is necessary because the high-level metrics cannot be measured directly from hardware. However, it can be periodically input to the controllers by the OS or the application. The transducer itself can be designed to model the relationship between the high-level metric and the observable low-level metric. To demonstrate this, we use SPECJBB and use transactions per second as our high level QoS metric. First, in Figure 15(a), we show how our model captures the relationship between the specified high-level QoS and the IPC. We run this benchmark with applu on our multicore with the baseline configuration (given in Table 3). Figure 15(b) shows how METE can track the high-level performance target. Our observation from this plot is that METE can successfully track a high level metric such as transactions per second. Further, Figure 15(c) shows that performance goals of both of the co-runner applications are satisfied in this case.

5.6 Evaluation of the Resource Broker

If the cumulative resource demands of applications are greater than what the available system resources can provide (i.e., Expression (1) is not satisfied), the resource broker is triggered and it arbitrates between the resource demands from the over-demanding or *greedy* applications. As a case study, we evaluated the efficacy of the resource broker when QoS target set by the application mixes is 1.8 IPC which is impossible to satisfy with the available resources. Figure 16 shows the result of this study. We evaluated two policies for the resource broker: (1) *Policy 1* penalizes each application equally i.e. if the core demands from each application is 4 but there are only 6 cores available, then this policy penalizes *each* application by a core (2) *Policy 2* (our default policy) penalizes each application in proportion to their demands, i.e., it penalizes each application in proportion to its demand. We observe that, using Pol-

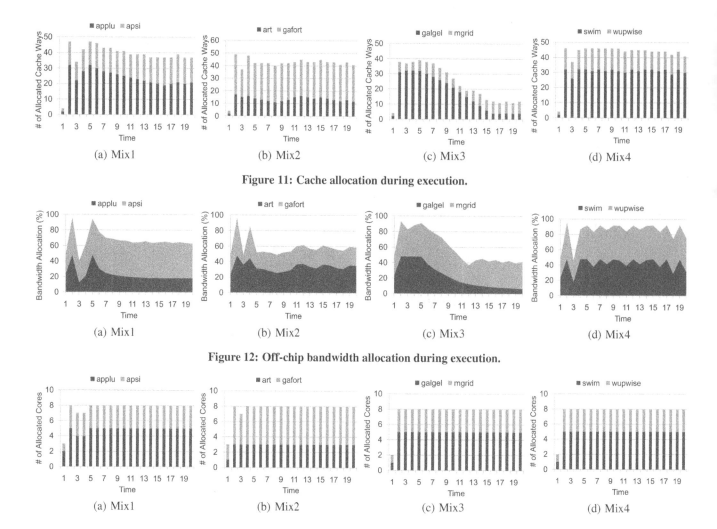

Figure 11: Cache allocation during execution.

Figure 12: Off-chip bandwidth allocation during execution.

Figure 13: Cores allocation during execution.

icy 1, none of the applications meets their specified target and penalizing each application equally can lead to undesirable behaviors since each resource has different implication for each application (see Figure 2). The overall *fair speedup*[4] achieved using Policy 2 is 4.9% better than Policy 1, implying that penalizing each application proportionately is better than a simplistic approach of penalizing them equally.

To further evaluate the efficacy of the resource broker, we evaluate a second case in which there exist resources in excess of what the applications specify. In Section 5.3, we evaluated a case where all performance targets where achieved but still few cache ways and some off-chip bandwidth were left un-allocated. Using our resource broker, such a scenario can be leveraged to provide further application level improvement. Figure 17(a) shows a case where the un-allocated system resources are partitioned equally among the applications, and Figure 17(b) shows the case where they are allocated based on policy mentioned in Section 4.5 (our default policy: resources are allocated based on their potential performance improvements with this additional resource allocation). In both cases we

find that the individual application performance improves but using our default policy, we observe that the FS metric is 4.8% better when compared to the scheme of redistributing the resources that oblivious of application behavior.

5.7 Sensitivity Study

Our goal in this section is to study sensitivity of our scheme to the values of some of the important parameters. The duration of the sampling periods (time intervals) is one of the important design parameters of our control scheme. To study the sensitivity of METE to this parameter, we performed experiments with the time intervals of 5-million and 20-million cycles. Figure 19 shows how well the measured IPC values for different applications track the specified IPC targets (as in Figure 10) when the time intervals are 5-million and 20-million cycles long. The results show that METE is not very sensitive to the execution intervals.

Smaller execution intervals can result in faster responses to the dynamic variations in application behaviors, and therefore, the magnitude of fluctuations may get reduced. In comparison, reducing the duration of time intervals, will increase the control scheme computation and enforcement overheads. Further, the intervals may not be long enough to see the impact of varying resource allocations in the next epoch that leads to inaccurate control decisions.

We next investigate the behavior of our scheme when the work-

---

[4]The Fair Speedup (FS) metric is defined as the harmonic mean of per application speedup with respect to the baseline equal resource share case [19] (i.e., $FS = N/\sum_{i=1}^{N}(IPC_{ai}(base)/IPC_{ai})$, where N is the number of applications). FS can be used to assess the overall improvement in IPC values across different schemes.

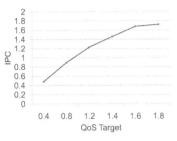

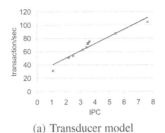

(a) Transducer model

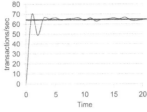

(b) Tracking transactions/sec metric

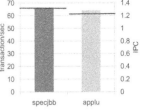

(c) Achieving two types of performance targets

Figure 14: QoS target sensitivity.

Figure 15: Transducer design for tracking high-level performance metrics.

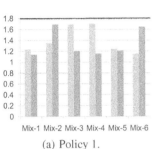

(a) Policy 1.

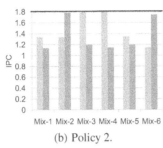

(b) Policy 2.

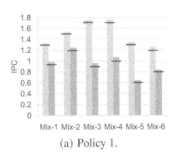

(a) Policy 1.

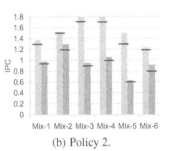

(b) Policy 2.

Figure 16: Resource Broker evaluation (lack of resources).

Figure 17: Resource Broker evaluation (use of excess resources).

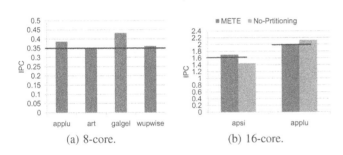

(a) 8-core.   (b) 16-core.

Figure 18: Results for 4 applications and 16-core simulations.

load size and core count are modified. Figure 18(a) plots both the IPC targets and the achieved IPC values when the workloads consists of 4 applications running together on 8 cores. We also tested METE on a multicore with 16 cores. As shown in Figure 18(b), the IPC targets are not achieved on the 16-core multicore when no partitioning scheme is used. By employing METE, these targets are satisfied through integrated partitioning of the available resources. As can be observed from these results, the specified targets are still achieved when we increase the number of running applications and cores and METE is scalable for more applications.

6. RELATED WORK

There has been extensive research on management and partitioning of the cache and off-chip memory bandwidth in multicores with the goal of improving the performance of hosted applications [5, 8, 9, 10, 11, 13, 14, 15]. Researchers have also explored various strategies to provide QoS in multicores [31, 32, 33, 34]. However, most prior studies have focused on the management of a single resource and have not considered multi-resource partitioning in multicores.

A multiple resource partitioning scheme called Symbiotic Resource Partitioning has been proposed in [18]. In this scheme, each of the shared cache space and off-chip memory bandwidth is partitioned dynamically based on the feedback from the partitioning of the other resource. The proposed scheme improves global per-

formance metrics and does not consider individual QoS requirements that each application may have. Bitirgan et al. [17] have proposed a framework to manage multiple shared resources on a multicore dynamically to achieve higher level performance objectives by using an artificial neural network based global resource manager that searches the design space of resource allocations by repeatedly querying the performance models followed by selecting the best candidate. Searching the allocation space is, in general, expensive and requires an efficient search mechanism.

Additionally, researchers have applied formal control theory in various domains of computer systems [36, 27] such as software services and performance [37, 38] and power management [20, 39]. A formal control theory approach is proposed in [40] to allocate shared virtualized resources to host application in order to meet QoS requirements.

In most of the prior schemes, the primary goal is to maximize the overall performance of a hosted workload. However, there may be applications that receive excess resources, whereas others might lack resources to achieve the specified targets. In contrast to this approach by prior works, in our work, the primary objective is to achieve the performance target of *each* individual application. Additionally, to our knowledge, ours is the first work that attempts to provide end-to-end QoS in multicore machines.

7. CONCLUDING REMARKS

In this paper, we propose a control theory centric scheme, called METE, to partition multiple shared resources in a multicore machine among concurrently-executing applications at runtime. In the current implementation of METE, we consider three types of shared resources: processing cores, shared cache space, and off-chip memory bandwidth. Assuming that each running application has a performance target to be satisfied, our main goal is to provide applications with sufficient resources to achieve the specified targets. For this, we propose a global resource broker for system wide resource management and a SIMO controller with an ARMA model for capturing the per-application demands. Our experimental results with various application workloads indicate that METE is able to partition the multi-level shared resources among co-running applications

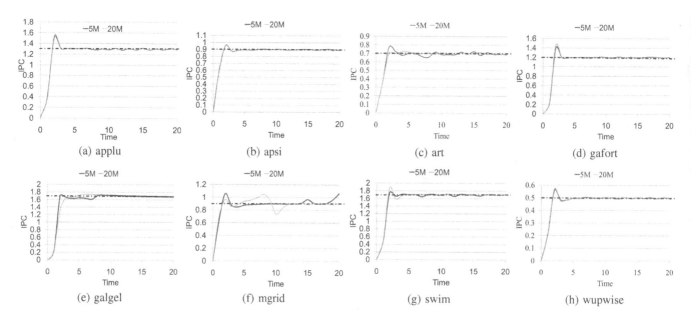

Figure 19: Sensitivity to execution interval.

in most cases, such that the specified QoS targets such as IPC and throughput are satisfied. In summary, our results make a strong case for using a feedback control based resource management scheme like METE for multicore architectures.

8. REFERENCES

[1] C. McNairy and R. Bhatia, "Montecito: A dual-core, dual-thread itanium processor," *IEEE Micro*, vol. 25, 2005.

[2] A. M. D. Inc, "AMD ATHLON processor technical brief," *Publication*, no. 22054, 2000.

[3] P. Kongetira, K. Aingaran, and K. Olukotun, "Niagara: A 32-way multithreaded SPARC processor," *IEEE Micro*. 2005.

[4] J. A. Kahle, et al, "Introduction to the CELL multiprocessor," *IBM J. Res. Dev.*, vol. 49, 2005.

[5] D. Chandra, et al, "Predicting Inter-Thread Cache Contention on a Chip Multi-Processor Architecture," in *HPCA*, 2005.

[6] J. Chang and G. S. Sohi, "Cooperative Cache Partitioning for Chip Multiprocessors," in *ICS*, 2007.

[7] L. R. Hsu, et al, "Communist, Utilitarian, and Capitalist Cache Policies on CMPs: Caches as a Shared Resource," in *PACT*, 2006.

[8] S. Kim, D. Chandra, and Y. Solihin, "Fair Cache Sharing and Partitioning in a Chip Multiprocessor Architecture," in *PACT*, 2004.

[9] B.-J. Ko, et al, "Scalable Service Differentiation in a Shared Storage Cache," in *ICDCS*, 2003.

[10] G. E. Suh, L. Rudolph, and S. Devadas, "Dynamic Partitioning of Shared Cache Memory," *J. Supercomput.*, vol.28, 2004.

[11] M. Hammoud, S. Cho, and R. Melhem, "Dynamic Cache Clustering for Chip Multiprocessors," in *SC*, 2009.

[12] E. Ipek, O. Mutlu, J. F. Martínez, and R. Caruana, "Self-optimizing memory controllers: A reinforcement learning approach," in *ISCA*, 2008.

[13] C. J. Lee, et al, "Prefetch-aware dram controllers," in *MICRO*, 2008.

[14] O. Mutlu and T. Moscibroda, "Stall-time fair memory access scheduling for chip multiprocessors," in *MICRO*, 2007.

[15] O. Mutlu and T. Moscibroda, "Parallelism-aware batch scheduling: Enhancing both performance and fairness of shared DRAM systems," in *ISCA*, 2008.

[16] K. J. Nesbit, et al, "Fair queuing memory systems," in *MICRO*, 2006.

[17] R. Bitirgen, E. Ipek, and J. F. Martinez, "Coordinated management of multiple interacting resources in chip multiprocessors: A machine learning approach," in *MICRO*, 2008.

[18] S. Srikantaiah and M. Kandemir, "SRP: Symbiotic resource partitioning of the memory hierarchy in CMPs." in *HiPEAC*, 2010.

[19] S. Srikantaiah, M. Kandemir, and Q. Wang, "Sharp control: controlled shared cache management in chip multiprocessors," in *MICRO*, 2009.

[20] Y. Wang, et al, "Temperature-constrained power control for chip multiprocessors with online model estimation," in *ISCA*, 2009.

[21] N. S. Nise, *Control Systems Engineering*. 1992.

[22] V. Bobal, et al, *Digital Self Tuning Controllers*. Springer, 2005.

[23] V. Aslot, et al, "SPECOMP: A new benchmark suite for measuring parallel computer performance," *IWOAT'01*, 2001.

[24] N. Rafique, W.-T. Lim, and M. Thottethodi, "Architectural Support for Operating System-Driven CMP Cache Management," in *PACT*, 2006.

[25] K. J. Nesbit, et al, "Fair Queuing Memory Systems," in *MICRO*, 2006.

[26] N. Rafique, W.-T. Lim, and M. Thottethodi, "Effective management of dram bandwidth in multicore processors," in *PACT*, 2007.

[27] J. L. Hellerstein, et al, *Feedback Control of Computing Systems*. John Wiley & Sons, 2004.

[28] K. J. Astrom and B. Wittenmark, *Adaptive Control*. Addison-Wesley Longman Publishing Co., Inc., 1994.

[29] "http://www.spec.org/jbb2000/."

[30] P. S. Magnusson, et al, "SIMICS: A full system simulation platform," *Computer*, vol. 35, no. 2, pp. 50–58, 2002.

[31] A. Herdrich, et al, "Rate-based QoS Techniques for Cache/Memory in CMP Platforms," in *SC*, 2009.

[32] R. Iyer, et al, "QoS Policies and Architecture for Cache/Memory in CMP Platforms," *SIGMETRICS Perform. Eval. Rev.*, 2007.

[33] R. Iyer, "CQoS: A Framework for Enabling QoS in Shared Caches of CMP Platforms," in *ICS*, 2004.

[34] F. Guo, et al, "From chaos to QoS: case studies in CMP resource management," *SIGARCH Comput. Archit. News*, 2007.

[35] X. Wang and M. Chen, "Cluster-level feedback power control for performance optimization," in *HPCA*, 2008.

[36] C. Karamanolis, M. Karlsson, and X. Zhu, "Designing controllable computer systems," in *HotOS*, 2005.

[37] T. F. Abdelzaher, et al, "Feedback performance control in software services," *IEEE Control Systems Magazine*, 2003.

[38] R. Zhang, et al, "Controlware: A middleware architecture for feedback control of software," in *ICDCS*, 2002.

[39] Q. Wu, et al, "Formal control techniques for power-performance management," *IEEE Micro*, 2005.

[40] P. Padala, et al, "Automated control of multiple virtualized resources," in *ECCS*, 2009.

Studying Inter-Core Data Reuse in Multicores*

Yuanrui Zhang, Mahmut Kandemir, and Taylan Yemliha
{yuazhang, kandemir}@cse.psu.edu, tyemliha@syr.edu
Pennsylvania State University & Syracuse University
University Park, PA 16802, USA

ABSTRACT

Most of existing research on emerging multicore machines focus on parallelism extraction and architectural level optimizations. While these optimizations are critical, complementary approaches such as data locality enhancement can also bring significant benefits. Most of the previous data locality optimization techniques have been proposed and evaluated in the context of single core architectures. While one can expect these optimizations to be useful for multicore machines as well, multicores present further opportunities due to shared on-chip caches most of them accommodate. In order to optimize data locality targeting multicore machines however, the first step is to understand data reuse characteristics of multithreaded applications and potential benefits shared caches can bring. Motivated by these observations, we make the following contributions in this paper. First, we give a definition for inter-core data reuse and quantify it on multicores using a set of ten multithreaded application programs. Second, we show that neither on-chip cache hierarchies of current multicore architectures nor state-of-the-art (single-core centric) code/data optimizations exploit available inter-core data reuse in multithreaded applications. Third, we demonstrate that exploiting all available inter-core reuse could boost overall application performance by around 21.3% on average, indicating that there is significant scope for optimization. However, we also show that trying to optimize for inter-core reuse aggressively without considering the impact of doing so on intra-core reuse can actually perform worse than optimizing for intra-core reuse alone. Finally, we present a novel, compiler-based data locality optimization strategy for multicores that balances both inter-core and intra-core reuse optimizations carefully to maximize benefits that can be extracted from shared caches. Our experiments with this strategy reveal that it is very effective in optimizing data locality in multicores.

*This work is supported in part by NSF grants #1017882, #0963839, CNS #0720645, CCF #0811687, and CCF #0702519, and a grant from Microsoft Corporation.

Categories and Subject Descriptors

D.3.4 [**Programming Languages**]: Processors—*compilers, optimization*

General Terms

Design, Performance, Experimentation, Algorithms

1. INTRODUCTION

Emerging multicore architectures offer a single processor package that contains two or more cores to enable parallel execution of multithreaded applications. These architectures are currently replacing traditional single-core machines that employ complex micro-architectures clocked at very high frequencies. All major chip vendors today have their multicore products on the market [1, 2, 3, 4] and trends indicate that the future multicores will have a large variety of on-chip configurations, in terms of the number of cores, on-chip cache topologies, and interconnect structures [5].

Unfortunately, in this multicore era, application developers can no longer rely on increasing clock speeds alone to speed up their sequential applications. Instead, they must be able to design and implement their applications to execute in a multithreaded environment. Clearly, the first step along this direction is to *parallelize* an application, i.e., creating a multithreaded version of it. While proper parallelization is critical to achieve good performance in emerging multicore architectures, this alone may *not* be sufficient for many applications. To gain a competitive advantage, application developers must also be able to exploit *on-chip cache hierarchies* of these new architectures. These hierarchies come in a variety of forms but most include some sort of shared component which can be accessed by two or more cores. Existence of shared last-level on-chip caches can play a very important role in application behavior [29, 11, 12, 46]. This is because missing in the last-level cache in a multicore architecture results in an off-chip memory access, which can be very costly from both performance and power consumption perspectives.

It needs to be noted that the performance of a multicore cache hierarchy is a function of both application characteristics and the underlying cache topology. As a result, it is of utmost importance to understand application characteristics regarding cache behavior and associate them with the cache topology information. Unfortunately, current state-of-the-art code analysis and optimization techniques for cache locality may not be sufficient in this context since they were developed in the context of single core machines which did not have the concept of shared caches. One of the significant impacts of shared caches is that they enable two cores/threads to share data using this cache space, which in turn brings up the concept of *inter-core data reuse*. This new reuse concept also brings with it the potential for a whole new set of optimization opportunities. Motivated by this observation, we make the following contributions in this work:

- We give a definition for inter-core data reuse and quantify it using a set of ten multithreaded application programs. Our results show that, while intra-core reuse distances are generally short, inter-core reuse distances tend to be much higher. Consequently, they may require/benefit from different optimization strategies than those available today. We further observe that both temporal and spatial inter-core reuses exhibit similar characteristics as far as reuse distances are concerned.

- We show that neither on-chip cache hierarchies of current multicore architectures nor state-of-the-art code/data optimizations exploit available inter-core data reuse in multithreaded applications. For example, while a three-layer on-chip cache hierarchy converts about 77.6% (51.8%) of available intra-core temporal (spatial) reuses into locality (hits in L2 or L3 levels), the same architecture is successful in converting only about 11.3% (4.1%) inter-core temporal (spatial) reuse into locality. Further, using a powerful set of data locality optimizations, we are able to convert only an additional 3.3% (3.2%) inter-core temporal (spatial) reuse into locality.

- We demonstrate that exploiting all available inter-core reuse could boost overall application performance by around 21.3% on average, indicating that there is significant scope for optimization. However, we also show that trying to optimize for inter-core reuse aggressively without considering the impact of doing so on intra-core reuse can actually perform worse than optimizing for intra-core reuse alone.

- Motivated by the observation in the previous item, we then present a novel, compiler-based data locality optimization strategy for multicores that *balances* both inter-core and intra-core reuse optimizations. Specifically, our approach implements an integrated mapping and scheduling strategy that maximizes both "vertical" and "horizontal" data reuses considering the on-chip cache hierarchy of the target architecture. The key component of this strategy is an intelligent weight assignment scheme that considers potential data reuses among different computation blocks. Our results collected using ten applications on an Intel multicore machine indicate that this new approach brings about 23.1% and 23.7% improvements in L2 and L3 cache hits, respectively, resulting in an average performance (execution time) improvement of 18.8%. Further, we study in detail several parameters used in our optimization strategy, and show that the proposed strategy brings consistent benefits under the different values of major experimental parameters.

The rest of this paper is organized as follows. The next section discusses on-chip cache behavior of multicores and Section 3 explains the concepts of data reuse, reuse distances and data locality, focusing in particular on multicore specific aspects. Section 4 describes our target architectures and the application programs used for quantifying intra-core and inter-core data reuses. Section 5 quantifies inter-core and intra-core data reuses in our original applications. Next, Section 6 gives the evaluation of conventional cache manage-

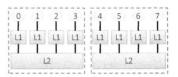

Figure 1: Harpertown architecture.

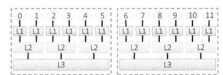

Figure 2: Dunnington architecture.

ment and state-of-the-art data locality optimizations, Section 7 discusses the potential and cost of inter-core reuse optimization, and Section 8 presents our compiler-based data locality optimization strategy that carefully balances inter-core and intra-core data reuses. Section 9 discusses the data locality improvements brought by our approach. Finally, Section 10 and Section 11 give related work and concluding remarks, respectively.

2. MULTICORE CACHE BEHAVIOR

In a multicore machine, two or more cores are integrated into a single circuit die. One of the distinguishing characteristics of multicore machines is their adoption of *on-chip caches*. These caches provide fast access to frequently-used data and thus help to reduce execution latencies. Many commercial multicore machines in the market today (e.g., [1, 3, 5]) employ *shared* on-chip caches, where a number of cores can access the same on-chip cache component. This cache space sharing, however, can be *constructive* or *destructive* [14]. In the former case, cores share data that reside in the same cache line (block) in a very efficient manner using this shared space. In the latter case, two cores can displace each other's data from the shared cache space, hurting application performance. Clearly, whether an execution experiences constructive sharing or destructive interferences depends on what threads are run on cores, what data they access, and what their data access/sharing patterns are.

Figures 1 and 2 show the high-level views of two commercial multicore architectures. Each of these machines has two sockets (delimited by dashed boxes in the figures). One of these machines, Intel Harpertown [22], has a two-level on-chip cache hierarchy (L1 and L2), and the other one, Intel Dunnington [21], has three levels of on-chip caches (L1, L2 and L3). In each of these multicore machines, performance of the last-level cache (L2 in Harpertown and L3 in Dunnington) is very important since a miss in this cache can be very costly (about 100 nsec in Harpertown and about 50 nsec in Dunnington). Consequently, one of the goals in mapping an application to a multicore architecture is to maximize the performance of the last-level cache.

One of the ways of improving cache performance, i.e., reducing destructive interferences while improving chances for constructive sharing is to reduce the distance (in terms of execution cycles) to shared data. This distance, called *reuse distance* and discussed in detail in the next section, is a critical metric to quantify for both the data accessed by a core exclusively and the data accessed (shared) by multiple cores. Note that reducing reuse distances minimizes intervening data accesses, thereby lowering chances for destructive interferences (as there are fewer potential candidates that can displace the data to be reused from the shared cache space) and increasing chances for constructive sharing (as we can catch the reused data in the shared cache space with a higher probability).

3. DATA REUSE, REUSE DISTANCES, AND DATA LOCALITY

In this paper, we define "temporal reuse" as the reuse of a previously accessed data element. On the other hand, "spatial reuse" can be defined as the access to a data element which falls into the same cache block boundary as a previously accessed data element. Note that, based on these definitions, temporal reuse can be considered as a special case of spatial reuse. The important point to emphasize is that the existence of a reuse does not tell much about the performance of the associated data reference. This latter characteristic is captured through the concept of "locality". More specifically, if, at the time of the reuse, the reused item is caught in the cache (as opposed to missing in the cache and being accessed from the main memory), we say that the reuse has been *converted* into locality.

Clearly, the success of an execution is directly related to the amount of data reuse that can be converted into locality. This conversion in turn is a function of both architectural parameters such as cache capacities, line (block) sizes, and associativities as well as a program characteristic called the "reuse distance". Specifically, shorter the reuse distance, higher the chances that the associated reuse will be exploited in the cache space. Therefore, one of the main goals of many previously-proposed code and data optimizations can be summarized as reducing the reuse distances.

As stated above, in a multicore architecture, on-chip caches can be shared across different cores, and consequently, one can think of two types of data reuses: *intra-core reuse* and *inter-core reuse*.[1] As illustrated in Figure 3, an intra-core reuse takes place if two successive accesses to a data element/block are from the same core. In contrast, an inter-core reuse is said to occur if two successive accesses to a data element/block are from different cores. It needs to be noted that while the concept of intra-core reuse is common to both single core and multicore machines, the concept of inter-core reuse is unique to multicore machines. Irrespective of whether we talk about intra-core or inter-core reuse however, reducing the reuse distances would be beneficial as far as cache performance is concerned because of the reasons explained earlier in Section 2.

4. TARGET ARCHITECTURES AND APPLICATION PROGRAMS

Most of our experiments in this paper have been conducted using the Intel Dunnington architecture, which is shown in Figure 2. We also report a set of results from another Intel architecture (Harpertown, shown in Figure 1) to demonstrate that our proposed scheme works well with different architectures. Table 1 gives the important characteristics of these two commercial architectures. The application programs used in this work are from the SPECOMP

---

[1]Since in our analysis in this paper, we assume one thread per core, we can use terms "intra-thread reuse" and "inter-thread reuse" in places of "intra-core reuse" and "inter-core reuse", respectively.

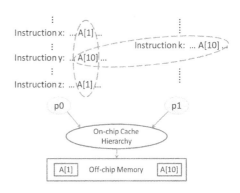

Figure 3: An example of inter-core and intra-core data reuses with respect to two array elements. There is an intra-core reuse of $A[1]$ between instructions x and z executed on core p0, and an inter-core reuse of $A[10]$ between instructions y and k, which are executed on cores p0 and p1, respectively.

	Harpertown	Dunnington
Number of Cores	8 cores (2 sockets)	12 cores (2 sockets)
Clock Frequency	3.20GHz	2.40GHz
L1 Cache	32KB, 8-way	32KB, 8-way
	64-byte line size	64-byte line size
	3 cycle latency	4 cycle latency
L2 Cache	6MB, 24-way	3MB, 12-way
	64-byte line size	64-byte line size
	15 cycle latency	10 cycle latency
L3 Cache	-	12MB, 16-way
		64-byte line size
		40 cycle latency
Off-Chip Latency	~100 ns	~50 ns

Table 1: Important parameters for our two Intel multicore machines.

benchmark suite [8]. We used all the benchmarks in this suite except wupwise which we could not compile in our multicore machines using the native compilers. The cache hit/miss statistics of these programs along with the total amount of data they manipulate are given in Table 2. All the reuse distance results presented in this work are collected using Simics-GEMS framework [34], which provides accurate timing models for multicore simulation. Specifically, using this platform, we simulated the configuration of Dunnington machine. The cache hit/miss statistics and execution time results on the other hand are collected using real execution on commercial machines (Dunnington and Harpertown).

5. QUANTIFYING INTRA-CORE AND INTER-CORE DATA REUSES

Our first set of results quantify the intra-core and inter-core reuses as well as temporal and spatial reuses in our applications and are presented in Figure 4. One can make two important observations from these results. First, most of data reuse is intra-core, which can be attributed to the fact that most of these applications have been parallelized such that inter-core data sharing is minimized to the maximum extent possible. An exception to this rule is fma3d, where inter-core reuse dominates. Our second observation is that, with the exception of equake, spatial reuse dominates the spectrum in both intra-core and inter-core reuses. This is particularly true in inter-core reuses as spatial reuses account for 82.2% of all inter-core reuses, whereas the corresponding figure in the case of intra-core reuses is about

Benchmark	Description	Data Set Size (MB)	Harpertown Miss Rates [%]		Dunnington Miss Rates [%]		
			L1	L2	L1	L2	L3
gafort	Genetic algorithm	28.6	3.9	37.4	2.9	41.0	31.1
swim	Shallow water modeling	20.5	3.1	27.7	4.4	29.0	23.6
mgrid	Multigrid solver in 3D potential field	18.6	6.6	49.7	7.2	44.2	39.6
applu	Parabolic/elliptic partial differential equations	24.3	5.1	52.8	5.3	55.3	43.6
galgel	Fluid dynamics: analysis of oscillatory instability	61.2	1.9	36.3	2.4	39.7	33.5
equake	Finite element simulation; earthquake modeling	47.4	8.1	32.9	7.7	38.2	29.3
apsi	Temperature, wind, velocity and distribution of pollutants	29.9	8.7	41.5	3.9	46.8	35.7
fma3d	Finite element crash simulation	18.2	4.1	56.3	6.8	40.1	41.1
art	Neural network simulation; adaptive resonance theory	26.1	6.7	38.9	7.3	47.7	39.4
ammp	Computational chemistry	36.1	4.1	48.3	8.7	46.0	46.3

Table 2: Benchmarks used in our study.

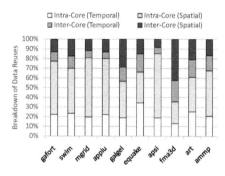

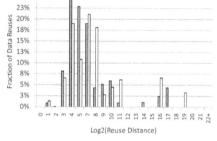

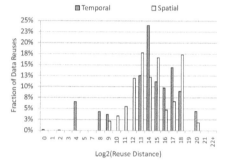

Figure 4: The breakdown of data reuses in our ten applications.

Figure 5: The distribution of intra-core reuse distances.

Figure 6: The distribution of inter-core reuse distances.

67.3%. This result means that, different cores mostly share cache blocks (lines) rather than individual data elements.

While the breakdown of data reuses into intra-core and inter-core components is clearly important, as discussed earlier, one of the main factors which plays an important role in determining whether a reuse would be converted into locality or not is the *reuse distance*. Figures 5 and 6 plot the distribution of reuse distances in our application programs for intra-core reuses and inter-core reuses separately. Note that, each graph represents *average statistics* over all the ten application programs we have. The x-axis represents the reuse distance in *log2* (of execution cycles) between references to the same data block, and the y-axis gives the fraction of the reuses. Maybe the most important observation from these results is that, *while intra-core reuse distances are generally short, inter-core reuse distances are much higher*. This result, which holds true in the case of both temporal and spatial reuses, is important and indicates that, when two different cores reuse the same data element or block, they do not reuse it within a short period of time. For example, about 85% and 98% of the temporal and spatial inter-core reuses, respectively, have a reuse distance of 1024 cycles or more, which are much higher than the corresponding percentage values (16% and 21%) in the case of intra-core data reuse.

These differences in reuse distance distributions across the intra-core and inter-core reuses can also be interpreted as an indication that we probably need different strategies for optimizing (taking advantage of) intra-core and inter-core reuses. For example, while a small increase in cache capacity can help us convert most of intra-core reuses into locality, to do the same with inter-core reuses would require a much larger increase in cache capacity.

Before we move to our detailed locality analysis, let us first discuss whether these intra-core and inter-core reuses belong to self or group reuses. In the context of this paper,

if two instructions that involve in a reuse are the same, the resulting reuse is termed as the "self-reuse", i.e., two different instances of the same static instruction touches the same data (temporal) or cache block (spatial); if they are different, they are called "group-reuse". The results presented in Figure 7 indicate that most of the intra-core reuses are actually self-reuses. It needs to be noted that all inter-core reuses are (by definition) group-reuses.

6. EVALUATION OF MULTI-LAYER CACHE HIERARCHY AND STATE-OF-THE-ART DATA LOCALITY OPTIMIZATIONS

Our goal in this section is two-fold. First, we want to measure the capability of the on-chip cache architecture in Dunnington in converting intra-core and inter-core data reuses into locality (hits in L2 and L3 caches). Second, we want to evaluate a set of well-known data locality optimization strategies originally developed in the context of single core machines with cache hierarchies, and quantify their success in converting intra-core and inter-core reuses into locality. Table 3 lists the set of optimizations considered in this work. The second column of this table gives a brief description of each optimization whereas the last column indicates the specific implementation employed in selecting the values of the important parameters used in the corresponding optimization. For example, in tiling, we used the strategy explained in [18] to select the tile sizes (also called blocking factors).

The y-axis in Figure 8 shows the fraction of data reuse that has been converted into locality (i.e., the fraction of the reused data elements/blocks that are caught in the cache at the time of their reuses). Note that we present these results for L2 and L3 caches separately. In this graph, the first group of bars (marked as "original") gives the results when original codes are used. The remaining groups correspond to the results obtained when using different data locality op-

Optimization	Brief Description	Reference
Linear	A general optimization strategy that represents a loop transformation using a linear matrix. The optimizations included are loop permutation, loop skewing and loop reversal.	[49]
Loop Scaling	Linear transformations augmented with loop scaling.	[32]
Tiling	A restructuring strategy that partitions a loop's iteration space into smaller chunks or blocks, so as to help ensure that data used in the loop remain in the cache until the reuse takes place.	[18]
Data Layout	Changing the memory layout of data (e.g., converting from row-major to column-major) to maximize spatial reuse.	[26]
Combined	This option implements all of the optimizations listed above.	

Table 3: The set of single-core centric data locality optimizations we evaluated on our multicore machine.

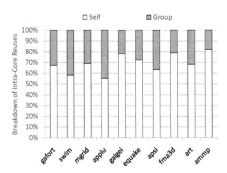
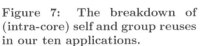

Figure 7: The breakdown of (intra-core) self and group reuses in our ten applications.

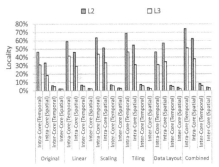

Figure 8: The fraction of data reuse converted into locality in L2 and L3 caches.

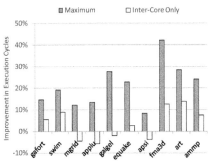

Figure 9: Ideal and practical application performance improvement by exploiting inter-core reuses.

timizations listed in Table 3. One can see from these results that, while these optimizations are effective in converting a majority of intra-core data reuse into locality, the same cannot be said for the inter-core data reuse. In fact, when considering all inter-core spatial reuses (i.e., all reuse distances), only 4.1% and 3.2% of them are converted into L2 and L3 hits, respectively, even when activating all these locality optimizations together. These numbers are much lower compared to 62.2% and 38% in the intra-core spatial reuse case when the same set of locality optimizations is used. Based on these results, we can conclude that the on-chip cache hierarchy of the Intel Dunnington machine (see Figure 2) fails to take advantage of inter-core data reuses (due to the high reuse distances experienced by data accesses). Further, even a state-of-the-art locality optimization suite is not successful in converting inter-core reuses into cache hits in L2 or L3. These observations certainly call for novel strategies to take advantage of inter-core reuses. However, at this point, there are two issues that need to be answered. First, it is not clear how much benefit optimizing for inter-core reuse would bring. Second and maybe more importantly, it is not clear how one can optimize for inter-core reuse without distorting intra-core reuse. Both these questions are addressed in the rest of this paper.

7. POTENTIAL AND COST OF INTER-CORE REUSE OPTIMIZATION

We start our discussion with the potential impact of improving inter-core data reuse. The first bar for each application in Figure 9 gives the performance improvement that can be achieved using a hypothetical scheme which removes all inter-core misses (both temporal and spatial) without affecting any hit coming from exploiting intra-core reuse. In these experiments, our baseline is a locality-optimized version of the applications (using the version called "Combined" which is explained in the previous section). We see from

these results that the maximum savings that could be obtained from exploiting inter-core reuse without harming any intra-core reuse is about 21.3% on average.

However, it needs to be noted that these results represent the maximum possible savings which may not be achieved in reality by a practical scheme. To see the difference between the two, we next present results from a scheme that tries to exploit inter-core data reuse without considering the impact of doing so on intra-core reuse. The basic idea behind this scheme is to ensure that inter-core reuses are exploited in the shared cache space even if doing so results in extra misses due to not exploiting intra-core data reuse fully. Specifically, this scheme first runs an instrumented version of the application and identifies data elements shared by different subsets of cores. Next, each load instruction in the code is tagged to indicate whether it accesses mostly core private data or data shared across cores. More specifically, we tag a load instruction as "shared" if at least 70% (a tunable parameter)[2] of the references it makes are to shared data. After that, the application is executed again. This time however, any data brought by a shared load into any of the shared caches in the system is prevented from being displaced by the access made by a non-shared (normal) load (this is implemented by disabling the cache access by the normal loads). In a sense, under this scheme, the shared data elements are prioritized over the private ones as far as shared caches are concerned. Our goal in performing experiments with this scheme is to measure the potential impact (in terms of both benefits and costs) of exploiting inter-core reuse aggressively.

The second bar for each application in Figure 9 gives the execution time improvement under this strategy. Our observation is that, this approach, which optimizes for inter-core data reuse aggressively, does not perform very well, resulting in an average execution time improvement of 4.4%. More importantly, this approach degrades the performance of four

---

[2]We also performed experiments with other ratios as well, and found that 70% generates better results than others.

applications (mgrid, applu, galgel, and apsi) as compared to the baseline version. Based on these results, we can conclude that an aggressive inter-core reuse centric strategy may not be the best option as far as overall application performance is concerned. Motivated by this, in the next section, we discuss a novel data locality optimization strategy that *balances* inter-core and intra-core reuse optimizations in an attempt to maximize shared cache performance and minimize application execution time.

8. BALANCING INTER-CORE AND INTRA-CORE DATA REUSES

In this section, we present and evaluate a compiler-directed strategy that considers both inter-core and intra-core data reuses in a balanced fashion. We used the SUIF compiler [48] from University of Stanford (as a source-to-source translator) to implement this compiler-based strategy. The operation of our compiler-based strategy can be summarized as follows. First, arrays accessed by the application are divided into equal-sized "data blocks" and each block is given a unique id. Second, for each core, the set of loop iterations assigned to it are divided into equal-sized "computation blocks". In this work, computation block is the unit for scheduling, i.e., we assign computation blocks to cores and schedule (in each core) one computation block at a time. Note that, computation blocks can come from different loop nests, and we capture data dependences and data sharing between them using two graph structures maintained by our compiler (these structures will be explained later in the paper). The key component of our strategy is the scheme we adopt to schedule computation blocks in both time (schedule slots) and space (cores). To select the computation block to be scheduled in a given slot and core, we consider data reuse between each of the potential candidates and a subset (explained below) of already scheduled computation blocks.

8.1 Integrated Mapping and Scheduling

Our goal is to fill in the entries of a "scheduling table", the high level structure of which is shown in Figure 10. An entry (x, y) in this scheduling table contains (when the scheduling is done) the id of the computation block scheduled at core x in slot y. One can think of two types of data reuses regarding this scheduling table. First, for a given core, iteration blocks scheduled at successive slots can have data reuse between them. Second, for a given slot, the iteration blocks scheduled at different cores can have data reuse among them. Clearly, to maximize application performance, data reuses in both these directions should be maximized to the greatest extent allowed by data dependences. In the rest of our discussion, we refer to these two types of reuse as "vertical reuse" and "horizontal reuse". It is important to note that exploiting vertical reuse helps to improve cache behavior at all levels of an on-chip cache hierarchy. In comparison, optimizing for horizontal reuse helps to improve the performance of shared caches. This is because when the computation blocks scheduled at different cores in the same slot have high data reuse, the data brought by one of the cores to a shared cache would most probably be reused by one or more other cores while they are still in the cache (due to short reuse distance).

Let $\Lambda_{i,t}$ be the computation block scheduled at core i in slot t, and $\Delta_{i,t}$ be the set of data blocks accessed by $\Lambda_{i,t}$.

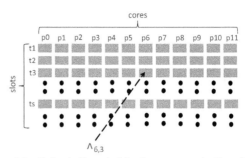

Figure 10: Scheduling table for computation blocks.

Based on these definitions, we can define our constraints for vertical and horizontal reuses as follows:

- *Vertical Constraint*
  $\forall i$: maximize $| \Delta_{i,t} \cap \Delta_{i,t-1} |$,[3] and
- *Horizontal Constraint*
  $\forall j$: maximize $| \Delta_{i,t} \cap \Delta_{j,t} |$ where $j \neq i$.

Considering the scheduling table, these constraints can be captured using a single expression:

$$Maximize\{\sum_{0 \leq j \leq (p-1)} \sum_{(t-K) \leq t_k < t} \pi_{j,t_k} \mid \Delta_{i,t} \cap \Delta_{j,t_k} \mid + \sum_{0 \leq j \leq (i-1)} \pi_{j,t} \mid \Delta_{i,t} \cap \Delta_{j,t} \mid\},$$

where π_s are coefficients that represent the weights for different reuses, i.e., how important a given reuse with respect to $\Lambda_{i,t}$. Note that this expression is for core i and schedule slot t. That is, we want to select the computation block to schedule at core i in slot t, and want to make this selection such that vertical and horizontal reuses could be maximized. There are several important observations regarding this expression. First, when we evaluate this expression, all the scheduling decisions for all cores in steps 1 through $t-1$ are assumed to have already been made. Further, the scheduling decisions for cores from 0 to $i-1$ at step t are also assumed to have been made.[4] As an example, Figure 11 illustrates the situation when we are about to schedule a computation block in core 7 at step 7. Second, the first part (the left operation of the addition operator) is there to capture reuses with respect to the schedule steps before t, whereas the second part is there to capture reuses with respect to the step t. Third, K represents how far we should go in considering the reuse (see Figure 11), that is, what is the maximum distance between two slots across which a data reuse can be considered? It is important to emphasize that we evaluate all possible candidates for a given schedule slot using the expression above, and select the one which maximizes its value. As an example, if $K = 1$, for $\Lambda_{7,7}$, the expression to maximize is:
$\pi_{0,6} \mid \Delta_{7,7} \cap \Delta_{0,6} \mid + \pi_{1,6} \mid \Delta_{7,7} \cap \Delta_{1,6} \mid + \pi_{2,6} \mid \Delta_{7,7} \cap \Delta_{2,6} \mid + \pi_{3,6} \mid \Delta_{7,7} \cap \Delta_{3,6} \mid + \pi_{4,6} \mid \Delta_{7,7} \cap \Delta_{4,6} \mid + \pi_{5,6} \mid \Delta_{7,7} \cap \Delta_{5,6} \mid + \pi_{6,6} \mid \Delta_{7,7} \cap \Delta_{6,6} \mid + \pi_{7,6} \mid \Delta_{7,7} \cap \Delta_{7,6} \mid + \pi_{8,6} \mid \Delta_{7,7} \cap \Delta_{8,6} \mid + \pi_{9,6} \mid \Delta_{7,7} \cap \Delta_{9,6} \mid + \pi_{10,6} \mid \Delta_{7,7} \cap \Delta_{10,6} \mid + \pi_{11,6} \mid \Delta_{7,7} \cap \Delta_{11,6} \mid + \pi_{0,7} \mid \Delta_{7,7} \cap \Delta_{0,7} \mid + \pi_{1,7} \mid \Delta_{7,7} \cap \Delta_{1,7} \mid + \pi_{2,7} \mid \Delta_{7,7} \cap \Delta_{2,7} \mid + \pi_{3,7} \mid \Delta_{7,7} \cap \Delta_{3,7} \mid + \pi_{4,7} \mid \Delta_{7,7} \cap \Delta_{4,7} \mid + \pi_{5,7} \mid \Delta_{7,7} \cap \Delta_{5,7} \mid + \pi_{6,7} \mid \Delta_{7,7} \cap \Delta_{6,7} \mid$.

There are two parameters one can study in the expression above: K and π. Clearly, a higher value of K indicates that we are considering reuses that span a larger distance (in time). In contrast, a smaller value means we only care

---

[3] $| \quad |$ denotes set cardinality and represents the number of common data blocks accessed by two computation blocks.
[4] The cores are ordered starting from 0 given the target multicore architecture.

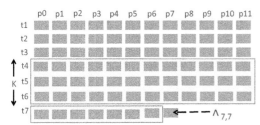

Figure 11: The computation blocks to be considered (indicated by the bounded rectangles) when scheduling computation block $\Lambda_{7,7}$.

for data reuses in a close proximity in time. On the other hand, weights (π values) indicate (for a given value of K) how important the different reuses are. One can adopt different strategies in assigning values to these weights, however, in principle, the closer reuses (in terms of both time and relative core locations) should have higher weights. In our work, in assigning these weights, we take into account the underlying on-chip cache topology of the target multicore architecture.

More specifically, we represent the on-chip cache hierarchy of the target multicore architecture using a *tree structure*, where the root denotes a shared last-level cache, the internal nodes are the caches that are connected to this last-level cache, and the leaves correspond to the cores. If there are more than one last-level cache, we have a disjoint union of trees, or equivalently, a forest. To precisely describe each core's location in the on-chip cache hierarchy, we assign ids to the caches at each level, and associate their corresponding internal nodes in the tree/forest structure with these ids, as illustrated in the example given in Figure 12, where there is only one shared last-level cache with id 0 (L3_0). Based on this, we employ a tuple of the form $< N_1, N_2, \cdots, N_{M-1}, N_M >$ to denote each path from the root to a leaf in an M-level tree, where N_i is the id of a node (cache or core) on that path. If we ignore the core id N_M, the *partial path* $< N_1, N_2, \cdots, N_{M-1} >$ provides us with a core's cache utilization information, i.e., which cache(s) a core accesses. For instance, in Figure 12, the partial paths for cores 0 and 1 are both $<0, 0, 0>$, whereas the partial paths for cores 2 and 3 are $<0, 0, 1>$. Note that, by comparing the partial paths of two cores, we can obtain the cache sharing information, i.e., the number of caches two cores both connect to. We define this as the *Core Sharing Degree* (CSD), and the following equation gives its mathematical formulation, where $\mathcal{P}_x$ represents the set of cache ids on the partial path for core x:

$$CSD(i,j) = | \mathcal{P}_i \cap \mathcal{P}_j |.$$

Continuing with Figure 12, it can be observed that the CSD of cores 0 and 1 is 3, whereas CSD(0, 2) equals to 2. Note that, if two cores reside in two different last-level cache hierarchies (or trees), their CSD will be 0.

Note further that, CSD gives us the weight information for the horizontal reuse between two computation blocks scheduled on different cores at any given slot. To capture the weight for the vertical reuse between two computation blocks scheduled in successive slots or two different slots within K distance, we define *Time (Slots) Sharing Degree* (TSD) as

$$TSD(t, t_k) = 1 - (t - t_k)/(K+1),$$

where t is the time slot under schedule, and t_k is a time

(a) An example multicore architecture

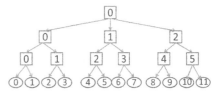

(b) The corresponding architecture tree

Figure 12: An example multicore architecture and its corresponding architecture tree.

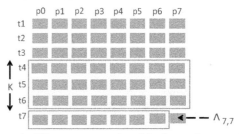

Figure 13: The computation blocks to be considered (indicated by the bounded rectangles) when scheduling computation block $\Lambda_{7,7}$, assuming the Harpertown architecture.

slot between t and $t - K$. Supposing $K = 3$, according to this definition, TSD(t, t) is 1, TSD($t, t-1$) is 0.75, TSD($t, t-2$) is 0.5, and TSD($t, t-3$) is 0.25. TSD reflects the fact that, closer the two computation blocks with data reuse are scheduled, higher the chance with which their data reuse can be converted into data locality in the cache, thanks to the shorter reuse distance. For any time slot t_k that is beyond the distance K of t, TSD(t, t_k) equals to 0, which means we do not consider the reuse between two computation blocks if the distance of their schedule slots is larger than K.

Based on these definitions, we now determine the weights (π values) according to the underlying on-chip cache topology for computation block $\Lambda_{i,t}$ at core i in slot t. Basically, we couple TSD and CSD to form the weights. In particular, the weight π_{j,t_k} for item $| \Delta_{i,t} \cap \Delta_{j,t_k} |$ in the target expression to be optimized is calculated as:

$$TSD(t, t_k) \times CSD(i, j).$$

Table 4 shows the weight assignment for computation block $\Lambda_{7,7}$ in Figure 11 using this strategy, assuming that the twelve cores are connected to a shared cache as depicted in Figure 12. Note that, with respect to the target computation block $\Lambda_{7,7}$, the computation blocks scheduled on cores 6 and 7 have higher data reuse weights than others, since their data will go through exactly the same set of caches at different levels. On the other hand, the computation blocks scheduled in slots t_6 and t_7 have higher data reuse weights than others, since the data touched by those recent computation blocks have a higher chance to be found in cache. In general, the weight values decrease as cores have less sharing with the target core i or as time (schedule) slots get further away from the target slot t. In addition, from Ta-

Weights	p0	p1	p2	p3	p4	p5	p6	p7	p8	p9	p10	p11
t_4	0.25	0.25	0.25	0.25	0.5	0.5	0.75	0.75	0.25	0.25	0.25	0.25
t_5	0.5	0.5	0.5	0.5	1	1	1.5	1.5	0.5	0.5	0.5	0.5
t_6	0.75	0.75	0.75	0.75	1.5	1.5	2.25	2.25	0.75	0.75	0.75	0.75
t_7	1	1	1	1	2	2	3	N/A	N/A	N/A	N/A	N/A

Table 4: The weight assignments for computation blocks under consideration when scheduling computation block $\Lambda_{7,7}$ in Figure 11 ($K = 3$).

Weights	p0	p1	p2	p3	p4	p5	p6	p7
t_4	0	0	0	0	0.25	0.25	0.25	0.5
t_5	0	0	0	0	0.5	0.5	0.5	1
t_6	0	0	0	0	0.75	0.75	0.75	1.5
t_7	0	0	0	0	1	1	1	N/A

Table 5: The weight assignments for computation blocks under consideration when scheduling computation block $\Lambda_{7,7}$ in Figure 13 ($K = 3$).

Input: Number of cores, N; Set of all computation blocks $\mathcal{C}$ to be scheduled; Computation block dependence graph, $CBDG(V,E)$; Distance, K; Id set of the partial path for each core x, $\mathcal{P}_x$.
Output: Computation blocks scheduled on each core.

```
 1: t = 1;
 2: while C != Empty do
 3:    S_t = FindSchedulableBlocks(t);
 4:    while S_t != Empty do
 5:       for i = 1 to i = N do
 6:          if S_t == Empty then
 7:             Λ_i,t = −1; //indicate synchronization
 8:             continue;
 9:          end if
10:          A = 0; //Record max data reuse between two
                     computation blocks
11:          B = 0; //Record the computation block selected
12:          for each computation block s in S_t do
13:             M = 0; //Record data reuse
14:             if t − K < 0 then
15:                t' = 0;
16:             else
17:                t' = t − K;
18:             end if
19:             for j = 0 to j = N − 1 do
20:                for t_k = t' to t_k = t do
21:                   if t_k == t and j >= i then
22:                      continue;
23:                   end if
24:                   π_{j,t_k} = TSD(t, t_k) × CSD(i, j);
25:                   M += π_{j,t_k} × | Δ_s ∩ Δ_{j,t_k} |;
26:                end for
27:             end for
28:             if M > A then
29:                A = M;
30:                B = s;
31:             end if
32:          end for
33:          Λ_i,t = B;
34:          S_t = S_t − B;
35:       end for
36:       t++;
37:    end while
38:    C = C − S_t;
39: end while
```

Figure 14: Pseudo-code of our mapping and scheduling algorithm.

ble 4, we can see that, intra-core reuses have high weights (e.g., weights on core 7), which is reasonable, since they are usually very short. As another example, Table 5 lists the weight assignments for computation blocks under consideration when scheduling computation block $\Lambda_{7,7}$ in Figure 13, assuming that the Harpertown architecture depicted in Figure 1 is used.

Next, we discuss the selection of parameter K. To choose a suitable value for K, we first construct an auxiliary data structure called the *Sharing Graph*. In this graph, each node corresponds to a computation block and there is an edge between two nodes if the corresponding computation blocks share data between them. After that, we set the value of K to the average *connectivity degree* in the graph, i.e., the average number of edges of a node. Clearly, this is a heuristic strategy. The motivation behind this is that, there exists a possible situation where all the neighboring nodes of a particular node (computation block) are scheduled at successive schedule slots on the same core right before this node. Note that, one can also set K to the highest connectivity degree in this graph, however, a larger K value will introduce more calculations and result in longer time when running our algorithm.

8.2 Our Algorithm and Implementation

Figure 14 gives a sketch of our algorithm that exploits both vertical and horizontal reuses to the maximum extent allowed by data dependences. With dependences, the set of computation blocks that can be scheduled at a given time in a given core is restricted. To capture dependences among computation blocks, we construct a *Computation Block Dependence Graph CBDG(V,E)*, where each node in the graph denotes a computation block and each edge represents a data dependence between two computation blocks. To determine $\Lambda_{i,t}$, we obtain the set of computation blocks that can be scheduled at slot t by calling a function named FindSchedulableBlocks(t). For each of the blocks, we then calculate its total data reuse with neighboring computation blocks in both vertical and horizontal directions within the region delimited by the K parameter (see lines 19-26 in Figure 14), and select the one that maximizes this value. If no computation block can be scheduled at a given slot due to data dependences, we put -1 into the corresponding entry of the scheduling table, to indicate that a synchronization across all the cores is needed at that point.

We want to emphasize that, although different computation blocks may have different execution times, since we have global synchronizations across the cores during application execution due to data dependences, even if the blocks with reuse are not processed exactly in the same scheduled slots as expected, the overall execution is close to our order captured in the scheduling table. In other words, one can expect significant benefits from our strategy even though cores do not execute in a lock-step fashion.

Our strategy for selecting the computation block size can

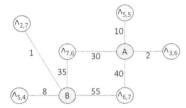

Figure 15: Sharing graph for two candidate computation blocks A and B.

Figure 19: Graphical illustration of Scheme-I through Scheme-V. Circles denote the target slots under consideration. In each figure, the shaded part indicates the region (slots) for which we have non-zero weights.

be summarized as follows. We start by assuming that the computation block size is S, an unknown parameter. After that, considering all references in the innermost loop position, we find an analytical expression that gives the total amount of data accessed by all the references (denoted by T). Then, we determine the value of S such that the resulting T is smaller than the L1 cache capacity of the target architecture. We found that, as long as this computation block size selection strategy is used, data block size does not matter too much, since the data accessed by inner loops will be captured in the cache. Note also that, both the computation block size parameter and the K parameter are inputs to our algorithm given in Figure 14.

8.3 Example

We now go over an example to illustrate the scheduling step of our algorithm. Let us consider the target schedule slot 7 at core 7 in Figure 13 on the Harpertown architecture. Assume that, at this point, by checking the dependence graph, we find two candidate computation blocks, A and B, which can be scheduled in this slot. The data sharing between these two computation blocks and other computation blocks is depicted in Figure 15 (the computation blocks that are not shown in the figure have no data sharing with computation blocks A and B). The weight of each edge denotes the number of data blocks shared by the connected nodes. Based on the π value assignments listed in Table 5 with $K = 3$, the total data reuse (including both vertical and horizontal) between computation block A and other computation blocks within its range K can be calculated as $1.5 \times 30 + 1 \times 40 + 0.5 \times 10 + 0 \times 2 = 90$, whereas the total data reuse for computation block B is $1.5 \times 35 + 1 \times 55 + 0.25 \times 8 + 0 \times 1 = 109.5$. Since the latter has higher data reuse, we select computation block B as $\Lambda_{7,7}$ to fill in the target slot, and proceed to the next slot.

9. EXPERIMENTAL EVALUATION

In this section, we present an experimental evaluation of the proposed data locality optimization algorithm that balances inter-core and intra-core data reuses. Most of our results are collected using the commercial Intel Dunnington multicore machine, whose important characteristics are given earlier in Section 4. Figure 16 gives improvements (reductions) in execution time under our algorithm (marked as "Balanced" in the graph) and six other strategies. These strategies differ from one another in how they assign weights. The weight assignment strategy our scheme employs has already been explained earlier in Section 8.1. Based on that strategy, we selected a K value of 3 for most of our applications except for equake and applu for which the values of 5 and 4 are selected, respectively. Also, for each application in our experimental suite, to determine the block size, we

adopted the approach discussed earlier. The selected computation block size (the number of iterations) turned out to be 2K for applications gafort, apsi, and fma3d, and 4K for the remaining applications.

We can summarize the weight assignment strategies used by other schemes tested as follows (we use the term "target slot" to refer to a slot for which we are scheduling a computation block, and also illustrate the graphic representations in Figure 19 for the first five schemes):

- *Scheme-I:* In this strategy, we do not consider inter-core reuse, and consequently, assign weights only to the slots in the same column as the target slot.
- *Scheme-II:* This strategy considers only short-term, inter-core reuse; so, only the slots that have already been scheduled in the same row as the target slot are assigned weights.
- *Scheme-III:* This scheme assigns equal weights to all (already) scheduled slots within the region.
- *Scheme-IV:* In assigning the weights, this scheme considers only the left and above neighbors of the target slot.
- *Scheme-V:* This is a combination of Scheme-I and Scheme II, that is, it considers only the row and the column of the target slot.
- *Scheme-VI:* This scheme considers all cache layers except for the last one. That is, in Dunnington, it decides the weights by considering L1 and L2 layers only. Our goal in making experiments with this version is to see how important to consider the entire cache hierarchy.

The most important observation from Figure 16 is that our scheme generates better results than the other six assignment strategies tested. It is important to note that Scheme-I in a sense represents the state-of-the-art data locality optimization for single-core architectures. To better explain why our scheme is better than Scheme-I and Scheme-II, we present in Figure 17, Figure 18 and Figure 20 reductions in cache misses at different layers by Scheme-I, Scheme-II and our scheme, respectively. It is important to observe that, as expected, Scheme-I improves L1 performance significantly. However, the relative improvements in L2 and L3 are not very significant. In contrast, Scheme-II results in better L2 and L3 performance but its L1 performance is relatively poor. In comparison, our scheme is able to optimize performance of the caches at all layers. More specifically, it brings 22.1%, 23.1% and 23.7% reductions, on average, in L1, L2 and L3 cache misses, respectively. The corresponding savings with Scheme-I are 26.6%, 10.2% and 9.8% and those with Scheme-II are 8.8%, 15.7% and 15.5%, in the same order.

Looking at the remaining schemes, as expected, Scheme-III does not perform well at all since giving equal weights to near and far reuses indiscriminately causes the compiler missing some important opportunities as far as converting

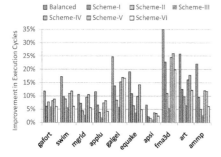

Figure 16: Performance improvements for each application under different strategies.

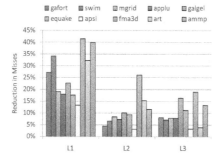

Figure 17: Reduction in cache misses at different layers by Scheme-I.

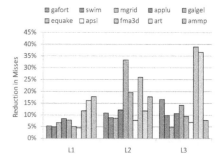

Figure 18: Reduction in cache misses at different layers by Scheme-II.

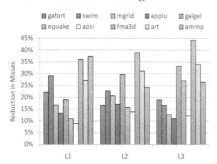

Figure 20: Reduction in cache misses at different layers by our scheme.

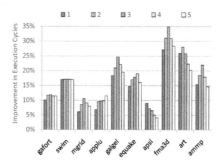

Figure 21: Performance improvements with different values of parameter K.

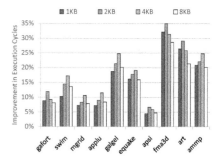

Figure 22: Performance improvements with different computation block sizes.

reuse into locality is concerned. Scheme-IV on the other hand performs better than schemes I, II and III, mainly because it focuses on the closest reuses. However, the scheme that comes closest to ours is Scheme V as it is able to optimize reuses in both horizontal and vertical directions. Finally, Scheme-VI does not perform very well, which indicates that, if we want to maximize locality improvements, *all* layers of the on-chip cache hierarchy should be considered.

We now study the impact of varying the value of parameter K on application performance. The results with different values of this parameter (from 1 to 5) are presented in Figure 21. We see from these results that, except for two applications (apsi and art), the values selected by our approach generated the best results. Based on these results, we can conclude that our approach to selecting the value of the K parameter is very successful in practice.

Our next set of experiments evaluate the impact of computation block sizes on application performance, which are given in Figure 22. One can observe from these results that the maximum savings are obtained when using the block sizes determined by the strategy explained in Section 8.2 except for art. In this application, a smaller block size performs better, most probably because the amount of data accessed by the computation block size selected by our strategy exceeded the L1 cache capacity, or caused extra conflict misses.

Our final set of results presented in Figure 23 are with the Harpertown machine. We see that, in general, the results with this architecture are lower than those obtained with Dunnington. This is mainly because the Dunnington machine has a more complex cache hierarchy than Harpertown, and this makes data locality optimization even more

critical for achieving maximum performance. The average performance improvement our scheme brings in Harpertown is about 16.3% (compared to 18.8% in Dunnington).

10. RELATED WORK

A data reuse theory for locality optimization is proposed by Wolf and Lam [49] in the context of single-core machines. They classify the data reuse into four classes: self-temporal reuse, self-spatial reuse, group-temporal reuse and group-spatial reuse. Wu et al [50] extend this intra-processor classification into eight types by introducing four more types of reuses. The reuse distance, also called LRU stack distance and first mentioned in [35], on the other hand, is a quantitative metric for data reuse in programs. Different reuse distance implementations have been presented in [6, 9, 37, 45] for single-core machines. [43], [24] and [31] propose multicore-aware reuse distance models, which can be used to collect statistics of the type shown in Figure 5 and Figure 6. In comparison, we present a detailed analysis of reuse distances for both inter-core and intra-core data reuses and propose a compiler-based optimization strategy for maximizing the performance of shared caches.

A few data locality optimizations targeting multicores have been proposed in recent years. Chen et al [13] discuss an application mapping strategy for multicores that tries to optimize data accesses from power and performance perspectives. Ascia et al [7] also employ a multi-objective algorithm for application mapping on multicores, but use evolutionary computing techniques. Sarkar and Tullsen present a data-cache aware compilation to find a layout for data objects which minimizes inter-object conflict misses [42]. Kandemir et al [27] discuss a multicore mapping strategy which does

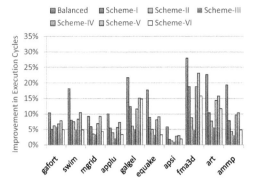

Figure 23: Performance improvements for each application under our algorithm and six other strategies on the Harpertown multicore machine.

not customize mapping based on target on-chip cache hierarchy. Zhang et al [52] evaluate the impact of cache sharing on parallel workloads. Zhang et al [51] study reference affinity and present a heuristic model for data locality. Chishti et al [15] propose a data mapping scheme that utilizes replication and capacity allocation techniques to improve locality. Lu et al [33] develop a compile-time framework for data locality optimization via non-cannicoal data layout transformation. In [41], the authors solve the allocation and scheduling problems of multicore through integer programming and constraint programming, respectively. Jin et al [25] implement a page-level data to L2 cache slice mapping for multicores. Chu et al [17] target codes with fine-grain parallelism by partitioning loop bodies in a locality-aware fashion. Chou et al [16] develop a run-time strategy for allocating the application tasks to platform resources in a network-on-chip. Cade and Qasem [10] present a model that captures the interaction between data locality and parallelism in the context of pipeline parallelism. These prior data locality optimizations do not consider target multicore cache hierarchies explicitly. Although the work in [28] also takes into account on-chip cache hierarchies, the vertical and horizontal reuses are exploited in separate steps. Compared to [28], our proposed strategy conducts an integrated mapping and scheduling for computation blocks, which maximizes the vertical and horizontal reuses at each schedule step at the same time.

In addition, there have been several hardware-based schemes for shared cache management. Kim et al [29] propose static and dynamic L2 cache partitioning algorithms that optimize fairness while improving throughput. Suh et al [46] measure cache utility for each application at runtime and dynamically vary the cache space for executing threads. Qureshi and Patt [39] monitor each application at runtime using a hardware circuit and partition a shared cache among threads based on their possible reductions in cache misses. Chang et al [12] use timeslicing as a means of cache partitioning to guarantee cache resources for each application for a certain time quantum. Prashanth et al [36] develop a dynamic cache partitioning scheme to alleviate intra-application conflicts. Other strategies rather than cache partitioning have also been explored to decrease interferences in shared caches, such as set pinning [44] and thread-aware replacement policies [23]. The modeling of cache sharing among applications include the work [11] and [38]. Prior efforts on reducing cache contention at the operating system (OS) level have explored two directions: software-based cache partitioning

[40, 47] and thread scheduling [30, 20, 19, 14]. Our compiler-based approach is complementary to most of these efforts. Further, our inter-core reuse distance analysis can be beneficial to some of these hardware and OS based schemes.

11. CONCLUDING REMARKS

In this paper, we have made four contributions. First, we have presented an in-depth investigation on the characteristics of inter-core and intra-core data reuses. Our observation is that, 1) while intra-core reuse distances are generally short, inter-core reuse distances tend to be much higher, and 2) both temporal and spatial inter-core reuses exhibit similar characteristics as far as reuse distances are concerned. Second, we have conducted a comprehensive study on how effective the on-chip cache hierarchies of current multicore architectures and state-of-the-art code/data optimizations are in exploiting available inter-core and intra-core data reuses in multithreaded applications separately. The conclusion is that neither of them is successful in converting inter-core reuses into data locality. Third, we have demonstrated that, although exploiting all available inter-core reuse can boost overall application performance by around 21.3% on average, trying to optimize for inter-core reuse without considering of doing so on intra-core reuse can actually perform worse than optimizing for intra-core reuse alone. Therefore, as the fourth contribution, we have developed a novel data locality optimization strategy for multicores that *balances* both inter-core and intra-core reuses. Specifically, our approach implements an integrated mapping and scheduling strategy that maximizes both "vertical" and "horizontal" reuses considering the on-chip cache hierarchy in the target architecture. Our results collected using ten applications indicate that this unified approach brings about 23.1% and 23.7% improvements in L2 and L3 cache hits, respectively, resulting in an average performance (execution time) improvement of 18.8%. Our results also show that the proposed strategy brings consistent benefits under different values of major experimental parameters.

12. REFERENCES

[1] AMD's Istanbul six-core Opteron processors. *http://techreport.com/articles.x/17005.*

[2] IBM Power7. *http://en.wikipedia.org/wiki/POWER7.*

[3] Intel core i7 processor. *http://www.intel.com/products/processor/corei7/specifications.htm.*

[4] Intel Xeon processors. *http://en.wikipedia.org/wiki/Xeon.*

[5] Platform 2015: Intel processor and platform evolution for the next decade. *http://epic.hpi.uni-potsdam.de/pub/Home/TrendsAndConceptsII2010/HW_Trends_borkar_2015.pdf,* 2005.

[6] G. Almasi et al. Calculating stack distances efficiently. *SIGPLAN Not.,* 2003.

[7] G. Ascia et al. Multi-objective mapping for mesh-based noc architectures. *Proc. of CODES+ISSS,* 2004.

[8] V. Aslot et al. SPECOMP: A new benchmark suite for measuring parallel computer performance. *OpenMP Shared Memory Parallel Programming, ISBN 978-3-540-42346-1,* 2001.

[9] B. Bennett and V.J.Kruskal. LRU stack processing. *IBM Journal of Research and Development*, 1975.

[10] M. J. Cade and A. Qasem. Balancing locality and parallelism on shared-cache multi-core systems. *Proc. of HPCC*, 2009.

[11] D. Chandra et al. Predicting inter-thread cache contention on a chip multi-processor architecture. *Proc. of HPCA*, 2005.

[12] J. Chang and G. S. Sohi. Cooperative cache partitioning for chip multiprocessors. *Proc. of ICS*, 2007.

[13] G. Chen et al. Application mapping for chip multiprocessors. *Proc. of DAC*, 2008.

[14] S. Chen et al. Scheduling threads for constructive cache sharing on cmps. *Proc. of SPAA*, 2007.

[15] Z. Chishti et al. Optimizing replication, communication, and capacity allocation in CMPs. *Proc. of ISCA*, 2005.

[16] C. L. Chou and R. Marculescu. User-aware dynamic task allocation in networks-on-chip. *Proc. of DATE*, 2008.

[17] M. Chu et al. Data access partitioning for fine-grain parallelism on multicore architectures. *Proc. of Micro*, 2007.

[18] S. Coleman and K. S. McKinley. Tile size selection using cache organization and data layout. *Proc. of PLDI*, 1995.

[19] A. Fedorova. Operating system scheduling for chip multithreaded processors. *PhD Thesis, Harvard University*, 2006.

[20] A. Fedorova et al. Cache-fair thread scheduling for multicore processors. *Technical Report, Harvard University*, 2006.

[21] P. P. Gelsinger. Intel architecture press briefing. *http://download.intel.com/pressroom/archive/reference/ Gelsinger_briefing_0308.pdf*, 2008.

[22] P. Gepner et al. Second generation quad-core Intel Xeon processors bring 45 nm technology and a new level of performance to HPC applications. *Proc. of ICCS, Part I*, 2008.

[23] A. Jaleel et al. Adaptive insertion policies for managing shared caches. *Proc. of PACT*, 2008.

[24] Y. Jiang et al. Is reuse distance applicable to data locality analysis on chip multiprocessors? *Proc. of CC*, 2010.

[25] L. Jin et al. A flexible data to L2 cache mapping approach for future multicore processors. *Proc. of MSPC*, 2006.

[26] M. Kandemir. A compiler technique for improving whole-program locality. *Proc. of POPL*, 2001.

[27] M. Kandemir et al. Optimizing shared cache behavior of chip multiprocessors. *Proc. of MICRO*, 2009.

[28] M. Kandemir et al. Cache topology aware computation mapping for multicores. *Proc. of PLDI*, 2010.

[29] S. Kim et al. Fair cache sharing and partitioning in a chip multiprocessor architecture. *Proc. of PACT*, 2004.

[30] R. Knauerhase et al. Using OS observations to improve performance in multicore systems. *IEEE Micro*, 2008.

[31] M. Kulkarni et al. Accelerating multicore reuse distance analysis with sampling and parallelization. *Proc. of PACT*, 2010.

[32] W. Li. Compiling for NUMA parallel machines. *Doctoral Dissertation, Cornell University*, 1993.

[33] A. Lu et al. Data layout transformation for enhancing data locality on nuca chip multiprocessors. *Proc. of PACT*, 2009.

[34] M. M. K. Martin et al. Multifacet's general execution-driven multiprocessor simulator (GEMS) toolset. *SIGARCH Comput. Archit. News*, 2005.

[35] R. Mattson et al. Evaluation techniques for storage hierarchies. *IBM Systems Journal*, 1970.

[36] S. Muralidhara et al. Intra-application shared cache partitioning for multithreaded applications. *Proc. of PPoPP*, 2010.

[37] F. Olken. Efficient methods for calculating the success function of fixed space replacement policies. *Technical Report, Lawrence Berkeley Laboratory*, 1981.

[38] P. Petoumenos et al. Modeling cache sharing on chip multiprocessor architectures. *Proc. of IEEE Internationl Symposium on Workload Characterization*, 2006.

[39] M. K. Qureshi and Y. N. Patt. Utility-based cache partitioning: a low-overhead, high-performance, runtime mechanism to partition shared caches. *Proc. of Micro*, 2006.

[40] N. Rafique et al. Architectural support for operating system-driven CMP cache management. *Proc. of PACT*, 2006.

[41] M. Ruggiero et al. Communication-aware allocation and scheduling framework for stream-oriented multi-processor systems-on-chip. *Proc. of DATE*, 2006.

[42] S. Sarkar and D. M. Tullsen. Compiler techniques for reducing data cache miss rate on a multithreaded architecture. *Proc. of HiPEAC*, 2008.

[43] D. Schuff et al. Multicore-aware reuse distance analysis. *Workshop on Performance Modeling, Evaluation, and Optimisation of Ubiquitous Computating and Networked Systems*, 2010.

[44] S. Srikantaiah et al. Adaptive set pinning: Managing shared caches in chip multiprocessors. *Proc. of ASPLOS*, 2008.

[45] R. Sugumar and S. Abraham. Multi-configuration simulation algorithms for the evaluation of computer architecture designs. *Technical Report, University of Michigan*, 1993.

[46] G. E. Suh et al. Dynamic partitioning of shared cache memory. *Journal of SuperComputing*, 2004.

[47] D. Tam et al. Managing shared L2 caches on multicore systems in software. *Proc. of WIOSCA*, 2007.

[48] R. Wilson et al. The suif compiler system: a parallelizing and optimizing research compiler. *Technical Report, University of Stanford*, 1994.

[49] M. E. Wolf and M. S. Lam. A data locality optimizing algorithm. *Proc. of PLDI*, 1991.

[50] J. Wu et al. Parallel data reuse theory for openmp applications. *Proc. of SNPD*, 2009.

[51] C. Zhang et al. A hierarchical model of data locality. *Proc. of POPL*, 2006.

[52] E. Zhang et al. Does cache sharing on modern CMP matter to the performance of contemporary multithreaded programs? *Proc. of PPOPP*, 2010.

Studying the Impact of Hardware Prefetching and Bandwidth Partitioning in Chip-Multiprocessors *

Fang Liu
fliu3@ece.ncsu.edu

Yan Solihin
solihin@ece.ncsu.edu

Department of Electrical and Computer Engineering
North Carolina State University
Raleigh, NC, USA

ABSTRACT

Modern high performance microprocessors widely employ hardware prefetching technique to hide long memory access latency. While very useful, hardware prefetching tends to aggravate the *bandwidth wall*, a problem where system performance is increasingly limited by the availability of the off-chip pin bandwidth in Chip Multi-Processors (CMPs).

In this paper, we propose an analytical model-based study to investigate how hardware prefetching and memory bandwidth partitioning impact CMP system performance and how they interact. The model includes a composite prefetching metric that can help determine under which conditions prefetching can improve system performance, a bandwidth partitioning model that takes into account prefetching effects, and a derivation of the weighted speedup-optimum bandwidth partition sizes for different cores. Through model-driven case studies, we find several interesting observations that can be valuable for future CMP system design and optimization. We also explore simulation-based empirical evaluation to validate the observations and show that maximum system performance can be achieved by selective prefetching, guided by the composite prefetching metric, coupled with dynamic bandwidth partitioning.

Categories and Subject Description
B.3.3 [**Hardware**]: Memory Structures-*Performance Analysis and Design Aids*;
C.4 [**Computer Systems Organization**]: Performance of Systems-*Performance Attributes*;
General Terms: Algorithm, Design, Management, Measurement, Performance
Keywords: Hardware Prefetching, Memory Bandwidth Partitioning, Analytical Model, Chip Multiprocessors

1. INTRODUCTION

Several decades of the persistent gap between microprocessor and DRAM main memory speed improvement has made it imperative for today's microprocessors to hide hundreds of processor clock cycles in memory access latency. In most high performance

---

*This research is in part supported by NSF grant CCF-0347425.

microprocessors today, this is achieved by employing several levels of caches augmented with *hardware prefetching* [2, 8, 9, 11]. Hardware prefetching works by predicting cache blocks that are likely needed by the processor in the near future, and fetching them into the cache early, allowing processor's memory accesses to hit (i.e. find data) in the cache. Since prefetching relies on prediction of future memory accesses, it is not 100% accurate in its prediction, implying that the latency hiding benefit of prefetching causes an increase in off-chip memory bandwidth usage and cache pollution.

In single core processor systems, for most workloads, off-chip bandwidth was rarely saturated from the use of prefetching, making prefetching almost always beneficial. However, the shift to multicore design has significantly altered the situation. Moore's Law continues to allow the doubling of the number of transistors (and hence number of cores) every approximately 2 years, increasing the off-chip bandwidth pressure at Moore's Law speed. However, the availability of off-chip bandwidth is only projected to grow at a much lower 15% annual rate, due to the limitations in pin density and power consumption [13]. This discrepancy leads to a problem called the *bandwidth wall*, where system performance is increasingly limited by the availability of off-chip bandwidth [7, 14, 15, 16, 17, 18, 22, 23, 30]. Hence, the demand for efficient use of off-chip bandwidth is tremendous and increasing.

At least two methods have been recently proposed to improve the efficiency of off-chip bandwidth usage. One method is to improve prefetching policies. Some studies proposed throttling or eliminating the useless/bad prefetches from consuming bandwidth [4, 5, 31, 33], and tweaking the memory scheduling policy to prioritize demand and profitable prefetch requests [4, 20]. Another method is to partition the off-chip bandwidth usage among cores [3, 12, 23, 25, 26, 27, 28, 32], with partition sizes chosen to optimize a particular goal, such as to maximize throughput or fairness. However, these studies suffer from several drawbacks. First, the studies address one technique but ignore the other: prefetching studies do not include bandwidth partitioning, whereas bandwidth partitioning studies assume systems that have no prefetching. As a result, the significant interaction between them was missed, and the opportunity for these techniques to work in synergy was left unexplored. Second, the studies were performed in an ad-hoc manner, yielding performance improvement but missing important insights.

To demonstrate the need for exploring prefetching and bandwidth partitioning jointly, Figure 1(a) shows how prefetching and bandwidth partitioning can affect each other. In the figure, system performance measured as weighted speedup [1] (referring to Equation 1) of three pairs of SPEC2006 [34] benchmarks running as a co-schedule on a dual-core CMP system is shown with four configurations: base system with no prefetching or bandwidth partitioning (Neither), hardware prefetching only (Pref), bandwidth partitioning only (PT), and both prefetching and bandwidth partitioning (Pref+PT) [1]. The three co-schedules highlight different interaction cases. For *hmmer-milc*, prefetching improves performance and bandwidth partitioning improves it further due to offsetting the effect of the prefetcher's increase in off-chip bandwidth usage. For *astar-gobmk* and *mcf-bzip2*, prefetching hurts performance due to high off-chip bandwidth consumption. For *mcf-bzip2*, applying bandwidth partitioning is not the right solution, since it cannot recover the lost performance due to prefetching (i.e. Pref+PT < Neither). Such a conclusion cannot be derived in prior studies, when only bandwidth partitioning was studied [3, 12, 23, 25, 26, 27, 28, 32], or when prefetchers were always turned on [4, 20]. The figure points out the need to understand when and under what situations the prefetcher of each core should be turned on or off, and how bandwidth partitioning should be implemented in order to optimize system performance.

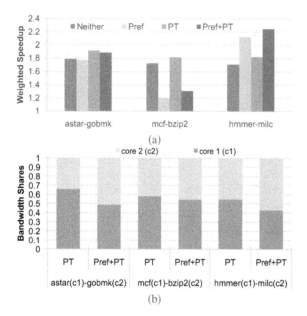

Figure 1: Weighted speedup (a) and optimum bandwidth allocation (b) for co-schedules running on a dual-core CMP.

Performing the studies in an ad-hoc manner often misses important insights. For example, it has been assumed that a core that enjoys useful prefetches should be rewarded with a higher bandwidth allocation, whereas a core for which prefetching is less useful should be constrained with a lower bandwidth allocation [4]. However, our experiments show the opposite. Maximum weighted speedup is achieved when a core with highly useful prefetching is given less bandwidth allocation, and the resulting excess bandwidth is given to cores with less useful prefetching. Figure 1(b) shows the bandwidth allocation for each core that maximizes the system throughput. The application that has more useful prefetching (higher prefetching coverage and accuracy) runs on Core 1. Comparing the two bars for each co-schedule, it is clear that in order to maximize system throughput, it is the applications that show less useful prefetching should receive higher bandwidth allocations.

The goal of this study is to *understand what factors contribute to the impact of prefetching and bandwidth partitioning on CMP system performance, and how they interact*. To arrive at the goal, we

propose an analytical model-based study, based on the Cycle Per Instruction (CPI) model [6] and queuing theory [21], taking various system parameters (CPU frequency, cache block size, and available bandwidth), and application cache behavior metrics (miss frequency, prefetching frequency, prefetching coverage and accuracy, and various CPIs) as input. Studying the model, coupled with empirical evaluation, we arrive at several interesting findings, among them are:

- Deploying prefetching makes the available bandwidth scarcer and therefore increases the effectiveness of bandwidth partitioning in improving system performance.

- The decision of turning prefetchers on or off should be made prior to employing bandwidth partitioning, because the performance loss due to prefetching in bandwidth-constrained systems cannot be fully repaired by bandwidth partitioning. In deciding whether to turn on or off the prefetcher for each core, traditional metrics such as coverage and accuracy are insufficient. Instead, we discover a new metric that works well for this purpose.

- The theoretical optimum bandwidth allocations can be derived, and a simplified version that is implementable in hardware can approximate it quite well.

- The conventional wisdom that rewards a core that has more useful prefetching with a larger bandwidth allocation is incorrect when prefetchers of all cores are turned on. Instead, its bandwidth allocation should be slightly more constrained. Our model explains why this is so.

The findings in our study carry significant implications for CMP design and performance optimization. As the number of cores on a chip continues to double every 18-24 months, versus 10-15% ITRS' projected growth in off-chip bandwidth [13], the off-chip bandwidth available per core will become increasingly scarcer, increasing the demand for better off-chip bandwidth management.

The remainder of this paper is organized as follows: Section 2 reviews the related work, Section 3 shows the construction of the analytical model, Section 4 discusses model-based exploration, Section 5 validates the findings obtained from the model through simulation based evaluation, and Section 6 concludes this paper.

2. RELATED WORK

Bandwidth partitioning. Researchers have proposed various bandwidth partitioning techniques to mitigate CMP memory bandwidth contention-related problems. The implication is to prioritize memory requests from different cores based on heuristics, in order to meet the objectives of Quality of Service (QoS) [27], fairness [25, 26, 28], or throughput [12]. Liu et al. [23] investigated the impact of bandwidth partitioning on CMP system performance and its interaction with shared cache partitioning. Srikantaiah and Kandemir [32] explored a symbiotic partitioning scheme on the shared cache and off-chip bandwidth via empirical models. None of those bandwidth partitioning techniques took prefetching into account.
Prefetching. Hardware prefetching is widely implemented in commercial microprocessors [2, 8, 9, 11] to hide the long memory access latency. Due to the imperfect accuracy, prefetching incurs cache pollution and increases off-chip bandwidth consumption. Prior studies have looked into how to make prefetching more effective in CMP. Techniques include throttling/filtering useless prefetching requests [20, 31, 33, 35] to reduce their extra bandwidth consumption, and a better hybrid prefetching algorithm [5]. All of the above

---

[1] A stream prefetcher similar to previous studies [19, 20] is used. Optimum bandwidth partitioning scheme from [23] is used. More details can be found in Section 5.1

studies ignore bandwidth contention that arises from demand and prefetch requests coming from different cores.

Prefetching and Bandwidth Partitioning. Only recently, prefetching and bandwidth partitioning in CMP were studied together as inter-related problems. Ebrahimi et al. [4] proposed to partition bandwidth usage in the presence of prefetching in CMP in order to reduce the inter-core interference. While their results show improved system performance, many questions are left unanswered. For example, what fundamental factors affect the effectiveness of prefetching and bandwidth partitioning? How do they interact with each other? Does combining prefetching and bandwidth partitioning always achieve better performance than using only one of them? What bandwidth shares can produce optimum system performance? The goal of this paper is to find out these answers, that are critical for designing a good policy for optimizing system performance. Due to the lack of understanding on these issues, the study [4] made a critical error of always keeping the prefetching engines of all cores on regardless of the situations. Figure 1 shows that in some cases, it is better to turn the prefetchers completely off.

3. ANALYTICAL MODELING

In this section, we discuss the assumptions used by our model (Section 3.1), derive a metric that determines whether prefetching benefits performance (Section 3.2), and present our prefetching and bandwidth partitioning model (Section 3.3).

3.1 Assumptions and Model Parameters

Assumptions. This study assumes a CMP with homogeneous cores, where each core has private L1 (instruction and data) and L2 (unified) caches. Each L2 cache has a hardware prefetcher that can be turned on or off, similar to the one used in IBM Power processors [2, 9, 11]. The off-chip bandwidth is shared by all cores through a single queue interface, where all off-chip memory requests are served in First-Ready First-Come-First-Serve (FR-FCFS) policy [29], a common base implementation in memory controllers. Our study focuses on multi-programmed workloads, hence we assume that single-threaded applications run on different cores and do not share data.

We define bandwidth partitioning as allocating fractions of off-chip bandwidth to different cores and enforcing these fractions as per-core quota. Thus, bandwidth partitioning reduces inter-core interference, without changing the underlying memory access scheduling policy. The bandwidth partitioning is implemented using token bucket algorithm [23], with the goal to optimize the system throughput expressed as weighted speedup, which is the sum of individual Instruction Per Cycle (IPC) speedup from each core [1] [2]:

$$WS = \sum_{i=1}^{N} \frac{IPC_i}{IPC_{alone,i}} = \sum_{i=1}^{N} \frac{CPI_{alone,i}}{CPI_i} \qquad (1)$$

In our model, we take into account the off-chip memory requests due to L2 cache misses and prefetches, but ignore memory traffic such as write backs and coherence messages. Besides of being much fewer than L2 cache misses and prefetches, write backs are not on the critical path of performance, hence they have no direct impact on weighted speedup. Off-chip coherence traffic is ignored since we only consider applications that do not share data.

---

[2] IPC_i and $IPC_{alone,i}$ are instruction throughput per cycle of thread i when it runs in a co-schedule and when it runs alone in the system, respectively. Weighted speedup is an optimization metric widely used in studying system performance, and includes some measure of fairness, in which speeding up one application at the expense of others will have some offsetting effect.

Model Parameters. The input to the model includes system parameters as well as per-thread parameters listed in Table 1.

Table 1: Input and parameters used in our model.

System parameters	
f	CPU clock frequency (Hz)
K	Cache block size (Bytes)
B	Peak off-chip memory bandwidth (Bytes/sec)
N	Number of cores in the CMP

Thread-specific parameters	
$CPI_{L2\infty,i}$	Thread i's CPI assuming infinite L2 cache size
$CPI_{alone,i}$	Thread i's CPI when it runs alone in the CMP
M_i	Thread i's L2 cache miss rate without prefetching
A_i	Thread i's L2 cache access frequency (#accesses/sec)
$M_{p,i}$	Thread i's L2 cache miss rate after prefetching
P_i	Thread i's L2 prefetching rate (#prefetches/#accesses)
c_i	Thread i's prefetching coverage
a_i	Thread i's prefetching accuracy
$T_{m,i}$	Thread i's average memory access latency (#cycles)
β_i	Fraction of bandwidth assigned to thread i

3.2 Composite Metric for Prefetching

Traditional metrics for prefetching performance include *coverage*, defined as the fraction of the original cache misses that are eliminated by prefetching; and *accuracy*, defined as the fraction of prefetch requests that successfully eliminate cache misses. These metrics cannot determine whether prefetching should be used or not in limited off-chip bandwidth environment because they do not take into account how much off-chip bandwidth is available, and how memory access latency is affected by prefetching.

To arrive at a new metric that can be used to determine whether prefetching is profitable for performance, taking into account the amount of available bandwidth, we start from the basic *Cycle per Instruction* (CPI) model [6] and add the effect of additional queueing delay due to prefetching traffic. We use Δt to represent the queueing delay on the bus and let T_m be the average access latency to the memory [3], the CPI becomes:

$$CPI = CPI_{L2\infty} + h_m \cdot (T_m + \Delta t) \qquad (2)$$

When prefetching is applied in the system, let CPI_p present the new CPI, Δt_p as the new queuing delay on the bus, $h_{m,p}$ as the new L2 misses per instruction, the CPI equation then becomes:

$$CPI_p = CPI_{L2\infty} + h_{m,p} \cdot (T_m + \Delta t_p) \qquad (3)$$

Let us examine how hardware prefetching affects CPI (Equation 3 vs. Equation 2). Prefetching may decrease the L2 miss per instruction, i.e. $h_{m,p} < h_m$, but increase the queueing delay, i.e. $\Delta t_p > \Delta t$ due to the extra traffic generated by prefetch requests.

Note that $h_{m,p}$ can be expressed as the multiplication of miss frequency ($M_p \cdot A_p$) and the average time taken to execute one instruction ($\frac{CPI_p}{f}$):

$$h_{m,p} = \frac{M_p \cdot A_p \cdot CPI_p}{f} \qquad (4)$$

Substituting Equation 4 into Equation 3, and solving CPI_p, we can arrive at:

$$CPI_p = \frac{CPI_{L2\infty}}{1 - \frac{M_p A_p}{f}(T_m + \Delta t_p)} \qquad (5)$$

Now we will derive Δt_p using Little's law. If we let λ_p denote the arrival rate of memory requests, then λ_p is equal to the sum of

---

[3] The average memory access latency T_m is an amortized value that implicitly includes the effect of memory bank and row buffer conflicts, Instruction Level Parallelism (ILP) as well as Thread Level Parallelism (TLP).

frequency of cache miss and prefetch requests:

$$\lambda_p = (M_p + P)A_p \tag{6}$$

Little's law [21] for a queuing system states that the average queue length (L_p) is equal to the arrival rate (λ_p) multiplied by the service time (T_p), i.e. $L_p = \lambda_p \cdot T_p$, while the service time on the off-chip bus is the cache block size (K) divided by the available bandwidth (B). Hence, the average number of memory requests arriving during the service time is:

$$L_p = \frac{K}{B} \cdot (M_p + P)A_p \tag{7}$$

If we assume memory requests are not bursty, i.e. requests are processed back to back, the average waiting time of a newly arriving request is equal to the L_p requests that are ahead of it in the queue, multiplied by the service time. Thus, the waiting time Δt_p (in cycles) can be expressed as:

$$\Delta t_p = f \cdot \frac{K}{B} \cdot L_p = f \cdot \frac{K^2}{B^2} \cdot (M_p + P)A_p \tag{8}$$

Substituting Equation 8 into Equation 5, expression for CPI_p is:

$$CPI_p = \frac{CPI_{L2\infty}}{1 - \frac{M_p A_p T_m}{f} - \frac{M_p(M_p+P)A_p^2 K^2}{B^2}} \tag{9}$$

Similarly, the system that does not employ prefetching has the CPI of:

$$CPI = \frac{CPI_{L2\infty}}{1 - \frac{MAT_m}{f} - \frac{M^2 A^2 K^2}{B^2}} \tag{10}$$

In order for prefetching to produce a net benefit in performance, the CPI after prefetching must be smaller than CPI without prefetching, i.e. $CPI_p < CPI$. From the definition of prefetching coverage and accuracy, we have (assuming L2 cache access frequency is not affected by prefetching, i.e. $A_p = A$):

$$c = \frac{MA - M_p A_p}{MA} = \frac{M - M_p}{M} \tag{11}$$

$$a = \frac{MA - M_p A_p}{PA_p} = \frac{M - M_p}{P} \tag{12}$$

Rearranging Equation 11 and Equation 12 to express M_p and P in terms of c and a, substituting them into the CPI_p expression in Equation 9, and simplifying the inequality $CPI_p < CPI$, we obtain the final expression for the inequality:

$$T_m > \frac{MAK^2}{B^2} f(c - 2 + \frac{1-c}{a}) \tag{13}$$

The right hand side of the inequality, $\frac{MAK^2}{B^2} f(c-2+\frac{1-c}{a})$, is the composite metric that takes into account prefetching coverage and accuracy, as well as cache block size, available bandwidth, and miss frequency. The left hand side of the inequality, T_m, measures the average exposed memory access latency. The inequality essentially provides a break-even point threshold for how large the average memory access latency should be for prefetching to be beneficial. It is easier to meet the inequality when the average memory access latency is large, the cache miss frequency is small, the available bandwidth is large, and the coverage and accuracy are large. All these factors make sense qualitatively, and Equation 13 captures their quantitative contributions. This leads us to:

OBSERVATION 1. *Whether prefetching improves or degrades performance cannot be measured just by its coverage or accuracy. Rather, a prefetching profitability criterion in Inequality 13 is needed, using input parameters that are easy to collect in hardware.*

Recall that in the model construction for the average total waiting time, we have assumed memory requests are not bursty and requests are contiguously processed back to back. This allows us to reach bandwidth utilization of 100% if the arrival rate of memory requests is high. However, in reality, due to the burstiness of memory requests, even a high arrival rate cannot achieve 100% bandwidth utilization. This introduces a small inaccuracy in our metric. Thus we can define a parameter $\alpha \in (0, 1)$ such that:

$$T_m > \frac{MAK^2}{\alpha B^2} f(c - 2 + \frac{1-c}{a}) \tag{14}$$

α loosely represents the degree of burstiness of memory requests and can be obtained from empirical evaluation (as shown in Section 5.2.1). Since $\alpha < 1$, the minimum value of the right hand side of the inequality is $\frac{MAK^2}{B^2} f(c - 2 + \frac{1-c}{a})$. Thus we can conclude:

OBSERVATION 2. *If an application running on a core satisfies $T_m < \frac{MAK^2}{B^2} f(c - 2 + \frac{1-c}{a})$, prefetching is harmful to performance. In addition, if $0 > \frac{MAK^2}{B^2} f(c - 2 + \frac{1-c}{a})$, prefetching improves performance.*

3.3 Memory Bandwidth Partitioning Model

This model extends the bandwidth partitioning model from [23] by taking into account not just demand fetches, but also prefetch requests, and prefetching coverage and accuracy. In a CMP system, multiple threads running on different cores will be generating their own cache misses and prefetch requests. Requests from multiple cores will compete for the off-chip bandwidth, resulting in queuing delay to access the main memory. Since there are multiple threads running simultaneously, we will denote the CPI expression from Equation 5 for thread i as:

$$CPI_{p,i} = \frac{CPI_{L2\infty,i}}{1 - \frac{M_{p,i}A_i}{f}(T_{m,i} + \Delta t_{p,i})} \tag{15}$$

$\Delta t_{p,i}$ is the queuing delay suffered by thread i on the shared bus. With a similar derivation method in [23], we can compute it using Little's law for the case where we do not apply bandwidth partitioning (i.e. requests from all cores contend with each other for bandwidth access naturally) and compare it against the case where we apply bandwidth partitioning (i.e. bandwidth fraction is allocated to each core for its own requests). The CPI of thread i in a system without bandwidth partitioning can be expressed as:

$$CPI_{p,i,nopt} = \frac{CPI_{L2\infty,i}}{1 - \frac{M_{p,i}A_i T_{m,i}}{f} - \frac{\left(\sum_{j=1}^{N}(M_{p,j}+P_j)A_j\right)^2 M_{p,i}K^2}{(M_{p,i}+P_i)B^2}} \tag{16}$$

Let β_i denote the fraction of bandwidth allocated to thread i. Using similar derivation, the CPI for thread i for a system with bandwidth partitioning will be:

$$CPI_{p,i,bwpt} = \frac{CPI_{L2\infty,i}}{1 - \frac{M_{p,i}A_i \cdot T_{m,i}}{f} - \frac{M_{p,i}(M_{p,i}+P_i)A_i^2 K^2}{\beta_i^2 \cdot B^2}} \tag{17}$$

Comparing Equation 17 and 16, we can conclude that Equation 16 is a special case of Equation 17 where:

$$\beta_i = \frac{(M_{p,i} + P_i)A_i}{\sum_{j=1}^{N}(M_{p,j} + P_j)A_j} \tag{18}$$

which leads us to the following observation:

OBSERVATION 3. *In a CMP system where off-chip bandwidth usage among multiple cores is unregulated, the off-chip bandwidth is naturally partitioned between cores, where the natural share of bandwidth a core uses is equal to the ratio of memory request frequency (including both cache misses and prefetch requests) of the core to the sum of all memory request frequencies from all cores.*

Substituting CPI from Equation 17 into Equation 1, we obtain:

$$WS_p = \sum_{i=1}^{N} C_i \left(1 - \frac{M_{p,i} A_i T_{m,i}}{f} - \frac{M_{p,i}(M_{p,i} + P_i)A_i^2 K^2}{\beta_i^2 B^2} \right) \tag{19}$$

where $C_i = \frac{CPI_{alone,i}}{CPI_{L2\infty,i}}$. Given that the first and second terms in the equation are not affected by bandwidth partitioning, to maximize weighted speedup, we need to minimize the sum of the third terms in the above equation, i.e.:

$$F(\beta_1, \dots, \beta_N) = \sum_{i=1}^{N} C_i \frac{M_{p,i}(M_{p,i} + P_i)A_i^2 K^2}{\beta_i^2 B^2} \tag{20}$$

Minimizing $F(\beta_1, \dots, \beta_N)$ is a constrained optimization problem with constraint of $\sum_{i=0}^{N} \beta_i = 1$. Solving via Lagrange multipliers [10], the bandwidth partition for thread i (β_i) is:

$$\beta_i = \frac{\left(C_i M_{p,i}(M_{p,i} + P_i)A_i^2 \right)^{1/3}}{\sum_{j=1}^{N} \left(C_j M_{p,j}(M_{p,j} + P_j)A_j^2 \right)^{1/3}} \tag{21}$$

leading us to the next observation:

OBSERVATION 4. *Weighted speedup-optimum bandwidth partition for a thread can be expressed as a function of all co-scheduled threads' miss and prefetch frequencies, infinite-L2 CPIs, and CPIs when each thread runs alone in the system, as in Equation 21* [4].

4. MODEL-DRIVEN STUDY

In this section, we will explore the bandwidth partitioning model derived in the previous section to gain insights into the how prefetching and bandwidth partitioning interact and affect system performance. To simplify the discussion, but without losing generality, we will assume dual-core CMP running two threads.

From Equation 21, we will assume that $C_i = \frac{CPI_{alone,i}}{CPI_{L2\infty,i}} = 1$. The reason is that C_i is a ratio of two CPIs, and the ratio tends to approach 1 in a system with many cores and a very large shared cache. Furthermore, bias of program behavior in terms of instruction level parallelism affects both the numerator and denominator. Hence ignoring C_i does not change the qualitative observations we will make in this section.

The model-driven study is split into three cases depending on what factors are varied: miss frequency, prefetching coverage, and prefetching accuracy. For all cases, we assume available bandwidth of $B = 1.6$GB/s, CPU clock frequency of $f = 3$GHz, average memory access latency of $T_m = 250$ cycles, cache block size of $K = 64$ bytes, and the miss frequency of Thread 1 of $M_1 A_1 = 2$ million/s. Note that these numbers are just one realistic and representative data point. Since we only make qualitative observations, it is the trends that matter, rather than the actual numbers.

4.1 The Impact of Miss Frequency

Figure 2(a) plots the optimum vs. natural bandwidth share for Thread 2 when miss frequency of Thread 2 is varied against that of Thread 1, with prefetching turned on (prefOpt vs. prefNat, in dashed lines) or turned off (Opt vs. Nat, in solid lines). The

---

[4]Note that the parameters in Equation 21 may vary due to the changes in an application's behavior throughout its execution. The equation does not assume them to be constant values, but assumes the parameters for any specific execution interval of the application are available.

prefetching coverage and accuracy are assumed to be $c_1 = 0.7$, $a_1 = 0.5$, $c_2 = 0.5$, and $a_2 = 0.2$.

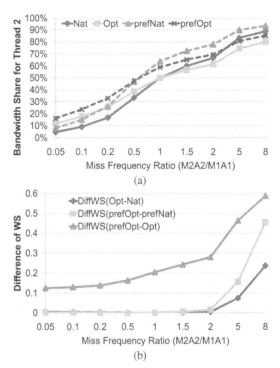

Figure 2: Bandwidth share for Thread 2 (a), and the resulting weighted speedup (b), as the miss frequency of Thread 2 varies.

Comparing Opt and Nat, they intersect at the point of equal miss frequencies ($\frac{M_2 A_2}{M_1 A_1} = 1$). At this intersection point, both of the natural bandwidth share already produces optimum weighted speedup. As we increase Thread 2's miss frequency by going to the right of the intersection along the x-axis, the natural and optimum bandwidth shares of Thread 2 increase, but the optimum bandwidth share increases at a slower pace. In essence, for optimum weighted speedup, the thread with higher miss frequency must be slightly (but not overly) constrained.

Comparing prefOpt and prefNat, they intersect at a point where the x-axis is roughly 0.5. At this point, the optimum bandwidth demand from misses and prefetches of both threads are equal. More specifically, according to Equation 21, when $\frac{M_{p,2}(M_{p,2}+P_2)A_2^2}{M_{p,1}(M_{p,1}+P_1)A_1^2} = 1$, $\frac{M_2 A_2}{M_1 A_1} = 0.583$. As we increase Thread 2's miss frequency by going to the right of the intersection along the x-axis, both of the natural and optimum bandwidth shares of Thread 2 increase. As before, the optimum bandwidth share increases at a slower pace. Thus we can make the following observation:

OBSERVATION 5. *With or without prefetching, to produce optimum weighted speedup, the threads that have higher bandwidth demand (higher cache miss and prefetch frequencies) must be slightly (but not overly) constrained, in effect preventing bandwidth hungry applications from dominating the bandwidth usage and starving other applications.*

Comparing Opt and PrefOpt, PrefOpt is always above Opt, implying that Thread 2 always receives a larger bandwidth allocation when prefetching is applied, regardless of its relative miss frequency. Conversely, Thread 1's optimum bandwidth allocation is reduced after prefetching applied. Given that Thread 1 has higher prefetching coverage and accuracy than Thread 2, we can make the following observation that is opposite to conventional wisdom:

OBSERVATION 6. *Compared to a system without prefetching, the optimum bandwidth partitioning for a system with prefetching tends to constrain the bandwidth usage of a core that has relatively more useful prefetches (higher prefetching coverage and accuracy), in favor of slightly increasing the allocations for other cores with lower prefetching coverage and accuracy.*

The intuition behind this is that a thread having higher prefetching coverage and accuracy tends to utilize the off-chip bandwidth more efficiently; hence this thread can donate some bandwidth allocation to other threads to improve the overall performance.

How does the slight constraint on bandwidth allocation for the thread with higher bandwidth demand impact weighted speedup? Figure 2(b) shows the difference in weighted speedup between various scenarios. DiffWS(Opt-Nat) represents the improvement in weighted speedup that comes from bandwidth partitioning, when prefetching is not applied. The curve shows an increasing trend as we increase Thread 2's miss frequency along the x-axis. This is because Thread 2's higher miss frequency begins to saturate the off-chip bandwidth.

DiffWS(prefOpt-prefNat) represents the weighted speedup improvement that comes from bandwidth partitioning, when prefetching is applied. The curve shows the same trend as DiffWS(Opt-Nat), but with steeper increase when $\frac{M_2 A_2}{M_1 A_1} >= 1.5$. The steeper increase is caused by the additional bandwidth consumption from prefetching, causing two effects: scarcer bandwidth, and larger difference in bandwidth demand from the two threads. To illustrate the latter effect, we note that after prefetching, the bandwidth demand ratio of the two threads becomes $\frac{M_{p,2}(M_{p,2}+P_2)A_2^2}{M_{p,1}(M_{p,1}+P_1)A_1^2} = \frac{(1-c_2)(1-c_2+c_2/a_2)}{(1-c_1)(1-c_1+c_1/a_1)} \cdot \frac{M_2^2 A_2^2}{M_1^2 A_1^2} = 2.94\frac{M_2^2 A_2^2}{M_1^2 A_1^2}$, where $\frac{M_2^2 A_2^2}{M_1^2 A_1^2}$ is the bandwidth demand ratio before prefetching.

Notice that while prefOpt reallocates about 10% of the available bandwidth from Thread 2 to Thread 1 as compared to prefNat (Figure 2(a)), it produces significant improvement in weighted speedup when the off-chip bandwidth is scarce. To summarize:

OBSERVATION 7. *Prefetching increases the magnitude of improvement in system performance from bandwidth partitioning, if it increases the difference in bandwidth demand from different cores and makes bandwidth scarcer. In contrast, the magnitude of improvement may decrease if prefetching reduces the difference of bandwidth demand from different cores.*

Analyzing DiffWS(prefOpt-Opt), we can conclude that deploying both prefetching and optimum bandwidth partitioning, the system can achieve better performance than only applying optimum bandwidth partitioning. An example of this effect can be seen in the co-schedule *hmmer-milc* (Figure 1(a)).

4.2 The Impact of Prefetching Coverage

Figure 3(a) shows Thread 2's natural and optimum bandwidth shares (prefNat and prefOpt) as its prefetching coverage varies along the x-axis. As for other parameters, Thread 1's coverage is set at 70% ($c_1 = 0.7$), while Thread 2's coverage varies from 7% to 98%. The prefetching accuracy for both threads is 70% ($a_1 = a_2 = 0.7$). The miss frequency ratio of two threads without prefetching is $\frac{M_2 A_2}{M_1 A_1} = 5$. This implies Thread 2's optimum bandwidth share without prefetching is 74.5% (the horizontal line labeled "Opt").

As prefetching coverage of Thread 2 increases along the x-axis, the off-chip bandwidth demand from Thread 2 increases, since an accuracy of 70% means that for every cache miss eliminated, 1.4 prefetch requests are generated. The increase in bandwidth demand increases Thread 2's natural bandwidth share (prefNat), but

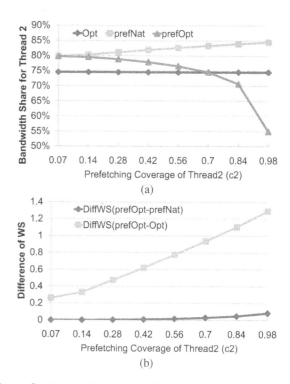

Figure 3: Bandwidth share for Thread 2 (a), and the resulting weighted speedup (b), as the prefetching coverage for Thread 2 varies.

notably decreases Thread 2's optimum bandwidth allocation (prefOpt). Such result seems to counter conventional wisdom, which may dictate that due to equal accuracy, prefetch requests from Thread 1 and Thread 2 are of equal importance. Consequently, higher prefetching coverage for Thread 2 should increase Thread 2's bandwidth allocation.

Our analytical model points out a flaw in the conventional wisdom. The reason why Thread 2's optimum bandwidth share decreases as its coverage increases is because Thread 2's performance improvement due to fewer cache misses comes at disproportionate decrease in Thread 1's performance, while Thread 1 has higher sensitivity to queueing delay for its memory requests. Thus, one cannot just consider prefetching coverage and accuracy of both threads, but must also consider the sensitivity of a thread's performance to the queuing delay.

Comparing Opt and prefOpt, they intersect at a point where Thread 1 and Thread 2 have an equal prefetching coverage ($c_2 = 0.7$), indicating that at equal prefetching coverage and accuracy, prefetching does not affect the optimum bandwidth partition sizes. As Thread 2's coverage increases further, its optimum bandwidth share decreases way below that before prefetching. The following observation summarizes the finding:

OBSERVATION 8. *The higher the prefetching coverage of a core, its bandwidth allocation must be decreased by a necessary amount in order to prevent it from dominating the bandwidth usage and starving other cores.*

How much does the optimum bandwidth partitioning improve weighted speedup? In Figure 3(b), DiffWS(prefOpt-prefNat)shows the weighted speedup improvement from bandwidth partitioning on a system with prefetching. The curve increases as Thread 2's coverage increases, due to both increasing scarcity of bandwidth, and increasing difference in bandwidth demand between the two threads, as concluded in Observation 7.

DiffWS(prefOpt-Opt) represents the weighted speedup improvement from prefetching at optimum bandwidth settings. The curve increases as Thread 2's coverage increases, because higher coverage implies more useful prefetching. Notice that DiffWS(prefOpt-Opt) is always above DiffWS(prefOpt-prefNat), because with relatively high prefetching accuracy ($a_1 = a_2 = 0.7$), prefetching makes larger impact on weighted speedup than optimum bandwidth partitioning, especially as Thread 2's coverage increases.

4.3 The Impact of Prefetching Accuracy

Figure 4(a) shows Thread 2's natural and optimum bandwidth share (prefNat and prefOpt) as its prefetching accuracy increases from 5% to 100%. Thread 1's accuracy is set at 10% ($a_1 = 0.1$). The prefetching coverage for both threads is 10% ($c_1 = c_2 = 0.1$). The miss frequency ratio of the two threads without prefetching is $\frac{M_2 A_2}{M_1 A_1} = 5$, implying that Thread 2's optimum bandwidth share without prefetching is 74.5% ("Opt").

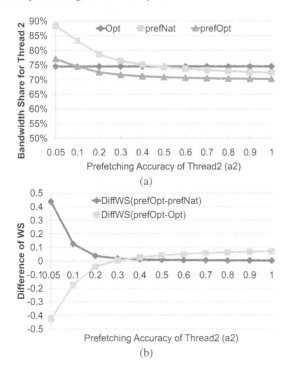

(a)

(b)

Figure 4: Bandwidth share for Thread 2 (a), and the resulting weighted speedup (b), as Thread 2's prefetching accuracy varies.

Analyzing prefNat and prefOpt in the figure, prefOpt is always below prefNat, indicating that Thread 2, which has higher miss and prefetch frequencies, is slightly constrained in order to achieve optimum weighted speedup (instantiating Observation 5).

Conventional wisdom may dictate that to produce maximal performance, a thread that has higher prefetching accuracy should be rewarded with a larger share of bandwidth, so that its prefetch requests are prioritized over prefetch requests from other threads with lower accuracy. Figure 4(a) shows that conventional wisdom is only partially correct and is overall incorrect. As Thread 2's prefetching accuracy increases along the x-axis, fewer prefetch requests are needed to eliminate the same number of cache misses. This causes a decline in bandwidth usage, decreasing the natural bandwidth share (prefNat) used by Thread 2. The optimum bandwidth share (prefOpt) also declines, but at a slower pace. This gap between prefNat and prefOpt narrows as Thread 2's accuracy increases, indicating that Thread 2's optimum bandwidth allocation is

less constrained with higher accuracy. While such narrowing supports conventional wisdom that more accurate prefetches should be given a higher priority because they use bandwidth more efficiently in eliminating cache misses, conventional wisdom is correct only in a relative sense. In an absolute sense, the bandwidth share allocated should decrease as prefetching accuracy increases.

Let us look at the optimum bandwidth partitioning after prefetching deployed (prefOpt) vs. without prefetching (Opt). They intersects at the point where Thread 2 and Thread 1's accuracy matches ($a_2 = a_1 = 0.1$). As Thread 2's accuracy increases along the x-axis, its optimum bandwidth share after prefetching falls below that before prefetching, while the opposite is true as we decrease Thread 2's accuracy. This indicates that when prefetching is highly accurate, the optimum bandwidth share should decrease. Thus:

OBSERVATION 9. *In an absolute term, the higher the prefetching accuracy for a core, the less bandwidth share should be allocated to it. In a relative term, more accurate prefetches should be given a relatively higher priority in bandwidth usage over less accurate prefetches.*

Figure 4(b) shows the impact of accuracy on weighted speedup. DiffWS(prefOpt-prefNat) represents the weighted speedup improvement due to bandwidth partitioning in a system with prefetching. The curve shows large improvement at low accuracy, but declines and flatlines with higher accuracy. This makes sense, because at high accuracy, bandwidth demand declines, making bandwidth less scarce. In addition, the difference of bandwidth demand between the two threads decreases ($\frac{M_{p,2}+P_2}{M_{p,1}+P_1}$ declines from 6.05 to 1.05). Both factors make bandwidth partitioning less effective (Observation 7). In contrast, DiffWS(prefOpt-Opt) increases along the higher prefetching accuracy. To summarize:

OBSERVATION 10. *As prefetching accuracy improves, prefetching becomes more effective, while bandwidth partitioning becomes less effective in improving system performance.*

Note that DiffWS(prefOpt-Opt) stays negative until Thread 2's accuracy exceeds 30%. This means that at low coverage and accuracy, prefetching may degrade performance so much that bandwidth partitioning cannot fully repair it. Only when prefetching is useful enough and the difference in miss and prefetch frequencies is high enough, can bandwidth partitioning fully repair the performance loss from prefetching. Thus:

OBSERVATION 11. *The decision to turn on or off prefetching, should be made prior to bandwidth partitioning, because bandwidth partitioning may not fully repair the performance loss due to low coverage and accuracy prefetching.*

This observation explains the reason for experimental results in Figure 1. Therefore, our prefetching profitability metric should be used to decide whether to selectively turn on/off prefetching for each core prior to making bandwidth partitioning decisions.

5. EMPIRICAL EVALUATION

5.1 Environment and Methodology

Simulation Parameters. We use a cycle-accurate full system simulator based on Simics [24] to model a CMP system with dual and quad cores. Each core has a scalar in-order issue pipeline with 4GHz clock frequency. To remove the effect of cache contention between cores, each core has private L1 and L2 caches. The L1 instruction cache and data caches are 16KB, 2-way associative, and have a 2-cycle access latency. The L2 cache is 512KB, 8-way associative, and has an 8-cycle access latency. All caches use a 64-byte block size, implement write-back policy, and LRU replacement. The bus to off-chip memory is a split transaction bus, with a peak bandwidth of 800MB/s for a single core system, 1.6GB/s for dual-core CMP and 3.2GB/s for quad-core CMP. The average main memory access latency is 300 cycles. The simulator allocates contiguous physical memory to each application. The CMP runs Linux OS that comes with Fedora Core 4 distribution.

Hardware Prefetchers. The L2 cache of each core is augmented with a typical stream prefetcher, similar to the hardware prefetchers used in previous studies [19, 20]. The stream buffers are commonly implemented in modern processors [2, 8, 9, 11] due to their low hardware cost and high effectiveness for a wide range of applications. Stream buffers can detect accesses to block addresses that form a sequential or stride pattern (called a *stream*), and prefetch the next few blocks in the stream in anticipation of continuing accesses from the stream. We implement a stream prefetcher with four streams, and up to four blocks prefetched for each stream.

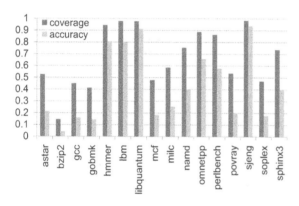

Figure 5: Benchmarks prefetch coverage and accuracy.

Workload Construction. We consider seventeen C/C++ benchmarks from the SPEC2006 benchmark suite [34]. We compile the benchmarks using `gcc` compiler with `O1` optimization level into `x86` binaries. We use the *ref* input sets, simulate 250 million instructions after skipping the initialization phase of each benchmark, by inserting breakpoints when major data structures have been initialized. We pair the benchmarks into co-schedules of two or four benchmarks. To reduce the number of co-schedules that we need to evaluate, we categorize the benchmarks based on the prefetching characteristics. Figure 5 shows the prefetch coverage and accuracy of each benchmark. From the figure, we pick up three representative benchmarks that have low (*bzip2*), medium (*astar*) and high (*hmmer*) coverage and accuracy, and pair each one with the other benchmarks to cover all representative co-schedules.

5.2 Experimental Results

5.2.1 Validating the Prefetching Metric

In this section, we investigate how well the composite prefetching metric in Equation 14 predicts prefetching performance profitability. We run each application on a single core system with available bandwidth of 800MB/s, and measure CPIs when prefetching is turned on (CPI_p) and when prefetching is turned off (CPI). Then we compute the difference ($\Delta CPI = CPI_p - CPI$) for each benchmark. A negative number represents performance improvement while a positive value represents degradation. Table 2 shows the applications sorted by their ΔCPIs. As a comparison, we compute our composite prefetching metric $\theta = \frac{MAK^2}{B^2}f(c - 2 + \frac{1-c}{a})$ and sort the applications in decreasing order of θ. Finally, conventional wisdom evaluates prefetching performance based on coverage or accuracy, so we also show the applications sorted in increasing order of accuracy. Note that Figure 5 shows that coverage and accuracy are highly correlated, hence we only show accuracy in the table. Applications whose ranks match with ones obtained from ΔCPI sorting are shown in bold.

Table 2: Ranking of applications based on ΔCPI, our composite metric θ, and prefetching accuracy a.

ΔCPI-sorted		θ-sorted		a-sorted
Benchmark	ΔCPI	Benchmark	θ	Benchmark
bzip2	4.837	**bzip2**	1375.77	**bzip2**
soplex	4.484	**soplex**	148.61	gobmk
mcf	4.463	**mcf**	145.88	gcc
gobmk	0.218	**gobmk**	85.44	soplex
gcc	0.207	**gcc**	78.25	mcf
povray	-0.006	astar	56.40	**povray**
namd	-0.012	milc	10.40	astar
omnetpp	-0.047	povray	0.83	milc
astar	-0.101	namd	-1.47	sphinx3
milc	-0.285	omnetpp	-7.92	namd
perlbench	-0.293	**perlbench**	-25.29	**perlbench**
hmmer	-1.364	**hmmer**	-43.11	omnetpp
sphinx3	-1.565	libquantum	-62.90	lbm
libquantum	-3.770	lbm	-69.39	hmmer
lbm	-4.196	sphinx3	-74.13	libquantum
sjeng	-13.820	**sjeng**	-76.86	**sjeng**

Let us compare the ranks of applications based on the actual performance improvement due to prefetching (ΔCPI), vs. based on our metric θ. The ranks of eight applications (shown in bold) out of sixteen exactly match. For the other eight applications, their ranks differ by at most three positions, indicating how well our metric θ correlates with the actual performance. If each application is given a rank number, and we compare ranks based on ΔCPI vs. θ, the correlation coefficient computes to 95%, indicating high correlation between them. In contrast, the correlation of ranks based on ΔCPI vs. accuracy a computes to 89%. From the rank comparison, it is clear that our composite metric correlates much better with the actual performance than conventional metrics such as accuracy or coverage.

In addition, conventional metrics cannot determine what level of accuracy or coverage is high enough to produce performance improvement, whereas our composite metric θ includes a performance profitability threshold (Equation 14): $T_m > \frac{\theta}{\alpha}$, where $\alpha \in (0, 1)$ is a number that reflects how bursty memory accesses are. Even when α is unknown, θ can still determine prefetching profitability unambiguously in some cases. For example, $\theta = 1375.77$ for *bzip2*, which is much larger than the fully exposed memory access latency $T_m = 300$ cycles, hence θ predicts unambiguously that prefetching will hurt performance (Observation 2). In addition, there are eight applications showing negative θ values in Table 2. θ predicts unambiguously that prefetching will improve performance. Only for seven out of sixteen cases, the actual value of α is needed to determine whether prefetching is profitable. Now we will show how α can be estimated.

If we choose $\alpha = 0.2$, all benchmarks ranked above *astar* satisfy $T_m \leq \frac{\theta}{\alpha}$, while all benchmarks ranked at *astar* and below satisfy $T_m > \frac{\theta}{\alpha}$. Thus, 0.2 provides a reasonable estimate for α. To validate the goodness of the estimate $\alpha = 0.2$, we double the available bandwidth to $B = 1.6$GB/s, and re-run all the benchmarks to identify which benchmarks can benefit from prefetching. Due to the increase in available bandwidth, now only *bzip2* suffers from performance degradation, while all other benchmarks enjoy performance

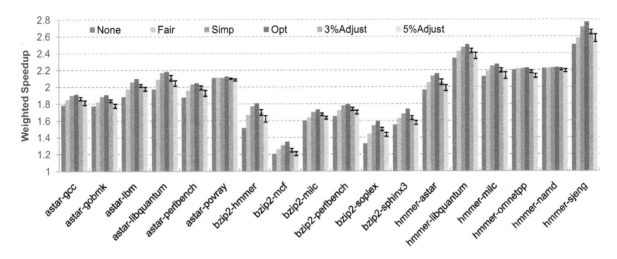

Figure 6: Weighted speedup for various partitioning schemes in a dual-core CMP system with prefetchers turned on.

improvement. Using $\alpha = 0.2$, θ correctly predicts this outcome: only for *bzip2*, $\theta = 469.57 > T_m$, while for all other benchmarks $\frac{\theta}{0.2} < T_m$. For further validation, we also tried another algorithm by controlling the prefetch aggressiveness, which directly changes the coverage and accuracy for all benchmarks. Again, $\alpha = 0.2$ predicts prefetching performance very well, and hence can be used to decide whether to turn on/off prefetching.

5.2.2 Approximating Optimum Bandwidth Partition

Recall that Equation 21 provides the weighted speedup optimum bandwidth shares for different cores with prefetchers turned on. Unfortunately, the equation cannot be implemented in hardware because the inputs $CPI_{alone,i}$ and $CPI_{L2\infty,i}$ cannot be easily obtained. To make a practical implementation, we assume $C_i = \frac{CPI_{alone,i}}{CPI_{L2\infty,i}} = 1$ and use it in the simplified partitioning scheme. The assumption no longer guarantees the optimality of performance, but we will demonstrate that the deviation from optimum is minor.

The bandwidth partitioning is enforced using token bucket algorithm [23], where a token generator distributes tokens to different per-core buckets at the rates proportional to the fraction of bandwidth allocated to different cores. Each cache miss or prefetch request is allowed to go to the off-chip interface only when the core generating the request has matching tokens in its bucket. In order to adapt to the changes in program behavior over time, we implement a dynamic partitioning scheme, where at the end of each interval of 1-million clock cycles, the miss and prefetch frequencies of various cores from the interval that just ended, are used to compute the new bandwidth shares for the next interval.

We test our bandwidth partitioning algorithm by comparing the weighted speedup with several schemes as shown in Figure 6: fair partitioning (Fair), which allocates the off-chip bandwidth equally among cores [27], simplified optimum partitioning (Simp), which assumes $C_i = 1$, and the true optimum partitioning (Opt), which relies on multiple simulation passes to collect the actual values of $CPI_{alone,i}$ and $CPI_{L2\infty,i}$, and allocations adjusted by 3% and 5% (x%Adjust) from Simp. Specifically, for each adjustment amount, we select one application and bump its bandwidth allocation by x%, and correspondingly reduce the allocation of the other by x%. There are two choices for each x% adjustment, so we show the average weighted speedup as a bar and the range (max and min) as a candle in the figure. For all cases, the prefetcher of each core is turned on.

The figure shows that compared to applying prefetching without bandwidth partitioning (None), fair partitioning (Fair) improves weighted speedup, primarily because to an extent it avoids pathological cases where one core dominates the bandwidth usage. However, our simplified bandwidth partitioning (Simp) outperforms Fair in all cases, because it dynamically chooses optimal bandwidth allocations. On average, the improvement in weighted speedup from Simp over None is twice as high as that from Fair, and is very close to the optimum partitioning (Opt), implying that assuming $C_i = 1$ does not cause Simp to deviate much from Opt.

When the bandwidth allocations are adjusted by even a small amount (3%) from the simplified allocations, weighted speedup degrades (or at best remains constant), comparing to Simp. The degradation increases with 5% adjustment. This implies that the bandwidth allocations achieved by Simp is within 3% deviation from Opt. Finally, the 3% and 5% adjustments also show that bandwidth partitioning can hurt performance if bandwidth allocations are not computed correctly, because bandwidth fragmentation may occur, in which memory requests that should have been served on the idle bus have to wait for new tokens, while other cores have tokens that they cannot utilize.

5.2.3 Validating Observations in Partitioning Model

In Section 4, we showed case studies using the bandwidth partition model and obtained several observations. In this section, we validate these observations through empirical evaluation. Figure 7 shows the weighted speedup and bandwidth share for various application co-schedules running on a dual-core CMP with four different configurations: no prefetching or bandwidth partitioning (Neither), prefetching for both cores but no bandwidth partitioning (Pref), no prefetching but simplified bandwidth partitioning (Simp), as well as prefetching for both cores and simplified bandwidth partitioning (Pref+Simp). The available memory bandwidth is 1.6GB/s.

The bandwidth shares show that when bandwidth partitioning is deployed, the application that has higher bandwidth demand is assigned smaller fraction of bandwidth, vs. when bandwidth partitioning is not used (Pref+Simp vs. Pref, and Simp vs. Neither). This agrees with Observation 5.

Comparing the bandwidth shares after prefetching vs. no prefetching (Pref+Simp vs. Pref), the application with higher prefetching coverage and accuracy receives smaller bandwidth share, validating Observation 6, Observation 8 and Observation 9.

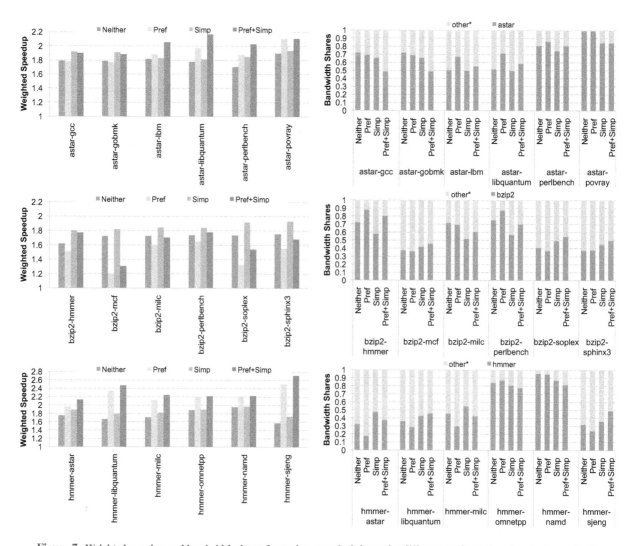

Figure 7: Weighted speedup and bandwidth shares for various co-schedules under different configurations in a dual-core CMP.

In Figure 7, we can see that in some cases (e.g. *astar-lbm* and *astar-libquantum*), Simp does not improve performance over Neither much. This is due to both applications in the co-schedules have roughly equal miss frequency (50%), hence their natural bandwidth shares already achieves optimum weighted speedup. However, after prefetching is applied, the weighted speedup improvement from bandwidth partitioning becomes large (Pref+Simp vs. Pref). The reason is because prefetching increases the difference in bandwidth demand of two cores, and therefore increases the impact of bandwidth partitioning on weighted speedup. This is also the case for most of the other co-schedules. In contrast, prefetching slightly decreases the difference in bandwidth demand (bandwidth shares Pref vs. Neither) in four co-schedules: *astar-gcc*, *astar-gobmk*, *bzip2-milc* and *bzip2-sphinx3*. This reduces the effectiveness of bandwidth partitioning, as can be seen from the smaller improvement of Pref+Simp over Pref, compared to the improvement of Simp over Neither. These results validate Observation 7.

For certain co-schedules such as *astar-povray*, *hmmer-omnetpp* and *hmmer-namd*, bandwidth partitioning does not affect performance much, regardless of prefetching (Simp vs. Neither, and Pref+Simp vs. Pref). The reason is that *povray*, *omnetpp* and *namd* are not bandwidth intensive due to the very few cache misses and

prefetches. This makes the available bandwidth plentiful enough that bandwidth partitioning is not needed.

Finally, comparing the weighted speedup of Pref with Simp, we can see cases where prefetching improves weighted speedup more than bandwidth partitioning, such as in all co-schedules *hmmer* runs in. This is due to the high prefetching coverage and accuracy of *hmmer*, consistent with Observation 10.

5.2.4 Co-Deciding Prefetching and Partitioning

In this section, we show results where our prefetching profitability metric in Inequality 14 guides the decision to selectively turn on/off prefetchers, coupled with dynamic bandwidth partitioning.

Figure 8 shows the weighted speedup for four system configurations a CMP system: no prefetching or bandwidth partitioning (Neither), only simplified bandwidth partitioning (Simp), all prefetchers turned on and bandwidth partitioning (AllPref+Simp), and selective activation of each core's prefetcher guided by prefetching profitability metric coupled with bandwidth partitioning (Ctrl-Pref+Simp). Specifically, we assume $\alpha = 0.2$ as discussed in Section 5.2.1. To make prefetching decision, we first run the applications on a CMP system with equal share of the available bandwidth for each core, and profile the hardware counters needed for computing θ. Based on the computed θ, we statically turn on/off the

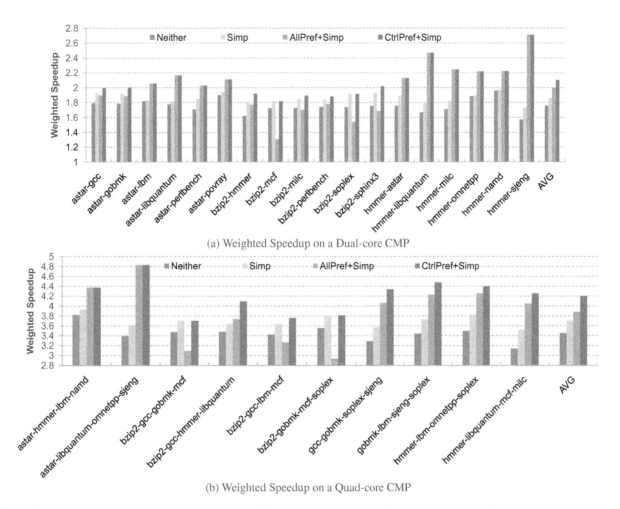

(a) Weighted Speedup on a Dual-core CMP

(b) Weighted Speedup on a Quad-core CMP

Figure 8: Weighted speedup of optimum bandwidth partitioning for no prefetching, all prefetching, vs. selectively turning on prefetchers using the composite prefetching metric on dual-core CMP with 1.6GB/s bandwidth (a), and quad-core CMP with 3.2GB/s bandwidth (b).

prefetcher of a core, and run the applications again to collect performance. Note that nothing prevents the prefetching decision to be performed dynamically at run time. However, making prefetching decision statically is sufficient to demonstrate the effectiveness of the prefetching profitability metric. The experiments are evaluated on a dual-core CMP with available bandwidth of 1.6GB/s and on a quad-core CMP with available bandwidth of 3.2GB/s respectively.

The figure shows that in many cases, turning on all prefetchers (AllPref+Simp) degrades performance over no prefetching (Simp) (i.e. 8 out of 16 co-schedules on a dual core CMP, and in 3 out of 10 co-schedules on a quad-core CMP). Worse, performance of All-Pref+Simp is even lower than the base case CMP without prefetching or bandwidth partitioning (Neither) in a majority of the above cases. This indicates that prefetching can be too harmful for bandwidth partitioning to offset, consistent with Observation 11.

In both figures, when we use our prefetching profitability criterion to guide the decision to turn on/off each core's prefetcher, coupled with dynamic bandwidth partitioning, the best weighted speedup can be achieved for all co-schedules. CtrlPref+Simp has at least the same performance as the best of Simp and AllPref+Simp, and in many cases outperforms both of them significantly. On average, over Neither, Simp, and AllPref+Simp, CtrlPref+Simp improves weighted speedup by 6.0%, 13.6% and 19.5%, respectively on a dual-core CMP, and 7.2%, 12.5% and 21.8%, respectively on a quad-core CMP.

6. CONCLUSIONS

The goal of this paper is to understand how hardware prefetching and memory bandwidth partitioning in CMP can affect system performance and interact with each other. We have presented an analytical model to achieve this goal. Firstly, we derived a composite prefetching metric that can help determine under which situations hardware prefetcher can improve system performance. Then we constructed a bandwidth partitioning model that can derive weighted speedup-optimum bandwidth allocations among different cores. We showed three case studies based on the partitioning model and arrived at several interesting observations. For instance, prefetching can increase the impact of bandwidth partitioning on system performance by increasing the difference of bandwidth demand from different cores and making the available bandwidth scarcer. When prefetchers are turned on for all cores, weighted speedup optimum partitioning tends to assign more bandwidth to the cores running applications with lower coverage and accuracy, compared to without using prefetching. Finally, we collected simulation results to validate the observations obtained from the analytical model, and show system performance improvement that can be achieved by co-deciding prefetching and bandwidth partitioning decisions using our prefetching metric and implementable dynamic bandwidth partitioning.

7. REFERENCES

[1] A. Snavely and D.M. Tullsen. Symbiotic Job Scheduling for a Simultaneous Multithreading Processor. In *Proc. of 19th Intl. Conf. on Architecture Support for Programming Language and Operating Systems(ASPLOS)*, 2000.

[2] B. Sinharoy and R.N. Kalla and J.M. Tendler and R.J. Eickemeyer and J.B. Joyner. POWER5 System Microarchitecture. *IBM Journal of Research and Development*, 49(4/5):505–521, 2005.

[3] R. Bitirgen, E. Ipek, and J. Martinez. Coordinated Management of Multiple Interacting Resources in Chip Multiprocessors: A Machine Learning Approach. In *Proc. of the 41th IEEE/ACM Intl. Symp. on Microarchitecture (MICRO)*, 2008.

[4] E. Ebrahimi, O. Mutlu, C. Lee, and Y. Patt. Coordinated Control of Multiple Prefetchers in Multi-Core Systems. In *Proc. of the 42th IEEE/ACM Intl. Symp. on Microarchitecture (MICRO)*, 2009.

[5] E. Ebrahimi, O. Mutlu, and Y. Patt. Techniques for Bandwidth-efficient Prefetching of Linked Data Structures in Hybrid Prefetching Systems. In *15th Intl. Symp. on High Performance Computer Architecture(HPCA)*, 2009.

[6] P. Emma. Understanding Some Simple Processor-Performance Limits. *IBM Journal of Research and Development*, 41(3), 1997.

[7] F. Liu and Y. Solihin. Understanding the Behavior and Implications of Context Switch Misses. *ACM Trans. on Architecture and Code Optimization (TACO)*, 7(4):21:1–28, 2010.

[8] G. Hinton and D. Sager and M. Upton and D. Boggs and D. Carmean and A. Kyker and P. Roussel. The Microarchitecture of the Pentium 4 Processor. *Intel Technology Journal*, (Q1), 2001.

[9] H.Q. Le and W.J. Starke and J.S. Fields and F.O. Connell and D.Q. Nguyen and B.J. Ronchetti and W.M Sauer and E.M. Schwarz and M.T. Waden. IBM Power6 Microarchitecture. *IBM Journal of Research and Development*, 51:639–662, 2007.

[10] I.B. Vapnyarskii. Numerical Methods of Solving Problems of the Mathematical Theory of Standardization. *USSR Computational Mathematics and Mathematical Physics*, 18(2):484–487, 1978.

[11] IBM. *IBM Power4 System Architecture White Paper*, 2002.

[12] E. Ipek, O. Mutlu, J. Martinez, and R. Caruana. Self-Optimizing Memory Controller: A Reinforcement Learning Approach. In *Proc.of the 35th Intl. Symp. on Computer Architecture (ISCA)*, 2008.

[13] ITRS. International Technology Roadmap for Semiconductors: 2005 Edition, Assembly and packaging. In *http://www.itrs.net/Links/2005ITRS/AP2005.pdf*, 2005.

[14] X. Jiang, N. Madan, L. Zhao, M. Upton, R. Iyer, S. Makineni, D. Newell, Y. Solihin, and R. Balasubramanian. CHOP: Adaptive Filter-Based DRAM Caching for CMP Server Platforms. In *Proc. of the 16th Intl. Symp. on High Performance Computer Architecture (HPCA)*, 2010.

[15] X. Jiang, N. Madan, L. Zhao, M. Upton, R. Iyer, S. Makineni, D. Newell, Y. Solihin, and R. Balasubramanian. CHOP: Integrating DRAM Caches for CMP Server Platforms. *IEEE Micro Top Picks*, 31(1):99–108, 2011.

[16] X. Jiang, A. Mishra, L. Zhao, R. Iyer, Z. Fang, S. Srinivasan, S. Makineni, P. Brett, and C. Das. ACCESS: Smart Scheduling for Asymmetric Cache CMPs. In *Proc. of the 17th Intl. Symp. on High Performance Computer Architecture (HPCA)*, 2011.

[17] X. Jiang and Y. Solihin. Architectural Framework for Supporting Operating System Survivability. In *Proc. of the 17th Intl. Symp. on High Performance Computer Architecture (HPCA)*, 2011.

[18] X. Jiang, Y. Solihin, L. Zhao, and R. Iyer. Architecture Support for Improving Bulk Memory Copying and Initialization Performance. In *Proc. of the 18th Intl. Conf. on Parallel Architecture and Compilation Techniques (PACT)*, 2009.

[19] N. Jouppi. Improving Direct-Mapped Cache Performance by the Addition of a Small Fully-Associative Cache and Prefetch Buffers. In *Proc. of the 17th Intl. Symp. on Computer Architecture*, 1990.

[20] C. Lee, O. Mutlu, V. Narasiman, and Y. Patt. Prefetch-Aware DRAM Controller. In *Proc. of the 41th IEEE/ACM Intl. Symp. on Microarchitecture (MICRO)*, 2008.

[21] J. Little. A Proof of Queueing Formula $L = \lambda W$. *Operations Research*, 9(383–387), 1961.

[22] F. Liu, F. Guo, S. Kim, A. Eker, and Y. Solihin. Characterizing and Modeling the Behavior of Context Switch Misses. In *Proc. of the 17th Intl. Conf. on Parallel Architecture and Compilation Techniques (PACT)*, 2008.

[23] F. Liu, X. Jiang, and Y. Solihin. Understanding How Off-Chip Memory Bandwidth Partitioning in Chip Multiprocessors Affects System Performance. In *16th Intl. Symp. on High Performance Computer Architecture*, 2010.

[24] P. S. Magnusson, M. Christensson, J. Eskilson, D. Forsgren, G. Hallberg, J. Hogberg, F. Larsson, A. Moestedt, and B. Werner. Simics: A Full System Simulation Platform. *IEEE Computer Society*, 35(2):50–58, 2002.

[25] O. Mutlu and T. Moscibroda. Stall-Time Fair Memory Access Scheduling for Chip Multiprocessors. In *Proc. of the 40th IEEE/ACM Intl. Symp. on Microarchitecture (MICRO)*, 2007.

[26] O. Mutlu and T. Moscibroda. Parallelism-Aware Batch Scheduling: Enhancing both Performance and Fairness of Shared DRAM Systems. In *Proc.of the 35th Intl. Symp. on Computer Architecture (ISCA)*, 2008.

[27] K. Nesbit, D. Aggarwal, J. Laudon, and J. Smith. Fair Queuing Memory System. In *Proc. of the 39th IEEE/ACM Intl. Symp. on Microarchitecture (MICRO)*, 2006.

[28] N. Rafique, W. Lim, and M. Thottethodi. Effective Management of DRAM Bandwidth in Multicore Processors. In *Proc. of the 16th Intl. Conf. on Parallel Architectures and Compilation Techniques(PACT)*, 2007.

[29] S. Rixner, W. Dally, U. Kapasi, P. Mattson, and J. Owens. Memory Access Scheduling. In *Proc.of the 27th Intl. Symp. on Computer Architecture (ISCA)*, 2000.

[30] B. Rogers, A. Krishna, G. Bell, X. Jiang, and Y. Solihin. Scaling the Bandwidth Wall: Challenges in and Avenues for CMP Scaling. In *Proc. of the 36th Intl. Conf. on Computer Architecture (ISCA)*, 2009.

[31] L. Spracklen, Y. Chou, and S. Spracklen. Effective Instruction Prefetching in Chip Multiprocessors for Modern Commercial Applications. In *11th Intl. Symp. on High Performance Computer Architecture(HPCA)*, 2004.

[32] S. Srikantaiah and M. Kandemir. SRP: Symbiotic Resource Partitioning of the Memory Hierarchy in CMPs. In *In Proc. of Intl. Conf. on High Performance Embedded Architectures and Compilers (HiPEAC)*, 2010.

[33] S. Srinath, O. Mutlu, H. Kim, and Y. Patt. Feedback Directed Prefetching: Improving the Performance and Bandwidth-efficiency of Hardware Prefetchers. In *13th Intl. Symp. on High Performance Computer Architecture(HPCA)*, 2007.

[34] Standard Performance Evaluation Corporation. Spec cpu2006 benchmarks. *http://www.spec.org*, 2006.

[35] X. Zhuang and H.-H. Lee. Reducing Cache Pollution via Dynamic Data Prefetch Filtering. *IEEE Trans. on Computers*, 56(1):18–31, 2007.

Stability Analysis of QCN: The Averaging Principle

Mohammad Alizadeh, Abdul Kabbani, Berk Atikoglu, and Balaji Prabhakar

Department of Electrical Engineering, Stanford University
{alizade, akabbani, atikoglu, balaji}@stanford.edu

ABSTRACT

Data Center Networks have recently caused much excitement in the industry and in the research community. They represent the convergence of networking, storage, computing and virtualization. This paper is concerned with the Quantized Congestion Notification (QCN) algorithm, developed for Layer 2 congestion management. QCN has recently been standardized as the IEEE 802.1Qau Ethernet Congestion Notification standard.

We provide a stability analysis of QCN, especially in terms of its ability to utilize high capacity links in the shallow-buffered data center network environment. After a brief description of the QCN algorithm, we develop a delay-differential equation model for mathematically characterizing it. We analyze the model using a linearized approximation, obtaining stability margins as a function of algorithm parameters and network operating conditions. A second contribution of the paper is the articulation and analysis of the Averaging Principle (AP)—a new method for stabilizing control loops when lags increase. The AP is distinct from other well-known methods of feedback stabilization such as higher-order state feedback and lag-dependent gain adjustment. It turns out that the QCN and the BIC-TCP (and CUBIC) algorithms use the AP; we show that this enables them to be stable under large lags. The AP is also of independent interest since it applies to general control systems, not just congestion control systems.

Categories and Subject Descriptors

C.2.2 [**Computer-Communication Networks**]: Network Protocols

General Terms

Algorithms, Performance, Theory

Keywords

Data center, Layer 2 congestion control, Ethernet, QCN

1. INTRODUCTION

Data centers pose interesting challenges in the areas of computing, storage and networking, and have caused the convergence of these disparate industries. Cloud computing platforms [14, 21, 3] need switching fabrics that simultaneously support latency sensitive high performance computing traffic, loss and latency sensitive storage traffic, and throughput intensive bulk data transfers. Similarly, the FCoE (Fiber Channel over Ethernet) standard [9] enables storage traffic to be carried over Ethernet. In order to facilitate this convergence, the IEEE 802.1 standards body has introduced several enhancements to classical Ethernet, notably the IEEE 802.1Qbb [24] and the IEEE 802.1Qau [23] standards. This work was undertaken by the Data Center Bridging Task Group [7].

The 802.1Qbb standard allows an Ethernet switch to pause transmission at its upstream neighbor switch on a per priority basis. This ensures that packets are not dropped, a feature that is critical for Fiber Channel traffic. However, since this can cause congestion to spread upstream and introduce spurious bottlenecks, the 802.1Qau standard enables an Ethernet switch to directly signal congestion to an Ethernet source in a manner similar to congestion control algorithms in the Internet.

This paper concerns the QCN (Quantized Congestion Notification) algorithm, which the authors have helped to develop as the IEEE 802.1Qau standard. The QCN algorithm has been described in previous work [2]; here, we are interested in analyzing the stability properties of the QCN feedback control loop.

There is an extensive literature on the design and analysis of congestion control algorithms in the Internet, especially for the high bandwidth–delay product regime [10, 18, 8, 27, 19, 28, 13]. In this regime, buffer occupancies become oscillatory (or the congestion control loop becomes "unstable"), causing link underutilization [20, 25]. The data center environment poses similar challenges, making it imperative that QCN ensure stable buffer occupancies. Specifically, data center Ethernet switches typically have buffers which are very small relative to the bandwidth-delay product and, hence, they can easily underflow or overflow. Furthermore, the number of flows which are simultaneously active on a link in a data center network is very small, typically fewer than 10. This makes it difficult to benefit from statistical multiplexing to reduce buffering requirements [4].[1]

---

[1]We revisit buffer sizing in Section 4 and refer to [2] for more discussion about the operating conditions in a data center.

The following are our main contributions:

(i) We obtain a delay-differential equation fluid model description of the QCN feedback control system. This model differs from conventional fluid models in that a QCN source needs *two* variables to describe its evolution as opposed to just one variable. We analyze this model using standard techniques and obtain the stability margins of the algorithm as a function of its design parameters and network conditions like link speeds, number of flows and round-trip time. These results complement the extensive investigation of QCN via simulation and experimentation conducted during the standardization process [23].

(ii) We describe the Averaging Principle (AP) which is a simple method for improving the stability of a control loop in the presence of increasing feedback delay. The QCN (and the BIC-TCP [28]) algorithm employs the AP, and we show that the AP is the underlying reason for the good stability properties of QCN. We also demonstrate the generality of the AP by applying it to various other feedback systems.

(iii) Finally, we analyze the AP and find that for linear control systems, it is *algebraically equivalent* to a PD (proportional-derivative) controller; that is, the AP controller and the PD controller are input-output equivalent. Since the PD controller is well-known to stabilize control loops when lags increase [11], this equivalence provides a precise characterization of the stability properties of the AP. This result is very useful in practice because the PD controller requires the switch to provide an *additional* derivative of the state—something difficult to achieve in practice since switches implement QCN functionality in hardware. The AP shows how an equivalent effect can be achieved without modifying switches.

Related literature on congestion control. Control theory prescribes two methods of feedback compensation and these have both been used to design stable congestion control algorithms as lags (round-trip times) increase. In one approach, an estimate of the RTT is used to find the correct "gains" for the loop to be stable. For example, this is the approach taken by FAST [27], XCP [18], RCP [8] and HSTCP [10].[2] The second approach improves stability by increasing the order of the feedback by sending higher order derivatives of the queue size. For instance, the active queue management schemes REM [5], and PI [15] compute a weighted sum of the queue size and its derivative (which equals input rate less output rate) as the congestion signal. This is also used in XCP and RCP.

On the other hand, BIC-TCP [28] operates stably in high bandwidth–delay product networks, even though it neither changes loop gains based on RTT nor uses higher order feedback. But it operates in the self-clocked universe of Internet congestion control schemes, where window size changes are made once every RTT. So there is the possibility that it implicitly exploits a knowledge of RTTs to derive stability. As we shall see, the QCN algorithm has no notion of RTTs. This and the similarity of operation of the BIC-TCP and QCN algorithms suggest there may be a more fundamental reason for their good stability. Our attempt to understand this reason has led us to the Averaging Principle.

---

[2]HSTCP does not explicitly use RTT estimates to adjust gains. Rather, it varies gains based on current window size, which implicitly depends on the RTT—the larger the RTT, the larger the current window.

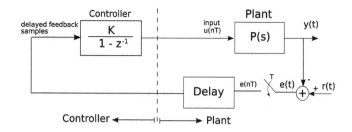

Figure 1: A generic sampled control system.

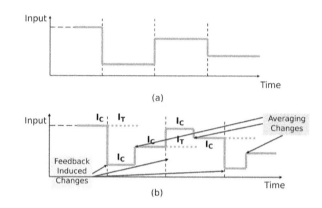

Figure 2: Plant input signal generated by (a) standard and (b) AP controller.

The Averaging Principle (AP). We explain the AP in the context of a generic control system such as the one shown in Fig. 1. The output of the system, $y(t)$, tracks a reference signal, $r(t)$, which is often a constant. The error, $e(t) = r(t) - y(t)$, is sampled with period T and fed back to the controller with some delay. The controller incrementally adjusts the input to the plant as follows:

$$u((n+1)T) = u(nT) + K\,e(nT), \qquad (1)$$

where K is the controller gain. The input is held constant between sampling times; i.e., $u(t) = u(nT)$ for $nT \le t < (n+1)T$. Fig. 2(a) illustrates the action of the controller just described. To translate this to the congestion control setting, the source (the controller) chooses a packet sending rate (i.e., the input $u(t)$). The output $y(t)$ is the queue size and rate information at a router or a switch. The error $e(t)$ is a deviation of the current queue size and rate from target values. The sampling period T is a function of the packet arrival rate, since most congestion control algorithms sample packets.

Fig. 2(b) shows the AP controller. This controller reacts to feedback messages it receives from the plant exactly as in (1), at times which are labelled "feedback-induced changes" in the figure. Note that feedback-induced changes occur every T units of time. At any time, let I_C (for current input) denote the value of the input, and let I_T (for target input) denote the value of the input *before* the last feedback induced change.

Precisely $T/2$ time units after every feedback-induced change, the AP controller performs an "averaging change", where the controller changes I_C as follows:

$$I_C \leftarrow \frac{I_C + I_T}{2}.$$

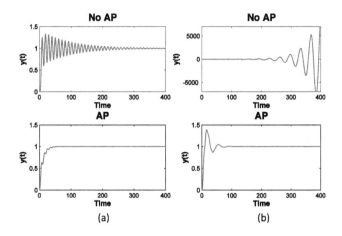

Figure 3: Unit step responses of the standard and AP controllers: (a) zero delay and (b) 8 secs delay. AP stabilizes the system.

The term "averaging" comes from the above equation: I_C moves to the average of its values before and after the last feedback-induced change. The BIC-TCP and the QCN algorithms perform averaging several times after receiving a congestion signal and we shall see that this results in their more stable operation.

To illustrate the effectiveness of the AP, let us consider an example linear, zero-delay stable control system with plant transfer function

$$P(s) = \frac{s+1}{s^3 + 1.6s^2 + 0.8s + 0.6},$$

controller gain $K = 1/8$, and sampling period $T = 1$s. We use a unit step function as the reference signal, and compare the stability of the control loop with and without AP as the delay increases. As shown in Fig. 3(a), when there is no delay, both schemes are stable. However, the AP controller induces less oscillations and settles faster. As the delay increases to $\tau = 8$s, the standard controller becomes unstable. However, the AP controller is more robust and continues to be stable. In fact, in this example, AP remains stable for delays up to $\tau = 15$s.

Organization of the paper. We briefly describe the salient features of the QCN algorithm and present the corresponding mathematical model (delay-differential equations) in Sections 2.1 and 2.2 respectively. We analyze a linearized approximation of this model in Section 2.3 to find the stability margins of the algorithm. We compare the stability of the linearized model with and without AP in Section 2.4 and find that the AP increases the stability margin. We analyze the AP in Section 3.1 and prove that, for linear control systems, it is algebraically equivalent to a PD (proportional-derivative) controller. We apply the AP to another congestion control algorithm, RCP [8], in Section 3.2 as an illustration of its wide applicability. We revisit the discussion in [4] in Section 4 and show that the AP reduces the buffering requirements at network switchs by reducing the *variance* in the sending rate of a source. We conclude in Section 5.

2. QCN

We begin with a brief overview of the QCN algorithm, focusing on those aspects which are relevant for the mathematical model.

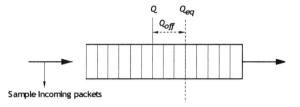

Figure 4: Congestion detection in QCN CP.

2.1 The QCN Algorithm

The QCN algorithm has two components: (i) the switch, or Congestion Point (CP) mechanism, and (ii) the source, or Reaction Point (RP) mechanism. The CP mechanism is concerned with measuring the extent of congestion at the switch buffer, and signaling this information back to the source(s). The RP mechanism is concerned with the actions that need to be taken when a congestion signal is received, and how sources must probe for available bandwidth when there is no congestion.

The CP Algorithm
The CP buffer is shown in Fig. 4. The goal of the CP is to maintain the buffer occupancy at a desired operating point, Q_{eq}. The CP computes a congestion measure F_b (defined below). With a probability p_s (1% by default), it randomly samples[3] an incoming packet and sends the value of F_b in a feedback message to the source of the sampled packet.

Let Q denote the instantaneous queue-size and Q_{old} denote the queue-size when the last packet was sampled. Let $Q_{off} = Q - Q_{eq}$ and $Q_\delta = Q - Q_{old}$. Then F_b is given by the formula:

$$F_b = Q_{off} + wQ_\delta,$$

where w is a positive constant (set to 2 by default).

The interpretation is that F_b captures a combination of queue-size excess (Q_{off}) and rate excess (Q_δ). Thus, when $F_b > 0$, either the buffer or the link or both are oversubscribed. A feedback message containing F_b, quantized to 6 bits, is sent to the source of the sampled packet *only* when $F_b > 0$; nothing is signaled when $F_b \leq 0$.

The RP Algorithm
The basic RP behavior is shown in Fig. 5. The RP algorithm maintains the following quantities:

- *Current Rate* (R_C): The sending rate at any time.

- *Target Rate* (R_T): The sending rate *just before* the arrival of the last feedback message.

Rate decrease. This occurs only when a feedback message is received, in which case R_C and R_T are updated as follows:

$$R_T \leftarrow R_C, \tag{2}$$

$$R_C \leftarrow R_C(1 - G_d F_b), \tag{3}$$

where the constant G_d is chosen so that $G_d F_{bmax} = \frac{1}{2}$; i.e. the sending rate can decrease by at most 50 %.

Rate increase. Since the RP is not given positive rate-increase signals by the network, it needs a mechanism for

---

[3]In the actual implementation, the sampling probability varies between 1-10% depending on the severity of congestion. We neglect this feature in this paper to keep the model tractable; refer to [2] and [17] for details.

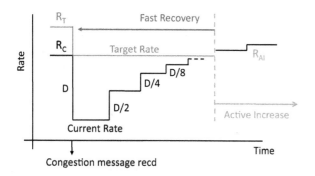

Figure 5: QCN RP operation.

increasing its sending rate on its own. This is achieved by using a *Byte Counter*, which counts the number of bytes transmitted by the RP.[4] Rate increase occurs in two phases: Fast Recovery and Active Increase.

Fast Recovery (FR). Immediately following a rate decrease episode, the Byte Counter is reset, and the RP enters the FR state. FR consists of 5 cycles; in each cycle 150 KBytes (100 packets, each 1500 Bytes long) of data are transmitted, as counted by the Byte Counter. At the end of each cycle, R_T remains unchanged while R_C is updated as follows:

$$R_C \leftarrow \frac{1}{2}(R_C + R_T).$$

Active Increase (AI). After 5 cycles of FR have completed, the RP enters the AI state where it probes for extra bandwidth on the path. In this phase, the RP increases its sending rate by updating R_T and R_C at the end of each cycle as follows:

$$R_T \leftarrow R_T + R_{AI},$$
$$R_C \leftarrow \frac{1}{2}(R_C + R_T),$$

where R_{AI} is a constant (5 Mbps by default).

Remark 1. Note that during the FR phase QCN performs *averaging*. The BIC-TCP algorithm is the first to use averaging. Indeed, the motives that led to BIC-TCP and QCN employing averaging are quite different and instructive to understand. As stated in [28], the additive increase portion of the TCP algorithm can be viewed as determining the correct window size through a *linear* search process, whereas the BIC-TCP (for Binary Increase TCP) algorithm performs the more efficient *binary* search. QCN takes a control-theoretic angle: a congestion control algorithm is zero-delay stable if the amount of rate increase after a drop is less than the amount of decrease during the drop. The rate before the last drop is check-pointed as the R_T. Since averaging ensures that $R_C < R_T$ throughout the FR phase, QCN is zero-delay stable (Section 2.3). In fact, Section 2.4 shows that averaging (or binary increase) is much more stable than simple additive increase in the face of large feedback delays.

Remark 2. The duration of Byte Counter cycles measured in seconds depends on the current sending rate, and can therefore become unacceptably large when R_C is small, jeopardizing the speed of bandwidth recovery (or respon-

siveness). Therefore, a *Timer* is also included in the standards implementation of QCN. The Byte Counter and Timer jointly determine rate increase times. The Timer is primarily used during transience, and since we are mainly interested in the steady state stability properties of QCN in this paper, we do not consider the Timer.

2.2 QCN Fluid Model

The fluid model presented below corresponds with the simplified version of QCN from the previous section. The derivation of the equations, for the most part, is part of the research literature [25]. The main difference is in our use of two variables, R_C and R_T, to represent source behavior. This is a necessary step, since although R_C and R_T are inter-dependent variables, neither can be derived from the other.

Consider a "dumb-bell topology" with N sources sharing a single link of capacity C. The RTT is assumed to be the same for all sources, equal to τ seconds. The source variables evolve according to the following differential equations:

$$\frac{dR_C}{dt} = -G_d F_b(t-\tau) R_C(t) R_C(t-\tau) p_r(t-\tau)$$
$$+ \left(\frac{R_T(t) - R_C(t)}{2}\right) \frac{R_C(t-\tau) p_r(t-\tau)}{(1-p_r(t-\tau))^{-100} - 1}, \quad (4)$$

$$\frac{dR_T}{dt} = -\left(R_T(t) - R_C(t)\right) R_C(t-\tau) p_r(t-\tau)$$
$$+ R_{AI} R_C(t-\tau) \frac{(1-p_r(t-\tau))^{500} p_r(t-\tau)}{(1-p_r(t-\tau))^{-100} - 1}, \quad (5)$$

where $p_r(t)$ is the "reflection"—not sampling, see equation (8)—probability at the switch, and $F_b(t)$ is the congestion measure. These quantities are related to the queue size, $Q(\cdot)$, at the switch and evolve as follows:

$$\frac{dQ}{dt} = \begin{cases} N R_C(t) - C & \text{if } q(t) > 0, \\ \max\left(N R_C(t) - C, 0\right) & \text{if } q(t) = 0, \end{cases} \quad (6)$$

$$F_b(t) = Q(t) - Q_{eq} + \frac{w}{C p_s}(N R_C(t) - C), \quad (7)$$

$$p_r(t) = p_s \mathbb{1}_{[F_b(t)>0]}, \quad (8)$$

where p_s is the sampling probability.

Equations (4) and (5) each consist of a negative (rate decrease) term, and a positive (rate increase) term. Let us first consider the simpler negative terms. These terms model the decrease in R_T and R_C due to negative feedback signals, corresponding to (2) and (3). Observing that feedback signals to each source arrive at rate $R_C(t-\tau) p_r(t-\tau)$ explains the negative terms.

Now consider the positive term in (4). A rate increase occurs each time 100 packets are sent and no negative feedback message is received.[5] The change in $R_C(t)$ at each such event is given by:

$$\Delta R_C(t) = \frac{R_C(t) + R_T(t)}{2} - R_C(t)$$
$$= \frac{R_T(t) - R_C(t)}{2}. \quad (9)$$

---

[4]Recall that due to the absence of ACKs in Ethernet, packet transmission isn't self-clocked like in TCP.

[5]The actual algorithm sets increases to occur every 50 packets in the Active Increase phase. For simplicity we use the 100 packet increment in both the FR and AI phases in the model.

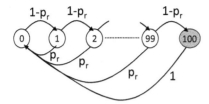

Figure 6: Markov chain corresponding to R_C rate increases.

To compute the rate at which such events occur, we consider the Markov Chain shown in Fig. 6. It is easy to see that if each packet is reflected with probability p_r, then the average number of packets that must be sent before an increase event occurs precisely equals the expected number of steps it takes to hit state 100 starting from state 0. This is easily computed:

$$\mathbb{E}_0(T_{100}) = \frac{(1 - p_r)^{-100} - 1}{p_r}.$$

Therefore, because packets from a source arrive at the switch with rate $R_C(t - \tau)$ at time t, the average time between increase events is:

$$\Delta T = \frac{(1 - p_r(t - \tau))^{-100} - 1}{R_C(t - \tau)p_r(t - \tau)}. \tag{10}$$

Dividing (9) by (10), we obtain the positive term in (4). The positive term in (5) is derived similarly.

Equations (6) and (7) are self-explanatory. Equation (8) captures the fact that sampled packets result in a reflected feedback message only when $F_b > 0$.[6]

Model validation. We have verified the fidelity of the model against packet-level simulations using the ns2 simulator [22]. An example run is shown in Fig. 7. As can be seen, the model and simulations match quite well.

2.3 Stability Analysis of Linearized Model

We now use the fluid model to analyze the stability of the QCN control loop in the presence of feedback delay. Define:

$$\eta(p_s) \triangleq \frac{p_s}{(1 - p_s)^{-100} - 1}, \quad \zeta(p_s) \triangleq \frac{(1 - p_s)^{500} p_s}{(1 - p_s)^{-100} - 1}.$$

It is easily verified that the fluid model (4)–(8) has the following unique fixed point:

$$R_C^* = \frac{C}{N},$$

$$R_T^* = \frac{C}{N} + \frac{\zeta(p_s) R_{AI}}{p_s},$$

$$Q^* = Q_{eq} + \frac{\eta(p_s)\zeta(p_s) N R_{AI}}{2p_s^2 G_d C}.$$

We are interested in understanding if, and under what conditions, is this fixed point locally stable. The standard approach we undertake is to linearize the system around the fixed point, and use tools from linear control theory to study its stability.

---

[6]It must be noted that when $p_r = 0$, the positive increase terms in (4) and (5) are to be interpreted as the resulting limits as $p_r \to 0$.

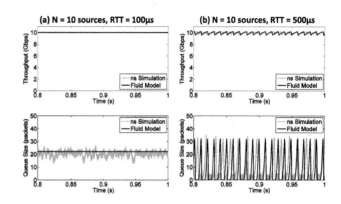

Figure 7: Comparison of QCN fluid model and ns2 simulation

The linearization of the differential equations is straightforward. Omitting the algebra, the linearized system describing the evolution of $\delta R_C(t) \triangleq R_C(t) - R_C^*$, $\delta R_T(t) \triangleq R_T(t) - R_T^*$, and $\delta Q(t) \triangleq Q(t) - Q^*$ is given by:

$$\frac{d\delta R_C}{dt} = -a_1 \delta R_C(t) + a_2 \delta R_T(t) - a_3 \delta R_C(t - \tau) - a_4 \delta Q(t - \tau), \tag{11}$$

$$\frac{d\delta R_T}{dt} = b\delta R_C(t) - b\delta R_T(t), \tag{12}$$

$$\frac{d\delta Q}{dt} = N\delta R_C(t), \tag{13}$$

where:

$$a_1 = \frac{\eta(p_s)}{2} R_C^* + \frac{\eta(p_s)\zeta(p_s)}{2p_s} R_{AI},$$

$$a_2 = \frac{\eta(p_s)}{2} R_C^*, \quad a_3 = G_d w R_C^*, \quad a_4 = p_s G_d R_C^{*\,2},$$

$$b = p_s R_C^*.$$

We have obtained a linear time-delayed system and can now study its stability through its characteristic equation whose roots constitute the poles of the system. The characteristic equation of (11)–(13), derived in Appendix A, is given by:

$$1 + G(s) = 0, \tag{14}$$

where

$$G(s) = e^{-s\tau} \frac{a_3(s + b)(s + \gamma)}{s(s^2 + \beta s + \alpha)}, \tag{15}$$

with $\gamma = Cp/w$, $\beta = b + a_1$, and $\alpha = b(a_1 - a_2)$.

Theorem 1. *Let*

$$\tau^* = \frac{1}{\omega^*}\left(\arctan(\frac{\omega^*}{b}) - \arctan(\frac{\omega^*}{\beta}) + \arctan(\frac{\omega^*}{\gamma})\right), \tag{16}$$

where

$$\omega^* = \sqrt{\frac{a_3^2}{2} + \sqrt{\frac{a_3^4}{4} + \gamma^2 a_3^2}}. \tag{17}$$

Then $\tau^* > 0$, and the system (11)–(13) is stable for all $\tau \leq \tau^*$.

PROOF. Using $\beta > b$, we have:

$$\arctan(\frac{\omega^*}{\beta}) < \arctan(\frac{\omega^*}{b}),$$

which implies $\tau^* > 0$. The proof of stability follows by applying the Bode stability criterion [11] to G(s). Define

$$r(\omega) = |G(j\omega)|, \quad \theta(\omega) = -\angle G(j\omega),$$

so that $G(j\omega) = r(\omega)e^{-j\theta(\omega)}$. We upper bound $r(\omega)$ as follows:

$$\begin{aligned} r(\omega)^2 &= \frac{a_3^2(\omega^2 + b^2)(\omega^2 + \gamma^2)}{\omega^2((\omega^2 - \alpha)^2 + \beta^2\omega^2)}, \\ &< \frac{a_3^2(\omega^2 + b^2)(\omega^2 + \gamma^2)}{\omega^4(\omega^2 + \beta^2 - 2\alpha)}, \\ &< \frac{a_3^2(\omega^2 + \gamma^2)}{\omega^4}. \end{aligned} \tag{18}$$

The last inequality holds because $\beta^2 - 2\alpha > b^2$, which is easily checked by plugging in $\beta = b + a_1$, $\alpha = b(a_1 - a_2)$. Now with ω^* given by (17), the bound (18) implies $r(\omega^*) < 1$. In particular, the 0-dB crossover frequency, ω_c, at which $r(\omega_c) = 1$ occurs for some $\omega_c < \omega^*$. Hence, the Bode stability criterion implies that if $\theta(\omega) < \pi$ for all $0 \le \omega < \omega^*$, the system is stable. But for $0 \le \omega < \omega^*$, using $\alpha > 0$ we have:

$$\begin{aligned} \theta(\omega) &= \pi + \omega\tau + \arctan\left(\frac{\omega^2 - \alpha}{\beta\omega}\right) - \arctan\left(\frac{\omega}{b}\right) - \arctan\left(\frac{\omega}{\gamma}\right), \\ &< \pi + \omega\tau + \arctan\left(\frac{\omega}{\beta}\right) - \arctan\left(\frac{\omega}{b}\right) - \arctan\left(\frac{\omega}{\gamma}\right), \\ &= \pi + \omega\tau - \arctan\left(\frac{(\beta - b)\omega}{\beta b + \omega^2}\right) - \arctan\left(\frac{\omega}{\gamma}\right), \\ &\le \pi + \omega\tau - \arctan\left(\frac{(\beta - b)\omega}{\beta b + \omega^{*2}}\right) - \arctan\left(\frac{\omega}{\gamma}\right), \tag{19} \end{aligned}$$

where in the last inequality, we use the fact that $\arctan(.)$ is an increasing function. Now let

$$\Psi(\omega) = \pi + \omega\tau - \arctan\left(\frac{(\beta - b)\omega}{\beta b + \omega^{*2}}\right) - \arctan\left(\frac{\omega}{\gamma}\right).$$

Note that $\Psi(0) = \pi$ and for $\tau \le \tau^*$, $\Psi(\omega^*) \le \pi$. Moreover, since $\arctan(x)$ is concave for $x \ge 0$, $\Psi(\omega)$ is convex on $\omega \in [0, \omega^*]$. Therefore $\Psi(\omega) \le \pi$ for all $0 \le \omega \le \omega^*$, and (19) implies $\theta(\omega) < \pi$, completing the proof. $\square$

Corollary 1 (ZERO-DELAY STABILTY). *If $\tau = 0$, system* (11)–(13) *is stable* .

PROOF. This follows because $\tau^* > 0$ in Theorem 1. $\square$

Corollary 1 confirms the intuitive argument given for zero-delay stability of QCN in Remark 1 of Section 2.1.

2.4 Averaging in QCN

As we have seen, the QCN Reaction Point averages R_C and R_T during the Fast Recovery phase. We now use fluid models to show that this averaging improves the robustness of QCN to increasing lags in the control loop.

Consider a modified QCN RP algorithm, henceforth called QCN-AIMD, where Active Increase begins *immediately* following a rate decrease, i.e. there is no Fast Recovery (see Fig 8 for an illustration). In Active Increase, the QCN-AIMD RP increases its sending rate each time the Byte Counter counts out 100 packets:

$$R_C \leftarrow R_C + R_{AI}.$$

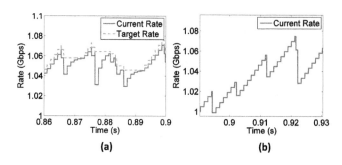

Figure 8: Rate evolutions for (a) QCN (b) QCN-AIMD

The CP algorithm remains the same as QCN.[7]

A fluid model for QCN-AIMD can be derived similarly as for QCN. In fact, since QCN-AIMD has no R_T variable, we only need to change the R_C equation (4) to the following:

$$\begin{aligned} \frac{dR_C}{dt} &= -G_d F_b(t - \tau)R_C(t)R_C(t - \tau)p_r(t - \tau) \\ &+ R_{AI}\frac{R_C(t - \tau)p_r(t - \tau)}{(1 - p_r(t - \tau))^{-100} - 1}. \end{aligned} \tag{20}$$

This, along with (6)–(8) constitute the QCN-AIMD fluid model. We can now linearize the QCN-AIMD model around its fixed point, and analyze its stability. This is done in Appendix B, where the following Theorem is proven:

Theorem 2. *Let*

$$\hat{\tau} = \frac{1}{\hat{\omega}}\left(\arctan\left(\frac{\hat{\omega}}{\gamma}\right) + \arctan\left(\frac{\hat{a}}{\hat{\omega}}\right)\right), \tag{21}$$

where

$$\hat{\omega} = \sqrt{\frac{a_3^2 - \hat{a}^2}{2} + \sqrt{\frac{(a_3^2 - \hat{a}^2)^2}{4} + \gamma^2 a_3^2}}. \tag{22}$$

Here a_3 and γ are the same constants found in the QCN model, and $\hat{a} = \eta(p_s)R_{AI}$. The linearized QCN-AIMD model (35)–(36) *is stable if and only if $\tau < \hat{\tau}$.*

Theorems 1 and 2 provide the largest feedback delay for which the linear models of QCN and QCN-AIMD control loops retain stability. The following theorem compares these two and proves that under mild conditions, the QCN system— with its use of averaging—remains stable for larger lags.

Theorem 3. *Let τ^* and $\hat{\tau}$ be given by* (16) *and* (21) *respectively. If*

$$\frac{R_{AI}}{C}\max\left(\frac{\eta(p_s)^2/p_s}{G_d}, \frac{2\eta(p_s) + 4p_s}{G_d}, \frac{\eta(p_s)w}{p_s}\right) < 0.1, \tag{23}$$

$$\frac{NR_{AI}}{C} < 0.2, \tag{24}$$

then $\tau^* > \hat{\tau}$.

PROOF. See Appendix C. $\square$

---

[7]QCN-AIMD and QCN are analogous to TCP and BIC-TCP respectively. However, an important distinction is that QCN-AIMD and QCN get multi-bit feedback from the network, allowing them to cut their rates by different factors corresponding to the amount of congestion.

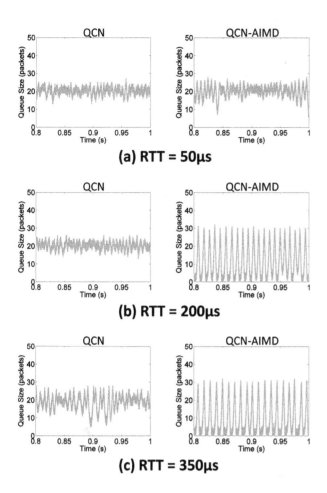

(a) RTT = 50μs

(b) RTT = 200μs

(c) RTT = 350μs

Figure 9: Queue size for QCN and AIMD-QCN with RTT of (a) 50μs (b) 200μs (c) 350μs. $N = 10$ sources share a single 10Gbps bottleneck. The desired operating point at the switch buffer, Q_{eq}, is set to 22 packets.

Remark 3. The required conditions of Theorem 3 are easily satisfied in practice. For instance, for the baseline QCN parameters $C = 10$Gbps, $R_{AI} = 5$Mbps, $G_d = 1/128$, $w = 2$, $p_s = 0.01$, (23) is satisfied and (24) is equivalent to $N < 400$, which is far more than the number of sources typically active on each path in the data center [2].

2.5 Simulations

We have verified the theoretical predictions of the previous sections using ns2 simulations. We briefly present a representative example.

We compare the stability of QCN-AIMD and QCN as RTT increases. Fig. 9 shows the queue size for the two schemes when 10 sources share a single 10Gbps bottleneck link. Note that according to (16) and (21), the *linearized* QCN and QCN-AIMD control loops are stable for RTTs less than $\tau^* = 249\mu s$ and $\hat\tau = 189\mu s$ respectively.

As shown, when the RTT is small (50μs), both schemes are able to keep the queue stable around Q_{eq}. But when RTT is increased to 200μs, QCN-AIMD can no longer control the oscillations and the queue underflows, while the queue size for QCN continues to be stable as predicted. Even with RTT equal to 350μs, which is beyond the stability mar-

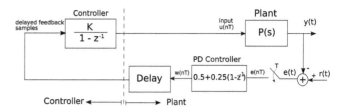

Figure 10: Equivalent PD control scheme to Averaging Principle.

gin, τ^*, of the linearized model, QCN continues to gracefully keep the queue occupancy closely hovering around 22 packets (albeit with an increase in the amplitude of oscillations). It is only after the RTT increases beyond 500μs that the queue size with QCN begins to underflow.

In the next section, we formally define the Averaging Principle for a generic sampled control system, and show that averaging improves the robustness of control loops to increasing lags in much more general settings.

3. THE AVERAGING PRINCIPLE

3.1 Analysis

Recall the sampled control system in Fig. 1, and the basic form of AP (see Fig. 2) composed of periodic *feedback-induced changes* given by:

$$I_T \leftarrow I_C,$$
$$I_C \leftarrow I_C + Ke(nT),$$

and *averaging changes* at the midpoints of the sampling periods:

$$I_C \leftarrow \frac{I_C + I_T}{2}.$$

Note: In the generic setting of Fig. 2, the feedback signal can take both positive and negative values. However, in some cases of interest, the feedback might be restricted to negative values only; QCN is such an example. The definition of AP is the same in either case: following every feedback-induced change, make (one or more) averaging changes.

We now address the question: Why does the AP improve the stability of the basic controller? To anticipate the answer, we find the AP controller behaves like a PD controller—which is well-known to improve the stability of control loops [11]—without explicitly computing a derivative. This last feature is very important since it avoids the switch having to compute derivatives, which can be very cumbersome to do in hardware.

Before proving the claimed equivalence of the AP and PD controllers, we demonstrate it using our example. Consider the PD control scheme of Fig. 10. Here the error samples are not directly fed back. Instead, the feedback samples are computed as:

$$w(nT) = \frac{1}{2}e(nT) + \frac{1}{4}(e(nT) - e((n-1)T)),$$
$$\approx \frac{1}{2}e(nT) + \frac{T}{4}\frac{d}{dt}e(nT).$$

Here, $w(nT)$ is a weighted sum of two terms: a *proportional* term, and a (discrete) *derivative* term. Hence this

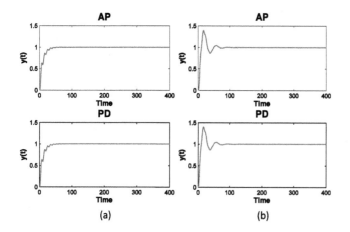

(a)   (b)

Figure 11: Step response for AP and PD controllers, with (a) zero delay (b) $\tau = 8$s delay.

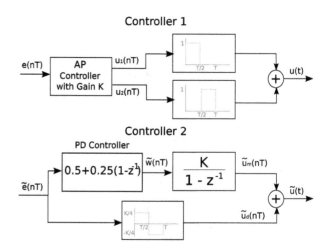

Figure 12: Two equivalent controllers.

is discrete-time PD control. The step response of this control loop is compared to the output of the AP controller in Fig. 11. As shown in the figure, the outputs of the AP and PD controllers are essentially identical.

Formally, consider the two controllers shown in Fig. 12. Both controllers map a sequence of error samples to an input signal driving the plant. Controller 1 is the AP controller, and Controller 2 is (essentially) the PD controller. The input-output relationships of the two controllers are given by the following equations:

Controller 1:

$$u_1(nT) = u_2((n-1)T) + Ke(nT)$$

$$u_2(nT) = \frac{u_1(nT) + u_2((n-1)T)}{2}$$

$$u(t) = \begin{cases} u_1(nT) & nT \le t < nT + \frac{T}{2} \\ u_2(nT) & nT + \frac{T}{2} \le t < nT + T \end{cases}$$

Controller 2:

$$\tilde{u}_m(nT) = \tilde{u}_m((n-1)T) + K\tilde{w}(nT) \qquad (25)$$

$$\tilde{w}(nT) = \frac{1}{2}\tilde{e}(nT) + \frac{1}{4}(\tilde{e}(nT) - \tilde{e}((n-1)T)) \qquad (26)$$

$$\tilde{u}_d(t) = \begin{cases} \frac{K}{4}\tilde{e}(nT) & nT \le t < nT + \frac{T}{2} \\ -\frac{K}{4}\tilde{e}(nT) & nT + \frac{T}{2} \le t < nT + T \end{cases} \qquad (27)$$

$$\tilde{u}(t) = \tilde{u}_m(t) + \tilde{u}_d(t) \qquad (28)$$

It should be noted $\tilde{u}_m(t) = \tilde{u}_m([\frac{t}{T}]T)$ in (28). For simplicity, we will not explicitly point out this conversion between discrete and continuous time signals each time.

Theorem 4. *Controllers 1 and 2 are algebraically equivalent; i.e., if they are given the same input sequences $e(nT) = \tilde{e}(nT)$ for all $n \ge 0$, and have the same initial condition $u(0) = \tilde{u}(0)$, then $u(t) = \tilde{u}(t)$ for all $t \ge 0$.*

PROOF. For $n \ge 0$, let $u_m(nT) = (u_1(nT) + u_2(nT))/2$. From the definition of Controller 1, we get that

$$u_m(nT) = u_2((n-1)T) + \frac{3K}{4}e(nT), \qquad (29)$$

and, in turn, that

$$u_1(nT) = u_m(nT) + \frac{K}{4}e(nT), \qquad (30)$$

$$u_2(nT) = u_m(nT) - \frac{K}{4}e(nT). \qquad (31)$$

Comparing (30) and (31) with (27) and (28), it suffices to establish: $u_m(nT) = \tilde{u}_m(nT)$ for all $n \ge 0$. We do this by showing that $u_m(\cdot)$ and $\tilde{u}_m(\cdot)$ satisfy the same recursion.

Equations (29) and (31) give

$$u_m(nT) = u_m((n-1)T) - \frac{K}{4}e((n-1)T) + \frac{3K}{4}e(nT)$$

$$= u_m((n-1)T) + Kw(nT), \qquad (32)$$

where

$$w(nT) = \frac{1}{2}e(nT) + \frac{1}{4}(e(nT) - e((n-1)T)). \qquad (33)$$

The recursion defined by (32) and (33) for $u_m(\cdot)$ in terms of $e(\cdot)$, is identical to the recursion defined by (25) and (26) for $\tilde{u}_m(\cdot)$ in terms of $\tilde{e}(\cdot)$. But, by hypothesis, $e(nT) = \tilde{e}(nT)$ for all $n \ge 0$ and $u_m(0) = \tilde{u}_m(0)$, and the proof is complete. □

Theorem 4 states that the AP controller is exactly equivalent to Controller 2. Since the effect of $\tilde{u}_d(t)$ is typically negligible (see below), we conclude that the AP controller is essentially equivalent to the top path of Controller 2. But, this is the same as the PD controller in Fig. 10.

The effect of $\tilde{u}_d(t)$ is negligible if the sampling time T is small compared to the rise time of the plant.[8] Intuitively, such a plant only reacts to the *mean* value of the input and not to the detailed variations of the input within a sampling interval. Since the mean of $\tilde{u}_d(t)$ in a sampling interval is zero, it doesn't affect the output of the plant. Thus, the AP and PD controllers are essentially identical, as seen in Fig. 11.

Remark 4. Extensions of the basic AP scheme are possible and are amenable to a complete theoretical analysis. These

---

[8]This is a fairly standard design criterion in digital control systems. For example, a simple rule of thumb is that the sampling time should be smaller than 10 % of the dominant time constant.

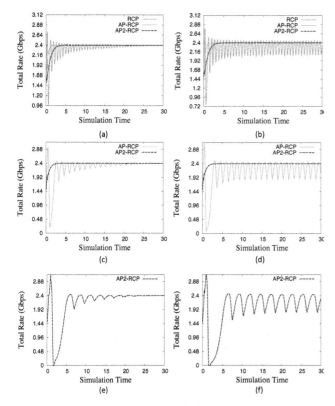

Figure 13: Total sending rate for RCP, AP-RCP and AP2-RCP with RTT of (a) 110ms (b) 115ms (c) 240ms (d) 250ms (e) 480ms (f) 490ms.

include: averaging by factors other than 1/2, for example

$$I_C \leftarrow (1 - \alpha)I_C + \alpha I_T \qquad (\text{for } 0 < \alpha < 1),$$

applying the averaging changes at points other than the midpoint, applying averaging more than once, etc.

Remark 5. The common tradeoff between stability and responsiveness exists with the AP as well: an AP-enhanced control scheme is more stable than the original, but it is also more sluggish. In practice, various techniques are used to improve the transient behavior of a system. Typically, these take the form of a temporary deviation from the normal controller behavior during times of transience. Some examples of this are BIC-TCP's *Fast Convergence* [28] and QCN's *Timer, Extra Fast Recovery,* and *Target Rate Reduction* [2].

3.2 The AP applied to another congestion control algorithm: RCP

As mentioned, the AP is a general technique and can be applied to any control loop. We now apply it to the congestion control scheme RCP [8]. In RCP, each router offers a rate, $R(t)$, to each flow passing through it. $R(t)$ is updated every T seconds:

$$R(t) = R(t - T)(1 + \frac{T}{d_0}F_b(t)), \qquad (34)$$

where d_0 is a moving average of the RTT measured across all packets, and:

$$F_b(t) = \frac{\alpha(C - y(t)) - \beta\frac{q(t)}{d_0}}{C} \approx \frac{-\alpha\dot{q}(t) - \beta\frac{q(t)}{d_0}}{C}.$$

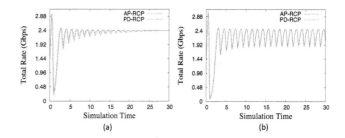

Figure 14: Comparison of AP-RCP and PD-RCP for (a) RTT = 240ms (b) 250ms.

Here $y(t)$ is the measured input traffic rate during the last update interval, $q(t)$ is the instantaneous buffer size, C is the link capacity, and α and β are non-negative constants. We refer the reader to [8] for details of RCP.

As seen in (34), RCP automatically adjusts the loop gain, d_0, based on the average RTT in the control loop. This automatic gain adjustment stabilizes RCP as RTT varies. To demonstrate the effect of the AP on RCP's stability, we disable the automatic gain adjustment of RCP; i.e., we consider the case where d_0 is held constant at the router while the actual RTT increases.[9]

In what follows, we compare RCP with two AP-enhanced versions of the algorithm: AP-RCP and AP2-RCP. AP-RCP is just the application of the basic form of AP to RCP. AP2-TCP makes two averaging changes within each update interval: at $T/3$ and $2T/3$ after the start of interval.

Stability. Using ns2 [22], we simulate RCP controlling 10 long-lived flows passing through a 2.4Gbps link. The RCP parameters are set to $\alpha = 0.1$, $\beta = 1$, the sampling period $T = 50$ms, and d_0 is fixed at 20ms.

The RTT is varied and the results are shown in Fig. 13. When the RTT is smaller than 110ms, both RCP and its AP modifications are stable. RCP becomes unstable when the RTT increases to 115ms, but AP-RCP and AP2-RCP both continue to be stable for RTTs up to 240ms. AP-RCP becomes unstable at an RTT of 250ms, but AP2-RCP remains stable even when the RTT equals 480 ms.

PD Equivalence to AP. We now apply a PD controller to RCP (PD-RCP), and compare it with AP-RCP. The rate update equation for PD-RCP is given by:

$$R(t) = R(t-T)\left(1 + \frac{T}{d_0}\left(\frac{1}{2}F_b(t) + \frac{1}{4}(F_b(t) - F_b(t - T))\right)\right).$$

Fig. 14 shows that AP-RCP and PD-RCP are both closely matched: both are stable at RTT = 240ms, unstable at RTT = 250ms, and exhibit very similar queue/rate oscillations.

4. BUFFER SIZING

The performance of congestion control algorithms crucially depends on the size of buffers at switches: if the buffers are small relative to the bandwidth–delay product of the flows they support, buffer occupancies will oscillate and can cause under-utilization of links. The TCP buffer

---

[9]It must be noted that this is only intended as a demonstration of how the AP can improve stability without gain adjustments; we are not suggesting a change to the RCP algorithm.

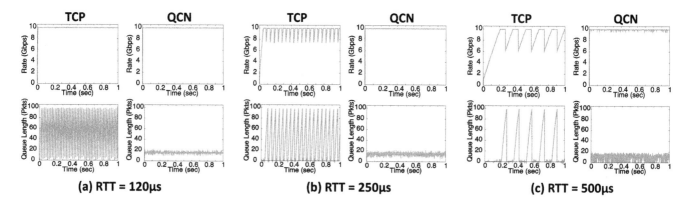

Figure 15: TCP vs. QCN utilization and queue occupancy as RTT increases. Switch buffer is 100 packets deep.

sizing "rule of thumb" states that a single TCP flow requires a bandwidth-delay product ($C \times RTT$) amount of buffering to fully utilize a link of capacity C [26]. For example, a 10Gbps network with a $500\mu s$ round-trip time (RTT) necessitates that switches have 625 Kbytes of buffering per priority per port.

On the other hand, the amount of buffering that *can be provided* in a data center switch is limited by cost (at 10Gbps line rates the low access time allowed per packet necessitate that expensive SRAMs be used to build switch buffers) and latency (having shallow buffers bounds the worst-case latency of a packet through a switch and, hence, end-to-end). Moreover, since these buffers are usually placed on-chip (to ensure low-latency), they will consume a large die area and dissipate a lot of heat. Thus, data center Ethernet switches typically have small buffers, usually around 2-10MB for 24-48 ports.

The above discussion illustrates there can be a mismatch in data centers between the amount of buffering that is needed and that which can be provided, and this is only likely to worsen as link speeds increase. (The Ethernet industry road map calls for the deployment of 40Gbps switched Ethernet in the near future.)

One way the buffering requirement at a switch can be smaller is if several flows are simultaneously traversing it: The paper by Appenzeller et. al. [4] shows that when N flows share the link, the required buffer size for TCP goes down by a factor of $\sqrt{N}$ ($C \times RTT/\sqrt{N}$). Essentially, as [4] explains, the variance of the total flow arrival rate is reduced due to statistical multiplexing, and this leads to a reduction in the required queue size. More precisely, if N flows are multiplexed, the variance of their aggregate sending rate equals

$$Var(\sum_{i=1}^{N} R_i) = \frac{Var(\widetilde{R})}{\sqrt{N}},$$

where $Var(\widetilde{R})$ is the variance in the sending rate when only 1 flow traverses the link. Note that the mean value of each R_i is C/N, but the mean value of $\widetilde{R}$ equals C.

However, the number of simultaneously active flows at a link in a data center network is very small, typically fewer than 10. Indeed, great pains are taken to ensure that flows are load balanced onto multiple paths so that they may fully utilize network bandwidth [16, 1, 12]. Therefore, it is hard

to obtain the benefit of statistical multiplexing in the data center environment and it appears that large buffers will be required.

Perhaps not. The amount of buffering a single source needs to occupy the link is dependent on the variance of the sending rate which, in turn, depends on the congestion control algorithm. Table 1 shows that over a 10Gbps link the standard deviation in the sending rate of a QCN source is significantly smaller than that of a TCP source as the RTT increases. QCN reduces the variance of the sending rate in two ways: (i) using a multi-bit feedback allows QCN sources to cut their sending rates by factors smaller than $1/2$ (as small as $1/128$), and (ii) employing the AP reduces the sending rate variance via averaging changes. Note that BIC-TCP also derives the benefit of (ii) (see also [6]), but is constrained to cut window sizes by a constant factor of 0.125 during congestion. So its variance, while smaller than TCP's, will be larger than QCN's.

Fig. 15 compares the throughput and queue occupancy of a TCP and a QCN flow traversing a 10Gbps link. The buffer size at the bottleneck switch is 150KBytes, which exactly equals the BDP for an RTT of $120\mu s$. Hence, as seen in part (a), both algorithms fully utilize the link. At higher RTTs ($250\mu s$ in part (b) and $500\mu s$ in part (c)), large queue oscillations cause TCP to lose throughput, whereas QCN remains stable.

Table 1: Standard deviation of sending rate

RTT	$120\mu s$	$250\mu s$	$500 \mu s$
TCP	265 Mbps	783 Mbps	1250 Mbps
QCN	14 Mbps	33 Mbps	95 Mbps

5. CONCLUSION

Data center networks present new opportunities and challenges for developing new networking technology. In this paper we studied one such technology: the L2 congestion control algorithm, QCN, developed for the IEEE 802.1Qau standard. We described the salient features of QCN and developed a high-fidelity fluid model corresponding to it. We determined the stability margins of the QCN algorithm using a linearization of the fluid model. We articulated the Averaging Principle (AP), and showed that it is the underlying reason for QCN's good stability properties. The AP applies to general control systems, not just congestion control systems. This aspect is worth pursuing further. The AP controller was analyzed from a control-theoretic point-of-view and found to be equivalent to a PD controller in a strong algebraic sense. Finally, we showed that QCN's use of the AP and of a multi-bit feedback signal allows it to use much smaller buffers when compared to TCP.

Acknowledgments

Mohammad Alizadeh is supported by a Caroline and Fabian Pease Stanford Graduate Fellowship. We thank our shepherd Yuliy Baryshnikov and the anonymous reviewers whose comments helped us improve the paper.

6. REFERENCES

[1] M. Al-Fares, A. Loukissas, and A. Vahdat. A scalable, commodity data center network architecture. In *SIGCOMM '08: Proceedings of the ACM SIGCOMM 2008 conference on Data communication*, pages 63–74, New York, NY, USA, 2008. ACM.

[2] M. Alizadeh, B. Atikoglu, A. Kabbani, A. Lakshmikantha, R. Pan, B. Prabhakar, and M. Seaman. Data center transport mechanisms: Congestion control theory and IEEE standardization. In *Allerton*, 2008.

[3] Amazon Web Services. http://aws.amazon.com.

[4] G. Appenzeller, I. Keslassy, and N. McKeown. Sizing router buffers. *SIGCOMM Comput. Commun. Rev.*, 34(4):281–292, 2004.

[5] S. Athuraliya, S. Low, V. Li, and Q. Yin. REM: active queue management. *Network, IEEE*, 15(3):48 –53, May 2001.

[6] H. Cai, D. Y. Eun, S. Ha, I. Rhee, and L. Xu. Stochastic Ordering for Internet Congestion Control and its Applications. In *INFOCOM*, May 2007.

[7] Data Center Bridging Task Group. http://www.ieee802.org/1/pages/dcbridges.html.

[8] N. Dukkipati, M. Kobayashi, R. Zhang-Shen, and N. McKeown. Processor sharing flows in the internet. In *IWQoS*, pages 271–285, 2005.

[9] Fiber Channel standard. http://www.t11.org/ftp/t11/pub/fc/bb-5/09-056v5.pdf.

[10] S. Floyd. HighSpeed TCP for Large Congestion Windows, 2003.

[11] G. F. Franklin, D. J. Powell, and A. Emami-Naeini. *Feedback Control of Dynamic Systems*. Prentice Hall PTR, Upper Saddle River, NJ, USA, 2001.

[12] A. Greenberg, J. R. Hamilton, N. Jain, S. Kandula, C. Kim, P. Lahiri, D. A. Maltz, P. Patel, and S. Sengupta. VL2: a scalable and flexible data center network. In *SIGCOMM '09: Proceedings of the ACM SIGCOMM 2009 conference on Data communication*, pages 51–62, New York, NY, USA, 2009. ACM.

[13] S. Ha, I. Rhee, and L. Xu. CUBIC: a new TCP-friendly high-speed TCP variant. *SIGOPS Oper. Syst. Rev.*, 42(5):64–74, 2008.

[14] B. Hayes. Cloud computing. *Commun. ACM*, 51(7):9–11, 2008.

[15] C. Hollot, V. Misra, D. Towsley, and W.-B. Gong. On designing improved controllers for AQM routers supporting TCP flows. In *INFOCOM 2001*, volume 3, pages 1726 –1734 vol.3, 2001.

[16] C. Hopps. Analysis of an Equal-Cost Multi-Path Algorithm, 2000.

[17] QCN pseudo code. http://www.ieee802.org/1/files/public/docs2008/au-rong-qcn-serial-hai-pseudo-code\%20rev2.0.pdf.

[18] D. Katabi, M. Handley, and C. Rohrs. Congestion control for high bandwidth-delay product networks. In *SIGCOMM '02: Proceedings of the 2002 conference on Applications, technologies, architectures, and protocols for computer communications*, pages 89–102, New York, NY, USA, 2002. ACM.

[19] T. Kelly. Scalable TCP: improving performance in highspeed wide area networks. *SIGCOMM Comput. Commun. Rev.*, 33(2):83–91, 2003.

[20] S. H. Low, F. Paganini, S. Adlakha, and J. C. Doyle. Dynamics of TCP/RED and a Scalable Control. In *IN PROCEEDINGS OF IEEE INFOCOM 2002*, pages 239–248, 2002.

[21] Microsoft Corporation. An Overview of Windows Azure. http://www.microsoft.com/downloads/en/details.aspx?displaylang=en&FamilyID=96d08ded-bbb9-450b-b180-b9d1f04c3b7f.

[22] The Network Simulator NS-2. http://www.isi.edu/nsnam/ns/.

[23] IEEE 802.1Qau. http://www.ieee802.org/1/pages/802.1au.html.

[24] IEEE 802.1Qbb. http://www.ieee802.org/1/pages/802.1bb.html.

[25] R. Srikant. *The Mathematics of Internet Congestion Control (Systems and Control: Foundations and Applications)*. SpringerVerlag, 2004.

[26] C. Villamizar and C. Song. High performance TCP in ANSNET. *SIGCOMM Comput. Commun. Rev.*, 24(5):45–60, 1994.

[27] D. X. Wei, C. Jin, S. H. Low, and S. Hegde. FAST TCP: motivation, architecture, algorithms, performance. *IEEE/ACM Trans. Netw.*, 14(6):1246–1259, 2006.

[28] L. Xu, K. Harfoush, and I. Rhee. Binary Increase Congestion Control (BIC) for Fast Long-Distance Networks. In *INFOCOM*, 2004.

APPENDIX

A. CHARACTERISTIC EQUATION OF LINEARIZED QCN FLUID MODEL

Taking the Laplace transform of (11)–(13), we have:

$$sR_C(s) - \delta R_C(0) = -a_1 R_C(s) + a_2 R_T(s)$$
$$- e^{-s\tau}\left(a_3 R_C(s) + a_4 Q(s)\right),$$
$$sR_T(s) - \delta R_T(0) = bR_C(s) - bR_T(s),$$
$$sQ(s) - \delta Q_0 = NR_C(s).$$

Solving for $Q(s)$ and $R_T(s)$ in terms of $R_C(s)$ and plugging into the first equation, we have:

$$\left(s + a_1 - \frac{a_2 b}{s+b} + e^{-s\tau}\left(a_3 + \frac{Na_4}{s}\right)\right)R_C(s)$$
$$= \delta R_C(0) + \frac{a_2 \delta R_T(0)}{s+b} - e^{-s\tau}\frac{a_4 \delta Q_0}{s}.$$

Multiplying both sides by $s(s+b)$, we see that the poles of the system are the given by the roots of:

$$s^2 + \beta s + \alpha + e^{-s\tau}a_3(s+b)(s+\gamma) = 0,$$

where $\beta = b + a_1$, and $\alpha = b(a_1 - a_2)$, and $\gamma = Na_4/a_3 = Cp/w$, which can equivalently be written as (14), (15).

B. STABILITY ANALYSIS OF THE QCN-AIMD FLUID MODEL

Recall the QCN-AIMD fluid model given by (20) and (6)–(8). We linearize the system around it unique fixed point:

$$\hat{R}_C = \frac{C}{N}, \quad \hat{Q} = Q_{eq} + \frac{\eta(p_s)NR_{AI}}{p_s G_d C}.$$

This leads to the following linear time-delay system:

$$\frac{d\delta R_C}{dt} = -\hat{a}\delta R_C(t) - a_3\delta R_C(t-\tau) - a_4\delta Q(t-\tau), \quad (35)$$

$$\frac{d\delta Q}{dt} = N\delta R_C(t). \quad (36)$$

The constants $a_3 = G_d w \hat{R}_C$, $a_4 = p_s G_d \hat{R}_C^2$, are the same as in the QCN linear model, and $\hat{a} = \eta(p_s)R_{AI}$. After taking the Laplace transform and rearranging, the characteristic equation of (35)–(36) is found to be:

$$1 + \hat{G}(s) = 0,$$

where

$$\hat{G}(s) = e^{-s\tau}\frac{a_3(s+\gamma)}{s(s+\hat{a})}.$$

To prove Theorem 2, we proceed by applying the Bode stability criterion to $\hat{G}(s)$. Let $\hat{G}(j\omega) = \hat{r}(\omega)\exp(-j\hat{\theta}(\omega))$. The 0-dB crossover frequency is found by solving the equation:

$$\hat{r}(\omega) = \frac{a_3\sqrt{\omega^2+\gamma^2}}{\omega\sqrt{\omega^2+\hat{a}^2}} = 1.$$

After squaring both sides, we have a quadratic equation in ω^2 which is easily solved, and we find that $\hat{\omega}$, given by (22), is the 0-dB crossover frequency. Therefore, we require $\hat{\theta}(\hat{\omega}) < \pi$ for the system to be stable. But:

$$\hat{\theta}(\omega) = \frac{\pi}{2} + \omega\tau + \arctan(\frac{\omega}{\hat{a}}) - \arctan(\frac{\omega}{\gamma}),$$

$$= \pi + \omega\tau - \arctan(\frac{\hat{a}}{\omega}) - \arctan(\frac{\omega}{\gamma}).$$

Therefore, $\hat{\theta}(\hat{\omega}) < \pi$ is equivalent to $\tau < \hat{\tau}$, completing the proof. $\square$

C. PROOF OF THEOREM 3

To prove $\tau^* > \tau$, we need to show:

$$\hat{\omega}\left(\arctan(\frac{\omega^*}{b}) - \arctan(\frac{\omega^*}{\beta}) + \arctan(\frac{\omega^*}{\gamma})\right)$$
$$> \omega^*\left(\arctan(\frac{\hat{\omega}}{\gamma}) + \arctan(\frac{\hat{a}}{\hat{\omega}})\right), \quad (37)$$

where ω^* and $\hat{\omega}$ are given by (17) and (22) respectively. We begin with two simple Lemmas.

Lemma 1. *If* (23) *and* (24) *are satisfied, then:*

$$\max\left(\frac{\hat{a}}{\gamma}, \frac{2\hat{a}b\beta}{\gamma a_3 a_1}\right) < 0.1, \quad (38)$$

$$\frac{\hat{a}}{a_1} < 0.4, \quad (39)$$

$$\frac{\hat{a}^2}{\gamma a_3} < 0.02. \quad (40)$$

PROOF. By direct substitution for $\hat{a}$, γ, a_3, b, β, and using $a_1 > \eta(p_s)C/(2N)$, it is easy to verify that (38) results from (23), and (39) results from (24). For (40), note that:

$$\frac{\hat{a}^2}{\gamma a_3} = \frac{NR_{AI}}{C} \times \frac{\eta(p_s)^2 R_{AI}}{p_s G_d C} < 0.2 \times 0.1 = 0.02 \quad \square$$

Lemma 2. *Let* ω^* *and* $\hat{\omega}$ *be given by* (17) *and* (22) *respectively. If* (23) *and* (24) *are satisfied, then:*

$$1 < \frac{\omega^*}{\hat{\omega}} < 1 + \epsilon,$$

where

$$\epsilon = \frac{3\hat{a}^2}{4\hat{\omega}^2} < 0.015.$$

PROOF. From (22) we have:

$$\hat{\omega}^2 = \frac{a_3^2 - \hat{a}^2}{2} + \sqrt{\frac{a_3^2}{4} + \gamma^2 a_3^2 + \frac{\hat{a}^4 - 2\hat{a}^2 a_3^2}{4}},$$

$$> \frac{a_3^2 - \hat{a}^2}{2} + \sqrt{\frac{a_3^2}{4} + \gamma^2 a_3^2}\sqrt{1 - \frac{2\hat{a}^2 a_3^2}{a_3^4 + 4\gamma^2 a_3^2}}.$$

Therefore, using $\sqrt{1-x} > 1 - x$ for $0 < x < 1$, we have:

$$\hat{\omega}^2 > \frac{a_3^2 - \hat{a}^2}{2} + \sqrt{\frac{a_3^4}{4} + \gamma^2 a_3^2}\left(1 - \frac{2\hat{a}^2 a_3^2}{a_3^4 + 4\gamma^2 a_3^2}\right),$$

$$= \frac{a_3^2}{2} + \sqrt{\frac{a_3^4}{4} + \gamma^2 a_3^2} - \frac{\hat{a}^2 a_3^2}{\sqrt{a_3^4 + 4\gamma^2 a_3^2}} - \frac{\hat{a}^2}{2},$$

$$> \omega^{*2} - \frac{3\hat{a}^2}{2}.$$

Therefore, using $\sqrt{1+x} < 1 + x/2$:

$$\frac{\omega^*}{\hat{\omega}} < \sqrt{1 + \frac{3\hat{a}^2}{2\hat{\omega}^2}} < 1 + \frac{3\hat{a}^2}{4\hat{\omega}^2}.$$

Let $\epsilon \triangleq 3\hat{a}^2/(4\hat{\omega}^2)$. Since $\hat{\omega}^2 > \gamma a_3$, using (40), we have $\epsilon < 0.015$. $\square$

We are now ready to prove (37). Using Lemma (2), it is enough to show:

$$\arctan(\frac{\omega^*}{b}) - \arctan(\frac{\omega^*}{\beta}) + \arctan(\frac{\omega^*}{\gamma})$$
$$> (1 + \epsilon)\left(\arctan(\frac{\hat{\omega}}{\gamma}) + \arctan(\frac{\hat{a}}{\hat{\omega}})\right),$$

and since $\omega^* > \hat{\omega}$, it is enough to show:

$$\arctan(\frac{\omega^*}{b}) - \arctan(\frac{\omega^*}{\beta}) > \epsilon\arctan(\frac{\hat{\omega}}{\gamma}) + (1 + \epsilon)\arctan(\frac{\hat{a}}{\hat{\omega}}).$$

However, using $\arctan(x) \le x$ for $x \ge 0$ and (38):

$$\epsilon\arctan(\frac{\hat{\omega}}{\gamma}) < \frac{\hat{a}^2}{\hat{\omega}^2}\left(\frac{\hat{\omega}}{\gamma}\right) < 0.1\left(\frac{\hat{a}}{\hat{\omega}}\right) < 0.2\arctan(\frac{\hat{a}}{\hat{\omega}}),$$

where the last inequality uses the fact: $x \le 2\arctan(x)$ for $0 \le x \le 1$. Therefore, it is enough to show:

$$\arctan(\frac{\omega^*}{b}) - \arctan(\frac{\omega^*}{\beta}) > 2\arctan(\frac{\hat{a}}{\hat{\omega}}).$$

After applying $\tan(\cdot)$ to both sides of this inequality and simplifying using $\omega^* > \omega$, we are left with:

$$a_1\hat{\omega}^2 - 2\hat{a}\omega^{*2} > a_1\hat{a}^2 + 2\hat{a}b\beta,$$

which can be further simplified using $\omega^* < (1 + \epsilon)\hat{\omega}$, and $\hat{\omega} > \gamma a_3$ to arrive at:

$$1 > \frac{\hat{a}^2}{\gamma a_3} + \frac{2\hat{a}b\beta}{\gamma a_3 a_1} + \frac{2\hat{a}}{a_1}(1 + \epsilon)^2.$$

This inequality holds because of (38)–(40) and $\epsilon < 0.015$. $\square$

Stochastic Networks with Multipath Flow Control: Impact of Resource Pools on Flow-level Performance and Network Congestion

Vinay Joseph and Gustavo de Veciana
The University of Texas at Austin
Austin, U.S.A.
vinayjoseph@mail.utexas.edu, gustavo@ece.utexas.edu

ABSTRACT

Multipath flow control has been proposed as a key way to improve the Internet's performance, reliability, and flexibility in supporting changing loads. Yet, at this point, there are very few tools to quantify the performance benefits; particularly in the context of a stochastic network supporting best effort flows, e.g., file transfers and web browsing sessions, where the metric of interest is transfer delay. This paper's focus is on developing analysis tools to evaluate flow-level performance and to support network design when multipath bandwidth allocation is based on proportional fairness. To overcome the analytical intractability of such systems we study closely related multipath approximations based on insensitive allocations such as balanced fairness. We obtain flow-level performance bounds on the mean per bit delay, exhibiting the role of resource pooling in the network, and use these to explore scenarios where increased path diversity need not result in high gains. While insightful these results are difficult to use to drive network design and capacity allocation. To that end, we study the large deviations for congestion events, i.e., accumulation of flows, in networks supporting multipath flow control. We show that such asymptotics are determined by certain critical resource pools, and study the sensitivity of congestion asymptotics to the pool's capacity and traffic loads. This suggests a disciplined approach to a capacity allocation problem in multipath networks based on a linear optimization problem.

Categories and Subject Descriptors

C.2.1 [**Computer Systems Organization**]: Computer-Communication Networks—*Network Architecture and Design*

General Terms

Design, Performance, Theory

1. INTRODUCTION

There has recently been substantial interest in redesigning the Internet's data transport mechanisms to support multipath flow control so as to exploit path diversity; see e.g., [10, 7, 14, 13, 22]. Key benefits of doing so might include: improved reliability through path/provider diversity, as well as improved performance and flexibility in supporting highly variable network loads through *resource pooling*. Resource pooling refers to making, possibly distributed, resources appear to users as a single possibly shared one, typically resulting in a higher effective capacity and better statistical multiplexing. Similarly, in the context of wireless networks one can expect that concurrently exploiting multiple interfaces, e.g., cellular and Wi-Fi, would lead to performance benefits. Additional intriguing scenarios are being considered where a high bandwidth residential wireless mesh is used to enable substantially higher uplink wireline capacity to the Internet by sharing multiple limited capacity upstream residential broadband wireline links. Fig. 1 shows two scenarios where one might expect to reap benefits from supporting sessions with multpath flow control.

While the potential for exploiting path diversity through multipath flow control is intuitively clear, there exist very few works in the literature that shed light on flow-level performance and network design. Herein we refer to flow-level performance, as measures of transfer delays or throughput achievable in a stochastic network supporting best effort flows, i.e., file transfers and web browsing sessions. If this paradigm is to be adopted, there are many fundamental questions that need to be answered, for example:

• What flow-level throughput gains can we expect over traditional networks? How sensitive are they to system loads, and peak rate constraints, e.g., due to DSL or TCP?

• Are there abstractions that can be used to understand the interaction of multipath sessions with others (e.g., resource pooling or cutset bounds) and how do these affect performance, routing and network dimensioning?

• What measures of robustness are gained when traffic with multipath flow control is supported?

• What fraction of the traffic needs the extra flexibility of multipath flow control to achieve the practical benefits?

• In the residential wireless mesh setting described above, given cost of relaying traffic across neighboring home networks, how far should traffic be relayed to enable effective sharing of limited uplink capacity?

Our goal in this paper is to make some progress towards developing the tools needed to partially answer these questions. For simplicity, we will focus on wireline networks though our models can also be interpreted in terms of shared wireless resources.

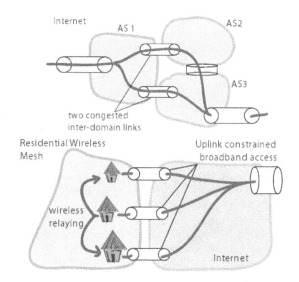

Figure 1: Top figure: Multipath routing could provide substantial benefits when there is limited shared inter-domain bandwidth among providers. Bottom figure: A residential wireless mesh network enables home users exploit multiple paths to overcome limited uplink links to the Internet.

Related Work.

There has been extensive recent work towards understanding how network protocols, e.g., TCP, allocate, or should allocate, bandwidth among competing flows. Much of this work has focused on associating a utility function with each user, and studying mechanisms to maximize the sum of the users' utilities. For a *fixed* set of users, the resulting allocation can be viewed as optimal in terms of optimizing network utility. The utility functions may be chosen to reflect users' valuation for allocated resources or can be used as a device to implement notions of fairness among competing flows, e.g., proportionally fair, max-min fair, α-fair, see e.g., [12, 1, 20]. Most notable among these are the allocations based on proportional fairness ([12]) due to its ease of implementation, and its performance, robustness and (approximate) insensitivity properties ([19], [11]). Note that an allocation is said to be insensitive if its steady state distribution is independent of all traffic characteristics except the average traffic loads.

Unfortunately, for networks supporting best effort flows, the relevant user perceived performance metrics will be averages taken over their sojourn in the network, such as file transfer delay or mean throughput, and the relationship between these flow averages and the utilities/fairness underlying the network design is not well understood. Early works in this area focused on the stability of such networks. See [23] for a survey of these results.

These early papers, however, do not provide concrete tools for assessing user perceived *performance* for network engineering. More recent work in [5, 3] provides substantial insights into why, attempting to do so directly is difficult, and attribute this difficulty mainly to the dependence of the steady state distribution of utility based allocations on detailed traffic characteristics, e.g., flow size distribution. In [5], the same researchers propose *balanced fair* allocation. They introduce it as the most efficient insensitive allocation, in the sense that it is the unique insensitive allocation for which a link is saturated or a peak rate constraint is met in every state with atleast one flow (see Section 2 for a detailed discussion of this allocation). Due to its insensitivity, flow level performance can either be explicitly computed, approximated or bounded, see e.g., [6, 4, 2].

The tractability of balanced fair allocation has been exploited to study the flow-level performance of intractable (sensitive) allocations like proportional fair allocation ([2]). Balanced fair allocation has been shown to be a good approximation of the proportional fair allocation especially at high loads ([3]). For a certain class of networks, balanced fair allocation coincides with proportional fair allocation ([5]). Further, [19] introduces modified proportional fair allocation that coincides with proportional fair allocation in an asymptotic sense, and shows that the modified proportional fair allocation and balanced fair allocation admit the same large deviation behavior.

Utility based allocations have been extended to accommodate multipath flow control to exploit the benefits of increased path diversity. However, most of the progress made in this area concerns the stability and distributed implementation for these allocations ([10, 7, 21]). Only the following works study flow-level performance in networks using multipath flow control: [17], [16], [11] and [9]. In [17] and [16], the main performance metric considered is the blocking probability for flows in a system with admission control that blocks a flow if it cannot be allocated a certain minimum bandwidth. However, a weakness of the approach in [17] and [16] is that it mostly relies on complex optimization formulations and simulations, and they fail to give insights into the elements in a network that are critical to the performance.

The performance metric considered in [11] is the mean delay experienced by flows in a network using multipath proportional fair allocation. Inspired by the relationship of this allocation to a related network of processor sharing queues, they propose an approximation for the mean delay experienced by a (possibly multipath) flow of class s

$$\sum_{j \in \mathcal{J}} \left(\frac{a_{js}}{\mu_s} \right) \frac{c_j}{c_j - \rho_j}$$

where $\mathcal{J}$ is a set of virtual resources, a_{js} is the capacity required on virtual resource j per unit of bandwidth allocated to class s, $(\mu_s)^{-1}$ is the mean flow size, and c_j and ρ_j are the capacity of and load on virtual resource $j \in \mathcal{J}$ respectively. The above approximation suggests that the delay experienced by a flow is dictated by certain virtual resources referred to as resource pools, and is related to the delay experienced by a flow that traverses the resource pools in a store and forward manner. Their approach is to transform the multipath network into an equivalent network with single path routing comprised of virtual resources. This transformation is computationally demanding for large networks ([15]). Also, [11] fails to give useful insights into the transformation, the constituent pools or even the terms

a_{js} and hence, the approximation above is difficult to use for engineering purposes like capacity allocation, design of multipath routing/flow control schemes etc. A concrete understanding of the resource pools affecting flow's delays is needed to enable the engineering of such networks. In [9], multipath network under proportional fair allocation is considered in a heavy-traffic regime. However, [9] also relies on the transformation of the multipath network into an equivalent network with single path routing.

Our Contributions.

The main goal of this paper is to develop tools to evaluate mean delay experienced by flows and support network design when multipath flow control allocation is based on proportional fairness. However, a study of flow level dynamics of proportional fair allocation is in general hard due to its sensitivity ([5]). Thus, we adopt an approach that involves studying a more tractable network that uses multipath balanced fair allocation, a multipath generalization of the balanced fair allocation introduced in [5]. We obtain lower and upper bounds on the mean per bit delay, exhibiting its relationship to the capacity and load associated with certain resource pools. Our bounds take into account competing multipath traffic in the network, and thus our results go beyond max flow like arguments. Proving these bounds is a challenging extension of the bounds obtained in [2] for networks with single path routing, in part due to a key feature of the multipath balanced fair allocation which modifies the splitting of traffic along different routes in accordance with the state of the network. We also use the bounds to explore scenarios where peak rate constraints are likely to hurt the performance gains achievable by adding more routes.

While insightful, the performance bounds are difficult to drive network design. Hence, we use the large deviations characteristics of balanced fair allocation obtained in [19] to zero in on a collection of resources referred to as a critical pool that plays the dominant role in determining the likelihood of congestion events involving accumulations of a large number of flows. Further, these critical resources indeed behave as a single pooled resource. We establish this by studying the sensitivity of the large deviations exponent to the pool's capacity. We also use the large deviation behavior to present a disciplined approach to a capacity allocation problem for such networks that is based on a linear optimization problem.

Main contributions of this paper are summarized below:
• We develop tools to study delays experienced by flows and support network design for a network under multipath proportional fair allocation.
• We obtain a stability condition for multipath balanced fair allocation.
• For multipath balanced fair allocation, we obtain bounds on mean per bit delay that exhibit the impact of the capacity and load associated with resource pools on performance.
• We explore scenarios where peak rate constraints can reduce the performance gains from the addition of more routes.
• We obtain the most likely mix of the flows of different classes when there is an accumulation of aggregate number of flows.
• For the multipath setting, we studied the large deviation for congestion events to identify critical resource pools.
• We present a disciplined approach to a capacity allocation problem in the form of a linear optimization problem.

Organization of the paper.

We discuss the system model in Section 2. In Section 3, we discuss two insensitive multipath allocations Random routing and multipath balanced fair allocations and study their stability. In Section 4, we obtain bounds on the mean per bit delay under multipath balanced fair allocation. In Section 5, we use the large deviation characteristics of multipath balanced fair allocation to identify and study critical resource pools and study their sensitivity to the pool's capacity. We present some conclusions drawn from the main discussion of the paper in Section 6.

2. SYSTEM MODEL

We begin by introducing some notation. Let $\mathbb{Z}_+$ denote the set of all non-negative integers. For any set $\mathcal{B}$, $|\mathcal{B}|$ denotes the number of elements in the set. For any vectors $\mathbf{b}, \mathbf{n}$ whose elements are indexed by some set $\mathcal{I}$, i.e., $\mathbf{b} = (b_i)_{i \in \mathcal{I}}$ and $\mathbf{n} = (n_i)_{i \in \mathcal{I}}$, let $\mathbf{b^n} = \prod_{i \in \mathcal{I}} b_i^{n_i}$ and $|\mathbf{a}| = \sum_{i \in \mathcal{I}} a_i$.

We consider a network where possibly multipath flows arrive, utilize network resources and leave. The network is comprised of a set $\mathcal{L}$ of links where each link $l \in \mathcal{L}$ has a capacity $c_l > 0$ bits per second. A flow ϑ arrives at some time t_ϑ^a, brings D_ϑ bits and leaves at some time t_ϑ^d given by $D_\vartheta = \int_{t_\vartheta^a}^{t_\vartheta^d} \sigma_\vartheta(t) dt$ where $\sigma_\vartheta(t)$ denotes the rate at which the flow ϑ is served at time t. We refer to D_ϑ as the size of flow ϑ.

Each flow is associated with some flow class $s \in \mathcal{S}$ where $\mathcal{S}$ denotes the set of all flow classes. The flows associated with a class $s \in \mathcal{S}$ arrive as a Poisson process of rate ξ_s with a mean flow size $(1/\nu_s)$ bits. Let $\rho_s = \xi_s/\nu_s$ bits per second be the traffic intensity of class $s \in \mathcal{S}$. Let $\boldsymbol{\rho} = (\rho_\mathbf{s})_{s \in \mathcal{S}}$. The flows associated with class s are peak rate constrained (e.g., by an access link, or by the transport mechanism like in TCP where the finite receiver buffer effectively acts as a peak rate constraint.) to a rate $a_s \in [0, \infty]$ bits per second, i.e., $\sigma_\vartheta(t) \leq a_s$ for any flow ϑ of class $s \in \mathcal{S}$. If there are no peak rate constraints for class s, we set $a_s = \infty$. For any $s \in \mathcal{S}$, let R_s denote the set of possible routes for class s flows where a route is a subset of $\mathcal{L}$. We refer to the important special case in which $|R_s| = 1 \ \forall \ s \in \mathcal{S}$ as the single path routing case. Let $\mathbf{A}$ be the route-link incidence matrix associated with the network, i.e., for $l \in \mathcal{L}$ and $r \in \cup_{s \in \mathcal{S}} R_s$, $A_{l,r} = 1$ if $l \in r$ (route r traverses link l) and 0 otherwise. The example in Fig. 2 should help the reader to get a feel for the notation (see the caption). The results presented in this paper are valid for a much more general model (see [5] for details) where the flows associated with each class are generated within sessions and the session arrivals correspond to independent Poisson processes. In this model, the flow size and number of flows per session of class s can have general distributions, and successive flow sizes can be correlated.

The network state is an integer valued $|\mathcal{S}|$-tuple whose s^{th} component is the number of flows of class $s \in \mathcal{S}$. For each $s \in \mathcal{S}$ and $r_s \in R_s$, let $\phi_{sr_s}(\mathbf{x})$ denote the bandwidth allocated to the route r_s of class s in network state $\mathbf{x}$. For each $s \in \mathcal{S}$, let $\phi_s(\mathbf{x}) = \sum_{r_s \in R_s} \phi_{sr_s}(\mathbf{x})$ denote the total bandwidth allocated to flows of class s in state $\mathbf{x}$, and assume it is shared equally among the x_s flows. Hence, there exists some $\mathbf{f}(\mathbf{x}) \in \mathcal{F}$ such that

$$\phi_{sr_s}(\mathbf{x}) = f_{sr_s}(\mathbf{x})\phi_s(\mathbf{x}), \forall s \in \mathcal{S}, r_s \in R_s,$$

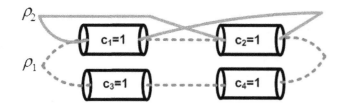

Figure 2: For the above network, $\mathcal{L} = \{1, 2, 3, 4\}$, $\mathcal{S} = \{1, 2\}$ $R_1 = \{r_{11}, r_{12}\}$, $R_2 = \{r_{21}, r_{22}\}$, $r_{11} = \{1, 2\}$, $r_{12} = \{3, 4\}$, $r_{21} = \{1\}$, $r_{22} = \{2\}$

where

$$\mathcal{F} = \prod_{s \in \mathcal{S}} \mathcal{F}_s,$$

$$\mathcal{F}_s = \{\mathbf{f}_s | f_{s,r_s} \geq 0, \forall r_s \in R_s; \sum_{r_s \in R_s} f_{s,r_s} = 1\} \text{ for each } s \in \mathcal{S}.$$

Thus, $(\boldsymbol{\phi}(\mathbf{x}), \mathbf{f}(\mathbf{x}))$ where $\boldsymbol{\phi}(\mathbf{x}) = (\phi_s(\mathbf{x}))_{s \in \mathcal{S}}$ fully characterizes the allocation in network state $\mathbf{x}$. We refer to $\mathbf{f} : \mathbb{Z}_+^{|\mathcal{S}|} \to \mathcal{F}$ as the splitting function. Here, the set $\mathcal{F}$ captures all possible ways to split the bandwidth allocated to various classes across their respective routes.

The allocated bandwidths satisfy the following linear capacity constraints

$$\sum_{s \in \mathcal{S}, r_s \in R_s} A_{l, r_s} \phi_{sr_s}(\mathbf{x}) \leq c_l, \forall l \in \mathcal{L}, \forall \mathbf{x} \in \mathbb{Z}_+^{|\mathcal{S}|}, \quad (1)$$

and peak rate constraints given by

$$\phi_s(\mathbf{x}) \leq a_s x_s, \forall s \in \mathcal{S}, \forall \mathbf{x} \in \mathbb{Z}_+^{|\mathcal{S}|}. \quad (2)$$

Let

$$\mathcal{C}_P^M(\mathbf{x}) = \{(\boldsymbol{\lambda}, \mathbf{f}) : \boldsymbol{\lambda} = (\lambda_s)_{s \in \mathcal{S}}, \mathbf{f} \in \mathcal{F},$$

$$\sum_{s \in \mathcal{S}, r_s \in R_s} A_{l, r_s} f_{sr_s} \lambda_s \leq c_l \ \forall l \in \mathcal{L}, \lambda_s \leq a_s x_s \forall s \in \mathcal{S}\}.$$

Then, (1) and (2) is equivalent to the condition

$$(\boldsymbol{\phi}(\mathbf{x}), \mathbf{f}(\mathbf{x})) \in \mathcal{C}_P^M(\mathbf{x}).$$

In systems where there are no peak rate constraints, i.e., $a_s = \infty \ \forall \ s \in \mathcal{S}$, the above condition simplifies to

$$(\boldsymbol{\phi}(\mathbf{x}), \mathbf{f}(\mathbf{x})) \in \mathcal{C}^M$$

where

$$\mathcal{C}^M = \{(\boldsymbol{\lambda}, \mathbf{f}) : \boldsymbol{\lambda} = (\lambda_s)_{s \in \mathcal{S}}, \mathbf{f} \in \mathcal{F} \text{ and}$$

$$\sum_{s \in \mathcal{S}, r_s \in R_s} A_{l, r_s} f_{sr_s} \lambda_s \leq c_l \ \forall l \in \mathcal{L}\}. \quad (3)$$

The multipath proportional fair allocation, for instance, satisfies (3) in which the allocation $(\boldsymbol{\lambda}^{PF}(\mathbf{x}), \mathbf{f}^{PF}(\mathbf{x}))$ in a network state $\mathbf{x}$ is a solution to the optimization problem MULTIPATH-PF given below

$$\max_{(\boldsymbol{\lambda}, \mathbf{f})} \left\{ \sum_{s \in \mathcal{S}} x_s \log(\lambda_s) \mid (\boldsymbol{\lambda}, \mathbf{f}) \in \mathcal{C}^M \right\}.$$

The steady state distribution of multipath proportional fair (more generally, utility function based allocations) are sensitive to the detailed traffic characteristics which makes an analysis of their flow level dynamics hard ([5]). Balanced fair allocation introduced in [5] for the single path routing setting is much more tractable due to its insensitivity properties.

The balanced fair allocation belongs to a much larger class of insensitive allocations. In [5], it is shown that any insensitive allocation corresponds to a positive function $\Phi : \mathbb{Z}_+^{|\mathcal{S}|} \to [0, \infty)$ where the allocation for class $s \in \mathcal{S}$ in network state $\mathbf{x}$ is given by

$$\phi_s(\mathbf{x}) = \frac{\Phi(\mathbf{x} - \mathbf{e}_s)}{\Phi(\mathbf{x})}$$

where the vector $\mathbf{e}_s \in \mathbb{Z}_+^{|\mathcal{S}|}$ has the uth coordinate equal to one for $u = s$ and 0 otherwise. Further, it is shown that if

$$\sum_{\mathbf{x} \in \mathbb{Z}_+^{|\mathcal{S}|}} \Phi(\mathbf{x}) \boldsymbol{\rho}^{\mathbf{x}} < \infty, \quad (4)$$

then the invariant distribution for a network state $\mathbf{x}$ is

$$\pi(\mathbf{x}) = \pi(\mathbf{0}) \Phi(\mathbf{x}) \boldsymbol{\rho}^{\mathbf{x}}$$

where $\pi(\mathbf{0})$ is the normalization constant of the distribution. In the rest of this section, we mainly focus on some of the important results for the single path routing setting. As each class is associated with a single route, in the rest of this section, we use s and the route associated with the class interchangeably. The balanced fair allocation for the single path routing setting is characterized by a balance function $\Phi : \mathbb{Z}_+^{|\mathcal{S}|} \to [0, \infty)$ given by ([5])

$$\Phi(\mathbf{x}) = \max \left\{ \max_{s \in \mathcal{S}: x_s > 0} \frac{\Phi(\mathbf{x} - \mathbf{e_s})}{a_s x_s}, \max_{l \in \mathcal{L}} \sum_{s \in \mathcal{S}} \frac{A_{l, s}}{c_l} \Phi(\mathbf{x} - \mathbf{e}_s) \right\}$$

for $\mathbf{x} \in \mathbb{Z}_+^{|\mathcal{S}|} \setminus \{\mathbf{0}\}$ with $\Phi(\mathbf{0}) = 1$, $\Phi(\mathbf{x}) = 0$ outside the positive quadrant. The balanced fair allocation for class s in network state $\mathbf{x}$ is then given by

$$\phi_s(\mathbf{x}) = \frac{\Phi(\mathbf{x} - \mathbf{e}_s)}{\Phi(\mathbf{x})}.$$

This allocation satisfies (1) and (2). In [5], it is shown that if $\boldsymbol{\rho}$ satisfies the following stability condition

$$\sum_{s \in \mathcal{S}, r_s \in R_s} A_{l, s} \rho_s < c_l \ \forall l \in \mathcal{L}, \quad (5)$$

then the invariant distribution for a network state $\mathbf{x}$ is

$$\pi(\mathbf{x}) = \pi(\mathbf{0}) \Phi(\mathbf{x}) \boldsymbol{\rho}^{\mathbf{x}} \quad (6)$$

where $\pi(\mathbf{0})$ is the normalization constant of the distribution. Note that the invariant distribution is *insensitive* to all the traffic characteristics except the traffic intensity. We refer to [5] for an extensive discussion on balanced fair allocation for the single path routing case. Except for certain networks ([6, 2, 4]), numerical evaluation of mean per-bit delay is intractable for large $|\mathcal{S}|$ due to state space explosion. The simple explicit bounds for the mean per bit delay τ_s of a class $s \in \mathcal{S}$ obtained in [2] become valuable in such settings.

The bounds are:

$$\tau_s \geq \max\left(\frac{1}{a_s}, \max_{l \in \mathcal{L}} \frac{A_{l,s}}{c_l - \alpha_l}\right),$$

$$\tau_s \leq \max\left(\frac{1}{a_s}, \max_{l \in \mathcal{L}} \frac{A_{l,s}}{c_l}\right) + \sum_{l \in \mathcal{L}} \frac{\alpha_l}{c_l} \frac{A_{l,s}}{c_l - \alpha_l} \quad (7)$$

where $\alpha_l = \sum_s A_{l,s} \rho_s$ for $l \in \mathcal{L}$. Note the intuition here is as follows. The lower bound is at least that associated with the peak rate constraint of class s, or that of the bottleneck link along the route of class s. The upper bound includes the peak rate constraint or capacity constraint of links along the path, and an additive term that roughly corresponds to sending the bits, in a store and forward manner over the links along the route of class s. Hence, we have a weighted summation of the mean per bit delays on each link on the route.

3. RANDOM ROUTING VS MULTPATH FLOW CONTROL

Our objective in this section and the next is to study and compare flow level delays in two systems. In the first system, for any class s, each flow of class s randomly chooses one route in R_s. We refer to this as *random routing*. In the second system, for any class s, each flow of class s can simultaneously use all the routes in the set R_s. The comparison allows us to gauge the benefits of balancing flow loads across paths vs balancing traffic (e.g., packet level) across multiple paths during the lifetime of a flow.

3.1 Random routing

A random routing policy corresponds to a $\mathbf{p} \in \mathcal{F}$ where each flow of class $s \in \mathcal{S}$ is routed to route $r_s \in R_s$ independently with probability p_{sr_s}. We could choose $\mathbf{p}$ to optimize a performance objective like load balancing. Since the route of each flow of any class s is chosen independently using $\mathbf{p}$, we can treat the traffic of class s on route $r_s \in R_s$ as that of an independent class indexed by (s, r_s) with traffic intensity $\rho_{(s,r_s)} = p_{sr_s}\rho_s$ and we let $\boldsymbol{\rho}^R = (\rho_{(s,r_s)})_{s \in \mathcal{S}, r_s \in R_s}$. The route level network state is a vector $\mathbf{x}^R \in \mathbb{Z}^{\sum_{s \in \mathcal{S}} |R_s|}$ where $x^R_{(s,r_s)}$ denotes the number of flows of class s routed along route $r_s \in R_s$. For a route level network state $\mathbf{x}^R$, let $\phi^R_{(s,r_s)}(\mathbf{x}^R)$ denote the total bandwidth allocated to flows of class s routed along $r_s \in R_s$, and assume this bandwidth is shared equitably by these flows. Further, the allocation must satisfy (1) and (2). For the route level balanced fair allocation, the allocation for the set of active flows of class s along route r_s is then given by

$$\phi^R_{(s,r_s)}(\mathbf{x}^R) = \frac{\Phi^R(\mathbf{x}^R - \mathbf{e}^R_{(s,r_s)})}{\Phi^R(\mathbf{x}^R)}.$$

We refer to the (single path routing) balanced fair allocation for this setting as the route level balanced fair allocation, where the allocation is characterized by the balance function $\Phi^R : \mathbb{Z}^{\sum_{s \in \mathcal{S}} |R_s|} \to [0, \infty)$ given by

$$\Phi^R(\mathbf{x}^R) = \max\left\{ \max_{s \in \mathcal{S}, r_s \in R_s : x_{(s,r_s)} > 0} \frac{\Phi^R(\mathbf{x}^R - \mathbf{e}^R_{(s,r_s)})}{a_s x_{(s,r_s)}}, \right.$$

$$\left. \max_{l \in \mathcal{L}} \sum_{s \in \mathcal{S}, r_s \in R_s} \frac{A_{l,r_s}}{c_l} \Phi^R\left(\mathbf{x}^R - \mathbf{e}^R_{(s,r_s)}\right) \right\} \quad (8)$$

for $\mathbf{x}^R \in \mathbb{Z}_+^{\sum_{s \in \mathcal{S}} |R_s|} \setminus \{\mathbf{0}\}$, $\Phi^R(\mathbf{0}) = 1$ and $\Phi^R(\mathbf{x}^R) = 0$ outside the positive quadrant. Here, $\mathbf{e}^R_{(s,r_s)} \in \mathbb{Z}^{\sum_{s \in \mathcal{S}} |R_s|}$ with 1 in the coordinate corresponding to the class (s, r_s) and zero otherwise.

The next result gives the stability condition and provides bounds on the mean per bit delay experienced by flows of a class $s \in \mathcal{S}$ under the route level balanced fair allocation. To that end, for a given $\mathbf{p}$, let

$$\Gamma(\mathbf{p}) = \left\{ \mu \in \mathbb{R}_+^{|\mathcal{S}|} : \sum_{s \in \mathcal{S}, r_s \in R_s} A_{l,r_s} p_{sr_s} \mu_s < c_l \ \forall l \in \mathcal{L}, \right\}.$$

Then, we have the following result.

THEOREM 1. *If $\boldsymbol{\rho} \in \Gamma(\mathbf{p})$, the following hold:*

(a) *The invariant distribution $\pi^R(\mathbf{x}^R)$ for the route level network state $\mathbf{x}^R$ is given by*

$$\pi^R(\mathbf{x}^R) = \pi^R(\mathbf{0}) \Phi^R(\mathbf{x}^R)(\boldsymbol{\rho}^R)^{\mathbf{x}^R} \quad (9)$$

where $\pi^R(\mathbf{0})$ is the normalization constant for the distribution.

(b) *The mean mean per bit delay τ_t for a class $t \in \mathcal{S}$ satisfies*

$$\tau_t \geq \sum_{r \in R_t} p_{tr} \left(\max\left\{ \frac{1}{a_t}, \max_{l \in \mathcal{L}} \frac{A_{l,r}}{c_l - \alpha_l} \right\} \right) \ and$$

$$\tau_t \leq \sum_{r \in R_t} p_{tr} \left(\max\left\{ \frac{1}{a_t}, \max_{l \in \mathcal{L}} \frac{A_{l,r}}{c_l} \right\} + \sum_{l \in \mathcal{L}} \frac{\alpha_l}{c_l} \frac{A_{l,r}}{(c_l - \alpha_l)} \right)$$

where for $l \in \mathcal{L}$,

$$\alpha_l = \sum_{s \in \mathcal{S}, r_s \in R_s} A_{l,r_s} p_{sr_s} \rho_s.$$

We skip the proof as it follows from (7). In particular, the bounds given above can be proved by noting that

$$\tau_t = \sum_{r_t \in R_t} p_{tr_t} \tau_{(t,r_t)}$$

and using the bounds given in (7) for the mean per bit delay.

3.2 Multipath flow control

Next, we consider the second system in which *each flow of class s can simultaneously use all the routes in the set R_s* by sending its data across on all the routes. Further, the splitting of the traffic corresponding to a class can change depending on the network state.

As pointed out in Section 2, corresponding to each insensitive allocation, there is a balance function. However, in the multipath setting, to fully characterize such an allocation, we need to further specify the splitting function $\mathbf{f}(\mathbf{x})$ for each network state $\mathbf{x}$. Thus, in the multipath setting, any insensitive allocation is fully characterized by a balance function and a splitting function defined for all network states. Then, the allocation for class s in network state $\mathbf{x}$ given by

$$\phi_s(\mathbf{x}) = \frac{\Phi(\mathbf{x} - \mathbf{e}_s)}{\Phi(\mathbf{x})} \quad (10)$$

and the bandwidth allocated on route $r_s \in R_s$ is given by

$$\phi_{s,r_s}(\mathbf{x}) = f_{s,r_s}(\mathbf{x})\phi_s(\mathbf{x}).$$

We define a multipath balanced fair allocation for this system as the insensitive allocation obtained using the balance function $\Phi : \mathbb{Z}^{|\mathcal{S}|} \to [0, \infty)$ defined as

$$\Phi(\mathbf{x}) = \max \left\{ \max_{s \in \mathcal{S}: x_s > 0} \frac{\Phi(\mathbf{x} - \mathbf{e_s})}{a_s x_s}, \right. \tag{11}$$
$$\left. \min_{\mathbf{f} \in \mathcal{F}} \max_{l \in \mathcal{L}} \left(\sum_{s \in \mathcal{S}, r_s \in R_s} \frac{A_{l,r_s}}{c_l} f_{s,r_s} \Phi(\mathbf{x} - \mathbf{e_s}) \right) \right\}$$

for $\mathbf{x} \in \mathbb{Z}^{|\mathcal{S}|} \setminus \{\mathbf{0}\}$, $\Phi(\mathbf{0}) = 1$ and $\Phi(\mathbf{x}) = 0$ outside the positive quadrant. For any network state $\mathbf{x}$, the splitting function $\mathbf{f}(\mathbf{x})$ is equal to $\mathbf{f}^*(\mathbf{x})$ which is a minimizer of the optimization problem given below:

$$\min_{\mathbf{f} \in \mathcal{F}} \max_{l \in \mathcal{L}} \left(\sum_{s \in \mathcal{S}, r_s \in R_s} \frac{A_{l,r_s}}{c_l} f_{s,r_s} \Phi(\mathbf{x} - \mathbf{e_s}) \right). \tag{12}$$

Note that the splitting function need not be unique. Also, note that such allocations satisfy (1) and (2). Further, note that the splitting function $\mathbf{f}^*(\mathbf{x})$ of the allocation is state-dependent and recursively defined. Also,

$$\Phi(\mathbf{x}) = \max \left\{ \max_{s \in \mathcal{S}: x_s > 0} \frac{\Phi(\mathbf{x} - \mathbf{e_s})}{a_s x_s}, \right. \tag{13}$$
$$\left. \max_{l \in \mathcal{L}} \left(\sum_{s \in \mathcal{S}, r_s \in R_s} \frac{A_{l,r_s}}{c_l} f^*_{s,r_s}(\mathbf{x}) \Phi(\mathbf{x} - \mathbf{e_s}) \right) \right\}.$$

The following result establishes that the balance function associated with multipath balanced fair allocation defined above is unique. A proof of the result is given in [8].

LEMMA 1. *For any balance function* $\tilde{\Phi} : \mathbb{Z}^{|\mathcal{S}|} \to [0, \infty)$ *with* $\tilde{\Phi}(\mathbf{0}) = 1$, *and splitting function* $\mathbf{f} : \mathbb{Z}^{|\mathcal{S}|} \to \mathcal{F}$, *if the corresponding insensitive allocation satisfies* (1) *and* (2), *then*

$$\Phi(\mathbf{x}) \le \tilde{\Phi}(\mathbf{x}), \ \forall \mathbf{x} \in \mathbb{Z}^{|\mathcal{S}|}.$$

Next, we study the stability of the multipath balanced fair allocation. Let

$$\Gamma^M = \left\{ \mu \in \mathbb{R}_+^{|\mathcal{S}|} : \mu \in \Gamma(\mathbf{f}) \text{ for some } \mathbf{f} \in \mathcal{F} \right\}. \tag{14}$$

The next result gives the stablity region. See [8] for a proof.

THEOREM 2. *If the offered load* $\boldsymbol{\rho} \in \Gamma^M$, *then the invariant distribution for a network state* $\mathbf{x}$ *is given by*

$$\pi(\mathbf{x}) = \pi(\mathbf{0})\Phi(\mathbf{x})\boldsymbol{\rho}^{\mathbf{x}} \tag{15}$$

where $\pi(\mathbf{0})$ *is the normalization constant of the distribution.*

From Lemma 1 and (15), we can conclude that the probability of having no flows in the system for the multipath balanced fair allocation is greater than or equal to that of any multipath insensitive allocation.

Also, note that $\Gamma(\mathbf{p}) \subseteq \Gamma^M$ for any $\mathbf{p} \in \mathcal{F}$. Thus, if a network using route level balanced fair allocation is stable, it will be stable when using multipath balanced fair allocation.

4. PERFORMANCE BOUNDS

In this section, we move beyond stability conditions and study the mean per bit delay for such a system. In this system too, the numerical evaluation of mean per bit delay for

the balanced fair allocation is intractable for large $|\mathcal{S}|$. Thus, we resort to bounding the mean per bit delay. We consider bounds that are based on pooled capacity constraints. The following definitions capture how such pooling is considered.

DEFINITION 1. *A (possibly multipath) flow class* s *is said to be* supported *by* $\mathcal{H} \subset \mathcal{L}$ *if for each* $r_s \in R_s$, $|r_s \cap \mathcal{H}| > 0$, *i.e., each route of class* s *traverses at least one link in* $\mathcal{H}$. *Let* $\mathcal{S}(\mathcal{H}) \subset \mathcal{S}$ *denote the set of flow classes that are supported by* $\mathcal{H}$.

DEFINITION 2. *A (possibly multipath) flow class* s *is said to be* partially supported *by* $\mathcal{H} \subset \mathcal{L}$ *if for some* $r_s \in R_s$, $|r_s \cap \mathcal{H}| > 0$, *i.e., at least one route of class* s *traverses at least one link in* $\mathcal{H}$. *We let* $\mathcal{P}(\mathcal{H}) \subset \mathcal{S}$ *denote the set of flow classes that are partially supported by* $\mathcal{H}$.

Note that $\mathcal{S}(\mathcal{H}) \subset \mathcal{P}(\mathcal{H})$, i.e., if a flow is supported by $\mathcal{H}$, then it is also partially supported by $\mathcal{H}$. Next, for each class $s \in \mathcal{S}$, we define the following collections of resource pools:

$$\mathcal{B}_s = \{\mathcal{H} \subseteq \mathcal{L} : s \in \mathcal{S}(\mathcal{H})\} \text{ and}$$
$$\mathcal{D}_s = \left\{ \mathcal{H} \in \mathcal{B}_s : \text{there exists no } \mathcal{H}' \in \mathcal{B}_s, \right.$$
$$\left. \mathcal{H}' \neq \mathcal{H} \text{ such that } \mathcal{H}' \subset \mathcal{H} \right\}.$$

Thus, $\mathcal{B}_s$ is the collection of resource pools that support flow class s. The set $\mathcal{D}_s$ corresponds to a minimal collection of pooled resources that support flow class s, i.e., pools which can not be reduced and still support class s. For the network in Fig. 2, $\mathcal{D}_1 = \{\{1, 3\}, \{1, 4\}, \{2, 3\}, \{2, 4\}\}$ and $\mathcal{D}_2 = \{\{1, 2\}\}$. In the next section, we will see that the bounds on mean per bit delay for a class $s \in \mathcal{S}$ will be dictated by the cumulative capacities and traffic associated the resource pools in $\mathcal{B}_s$ and $\mathcal{D}_s$.

In general, a multipath flow may traverse a *set* of links $\mathcal{H}$ multiple times, or may have constituent routes that traverse those resources different numbers of times. To account for these we define the following.

DEFINITION 3. *For any flow class* s, *route* $r_s \in R_s$ *and set* $\mathcal{H} \subseteq \mathcal{L}$, *let* $n_{s,r_s}(\mathcal{H}) = |r_s \cap \mathcal{H}|$, *i.e.,* $n_{s,r_s}(\mathcal{H})$ *denotes the number of links (possibly zero) in* $\mathcal{H}$ *that* r_s *traverses. Let* $n_s(\mathcal{H}) = \min_{r \in R_s} n_{s,r}(\mathcal{H})$ *be the minimum multiplicity with which the class* s *is supported by* $\mathcal{H}$. *Similarly, let* $\overline{n}_s(\mathcal{H}) = \max_{r \in R_s} n_{s,r}(\mathcal{H})$ *be the maximum multiplicity with which the class* s *is supported by* $\mathcal{H}$.

For the network in Fig. 2, if $\mathcal{H} = \{1, 2\}$, then $n_1(\mathcal{H}) = 0$, $\overline{n}_1(\mathcal{H}) = 2$ and $n_2(\mathcal{H}) = \overline{n}_2(\mathcal{H}) = 1$. Finally, let

$$c(\mathcal{H}) = \sum_{l \in \mathcal{H}} c_l$$

denote the pooled capacity of an $\mathcal{H} \subset \mathcal{L}$,

$$\rho(\mathcal{H}) = \sum_{s \in \mathcal{S}(\mathcal{H})} n_s(\mathcal{H})\rho_s$$

denote the aggregate load of classes supported by $\mathcal{H}$ accounting for multiplicities, and

$$\overline{\rho}(\mathcal{H}) = \sum_{s \in \mathcal{P}(\mathcal{H})} \overline{n}_s(\mathcal{H})\rho_s$$

be an upper bound on the aggregate load partially supported by $\mathcal{H}$ also accounting for multiplicities.

In this section, we obtain bounds on the mean per bit delay of a flow of class $t \in \mathcal{S}$ under balanced fair allocation with multipath flow control assuming that the stability condition holds, i.e., the offered load $\rho \in \Gamma^M$. From Little's theorem and (15), the mean per bit delay τ_t for any class $t \in \mathcal{S}$ satisfies

$$\tau_t = \frac{E[X_t]}{\rho_t} = \frac{1}{\rho_t} \sum_{\mathbf{x}} x_t \pi(\mathbf{x}) = \frac{1}{\rho_t} \frac{\sum_{\mathbf{x}} x_t \Phi(\mathbf{x}) \rho^{\mathbf{x}}}{\sum_{\mathbf{x}} \Phi(\mathbf{x}) \rho^{\mathbf{x}}}$$

where $\sum_{\mathbf{x}}$ stands for $\sum_{\mathbf{x} \in \mathbb{Z}_+^{|\mathcal{S}|}}$. The numerical evaluation of mean per bit delay using the above expression becomes intractable as the number of classes of flows becomes large. Also, note that evaluation of $\Phi(\mathbf{x})$ using (11) involves linear programming for each network state $\mathbf{x}$. Hence, the simple explicit bounds on mean per bit delay obtained in the rest of this section are invaluable towards understanding for the flow level performance in a general network with multipath routes and flow control. These bounds are generalizations of those in [2] which only consider the single path routing setting. The proofs of the bounds presented in this section use ideas from [2], but require substantial additional development to show, due to the state dependent nature of the splitting function $\mathbf{f}^*(\mathbf{x})$.

4.1 Lower bound

The following theorem gives a lower bound on the mean per bit delay τ_t of a class $t \in \mathcal{S}$.

THEOREM 3. *For any class* $t \in \mathcal{S}$,

$$\tau_t \geq \max \left\{ \frac{1}{a_t}, \max_{\mathcal{H} \in \mathcal{B}_t} \left(\frac{n_t(\mathcal{H})}{c(\mathcal{H}) - \rho(\mathcal{H})} \right) \right\}.$$

PROOF. For an $\mathcal{H} \subset \mathcal{L}$, consider a link $l \in \mathcal{H}$. From (13),

$$\Phi(\mathbf{x}) \geq \sum_{s \in \mathcal{S}, r \in R_s} \frac{A_{l,r}}{c_l} f_{s,r}^*(\mathbf{x}) \Phi(\mathbf{x} - \mathbf{e}_s).$$

Using (15), for any link $l \in \mathcal{H}$, we have

$$\pi(\mathbf{x}) \geq \sum_{s \in \mathcal{S}, r \in R_s} \frac{A_{l,r}}{c_l} f_{s,r}^*(\mathbf{x}) \rho_s \pi(\mathbf{x} - \mathbf{e}_s).$$

Further, we can write

$$
\begin{aligned}
\pi(\mathbf{x}) &= \sum_{l \in \mathcal{H}} \frac{c_l}{c(\mathcal{H})} \pi(\mathbf{x}) \\
&\geq \sum_{l \in \mathcal{H}} \frac{c_l}{c(\mathcal{H})} \sum_{s \in \mathcal{S}, r \in R_s} \frac{A_{l,r}}{c_l} f_{s,r}^*(\mathbf{x}) \rho_s \pi(\mathbf{x} - \mathbf{e}_s) \\
&\geq \frac{1}{c(\mathcal{H})} \sum_{s \in \mathcal{S}, r \in R_s} n_{s,r}(\mathcal{H}) f_{s,r}^*(\mathbf{x}) \rho_s \pi(\mathbf{x} - \mathbf{e}_s) \\
&\geq \frac{1}{c(\mathcal{H})} \sum_{s \in \mathcal{S}(\mathcal{H})} n_s(\mathcal{H}) \rho_s \pi(\mathbf{x} - \mathbf{e}_s).
\end{aligned}
$$

Thus, we have (using $\sum_{\mathbf{x}}$ for $\sum_{\mathbf{x} \in \mathbb{Z}_+^{|\mathcal{S}|}}$)

$$
\begin{aligned}
E[X_t] &= \sum_{\mathbf{x}} x_t \pi(\mathbf{x}) \geq \sum_{\mathbf{x}} \frac{x_t}{c(\mathcal{H})} \sum_{s \in \mathcal{S}(\mathcal{H})} n_s(\mathcal{H}) \rho_s \pi(\mathbf{x} - \mathbf{e}_s) \\
&= \sum_{s \in \mathcal{S}(\mathcal{H})} \frac{n_s(\mathcal{H}) \rho_s}{c(\mathcal{H})} \sum_{\mathbf{x}} x_t \pi(\mathbf{x} - \mathbf{e}_s) \\
&= \sum_{s \in \mathcal{S}(\mathcal{H}) \setminus \{t\}} \frac{n_s(\mathcal{H}) \rho_s}{c(\mathcal{H})} \sum_{\mathbf{x}} x_t \pi(\mathbf{x} - \mathbf{e}_s) \\
&\quad + \frac{n_t(\mathcal{H}) \rho_t}{c(\mathcal{H})} \left(\sum_{\mathbf{x}} (x_t - 1) \pi(\mathbf{x} - \mathbf{e}_t) + \sum_{\mathbf{x}} \pi(\mathbf{x} - \mathbf{e}_t) \right) \\
&= \sum_{s \in \mathcal{S}(\mathcal{H}) \setminus \{t\}} \frac{n_s(\mathcal{H}) \rho_s}{c(\mathcal{H})} E[X_t] + \frac{n_t(\mathcal{H}) \rho_t}{c(\mathcal{H})} \left(E[X_t] + 1 \right) \\
&= \frac{\rho(\mathcal{H})}{c(\mathcal{H})} E[X_t] + \frac{n_t(\mathcal{H}) \rho_t}{c(\mathcal{H})}.
\end{aligned}
$$

From the above inequality, we conclude

$$\tau_t = \frac{E[X_t]}{\rho_t} \geq \frac{n_t(\mathcal{H})}{c(\mathcal{H}) - \rho(\mathcal{H})}.$$

Since the above inequality holds for any subset $\mathcal{H}$ of $\mathcal{L}$, $n_t(\mathcal{H}) = 0$ for $\mathcal{H} \notin \mathcal{B}_t$, and $\tau_t \geq 1/a_t$, the theorem follows. $\square$

Intuitively, the lower bound for mean per bit delay is at least that associated with the peak rate constraint of class t, or that of the bottleneck resource pool associated with the routes of class t. We consider the network in Fig. 2 to stress that a lower bound based on pools in $\mathcal{D}_t$ alone may not be tight. Let $\rho_1 = 1$ and $\rho_2 = 2 - \epsilon$. Suppose we are interested in bounding the performance of flow class 1. Any lower bound for flow class 1 using a pool in $\mathcal{D}_1$, involves two resources with sum capacity 2, say link 1 and link 3, i.e., $\mathcal{H} = \{1, 3\}$, whence $c(\mathcal{H}) = 2$ and $\rho(\mathcal{H}) = 1$ since only flow class 1 is supported by $\mathcal{H}$. The lower bound is thus

$$\tau_1 \geq \frac{1}{c(\mathcal{H}) - \rho(\mathcal{H})} = 1.$$

Now consider the set $\mathcal{H}' = \{1, 2, 3\}$. Both flow classes are supported by $\mathcal{H}'$ and thus we get a much tighter lower bound

$$\tau_1 \geq \frac{n_1(\mathcal{H}')}{c(\mathcal{H}') - \rho(\mathcal{H}')} = \frac{1}{3 - 1 - (2 - \epsilon)} = \frac{1}{\epsilon}.$$

4.2 Upper bound

One can also show an upper bound on the mean per bit delay of a class $t \in \mathcal{S}$. Let

$$b_t = \max \left\{ \frac{1}{a_t}, \left(\max_{\mathcal{H} \in \mathcal{D}_t} \frac{\bar{n}_t(\mathcal{H})}{c(\mathcal{H})} \right) \right\}$$

where b_t roughly is the bottleneck resource/peak rate constraint. Our upper bound is given in the following theorem:

THEOREM 4. *For any* $t \in \mathcal{S}$, *if* $\bar{\rho}(\mathcal{H}) < c(\mathcal{H}) \ \forall \ \mathcal{H} \in \mathcal{D}_t$, *then*

$$\tau_t \leq b_t + \sum_{\mathcal{H} \in \mathcal{D}_t} \frac{\bar{\rho}(\mathcal{H})}{c(\mathcal{H})} \left(\frac{\bar{n}_t(\mathcal{H})}{c(\mathcal{H}) - \bar{\rho}(\mathcal{H})} \right).$$

See [8] for a proof. We can see that the upper bound includes the peak rate constraint or capacity constraint of pooled resources along the path, and an additive term that roughly corresponds to sending the bits, in a store and forward manner over the pooled resources along the route of class s. The expression for the upper bound provides some rough insights into how a flow is delayed in such a system.

Though the bound can be loose (especially when $|\mathcal{D}_t|$ is large or when $\bar{\rho}(\mathcal{H})$ is close to $c(\mathcal{H})$ for some $\mathcal{H} \in \mathcal{D}_t$), it is the only non-trivial upper bound available for mean per bit delay in a system using multipath routing with multipath flow control. Further, we can use the upper bound to provide mean delay guarantees to a class in such a system.

Another approach to obtain bounds on performance for networks using multipath routing with multipath flow control is to transform the original network to an equivalent network (for e.g., see [11], [9]) with single path routing, and apply bounds in [2] to it. We feel that our lower bound is going to be close to the lower bound obtained using this approach. However, the upper bound obtained for the equivalent network can be much better than our upper bound. But, as pointed out in Section 1, this approach is computationally demanding for large networks.

4.3 Comparisons and examples

In Section 3, we compared the throughput of a system using random routing with balanced fair allocation against a system using multipath routing and multipath flow control with balanced fair allocation. We saw that the latter has a larger stability region. In this section, we compare mean per bit delay for the two systems using the bounds obtained in the previous sections.

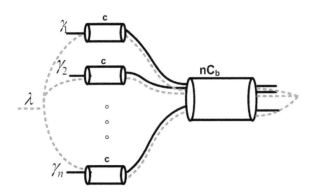

Figure 3: Example: One multipath class competing with n unipath classes

Consider the network shown in Fig. 3 being shared by one multipath class with peak rate constraint a and n unipath classes without any peak rate constraints. Each route in the network comprises a link of capacity c and a link of capacity c_b where $c << c_b$. The routes used by the classes should be clear from the figure: the multipath class is using n routes and each unipath class is using a different route. Note that the above network captures a scenario that can arise in the residential wireless mesh network in Fig. 1 in which there is only one home user using multipath routing.

If the network uses random routing where the multipath class chooses a route for a flow independently and with equal

probability, the following upper bound τ_r^{UB} on mean per bit delay τ_r of the multipath class can be obtained using Theorem 1

$$\tau_r \leq \tau_r^{UB} = \max\left(\frac{1}{a}, \frac{1}{c}\right) + \left(\frac{1}{c}\right)\frac{\gamma+\lambda}{c-(\gamma+\lambda)} \quad (16)$$
$$+ \left(\frac{1}{nc_b}\right)\frac{\gamma+\lambda}{c_b-(\gamma+\lambda)}.$$

If the network uses multipath flow control, the following lower bound on mean per bit delay τ_m of the multipath class can be obtained using Theorem 3

$$\tau_m \geq \max\left(\frac{1}{a}, \frac{1}{n\left(c-(\gamma+\lambda)\right)}\right).$$

The improvement in delay by using multipath flow control is captured by $G = \frac{\tau_r}{\tau_m}$ which can be upper bounded using the above bounds as given below

$$G \leq \min\left(a, n\left(c-(\gamma+\lambda)\right)\right)\tau_r^{UB}.$$

Intuitively, we would expect G to increase with the number of routes n of the multipath class due to increased statistical multiplexing. However, this need not be the case always as shown below. Since $c << c_b$, the first two terms in (16) dominate τ_r^{UB} and thus, τ_r^{UB} does not change much with n. From the above expression, we can conclude that we can expect a linear improvement in mean per bit delay for multipath flow control only if $a > n\left(c-(\gamma+\lambda)\right)$. Thus, as far as improvement in delay performance with multipath flow control is concerned, a key factor is whether the peak rate constraint exceeds the average spare capacity $n\left(c-(\gamma+\lambda)\right)$. Thus, adding more routes to a system may not always help.

This can also be inferred from Fig. 4 where we compare the mean per bit delay of the multipath class for $n = 2$ and $n = 4$. The data points are obtained from a discrete event simulation (an event comprises of an arrival or a departure of a flow) carried out for different values of traffic intensity λ of the multipath class. The active flows are served at a rate determined by the balanced fair allocation. Each data point corresponds to a simulation run involving roughly 10^5 flows of each class. We set $c = 1$, $c_b = 2$, $a = 0.5$ and $\gamma = 0.25$ and simulated the networks with multipath balanced fair allocation. We can see that the improvement in delay performance by adding two more routes is minimal for low loads where the peak rate constraints and the average spare capacity are comparable whereas the improvement for larger loads where the peak rate constraint dominates the spare capacity. We have also plotted the lower and upper bounds for the mean per bit delay of the multipath class obtained using Theorem 3 and 4 which are quite good for this example.

5. BALANCED FAIR: LARGE DEVIATIONS

In this section, we use the large deviation characteristics of networks under single path and multipath balanced fair allocations to obtain insights that are useful in network design. As we have seen in the previous sections, directly studying the mean delay is often very difficult and hence, we consider meaningful alternatives. We focus on the events in a network where there are accumulations in the aggregate number of flows. Accumulation of flows in the network would loosely translate to an increase in the delay seen by the flows. However, large deviations in delays could be due to several other

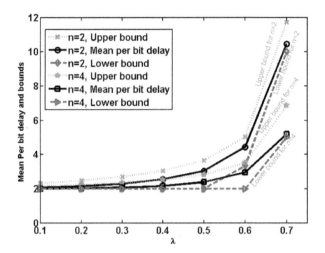

Figure 4: A comparison of mean per bit delay of the multipath class for different n

reasons too (see [18]). In Sections **5.1** and **5.2**, we study large deviations in the total number of flows. Though single path routing is a special case of multipath routing, for clarity, we start by considering it on its own. The notation used for the two settings are similar and hence, we use a superscript or (sometimes) subscript U for the terms associated with single path routing, and a superscript or (sometimes) subscript M is used for the multipath setting. Also, in this section, we assume that there are no peak rate constraints, i.e., $a_s = \infty$, $\forall \, s \in \mathcal{S}$ and hence, we ignore them.

5.1 Single route networks

We consider the single path routing setting where each class is associated with a single route. In the following, we use s and the route associated with the class interchangeably. Let

$$\Lambda^U = \left\{ \lambda \in \mathbb{R}^{|\mathcal{S}|} : \sum_{s \in \mathcal{S}} A_{ls} \lambda_s \leq c_l \; \forall l \in \mathcal{L} \right\}.$$

Define set $\mathcal{K}^U \subset \mathbb{R}_+^{|\mathcal{S}|}$ as follows:

$$\gamma = (\gamma_s)_{s \in \mathcal{S}} \in \mathcal{K}^U \iff \{e^{\gamma_s}\}_{s \in \mathcal{S}} \in \Lambda^U.$$

Let the function $\delta_{\mathcal{K}^U}$ be given by

$$\delta_{\mathcal{K}^U}(\gamma) = \begin{cases} 0, & \gamma \in \mathcal{K}^U, \\ \infty, & \gamma \notin \mathcal{K}^U. \end{cases}$$

Let $\delta_{\mathcal{K}^U}^*$ denote the convex conjugate function of $\delta_{\mathcal{K}^U}$, i.e.,

$$\delta_{\mathcal{K}^U}^*(\mathbf{x}) = \sup_{\gamma \in \mathbb{R}^{|\mathcal{S}|}} (<\gamma, \mathbf{x}> - \delta_{\mathcal{K}^U}(\gamma)).$$

Note that $\delta_{\mathcal{K}^U}^*(\mathbf{x})$ is simply an alternative way to write the maximum value of sum log utility subject to the capacity constraints Λ^U. A proportional fair allocation (note that proportional fair allocation need not be unique for a state $\mathbf{x}$ with $x_s = 0$ for some $s \in \mathcal{S}$ as the choice of allocation for class s will not affect the objective function as long as we do not violate any capacity constraints) $\left(\lambda_s^{PF}(\mathbf{x})\right)_{s \in \mathcal{S}}$ in state

$\mathbf{x}$ is an optimizer to the above problem and hence,

$$\delta_{\mathcal{K}^U}^*(\mathbf{x}) = \sum_{s \in \mathcal{S}} x_s \log\left(\lambda_s^{PF}(\mathbf{x})\right).$$

In [19], the following large deviation result was proved for the single path routing setting:

$$\lim_{n \to \infty} \frac{\log\left(\pi_{BF}^U(n\mathbf{x})\right)}{n} = -L^U(\mathbf{x}). \qquad (17)$$

where $\pi_{BF}^U()$ denotes the steady state distribution under balanced fair allocation and

$$L^U(\mathbf{x}) = \delta_{\mathcal{K}^U}^*(\mathbf{x}) - \sum_{s \in \mathcal{S}} x_s \log(\rho_s).$$

The above result presents an interesting relationship between the large deviation characteristics of balanced fair allocation and the proportional fair allocation. Hence,

$$\pi_{BF}^U(n\mathbf{x}) = \zeta^U(n)e^{-nL^U(\mathbf{x})} \text{ for large } n \qquad (18)$$

and some sub-exponential function $\zeta^U(n)$. Thus, the likelihood of accumulating a large number of flows, and the associated mix is determined by

$$\mathbf{x}^* = \operatorname{argmin}_{\{\mathbf{x}: x_s \geq 0 \; \forall s \in \mathcal{S} \text{ and } \sum_{s \in \mathcal{S}} x_s = 1\}} L^U(\mathbf{x}) \qquad (19)$$

This mix is a useful vector which helps us to find the classes and resources that require attention from the capacity allocation point of view. For instance, if $|\mathcal{S}| = 3$ and $\mathbf{x}^* = [0.2 \; 0.8 \; 0]$, then a typical congestion event will involve a large number of flows of the second class, and thus we can take steps to remedy this. Also, from (18), $L^U(\mathbf{x}^*)$ is roughly the negative of the rate of exponential decay along the direction $\mathbf{x}^*$. We will refer to $L^U(\mathbf{x}^*)$ as the LD exponent. The next result gives an expression for $\mathbf{x}^*$ and $L^U(\mathbf{x}^*)$.

THEOREM 5. *For the single path routing setting,*

$$x_s^* = b^U n_s^U \rho_s \; \forall s \in \mathcal{S} \text{ and } L^U(\mathbf{x}^*) = \log(d_U^*),$$

where $b^U = \dfrac{1}{\sum_{u \in \mathcal{S}} n_u^U \rho_u}$, $n_s^U = \displaystyle\sum_{l \in \mathcal{L}_{crit}^U} A_{ls}$,

$$\mathcal{L}_{crit}^U = \left\{ l : \sum_{s \in \mathcal{S}} A_{ls} \rho_s d_U^* = c_l \right\}, \quad d_U^* = \min_{l \in \mathcal{L}} \left(\frac{c_l}{\sum_{s \in \mathcal{S}} A_{ls} \rho_s} \right).$$

The above result can be proved using following three facts:
(i) $\delta_{\mathcal{K}^U}^*(.)$ is a convex function and hence, optimization problem in (19) is convex.
(ii) From [19], the subgradient set of $\delta_{\mathcal{K}^U}^*(.)$ satisfies

$$\left\{ \gamma : [e^{\gamma_s}]_{s \in \mathcal{S}} \in \Lambda^{PF}(\mathbf{x}^*) \right\} \subset \partial \delta_{\mathcal{K}^U}^*(\mathbf{x}^*)$$

where

$$\Lambda_{PF}^U(\mathbf{x}^*) = \{\boldsymbol{\lambda} : \boldsymbol{\lambda} \text{ is a proportional fair allocation}$$
$$\text{in the state } \mathbf{x}^*\}.$$

(iii) A proportional fair allocation $\boldsymbol{\lambda}$ for state $\mathbf{x}^*$ satisfies ([12])

$$\lambda_s = \frac{x_s^*}{\sum_{l \in \mathcal{L}} A_{lr_s} p_l} \forall s \in \{u : x_u^* > 0\}$$

where $\forall\ l \in \mathcal{L}$, $p_l \geq 0$ and $(\mathbf{A}\boldsymbol{\lambda})_l \leq c_l$, and $\sum_{l \in \mathcal{L}} p_l(c_l - (\mathbf{A}\boldsymbol{\lambda})_l) = 0$.

The result suggests that for a class $s \in \mathcal{S}$, the traffic intensity ρ_s and the number of links in $\mathcal{L}_{crit}^U$ traversed by the class are the two critical factors that decide its contribution to accumulation in aggregate number of flows.

This large deviation characterization motivates an approach to capacity allocation. Here, we consider the problem of assigning link capacities c_l to maximize the LD exponent so that $\sum_{l \in \mathcal{L}} c_l \leq c_{tot}$ for some $c_{tot} > 0$. Thus, we are roughly minimizing the probability that a large number of flows accumulate. Since $L^U(\mathbf{x}^*) = \log(d_U^*)$, we can use the definition of d_U^* to get an equivalent linear optimization problem:

$$\min_{k,(c_l)_{l \in \mathcal{L}}} \left\{ k \mid \sum_{l \in \mathcal{L}} c_l = c_{tot}, k \sum_{s \in \mathcal{S}} A_{ls}\rho_s \geq c_l \text{ for all } l \in \mathcal{L} \right\}.$$

It can be shown (using the KKT optimality conditions) that the optimal allocation is given by $c_l^* = k^* \sum_{s \in \mathcal{S}} A_{ls}\rho_s\ \forall\ l \in \mathcal{L}$ where $k^* > 0$ is chosen so that $\sum_{l \in \mathcal{L}} c_l^* = c_{tot}$. The result suggests a simple rule of thumb: allocating bandwidth in proportion to the load being carried by the links minimizes the likelihood of network congestion.

5.2 Multipath networks

Here, we consider a more general setting where the classes can send their traffic through more than one route. Let

$$\Lambda^M = \left\{ \boldsymbol{\lambda} \in \mathbb{R}_+^{|\mathcal{S}|} : \text{for some } \mathbf{f} \in \mathcal{F}, (\boldsymbol{\lambda}, \mathbf{f}) \in \mathcal{C}^M \right\}.$$

As done above, we define the set $\mathcal{K}^M \subset \mathbb{R}^{|\mathcal{S}|}$ as follows:

$$\gamma = \{\gamma_s\}_{s \in \mathcal{S}} \in \mathcal{K}^M \Leftrightarrow \boldsymbol{\lambda} = \{e^{\gamma_s}\}_{s \in \mathcal{S}} \in \Lambda^M.$$

Let the function $\delta_{\mathcal{K}^M}$ be given by

$$\delta_{\mathcal{K}^M}(\gamma) = \begin{cases} 0, & \gamma \in \mathcal{K}^M, \\ \infty, & \gamma \notin \mathcal{K}^M. \end{cases}$$

Let $\delta_{\mathcal{K}^M}^*$ denote the convex conjugate function of $\delta_{\mathcal{K}^M}$, i.e.,

$$\delta_{\mathcal{K}^M}^*(\mathbf{x}) = \sup_{\gamma \in \mathbb{R}^{|\mathcal{S}|}} (<\gamma, \mathbf{x}> - \delta_{\mathcal{K}^M}(\gamma)).$$

An optimizer to the above problem corresponds to a solution $\left(\lambda_s^{PF}(\mathbf{x})\right)_{s \in \mathcal{S}}$ of the optimization problem MULTIPATH-PF given in Section 2.

Although (17) is proved in [19] for the case where a flow class uses only a single route, it can be shown that a similar result holds for the case where each flow class routes its traffic through multiple routes, i.e.,

$$\lim_{n \to \infty} \frac{\log\left(\pi_{BF}^M(n\mathbf{x})\right)}{n} = -L^M(\mathbf{x})$$

where $L^M(\mathbf{x}) = \delta_{\mathcal{K}^M}^*(\mathbf{x}) - \sum_{s \in \mathcal{S}} x_s \log(\rho_s)$,

and π_{BF}^M denotes the steady state distribution of the multipath balanced fair allocation obtained in Section 3.2. Thus, the most likely mix $\mathbf{x}^*$ of the flows of different classes when there is an accumulation in the aggregate number of flows is given by

$$\mathbf{x}^* = \text{argmin}_{\{\mathbf{x}: x_s \geq 0\ \forall s \in \mathcal{S} \text{ and } \sum_{s \in \mathcal{S}} x_s = 1\}} L^M(\mathbf{x}).$$

Next we consider the following linear optimization problem referred to as OPT-MAXMIN in the sequel:

$$\max_{d_M, \mathbf{f}} d_M \text{ such that}$$

$$\sum_{s \in \mathcal{S}} \sum_{r_s \in R_s} A_{lr_s} f_{sr_s} \rho_s \leq c_l\ \forall l \in \mathcal{L}; \tag{20}$$

$$\sum_{r_s \in R_s} f_{sr_s} = d_M\ \forall s \in \mathcal{S}; \tag{21}$$

$$f_{sr_s} \geq 0\ \forall r_s \in R_s, \forall s \in \mathcal{S}. \tag{22}$$

Let $\left(d_M^*, \mathbf{f}'\right)$ be a solution to the above problem, and let $\left(p_l'\right)_{l \in \mathcal{L}}$, $(\alpha_s)_{s \in \mathcal{S}}$ and $(\beta_{sr_s})_{s \in \mathcal{S}, r_s \in R_s}$ be corresponding optimal Lagrange multipliers associated with (20), (21) and (22) respectively. Then, the next result gives the most likely direction for overflow. We skip a discussion of the proof as it is similar in flavor to that for the single path routing setting.

THEOREM 6. *For the multipath routing setting,*

$$x_s{}^* = b^M n_s^M \rho_s\ \forall s \in \mathcal{S} \text{ and } L^M(\mathbf{x}^*) = \log(d_M^*)$$

where $b^M = \dfrac{1}{\sum_{u \in \mathcal{S}} n_u \rho_u}$, $n_s^M = \sum_{l \in \mathcal{L}} p_l' \sum_{r_s \in R_s} A_{lr_s} f'_{sr_s}$ *and*

d_M^* *is the maximum value of the objective function in OPT-MAXMIN.*

Let $\mathcal{L}_{crit}^M = \left\{ l \in \mathcal{L} : p_l' > 0 \right\}$ be the set of links that are critical to the exponent. Similar to the single path setting, for a class $s \in \mathcal{S}$, the traffic intensity ρ_s and the number of critical links traversed by the class are the two factors that decide its contribution to an accumulation in the aggregate number of flows. As the classes can split their traffic along multiple routes, there is more interdependence between the flow classes. Hence, we can expect more critical links and classes to contribute to the most likely mix than in the single path setting.

Like in the single path routing case, we use the large deviation behavior of balanced fair allocation to design networks in which the probability of overflows in the aggregate number of flows is less. We consider the problem of assigning link capacities c_l to maximize the LD exponent so that $\sum_{l \in \mathcal{L}} c_l \leq c_{tot}$ for some $c_{tot} > 0$. Since $L^M(\mathbf{x}^*) = \log(d_M^*)$ and d_M^* is obtained by optimizing OPT-MAXMIN, we can maximize $L^M(\mathbf{x}^*)$ by solving the following linear program:

$$\max_{d_M,(c_l)_{l \in \mathcal{L}}, \mathbf{f}} d_M \text{ such that}$$

$$\sum_{s \in \mathcal{S}} \sum_{r_s \in R_s} A_{lr_s} f_{sr_s} \rho_s \leq c_l\ \forall l \in \mathcal{L}; \quad \sum_{r_s \in R_s} f_{sr_s} = d_M\ \forall s \in \mathcal{S};$$

$$f_{sr_s} \geq 0\ \forall r_s \in R_s, \forall s \in \mathcal{S}; \quad \sum_{l \in \mathcal{L}} c_l = c_{tot}.$$

5.3 Sensitivity of LD exponent

In this section, we study the sensitivity of the LD exponent to link capacities and the capacity of collections (pools) of links. This study of sensitivity will help us to identify the resources/pools of resources that are critical to the LD exponent and thus, to the accumulation of flows in the network. It is intuitive to expect that addition of capacity to certain links or resource pools should reduce the likelihood of congestion. However, we show that the rate of increase in the exponent decreases with the capacity of associated link/resource pool. One can also show that the LD exponent is insensitive to the capacities of links $l \notin \mathcal{L}_{crit}^U$ for the single path routing setting and to the capacities of links $l \notin \mathcal{L}_{crit}^M$ in the multipath routing setting. We are now left to study the relationship between LD exponent and the remaining links.

First, we consider a simple but insightful example shown in Fig. 5. For all positive values of c and ρ_s for $s \in \mathcal{S}$, $L(\mathbf{x}^*) = \log(d_U^*) = \log\left(\frac{c}{\sum_{u \in \mathcal{S}} \rho_u}\right)$ is a differentiable function of c and ρ_s . Hence,

$$\frac{\partial L^U(\mathbf{x}^*)}{\partial c} = \frac{1}{c} \text{ and } \frac{\partial L^U(\mathbf{x}^*)}{\partial \rho_s} = -\frac{1}{\sum_{u \in \mathcal{S}} \rho_u}.$$

Thus the rate of decrease of $L^U(\mathbf{x}^*)$ with c decreases as we increase c. Thus if the link already has a large capacity, we require a large addition of capacity to obtain a significant increase in the LD exponent. From the above result, we can also infer that if the cumulative traffic intensity is high, we need a large decrease in the offered load to achieve a significant reduction in the LD exponent.

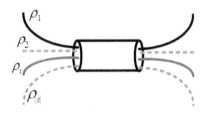

Figure 5: Example: A link shared by $|\mathcal{S}|$ classes

A similar result holds for the single path routing setting when $\left|\mathcal{L}_{crit}^U\right| = 1$, i.e., there is only a single critical link. Let $\mathcal{L}_{crit}^U = \{l_B\}$. Then, using Theorem 5, we can show that $d_U^* = \log\left(\frac{c_{l_B}}{\sum_{s \in \mathcal{S}} A_{ls} \rho_s}\right)$, and that we can partially differentiate d_U^* with respect to c_{l_B} at c_{l_B} to obtain

$$\frac{\partial L(\mathbf{x}^*)}{\partial c_{l_B}} = \frac{1}{c_{l_B}} \text{ and } \frac{\partial L(\mathbf{x}^*)}{\partial c_l} = 0 \ \forall \ l \in \mathcal{L} \setminus \{l_B\},$$

and that we can partially differentiate d_M^* with respect to ρ_s for $s \in \mathcal{S}$ at ρ_s to obtain

$$\frac{\partial L(\mathbf{x}^*)}{\partial \rho_s} = -\frac{A_{ls}}{\sum_{u \in \mathcal{S}} A_{lu} \rho_u}.$$

We close the discussion for the single path routing setting by pointing out that for the case in which $\left|\mathcal{L}_{crit}^U\right| > 1$, any small decrease in the capacity of a link $l \in \mathcal{L}_{crit}^U$ will result in a network with only l as the critical link.

5.3.1 Resource pools in the multipath routing setting

Next, let us consider the multipath flow control setting and obtain a collection of links $\mathcal{P}(\rho) \subset \mathcal{L}$ which behaves almost like a single pooled resource as far as LD exponents are concerned. This is a key feature associated with the notion of resource pooling discussed in [22]. As we will see, the pools can vary with changes in the offered load and hence, the dependence on ρ. However, for notation simplicity, we

use $\mathcal{P}$ for $\mathcal{P}(\rho)$. In the sequel, we obtain $\mathcal{P} \subset \mathcal{L}$ such that

$$\frac{\partial L(\mathbf{x}^*)}{\partial c_l} = \frac{1}{\sum_{l' \in \mathcal{P}} c_{l'}} \ \forall \ l \in \mathcal{P}.$$

On comparing above expression with (23), we see that it is as if there is a single shared resource $\mathcal{P}$ with capacity $c_\mathcal{P} = \sum_{l' \in \mathcal{P}} c_{l'}$ such that

$$\frac{\partial L(\mathbf{x}^*)}{\partial c_\mathcal{P}} = \frac{1}{c_\mathcal{P}}.$$

In the following, we refer to $\mathcal{P}$ as the critical pool in the network.

Let $\mathcal{S}_{crit} = \{s \in \mathcal{S} : x_s^* > 0\}$. From Theorem 6, we have

$$\mathcal{S}_{crit} = \left\{ s \in \mathcal{S} : \rho_s > 0, \sum_{l \in \mathcal{L}} p_l' \sum_{r_s \in R_s} A_{lr_s} f_{sr_s}' > 0 \right\}. \quad (23)$$

For a class $s \in \mathcal{S}_{crit}$, we define the set of links critical with respect to class s as

$$\mathcal{L}_{crit}(s) = \left\{ l \in \mathcal{L} : p_l' \sum_{r_s \in R_s} A_{lr_s} f_{sr_s}' > 0 \right\}.$$

From (23), we see that $\mathcal{L}_{crit}(s)$ is non-empty for any $s \in \mathcal{S}_{crit}$. Further, we can show that $\cup_{s \in \mathcal{S}_{crit}} \mathcal{L}_{crit}(s) = \mathcal{L}_{crit}$. We define the Class Coupling Graph (CCG) as $(\mathcal{S}_{crit}, E)$ where for $s_1, s_2 \in \mathcal{S}_{crit}$, $E_{s_1,s_2} = 1$ if $|\mathcal{L}_{crit}(s_1) \cap \mathcal{L}_{crit}(s_2)| > 0$, i.e, the classes s_1 and s_2 share a critical link.

To obtain the single resource pool, we make the following assumptions:

A1: The CCG is strongly connected.
A2: For any $s \in \mathcal{S}_{crit}$, $A_{lr_s} \in \{0, 1\} \ \forall \ l \in \mathcal{L}$ and $r_s \in R_s$.
A3: For any $s \in \mathcal{S}_{crit}$, $f_{s,r_s}' > 0 \ \forall r_s \in R_s$.
A4: For any $s \in \mathcal{S}_{crit}$ and any $r_s \in R_s$, $|r_s \cap \mathcal{L}_{crit}(s)| = 1$.

For $s \in \mathcal{S}_{crit}$ and $r_s \in R_s$, let $l^*(r_s)$ be the element in $r_s \cap \mathcal{L}_{crit}(s)$. The next result gives the critical pool. The proof is long and due to space constraints, we are not able to include it in the paper.

THEOREM 7. (*Single critical pool: Sensitivity*) *Under Assumptions A1-A4,*

$$d_M^* = \frac{\sum_{l \in \mathcal{L}_{crit}} c_l}{\sum_{s \in \mathcal{S}_{crit}} \rho_s} \text{ and } x_s^* = \begin{cases} \frac{\rho_s}{\sum_{u \in \mathcal{S}_{crit}} \rho_u} & , \forall s \in \mathcal{S}_{crit}, \\ 0 & , \forall s \notin \mathcal{S}_{crit}. \end{cases}$$

Further, there is a collection of links $\mathcal{P} = \{l^*(r_s) : r_s \in R_s \text{ for some } s \in \mathcal{S}_{crit}\}$ *that satisfies*

$$\frac{\partial L(\mathbf{x}^*)}{\partial c_l} = \frac{1}{\sum_{l' \in \mathcal{P}} c_{l'}} \ \forall \ l \in \mathcal{P} \text{ and } \frac{\partial L(\mathbf{x}^*)}{\partial c_l} = 0 \ \forall \ l \notin \mathcal{P}.$$

Assumptions A1 and A3 together ensure that for a small enough change in the capacity of a link in $\mathcal{P}$, traffic going through other links in $\mathcal{P}$ can be shifted so that the effect of the change in capacity gets spread over all the links in $\mathcal{P}$. Consider the example in Fig. 6 where three multipath classes of traffic intensities 2 , 1 and 1 bits per second are sharing the network. The capacities (measured in bits per second) of the links are indicated near the link in the figure. Using Theorem 7, we can show that the shaded links form the critical resource pool. This example illustrates the usefulness of Theorem 7: intuition would only suggest that we need to allocate more capacities to links being used by class

1. However, the critical pool contains the starred link too which can be attributed to the coupling between flow classes 1 and 2.

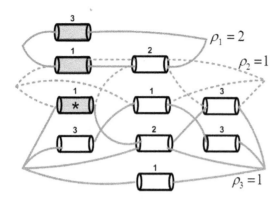

Figure 6: Example: $x^* = [0.6667, 0.3333, 0]$ and the critical links are shaded.

6. CONCLUSIONS

We developed the first flow level performance bounds for networks supporting multipath flow control. Further, we studied large deviation for congestion events, and presented a possible approach to capacity allocation for such networks. Some practical implications of our work are listed below:

(a) Theorem 3 and Section 4.3 suggest that when the spare capacity in the most congested resource pool of a multpath class is close to the access rate constraint of that class, gains from additional routes will be negligible.

(b) Theorems 3 and 4 suggest that the resource pools in $\mathcal{B}_t$ play a critical role in determining the performance of class t, and the spare capacity($\approx c(\mathcal{H}) - \rho(\mathcal{H}) \approx c(\mathcal{H}) - \bar{\rho}(\mathcal{H})$) loosely captures the role of a pool $\mathcal{H} \in \mathcal{B}_t$.

(c) Using Theorem 7, we can obtain the resource pool that is most critical in terms of resulting in an accumulation of the aggregate number flows in the network.

(d) Section 5.2 provides a simple, intuitive capacity allocation scheme that minimizes the chances of an accumulation of the aggregate number of flows in the network. The scheme essentially allocates capacity in proportion to the load carried by links under an optimized multipath flow allocation.

This work provides initial steps towards tackling the many open questions (see Section 1) associated with possible adoption of mulipath flow control in future networks. Addressing these challenging questions will be part of our future work.

7. ACKNOWLEDGMENTS

This research was supported in part by National Science Foundation Award CNS-0917067. Prof. de Veciana would like to thank IMDEA Networks for hosting him when this work took birth, as well as Drs Banchs and Serrano for valuable discussions. We would also like to thank Dr. B. Godfrey for his comments which have served to improve this work.

8. REFERENCES

[1] D. Bertsekas and R. Gallager. *Data networks*. Prentice-Hall, Inc., 1992.

[2] T. Bonald. Throughput performance in networks with linear capacity constraints. In *Proc. CISS 2006*.

[3] T. Bonald, L. Massoulié, A. Proutière, and J. Virtamo. A queueing analysis of max-min fairness, proportional fairness and balanced fairness. *Queueing Systems*, 53:65–84, 2006.

[4] T. Bonald, A. Penttinen, and J. Virtamo. On light and heavy traffic approximations of balanced fairness. In *Proceedings of SIGMETRICS/Performance 2006*, pages 109–120, June 2006.

[5] T. Bonald and A. Proutière. Insensitive bandwidth sharing in data networks. *Queueing Systems*, 44:69–100, 2003.

[6] T. Bonald and J. Virtamo. Calculating the flow level performance of balanced fairness in tree networks. *Performance Evaluation*, 58:1–14, 2004.

[7] H. Han, S. Shakkottai, C. V. Hollot, R. Srikant, and D. Towsley. Multi-path TCP: a joint congestion control and routing scheme to exploit path diversity in the internet. *IEEE/ACM Trans. Netw.*, 14:1260–1271, December 2006.

[8] V. Joseph and G. de Veciana. Stochastic Networks with Multipath Flow Control: Impact of Resource Pools on Flow-level Performance and Network Congestion. Extended version, Mar 2011. http://users.ece.utexas.edu/~gustavo/publications.php.

[9] W. N. Kang, F. P. Kelly, N. H. Lee, and R. J. Williams. State space collapse and diffusion approximation for a network operating under a fair bandwidth sharing policy. *Annals of Applied Probability*, 19:1719–1780, 2009.

[10] F. Kelly and T. Voice. Stability of end-to-end algorithms for joint routing and rate control. *Queueing Systems*, 35:5–12, 2005.

[11] F. P. Kelly, L. Massoulie, and N. S. Walton. Resource pooling in congested networks: proportional fairness and product form. *Queueing Syst. Theory Appl.*, 63:165–194, December 2009.

[12] F. P. Kelly, A. Maulloo, and D. Tan. Rate control for communication networks: Shadow prices, proportional fairness and stability. *Journal of Operation Research*, 49(3):237–252, 1998.

[13] P. Key, L. Massoulié, and D. Towsley. Multipath routing, congestion control and dynamic load balancing. In *Proc. ICASSP*, pages 109–120, April 2007.

[14] P. Key, L. Massoulié, and D. Towsley. Path selection and multipath congestion control. In *Proc. IEEE INFOCOM*, pages 109–120, May 2007.

[15] C. N. Laws. Resource pooling in queueing networks with dynamic routing. *Advances in Applied Probability*, 24:699–726, 1992.

[16] J. Leino and J. Virtamo. Insensitive traffic splitting in data networks. In *Proceedings of ITC*, pages 1355–1364, Beijing, China, 2005.

[17] J. Leino and J. Virtamo. Insensitive load balancing in data networks. *Comput. Netw.*, 50:1059–1068, June 2006.

[18] M. Mandjes and B. Zwart. Large deviations of sojourn times in processor sharing queues. *Queueing Syst. Theory Appl.*, 52(4):237–250, 2006.

[19] L. Massoulie. Structural properties of proportional fairness: Stability and insensitivity. *Annals of Applied Probability*, 2007.

[20] J. Mo and J. Walrand. Fair end-to-end window-based congestion control. *IEEE/ACM Transactions on Networking*, 8:556–567, October 2000.

[21] W. H. Wang, M. Palaniswami, and S. H. Low. Optimal flow control and routing in multi-path networks. *Perform. Eval.*, 52:119–132, April 2003.

[22] D. Wischik, M. Handley, and M. B. Braun. The resource pooling principle. *SIGCOMM Comput. Commun. Rev.*, 38:47–52, September 2008.

[23] Y. Yi and M. Chiang. Stochastic network utility maximization. *European Transactions on Telecommunications*, 19:421–442, June 2008.

Analysis of DCTCP: Stability, Convergence, and Fairness

Mohammad Alizadeh, Adel Javanmard, and Balaji Prabhakar

Department of Electrical Engineering, Stanford University
{alizade, adelj, balaji}@stanford.edu

ABSTRACT

Cloud computing, social networking and information networks (for search, news feeds, etc) are driving interest in the deployment of large data centers. TCP is the dominant Layer 3 transport protocol in these networks. However, the operating conditions—very high bandwidth links, low round-trip times, small-buffered switches—and traffic patterns cause TCP to perform very poorly. The Data Center TCP (DCTCP) algorithm has recently been proposed as a TCP variant for data centers and addresses these shortcomings.

In this paper, we provide a mathematical analysis of DCTCP. We develop a fluid model of DCTCP and use it to analyze the throughput and delay performance of the algorithm, as a function of the design parameters and of network conditions like link speeds, round-trip times and the number of active flows. Unlike fluid model representations of standard congestion control loops, the DCTCP fluid model exhibits limit cycle behavior. Therefore, it is not amenable to analysis by linearization around a fixed point and we undertake a direct analysis of the limit cycles, proving their stability. Using a hybrid (continuous- *and* discrete-time) model, we analyze the convergence of DCTCP sources to their fair share, obtaining an explicit characterization of the convergence rate. Finally, we investigate the "RTT-fairness" of DCTCP; i.e., the rate obtained by DCTCP sources as a function of their RTTs. We find a very simple change to DCTCP which is suggested by the fluid model and which significantly improves DCTCP's RTT-fairness. We corroborate our results with ns2 simulations.

Categories and Subject Descriptors:
C.2.2 [Computer-Communication Networks]: Network Protocols

General Terms:
Algorithms, Performance, Theory

Keywords:
Data center network, Congestion control, Analysis, TCP

1. INTRODUCTION

1.1 Background and Motivation

TCP is the dominant transport protocol in the Internet and has proven to be scalable and robust to network operating conditions. It is also the dominant Layer 3 protocol in the data center environment, notably in data centers associated with cloud computing, social networking and information networks delivering services such as search, news, advertisement, etc. Its performance in data center environments, however, is quite poor. As detailed in [1], this is mainly because data centers have switches with very small buffers, high speed links, and low round-trip times. Moreover, the nature of traffic and the requirements of applications in data centers are quite different from that in the wide area Internet; data center applications generate a mixture of bursty query traffic, delay-sensitive short messages, and throughput-intensive long flows and often have strict deadlines for the completion of flows.

These differences in operating conditions have caused TCP to underperform in the following ways: (i) It requires large buffers so as to not under-run links, and these buffers can be expensive at high line rates. (ii) It uses all the available buffering; therefore, it induces unacceptably large queuing delays. (iii) It does not handle bursty traffic well, especially under 'Incast' [20] scenarios. See [1] for a more detailed discussion of TCP performance in data centers.

Data Center TCP (DCTCP) has been proposed in [1] to address these shortcomings of TCP. Figure 1, taken from [1], compares the operation of TCP and DCTCP in an actual hardware testbed. It is seen that DCTCP achieves full throughput (the buffer does not underflow) while maintaining a very low buffer occupancy compared to TCP. This allows DCTCP to simultaneously provide low latency and good burst tolerance for the short flows, and high throughput for the long flows.

The key mechanisms used by DCTCP are a simple active queue management scheme at the switch, based on Explicit Congestion Notification (ECN) [16], and a window control scheme at the source which reacts to ECN marks by reducing the window size in proportion to the *fraction* of packets that are marked (contrast this with TCP which *always* cuts the window by half if at least one packet is marked). The performance of DCTCP is determined by two parameters: (i) K, the marking threshold on the queue at the switch above which all packets are marked; and (ii) g, the weight used for exponentially averaging ECN mark values at the source. See Section 2.1 for details.

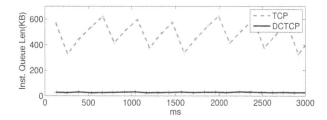

Figure 1: Taken from [1]. Queue length measured on a Broadcom Triumph switch. Two long flows are launched from distinct 1Gbps ports to a common 1Gbps port. The switch allocates about 600KB of buffer to the congested port.

1.2 Main Contributions and Organization

This paper undertakes a rigorous analysis of DCTCP. The following are our main contributions:

1. DCTCP fluid model. We briefly review the DCTCP algorithm and derive a fluid model for it in Section 2. The model comprises of a system of nonlinear delay-differential equations. Using ns2 [15] simulations, we find that the fluid model is very accurate and that it is more accurate across a wider range of parameters than a simple model presented in [1]. A key step in developing the fluid model is accurately capturing the bursty (0–1 type) marking at the switch which DCTCP employs.[1]

2. Steady state. We analyze the steady state behavior of DCTCP using the fluid model in Section 3. Due to its 0–1 style marking function, the fluid model does not have a fixed point. Instead, it exhibits a (periodic) limit cycle behavior in steady state. Theorem 1 provides a necessary and sufficient condition for local stability of the limit cycles using the so-called *Poincaré map* technique [4, 10, 14, 22]. We verify this condition (numerically) for a wide range of parameter values. We then explore the throughput and delay performance of DCTCP by explicitly evaluating the limit cycle solutions. Here we find that for DCTCP to achieve 100% throughput, the marking threshold, K, needs to be about 17% of the bandwidth-delay product. For smaller values of K, we determine the throughput loss; i.e., we obtain the throughput-delay tradeoff curve. A key result is that DCTCP's throughput remains higher than 94% even as $K \to 0$. This is much higher than the limiting throughput of 75% for a TCP source as the buffer size goes to zero [21].

3. Convergence. We analyze how quickly DCTCP flows converge to their fair equilibrium window sizes (equivalently, sending rates) in Section 4. This is important to determine since DCTCP reduces its sending rate by factors much smaller than TCP; therefore, DCTCP sources may take much longer to converge. Theorem 2 gives the following explicit characterization: For N flows (with identical RTTs) sharing a single bottleneck link, the window sizes at the nth congestion episode, $W_i(T_n)$, converge to the fair share, W^*, as follows:

$$|W_i(T_n) - W^*| < O(n^2) \exp\left(-\beta_{DCTCP} T_n\right),$$

where an explicit expression is given for β_{DCTCP}. Using this, we compare the rate of convergence of TCP and DCTCP

---

[1]This is similar to the difficulty of modeling TCP–Drop-tail using fluid models.

and obtain the following bounds

$$\beta_{DCTCP} < \beta_{TCP} < 1.4 \times \beta_{DCTCP}.$$

Thus, even though DCTCP converges slower than TCP, it is at most 1.4 times slower.

We note that the convergence results are obtained using a different model from the fluid model, since the fluid model is not suitable for conducting transient analyses. This new model of DCTCP, which we call the Hybrid Model, employs continuous- and discrete-time variables and is similar to the AIMD models used in the analysis of TCP–Drop-tail [5, 17, 18]. While the AIMD models are linear and can be used to determine convergence rates via an analysis of the eigenvalues of linear operators [17, 18], the Hybrid Model is more challenging because it is nonlinear.

4. RTT-fairness. We investigate the fairness properties of DCTCP for flows with diverse RTTs in Section 5. RTT-fairness is defined as the ratio of the throughput achieved by two groups of flows as a function of the ratio of their RTTs [23, 11, 6, 2]. Using ns2 simulations, we find that DCTCP's RTT-fairness is better than TCP–Drop-tail but worse than TCP with RED [7] marking. We identify a very simple change to the DCTCP algorithm, suggested by the fluid model, which considerably improves its RTT-fairness. The modified DCTCP is shown to have linear RTT-fairness ($Throughput \propto RTT^{-1}$) and achieve a better fairness than TCP–RED.

5. DCTCP Parameter Guidelines. Our analysis of DCTCP's steady state and convergence properties yields guidelines for choosing algorithm parameters. Let C and d respectively denote the bottleneck capacity (in packets/sec) and propagation delay (in sec). Then,

$$K \approx 0.17Cd, \tag{1}$$

$$\frac{5}{Cd + K} \lesssim g \lesssim \frac{1}{\sqrt{Cd + K}}. \tag{2}$$

For example, when $C = 10$Gbps and $d = 300\mu$s, assuming 1500Byte packets, K needs to be about 42 packets and $0.02 \lesssim g \lesssim 0.06$.

2. DCTCP: ALGORITHM AND MODEL

2.1 The Algorithm

First, we briefly review the DCTCP algorithm. We focus on those aspects relevant to this paper and refer to [1] for more details.

Switch Side. DCTCP uses a very simple active queue management scheme: When a packet arrives at the switch buffer and the buffer occupancy is at least K packets, the packet is "marked" using the ECN mechanism. Note that the arriving packet is marked if (and only if) it finds the *instantaneous* buffer occupancy to be larger than K packets.

Source Side. DCTCP is designed to simultaneously achieve high throughput and very low queue occupancies. It does this by reducing its current window (hence, sending rate) in proportion to the *extent* of congestion. Specifically, a DCTCP source reduces its window by a factor that is proportional to the *fraction* of marked packets: the larger the fraction, the larger the decrease factor. This is in contrast to the behavior a TCP source which reacts to marked packets by *always halving* its window size.

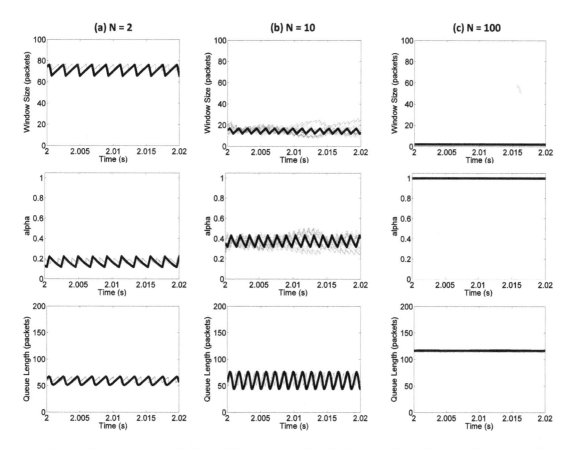

Figure 2: Comparison between fluid model and ns2. The fluid model results are shown in solid black.

Operationally, the source maintains a running estimate of the fraction of its packets that are marked. This estimate, α, is updated once for every window of data (roughly each round-trip time) as follows:

$$\alpha \leftarrow (1-g)\alpha + gF, \tag{3}$$

where F is the *fraction* of packets that were marked in the most recent window of data, and $g \in (0,1)$ is a fixed parameter. DCTCP uses α to cut its window size in response to a marked ACK as follows:

$$W \leftarrow (1-\frac{\alpha}{2})W. \tag{4}$$

Thus when α is close to 0 (low congestion), the window is only slightly reduced, whereas when α is close to 1 (high congestion), the window is cut nearly in half. It is important to note that, as in TCP, DCTCP cuts its window size at most once per window of data (or round-trip time) [16].

This is the only difference between a DCTCP source and a TCP source. Other aspects of the TCP algorithm, such as slow start, additive increase during congestion avoidance, or recovery from packet loss remain unchanged.

2.2 The Fluid Model

We now develop a fluid model for DCTCP by considering N long-lived flows traversing a single bottleneck switch port with capacity C. The following non-linear, delay-differential equations describe the dynamics of $W(t)$, $\alpha(t)$, and the queue size at the switch, $q(t)$:

$$\frac{dW}{dt} = \frac{1}{R(t)} - \frac{W(t)\alpha(t)}{2R(t)}p(t-R^*), \tag{5}$$

$$\frac{d\alpha}{dt} = \frac{g}{R(t)}\left(p(t-R^*) - \alpha(t)\right), \tag{6}$$

$$\frac{dq}{dt} = N\frac{W(t)}{R(t)} - C. \tag{7}$$

Here $p(t)$ indicates the packet marking process at the switch and is given by

$$p(t) = \mathbb{1}_{\{q(t)>K\}}, \tag{8}$$

and $R(t) = d + q(t)/C$ is the round-trip time (RTT), where d is the propagation delay (assumed to be equal for all flows), and $q(t)/C$ is the queueing delay.

Equations (5) and (6) describe the DCTCP source, while (7) and (8) describe the queue process at the switch and the DCTCP marking scheme. The source equations are coupled with the switch equations through the packet marking process $p(t)$ which gets fed back to the source with some delay. This feedback delay is the round-trip time $R(t)$, and varies with $q(t)$. However, as a simplification—and following [9] and [12]—we use the approximate fixed value $R^* = d + K/C$ for the delay. The approximation aligns well with DCTCP's attempt to strictly hold the queue size at around K packets.

Equation (5) models the window evolution and consists of the standard additive increase term, $1/R(t)$, and a multiplicative decrease term, $-W(t)\alpha(t)/2R(t)$. The latter term models the source's reduction of its window size by a factor $\alpha(t)/2$ when packets are marked (i.e., $p(t - R^*) = 1$), and this occurs once per RTT. Equation (6) is a continuous approximation of (3). Finally, equation (7) models the queue evolution: $N \cdot W(t)/R(t)$ is the net input rate and C is the service rate.

Remark 1. In standard TCP fluid models [19, 13, 8, 12], the multiplicative decrease term is given by

$$-\frac{W(t)}{2}\frac{W(t - R^*)}{R(t - R^*)}p(t - R^*), \qquad (9)$$

with the interpretation that $W(t-R^*)/R(t-R^*) \times p(t-R^*)$ is the rate at which marked ACKs arrive at the source, each causing a window reduction of $W(t)/2$. As explained in [13], this model is accurate when the packet marks can be assumed to occur as a Poisson process, for example, when the RED algorithm [7] marks packets. In DCTCP, the marking process is bursty, as captured by the function $p(t)$ at equation (8). Hence, the natural adaptation of (9):

$$-\frac{W(t)\alpha(t)}{2}\frac{W(t - R^*)}{R(t - R^*)}p(t - R^*), \qquad$$

is not valid for DCTCP.

Simulation comparison of the model. Fig. 2 compares the fluid model with packet-level simulations using the ns2 simulator [15]. The parameters used are: $C = 10$Gbps, $d = 100\mu$s, $K = 65$ packets, and $g = 1/16$ (K and g are chosen to match those of the 10Gbps experiments in [1]). The fluid model plots correspond to the evolution of $W(\cdot)$ and $\alpha(\cdot)$, whereas the ns2 plots show the evolutions of the window size and α of *each* of the N sources, for $N = 2, 10, 100$. In the case $N = 100$, the queue size climbs to about 120 packets, even though the marking threshold, K, is 65. Thus *every* arriving packet is marked at the switch buffer (captured by $\alpha = 1$) to signal congestion to each of the 100 sources. The window size at each source is reduced to the minimum, equal to 2 packets, corresponding to a sending rate of 100 Mbps per source.[2]

As can be seen, the fluid model matches the simulations quite well. We have also compared the model with simulations for a wide range of line speeds, propagation delays, number of sources and DCTCP parameters. Our findings are that the model has very good fidelity and that, as is typical, the fidelity increases with the number of sources.

Comparison with the Sawtooth model. The DCTCP paper [1] presents a simplified model of the steady state behavior of long-lived DCTCP flows sharing a single bottleneck. We call this the 'Sawtooth' model. It is based on the assumption that the window sizes of the N flows and the queue size can be thought of as being perfectly synchronized, described by periodic sawtooth processes. This makes it possible to compute the steady state fraction of packets marked at the switch, which can be used to completely specify the sawtooth processes in the model. See [1] for details.

The Sawtooth model provides simple closed form approximations to quantities of interest, such as the amplitude of queue oscillations, leading to some guidelines on how to set the DCTCP parameters. But the accuracy of the Sawtooth

---

[2]Note that, when $N = 100$, the RTT equals 240 microseconds, since $d = 100$ microseconds and $q/C = 140$ microseconds. With these numbers, the sending *rate* of each source, W/RTT, equals 100 Mbps, as required.

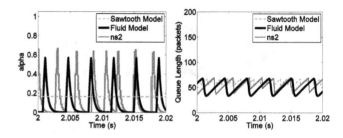

Figure 3: Comparison of the fluid and Sawtooth models with ns2 simulations.

model rests heavily on the validity of the synchronization assumption. As mentioned in [1], this holds when N is small, typically less than 10. Further, the Sawtooth model assumes that sources know the exact fraction of marked packets and does not include the variations in α resulting from the exponentially weighted moving average at equation (3). In particular, the model is only accurate for small values of g and does not capture the effect of g on system dynamics.

This is demonstrated in Fig. 3, which repeats the previous simulation with $N = 2$, this time setting $g = 0.4$. Because the Sawtooth model assumes α is a constant, its prediction of the queue size evolution is very poor. The fluid model presented above captures the fluctuations in α and is, therefore, much more accurate.

3. ANALYSIS: STEADY STATE

3.1 The Normalized Fluid Model

We change variables

$$\tilde{W}(t) = W(R^*t), \quad \tilde{\alpha}(t) = \alpha(R^*t), \quad \tilde{q}(t) = \frac{q(R^*t) - K}{CR^*}, \quad (10)$$

and rewrite the fluid model equations (5)–(8):

$$\frac{d\tilde{W}}{dt} = \frac{1}{1 + \tilde{q}(t)}(1 - \frac{\tilde{W}(t)\tilde{\alpha}(t)}{2}\tilde{p}(t - 1)), \qquad (11)$$

$$\frac{d\tilde{\alpha}}{dt} = \frac{g}{1 + \tilde{q}(t)}(\tilde{p}(t - 1) - \tilde{\alpha}(t)), \qquad (12)$$

$$\frac{d\tilde{q}}{dt} = \frac{1}{\bar{w}}\frac{\tilde{W}(t)}{(1 + \tilde{q}(t))} - 1. \qquad (13)$$

Here

$$\tilde{p}(t) = \mathbb{1}_{\{\tilde{q}(t) > 0\}}, \qquad (14)$$

and $\bar{w} = (Cd + K)/N$ is the average per-flow window size. Henceforth, we refer to this as the normalized fluid model. The normalized model immediately reveals that while the DCTCP fluid model has 5 parameters (C, N, d, K and g), the system dynamics is completely determined by: (i) the average per-flow window size $\bar{w}$, and (ii) the parameter g.

We now discuss the existence of possible fixed points for the normalized fluid model. A fixed point of the system, $(\tilde{W}, \tilde{\alpha}, \tilde{q})$, must satisfy the following equations:

$$1 - \frac{\tilde{W}\tilde{\alpha}}{2}\tilde{p} = 0, \quad \tilde{p} - \tilde{\alpha} = 0, \quad \frac{1}{\bar{w}}\frac{\tilde{W}}{(1 + \tilde{q})} - 1 = 0, \quad (15)$$

where $\tilde{p} = \mathbb{1}\{\tilde{q} > 0\}$. The above equations have a solution only if $\bar{w} \leq 2$. Therefore, we have the following two operating regimes:

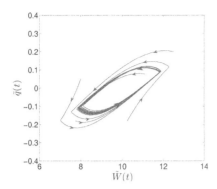

Figure 4: Phase diagram showing occurrence of limit cycle for $\bar{w} = 10$, $g = 1/16$ (the projection on the $\tilde{W}$–$\tilde{q}$ plane is shown).

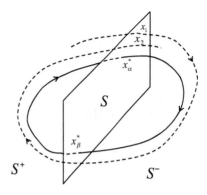

Figure 5: Periodic system trajectory and the Poincaré map.

(i) $\bar{w} \leq 2$: In this regime, the normalized model has a unique fixed point, namely $(\tilde{W}, \tilde{\alpha}, \tilde{q}) = (2, 1, \frac{2}{\bar{w}} - 1)$. Equivalently, (5)–(8) has the fixed point $(W, \alpha, q) = (2, 1, 2N - Cd)$. This regime corresponds to the large N case, where the system has a very simple steady state behavior: each source transmits two packets per RTT, of which Cd fill the link capacity, and the remaining $2N - Cd$ build up a queue. All packets are marked as the queue constantly remains larger than K. The $N = 100$ case of Fig. 2 is in this regime.

(ii) $\bar{w} > 2$: In this regime, the system does not have a fixed point. Rather, it has a periodic solution or limit cycle,[3] characterized by a closed trajectory in state space. Figure 4 shows a sample phase diagram of the limit cycle projected onto the $\tilde{W}$–$\tilde{q}$ plane for $\bar{w} = 10$ and $g = 1/16$. As shown, all trajectories evolve toward the orbit of the limit cycle. Both the $N = 2$ and $N = 10$ cases of Fig. 2 are in this regime.

The regime $\bar{w} \leq 2$ will no longer be discussed since it is trivial to show that the system converges to the unique fixed point. In the next two sections, we study the stability and structure of the limit cycle solution when $\bar{w} > 2$.

3.2 Stability of Limit Cycle

The analysis of the stability of limit cycles is complicated and few analytical tools exist. Fortunately, a wealth of computational tools are available [14], and it is possible to compute the periodic solution of the system and determine its stability properties numerically. A limitation of the computational approach is that it requires sweeping the different parameters of the model to completely characterize the dynamics. However, our task is greatly simplified by the fact that the dynamics of the normalized model is completely determined by the two parameters $\bar{w}$, and g. We proceed by defining stability of limit cycles.

Let X^* denote the set of points in the state space belonging to the limit cycle. We define an ϵ-neighborhood of X^* by

$$U_\epsilon = \{x \in \mathbb{R}^n \mid dist(x, X^*) < \epsilon\},$$

where $dist(x, X^*)$ is the minimum distance from x to a point in X^*; i.e., $dist(x, X^*) = \inf_{y \in X^*} ||x - y||$.

---

[3]Formally, a periodic solution is said to be a limit cycle if there are no other periodic solutions sufficiently close to it. In other words, a limit cycle corresponds to an isolated periodic orbit in the state space [14].

Definition 1. *The limit cycle X^* is*

(i) **stable** *if for any $\epsilon > 0$, there exists a $\delta > 0$ such that*

$$x(0) \in U_\delta \Rightarrow x(t) \in U_\epsilon, \ \forall t \geq 0.$$

(ii) **locally asymptotically stable** *if it is stable and δ can be chosen such that*

$$x(0) \in U_\delta \Rightarrow \lim_{t \to \infty} dist(x(t), X^*) = 0.$$

Figure 4 illustrates the local asymptotical stability of our system for a choice of parameters: orbits initiated from points close enough to the limit cycle are attracted to it.

To proceed, let $x(t) = (\tilde{W}(t), \tilde{\alpha}(t), \tilde{q}(t))^T$ denote the state space of the fluid model equations at (11)–(14). It is convenient to represent the fluid model as:

$$\dot{x}(t) = F(x(t), u(t-1)), \quad u(t) = \mathbb{1}_{\{cx(t) > 0\}}, \quad (16)$$

where $c = [0, 0, 1]$ and $u(t) = \tilde{p}(t)$ is the system feedback.

Poincaré map. We analyze the stability of the limit cycle via the 'Poincaré map', which we introduce after making some definitions. Define the *switching plane* as $S = \{x \in \mathbb{R}^3 : cx = 0\}$ and let $S^+ = \{x \in \mathbb{R}^3 : cx > 0\}$ and $S^- = \{x \in \mathbb{R}^3 : cx < 0\}$ (see Fig. 5 for an illustration). Note that the switching plane is the $\tilde{q} = 0$ (equivalently, $q = K$) plane and corresponds to the DCTCP marking threshold. The limit cycle crosses the switching plane twice in each period, once from S^+ (at the point x_α^*) and once from S^- (at the point x_β^*).

The Poincaré map traces the evolution of the system at the times when its trajectory crosses the switching plane in a given direction. More precisely, let the successive intersections of the trajectory $x(t)$ with S in direction S^+ to S^- be denoted by x_i. The Poincaré map $x_{i+1} = P(x_i)$, maps the ith intersection to the subsequent one. Note that the Poincaré map is well-defined for our system, because equations (11)–(14) guarantee that starting from any point in S^+ or S^-, the trajectory will eventually intersect with S.

The fixed point of the Poincaré map corresponds to the intersection of the limit cycle with the switching plane, say at x_α^*. Therefore, local stability of the Poincaré map at x_α^* implies local stability of the limit cycle. We refer to [4, 10, 14, 22] for more details on the Poincaré map technique.

Next, there are two main steps to establish:

Step 1. The Poincaré map is locally stable. Theorem 1,

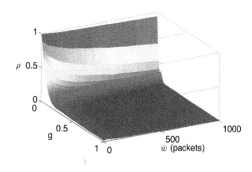

Figure 6: Limit cycle stability (Theorem 1).

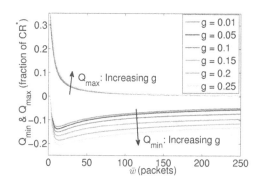

Figure 7: Queue undershoot and overshoot.

which is an adaptation of Theorem 3.3.1 in [22] to our setting, provides a necessary and sufficient condition for local stability of the Poincaré map, and consequently, the limit cycle.

Step 2. Verify that our system satisfies the condition of Theorem 1 for a wide range of $\bar{w}$ and g.

Before proceeding with the statement of Theorem 1, we need the following definitions. Let $x^*(t)$ denote the trajectory of the limit cycle of system (16). Assume that $x^*(t)$ traverses the switching plane from S^+ to S^- at time $t_0 = 0$; i.e., $x^*(0) = x_\alpha^*$, and that the period of the limit cycle is $T = (1 + h_\alpha) + (1 + h_\beta)$ with $h_\alpha > 0$ and $h_\beta > 0$, where $1 + h_\alpha$ (resp. $1 + h_\beta$) is the time taken for the trajectory to move from x_α^* to x_β^* (resp. from x_β^* to x_α^*). For notational convenience, define $u_\alpha = 0$ and $u_\beta = 1$. Let

$$Z_1 = \left(I - \frac{F(x_\alpha^*, u_\beta)c}{cF(x_\alpha^*, u_\beta)} \right) \exp\left(\int_{1+h_\alpha}^{T} J_F(x^*(s), u(s-1))ds \right),$$

$$Z_2 = \left(I - \frac{F(x_\beta^*, u_\alpha)c}{cF(x_\beta^*, u_\alpha)} \right) \exp\left(\int_0^{1+h_\alpha} J_F(x^*(s), u(s-1))ds \right),$$

where J_F is the Jacobian matrix of F with respect to x, and I is the identity matrix. The integral of the matrix J_F is entry wise. We assume that $cF(x_\alpha^*, u_\beta) \neq 0$ and $cF(x_\beta^*, u_\alpha) \neq 0$; i.e., $x^*(t)$ is nontangent with the switching plane at the traversing points. Note that Z_1 and Z_2 are 3×3 matrices.

Theorem 1. *The Poincaré map (and its associated limit cycle) is locally asymptotically stable if and only if*

$$\rho(Z_1 Z_2) < 1.$$

Here, $\rho(\cdot)$ is the spectral radius.

A proof sketch is provided in Appendix A of the full version of this paper [24].

Verification. We use Theorem 1 to verify the stability of DCTCP's limit cycle. Since Z_1 and Z_2 do not have a closed form, we sweep the parameters $\bar{w}$ and g in the ranges of interest and compute $\rho(Z_1 Z_2)$ numerically. This has been done in Fig. 6 for the range $g \in [0.001, 1]$, and $\bar{w} \in [2.01, 1000]$. Throughout this range, $\rho < 1$, and (local) stability is verified. We conjecture that the limit cycle is actually globally stable for all $g \in (0, 1]$, $\bar{w} > 2$.

3.3 Steady State Throughput & Delay

In this section, we study the key performance metrics of throughput and delay of DCTCP, by analyzing the limit cycle solution of equations (11)–(14).

A standard method for approximately determining the amplitude and frequency of limit cycles is the so-called 'Describing Function (DF) Method' [10]. Unfortunately, the DF method applied to system (11)–(14) yields very poor results. This is because a key assumption of the DF method—that the limit cycle can be well-approximated by a single frequency sinusoid—does not hold for this system. We therefore evaluate the exact limit cycle solutions numerically.

3.3.1 100% Throughput

The first question we consider is: How much buffering is required for DCTCP to achieve 100% throughput? Since queue underflow must be avoided for 100% throughput, we need to determine how large the queue size oscillations are about the operating point K.

Assume $\{(\tilde{W}(t), \tilde{\alpha}(t), \tilde{q}(t)) | 0 \leq t < T\}$ is the limit cycle of our system (with period T). Define $Q_{min} = \min_{0 \leq t < T} \tilde{q}(t)$, and $Q_{max} = \max_{0 \leq t \leq T} \tilde{q}(t)$ to be the maximum and minimum excursions of the (normalized) queue size during a period. In Fig. 7, we plot Q_{min} and Q_{max} against $\bar{w}$ for some values of g.

There are three key observations:

(i) The queue overshoot is not sensitive to g and increases as $\bar{w}$ decreases. This follows because the queue overshoot is primarily determined by the rate at which flows increase their window size, and as $\bar{w}$ decreases, the window increase rate of 1 packet/RTT per source becomes increasingly large compared to the bandwidth-delay product.

(ii) There is a worst case $\bar{w}$ (about 12-16 packets for the range of g values shown in Fig. 7) at which the queue undershoot is maximized. This implies an interesting property of DCTCP: as per-flow window sizes increase—for example, due to higher and higher link speeds—DCTCP requires less buffers as a fraction of the bandwidth-delay product to achieve high utilization.

(iii) The amplitude of queue undershoot increases as g increases. This is to be expected: high values of g cause large fluctuations in α which inhibit DCTCP's ability to maintain a steady sending rate (see Fig. 3 for an example).[4]

Choosing K. As seen in Fig. 7, $Q_{min} \gtrsim -0.15$ when g is sufficiently small (the choice of g is discussed next). Therefore, to avoid queue underflow, we require $K > |Q_{min}|CR^* \gtrsim 0.15CR^*$. Substituting $R^* = d + K/C$ in this inequality gives

---

[4]It is important to note that although α will cease to oscillate as $g \to 0$, queue size oscillations cannot be made arbitrary small by lowering g. In fact in Fig. 7, all $g \leq 0.01$ values basically produce the same curve.

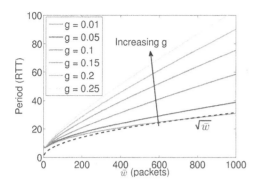

Figure 8: Limit cycle period of oscillations.

the following guideline:

$$K \approx 0.17Cd. \tag{17}$$

In words, about 17% of the bandwidth-delay product of buffering is needed for 100% throughput; any more available buffer can be used as headroom to absorb bursts. Note that this value for K is quite close to the guideline $K > (1/7)Cd$, suggested in [1]. This also confirms the validity of the simple sawtooth model for small g.

Limit cycle period & an upper limit for g. Figure 8 plots the period of oscillations of the limit cycle. The figure suggests that the period grows as $\sqrt{\bar{w}}$ (for small g). Now, the marking process $\{p(t-1)\}$ is a periodic 'signal' (with period equal to the period of the limit cycle), which is input to the low-pass filter defined at equation (12). Since the filter has a cutoff frequency of about g, for it to be effective, it is necessary that g be smaller than the primary oscillation frequency of the signal, $1/\sqrt{\bar{w}}$. But $\bar{w} = (Cd + K)/N$ and is maximized for $N = 1$. Therefore, we get the following bound:

$$g \lesssim \frac{1}{\sqrt{Cd + K}}. \tag{18}$$

Appendix C of [24] provides a different justification for (18) based on the Hybrid Model, which we introduce in Section 4. We will revisit the matter of choosing g in Section 4.2, where we obtain a lower limit for g.

3.3.2 Throughput-Delay Tradeoff

We have seen that if K is at least 17% of the bandwidth-delay product, DCTCP achieves 100% throughput. However, when we require very low queueing delays, or when switch buffers are extremely shallow, it may be desirable to choose K even smaller than this. Inevitably, this will result in some loss of throughput. We are interested in quantifying how much throughput is lost, and in effect, deriving a throughput-delay tradeoff curve for DCTCP.

A more accurate model of the switch queue is needed to study throughput loss. Equation (13) ignores the fact that a real queue will never become negative. To account for this and capture the correct behavior when queues underflow, we define $\psi \triangleq K/(Cd)$, and replace (13) with:

$$\frac{d\tilde{q}}{dt} = \begin{cases} \frac{1}{\bar{w}}\frac{\tilde{W}(t)}{(1+\tilde{q}(t))} - 1 & \tilde{q}(t) > \frac{-\psi}{1+\psi}, \\ \max\left(\frac{1}{\bar{w}}\frac{\tilde{W}(t)}{(1+\tilde{q}(t))} - 1, 0\right) & \tilde{q}(t) = \frac{-\psi}{1+\psi}. \end{cases}$$

We can now explore the limit cycle solution as we vary ψ,

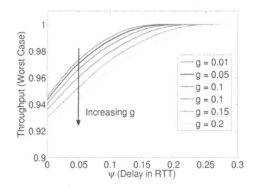

Figure 9: Worst Case Throughput vs Delay.

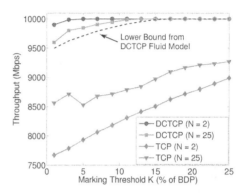

Figure 10: Throughput vs marking threshold K in ns2 simulation; K is varied from 4 to 100 packets (1-25% of the BDP). Note that as predicted by the analysis, the throughput remains higher than 94% even for K as small as 1% of the BDP.

and compute the average throughput (over period T):

$$Throughput = \frac{1}{T}\int_0^T \frac{\tilde{W}(t)}{\bar{w}(1+\tilde{q}(t))}dt.$$

In Fig. 9, we plot the worst case throughput as ψ is varied. At each value of ψ, the value of $\bar{w}$ which yields the lowest throughput is used. It should be noted that since the queue size is maintained near the marking threshold, the ψ axis also (roughly) corresponds to the average queueing delay. As expected, when $\psi \gtrsim 0.17$, 100% throughput is achieved (for small g). As ψ is lowered, the throughput decreases, but **is always at least 94%** for $g < 0.1$. This indicates that very small marking thresholds can be used in DCTCP, with only a minor loss in throughput. We verify this next through ns2 simulations.

3.3.3 Simulations

We use ns2 simulations to evaluate the throughput achieved as the marking threshold K is varied. We choose $C = 10$Gbps and $d = 480\mu$s, for a bandwidth-delay product of 400 packets (each 1500 Bytes), and set $g = 0.05$. We consider two cases with $N = 2$ and $N = 25$ long-lived flows. The results are shown in Fig. 10. For reference, we also report the results for TCP in the same scenarios.

The simulations clearly show that DCTCP achieves high throughput, even with marking threshold as low as 1% of the bandwidth-delay product. In all cases, we find the throughput is indeed higher than the worst case lower bound predicted by the fluid model. Of course, we see a much worse throughput loss with TCP. An interesting observation is that unlike TCP, whose throughput improves as we increase the number of flows, DCTCP gets lower throughput with $N = 25$ flows than $N = 2$ flows. This is expected from our analysis, because with DCTCP, the worst case queue size fluctuations (and throughput loss) occur when the per-flow window size is around 10-20 packets (see Fig. 7 and observation (ii) in Section 3.3.1).

4. ANALYSIS: CONVERGENCE

DCTCP uses the multi-bit information derived from estimating the fraction of marked packets to reduce its window by factors smaller than two. As we have seen in the previous section, this allows it to very efficiently utilize shallow buffers, achieving both high throughput and low queueing delays. However, the reduced multiplicative decrease factors mean slower convergence times: it takes longer for a flow with a large window size to relinquish bandwidth to a flow with a small window size.

Since the convergence time is proportional to the RTT for window-based algorithms and the RTTs in a data center are only a few 100s of microseconds, it is argued in [1] the actual time to converge is not substantial relative to the transfer time of large data files. But an analysis of convergence time has not been conducted in [1]. Based on simulations, [1] reports that the convergence time of DCTCP is a factor 2-3 slower than TCP. The results of this section show that this is, indeed, correct in general.

Our aim in this section is to derive rigorous bounds for the rate of convergence of DCTCP. We consider how fast N DCTCP flows with identical RTTs[5], starting with arbitrary window sizes and values of α, converge to their share of the bottleneck bandwidth. Since this is an analysis of the system in transience, the fluid model of the previous section is inadequate. Instead, we use a hybrid (continuous- and discrete-time) model based on the AIMD models introduced in [5, 17]. A key difference between our model and the AIMD models is that ours is non-linear because it models the DCTCP-style multiplicative decrease, whereas the models in [5, 17] and are linear since they correspond to a constant decrease factor (equal to 2 for TCP).

4.1 Hybrid Model

Consider N DCTCP flows whose window size and value of α at time t (measured in units of RTT) are denoted by $W_i(t)$ and $\alpha_i(t)$. Assume the window sizes of the N flows are synchronized; i.e., each flow reduces its window at every congestion event. See Fig. 11 for an illustration.

Let $W_{max} = Cd + K$. When $\sum_{i=1}^{N} W_i(t) < W_{max}$, all window sizes increase linearly with slope 1 packet/RTT. Once $\sum_{i=1}^{N} W_i(t) = W_{max}$, a congestion event occurs and each flow cuts its window size according to (4) using its current value of α. Note that packets are marked ($p(t) = 1$) for 1 RTT after the window reductions because of the feedback delay. Assume the kth congestion event occurs at time T_k. Since the total reduction in $\sum_{i=1}^{N} W_i(t)$ at T_k is equal to $\sum_{i=1}^{N} W_i(T_k)\alpha_i(T_k)/2$, which is regained at the rate of N

[5]This ensures that in equilibrium, each flow gets $(1/N)^{th}$ of the bottleneck bandwidth. See Section 5 for a discussion of the bias against flows with longer RTTs.

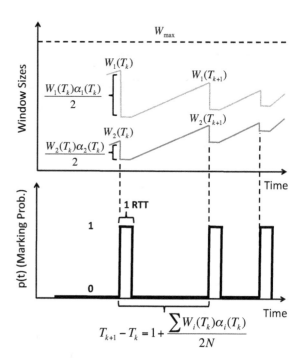

Figure 11: Hybrid Model. The window sizes are shown for 2 flows. Note that $\sum W_i(T_k) = W_{max}$ for all k.

packets/RTT, the duration of the kth "congestion epoch" is

$$\Delta T_k \triangleq T_{k+1} - T_k = 1 + \frac{\sum_{i=1}^{N} W_i(T_k)\alpha_i(T_k)}{2N}, \qquad (19)$$

and we have:

$$W_i(T_{k+1}) = (1 - \frac{\alpha_i(T_k)}{2})W_i(T_k) + \Delta T_k - 1. \qquad (20)$$

It only remains to specify the evolution of $\alpha_i(t)$. This is simply given by:

$$\frac{d\alpha_i}{dt} = g(p(t) - \alpha_i(t)).$$

In particular, $\alpha_i(T_{k+1})$ is the solution of the following initial value problem at time ΔT_k:

$$\frac{dx}{dt} = g(p(t) - x(t)), \quad x(0) = \alpha_i(T_k)$$

$$p(t) = \begin{cases} 1 & 0 \le t < 1 \\ 0 & t \ge 1 \end{cases}$$

Using this, it is not difficult to show:

$$\alpha_i(T_{k+1}) = e^{-g\Delta T_k}(e^g - 1 + \alpha_i(T_k)). \qquad (21)$$

4.2 Rate of Convergence

We make the following assumptions regarding the system parameters:

$$N \ge 2, \quad W_{max} \ge 2N, \quad g \le \frac{1}{\sqrt{W_{max}}}. \qquad (22)$$

The first two assumptions are natural for studying convergence, and the third is in accordance with the guidelines of the previous section regarding steady state. Let $W^* = W_{max}/N$. The main result of this section is given by the following theorem.

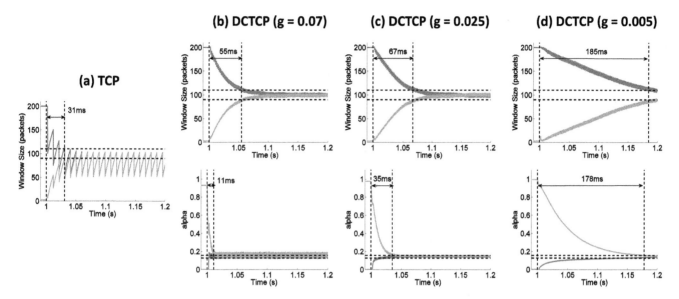

Figure 12: ns2 simulation of convergence time for 2 flows. The chosen g values for DCTCP correspond to: (b) $1/\sqrt{W_{max}}$, (c) $5/W_{max}$, and (d) $1/W_{max}$.

Theorem 2. *Consider N DCTCP flows evolving according to (20) and (21), with parameters satisfying (22). Suppose that $W_i(0)$ and $\alpha_i(0)$ are arbitrary. Let $0 < \alpha^* \leq 1$ be the unique positive solution of*

$$\alpha^* = e^{-g(1+W^*\alpha^*/2)}(e^g - 1 + \alpha^*). \quad (23)$$

Then $W_i(T_n) \to W^*$ (defined above), and $\alpha_i(T_n) \to \alpha^*$ for all $1 \leq i \leq N$ as $n \to \infty$. Moreover:

$$|W_i(T_n) - W^*| < 2W_{max}\left(1 + g^6 n^2\right)e^{-\beta(T_n - T_{P2})}, \quad (24)$$

for all $1 \leq i \leq N$, where:

$$\beta = \min\left(g, \frac{-\log(1 - \alpha^*/2)}{1 + W^*\alpha^*/2}\right), \quad (25)$$

$$T_{P2} = \frac{\log(2W^*/g^6)}{g} + 2(1 + W^*/2). \quad$$

The proof of Theorem 2 is given in Section 4.4. Here, we make a few remarks about the convergence rate. The crucial term in (24) is the exponential decay $e^{-\beta T_n}$. The convergence rate is therefore chiefly determined by (25), which has the following interpretation. Two things occur (simultaneously) during convergence of DCTCP: (i) the $\alpha_i(T_n)$ converge to α^*, and (ii) the $W_i(T_n)$ converge to W^*. It is shown in the proof of Theorem 2 that (i) happens with rate g, and (ii) with rate $\gamma = -\log(1 - \alpha^*/2)/(1 + W^*\alpha^*/2)$. The overall convergence rate is determined by the slower of the two.

Lower limit for g. We have seen that g should be smaller than $1/\sqrt{W_{max}}$ to not adversely affect steady state performance. Equation (25) suggests a lower bound for g, in order to not slow down convergence. Note that:

$$\frac{1}{W^*} < \gamma \approx \frac{-2\log(1 - \alpha^*/2)}{W^*\alpha^*} < \frac{2\log 2}{W^*}. \quad (26)$$

Therefore if $g > (2\log 2)/W^*$, it will not limit the convergence rate. Of course, in practice, we don't know the number

of flows N, and so don't know W^*. However, in data centers, there are typically a small number of large active flows on a path[6]. Therefore, we mainly need to focus on the small N case, for which convergence is also slowest. With these considerations, we propose the following guideline:

$$\frac{5}{W_{max}} \lesssim g \lesssim \frac{1}{\sqrt{W_{max}}}. \quad (27)$$

Comparison with TCP. As mentioned in the beginning of this section, DCTCP converges slower than TCP. But how much slower is DCTCP? It is straight forward to show that the convergence rate of TCP is given by:

$$\beta_{TCP} = \frac{\log 2}{1 + W^*/2} \approx \frac{2\log 2}{W^*}.$$

Therefore, (25) and (26) imply that for g properly chosen large enough:

$$\beta_{DCTCP} < \beta_{TCP} < (2\log 2)\beta_{DCTCP} \approx 1.4 \times \beta_{DCTCP}.$$

This means that the DCTCP convergence rate is at most 40% slower than TCP. It is important to note however that this is a statement about the *asymptotic* rate of convergence. In practice, all the terms present in (24) affect the convergence time. Therefore, in simulations, the actual time to converge is about a factor 1.5-2 larger (see also [1]).

Bounds on α^*. The following bounds are proven in Appendix C of the full version of this paper [24].

$$\frac{1}{2}\sqrt{\frac{2}{W^*}} - g < \alpha^* < \sqrt{\frac{2}{W^*}} + g.$$

4.3 Simulations

We have verified the results of our analysis using extensive ns2 simulations. Figure 12 shows a representative example

---

[6]For example, measurements reported in [1] show at most 4 flows larger than 1MB concurrently active at a server in any 50ms period. Note that only the large flows need to be considered, as only they can possibly converge.

with 2 flows. The choice of parameters $C = 10\text{Gbps}$, $d = 200\mu s$, and $K = 35$ (or 17% of the BDP) gives $W_{max} \approx 200$ packets. One flow starts at the beginning of the simulation, and grabs all the available capacity (its window size reaches 200). At time 1sec, a second flow begins with a window of 1 packet, and we are interested in how long it takes for both window sizes to get within 10% of the fair share value (100 packets) for the first time. In order to have the worst case convergence time with DCTCP, we begin the second flow with $\alpha = 1$, whereas the first flow has $\alpha = 0$ before time 1sec; so the second flow actually cuts its window by much larger factors initially.

We test three values of g for DCTCP. With $g = 1/\sqrt{W_{max}}$, as expected from the analysis, the α variables converge much quicker than the window sizes (about 5x faster). Reducing g to $5/\sqrt{W_{max}}$, the convergence times of the α and window sizes get closer, with the α still converging about twice as fast. Here, the increase in convergence time is small (67ms up from 55ms). But when g is further reduced to $1/W_{max}$, the convergence of α and window sizes take about the same amount of time, showing that the limiting factor is now the convergence of α. In this case, the small value of g significantly increases the total convergence time (185ms). A final observation is that when g is appropriately chosen according to (27), the convergence time of DCTCP is indeed up to about a factor of 2 longer than TCP.

4.4 Proof of Theorem 2

The key idea in proving Theorem 2 is to consider convergence as happening in three separate phases.

Phase 1. Initially, the α_i values get close to each other. In fact (21) implies that for any i and j:

$$|\alpha_i(T_n) - \alpha_j(T_n)| \le e^{-gT_n}|\alpha_i(T_0) - \alpha_j(T_0)| \le e^{-gT_n} \quad (28)$$

We have the following simple Lemma.

Lemma 1. *Let $\bar{\alpha}(T_k) = \sum_{i=1}^{N} \alpha_i(T_k)/N$. Then:*

$$|\alpha_i(T_n) - \bar{\alpha}(T_n)| \le e^{-gT_n}$$

for all $1 \le i \le N$.

PROOF. This follows by applying the triangle inequality and using (28). □

We take Phase 1 to last until time $T_{P1} \triangleq log(2W^*)/g$, so that:

$$|\alpha_i(T_k) - \bar{\alpha}(T_k)| \le e^{-gT_k} = \frac{1}{2W^*}e^{-g(T_k - T_{P1})}. \quad (29)$$

Phase 2. The second phase begins with $T_k \ge T_{P1}$. In this phase, the α_i converge to a positive constant α^*. The following proposition is the main convergence result for Phase 2 and is proved in Appendix B of [24].

Proposition 1. *For $n \ge 1$, and all $1 \le i \le N$:*

$$|\alpha_i(T_n) - \alpha^*| \le A_0 n e^{-g(T_n - T_{P1})}, \quad (30)$$

where $A_0 = e^{2g(1+W^*/2)}$.

We take Phase 2 to last until time

$$T_{P2} \triangleq T_{P1} + 2(1 + W^*/2) - 6\log(g)/g,$$

so that:

$$|\alpha_i(T_k) - \alpha^*| \le A_0 k e^{-g(T_k - T_{P1})} = g^6 k e^{-g(T_k - T_{P2})}. \quad (31)$$

In particular, it is easy to check that given (22), $g^6 T_{P2} \le g$, which implies that for $T_k \ge T_{P2}$:

$$\zeta_k \triangleq g^6 k e^{-g(T_k - T_{P2})} \le g^6 T_k e^{-g(T_k - T_{P2})} \le g. \quad (32)$$

Phase 3. The third and final phase begins with $T_k \ge T_{P2}$. In Phase 3, the α_i values are all close to α^*, and the sources essentially perform AIMD with a decrease factor of $\alpha^*/2$.

The following Lemma is the key ingredient for convergence in Phase 3.

Lemma 2. *For $T_k \ge T_{P2}$, and any $1 \le i, j \le N$:*

$$|W_i(T_{k+1}) - W_j(T_{k+1})| \le e^{-\gamma \Delta T_k}|W_i(T_k) - W_j(T_k)| + 2W_{max}\zeta_k, \quad (33)$$

where $\gamma = -\log(1 - \alpha^*/2)/(1 + W^*\alpha^*/2)$.

PROOF. Using (20), (31), and (32), we have:

$$|W_i(T_{k+1}) - W_j(T_{k+1})| \le (1 - \frac{\alpha^*}{2})|W_i(T_k) - W_j(T_k)| +$$
$$\frac{|W_i(T_k)|}{2}|\alpha_i(T_k) - \alpha^*| + \frac{|W_j(T_k)|}{2}|\alpha_j(T_k) - \alpha^*|,$$
$$\le (1 - \frac{\alpha^*}{2})|W_i(T_k) - W_j(T_k)| + W_{max}\zeta_k.$$

Noting that

$$\Delta T_k \le 1 + W^*\alpha^*/2 + W^*\zeta_k/2, \quad (34)$$

the result follows from:

$$(1 - \alpha^*/2) \le e^{-\gamma(\Delta T_k - W^*\zeta_k/2)} \le e^{-\gamma \Delta T_k}(1 + \zeta_k),$$

where the last inequality is true because:

$$e^{\gamma W^*\zeta_k/2} \le e^{-\zeta_k \log(1-\alpha^*/2)/\alpha^*}$$
$$\le e^{\zeta_k \log 2} = 2^{\zeta_k} \le 1 + \zeta_k. \quad (35)$$

This holds for $\zeta_k \le 1$, which we have from (32). □

We can now prove Theorem 2. Let $r \triangleq \inf\{k|T_k \ge T_{P2}\}$ and $\beta \triangleq \min(g, \gamma)$. Similar as we did for Proposition 1, we iterate (33) backwards starting from $n \ge r$ to get:

$$|W_i(T_n) - W_j(T_n)|$$
$$\le W_{max}\left(e^{\beta(T_r - T_{P2})} + 2g^6 \sum_{k=r}^{n-1} k e^{\beta \Delta T_k}\right)e^{-\beta(T_n - T_{P2})}.$$

But:

$$e^{\beta(T_r - T_{P2})} \le e^{\gamma(1+W^*/2)} \le e^{-\log(1-\alpha^*/2)/\alpha^*} \le e^{\log 2} = 2,$$

and using (34), (35), and (32):

$$\sum_{k=r}^{n-1} k e^{\beta \Delta T k} \le \sum_{k=r}^{n-1} k e^{\gamma(1+W^*\alpha^*/2)} e^{\gamma W^*\zeta_k/2}$$
$$\le (1 - \alpha^*/2)(1 + g)\sum_{k=r}^{n-1} k < n^2.$$

Noting that $|W_i(T_n) - W^*| \le \frac{1}{N}\sum_{j=1}^{N}|W_i(T_n) - W_j(T_n)|$, we have established (24) for $n \ge r$. The result is trivial for $n < r$, completing the proof. □

5. RTT-FAIRNESS

It is well-known that TCP has a bias against flows with long round-trip times; i.e., flows with longer RTTs get a lower share of the bottleneck bandwidth when competing with flows with shorter RTTs [11, 6, 2, 3, 23]. This is due to the fact that the rate at which flows increase their window size is inversely proportional to their RTT (one packet per RTT). Therefore, flows with short RTTs grab bandwidth much more quickly than flows with long RTTs and settle at a higher rate in steady-state. In fact, it has been shown that the throughput achieved by a TCP flow is inversely proportional to RTT^θ with $1 \leq \theta \leq 2$ [11].

Another important factor which affects RTT-fairness is synchronization between flows. Typically, higher synchronization, in terms of detecting a loss or mark event, leads to worse RTT-fairness. In fact, it has been argued that active queue management (AQM) schemes like RED [7] which avoid synchronization by probabilistically dropping (or marking) packets improve RTT fairness compared to Drop-tail queues [2, 23].

Since DCTCP employs the same additive increase mechanism used by TCP, it is expected that DCTCP also exhibits a bias against flows with longer RTTs. Moreover, the active queue management of DCTCP is (by design) similar to Drop-tail (albeit with marking instead of dropping) and prone to causing synchronization. This makes a study of how well DCTCP handles RTT diversity important.

5.1 Simulations

We consider the following ns2 simulation to investigate RTT-fairness. Four flows share a single 10Gbps bottleneck link in a "dumbbell" topology. The first two of these flows have a fixed RTT of 100μs. The RTT of the other two flows is varied from 100μs to 1ms. We measure the throughput for all flows in each test, and compute the ratio of the throughput of the first two flows to that of the second two flows, as a function of the RTT ratio.

The DCTCP parameters chosen are $K = 35$ packets and $g = 1/16$. For reference, we compare the results with TCP using the DCTCP style "Drop-tail" (0–1) marking, and also TCP with RED marking[7]. The results are shown in Fig. 13. The algorithm labeled "DCTCP–Improved Fairness" is described in the next section.

As expected, DCTCP does exhibit a bias against flows with longer RTTs. The simulations indicate that DCTCP's RTT-fairness is better than TCP–Drop-tail, which has approximately squared RTT-fairness ($Throughput \propto RTT^{-2}$), but worse than TCP–RED, which has approximately linear RTT-fairness ($Throughput \propto RTT^{-1}$). In this and other simulations not reported here, we observed that when the RTT ratio is moderate, DCTCP exhibits slightly worse than linear RTT-fairness, but tends to squared RTT-fairness as the RTT ratio becomes large. Apparently, the smooth window adjustments made by DCTCP help alleviate some of the synchronization effects caused by the 0–1 marking strategy, thereby improving DCTCP's RTT-fairness.

---

[7]For RED, the marking probability increases linearly from 0 to 10% as the *average* queue length (EWMA with weight 0.1) increases from 30 to 100 packets. These parameters are chosen to ensure stability of RED in this configuration and yield roughly the same queue lengths as DCTCP.

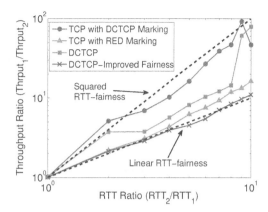

Figure 13: RTT-fairness in ns2 simulation: 2 groups each with 2 flows are activated. Flows in group 1 have $RTT_1 = 100\mu s$. The RTT for flows in group 2 (RTT_2) is varied from $100\mu s$ to $1ms$. Note the log-log scale.

5.2 DCTCP–Improved Fairness

The DCTCP fluid model (Section 2.2) suggests a very simple change which considerably improves the RTT-fairness of DCTCP. We will first state this change, contrasting it with the DCTCP algorithm defined in Section 2.1. We will then explain how the fluid model suggests this change.

Recall that the DCTCP algorithm reduces the window size according to

$$W \leftarrow W(1 - \alpha/2)$$

in response to a marked ACK, and that this is done at most once for each window of data. Instead, we propose subtracting $\alpha/2$ from the window size for each marked ACK, resulting in the following simple window update equation:

`for each received ACK:`

$$W \leftarrow W + \begin{cases} 1/W & \text{if ECN} = 0 \\ 1/W - \alpha/2 & \text{if ECN} = 1 \end{cases} \quad (36)$$

Note that a full window of marked ACKs will cause a reduction of about $W\alpha/2$, which is the same amount DCTCP would reduce the window size upon receiving a mark. A nice feature is that since (36) applies to every ACK, it does not require maintaining extra state to prevent window reductions from happening more than once per window of data.

The simulation results in Fig. 13 confirm that this simple change significantly improves RTT-fairness (especially at high RTT ratios), and does indeed achieve linear RTT-fairness. In fact, it even achieves a slightly better RTT-fairness than TCP–RED.

Connection with Fluid Model. Consider N flows with round-trip times RTT_i ($1 \leq i \leq N$) in steady-state. Recall the source side equations:

$$\frac{dW_i}{dt} = \frac{1}{RTT_i} - \frac{W_i(t)\alpha_i(t)}{2RTT_i}p(t - RTT_i), \quad (37)$$

$$\frac{d\alpha_i}{dt} = \frac{g}{RTT_i}\left(p(t - RTT_i) - \alpha_i(t)\right), \quad (38)$$

where, for simplicity, we neglect the contribution of the (time-varying) queueing delay to the RTT. Note that each flow sees a time-delayed version of the common marking process $p(\cdot)$. Therefore, the $\alpha_i(\cdot)$ processes—each given by passing $p(\cdot)$ through a low pass filter—all oscillate around the same value, namely, the duty cycle of $p(\cdot)$. This leads to the following key observation based on (37): the *average* window size for flow i does not depend on RTT_i; i.e., the fluid model suggests that all flows should on average have the same window size, thereby achieving linear RTT-fairness (because $Throughput_i = W_i/RTT_i$).

However, as seen in Fig. 13, simulation results indicate that the actual RTT-fairness is worse than linear. The key source of discrepancy between the fluid model and simulations lies in the *continuous* dynamics present in the fluid model.[8] In particular, let us consider the manner in which the window size decreases in (37). While $p(t - RTT_i) = 1$, the window steadily decreases with rate $W_i(t)\alpha_i(t)/(2RTT_i)$. In contrast, the packet-level algorithm reduces its window *instantaneously* upon receiving a mark. This suggests the change previously discussed to the DCTCP algorithm in equation (36), which bridges the gap between the packet-level and fluid dynamics.

Intuitively, this change improves the RTT-fairness by allowing flows with long RTTs to reduce their window sizes (on average) by a smaller factor compared to flows with short RTTs. This is because in a typical congestion event, flows with short RTTs receive marks earlier and reduce their window sizes, thereby relieving congestion. In such cases, less than a full window of packets from a flow with a long RTT will be marked, and therefore, the net decrease to its window size based on (36) will be smaller than the standard DCTCP window reduction, $W\alpha/2$.

6. FINAL REMARKS

We analyzed DCTCP, a TCP variant for data centers which has recently been proposed in [1]. Our analysis shows that DCTCP can achieve very high throughput while maintaining low buffer occupancies. Specifically, we found that with a marking threshold, K, of about 17% of the bandwidth-delay product, DCTCP achieves 100% throughput, and that even for values of K as small as 1% of the bandwidth-delay product, its throughput is at least 94%. While DCTCP converges slower than TCP, we found that its convergence rate is no more than a factor 1.4 slower than TCP. We also evaluated the RTT-fairness of DCTCP, and found a simple change to the algorithm, which considerably improves its RTT-fairness.

In future, it is worth understanding the behavior of DCTCP in general networks. The work in this paper has focused on the case where there is a single bottleneck.

Acknowledgments

Mohammad Alizadeh and Adel Javanmard are supported by Caroline and Fabian Pease Stanford Graduate Fellowships. We thank the anonymous reviewers whose comments helped us improve the paper.

7. REFERENCES

[1] M. Alizadeh, A. Greenberg, D. A. Maltz, J. Padhye, P. Patel, B. Prabhakar, S. Sengupta, and M. Sridharan. Data center TCP (DCTCP). In *Proceedings of SIGCOMM '10*, pages 63–74, New York, NY, USA, 2010. ACM.

[2] E. Altman, C. Barakat, E. Laborde, P. Brown, and D. Collange. Fairness analysis of TCP/IP. In *Proceedings of the 39th IEEE Conference on Decision and Control, 2000.*, volume 1, pages 61 –66 vol.1, 2000.

[3] E. Altman, T. Jiménez, and R. Núñez Queija. Analysis of two competing TCP/IP connections. *Perform. Eval.*, 49:43–55, September 2002.

[4] K. Astrom, G. Goodwin, and P. Kumar. *Adaptive Control, Filtering, and Signal Processing.* SpringerVerlag, 1995.

[5] F. Baccelli and D. Hong. AIMD, fairness and fractal scaling of TCP traffic. In *INFOCOM*, 2002.

[6] P. Brown. Resource sharing of TCP connections with different round trip times. In *INFOCOM*, 2000.

[7] S. Floyd and V. Jacobson. Random early detection gateways for congestion avoidance. *IEEE/ACM Trans. Netw.*, 1(4):397–413, 1993.

[8] C. V. Hollot, V. Misra, D. Towsley, and W. bo Gong. A control theoretic analysis of RED. In *Proceedings of IEEE INFOCOM*, pages 1510–1519, 2001.

[9] C. V. Hollot, V. Misra, D. Towsley, and W. Gong. Analysis and Design of Controllers for AQM Routers Supporting TCP Flows. *IEEE Transactions on Automatic Control*, 47:945–959, 2002.

[10] H. Khalil. *Nonlinear Systems.* Prentice Hall, 2002.

[11] T. Lakshman and U. Madhow. The performance of TCP/IP for networks with high bandwidth-delay products and random loss. *Networking, IEEE/ACM Transactions on*, 5(3):336 –350, June 1997.

[12] H. Low, O. Paganini, and J. C. Doyle. Internet congestion control. *IEEE Control Systems Magazine*, 22:28–43, 2002.

[13] V. Misra, W.-B. Gong, and D. Towsley. Fluid-based analysis of a network of AQM routers supporting TCP flows with an application to RED. *SIGCOMM Comput. Commun. Rev.*, 30(4):151–160, 2000.

[14] A. H. Nayfeh and B. Balachandran. *Applied Nonlinear Dynamics: Analytical, Computational, and Experimental Methods.* Wiley-VCH, 2007.

[15] The Network Simulator NS-2. http://www.isi.edu/nsnam/ns/.

[16] K. Ramakrishnan, S. Floyd, and D. Black. RFC 3168: the addition of explicit congestion notification (ECN) to IP.

[17] R. Shorten, D. Leith, J. Foy, and R. Kilduff. Analysis and design of AIMD congestion control algorithms in communication networks. *Automatica*, 41(4):725 – 730, 2005.

[18] R. Shorten, F. Wirth, and D. Leith. A positive systems model of TCP-like congestion control: asymptotic results. *IEEE/ACM Trans. Netw.*, 14(3):616–629, 2006.

[19] R. Srikant. *The Mathematics of Internet Congestion Control (Systems and Control: Foundations and Applications).* SpringerVerlag, 2004.

[20] V. Vasudevan, A. Phanishayee, H. Shah, E. Krevat, D. G. Andersen, G. R. Ganger, G. A. Gibson, and B. Mueller. Safe and effective fine-grained TCP retransmissions for datacenter communication. In *Proceedings of SIGCOMM '09*, pages 303–314, New York, NY, USA, 2009. ACM.

[21] A. Vishwanath, V. Sivaraman, and M. Thottan. Perspectives on router buffer sizing: recent results and open problems. *SIGCOMM Comput. Commun. Rev.*, 39:34–39, March 2009.

[22] Q.-G. Wang, T. H. Lee, and C. Lin. *Relay Feedback: Analysis, Identification and Control.* SpringerVerlag, 2003.

[23] L. Xu, K. Harfoush, and I. Rhee. Binary Increase Congestion Control (BIC) for Fast Long-Distance Networks. In *INFOCOM*, 2004.

[24] M. Alizadeh, A. Javanmard, and B. Prabhakar. Analysis of DCTCP: Stability, Convergence, and Fairness. http://www.stanford.edu/~alizade/Site/Publications_files/dctcp_analysis-full.pdf.

---

[8]We emphasize that the mentioned discrepancy affects the accuracy of the fluid model only for heterogenous RTTs. As shown in Section 2.2, the fluid model is very accurate when sources have identical RTTs.

Soft Error Benchmarking of L2 Caches with PARMA

Jinho Suh, Mehrtash Manoochehri, Murali Annavaram and Michel Dubois
Ming Hsieh Department of Electrical Engineering
University of Southern California, Los Angeles
{jinhosuh, mmanooch, annavara}@usc.edu, dubois@paris.usc.edu

ABSTRACT

The amount of charge stored in an SRAM cell shrinks rapidly with each technology generation thus increasingly exposing caches to soft errors. Benchmarking the FIT rate of caches due to soft errors is critical to evaluate the relative merits of a plethora of protection schemes that are being proposed to protect against soft errors. The benchmarking of cache reliability introduces a unique challenge as compared to internal processor storage structures, such as the load/store queue. In the case of internal processor structures the time a data bit resides in the structure is so short that it is generally safe to assume that no more than one soft error strike can occur. Thus the reliability of such structures is overwhelmingly dominated by single bit errors. By contrast, a memory block may reside for millions of cycles in a last level cache. In this case it is important to consider the impact of the spatial and temporal distribution of multiple errors within the lifetime of a cache block in the presence of error protection.

This paper introduces a unified reliability benchmarking framework called PARMA (Precise Analytical Reliability Model for Architecture). PARMA is a rigorous analytical framework that accurately accounts for the distribution of multiple errors to measure the failure rate under any protection scheme. In a single simulation run PARMA provides a precise FIT rate (expected number of failures in one billion hours) measurement for storage structures where the effect of multiple errors cannot be neglected. We have implemented the PARMA framework on top of a cycle-accurate out-of-order processor simulator (sim-outorder) to benchmark L2 cache failure rates for a set of CPU 2000 benchmarks. The effectiveness of three protection schemes are compared in terms of L2 cache FIT rate: parity, word-level Single Error Correcting Double Error Detecting (SECDED) code and block-level SECDED.

Exploiting the accuracy of PARMA, we demonstrate that current techniques to evaluate cache FIT rates in the presence of SECDED, such as accelerated fault injection simulations and first-principle derivations based on Architectural Vulnerability Factor (AVF), can overestimate FIT rates by vast amounts. Based on the insights gained during this research we also introduce a new approximate analytical model that can quickly and more accurately estimate cache FIT rate in the presence of SECDED.

Categories and Subject Descriptors

C.4 [**PERFORMANCE OF SYSTEMS**]: *Reliability, availability and serviceability*

General Terms

Measurement, Reliability

Keywords

Soft Error, Reliability, Cache

1. INTRODUCTION

Roughly 50% of chip real estate today is occupied by caches. To reduce static power dissipation, caches are operated at low voltage using techniques such as drowsy supply voltages [8] and sub-threshold voltage operation [7]. Lower supply voltages during drowsy operation, for instance, reduce the amount of charge held in a SRAM cell thereby making it highly susceptible to single event upsets (SEUs) and soft errors. The impact of SEUs is even more pronounced when chips are deployed in space electronic systems where the intensity of cosmic rays is much higher. In space, under the GEO solar flare model, the failure rate rises by 10 orders of magnitude [3]. Therefore, the resilience of a system to soft errors must be considered and measured during the design phase. Based on these measurements, appropriate error protection mechanisms must be added to every component where required in order to meet the system reliability goals.

Existing research on the impact of SEUs often assumes that soft errors resulting from SEUs are Poisson distributed. While SEUs follow a Poisson process, the resulting soft errors may not be Poisson distributed, as previously noted in [12], especially with higher SEU rates. Some specific reasons include: (1) accesses to memory bits are determined by program behavior or microarchitectural status, (2) faults are masked due to timing, logical, architectural, and microarchitectural factors, and (3) error protection codes change the constant Poisson rate into a time-varying rate.

Several recent studies have focused on computing the FIT rate due to SEUs [1][4][13][16][26]. FIT is a commonly used metric that measures the average number of failures in one billion hours. These studies are rooted in AVF (Architectural Vulnerability Factor) analysis which assumes that no more than one soft error strike can occur during the time a data bit resides in a processor structure. This single-bit fault assumption works well for the vulnerability of processor storage buffers such as load/store queues (LSQ) or reorder buffers (ROBs). Indeed, data resides in these structures for very short periods of time and hence the occurrence of more than one SEU during the residence time has, for all practical purposes, a probability of zero. As such these prior AVF-based approaches are preferred for computing the FIT rate of processor buffers. By contrast, in caches, particularly large last-level caches, a block of data can potentially reside for millions of cycles between two consecutive accesses to it. When residence time is long each byte, word or block becomes vulnerable to more than one single SEU strike. Hence, it is necessary to complement existing approaches to account for the possibility of multiple errors in large last-level caches. Under the single-bit error dominant assumption, which is the state of the art, the amount of protection against multi-bit errors afforded by simple schemes such as Single Error Correcting Double Error Detecting (SECDED) code cannot be estimated. In the presence of multi-bit errors, it is important to consider the cost/benefit tradeoffs of various protection schemes because error protection mechanisms are expensive in terms of silicon area, energy and performance penalty. Given the likely predominance of multiple errors in large caches, this paper focuses on benchmarking L2 cache vulnerability to soft errors.

One common approach to model and estimate the vulnerability of various components is fault injection. Faults are statistically injected into the detailed RTL model or simulation of the system under study [11][20][29][30]. While this framework is conceptually simple and can model any type of error, including multiple errors, it requires an astronomical number of extremely long simulation experiments to obtain statistically meaningful results: With the current SEU rate of the order of 10^{-25} per bit per cycle, no current benchmark that we are aware of is long enough to register even one single SEU during one of its execution. Even if fault injections are accelerated by orders upon orders of magnitude the procedure still requires massive amounts of test time and only produces statistical estimates. Furthermore the artificial acceleration of faults distorts the results of the test, as we will show at the end of this paper, and accurately correcting for these distortions is a daunting problem.

Given these challenges, we introduce PARMA (Precise Analytical Reliability Model for Architecture). PARMA uses a rigorous fault generation model to address temporal multi-bit errors (MBEs), starting with the probability of SEUs on a single-bit and then expounding the probabilities in both temporal and spatial dimensions while taking error protection schemes into consideration. In the temporal dimension PARMA accounts for the probability of multiple SEU strikes to the same bit during the bit's residency in cache while taking into account scenarios such as processor Stores into L1, and writebacks from L1 to L2 and from L2 to memory. In the spatial dimension PARMA derives the probabilities of one or more errors in bytes, words and finally blocks.

Currently PARMA does not handle the case where a single particle hit causes multiple bit errors (spatial MBEs). This is essentially due to the lack of a proven physical fault model on which we can build. Several studies [9][24] report on spatial MBEs in an array of RAM cells. To the best of our knowledge, only one model, which uses compound Poisson process [2], exists for deciding on the interleaving distance of SECDED code to suppress spatial MBEs. A compound Poisson process models multiple Poisson arrivals (or upsets) simultaneously. The test scheme used in this work is to observe every single spatial MBE and to declare whether this spatial MBE causes a failure or not, based on the interleaving distance of SECDED code. However, modeling various geometric upset patterns resulting from interactions of multiple spatial MBEs, temporal MBEs and multiple single bit errors in a single model is an unanswered, challenging. This is an open and important research area, since such a model would enable accurate evaluation of multi-bit error correcting schemes in the presence of spatial MBEs.

The contributions of our paper are as follows:

- We derive an analytical fault generation and propagation model that captures soft error events rigorously in SRAM arrays.

- We introduce PARMA, a unified framework to measure the reliability of SRAM arrays protected by any possible error protection scheme when temporal multi-bit soft errors exist.

- We show how PARMA can compare the reliability of various protection schemes from benchmark executions.

- By exploiting the accuracy of PARMA, we demonstrate that known techniques to evaluate cache FIT rates in the presence of SECDED, such as accelerated fault injection simulations and first-principle derivations based on Architectural Vulnerability Factor (AVF), can overestimate FIT rates by vast amounts.

- We introduce a new approximate analytical model for measuring the FIT rate of caches protected by word-level SECDED codes. Our new approximate model can quickly and more accurately estimate cache FIT rates in the presence of SECDED.

The rest of this paper is organized as follows. Section 2 develops the PARMA framework in detail and applies it to L2 caches to calculate the FIT rates of various error types under various error protection schemes. Section 3 describes our implementation of the framework on top of SimpleScalar [6]. Results are presented in Section 3.2. Comparison of PARMA with previous proposed schemes such as fault injection and AVF-based approaches are discussed in Section 4. The new approximate model is also presented in Section 4.2.2. Section 5 provides an overview of prior work. We conclude in Section 6.

2. THE PARMA MODEL

Not every SEU in an SRAM cell translates into an error. The impact of an SEU in a cache can be masked due to a variety of reasons such as: the cache line is invalid, the corrupted cache line is overwritten before it is read, the cache line is empty, or the block in the cache line is not referenced again. In general errors can be classified into three categories: Recoverable Errors (RE), Detected Unrecoverable Errors (DUE), and Silent Data Corruption errors (SDC).

Recoverable errors do not impact system integrity and are ignored. DUE FIT rates are further classified into TRUE DUE FIT rates and FALSE DUE FIT rates [26]. An SDC or a TRUE DUE happens when a fault affects the architectural state of the processor and finally corrupts the outcome of an execution. In this paper, we use a simple fault propagation model whereby a fault translates into an error when the fault corrupts the architectural state of the processor. This happens when the processor commits an instruction with at least one faulty bit in the instruction itself (e.g., in its opcode), or when a Load returns data from memory with at least one faulty bit and commits the data value to one of its architectural registers. When this happens, we say that the processor has *consumed* a faulty bit. Note that, to *consume* a faulty bit, the processor must commit the instruction or the Load value, not just fetch it. Thus we track cache errors up until instructions retire in the processor before we deem them SDC, TRUE DUE or FALSE DUE.

When a fault cannot be corrected or masked, we call it *failure*. Well-developed fault propagation models exist [4][13] that may track a fault all the way to I/O or some user-perceived stated, but many studies use simple fault propagation models [1][23] similar to ours to make the problem more tractable. This limitation can be lifted in the PARMA framework, but this is beyond the scope of this paper.

In every cycle, we measure the probability of any component failure in a system, assuming that no more than one failure of the same component can occur in the same cycle.

Let's index each processor cycle by j (where $1 \leq j \leq T_{exe}$). Then $h_{ERR}(j)$, the discrete time failure probability mass at the jth cycle, is defined as:

$$h_{ERR}(j) = \Pr(\text{Type } ERR \text{ failure at } j \\ | \text{ system survived all faults until } j) \tag{1}$$

This is the *conditional* probability that a failure of type *ERR* (*ERR* can be SDC, TRUE DUE or FALSE DUE) has occurred at the jth cycle, given that the system survived all types of faults up to the jth cycle. Thus the total expected number of failures of type *ERR* observed during the execution time T_{exe} of a benchmark is:

$$H_{ERR}(T_{exe}) = \sum_{j=1}^{T_{exc}} h_{ERR}(j) = E[ERR] \tag{2}$$

$H_{ERR}(T_{exe})/T_{exe}$ is the failure rate for errors of type *ERR*. We can extrapolate the observed failure rate to the more familiar FIT rate, simply by scaling time. Then, the average FIT rate for a set of applications running one after another, independently on a processor is calculated as:

$$\overline{FIT_{ERR}} = \sum_{\forall \text{ benchmark } i} f_i \times FIT_{i,ERR}$$
$$= \sum_{\forall \text{ benchmark } i} f_i \times \frac{E_i[ERR]}{(T_{exe})_i \times CyclePeriod} \times 3600 \times 10^9 \tag{3}$$
$$= \frac{\sum_{\forall \text{ benchmark } i} E_i[ERR]}{T_{exe} \times CyclePeriod} \times 3600 \times 10^9$$

where f_i ($=T_{exe,i}/T_{exe,all}$) is the fraction of time taken by the execution of benchmark i. $FIT_{i,ERR}$ is the FIT rate extrapolated from $E_i[ERR]$. We will use (3) to report our results in FIT rates.

2.1 Physical Model – Target System

The system considered in this paper is shown in Figure 1. The L2 cache in the dotted frame is the only component vulnerable to soft errors. All other system components are assumed to be totally fault-free (bullet-proof). This approach isolates the contribution of the L2 cache to the overall FIT rates of the entire system.

2.2 Physical Model – SEU Model

PARMA uses one bit of data and one clock cycle as the minimum units of space and time. The probability that one bit is upset in one cycle is denoted p. We make two basic assumptions about the physical fault model: (i) All clock cycles are independent: whether a bit is struck or not at clock cycle i is independent of whether or not it was hit in cycles $k = 1$ to i-1 (This allows us to consider SEUs as a renewal process, so that the probability distribution of SEUs is always the same after every cycle.), and (ii) all cache bits are independent: there is no correlation between SEUs affecting any two cache bits.

2.3 Vulnerability Clock

In between two consecutive accesses to a memory block in the L2 cache, the block is vulnerable to SEUs. Memory is byte-addressable

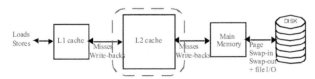

Figure 1. Memory hierarchy model

and therefore PARMA must track the integrity of a memory unit no less than one byte. To this effect, in PARMA, each byte of memory is associated with a *vulnerability clock* which is initialized to zero and which keeps track of the time the byte is exposed to SEUs in L2 while taking into consideration Stores to L1, and writebacks from L1 to L2 and from L2 to memory. In this section, we briefly explain how vulnerability clocks are managed in the PARMA framework.

As soon as a block of data is brought from memory into L2 all the bytes in this block become vulnerable and the vulnerability clock of each byte ticks up in every clock cycle, while the block resides in the L2 cache. At the time when a block is loaded from L2 to L1 there is no knowledge as yet of which bytes are actually going to be consumed by the processor. Hence, we save the snapshot of L2 vulnerability clocks for future use as soon as the L1 copy is filled-in. When the processor accesses L1 and consumes a subset of bytes then we mark the consumed bytes. Eventually when the L1 block is evicted (or when the program finishes) we then compute SDC FIT rates or TRUE DUE FIT rates using information from the saved snapshot of L2 vulnerability cycles and the bytes consumed by the processor. In addition, eviction from L1 can change the vulnerability status of the L2 copy. When a block is loaded in L1 two copies of the same block coexist, one in L1 and one in L2. The copy in L1 is bullet-proof to any strike, but the copy in L2 is still vulnerable. Thus we must keep track of two cases: (i) the block copy in L1 is modified, in which case it will be written back and the vulnerability clocks of every byte of the L2 copy will be reset to zero so that PARMA does not count the same error twice, or (ii) the block copy in L1 is not modified, in which case the block will not be written back to L2. In this latter case, the block copy in L2 remains vulnerable during the entire stay of the block in L1 and the vulnerability clocks of its bytes will not be reset when the block is silently replaced in L1.

When a block is replaced in L2, it is either replaced silently, i.e. the block is not written back to main memory since the block is clean, or it is written back to main memory if it is dirty. If it is replaced silently, then the vulnerability clocks for all the bytes in the block remain unchanged in the main memory as if they had never been loaded in L2 before. If it is written back to main memory because it was modified, then each byte in the L2 block carries its corresponding vulnerability clock with it to main memory but the clocks stop ticking in memory (since memory is also assumed to be bullet-proof) and will restart later on when the block is reloaded in the L2 cache on a miss.

We update failure metrics every time a cache line is accessed. At these times, we calculate the conditional probability of various failure types, called discrete failure probability mass, based on the vulnerability clock in each byte of the block. The first step towards this goal is to calculate the distribution of bit faults in a set of bytes.

2.4 Overview of PARMA Probability Calculations

Figure 2 overviews PARMA's calculations of the failure rates. PARMA starts with the probability p that one bit is flipped in one processor cycle. Then, exploiting the basic assumption that the rate of SEUs is time-independent, PARMA expands the probability p into $q(N_c)$, the probability that a given bit is faulty after N_c vulnerability cycles. This is illustrated in Figure 2(a), and will be explained in Section 2.5.1. Then, exploiting the assumption that SEUs are spatially independent, PARMA expands the probability $q(N_c)$ into $q_b(k)$, the probability that a byte has k faulty bit(s) after N_c

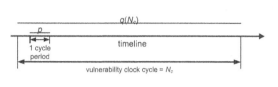

(a) Temporal expansion of failure probability:
from 1 cycle period to N_c vulnerability clock cycle period on 1 bit

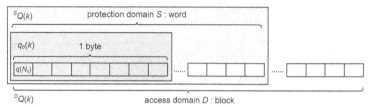

(b) Spatial expansion of failure probability: from 1 bit to 1 byte to 1 word to 1 block

Figure 2. Temporal and spatial expansions of probability calculations when every individual word is protected

vulnerability cycles. This is illustrated in Figure 2(b), and will be explained in Section 2.5.2.

We call a set of bytes that are bundled together as a *domain*. Let's denote an arbitrary domain as A. Then the goal of PARMA is to calculate ${}^AQ(k)$, the probability that there are k faulty bit(s) after N_c vulnerability cycles in a domain A, whenever A is accessed. Once we have ${}^AQ(k)$, PARMA determines what k should be in order to have an error in that domain, considering the kind of protection scheme covering a domain (for example, an unprotected domain will have one SDC whenever $k > 0$). Throughout the benchmark execution, PARMA keeps measuring the probabilities of having errors in the domain. Finally, based on the number of errors expected whenever the domain is accessed, PARMA accumulates the expected numbers of faults using ${}^AQ(k)$s measured during the benchmark execution.

Let's call a set of bytes that are accessed together an *access domain* (denoted D), and a set of bytes that are protected together by the same code under any specific protection scheme a *protection domain* (denoted S). Access domain and protection domain can be the same or one can be a subset of the other. For example the cache block is the access domain when the L2 cache writes back to main memory since the transfer happens at the block -level, but the protection domain is a word if a word-level SECDED code is used. In this case, one faulty bit will be corrected and two faulty bits will be detected within a word. In general, the protection domain can be a word, a block, or a set of bytes that are protected together as in interleaved SECDED [17]. In the following we assume that the access domain is an L2 cache block and that the protection domain is a subset of the access domain.

Figure 2(b) illustrates how PARMA calculates ${}^SQ(k)$, the probability that the set of bytes in a protection domain S has k faulty bit(s) after N_c vulnerability cycles, from probability $q_b(k)$, by exploiting the spatial-independence assumption further. This expansion will be explained in Section 2.5.3. In the example of Figure 2(b), the protection domain is one word.

2.5 Fault Generation Model: Probability Distribution of Faults in a Set of Bytes

2.5.1 Temporal Expansion from 1 to N_c Vulnerability Clock Cycles in a Bit

We first calculate the probability of i SEUs on one cache bit in N_c vulnerability clock cycles.

$$P_i(N_c) = \binom{N_c}{i} p^i (1-p)^{N_c - i}, i = 0,..., N_c \tag{4}$$

This result is based on the fact that, in any cycle, one SEU can cause a bit to flip, with probability p. A bit can flip i times up to N_c times

in N_c vulnerability cycles, and bit flips may happen in any one set of i cycles amongst the N_c vulnerability cycles.

With (4), we can calculate the probability q that a given cache bit will be faulty after N_c vulnerability cycles, knowing that a bit is faulty if it is flipped an odd number of times during N_c cycles.

$$q(N_c) = \sum_{i=0}^{\lfloor N_c/2 \rfloor} P_{2i+1}(N_c) \tag{5}$$

2.5.2 Spatial Expansion from 1 Bit to 1 Byte

Given the value of $q(N_c)$ we calculate the probabilities $q_b(k)$ that a byte residing in an L2 cache line will experience k bit errors in N_c vulnerability cycles, where $k = 0$ to 8 (the number of errors can be from 0 to 8). We first choose any k out of 8 bits and then compute the probability of errors in these k bits while the remaining (8-k) bits are fault-free.

$$q_b(k) = \binom{8}{k} q(N_c)^k (1 - q(N_c))^{8-k}, k = 0,...,8 \tag{6}$$

To simplify the notation, $q_b(k)$ is an implicit function of N_c.

2.5.3 Spatial Expansion from 1 Byte to the Whole Protection Domain

We can now calculate the probability distribution of k bit faults ($k = 0$ to $8N_S$) in a protection domain S of N_S bytes. To do this, we index each byte by j, $j = 1$ to N_S. We use the notation $\{j\} \in S$ to sweep all bytes in protection domain S. A vulnerability clock with value N_c is associated with each byte and is implicit in the notation $q_{b,j}(k)$. The probability of k faulty bits within the protection domain can be expressed as a function of all $q_{b,j}(k)$'s as follows:

$$^SQ_m(k) = \sum_{(\sum l_j = k)} \prod_{\{j\} \in S} q_{b,j}(l_j) \tag{7}$$

where m is an optional index characterizing the protection domain in the access domain. In (7), we choose all the cases in which S has k faulty bits among N_S bytes and compose the probability accordingly. m is omitted in the notation if the access domain holds only one protection domain. We do not need to calculate the probability distributions at the granularity of an access domain, as error types such as DUE or SDC are calculated for each protection domain. Because errors in different protection domains are independent of each other, they are additive. For instance, if L2 blocks are protected by parity then the summation of (7) over all odd k values and all cache blocks gives the L2 DUE. This calculation is performed whenever a block is fetched from L2 to L1. We now show how to classify errors into SDC and TRUE DUE based on how the data is accessed in L1.

Table 1. Errors as a function of k and N_S

	No Parity	1-bit Parity		SECDED			
				TRUE DUE		SDC	
	SDC	TRUE DUE	SDC	word-level	block-level	word-level	block-level
D: Access Domain	Block	Block	Block	Blk containing M words	Block	Blk containing M words	Block
S: Protection Domain	N/A	Block	Block	Word	Block	Word	Block
Faulty bits	≥ 1 in C	$\forall$ odd in S, ≥ 1 in C	$\forall$ even >0 in S, ≥ 1 in C	2 in any S_m, ≥ 1 in that C_m	2 in S, ≥ 1 in C	≥ 3 in any S_m, ≥ 1 in that C_m	≥ 3 in S, ≥ 1 in C
Notation	$^B E^{NP,SDC}$	$^B E^{P1B,TRUE\_DUE}$	$^B E^{P1B,SDC}$	$^W E^{SW,TRUE\_DUE}$	$^B E^{SB,TRUE\_DUE}$	$^W E^{SW,SDC}$	$^B E^{SB,SDC}$

2.6 Fault Propagation Model: SDC FIT Rates and DUE FIT Rates in Each Error Protection Scheme

2.6.1 Probability Calculations of Generic SDC Errors and TRUE DUE Errors

Even if a corrupted L2 cache block reaches the first level cache, the execution may still be correct. Indeed, if no bit in the block is *consumed* during the sojourn of the block in L1, then faults in an L2 cache block cause no error and, if it was detected as an L2 DUE, it becomes a FALSE DUE. The first time a faulty bit is *consumed* from the block residing in L1, the bit fault turns into either an SDC or a TRUE DUE. If the processor stores a value in an L1 byte before the byte is read then that byte becomes error-free. We need to consider all the above scenarios to compute TRUE DUE and SDC.

Let's denote the set of consumed bytes in the L1 copy of a protection domain as C. Then the complement set $\overline{C}$ contains all the *unconsumed* bytes in the same domain. C and $\overline{C}$ are illustrated in Figure 3. $\overline{C}$ is the set of unconsumed bytes when the L1 copy is evicted. The union of C and $\overline{C}$ is the protection domain. We use the same notation as in (7). The probability of having k faulty bits *only* in $\overline{C}$, but having no faulty bit in C is obtained as:

$$^{C_m}Q_m(0) \times {}^{\overline{C_m}}Q_m(k) \qquad (8)$$

where m is an optional index for a protection domain in the access domain. When the protection domain is the same as the access domain, we drop the optional index m from (8). (8) simply states that C has no fault and $\overline{C}$ has k faults. $\overline{C}$ is not known until the block is replaced in L1, or until the end of the execution, whichever comes first. (8) is used to calculate SDC and TRUE DUE FIT rates in the following subsections.

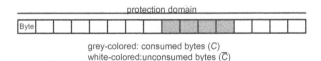

grey-colored: consumed bytes (C)
white-colored: unconsumed bytes ($\overline{C}$)

Figure 3. C : A set of consumed bytes in a protection domain

2.6.2 Protection Schemes

We have shown the generality of the approach with any granularity of protection and access domains. In the balance of this paper, we restrict the protection domain to either a word (W) or a block (B), and the access domain to a block. We consider four schemes: no error detection or correction (NP), 1 bit parity (P1B), SECDED per block (SB) and SECDED per word (SW). Table 1 summarizes SDC, TRUE DUE and FALSE DUE classifications in different protection schemes. The number of faulty bits necessary to diagnose DUE or SDC are shown in Table 1 for all scenarios. For example, when the L2 cache is protected with word-level SECDED, it encounters an SDC when (i) three or more faulty bits are in the protection domains (word) when an L2 block is accessed, and (ii) the processor *consumes* at least one bit among these faulty bits. In the following subsections, we show how to calculate SDC FIT rates and DUE FIT rates using (7) and (8).

2.6.3 SDC Errors

If an L2 block is copied to L1 with at least one undetected faulty bit, then one SDC is counted for all cases when any one of the faulty bit(s) is consumed. As shown in Table 1 (row "faulty bits"), the SDC FIT rate depends on the protection scheme in L2. To compute the probability of an SDC, we simply subtract the probability of having undetected faulty bit(s) in C only, from the probability of having undetected faulty bit(s) in the entire block. Thus, the expected number of SDCs under no-protection (NP) is as follows:

$$^B E^{NP,SDC} = \sum_{k=1}^{8N_B} {}^B Q(k) - {}^C Q(0) \times \sum_{i=1}^{8N_{\overline{C}}} {}^{\overline{C}}Q(i) \qquad (9)$$

The first summation term is the probability of any number of faults in the block and the second term is the probability of no fault in C multiplied by the probability of any number of faults in $\overline{C}$. Similarly, with single error detection per block (denoted as P1B), all odd numbers of error are detected but even numbers of error go undetected. So the expected number of SDCs is:

$$^B E^{P1B,SDC} = \sum_{\forall even\, k>0}^{8N_B} {}^B Q(k) - {}^C Q(0) \times \sum_{\forall even\, i>0}^{8N_{\overline{C}}} {}^{\overline{C}}Q(i) \qquad (10)$$

Consider now the case of an L2 cache with SECDED per block (denoted as SB). The expected numbers of SDCs is:

$$^B E^{SB,SDC} = \sum_{k=3}^{8N_B} {}^B Q(k) - {}^C Q(0) \times \sum_{i=3}^{8N_{\overline{C}}} {}^{\overline{C}}Q(i) \qquad (11)$$

Finally, consider the case of an L2 cache with SECDED per word (denoted as SW). Let N_W be the number of bytes in a word and M be the number of words in a block. Up to M faulty bits can be corrected in a block and we need to include all M words whenever a block is accessed. Let's index each word in the block by m, where $m = 1$ to M. The expected number of SDCs with word-level SECDED (denoted as SW) is:

$$^B E^{SW,SDC} = \sum_{m=1}^{M} {}^W E_m^{SW,SDC}$$

$$= \sum_{m=1}^{M} \sum_{k=3}^{8N_W} {}^W Q_m(k) - \sum_{m=1}^{M} \left[{}^{C_m} Q_m(0) \times \sum_{i=3}^{8N_{\overline{C_m}}} {}^{\overline{C_m}} Q_m(i) \right] \quad (12)$$

Whenever an L2 cache line is filled from memory, an L2 block is accessed due to an L1 miss, or an L1 block is evicted (discarded or written back to L2), (9)-(12) are invoked to yield the expected number of SDC faults since the last access to the block. These expected numbers of failures are accumulated until the simulation ends.

2.6.4 DUE Errors

Unlike for SDC errors, DUE FIT rates are further classified as TRUE DUE FIT rates and FALSE DUE FIT rates. As shown in Table 1, DUE FIT rates are classified differently in different protection schemes. DUEs are raised if and as soon as they are detected – i.e., when an L2 block is fetched if it is protected by a protection code with error detection capabilities. Just as for SDC FIT rates, PARMA counts them as TRUE DUE FIT rates if at least one faulty bit is consumed by the processor after the DUE has been raised. FALSE DUE FIT rates are computed as the probability that all faulty bits fall in $\overline{C}$ only. TRUE DUE FIT rates are obtained by subtracting the probability of FALSE DUE from the total probability that the faulty bits fall anywhere in the protection domain. There is no DUE under NP. With P1B, DUE FIT rates are calculated as:

$$^B E^{P1B,FALSE\_DUE} = {}^C Q(0) \times \sum_{\forall odd\ i}^{8N_{\overline{C}}} {}^{\overline{C}} Q(i) \quad (13)$$

$$^B E^{P1B,TRUE\_DUE} = \sum_{\forall odd\ k}^{8N_B} {}^B Q(k) - {}^C Q(0) \times \sum_{\forall odd\ i}^{8N_{\overline{C}}} {}^{\overline{C}} Q(i) \quad (14)$$

With block-level SECDED, the expected number of DUEs is:

$$^B E^{SB,FALSE\_DUE} = {}^C Q(0) \times {}^{\overline{C}} Q(2) \quad (15)$$

$$^B E^{SB,TRUE\_DUE} = {}^B Q(2) - {}^C Q(0) \times {}^{\overline{C}} Q(2) \quad (16)$$

With word-level SECDED, the expected number of DUEs is:

$$^B E^{SW,FALSE\_DUE} = \sum_{m=1}^{M} {}^W E_m^{SW,FALSE\_DUE}$$

$$= \sum_{m=1}^{M} \left[{}^{C_m} Q_m(0) \times {}^{\overline{C_m}} Q_m(2) \right] \quad (17)$$

$$^B E^{SW,TRUE\_DUE} = \sum_{m=1}^{M} {}^W E_m^{SW,TRUE\_DUE}$$

$$= \sum_{m=1}^{M} {}^W Q_m(2) - \sum_{m=1}^{M} \left[{}^{C_m} Q_m(0) \times {}^{\overline{C_m}} Q_m(2) \right] \quad (18)$$

3. PARMA SIMULATIONS

3.1 Parameters in PARMA Simulations

We have implemented PARMA on top of the SimpleScalar/Alpha simulator [6] to measure FIT rates for various benchmarks. The PARMA model starts with a probability p representing the probability that any one bit is flipped during one clock period. To calculate p, we use the Poisson rate λ projected by ITRS 2007 [22], which is 1,150 SEU FIT rates (equivalent to SER in 10^9 hours) for a 1Mbit SRAM in 65nm technology. The target processor frequency is 3GHz, so the value of p is 1.0155×10^{-25} from the Poisson probability mass function by summing the probabilities of all the odd numbers of SEU arrivals during a cycle.

In our simulations we add the time to decode the protection check bits to the latency of a block access. 1-bit parity causes little performance penalty and hence the access latency with 1-bit parity is same as no protection scheme. On the other hand, both space (number of check bits) and time (decoding delays) overheads are incurred for SECDED. Naseer, et al. [18] reported the decoder delays for various protection codes in a 90nm technology. We have extrapolated the reported SECDED decoder delays from [18] and scaled it to our 65nm technology. In summary, 4-byte word-level SECDED has 7 check bits with 0.827ns decoder delay. Similarly, 32-byte block-level SECDED has 11 check bits overhead with 1.244ns decoder delay. The resulting L2 access latencies as calculated by Cacti [25] for different protection schemes are shown in Table 2.

Table 2. Cache hierarchy parameters

Cache	Size	Associativity	Latency [cycles]		
IL1	16KB	1-way	2		
DL1	16KB	4-way	3		
UL2	256KB	8-way	NP/P1B: 10	SW (4B): 13	SB (32B): 14

The target processor simulated in our 65nm technology is a 4-wide out-of-order processor with 64-entry ROB, 32-entry LSQ, and McFarling's hybrid branch predictor. The processor runs at 3GHz with 150 cycles of latency to off-chip main memory. L1-I, L1-D and unified L2 caches all have 32-byte lines. All the caches are non-blocking, write-back caches. All the cache parameters shown in Table 2 are obtained from Cacti 5 [25]. The delay for fetching and decoding ECC check bits is included in the L2 latencies.

The benchmarks are execution samples of 100 million committed instructions obtained from 18 SPEC2K benchmarks compiled for the alpha ISA and shown in Table 3. Every sample was selected using SimPoint [19], which is a well-know method for selecting the most representative sample sequence of instructions to simulate.

Table 3. FIT rates in various protection schemes

(a) NP_ SDC: no-protection/SDC
  P1B_TRUE_DUE:1bit parity/TRUE DUE
(b) P1B_FALSE_DUE:1bit parity/FALSE DUE
(c) P1B_ SDC: 1bit parity/SDC
(d) SB_TRUE_DUE: block-level 1bit SECDED/TRUE DUE
(e) SB_FALSE_DUE: block-level 1bit SECDED /FALSE DUE

(f) SB_SDC: block-level 1bit SECDED /SDC
(g) SW_TRUE_DUE: word-level 1bit SECDED /TRUE DUE
(h) SW_FALSE_DUE: word-level 1bit SECDED /TRUE DUE
(i) SW_SDC: word-level 1bit SECDED /SDC
(j) AVF_SDC: SDC calculated by AVF method
(k) %_Diff: Percentage difference of SDC (PARMA/AVF)

Bench	(a)	(b)	(c)	(d)	(e)	(f)	(g)	(h)	(i)	(j)	(k)
ammp	320.32	419.27	2.50E-14	2.53E-14	1.53E-14	1.32E-29	1.99E-15	2.92E-15	1.02E-31	320.32	0.000%
art	48.76	16.74	1.22E-16	1.22E-16	3.70E-17	3.89E-34	1.03E-17	9.01E-18	3.21E-36	48.76	0.000%
crafty	429.47	716.45	1.99E-14	2.34E-14	4.74E-14	4.24E-30	1.85E-15	6.41E-15	2.83E-32	429.47	0.000%
eon	382.25	298.23	1.45E-14	1.63E-14	6.03E-15	2.72E-30	1.69E-15	9.77E-16	3.57E-32	382.25	0.000%
facerec	98.08	0.59	9.80E-17	9.79E-17	1.37E-18	8.88E-35	1.18E-17	2.45E-19	1.22E-36	98.08	0.000%
galgel	60.35	77.61	9.52E-17	9.52E-17	8.53E-17	3.54E-34	8.15E-18	1.38E-17	2.72E-36	60.35	0.000%
gap	138.59	22.27	3.32E-16	3.94E-16	5.26E-17	2.34E-33	4.30E-17	8.80E-18	2.59E-35	138.59	0.000%
gcc	349.11	229.96	3.76E-15	4.86E-15	3.25E-15	1.89E-31	4.65E-16	4.68E-16	1.86E-33	349.11	0.000%
gzip	547.53	1115.56	1.05E-14	1.17E-14	9.56E-15	2.86E-31	1.30E-15	1.24E-15	3.67E-33	547.53	0.000%
mcf	14.71	14.43	1.28E-17	1.28E-17	3.23E-17	2.93E-35	1.13E-18	4.35E-18	1.89E-37	14.71	0.000%
mesa	460.52	112.19	4.50E-15	5.03E-15	8.57E-16	4.01E-32	5.44E-16	1.52E-16	4.73E-34	460.52	0.000%
parser	138.54	380.34	1.86E-15	2.00E-15	4.12E-15	4.59E-32	1.47E-16	5.82E-16	2.97E-34	138.54	0.000%
perlbmk	100.82	315.37	2.74E-15	2.97E-15	8.85E-15	6.96E-32	2.36E-16	1.17E-15	4.46E-34	100.82	0.000%
sixtrack	76.24	7.92	3.75E-16	3.91E-16	1.39E-16	9.70E-33	4.26E-17	2.14E-17	1.12E-34	76.24	0.000%
twolf	193.40	419.25	1.52E-15	1.56E-15	2.88E-15	1.45E-32	1.24E-16	4.11E-16	1.06E-34	193.40	0.000%
vortex	831.26	324.74	8.57E-15	9.63E-15	2.80E-15	1.70E-31	1.04E-15	4.31E-16	1.93E-33	831.26	0.000%
vpr	184.31	369.25	2.16E-15	2.18E-15	3.27E-15	3.04E-32	1.83E-16	4.79E-16	2.45E-34	184.31	0.000%
wupwise	146.69	130.00	1.99E-15	2.02E-15	7.28E-16	1.75E-32	1.63E-16	1.70E-16	1.42E-34	146.69	0.000%
Avg	155.66	217.17	2.53E-15	3.45E-15	3.59E-15	8.34E-31	2.25E-16	4.07E-16	2.92E-33	155.66	0.000%

3.2 Simulation Results

Table 3 shows the FIT rates extrapolated from the failure rates measured in our simulations. The average FIT rates in the last row are derived from (3). Without any error protection the SDC FIT rate (Table 3(a)) is still very high, varying from 15 to 832, which is not acceptable for most manufacturers today. With 1-bit parity, SDC FIT rates are in effect turned into TRUE DUE FIT rates. The SDC FIT rate with 1-bit parity is 16 orders of magnitude smaller than the SDC FIT rate with no protection. Hence, 1-bit parity is more than sufficient to satisfy the stringent SDC FIT rate requirements of most manufacturers. However the DUE FIT rate may not be within the reliability budget for an L2 cache. By upgrading to block-level SECDED (column (d) and (e) in Table 3) or word-level SECDED (column (g) and (h) in Table 3), the average DUE FIT rates drop by a factor of 5.30×10^{16} and 5.90×10^{17} respectively. Due to different memory footprints, and different memory behaviors in each benchmark, the FIT rate varies widely amongst programs, as shown in Table 3. Note that the SDC FIT rates calculated by PARMA match AVF FIT rates down to 10 decimal points, giving 0% differences in all cases in Table 3(column (k)). This is expected.

One distinct advantage of word-level SECDED over block-level SECDED is that word-level SECDED can correct more words and

thus yields lower DUE FIT rates than block-level SECDED. The numbers show that word-level SECDED capable of correcting one faulty bit in every four-byte word is on average about 11.14 times stronger than block-level SECDED capable of correcting one faulty bit in every 32-byte block. However, word-level SECDED has bit overhead for a 256KB cache. Because the block-level SECDED DUE is already very tiny ($10^{-15} \sim 10^{-17}$), reducing the failure rate again by an order of magnitude may not be a critical reliability gain, although using more silicon with word-level SECDED as compared to block-level SECDED might need stronger justification. If the reduction of the failure rate is the sole purpose of a (stronger) word-level SECDED, investing more in silicon may not be justified.

4. COMPARISON WITH PREVIOUS MODELS

Current popular models to estimate FIT rates in the presence of error protection codes include accelerated fault injection simulations and approximate analytical models. In this section we demonstrate that previous models can vastly overestimate FIT rates for a variety of reasons. Therefore PARMA is a necessary tool to reach accurate design decisions.

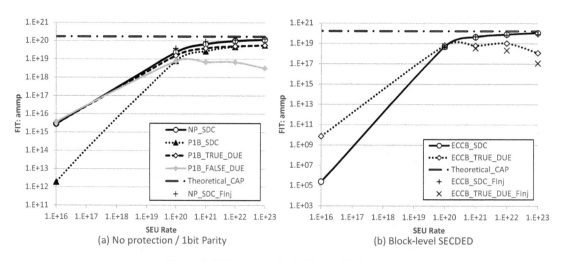

(a) No protection / 1bit Parity (b) Block-level SECDED

Figure 4. FIT rates under different SEU rates

4.1 Accelerated Fault Injection Simulations

Fault injection simulations are common for reliability studies. They have the advantage to handle various fault scenarios in a fairly simple framework. For example, the effectiveness of error correction codes can be measured with fault injection simulation. Unfortunately fault injection simulations require greatly accelerated SEU rates in order to benchmark the vulnerability of caches because the benchmarks' execution times are extremely short compared to the expected time between two SEUs in the real world. In order to observe at least several SEUs that are not architecturally masked during one benchmark execution, one need to raise the SEU rate to the order of 10^{20} SEUs per 10^9 hours, an astronomical 17 orders of magnitude acceleration. 10^{20} SEUs corresponds roughly to $p=10^{-8}$ and generates about 10 SEUs during a 1 billion cycle simulation run, and fewer than 10 errors when accounting for architectural masking effect. Accelerating injection rates is problematic because it causes distortions in the results and no credible methodology exists to scale the results to the real SEU rate. This is true both for quantitative *and* qualitative design explorations.

Figure 4 shows the FIT rates measured by accurate PARMA simulations for the SimPoint of the SPEC ammp benchmark for a range of accelerated SEU rates, which includes the fault injection rates range compatible with feasible simulations (i.e., SEU rate >> 10^{20}). PARMA measurements of SDC FIT rates and TRUE DUE FIT rates under 1-bit Parity and block-level SECDED in this SEU range are shown in Figure 4(a) and (b). Several fault injection test results are also displayed in Figure 4 with suffix 'FInj'. The horizontal line labeled 'Theoretical_CAP' shows the maximum possible failure rates obtained when every access to any L2 block with a non-zero vulnerability clock is counted as one failure with probability one. With highly accelerated SEU rates, FIT rate measurements from fault injection simulations converge to this cap. As shown in the figure, under very high SEU rates, SDC FIT rates catch up with DUE FIT rates under Parity to a point that they become equal, which is a highly unrealistic result in reality.

The distortions are even more serious under block-level ECC (Figure 4(b)). We observe that in the lower SEU rate range TRUE

DUE FIT rates dominate SDC FIT rates (as is expected in the real world). However, as the SEU rate increases, an inversion occurs, in which SDC FIT rates dominate TRUE DUE FIT rates, both a non-intuitive and incorrect observation. The basic reason for these distortions can be illustrated with a simple example. Consider the case that a block is protected with 1-bit parity. This block will experience SDCs only when an even number of bits are flipped, and all odd numbers of bit flips will turn into DUE. Since 1-bit flips are the most common case one would expect that SDC FIT rates would be much lower than TRUE DUE rates. However, with highly accelerated SEU rates, the probability of having an even number of faulty bits becomes almost the same as the probability of having an odd number of faulty bits. Hence, the SDC FIT rate and DUE FIT rate converge. Similarly, in the case of SECDED the probability of having more than two faulty bits overwhelms the probability of having two faulty bits and hence SDC and TRUE DUE FIT rates converge even with SECDED protection.

The main lesson to learn from Figure 4 is that FIT rate distortions are high in the high SEU rate range compatible with fault injection rates typically used in simulations. With SEU rates higher than 10^{20} SEUs per 10^9 hours, the measured FIT is limited by the theoretical cap, and the non-linear effects in the relation between SDC FIT rates or DUE FIT rates and SEU rates lead to incorrect *qualitative* conclusions. These observations show the importance of an accurate tool such as PARMA to evaluate the relative strength of various error protection schemes.

4.2 Approximate Analytical Models for ECC-Protected Caches

PARMA provides accurate FIT rate measurements. With PARMA we can now validate prior approaches taken to compare the strength of various error protection codes. We have just shown that fault injection simulations can distort the observations. We now evaluate the effectiveness of existing approximate analytical models to compute the FIT rates of caches protected by SECDED, and then propose a better one.

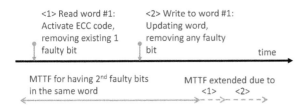

<1> Read word #1:
Activate ECC code, removing existing 1 faulty bit

<2> Write to word #1:
Updating word, removing any faulty bit

time

MTTF for having 2nd faulty bits in the same word

MTTF extended due to <1> <2>

Figure 5. MTTF for SECDED protected cache [17][20] affected by cache accesses

Approximate analytical models have been proposed in the past to evaluate the Mean Time To Failure (MTTF) and FIT rates of caches protected by SECDED [17][20]. We will now compare the FIT rates measured by PARMA with FIT rates computed by these approximate models and show why these prior approaches overestimate FIT rates significantly. The main reason for this vast discrepancy is that these existing approximate models overlook the fact that, between two successive SEU strikes in a word, several fault mitigating events can occur. Every time a word is accessed, error correction is invoked and a single fault can be corrected multiple times, thus prolonging the MTTF by vast amounts of time (see Figure 5). Therefore these approximate models underestimate the MTTF and overestimate the FIT rates. Based on this insight we have developed a more rigorous approximate model for cache failures under SECDED protection. This new model predicts FIT rates that are much closer to the accurate values computed by PARMA than existing approximate models.

4.2.1 Previous Approximate Models

The calculation of FIT using AVF is as follows [5][12]:

$$\text{Soft Error Rate}_{component}$$
$$= \text{AVF}_{component} \times \text{intrinsic Soft Error Rate}_{component} \quad (19)$$

To apply (19) in the case of a cache where words are protected by SECDED, we need to find first the intrinsic SER (Soft Error Rate) of a word-level SECDED protected cache. To compute the intrinsic SER for a word-level SECDED protected cache it is necessary to estimate the expected time for having two faulty bits in a word. Models for such estimation were proposed in [17] and [20] in the context of cache scrubbing. There the goal was to determine the optimal cache scrubbing interval such that only a maximum of one fault is expected to occur between scrubbing intervals so that scrubbing provides a guard mechanism against the occurrence of SDC faults. These models, in effect, calculate the intrinsic SER for caches protected by SECDED.

These models calculate the expected time of a second SEU strike given that there has been a first SEU strike already. The most critical information that was overlooked in these studies is that in between any two SEU strikes single-bit faults will be corrected by SECDED if there is at least one access to the cache in between the two strikes. Figure 5 illustrates how cache accesses affect the The first read activates SECDED for the word and the following write overwrites the word. The effect in these two cases is to improve (reduce) the intrinsic SER.

In order to evaluate how cache accesses and corrections affect the MTTF under SECDED protection we now compare PARMA results with results obtained by the approximate model in [20]. Note that the authors in [17] compared their model with the closed form MTTF formula in [20] and concluded that both models have very

similar outcomes. Hence, our comparison results with [20] and the resulting conclusions also hold well against [17].

In [20] the authors provided a closed-form MTTF analytical model for caches protected by word-level SECDED as:

$$\text{MTTF} = \frac{1}{L}\sqrt{\frac{\pi}{2M}} \quad (20)$$

where L is the soft error rate in the protection domain and M is the total number of protection domains in the cache.

Table 4 DUE FIT rates in word-level SECDED protected cache

Name	AVF	AVFxFIT from (20)	FIT from Eq (23)	FIT from PARMA
ammp	40.977%	2.9374	8.4182E-14	4.9114E-15
art	2.849%	0.2042	4.5179E-16	1.93476E-17
crafty	61.078%	4.3784	3.3463E-14	8.25685E-15
eon	99.049%	7.1003	1.3441E-13	2.67121E-15
facerec	4.319%	0.3096	1.3138E-15	1.20444E-17
galgel	6.010%	0.4308	7.0577E-16	2.19513E-17
gap	7.118%	0.5103	4.5248E-16	5.18293E-17
gcc	27.658%	1.9827	7.7612E-15	9.33375E-16
gzip	83.466%	5.9832	6.9763E-14	2.53328E-15
mcf	1.267%	0.0908	2.9364E-16	5.47892E-18
mesa	30.070%	2.1555	1.6881E-14	6.96557E-16
parser	22.983%	1.6475	1.8796E-14	7.28453E-16
perlbmk	31.621%	2.2667	2.9209E-14	1.41053E-15
sixtrack	3.916%	0.2807	5.9788E-16	6.39658E-17
twolf	26.750%	1.9176	2.2392E-14	5.35443E-16
vortex	53.171%	3.8115	3.6437E-14	1.4704E-15
vpr	24.232%	1.7371	4.0074E-14	6.61992E-16
wupwise	12.183%	0.8733	1.1242E-14	3.33145E-16
Average	27.333%	2.1454	2.8246E-14	6.31707E-16

With (20), we calculate the FIT rate of our target cache with word-level SECDED and we multiply it by the AVF ([1][4]) we measured on our target system executing the target benchmarks. Table 4 shows the results (3rd column).

We observe that the model in [20] (and [17] as well) overestimates the FIT rate of the cache. The PARMA FIT estimates (5th column) are 16 *orders of magnitude* smaller. Tens of millions of L2 cache accesses are made during the execution, each of which may correct single faults in words, thus prolonging the MTTF.

4.2.2 A New Approximate Model

PARMA is not just a benchmarking tool; it also provides deeper insights into the reliability of cache structures. Prior analytical models overestimate FIT rates by not considering how intermediate accesses may activate ECC to clean single-bit faults before a second SEU strike. In this section our goal is to introduce a new approximate analytical model using AVF methodology [4] to estimate the DUE FIT rate of SECDED caches while taking into account ECC activation effects as well as the architectural masking effects.

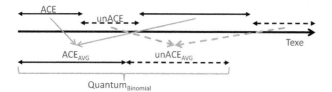

Figure 6. Alternance between ACE and unACE intervals

The L2 cache AVF is computed as:

$$AVF_{Cache} = \frac{1}{n \times T_{exe}} \times \sum_{\forall n \text{ words in a cache}} T_{ACE,n} = \frac{T_{ACE\_cache}}{n \times T_{exe}} \quad (21)$$

Thus, from $T_{ACE\_cache} = AVF_{Cache} \times n \times T_{exe}$, we compute the average ACE cycles for a single word in that cache, called T_{ACE_word}, by dividing T_{ACE_cache} by the total number of accesses to n words in L2.

T_{ACE_word} is the average number of cycles between two accesses to a word. Since ECC is activated on each access T_{ACE_word} is also the average interval when SECDED may correct a single faulty bit in a word. In order to compute the DUE FIT rate with word-level SECDED our goal now is to calculate the probability that *exactly two* temporal faults on the same word happen during T_{ACE_word}. After T_{ACE_word} there are only two outcomes: failure or survival. Hence, we calculate the probability of having a failure in a word using a geometric distribution where each word access becomes a Bernoulli trial. During T_{ACE_word} the SER rate is λ_{ACE_word} (which can be easily computed from ITRS2007 SEU FIT rates).

Using the Poisson probability mass function, we can get the probability that a word has *exactly two* SEUs (i.e., the probability of a DUE with SECDED) during T_{ACE_word}. This probability is given by:

$$P_{DUE} = \frac{(\lambda_{ACE\_word})^2}{2!} e^{-\lambda_{ACE\_word}} \quad (22)$$

Then from the geometric distribution, the expected number of attempts to see a DUE in a word under SECDED is $1/P_{DUE}$. Note that the duration of each attempt here is not T_{ACE_word}, rather it is T_{ACE_word}/AVF_{Cache} to correctly account for the total benchmark execution time, which also includes unACE time. This effect is illustrated in Figure 6, where each binomial attempt should include two different intervals: average ACE time and unACE time. We can then compute $MTTF_{SW}$ as:

$$MTTF_{SW} = \frac{1}{P_{DUE}} \times \frac{T_{word}(ACE)}{AVF_{Cache}} [sec] \quad (23)$$

We calculated the $MTTF_{SW}$ and converted it to FIT_{SW} and show it in the 4th column of Table 4. As can be seen, the new approximate model that takes the SECDED correction effects into account yields much better estimates of the DUE FIT rates compared to prior approaches such as [20]. However, the approximate method still overestimates the DUE FIT rates as compared to PARMA by 1 to 2 orders of magnitude. This residual error comes from various For instance, T_{ACE_word} is the average over time and words instead of the instantaneous ACE time per each word. Because the right side of (23) is a convex function, the average of the function values calculated for each interval is greater or equal to the function value calculated for the average of all intervals, meaning that the estimated MTTF from (23) can be smaller than the accurate estimate.

To the best of our knowledge, PARMA is the *only* framework that can accurately measure the SDC FIT rates or DUE FIT rates of SRAM arrays that are protected by various protection schemes, by correctly addressing the non-linear effects caused by error correction.

5. RELATED WORK

Recognizing the drawbacks of fault injection simulations, researchers have proposed methods to accelerate reliability estimation, particularly for processor internal buffers such as ROBs and LSQs. In this regard, two approaches are particularly relevant: SoftArch [13] and AVF [16]. These techniques use a simple fault generation model assuming that all SEUs are converted to faulty bits; thus soft errors are Poisson distributed. This approximated generation model [12] is valid in environments dominated by single-bit errors since the expected residence time of bits in the target structures is extremely short and hence the likelihood of multiple errors to a word during its vulnerability window is negligibly small. Both approaches focus on measuring SDC FIT rates without error protection scheme. PARMA is a complementary approach targeting large memory structures where the vulnerability window may extend to millions of cycles and hence demands more extensive analytical models. PARMA models soft errors with a binomial process which can account for all possible spatial or temporal patterns of faults over a period of time. This detailed model allows PARMA to consider and quantify the effect of multi-bit error protection schemes.

Studies in [17][20] developed approximate analytical models to estimate the expected time for two-bit errors in a word, in order to decide on an effective scrubbing rate. These methods consider fault rates closer to *intrinsic* rates as mentioned in the previous section. The expected time that any word may have *exactly* two temporal faulty bits without considering masking effects conservatively estimates the scrubbing interval so as to prevent the second fault from occurring. But in the presence of error protection schemes caches can have non-trivial derating factors as reported in [4] and as confirmed by PARMA. Resultantly, we can relax the scrubbing rate significantly based on the much lower DUE FIT rates obtained with PARMA. Further scrubbing rate relaxation may therefore be possible.

Under low operating voltages, gates behave erratically due to process variations and their failure rate soars by nine orders of magnitude [7]. In [27], the authors showed that the probability of having retention errors increases by multiple orders of magnitude when reducing the refresh rates of eDRAM caches to save power. PARMA is applicable to these techniques, although we only have demonstrated PARMA to measure soft error rates in SRAM structures.

The study in [5] showed that the DUE FIT rate of write-back caches increases superlinearly when the cache size is doubled due to the parity-protected TAG vulnerability on dirty lines. In their work, the authors introduced the notion of DUE AVF which is different from the well-known (SDC) AVF. The DUE AVF is empirically measured from real machine tests by reading error logs on a real system exposed to accelerated beam tests. We believe that PARMA can be extended to include reliability effects on TAG and state bits but this requires significant future research.

6. CONCLUSION AND FUTURE WORK

The cache reliability problem caused by soft errors has become a cause for significant concern leading to the introduction of sophisticated error protection schemes. Cache FIT rates must be accurately measured in order to evaluate and compare the merits of various protection schemes. PARMA enumerates all possible temporal and spatial fault patterns to address temporal MBEs and derives accurate expected failure rates. The rigorous, fundamental approach adopted in PARMA is potentially applicable to the reliability benchmarking of any memory structure with any protection scheme. PARMA models provide an accurate quantitative basis to trade-off various design targets such as reliability, power and performance. Furthermore, PARMA can measure the reliability of caches protected by such schemes as CPPC [15] that are hard to model using classical approaches.

PARMA can work as a standard to check the accuracy of popular techniques used up to now to evaluate the reliability of caches. We have shown that non-linear effects distort the observations obtained from highly accelerated fault injection simulations. Hence the results from highly accelerated reliability simulations cannot be trusted in actual design decisions, even from a purely qualitative viewpoint. Using PARMA we have also shown that prior approximate analytical models to evaluate the FIT rates of memories with error correction codes were totally inaccurate. Using the insights gained from the comparison of the PARMA model with prior approximate analytical models we have introduced a new approximate analytical model based on a refined AVF methodology to estimate the DUE FIT rate of SECDED protected caches. The FIT rates obtained with our new model are closer to PARMA FIT rates although they are still off by one or two orders of magnitude. The advantage of the new approximate model over PARMA models is that it can be evaluated much faster than PARMA and thus is worth considering for rapid comparisons of FIT rates with different protection schemes.

In our simulator, sim-outorder is augmented with a Binary Search Tree (BST) to keep track of the entire memory footprint of a program. In this structure, the simulator records the vulnerability clock at the byte level. As a result, the memory overhead of PARMA is about 35x the total simulated memory footprint. Additionally the computation of probabilities at each cache access has a complexity of $O(n^3)$, where n is the number of bits in the access domain. As a result of the lengthy, random searches in the large data structure keeping track of vulnerability clocks and of the complex floating-point operations computing probabilities, the sim-outorder/PARMA simulation is, on the average, slower than the basic sim-outorder simulation by a factor of about 25x for 100M SimPoint simulations.

We are currently exploring sampling techniques to speedup PARMA using cache set sampling [14] and access interval sampling. In access interval sampling, we select the intervals between cache accesses that we keep track of at random. This reduces both the size of the data structure keeping track of vulnerability clocks and the number of probability calculations. It reduces memory pressure and speeds up the simulations. Preliminary results based on set sampling only show great promise. By sampling 10% of the cache sets we have been able to cut the slowdown factor down to seven, with an acceptable average loss of accuracy of 6% on the FIT rate across the benchmarks we have considered.

7. ACKNOWLEDGMENTS

This material is based upon work supported by the National Science Foundation under Grants No. CSR-0615428 and CCF-0834798.

8. REFERENCES

[1] H. Asadi, V. Sridharan, M.B. Tahoori, and D. Kaeli. Vulnerability analysis of L2 cache elements to single event upsets. In *Proceedings of the Design, Automation and Test in Europe,* 1276-1281, 2006.

[2] S. Baeg, S. Wen, R. Wong, SRAM Interleaving Distance Selection With a Soft Error Failure Model, *Nuclear Science, IEEE Transactions on* , vol.56, no.4, pp.2111-2118, Aug. 2009

[3] M.A. Bajura, Y. Boulghassoul, R. Naseer, S. DasGupta, A.F. Witulski, J. Sondeen, S.D. Stansberry, J. Draper, L.W. Massengill, J.N. Damoulakis. Models and Algorithmic Limits for an ECC-Based Approach to Hardening Sub-100-nm SRAMs. In *IEEE Transactions on Nuclear Science*, 54(4), 935-945, 2007.

[4] A. Biswas, P. Racunas, R. Cheveresan, J. Emer, S. Mukherjee, R Rangan, Computing Architectural Vulnerability Factors for Address-Based Structures, In *Proceedings of the 32nd International Symposium on Computer Architecture*, 532-543, 2005

[5] Arijit Biswas, Charles Recchia, Shubhendu S. Mukherjee, Vinod Ambrose, Leo Chan, Aamer Jaleel, Mike Plaster, and Norbert Seifert, Explaining Cache SER Anomaly Using Relative DUE AVF Measurement, In *Proceedings of the 16th IEEE International Symposium on High-Performance Computer Architecture (HPCA)*, 2010

[6] D. Burger and T. M. Austin. The SimpleScalar Tool Set Version 2.0. Technical Report 1342, CS Department, University of Wisconsin-Madison.

[7] D. Ernst, N. Kim, S. Das, S. Pant, R. Rao, T. Pham, C. Ziesler, D. Blaauw, T. Austin, K. Flautner, and T. Mudge. Razor: a low-power pipeline based on circuit-level timing speculation. In *Proceedings of the 36th International Symposium on Microarchitecture*, pages 7-18, 2003.

[8] K. Flautner, N.S. Kim, S. Martin, D. Blaauw, and T. Mudge. Drowsy caches: simple techniques for reducing leakage power. In *Proceedings of the 29th International Symposium on Computer Architecture*, 148-157, 2002.

[9] E. Ibe, S.S. Chung, S. Wen, H Yamaguchi, Y Yahagi, H Kameyama, S Yamamoto, T Akioka, "Spreading Diversity in Multi-cell Neutron-Induced Upsets with Device Scaling," *Custom Integrated Circuits Conference*, 2006. CICC '06. IEEE , vol., no., pp.437-444, 10-13 Sept. 2006

[10] J.W. Kellington, R. McBeth, P. Sanda, and R.N. Kalla. IBM POWER6 Processor Soft Error Tolerance Analysis Using Proton Irradiation. In *Proceedings of the 3rd IEEE Workshop on Silicon Errors in Logic System Effects*, 2007.

[11] M. Li, P. Ramachandran, R.U. Karpuzcu, S.K.S Hari, S. Adve. Accurate Microarchitecture-Level Fault Modeling for Studying Hardware Faults. In *Proceedings of the International Conference on High Performance Computer Architecture*, 105-116, 2009.

[12] X. Li, S. Adve, P. Bose, and J.A. Rivers. Architecture-Level Soft Error Analysis: Examining the Limits of Common Assumptions. In *Proceedings of the International Conference on Dependable Systems and Networks*, 266-275, 2007.

[13] X. Li, S. Adve, P. Bose, and J.A. Rivers. SoftArch: An Architecture Level Tool for Modeling and Analyzing Soft

Errors. In *Proceedings of the International Conference on Dependable Systems and Networks*, 496-505, 2005.

[14] Liu, L.; Peir, J.K.; , Cache sampling by sets, *Very Large Scale Integration (VLSI) Systems, IEEE Transactions on* , vol.1, no.2, pp.98-105, Jun 1993

[15] M. Manoochehri, M. Annavaram, M. Dubois. CPPC: Correctable Parity Protected Cache, In *Proceedings of the 38th International Symposium on Computer Architecture*, 2011

[16] S. S. Mukherjee, C. Weaver, J. Emer, S. K. Reinhardt, and T.Austin. A systematic methodology to calculate the architectural vulnerability factors for a high-performance microprocessor. In *Proceedings of the 36th International Symposium on Microarchitecture*, pages 29-40, 2003.

[17] S. S. Mukherjee, J. Emer, T. Fossum, and S. K. Reinhardt. Cache Scrubbing in Microprocessors: Myth or Necessity? In *Proceedings of the 10th IEEE Pacific Rim Symposium on Dependable Computing*, 37-42, 2004.

[18] R. Naseer, Y. Boulghassoul, J. Draper, S. DasGupta, A. Witulski. Critical Charge Characterization for Soft Error Rate Modeling in 90nm SRAM. In *Proceedings of the IEEE Symposium on Circuits and Systems*, 1879-1882, 2007.

[19] E. Perelman, G. Hamerly, M. Van Biesbrouck, T. Sherwood, and B. Calder. Using SimPoint for Accurate and Efficient Simulation. In *Proceedings of the ACM SIGMETRICS International Conference on Measurement and Modeling of Computer Systems*, 318-319, 2003.

[20] M. Rebaudengo, M. S. Reorda, and M. Violante. An Accurate Analysis of the Effects of Soft Errors in the Instruction and Date Caches of a Pipelined Microprocessor. In *Proceedings of the Design, Automation and Test in Europe*, 602-607, 2003.

[21] A.M.Saleh, J.J.Serrano, and J.H.Patel. Reliability of Scrubbing Recovery Techniques for Memory Systems. In *IEEE Transactions on Reliability*, 39(1), 114-122, 1990.

[22] Semiconductor Industries Association, International Technology Roadmap for Semiconductors.

[23] Sridharan, V., Asadi, H., Tahoori, M. B., and Kaeli, D. 2006. Reducing Data Cache Susceptibility to Soft Errors. *IEEE Trans. Dependable Secur. Comput.* 3, 4 Oct. 2006, 353-364.

[24] Tosaka, Y., Satoh, S., Itakura, T., Suzuki, K., Sugii, T., Ehara, H., Woffinden, G.A., Cosmic ray neutron-induced soft errors in sub-half micron CMOS circuits, *Electron Device Letters, IEEE* , vol.18, no.3, pp.99-101, Mar 1997

[25] S. Thoziyoor, N. Muralimanohar, J. H. Ahn, and N. P. Jouppi. Cacti 5.1. HP Report HPL-2008-20.

[26] C. Weaver, J. Emer, S.S. Mukherjee, and S.K. Reinhardt. Techniques to Reduce the Soft Error Rate of a High-Performance Microprocessor. In *Proceedings of the International Symposium on Computer Architecture*, 264-274, 2004.

[27] Wilkerson, C., Alameldeen, A. R., Chishti, Z., Wu, W., Somasekhar, D., and Lu, S. 2010. Reducing cache power with low-cost, multi-bit error-correcting codes. In *Proceedings of the 37th Annual international Symposium on Computer Architecture*. ISCA '10., 83-93.

[28] Wunderlich, R. E., Wenisch, T. F., Falsafi, B., and Hoe, J. C. "SMARTS: accelerating microarchitecture simulation via rigorous statistical sampling." In *Proceedings of the 30th Annual international Symposium on Computer Architecture*. ISCA '03., 84-97.

[29] B. Zandian, M. Annavaram. Cross-layer Resilience Using Wearout Aware Design Flow. *Dependable Systems and Networks* (DSN), 2011.

[30] B. Zandian, W. Dweik, S. Kang, T. Punihaole, and M. Annavaram. WearMon: Reliability Monitoring Using Adaptive Critical Path Testing. *Dependable Systems and Networks* (DSN), pages 151-160, 2010.

Network Architecture for Joint Failure Recovery and Traffic Engineering

Martin Suchara
Dept. of Computer Science
Princeton University, NJ 08544
msuchara@princeton.edu

Dahai Xu
AT&T Labs Research
Florham Park, NJ 07932
dahaixu@research.att.com

Robert Doverspike
AT&T Labs Research
Florham Park, NJ 07932
rdd@research.att.com

David Johnson
AT&T Labs Research
Florham Park, NJ 07932
dsj@research.att.com

Jennifer Rexford
Dept. of Computer Science
Princeton University, NJ 08544
jrex@princeton.edu

ABSTRACT

Today's networks typically handle *traffic engineering* (e.g., tuning the routing-protocol parameters to optimize the flow of traffic) and *failure recovery* (e.g., pre-installed backup paths) independently. In this paper, we propose a unified way to balance load efficiently under a wide range of failure scenarios. Our architecture supports flexible splitting of traffic over multiple precomputed paths, with efficient path-level failure detection and automatic load balancing over the remaining paths. We propose two candidate solutions that differ in how the routers rebalance the load after a failure, leading to a trade-off between router complexity and load-balancing performance. We present and solve the optimization problems that compute the configuration state for each router. Our experiments with traffic measurements and topology data (including shared risks in the underlying transport network) from a large ISP identify a "sweet spot" that achieves near-optimal load balancing under a variety of failure scenarios, with a relatively small amount of state in the routers. We believe that our solution for joint traffic engineering and failure recovery will appeal to Internet Service Providers as well as the operators of data-center networks.

Categories and Subject Descriptors

C.2.3 [**Computer-communication Networks**]: Network Operations—*Network Management*

General Terms

Reliability, Algorithms, Experimentation

Keywords

network architecture, failure recovery, optimization

1. INTRODUCTION

To ensure uninterrupted data delivery, communication networks must distribute traffic efficiently even as links and routers fail and recover. By tuning routing to the offered traffic, *traffic engineering* [27] improves performance and allows network operators to defer expensive outlays of new capacity. Effective *failure recovery* [28,34]—adapting to failures by directing traffic over good alternate paths—is also important to avoid performance disruptions. However, today's networks typically handle failure recovery and traffic engineering independently, leading to more complex routers and less efficient paths after failures. In this paper, we propose an integrated solution with much simpler routers that balances load effectively under a range of failure scenarios.

We argue that traffic engineering and failure recovery can be achieved by the same underlying approach—dynamically rebalancing traffic across diverse end-to-end paths in response to individual failure events. This reduces the complexity of the routers by moving most functionality to the management system—an algorithm run by the network operator. Our network architecture has three key features:

Precomputed multipath routing: Traffic between each pair of edge routers is split over multiple paths that are configured in advance. The routers do *not* compute (or recompute) paths, reducing router overhead and improving path stability. Instead, the management system computes paths that offer sufficient diversity across a range of failure scenarios, including correlated failures of multiple links.

Path-level failure detection: The ingress routers perform failure recovery based only on which *paths* have failed. A minimalist control plane performs path-level failure detection and notification, in contrast to the link-level probing and network-wide flooding common in today's intradomain routing protocols. This leads to simpler, cheaper routers.

Local adaptation to path failures: Upon detecting path failures, the ingress router rebalances the traffic on the remaining paths, based only on which path(s) failed—*not* on load information. This avoids having the routers distribute real-time updates about link load and prevents instability. Instead, the management system *precomputes* the reactions to path failures and configures the routers accordingly.

The first two features—multiple precomputed paths and path-level monitoring—are ideas that have been surfacing (sometimes implicitly) in the networking literature over the past few years (e.g., [4, 14, 24, 39], and many others). Our architecture combines these two ideas in a new way, through (i) a specific proposal for the "division of labor" between the routers and the management system and (ii) an integrated view of traffic engineering and failure recovery within a single administrative domain. To support the simple network elements, the management system makes *network-wide* decisions based on the expected traffic, the network topology, and the groups of links that can fail together. The management system does *not* need to make these decisions in real time—quite the contrary, offline algorithms can compute the paths and the adaptations to path failures.

Our architecture raises important questions about (i) what configuration state the routers should have to drive their local reactions to path failures and (ii) how the management system should compute this state, and the underlying paths, for good traffic engineering and failure recovery. In addressing these questions, we make four main contributions:

Simple architecture for joint TE and failure recovery (Section 2): We propose a joint solution for traffic engineering and failure recovery, in contrast to today's networks that handle these problems separately. Our minimalist control plane has routers balance load based only on path-failure information, in contrast to recent designs that require routers to disseminate link-load information and compute new path-splitting parameters in real time [18, 23].

Network-wide optimization across failure scenarios (Section 3): We formulate and solve network-wide optimization problems for configuring the routers. Our algorithms compute (i) multiple paths that distribute traffic efficiently under a range of failure scenarios and (ii) the state for each ingress router to adapt to path failures. We present algorithms for two router designs that strike a different trade-off between router state and load-balancing performance.

Experiments with measurement data from a large ISP (Section 4): We evaluate our algorithms on measurement data from a tier-1 ISP network. Our simulation achieves a high degree of accuracy by utilizing the real topology, link capacities, link delays, hourly traffic matrices, and Shared Risk Link Groups (SRLGs) [13]. Our experiments show that one of our candidate router designs achieves near-optimal load balancing across a wide range of failure scenarios, even when the traffic demands change *dynamically*.

Deployability in ISP and data-center networks (Section 5): While our architecture enables simpler routers and switches, existing equipment can support our solutions. ISP backbones can use RSVP to signal multiple MPLS [29] paths, with hash-based splitting of traffic over the paths. In data centers, the fabric controller can configure multiple paths through the network, and the server machines can encapsulate packets to split traffic in the desired proportions.

The paper ends with related work in Section 6, conclusion in Section 7, and supporting proofs in an Appendix.

2. SIMPLE NETWORK ARCHITECTURE

Our architecture uses simple, cheap routers to balance load before, during, and after failures by placing most functionality in a management system that performs offline optimization. The network-management system computes multiple diverse paths between each pair of edge routers, and tells each ingress router how to split traffic over these paths under a range of failure scenarios. Each edge router simply

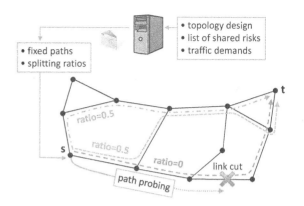

Figure 1: **The management system calculates a fixed set of paths and splitting ratios, based on the topology, traffic demands, and potential failures. The ingress router learns about path failures and splits traffic over the remaining paths, based on pre-configured splitting ratios.**

detects path-level failures and uses this information to adjust the splitting of traffic over the remaining paths, as shown in Figure 1. The main novel feature of our architecture is the way routers split traffic over the working paths; we propose two approaches that introduce a trade-off between router state and load-balancing performance.

2.1 Precomputed Multipath Routing

Many existing routing protocols compute a single path between each pair of routers, and change that path in response to topology changes. However, dynamic routing has many downsides, including the overhead on the routers (to disseminate topology information and compute paths) and the transient disruptions during routing-protocol convergence. Techniques for making convergence faster tend to increase the complexity of the routing software and the overhead on the routers, by disseminating more information or updating it more quickly. Rather than trying to reduce convergence time, or add mechanisms to detect transient loops and blackholes, we avoid dynamic routing protocols entirely [4].

Our architecture uses multiple *preconfigured* paths between each pair of edge routers, allowing ingress routers to adapt to failures by shifting traffic away from failed path(s). With multiple paths through the network, the routers do not need to recompute paths dynamically—they simply stop using the failed paths until they start working again. This substantially reduces router software complexity and protocol overheads (e.g., bandwidth and CPU resources), while entirely side-stepping the problem of convergence. Instead, the management system computes these paths, based on *both* traffic-engineering and failure-recovery goals, and installs the paths in the underlying routers. The management system can select diverse paths that ensure connectivity in the face of failures, including multiple correlated failures.

Using multiple paths also leads to better load balancing, whether or not failures occur. Today's shortest-path routing protocols (like OSPF and IS-IS) use a single path, or (at best) only support *even* splitting of traffic over multiple *shortest* paths. Our architecture (like other recent proposals for multipath load balancing [6, 14, 17, 37]) allows flexible splitting of traffic over multiple paths. However, we do

	Optimal (Baseline)	State-Dependent Splitting	State-Independent Splitting
Router state	Exponential in total # of links	Exponential in # of pre-configured paths between two routers	Linear in # of pre-configured paths between two routers
Failure information	Link level	Path level	Path level
Optimality	Optimal	Nearly-optimal	Good

Table 1: Properties of the candidate solutions. The solutions differ in the amount of configuration state that must be stored in the routers, the information the routers must obtain about each failure, and the achieved traffic-engineering performance.

not require dynamic adaptation of the traffic splitting. Instead, the ingress router has a simple static configuration that determines the splitting of traffic over the available paths, while intermediate routers merely forward packets over pre-established paths. The management system optimizes this configuration *in advance* based on a network-wide view of the expected traffic and likely failures. This avoids the protocol overhead and stability challenges of distributed, load-sensitive routing protocols. Also, the management system can use knowledge about shared risks and anticipated traffic demands—information the routers do not have.

2.2 Path-Level Failure Detection

Most routing protocols detect failures by exchanging "hello" messages between neighboring routers and flooding the topology changes through the network. This approach requires small timers for fast failure detection, imposing additional overhead on the routers. In addition, many failures are triggered by planned maintenance [21], leading to *two* convergence events—one for the link failure(s), and another for the recovery—that both cause transient disruptions. In addition, "hello" messages do not detect all kinds of failures—some misconfigurations (e.g., having a maximum packet size that is too small) and attacks (e.g., an adversary selectively dropping packets) do not lead to lost "hello" messages.

Instead, our architecture relies on *path-level* failure detection. Each ingress-egress router pair has a session to monitor each of its paths (e.g., as in BFD [15]). The probes can be piggybacked on existing data traffic, obviating the need for separate "hello" messages when the path is carrying regular data traffic. This enables fast failure detection without introducing extra probe traffic, and the "implicit probes" provide a more realistic view of the reliability of a path [3, 11], since the packets vary in size, addresses, and so on. Another advantage is that the packets are handled by the hardware interfaces and, as such, do not consume processing resources (or experience software processing delays) at intermediate routers. (Still, the propagation delay along a path does impose limits on detection time in large topologies, an issue we discuss in more detail in Section 5.)

Although the ingress router doesn't learn which *link* failed, knowledge of the *path* failures is sufficient to avoid the failed path. In fact, since the routers need not be aware of the topology, no control protocol is needed to exchange topology information. In fact, only some of the ingress routers need to learn about the failure—only the routers that have paths traversing the failed edge. The other ingress routers, and the intermediate routers, can remain unaware of the link failure. Of course, the *management system* ultimately needs to know about topology changes, so failed equipment

can be fixed or replaced. But this detection problem can be handled on a much longer timescale since it does not affect the failure-recovery time for data traffic.

2.3 Local Adaptation to Path Failures

In our architecture, a router is a simple device that does not participate in a routing protocol, collect congestion feedback, or solve any computationally difficult problems. Still, the routers do play an important role in adapting the distribution of traffic when paths fail or recover, at the behest of the management system. We propose two different ways the routers can split traffic over the working paths: (i) state-independent splitting which has minimal router state and (ii) state-dependent splitting which introduces more state in exchange for near-optimal performance, as summarized (and compared to an idealized solution) in Table 1.

Optimal load balancing: This idealized solution calculates the optimal paths and splitting ratios separately for each possible failure state, i.e., for each combination of link failures. This approach achieves the best possible load balancing. However, the approach is impractical because the routers must (i) store far too much state and (ii) learn about all link failures—even on links the router's paths do not traverse. Therefore, this solution would violate our architecture. However, the solution is still interesting as it provides a lower bound on the amount of congestion achievable by the other two schemes.

State dependent splitting: In this solution, each ingress router has a separate configuration entry with path-splitting weights for each combination of *path* failures to a particular egress router. For example, suppose a router has three paths to an egress router. Then, the router configuration contains seven entries—one for each of the $2^3 - 1$ combinations of path failures. Each configuration entry, computed ahead of time by the management system, consists of three weights—one per path, with a 0 for any failed paths. Upon detecting path failures, the ingress router inspects a pre-configured table to select the appropriate weights for splitting the traffic destined to the egress router. Our experiments in Section 4 show that, even in a large ISP backbone, having three or four paths is sufficient, leading to modest state requirements on the router in exchange for near-optimal load balancing.

State independent splitting: This solution further simplifies the router configuration by having a *single* set of weights across all failure scenarios. So, an ingress router with three paths to an egress router would have only *three* weights, one for each path. If any paths fail, the ingress router simply renormalizes the traffic on the remaining paths. As such, the management system must perform a *robust* optimization of the limited configuration parameters to achieve good load-balancing performance across a range of failure scenarios. Our experiments in Section 4 show that this simple approach can perform surprisingly well, but understandably not as well as state-dependent splitting.

3. NETWORK-WIDE OPTIMIZATION

In our architecture, the network-management system performs network-wide optimization to compute paths and traffic-splitting ratios that balance load effectively across a range of failure scenarios. In this section, we first discuss the information the management system has about the network topology, traffic demands, and shared risks. Then, we explain how the management system computes the multiple diverse paths and the traffic-splitting ratios, for both state-dependent and state-independent splitting. We solve all optimization problems either by formulating them as convex optimizations solvable in polynomial time, or by providing heuristics for solving NP-hard problems. Table 2 summarizes the notation.

3.1 Network-Wide Visibility and Control

The management system computes paths and splitting ratios based on a network-wide view:

Fixed topology: The management system makes decisions based on the designed topology of the network—the routers and links that have been deployed. The topology is represented by a graph $G(V, E)$ with a set of vertices V and directed edges E. The capacity of edge $e \in E$ is denoted by c_e, and the propagation delay on the edge is y_e.

Shared risk link groups: The management system knows which links share a common vulnerability, such as connecting to the same line card or router or traversing the same optical fiber or amplifier [13]. The shared risks are denoted

Variable	Description
$G(V,E)$	network with vertices V and directed edges E
c_e	capacity of edge $e \in E$
y_e	propagation delay on edge $e \in E$
S	family of network failure states
s	network failure state (set of failed links)
w^s	weight of network failure state $s \in S$
D	set of demands
u_d	source of demand $d \in D$
v_d	destination of demand $d \in D$
h_d	flow requirement of demand $d \in D$
P_d	paths available to demand $d \in D$
α_p	fraction of the demand assigned to path p
O_d	family of observable failure states for node u_d
$o_d(s)$	state observable by u_d in failure state $s \in S$
P_d^o	paths available to u_d in failure state $o \in O_d$
f_p^s	flow on path p in failure state $s \in S$
f_p^o	flow on path p in failure state $o \in O_d$
l_e^s	total flow on edge e in failure state s
$l_{e,d}^s$	flow of demand d on edge e in failure state s

Table 2: Summary of notation

by the set S, where each $s \in S$ consists of a set of edges that may fail together. For example, a router failure is represented by the set of its incident links, a fiber cut is represented by all links in the affected fiber bundle, and the failure-free case is represented by the empty set $\emptyset$. Operators also have measurement data from past failures to produce estimates for the likelihood of different failures (e.g., an optical amplifier may fail less often than a line card). As such, each failure state s has a weight w^s that represents its likelihood or importance.

Expected traffic demands: The management system knows the anticipated traffic demands, based on past measurements and predictions of traffic changes. Each traffic demand $d \in D$ is represented by a triple (u_d, v_d, h_d), where $u_d \in V$ is the traffic source (ingress router), $v_d \in V$ is the destination (egress router), and h_d is the flow requirement (measured traffic). For simplicity, we assume that all demands remain connected for each failure scenario; alternatively, a demand can be omitted for each failure case that disconnects it. In practice, the management system may have a time sequence of traffic demands (e.g., for different hours in the day), and optimize the network configuration across all these demands, as we discuss in Section 4.3.

The management system's output is *set of paths* P_d for each demand d and the *splitting ratios* for each path. In each failure state s, the traffic splitting by ingress router u_d depends only on which *paths* have failed, not which failure scenario s has occurred; in fact, multiple failure scenarios may affect the same subset of paths in P_d. To reason about the handling of a particular demand d, we consider a set O_d of "observable" failure states, where each observable state $o \in O_d$ corresponds to a particular $P_d^o \subset P_d$ representing the available paths. For ease of expression, we let the function $o_d(s)$ map to the failure state observable by node u_d when the network is in failure state $s \in S$. The amount of flow assigned to path p in observable failure state $o \in O_d$ is f_p^o. The total flow on edge e in failure state s is l_e^s, and the flow on edge e corresponding to demand d is $l_{e,d}^s$.

The management system's goal is to compute paths and splitting ratios that minimize congestion over the range of possible failure states. A common traffic-engineering objective [9] is to minimize $\sum_{e \in E} \Phi(l_e^s/c_e)$ where l_e is the load on edge e and c_e is its capacity. $\Phi()$ could be a convex function of link load [9], to penalize the most congested links while still accounting for load on the remaining links. The final objective minimizing congestion across failure scenarios is

$$obj(l_{e_1}^{s_1}/c_{e_1}, ...) = \sum_{s \in S} w^s \sum_{e \in E} \Phi(l_e^s/c_e). \quad (1)$$

Minimizing this objective function is the goal of all the candidate solutions in the following section. The constraints that complete the problem formulation differ depending on the functionality placed in the underlying routers.

3.2 Computing Multiple Diverse Paths

The management system must compute multiple diverse paths that ensure good load balancing—and (most importantly) continued connectivity—across a range of failure scenarios. However, as shown later, computing the optimal paths for state-dependent and state-independent splitting is NP-hard. Instead, we propose a heuristic: using the collection of paths computed by the optimal solution that optimizes for each failure state independently. This guarantees that the paths are sufficiently diverse to ensure traffic delivery in all failure states, while also making efficient use of network resources.

The idealized optimal solution has a separate set of paths and splitting ratios in each failure state s. To avoid having variables for exponentially many paths, we formulate the problem in terms of the amount of flow $l_{e,d}^s$ from demand d traversing edge e for failure state s. The optimal edge loads are obtained by solving the convex optimization:

$$
\begin{aligned}
\min \quad & obj(l_{e_1}^{s_1}/c_{e_1}, ...) \\
\text{s.t.} \quad & l_e^s = \textstyle\sum_{d \in D} l_{e,d}^s && \forall s, e \\
& 0 = \textstyle\sum_{i:e=(i,j)} l_{e,d}^s - \sum_{i:e=(j,i)} l_{e,d}^s && \forall d, s, j \neq u_d, v_d \\
& h_d = \textstyle\sum_{i:e=(u_d,i)} l_{e,d}^s - \sum_{i:e=(i,u_d)} l_{e,d}^s && \forall d, s \\
& h_d = \textstyle\sum_{i:e=(i,v_d)} l_{e,d}^s - \sum_{i:e=(v_d,i)} l_{e,d}^s && \forall d, s \\
& 0 \leq l_{e,d}^s && \forall d, s, e,
\end{aligned}
\tag{2}
$$

where l_e^s and $l_{e,d}^s$ are variables. The first constraint defines the load on edge e, the second constraint ensures flow conservation, the third and fourth constraints ensure that the demands are met, and the last constraint guarantees flow non-negativity. An optimal solution can be found in polynomial time using conventional techniques for solving multi-commodity flow problems.

After obtaining the optimal flow on each edge for all the failure scenarios, we use a standard decomposition algorithm to determine the corresponding paths P_d and the flow f_p^s on each of them. The decomposition starts with a set P_d that is empty. New unique paths are added to the set by performing the following decomposition for each failure state s. First, annotate each edge e with the value $l_{e,d}^s$. Remove all edges that have 0 value. Then, find a path connecting u_d and v_d. Although we could choose any of the paths from u_d to v_d, our goal is to obtain paths that are as short as possible. So, if multiple such paths exist, we use the path p with the smallest propagation delay. Add this path p to the set P_d and assign to it flow f_p^s equal to the smallest value of the edges on path p. Reduce the values of these edges accordingly. Continue in this fashion, removing edges with zero value and finding new paths, until there are no remaining edges in the graph.

Note that we can show by induction that this process completely partitions the flow $l_{e,d}^s$ into paths. The decomposition yields at most $|E|$ paths for each network failure state s because the value of at least one edge becomes 0 whenever a new path is found. Hence the total size of the set P_d is at most $|E||S|$. It is difficult to obtain a solution that restricts the number of paths as we prove in the appendix that it is NP-hard to solve problem (2) when the number of allowed paths is bounded by a constant J. In practice, the algorithm produces a relatively small number of paths between each pair of edge routers, as shown later in Section 4.

3.3 Optimizing the Traffic-Splitting Ratios

Once the paths are computed, the network-management system can optimize the path-splitting ratios for each ingress-egress router pair. The optimization problem and the resulting solution depend on whether the routers perform state-dependent or state-independent splitting.

3.3.1 State-Dependent Splitting

In state-dependent splitting, each ingress router u_d has a set of splitting ratios for each *observable* failure state $o \in O_d$.

Since the path-splitting ratios depend on *which* paths in P_d have failed, the ingress router must store splitting ratios for $min(|S|, 2^{|P_d|})$ scenarios; fortunately, the number of paths $|P_d|$ is typically small in practice. When the network performs such *state-dependent splitting*, the management system's goal is to find a set of paths P_d for each demand and the flows f_p^o on these paths in all observable states $o \in O_d$. If the paths P_d are known and fixed, the problem can be formulated as a convex optimization:

$$
\begin{aligned}
\min \quad & obj(l_{e_1}^{s_1}/c_{e_1}, ...) \\
\text{s.t.} \quad & l_e^s = \sum_{d \in D} \sum_{p \in P_d^o, e \in p} f_p^o && \forall e, s, o = o_d(s) \\
& h_d = \textstyle\sum_{p \in P_d^o} f_p^o && \forall d, o \in O_d \\
& 0 \leq f_p^o && \forall d, o \in O_d, p \in P_d,
\end{aligned}
\tag{3}
$$

where l_e^s and f_p^o are variables. The first constraint defines the load on edge e, the second constraint guarantees that the demand d is satisfied in all observable failure states, and the last constraint ensures non-negativity of flows assigned to the paths. The solution of the optimization problem (3) can be found in polynomial time.

Finding the optimal set of paths $\{P_d\}$ in problem (3) is NP-hard. The Appendix shows that it is NP-hard to construct a path (if one exists) that allows the ingress router to distinguish the failure state s. This is required to decide how to best balance the load. All our formulations where the routers cannot directly observe link failures are NP-hard. Therefore, we use the paths that are found by the decomposition of the optimal solutions (2), as outlined in the previous subsection. Since these paths allow optimal load balancing for the optimal solutions (2), they are also likely to enable good load balancing for the optimization problem (3).

3.3.2 State-Independent Splitting

In state independent splitting, each ingress router has a *single* configuration entry containing the splitting ratios that are used under any combination of path failures. Each path p is associated with a splitting fraction α_p. When one or more paths fail, the ingress router u_d observes state o and uses $\frac{\alpha_p}{\sum_{q \in P_d^o} \alpha_q}$ as the splitting ratio for path p (and 0 for all the failed paths). If the network elements implement such *state-independent splitting*, and the paths P_d are known and fixed, the management system needs to solve the following non-convex optimization problem:

$$
\begin{aligned}
\min \quad & obj(l_{e_1}^{s_1}/c_{e_1}, ...) \\
\text{s.t.} \quad & f_p^o = h_d \frac{\alpha_p}{\sum_{q \in P_d^o} \alpha_q} && \forall d, o \in O_d, p \in P_d \\
& l_e^s = \sum_{d \in D} \sum_{p \in P_d^o, e \in p} f_p^o && \forall e, s, o = o_d(s) \\
& 0 \leq f_p^o && \forall d, o \in O_d, p \in P_d,
\end{aligned}
\tag{4}
$$

where l_e^s, f_p^o and α_p are variables. The first constraint ensures that the flow assigned to every available path p is proportional to α_p. The other three constraints are the same as in (3).

Unfortunately, no standard optimization techniques allow us to compute an optimal solution efficiently, even when the paths P_d are fixed. Therefore, we have to rely on heuristics to find both the candidate paths P_d and the splitting ratios α_p. To find the set of candidate paths P_d, we again use the optimal paths obtained by decomposing (2). To find the splitting ratios we mimic the behavior of the optimal solution as closely as possible. We find the splitting ratios for all paths p by letting $\alpha_p = \sum_{s \in S} \frac{w^s f_p^s}{h_d}$ where f_p^s is the flow assigned by the optimal solution to path p in network failure state s. Since $\sum w^s = 1$, the calculated ratio is the weighted average of the splitting ratios used by the optimal solutions (2).

4. EXPERIMENTAL EVALUATION

To evaluate the algorithms described in the previous section, we wrote a simulator in C++ that calls the CPLEX linear program solver in AMPL and solves the optimization problems (2) and (3). We compare our two heuristics to the optimal solution, a simple "equal splitting" configuration, and OSPF with the link weights set using state-of-the-art optimization techniques. We show that our two heuristics require few paths resulting in compact routing tables, and the round-trip propagation delay does not increase. Finally, using real traffic traces obtained during a 24-hour measurement in the network of a tier-1 ISP we show that our solutions achieve excellent results without the need to perform any reoptimizations even in the presence of a changing traffic matrix.

Our experimental results show that the **objective value of state-dependent splitting very closely tracks the optimal objective**. For this reason, this solution is our favorite. Although state-independent splitting has somewhat worse performance especially as the network load increases beyond current levels, it is also attractive due to its simplicity.

4.1 Experimental Setup

Our simulations use a variety of synthetic topologies, the Abilene topology, as well as the city-level IP backbone topology of a tier-1 ISP with a set of failures provided by the network operator. The parameters of the topologies we used are summarized in Table 3.

Synthetic topologies: The synthetic topologies include 2-level hierarchical graphs, purely random graphs, and Waxman graphs. 2-level hierarchical graphs are produced using the generator GT-ITM [40], for random graphs the probability of two edges being connected is constant, and the probability of having an edge between two nodes in the Waxman graph decays exponentially with the distance of the nodes. These topologies also appear in [8].

Abilene topology: The topology of the Abilene network and a measured traffic matrix are used. We use the true edge capacities of 10 Gbps.

Tier-1 IP backbone: The city-level IP backbone of a tier-1 ISP is used. In our simulations, we use the real link capacities and measured traffic demands. We also obtained the link round-trip propagation delays.

The collection of network failures S for the synthetic topologies and Abilene contains single edge failures and the no-failure case. Two experiments with different collections of failures are performed on the tier-1 IP backbone. In the first experiment, single edge failures are used. In the second experiment, the collection of failures also contains Shared Risk Link Groups (SRLGs), link failures that occur simultaneously. SRLGs were obtained from the network operator's database that contains 954 failures with the largest failure affecting 20 links simultaneously. For each potential line

card failure, a complete router failure, or a link cut there is a corresponding record in the SRLG database. Therefore, failures that do not appear in the database are rare. The weights w^s in the optimization objective (1) were set to 0.5 for the no-failure case, and all other failure weights are equal and sum to 0.5.

The set of demands D in the Abilene and tier-1 networks were obtained by sampling Netflow data measured on Nov. 15th 2005 and May 22nd 2009, respectively. For the synthetic topologies, we chose the same traffic demands as in [8].

To simulate the algorithms in environments with increasing congestion, we repeat all experiments several times while uniformly increasing the traffic demands. For the synthetic topologies we start with the original demands and scale them up to twice the original values. As the average link utilization in Abilene and the tier-1 topology is lower than in the synthetic topologies, we scale the demands in these realistic topologies up to three times the original value.

In our experiments we use the piecewise linear penalty function defined by $\Phi(0) = 0$ and its derivatives:

$$\Phi'(\ell) = \begin{cases} 1 & \text{for} & 0 \le \ell < 0.333 \\ 3 & \text{for} & 0.333 \le \ell < 0.667 \\ 10 & \text{for} & 0.667 \le \ell < 0.9 \\ 70 & \text{for} & 0.9 \le \ell < 1 \\ 500 & \text{for} & 1 \le \ell < 1.1 \\ 5000 & \text{for} & 1.1 \le \ell < \infty \end{cases}$$

This penalty function was introduced in [9], and allows one to formulate the optimizations (2) and (3) as linear programs by adding auxiliary variables. The function can be viewed as modeling retransmission delays caused by packet losses. The cost is small for low utilization, and increases steeply as the utilization exceeds 100%.

Our simulation calculates the objective value of the optimal solution, state-independent and state-dependent splitting, and equal splitting. Equal splitting is a variant of state-independent splitting that splits the flow evenly on the available paths. We also calculate the objective achieved by the shortest path routing of OSPF with optimized link weights. These link weights were calculated using the state-of-the-art optimizations of [8], and these optimizations take into consideration the set of failure states S and the corresponding failure weights w^s.

Our simulations were performed using CPLEX version 11.2 on a 1.5 GHz Intel Itanium 2 processor. Solving the linear program for (2) for a particular failure case in the tier-1 topology takes 4 seconds, and solving the linear pro-

Name	Topology	Nodes	Edges	Demands
hier50a	hierarchical	50	148	2,450
hier50b	hierarchical	50	212	2,450
rand50	random	50	228	2,450
rand50a	random	50	245	2,450
rand100	random	100	403	9,900
wax50	Waxman	50	169	2,450
wax50a	Waxman	50	230	2,450
Abilene	backbone	11	28	110
tier-1	backbone	50	180	625

Table 3: Synthetic and realistic network topologies.

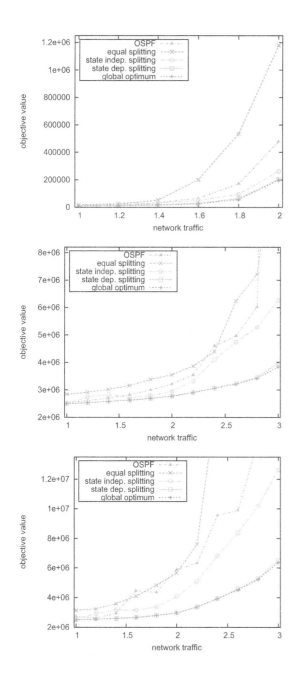

Figure 2: From top to bottom the traffic engineering objective as a function of an increasing traffic load in the hierarchical topology hier50a, tier-1 topology with single edge failures, and tier-1 topology with SRLGs, respectively. The performance of the optimal solution and state-dependent splitting is nearly identical.

gram (3) takes about 16 minutes. A tier-1 network operator can perform calculations for its entire city-level topology in less than 2 hours.

4.2 Performance with Static Traffic

Avoiding congestion and packet losses during planned and unplanned failures is the central goal of traffic engineering. Our traffic engineering objective measures congestion across all the considered failure cases. The objective as a function

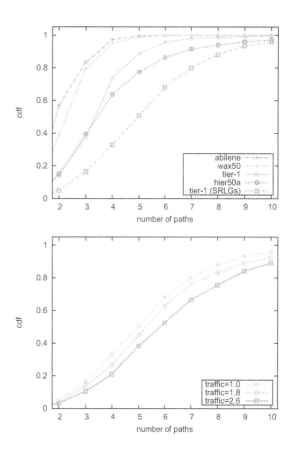

Figure 3: The number of paths used in various topologies at the top, and in the tier-1 topology with SRLGs at the bottom. The cumulative distribution function shows that the number of paths is almost independent of the traffic load in the network, but is larger for bigger, more well-connected topologies.

of the scaled-up demands is depicted in Figure 2. The results which were obtained on the hierarchical and tier-1 topologies are representative, we made similar observations for all the other topologies. In Figure 2, the performance of state-dependent splitting and the optimal solution is virtually indistinguishable in all cases. State-independent splitting is less sophisticated and does not allow custom load balancing ratios for distinct failures, and therefore its performance is worse compared to the optimum. It is not surprising that the equal splitting algorithm achieves the worst performance.

We observe that OSPF achieves a somewhat worse performance than state-independent and state-dependent splitting as the load increases. However, we should note that in OSPF, each router is restricted to sending all its traffic on the single path with the smallest weight, or splitting the traffic evenly if multiple smallest-weight paths exist. This approach does not allow the same flexibility in choosing routes and splitting ratios as our solution, and, therefore, OSPF should not be expected to achieve the same performance even for an optimal choice of OSPF link weights.

Solutions with few paths are preferred as they decrease the number of tunnels that have to be managed, and reduce the size of the router configuration. However, a sufficient number of paths must be available to avoid failures and to

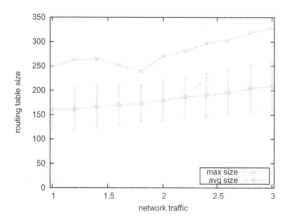

Figure 4: Size of the compressed routing tables in the tier-1 topology with SRLGs. The largest and average routing table sizes (± one standard deviation) in the backbone routers are shown.

reduce congestion. We observe that the number of paths used by our algorithms is small. We record the number of paths used by each demand, and plot the distribution in Figure 3. Not surprisingly, the number of paths is greater for larger and more diverse topologies. 92% of the demands in the hierarchical topology use 7 or fewer paths, and fewer than 10 paths are needed in the tier-1 backbone topology for almost all demands. Further, Figure 3 shows that the number of paths only increases slightly as we scale up the amount of traffic in the networks. This small increase is caused by shifting some traffic to longer paths as the short paths become congested.

A practical solution uses few MPLS labels in order to reduce the size of routing tables in the routers. Our experimental results reveal that when we use MPLS tunnels in the tier-1 topology, a few thousand tunnels can pass through a single router. However, a simple routing table compression technique allows us to reduce the routing table size to a few hundred entries in each router. Such compression is important because it reduces the memory requirements imposed on the simple routers whose use we advocate, and it improves the route lookup time.

Routing tables can be compressed by using the same MPLS labels for routes with a common path to the destination. Specifically, if two routes to destination t pass through router r, and these routes share the same path between the router r and the destination t, the same outbound label should be used in the routing table of router r. The resulting routing table sizes as a function of the network load are depicted in Figure 4. The curve on the top shows the size of the largest routing table, and the curve on the bottom shows the average routing table size among all the backbone routers.

Minimizing the delay experienced by the users is another important goal of network operators. We calculated the average round-trip propagation delays of all the evaluated algorithms. The calculated delays include delays in all failure states weighted by the corresponding likelihood of occurrence, but exclude congestion delay which is negligible. The delays are summarized in Table 4. We observe that the round-trip delay of all algorithms except equal splitting is almost identical at around 31 ms. These values would satisfy the 37 ms requirement specified in the SLAs of the tier-1

network. Moreover, these values are not higher than these experienced by the network users today. To demonstrate this, we repeated our simulation on the tier-1 topology using the real OSPF weights which are used by the network operator. These values are chosen to provide a tradeoff between traffic engineering and shortest delay routing. The results which appear in Table 4 in the row titled OSPF (current) show that the current delays are 31.38 ms for each of the two tier-1 failure sets.

Algorithm	Single edge	SRLGs
Optimal load balancing	31.75 ± 0.26	31.80 ± 0.25
State dep. splitting	31.51 ± 0.17	31.61 ± 0.16
State indep. splitting	31.76 ± 0.26	31.87 ± 0.25
Equal splitting	34.83 ± 0.33	40.85 ± 0.86
OSPF (optimized)	31.18 ± 0.40	31.23 ± 0.40
OSPF (current)	31.38 ± 0	31.38 ± 0

Table 4: Round-trip propagation delay in ms (average ± one standard deviation) in the tier-1 backbone network for single edge failures and SRLG failures.

4.3 Robust Optimization for Dynamic Traffic

Solving the optimization problems repeatedly as the traffic matrix changes is undesirable due to the need to update the router configurations with new paths and splitting ratios. We explore the possibility of using a single router configuration that is robust to diurnal changes of the demands.

To perform this study we collected hourly netflow traffic traces in the tier-1 network on September 29, 2009. We denote the resulting 24 hourly traffic matrices $D^0, D^1, ..., D^{23}$. Figure 5 depicts the aggregate traffic volume, as well as example of the traffic between three ingress-egress router pairs. The aggregate traffic volume is the lowest at 9 a.m. GMT and peaks with 2.5 times as much traffic at midnight and 8 p.m. GMT. Comparison to the three depicted ingress-egress router demands reveals that the traffic during a day cannot be obtained by simple scaling as the individual demands peak at different times. This makes the joint optimization challenging.

The first step in the joint optimization is to calculate a single set of paths that guarantee failure resilience and load balancing for each of the 24 traffic matrices. There are several approaches we can take. In the first approach, we solve the linear program for (2) for each traffic matrix D^i separately and use the union of the paths obtained for each matrix. The second approach is to calculate the average traffic matrix $D = \frac{1}{24} \sum_i D^i$. The linear program for (2) is then solved for the average traffic matrix. In the third approach we use the envelope of the 24 traffic matrices instead of the average, i.e., we let $D_{jk} = max_i D^i_{jk}$.

In our simulations we chose the last method. Compared to the first method, it results in fewer paths. Compared to the second method, it allows better load balancing because demands between ingress-egress pairs with high traffic variability throughout the day are represented by the peak traffic.

The second step is to calculate router configuration robust to traffic changes. We again use the envelope $D_{jk} = max_i D^i_{jk}$ as the input traffic matrix and repeat the opti-

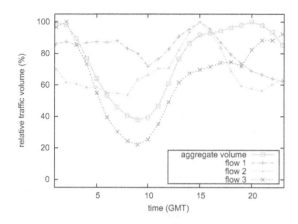

Figure 5: The aggregate traffic volume in the tier-1 network has peaks at midnight GMT and 8 p.m. GMT. Examples of three demands show that their peaks occur at different times of the day.

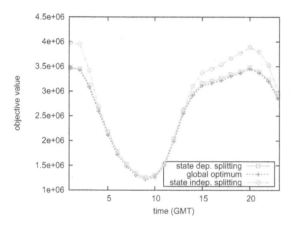

Figure 6: The traffic engineering objective in the tier-1 topology with SRLGs. The state dependent and state independent splitting algorithms use a single configuration throughout the day. The optimal solution uses a custom configuration for each hour.

mizations from the previous section. Then we test the solution by simulating the varying traffic demand during one day period. The resulting objective value of state dependent splitting and state independent splitting is depicted in Figure 6. The optimal objective in Figure 6 represents the performance of the best possible solution that uses custom configuration updated hourly. We observe that state dependent splitting with a single configuration is robust to diurnal traffic changes and the value of its objective closely tracks the optimum. State independent splitting is also close to optimal during low congestion periods, but becomes suboptimal during the peak hours.

5. DEPLOYMENT SCENARIOS

Although our architecture enables the use of new simpler routers, we can readily deploy our solutions using existing protocols and equipment, as summarized in Table 5. An ISP can deploy our architecture using Multi-Protocol Label Switching (MPLS) [29]. Data centers could use the same

	ISP Backbone	Data Center
Network element	MPLS router	Ethernet switch
Path installation	RSVP	VLAN trunking
Traffic splitting	Ingress router	End host
Failure detection	BFD	Host probing
Fast recovery	Ingress router	End host
Traffic demand	MPLS MIB	Host/VLAN counter

Table 5: Existing tools and protocols that can be used to deploy our architecture.

solution, or leverage existing Ethernet switches and move some functionality into the end-host machines.

5.1 ISP Backbone Using MPLS

Installing MPLS paths with RSVP: MPLS is particularly suitable because ingress routers encapsulate packets with labels and direct them over pre-established Label-Switched Paths (LSPs). This enables flexible routing when multiple LSPs are established between each ingress-egress router pair. Our solution, then, could be viewed as a particular application of MPLS, where the management system computes the LSPs, instructs the ingress routers to establish the paths (say, using RSVP), and disables any dynamic recalculation of alternate paths when primary paths fail.

Hash-based splitting at ingress routers: Multipath forwarding is supported by commercial routers of both major vendors [2, 27]. The routers can be configured to hash packets based on port and address information in the headers into several groups and forward each group on a separate path. This provides path splitting with relatively fine granularity (e.g., at the 1/16th level), while preventing out-of-order packet delivery by ensuring that packets belonging to the same TCP or UDP flow traverse the same path.

Path-level failure detection using BFD: Fast failure detection can be done using Bidirectional Forwarding Detection (BFD) [15]. A BFD session can monitor each path between two routers, by piggybacking on the existing data traffic. (Backbones covering a large geographic region may also use existing link-level detection mechanisms for even faster recovery. For example, *local path protection* [28] installs a short alternate path between two adjacent routers, for temporary use after the direct link fails. However, local protection cannot fully exploit the available path diversity, leading to suboptimal load balancing; instead, local protection can be used in conjunction with our design.)

Failure recovery at ingress router: The ingress router adapts to path failures by splitting traffic over the remaining paths. In state-independent splitting, the ingress router has a single set of traffic-splitting weights, and automatically renormalizes to direct traffic over the working paths. State-dependent splitting requires modification to the router software to switch to alternate traffic-splitting weights in the data plane; no hardware modifications are required.

Measuring traffic demands using SNMP: MPLS has SNMP counters (called Management Information Bases) that measure the total traffic traversing each Label-Switched Path. The management system can poll these counters to measure the traffic demands. Alternative measurement techniques, such as Netflow or tomography, may also be used.

5.2 Data Center Using Hosts and Switches

While a data center could easily use the same MPLS-based solution, control over the end host and the availability of cheaper commodity switches enable another solution.

End-host support for monitoring and traffic splitting: The server machines in data centers can perform many of the path-level operations in our architecture. As in the VL2 [12] and SPAIN [24] architectures, the end host can encapsulate the packets (say, using a VLAN tag) to direct them over a specific path. This enables much finer-grain traffic splitting. In addition, the end host can perform path-level probing in the data plane, by piggybacking on existing data traffic and sending additional active probes when needed. Upon detecting path failures, the end host can change to new path-splitting percentages based on the precomputed configuration installed by the controller. The end host could also measure the traffic demands by keeping counts of the traffic destined to each egress switch. These functions can be implemented in the hypervisor, such as the virtual switch that often runs on server machines in data centers.

Multiple VLANs or OpenFlow rules for forwarding: The remaining functions can be performed by the underlying switches. For example, the management system can configure multiple paths by merging these paths into a set of trees, where each tree corresponds to a different VLAN [24]. Or, if the switches support the emerging Open-Flow standard [1,22], the management system could install a forwarding-table rule for each hop in each path, where the rule matches on the VLAN tag, and forwards the packet to the appropriate output port. Since OpenFlow switches maintain traffic counters for each rule, the management system can measure the traffic demands by polling the switches, in lieu of the end hosts collecting these measurements.

6. RELATED WORK

Traffic engineering: Most of the related work treats failure recovery and traffic engineering independently. Traffic engineering without failure recovery in the context of MPLS is studied in [5, 6, 19, 32, 37]. The work in [5] utilizes traffic splitting to minimize end-to-end delay and loss rates; however, an algorithm for optimal path selection is not provided. The works in [19] and [32] minimize the maximum link utilization while satisfying the requested traffic demands. Other papers [6, 14, 17, 37] prevent congestion by adaptively balancing the load among multiple paths based on measurements of congestion, whereas our solution *precomputes* traffic-splitting configurations based on both the offered traffic and the likely failures.

Failure recovery: Local and global path protection are popular failure recovery mechanisms in MPLS. In local protection the backup path takes the shortest path that avoids the outage location from a point of local repair to the merge point with the primary path. The IETF RFC 4090 [28] focuses on defining signaling extensions to establish the backup paths, but leaves the issues of bandwidth reservation and optimal route selection open. In [35] the shortest path that avoids the failure is used. While [31] and [36] attempt to find optimal backup paths with the goal of reducing congestion, local path protection is less suitable for traffic engineering than global path protection, which allows rerouting on end-to-end paths [34]. Other work describes how to manage restoration bandwidth and select optimal paths [16, 20].

While our solution also uses global protection to reroute around failures, the biggest difference is that most of the related work distinguishes primary and backup paths and only uses a backup path when the primary path fails. In contrast, our solution balances the load across multiple paths even before failures occur, and simply adjusts the splitting ratios in response to failures.

Integrated failure recovery and TE: Some proposals only use alternate paths when primary routes fail [30], or they require explicit congestion feedback and do not provide algorithms to find the optimal paths [18, 23]. YAMR [10] constructs a set of diverse paths in the interdomain routing setting that are resilient against a specified set of failures, but without regard to load balancing. In [41] they integrate failure recovery with load balancing, but their focus is different—they guarantee delivery of a certain fraction of the traffic after a single edge failure, whereas our goal is to deliver *all* traffic for a known set of multi-edge failures. In [38] they propose an architecture that handles up to F link failures by using local rerouting, subject to link capacity constraints. Unlike [38], our work uses end-to-end routing, and does not require link state flooding and dynamic router reconfigurations. Proposals that optimize OSPF or IS-IS link weights with failures in mind, such as [8] and [26], must rely on shortest path IGP routing and therefore cannot fully utilize the path diversity in the network.

Failure recovery and TE with multiple spanning trees: Enterprise and data-center networks often use Ethernet switches, which do not scale well because all traffic flows over a single spanning tree, even if multiple paths exist. Several papers propose more scalable Ethernet designs that use multiple paths. The work of Sharma et al. uses VLANs to exploit multiple spanning trees to improve link utilization, and achieve improved fault recovery [33]. Most of the designs such as VL2 [12], and PortLand [25] rely on equal splitting of traffic on paths with the same cost. SPAIN [24] supports multipath routing through multiple spanning trees, with end hosts splitting traffic over the multiple paths. However, the algorithm for computing the paths does not consider the traffic demands, and the end hosts must play a stronger role in deciding which path to use for each individual flow based on the observed performance.

7. CONCLUSION

In this paper we propose a mechanism that combines path protection and traffic engineering to enable reliable data delivery in the presence of link failures. We formalize the problem by providing several optimization-theoretic formulations that differ in the capabilities they require of the network routers. For each of the formulations, we present algorithms and heuristics that allow the network operator to find a set of optimal end-to-end paths and load balancing rules.

Our extensive simulations on the IP backbone of a tier-1 ISP and on a range of synthetic topologies demonstrate the attractive properties of our solutions. First, state-dependent splitting achieves load balancing performance close to the theoretical optimum, while state-independent splitting often offers comparable performance and a very simple setup. Second, using our solutions does not significantly increase propagation delay compared to the shortest path routing of OSPF. Finally, our solution is robust to diurnal traffic changes and a single configuration suffices to provide good performance.

In addition to failure resilience and favorable traffic engineering properties, our architecture has the potential to simplify router design and reduce operation costs for ISPs as well as operators of data centers and enterprise networks.

8. ACKNOWLEDGMENTS

We thank Adel Saleh, DARPA Program Manager, for his guidance and support of our participation in the DARPA CORONET Program, Contract N00173-08-C-2011. We also acknowledge the suggestions received from Olivier Bonaventure, Quynh Nguyen, Kostas Oikonomou, Rakesh Sinha, Robert Tarjan, Kobus van der Merwe, and Jennifer Yates.

9. REFERENCES

[1] OpenFlow Switch Consortium. http://www.openflowswitch.org/.

[2] JUNOS: MPLS fast reroute solutions, network operations guide, 2007.

[3] I. Avramopoulos and J. Rexford. Stealth probing: Securing IP routing through data-plane security. In *Proc. USENIX Annual Technical Conference*, June 2006.

[4] M. Caesar, M. Casado, T. Koponen, J. Rexford, and S. Shenker. Dynamic route computation considered harmful. *SIGCOMM Comput. Commun. Rev.*, Apr. 2010.

[5] E. Dinan, D. Awduche, and B. Jabbari. Analytical framework for dynamic traffic partitioning in MPLS networks. In *IEEE International Conference on Communications*, volume 3, pages 1604–1608, 2000.

[6] A. Elwalid, C. Jin, S. Low, and I. Widjaja. MATE: MPLS adaptive traffic engineering. In *Proc. INFOCOM*, volume 3, pages 1300–1309, 2001.

[7] S. Fortune, J. Hopcroft, and J. Wyllie. The directed subgraph homeomorphism problem. *Theor. Comput. Sci.*, 10(2):111–121, 1980.

[8] B. Fortz and M. Thorup. Optimizing OSPF/IS-IS weights in a changing world. *IEEE Journal on Selected Areas in Communications*, 20(4):756–767, 2002.

[9] B. Fortz and M. Thorup. Increasing Internet capacity using local search. *Computational Optimization and Applications*, 29(1):13–48, 2004.

[10] I. Ganichev, B. Dai, B. Godfrey, and S. Shenker. YAMR: Yet another multipath routing protocol. *SIGCOMM Comput. Commun. Rev.*, 40(5):14–19, 2010.

[11] S. Goldberg, D. Xiao, E. Tromer, B. Barak, and J. Rexford. Path-quality monitoring in the presence of adversaries. In *Proc. ACM SIGMETRICS*, June 2008.

[12] A. Greenberg et al. VL2: A scalable and flexible data center network. In *Proc. ACM SIGCOMM*, pages 51–62, 2009.

[13] I. P. Kaminow and T. L. Koch. *The Optical Fiber Telecommunications IIIA*. Academic Press, New York, 1997.

[14] S. Kandula, D. Katabi, B. Davie, and A. Charny. Walking the tightrope: Responsive yet stable traffic engineering. In *Proc. ACM SIGCOMM*, pages 253–264, 2005.

[15] D. Katz and D. Ward. Bidirectional forwarding detection (BFD). IETF RFC 5880, 2010.

[16] M. Kodialam and T. V. Lakshman. Dynamic routing of restorable bandwidth-guaranteed tunnels using aggregated network resource usage information. *IEEE/ACM Trans. Netw.*, 11(3):399–410, 2003.

[17] A. Kvalbein, C. Dovrolis, and C. Muthu. Multipath load-adaptive routing: Putting the emphasis on robustness and simplicity. In *IEEE ICNP*, 2009.

[18] C. M. Lagoa, H. Che, and B. A. Movsichoff. Adaptive control algorithms for decentralized optimal traffic engineering in the Internet. *IEEE/ACM Trans. Netw.*, 12(3):415–428, 2004.

[19] Y. Lee, Y. Seok, Y. Choi, and C. Kim. A constrained multipath traffic engineering scheme for MPLS networks. In *IEEE International Conference on Communications*, volume 4, pages 2431–2436, 2002.

[20] Y. Liu, D. Tipper, and P. Siripongwutikorn. Approximating optimal spare capacity allocation by successive survivable routing. *IEEE/ACM Trans. Netw.*, 13(1):198–211, 2005.

[21] A. Markopoulou et al. Characterization of failures in an operational IP backbone network. *IEEE/ACM Trans. Netw.*, 16(4):749–762, 2008.

[22] N. McKeown et al. OpenFlow: enabling innovation in campus networks. *SIGCOMM Comput. Commun. Rev.*, 38:69–74, 2008.

[23] B. A. Movsichoff, C. M. Lagoa, and H. Che. End-to-end optimal algorithms for integrated QoS, traffic engineering, and failure recovery. *IEEE/ACM Trans. Netw.*, 15(4):813–823, 2007.

[24] J. Mudigonda, P. Yalagandula, M. Al-Fares, and J. C. Mogul. SPAIN: COTS data-center ethernet for multipathing over arbitrary topologies. In *Proc. Networked Systems Design and Implementation*, Apr. 2010.

[25] N. Mysore et al. Portland: A scalable fault-tolerant layer 2 data center network fabric. In *Proc. ACM SIGCOMM*, pages 39–50, 2009.

[26] A. Nucci, S. Bhattacharyya, N. Taft, and C. Diot. IGP link weight assignment for operational tier-1 backbones. *IEEE/ACM Trans. Netw.*, 15(4):789–802, 2007.

[27] E. Osborne and A. Simha. *Traffic Engineering with MPLS*. Cisco Press, Indianapolis, IN, 2002.

[28] P. Pan, G. Swallow, and A. Atlas. Fast reroute extensions to RSVP-TE for LSP tunnels. IETF RFC 4090, 2005.

[29] E. Rosen, A. Viswanathan, and R. Callon. Multiprotocol label switching architecture. IETF RFC 3031, 2001.

[30] H. Saito, Y. Miyao, and M. Yoshida. Traffic engineering using multiple multipoint-to-point LSPs. In *Proc. INFOCOM*, volume 2, pages 894–901, 2000.

[31] H. Saito and M. Yoshida. An optimal recovery LSP assignment scheme for MPLS fast reroute. In *International Telecommunication Network Strategy and Planning Symposium (Networks)*, pages 229–234, 2002.

[32] Y. Seok, Y. Lee, Y. Choi, and C. Kim. Dynamic constrained multipath routing for MPLS networks. In *International Conference on Computer Communications and Networks*, pages 348–353, 2001.

[33] S. Sharma, K. Gopalan, S. Nanda, and T. Chiueh. Viking: A multi-spanning-tree ethernet architecture for metropolitan area and cluster networks. In *Proc. INFOCOM*, volume 4, pages 2283 – 2294, 2004.

[34] V. Sharma and F. Hellstrand. Framework for multi-protocol label switching (MPLS)-based recovery. IETF RFC 3469, 2003.

[35] J.-P. Vasseur, M. Pickavet, and P. Demeester. *Network Recovery: Protection and Restoration of Optical, SONET-SDH, IP, and MPLS*, pages 397–422. Morgan Kaufmann Publishers Inc., San Francisco, CA, 2004.

[36] D. Wang and G. Li. Efficient distributed bandwidth management for MPLS fast reroute. *IEEE/ACM Trans. Netw.*, 16(2):486–495, 2008.

[37] J. Wang, S. Patek, H. Wang, and J. Liebeherr. Traffic engineering with AIMD in MPLS networks. In *IEEE International Workshop on Protocols for High Speed Networks*, pages 192–210, 2002.

[38] Y. Wang et al. R3: Resilient routing reconfiguration. In *Proc. ACM SIGCOMM*, pages 291–302, 2010.

[39] D. Wendlandt, I. Avramopoulos, D. Andersen, and J. Rexford. Don't secure routing protocols, secure data delivery. In *Proc. ACM SIGCOMM Workshop on Hot Topics in Networks*, Nov. 2006.

[40] E. W. Zegura. GT-ITM: Georgia Tech internetwork topology models (software), 1996.

[41] W. Zhang, J. Tang, C. Wang, and S. de Soysa. Reliable adaptive multipath provisioning with bandwidth and differential delay constraints. In *Proc. INFOCOM*, pages 2178–2186, 2010.

APPENDIX

A. PROOFS

This Appendix shows that two problems are NP-hard:

FAILURE STATE DISTINGUISHING
INSTANCE: A directed graph $G = (V, E)$, source and destination vertices $u, v \in V$, and a sets $s \subseteq E$.
QUESTION: Is there a simple directed path P from u to v that is up if the edges in s do not fail and down if they fail?

BOUNDED PATH LOAD BALANCING
INSTANCE: A directed graph $G = (V, E)$ with a positive rational capacity c_e for each edge $e \in E$, a collection S of subsets $s \subseteq E$ of *failure states* with a rational weight w^s for each $s \in S$, a set of triples (u_d, v_d, h_d), $1 \leq d \leq k$, corresponding to *demands*, where h_d units of demand d need to be sent from source vertex $u_d \in V$ to destination vertex $v_d \in V$, an integer bound J on the number of paths that can be used between any source-destination pair, a piecewise-linear increasing cost function $\Phi(\ell)$ mapping edge loads ℓ to rationals, and an overall cost bound B.
QUESTION: Are there J (or fewer) paths between each source-destination pair such that the given demands can be assigned to the paths so that the cost (sum of $\Phi(\ell)$ over all edges and weighted failure states as described in the text) is B or less?

To prove that a problem X is NP-hard, we must show that for some known NP-hard problem Y, any instance y of Y can be transformed into an instance x of X in polynomial time, with the property that the answer for y is yes if and only if the answer for x is yes. Both our problems can be proved NP-hard by transformations from the following problem, proved NP-hard by Fortune, Hopcroft, and Wyllie [7].

DISJOINT DIRECTED PATHS
INSTANCE: A directed graph $G(V, E)$ and distinguished vertices $u_1, v_1, u_2, v_2 \in V$.
QUESTION: Are there directed paths P_1 from u_1 to v_1 and P_2 from u_2 to v_2 such that P_1 and P_2 are vertex-disjoint?

THEOREM 1. *The* FAILURE STATE DISTINGUISHING *problem is NP-hard.*

Proof. Suppose we are given an instance $G = (V, E), u_1, v_1, u_2, v_2$ of DISJOINT DIRECTED PATHS. Our constructed instance of FAILURE STATE DISTINGUISHING consists of the graph $G' = (V, E')$, where $E' = E \cup \{(v_1, u_2)\}$, with $u = u_1$, $v = v_2$, and $s = \{(v_1, u_2)\}$.

Given this choice of s, a simple directed path from u to v that is up only if the edge (v_1, u_2) is up must contain that edge. We claim that such a path exists if and only if there are vertex-disjoint directed paths P_1 from u_1 to v_1 and P_2 from u_2 to v_2. Suppose a distinguishing path P exists. Then it must consist of of three segments: a path P_1 from $u = u_1$ to v_1, the edge (v_1, u_2), and then a path P_2 from u_2 to $v = v_2$. Since it is a simple path, P_1 and P_2 must be vertex-disjoint. Conversely, if vertex-disjoint paths P_1 from u_1 to v_1 and P_2 from u_2 to v_2 exist, then the path P that concatenates P_1 followed by (v_1, u_2) followed by P_2 is our desired distinguishing path. ∎

THEOREM 2. *The* BOUNDED PATH LOAD BALANCING *problem is NP-hard even if there are only two commodities ($k = 2$), only one path is allowed for each ($J = 1$), and there is only one failure state s.*

Proof. For this result we use the variant of DISJOINT DIRECTED PATHS in which we ask for edge-disjoint rather than vertex-disjoint paths. The NP-hardness of this variant is easy to prove, using a construction in which each vertex x of G is replaced by a pair of new vertices in_x and out_x connected by the edge (in_x, out_x), and each edge (x, y) of G is replaced by the edge (out_x, in_y).

Suppose we are given an instance $G = (V, E), u_1, v_1, u_2, v_2$ of the edge-disjoint variant of DISJOINT DIRECTED PATHS. Our constructed instance of BOUNDED PATH LOAD BALANCING is based on the same graph, with each edge e given capacity $c_e = 1$, with the single failure state $s = \phi$ (i.e., the state with no failures), with $w^s = 1$, and with demands represented by $(u_1, v_1, 1)$ and $(u_2, v_2, 1)$. The cost function Φ has derivative $\Phi'(\ell) = 1$, $0 \leq \ell \leq 1$, and $\Phi'(\ell) = |E| + 1$, $\ell > 1$. Our target overall cost bound is $B = |E|$.

If the desired disjoint paths exist, we can use P_1 to send the required unit of traffic from u_1 to v_1, and P_2 to send the traffic from u_2 to v_2. Since the paths are edge-disjoint, no edge will carry more than one unit of traffic, so the cost per edge used is 1, and the total number of edges used is at most $|E|$. Thus the specified cost bound $B = |E|$ is met. On the other hand, if no such pair of paths exist, then we must choose paths P_1 and P_2 that share at least one edge, which will carry two units of flow, for a cost of at least $|E| + 1$, just for that edge. Thus if there is a solution with cost $|E|$ or less, the desired disjoint paths must exist. ∎

Adding more paths, failure states, or commodities cannot make the problem easier. Note, however, that this does not imply that the problem for the precise cost function Φ presented in the text is NP-hard. It does, however, mean that, assuming P $\neq$ NP, any efficient algorithm for that Φ would have to exploit the particular features of that function.

Record and Transplay: Partial Checkpointing for Replay Debugging Across Heterogeneous Systems

Dinesh Subhraveti
Columbia University
dinesh@cs.columbia.edu

Jason Nieh
Columbia University
nieh@cs.columbia.edu

ABSTRACT

Software bugs that occur in production are often difficult to reproduce in the lab due to subtle differences in the application environment and nondeterminism. To address this problem, we present TRANSPLAY, a system that captures production software bugs into small per-bug recordings which are used to reproduce the bugs on a completely different operating system without access to any of the original software used in the production environment. TRANSPLAY introduces *partial checkpointing*, a new mechanism that efficiently captures the partial state necessary to reexecute just the last few moments of the application before it encountered a failure. The recorded state, which typically consists of a few megabytes of data, is used to replay the application without requiring the specific application binaries, libraries, support data, or the original execution environment. TRANSPLAY integrates with existing debuggers to provide standard debugging facilities to allow the user to examine the contents of variables and other program state at each source line of the application's replayed execution. We have implemented a TRANSPLAY prototype that can record unmodified Linux applications and replay them on different versions of Linux as well as Windows. Experiments with several applications including Apache and MySQL show that TRANSPLAY can reproduce real bugs and be used in production with modest recording overhead.

Categories and Subject Descriptors

C.4 [**Performance of Systems**]: Reliability, availability, serviceability; D.2.5 [**Software Engineering**]: Testing and Debugging; D.4.5 [**Operating Systems**]: Reliability

General Terms

Design, Experimentation, Performance, Reliability.

Keywords

Record-Replay, Virtualization, Checkpoint-Restart.

1. INTRODUCTION

When core business processes of a customer are suspended due to an application failure, quickly diagnosing the problem and putting the customer back in business is of utmost importance. Resolving a bug typically starts with reproducing it in the lab. However, reproducing a software bug is one of the most time consuming and difficult steps in the resolution of a problem. Reproducibility of a bug is impacted by heterogeneity of the application environments. A variety of operating systems, corresponding libraries and their many versions, application tiers supplied by different ISVs, and network infrastructure with varied configuration settings make application environments complex and bugs hard to reproduce. The source of the problem might be an incorrect assumption implicitly made by the application about the availability or configuration of local services such as DNS, or about co-deployed applications and their components, or it may surface only when a particular library version is used [33]. Furthermore, nondeterministic factors such as timing and user inputs contribute to the difficulty in reproducing software bugs.

Because the common approach of conveying a bug report is often inadequate, record-replay approaches [29, 28, 31, 19, 24, 2, 13] have been proposed to capture and reproduce hard-to-find application bugs. By directly recording the application and capturing the bug as it occurs, the burden of repeated testing to reproduce the bug is removed. Despite its potential for simplifying bug reproduction and debugging, the fundamental limitation of previous record-replay approaches is that they require the availability or replication of the production application environment during replay. All previous approaches require at minimum the availability of all original code executed as a part of the recording, including not just the buggy application binary, but also any other software executed, such as other applications, libraries, utilities, and the operating system. The original code is required to generate the instructions that will be executed during replay.

This is problematic in practice for several reasons. First, customers are generally unwilling to make available their actual production environment to vendors for debugging purposes given that keeping it up and running in production is crucial for business. Second, customers are often unwilling to even make replicas available since they may contain custom proprietary software and data that they do not want to provide in their entirety, or applications from other vendors which they are not allowed to provide to a competing vendor. Third, even if customers provide detailed information to allow vendors to create replicas, it is quite difficult for them to get all the versions and configurations of all software right to replay a bug that occurred in a complex production environment. Fourth, even if an exact replica of a production environment could be created for debugging purposes, its creation may be prohibitively expensive in terms of both hardware and software requirements for complex production environments. Finally, bugs can be data dependent and all necessary data is typically not available outside of the original production environment. While it may be possible to record every single instruction executed along with all data arguments so that they can be replayed without need for the production environment, such a recording would be prohibitively expensive to do, impose excessive storage requirements, and result in unacceptable recording overhead in production.

We introduce TRANSPLAY, a software failure diagnosis tool that can package up the minimum amount of data necessary to correctly reproduce production software bugs on a stateless target machine in the developer environment. Exclusively relying on a per-bug lightweight recording, TRANSPLAY deterministically reproduces the captured bug on a different operating system, without access to any originally executed binaries or support data. At the target lab, there is no need to install or configure the original application, support libraries, other applications, or the operating system to reproduce the failure. Portions of the application environment, including bits of application and library code necessary to reproduce the failure, are automatically detected and recorded.

TRANSPLAY introduces *partial checkpointing*, a simple technique based on the premise of short error propagation distances [21, 32] that captures the buggy execution of the application in its last few seconds prior to failure. Instead of the traditional approach of taking a full application checkpoint representing its cumulative state until that point, followed by a log of external inputs, partial checkpointing completely ignores the application's previous execution and focuses on state accessed by the application within the interval of interest. Every piece of required data, including the instructions executed within its binary and other libraries, is captured. In this model, the application is treated as a state machine with the processor context as its only internal state, with all other state captured on initial access.

Partial checkpointing provides two guarantees by design. First, all state necessary to replay the interval of execution is captured. As TRANSPLAY monitors every interface through which the application could access external data, any data required by the application during its deterministic reexecution is guaranteed to be available. This completeness also decouples replay from the target environment by providing necessary state from the self-contained log. Second, any state not directly accessed by the application is not included in the recording. Since TRANSPLAY only captures state actually accessed by the application, any extraneous state such as unaccessed parts of the application's address space or its binaries, are not included, leading to a small per-bug recording.

TRANSPLAY allows playing back the bug captured within a partial checkpoint in a different environment by decoupling replay from the target environment. The application is decoupled from its binaries and memory state by trapping accesses to the code pages and mapping the actual pages captured at the source, thus avoiding any version discrepancies. Relevant pages from potentially large memory mapped data files are presented back to the application as needed. Replay is decoupled from the operating system by replaying the system call results instead of reexecuting them. Processes of an application are decoupled from one another as well so that replay can be done on a subset of processes, rather than needing to replay an entire application. Applications are decoupled from the memory address space through a lightweight binary translation technique designed specifically for user code that enables the application to be restored on a different operating system. Applications are decoupled from processor MMU structures such as segment descriptor tables by trapping and emulating the offending instructions during replay.

TRANSPLAY achieves the record-replay functionality while meeting four important goals. First, TRANSPLAY does not require source code modifications, relinking, or other assistance from the application. Second, TRANSPLAY does not require specialized hardware modifications which limit its use and are expensive to implement. Third, recorded state is per bug and small enough to be easily shared with the developer. Having to share large amounts of data, as in the case of VM images, adversely impacts ease of use and privacy. Fourth, TRANSPLAY's recording overhead is low enough that it can be used in production. Allowing TRANSPLAY's instrumentation to be enabled while the application is running in production also side steps the probe effect problem.

We have implemented a TRANSPLAY prototype that integrates with standard interactive debuggers. Our prototype can record application execution on one Linux system and replay it on different Linux distributions or on Windows without any of the original application binaries or libraries. Using several real multi-process and multi-threaded applications, we demonstrate TRANSPLAY's ability to record and deterministically replay execution across completely different Linux environments and across Linux and Windows operating systems, capturing the root cause of various types of real software bugs in desktop and server applications. Recording overhead is less than 3% for most applications including Apache, and less than 17% in all cases, with respective partial checkpoints consuming less than 5 MB.

2. USAGE MODEL AND SYSTEM OVERVIEW

TRANSPLAY is a tool for recording and replaying specified intervals of the execution of a group of processes and threads. We refer to a group of processes and threads being recorded or replayed as a *session*. A session can consist of multiple processes that make up an application or a set of applications, where each process may contain threads that share the address space of the process. Once TRANSPLAY is installed on the same machine as a production application, it continuously records its execution. When a fault occurs, TRANSPLAY outputs a set of partial checkpoints and logs taken before the fault. A partial checkpoint is the partial state of a session which needs to be restored initially to replay the session's execution for a specified time interval. A log contains the events recorded over the interval that works together with a partial checkpoint to enable deterministic replay. When recording multiple processes, partial checkpoints and logs are saved separately for each process, along with information identifying the process that had the failure.

TRANSPLAY divides the recording of an application into periodic, contiguous time intervals. For each time interval, it records a partial checkpoint and log for each application process that executes during that interval. A recording interval can be configured to be of any length. As the application executes, a series of partial checkpoints and logs are generated and the most recent set of checkpoints and logs are stored in a fixed size memory buffer. Storing a set of partial checkpoints and logs rather than just the most recent one ensures that a certain minimum amount of execution context is available when a failure occurs. Partial checkpoints and logs are maintained in memory to avoid disk I/O and minimize runtime overhead. Older partial checkpoints and logs are discarded to make room for the new ones. Partial checkpoints and logs in memory can be written to disk at any time by stopping the current recording interval, causing the accumulated partial checkpoints and logs in memory to be written to disk. TRANSPLAY has built-in support for detecting explicit faults such as a segmentation violation and divide by zero, and provides an interface to integrate with external fault sensors.

When a failure occurs, the recording can be made available to the developer in lieu of, or as an attachment to a bug report. The bug can then be directly replayed on any hardware in the developer's environment using TRANSPLAY. Although the failure may involve the interaction of multiple tiers of software, the developer does not need access to any of that software to reproduce the failure. This is important since an application developer may have access to only his application software, not other software required to reproduce the failure. Since TRANSPLAY captures architecture dependent binary instructions of the application as a part of its partial checkpoint, the target CPU where replay is performed is required to be the same type as the original CPU. Other hardware attributes are not required to be the same.

Using partial checkpoints, a developer does not need to replay an entire multi-process application or a set of applications. The developer could just select the process where the fault occurs to simplify problem diagnosis, and TRANSPLAY will replay just that process, with its interactions with other application processes virtualized. If the selected process uses shared memory, TRANSPLAY will also simultaneously replay other processes that share memory with the selected process to provide deterministic replay.

TRANSPLAY integrates with the GNU Project Debugger (GDB) to closely monitor and analyze the execution of the application being replayed. Any inputs needed by the replay are provided from the recorded partial checkpoint and log, and any outputs generated by the replay are captured into an output file and made available to the user. If the application writes into a socket, for instance, the user would be able to examine the contents of the buffer passed to the `write` system call and also see how the content of the buffer is generated during the steps leading to the system call. For root cause analysis, TRANSPLAY allows the programmer to set breakpoints at arbitrary functions or source lines, single step the instructions, watch the contents of various program variables at each step, and monitor the application's original recorded interactions with the operating system and other processes. Reverse debugging can also be done by resuming the application from an earlier partial checkpoint with a breakpoint set to a desired point of execution in the past.

A partial checkpoint file itself does not contain any symbol information, so the debugger retrieves it from a separately provided symbol file. Typically, application binaries are stripped of their symbol table and debugging sections before they are shipped to the user. However, the symbol and debugging information is preserved in respective formats [1] separately in a symbol file which would be accessible to developers.

3. PARTIAL CHECKPOINTING

The traditional approach for recording an interval of an application's execution is to checkpoint the initial state of the application at the beginning of the interval, followed by logging events that guide replay. The initial checkpoint represents the cumulative execution until the beginning of the interval and the log represents data inputs and events required to guide replay. Such an approach may include data which is not relevant for reproducing the recorded bug. For example, the checkpoint may contain pages in the memory address space which will not be used at replay.

TRANSPLAY uses a different approach called partial checkpointing, to capture minimal but complete state required for replay. Treating the application as a state machine with the processor context as the only internal state, TRANSPLAY continuously monitors its interfaces to intercept and record every piece of state that crosses the application boundary. Any previous execution, and state accumulated as a result, is ignored. In addition to recording the system call results and other events required for deterministic replay, TRANSPLAY monitors accesses and changes to the address space pages and captures relevant information to create a self-contained recording of the application bug.

A partial checkpoint has four key characteristics. First, the state captured is completely decoupled from the underlying application binaries and the operating system. Second, it is defined only for a specific interval of an application's execution and contains only the portion of state accessed by the application in that interval. The space needed to store a partial checkpoint can be small since it is used only for recording execution of a brief interval of time. Even though an application itself may be large in its memory footprint and processing large quantities of data, it only accesses a fraction of itself during a brief interval of time. In contrast, regular checkpointing mechanisms [26, 23, 12], including virtual machine snapshots [5], rely on the availability of complete file system state or virtual machine images, including all software code and additional file snapshots, to resume execution. Third, it is only useful for deterministically replaying the specific time interval, not for running the application normally. When the application is replayed, it does not perform any useful work, except that its execution can be analyzed using tools such as debuggers and profilers. Fourth, it is captured over the specified time interval, not at a single point in time. A particular piece of state is included in the partial checkpoint when it is first accessed within the interval. For instance, a shared library page is included in the partial checkpoint when the application calls a function located in that page. Similarly, the state of an installed signal handler is included when the respective signal is delivered to a thread. Partial checkpointing further provides an efficient

Algorithm 1: Partial checkpointing mechanism implemented within the page fault handler

```
1  if partial flag in the PTE is set then
2  |  if page is shared then
3  |  |  add (page address, page content) to the corresponding shared_memory_object;
4  |  |  add (region's start address, corresponding shared_memory_object) to the process shared_maps;
5  |  else
6  |  |  if page is mapped within current recording interval then
7  |  |  |  add page and page content to the list of saved pages in the respective system call event_record;
8  |  |  else
9  |  |  |  add page to the initial_page_list;
10 |  |  end
11 |  end
12 end
```

representation that minimizes the information necessary to replay the application over a fixed time interval.

Partial checkpointing is substantially different from incremental checkpointing [27]. Incremental checkpointing assumes the existence of an earlier full checkpoint, and saves only the execution state that has changed since the prior checkpoint. To resume execution from an incremental checkpoint, the state from the full checkpoint must be restored, as well as the state from the subsequent incremental checkpoint. Partial checkpointing differs in at least three ways. First, partial checkpointing does not require saving or restoring any full checkpoint. All checkpointed state necessary to use a partial checkpoint is completely contained within the partial checkpoint. Second, a partial checkpoint is completed after a time interval to enable deterministic replay over only the previous time interval. In contrast, an incremental checkpoint occurs after a time interval to enable normal execution to be resumed after that time interval going forward. Third, a partial checkpoint contains state that has been read during a time interval, while an incremental checkpoint contains state that has been modified.

3.1 Partial Checkpointing Mechanism

We will use Linux semantics to describe how partial checkpointing and logging are done in further detail. A partial checkpoint broadly consists of session state accessed by processes and threads in the session, per process state, and per thread state. Per session state consists of global shared memory objects accessed during the interval and not tied to any process, such as shared mapped files and System V shared memory. Per process state consists of the initial set of memory pages needed to enable replay and mappings for global shared memory objects. Per thread state consists of CPU, FPU, and MMU state. To start recording a partial checkpoint for a time interval, TRANSPLAY forces all threads in the session to reach a synchronization barrier at their next entry into the kernel. The barrier is required to produce a globally consistent partial checkpoint across all threads. The last thread to reach the barrier records the CPU, FPU and MMU state of each thread, including the processor register state and the user created entries in the global and local descriptor tables. A status flag indicating that the session is in recording mode is set and all threads waiting at the barrier are woken up.

For both per process and per session memory state, only pages that were read during a recording interval need to be saved in a partial checkpoint. If a process only writes to a page, but does not read from it, such a page is not required from the partial checkpoint during replay. However, page table status flags provided by most processors are not sufficient to determine if a written page has also been read. We conservatively include all pages accessed during the interval in the partial checkpoint even though the application may not have read from some of them. This approximation works well in most cases as most pages that are written by an application are also read.

To save per process memory state in a partial checkpoint, TRANSPLAY must determine the memory pages that are read by the threads associated with the process during the interval of execution. Similarly, TRANSPLAY must also account for per session state corresponding to memory objects that are shared across multiple processes and not necessarily associated with any individual process. To save per session state in a partial checkpoint, TRANSPLAY must determine the memory pages of global shared memory objects that are read by the threads during the interval of execution. Algorithm 1 illustrates the partial checkpointing mechanism and Table 1 describes the data structures involved.

TRANSPLAY uses two types of objects to store the contents of accessed pages during the recording interval. A per process initial_page_set is allocated for memory regions private to a process. Each record in the set contains a page address and content. A per session shared_memory_object is allocated for each shared memory region accessed within a recording interval and contains the subset of pages accessed by any process or thread in the session in that interval. Each record in the set contains the offset of the page within the region and its content as of the first access to that page by any process or thread in that recording interval. The pages in the shared_memory_object may be mapped at different addresses by different processes.

To track which pages are accessed, TRANSPLAY utilizes the present bit available in the page table entry. It cooperatively shares its use with the kernel by keeping track of kernel use of and changes to these bits by using one of the unused bits available in the page table entry as a *partial flag*. At the beginning of the recording interval, TRANSPLAY clears the present bit for each page in the process address space that is present, using the partial flag to store the original value of the present bit. TRANSPLAY also clears the present bit and sets the partial flag whenever a new page table entry is added. When a thread accesses a page which does not have its present bit set, a page fault is generated. As a part of the page fault handler, TRANSPLAY checks the partial flag to see if it is set. If it is set, the page was originally present and needs to be recorded.

If the page belongs to a shared memory region, TRANSPLAY adds a record containing the offset of the page within the shared memory region and the page content to the `shared_memory_object` that represents the shared memory region. It updates a per process set of shared memory regions, `shared_maps`, that represents the mapped instances of the `shared_memory_object`s for that process. Otherwise, TRANSPLAY copies the page address and contents to the process's `initial_page_set`.

Each accessed page is copied just once when it is first accessed during the interval. Memory shared among threads associated with a process is automatically taken care of as a part of this simple mechanism. If a process is created via `fork` during the recording interval, its initially mapped pages at the time of creation that are accessed during the recording interval are also included in the partial checkpoint. This is done by performing the same operations to the process at creation time as were done to other processes already created at the beginning of the recording interval, namely clearing the present bit for each page in the process address space that is present, and using the partial flag to store the original value of the present bit. Note that for pages not corresponding to a shared memory region, TRANSPLAY only includes pages in the partial checkpoint that are already mapped at the beginning of the recording interval or at process creation.

Changes in Memory Region Geometry. The threads of an application may map, remap or unmap memory regions within a recording interval. TRANSPLAY must capture sufficient state to reproduce these events at replay. TRANSPLAY keeps track of the system calls made by each thread in a per-thread queue of `event_record` structures. In addition, TRANSPLAY keeps track of the system calls that map memory in the current recording interval in a per process stack called `recent_maps`, including a reference to the respective system call `event_record`. When a page is first accessed that was mapped during the recording interval, a page fault occurs and TRANSPLAY searches the `recent_maps` stack to find the most recently mapped memory region corresponding to the page, which is the current mapping being used by the thread. The page is then added to the respective system call `event_record` or to the respective `shared_memory_object` if it is for a shared memory region. If the page happens to be a global shared page, a record containing a pointer to its `shared_memory_object`, and the starting address where the shared memory region is mapped in the process address space is added to the `event_record` of the system call event that mapped the shared memory region. If the page was not mapped within the current recording interval, the record is added to the `shared_maps` set of the process. When a failure is detected and a partial checkpoint is emitted, the pages associated with the system call are saved along with the `event_record`.

An incremental partial checkpointing mechanism could be used to reduce storage requirements and copying overhead. Pages already copied as part of previous partial checkpoints that are still stored in memory do not need to be copied again in the current partial checkpoint if the contents remain the same. However, Section 5 shows that the additional complexity of incremental partial checkpointing is not needed as the storage requirements and copying overhead of regular partial checkpoints is modest.

3.2 Logging

TRANSPLAY performs logging to collect necessary information and application state to deterministically replay each thread and process in a session from an initial state defined by the partial checkpoint through the end of the recording interval. Logging serves two purposes. First, it records necessary data which may not be available at the target environment. Second, it captures information related to the outcomes of nondeterministic events to ensure a deterministic replay. Our logging mechanism builds on SCRIBE [13], a low-overhead operating system mechanism for deterministic record-replay that supports multi-threaded and multi-process applications on multiprocessors. TRANSPLAY leverages SCRIBE's mechanisms for handling nondeterminism due to signals, shared memory interleavings and instructions such as `rdtsc`. We omit further details about addressing these sources of nondeterminism due to space constraints. Unlike SCRIBE, TRANSPLAY provides a different system call logging mechanism which records all system call results rather than reexecuting them at replay. This is done to support replay debugging across heterogeneous systems.

4. PARTIAL REPLAY

To replay a piece of previously recorded application, the user chooses a process and an interval of execution to replay by selecting the corresponding partial checkpoints. To reproduce a deterministic replay of interleaved shared memory accesses among application processes, TRANSPLAY computes a *shared memory closure* of the selected process and replays all processes in the closure together as a session. A shared memory closure of a process `p` is the smallest set of processes consisting of `p`, such that no process within the set shares memory with a process outside the set. All threads within each process in the closure are included in the session and replayed together. To aid debugging, replay can also be done across consecutive recording intervals by coalescing the partial checkpoints and concatenating the respective logs; details are omitted due to space constraints.

Partial replay consists of two phases: *Load phase*, where the coalesced partial checkpoint of each process in the session is restored, and *Replay phase*, where the application threads are deterministically reexecuted within TRANSPLAY's control. Transition from load to replay phase occurs when control is transferred to the application code. We first describe the general mechanism of each of these phases, and then describe in further detail how the mechanism works for replaying specifically on Linux and Windows.

4.1 Partial Replay Mechanism

4.1.1 Load Phase

As a part of the load phase, TRANSPLAY prepares the process context required for the application to run independent of the target. It includes creating and populating the memory regions, creating the application processes and threads, and loading user created segment descriptor table entries. The x86 architecture provides global (GDT) and local (LDT) descriptor tables, which describe user accessible memory segments in its segmented memory model. Typical multi-threaded applications create private memory segments by adding segment descriptor entries to these tables and execute instructions that reference their entries. If the target operating system's segment layout matches with that

Data structure	Function
event_record	Entry describing system call state in per-thread system call queue
recent_maps	Stack of system call event_records that map memory regions within current recording interval
initial_page_set	Per-process set of pages initially restored at replay
shared_memory_object	Set of (page offset, page content) records describing a sparse shared memory region
shared_maps	Set of (page offset, shared_memory_object) records indicating shared memory regions mapped within a process
segment_selector	Key-value table that maps a segment register to the selector it contains during replay phase
selector_base	Key-value table that maps a selector to the base linear address of the segment it points to

Table 1: Key Transplay data structures

of the source and it provides an API to access the tables, TRANSPLAY loads the entries into the tables. If not, emulation of instructions that explicitly reference the segments must be done as described in Section 4.3.

A key requirement for heterogeneous replay is that the same address space regions used by the application during recording be available to the application during replay. Since TRANSPLAY captures non-relocatable chunks of application binaries directly from application's memory, they have to be loaded at the same address offsets at replay. However, in the general case, the required address regions may not be available on the target system, because they may be reserved for the operating system or system libraries. For example, the default Linux/x86 configuration makes 3 GB of address space available to the user space, but the default Windows configuration does not use the same size address space. Furthermore, system libraries such as Windows' kernel.dll and Linux's Virtual Dynamic Shared Object (VDSO) reserve specific address offsets for themselves, preventing the use of their address regions by the application.

Virtual machines and emulators decouple the user code from the target system by running it on a virtual MMU, but TRANSPLAY avoids full emulation of the processor MMU by making a reasonable assumption that the address regions required by application's memory pages are available to the user at replay. Common operating systems share the basic memory layout on a given architecture and typically allow the user to configure the way the linear address space is partitioned between the user and kernel space using a boot-time switch. For example, to record Linux/x86 applications and replay them on Windows/x86, a simple way to avoid conflicts is to configure Linux/x86 and Windows/x86 to allocate the bottom 2 GB and 3 GB, respectively, of address space to application programs. In this way, Windows system libraries, which only occupy a small region immediately below the kernel region, will not conflict with an application's pages in the bottom 2 GB of address space.

4.1.2 Replay Phase

The replay phase executes the instructions produced by the application during replay and decouples them from the target system. Most instructions dispatched by the application are executed natively. Note that TRANSPLAY does not need to process privileged instructions since a partial checkpoint never contains them. TRANSPLAY only tracks pages within the application address space. Any privileged instructions such as in or cli, which may be executed as a part of the system calls, are not included. However, there are two classes of instructions that TRANSPLAY may need to emulate: 1. instructions explicitly referencing user created segments, and 2. instructions that invoke a system call. Instructions that reference the user segments are emulated using a simple binary translation mechanism. Because the GDT and LDT may be managed differently by different operating sys-

tems, TRANSPLAY virtualizes an application's access to the tables.

TRANSPLAY emulates the system calls by intercepting the instructions used to invoke a system call, and emulating the call itself. For example, on the x86 architecture, Linux applications invoke the system calls using the sysenter or int x80 instruction. TRANSPLAY intercepts these instructions and emulates the respective system call based on techniques developed in RR [3]. For most system calls, emulation is done by simply returning the results of the system call from the recording, bypassing kernel execution. There are three classes of system calls that require further emulation: system calls for process control, system calls that modify the address space geometry, and system calls related to the MMU context. We discuss these in further detail in Sections 4.2 and 4.3. Replaying the system call results is done in an operating system independent way by TRANSPLAY on behalf of the application. The application never directly contacts the target operating system, thereby decoupling the replayed application from the operating system services of the target.

4.1.3 Integration with the Debugger

TRANSPLAY integrates with GDB by providing a GDB script that directs the load phase until the application is fully initialized for the user to start interacting through the debug interface. It also contains the necessary GDB directives to load the symbol information for the application being debugged. The script begins the debugging session with the invocation of the program that performs the load phase as the debuggee, which reads the partial checkpoint files, reconstructs their address space and initializes their threads. The debugger does not intervene during this process. The latency of the load phase is usually imperceptible to the user. After the application is loaded, a single forward step within the GDB script transfers control to the application code. The application is presented to the user in a stopped state while the debugger shows the register state and the source line of the application a few moments prior to the failure. The user can then set break points, single step through the source lines to examine program variables and monitor application's interactions with the operating system and other processes, to analyze the root cause. Any inputs needed by the application are automatically provided by TRANSPLAY. For instance, when the application attempts to read from the console, the input is directly provided from the log rather than waiting for user input. When the application executes the system call interrupt instruction in a debugging session, the perceived state of the application's registers and memory after returning from the instruction would be identical to its state at the corresponding point during recording.

4.2 Partial Replay Across Linux

Load Phase. The load phase is performed by a statically linked program, *partial checkpoint loader*, which cre-

Category	System Call	Linux	Windows
Process control	`fork`	emulate with `fork`	emulate with `CreateProcess`
	`clone`	forward to the OS	emulate with `CreateThread`
	`exit_group`	wait for other threads	wait for other threads
Memory geometry	`mmap, brk, execve`	emulate with `mmap` and `munmap`	emulate with `VirtualAlloc`
	`shmat, mmap` with `MAP_SHARED` flag	emulate with `shmat`	emulate with `MapViewOfFile`
	`munmap`	forward to the OS	emulate with `UnmapViewOfFile`
MMU context	`set_thread_area, modify_ldt`	forward to the OS	update `selector_base` table

Table 2: Transplay system call emulation

ates the application processes, restores their address space and finally transfers control to the application code. The partial checkpoint loader itself is built to be loaded at an unconventional address region to avoid conflicting with the pages of the application and does not use the standard program heap or stack. The partial checkpoint loader begins by creating the per session shared memory regions as defined by the `shared_memory_objects`, and mapping them into its address space. The sparse set of memory pages in each `shared_memory_object` are then loaded into respective shared memory regions, and the regions are unmapped.

A set of processes, each to become one of the processes recorded in the partial checkpoint, are recursively created with unconventional address regions used as their stacks, to avoid conflict with the application's stack pages. Each process begins restoring itself by attaching to the shared memory regions indicated by the `shared_maps` set in its partial checkpoint. Each page in the `initial_page_set` is then mapped as an independent, private, anonymous, writable region and its initial page content is loaded. After the page content is loaded, its protection flags are set to their original recorded values through `mprotect` system call. For example, if the page was originally a file map of a read-only shared library, it is first mapped as a writable anonymous region to load its contents, and the original page permissions are restored afterwards.

After the process address space is prepared, each process recursively creates its threads. Each process and thread loads respective descriptor table entries using the Linux API, and enters a `futex` barrier. Once all threads reach the barrier, the main replay thread invokes TRANSPLAY to attach to the threads and start replaying. Each thread then executes the instructions to restore the processor registers. When the instruction pointer is finally restored through a `jmp` instruction, the thread starts running the application code.

Replay Phase. During the replay phase, instructions explicitly referencing the user segments can be natively executed without any emulation because different Linux versions manage the GDT and LDT in the same way, and provide the API to load the entries required by the application. Most system calls made by the application are handled by simply copying the data from the respective `event_record`s. Table 2 lists three main classes of exceptions, where further processing is performed beyond data copy. In particular, for the `fork` system call, TRANSPLAY creates a new child process and preloads the pages indicated in the `event_record`. These pages include the pages accessed by the child process in the recording interval which were not present in the parent's address space. For the `exit_group` system call, TRANSPLAY defers its execution until all other threads in that process exhaust their `event_record`s, to avoid their premature termination. For system calls that map a new memory region (`mmap, brk, execve` etc.), the pages indicated in the system call's `event_record` are mapped and preloaded into memory.

For system calls that map a System V shared memory region or a shared memory mapped file, the `shared_memory_object` indicated in the `event_record` of the system call is mapped. For `clone`, `set_thread_area` and `modify_ldt` system calls, the system call is simply forwarded to the underlying kernel. The interleaving of shared memory accesses as recorded in the event stream is enforced among replaying processes and threads and any signals received by the application within the interval are delivered at respective points using the SCRIBE [13] mechanisms.

4.3 Partial Replay on Windows

TRANSPLAY's mechanism for replaying Linux applications on Windows is based on Pin instrumentation [16], but is conceptually similar to replaying on Linux as discussed in Section 4.2. We highlight the steps which are different below.

Load Phase. The load phase is performed by the Windows version of the partial checkpoint loader in user space using the Windows API. To replay the application, the partial checkpoint loader itself is started under the control of TRANSPLAY *pintool* [16]. TRANSPLAY pintool does not interfere with the loading process performed by the partial checkpoint loader. The creation of processes, partial reconstruction of their address space and creation of threads within them is performed as already outlined, except using equivalent Windows APIs. Once the partial checkpoints are loaded, each thread leaves the synchronization barrier and makes a special system call, which is normally undefined in Linux and Windows. The system call activates TRANSPLAY pintool by notifying it of the completion of the load phase and transition into replay phase. TRANSPLAY pintool reads the respective log file of the thread to obtain its saved processor context and loads it using Pin's `PIN_ExecuteAt` API function, which turns the control over to the application code.

Replay Phase. TRANSPLAY pintool continues with the replay phase to monitor the application to satisfy the requests it makes. In particular, TRANSPLAY emulates the key categories of the Linux system calls listed in Table 2 using equivalent Windows APIs. For other system calls, TRANSPLAY pintool traps the system call interrupt instruction, copies system call return data to the application, increments the instruction pointer to skip the system call instruction and allows the application to continue normally. In the absence of such a mechanism, executing the Linux system call interrupt instruction would cause a general protection fault on Windows. When new memory regions are mapped, respective memory pages that will be accessed by the application in its future execution are brought into memory in a way similar to Linux replay, except using the Windows semantics. For instance, Windows treats memory address space and the physical memory that backs it as separate resources, whereas Linux transparently associates physical pages to memory mapped regions. To emulate the Linux system calls that map new memory regions, TRANSPLAY reserves both the address space and the memory together.

Instructions explicitly referencing user segment registers are treated through a trap and emulate mechanism. Windows configures the CPU descriptor tables based on its memory layout which is different from that of Linux. A segment selector, which is an index into the segment descriptor table, used by the Linux application may point to a different region of memory on Windows or may not be valid at all. Any attempts to update the Windows descriptor tables may result in a conflict with the way Windows uses its resources. TRANSPLAY resolves these conflicts by intercepting and emulating the offending instructions within the Linux application's binary and the system calls that modify the descriptor tables.

TRANSPLAY uses two key-value table data structures, `segment_selector` and `selector_base`, to emulate the instructions with segment register operands. At any time during replay, the `segment_selector` table maps a segment register to the selector it contains, and the `selector_base` table maps a selector to the base linear address of the segment that it points to. When an instruction which refers to its operands through a segment register is encountered during replay, TRANSPLAY computes the location of each operand in the flat address space using the formula, `(segment base + operand base + displacement + index*scale)`, where `segment base` is the base address of the segment and is obtained by joining the two tables on the selector and the remaining terms have instruction semantics and are obtained from the instruction. TRANSPLAY then rewrites the original instruction such that the final linear address of the operand is used rather than referencing the segment register. The tables are initialized based on the descriptor table state captured in the partial checkpoint. As the application executes during replay, the `segment_selector` table is updated by intercepting the `mov` instructions that load the segment registers with selectors and the `segment_selector` table is updated by intercepting the `set_thread_area` and `modify_ldt` system calls which provide the mapping between the segment base address and the selector.

5. EXPERIMENTAL RESULTS

We have implemented TRANSPLAY as a kernel module and associated user-level tools on Linux which can record and replay partial checkpoints of multi-threaded and multi-process Linux applications across different Linux distributions. We have also implemented a user-level replay tool for Windows based on Pin binary instrumentation [16], which currently only replays partial checkpoints of non-threaded Linux applications on Windows. Our unoptimized prototype works with unmodified applications without any library or base kernel modifications. Using our prototype, we evaluate TRANSPLAY's effectiveness in (1) replaying partial checkpoints across environments differing in software installation, operating system and hardware, (2) minimizing runtime overhead and storage requirements of recording applications, and (3) capturing the root cause of various types of real software bugs on server and desktop applications.

Recording was done on a blade in an IBM HS20 eServer BladeCenter, each blade with dual 3.06 GHz Intel Xeon CPUs with hyperthreading, 2.5 GB RAM, a 40 GB local disk, and interconnected with a Gigabit Ethernet switch. Each blade was running the Debian 3.1 distribution and the Linux 2.6.11 kernel and appears as a 4-CPU multiprocessor to the operating system. For server application workloads that also required clients, we ran the clients on another blade. Replay was done in three different environments: (1) a different blade in the BladeCenter running Debian 3.1, (2) a Lenovo T61p notebook with an Intel Core 2 Duo 2.4 GHz CPU, 2 GB RAM, and a 160 GB local disk running Windows XP 3.0 with Pin-25945, and (3) a VMware virtual machine with 2 CPUs, 512 MB RAM, and an 8 GB virtual disk running Linux Gentoo 1.12 using VMware Player 3.0 on the Lenovo notebook. None of the recorded application binaries were installed or available in any of the environments used for replay. Furthermore, the Windows and Gentoo replay environments had completely different software stacks from the Debian recording environment.

Table 3 lists the application workloads we recorded and replayed using TRANSPLAY. The server applications were the Apache web server in both multi-process (`apache-p`) and multi-threaded (`apache-t`) configurations, the MySQL server (`mysql`), and the Squid web cache proxy server (`squid`). `httperf-0.9` was used as the benchmark for the web servers and web proxy to generate 20,000 connection requests. The desktop applications were a media player (`mplayer`) and various compute and compression utilities (`gzip`, `bc`, and `ncomp`). The applications were all run with their default configurations. We recorded each application workload by taking partial checkpoints at three different intervals: 5, 10, and 15 seconds. All of the applications were recorded and deterministically replayed correctly across all three different replay environments except for `mysql` and `apache-t`, which were replayed in the two different Linux environments but not in Windows due to threading.

5.1 Performance and Storage Overhead

Table 3 lists the execution time for each application workload when run natively on Linux without TRANSPLAY, and Figure 1 shows the normalized runtime overhead of recording the application workloads compared to native execution. As a conservative measure and due to space constraints, we show the recording overhead for the shortest of the intervals used, 5 seconds. Overhead for the 10 and 15 seconds was smaller due to the longer recording intervals. For the 5 second intervals, the recording overhead was under 3% for all workloads except for `squid` and `mysql`, where the overhead was 9% and 17%, respectively.

Figure 1 also shows the speedup of replay on Linux and Windows for 5 second replay intervals. Replay results are shown for 5 second intervals for Linux using the blade and Windows using the notebook; other results are omitted due to space constraints. Replay was generally faster than recording, several times faster in some cases. Two factors contribute to replay speedup: omitted in-kernel work due to system calls partially or entirely skipped (e.g. network output), and time compressed due to skipped waiting at replay (e.g. timer expiration). `bc` did not show any speedup because it is a compute-bound workload which performs few system calls. Speedups on Windows were smaller due to the additional overhead of binary instrumentation and emulation required to replay on Windows. The binary instrumentation overhead was less for longer replay intervals as Pin's overhead of creating the initial instruction cache for emulation is amortized over the replay interval.

Figure 2 shows a measure of partial checkpoint latency,

Name	Workload	Time	Bug	Memory	Partial	Log
mysql	MySQL 3.23.56, 10 threads, run `sql-bench`	105 s	data race	121 MB	538 KB	29 KB
apache-t	Apache 2.0.48, 57 threads, run `httperf 0.9`	57 s	atomicity violation	221 MB	1305 KB	2284 KB
apache-p	Apache 2.0.54, 6 processes, run `httperf 0.9`	59 s	library incompatibility	4188 KB	935 KB	2570 B
squid	Squid 2.3, run `httperf 0.9`	82 s	heap overflow	7192 KB	991 KB	4 KB
bc	bc 1.06, compute π to 5000 decimal places	55 s	heap overflow	2172 KB	349 KB	2714 B
gzip	Gzip 1.2.4, compress 200 MB /dev/urandom data	68 s	global buffer overflow	1820 KB	321 KB	1341 B
ncomp	Ncompress 4.2, compress 200 MB /dev/urandom data	82 s	stack smash	1440 KB	293 KB	1229 B
mplayer	Mplayer 1.0rc2, play 10 MB 1080p HDTV video at 24 fps	40 s	device incompatibility	44 MB	1393 KB	9513 KB

Table 3: Application workloads and bugs

the average time it takes to atomically finish recording one interval and start recording a subsequent recording interval while doing a periodic recording of the applications. It includes the time taken for the application threads to reach the synchronization barrier so that a consistent initial state of the application for the partial checkpoint can be recorded. The application is not completely stopped during this time. Some of the application threads may still be running application code while others reach the barrier. The barrier is created in the kernel when checkpoint request arrives and each application thread reaches the barrier the next time it enters the kernel. Once all threads reach the barrier, the rest of the processing is done. The latency is less than a few hundred milliseconds in all cases. The average latency was the same for the 5, 10, and 15 second recording intervals.

We saved the last three partial checkpoints and their associated logs for each application and characterized their size and composition. For mplayer, only the last two partial checkpoints and logs were saved for the 15 second recording interval due to its relatively short execution time. We only considered complete intervals, so if 5 second recording intervals were used and an application had a partial checkpoint at the end of its execution accounting for the last 2 seconds of execution, that partial checkpoint was not included in this characterization.

Figure 3 shows the average total size of partial checkpoints across all processes of each workload for 5, 10 and 15 second recording intervals. Partial checkpoint sizes are modest in all cases, no more than roughly 5 MB even for the longest recording intervals. Most of an application's memory pages are not accessed during any particular interval of execution. For example, the largest partial checkpoint was roughly 5 MB for mysql, which had a virtual memory footprint of well over 100 MB. Figure 3 also shows the size of the partial checkpoints when compressed using lzma, as denoted by the patterned bars. In addition to the fact that the partial checkpoint data compressed well, the high compression ratios indicated were also due to our unoptimized prototype which will end up storing duplicate code pages with the same content for multi-process applications. While the cost of taking regular full checkpoints is usually highly correlated with checkpoint size due to the large amount of memory state that needs to be saved, Figures 2 and 3 show that partial checkpoint latency is not correlated with partial checkpoint size because the sizes are quite small.

Figure 4 shows the total size of logs generated by all processes of each application for 5, 10 and 15 second recording intervals. mysql had the most log data due to the high density of system call events carrying input data presented by sql-bench. For a 5 second recording interval, the log size was 59 MB. While this is significant storage overhead, the log does not accumulate over time. Even though TRANSPLAY continuously records the application, it only stores the most

recent execution history within a buffer of fixed size. bc was mostly compute bound and had the least log data, less than 1 KB, which is not visible in Figure 4. Figure 4 also shows the compressed log sizes, as denoted by the patterned bars. The logs of most workloads compressed well, except for gzip, ncomp and mplayer, for which negligible compression was obtained and hence the compressed values are not visible. The log of gzip and ncomp mostly contained the 200 MB of random data, which does not compress well. The log of mplayer was dominated by the compressed video file, which also does not compress well.

Figure 5 shows the composition of each application's log. The three bars shown for each application correspond from left to right to the 5, 10, and 15 second recording intervals, respectively. The log data is classified into four categories: sys is system call records and integer return values, output is the data returned from system calls, mmap is pages mapped during the recording interval, and shm are events corresponding to page ownership management of shared memory. In most cases, the log was dominated by output data which is returned to the replayed application through system calls. One of the primary goals of TRANSPLAY is to decouple the application from its source environment and TRANSPLAY meets this goal in part by logging more data than other record-replay systems that require an identical replay environment. bc produced a small log, mostly containing the system call records. apache-t shows many page ownership management events in its log since it is a multi-threaded application with many threads. mysql has fewer threads and less page ownership management events. Log data due to memory mapped pages was generally small relative to other constituents of the log because most of the memory mappings occurred at the beginning of the applications and the logs are for the last few complete intervals of application execution.

5.2 Software Bugs

Table 3 also lists with each application the real-life software bugs that we used to measure TRANSPLAY's ability to capture and reproduce failures. All of the application bugs were taken from BugBench [15], except for the bugs for apache-p and mplayer, which were collected from Internet forums where they were reported. The bugs include nondeterministic data race bugs, different types of memory corruption issues such as buffer overflow, and issues due to incompatible interactions with the target environment where the application was run. We recorded each faulty application while the bug is triggered. In some cases, the experiment had to be repeated many times before the bug manifested. mysql and apache-t bugs were nondeterministic data race bugs. The apache-t bug was triggered by running two concurrent instances of the httperf benchmark and the mysql bug was triggered using mysql's rpl_max_relay_size test.

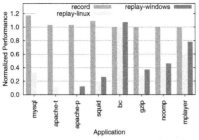

Figure 1: Recording overhead

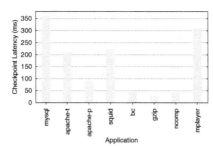

Figure 2: Checkpoint latency

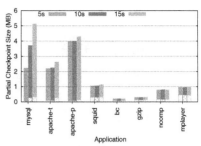

Figure 3: Partial checkpoint size

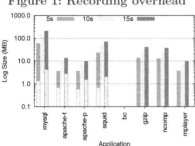

Figure 4: Log size

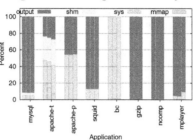

Figure 5: Log composition

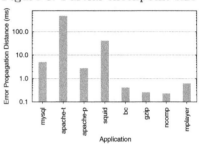

Figure 6: Error propagation distance

For most other applications, the bug is triggered using malformed input. For example, the bug for bc is triggered using a malformed bc script, the bug for squid is triggered using a malformed client request, and the bugs for gzip and ncompress are triggered using malformed command line input.

Table 3 shows the partial checkpoint and log sizes for TRANSPLAY to capture and reproduce each bug. We also measured the virtual memory footprint of each application as reported by the top command to provide a rough measure of the amount of state required to run it. In practice, applications typically require more data than the content of their virtual memory. They also indirectly rely on the state represented by their environment and the operating system. In all cases, the size of the sum of the partial checkpoint and log is much less than the virtual memory footprint of each application. Within the same recording interval where the mplayer bug was triggered, it was also mapping various codec libraries and accessing their pages to initialize them. This additional noise accounts for the large log size produced by the mplayer bug. Note that the partial checkpoints and logs required to capture the bugs are in general much less than what was required to record the more resource-intensive application workloads shown in Figures 3 and 4.

Once a recording of the bug occurrence was captured, TRANSPLAY was able to deterministically replay the bug every time, even on a different platform, and was useful to diagnose the root cause of each bug. For example, for the mysql and apache-t nondeterministic data race bugs, TRANSPLAY correctly captured the specific interleaving of shared memory accesses required to reproduce the bug. TRANSPLAY was able to capture all data required to reproduce these bugs with partial checkpoint and log sizes orders of magnitude smaller than the application's memory footprint. In general, TRANSPLAY captured the bug-triggering conditions and input required to reproduce all bugs. For instance, the malformed client request which caused squid to fail and the relevant code snippet from the input program that triggered a heap overflow in bc were part of the log recorded by TRANSPLAY. In the case of apache-p and mplayer, the bugs occurred due to incompatibility with the target environment. For apache-p, one of the processes would silently exit when it notices unexpected behavior from a function in one of the libraries it uses due to an incompatible version. Since TRANSPLAY captured the code page in the library where the offending function existed, TRANSPLAY was able to reproduce the faulty behavior even on the system where the right version of the library was installed. Other record-replay tools which only record at the system call interface would not be able to capture these types of bugs. Similarly, TRANSPLAY correctly captured the root cause of the problem for mplayer, which failed due to an incompatible audio device at the target system.

Figure 6 shows the error propagation distance for each bug listed in Table 3. To measure error propagation distance, we instrumented TRANSPLAY to log the value of the time stamp counter along with each recorded event, and calculated the time between two closest events that encompass the root cause of the bug and the appearance of its symptom. In all cases, the observed value was less than half a second, supporting TRANSPLAY's assumption and demonstrating that a modest recording interval of 5 seconds as used in our experiments is sufficient to reproduce the bugs. Bugs with longer propagation distances may be captured by dedicating more storage space to store longer intervals of execution.

6. RELATED WORK

Many diagnosis and debugging tools have been developed. While interactive debugging tools [8] are helpful for analyzing bugs that can be easily reproduced, they do not assist with reproducing bugs. Techniques for compile-time static checking [7] and runtime dynamic checking [11] are useful in detecting certain types of bugs, but many bugs escape these detection methods and surface as failures, to be reproduced and debugged in the developer environment. Bug reporting mechanisms [18, 10] collect information when a failure occurs, but they are often limited in their ability to provide insight into the root cause of the problem because they represent the aftermath of the failure, not the steps that lead to it.

Many record-replay approaches have been proposed to improve bug reproducibility and debugging [14, 29, 28, 31, 19, 24, 2, 13]. All of these approaches impose crucial dependencies between the environment at the time of replay and the original production recording environment. Although some approaches claim to be able to replay in a different environment from which recording occurs, all previous approaches assume the availability during replay of all software code used during recorded execution. Hardware mechanisms [34, 20, 17] record data accesses at an instruction granularity, but do not record code and rely on the availability of binaries to replay instructions. Netzer and Weaver [22] proposed a tracing mechanism that has some similarities to partial checkpointing. Tracing creates a checkpoint for replaying from some starting point by recording values of memory locations when they are initially read, then restoring all of those values upon replay. Tracing differs fundamentally from partial checkpointing as it does not support replay in a different environment and requires the availability of the same instrumented application code. BugNet [21] uses a similar approach at the hardware level to record the operand values accessed by load instructions at the hardware level to replay the execution. Partial checkpointing is conceptually different from this approach because TRANSPLAY considers all data including the instruction opcodes as external inputs in order to produce a self-contained recording.

Virtual machine mechanisms [6, 4] may allow replay on a different host environment from recording, but require the availability of the same virtual machine image at record and replay time, including all application, library, and operating system binaries. Not only does this require a large amount of data, but this is often impractical for bug reproducibility as customers are unlikely to allow application vendors to have an entire replica of all of their custom proprietary software. Crosscut [5] aims to extract a subset of data offline from a complete recording of a VM to reduce the size. However, it still requires a heavy weight instrumentation during recording and the original log it generates is large. Operating system mechanisms [29, 31] may record input data through system calls, but still require the availability of all files, including application binaries, during replay. For example, consider use of a memory mapped file or access to a memory mapped device, both of which would impose dependencies on devices and files from the original recording envionment. Neither of these types of data would be included by recording system call arguments or results, as has been previous proposed. Application, library, and programming language mechanisms [28, 9] not only require access to binaries during replay, but they also require access to source code to modify applications to provide record-replay functionality. In contrast, TRANSPLAY requires no access to any software from the production recording environment, including application, library, or operating system binaries.

Combining the key features of transparency, determinism, and low overhead has been difficult to achieve with record-replay, especially for multi-threaded applications on multi-processors. Hardware mechanisms face a high implementation barrier and do not support record-replay on commodity hardware. Application, library, and programming language mechanisms require application modifications, lacking transparency. Virtual machine mechanisms incur high overhead on multiprocessors, making them impractical to use in production environments [6]. To reduce recording overhead, various mechanisms propose record-replay that is not deterministic [2, 24]. Building on SCRIBE [13], TRANSPLAY addresses these shortcomings using a lightweight operating

system mechanism to provide transparent, fully deterministic record-replay for multi-threaded applications on multi-processors with low overhead.

A number of speculative tools leverage record-replay or checkpointing. Triage [32] proposes a diagnosis protocol to automatically determine the root cause of a software failure in production. ASSURE [30] and ClearView [25] attempt to automatically diagnose a failure and automatically patch the software, with a goal of quickly responding to vulnerabilities. While such techniques may work for a limited set of well characterized bugs, they are generally not suitable for many common bugs which require intuitive faculties and application-specific knowledge of a human programmer. For instance, the right set of program inputs and environment manipulations to be used for each repetition of the execution heavily depends on the application and is generally not possible to automatically generate.

7. CONCLUSIONS

TRANSPLAY is the first system which can capture production software bugs and reproduce them deterministically in a completely different environment, without access to any of the original software used in the production environment. TRANSPLAY accomplishes this by relying only on a lightweight per-bug recording; there is no need for access to any originally executed binaries or support data, no need to run the same operating system, and no need to replicate the original setup or do repeated testing. TRANSPLAY introduces partial checkpointing, a simple and novel mechanism to record the complete state required to deterministically replay an application, including relevant pieces of its executable files, for a brief interval of time before its failure. Partial checkpointing minimizes the amount of data to be recorded and decouples replay from the original execution environment while ensuring that all information necessary to reproduce the bug is available. TRANSPLAY integrates with a standard unmodified debugger to provide debugging facilities such as breakpoints and single-stepping through source lines of application code while the application is replayed. The captured state, which typically amounts to a few megabytes of data, can be used to deterministically replay the application.s execution to expose the steps that lead to the failure. No source code modifications, relinking or other assistance from the application is required.

Our experimental analysis on real applications running on Linux shows that TRANSPLAY (1) can capture the root cause of real-life software bugs and the necessary bug triggering data and events, (2) can capture partial checkpoints of unmodified Linux applications and deterministically replay them on other Linux distributions and on Windows, and (3) is able to generate partial checkpoints of applications such as Apache and MySQL with modest recording overhead and storage requirements. These results demonstrate that TRANSPLAY is a valuable tool that can simplify the root cause analysis of production application failures.

8. ACKNOWLEDGEMENTS

This work was supported in part by NSF grants CNS-09025246, CNS-0914845, and CNS-1018355, AFOSR MURI grant FA9550-07-1-0527, and IBM. Oren Laadan and Nicolas Viennot provided invaluable help with SCRIBE source code for implementing TRANSPLAY.

9. REFERENCES

[1] T. Allen et al. DWARF Debugging Information Format, Version 4, Jun 2010.

[2] G. Altekar and I. Stoica. ODR: Output-Deterministic Replay for Multicore Debugging. In *Proceedings of the 22nd Symposium on Operating Systems Principles (SOSP)*, Oct 2009.

[3] P. Bergheaud, D. Subhraveti, and M. Vertes. Fault Tolerance in Multiprocessor Systems via Application Cloning. In *Proceedings of the 27th International Conference on Distributed Computing Systems (ICDCS)*, Jun 2007.

[4] J. Chow, T. Garfinkel, and P. Chen. Decoupling Dynamic Program Analysis from Execution in Virtual Environments. In *Proceedings of the 2008 USENIX Annual Technical Conference*, Jun 2008.

[5] J. Chow, D. Lucchetti, T. Garfinkel, G. Lefebvre, R. Gardner, J. Mason, S. Small, and P. M. Chen. Multi-Stage Replay With Crosscut. In *Proceedings of the 6th International Conference on Virtual Execution Environments (VEE)*, Mar 2010.

[6] G. W. Dunlap, D. G. Lucchetti, M. A. Fetterman, and P. M. Chen. Execution Replay of Multiprocessor Virtual Machines. In *Proceedings of the 4th International Conference on Virtual Execution Environments (VEE)*, Mar 2008.

[7] D. Evans, J. Guttag, J. Horning, and Y. M. Tan. LCLint: A Tool For Using Specifications to Check Code. In *Proceedings of the 2nd Symposium on Foundations of Software Engineering (SIGSOFT)*, Dec 1994.

[8] GNU. GDB: The GNU Project Debugger, http://www.gnu.org/software/gdb/.

[9] Z. Guo, X. Wang, J. Tang, X. Liu, Z. Xu, M. Wu, M. F. Kaashoek, and Z. Zhang. R2: An Application-Level Kernel for Record and Replay. In *Proceedings of the 8th Symposium on Operating Systems Design and Implementation (OSDI)*, Dec 2008.

[10] IBM. WebSphere Application Server V6: Diagnostic Data, http://www.redbooks.ibm.com/redpapers/pdfs/redp4085.pdf.

[11] Intel. Assure, http://developer.intel.com/software/products/assure/.

[12] O. Laadan and J. Nieh. Transparent Checkpoint-Restart of Multiple Processes on Commodity Operating Systems. In *In Proceedings of the 2007 USENIX Annual Technical Conference*, Jun 2007.

[13] O. Laadan, N. Viennot, and J. Nieh. Transparent, Lightweight Application Execution Replay on Commodity Multiprocessor Operating Systems. In *Proceedings of the International Conference on Measurement and Modeling of Computer Systems (SIGMETRICS)*, Jun 2010.

[14] T. LeBlanc and J. Mellor-Crummey. Debugging Parallel Programs with Instant Replay. *IEEE Transactions on Computers*, C-36(4), Apr 1987.

[15] S. Lu, Z. Li, F. Qin, L. Tan, P. Zhou, and Y. Zhou. BugBench: Benchmarks for Evaluating Bug Detection Tools. In *PLDI Workshop on the Evaluation of Software Defect Detection Tools*, Jun 2005.

[16] C. Luk, R. Cohn, R. Muth, H. Patil, A. Klauser, G. Lowney, S. Wallace, V. J. Reddi, and K. Hazelwood. Pin: Building Customized Program Analysis Tools with Dynamic Instrumentation. In *Proceedings of the SIGPLAN Conference on Programming Language Design and Implementation (PLDI)*, Jun 2005.

[17] P. Montesinos, M. Hicks, S. T. King, and J. Torrellas. Capo: A Software-Hardware Interface for Practical Deterministic Multiprocessor Replay. In *Proceedings of the 14th International Conference on Architectural Support for Programming Languages and Operating Systems (ASPLOS)*, Mar 2009.

[18] Mozilla.org. Quality Feedback Agent, http://kb.mozillazine.org/Quality_Feedback_Agent.

[19] M. Musuvathi, S. Qadeer, T. Ball, G. Basler, P. Nainar, and I. Neamtiu. Finding and Reproducing Heisenbugs in Concurrent Programs. In *Proceedings of the 8th Symposium on Operating Systems Design and Implementation (OSDI)*, Dec 2008.

[20] S. Narayanasamy, C. Pereira, and B. Calder. Recording Shared Memory Dependencies Using Strata. In *Proceedings of the 12th International Conference on Architectural Support for Programming Languages and Operating Systems (ASPLOS)*, Oct 2006.

[21] S. Narayanasamy, G. Pokam, and B. Calder. BugNet: Continuously Recording Program Execution for Deterministic Replay Debugging. In *Proceedings of the 32nd International Symposium on Computer Architecture (ISCA)*, Jun 2005.

[22] R. Netzer and M. Weaver. Optimal Tracing and Incremental Reexecution for Debugging Long-Running Programs. In *Proceedings of the SIGPLAN Conference on Programming Language Design and Implementation (PLDI)*, Jun 1994.

[23] S. Osman, D. Subhraveti, G. Su, and J. Nieh. The Design and Implementation of Zap: A System for Migrating Computing Environments. In *Proceedings of the 5th Symposium on Operating System Design and Implementation (OSDI)*, Dec 2002.

[24] S. Park, Y. Zhou, W. Xiong, Z. Yin, R. Kaushik, K. H. Lee, and S. Lu. PRES: Probabilistic Replay With Execution Sketching on Multiprocessors. In *Proceedings of the 22nd Symposium on Operating Systems Principles (SOSP)*, Oct 2009.

[25] J. H. Perkins, S. Kim, S. Larsen, S. Amarasinghe, J. Bachrach, M. Carbin, C. Pacheco, F. Sherwood, S. Sidiroglou, G. Sullivan, W.-F. Wong, Y. Zibin, M. D. Ernst, and M. Rinard. Automatically Patching Errors in Deployed Software. In *Proceedings of the 22nd Symposium on Operating Systems Principles (SOSP)*, Oct 2009.

[26] J. Plank. An Overview of Checkpointing in Uniprocessor and Distributed Systems, Focusing on Implementation and Performance. Technical Report UT-CS-97-372, University of Tennessee, Jul 1997.

[27] J. Plank, J. Xu, and R. Netzer. Compressed Differences: An Algorithm for Fast Incremental Checkpointing. Technical Report UT-CS-95-302, University of Tennessee, Aug 1995.

[28] M. Ronsse and K. De-Bosschere. RecPlay: A Fully Integrated Practical Record/Replay System. *ACM Transactions on Computer Systems*, 17(2), May 1999.

[29] Y. Saito. Jockey: A User-space Library for Record-Replay Debugging. In *Proceedings of the 6th International Symposium on Automated Analysis-Driven Debugging (AADEBUG)*, Sep 2005.

[30] S. Sidiroglou, O. Laadan, C. Perez, N. Viennot, J. Nieh, and A. D. Keromytis. ASSURE: Automatic Software Self-Healing Using Rescue Points. In *Proceedings of the 14th International Conference on Architectural Support for Programming Languages and Operating Systems (ASPLOS)*, Mar 2009.

[31] S. Srinivasan, S. Kandula, C. Andrews, and Y. Zhou. Flashback: A Lightweight Extension for Rollback and Deterministic Replay for Software Debugging. In *Prooceedings of the 2004 USENIX Annual Technical Conference*, Jun 2004.

[32] J. Tucek, S. Lu, C. Huang, S. Xanthos, and Y. Zhou. Triage: Diagnosing Production Run Failures at the User's Site. In *Proceedings of the 21st Symposium on Operating Systems Principles (SOSP)*, Oct 2007.

[33] Wikipedia. Dependency Hell, http://en.wikipedia.org/wiki/Dependency_hell.

[34] M. Xu, R. Bodik, and M. Hill. A Flight Data Recorder for Enabling Full-system Multiprocessor Deterministic Replay. In *Proceedings of the 30th International Symposium on Computer Architecture (ISCA)*, Jun 2003.

On the Power of (even a little) Centralization in Distributed Processing

John N. Tsitsiklis [*]
MIT, LIDS
Cambridge, MA 02139
jnt@mit.edu

Kuang Xu [*]
MIT, LIDS
Cambridge, MA 02139
kuangxu@mit.edu

ABSTRACT

We propose and analyze a multi-server model that captures a performance trade-off between centralized and distributed processing. In our model, a fraction p of an available resource is deployed in a centralized manner (e.g., to serve a most-loaded station) while the remaining fraction $1 - p$ is allocated to local servers that can only serve requests addressed specifically to their respective stations.

Using a fluid model approach, we demonstrate a surprising *phase transition* in *steady-state delay*, as p changes: in the limit of a large number of stations, and when *any amount* of centralization is available ($p > 0$), the average queue length in steady state scales as $\log_{\frac{1}{1-p}} \frac{1}{1-\lambda}$ when the traffic intensity λ goes to 1. This is *exponentially smaller* than the usual $M/M/1$-queue delay scaling of $\frac{1}{1-\lambda}$, obtained when all resources are fully allocated to local stations ($p = 0$). This indicates a strong qualitative impact of even a small degree of centralization.

We prove convergence to a fluid limit, and characterize both the transient and steady-state behavior of the finite system, in the limit as the number of stations N goes to infinity. We show that the queue-length process converges to a *unique* fluid trajectory (over any finite time interval, as $N \to \infty$), and that this fluid trajectory converges to a unique invariant state $\mathbf{v}^I$, for which a simple closed-form expression is obtained. We also show that the steady-state distribution of the N-server system concentrates on $\mathbf{v}^I$ as N goes to infinity.

Categories and Subject Descriptors

G.3 [**Probability and Statistics**]: Queuing theory, Markov processes; C.2.1 [**Network Architecture and Design**]: Centralized networks, Distributed networks

* Research supported in parts by an MIT Jacobs Presidential Fellowship, an MIT-Xerox Fellowship, a Siebel Scholarship, and NSF grant CCF-0728554.

General Terms

Performance, Theory

Keywords

Phase transition, Dynamic resource allocation, Partial centralization

1. INTRODUCTION

The tension between *distributed* and *centralized* processing seems to have existed ever since the inception of computer networks. Distributed processing allows for simple implementation and robustness, while a centralized scheme guarantees optimal utilization of computing resources at the cost of implementation complexity and communication overhead. A natural question is how performance varies with the *degree of centralization*. Such understanding is of great interest in the context of, for example, infrastructure planning (static) or task scheduling (dynamic) in large server farms or cloud clusters, which involve a trade-off between performance (e.g., delay) and cost (e.g., communication infrastructure, energy consumption, etc.). In this paper, we address this problem by formulating and analyzing a multi-server model with an *adjustable* level of centralization. We begin by describing informally two motivating applications.

1.1 Primary Motivation: Server Farm with Local and Central Servers

Consider a server farm consisting of N stations, depicted in Figure 1. Each station is fed by an independent stream of tasks, arriving at a rate of λ tasks per second, with $0 < \lambda < 1$.[1] Each station is equipped with a *local server* with identical performance; the server is local in the sense that it only serves its own station. All stations are also connected to a single *centralized server* which will serve a station with the longest queue whenever possible.

We consider an N-station system. The system designer is granted a total amount of N divisible *computing resources* (e.g., a collection of processors). In a loose sense (to be formally defined in Section 2.1), this means that the system is capable of processing N tasks per second when fully loaded. The system designer is faced with the problem of allocating computing resources to local and central servers. Specifically, for some $p \in (0,1)$, each of the N local servers is able to process tasks at a maximum rate of $1 - p$ tasks per second, while the centralized server, equipped with the

---

[1] Without loss of generality, we normalize so that the largest possible arrival rate is 1.

remaining computing power, is capable of processing tasks at a maximum rate of pN tasks per second. The parameter p captures the amount of centralization in the system. Note that since the total arrival rate is λN, with $0 < \lambda < 1$, the system is underloaded for any value $p \in (0, 1)$.

When the arrival process and task processing times are random, there will be times when some stations are empty while others are loaded. Since a local server cannot help another station process tasks, the total computational resources will be better utilized if a larger fraction is allocated to the central server. However, a greater degree of centralization (corresponding to a larger value of p) entails more frequent communications and data transfers between the local stations and the central server, resulting in higher infrastructure and energy costs.

How should the system designer choose the coefficient p to optimize system performance? Alternatively, we can ask an even more fundamental question: is there any significant difference between having a small amount of centralization (a small but positive value of p), and complete decentralization (no central server and $p = 0$)?

1.2 Secondary Motivation: Partially Centralized Scheduling

Consider the system depicted in Figure 2. The arrival assumptions are the same as in the Section 1.1. However, there is no local server associated with a station; all stations are served by a single central server. Whenever the central server becomes free, it chooses a task to serve as follows. With probability p, it processes a task from a most loaded station. Otherwise, it processes a task from a station selected uniformly at random; if the randomly chosen station is empty, the current round is in some sense "wasted" (to be formalized in Section 2.1).

This second interpretation is intended to model a scenario where resource allocation decisions are made at a centralized location on a *dynamic* basis, but *communications* between the decision maker (central server) and local stations are costly or simply unavailable from time to time. Hence, while it is intuitively obvious that longest-queue-first (LQF) scheduling is more desirable, it may not always be possible to obtain up-to-date information on the system state (i.e., the queue lengths at all stations). Thus, the central server may be forced to allocate service blindly. In this setting, a system designer is interested in setting the optimal *frequency* (p) at which global state information is collected so as to balance performance and communication costs.

As we will see in the sequel, the system dynamics in the two applications are captured by the *same* mathematical structure under appropriate stochastic assumptions on task arrivals and processing times, and hence will be addressed jointly in the current paper.

1.3 Overview of Main Contributions

We provide here an overview of the main contributions. Exact statements of our results will be provided in Section 3 after the necessary terminology has been introduced.

Our goal is to study the performance implications of varying degrees of centralization, as expressed by the coefficient p. To accomplish this, we use a so-called *fluid approximation*, whereby the queue length dynamics at the local stations are approximated, as $N \to \infty$, by a deterministic *fluid*

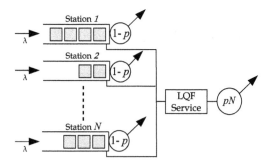

Figure 1: Server Farm with Local and Central Servers

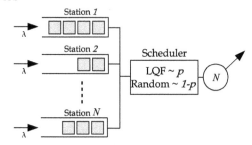

Figure 2: Centralized Scheduling with Communication Constraints

model, governed by a system of ordinary differential equations (ODEs).

Fluid approximations typically lead to results of two flavors: qualitative results derived from the fluid model that give insights into the performance of the original finite stochastic system, and technical convergence results (often mathematically involved) that justify the use of such approximations. We summarize our contributions along these two dimensions:

1. On the **qualitative end**, we derive an exact expression for the invariant state of the fluid model, for any given traffic intensity λ and centralization coefficient p, thus characterizing the steady-state distribution of the queue lengths in the system as $N \to \infty$. This enables a system designer to use any performance metric and analyze its sensitivity with respect to p. In particular, we show a surprising *exponential phase transition* in the scaling of average system delay as the load approaches capacity ($\lambda \to 1$) (Corollary 3): when an *arbitrarily small* amount of centralized computation is applied ($p > 0$), the average queue length in the system scales as [2]

$$\mathbb{E}(Q) \sim \log_{\frac{1}{1-p}} \frac{1}{1-\lambda}, \qquad (1)$$

as the traffic intensity λ approaches 1. This is *drastically smaller* than, the $\frac{1}{1-\lambda}$ scaling obtained if there is no centralization ($p = 0$).[3] In terms of the question raised at the end of Section 1.1, this suggests that for large systems, even a small degree of centralization in-

---

[2] The $\sim$ notation used in this paper is to be understood as *asymptotic closeness* in the following sense: $f(x) \sim g(x)$, as $x \to 1 \Leftrightarrow \lim_{x \to 1} \frac{f(x)}{g(x)} = 1$.

[3] When $p = 0$, the system degenerates into N independent queues. The $\frac{1}{1-\lambda}$ scaling comes from the mean queue length expression for $M/M/1$ queues.

deed provides significant improvements in the system's delay performance, in the heavy traffic regime.

2. On the **technical end**, we show:

   (a) Given any finite initial queue sizes, and with high probability, the evolution of the queue length process can be approximated by the unique solution to a fluid model, over any finite time interval, as $N \to \infty$.

   (b) All solutions to the fluid model converge to a unique invariant state, as time $t \to \infty$, for any finite initial condition (global stability).

   (c) The steady-state distribution of the finite system converges to the invariant state of the fluid model as $N \to \infty$.

The most notable technical challenge comes from the fact that the longest-queue-first policy used by the centralized server causes discontinuities in the drift in the fluid model (see Section 3.1 for details). In particular, the classical approximation results for Markov processes (see, e.g., [2]), which rely on a Lipschitz-continuous drift in the fluid model, are hard to apply. Thus, in order to establish the finite-horizon approximation result (a), we employ a sample-path based approach: we prove tightness of sample paths of the queue length process and characterize their limit points. Establishing the convergence of steady state distributions in (c) also becomes non-trivial due to the presence of discontinuous drifts. To derive this result, we will first establish the uniqueness of solutions to the fluid model and a uniform speed of convergence of stochastic sample paths to the solution of the fluid model over a compact set of initial conditions.

1.4 Related Work

To the best of our knowledge, the proposed model for the splitting of computing resources between distributed and central servers has not been studied before. However, the fluid model approach used in this paper is closely related to, and partially motivated by, the so-called supermarket model of randomized load-balancing. In that literature, it is shown that by routing tasks to the shorter queue among a small number ($d \geq 2$) of randomly chosen queues, the probability that a typical queue has at least i tasks (denoted by s_i) decays as $\lambda^{\frac{d^i-1}{d-1}}$ (super-geometrically) as $i \to \infty$ ([3],[4]); see also the survey paper [8] and references therein. A variation of this approach in a scheduling setting with channel uncertainties is examined in [5], but s_i no longer exhibits super-geometric decay and only moderate performance gain can be harnessed from sampling more than one queue.

In our setting, the system dynamics causing the exponential phase transition in the average queue length scaling are significantly different from those for the randomized load-balancing scenario. In particular, for any $p > 0$, the tail probabilities s_i become zero for sufficiently large finite i, which is significantly faster than the super-geometric decay in the supermarket model.

On the technical side, arrivals and processing times used in supermarket models are often memoryless (Poisson or Bernoulli) and the drifts in the fluid model are typically continuous with respect to the underlying system state. Hence

convergence results can be established by invoking classical approximation results, based on the convergence of the generators of the associated Markov processes. An exception is [7], where the authors generalized the supermarket model to arrival and processing times with general distributions. Since the queue length process is no longer Markov, the authors reply on an asymptotic independence property of the limiting system and use tools from statistical physics to establish convergence.

Our system remains Markov with respect to the queue lengths, but a significant technical difference from the supermarket model lies in the fact that the longest-queue-first service policy introduces *discontinuities* in the drifts. For this reason, we need to use a more elaborate set of techniques to establish the connection between stochastic sample paths and the fluid model. Moreover, the presence of discontinuities in the drifts creates challenges even for proving the uniqueness of solutions for the deterministic fluid model. (Such uniqueness is needed to establish convergence of steady-state distributions.) Our approach is based on a state representation that is different from the one used in the popular supermarket models, which turns out to be surprisingly more convenient to work with for establishing the uniqueness of solutions to the fluid model.

Besides the queueing-theoretic literature, similar fluid model approaches have been used in many other contexts to study systems with large populations. Recent results in [6] establish convergence results for finite-dimensional symmetric dynamical systems with drift discontinuities, using a more probabilistic (as opposed to sample path) analysis, carried out in terms of certain conditional expectations. We believe it is possible to prove our results using the methods in [6], with additional work. However, the coupling approach used in this paper provides strong physical intuition on the system dynamics, and avoids the need for additional technicalities from the theory of multi-valued differential inclusions.

Finally, there has been some work on the impact of service flexibilities in routing problems motivated by applications such as multilingual call centers. These date back to the seminal work of [9], with a more recent numerical study in [10]. These results show that the ability to route a portion of customers to a least-loaded station can lead to a constant-factor improvement in average delay under diffusion scaling. This line of work is very different from ours, but in a broader sense, both are trying to capture the notion that system performance in a random environment can benefit significantly from even a small amount of centralized coordination.

1.5 Organization of the Paper

Section 2 introduces the precise model to be studied, our assumptions, and the notation to be used throughout. The main results are summarized in Section 3, where we also discuss their implications along with some numerical results. The remainder of the paper is devoted to proofs, and the reader is referred to Section 4 for an overview of the proof structure. Due to space limitations, some of the proofs are sketched, omitted, or relegated to [11].

2. MODEL AND NOTATION

2.1 Model

We present our model using language that corresponds to

the server farm application in Section 1.1. Time is assumed to be continuous.

1. **System.** The system consists of N parallel stations. Each station contains a queue which stores the tasks to be processed. The queue length (i.e., number of tasks) at station i at time t is denoted by $Q_i(t)$, $i \in \{1, 2, \ldots, N\}$. For now, we do not make any assumptions on the queue lengths at time $t = 0$, other than that they are finite.

2. **Arrivals.** Stations receive streams of incoming tasks according to independent Poisson processes with a common rate $\lambda \in [0, 1)$.

3. **Task Processing.** We fix a centralization coefficient $p \in [0, 1]$.

    (a) **Local Servers.** The local server at station i is modeled by an independent Poisson clock with rate $1 - p$ (i.e., the times between two clock ticks are independent and exponentially distributed with mean $\frac{1}{1-p}$). If the clock at station i ticks at time t, we say that a **local service token** is generated at station i. If $Q_i(t) \neq 0$, exactly one task from station i "consumes" the service token and leaves the system immediately. Otherwise, the local service token is wasted and has no impact on the future evolution of the system.[4]

    (b) **Central Server.** The central server is modeled by an independent Poisson clock with rate Np. If the clock ticks at time t at the central server, we say that a **central service token** is generated. If the system is non-empty at t (i.e., $\sum_{i=1}^{N} Q_i(t) > 0$), exactly one task from some station i, chosen uniformly at random out of the stations with a *longest queue* at time t, consumes the service token and leaves the system immediately. If the whole system is empty, the central service token is wasted.

Equivalence between two the interpretations. We comment here that the scheduling application in Section 1.2 corresponds to the same mathematical model. The arrival statistics to the stations are obviously identical in both models. For task processing, note that we can equally imagine all service tokens as being generated from a single Poisson clock with rate N. Upon the generation of a service token, a coin is flipped to decide whether the token will be directed to process a task at a random station (corresponding to a *local service token*), or a station with a longest queue (corresponding to a *central service token*). Due to the Poisson splitting property, this produces identical statistics for the generation of local and central service tokens as described above.

2.2 System State

Let us fix N. Since all events (arrivals of tasks and service tokens) are generated according to independent Poisson processes, the queue length vector at time t, $(Q_1(t), Q_2(t),$

---

[4]The generation of a token can also be thought of as a completion of a previous task, so that the server "fetches" a new task from the queue to process, hence decreasing the queue length by 1. The same interpretation holds for the central service token.

$\ldots, Q_N(t))$, is Markov. Moreover, the system is fully symmetric, in the sense that all queues have identical and independent statistics for the arrivals and local service tokens, and the assignment of central service token does not depend on the specific identity of stations besides their queue lengths. Hence we can use a Markov process $\left\{ \mathbf{S}_i^N(t) \right\}_{i=0}^{\infty}$ to describe the evolution of a system with N stations, where

$$\mathbf{S}_i^N(t) \triangleq \frac{1}{N} \sum_{k=1}^{N} \mathbb{I}_{[i,\infty)}\left(Q_k(t)\right), \quad i \geq 0. \qquad (2)$$

Each coordinate $\mathbf{S}_i^N(t)$ represents the fraction of queues with at least i tasks. We call $\mathbf{S}^N(t)$ the **normalized queue length process**. We also define the **aggregate queue length process** as

$$\mathbf{V}_i^N(t) \triangleq \sum_{j=i}^{\infty} \mathbf{S}_j^N(t), \quad i \geq 0. \qquad (3)$$

Note that $\mathbf{S}_i^N(t) = \mathbf{V}_i^N(t) - \mathbf{V}_{i+1}^N(t)$, and that $\mathbf{V}_1^N(t) = \sum_{j=1}^{\infty} \mathbf{S}_j^N(t)$ is equal to the *average queue length* in the system at time t. When the total number of tasks in the system is finite (hence all coordinates of $\mathbf{V}^N$ are finite), there is a straightforward bijection between $\mathbf{S}^N$ and $\mathbf{V}^N$. Hence $\mathbf{V}^N(t)$ is Markov and also serves as a valid representation of the system state. While the $\mathbf{S}^N$ representation admits a more intuitive interpretation as the "tail" probability of a typical station having at least i tasks, it turns out the $\mathbf{V}^N$ representation is significantly more convenient to work with, especially in proving uniqueness of solutions to the associated fluid model. For this reason, we will be working mostly with the $\mathbf{V}^N$ representation, but will in some places state results in terms of $\mathbf{S}^N$, if doing so provides a better physical intuition.

2.3 Notation

The following sets will be used throughout the paper (where M is a positive integer):

$$\mathcal{S} \triangleq \left\{ \mathbf{s} \in [0,1]^{\mathbb{Z}^+} : 1 = \mathbf{s}_0 \geq \mathbf{s}_1 \geq \cdots \geq 0 \right\},$$

$$\overline{\mathcal{S}}^M \triangleq \left\{ \mathbf{s} \in \mathcal{S} : \sum_{i=1}^{\infty} \mathbf{s}_i \leq M \right\}, \quad \overline{\mathcal{S}}^\infty \triangleq \left\{ \mathbf{s} \in \mathcal{S} : \sum_{i=1}^{\infty} \mathbf{s}_i < \infty \right\},$$

$$\overline{\mathcal{V}}^M \triangleq \left\{ \mathbf{v} : \mathbf{v}_i = \sum_{j=i}^{\infty} \mathbf{s}_j, \text{ for some } \mathbf{s} \in \overline{\mathcal{S}}^M \right\},$$

$$\overline{\mathcal{V}}^\infty \triangleq \left\{ \mathbf{v} : \mathbf{v}_i = \sum_{j=i}^{\infty} \mathbf{s}_j, \text{ for some } \mathbf{s} \in \overline{\mathcal{S}}^\infty \right\},$$

$$\mathcal{Q}^N \triangleq \left\{ \mathbf{x} \in \mathbb{R}^{\mathbb{Z}^+} : \mathbf{x}_i = \frac{K}{N}, \text{ for some } K \in \mathbb{Z}, \forall i \right\}.$$

We define the weighted L_2 norm $\| \cdot \|_w$ on $\mathbb{R}^{\mathbb{Z}^+}$ as

$$\|\mathbf{x} - \mathbf{y}\|_w^2 = \sum_{i=0}^{\infty} \frac{|\mathbf{x}_i - \mathbf{y}_i|^2}{2^i}, \quad \mathbf{x}, \mathbf{y} \in \mathbb{R}^{\mathbb{Z}^+}. \qquad (4)$$

We will be using bold letters to denote vectors, and either bold or ordinary letters for scalars. Upper-case letters are in general reserved for random variables (e.g., $\mathbf{V}^{(0,N)}$) or scholastic processes (e.g., $\mathbf{V}^N(t)$), and lower-case letters are used for constants (e.g., $\mathbf{v}^0$) and deterministic functions (e.g., $\mathbf{v}(t)$). Finally, a function is in general denoted by $x(\cdot)$, but is sometimes written as $x(t)$ to emphasize the type of its argument.

3. SUMMARY OF MAIN RESULTS

3.1 Definition of Fluid Model

Before introducing the main results, we first define the fluid model, with some intuitive justification.

Definition 1. (Fluid Model) *Given an initial condition* $\mathbf{v}^0 \in \overline{\mathcal{V}}^\infty$, *a function* $\mathbf{v}(t) : [0, \infty) \to \overline{\mathcal{V}}^\infty$ *is said to be a* **solution to the fluid model** *(or fluid solution for short) if:*

(1) $\mathbf{v}(0) = \mathbf{v}^0$

(2) For all $t \geq 0$, $\mathbf{v}_0(t) - \mathbf{v}_1(t) = 1$ *and* $1 \geq \mathbf{v}_i(t) - \mathbf{v}_{i+1}(t) \geq \mathbf{v}_{i+1}(t) - \mathbf{v}_{i+2}(t) \geq 0$ *for all* $i \geq 0$.

(3) For almost all $t \in [0, \infty)$, *every* $\mathbf{v}_i(t)$ *is differentiable and satisfies*

$$\dot{\mathbf{v}}_i(t) = \lambda(\mathbf{v}_{i-1} - \mathbf{v}_i) - (1-p)(\mathbf{v}_i - \mathbf{v}_{i+1}) - g_i(\mathbf{v}), \quad (5)$$

where

$$g_i(\mathbf{v}) = \begin{cases} p, & \mathbf{v}_i > 0, \\ \min\{\lambda\mathbf{v}_{i-1}, p\}, & \mathbf{v}_i = 0, \mathbf{v}_{i-1} > 0, \\ 0, & \mathbf{v}_i = 0, \mathbf{v}_{i-1} = 0, \end{cases} \quad (6)$$

We can write Eq. (5) more compactly as

$$\dot{\mathbf{v}}(t) = \mathbf{F}(\mathbf{v}), \quad (7)$$

where $\mathbf{F}(\mathbf{v})$ is called the drift at point $\mathbf{v}$.

Interpretation of the fluid model. The solution to the fluid model, $\mathbf{v}(t)$, can be thought of as a deterministic approximation to the sample paths of $\mathbf{V}^N(t)$ for large values of N. Conditions (1) and (2) correspond to initial and boundary conditions, respectively. Before rigorously establishing the validity of approximation, we provide some intuition for each of the drift terms in Eq. (5):

I. $\lambda(\mathbf{v}_{i-1} - \mathbf{v}_i)$: This term corresponds to arrivals. When a task arrives at a station with $i-1$ tasks, the system has one more queue with i tasks, and $\mathbf{S}_i^N$ increases by $\frac{1}{N}$. However, the number of queues with at least j tasks, for $j \neq i$, does not change. Thus, $\mathbf{S}_i^N$ is the only one that is incremented. Since $\mathbf{V}_i^N \triangleq \sum_{k=i}^{\infty} \mathbf{S}_k^N$, this implies that $\mathbf{V}_i^N$ is increased by $\frac{1}{N}$ if and only if a task arrives at a queue with at least $i-1$ tasks. Since all stations have an identical arrival rate λ, the probability of $\mathbf{V}_i^N$ being incremented upon an arrival to the system is equal to the fraction of queues with at least $i-1$ tasks, which is $\mathbf{V}_{i-1}^N(t) - \mathbf{V}_i^N(t)$. We take the limit as $N \to \infty$, and multiply by the total arrival rate, $N\lambda$, times the increment due to each arrival, $\frac{1}{N}$, to obtain the term $\lambda(\mathbf{v}_{i-1} - \mathbf{v}_i)$.

II. $(1-p)(\mathbf{v}_i - \mathbf{v}_{i+1})$: This term corresponds to the completion of tasks due to *local* service tokens. The argument is similar to that for the first term.

III. $g_i(\mathbf{v})$: This term corresponds to the completion of tasks due to *central* service tokens.

1. $g_i(\mathbf{v}) = p$, if $\mathbf{v}_i > 0$. If $i > 0$ and $\mathbf{v}_i > 0$, then there is a positive fraction of queues with at least i tasks. Hence the central server is working at full capacity, and the rate of decrease in $\mathbf{v}_i$ due to central service tokens is equal to the maximum rate of the central server, namely p.

2. $g_i(\mathbf{v}) = \min\{\lambda\mathbf{v}_{i-1}, p\}$, if $\mathbf{v}_i = 0, \mathbf{v}_{i-1} > 0$. This case is more subtle. Note that since $\mathbf{v}_i = 0$, the term $\lambda\mathbf{v}_{i-1}$ is equal to $\lambda(\mathbf{v}_{i-1} - \mathbf{v}_i)$, which is the rate at which $\mathbf{v}_i$ increases due to arrivals. Here the central server serves queues with at least i tasks whenever such queues arise to keep $\mathbf{v}_i$ at zero. Thus, the total rate of central service tokens dedicated to $\mathbf{v}_i$ matches exactly the rate of increase of $\mathbf{v}_i$ due to arrivals.[5]

3. $g_i(\mathbf{v}) = 0$, if $\mathbf{v}_i = \mathbf{v}_{i-1} = 0$. Here, both $\mathbf{v}_i$ and $\mathbf{v}_{i-1}$ are zero and there are no queues with $i-1$ or more tasks. Hence there is no positive rate of increase in $\mathbf{v}_i$ due to arrivals. Accordingly, the rate at which central service tokens are used to serve stations with at least i tasks is zero.

Note that, as mentioned in the introduction, the discontinuities in the fluid model come from the term $g(\mathbf{v})$, which reflects the presence of a central server.

3.2 Analysis of the Fluid Model

The following theorem characterizes the invariant state for the fluid model. It will be used to demonstrate an *exponential improvement* in the rate of growth of the average queue length as $\lambda \to 1$ (Corollary 3).

Theorem 2. *The drift* $\mathbf{F}(\cdot)$ *in the fluid model admits a unique invariant state* $\mathbf{v}^I$ *(i.e.* $\mathbf{F}(\mathbf{v}^I) = 0$). *Letting* $\mathbf{s}_i^I \triangleq \mathbf{v}_i^I - \mathbf{v}_{i+1}^I$ *for all* $i \geq 0$, *the exact expression for the invariant state is given as follows:*

(1) If $p = 0$, *then* $\mathbf{s}_i^I = \lambda^i$, $\forall i \geq 1$.

(2) If $p \geq \lambda$, *then* $\mathbf{s}_i^I = 0$, $\forall i \geq 1$.

(3) If $0 < p < \lambda$, *and* $\lambda = 1 - p$, *then*

$$\mathbf{s}_i^I = \begin{cases} 1 - \left(\frac{p}{1-p}\right)i, & 1 \leq i \leq \tilde{i}^*(p, \lambda), \\ 0, & i > \tilde{i}^*(p, \lambda), \end{cases}$$

where $\tilde{i}^*(p, \lambda) \triangleq \left\lfloor \frac{1-p}{p} \right\rfloor$.[6]

(4) If $0 < p < \lambda$, *and* $\lambda \neq 1 - p$, *then*

$$\mathbf{s}_i^I = \begin{cases} \frac{1-\lambda}{1-(p+\lambda)}\left(\frac{\lambda}{1-p}\right)^i - \frac{p}{1-(p+\lambda)}, & 1 \leq i \leq i^*(p, \lambda), \\ 0, & i > i^*(p, \lambda), \end{cases}$$

where

$$i^*(p, \lambda) \triangleq \left\lfloor \log_{\frac{\lambda}{1-p}} \frac{p}{1-\lambda} \right\rfloor, \quad (8)$$

PROOF. The proof consists of simple algebra to compute the solution to $\mathbf{F}(\mathbf{v}^I) = 0$. See Appendix A.1 in [11] for a proof. $\blacksquare$

Case 4 in the above theorem is particularly interesting, as it reflects the system's performance under heavy load (λ close to 1). Note that since $\mathbf{s}_1^I$ represents the probability of a typical queue having at least i tasks, the quantity $\mathbf{v}_1^I \triangleq$

---

[5]Technically, the minimization involving p is not necessary: if $\lambda\mathbf{v}_{i-1}(t) > p$, then $\mathbf{v}_i(t)$ cannot stay at zero and will immediately increase after t. We keep the minimization just to emphasize that the maximum rate of increase in $\mathbf{v}_i$ due to central service tokens cannot exceed the central service capacity p.

[6]Here $\lfloor x \rfloor$ is defined as the largest integer that is less than or equal to x.

$\sum_{i=1}^{\infty} \mathbf{s}_i^I$ represents the *average queue length*. The following corollary, which characterizes the average queue length in the invariant state for the fluid model, follows from Case 4 in Theorem 2 by some straightforward algebra.

Corollary 3. (Phase Transition in Average Queue Length Scaling) *If $0 < p < \lambda$ and $\lambda \neq 1 - p$, then*

$$\mathbf{v}_1^I \triangleq \sum_{i=1}^{\infty} \mathbf{s}_i^I = \frac{(1-p)(1-\lambda)}{(1-p-\lambda)^2}\left[1 - \left(\frac{\lambda}{1-p}\right)^{i^*(p,\lambda)}\right]$$
$$- \frac{p}{1-p-\lambda}i^*(p,\lambda), \qquad (9)$$

with $i^*(p,\lambda) = \left\lfloor \log_{\frac{\lambda}{1-p}} \frac{p}{1-\lambda} \right\rfloor$. In particular, this implies that for any fixed $p > 0$, $\mathbf{v}_1^I$ scales as

$$\mathbf{v}_1^I \sim i^*(p,\lambda) \sim \log_{\frac{1}{1-p}} \frac{1}{1-\lambda}, \quad as \ \lambda \to 1. \qquad (10)$$

The scaling of the average queue length in Eq. (10) with respect to arrival rate λ is contrasted with (and is *dramatically better* than) the familiar $\frac{1}{1-\lambda}$ scaling when no centralized resource is available ($p = 0$).

Intuition for Exponential Phase Transition. The exponential improvement in the scaling of $\mathbf{v}_1^I$ is surprising, because the expressions for $\mathbf{s}_i^I$ look ordinary and do not contain any super-geometric terms in i. However, a closer look reveals that for any $p > 0$, the tail probabilities $\mathbf{s}^I$ have **finite support**: $\mathbf{s}_i^I$ "dips" down to 0 as i increases to $i^*(p,\lambda)$, which is even faster than a super-geometric decay. Since $0 \leq \mathbf{s}_i^I \leq 1$ for all i, it is then intuitive that $\mathbf{v}_1^I = \sum_{i=1}^{i^*(p,\lambda)} \mathbf{s}_i^I$ is upper-bounded by $i^*(p,\lambda)$, which scales as $\log_{\frac{1}{1-p}} \frac{1}{1-\lambda}$ as $\lambda \to 1$. Note that a tail probability with "finite-support" implies that the fraction of stations with more than $i^*(p,\lambda)$ tasks *decreases to zero* as $N \to \infty$. For example, we may have a strictly positive fraction of stations with, say, 10 tasks, but stations with more than 10 tasks hardly exist. While this may appear counterintuitive, it is a direct consequence of centralization in the resource allocation schemes. Since a fraction p of the total resource is constantly going after the longest queues, it is able to prevent long queues (i.e., queues with more than $i^*(p,\lambda)$ tasks) from even appearing. The thresholds $i^*(p,\lambda)$ increasing to infinity as $\lambda \to 1$ reflects the fact that the central server's ability to annihilate long queues is compromised by the heavier traffic loads; our result essentially shows that the increase in $i^*(\lambda,p)$ is surprisingly slow. $\diamond$

Numerical Results: Figure 3 compares the invariant state vectors for the case $p = 0$ (stars) and $p = 0.05$ (diamonds). When $p = 0$, $\mathbf{s}_i^I$ decays exponentially as λ^i, while when $p = 0.05$, $\mathbf{s}_i^I$ decays much more quickly, and reaches zero at around $i = 40$. Figure 4 demonstrates the exponential phase transition in the average queue length as the traffic intensity reaches 1, where the solid curve, corresponding to a positive p, increases significantly slower than the usual $\frac{1}{1-\lambda}$ delay scaling (dotted curve). Simulations show that the theoretical model offers good predictions for even a moderate number of servers ($N = 100$)[7]. Table 1 gives examples of the values for $i^*(p,\lambda)$; note that these values in some sense correspond to the *maximum delay* an average customer could experience in the system. $\diamond$

---

[7]The detailed simulation setup can be found in Appendix C in [11].

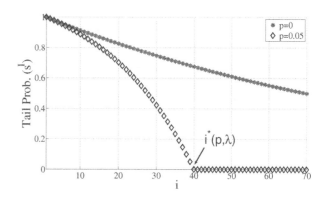

Figure 3: Values of $\mathbf{s}_i^I$, as a function of i, for $p = 0$ and $p = 0.05$, with traffic intensity $\lambda = 0.99$.

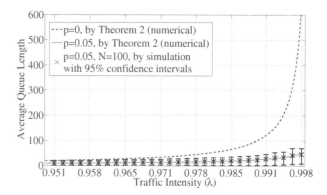

Figure 4: Illustration of the exponential improvement in average queue length from $O(\frac{1}{1-\lambda})$ to $O(\log \frac{1}{1-\lambda})$ as $\lambda \to 1$, when we compare $p = 0$ to $p = 0.05$.

Theorem 2 characterizes the invariant state of the fluid model, without saying if and how a solution of the fluid model reaches it. The next two results state that given any finite initial condition, the solution to the fluid model is unique and converges to the unique invariant state as time goes to infinity.

Theorem 4. (Uniqueness of Solutions to Fluid Model) *Given any initial condition $\mathbf{v}^0 \in \overline{\mathcal{V}}^{\infty}$, the fluid model has a unique solution $\mathbf{v}(t)$, $t \in [0, \infty)$.*

PROOF. See Section 7.1.

Theorem 5. (Global Stability of Fluid Solutions) *Given any initial condition $\mathbf{v}^0 \in \overline{\mathcal{V}}^{\infty}$, and with $\mathbf{v}(\mathbf{v}^0, t)$ the unique solution to the fluid model, we have*

$$\lim_{t \to \infty} \left\| \mathbf{v}\left(\mathbf{v}^0, t\right) - \mathbf{v}^I \right\|_w = 0, \qquad (11)$$

where $\mathbf{v}^I$ is the unique invariant state of the fluid model given in Theorem 2.

PROOF. See Section 7.3.

3.3 Convergence to a Fluid Solution - Finite-time and Steady-state

The two theorems in this section justify the use of the fluid model as an approximation for the finite stochastic system. The first theorem states that with high probability, the

$p = \backslash\ \lambda =$	0.1	0.6	0.9	0.99	0.999
0.002	2	10	37	199	692
0.02	1	6	18	68	156
0.2	0	2	5	14	23
0.5	0	1	2	5	8
0.8	0	0	1	2	4

Table 1: Values of $i^*(p, \lambda)$ for various combinations of (p, λ).

evolution of the aggregated queue length process $\mathbf{V}^N(t)$ is uniformly close, over any finite time horizon $[0, T]$, to the unique solution of the fluid model as $N \to \infty$.

Theorem 6. (Convergence to Fluid Solutions over a Finite Horizon) *Consider a sequence of systems as the number of servers $N \to \infty$. Fix any $T > 0$. If for some $\mathbf{v}^0 \in \overline{\mathcal{V}}^\infty$,*

$$\lim_{N \to \infty} \mathbb{P}\left(\|\mathbf{V}^N(0) - \mathbf{v}^0\|_w > \gamma \right) = 0, \quad \forall \gamma > 0, \quad (12)$$

then

$$\lim_{N \to \infty} \mathbb{P}\left(\sup_{t \in [0,T]} \|\mathbf{V}^N(t) - \mathbf{v}(\mathbf{v}^0, t)\|_w > \gamma \right) = 0, \quad \forall \gamma > 0. \quad (13)$$

where $\mathbf{v}(\mathbf{v}^0, t)$ is the unique solution to the fluid model given initial condition $\mathbf{v}^0$.

PROOF. See Section 7.2.

Note that if we combine Theorem 6 with the convergence of $\mathbf{v}(t)$ to $\mathbf{v}^I$ in Theorem 5, we see that the finite system ($\mathbf{V}^N$) is approximated by the invariant state of the fluid model $\mathbf{v}^I$ after a fixed time period. In other words, we now have

$$\lim_{t \to \infty} \lim_{N \to \infty} \mathbf{V}^N(t) = \mathbf{v}^I, \text{ in distribution.} \quad (14)$$

If we switch the order in which the limits over t and N are taken in Eq. (14), the question becomes to describe the limiting behavior of the *sequence of steady-state distributions* (if they exist) as the system size grows large. Indeed, in practice it is often of great interest to obtain a performance guarantee for the steady state of the system, if it were to run for a long period of time. In light of Eq. (14), we may expect that

$$\lim_{N \to \infty} \lim_{t \to \infty} \mathbf{V}^N(t) = \mathbf{v}^I, \text{ in distribution.} \quad (15)$$

The following theorem shows that this is indeed the case, i.e., that a unique steady-state distribution of $\mathbf{v}^N(t)$ (denoted by π^N) exists for all N, and that the sequence π^N concentrates on the invariant state of the fluid model ($\mathbf{v}^I$) as N grows large.

Theorem 7. (Convergence of Steady State Distributions to $\mathbf{v}^I$) *For any N, the system is positive recurrent, and $\mathbf{V}^N(t)$ admits a unique steady-state distribution π^N. Moreover,*

$$\lim_{N \to \infty} \pi^N = \mathbf{v}^I, \text{ weakly.} \quad (16)$$

PROOF. The proof is based on the tightness of the sequence of steady-state distributions π^N, and a uniform rate of convergence of $\mathbf{V}^N(\cdot)$ to $\mathbf{v}(\cdot)$ over any compact set of initial conditions. See Appendix B in [11] for a proof.

Figure 5 summarizes the relationships between the convergence to the solution of the fluid model over a finite time horizon (Theorem 5 and Theorem 6) and the convergence of the sequence of steady state distributions (Theorem 7).

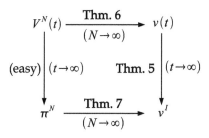

Figure 5: Relationships between convergence results.

4. PROOF OVERVIEW

The remainder of the paper will be devoted to proving the results summarized in Section 3. We begin by coupling the sample paths of processes of interest (e.g., $\mathbf{V}^N$) with those of two fundamental processes that drive the system dynamics (Section 5). This approach allows us to link deterministically the convergence properties of the sample paths of interest to the convergence of the fundamental processes, on which probabilistic arguments are easier to apply (such as the Functional Law of Large Numbers). Using this coupling framework, we show in Section 6 that almost all sample paths of $\mathbf{V}^N$ are "tight" in the sense that they are uniformly approximated by a set of Lipschitz-continuous trajectories, which we refer to as the fluid limits, as $N \to \infty$, and that all such fluid limits are valid solutions to the fluid model. This makes the connection between the finite stochastic system and the deterministic fluid solutions. Section 7 studies the properties of the fluid model, and provides proofs for Theorem 4 and 5. Note that Theorem 6 (convergence of $\mathbf{V}^N$ to the unique fluid solution, over a finite time horizon) now follows from the tightness results in Section 6 and the uniqueness of fluid solutions (Theorem 4). The proof of Theorem 2 stands alone, and due to space constraints, is included in Appendix A.1 in [11]. Finally, the proof of Theorem 7 (convergence of steady state distributions to $\mathbf{v}^I$), which is more technical, is given in Appendix B of [11].

5. PROBABILITY SPACE AND COUPLING

The goal of this section is to formally define the probability spaces and stochastic processes with which we will be working in the rest of the paper. Specifically, we begin by introducing two *fundamental processes*, from which all other processes of interest (e.g., $\mathbf{V}^N(t)$) can be derived on a per sample path basis.

5.1 Definition of Probability Space

Definition 8. (Fundamental Processes and Initial Conditions)

(1) **The Total Event Process** $W(t)$, *defined on a probability space $(\Omega_W, \mathcal{F}_W, \mathbb{P}_W)$, is a Poisson process with rate $\lambda + 1$, where each jump marks the* time *when an "event" takes place in the system.*

(2) **The Selection Process** $U(n)$, *defined on a probability space $(\Omega_U, \mathcal{F}_U, \mathbb{P}_U)$, is a discrete-time process, where each $U(n)$ is independent and uniformly distributed in $[0, 1]$. This process, along with the current system state, determines the type of each event (i.e., whether it is an arrival, a local token generation, or a central token generation).*

(3) **The (Finite) Initial Conditions** $\{\mathbf{V}^{(0,N)}\}$ *is a sequence of random variables defined on a common probability space* $(\Omega_0, \mathcal{F}_0, \mathbb{P}_0)$*, with* $\mathbf{V}^{(0,N)}$ *taking values in* $\overline{\mathcal{V}}^\infty \cap \mathcal{Q}^N$. [8] $\mathbf{V}^{(0,N)}$ *represents the initial queue length distribution.*

For the rest of the paper, we will be working with the probability space $(\Omega, \mathcal{F}, \mathbb{P})$ defined as the **product space** of $(\Omega_W, \mathcal{F}_W, \mathbb{P}_W)$, $(\Omega_U, \mathcal{F}_U, \mathbb{P}_U)$ and $(\Omega_0, \mathcal{F}_0, \mathbb{P}_0)$. With a slight abuse of notation, we use the same symbols $W(t)$, $U(n)$ and $\mathbf{V}^{(0,N)}$ for their corresponding *extensions* on Ω, i.e. $W(\omega, t) \stackrel{\triangle}{=} W(\omega_W, t)$, where $\omega \in \Omega$ and $\omega = (\omega_W, \omega_U, \omega_0)$. The same holds for U and $\mathbf{V}^{(0,N)}$.

5.2 A Coupled Construction of Sample Paths

Recall the interpretation of the fluid model drift terms in Section 3.1. Mimicking the expression of $\dot{v}_i(t)$ in Eq. (5), we would like to decompose $\mathbf{V}_i^N(t)$ into three non-decreasing right-continuous processes,

$$\mathbf{V}_i^N(t) = \mathbf{V}_i^N(0) + \mathbf{A}_i^N(t) - \mathbf{L}_i^N(t) - \mathbf{C}_i^N(t), \quad i \geq 1, \quad (17)$$

so that $\mathbf{A}_i^N(t)$, $\mathbf{L}_i^N(t)$, and $\mathbf{C}_i^N(t)$ correspond to the *cumulative changes* in $\mathbf{V}_i^N$ due to arrivals, local service tokens and central service tokens, respectively. We will define processes $\mathbf{A}^N(t), \mathbf{L}^N(t), \mathbf{C}^N(t)$, and $\mathbf{V}^N(t)$ on the common probability space $(\Omega, \mathcal{F}, \mathbb{P})$, and *couple* them with the sample paths of the fundamental processes $W(t)$ and $U(n)$ and the value of $\mathbf{V}^{(0,N)}$, for each sample $\omega \in \Omega$. First, note that since the N-station system has N independent Poisson arrival streams, each with rate λ, and an exponential server with rate N, the total event process for this system is a Poisson process with rate $N(1 + \lambda)$. Hence, we define $W^N(\omega, t)$, the Nth event process, by $W^N(\omega, t) \stackrel{\triangle}{=} W(\omega, Nt)$, $\forall t \geq 0$, $\omega \in \Omega$.

The coupled construction is intuitive: whenever there is a jump in $W^N(\omega, \cdot)$, we decide the type of event by looking at the value of the corresponding selection variable $U(\omega, n)$ and the current state of the system $\mathbf{V}^N(\omega, t)$. Fix ω in Ω, and let $t_k, k \geq 1$, denote the time of the kth jump in $W^N(\omega, \cdot)$. We first set all of $\mathbf{A}^N$, $\mathbf{L}^N$, and $\mathbf{C}^N$ to zero for $t \in [0, t_1)$. Starting from $k = 1$, repeat the following steps for increasing values of k:

(1) If $U(\omega, k) \in \frac{\lambda}{1+\lambda} \left[0, \mathbf{V}_{i-1}^N(\omega, t_k-) - \mathbf{V}_i^N(\omega, t_k-) \right)$ for some $i \geq 1$,[9] the event corresponds to an **arrival** to a station with at least $i - 1$ tasks. Hence we increase $\mathbf{A}_i^N(\omega, t)$ by $\frac{1}{N}$ at all such i.

(2) If $U(\omega, k) \in \frac{\lambda}{1+\lambda} + \frac{1-p}{1+\lambda} \left[0, \mathbf{V}_i^N(\omega, t_k-) - \mathbf{V}_{i+1}^N(\omega, t_k-) \right)$ for some $i \geq 1$, the event corresponds to the **completion** of a task at a station with at least i tasks due to a **local service token**. We increase $\mathbf{L}_i^N(\omega, t)$ by $\frac{1}{N}$ at all such i. Note that $i = 0$ is *not* included here, reflecting the fact that if a local service token is generated at an empty station, it is immediately wasted and has no impact on the system.

(3) For all other values of $U(\omega, k)$, the event corresponds to the generation of a **central service token**. Since the central service token is alway sent to a station with the longest queue length, we will have a task completion in a most-loaded station, unless the system is empty. Let $i^*(t)$ be the last positive coordinate of $\mathbf{V}^N(\omega, t-)$, i.e., $i^*(t) = \sup\{i : \mathbf{V}_i^N(\omega, t-) > 0\}$. We increase $\mathbf{C}_j^N(\omega, t)$ by $\frac{1}{N}$ for all j such that $1 \leq j \leq i^*(t_k)$.

To finish, we set $\mathbf{V}^N(\omega, t)$ according to Eq. (17), and keep the values of all processes unchanged between t_k and t_{k+1}. We set $\mathbf{V}_0^N \stackrel{\triangle}{=} \mathbf{V}_1^N + 1$, just to stay consistent with the definition of $\mathbf{V}_0^N$.

6. FLUID LIMITS OF STOCHASTIC SAMPLE PATHS

In the sample-path-wise construction in Section 5.2, all randomness is attributed to the initial condition $\mathbf{V}^{(0,N)}$ and the two fundamental processes $W(\cdot)$ and $U(\cdot)$. Everything else, including the system state $\mathbf{V}^N$ that we are interested in, can be derived from a deterministic mapping, given a particular realization of $\mathbf{V}^{(0,N)}$, $W(\cdot)$, and $U(\cdot)$. With this in mind, the approach we will take to prove convergence to a fluid limit, over a finite time interval $[0, T]$, can be summarized as follows:

(1) Find a subset $\mathcal{C}$ of the sample space Ω, such that $\mathbb{P}(\mathcal{C}) = 1$ and the sample paths of W and U are sufficiently "nice" for every $\omega \in \mathcal{C}$.

(2) Show that for all ω in this nice set, the derived sample paths $\mathbf{V}^N$ are also "nice", and contain a subsequence converging to a Lipschitz-continuous trajectory $\mathbf{v}(\cdot)$, as $N \to \infty$.

(3) Characterize the derivative at any regular point[10] of $\mathbf{v}(\cdot)$ and show that it is identical to the drift in the fluid model. Hence $\mathbf{v}(\cdot)$ is a solution to the fluid model.

(4) Finally, show that given any finite initial condition, $\mathbf{v}(t)$ converges to a unique invariant state $\mathbf{v}^I$ as $t \to \infty$.

The proof will be presented according to the above order.

6.1 Tightness of Sample Paths over a Nice Set

We begin by proving the following lemma which characterizes a "nice" set $\mathcal{C} \subset \Omega$ whose elements have desirable convergence properties.

Lemma 9. *Fix $T > 0$. There exists a measurable set $\mathcal{C} \subset \Omega$ such that $\mathbb{P}(\mathcal{C}) = 1$ and for all $\omega \in \mathcal{C}$,*

$$\lim_{N \to \infty} \sup_{t \in [0,T]} \left| W^N(\omega, t) - (1 + \lambda) t \right| = 0, \quad (18)$$

$$\lim_{N \to \infty} \frac{1}{N} \sum_{i=1}^N \mathbb{I}_{[a,b)} (U(\omega, i)) = b - a, \ \forall [a, b) \subset [0, 1]. \quad (19)$$

PROOF. Eq. (18) is based on the Functional Law of Large Numbers and Eq. (19) is a consequence of the Glivenko-Cantelli theorem. See Appendix A.2 in [11] for a proof.

---

[8]For a finite system of N stations, the measure induced by $\mathbf{V}_i^N(t)$ is discrete and takes positive values only in the set of rational numbers with denominator N.

[9]Throughout the paper, we use the short-hand notation $f(t-)$ to denote the left limit $\lim_{s \uparrow t} f(s)$.

[10]Regular points are points where the derivative exists. Since the trajectories are Lipschitz-continuous, almost all points are regular.

Definition 10. *We call the 4-tuple,* $\mathbf{X}^N \stackrel{\triangle}{=} \left(\mathbf{V}^N, \mathbf{A}^N, \mathbf{L}^N, \mathbf{C}^N \right)$, *the Nth system. Note that all four components are infinite-dimensional processes.* [11]

Consider the space of functions from $[0, T]$ to $\mathbb{R}$ that are right-continuous-with-left-limits (RCLL), denoted by $D[0,T]$, and let it be equipped with the uniform metric, $d(\cdot, \cdot)$:

$$d(x,y) \stackrel{\triangle}{=} \sup_{t \in [0,T]} |x(t) - y(t)|, \; x, y \in D[0,T]. \quad (20)$$

Denote by $D^\infty[0,T]$ the set of functions from $[0,T]$ to $\mathbb{R}^{\mathbb{Z}^+}$ that are RCLL on every coordinate. Let $d^{\mathbb{Z}^+}(\cdot, \cdot)$ denote the uniform metric on $D^\infty[0,T]$:

$$d^{\mathbb{Z}^+}(\mathbf{x}, \mathbf{y}) \stackrel{\triangle}{=} \sup_{t \in [0,t]} \|\mathbf{x}(t) - \mathbf{y}(t)\|_w, \mathbf{x}, \mathbf{y} \in D^{\mathbb{Z}^+}[0,T], \quad (21)$$

with $\|\cdot\|_w$ defined in Eq. (4).

The following proposition is the main result of this section. It shows that for sufficiently large N, the sample paths are sufficiently close to some absolutely continuous trajectory.

Proposition 11. *Assume that there exists some $\mathbf{v}^0 \in \overline{\mathcal{V}}^\infty$ such that*

$$\lim_{N \to \infty} \|\mathbf{V}^N(\omega, 0) - \mathbf{v}^0\|_w = 0, \quad (22)$$

for all $\omega \in \mathcal{C}$. Then for all $\omega \in \mathcal{C}$, any subsequence of $\left\{ \mathbf{X}^N(\omega, \cdot) \right\}$ contains a further subsequence, $\left\{ \mathbf{X}^{N_i}(\omega, \cdot) \right\}$, that converges to some coordinate-wise Lipschitz-continuous function $\mathbf{x}(t) = (\mathbf{v}(t), \mathbf{a}(t), \mathbf{l}(t), \mathbf{c}(t))$, with $\mathbf{v}(0) = \mathbf{v}^0$, $\mathbf{a}(0) = \mathbf{l}(0) = \mathbf{c}(0) = 0$ and

$$|\mathbf{x}_i(a) - \mathbf{x}_i(b)| \le L|a - b|, \quad \forall a, b \in [0,T], \, i \in \mathbb{Z}^+, \quad (23)$$

where $L > 0$ is a universal constant, independent of the choice of ω, $\mathbf{x}$ and T. Here the convergence refers to $d^{\mathbb{Z}^+}(\mathbf{V}^{N_i}, \mathbf{v})$, $d^{\mathbb{Z}^+}(\mathbf{A}^{N_i}, \mathbf{a})$, $d^{\mathbb{Z}^+}(\mathbf{L}^{N_i}, \mathbf{l})$, and $d^{\mathbb{Z}^+}(\mathbf{C}^{N_i}, \mathbf{c})$ all converging to 0, as $i \to \infty$.

For the rest of the paper, we will refer to such a limit point $\mathbf{x}$, or any subset of its coordinates, as a **fluid limit**.

Proof outline: We first show that for all $\omega \in \mathcal{C}$, and for every coordinate i, any subsequence of $\left\{ X_i^N(\omega, \cdot) \right\}$ has a convergent further subsequence with a Lipschitz-continuous limit. We then use this coordinate-wise convergence result to construct a limit point in the space $D^{\mathbb{Z}^+}$. To establish coordinate-wise convergence, we use a tightness technique previously used in the literature of multiclass queuing networks (see, e.g., [1]). A key realization in this case, is that the total number of jumps in any derived process $\mathbf{A}^N$, $\mathbf{L}^N$, and $\mathbf{C}^N$ cannot exceed that of the event process $W^N(t)$ for a particular sample. Since $\mathbf{A}^N, \mathbf{L}^N$, and $\mathbf{C}^N$ are non-decreasing, we expect their sample paths to be "smooth" for large N, due to the fact that the sample path of $W^N(t)$ does become "smooth" for large N, for all $\omega \in \mathcal{C}$ (Lemma 9). More formally, it can be shown that for all $\omega \in \mathcal{C}$ and $T > 0$, there exist diminishing positive sequences $M_N \downarrow 0$ and $\gamma_N \downarrow 0$, such that the sample path along any coordinate of $\mathbf{X}^N$ is γ_N-approximately-Lipschitz continuous with a uniformly bounded initial condition, i.e., for all i,

$$\left| \mathbf{X}_i^N(\omega, 0) - x_i^0 \right| \le M_N \text{ and}$$

$$\left| \mathbf{X}_i^N(\omega, a) - \mathbf{X}_i^N(\omega, b) \right| \le L|a - b| + \gamma_N, \quad \forall a, b \in [0,T]$$

[11] If necessary, $\mathbf{X}^N$ can be enumerated by writing it explicitly as $\mathbf{X}^N = \left(\mathbf{V}_0^N, \mathbf{A}_0^N, \mathbf{L}_0^N, \mathbf{C}_0^N, \mathbf{V}_1^N, \mathbf{A}_1^N, \dots \right)$.

where L is the Lipschitz constant, and $T < \infty$ is a fixed time horizon. Using a linear interpolation argument, we then show that sample paths of the above form can be uniformly approximated by a set of L-Lipschitz-continuous function on $[0, T]$. We finish by using the Arzela-Ascoli theorem (sequential compactness) along with closedness of this set, to establish the existence of a convergent further subsequence along any subsequence (compactness) and that any limit point must also L-Lipschitz-continuous (closedness). This completes the proof for coordinate-wise convergence.

Using this coordinate-wise convergence, we now construct the limit points of $\mathbf{X}^N$ in the space $D^{\mathbb{Z}^+}[0,T]$. Let $\mathbf{v}_1(\cdot)$ be any L-Lipschitz-continuous limit point of $\mathbf{V}_1^N$, so that a subsequence $\mathbf{V}_1^{N_j^1}(\omega, \cdot) \to \mathbf{v}_1(\cdot)$, as $j \to \infty$, with respect to $d(\cdot, \cdot)$. Then, we proceed recursively by letting $\mathbf{v}_{i+1}(\cdot)$ be a limit point of a subsequence of $\left\{ \mathbf{V}_{i+1}^{N_j^i}(\omega, \cdot) \right\}_{j=1}^\infty$, where $\{N_j^i\}_{j=1}^\infty$ are the indices for the ith subsequence. We claim that $\mathbf{v}$ is indeed a limit point of $\mathbf{V}^N$ under the norm $d^{\mathbb{Z}^+}(\cdot, \cdot)$. Note that since $\mathbf{v}_1(0) = \mathbf{v}_1^0$, $0 \le \mathbf{V}_i^N(t) \le \mathbf{V}_1^N(t)$, and $\mathbf{v}_1(\cdot)$ is L-Lipschitz-continuous, we have that

$$\sup_{t \in [0,T]} |\mathbf{v}_i(t)| \le \sup_{t \in [0,T]} |\mathbf{v}_1(t)| \le |\mathbf{v}_1^0| + LT, \quad \forall i \in \mathbb{Z}^+. \quad (24)$$

Set $N_1 = 1$, and let, for $k \ge 2$,

$$N_k = \min \left\{ N \ge N_{k-1} : \sup_{1 \le i \le k} d(\mathbf{V}_i^N(\omega, \cdot), \mathbf{v}_i) \le \frac{1}{k} \right\}. \quad (25)$$

Note that the construction of $\mathbf{v}$ implies that N_k is well defined and finite for all k. From Eqs. (24) and (25), we have, for all $k \ge 2$,

$$\begin{aligned} d^{\mathbb{Z}^+}\left(\mathbf{V}^{N_k}(\omega, \cdot), \mathbf{v} \right) &= \sup_{t \in [0,T]} \sqrt{\sum_{i=0}^\infty \frac{\left| \mathbf{V}_i^{N_k}(\omega, t) - \mathbf{v}_i(t) \right|^2}{2^i}} \\ &\le \frac{1}{k} + \sqrt{\left(|\mathbf{v}_1^0| + LT \right)^2 \sum_{i=k+1}^\infty \frac{1}{2^i}} \\ &= \frac{1}{k} + \frac{1}{2^{k/2}} \left(|\mathbf{v}_1^0| + LT \right). \quad (26) \end{aligned}$$

Hence $d^{\mathbb{Z}^+}\left(\mathbf{V}^{N_k}(\omega, \cdot), \mathbf{v} \right) \to 0$, as $k \to \infty$. The existence of the limit points $\mathbf{a}(t)$, $\mathbf{l}(t)$ and $\mathbf{c}(t)$ can be established by an identical argument. This completes the proof. $\square$

6.2 Derivatives of the Fluid Limits

The previous section established that any sequence of "good" sample paths ($\left\{ \mathbf{X}^N(\omega, \cdot) \right\}$ with $\omega \in \mathcal{C}$) eventually stays close to some Lipschitz-continuous, and therefore absolutely continuous, trajectory. In this section, we will characterize the derivatives of $\mathbf{v}(\cdot)$ at all regular (differentiable) points of such limiting trajectories. We will show, as we might expect, that they are the same as the drift terms in the fluid model. This means that all fluid limits of $\mathbf{V}^N(\cdot)$ are in fact solutions to the fluid model.

Proposition 12. (Fluid Limits and Fluid Model) *Fix $\omega \in \mathcal{C}$ and $T > 0$. Let $\mathbf{x}$ be a limit point of some subsequence of $\mathbf{X}^N(\omega, \cdot)$, as in Proposition 11. Let t be a point of* *differentiability of all coordinates of* $\mathbf{x}$*. Then, for all* $i \in \mathbb{N}$,

$$\dot{\mathbf{a}}_i(t) = \lambda(\mathbf{v}_{i-1} - \mathbf{v}_i), \qquad (27)$$

$$\dot{\mathbf{l}}_i(t) = (1-p)(\mathbf{v}_i - \mathbf{v}_{i+1}), \qquad (28)$$

$$\dot{\mathbf{c}}_i(t) = g_i(\mathbf{v}), \qquad (29)$$

where g *was defined in Eq. (6), with the initial condition* $\mathbf{v}(0) = \mathbf{v}^0$ *and boundary condition* $\mathbf{v}_0(t) - \mathbf{v}_1(t) = 1, \forall t \in [0, T]$*. In other words, all fluid limits of* $\mathbf{V}^N(\cdot)$ *are solutions to the fluid model.*

PROOF. We fix some $\omega \in \mathcal{C}$ and for the rest of this proof we will suppress the dependence on ω in our notation. The existence of Lipschitz-continuous limit points for the given $\omega \in \mathcal{C}$ is guaranteed by Proposition 11. Let $\{\mathbf{X}^{N_k}(\cdot)\}_{k=1}^{\infty}$ be a convergent subsequence such that $\lim_{k \to \infty} d^{\mathbb{Z}^+}(\mathbf{X}^{N_k}(\cdot), \mathbf{x}) = 0$. We now prove each of the three claims (Eqs. (27)-(29)) separately, and index i is always fixed unless otherwise stated.

Claim 1: $\dot{\mathbf{a}}_i(t) = \lambda(\mathbf{v}_{i-1}(t) - \mathbf{v}_i(t))$. Consider the sequence of trajectories $\{A^{N_k}(\cdot)\}_{k=1}^{\infty}$. By construction, $\mathbf{A}_i^N(t)$ receives a jump of magnitude $\frac{1}{N}$ at time t if and only if an event happens at time t and the corresponding selection random variable, $U(\cdot)$, falls in the interval $\frac{\lambda}{1+\lambda}\left[0, \mathbf{V}_{i-1}^N(t-) - \mathbf{V}_i^N(t-)\right)$. Therefore, we can write:

$$\mathbf{A}_i^{N_k}(t+\epsilon) - \mathbf{A}_i^{N_k}(t) = \frac{1}{N_k} \sum_{j=N_k W^{N_k}(t)}^{N_k W^{N_k}(t+\epsilon)} \mathbb{I}_{I_j}(U(j)), \qquad (30)$$

where $I_j \triangleq \frac{\lambda}{1+\lambda}\left[0, \mathbf{V}_{i-1}^{N_k}(t_j^{N_k}-) - \mathbf{V}_i^{N_k}(t_j^{N_k}-)\right)$ and t_j^N is defined to be the time of the jth jump in $W^N(\cdot)$, i.e.,

$$t_j^N \triangleq \inf\left\{t \geq 0 : W^N(t) \geq \frac{j}{N}\right\}. \qquad (31)$$

Note that by the definition of a fluid limit, we have that

$$\lim_{k \to \infty} \left(\mathbf{A}_i^{N_k}(t+\epsilon) - \mathbf{A}_i^{N_k}(t)\right) = \mathbf{a}_i(t+\epsilon) - \mathbf{a}_i(t). \qquad (32)$$

The following lemma bounds the change in $\mathbf{a}_i(t)$ on a small time interval.

Lemma 13. *Fix* i *and* t*. For all sufficiently small* $\epsilon > 0$

$$|\mathbf{a}_i(t+\epsilon) - \mathbf{a}_i(t) - \epsilon \lambda(\mathbf{v}_{i-1}(t) - \mathbf{v}_i(t))| \leq 2\epsilon^2 L \qquad (33)$$

Proof outline: The proof is based on the fact that $\omega \in \mathcal{C}$. Using Lemma 9, Eq. (33) follows from Eq. (30) by applying the convergence properties of $W^N(t)$ (Eq. (18)) and $U(n)$ (Eq. (19)). See Appendix A.3 in [11] for a proof. $\square$

Since by assumption $\mathbf{a}(\cdot)$ is differentiable at t, Claim 1 follows from Lemma 13 by noting $\dot{\mathbf{a}}_i(t) \triangleq \lim_{\epsilon \downarrow 0} \frac{\mathbf{a}_i(t+\epsilon)-\mathbf{a}_i(t)}{\epsilon}$.

Claim 2: $\dot{\mathbf{l}}_i(t) = (1-p)(\mathbf{v}_i(t) - \mathbf{v}_{i+1}(t))$. Claim 2 can be proved using an identical approach to the one used to prove Claim 1. The proof is hence omitted.

Claim 3: $\dot{\mathbf{c}}_i(t) = g_i(\mathbf{v})$. We prove Claim 3 by considering separately the three cases in the definition of $\mathbf{v}$.

(1) **Case 1**: $\dot{\mathbf{c}}_i(t) = 0$, if $\mathbf{v}_{i-1} = 0, \mathbf{v}_i = 0$. Write

$$\dot{\mathbf{c}}_i(t) = \dot{\mathbf{a}}_i(t) - \dot{\mathbf{l}}_i(t) - \dot{\mathbf{v}}_i(t). \qquad (34)$$

We calculate each of the three terms on the right-hand side of the above equation. By Claim 1, $\dot{\mathbf{a}}_i(t) = \lambda(\mathbf{v}_{i-1} - \mathbf{v}_i) = 0$, and by Claim 2, $\dot{\mathbf{l}}_i(t) = \lambda(\mathbf{v}_i - \mathbf{v}_{i+1}) = 0$. To obtain the value for $\dot{\mathbf{v}}_i(t)$, we use the following trick:

since $\mathbf{v}_i(t) = 0$ *and* $\mathbf{v}_i$ *is non-negative*, the *only* possibility for $\mathbf{v}_i(t)$ to be differentiable at t is that $\dot{\mathbf{v}}_i(t) = 0$. Since $\dot{\mathbf{a}}_i(t)$, $\dot{\mathbf{l}}_i(t)$, and $\dot{\mathbf{v}}_i(t)$ are all zero, we have that $\dot{\mathbf{c}}_i(t) = 0$.

(2) **Case 2**: $\dot{\mathbf{c}}_i(t) = \min\{\lambda \mathbf{v}_{i-1}, p\}$, if $\mathbf{v}_i = 0, \mathbf{v}_{i-1} > 0$.

In this case, the fraction of queues with at least i tasks is zero, hence $\mathbf{v}_i$ receives no drift from the local portion of the service capacity by Claim 2. First consider the case $\mathbf{v}_{i-1}(t) \leq \frac{p}{\lambda}$. Here the line of arguments is similar to the one in Case 1. By Claim 1, $\dot{\mathbf{a}}_i(t) = \lambda(\mathbf{v}_{i-1} - \mathbf{v}_i) = \lambda \mathbf{v}_{i-1}$, and by Claim 2, $\dot{\mathbf{l}}_i(t) = \lambda(\mathbf{v}_i - \mathbf{v}_{i+1}) = 0$. Using again the same trick as in Case 1, the non-negativity of $\mathbf{v}_i$ and the fact that $\mathbf{v}_i(t) = 0$ together imply that we must have $\dot{\mathbf{v}}_i(t) = 0$. Combining the expressions for $\dot{\mathbf{a}}_i(t)$, $\dot{\mathbf{l}}_i(t)$, and $\dot{\mathbf{v}}_i(t)$, we have

$$\dot{\mathbf{c}}_i(t) = -\dot{\mathbf{v}}_i(t) + \dot{\mathbf{a}}_i(t) - \dot{\mathbf{l}}_i(t) = \lambda \mathbf{v}_{i-1}. \qquad (35)$$

Intuitively, here the drift due to random arrivals to queues with $i-1$ tasks, $\lambda \mathbf{v}_{i-1}$, is "absorbed" by the central portion of the service capacity.

If $\mathbf{v}_{i-1}(t) > \frac{p}{\lambda}$, then the above equation would imply that $\dot{\mathbf{c}}_i(t) = \lambda \mathbf{v}_{i-1}(t) > p$, if $\dot{\mathbf{c}}_i(t)$ exists. But clearly $\dot{\mathbf{c}}_i(t) \leq p$. This simply means $\mathbf{v}_i(t)$ cannot be differentiable at time t, if $\mathbf{v}_i(t) = 0, \mathbf{v}_{i-1}(t) > \frac{p}{\lambda}$. Hence we have the claimed expression.

(3) **Case 3**: $\dot{\mathbf{c}}_i(t) = p$, if $\mathbf{v}_i > 0, \mathbf{v}_{i+1} > 0$.

Since there is a positive fraction of queues with more than i tasks, it follows that $\mathbf{V}_i^N$ is decreased by $\frac{1}{N}$ *whenever* a central token becomes available. Formally, for some small enough ϵ, there exists K such that $\mathbf{V}_i^{N_k}(s) > 0$ for all $k \geq K$, $s \in [t, t+\epsilon]$. Given the coupling construction, this implies for all $k \geq K$, $s \in [t, t+\epsilon]$

$$\mathbf{V}_i^{N_k}(s) - \mathbf{V}_i^{N_k}(t) = \frac{1}{N_k} \sum_{j=N_k W^{N_k}(t)}^{N_k W^{N_k}(s)} \mathbb{I}_{[1-\frac{p}{1+\lambda}, 1)}(U(j)).$$

Using the same arguments as in the proof of Lemma 13, we see that the right-hand side of the above equation converges to $(s-t)p + o(\epsilon)$ as $k \to \infty$. Hence, $\dot{\mathbf{v}}_i(t) = \lim_{\epsilon \downarrow 0} \lim_{k \to \infty} \frac{\mathbf{V}_i^{N_k}(t+\epsilon) - \mathbf{V}_i^{N_k}(t)}{\epsilon} = p$.

Finally, note that the boundary condition $\mathbf{v}_0(t) - \mathbf{v}_1(t) = 1$ is a consequence of the fact that $\mathbf{V}_0^N(t) - \mathbf{V}_1^N(t) \triangleq \mathbf{S}_1^N(t) = 1$ for all t. This concludes the proof of Proposition 12. $\square$

7. PROPERTIES OF THE FLUID MODEL

7.1 Uniqueness of Fluid Limit & Continuous Dependence on Initial Conditions

We now prove Theorem 4, which states that given an initial condition $\mathbf{v}^0 \in \overline{\mathcal{V}}^{\infty}$, a solution to the fluid model exists and is unique. As a direct consequence of the proof, we obtain an important corollary, that the unique solution $\mathbf{v}(t)$ depends *continuously* on the initial condition $\mathbf{v}^0$.

The uniqueness result justifies the use of the fluid approximation, in the sense that the evolution of the stochastic system is close to a *single* trajectory. The uniqueness along with the continuous dependence on the initial condition will be used to prove convergence of steady-state distributions to $\mathbf{v}^I$ (Theorem 7).

130

PROOF. (**Theorem 4**) The existence of a solution to the fluid model follows from the fact that $\mathbf{V}^N$ has a limit point (Proposition 11) and that all limit points of $\mathbf{V}^N$ are solutions to the fluid model (Proposition 12). We now show uniqueness. Define $i^p(\mathbf{v}) \overset{\triangle}{=} \sup\{i : \mathbf{v}_i > 0\}$.[12] Let $\mathbf{v}(t), \mathbf{w}(t)$ be two solutions to the fluid model such that $\mathbf{v}(0) = \mathbf{v}^0$ and $\mathbf{w}(0) = \mathbf{w}^0$, with $\mathbf{v}^0, \mathbf{w}^0 \in \overline{\mathcal{V}}^\infty$. At any regular point $t \geq 0$, where all coordinates of $\mathbf{v}(t), \mathbf{w}(t)$ are differentiable, without loss of generality, assume $i^p(\mathbf{v}(t)) \leq i^p(\mathbf{w}(t))$ with equality holding if both are infinite. Denoting by $\mathbf{a}^{\mathbf{v}}$ the arrival process $\mathbf{a}$ corresponding to the fluid limit $\mathbf{v}$ (and similarly for $\mathbf{l}$ and $\mathbf{c}$), we have:

$$\frac{d}{dt}\|\mathbf{v}-\mathbf{w}\|_w^2 \overset{\triangle}{=} \frac{d}{dt}\sum_{i=0}^\infty \frac{|\mathbf{v}_i - \mathbf{w}_i|^2}{2^i} \overset{(a)}{=} \sum_{i=0}^\infty \frac{(\mathbf{v}_i - \mathbf{w}_i)(\dot{\mathbf{v}}_i - \dot{\mathbf{w}}_i)}{2^{i-1}}$$

$$= \sum_{i=0}^\infty \frac{(\mathbf{v}_i - \mathbf{w}_i)[(\dot{\mathbf{a}}_i^{\mathbf{v}} - \dot{\mathbf{l}}_i^{\mathbf{v}}) - (\dot{\mathbf{a}}_i^{\mathbf{w}} - \dot{\mathbf{l}}_i^{\mathbf{w}})]}{2^i}$$
$$- \sum_{i=0}^\infty \frac{(\mathbf{v}_i - \mathbf{w}_i)(\dot{\mathbf{c}}_i^{\mathbf{v}} - \dot{\mathbf{c}}_i^{\mathbf{w}})}{2^{i-1}}$$

$$\overset{(b)}{\leq} C\|\mathbf{v}-\mathbf{w}\|_w^2 - \sum_{i=0}^\infty \frac{(\mathbf{v}_i - \mathbf{w}_i)(\dot{\mathbf{c}}_i^{\mathbf{v}} - \dot{\mathbf{c}}_i^{\mathbf{w}})}{2^{i-1}}$$

$$= C\|\mathbf{v}-\mathbf{w}\|_w^2 - \sum_{i=0}^{i^p(\mathbf{v})} \frac{1}{2^{i-1}}(\mathbf{v}_i - \mathbf{w}_i)(p-p)$$
$$- \frac{1}{2^{i^p(\mathbf{v})}}(0 - \mathbf{w}_{i^p(\mathbf{v})+1})(\min\{\lambda\mathbf{v}_{i^p(\mathbf{v})}, p\} - p)$$
$$- \sum_{i=i^p(\mathbf{v})+2}^{i^p(\mathbf{w})} \frac{1}{2^{i-1}}(0 - \mathbf{w}_i)(0 - p)$$
$$- \sum_{j=i^p(\mathbf{w})+1}^\infty \frac{1}{2^{i-1}}(0 - 0)(\dot{\mathbf{c}}_i^{\mathbf{v}} - \dot{\mathbf{c}}_i^{\mathbf{w}})$$

$$\leq C\|\mathbf{v}-\mathbf{w}\|_w^2, \qquad (36)$$

where $C = 6(\lambda + 1 - p)$. The existence of the derivative $\frac{d}{dt}\|\mathbf{v}-\mathbf{w}\|_w^2$ and the exchange of limits in (a) require some care, but they are based on the fact that $\mathbf{v}_i(t)$ and $\mathbf{w}_i(t)$ are L-Lipschitz for all i[13]. Step (b) follows from the fact that $\dot{\mathbf{a}}$ and $\dot{\mathbf{l}}$ are both continuous and linear in $\mathbf{v}$ (see Eqs. (27) – (29)). The specific value of C can be derived after some simple algebra. Now suppose that $\mathbf{v}^0 = \mathbf{w}^0$. By Gronwall's inequality and Eq. (36), we have

$$\|\mathbf{v}(t) - \mathbf{w}(t)\|_w^2 \leq \|\mathbf{v}(0) - \mathbf{w}(0)\|_w^2 \, e^{Ct} = 0, \; \forall t \in [0, \infty), \quad (37)$$

which establishes uniqueness of the fluid limit on $[0, \infty)$. $\square$

The following Corollary is an easy, but very important, consequence of the uniqueness proof.

Corollary 14. (Continuous Dependence on Initial Conditions) *Denote by* $\mathbf{v}(\mathbf{v}^0, \cdot)$ *the unique solution to the fluid model given initial condition* $\mathbf{v}^0 \in \overline{\mathcal{V}}^\infty$. *If* $\mathbf{w}^n \in \overline{\mathcal{V}}^\infty, \forall n$, *and* $\|\mathbf{w}^n - \mathbf{v}^0\|_w \to 0$ *as* $n \to \infty$, *then for all* $t \geq 0$,

$$\lim_{n\to\infty} \|\mathbf{v}(\mathbf{w}^n, t) - \mathbf{v}(\mathbf{v}^0, t)\|_w = 0. \qquad (38)$$

---

[12] $i^p(\mathbf{v})$ can be infinite if all coordinates of $\mathbf{v}$ are positive.

[13] In particular, this implies that there exists $L' > 0$ such that $h_i(t) \overset{\triangle}{=} |\mathbf{v}_i(t) - \mathbf{w}_i(t)|^2$ are L'-Lipschitz in a small neighborhood around t for all i, i.e. $\left|\frac{h_i(t+\epsilon)-h_i(t)}{\epsilon}\right| \leq L'$ for all i and all sufficiently small ϵ. The existence of $\frac{d}{dt}\|\mathbf{v}-\mathbf{w}\|_w^2$ and the exchange of limits then follow from the dominated convergence theorem. See a more elaborate version of this proof in [11] for details.

PROOF. The continuity with respect to the initial condition is a direct consequence of Eq. (37): if $\mathbf{v}(\mathbf{w}^n, \cdot)$ is a sequence of fluid limits with initial conditions $\mathbf{w}^n \in \overline{\mathcal{V}}^\infty$ and if $\|\mathbf{w}^n - \mathbf{v}^0\|_w^2 \to 0$ as $N \to \infty$, then for all $t \in [0, \infty)$,

$$\|\mathbf{v}(\mathbf{v}^0, t) - \mathbf{v}(\mathbf{w}^n, t)\|_w^2 \leq \|\mathbf{v}^0 - \mathbf{w}^n\|_w^2 \, e^{Ct} \to 0, \; \text{as } n \to \infty.$$

This completes the proof. $\square$

$\mathbf{V}^N(t)$ **versus** $\mathbf{S}^N(t)$: The above uniqueness proof (Theorem 4) demonstrates the power of using $\mathbf{V}^N(t)$ and $\mathbf{v}(t)$ as a state representation. The proof technique exploits a property of the drifts, also known as the one-sided-Lipschitz condition in the dynamical systems literature. In fact, if we instead use $\mathbf{s}(t)$ to construct the fluid mode, the resulting drift terms, given by the relation $\mathbf{s}_i(t) = \mathbf{v}_i(t) - \mathbf{v}_{i+1}(t)$, fail to be one-sided-Lipschitz-continuous. The uniqueness result should still hold, but the proof would be much more difficult, requiring an examination of all points of discontinuity in the space. The intuitive reason is that the total drifts of the $\mathbf{s}_i$'s provided by the centralized service remains *constant* as long as the system is non-empty; hence, by adding up all the coordinates of $\mathbf{s}_i$, we eliminate many of the drift discontinuities. The fact that such a simple linear transformation can create one-sided-Lipschitz continuity and greatly simplify the analysis seems interesting in itself.

7.2 Proof of Theorem 6

PROOF. (**Theorem 6**) The proof follows from the sample-path tightness in Proposition 11 and the uniqueness of the fluid limit from Theorem 4. By assumption, the sequence of initial conditions $\mathbf{V}^{(0,N)}$ converges to some $\mathbf{v}^0 \in \overline{\mathcal{V}}^\infty$, in probability. Since the space $\overline{\mathcal{V}}^\infty$ is separable and complete under the $\|\cdot\|_w$ metric, by Skorohod's representation theorem, we can find a probability space $(\Omega_0, \mathcal{F}_0, \mathbb{P}_0)$ on which $\mathbf{V}^{(0,N)} \to \mathbf{v}^0$ almost surely. By Proposition 11 and Theorem 4, for almost every $\omega \in \Omega$, any subsequence of $\mathbf{V}^N(\omega, t)$ contains a further subsequence that converges to the unique fluid limit $\mathbf{v}(\mathbf{v}^0, t)$ uniformly on any compact interval $[0, T]$. Therefore for all $T < \infty$,

$$\lim_{N\to\infty} \sup_{t\in[0,T]} \|\mathbf{V}^N(\omega, t) - \mathbf{v}(\mathbf{v}^0, t)\|_w = 0, \; \mathbb{P}\text{-almost surely}, \quad (39)$$

which implies convergence in probability, and Eq. (13) holds. $\square$

7.3 Convergence to the Invariant State $\mathbf{v}^I$ (Proof of Theorem 5)

In this section, we will switch to the alternative state representation, $\mathbf{s}(t)$, where

$$\mathbf{s}_i(t) \overset{\triangle}{=} \mathbf{v}_{i+1}(t) - \mathbf{v}_i(t), \; \forall i \geq 0 \qquad (40)$$

to study the evolution of a fluid solution as $t \to \infty$. It turns out that a nice monotonicity property of the evolution of $\mathbf{s}(t)$ induced by the drift structure will help establish the convergence to an invariant state. We note that $\mathbf{s}_0(t) = 1$ for all t, and that for all points where $\mathbf{v}$ is differentiable,

$$\dot{\mathbf{s}}_i(t) = \dot{\mathbf{v}}_i(t) - \dot{\mathbf{v}}_{i+1}(t) = \lambda(\mathbf{s}_{i-1} - \mathbf{s}_i) - (1-p)(\mathbf{s}_i - \mathbf{s}_{i+1}) - g_i^s(\mathbf{s}),$$

for all $i \geq 1$, where $g_i^s(\mathbf{s}) \overset{\triangle}{=} g_i(\mathbf{v}) - g_{i+1}(\mathbf{v})$. Throughout this section, we will use both representations $\mathbf{v}(t)$ and $\mathbf{s}(t)$ to refer to the *same* fluid solution, with their relationship specified in Eq. (40).

The approach we will be using is essentially a variant of the convergence proof given in [3]. The idea is to partition the space $\overline{\mathcal{S}}^{\infty}$ into dominating classes, and show that (i) dominance in initial conditions is preserved by the fluid model, and (ii) any solution $\mathbf{s}(t)$ to the fluid model with an initial condition that dominates or is dominated by the invariant state $\mathbf{s}^I$ converges to $\mathbf{s}^I$ as $t \to \infty$. Properties (i) and (ii) together imply the convergence of the fluid solution $\mathbf{s}(t)$ to $\mathbf{s}^I$, as $t \to \infty$, for any finite initial condition. It turns out that such dominance in $\mathbf{s}$ is much stronger than a similarly defined relation for $\mathbf{v}$. For this reason we cannot use $\mathbf{v}$ but must rely on $\mathbf{s}$ to establish the result.

Definition 15. (Coordinate-wise Dominance) *For any* $\mathbf{s}, \mathbf{s}' \in \overline{\mathcal{S}}^{\infty}$, *we write* $\mathbf{s} \succeq \mathbf{s}'$ *if* $\mathbf{s}_i \geq \mathbf{s}'_i$, *for all* $i \geq 0$.

The following lemma states that $\succeq$-dominance in initial conditions is preserved by the fluid model.

Lemma 16. *Let* $\mathbf{s}^1(\cdot)$ *and* $\mathbf{s}^2(\cdot)$ *be two solutions to the fluid model such that* $\mathbf{s}^1(0) \succeq \mathbf{s}^2(0)$. *Then* $\mathbf{s}^1(t) \succeq \mathbf{s}^2(t), \forall t \geq 0$.

The proof of Lemma 16 consists of checking the drift terms of the fluid model. It is straightforward and is omitted. We are now ready to prove Theorem 5.

PROOF. **(Theorem 5)** Let $\mathbf{s}(\cdot), \mathbf{s}^u(\cdot)$ and $\mathbf{s}^l(\cdot)$ be three fluid limits with initial conditions in $\overline{\mathcal{S}}^{\infty}$ such that $\mathbf{s}^u(0) \succeq \mathbf{s}(0) \succeq \mathbf{s}^l(0)$ and $\mathbf{s}^u(0) \succeq \mathbf{s}^I \succeq \mathbf{s}^l(0)$. By Lemma 16, we must have $\mathbf{s}^u(t) \succeq \mathbf{s}^I \succeq \mathbf{s}^l(t)$ for all $t \geq 0$. Hence it suffices to show that $\lim_{t \to \infty} \|\mathbf{s}^u(t) - \mathbf{s}^I\|_w = \lim_{t \to \infty} \|\mathbf{s}^l(t) - \mathbf{s}^I\|_w = 0$. Recall, for any regular $t > 0$,

$$
\begin{aligned}
\dot{\mathbf{v}}_i(t) &= \lambda(\mathbf{v}_{i-1} - \mathbf{v}_i) - (1-p)(\mathbf{v}_i - \mathbf{v}_{i+1}) - g_i(\mathbf{v}) \\
&= \lambda \mathbf{s}_{i-1} - (1-p)\mathbf{s}_i - g_i(\mathbf{v}) \\
&= (1-p)\left(\frac{\lambda \mathbf{s}_{i-1} - g_i(\mathbf{v})}{1-p} - \mathbf{s}_i\right).
\end{aligned}
\tag{41}
$$

Recall, from the expressions for $\mathbf{s}^I$ in Theorem 2, that $\mathbf{s}^I_{i+1} \geq \frac{\lambda \mathbf{s}^I_i - p}{1-p}$, $\forall i \geq 0$. From Eq. (41) and the fact that $\mathbf{s}^u_0 = \mathbf{s}^I_0 = 1$, we have

$$
\dot{\mathbf{v}}^u_1(t) = (1-p)\left(\frac{\lambda - g_1(\mathbf{v}^u)}{1-p} - \mathbf{s}^u_1\right) \leq (1-p)\left(\mathbf{s}^I_1 - \mathbf{s}^u_1\right), \tag{42}
$$

for all regular $t \geq 0$. To see why the above inequality holds, note that $\frac{\lambda - g_1(\mathbf{v}^u)}{1-p} = \frac{\lambda - p}{1-p} \leq \mathbf{s}^I_1$ whenever $\mathbf{s}^u_1(t) > 0$, and $\frac{\lambda - g_1(\mathbf{v}^u)}{1-p} = \mathbf{s}^I_1(t) = 0$ whenever $\mathbf{s}^u_1(t) = \mathbf{s}^I_1 = 0$.

Since $\mathbf{v}^u_1(0) < \infty$ and $\mathbf{v}^u_1(t) \geq 0$ for all $t \geq 0$, it is not hard to show that Eq. (42) implies that $\lim_{t \to \infty} |\mathbf{s}^u_1(t) - \mathbf{s}^I_1| = 0$.

We then proceed by induction. Suppose $\lim_{t \to \infty} |\mathbf{s}^u_i(t) - \mathbf{s}^I_i| = 0$ for some $i \geq 1$. By Eq. (41), we have

$$
\begin{aligned}
\dot{\mathbf{v}}^u_{i+1} &= (1-p)\left(\frac{\lambda \mathbf{s}^u_i - g_i(\mathbf{v}^u)}{1-p} - \mathbf{s}^u_{i+1}\right) \\
&= (1-p)\left(\frac{\lambda \mathbf{s}^I_i - g_i(\mathbf{v}^u)}{1-p} - \mathbf{s}^u_{i+1} + \epsilon^u_i\right) \\
&\leq (1-p)\left(\mathbf{s}^I_{i+1} - \mathbf{s}^u_{i+1} + \epsilon^u_i\right),
\end{aligned}
\tag{43}
$$

where $\epsilon^u_i \triangleq \frac{\lambda}{1-p}\left(\mathbf{s}^u_i(t) - \mathbf{s}^I_i\right) \to 0$ as $t \to \infty$ by the induction hypothesis. With the same argument as the one for $\mathbf{s}_1$, we obtain $\lim_{t \to \infty} |\mathbf{s}^u_{i+1}(t) - \mathbf{s}^I_{i+1}| = 0$. This establishes the convergence of $\mathbf{s}^u(t)$ to $\mathbf{s}^I$ along all coordinates, which implies $\lim_{t \to \infty} \|\mathbf{s}^u(t) - \mathbf{s}^I\|_w = 0$. Using the same set of arguments we can show that $\lim_{t \to \infty} \|\mathbf{s}^l(t) - \mathbf{s}^I\|_w = 0$. This completes the proof. $\square$

8. CONCLUSIONS

The overall theme of this paper is to study how the degree of centralization in allocating computing or processing resources impacts performance. This investigation was motivated by applications in server farms, cloud centers, as well as more general scheduling problems with communication constraints. Using a fluid model and associated convergence theorems, we showed that any small degree of centralization induces an exponential performance improvement in the steady-state scaling of system delay, for sufficiently large systems. Simulations show good accuracy of the model even for moderate-sized finite systems ($N = 100$).

For future work, some current modeling assumptions could be restrictive for practical applications. For example, the transmission delays between the local and central stations are assumed to be negligible compared to processing times; this may not be true for data centers that are separated by significant geographic distances. Also, the arrival and processing times are assumed to be Poisson, while in reality more general traffic distributions (e.g., heavy-tailed traffic) are observed. Finally, the speed of the central server may not be able to scale linearly in N for large N. Further work to extend the current model by incorporating these realistic constraints could be of great interest, although obtaining theoretical characterizations seems quite challenging. Lastly, the surprisingly simple expressions in our results make it tempting to ask whether similar performance characterizations can be obtained for other stochastic systems with partially centralized control laws; insights obtained here may find applications beyond the realm of queueing theory.

9. REFERENCES

[1] M. Bramson. State space collapse with application to heavy traffic limits for multiclass queueing networks. *Queueing Systems: Theory and Applications*, 30: pp. 89–148, 1998.

[2] S.N. Ethier and T.G. Kurtz. *Markov Processes: Characterization and Convergence (2nd edition)*. Wiley-Interscience, 2005.

[3] N.D. Vvedenskaya, R.L. Dobrushin, and F.I. Karpelevich. Queueing system with selection of the shortest of two queues: An asymptotic approach. *Probl. Inf. Transm*, 32(1): pp. 20–34, 1996.

[4] M. Mitzenmacher. The power of two choices in randomized load balancing. *Ph.D. thesis, U.C. Berkeley*, 1996.

[5] M. Alanyali and M. Dashouk. On power-of-choice in downlink transmission scheduling. *Inform. Theory and Applicat. Workshop*, U.C. San Diego, 2008.

[6] N. Gast and B. Gaujal. Mean field limit of non-smooth systems and differential inclusions. *INRIA Research Report*, 2010.

[7] M. Bramson, Y. Lu, and B. Prabhakar. Randomized load balancing with general service time distributions. *ACM Sigmetrics*, New York, 2010.

[8] M. Mitzenmacher, A. Richa, and R. Sitaraman. The power of two random choices: A survey of techniques and results. *Handbook of Randomized Computing: Volume 1*, pp. 255–312, 2001.

[9] G.J. Foschini and J. Salz. A basic dynamic routing problem and diffusion. *IEEE Trans. on Comm.* 26: pp. 320–327, 1978.

[10] Y.T. He and D.G. Down, On accommodating customer flexibility in service systems. *INFOR*, 47(4): pp. 289–295, 2009.

[11] J.N. Tsitsiklis and K. Xu, On the power of (even a little) centralization in distributed processing (Technical Report). http://web.mit.edu/jnt/www/Papers/TXSIG11.pdf.

Weighted Proportional Allocation

Thành Nguyen*
Northwestern University
Evanston, IL, USA
thanh@eecs.northwestern.edu

Milan Vojnović
Microsoft Research
Cambridge, UK
milanv@microsoft.com

ABSTRACT

We consider a weighted proportional allocation of resources that allows providers to discriminate usage of resources by users. This framework is a generalization of well-known proportional allocation by accommodating allocation of resources proportional to weighted bids or proportional to submitted bids but with weighted payments.

We study a competition game where *everyone is selfish*: providers choose user discrimination weights aiming at maximizing their individual *revenues* while users choose their bids aiming at maximizing their individual payoffs. We analyze revenue and social welfare of this game. We find that the revenue is lower bounded by $k/(k+1)$ times the revenue under standard price discrimination scheme, where a set of k users is excluded. For users with linear utility functions, we find that the social welfare is at least $1/(1+2/\sqrt{3})$ of the maximum social welfare (approx. 46%) and that this bound is tight. We extend this efficiency result to a broad class of utility functions and multiple competing providers. We also describe an algorithm for adjusting discrimination weights by providers without a prior knowledge of user utility functions and establish convergence to equilibrium points of the competition game.

Our results show that, in many cases, weighted proportional sharing achieves competitive revenue and social welfare, despite the fact that everyone is selfish.

Categories and Subject Descriptors

K.6.0 [**Management of Computing and Information Systems**]: General—*Economics*; C.2.3 [**Network Architecture Design**]: Network Operations

General Terms

Algorithms, Economics, Theory

---

*Work performed in part while an intern with Microsoft Research.

1. INTRODUCTION

Auction-based Resource Allocation. Use of *pay-per-use pricing* to offer communication and computer services has much proliferated over recent years. For example, cloud computing services are offered through using either fixed pricing or auctions to sell compute instances. The two forms of sales have their own advantages and disadvantages. While fixed pricing schemes are simple to implement, in many scenarios they are neither robust nor flexible enough. For instance, when the user demand is inelastic, a small change in price can translate to a dramatic change in the demand, which can cause congestion and system failure. Furthermore, in order to update prices, providers usually need to gather enough data from sales and this inflexibility can cause system inefficiency and result in low revenue. In recent years, using auction-based schemes for allocating and selling resources in computing systems has become more popular. Sales using auctions are known to be more flexible and can extract information from users. The fact that users can adjust their bids and providers can change the auction parameters in a dynamic fashion yields tremendous improvements of the system efficiency or the revenue extracted by providers. Moreover, the disadvantages of the auction-based approaches such as the difficulty for users to find optimal strategies and for providers to change their platforms have been greatly improved with availability of software that helps users to optimize their bidding strategies and several online services offering auction platforms.

Examples of using auctions for resource allocation include selling of Amazon EC2 spot instances [1], selling of *sponsored search ad slots* to advertisers by major providers of online services, and are of wide interest across engineering systems, e.g. the *electricity markets* [23] that have been of raising interest due to variable supply from renewable energy sources. Furthermore, numerous auction-based allocations of system resources have been proposed such as allocation of disk I/O in storage systems [6], allocation of computational resources [3], and it was even showed that sharing of the Internet bandwidth by TCP connections may be seen as an auction [11, 9].

User Differentiation. In practice providers often apply different prices to different users for selling identical goods or services, which is commonly referred to as *price discrimination*. It is not surprising that similar discrimination schemes are also extensively used in auction-based allocations. There are two main reasons for using such a discriminative framework. First, different users may require different subsets of resources owned by the provider, e.g. bandwidth over different paths in a communication network, and thus, the provider may improve the system efficiency by differentiating users. Second, different users may have different valuations for the amount of resource received, e.g. different valuation for the amount of network bandwidth received; in this case, once having learned this information, the provider may naturally try to take advantage to increase the revenue by differentiating users.

The most well known example of an auction that differentiates users is the generalized second price auction that is in common use by search engines for allocating ads. In this mechanism, providers (search engines) assign different weights to different users (advertisers) and the mechanism is run based on weighted bids.

The Framework. In this paper, we consider a class of auctions that allows for user differentiation. Specifically, we are interested in auctions that are simple in terms of the information provided by users and are easy to describe to users. We consider two natural instances of weighted proportional allocation: (1) *weighted bid auction* where for a user the allocation is proportional to the product of the bid submitted by this user and the user-specific discrimination weight selected by the provider, and the payment is equal to the bid; (2) *weighted payment auction* where the allocation to a user is proportional the bid of this user and the payment is equal to the product of the bid of this user and the user-specific discrimination weight selected by the provider. The weighted bid auction is a novel proposal while the weighted payment auction was previously considered in Ma et al [15].

As standard in the network pricing literature [18], we consider these allocation mechanisms in the *full information* setting. The justification lies in the fact that in practice allocation auctions are run repeatedly and, thus, providers can learn about the behavior and private information of users. As discussed in the beginning of this section, even in this setting there are advantages of using proportional sharing-like auctions over fixed price schemes. Both auctions that we consider are akin and natural generalizations of the well-known proportional allocation (e.g. [11, 9, 7], see related work discussed later in this section). Therefore, this class of auctions inherits many natural properties of the traditional proportional sharing rule, making it *easy and robust to implement* in practice. Specifically, these mechanisms are simple for bidders as they only need to know the total of others' bids and the allocation is a continuous function of the bids which facilitates robust implementation in a distributed system as will show later in the paper.

Another important reason that motivates us to study the weighted proportional allocation rules is the fact that in settings where provider's goal is to *maximize revenue*, the weighted proportional sharing is preferred over traditional proportional sharing. As it will be shown later, while weighted proportional sharing can provide near-optimal revenue, this is not guaranteed by traditional proportional sharing, which in this regard can be arbitrarily bad.

We study the allocation in *general convex environments* that capture many special cases of resource constraints including those of communication networks, sponsored search, and scheduling of computing resources (see Figure 1 for an illustration).

We describe the weighted proportional schemes considered in this paper in more detail as follows. We consider a single provider and a set of $n \geq 1$ users and denote with $U = \{1, 2, \ldots, n\}$ the set of users. The vectors of allocations and payments are denoted by $\vec{x} = (x_1, x_2, \ldots, x_n)$ and $\vec{q} = (q_1, q_2, \ldots, q_n)$, respectively. The resource owned by the provider is an arbitrary infinitely divisible resource with the constraints specified by the convex set $\mathcal{P} \in \mathbb{R}_+^n$. An allocation vector $\vec{x}$ is said to be *feasible* if and only if $\vec{x} \in \mathcal{P}$. The provider assigns *discrimination weight* $C_i \geq 0$ to each user i. We denote with $w_i \geq 0$ the bid submitted by user i.

The weighted bid auction is specified by the following allocation and payment rules:

WEIGHTED BID AUCTION

For user i with bid w_i:

$$\text{Allocation} \quad x_i = C_i \frac{w_i}{\sum_{j \in U} w_j}$$

$$\text{Payment} \quad q_i = w_i$$

where the discrimination weights $\vec{C}$ are chosen such that $\vec{x}$ is feasible. We may interpret the discrimination weight C_i as the maximum allocation that is assigned by the provider to user i and x_i as the actual allocation that is the fraction $w_i / \sum_{j \in U} w_j$ of the user-specific maximum allocation C_i.

In turn, the weighted payment auction is specified by the allocation and payment rules defined as follows:

WEIGHTED PAYMENT AUCTION

For user i with bid w_i:

$$\text{Allocation} \quad x_i = C \frac{w_i}{\sum_{j \in U} w_j}$$

$$\text{Payment} \quad q_i = C_i w_i$$

where C is the maximum allocation that is assigned to every user and the discrimination weight C_i determines the payment by user i.

Compared with the traditional proportional allocation, the weighted bid auction is more suitable for general convex resource constraints. This is not the case for the weighted payment auction: while the relative allocation across users can be arbitrary by appropriate choice of the user bids, the implicit assumption of the allocation rule is that $\sum_i x_i = C$, i.e. the provider is required to a priori commit to allocate the total amount of resource C. While this is not restrictive for allocating an infinitely divisible resource of capacity C, this allocation rule cannot accommodate more general polyhedral constraints. Thus, in this paper we will mainly focus on the weighted bid auction but also consider some properties of the weighted payment auction, as it is an alternative auction that allows for user discrimination, albeit for special type of resource constraints.

Questions Studied in this Paper. We consider a competitive setting with multiple providers and users where *everyone is selfish*: each provider aims at maximizing own revenue and each user aims at maximizing own payoff. Ideally, an allocation mechanism would guarantee high *revenue* to the provider and high *efficiency* where by efficiency we mean social welfare (i.e. the total utility across all users) compared with the best possible social welfare. In the competitive setting where everyone is selfish, it is rather unclear whether the two goals could be achieved simultaneously. Intuitively, one would expect that selfishness of providers and

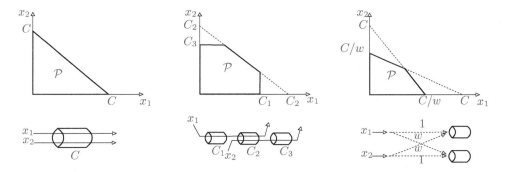

Figure 1: Examples of polyhedron constraints: (left) single link, (middle) a network of links, (right) assignment costs of a workflow to machines.

users may well result in either low revenue or efficiency. For example, providers that aim at maximizing their revenue may well have an incentive to misreport availability of their resources[1]. The main questions that we consider in this paper are:

Q1: *How much of the revenue can be guaranteed using the weighted proportional sharing?*

Q2: *What is the efficiency loss in competitive systems where everyone is selfish?*

Summary of Results. We summarize our results in the following points:

• *Revenue*: We show that the revenue of weighted bid auction is at least $k/(k+1)$ times the revenue under standard price discrimination scheme with a set of k users excluded, which we describe in more detail in Section 3. The comparison of the revenue of a mechanism with the maximum revenue obtained under another mechanism where some users are excluded is standard in the mechanism design literature (e.g. [8]) and in this context, our revenue comparison result is novel and may be of general interest. The result enables us to understand conditions under which the revenue of weighted bid auction is competitive to that under the benchmark pricing scheme, e.g. the case of many users.

• *Efficiency*: We establish that for linear user utility functions, the social welfare under weighted bid auction is at least $1/(1+2/\sqrt{3}) \approx 0.46$-factor of the maximum social welfare and this bound is tight. We also show a tight efficiency bound of $1/2$ for the weighed payment auctions. We extend our efficiency result of the weighed bid auction to a broad class of utility functions, we call δ-utility functions, where $\delta \geq 0$. We show that many utility functions found in literature are δ-utility functions, in many cases with $\delta \leq 2$, and show that this class of utility functions is closed to addition and multiplication with a positive constant. For the class of δ-utility functions, we show that the social welfare is at least $1/(1+2/\sqrt{3}+\delta)$-factor of the maximum social welfare and establish that this guarantee holds also for the case of multiple competing providers. A similar extension for the weighted payment auction is also shown.

• *Convergence and distributed algorithms*: We describe how the provider can adjust discrimination weights in an online fashion so that user allocations and payments converge to equilibrium points of the underlying competition game. This shows that the information about user utility functions needed by the provider can be estimated from the bids submitted by users in an online fashion. We describe a distributed iterative scheme and prove convergence to Nash equilibrium points for the case of linear user utility functions.

Related Work. The allocation of resources in proportion to user-specific weights has a long and rich history in the context of computer systems and services. For example, it underlies the objective of generalized processor sharing [19, 2], sharing of bandwidth in communication networks [11], and has been considered for allocation of various types of resources, including storage [6] and compute instances [3]. The weighted bid auction considered in this paper could be seen as a generalization of traditional proportional allocation to allow for user differentiation and general convex resource constraints.

Previous work primarily focused on analyzing social efficiency of proportional allocation in competitive environments where only users are assumed to be selfish. Kelly [11] showed that under price taking users, where each user submits a scalar bid for a set of resources of interest (e.g. allocation of bandwidth at each link along the path of a network connection), the proportional allocation guarantees 100% efficiency. In subsequent work, Johari and Tsitsiklis [9] showed that the social efficiency is at least 75% under so called price anticipating users and assumption that each user submits an individual bid for each individual resource of interest (e.g. an individual bid submitted for each link along the path of a network connection). The latter result was extended by Nguyen and Tardos [16] to more general polyhedral constraints. Furthermore, Yang and Hajek [7] showed that the worst-case efficiency is 0% if users are restricted to submitting a scalar bid for the set of resources of interest. Our work is different from all this work in that we consider a competitive environment where everyone is selfish.

The weighted payment auction was considered by Ma et al [15] where the focus was on the efficiency with respect to the social welfare. Our work provides new results for this type of auctions with regard to the revenue and efficiency in competitive environments where everyone is selfish.

The setting of multiple providers considered in this paper bears quite some similarity with that found in the context of

---

[1]A famous example of such a market manipulation is *California electricity crises* where in 2000 and 2001 there was a shortage of electricity because energy traders were gratuitously taking their plants offline at peak demand in order to sell at higher prices [24].

ISP multihoming, e.g. [5, 20], multi-path congestion control, e.g. [4], and may also inform about the competition in time-varying markets using the approach in [13].

Outline of the Paper. Section 2 introduces the resource competition game. Section 3 presents our main revenue comparison result (Theorem 3.1). In Section 4, we present our results on the efficiency guarantees for the case of a single provider and users with linear utility functions (Theorem 4.1). Section 5 extends the efficiency result to more general class of user utility functions and more general setting of multiple providers (Theorem 5.1). We discuss convergence to Nash equilibrium points and distributed schemes in Section 6. In Section 7, we conclude.

2. THE RESOURCE ALLOCATION GAME WHERE EVERYONE IS SELFISH

We consider a system of $n \geq 1$ users competing for resources of a single provider; we introduce the setting with multiple providers later in Section 5.1. Recall that $\vec{x} = (x_1, x_2, \ldots, x_n)$ and $\vec{q} = (q_1, q_2, \ldots, q_n)$ denote the vectors of allocations and payments by users, respectively. The allocation vector $\vec{x}$ is feasible if and only if $\vec{x} \in \mathcal{P}$ where $\mathcal{P}$ is a convex set of the form $\mathcal{P} = \{\vec{x} \in \mathbb{R}_+^n : A\vec{x} \leq \vec{b}\}$ for some matrix A and vector $\vec{b}$ with non-negative elements. (Note that A and $\vec{b}$ can have arbitrarily many rows, so we will often refer to "convex" constraints instead to polyhedrons.)

Suppose that $U_i(x_i)$ is the utility of allocation x_i to user i. Throughout this paper we assume that for every i, $U_i(x)$ is a non-negative, non-decreasing and continuously differentiable concave function. The payoffs for the provider and users are defined as follows. The payoff of the provider is equal to the revenue, i.e. the total payments received from all users, $R = \sum_i q_i$. The payoff for user i is equal to the utility minus the payment, i.e. $U_i(x_i) - q_i$.

The competition game that we study can be seen as the following *two-stage Stackelberg game*: in the first stage, the provider announces the discrimination weights $\vec{C}$ and then, in the second stage, users adjust their bids in a selfish way aiming at maximizing their individual payoffs. In the first stage, the provider anticipates how users would react to given discrimination weights $\vec{C}$ and sets these weights in a selfish way aiming at maximizing the revenue. In a dynamic setting, the two stages of this game would alternate over time (we discuss this in Section 6).

In the reminder of this section, we characterize the Nash equilibria for weighted-bid and weighted-payment auction.

Equilibrium of Weighted Bid Auction. We show a relation between the revenue and the allocation of an outcome. Given discrimination weight C_i and sum of the bids $\sum_j w_j$, user i selects bid w_i that maximizes his surplus, i.e. solves

$$\text{USER:} \quad \max_{w_i \geq 0} U_i\left(\frac{w_i}{\sum_{j \neq i} w_j + w_i} C_i\right) - w_i. \quad (1)$$

Under the assumed user behavior, one can analyze the Nash equilibrium of the game. It turns out that Nash equilibrium exists and is unique, and at Nash equilibrium, the relation between the revenue and allocation is captured by an implicit function, which we show in the following lemma.

LEMMA 2.1. *Given a vector of discrimination weights $\vec{C}$, there is a unique allocation $\vec{x}$ corresponding to unique Nash equilibrium. Conversely, given an equilibrium allocation vector $\vec{x}$, there is a unique vector of discrimination weights $\vec{C}$. Furthermore, the corresponding revenue $R(\vec{x})$ is a function of the allocation vector $\vec{x}$ given by*

$$\sum_i \frac{U_i'(x_i) x_i}{U_i'(x_i) x_i + R(\vec{x})} = 1, \quad (2)$$

where $U_i'(x_i)$ is the derivative of U_i at x_i.

Given this result, we obtain the following optimization problem for the provider.

PROVIDER: maximize $R(\vec{x})$ over $\vec{x} \in \mathcal{P}$. (3)

In the rest of this section we prove Lemma 2.1.

PROOF OF LEMMA 2.1. We have

$$x_i = C_i \frac{w_i}{\sum_j w_j} \quad (4)$$

and USER problem can be written as:

$$\text{maximize } U_i\left(\frac{w_i}{\sum_{j \neq i} w_j + w_i} C_i\right) - w_i \text{ over } w_i \geq 0. \quad (5)$$

Note that the objective function in (5) is concave in w_i, hence, at an optimum solution either $w_i = 0$ or the derivative of the objective function is zero. Setting the derivative to zero is equivalent to:

$$U_i'(x_i) \cdot C_i \frac{\sum_{j \neq i} w_j}{(\sum_j w_j)^2} = 1, \text{ for } x_i > 0.$$

It follows

$$U_i'(x_i) = \frac{(\sum_j w_j)^2}{C_i \sum_{j \neq i} w_j} = \frac{R^2}{C_i(R - w_i)} \quad (6)$$

where recall that the revenue is equal to the sum of payments made by users, i.e. $R = \sum_j w_j$. Combining with $w_i = x_i R/C_i$, which follows from (4), we have

$$U_i'(x_i) = \frac{R}{C_i - x_i} \Leftrightarrow C_i U_i'(x_i)\left(1 - \frac{x_i}{C_i}\right) = R. \quad (7)$$

Now, $\sum \frac{x_i}{C_i} = 1$, thus, condition (7) is exactly the optimality condition for the following problem

$$\text{maximize } \sum_i \int_0^{x_i} C_i U_i'(t_i)\left(1 - \frac{t_i}{C_i}\right) dt_i$$
$$\text{over } \vec{x} \in \mathbb{R}_+^n$$
$$\text{subject to } \sum_i \frac{x_i}{C_i} = 1.$$

Since $\int_0^{x_i} C_i U_i'(t_i)\left(1 - \frac{t_i}{C_i}\right) dt_i$ is a strictly concave function with respect to x_i, there exists a unique Nash equilibrium.

It remains to show that for an equilibrium allocation $\vec{x}$, the revenue R is given by

$$\sum_i \frac{U_i'(x_i) x_i}{U_i'(x_i) x_i + R} = 1. \quad (8)$$

From (7), we have

$$U_i'(x_i) = \frac{R}{C_i - x_i} \Rightarrow \frac{C_i}{x_i} - 1 = \frac{R}{U_i'(x_i) x_i}$$

$$\Rightarrow \frac{x_i}{C_i} = \frac{U_i'(x_i)x_i}{U_i'(x_i)x_i + R}.$$

Combining with $\sum_i x_i/C_i = 1$, which follows from (4), we obtain (8). Note that all the formulas above are applied for the case $x_i > 0$ only; nevertheless, if $x_i = 0$, we have $U_i'(x_i)x_i = 0$, and therefore, the equation (8) holds for any optimum allocation vector $\vec{x}$.

Finally, we note that in equilibrium, the vector of discrimination weights $\vec{C}$ and the vector of bids $\vec{w}$ are functions of the equilibrium allocation $\vec{x}$ given as follows: for every i,

$$C_i = x_i + \frac{R(\vec{x})}{U_i'(x_i)} \text{ and } w_i = \frac{R(\vec{x})}{U_i'(x_i)x_i + R(\vec{x})}U_i'(x_i)x_i.$$

$\square$

Equilibrium of Weighted Payment Auction. The analysis follows similar steps as for weighted bid auction. In this case, the revenue in Nash equilibrium can be represented as an explicit function of the allocation vector $\vec{x}$. Given discrimination weight C_i, user i solves the following surplus maximization problem:

$$\textbf{USER:} \quad \max_{w_i \geq 0} U_i\left(\frac{w_i}{\sum_{j \neq i} w_j + w_i}C\right) - C_i w_i. \quad (9)$$

LEMMA 2.2. *Given a vector of discrimination weights $\vec{C}$, there is a unique allocation $\vec{x}$ corresponding to the unique Nash equilibrium. Conversely, given an allocation $\vec{x}$, such that $\sum_i x_i = C$, there is a vector $\vec{C}$ of discrimination weights such that $\vec{x}$ is an outcome. Furthermore, the corresponding revenue $R(\vec{x})$ is given by*

$$R(\vec{x}) = \sum_i U_i'(x_i)\frac{x_i}{C}\left(1 - \frac{x_i}{C}\right).$$

The proof of this lemma is provided in [17].

3. REVENUE

Revenue of Proportional Sharing. We provide an example showing that traditional proportional sharing can perform poorly with respect to the revenue. The example is for the parking-lot network scenario that has been extensively used in the context of networking; see Figure 2 for an illustration. The resource consists of a series of $n \geq 1$ links, each of capacity $C > 0$ (without loss of generality we assume $C = 1$). The example consists of $n + 1$ users; user 0 is a *multi-hop user* that requires a connection through all links $1, 2, \ldots, n$ while user i is a *single-hop user* that requires a connection through link i. User utility functions are assumed to be α-fair, i.e. for $\alpha > 0$ and $\alpha \neq 1$, we have $U_i(x) = \frac{\gamma_i^\alpha}{1-\alpha}x^{1-\alpha}$, and $U_i(x) = \gamma_i \log(x)$, for $\alpha = 1$, where $\gamma_i > 0$ (in our example, we consider symmetric case where $\gamma_i = 1$, for every user i). The resource constraints in this example are $x_i + x_0 \leq 1$, for every link i.

Under proportional sharing mechanism, user 0 submits an individual bid for each link while user $i > 0$ only bids for link i. Using the known conditions for Nash equilibrium of the underlying game (e.g. [9, 16]), one can show that there is a unique equilibrium with the allocation vector, solution

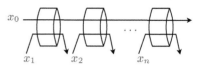

Figure 2: Parking-lot example.

of the following problem:

$$\text{maximize } \sum_{i=0}^{n} \int_0^{x_i} U_i'(y)(1-y)dy$$

$$\text{over } \vec{x} \in \mathbb{R}_+^{n+1}$$

$$\text{subject to } x_i + x_0 \leq 1, \; i = 1, 2, \ldots, n.$$

It is known that in Nash equilibrium, the sum of bids submitted to link i is equal to $U_i'(x_i)(1-x_i)$ [16]. Therefore, the revenue of proportional sharing in Nash equilibrium is $\sum_{i=1}^{n} U_i'(x_i)(1-x_i)$. By straightforward calculations, one can show that in Nash equilibrium, the allocation is x_0 to user 0 and $1 - x_0$ to each user $i > 1$, where $x_0 = \frac{1}{1+n^{1/(\alpha+1)}}$, and the revenue is $\frac{nx_0}{(1-x_0)^\alpha}$. For large network size n, the revenue in Nash equilibrium is $O(n^{\frac{\alpha}{\alpha+1}})$, therefore, $o(n)$, for every fixed $\alpha > 0$. The intuition behind why the revenue is low is: for large network size n, user 0 competes against many users and, therefore, the payment that this user can afford at each link is small. Consequently, the competition at each link is low which results in low revenue.

On the other hand, using fixed pricing, the provider can charge the price per unit resource of 1 on each link and receive the revenue of n.

The question that we investigate in this section is how large revenue the weighted bid auction can achieve, in comparison with the best fixed pricing scheme (with price discrimination). We will answer this question in the remainder of this section.

Revenue of Weighted Bid Auction. We will compare the revenue of weighted bid auction with that of a benchmark that consists of standard fixed price scheme [22]. In this pricing scheme, the provider charges user-specific prices per unit of resource for different users. Suppose that provider charges user i, the price per unit resource p_i. Then, user i surplus maximization problem is $\max U_i(x_i) - p_i x_i$ over $x_i \geq 0$. The solution of this problem is given by $U_i'(x_i) = p_i$. Therefore, the revenue of the provider is $R = \sum_i p_i x_i = \sum_i U_i'(x_i)x_i$. Hence, the optimal revenue is

$$R^* = \max\left\{\sum_i U_i'(x_i)x_i : \vec{x} \in \mathcal{P}\right\}.$$

Comparing with such a benchmark would be too ambitious because with auction-based allocation, the provider cannot announce fixed prices, but instead prices are induced from user demand. Thus, instead, we will compare with the revenue R^* where *some users are excluded*. That is, we will compare the revenue achieved by an auction for n users with the revenue achieved by the fixed pricing scheme for $n - k$ users, for $0 < k < n$. Note that using as a benchmark a scheme with some users excluded is standard in the theory of auctions [8].

In the parking-lot example introduced above, if we consider n large enough, then the optimal revenue is of the order n, which can be achieved if the provider charges every single-hop user the price per unit of resource of 1 and charges the multi-hop user the price per unit of resource of n. Now, if we exclude an arbitrary set of $k < n$ users, then the optimal revenue is $n - k$. Therefore, if k is much smaller compared with n, then one can think of this as a *large market* regime where the effect of removing a few users from the market is negligible.

Having discussed the intuition, we can now state our main result on the revenue guarantee of weighted bid auctions. Let R_{n-k}^* be the optimal revenue under our benchmark, i.e.

$$R_{n-k}^* = \min_{S \subset \{1,\ldots,n\}: \, |S| = n-k} \, \max_{\vec{x} \in \mathcal{P}} \sum_{i \in S} U_i'(x_i) x_i.$$

The revenue guarantee of weighted bid auctions is stated as follows.

THEOREM 3.1. *Suppose that for each user i, $U_i'(x)x$ is a concave function. Let R be the optimum revenue of the weighted bid allocation mechanism, then*

$$\text{for every } 1 \leq k < n: \ R \geq \frac{k}{k+1} R_{n-k}^*.$$

The proof of the theorem is based on an induction argument over k and is provided in [17]. It is noteworthy that the proof admits weak assumptions about the structure of the underlying auction. For example, using an analogue argument, we can also prove similar revenue guarantee for weighted payment auctions, which is provided in [17].

Finally, note that the revenue guarantee of the theorem above is rather strong. In particular, by taking as a benchmark the system with just one user excluded, we obtain that the revenue under weighted bid auction is at least $1/2$ of the revenue under the price discrimination scheme with one user excluded (whose exclusion reduces the revenue the most). Informally, the result tells us that for systems with many users with comparable utility functions, the revenue under weighted bid auction is nearly the same as under standard price discrimination. As discussed above, such a guarantee cannot be provided by proportional sharing.

4. EFFICIENCY FOR LINEAR USER UTILITY FUNCTIONS

In this section, we analyze the efficiency for the case of single provider and linear user utility functions. The analysis in this section provides us with basic techniques that are applied to the more general setting in Section 5.

4.1 Efficiency of Weighted Bid Auction

We show the following theorem.

THEOREM 4.1. *Assume that the provider maximizes the revenue and for each user i the utility function is linear, $U_i(x) = v_i x$, for some $v_i > 0$. Then, the worst-case efficiency is $1/(1 + 2/\sqrt{3})$ (approx. 46%). Furthermore, this bound is tight.*

Remark Before proving the theorem, we note that the worst-case efficiency can be achieved asymptotically as the number of users n tends to infinity. An example is for the resource constraint $\sum_i x_i \leq 1$ and the user valuations such that there is a unique user with the largest marginal utility, say this is

user 1, and all other users with identical marginal utilities equal to $(2-\sqrt{3})^2 v_1 \approx 0.0718 v_1$. In Nash equilibrium, user 1 obtains 42.26% of the resource and the rest is equally shared by other users. One can show that with higher user competitiveness, the efficiency increases. Specifically, if there are at least k users with the largest marginal utility, then the efficiency is at least $1 - \frac{1}{2k} + o(1/k)$. The proof of this result is in [17].

We first need the following lemma about the *quasi-concavity* of the objective function optimized by the provider. Recall that $R(\vec{x})$ is the function given by (2). Let R^* be the optimum revenue, i.e. $R^* = \max\{R(\vec{x}) : \vec{x} \in \mathcal{P}\}$. We note the following fact.

LEMMA 4.1. *The set $\mathcal{L}_\mu := \{\vec{x} \in \mathbb{R}_+^n : R(\vec{x}) \geq \mu\}$ is convex, for every $\mu \in [0, R^*]$.*

The proof of this lemma is straightforward and thus omitted (see [17]). In the remainder of this section, we prove Theorem 4.1.

PROOF OF THEOREM 4.1. An example showing that the bound is tight was already given in the remark above; it remains to prove that the efficiency is at least $1/(1 + 2/\sqrt{3})$.

Recall that R^* is the optimal revenue, thus for every $\vec{x} \in \mathcal{P}$, $R(\vec{x}) \leq R^*$. Consider the two convex sets $\mathcal{L}_{R^*}$ and $\mathcal{P}$. These two sets intersect at $\vec{x}$ where $R(\vec{x}) = R^*$ and do not have common interior points. Let H be the hyperplane that weakly separates these two sets, defined by $\gamma_i \geq 0$, for every i and

$$\sum_i \gamma_i x_i = 1. \qquad (10)$$

Consider the game where the provider has the feasible set $\mathcal{Q} = \{\vec{x} \in \mathbb{R}_+^n : \sum_i \gamma_i x_i \leq 1\}$, then the allocation that maximizes the revenue over $\mathcal{Q}$ is the same as in the original game. Since $\mathcal{P} \subset \mathcal{Q}$, the optimal social welfare of the new game is at least the social welfare of the original game. Therefore, it is enough to prove a lower bound on the efficiency for the class of games where the provider has the feasible set $\mathcal{Q}$. See Figure 3 for an illustration.

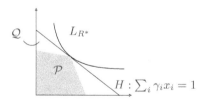

Figure 3: Reduction to a simpler constraint.

The observation above allows us to consider a simpler optimization problem. In particular, the optimal social welfare in the new game is $\max_i v_i/\gamma_i$; the condition for Nash equilibrium, as argued above, is the condition for $\vec{x}$ to maximize $R(\vec{x})$ over $\vec{x} \in \mathbb{R}_+^n$ such that $\sum_i \gamma_i x_i = 1$, which we derive in the following. Taking partial derivative with respect to x_j to both sides in (2), with $U_i(x_i) = v_i x_i$, we have

$$\frac{\partial}{\partial x_j} \sum_i \frac{v_i x_i}{v_i x_i + R} = 0 \Leftrightarrow$$

$$\Leftrightarrow \frac{\partial}{\partial x_j} \frac{v_j x_j}{(v_j x_j + R)} - \sum_{i \neq j} \frac{\partial R}{\partial x_j} \frac{v_j x_i}{(v_i x_i + R)^2} = 0.$$

Now, note that

$$\frac{\partial}{\partial x_j} \frac{v_j x_j}{v_j x_j + R} = \frac{R v_j}{(v_j x_j + R)^2} - \frac{\partial R}{\partial x_j} \frac{v_j x_j}{(v_j x_j + R)^2}.$$

Thus, we have

$$\frac{R v_j}{(v_j x_j + R)^2} = \frac{\partial R}{\partial x_j} \cdot \sum_i \frac{v_i x_i}{(v_i x_i + R)^2}.$$

Since $R(\vec{x})$ achieves the optimum value R^* over the set $\{\vec{x} \in \mathbb{R}_+^n : \sum_i \gamma_i x_i \leq 1\}$, we have either $x_j = 0$ or $\frac{\partial}{\partial x_j} R = \lambda \gamma_j$ where $\lambda \geq 0$ is the Lagrange multiplier associated to the constraint $\sum_i \gamma_i x_i \leq 1$. It follows that for $p > 0$,

either $x_i = 0$

$$\text{or } \frac{v_i / \gamma_i}{(v_i x_i + R^*)^2} = \frac{\lambda}{R^*} \sum_i \frac{v_i x_i}{(v_i x_i + R^*)^2} = p. \quad (11)$$

From this, we obtain that at in Nash equilibrium, if $x_i > 0$, then $\frac{v_i / \gamma_i}{(v_i x_i + R^*)^2}$ is equal to p, for every i. Therefore, if v_i / γ_i is large, then the denominator $(v_i x_i + R^*)^2$ needs to be large as well. At the same time, the optimal solution of social welfare distributes all the resource to users with the highest value of v_i / γ_i. This is the intuition for the fact that the efficiency is bounded by a constant.

First, we will use the change of variables to make equations easier to follow: $z_i = \gamma_i x_i$ and $a_i = v_i / \gamma_i$. One way to think about these new variables is to think of another game where the resource constraint is $\sum_i z_i = 1$ and user i's utility is $a_i z_i$. Without loss of generality, we assume that $a_1 = \max_i a_i$. The optimal social welfare is

$$W_{\text{OPT}} = \max_{\vec{x} : \sum_i \gamma_i x_i = 1} \sum_i v_i x_i = \max_{\vec{z} : \sum_i z_i = 1} \sum_i a_i z_i = a_1.$$

We also introduce variables y_i defined by

$$y_i = \frac{v_i x_i}{v_i x_i + R^*} = \frac{a_i z_i}{a_i z_i + R^*}.$$

Because of (2), we have $\sum_i y_i = 1$. The goal of introducing these variables is to bound the optimal social welfare and the social welfare in Nash equilibrium as functions of y_i. From $y_i = a_i z_i / (a_i z_i + R^*)$, we have

$$a_i z_i = R^* \frac{y_i}{1 - y_i} \quad \text{and} \quad z_i = R^* \frac{y_i}{a_i(1 - y_i)}.$$

Next, we are going to bound the social welfare of Nash equilibrium and the optimal solution.

The social welfare in Nash equilibrium, which we denote as W_{NASH}, can be bounded as follows

$$\begin{aligned} W_{\text{NASH}} &= \sum_i a_i z_i = R^* \sum_i \frac{y_i}{1 - y_i} \\ &\geq R^* \left(\frac{y_1}{1 - y_1} + \sum_{i \geq 2} y_i \right) = R^* \left(\frac{y_1}{1 - y_1} + 1 - y_1 \right) \\ &\geq R^* \frac{y_1^2 - y_1 + 1}{1 - y_1}. \end{aligned} \quad (12)$$

The optimal social welfare, as argued above, is

$$W_{\text{OPT}} = \max_i a_i = a_1.$$

In order to bound a_1 with a function of y_i, we multiply a_1 with $\sum_i z_i$, which is 1, and use the relation between z_i and

y_i to have W_{OPT} as a function of y_i. Specifically,

$$W_{\text{OPT}} = a_1 = a_1 \left(\sum_i z_i \right) = a_1 R^* \sum_i \frac{y_i}{a_i(1 - y_i)}. \quad (13)$$

Now, we use the condition for Nash equilibrium. (Note that this is the only place in the proof that uses (11).) First we rewrite the condition for the variables z_i and a_i. Replacing $a_i = v_i / \gamma_i$ and $v_i x_i = a_i z_i = R^* \frac{y_i}{1 - y_i}$ in the condition for Nash equilibrium (11), we derive

$$\text{either } y_i = 0 \text{ or } \frac{a_i(1 - y_i)^2}{R^{*2}} = p > 0.$$

From this condition, we have $a_i(1 - y_i)^2 = a_1(1 - y_1)^2$ whenever $y_1, y_i > 0$, hence $a_i(1 - y_i) = \frac{a_1(1 - y_1)^2}{1 - y_i}$. Replacing this equality in the optimal social welfare (13), we have

$$\begin{aligned} W_{\text{OPT}} &= a_1 R^* \sum_i \frac{y_i}{a_i(1 - y_i)} = \frac{R^*}{(1 - y_1)^2} \sum_i y_i(1 - y_i) \\ &\leq \frac{R^*}{(1 - y_1)^2} \left(y_1(1 - y_1) + \sum_{i \geq 2} y_i \right). \end{aligned}$$

Using this and replacing $\sum_{i \geq 2} y_i = 1 - y_1$, we obtain

$$W_{\text{OPT}} \leq \frac{R^*}{(1 - y_1)^2}(y_1(1 - y_1) + 1 - y_1) = R^* \frac{1 - y_1^2}{(1 - y_1)^2}. \quad (14)$$

From (12) and (14), we have the following lower bound for the efficiency

$$\frac{W_{\text{NASH}}}{W_{\text{OPT}}} \geq \frac{y_1^2 - y_1 + 1}{y_1 + 1}.$$

By simple calculus, one can show that the right-hand side is at least $1/(1 + 2/\sqrt{3})$, which is what we needed to prove. $\square$

4.2 Efficiency of Weighted Payment Auction

For weighted payment auction, we have the following result.

THEOREM 4.2. *Assuming that the provider maximizes the revenue, the efficiency is at least $1/2$ for weighted payment auction and this bound is tight.*

The proof of this theorem is provided in [17]. We note that the weighted payment auction admits much simpler resource constraint and, therefore, the proof of this theorem is much simpler than that for weighted bid auctions, which we presented above.

5. EXTENSION TO MULTIPLE PROVIDERS AND GENERAL USER UTILITIES

In this section, we will extend the efficiency result of the previous section to the more general setting that consists of multiple competing providers and more general class of utility functions. Perhaps surprisingly, we will show that even in such more complex competitive environments, the efficiency can be bounded by a positive constant that is independent of the number of providers and the number of users. We first define the framework in Section 5.1 and Section 5.2, and then present our main result in Section 5.3.

5.1 Multiple Providers

We consider a system of multiple providers where each provider allocates resources according to the weighted proportional allocation. We assume that each provider k is endowed with resource constraints specified by the convex set $\mathcal{P}_k$. We assume that each user can receive resources from any provider and is concerned only about the total amount of resource received across all providers. We will use the following notation. We denote with x_i^k the allocation to user i by provider k. Let $x_i = \sum_k x_i^k$ denote the total allocation to user i over all providers. For each user i, the utility of allocation $(x_i^k,\ k = 1, \ldots, m)$ is $U_i(x_i)$. We denote with $x_i^{-k} = x_i - x_i^k$, the total allocation to user i over all providers except provider k. See Fig. 4 for an illustration.

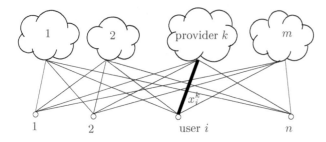

Figure 4: The setting of multiple providers.

Let $\vec{x} = (x_i^k,\ i = 1, \ldots, n,\ k = 1, \ldots, m)$ be an allocation under weighted proportional sharing mechanism. By same arguments as in Section 2, we note that each provider k can find discrimination weights $(C_1^k, C_2^k, \ldots, C_n^k)$ such that $\vec{x}$ is the equilibrium of the weighted proportional sharing in the multiple provider setting. We denote with w_i^k the bid of user i to provider k and this is the payment from user i to provider k. The user i goal is to maximize the payoff $U_i(\sum_k x_i^k) - \sum_k w_i^k$, where $x_i^k = C_i^k w_i^k / \sum_i w_i^k$. On the other hand, provider k obtains the revenue R^k, which satisfies the following

$$\sum_{i=1}^n \frac{U_i'(x_i^{-k} + x_i^k) x_i^k}{U_i'(x_i^{-k} + x_i^k) x_i^k + R^k} = 1. \qquad (15)$$

In order to gain some intuition, note that if for every user i, $U_i(x)$ is a strictly concave function, then $U_i'(x_i^{-k} + x_i^k)$ decreases with x_i^{-k}. In other words, the larger the amount of resource allocated to user i from providers other than k, the smaller the marginal utility for user i to receive an allocation from provider k. As a result, provider k may extract smaller revenue due to competition with other providers. With this in mind, we now define the equilibrium for the case of multiple providers.

DEFINITION 1. *We call $\vec{x}$ an equilibrium allocation if for every provider k, the allocation vector $\vec{x}^k = (x_1^k, \ldots, x_n^k)$ maximizes R^k given by (15) over the set $\mathcal{P}_k$.*

We note that in the multiple provider setting, we can think of the game as the provider k's strategy set is $\mathcal{P}_k$. The discrimination weights and the revenue then can be calculated according to the allocation vector $\vec{x}$ of all providers. With these discrimination weights, under users' selfish behavior, $\vec{x}$ will be an outcome of the game. From the providers' perspective, an equilibrium allocation is an allocation $\vec{x}$ where

no provider has an incentive to unilaterally change its allocation vector. Note that if there is only one provider, the game boils down to the same two-stage Stackelberg game considered in Section 2.

5.2 A Class of Utility Functions

We introduce the class of δ-utility functions in the following definition.

DEFINITION 2. *Let $U(x)$ be a non-negative, increasing, and concave utility function and let $x_0 \geq 0$ be the value maximizing $U'(x)x$. We say $U(x)$ is a δ-utility, if in addition the following two conditions hold:*

(i) $U'(x)x$ is a concave function over $[0, x_0]$, and

(ii) there exists $\delta \in [0, \infty)$, such that, for every $a \in [0, x_0]$,

$$U(b) - [U'(a)a]'b \leq \delta U(a)$$

where $b \geq 0$ is such that $U'(b) = [U'(a)a]' = U'(a) + U''(a)a \geq 0$.

The class of δ-utility functions is intimately related with the theory of price discrimination [22], which we discuss in [17]. Furthermore, the class accommodates many utility functions considered in literature. For example, we can show that a linear or a truncated linear function is a 0-utility function, polynomial $(c + x)^\alpha$, for $c \geq 0$ is a $\frac{c}{2}$-utility function, for any $0 \leq \alpha \leq 1$, and a logarithmic utility function is a 2-utility function; we provide a detailed list and proofs in [17]. We remark that truncated linear utility functions or logarithmic functions were considered representative of real-time traffic sources in communication networks [21], polynomial utility functions were widely used in economic theory [22], α-fair utility functions were widely used in the context of communication networks [12, 10].

Finally, we note the following result whose proof is provided in [17].

LEMMA 5.1. *If f and g are δ-utility functions, then so are: $c \cdot f$, for $c > 0$ and $f + g$.*

Consequently, every polynomial of the form $\sum_i a_i x^{\alpha_i}$ where $a_i > 0$ and $0 \leq \alpha_i \leq 1$ is a $\frac{e}{2}$-utility function.

5.3 Efficiency Bound

We now state and then prove our main theorem on the efficiency of weighted bid auctions.

THEOREM 5.1. *Assume that for every user i and every $a \geq 0$, $U_i'(x + a)x$ is a continuous and concave function. Then, there exists an equilibrium in the case of multiple providers defined as above. Furthermore, if $U_i(a + x)$ are δ-utility functions, then the efficiency at any equilibrium is at least $1/(1 + 2/\sqrt{3} + \delta)$.*

For the special case of linear utility functions $\delta = 0$ and the above theorem yields the same bound as in Theorem 4.1. The result of Theorem 5.1 is perhaps surprising as it is not a priori clear that in complex competitive environments where both providers and users are selfish in trying to maximize their individual payoffs (objectives which often conflict with each other), the efficiency would be bounded by a positive constant that is independent of the number of providers and the number of users.

Before going into the proof of Theorem 5.1, we outline the main ideas. The key idea of the proof is to bound the social welfare of the system, which is a complicated optimization problem over allocations in the Minkowski sum of the sets $\mathcal{P}_k$. If the utility functions are linear, then this optimization problem can be *separated* into optimization problems for individual providers, and the optimal value is the sum of these optimal values. Using this idea, we will bound the utility function by an affine function that is a tangent to the concave utility function at particular allocation in Nash equilibrium. This idea is illustrated in Figure 5. It will be shown that because of the property of δ-utility functions, the value a_i in the figure is at most $\delta U_i(x_i)$, which will be the key inequality of the proof.[2]

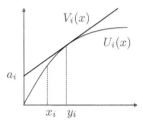

Figure 5: The key bounding of $U_i(x)$ with the affine function $V_i(x)$ such that $V_i'(y_i) = U_i'(x_i) + U_i''(x_i)\max_k x_i^k$ and $V_i(y_i) = U_i(y_i)$.

PROOF OF THEOREM 5.1. The proof of the first part of the theorem about existence of Nash equilibrium is based on standard fixed point theorem and is provided in [17].

For the second part, the key idea of the proof is to bound the social welfare by an affine function which allows separating the maximization over $(\vec{x}^1, \ldots, \vec{x}^m) \in \sum_k \mathcal{P}_k$ to maximizations over sets $\mathcal{P}_k$, where $\sum_k \mathcal{P}_k$ is the Minkowski sum defined by $\{\vec{z}^1 + \cdots + \vec{z}^m : \vec{z}^k \in \mathcal{P}_k, k = 1, \ldots, m\}$. Once the optimization problem is separated, we can use similar bound as in Section 4 (see Lemma 5.2 below) as a subroutine to prove the theorem.

Let us define

$$v_i^k = U_i'(x_i) + U_i''(x_i)x_i^k \text{ and } v_i = \min_k v_i^k.$$

Since for every i, $U_i(x)$ is a concave function, we have

$$v_i = U_i'(x_i) + U_i''(x_i)(\max_k x_i^k) \geq U_i'(x_i) + U_i''(x_i)x_i.$$

Now, let us define $V_i(x) = a_i + v_i x$ where a_i is chosen such that $V_i(x)$ is a tangent to $U_i(x)$. Let y_i be the point at $V_i(x)$ and $U_i(x)$ intersect. We will use $V_i(x)$ as an upper bound for $U_i(x)$, for every $x \geq 0$. Notice that $a_i = U_i(y_i) - (U_i'(x_i) + U_i''(x_i)x_i)y_i$.

By definition of δ-utility functions, $a_i \leq \delta U_i(x_i)$. Therefore,

$$\sum_i a_i \leq \delta \sum_i U_i(x_i). \quad (16)$$

---

[2]We note that our proof technique is rather general and that similar result for weighted payment auctions can also be obtained using this framework. However, we omit details as our focus is on weighted bid auctions, which allow for much more general resource constraints.

Since $U_i(x)$ is a non-negative concave function, we have $U_i(x) \leq V_i(x)$. Hence,

$$\max_{\vec{z} \in \sum_k \mathcal{P}_k} \sum_i U_i(z_i) \leq \max_{\vec{z} \in \sum_k \mathcal{P}_k} \sum_i V_i(z_i) =$$
$$= \sum_i a_i + \max_{\vec{z} \in \sum_k \mathcal{P}_k} \sum_i v_i z_i$$
$$= \sum_i a_i + \sum_k \max_{\vec{z} \in \mathcal{P}_k} \sum_i v_i z_i. \quad (17)$$

The last inequality enables us to use the fact that $v_i z_i$ are linear functions, therefore, instead of considering the maximization over the set $\sum_k \mathcal{P}_k$, we can bound $\sum_i v_i z_i$ over each $\mathcal{P}_k$.

By similar arguments as in the proof of Theorem 4.1, we can prove the following lemma whose proof is provided in [17].

LEMMA 5.2. *For ever k,*

$$\sum_i U_i'(x_i)x_i^k \geq \frac{1}{1 + 2/\sqrt{3}} \max_{z \in \mathcal{P}_k} \sum_i v_i^k z_i. \quad (18)$$

We use this lemma to prove our main result. On the one hand, if we sum the left-hand side of (18) over all k, we have

$$\sum_{k,i} U_i'(x_i)x_i^k = \sum_i U_i'(x_i)x_i \leq \sum_i U_i(x_i) \quad (19)$$

where the last inequality is true because $U_i(x)$ is a non-negative and concave function for every i. On the other hand, if we sum the right-hand side of (18) over all k, we obtain

$$\frac{\sum_k \max_{z \in \mathcal{P}_k} \sum_i v_i^k z_i}{1 + 2/\sqrt{3}} \geq \frac{\sum_k \max_{z \in \mathcal{P}_k} \sum_i v_i z_i}{1 + 2/\sqrt{3}} \quad (20)$$

where in the last inequality, v_i^k are replaced by v_i, which recall is equal to $\min_k v_i^k$.

Combining (18)–(20), we derive

$$\sum_i U_i(x_i) \geq \frac{1}{1 + 2/\sqrt{3}} \sum_k \max_{z \in \mathcal{P}_k} \sum_i v_i z_i$$

$$\Rightarrow (1 + 2/\sqrt{3}) \sum_i U_i(x_i) \geq \sum_k \max_{z \in \mathcal{P}_k} \sum_i v_i z_i. \quad (21)$$

Finally, from (16), (17) and (21), we have

$$\max_{\vec{z} \in \sum_k \mathcal{P}_k} \sum_i U_i(z_i) \leq (\delta + 1 + 2/\sqrt{3}) \sum_i U_i(x_i)$$

which establishes the asserted result. $\square$

6. CONVERGENCE AND DISTRIBUTED ALGORITHMS

In this section, we show how a provider may adjust user discrimination weights by an iterative algorithm whose limit points are Nash equilibrium points of the resource competition game studied in earlier sections. We focus on weighted bid auctions but note that similar type of analysis can be carried out for weighted payment auctions. Our aim in this section is to show how such iterative algorithms can be designed in principle.[3]

---

[3]It is beyond the scope of this paper to fully specify implementation details such as online estimation of the elasticity of user utility functions and address the stability in presence of feedback delays.

We replace the polyhedron constraints by incorporating *penalty* function $P(\vec{x})$ in the objective function, which is chosen to confine the allocation vector $\vec{x}$ in the feasible set specified by the polyhedron constraints. Informally, the function $P(\vec{x})$ would assume small values for every feasible allocation vector $\vec{x}$ that is sufficiently away from the boundary of the feasible set and would grow large as the allocation vector $\vec{x}$ approaches the boundary of the feasible set. We assume that $P(\vec{x})$ is a continuously differentiable and convex function. Specifically, we assume that for a collection of functions P_l, one for each of the constraints, we have

$$P(\vec{x}) = \sum_l P_l \left(\sum_j a_{l,j} x_j \right).$$

Indeed, if P_l is a continuously differentiable and convex function for every l, then so is P. We define $V(\vec{x}) = R(\vec{x}) - P(\vec{x})$ where $R(\vec{x})$ is the revenue given by (2). The provider problem is redefined to

PROVIDER$'$: maximize $V(\vec{x})$ over $\vec{x} \in \mathbb{R}^n_+$.

We first show how the provider may adjust the user discrimination weights, assuming that the provider knows user utility functions and establish convergence to the Nash equilibrium points in this case. This provides a baseline dynamics that we then approximate as follows. We consider a provider who a priori does not know user utility functions but estimates the needed information in an online fashion while adjusting the discrimination weights. The main idea here is to use an argument based on *separation of timescales* where the provider adjusts the discrimination weights at a slow timescale in comparison with the rate at which bids are received from users, allowing the provider to estimate the needed information about the user utility functions for every given set of discrimination weights. We will formulate iterative algorithms as dynamical systems in continuous time as this is standard in previous work, e.g. [11], and it readily suggests practical distributed algorithms.

User Utility Functions a Priori Known. Suppose that user utility functions are a priori known by the provider (this may be the case if profiles of users are known to the provider, e.g. from the history of previous interactions). The provider announces discrimination weights $\vec{C}(t)$ at every time $t \geq 0$ that are adjusted as follows. The provider computes the allocation vector $\vec{x}(t)$ according to the following system of ordinary differential equations, for some $\alpha > 0$,

$$\frac{d}{dt} x_i(t) = \alpha x_i(t) \frac{\partial}{\partial x_i} V(\vec{x}(t)), \ i = 1, 2, \ldots, n. \quad (22)$$

For every time $t \geq 0$, the provider announces to users the discrimination weights $\vec{C}(t)$ where the discrimination weight for user i is:

$$C_i(t) = x_i(t) + \frac{R(\vec{x}(t))}{U'_i(x_i(t))}.$$

Notice that the right-hand side in (22) requires knowledge of the gradient of the revenue function $R(\vec{x})$, which is given by

$$\frac{\partial}{\partial x_i} R(\vec{x}) = \phi(\vec{x}) \frac{[U'_i(x_i)x_i]'}{(U'_i(x_i)x_i + R(\vec{x}))^2} \quad (23)$$

where

$$\phi(\vec{x}) = \frac{R(\vec{x})}{\sum_j \frac{U'_j(x_j)x_j}{(U'_j(x_j)x_j + R(\vec{x}))^2}}.$$

The convergence to optimal solution of PROVIDER' is showed in the following theorem.

THEOREM 6.1. *Suppose that for every user i, $U'_i(x)x$ is a continuously differentiable and concave function and that $P(\vec{x})$ is a strictly convex function. Then, every trajectory $(\vec{x}(t), \ t \geq 0)$ of the system (22) converges to the maximizer of function $V(\vec{x})$.*

The proof is based on standard application of Lyapunov stability theorem and is thus omitted. It amounts to showing that the function V is a Lyapunov function for system (22), which increases along every trajectory $\vec{x}(t)$, and thus implying convergence to unique maximizer of V.

User Utility Functions a Priori Unknown. We discuss how the user discrimination weights may be adjusted by provider who does not a priori know the user utility functions. The key idea is to use *separation of timescales*: the provider adjusts the discrimination weights at a slower timescale than the timescale at which bids are adjusted by users. Informally speaking, this allows the provider to act as if for every fixed set of discrimination weights, users adjust their bids instantly to the Nash equilibrium bids.

From (6) and the allocation rule $x_i = C_i w_i / \sum_j w_j$, we readily observe that the following identities hold in Nash equilibrium:

$$U'_i(x_i)x_i = \frac{Rw_i}{R - w_i} \text{ and } U'_i(x_i)x_i + R = \frac{R^2}{R - w_i}$$

where $R = \sum_j w_j$. Using these identities, we note that the gradient in (23) can be expressed as follows

$$\frac{\partial}{\partial x_i} R = R \frac{\frac{w_i}{R} \left(1 - \frac{w_i}{R} \right) \frac{1}{x_i} + \left(1 - \frac{w_i}{R} \right)^2 \frac{U''_i(x_i)x_i}{R}}{\sum_j \frac{w_j}{R} \left(1 - \frac{w_j}{R} \right)}. \quad (24)$$

Notice that the gradient is fully expressed as a function of the vector of bids $\vec{w}$ except for the term that involves the second derivative of the user utility function. For the case of linear user utility functions, we have $U''_i(x_i) = 0$ for every i, and thus, in this case the gradient of the revenue $R(\vec{x})$ is fully described by the vector of bids $\vec{w}$.

In general, we assume that at every time $t \geq 0$, the provider sets the user discrimination weight for user i as follows

$$C_i(t) = \frac{R(\vec{w}(t))}{w_i(t)} x_i(t).$$

For the case of linear utility function, $\vec{x}(t)$ is assumed to evolve according to the following system of ordinary differential equations, for $\alpha > 0$ and every $i = 1, 2, \ldots, n$,

$$\frac{d}{dt} x_i(t) = \alpha \left[v_i(w_i(t), R(\vec{w}(t))) - x_i(t)p_i(\vec{x}(t)) \right] \quad (25)$$

where

$$v_i(w_i, R) = R \frac{\frac{w_i}{R} \left(1 - \frac{w_i}{R} \right)}{\sum_j \frac{w_j}{R} \left(1 - \frac{w_j}{R} \right)}$$

$$p_i(\vec{x}) = \sum_l a_{l,i} P'_l \left(\sum_j a_{l,j} x_j(t) \right).$$

Furthermore, we assume natural dynamics for solving USER problem that amounts to adjusting bid $w_i(t)$ by user i according to the following system

$$\frac{d}{dt}w_i(t) = U_i'(x_i(t))x_i(t) - R(\vec{w}(t))\frac{\frac{w_i(t)}{R(\vec{w}(t))}}{1 - \frac{w_i(t)}{R(\vec{w}(t))}}. \quad (26)$$

The convergence for the case of linear user utility functions is established in the following theorem.

THEOREM 6.2. *Suppose that user utility functions are linear. For every sufficiently small $\alpha > 0$, the allocation vector under system (25)-(26) approximates that of the system (22) with an approximation error that diminishes with α.*

The proof is based on applying the *averaging theory* of non-linear dynamical systems [14] and is provided in [17]. It is noteworthy that part of the proof establishes global asymptotic stability of system (26), for the allocation vector $\vec{x}(t)$ fixed to an arbitrary feasible allocation vector $\vec{x}$ for every $t \geq 0$, which is of independent interest as it applies to more general class of utility functions.

Same approach applies more generally to non-linear user utility functions, but the second derivative of the utility function in (24) would need to be estimated in an online fashion from the observed bids submitted by users.[4] In principle, this can be done by observing the effect of perturbing the allocation for a user on the bid submitted by this user, which we briefly discuss in the following. From (6) and the allocation rule $x_i = C_i w_i / \sum_j w_j$, we have $U_i'(x_i) = \frac{R}{x_i}\frac{w_i}{R}/(1 - \frac{w_i}{R})$. Taking the derivative with respect to x_i, we obtain

$$U_i''(x_i)x_i = \frac{\frac{w_i}{R}}{1 - \frac{w_i}{R}}\left(\frac{\partial}{\partial x_i}R - \frac{1}{x_i}R\right) + R\frac{1}{\left(1 - \frac{w_i}{R}\right)^2}\frac{\partial}{\partial x_i}\left(\frac{w_i}{R}\right).$$

Plugging this in (24), we have

$$\frac{\partial}{\partial x_i}R = \frac{R}{\sum_j \frac{w_j}{R}\left(1 - \frac{w_j}{R}\right) - \frac{w_i}{R}\left(1 - \frac{w_i}{R}\right)}\frac{\partial}{\partial x_i}\left(\frac{w_i}{R}\right).$$

Therefore, the gradient of the revenue can be fully expressed in terms of the bids $\vec{w}$ and $(\partial/\partial x_i)(w_i/R)$, where the latter term can be estimated in an online fashion by perturbing the allocation of user i and observing the resulting change of w_i/R.

Parking-Lot Example. We demonstrate convergence of the iterative scheme (25)-(26) for the example of parking-lot network that we introduced in Section 3 (Figure 2). Recall that the resource consists of $n \geq 1$ links, each of capacity 1, with a multi-hop user 0 with allocation x_0 at each link and a single-hop user with allocation x_i at link i. User utility functions are assumed to be linear $U_i(x) = v_i x$, for $x \geq 0$, where $v_i = v_1$, for $i = 1, 2, \ldots, n$, and $v_0, v_1 > 0$.

The Nash equilibrium allocation and the corresponding revenue are specified by the following lemma whose proof is simple and thus omitted.

LEMMA 6.1. *Let $\eta = \frac{n-1}{2\sqrt{n}}\sqrt{\frac{v_1}{v_0}}$. For the parking-lot scenario, the Nash equilibrium allocation is $1 - x_1$ for user*

---

[4]Notice that the need to infer the second derivatives of utility functions is intrinsic to the revenue maximization objective and is not an artifact of our auction scheme.

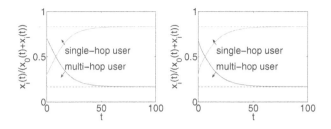

Figure 6: Convergence to equilibrium points for the parking-lot example: (Left) a priori known utility functions and (Right) a priori unknown utility functions.

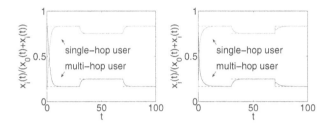

Figure 7: Another example for the convergence to equilibrium points for the parking-lot: (Left) a priori known utility functions and (Right) a priori unknown utility functions.

0 *and* x_1 *for each user* $i = 1, 2, \ldots, n$, *where*

$$x_1 = \begin{cases} \frac{1}{2(1-\eta)}, & \text{for } \eta < 1/2 \\ 1, & \text{for } \eta \geq 1/2 \end{cases}. \quad (27)$$

The revenue in Nash equilibrium is given by

$$R = \begin{cases} \frac{1}{4\eta(1-\eta)}(n-1)v_1, & \text{for } \eta < 1/2 \\ (n-1)v_1, & \text{for } \eta \geq 1/2. \end{cases}$$

We note that in Nash equilibrium, the allocation to any single-hop user is increasing with the ratio of the valuations v_1/v_0, from $1/2$ for $v_1/v_0 = 0$ to 1 for $v_1/v_0 = n/(n-1)^2$ and beyond this the single-hop user is allocated the entire link capacity.

Numerical examples. We illustrate convergence for two particular cases. In either case, we consider the parking-lot network with $n = 5$ links and linear utility functions specified by $v_0 = 5$ and $v_1 = v_2 = \cdots = v_n = 1$. The link cost functions are defined as

$$P_l'(x) = \begin{cases} 0, & 0 \leq x \leq \rho_0, \\ \left(\frac{1}{x} - \frac{1}{1-\rho_0}\right)^p, & \rho_0 < x \leq 1 \end{cases}$$

where $p > 0$ and, in particular, we use $p = 2$ and $\rho_0 = 0.8$. We show results for initial allocation $\vec{x}(0)$ such that $x_1(0) = x_2(0) = \cdots = x_n(0)$, so that due to symmetry $x_1(t) = x_2(t) = \cdots = x_n(t)$, for every $t \geq 0$. This simplifies the exposition. We validated convergence for various other choices for initial values and other parameters, but for space reasons we confine to the above asserted setting.

In our first case, we consider a closed system with a fixed set of users. In Figure 6, we show trajectories of the allocations $x_0(t)$ and $x_1(t)$ for both a priori known utility functions (left) and a priori unknown utility functions (right), with α set to 0.1. The results indeed validate convergence to the Nash equilibrium allocation, which are indicated with dashed lines.

Finally, in our second case, we consider an open system where at time $t_1 \geq 0$, a single-hop user departs the system and then another such user arrives at time $t_2 > t_1$. In particular, we use the values $t_1 = 30$, $t_2 = 70$, and $\alpha = 0.8$. Figure 6 well validates convergence to the Nash equilibrium allocation in this case.

7. CONCLUSION

We considered a simple mechanism for allocation of resources that allows for user differentiation and general convex resource constraints. We showed that in a competitive framework where everyone is selfish, the mechanism can guarantee nearly optimal revenue to the provider and competitive social efficiency (including a setting with multiple providers). Besides analysis of equilibrium points of the underlying competition game, we showed how one would design an iterative algorithm that converges to equilibrium points.

The work suggests several interesting directions for future research. First, it would be of interest to study revenue and efficiency properties for classes of user utility functions that are not accommodated in our work. Second, it would be of interest to further explore the space of iterative schemes that are practical and converge to equilibrium points. Finally, one may consider more general settings of multiple competing providers where each user can receive the service only from a subset of providers.

8. REFERENCES

[1] Amazon Web Services. Amazon EC2 Spot Instances. http://aws.amazon.com/ec2/spot-instances, 2010.

[2] A. Demers, S. Keshav, and S. Shenker. Analysis and simulation of a fair queueing algorithm. *Internetworking: Research and Experience*, 1:3–26, 1990.

[3] M. Feldman, K. Lai, and L. Zhang. A price-anticipating resource allocation mechanism for distributed shared clusters. In *Proc. of ACM EC*, 2005.

[4] R. J. Gibbens and F. P. Kelly. On packet marking at priority queues. *IEEE Trans. on Automatic Control*, 47:1016–1020, 2002.

[5] D. K. Golldenberg, L. Qiuy, H. Xie, Y. R. Yang, and Y. Zhang. Optimizing cost and performance for multihoming. In *Proc. of ACM Sigcomm'04*, Portland, Oregon, USA, 2004.

[6] A. Gulati, I. Ahmad, and C. A. Waldspurger. Parda: proportional allocation of resources for distributed access. In *Proc. of FAST'09*, San Francisco, CA, 2009.

[7] B. Hajek and S. Yang. Strategic buyers in a sum bid game for flat networks. In *IMA Workshop*, March 2004.

[8] J. Hartline and A. Karlin. *Algorithmic Game Theory*, chapter Profit Maximization in Mechanism Design, pages 331–362. editors N. Nisan, T. Roughgarden, E. Tardos, and V. V. Vazirani, Cambridge University Press, 2007.

[9] R. Johari and J. N. Tsitsiklis. Efficiency loss in a network resource allocation game. *Mathematics of Operations Research*, 29(3):402–435, 2004.

[10] F. Kelly. *Mathematics Unlimited - 2001 and Beyond*, chapter Mathematical modelling of the Internet, pages 685–702. editors B. Engquist and W. Schmid. Springer-Verlag, Berlin, 2001.

[11] F. P. Kelly. Charging and rate control for elastic traffic. *European Trans. on Telecommunications*, 8:33–37, 1997.

[12] F. P. Kelly, A. K. Maulloo, and D. K. H. Tan. Rate control for communication networks: Shadow prices, proportional fairness and stability. *Journal of the Operational Research Society*, 49, 1998.

[13] P. Key, L. Massoulie, and M. Vojnović. Farsighted users harness network time-diversity. In *Proc. of IEEE Infocom 2005*, Miami, FL, USA, 2005.

[14] H. K. Khalil. *Nonlinear Systems*. Prentice Hall, 3 edition, 2001.

[15] R. T. Ma, D. M. Chiu, J. C. S. Lui, V. Misra, and D. Rubenstein. On resource management for cloud users: A generalized kelly mechanism approach. Technical report, Technical Report, Electrical Engineering, May 2010.

[16] T. Nguyen and E. Tardos. Approximately maximizing efficiency and revenue in polyhedral environments. In *Proc. of ACM EC'07*, pages 11–19, 2007.

[17] T. Nguyen and M. Vojnović. The weighted proportional allocation mechanism. Technical Report MSR-TR-2010-145, Microsoft Research, 2010.

[18] A. Ozdaglar and R. Srikant. *Algorithmic Game Theory*, chapter Incentives and Pricing in Communication Networks. editors N. Nisan, T. Roughgarden, E. Tardos, and V. V. Vazirani, Cambridge University Press, 2007.

[19] A. K. Parekh and R. G. Gallager. A generalized processor sharing approach to flow control in integrated services networks: The multi node case. *IEEE/ACM Trans. on Networking*, 2:137–150, April 1994.

[20] S. Shakkottai and R. Srikant. Economics of network pricing with multiple isps. *IEEE/ACM Trans. on Networking*, 14(6):1233–1245, 2006.

[21] S. Shakottai, R. Srikant, A. Ozdaglar, and D. Acemoglu. The price of simplicity. *IEEE Journal on Selected Areas in Communications*, 26(7):1269–1276, 2008.

[22] J. Tirole. *The Theory of Industrial Organization*. The MIT Press, 2001.

[23] G. Wang, A. Kowli, M. Negrete-Pincetic, E. Shafieepoorfard, and S. Meyn. A control theorist's perspective on dynamic competitive equilibria in electricity markets. In *Proc. 18th World Congress of the International Federation of Automatic Control (IFAC)*, Milano, Italy, 2011.

[24] Wikipedia. California electricity crises. http://en.wikipedia.org/wiki/California_electricity_crisis, 2010.

On the Optimal Trade-off between SRPT and Opportunistic Scheduling

Samuli Aalto
Aalto University
Finland
samuli.aalto@tkk.fi

Aleksi Penttinen
Aalto University
Finland
aleksi.penttinen@aalto.fi

Pasi Lassila
Aalto University
Finland
pasi.lassila@tkk.fi

Prajwal Osti
Aalto University
Finland
prajwal.osti@aalto.fi

ABSTRACT

We consider service systems where new jobs not only increase the load but also improve the service ability of such a system, cf. opportunistic scheduling gain in wireless systems. We study the optimal trade-off between the SRPT (Shortest Remaining Processing Time) discipline and opportunistic scheduling in the systems characterized by compact and symmetric capacity regions. The objective is to minimize the mean delay in a transient setting where all jobs are available at time 0 and no new jobs arrive thereafter. Our main result gives conditions under which the optimal rate vector does not depend on the sizes of the jobs as long as their order (in size) remains the same. In addition, it shows that in this case the optimal policy applies the SRPT principle serving the shortest job with the highest rate of the optimal rate vector, the second shortest with the second highest rate etc. We also give a recursive algorithm to determine both the optimal rate vector and the minimum mean delay. In some special cases, the rate vector, as well as the minimum mean delay, have even explicit expressions as demonstrated in the paper. For the general case, we derive both an upper bound and a lower bound of the minimum mean delay.

Categories and Subject Descriptors

C.4 [**Performance of Systems**]: Performance attributes; F.2.2 [**Nonnumerical Algorithms and Problems**]: Sequencing and scheduling; C.2.1 [**Network Architecture and Design**]: Wireless communication

General Terms

Performance, Theory

Keywords

Opportunistic scheduling, SRPT, mean delay, capacity region

1. INTRODUCTION

Modern wireless cellular systems allow highly sophisticated scheduling algorithms to be used for sharing the radio resources among the users. These systems operate in slotted time with a very short time slot duration (at millisecond time scale). The base station also has access to information about the instantaneous transmission reception conditions of every user, essentially the instantaneous transmission rates, which are randomly varying over time due to various fading phenomena. This has given rise to *opportunistic scheduling*, where the idea is to favor those users with instantaneously high transmission rates. It is clear that the more users there are in the system, the more likely it is to have some user in a good state. Thus, the overall service rate of the system increases with the number of users, i.e., there is opportunistic scheduling gain (also sometimes referred to as multiuser diversity gain).

A well-known example of opportunistic scheduling is the PF (Proportionally Fair) scheduler [3, 10, 21], which combines information about the instantaneous rates with the throughput. PF belongs to a more general class of utility-based α-fair schedulers [19, 8]. Other examples of opportunistic schedulers include maxweight schedulers that combine the channel information with the queue lengths or delays [18], or rate-based schedulers that only use information about the channel-statistics [4, 5, 12]. Maxweight and utility-based schedulers have been analyzed at the time-slot level (or packet level) by assuming a fixed population of users and they have been shown to exhibit certain optimality properties, see [18, 19].

In reality the number of active users varies in the system. Models that take this into account are called flow-level models. Flows roughly represent file transfers controlled by TCP (elastic data) and the performance at flow-level characterizes, e.g., the mean delay of file transfers. An approach often utilized in the flow-level modeling is the assumption of *time scale separation* between the flow-level dynamics and the time-slot level channel dynamics, see also [7, 6, 16]. This implies that, at the flow level, the flows observe the time-average throughput provided by the time-slot level scheduler. For a given number of flows in the system, the set of achievable rate vectors that the time-slot level scheduler can support is characterized by the notion of the *capacity region*, see [7, 6, 16]. The general scheduling problem at the flow-level is then to determine the rate vector to be used within the capacity region given the current state at the flow-level so that, e.g., the mean flow delay is minimized.

In the *dynamic setting* the system at the flow level consists of random flow arrivals and departures. In this setting the existing provable properties of opportunistic scheduling policies are limited to results on their stability properties, see [7, 8, 6, 1]. Utility-based policies of the throughput have been shown to achieve the maximal stability region [8], while rate-based policies may suffer from instability [7, 1].

Size-based scheduling is known to be a good choice for the systems *without* any opportunistic gain. For example, for classical single-server queues, it is well-known that the SRPT (Shortest-Remaining-Processing-Time) discipline is optimal minimizing the mean delay [17]. The idea of SRPT is to minimize the delay by getting rid of flows as soon as possible. However, with fewer flows part of the opportunistic gain is lost. As a result, combining the advantages of size-based scheduling with opportunistic scheduling gain has proven very challenging. Results on the optimal policy to minimize the mean flow-level delay in the dynamic setting for the systems with opportunistic scheduling gain are not available, owing to the difficulty of the problem. Only some heuristic algorithms have been proposed and experimented with that try to combine opportunistic scheduling gain with size-based scheduling [9, 11, 16, 2].

All optimality results concerning the minimization of the mean flow-level delay under opportunistic scheduling gain are related to the *transient system*, where there are initially n flows with given sizes but no new arrivals. It has been shown that the optimal scheduling problem in the time slot level (without the time scale separation assumption) can be formulated as a dynamic program [20]. However, the dynamic program does not allow to extract any structural properties of the optimal policy. More structure for the (nearly) optimal time slot level scheduler is provided in a recent paper [2], where the theory of restless bandits is applied to the transient system. The approach requires a Markovian description of the system and is therefore limited to geometric flow size distributions with the memoryless property.

A structural optimality result that utilizes the time scale separation assumption appeared recently in [16], where the authors show that when the capacity regions are nested polymatroids and the opportunistic gain γ_n is increasing and concave in the number n of flows, the optimal policy is an SRPT-type discipline such that the shortest flow is served with the highest possible rate γ_1, the second shortest with the second highest rate $\gamma_2 - \gamma_1$, etc. Importantly, the optimal rate vector does *not* depend on the sizes of the flows as long as their order (in size) remains the same. In their proof, the authors of [16] utilize the known optimality result of the SRPT-FM (SRPT-Fastest-Machine) discipline for the heterogeneous multiserver queues [13]. In fact, a similar result, related to Gaussian multiple access channels, already appeared in [14].

As in [16], we make the the time scale separation assumption and consider the optimal scheduling problem under opportunistic scheduling gain in the transient setting. We focus on the situation, where the capacity regions are compact and symmetric (including, e.g., all nested polymatroids). From the wireless channel point of view, the symmetry assumption implies that the random variations at the time slot level experienced by the flows are statistically identical, see [7]. Our aim is to minimize the mean flow-level delay by determining the optimal trade-off between SRPT and opportunistic scheduling.

Our main result gives conditions under which the optimal rate vector does not depend on the sizes of the flows as long as their order (in size) remains the same. In addition, it shows that in this case the optimal policy applies the SRPT principle serving the shortest flow with the highest rate of the optimal rate vector, the second shortest with the second highest rate etc. We also give a recursive algorithm to determine both the optimal rate vector and the minimum mean delay. In addition to the theoretic value, the presented approach provides a vast improvement over any general optimization method for numerical evaluation of the optimal scheduling problem. Since we specify the conditions for *any* family of compact and symmetric capacity regions, the result is also essentially more general than the result given in [16] (concerning only nested polymatroids). In some special cases, the rate vector, as well as the minimum flow time, have even explicit expressions as demonstrated in the paper. In addition to the lower bound (i.e., an optimistic estimate) given already in [16], we derive an upper bound (i.e., a conservative estimate) of the minimum mean delay in the general case. Numerically, the upper bound seems to be closer to the optimum value.

The rest of the paper is organized as follows. The optimal scheduling problem is formulated and some important operating policies are introduced in Section 2. Section 3 includes the main theoretic results for compact and symmetric capacity regions. In Section 4, we demonstrate that the optimality result for nested polymatroids given in [16] is essentially a special case of our main result. Nested polymatroids are also used to determine an optimistic estimate for the minimum mean delay. Section 5 considers another family of polytopes for which the optimality result is a special case of our main result. These polytopes can be utilized to determine a conservative estimate for the minimum mean delay. In Section 6, to demonstrate the applicability of the theoretical results, we consider a parametric family of capacity regions (so-called α-balls) for which the optimal rate vector and the minimum flow time have explicit expressions. We also work out some numerical examples for illustrative purposes. Section 7 concludes the paper and also discusses some future research directions.

2. PROBLEM FORMULATION

Consider a service system where the service capacity is adjustable depending on the current number of jobs.[1] More precisely said, when there are k jobs in the system (indexed with $i = 1, \dots, k$), the operator (of the system) chooses a rate vector $\mathbf{c} = (c_1, \dots, c_k)$ from the capacity region $\mathcal{C}_k \subset \mathbb{R}_+^k$. From that on, each job i is served with rate c_i until the number of jobs again changes, and a new rate vector is

---

[1]Since the concept job is often used in scheduling literature rather than flow, we will subsequently use the words job/flow interchangeably.

chosen. We assume that when choosing the rate vector the operator is aware of the (remaining) sizes of the jobs.

Assume now that, at time 0, there are n jobs in the system with sizes

$$s_1 \geq \ldots \geq s_n.$$

We consider the transient system, i.e., we do not allow any further arrivals.

An *operating policy* π is defined by a sequence of vectors $\mathbf{c}_k = (c_{k1}, \ldots, c_{kk}) \in \mathcal{C}_k$ for all $k = 1, \ldots, n$, where $\mathbf{c}_k$ refers to the rate vector that the operator applies when there are k jobs in the system (called hereafter *phase k*). It is assumed that when a job completes, the remaining $k - 1$ jobs are *re-indexed* in such a way that the remaining sizes $s_{k-1,i}$ again satisfy

$$s_{k-1,1} \geq \ldots \geq s_{k-1,k-1}.$$

Thus, in the next step, the longest job is served with rate $c_{k-1,1}$, the second longest with rate $c_{k-1,2}$, etc. Let Π_n denote the family of all operating policies,

$$\Pi_n = \{\pi = (\mathbf{c}_1, \ldots, \mathbf{c}_n) : \mathbf{c}_k \in \mathcal{C}_k \text{ for all } k\}.$$

Let then t_i^π denote the time when the job with original index i completes under policy π. As usual in scheduling literature, the *flow time T^π* (a.k.a. total completion time) is defined as

$$T^\pi = \sum_{i=1}^{n} t_i^\pi.$$

Note that the mean delay of a job is now given by T^π/n.

In this paper, we consider the scheduling problem in which the optimal operating policy minimizes the flow time (or the mean delay, as well). Let π^* denote such an optimal policy. Thus,

$$T^{\pi^*} = \min_{\pi \in \Pi_n} T^\pi,$$

where the minimization is taken over all operating policies defined by the n fixed capacity regions $\mathcal{C}_1, \ldots, \mathcal{C}_n$.

Finally we define an important category of operating policies. Policy π belongs to the class of *SRPT-HPR* (SRPT-Highest-Possible-Rate) *policies* if the corresponding rate vectors $(\mathbf{c}_1, \ldots, \mathbf{c}_n)$ satisfy the following condition, for all k and j,

$$c_{k,j} \leq c_{k,j+1}.$$

An example is given by the ordinary *SRPT* discipline that serves only the shortest job so that the rate vectors $\mathbf{c}_k$ take the form

$$\mathbf{c}_k = (0, \ldots, 0, \gamma_1),$$

where $\gamma_1 > 0$. Another example is given by the *OPS* (Opportunistic Processor Sharing) discipline, which takes the most out of the opportunistic gain in a fair way and which has been used to model the behaviour of the PF scheduler at the flow level under certain circumstances, see [7, 16]. For the OPS discipline the rate vectors $\mathbf{c}_k$ are of form

$$\mathbf{c}_k = (\frac{\gamma_k}{k}, \ldots, \frac{\gamma_k}{k}),$$

where γ_k is an increasing positive sequence referring to the opportunistic gain. An intermediate version of the two (extreme) policies, called *SRPT-OPS*, was introduced in [16].

For the SRPT-OPS discipline the rate vectors $\mathbf{c}_k$ read as

$$\mathbf{c}_k = (0, \ldots, 0, \frac{\gamma_{j_k}}{j_k}, \ldots, \frac{\gamma_{j_k}}{j_k})$$

with j_k non-zero elements, where γ_k is an increasing positive sequence referring to the opportunistic gain and j_k indicates the number of jobs (out of k) that share the service capacity available.

3. SYMMETRIC CAPACITY REGIONS

In this section we assume that the capacity regions $\mathcal{C}_k$ have the following two properties for all $k = 1, \ldots, n$:

(i) $\mathcal{C}_k$ is a compact region of $\mathbb{R}_+^k$, i.e., $\mathcal{C}_k$ is closed and bounded;

(ii) $\mathcal{C}_k$ is *symmetric*, i.e., if $\mathbf{c} \in \mathcal{C}_k$, then any permutation $\tilde{\mathbf{c}}$ of its components also lies in $\mathcal{C}_k$.

If there is only one job, $n = 1$, then the optimal policy π^* is clearly defined by the maximal service capacity

$$c_1^* = \max\{c \in \mathcal{C}_1\},$$

the existence of which is guaranteed by the compactness property (i) above. We note that the optimal policy π^* is independent of the size s_1 of the job.

Now we consider the general case where there is any number of jobs, $n \geq 1$. An operating policy π is defined by a sequence of vectors $\mathbf{c}_k = (c_{k1}, \ldots, c_{kk}) \in \mathcal{C}_k$ for $k = 1, \ldots, n$. The flow time of π reads as

$$T^\pi = \sum_{k=1}^{n} k T_k^\pi,$$

where T_k^π refers to the length of phase k for policy π.

Let $g_1, \ldots, g_n$ be a sequence of functions with $g_k(\mathbf{c}_k)$ defined on $\mathcal{C}_k$ for all k, $G_1^*, \ldots, G_n^*$ a sequence of scalars, and $\mathbf{c}_1^*, \ldots, \mathbf{c}_n^*$ a sequence of vectors with $\mathbf{c}_k^* \in \mathcal{C}_k$ for all k. These sequences are defined recursively as follows:

$$\begin{aligned}
& g_1(c_1) = \frac{1}{c_1}, \\
& G_1^* = g_1(c_1^*) = \min_{c_1 \in \mathcal{C}_1} g_1(c_1), \\
& g_k(\mathbf{c}_k) = \frac{1}{c_{kk}}\left(k - \sum_{j=1}^{k-1} c_{kj} G_j^*\right), \\
& G_k^* = g_k(\mathbf{c}_k^*) = \min_{\mathbf{c}_k \in \mathcal{C}_k} g_k(\mathbf{c}_k), \quad k = 2, \ldots, n.
\end{aligned} \tag{1}$$

Note that the existence of the minimum values G_k^* is guaranteed by the compactness of capacity regions $\mathcal{C}_k$ (Property (i)). Note also that functions $g_k(\mathbf{c}_k)$ do not depend on the sizes $s_1, \ldots, s_n$ of the jobs.

We further note that G_k^* are positive at least if the symmetric and compact capacity regions $\mathcal{C}_k$ are *nested*, i.e., for all $k = 2, \ldots, n$ and $\mathbf{c}_k \in \mathcal{C}_k$,

$$(c_{k1}, \ldots, c_{k,k-1}) \in \mathcal{C}_{k-1},$$

which is easily verified. However, this is not a necessary condition as demonstrated below after Theorem 1.

PROPOSITION 1. *If the capacity regions $\mathcal{C}_1, \ldots, \mathcal{C}_n$ are such that*

$$G_1^* < \ldots < G_n^*,$$

then $c_{k,j+1}^* \geq c_{k,j}^*$ for all $k = 2, \ldots, n$ and $j = 1, \ldots, k-1$.

PROOF. $1°$ Let $k \in \{2, \ldots, n\}$ and $j \in \{1, \ldots, k-2\}$. In addition, let $\tilde{\mathbf{c}}_k^*$ denote the modification of $\mathbf{c}_k^*$ where the service rates $c_{k,j}^*$ and $c_{k,j+1}^*$ have changed their places,

$$\tilde{\mathbf{c}}_k^* = (c_{k,1}^*, \ldots, c_{k,j-1}^*, c_{k,j+1}^*, c_{k,j}^*, c_{k,j+2}^*, \ldots, c_{k,k}^*).$$

Note that $\tilde{\mathbf{c}}_k^* \in \mathcal{C}_k$, since $\mathcal{C}_k$ is symmetric (Property (ii)). Now

$$\begin{aligned}
& c_{kk}^* \left(g_k(\mathbf{c}_k^*) - g_k(\tilde{\mathbf{c}}_k^*) \right) \\
&= c_{k,j+1}^* G_j^* + c_{k,j}^* G_{j+1}^* - c_{k,j}^* G_j^* - c_{k,j+1}^* G_{j+1}^* \\
&= (c_{k,j}^* - c_{k,j+1}^*)(G_{j+1}^* - G_j^*).
\end{aligned}$$

Since $c_{kk}^* \left(g_k(\mathbf{c}_k^*) - g_k(\tilde{\mathbf{c}}_k^*) \right) \leq 0$ by definition, and $G_{j+1}^* - G_j^* > 0$ by the assumption, we conclude that

$$c_{k,j}^* - c_{k,j+1}^* \leq 0.$$

$2°$ Consider now the remaining case where $k \in \{2, \ldots, n\}$ and $j = k-1$. If $c_{k,k-1}^* = 0$, then $c_{k,k-1}^* - c_{kk}^* \leq 0$ for sure. Thus, we may assume that $c_{k,k-1}^* > 0$. Now, let $\tilde{\mathbf{c}}_k^*$ denote the modification of $\mathbf{c}_k^*$ where the service rates $c_{k,k-1}^*$ and $c_{k,k}^*$ have changed their places,

$$\tilde{\mathbf{c}}_k^* = (c_{k,1}^*, \ldots, c_{k,k-2}^*, c_{k,k}^*, c_{k,k-1}^*).$$

Note again that $\tilde{\mathbf{c}}_k^* \in \mathcal{C}_k$, since $\mathcal{C}_k$ is symmetric (Property (ii)). Now

$$\begin{aligned}
& c_{kk}^* c_{k,k-1}^* \left(g_k(\mathbf{c}_k^*) - g_k(\tilde{\mathbf{c}}_k^*) \right) \\
&= c_{k,k-1}^* \left(k - \sum_{j=1}^{k-2} c_{kj}^* G_j^* - c_{k,k-1}^* G_{k-1}^* \right) \\
& \quad - c_{kk}^* \left(k - \sum_{j=1}^{k-2} c_{kj}^* G_j^* - c_{kk}^* G_{k-1}^* \right) \\
&= (c_{k,k-1}^* - c_{kk}^*) \left(k - \sum_{j=1}^{k-1} c_{kj}^* G_j^* - c_{kk}^* G_{k-1}^* \right) \\
&= (c_{k,k-1}^* - c_{kk}^*) (c_{kk}^* G_k^* - c_{kk}^* G_{k-1}^*) \\
&= c_{kk}^* (c_{k,k-1}^* - c_{kk}^*)(G_k^* - G_{k-1}^*).
\end{aligned}$$

Since $c_{kk}^* c_{k,k-1}^* \left(g_k(\mathbf{c}_k^*) - g_k(\tilde{\mathbf{c}}_k^*) \right) \leq 0$ by definition, and $G_k^* - G_{k-1}^* > 0$ by the assumption, we conclude that

$$c_{k,k-1}^* - c_{kk}^* \leq 0,$$

which completes the proof. $\square$

THEOREM 1. *If the capacity regions $\mathcal{C}_1, \ldots, \mathcal{C}_n$ are such that*

$$G_1^* < \ldots < G_n^*,$$

then the optimal operating policy is $\pi^* = (\mathbf{c}_1^*, \ldots, \mathbf{c}_n^*)$ for all sizes $s_1 \geq \ldots \geq s_n$, where the optimal rate vectors $\mathbf{c}_k^*$ are defined recursively in (1). In this case, the minimum flow time T^{π^*} satisfies

$$T^{\pi^*} = \sum_{k=1}^{n} s_k G_k^*. \tag{2}$$

In addition, $c_{k,j+1}^* \geq c_{k,j}^*$ for all $k = 2, \ldots, n$ and $j = 1, \ldots, k-1$ so that the optimal policy belongs to the SRPT-HPR category.

PROOF. The result is proved by induction. For $n = 1$, the result is clearly true:

$$T^{\pi^*} = \frac{s_1}{c_1^*} = \min_{c_1 \in \mathcal{C}_1} \frac{s_1}{c_1} = \min_{\pi} T^{\pi}.$$

In addition, $G_1^* = \frac{1}{c_1^*}$ so that $T^{\pi^*} = s_1 G_1^*$ as claimed.

Assume now that $n \geq 2$ and the result is true for all values $1, \ldots, n-1$. We will show that it is also true for value n.

It follows from the induction assumption that the optimal policy applies rate vectors $\mathbf{c}_k^*$ for all $k = 1, \ldots, n-1$. Thus, for any policy $\pi = (\mathbf{c}_1, \ldots, \mathbf{c}_n) \in \Pi_n$, the modified policy $\tilde{\pi} = (\mathbf{c}_1^*, \ldots, \mathbf{c}_{n-1}^*, \mathbf{c}_n) \in \Pi_n$ results in a smaller flow time so that

$$\begin{aligned}
T^{\pi} &\geq T^{\tilde{\pi}} \\
&= n T_n^{\tilde{\pi}} + \sum_{k=1}^{n-1} k T_k^{\tilde{\pi}} \\
&= n T_n^{\tilde{\pi}} + \sum_{k=1}^{n-1} \left(s_{i(k)} - T_n^{\tilde{\pi}} c_{n,i(k)} \right) G_k^* \\
&= n \frac{s_{i(n)}}{c_{n,i(n)}} + \sum_{k=1}^{n-1} \left(s_{i(k)} - \frac{s_{i(n)}}{c_{n,i(n)}} c_{n,i(k)} \right) G_k^* \\
&= \frac{s_{i(n)}}{c_{n,i(n)}} \left(n - \sum_{k=1}^{n-1} c_{n,i(k)} G_k^* \right) + \sum_{k=1}^{n-1} s_{i(k)} G_k^* \\
&= s_{i(n)} g_n((c_{n,i(1)}, \ldots, c_{n,i(n)})) + \sum_{k=1}^{n-1} s_{i(k)} G_k^*,
\end{aligned}$$

where $i(k)$ refers to the original index of the job that completes at the end of phase k under policy $\tilde{\pi}$. Note that $(c_{n,i(1)}, \ldots, c_{n,i(n)}) \in \mathcal{C}_n$, since $\mathbf{c}_n = (c_{n1}, \ldots, c_{nn}) \in \mathcal{C}_n$ and $\mathcal{C}_n$ is symmetric (Property (ii)). Thus,

$$g_n((c_{n,i(1)}, \ldots, c_{n,i(n)})) \geq G_n^*$$

implying that

$$T^{\pi} \geq \sum_{k=1}^{n} s_{i(k)} G_k^* \geq \sum_{k=1}^{n} s_k G_k^*,$$

where the latter inequality follows from the facts that $s_1 \geq \ldots \geq s_n$ and $G_1^* < \ldots < G_n^*$.

Consider then policy $\pi^* = (\mathbf{c}_1^*, \ldots, \mathbf{c}_n^*)$ and let $i^*(k)$ denote the original index of the job that completes at the end of phase k under this policy π^*. It follows from Proposition 1 that $i^*(k) = k$ for all k. Thus,

$$\begin{aligned}
T^{\pi^*} &= n T_n^{\pi^*} + \sum_{k=1}^{n-1} k T_k^{\pi^*} \\
&= n \frac{s_n}{c_{nn}^*} + \sum_{k=1}^{n-1} \left(s_k - \frac{s_n}{c_{nn}^*} c_{nk}^* \right) G_k^* \\
&= \frac{s_n}{c_{nn}^*} \left(n - \sum_{k=1}^{n-1} c_{nk}^* G_k^* \right) + \sum_{k=1}^{n-1} s_k G_k^* \\
&= s_n g_n(\mathbf{c}_n^*) + \sum_{k=1}^{n-1} s_k G_k^* \\
&= \sum_{k=1}^{n} s_k G_k^*
\end{aligned}$$

so that $T^{\pi} \geq T^{\pi^*}$ for any $\pi \in \Pi_n$. $\square$

We would emphasize that all the results in this section are achieved with very general assumptions. Unlike in [16], no convexity nor coordinate-convexity is required from the capacity regions. It is only assumed that the capacity regions are compact and symmetric.

The capacity regions do not even need to be nested. An easy example can be found for $n = 2$. If $\mathcal{C}_1 = [0, 1]$ and $\mathcal{C}_2 \subset \mathbb{R}_+^2$ is a compact and symmetric region such that $c_{21} + c_{22} < 2$ for all $\mathbf{c}_2 \in \mathcal{C}_2$, then $G_1^* = 1$ and

$$G_2^* = \frac{1}{c_{22}^*}(2 - c_{21}^*) > 1 = G_1^*$$

so that Theorem 1 can be applied to determine the optimal policy.

However, if $\mathcal{C}_1 = [0, 1]$ and $\mathcal{C}_2 = \{\mathbf{c}_2 \in \mathbb{R}_+^2 : c_{21} + c_{22} \leq 2\}$, then $G_1^* = G_2^* = 1$. Furthermore, for any $\mathcal{C}_2 = \{\mathbf{c}_2 \in \mathbb{R}_+^2 : \min\{ac_{21} + c_{22}, c_{21} + ac_{22}\} \leq 2\}$ with $0 < a < 1$, we have $G_1^* = 1 > a = G_2^*$.

Note also that (1) gives a recursive algorithm to determine both the optimal rate vector and the minimum mean delay. The explicit expression (2) for the minimum flow time nicely generalizes the result derived for nested polymatroids, cf. [16, Equation (5)].

In addition, the proposed approach vastly facilitates the numerical evaluation of the optimal scheduling problem for any family of capacity regions that meet the presented conditions. The general optimization problem is difficult: (i) The number of possible service orders becomes quickly overwhelming when the number of flows increases, (ii) optimization on a high-dimensional capacity set may be computationally tedious, e.g., when the capacity region is a solution space of some packet level scheduling problem, and (iii) the problem needs to be solved separately for each set of flow sizes. The proposed approach avoids the combinatorial problems altogether, minimizes the need for numerical optimization on capacity sets and produces results that can be readily recycled for different flow sizes.

4. SYMMETRIC POLYMATROIDS

Capacity regions $\mathcal{C}_k$, $k = 1, \ldots, n$, are nested and symmetric *polymatroids* if there is an increasing sequence $\gamma_k \in \mathbb{R}_+$ (referring to the opportunistic gain) such that, for all k,

$$\mathcal{C}_k = \{\mathbf{c}_k \in \mathbb{R}_+^k : \sum_{i \in \mathcal{I}} c_{ki} \leq \gamma_{|\mathcal{I}|} \text{ for all } \mathcal{I} \in \{1, \ldots, n\}\}.$$

Sadiq and de Veciana [16] proved that the optimal policy belongs to the SRPT-HPR category when the capacity regions are nested and symmetric polymatroids and the gain function γ_k is increasing and concave, i.e., $\gamma_{k+1} - \gamma_k$ is decreasing. In fact, a similar result already appeared in [14]. In this section, we demonstrate that (with a minor additional assumption) this result is, in fact, a special case of our Theorem 1.

Given an increasing sequence γ_k, let $\theta_1, \ldots, \theta_n$ denote a sequence of positive real numbers defined recursively as follows:

$$\theta_1 = \frac{1}{\gamma_1},$$
$$\theta_k = \frac{1}{\gamma_1}\left(k - \sum_{j=1}^{k-1}(\gamma_{k+1-j} - \gamma_{k-j})\theta_j\right), \quad k = 2, \ldots, n.$$
(3)

Sadiq [15, Proof of Theorem 5.1] has shown that the sequence θ_k is increasing when the sequence γ_k is concave, i.e., $\gamma_{k+1} - \gamma_k$ is decreasing as a function of k. Below we show that it is strictly increasing when the sequence γ_k is

strictly concave, i.e.,

$$\gamma_1 > \gamma_2 - \gamma_1 > \ldots > \gamma_n - \gamma_{n-1}.$$

PROPOSITION 2. *If the increasing sequence γ_k is strictly concave, then*

$$\theta_1 < \ldots < \theta_n.$$

PROOF. The result is proved by induction. For $n = 1$, the result is trivially true.

Assume now that $n \geq 2$ and the result is true for all values $1, \ldots, n - 1$. We will show that it is also true for value n.

Let us denote $\gamma_0 = \theta_0 = 0$. It follows from the definition of θ_n that

$$n = \sum_{k=0}^{n-1}(\gamma_{k+1} - \gamma_k)\theta_{n-k}.$$

Correspondingly, by the definition of θ_{n-1},

$$n - 1 = \sum_{k=0}^{n-2}(\gamma_{k+1} - \gamma_k)\theta_{n-1-k}.$$

The difference of these two equations gives thus

$$1 = \sum_{k=0}^{n-1}(\gamma_{k+1} - \gamma_k)(\theta_{n-k} - \theta_{n-1-k}).$$

By substituting n with $n - 1$, we get

$$1 = \sum_{k=0}^{n-2}(\gamma_{k+1} - \gamma_k)(\theta_{n-1-k} - \theta_{n-2-k}).$$

Since $\gamma_{k+2} - \gamma_{k+1} < \gamma_{k+1} - \gamma_k$ for all k, it follows that

$$\begin{aligned}
1 &= \sum_{k=0}^{n-1}(\gamma_{k+1} - \gamma_k)(\theta_{n-k} - \theta_{n-1-k}) \\
&= \gamma_1(\theta_n - \theta_{n-1}) + \sum_{k=0}^{n-2}(\gamma_{k+2} - \gamma_{k+1})(\theta_{n-1-k} - \theta_{n-2-k}) \\
&< \gamma_1(\theta_n - \theta_{n-1}) + \sum_{k=0}^{n-2}(\gamma_{k+1} - \gamma_k)(\theta_{n-1-k} - \theta_{n-2-k}) \\
&= \gamma_1(\theta_n - \theta_{n-1}) + 1.
\end{aligned}$$

Thus, $\gamma_1(\theta_n - \theta_{n-1}) > 0$, implying that $\theta_n > \theta_{n-1}$, since $\gamma_1 > 0$. □

To prove the main result of this section (given below in Theorem 2) we need the following auxiliary result.

PROPOSITION 3. *If the increasing sequence γ_k is strictly concave, then, for all $k = 2, \ldots, n$ and $\mathbf{c}_k \in \mathcal{C}_k$,*

$$\sum_{j=1}^{k-2} c_{kj}\theta_j + (c_{k,k-1} + c_{kk})\theta_{k-1} \leq \sum_{j=1}^{k-2}(\gamma_{k-j+1} - \gamma_{k-j})\theta_j + \gamma_2\theta_{k-1}.$$

PROOF. The result follows easily from the facts that

$$0 < \theta_1 < \ldots < \theta_{k-1}$$

and

$$\sum_{j=k-k'+1}^{k} c_{ki} \leq \gamma_{k'} = \sum_{j=3}^{k'}(\gamma_j - \gamma_{j-1}) + \gamma_2$$

for all $k' = 2, \ldots, k$. The former is due to Proposition 2 and the latter follows from the properties of polymatroid $\mathcal{C}_k$. □

THEOREM 2. *If the capacity regions $\mathcal{C}_k$, $k = 1, \ldots, n$, are nested and symmetric polymatroids generated by an increasing and strictly concave sequence γ_k, then the optimal operating policy, for all sizes $s_1 \geq \ldots \geq s_n$, is $\pi^* = (\mathbf{c}_1^*, \ldots, \mathbf{c}_n^*)$, where*

$$\mathbf{c}_k^* = (\gamma_k - \gamma_{k-1}, \ldots, \gamma_2 - \gamma_1, \gamma_1)$$

for all k. In this case, the minimum flow time T^{π^*} satisfies

$$T^{\pi^*} = \sum_{k=1}^{n} s_k \theta_k,$$

where θ_k's are defined in (3). In addition, $c_{k,j+1}^* > c_{k,j}^*$ for all $k = 2, \ldots, n$ and $j = 1, \ldots, k - 1$ so that the optimal policy belongs to the SRPT-HPR category.

PROOF. By Theorem 1 and Proposition 2, it is sufficient to prove that, for all k,

$$\theta_k = \min_{\mathbf{c}_k \in \mathcal{C}_k} g_k(\mathbf{c}_k),$$

where functions g_k are defined in (1).

The result is proved by induction. For $k = 1$, the result is clearly true.

Assume now that $k \geq 2$ and the result is true for all values $1, \ldots, k - 1$. We will show that it is also true for value k.

Note first that

$$\theta_k - \theta_{k-1} = \frac{1}{\gamma_1}\left(k - \sum_{j=1}^{k-2}(\gamma_{k-j+1} - \gamma_{k-j})\theta_j - \gamma_2\theta_{k-1}\right) > 0$$

by Proposition 2. In addition, by the induction assumption, for any $j = 1, \ldots, k - 1$,

$$\theta_j = \min_{\mathbf{c}_j \in \mathcal{C}_j} g_j(\mathbf{c}_j) = G_j^*.$$

Thus, for any $\mathbf{c}_k \in \mathcal{C}_k$,

$$\begin{aligned}
&g_k(\mathbf{c}_k) - g_k(\mathbf{c}_k^*) \\
&= \frac{1}{c_{kk}}\left(k - \sum_{j=1}^{k-1}c_{kj}\theta_j\right) \\
&\quad - \frac{1}{\gamma_1}\left(k - \sum_{j=1}^{k-1}(\gamma_{k-j+1} - \gamma_{k-j})\theta_j\right) \\
&= \frac{1}{c_{kk}}\left(k - \sum_{j=1}^{k-2}c_{kj}\theta_j - (c_{k,k-1} + c_{kk})\theta_{k-1}\right) \\
&\quad - \frac{1}{\gamma_1}\left(k - \sum_{j=1}^{k-2}(\gamma_{k-j+1} - \gamma_{k-j})\theta_j - \gamma_2\theta_{k-1}\right) \\
&\geq \frac{1}{c_{kk}}\left(k - \sum_{j=1}^{k-2}(\gamma_{k-j+1} - \gamma_{k-j})\theta_j - \gamma_2\theta_{k-1}\right) \\
&\quad - \frac{1}{\gamma_1}\left(k - \sum_{j=1}^{k-2}(\gamma_{k-j+1} - \gamma_{k-j})\theta_j - \gamma_2\theta_{k-1}\right) \\
&= \left(\frac{1}{c_{kk}} - \frac{1}{\gamma_1}\right)\gamma_1(\theta_k - \theta_{k-1}) \geq 0,
\end{aligned}$$

where the inequality is justified by Proposition 3. $\square$

Note that the result given above is valid even for more general capacity regions, which include the operating points $\mathbf{c}_k^* = (\gamma_k - \gamma_{k-1}, \ldots, \gamma_2 - \gamma_1, \gamma_1)$ and which are subsets of the corresponding polymatroids. Note also that such capacity regions are not required to be symmetric.

As already shown in [16], symmetric polymatroids can be utilized to determine a lower bound (i.e., an *optimistic estimate*) for the flow time whenever the original capacity regions are compact, convex and symmetric, cf. Figure 1 in Section 6.

5. SYMMETRIC OPS-LIMITED POLYTOPES

Capacity regions $\mathcal{C}_k$, $k = 1, \ldots, n$, are nested and symmetric *OPS-limited polytopes* if there is an increasing sequence $\gamma_k \in \mathbb{R}_+$ (referring to the opportunistic gain) such that, $\mathcal{C}_k$ is the convex hull of the points $\mathcal{V}_k \subset \mathbb{R}_+^k$ for all k, where

$$\mathcal{V}_k = \bigcup_{j=0}^{k} \mathcal{V}_{kj}$$

and $\mathcal{V}_{kj}$ consists of all permutations of the rate vector

$$(0, \ldots, 0, \frac{\gamma_j}{j}, \ldots, \frac{\gamma_j}{j})$$

with j non-zero elements. Note that these permutations correspond to rate vectors for the OPS policy when applied to j jobs (out of k). It follows that

$$\mathcal{C}_k = \{\sum_{i=1}^{|\mathcal{V}_k|}\alpha_i\mathbf{v}_{ki} : \mathbf{v}_{ki} \in \mathcal{V}_k, \alpha_i \geq 0, \sum_{i=1}^{|\mathcal{V}_k|}\alpha_i = 1\}.$$

It is also easy to see that $|\mathcal{V}_k| = 2^k$ and $|\mathcal{V}_{kj}| = \frac{k!}{j!(k-j)!}$.

Given an increasing sequence γ_k, let $\eta_1, \ldots, \eta_n$ denote a sequence of positive real numbers defined recursively as follows:

$$\begin{aligned}
\eta_1 &= \frac{1}{\gamma_1}, \\
\eta_k &= \min_{j\in\{1,\ldots,k\}}\left(\frac{jk}{\gamma_j} - \sum_{i=k+1-j}^{k-1}\eta_i\right), \quad k = 2, \ldots, n.
\end{aligned}$$
(4)

PROPOSITION 4. *If the increasing sequence γ_k is such that*

$$\eta_1 < \ldots < \eta_n,$$

then, for all $k = 1, \ldots, n$ and $\mathbf{v}_k = (v_{k1}, \ldots, v_{kk}) \in \mathcal{V}_k$,

$$\sum_{j=1}^{k}v_{kj}\eta_j \leq k.$$

PROOF. For $\mathbf{v}_k = (0, \ldots, 0) \in \mathcal{V}_k$ the result is trivially true. Let then $\mathbf{v}_k \in \mathcal{V}_k$ such that

$$\mathbf{v}_k = (0, \ldots, 0, \frac{\gamma_j}{j}, \ldots, \frac{\gamma_j}{j})$$

with $j \in \{1, \ldots, k\}$ non-zero elements. It follows from (4) that

$$\eta_k \leq \left(\frac{jk}{\gamma_j} - \sum_{i=k+1-j}^{k-1}\eta_i\right),$$

which is equivalent with

$$\sum_{j=1}^{k}v_{kj}\eta_j \leq k.$$

Consider then any permutation $\tilde{\mathbf{v}}_k = (\tilde{v}_{k1}, \ldots, \tilde{v}_{kk})$ of $\mathbf{v}_k$. The assumption

$$\eta_1 < \ldots < \eta_n$$

implies that

$$\sum_{j=1}^{k} \tilde{v}_{kj}\eta_j \leq \sum_{j=1}^{k} v_{kj}\eta_j \leq k,$$

which completes the proof. $\square$

THEOREM 3. *If the capacity regions $\mathcal{C}_k$, $k = 1, \ldots, n$, are nested and symmetric OPS-limited polytopes generated by an increasing sequence γ_k such that*

$$\eta_1 < \ldots < \eta_n,$$

then the optimal operating policy, for all sizes $s_1 \geq \ldots \geq s_n$, is the SRPT-OPS policy $\pi^* = (\mathbf{c}_1^*, \ldots, \mathbf{c}_n^*)$, where, for all k,

$$\mathbf{c}_k^* = (0, \ldots, 0, \frac{\gamma_{j_k^*}}{j_k^*}, \ldots, \frac{\gamma_{j_k^*}}{j_k^*})$$

with j_k^* non-zero elements, where j_k^* is the optimal index in (4). In this case, the minimum flow time T^{π^*} satisfies

$$T^{\pi^*} = \sum_{k=1}^{n} s_k \eta_k.$$

PROOF. By Theorem 1, it is sufficient to prove that, for all k,

$$\eta_k = \min_{\mathbf{c}_k \in \mathcal{C}_k} g_k(\mathbf{c}_k),$$

where functions g_k are defined in (1).

The result is proved by induction. For $k = 1$, the result is clearly true.

Assume now that $k \geq 2$ and the result is true for all values $1, \ldots, k-1$. We will show that it is also true for value k.

Let $\mathbf{c}_k = (c_{k1}, \ldots, c_{kk}) \in \mathcal{C}_k$. There are $\alpha_i \geq 0$ such that

$$\sum_{i=1}^{|\mathcal{V}_k|} \alpha_i = 1 \quad \text{and} \quad \mathbf{c}_k = \sum_{i=1}^{|\mathcal{V}_k|} \alpha_i \mathbf{v}_{ki},$$

where $\mathbf{v}_{ki} = (v_{ki1}, \ldots, v_{kik}) \in \mathcal{V}_k$. By Proposition 4,

$$\sum_{j=1}^{k} c_{kj}\eta_j = \sum_{j=1}^{k} \sum_{i=1}^{|\mathcal{V}_k|} \alpha_i v_{kij}\eta_j = \sum_{i=1}^{|\mathcal{V}_k|} \alpha_i \sum_{j=1}^{k} v_{kij}\eta_j \leq k,$$

implying, by the induction assumption, that

$$g_k(\mathbf{c}_k) = \frac{1}{c_{kk}}\left(k - \sum_{j=1}^{k-1} c_{kj}G_j^*\right) = \frac{1}{c_{kk}}\left(k - \sum_{j=1}^{k-1} c_{kj}\eta_j\right) \geq \eta_k.$$

On the other hand, by (4),

$$\sum_{j=1}^{k} c_{kj}^*\eta_j = \frac{\gamma_{j^*(k)}}{j^*(k)} \sum_{j=k+1-j^*(k)}^{k} \eta_j = k,$$

implying that

$$g_k(\mathbf{c}_k^*) = \frac{1}{c_{kk}^*}\left(k - \sum_{j=1}^{k-1} c_{kj}^*G_j^*\right) = \frac{1}{c_{kk}^*}\left(k - \sum_{j=1}^{k-1} c_{kj}^*\eta_j\right) = \eta_k,$$

which completes the proof. $\square$

In fact, the result given above is valid for more general capacity regions $\mathcal{C}_k$ that include the points in $\mathcal{V}_k$ and that are bounded by the corresponding polytopes $\mathcal{T}_k$, i.e., $\mathcal{V}_k \subset \mathcal{C}_k \subset \mathcal{T}_k$. Note that such capacity regions are not required to be symmetric.

It is also important to observe that symmetric OPS-limited polytopes can easily be utilized to determine an upper bound (i.e., a *conservative estimate*) for the flow time whenever the original capacity regions are compact, convex and symmetric, cf. Figure 1 in Section 6.

An interesting open question is to determine sufficient conditions for the increasing sequence γ_k such that

$$\eta_1 < \ldots < \eta_n.$$

We believe that the concavity of the sequence γ_k would be such a condition, but, until now, we have managed to prove the claim only for $n = 2$ and $n = 3$.

Next we show that it is possible to find a nested family of symmetric OPS-limited polytopes $\mathcal{T}_k$ guaranteeing the optimality of the ordinary SRPT discipline (serving always just the shortest job with fixed rate γ_1) whenever the (original) capacity regions $\mathcal{C}_k$ are bounded by the corresponding polytopes $\mathcal{T}_k$. Note again that such capacity regions are not required to be symmetric.

THEOREM 4. *Consider a sequence of compact capacity regions $\mathcal{C}_k \subset \mathbb{R}_+^k$, $k = 1, \ldots, n$. Denote*

$$\gamma_1 = \max\{c \in \mathcal{C}_1\}.$$

Let $\mathcal{T}_k$, $k = 1, \ldots, n$, denote the symmetric OPS-limited polytopes generated by the increasing sequence γ_k defined by

$$\gamma_k = \frac{2n}{2n+1-k}\,\gamma_1. \tag{5}$$

If $(0, \ldots, 0, \gamma_1) \in \mathcal{C}_k$ and $\mathcal{C}_k \subset \mathcal{T}_k$ for all k, then the optimal operating policy, for all sizes $s_1 \geq \ldots \geq s_n$, is the SRPT policy $\pi^* = (\mathbf{c}_1^*, \ldots, \mathbf{c}_n^*)$, where, for all k,

$$\mathbf{c}_k^* = (0, \ldots, 0, \gamma_1).$$

In this case, the minimum flow time T^{π^*} satisfies

$$T^{\pi^*} = \frac{1}{\gamma_1} \sum_{k=1}^{n} k s_k.$$

PROOF. $1°$ Assume first that $\mathcal{C}_k = \mathcal{T}_k$ for all k. By Theorem 3, it is sufficient to prove that, for all k,

$$\eta_k = \frac{k}{\gamma_1} = \min_{j \in \{1, \ldots, k\}}\left(\frac{jk}{\gamma_j} - \sum_{i=k+1-j}^{k-1} \eta_i\right).$$

Note that in this case, we certainly have

$$\eta_1 < \ldots < \eta_n.$$

The result is proved by induction in $k = 1, \ldots, n$. For $k = 1$, the result is trivially true since $\eta_1 = 1/\gamma_1$ by definition.

Assume now that $k \geq 2$ and the result is true for $j = 1, \ldots, k-1$. We will show that the result is valid for $j = k$.

Since $k \leq n$ and $2x/(2x+1-j)$ is a decreasing function of x for $j > 1$, we have, for all $j \in \{2, \ldots, k\}$,

$$\frac{\gamma_j}{\gamma_1} = \frac{2n}{2n+1-j} \leq \frac{2k}{2k+1-j}. \tag{6}$$

On the other hand, by (4), $\eta_k = k/\gamma_1$ if

$$\frac{k}{\gamma_1} \leq \frac{jk}{\gamma_j} - \sum_{i=k+1-j}^{k-1} \eta_i$$

151

By applying the induction assumption, the condition reads as

$$\frac{k}{\gamma_1} \leq \frac{jk}{\gamma_j} - \frac{1}{\gamma_1}\left((k+1-j) + \ldots + (k-1)\right),$$

which is easily seen to be equivalent with condition

$$\frac{\gamma_j}{\gamma_1} \leq \frac{2k}{2k+1-j},$$

which is satisfied by (6). Thus, $\eta_k = k/\gamma_1$.

2° Assume now that $(0, \ldots, 0, \gamma_1) \in \mathcal{C}_k \subset \mathcal{T}_k$ for all $k = 1, \ldots, n$. Since $\mathbf{c}_k^* = (0, \ldots, 0, \gamma_1)$ is the optimal operating point in $\mathcal{T}_k$ and $\mathbf{c}_k^* \in \mathcal{C}_k \subset \mathcal{T}_k$ for all k, it must be the optimal operating point in $\mathcal{C}_k$, as well. □

It is interesting to observe that the increasing sequence γ_k defined by (5) is convex and bounded ($\gamma_k \leq 2\gamma_1$ for all k).

Note also that if $\mathcal{C}_n \not\subset \mathcal{T}_n$, then applying the ordinary SRPT discipline is no longer optimal.

6. EXAMPLES AND NUMERICAL RESULTS

In this section we study a particular parametric family of capacity regions $\mathcal{C}_k$, for which the optimal rate vector and the minimum delay have explicit expressions. The minimum delay is compared against the results given by bounding the capacity region either by the tightest polymatroid (lower bound for the mean delay) or OPS-limited polytope (upper bound for the mean delay).

6.1 Optimum solutions

Let $\alpha > 1$, and consider the symmetric capacity regions $\mathcal{C}_k$ defined as follows:

$$\mathcal{C}_k = \{\mathbf{c} \in \mathbb{R}_+^k : \sum_{j=1}^{k} c_j^\alpha \leq 1\}.$$

In the special case when $\alpha = 2$, the above regions represent the k-dimensional balls (sphere), and thus we refer to the above regions as α-balls, for short. The α-ball serves as a suitable example of a capacity region where the degree of scheduling gain can be easily parameterized between the extreme cases of a linear capacity region ($\alpha = 1$) and a hypercube ($\alpha \to \infty$).

To obtain the minimum delay T^{π^*} under the α-ball capacity region for n jobs, the optimizing values G_k^*, $k = 1, \ldots, n$, need to be determined recursively by applying (1). Thus, at each stage k the following optimization problem is solved to determine the optimal rate vector $\mathbf{c}^* = (c_1^*, \ldots, c_k^*) \in \mathcal{C}_k$ and the associated G_k^*,

$$G_k^* = \min_{\mathbf{c}} g_k(\mathbf{c}) = \frac{1}{c_k}\left(k - \sum_{j=1}^{k-1} c_j G_j^*\right)$$
$$\text{s.t. } \sum_{j=1}^{k} c_j^\alpha \leq 1.$$

Recall that the optimizing values $G_1^*, \ldots, G_{k-1}^*$ are fixed constants that were determined already in the earlier stages. The above nonlinear optimization problem can be solved explicitly by an appropriate geometrical interpretation of the problem.

Let us denote $x = G_k^*$. The function $g(\mathbf{c}) = x$ represents a hyperplane with respect to $\mathbf{c}$,

$$x c_k + \sum_{j=1}^{k-1} c_j G_j^* = k. \quad (7)$$

The solution to the optimization problem is given by determining the value of the unknown constant x such that the hyperplane $g(\mathbf{c}) = x$ touches the boundary of the capacity region $\mathcal{C}_k$ given by

$$\sum_{j=1}^{k} c_j^\alpha = 1. \quad (8)$$

This means that at the optimal rate vector $\mathbf{c} = \mathbf{c}^*$, the outer normal vectors to the capacity boundary (8) and the hyperplane (7) must be equal up to a constant y, which gives us componentwise the following equations,

$$\begin{aligned} y\, c_j^{\alpha-1} &= G_j^*, \quad j = 1, \ldots, k-1, \\ y\, c_k^{\alpha-1} &= x. \end{aligned} \quad (9)$$

Thus, we have $k + 2$ unknowns and $k + 2$ equations, i.e., (7), (8) and (9). The solution for G_k^*, i.e., x, is readily obtained in recursive form

$$G_k^{*\frac{\alpha}{\alpha-1}} = \left(k^{\frac{\alpha}{\alpha-1}} - \sum_{j=1}^{k-1} G_j^{*\frac{\alpha}{\alpha-1}}\right).$$

The above recursive formula can be solved by reapplying the recursion to the $(k-1)$th term on the right hand side which finally gives

$$G_k^* = \left(k^{\frac{\alpha}{\alpha-1}} - (k-1)^{\frac{\alpha}{\alpha-1}}\right)^{\frac{\alpha-1}{\alpha}}. \quad (10)$$

The associated optimal rate vector $\mathbf{c}^* = (c_1^*, \ldots, c_k^*)$ as given by (9) satisfies, for all $j = 1, \ldots, k$,

$$c_j^* = k^{\frac{-1}{\alpha-1}}\left(j^{\frac{\alpha}{\alpha-1}} - (j-1)^{\frac{\alpha}{\alpha-1}}\right)^{\frac{1}{\alpha}},$$

and the minimum flow time T^{π^*} for n jobs of sizes $s_1 \geq \ldots \geq s_n$ is given by

$$T^{\pi^*} = \sum_{k=1}^{n} s_k \left(k^{\frac{\alpha}{\alpha-1}} - (k-1)^{\frac{\alpha}{\alpha-1}}\right)^{\frac{\alpha-1}{\alpha}}.$$

For the polymatroid and the polytope bounds, the opportunistic gain γ_k is needed. The gain function corresponds in the capacity region to the point where the sum of the rates is maximized, i.e., one needs to solve

$$\begin{aligned} \gamma_k = \ &\max_{\mathbf{c}} c_1 + \cdots + c_k \\ &\text{s.t. } \sum_{j=1}^{k} c_j^\alpha = 1. \end{aligned} \quad (11)$$

Due to the symmetry of the capacity region, the optimal solution to (11) is clearly found to be $c_j = k^{-1/\alpha}$ for all $j = 1, \ldots, k$, so that the gain function is

$$\gamma_k = k^{\frac{\alpha-1}{\alpha}}.$$

Note that the sequence γ_k, $k = 1, \ldots, n$, is easily verified to be increasing and concave.

6.2 Numerical results

Next we give some numerical results on the delay performance in the α-ball capacity regions. We study the SRPT-HPR-type optimal policy in the actual α-ball capacity region and compare it against the lower bound given by the SRPT-HPR-type optimal policy in the tightest polymatroid capacity regions (covering the α-balls) and the upper bound given by the optimal SRPT-OPS policy in the tightest OPS-limited polytope capacity regions (inside the α-balls). These

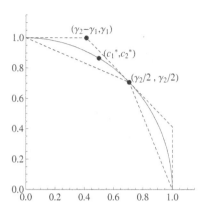

Figure 1: The capacity regions for $n = 2$ jobs with $\alpha = 2$. The actual α-ball capacity region is shown with solid line and the polymatroid and the OPS-limited polytope capacity regions are the outer and inner bounding dashed lines, respectively.

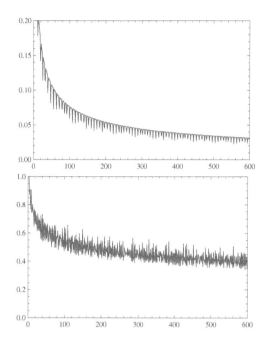

Figure 2: The differences $\eta_k - \eta_{k-1}$ in OPS-limited polytopes as a function of number of jobs for $\alpha = 2$ (upper panel) and $\alpha = 1.2$ (lower panel) remain positive, i.e., the η_k are an increasing sequence.

capacity regions are illustrated in Figure 1 for $n = 2$ and $\alpha = 2$, where the solid line represents the actual capacity region. The polymatroid capacity region is the outer bounding dashed line (i.e., capacity region is larger than original and hence it gives a lower bound for delay) and the inner bounding dashed line corresponds to the OPS-limited polytope capacity region (i.e., capacity region is smaller and hence it gives an upper bound on the delay). In the figure, we have also indicated (i) the rate vector $(c_1^*, c_2^*) = (\frac{1}{2}, \frac{\sqrt{3}}{2})$ associated with the optimal policy in the α-ball, (ii) the rate vector $(\gamma_2 - \gamma_1, \gamma_1) = (\sqrt{2} - 1, 1)$ associated with the optimal policy in the polymatroid capacity region, and (iii) the rate vector $(\frac{\gamma_2}{2}, \frac{\gamma_2}{2}) = (\frac{\sqrt{2}}{2}, \frac{\sqrt{2}}{2})$ associated with the optimal policy in the OPS-limited polytope capacity region.

Note that the optimal policy in the OPS-limited polytope capacity region, i.e., SRPT-OPS, considered in Section 5 represents the size-based optimal policy when the opportunistic scheduler is only able to achieve the gain given by the PF scheduler. For this optimality, it was required that the sequence η_k is strictly increasing. This is verified in Figure 2 for the α-ball capacity region, which depicts the difference $\eta_k - \eta_{k-1}$ as a function of the number of jobs k for $\alpha = 2$ (upper panel) and $\alpha = 1.2$ (lower panel). The reason for the somewhat irregular behavior is the minimum operation required in solving (4), which makes it also difficult to analytically prove the increasing property. However, numerically we can observe that the differences remain positive (i.e., the sequence is increasing) and the figure also suggests that the differences will remain positive for any value of k.

To study the performance of the different policies, we consider the mean delay per job as a function of the number of jobs in the system. We simulated the system with random initial sizes of the jobs taken from an exponential distribution with unit mean, and the results were obtained as an average over 10^5 such realizations. Note that in the simulations there are no new arrivals and thus the only randomness comes from the random initial sizes. In the results, we additionally show the mean delay of the OPS policy representing a practical point of reference, which corresponds to the size-oblivious fair policy that serves, given n jobs in the system, all jobs in parallel at rate γ_n/n.

The results are given in Figure 3, where the upper panel corresponds to the case with $\alpha = 2$ and the lower panel to the case with $\alpha = 1.2$. The curves in each figure from bottom up correspond to (i) the polymatroid lower bound, (ii) the minimum mean delay in the α-ball capacity regions, (iii) the polytope upper bound, and (iv) the mean delay for the OPS policy. We can observe that the polymatroid lower bound becomes more loose for smaller values of α, while the polytope upper bound remains quite accurate and seems to give a good approximation to the actual optimum delay. Also, at small values of α there is less scheduling gain and OPS gives significantly poorer performance than the size-based optimum policy.

Finally, we consider the performance of the OPS policy relative to the SRPT-HPR-type optimal policy in the α-balls. Similarly as before, each simulation consisted of averaging over 10^5 realizations of random initial sizes drawn from an exponential distribution with unit mean. The results are shown in Figure 4, which gives the mean delay ratio of the OPS policy relative to the optimal policy in the α-balls as a function of the number of jobs. The curves from the bottom up correspond to $\alpha = \{2, 1.3, 1.1\}$, respectively. As can be seen, the gain from the optimal policy increases the smaller α is, e.g., for $\alpha = 2$ the benefit is only marginal. However, for smaller values of α the gain can be more than 40%.

7. CONCLUSIONS

We have considered the minimization of the mean flow-level delay in a transient setting for service systems where the service ability can improve as the number of jobs increases. The situation reflects the opportunistic scheduling gain observed, e.g., in modern wireless cellular networks.

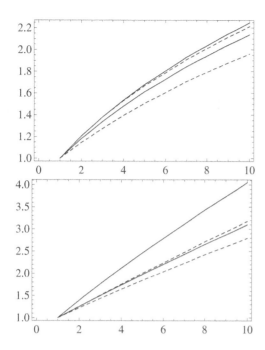

Figure 3: The mean delay as a function of number of jobs for $\alpha = 2$ (upper panel) and $\alpha = 1.2$ (lower panel). The curves from bottom up correspond to the polymatroid lower bound, the minimum mean delay for the α-balls, the polytope upper bound, and the mean delay for OPS.

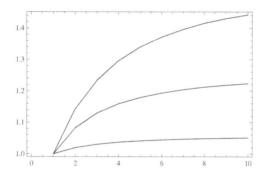

Figure 4: The mean delay ratio of the OPS policy relative to optimal policy as a function of number of jobs. The curves from bottom up correspond to $\alpha = \{2, 1.3, 1.1\}$, respectively.

Our key result is that under the given conditions the SRPT principle is optimal in a sense that the shortest flow is served at the highest rate of the optimal rate vector, the second shortest at the second highest rate etc. Importantly, the optimal rate vector does not depend on the sizes of the flows. We provided a recursive algorithm to determine the optimal rate vector as well as the minimum mean delay. Also upper and lower bounds for the delay were derived by applying the main result to systems with specific polytope capacity regions. The results even allow solving the optimal scheduling problem in closed form for certain special cases and vastly facilitate numerical evaluation in the general case.

We restricted ourselves to the operating policies where the rate vector is kept unchanged until the number of jobs is de-

creased. However, our results give strong indication that the optimal operating policy would be the same even if we allowed *continuous* control over the rate vector. This kind of generalization might be approached by dynamic programming techniques.

While we used modern wireless cellular systems as an example of systems with opportunistic scheduling gain, where the overall service rate of the system increases with the number of users, there are many more examples as well. A similar phenomenon can be observed, e.g., in peer-to-peer file sharing systems due to the double-role of leechers as being customers and servers at the same time. Or one may consider a multi-server queue with m parallel servers and n jobs, where the total service capacity is $\gamma_n = \min\{n, m\}$. As long as there are free servers, each new job activates a new server increasing thus the whole service capacity of the system. Queueing systems with opportunistic scheduling gain may briefly be called *scalable queues*.

In the future we plan to study the optimal scheduling problems related to various scalable queues in the dynamic setting. Even for the multi-server queue this is an open problem. It is only known that the SRPT-FM discipline minimizes the mean delay in the transient system starting with a fixed number of jobs but not allowing any (further) arrivals [13].

Another promising research direction is to consider systems where the flow level capacity regions are not explicitly defined but rather result from some adjustable packet level scheduling schemes. Combining the optimization tasks of the flow level and the packet level seems to allow solving optimal scheduling problems even in cases where determining the capacity sets would be otherwise tedious or difficult, especially at higher dimensions. An example of such a system is a weighted PF scheduler.

8. ACKNOWLEDGMENTS

This research has been partially supported by the AWA (Advances in Wireless Access) project, funded by Ericsson, Nokia-Siemens Networks and TEKES. The anonymous referees are acknowledged for the instructive comments that helped in improving the final version of the paper.

9. REFERENCES

[1] S. Aalto and P. Lassila. Flow-level stability and performance of channel-aware priority-based schedulers. In *Proceedings of NGI*, June 2010.

[2] U. Ayesta, M. Erausquin, and P. Jacko. A modeling framework for optimizing the flow-level scheduling with time-varying channels. *Performance Evaluation*, 67:1014–1029, 2010.

[3] P. Bender, P. Black, M. Grob, R. Padovani, N. Sindhushyana, and S. Viterbi. CDMA/HDR: a bandwidth efficient high speed wireless data service for nomadic users. *IEEE Communications Magazine*, 38(7):70–77, 2000.

[4] F. Berggren and R. Jäntti. Asymptotically fair transmission scheduling over fading channels. *IEEE Transactions on Wireless Communications*, 3:326–336, 2004.

[5] T. Bonald. A score-based opportunistic scheduler for fading radio channels. In *Proceedings of European Wireless*, pages 283–292, February 2004.

[6] T. Bonald, S. Borst, N. Hegde, M. Jonckheere, and A. Proutiére. Flow-level performance and capacity of wireless networks with user mobility. *Queueing Systems*, 63:131–164, 2009.

[7] S. Borst. User-level performance of channel-aware scheduling algorithms in wireless data networks. *IEEE/ACM Transactions on Networking*, 13:636–647, 2005.

[8] S. Borst and M. Jonckheere. Flow-level stability of channel-aware scheduling algorithms. In *Proceedings of WiOpt*, April 2006.

[9] M. Hu, J. Zhang, and J. Sadowsky. Traffic aided opportunistic scheduling for wireless networks: algorithms and performance bounds. *Computer Networks*, 46:505–518, 2004.

[10] A. Jalali, R. Padovani, and R. Pankaj. Data throughput of CDMA-HDR a high efficiency-high data rate personal communication wireless system. In *Proceedings of IEEE VTC 2000-Spring Conference*, pages 1854–1858, May 2000.

[11] P. Lassila and S. Aalto. Combining opportunistic and size-based scheduling in wireless systems. In *Proceedings of ACM MSWiM*, pages 323–332, October 2008.

[12] D. Park, H. Seo, H. Kwon, and B. Lee. Wireless packet scheduling based on the cumulative distribution function of user transmission rates. *IEEE Transactions on Communications*, 53:1919–1929, 2005.

[13] M. Pinedo. *Scheduling: Theory, Algorithms and Systems*. Springer, 3rd edition, 2008.

[14] S. Raj, E. Telatar, and D. Tse. Job scheduling and multiple access. In *Advances in Network Information Theory*. AMS, 2004.

[15] B. Sadiq. *Optimality and Robustness in Opportunistic Scheduler Design for Wireless Networks*. PhD thesis, University of Texas at Austin, USA, August 2010.

[16] B. Sadiq and G. de Veciana. Balancing SRPT prioritization vs opportunistic gain in wireless systems with flow dynamics. In *Proceedings of ITC-22*, September 2010.

[17] L. Schrage. A proof of the optimality of the shortest remaining processing time discipline. *Operations Research*, 16:687–690, 1968.

[18] A. Stolyar. Maxweight scheduling in a generalized switch: state space collapse and equivalent workload minimization in heavy traffic. *Annals of Applied Probability*, 14:1–53, 2004.

[19] A. Stolyar. On the asymptotic optimality of the gradient scheduling algorithm for multiuser throughput allocation. *Operations Research*, 53:12–25, 2005.

[20] B. Tsybakov. File transmission over wireless fast fading downlink. *IEEE Transactions on Information Theory*, 48:2323–2337, 2002.

[21] P. Viswanath, D. Tse, and R. Laroia. Opportunistic beamforming using dumb antennas. *IEEE Transactions on Information Theory*, 48:1277–1294, 2002.

Structure-Aware Sampling on Data Streams

Edith Cohen, Graham Cormode, Nick Duffield
AT&T Labs–Research
180 Park Avenue
Florham Park, NJ 07932, USA
edith,graham,duffield@research.att.com

ABSTRACT

The massive data streams observed in network monitoring, data processing and scientific studies are typically too large to store. For many applications over such data, we must obtain compact summaries of the stream. These summaries should allow accurate answering of post hoc queries with estimates which approximate the true answers over the original stream. The data often has an underlying structure which makes certain subset queries, in particular *range queries*, more relevant than arbitrary subsets. Applications such as access control, change detection, and heavy hitters typically involve subsets that are ranges or unions thereof.

Random sampling is a natural summarization tool, being easy to implement and flexible to use. Known sampling methods are good for arbitrary queries but fail to optimize for the common case of range queries. Meanwhile, specialized summarization algorithms have been proposed for range-sum queries and related problems. These can outperform sampling giving fixed space resources, but lack its flexibility and simplicity. Particularly, their accuracy degrades when queries span multiple ranges.

We define new stream sampling algorithms with a smooth and tunable trade-off between accuracy on range-sum queries and arbitrary subset-sum queries. The technical key is to relax requirements on the variance over all subsets to enable better performance on the ranges of interest. This boosts the accuracy on range queries while retaining the prime benefits of sampling, in particular flexibility and accuracy, with tail bounds guarantees. Our experimental study indicates that structure-aware summaries can drastically improve range-sum accuracy with respect to state-of-the-art stream sampling algorithms and outperform deterministic methods on range-sum queries and hierarchical heavy hitter queries.

Categories and Subject Descriptors: G.3 [**Probability and Statistics**] : Statistical Computing

General Terms: Algorithms, Measurement, Performance

Keywords: Structure-aware sampling, VarOpt, Data Streams, Approximate query processing

1. INTRODUCTION

Many applications, such as high speed networks, transaction processing, and scientific experiments, generate large quantities of data in the form of high-volume streams. These streams of ephemeral observations are too large to store in their entirety, so instead we must create a compact summary that captures the core properties of the data. These summaries must enable a variety of post hoc analyses of the data, to identify structure, patterns and anomalies.

As a motivating example, consider the massive transient data that arises in IP networks. Each network element observes a huge number of events, in the form of packets traveling across the network. Certainly, no router keeps a copy of the packets that it sees, but modern devices can maintain aggregate records of the traffic they have routed, in the form of NetFlow logs. These describe flows, in terms of the source and destination addresses, ports, duration and size. For a high speed link, these logs themselves represent high-volume streams, and across a large network add up to a vast amount of data. The network operator needs to collect summaries of these logs to enable analysis of the network health and operation, and to detect anomalies, misconfigurations or attacks in near-real time. These high-level analyses rely on being able to accurately estimate volumes of traffic in various projections of the data: from particular sources, to collections of subnetworks, between particular port combinations and so on. Importantly, the summaries should give high accuracy in small space, so that the cost of collecting, transporting, storing and analyzing them is minimized.

The state of the art for these tasks are techniques based on random sampling. The problem is abstracted as receiving a stream of multi-dimensional keys (the identifying addresses, ports, timestamps) each associated with a weight (the size of the flow). The sample enables estimating the total weight associated with an arbitrary subset of keys. This primitive is the basis of higher-lever analysis: extracting order statistics (quantiles), heavy hitters, patterns and trends. The estimates produced from the samples are unbiased, have low variance, and are subject to well-understood exponential tail bounds (Chernoff bounds). This ensures that they have good properties for the composition of several samples and queries, and so the relative estimation error decreases for queries that span multiple samples or larger subsets.

There are many other advantages to working with sampled data: the sampled keys are drawn from the original data (so, for example, within a subnetwork identified as generating an unusual volume of traffic, full details of typical flows from this subnet are captured), and these keys can be further examined or analyzed as needed. The sample itself resembles a smaller (reweighted) snapshot of the original data, and so can be directly manipulated with existing tools.

But a limitation of existing techniques is their failure to use the inherent *structure* that is present in the space of the keys. In our network data example there is significant structure in several forms. There is *order* across the timestamps, durations, and other attributes which have a natural total order. There are multiple *hierarchies*: on geographic locations, on network addresses, and on time values. Lastly, the keys are formed as the *product* of multiple attributes, each of which has certain (one-dimensional) structure. This structure fundamentally determines the kind of queries which are most important to the users: the class of *range queries* are those which are structure respecting, where the ranges correspond to contiguous keys in the ordered case, nodes in the hierarchy, or products of ranges in the multi-dimensional case (i.e. axis-parallel boxes, or hyper-rectangles).

Almost all queries posed to data are range queries, or collections of ranges. But existing stream sampling techniques are completely *oblivious* to this structure! They treat each key independently, and so consider any query as a *subset-sum* query: an arbitrary collection of keys. The guarantees for these samples assume that any subset is equally likely. But, on one-dimensional data, there are exponentially many possible subsets, while at most quadratically many of these are the more important ranges. By assuming uniformity over this larger space of queries, existing methods are missing the opportunity to optimize for the more common case of range queries.

The prior work on sampling has shown how to draw a sample from a stream of keys to build unbiased estimators with low variance. For particular classes of queries, such as subset-sum queries, the goal is *variance optimality*: achieving variance over the queries that is provably the smallest possible for any sample of that size. Classic sample-based summaries are based on Poisson sampling, where keys are sampled independently. Choosing inclusion probabilities which are proportional to the weight of a key (IPPS) [12] and using Horvitz-Thompson estimators [13] is known to minimize the sum of per-key variances. "VarOpt" summaries [2, 18, 5] improve on Poisson sampling by having a fixed sample size and better accuracy on subset-sum queries. SVarOpt [5] efficiently computes VarOpt summaries over a data stream and is a weighted generalization of reservoir sampling [19].

Classic sample-based summaries are optimized for the uniform workload of arbitrary subset-sum queries, and so do not adapt to the structure in data. Instead, for specific applications, such as (hierarchical) heavy hitters and quantiles, tailored solutions have been proposed [1, 10, 20]. For example, the popular Q-digest gives deterministic guarantees for range queries, with error bounded by a constant fraction of the total weight of all keys [15]. Such summaries are less flexible than samples, since they target a particular goal. Since they are not unbiased, combining the information for multiple subranges (as happens for HHHs) quickly loses accuracy. They cannot support non-range queries, and do not provide any "representative" keys from the input. Lastly, adapting these summaries to multiple dimensions is complex, and the size tends to grow exponentially with the dimensionality.

In the context of the IP flow example, deterministic summaries taken with respect to source IP addresses work well for capturing the volume under all sufficiently large prefixes. But if we are interested in a union of prefixes (say, associated with a certain geographic location or type of customer) or in gleaning from daily summaries the total monthly volume of a certain prefix, errors add up and the relative accuracy deteriorates. In contrast, under unbiased sample-based summaries, the relative error can decrease. For similar reasons, in estimating the total amount of traffic of many low-volume addresses, deterministic summaries can perform poorly with no useful guarantee, while the unbiased sample promises a good estimate if the total volume is large enough.

In recent work, we introduced offline structure-aware VarOpt sampling, as an improvement to structure-oblivious VarOpt that boosts accuracy on ranges. Our structure-aware summaries are built on a choice of VarOpt sample distributions in the offline setting to construct VarOpt samples with better accuracy on ranges [4]. Because the samples are VarOpt, they retain the desirable qualities of traditional sample-based summaries: unbiasedness, tail bounds on arbitrary subset-sums, and support for representative samples.

Our aim in this paper is to considerably extend this line of work,

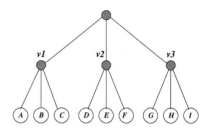

Figure 1: Hierarchy structure example.

to produce methods for structure-aware stream sampling. This requires substantially different techniques to any that have been proposed before. Stream sampling algorithms are constrained in that the sample must include at most k keys from the prefix of the stream seen so far. When a new key is added to the sample, one key must be discarded. We refer to this (randomized) action by the stream sampling algorithm as a *pivot* step. SVarOpt turns out to be inherently inflexible—there is a unique pivot at each step that results in a VarOpt sample [2, 5]. Thus in contrast to the offline setting, it is not possible to design stream sampling algorithm that compute VarOpt and structure-aware samples. Instead, we describe how to relax our requirements and find samples that are approximately VarOpt.

The next example illustrates the limitations of existing sampling methods for range queries, and the potential for a better solution.

EXAMPLE 1. *Consider the hierarchy structure depicted in Figure 1. There are 9 leaf nodes (keys) with unit weights. In a hierarchy, the ranges correspond to the leaf descendants of any internal node: here, they are the sets $v_1 = \{A, B, C\}$, $v_2 = \{D, E, F\}$, and $v_3 = \{G, H, I\}$, as well the individual leaves themselves. We may also be interested in querying other subsets, such as $\{A, E, H\}$, based on some selection criteria that is not captured by the structure, but such queries are considered less likely.*

When the desired sample size is 3, since keys have uniform weights, we include each key with probability $1/3$. The summary S includes the sampled keys and associates an adjusted weight of 3 with each key – to estimate the weight of a query set Q, we add up the adjusted weights of keys in $S \cap Q$. In our example, the estimate is $3|Q \cap S|$. The expected number of samples from each of v_1, v_2, v_3 is 1. When there is exactly one sample, the estimate is exact.

Poisson sampling (which for unit weights is Bernoulli sampling) picks each leaf independently. The sample size $|S|$ is Binomial, with mean 3, and clearly, has no relation to the structure. The probability that S will include exactly one key from v_1, yielding an exact value of 3 for the estimate on the weight of v_1, is $4/9$.

Reservoir sampling [19] (which in our case of uniform weights is the same as SVarOpt), uniformly selects a subset of size 3. The probability that v_1 contains exactly one sample is the same as for any other subset of size 3, i.e. $15/28$.

A deterministic summary such as Q-digest associates values with both leaf and internal nodes which allow to obtain estimates with given absolute error. When ranges are combined, errors add up.

There is an optimal structure-aware VarOpt sample distribution for any hierarchy [4]—the number of samples at each internal node is between the floor and ceiling of its expectation. Since the sample is VarOpt, estimates on arbitrary queries are at least as good as with Poisson sampling in terms of variance and tail bounds. In our example, one key is selected uniformly from each of v_1, v_2, and v_3, yielding a sample that is optimal for ranges – exact estimates of 3 on the weights of v_1, v_2, and v_3. As explained above, however, this sample can not be realized under stream constraints.

1.1 Our Contributions

We present a class of stream sampling schemes with a parametrized tradeoff between accuracy on ranges and tightness of tail bounds on arbitrary subsets. VAROPT summaries form one end of this tradeoff, being optimal for arbitrary subset-sums but structure-oblivious.

The first component of our solution is the introduction of *weight-bounded summaries*, which generalize VAROPT summaries via a tunable *tightness parameter*. This generalization facilitates a choice of pivots in stream summarization. The tightness parameter controls a tradeoff: the choice of pivots increases with tightness parameter while accuracy on arbitrary subset queries degrades. Specifically, the degradation is tightly controlled: we establish analytically that variance and tail bounds of weight-bounded summaries are at least as good as those of VAROPT summaries of a smaller sample size. The size of that smaller sample is determined by the value of the tightness parameter. *In the context of Example 1, a weight-bounded summary, just like* SVAROPT *summary, contains 3 keys and the expected value of each adjusted weight is 1. Adjusted weights values, however, may vary, but may not exceed a value determined by the tightness parameter.*

The second component of our solution is methods and heuristics for *structure aware* choice of pivots. We propose various local optimality criteria for this selection. For applications where each new update must be processed quickly, we present fast heuristics with a more limited search space for the best structure-aware step.

Practicality. We perform an experimental study of the tradeoffs between performance on ranges and on arbitrary subsets of our structure-aware summaries and various heuristics. We find that our new structure-aware summaries can be dramatically more accurate than SVAROPT or tailored deterministic summaries (Q-digest) on range queries. This makes the new approach highly suited for summarizing large streaming data. On arbitrary subset queries, which are poorly supported by deterministic summaries, the accuracy is similar to that of VAROPT and exceeds theoretical guarantees.

Outline. Section 3 introduces *weight-bounded summaries*, and Section 3.2 presents an iterative template algorithm for computing weight-bounded summaries, where in each step a subset $X \subset S$ of the keys is selected and we sample out one key out of X. We refer to X as the *pivot set*. Each pivot choice is associated with some adjusted weight value, and we are restricted to pivots where this value is below some weight bound.

In Section 4 we define a *range-cost* measure of each pivot choice X, which captures average variance over ranges resulting from pivoting on X. Since finding a pivot with minimum range cost can be computationally intensive, we propose in Section 5 various efficient heuristics for pivot selection.

Finally, Section 6 contains an experimental evaluation, which shows the effectiveness of range-aware stream sampling, both for the basic problem of range queries, and in its application to more complex data mining.

2. PRELIMINARIES

We review some central concepts from the sampling literature. Given a set of keys $[n]$, where each key $i \in [n]$ has weight w_i, a *sample-based summary* is a random subset of keys $S \subset [n]$, together with an *adjusted weight* a_i assigned to each sampled key $i \in S$ (we define $a_i \equiv 0$ for $i \notin S$). Using the summary, the estimate of the weight $w_J = \sum_{i \in J} w_i$ of a subset J of keys is $a_J = \sum_{i \in J} a_i = \sum_{i \in S \cap J} a_i$, i.e., the sum of the adjusted weights of sampled keys that are members of J. In particular, a_i is an estimate of w_i. We use adjusted weights which are unbiased estimators of the original weights: for all i, $\mathsf{E}[a_i] = w_i$. Hence, from linearity

of expectation, for all subsets J, $\mathsf{E}[a_J] = w_J$. Unbiasedness is important when estimates are combined (such as aggregating across time periods or measurement points). If the combined estimates are independent or non-positively correlated, the relative error on the sum estimate decreases.

Stream Summarization: The input is an (unordered) stream of distinct[1] keys with weight values $(w_1, w_2, \ldots)$ (key labels are identified with their position in the stream). The algorithm maintains a summary of $(w_1, \ldots, w_i)$ containing at most k keys from $[i]$: when processing key i, the algorithm computes a size-k summary of $(w_1, \ldots, w_i)$ using w_i and the summary of $(w_1, \ldots, w_{i-1})$.

Inclusion Probability Proportional to Size (IPPS) [12]: A weighted sampling method where the inclusion probability of each key in the sample is proportional to its weight, but truncated as not to exceed 1. Formally, when defined with respect to a parameter $\tau > 0$, the inclusion probability of i is $p_i = \min\{1, w_i/\tau\}$. The (expected) size of the sample is $k = \sum_i p_i$. The relation between k and $\tau \equiv \tau_k$ is expressed by the equality

$$\sum_i \min\{1, w_i/\tau_k\} = k \ . \tag{1}$$

The value of τ_k on the observed part of the stream can be maintained by an algorithm which uses $O(k)$ storage: The algorithm adjusts τ_k upwards on the go, maintaining all observed keys with $w_i \geq \tau_k$ in a heap (there are at most k such keys), and tracking the total weight of all other keys. From this information, we can also compute the value $\tau_{k'}$ for any $k' < k$.

The Horvitz-Thompson (HT) estimator [13] assigns the adjusted weight $a_i = w_i/p_i$ to a key $i \in S$ with inclusion probability p_i. HT adjusted weights are optimal for the particular inclusion probability p_i in that they minimize the variance $\mathsf{Var}[a_i]$ over all assignments of adjusted weights.

Under IPPS, the HT adjusted weight of $i \in S$ is τ if $w_i \leq \tau$ and w_i otherwise. The variance is $\mathsf{Var}[a_i] = w_i^2(1/p_i - 1) \equiv w_i(\tau - w_i)$ if $w_i \leq \tau$ and 0 otherwise. HT adjusted weights with IPPS inclusion probabilities are optimal in that they minimize the sum $\sum_i \mathsf{Var}[a_i]$ of per-key variances for a given expected sample size, over all sample-based summaries.

Poisson sampling is such that inclusions of different keys are independent. With HT adjusted weights we have $\mathsf{Var}[a_J] = \sum_{i \in J} \mathsf{Var}[a_i]$ for any subset J. A Poisson IPPS sample of a expected size k can be computed by a simple stream algorithm. A drawback of Poisson sampling is that the sample size varies, whereas we would like to keep it fixed to make the best use of the space available.

VAROPT **summaries** [2, 18, 5] use IPPS inclusion probabilities (i.e. $p_i = \min\{1, w_i/\tau\}$) and HT adjusted weights (i.e. for $i \in S$, $a_i = \max\{w_i, \tau\}$). The underlying sample distribution meets the VAROPT criteria:

(a) The sample size is *exactly* $k = \sum_{i \in [n]} p_i$.

(b) *High-order inclusion and exclusion probabilities are bounded by products of first-order probabilities*: for any $J \subseteq [n]$,

$$\text{(I):} \qquad \mathsf{E}\left[\prod_{i \in J} X_i\right] \quad \leq \quad \prod_{i \in J} p_i$$

$$\text{(E):} \qquad \mathsf{E}\left[\prod_{i \in J}(1 - X_i)\right] \quad \leq \quad \prod_{i \in J}(1 - p_i)$$

where X_i is the indicator variable for i being included in the sample: $X_i = 1$ if $i \in S$ and $X_i = 0$ otherwise. The product $\prod_{i \in J} X_i$

---

[1] Our analysis and evaluation assume that keys are distinct but this requirement can be waved in our algorithms.

is the joint inclusion probability of all keys $i \in J$ and symmetrically, $\prod_{i \in J}(1 - X_i)$ is the joint exclusion probability.

Poisson sampling satisfies (b) (with equalities) but does not satisfy (a). VAROPT improves over Poisson IPPS by fixing the size of the summary. When τ_k is fixed, the variance of any subset-sum estimate of a VAROPT summary is at most that of a Poisson IPPS summary. This is because for a VAROPT summary, for all subsets J, $\mathsf{Var}[a_J] \leq \sum_{i \in J} \mathsf{Var}[a_i]$, which is implied by the joint inclusion property for subsets of size 2 (equivalently, covariances are nonpositive) whereas with Poisson IPPS, $\mathsf{Var}[a_J] = \sum_{i \in J} \mathsf{Var}[a_i]$.

VAROPT summaries are optimal for arbitrary subset-sum queries in that for *any* subset size, they minimize the expected variance of the estimates [17, 5]. This follows from VAROPT minimizing both $\sum_{i \in [n]} \mathsf{Var}[a_i]$ (by using IPPS) and $\mathsf{Var}[\sum_{i \in [n]} a_i] = 0$, and from [17] which established that the expected variance depends only on these two quantities. The notation VAROPT_k denotes a VAROPT summary of size k.

Stream Sampling. The SVAROPT method [5] efficiently computes a VAROPT_k summary of a data stream of weighted keys. The algorithm maintains a VAROPT_k summary S of the processed prefix of the stream, which we can view as a vector a with entry $a_i > 0$ if and only if $i \in S$. For each new key n, its adjusted weight is initialized to its weight value $a_n \leftarrow w_n$. The vector a now has $k + 1$ positive entries, for keys $S \cup \{n\}$. We apply $a \leftarrow \text{VAROPT}_k(a)$ to obtain a summary of size k. In sampling terms, one of the $k + 1$ keys in $S \cup \{n\}$ is ejected from the sample and weights of remaining keys are adjusted. We call the operation of VAROPT sampling out of a single key a *pivot*. The pivot performed by SVAROPT is $\text{PIVOT}(a, S \cup \{n\})$ (Algorithm 1).

While VAROPT_k is a family of sample distributions satisfying some constraints, SVAROPT is the unique way to maintain a VAROPT_k sample of the prefix of the stream – the pivot $\text{PIVOT}(a, S \cup \{n\})$ is the only way to obtain a VAROPT_k summary given a new key and a VAROPT_k summary of previously-seen keys. When keys have uniform weights, SVAROPT is isomorphic to reservoir sampling [19] and the sample distribution is a uniform selection of a k-tuple.

Chernoff bounds. Given a (query) subset J and a Poisson or VAROPT sample S the size of $J \cap S$, the number of samples from J satisfies exponential tail bounds [3, 14, 16, 11, 7]. Let $X_J = \sum_{i \in J} X_i$, where X_i is the indicator variable for $i \in S$ as before. When inclusion probabilities are IPPS and we use HT adjusted weights, Chernoff bounds imply bounds on a_J: Observe that it suffices to consider J such that $\forall i \in J, p_i < 1$ (as we have the exact weight of keys with $p_i = 1$). For such a J, the estimate is $a_J = \tau X_J = \tau|J \cap S|$. We bound a_J by substituting $X_J = a_J/\tau$ into the basic form of Chernoff bounds, and obtain

$$\Pr[a_J \leq v], \; \Pr[a_J \geq v] \leq e^{(v - w_J)/\tau}(w_J/v)^{v/\tau}. \quad (2)$$

3. WEIGHT-BOUNDED SUMMARIES

3.1 WB Summary Definition and Properties

We introduce the concept of weight-bounded (WB) summaries which facilitates our streaming algorithms. Weight-bounded summaries generalize VAROPT summaries by replacing the function τ_k with a (larger) value M. This allows us to bound the accuracy relative to a smaller VAROPT summary of size k^* while giving more freedom to choose which elements to retain at each step.

DEFINITION 1 (WEIGHT-BOUNDED SUMMARY). *A random weight vector $a \geq 0$ is an M-bounded summary of weight vector $w = (w_1 \ldots w_n) \geq 0$ if:*

Algorithm 1 $\text{PIVOT}(a, X)$

Require: $|X| \geq 2$
1: $A \leftarrow \text{CAND}(a, X)$
2: $M \leftarrow M(a, X) := \frac{\sum_{i \in A} a_i}{|A| - 1}$
3: Select $i \in A$ with probability $q_i = 1 - \frac{a_i}{M}$
     $\triangleright$ IPPS probability for excluding i
4: $a_i \leftarrow 0;$
5: **for all** $j \in A \setminus \{i\}$ **do**
6:     $a_j \leftarrow M$
7: **end for**
8: **return** a

---

1. $\forall i \in [n]$, $\mathsf{E}[a_i] = w_i$.
2. $\sum_{i \in [n]} a_i = \sum_{i \in [n]} w_i$
3. $\forall i \in [n]$, if $w_i \geq M$ then $a_i \equiv w_i$, otherwise $a_i \leq M$.
4. For any $J \subseteq [n]$ and an upper bound $\overline{M} \geq \max_{i \in J} a_i$ (over all possible outcomes).

$$\text{(I):} \qquad \mathsf{E}[\prod_{i \in J} a_i] \leq \prod_{i \in J} w_i \qquad (3)$$

$$\text{(E):} \qquad \mathsf{E}[\prod_{i \in J}(\overline{M} - a_i)] \leq \prod_{i \in J}(\overline{M} - w_i) \qquad (4)$$

The size of a weight-bounded summary is said to be k if there are k non-zero weights in it, i.e. a set of keys S with $|S| = k$.

A VAROPT_k summary is a τ_k-bounded summary where a has exactly k positive entries, so all positive entries in a with $w_i < \tau_k$ have $a_i = \tau_k$. From Section 2, τ_k for a given set of input keys and weights is the threshold such that the corresponding IPPS probabilities sum to k.

The property of being a weight-bounded summary is transitive:

LEMMA 2. *If $a^{(1)}$ is an $M^{(1)}$-bounded summary of $a^{(0)}$ and $a^{(2)}$ is an $M^{(2)}$-bounded summary of $a^{(1)}$, then $a^{(2)}$ is an M^*-bounded summary of $a^{(0)}$, where $M^{(*)}$ is the maximum value of $M^{(1)}$ and $M^{(2)}$ over all outcomes.*

Let $k^*(M)$ be the maximum k' such that $\tau_{k'} \geq M$. In other words, M is approximately the threshold that would give an VAROPT sample of size $k^*(M)$. We show that the quality of an M-bounded summary of size $k > k^*(M)$, in terms of tail bounds and average variance measures, is at least that of a $\text{VAROPT}_{k^*(M)}$ summary. Average-case variance is determined by $V\Sigma = \mathsf{Var}[\sum_i a_i]$ and $\Sigma V = \sum_i \mathsf{Var}[a_i]$. Like VAROPT summaries, weight-bounded summaries have optimal $V\Sigma = 0$, and therefore it suffices to bound ΣV. We state the results below; full proofs are in the Appendix.

THEOREM 3. *For any key i, the variance in the adjusted weight of i under an M-bounded summary is at most the variance under $\text{VAROPT}_{k^*(M)}$.*

THEOREM 4. *For any subset J of keys, the estimate a_J of w_J under an M-bounded summary satisfies the tail bounds obtained for $\text{VAROPT}_{k^*(M)}$.*

In the evaluations we find that in practice we get much smaller errors than suggested by these worst-case bounds. When $k^*(M) = k/2$, the performance is closer to VAROPT_k than to $\text{VAROPT}_{k^*(M)}$. This is because the adjusted weight of most included keys in an M-bounded summary is usually much smaller than M.

3.2 Computing WB summaries

We first define an (offline) iterative randomized process that manipulates a weight vector a, initialized with the original weight vector w. The number of non-zero entries decreases by one each iteration—after $(n-k)$ iterations we have a summary of size k. In each iteration we select a subset $X \subset [n]$ of the positive entries, and choose one of these to remove. Essentially, we treat X as a set of weighted keys and apply the IPPS procedure to X to compute a VarOpt summary of size $|X| - 1$. We later discuss criteria for choosing X based on structural considerations.

Candidate Set and Pivot Threshold. Recall from Section 2 that for any set of weighted keys there is a unique threshold τ_k which produces a sample of size k. Applying IPPS to the set of keys X with associated weights a, the threshold is $\tau_{|X|-1}(M)$ for X, which we call the *pivot threshold*, $M(a, X)$. This can be computed efficiently as described in Section 2. We then define the *candidate set*, $\text{CAND}(a, X)$ as the (unique) subset of X which are candidates for ejection (under IPPS with threshold $M(a, X)$: $\text{CAND}(a, X)$ is the subset of keys with weight $a_i < M(a, X)$, that is, they have retention probability < 1. The remaining keys in X have sufficient weight to ensure that they will not be removed in this pivot step. Observe that $\text{CAND}(a, X)$ is of size at least 2 when $|X| \geq 2$ since the two smallest weight keys are always candidates for ejection.

PIVOT **Algorithm.** To perform the pivot, we use the pivot threshold to sample an element to eject from the candidate set. This is implemented in Algorithm 1: $\text{PIVOT}(a, X)$. The algorithm computes a VarOpt summary of X of size $|X| - 1$. One can verify that the exclusion probabilities in line 3 sum to 1. After the pivot operation, one of the candidate keys has adjusted weight 0 and the others have their new adjusted weight set to $M(a, X)$, which is equal to $\frac{\sum_{i \in \text{CAND}(a,X)} a_i}{|\text{CAND}(a,X)| - 1}$.

LEMMA 5. *The output of* $\text{PIVOT}(a, X)$ *is an* $M(a, X)$-*bounded summary of* a.

Consider such a process with input weight vector $a^{(0)} = w$. For $\ell \geq 1$, the ℓth iteration has input $(a^{(\ell-1)}, X^{(\ell-1)})$ —a weight vector and a pivot set—and outputs weight vector $a^{(\ell)}$. Let $M^{(\ell)} = M(a^{(\ell-1)}, X^{(\ell-1)})$. Define $\overline{M^{(\ell)}}$ to be the maximum of $\max_{h \leq \ell} M^{(h)}$ in all possible outcomes of the first ℓ iterations. From Lemma 2 and Lemma 5, we obtain:

THEOREM 6. $\forall \ell$, $a^{(\ell)}$ *is an* $\overline{M^{(\ell)}}$-*bounded summary of* w.

3.3 Stream WB summarization

In the streaming setting, we must ensure that the total number of stored keys at any time is small enough to fit in the available memory. The keys that must be stored when the ℓth element is processed are those amongst the first ℓ elements (the elements seen so far) that have positive adjusted weights.

Therefore for stream weight-bounded summarization, we apply a pivot operation after each arrival following the kth stream element. The ℓth pivoting iteration is performed after the $k + \ell$th stream arrival and the stored keys are $S^{(\ell)} = \{i | a_i^{(\ell)} > 0 \wedge i \leq \ell + k\}$. As each iteration sets the adjusted weight of one key to zero, the total number of stored keys is kept to k.

Algorithm 2 takes as input a data stream with weights $w_1, w_2, \ldots$ and a *tightness parameter* $c \geq 1$. This parameter controls the flexibility with which the algorithm can deviate from strict VarOpt and is described in more detail below. The algorithm maintains a set S of (at most k) keys and adjusted weights a_S. It has the property that at any point, a is a weight-bounded summary of the processed prefix of the data stream:

Algorithm 2 STREAMWBSUMMARY$(c, w_1, w_2, \ldots)$

1: $S \leftarrow \emptyset$ ▷ Initialize
2: **for** $i = 1, \ldots$ **do**   ▷ Process key i
3:     $S \leftarrow S \cup \{i\}$
4:     $a_i \leftarrow w_i$
5:     **if** $i > k$ **then**
6:        $a \leftarrow \text{PIVOT}(a, X)$, for some $X \subset S$ such that:
          • X satisfies some structure-aware selection criteria
          • $M(a, X) \leq \tau_{k/c}(S)$;
7:        $S \leftarrow \{i : a_i > 0\}$
8:     **end if**
9: **end for**

LEMMA 7. *Defining* $a_i \equiv 0$ *for* $i \notin S$, *vector* a *is a* $\tau_{k/c}(w_1, \ldots, w_\ell)$-*bounded summary of* $(w_1, \ldots, w_\ell)$

The smaller c is, the less flexibility we have in choosing the pivot set X. Since τ_k is decreasing in k, as c decreases, $\tau_{k/c}$ decreases, providing less scope for choosing X. At the extreme, if $c = 1$, every X with $M(a, X) \leq \tau_k$ must include all of $\text{CAND}(a, S)$ and the algorithm becomes identical to SVAROPT [5]. SVAROPT also minimizes the "local" variance cost, which is the variance of $a^{(\ell)}$ with respect to $a^{(\ell-1)}$:

$$\Sigma V(X) \equiv \sum_{i \in X} \text{Var}[a_i^{(\ell)}] = \sum_{i \in X} a_i^{(\ell-1)} \left(\frac{\sum_{i \in X} a_i^{(\ell-1)}}{|X| - 1} - a_i^{(\ell-1)} \right). \quad (5)$$

When we set $c > 1$ (e.g. to a small constant such as 2), we have greater freedom in choosing the pivot set X meeting the constraints on $M(a, X)$. We will use this flexibility to make a "structure-aware" selection (we formalize this notion in the next section). That is, we can choose a subset of keys on which to pivot such that the keys are "close" under the assumed structure (e.g. close in the hierarchy). This way, by keeping the necessary shifting of weight due to pivoting localized, crossing fewer range boundaries, we are more likely to end up with a summary such that the adjusted weight of ranges is closer to their actual weight. Figure 2 compares the actions of SVAROPT (which is structure oblivious) and STREAMWBSUMMARY (with an intuitive structure-aware pivot selection) on a stream of keys from the example hierarchy structure of Figure 1.

An alternative to constraining pivot selection is to compute the *effective* tightness for a chosen pivot, i.e., the value of c that yields equality in line 6 of Algorithm 2. Tail bounds for estimation are then governed by the maximum effective tightness over the stream.

4. RANGE COST

In this section, we formalize "structure-awareness" by associating a "range cost" with each possible choice, and striving to select a pivot with low range cost. Our *range cost* $\rho(X)$ of a pivot X measures the variance local to the iteration, averaged over "range boundaries." By local we mean that we consider the variance of the adjusted weights a' at the end of the iteration with respect to the adjusted weights a that are the input to the iteration. This local view follows from restrictions imposed by the streaming context and is inspired by SVAROPT, where the selected pivot locally minimizes the "structure oblivious" variance ΣV (5).

For a range $R \in \mathcal{R}$, the change in its estimated weight following a pivot step is the random variable $\Delta_R = |a'_R - a_R|$. Because both sets of weights are unbiased, $\mathsf{E}[\Delta_R] = 0$ and the variance of this change is $\mathsf{E}[\Delta_R^2]$. Generally, there is no one pivot which simultaneously minimizes variance for all ranges in $\mathcal{R}$. Next we

SVarOpt:

	A	D	E	G	B	C	H	I	F	τ
3	1	1	1							1
4	$\frac{4}{3}$	0	$\frac{4}{3}$	$\frac{4}{3}$						$\frac{4}{3}$
5	0	0	$\frac{5}{3}$	$\frac{5}{3}$	$\frac{5}{3}$					$\frac{5}{3}$
6	0	0	2	2	2	0				2
7	0	0	$\frac{7}{3}$	$\frac{7}{3}$	0	0	$\frac{7}{3}$			$\frac{7}{3}$
8	0	0	$\frac{8}{3}$	$\frac{8}{3}$	0	0	$\frac{8}{3}$	0		$\frac{8}{3}$
9	0	0	3	3	0	0	3	0	0	3

StreamWBSummary:

	X	A	D	E	G	B	C	H	I	F	τ
3		1	1	1							1
4	$\{D, E\}$	1	0	2	1						$\frac{4}{3}$
5	$\{A, B\}$	0	0	2	1	2					$\frac{5}{3}$
6	$\{B, C\}$	0	0	2	1	3	0				2
7	$\{G, H\}$	0	0	2	0	3	0	2			$\frac{7}{3}$
8	$\{H, I\}$	0	0	2	0	3	0	3	0		$\frac{8}{3}$
9	$\{E, F\}$	0	0	3	0	3	0	3	0	0	3

Figure 2: Selecting a sample of size 3 from a stream of 9 unit weight keys. Each row corresponds to a new arrival (starting with the 4th arrival). The table entries are adjusted weights at the end of the iteration. The rightmost column shows the IPPS threshold τ_3 on the prefix of the stream. The tables show possible execution of the randomized algorithms. SVarOpt (top): The pivot set is always of size 4, containing the 3 participants in the current summary S and the new arrival. The final summary contains the keys $S = \{E, G, H\}$, all with adjusted weights 3. StreamWBSummary with $c = 3/2$ (bottom): According to the structure (Figure 1), we prioritize pivot sets with lower LCA. This pivot selection rule is intuitively structure aware as it tends to preserve the weight under internal nodes. In this particular case, all outcomes constitute an optimal structure-aware sample, containing exactly one sample from each of v_1, v_2, and v_3.

propose ways to measure the overall impact of a pivot in different types of structure, and to pick pivots with minimum impact.

4.1 Partition

When the structure is a partition of keys, the ranges are parts in this partition and are disjoint. We define range cost as the sum of variances over individual ranges:

$$\rho(X) = \sum_{R \in \mathcal{R}} \mathsf{E}[\Delta_R^2] = \mathsf{E}[\sum_{R \in \mathcal{R}} \Delta_R^2] .$$

Defining $L_R = \sum_{i \in \text{CAND}(X) \cap R} a_i - M(a, X) \lfloor \frac{\sum_{i \in \text{CAND}(X) \cap R} a_i}{M(a, X)} \rfloor$, the portion of the weight in range R that will be rounded up to $M(a, X)$ or down to 0 when pivoting on X, we get

$$\rho(X) = \sum_{R \in \mathcal{R}} L_R(M(a, X) - L_R) .$$

In the degenerate case when each range contains a single key, $\rho(X) \equiv \Sigma V(X)$ (see (5)) and therefore minimizing the range cost is equivalent to VarOpt sampling.

For the general case, $\rho(X) = 0$ if and only if $X \subset R$ for some range R (i.e. X is fully contained in some range R). Between pivot choices with $\rho(X) = 0$, we propose to use a pivot with minimum $M(a, X)$, which must be of the form $S \cap R$ for some range R. In summary, we propose to pick $X = S \cap R$ with minimum $M(a, X)$ if $M(a, X) \leq \tau_{k/c}$. Else, pick the whole sample S as the pivot X.

4.2 Order

When there is a natural total order over the keys in the data, we define the range cost to be a weighted average of the variance over

prefixes (a.k.a. 1-d halfspaces). Appropriate weighting of prefixes prevents regions with many small weights from dominating those with few larger weights. Considering the linearly many prefixes rather than the quadratically many intervals simplifies analysis and prevents smaller intervals from dominating fewer larger ones. As the weight of an interval (range of contiguous keys) is the difference of weights of two prefixes, the (additive) estimation error on an interval is at most the sum of estimation errors on two prefixes.

To analyze the range cost, we study how a pivot changes the distribution of weights in the sample. Formally, for $0 \leq q \leq 1$, the *q-quantile point* of the sample S is the prefix of ordered points that contains a q fraction of the total adjusted weight, a_S. Key i from the ordered universe has adjusted weight a_i, and if $i \in S$, this key covers a range of quantile points. We write i_q to denote the index of the key which includes the q-quantile, i.e. the index i that satisfies

$$q \in \left(\frac{\sum_{j < i} a_j}{a_S}, \frac{a_i + \sum_{j < i} a_j}{a_S} \right] .$$

For a subset X and q, let Δ_q be the random variable corresponding to the (absolute value) of the weight that "moves" across the half-space induced by i_q as a result of $a' \leftarrow \text{PIVOT}(a, X)$.

If $i_q \notin X$, then this is just the difference in weight below the key before and after the pivot:

$$\Delta_q = \big| \sum_{i \in S | i < i_q} a_i - \sum_{i \in S | i < i_q} a_i' \big| .$$

If $i_q \in X$, we treat the distribution as a continuous one with the weight of each key spread across an interval (the cost is invariant to the size of the interval). The fraction of the weight a_{i_q} of i_q that lies "below" the quantile point is

$$\delta_q = \frac{1}{a_{i_q}}(q a_S - \sum_{i \in S | i < i_q} a_i) ,$$

and so the change in weight across q is

$$\Delta_q = \big| \big(\delta_q a_{i_q} + \sum_{i \in S | i < i_q} a_i\big) - \big(\delta_q a_{i_q}' + \sum_{i \in S | i < i_q} a_i'\big) \big|$$

The range cost is defined as the sum (integral) of variances $\mathsf{E}[\Delta_q^2]$ across all half-spaces, i.e. all quantiles $0 \leq q \leq 1$ of S.

$$\rho(X) = \mathsf{E}[\int_0^1 \Delta_q^2 dq] \equiv \int_0^1 E[\Delta_q^2] dq .$$

In the full version of this paper, we show that this cost is minimized when the pivot set X is a pair of keys (i.e. $X = \{i_1, i_2\}$) and that the range cost is

$$\rho(\{i_1, i_2\}) = a_{i_1} a_{i_2} (\tfrac{1}{3}(a_{i_1} + a_{i_2}) + a_{S_M}) , \qquad (6)$$

where $S_M = \{i : i_1 < i < i_2\}$ is the subset of all keys in S that lie strictly between i_1 and i_2.

The range cost can be computed efficiently: Algorithm 3 presents pseudocode of an algorithm which finds $\rho(X)$ in $O(|X|)$ time. It first computes prefix sums W_j of the weights of keys in X (line 6), and values y_j which are the sums of weights between the jth and $j + 1$th keys in X (line 9): computing each takes constant time, assuming that we have access to the prefix sums of weights in S. Then lines 13 and 14 use these values to compute the range cost, following our (omitted) analysis Consequently, we can find the range cost of *every* pair i_1, i_2 in time $O(|S|^2)$, and pick the best to pivot on. Section 5 discusses choices which compromise on picking the best pair to reduce this time cost.

4.3 Hierarchy

We use the above analysis of order to analyze the hierarchy case. There are many possible ways to linearize a hierarchy to produce an order. Here we consider *all* possible linearizations, and take

Algorithm 3 RANGE-COST(X)

Require: $|X| \geq 2$
1:   $X \leftarrow \text{CAND}(a, X)$
2:   $M \leftarrow M(a, X)$
Require: $X = \{i_1, \ldots, i_{|X|}\}, i_1 < i_2 < \cdots < i_{|X|}$

3:   $W_0 \leftarrow 0$
4:   **for** $j = 1, \ldots, |X|$ **do**
5:      $w_j \leftarrow a_{i_j}$ ▷ weight of key i_j.
6:      $W_j \leftarrow W_{j-1} + w_j$ ▷ weight of j smallest keys in X
7:   **end for**
8:   **for** $j = 1, \ldots, |X| - 1$ **do**
9:      $y_j \leftarrow \sum_{h \in S \setminus X | i_j < h < i_{j+1}} a_h$
         ▷ Weight of keys in S that are between i_j and i_{j+1}.
10:   **end for**
11:   $R \leftarrow 0$ ▷ Initialize
12:   **for** $\ell = 0, \ldots, |X| - 1$ **do**
13:      $R \leftarrow R + y_\ell (M\ell - W_\ell)(W_\ell - (\ell - 1)M)$
        ▷ contribution of q when $i_q \in S \setminus X$ is between i_ℓ and $i_{\ell+1}$.
14:      $R \leftarrow R + w_{\ell+1}(\ell M - W_\ell)(W_{\ell+1} - \ell M) + \frac{w_{\ell+1}^2}{3}(M - w_{\ell+1})$
        ▷ contribution of q such that $i_q = i_{\ell+1}$.
15:   **end for**
16:   **return** R/a_S

---

the average of the range costs of the corresponding order structure. When the pivot set X is two leaf nodes u, v we use (6) and obtain

$$\rho(\{u, v\}) = a_u a_v \left(\tfrac{1}{3}(a_u + a_v + a_{S_M}) + \tfrac{1}{2} a_{S_C}\right). \quad (7)$$

To define these terms, we let $r = \text{LCA}(u, v)$ be the lowest common ancestor of u and v. Then S_M is the set of leaf nodes in the subtree of r but which share no other ancestors below r, i.e. $y \in S \setminus \{u, v\}$ such that y is a descendant of r and $\text{LCA}(u, y) \equiv \text{LCA}(v, y) \equiv r$. Any $y \in S_M$ is placed between u and v in exactly a $1/3$ fraction of all possible linearizations. S_C corresponds to the remaining leaf nodes in the same subtree of r: the keys $y \in S \setminus \{u, v\}$ such that y is a descendant of $\text{LCA}(u, v)$ and either $\text{LCA}(u, y) \neq r$ or $\text{LCA}(v, y) \neq r$. In this case, the probability, over linearizations, that y lies between u and v is $1/2$.

We use these costs (7) to guide our selection of a pivot set X. Below we discuss how to do so efficiently.

4.4 Product space

Our results extend to the case when we have a multi-dimensional key space and each dimension is itself a partition, order and/or hierarchy. For such product spaces, we define the range cost as the average over dimensions of the 1-dimensional range costs. This corresponds to averaging over all axis-parallel halfspaces, treating all dimensions as equally important. The expressions for range cost rapidly become complex, and the search for an optimal pivot set at each step becomes costly, so we omit detailed analysis and instead identify fast heuristics to find pivot sets.

5. PIVOT SELECTION

In the previous section, we showed that the range cost of a subset X is well-defined and, given X, can be computed efficiently. However, naively searching over all $2^{|S|}$ subsets to find an applicable pivot $X \subset S$ with minimum range-cost is clearly prohibitive; we must find a pivot for every new key in the stream: this does not scale to high-volume streaming environments. The range cost $\rho(X)$ is non-decreasing when keys are added to X, while $M(a, X)$

is non-increasing. Thus, although we might find an X which minimizes $\rho(X)$, it may not be a valid pivot given the requirement on $M(a, X)$ in Algorithm 2. This strict upper bound on $M(a, X)$ forces us to consider a broader range of possible pivots. Here, we propose and evaluate heuristics for finding valid pivots with good range cost, and compare them empirically in our experiments.

5.1 Pair heuristics

Our analysis (details omitted for brevity) suggests that range cost on order structures is minimized for a pair of keys. A pair $\{i_1, i_2\}$ is applicable if and only if $w_{i_1} + w_{i_2} \leq \tau_{k/c}$. However, when $c \geq 2$, we can guarantee that there are always applicable pairs of keys in the sample (below, we show a stronger result, that there are always applicable pairs which are close together). Inspired by this, we propose some heuristics to choose pairs to pivot on.

Best pair: Select the applicable pair $\{i_1, i_2\}$ with least range cost.

For an order, Eq. (6) allows quick elimination in finding such a pair: to identify an applicable pair with minimum range cost, it suffices to consider pairs $i_1 < i_2$ such that

$$\forall i_3 \text{ such that } i_1 < i_3 < i_2, \; w_{i_3} > \max\{w_{i_1}, w_{i_2}\} \quad (8)$$

To see that this is a necessary condition, consider a triple i_1, i_2, i_3 for which this does not hold. By replacing the heavier key among i_1, i_2 with i_3, we obtain an applicable pair with a lower range cost that i_1, i_2. Consequently, any range of keys in the sample must be either disjoint or in a containment relation, and so there are at most $O(|S|)$ pairs that satisfy (8). We can find them quickly by initializing the set of candidate with all adjacent pairs. We then try to extend each candidate it turn by merging with its left or right neighbor (at most one is possible). This finds all possibilities with $O(|S|)$ work.

For a hierarchy, we maintain for each internal node the total adjusted weight under the node, and the two smallest weight keys in the subtree. In general there are many nodes in the hierarchy, but we only need to monitor those subtrees with at least two keys in the sample, and can also ignore nodes where only one descendant tree is populated. On receiving each new key, we update the stored data to meet the requirements, and pivot on the pair with lowest range cost. Updating subsequent to a pivot is fast, since the cost is proportional to the depth of the hierarchy.

For a product space, it suffices to consider only those pairs such that both keys have smaller weight than any other key in the bounding box containing them. A key is in the bounding box of two keys if on order dimensions, it lies between them, and in a hierarchy dimension, it is a descendant of their LCA. In the worst case, however, there can still be $\Omega(|S|^2)$ such pairs even for $d = 2$, so other heuristics are needed to more quickly find pivots.

Simple Nearest Neighbors heuristic (SNN). Typically, the structures we consider have a natural notion of proximity: the number of intervening keys in an order, distance to a lowest common ancestor in a hierarchy. The SNN heuristic considers one pivot pair for each sampled key i, which is its nearest neighbor in the sample. This is a good heuristic, but does not necessarily find the pair with smallest range cost. Pivoting on NN pairs gives intuitive structure awareness because the movement of weight is localized. Specifically, for order we consider the neighbors of each key; for hierarchy, the key in the same subtree as i with smallest weight; for product spaces, we maintain a KD-tree and treat it as a hierarchy. When $c \geq 2$, there must exist an applicable pair X of NN keys. To see this under order, assume k is odd, and consider the pairs of keys in the sample with non-zero weights, indexed $i_1, i_2 \ldots i_{k+1}$. Consider their IPPS

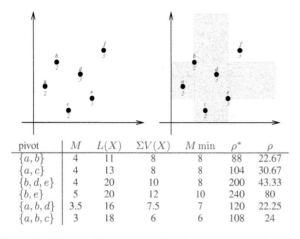

pivot	M	$L(X)$	$\Sigma V(X)$	M min	ρ^*	ρ
$\{a,b\}$	4	11	8	8	88	22.67
$\{a,c\}$	4	13	8	8	104	30.67
$\{b,d,e\}$	4	20	10	8	200	43.33
$\{b,e\}$	5	20	12	10	240	80
$\{a,b,d\}$	3.5	16	7.5	7	120	22.25
$\{a,b,c\}$	3	18	6	6	108	24

Figure 3: 5 keys with structure that is the product of two orders. Right: Span of $\{b,e\}$: keys b,d,e are counted twice in the span weight, keys a,c are counted once. The span of $\{b,e\}$ and $\{b,d,e\}$ is the same and the span weight is $L(\{b,e\}) \equiv L(\{b,d,e\}) = 20$. The table shows for pivot sets the weight-bound, span weight, ΣV, $M(a,X)\min_{i\in X}a_i$, and (unnormalized, multiplied by $2a_S$) span cost and range cost.

probabilities under $\tau_{k/2}$ in adjacent non-overlapping pairs:

$$\max\{\frac{w_{i_{2j-1}}}{\tau_{k/2}},1\} + \max\{\frac{w_{i_{2j}}}{\tau_{k/2}},1\}$$

Observe that over all $(k+1)/2$ pairs, these sums total $k/2$, and hence the mean is less than 1. Therefore there must be an applicable pair of some key and its left or right NN.

Among applicable NN pairs we can select one (i) arbitrarily (ii) with minimum range cost (iii) with minimum a_1a_2 (minimizing the ΣV variance cost), or (iv) with minimum $M(a,X) = a_1 + a_2$ (automatically ensuring that $c \leq 2$). These variations have differing costs, and we compare their cost and quality experimentally.

5.2 Span cost approximation

We define the *span cost* of a pivot X as an alternative to range cost that is easier to compute. The span cost

$$\rho^*(X) = M(a,X)(\min_{i\in X} a_i)\frac{L(X)}{d \cdot a_S} . \quad (9)$$

is a product of two main components. The first one, the *span-weight* $L(X)$ (defined below), is structure-sensitive—the more "spread out" X is, the larger it is. It captures the halfspaces impacted by pivoting on X. The second component $M(a,X)(\min_{i\in X} a_i)$ is oblivious to the structure. It is non increasing when keys are added to X since this holds for both $M(a,X)$ and $\min_{i\in X} a_i$. It captures the maximum expected variance of the pivot over a subset of X.

We now show how we define the span-weight $L(X)$: For order structures, $L(X)$ is the weight of all keys in X and all keys in $S \setminus X$ that lie between keys in X, i.e. $L(X) = \sum_{j\in S:\min(X)\leq j\leq\max(X)} a_j$. For a hierarchy, $L(X)$ is the weight under $\mathrm{LCA}(X)$, i.e. $L(X) = \sum_{j\in S:\mathrm{LCA}(j)=\mathrm{LCA}(X)} a_j$. For a product space, it is the sum over dimensions of the 1-dimensional span weights. The normalized span weight is $0 \leq \frac{L(X)}{d \cdot a_S} \leq 1$, where d is the dimension ($d = 1$ for a single order or hierarchy). It upper bounds $\frac{L(\mathrm{CAND}(X))}{d \cdot a_S}$, the fraction of halfspaces impacted by pivoting on X.[2] Similarly, the range

---

[2]However, if $L(\mathrm{CAND}(X)) < L(X)$, then there is a smaller range containing $\mathrm{CAND}(X)$ with span weight $L(\mathrm{CAND}(X))$. This range

cost $\rho(X)$, defined as the average variance over halfspaces, is also upper bounded by the span cost. An example span cost computation in shown in Figure 3.

A helpful property in searching for an applicable pivot with minimum span cost is that amongst all pivots with same span $L(X)$, the span cost is minimized by the most inclusive pivot. Consequently, it suffices to consider *complete ranges*: That is, in an order, we include all keys between the least and greatest key in the pivot. For a hierarchy, we consider only pivots that corresponds to *all* descendants of a node in the hierarchy. In a product space, products of complete ranges capture all keys within a box.

Approximate Span Cost. For product spaces, where searching through all ranges can be prohibitive, we can further limit the search space by settling for approximation. We can limit the number of 1-dimension projections, considering a subset of those where a range is included only if its weight is smaller by a factor of at least $(1+\epsilon)$ from the weight of an included range that contains it. It also suffices to consider "boxes" (products of 1-d ranges) where the span weights of each dimension are within ϵ to $1/\epsilon$ factor of each other.

6. EXPERIMENTAL EVALUATION

In this section we describe our experimental study of representative structure-aware sampling methods for summarization. We consider datasets in the 1-dimensional case when the keys take values in a hierarchies, and the 2-dimensional case when keys take values in a product of two hierarchies. We explore the behavior of several heuristics described in Section 5. We compare their performance against existing approaches, namely structure-oblivious VAROPT sampling, and the deterministic Q-digest.

6.1 Data and Hierarchy Description

Our evaluations used IP flow statistics compiled from flows observed at a router attached to network peering point. Each flow record contains 32-bit source and destination IPv4 address, taking values in the natural binary IP address hierarchy. For the 1-dimensional experiment, we projected the data set on the source address, and used both source and destination for the 2-dimensional experiments. There were 63K sources and 50K destinations, and a total of 196K pairs active in the data. These data sets are large enough to show the relative performance of different methods but small enough to enable us to compare the accuracy to methods that are less scalable. In our experiments, the keys were the (distinct) 1- and 2- dimensional addresses, and the weights were the total recorded bytes associated with each key.

6.2 Summarization Algorithms and Heuristics

We next describe the set of summarization algorithms studied. We first present the existing algorithms used as reference in the 1-dim and 2-dim cases, then the structure-aware sampling heuristics specific to each of those cases.

In choosing efficient heuristics to work with, we aim to pick methods which are comparable to existing methods in terms of their computational costs. The cost of $\mathrm{SVAROPT}_k$ is at worst $O(\log k)$ per insertion, and an amortized $O(\log \log k)$ implementation exists [5]. In order to be computationally competitive for large sample sizes, we aim to have algorithms which are no worse than $O(\log k)$. However, we also evaluate some heuristics with higher computational cost in order to determine the potential benefits in accuracy which might be achievable.

---

will have the same variance component, and hence, lower span cost. It is therefore not useful to replace $L(X)$ by (the harder to compute) $L(\mathrm{CAND}(X))$ in the span cost formula.

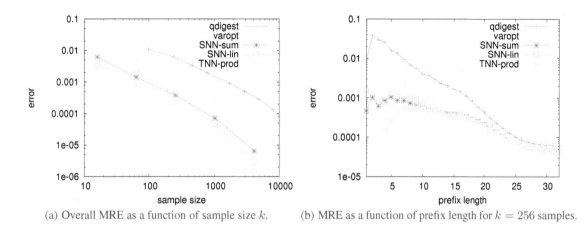

(a) Overall MRE as a function of sample size k.　　(b) MRE as a function of prefix length for $k = 256$ samples.

Figure 4: Accuracy: 1-dimension.

6.2.1　Existing Algorithms

Q-digest. The Q-digest data structure [15] imposes a (conceptual) binary tree over a domain of size U, and associates counts with a subset of nodes in the tree. A top-down version of the maintenance algorithm handles an update of weight w to key i by sharing the weight among the path of nodes from root to i so that the prefix of nodes all have count exactly $\lfloor \epsilon N / \log U \rfloor$ [9]. Here, N denotes the sum of weights observed so far, and ϵ is an error parameter. The algorithm guarantees (deterministically) that the frequency of any key or node can be estimated from the stored counts with error at most ϵN. By periodically moving weight from nodes back along their path to the root (while respecting the $\lfloor \epsilon N / \log U \rfloor$ condition on weights), the algorithm guarantees that the space required is $O(1/\epsilon \log U)$ In comparison to randomized "sketch" algorithms, the Q-digest has been observed to give much more accurate answers given the same space allocation [8].

The Q-digest approach is closely related to other Heavy Hitter focused summarization, as discussed in Section 1. For example, the trie-based solution of Zhang *et al.* [20] is essentially identical, but omits the rebalancing step since it is assumed that the total weight of keys is known in advance. For this reason, we take Q-digest as the sole representative of this class of methods.

In two dimensions (i.e. $U \times U$), the data structure performs the same algorithm on the data projected on the first dimension. But in addition to updating the weight at nodes in the tree, it also keeps a secondary Q-digest data structure at each node, and updates these with the second dimension of the key and corresponding weight. From these, it is possible to estimate the weight of any rectangle with error ϵN in space $O(1/\epsilon \log^2 U)$.

VarOpt: We compared to an implementation of the structure oblivious stream sampling scheme $\mathrm{SVAROPT}_k$ [5]. Each key observed in the data stream is added to the sample, then one is chosen for ejection to maintain a summary size of k.

6.2.2　Structure Aware Sampling in One Dimension

Based on the discussion in Section 5, we compared a variety of heuristics for pivot selection. Here, we describe how they were implemented to ensure fast per-key processing.

SNN: Simple Nearest Neighbor. As described in Section 5, the SNN heuristic restricts the pivot to be a pair. In one-dimension we maintain the IP addresses present in the sample in a binary search tree (BST) ordered by treating the key as a 32-bit integer; for simplicity we allow both left and right neighbors of a given element

to constitute a pair with it. (Note this method generalizes to pairing with nodes that are siblings in the IP address hierarchy of a left or right neighbor, but happen to be further away numerically). To allow quickly finding the best pair to pivot on, the range cost associated with each pair is maintained in an ascending order priority queue. The lowest cost pair is selected as the pivot at each step. We discuss specific range cost variants below. Updates to the BST are $O(\log k)$ in complexity, and updates to the priority queue have the same cost (since there are $O(k)$ NN pairs).

We consider the following SNN variants based on how we define the cost of a pair.

- **SNN-Sum:** the cost is set as the sum of the weights of the pair elements. We also tried using the product of the weights as the cost; the results were similar to SNN-SUM, and are omitted.

- **SNN-Lin:** uses the average range cost over all linearizations of the hierarchy, as given by (7). This is a way of adding further structure awareness to SNN. A pitfall of SNN described above is that an SNN pair can be quite distant in the IP hierarchy. The linearization cost penalizes pairs (x, y) that are distant in the hierarchy by including the weight of other descendants of $\mathrm{LCA}(x, y)$.

TNN-Prod: True Nearest Neighbor. For each node we find its nearest neighbor of minimum weight, then minimize the cost over all such pairs. The pair cost was set as the product of weights, i.e., the estimation variance associated with VAROPT sampling from a pair. Note that implementing this algorithm is more costly than the SNN approaches; we include it to compare accuracy.

6.2.3　Structure Aware Sampling in Two Dimensions

VSNN: Very Simple Nearest Neighbor. As described in Section 5.1, IPv4 address pairs are represented as points in a KD-Tree. Ideally we would want to determine true NN pairs using distance based on the IP4v hierarchy, e.g.,

$$\mathcal{D}((s_1, d_1), (s_2, d_2)) = (32 - \mathrm{PRE}(s_1, s_2)) + (32 - \mathrm{PRE}(d_1, d_2))$$

were $\mathrm{PRE}(\cdot, \cdot)$ returns the longest common prefix length. However, finding a nearest neighbor in a KD-Tree can take time linear in the number of keys stored, so we adopt a simpler approach. The VSNN of a given node is determined by finding the element in the KD-tree of minimum $\mathcal{D}$ distance, when testing all nodes (except the node itself) on the path that would be followed by a fresh insertion of the node. We then use the weight product pair cost, maintained over all

VSNN pairs in a priority queue. Similarly to the 1-dim SNN case, the complexity is $O(\log k)$ per key.

SpanApprox. This is a heuristic related to span cost in Section 5.2. In each dimension we compute internal nodes s and d in the respective spanning tree IPv4 hierarchies of the addresses of the nodes currently stored. Let S_s and D_d be the keys in the sample with source address (respectively, destination) in the subtree of s (resp., d). To choose a pivot set, then for each pair (s, d) we search for an applicable set in $S_s \cap D_d$ which induces the minimal value of the tightness parameter c in Section 3.3. The range cost associated with this set is then $W(S_s) + W(D_d)$; this is minimized over all such pairs (s, d) to select the actual pivot. This algorithm is clearly expensive computationally; we include it to compare accuracy.

6.3 Evaluation Metrics

Our principle metric for evaluating summarization accuracy is the error of the estimated weight a_J of a given node or nodes J, as compared with the actual weights w_J. This is normalized by the total weight of the whole dataset, which is equivalent to a_S. The corresponding elementary error value is $\epsilon = |a_J - w_J|/a_S$.

A given set of unsampled data is represented as leaf weights w_j. We consider the set of aggregates of these weights up the tree, i.e., $w_v = \sum_{j \in L_v} w_j$ where L_v is the set of leaf nodes descended from v. For each internal node v with non-zero actual aggregate w_v, we calculate the corresponding error ϵ_v. In order to understand the dependence of accuracy on level in the address hierarchy, we average errors of non-zero aggregates at each prefix prefix length, as the Mean Relative Error (MRE). In the two-dimensional case we consider prefixes of the same length in each of the two dimensions. Finally, we construct a global average of the length-wise error over all prefix lengths.

In the one-dimensional case, we also evaluated performance in identifying hierarchical heavy hitters (HHH). Specifically, we considered prefixes whose true aggregate weight exceeded a given threshold fraction (after discounting the weight all such prefixes under them), then calculated the Root Mean Square relative estimation error over all such nodes, over the set of runs.

6.4 Experimental Results

We extracted from our trace 10 subsets of 16,384 flows each. We employed sample sizes of $k = 64$, 256, 1024 and $4,096$, corresponding to sampling rates of 1 in $256, 64, 16$ and 4 respectively. We computed the error measured described above, averaged over the 10 runs. The algorithm implementations were constructed using Python and Perl.

One-dimensional Results. Figure 4(a) shows the global MRE in the one-dimensional case as the sample size is varied. We observe that although designed to give accurate answers for these kinds of range queries, the Q-digest approach is clearly less accurate than sampling methods on this data. This is due to the method's dependence on $\log U$, the logarithm of the domain size: in this case, it contributes a factor of 32 to the space cost. Beyond this, we still see much variation in the behavior of the sampling-based methods (note that the plot is on a log scale). SVarOpt, the state-of-the-art stream sampling method, can be improved on by up to an order of magnitude by methods which are structure-aware. Across sample sizes, the TNN-prod method consistently achieves the best (or approximately best) accuracy, since it puts more effort into finding the best NN pair to pivot on. The two SNN methods were appreciably faster to process the data, and the simplest SNN-sum method still achieves a clear improvement over SVarOpt while having low computational complexity.

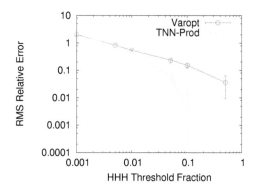

Figure 5: HHH Detection: Relative Error vs. Threshold

The MRE is broken down by prefix length in Figure 4(b) for $k = 256$ samples. For the longer prefixes, which have very low associated weight, our implementation of Q-digest essentially estimates their weight as 0. We see that even here, sampling methods can achieve better accuracy. Structure aware sampling is more accurate than structure-oblivious down to a prefix length of about 16, corresponding to ranges that are only a $1/2^{16}$ fraction of the data domain size and (roughly) the corresponding fraction of the data weight. Even the least costly computational methods (SNN) have accuracy up to an order of magnitude better than SVarOpt, with even greater gains possible for the more computationally intensive TNN. As expected SVarOpt is (barely) the most accurate for long prefixes; it has optimal variance for the case of leaf nodes. This confirms our claims, that for the common case of range queries, there are considerable benefits to making sampling structure aware.

We show an example of how improved sampling can assist data mining applications, in this example, detection of Hierarchical Heavy Hitters (HHH). Figure 5 displays the Root Mean Square relative estimation error of HHH weights for SVarOpt and TNN-prod, as a function of the HHH detection threshold. The central observation here is that the structure-aware sampling can be substantially more accurate than the structure-oblivious approach.

Two-dimensional Results. Figure 6(a) shows the global MRE in the two-dimensional case. Here, even with large values of the parameter ϵ, the Q-digest approach needs to build a summary of size 10^5 or higher to achieve good accuracy. Hence the difference between Q-digest and the sampling-based methods is more striking, being over 2 orders of magnitude on comparable sample sizes. Again, there is a clear improvement of structure aware sampling over structure oblivious. The VSNN method has less than half the error of SVarOpt for moderate sample sizes (from 10s to 1000s of sampled keys). The partial results for SpanApprox indicate that there is room for a further factor of 2 improvement. However, the more extensive search for NN pairs means that the computational cost becomes prohibitive for a sample size of more than 100.

When we compare the accuracy over different prefix lengths (Figure 6(b), we see similar behavior to the 1-dimensional case, but accentuated. Recall that here we compare queries over square ranges, corresponding to prefixes of the same length on each dimension. There is a clear benefit for VSNN over SVarOpt when the prefixes are short, corresponding to queries with an appreciable fraction of the weight. The cross-over point comes when the prefix length is about 8: this corresponds to a $2^{-16} = 1.5 \times 10^{-5}$ fraction of the toal area. So with a sample of 1024 keys, the structure-aware approach still obtains good accuracy for queries down to ranges which touch a relatively small fraction of the data. We also conducted a

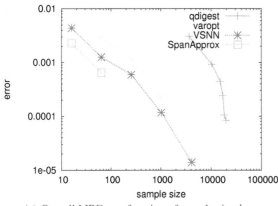

(a) Overall MRE as a function of sample size k.

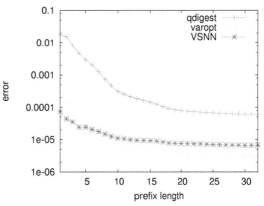

(b) MRE as a function of prefix length for $k = 1024$ samples.

Figure 6: Accuracy: 2-dimensions.

single set of experiments on the full set of 196K pair flows, comparing SVAROPT and VSNN. The behavior was similar to that just described, with VSNN outperforming SVAROPT in accuracy on queries over square ranges down to prefix lengths of 10.

Discussion. In both the one-dimensional and two-dimensional cases we saw (i) the smaller accuracy of Q-digest, relative to other methods; (ii) the greatest accuracy of the most costly heuristics; (iii) The computationally cheapest structure aware approaches based on SNN still give an considerable increase in accuracy relative to SVAROPT, down to prefix length 16 in the 1-dimensional case. That the structure-aware SSN heuristic is most accurate on queries with high weight is a factor in its favor as compared with existing methods. As expected, SVAROPT is more accurate on very small ranges. However, the penalty paid by structure aware sampling in error relative to SVAROPT in these cases is not great, making it a good general-purpose summary.

7. CONCLUDING REMARKS

We have presented a new class of algorithms for stream sampling that is *structure aware*. Structure-aware sampling combines the principal benefits of sampling, as traditionally used in a structure-oblivious manner, and of dedicated summaries designed specifically for range-sum queries and applications such as heavy hitter detection. Our summaries retain the ability to answer arbitrary subset queries and produce unbiased estimates with tail bounds on the error. These have guaranteed performance at least as good as that of smaller VAROPT summaries. At the same time, we can optimize for the structure present in the data which makes range queries much more likely than other subset queries, achieving superior accuracy on such queries. In practice this can be achieved at a low computational cost: $O(\log k)$ per new key in a buffer of k keys.

For our analysis, we used the assumption that the streams are aggregated, i.e. each key appears at most once. Our algorithms naturally extend to handle unaggregated streams, following the structure-oblivious setting [6]: if the key of the stream element is already in S, the adjusted weight is increased by new value (no need to pivot). Our analysis, however, does not cover this case. In future work, we plan to study structure-aware summarization of unaggregated data streams, where keys may appear multiple times and the weight of a key is the sum of weights over occurrences.

8. REFERENCES

[1] C. Buragohain and S. Suri. Quantiles on streams. In *Encyclopedia of Database Systems*. Springer, 2009.

[2] M. T. Chao. A general purpose unequal probability sampling plan. *Biometrika*, 69(3):653–656, 1982.

[3] H. Chernoff. A measure of the asymptotic efficiency for test of a hypothesis based on the sum of observations. *Annals of Math. Statistics*, 23:493–509, 1952.

[4] E. Cohen, G. Cormode and N. Duffield. Structure-aware sampling: Flexible and accurate summarization. arXiv:1102.5146, 2011.

[5] E. Cohen, N. Duffield, H. Kaplan, C. Lund, and M. Thorup. Stream sampling for variance-optimal estimation of subset sums. In *ACM-SIAM SODA*, 2009.

[6] E. Cohen, N. Duffield, H. Kaplan, C. Lund, and M. Thorup. Composable, Scalable, and Accurate Weight Summarization of Unaggregated Data Sets In *VLDB*, 2009.

[7] E. Cohen, N. Duffield, C. Lund, M. Thorup, and H. Kaplan. Variance optimal sampling based estimation of subset sums. Tech. report arXiv:0803.0473v1 [cs.DS], 2008.

[8] G. Cormode and M. Hadjieleftheriou. Finding frequent items in data streams. In *VLDB*, 2008.

[9] G. Cormode, F. Korn, S. Muthukrishnan, and D. Srivastava. Space- and time-efficient deterministic algorithms for biased quantiles over data streams. In *ACM PODS*, 2006.

[10] G. Cormode, F. Korn, S. Muthukrishnan, and D. Srivastava. Finding hierarchical heavy hitters in streaming data. *ACM Trans. Knowl. Discov. Data*, 1(4):1–48, 2008.

[11] R. Gandhi, S. Khuller, S. Parthasarathy, and A. Srinivasan. Dependent rounding and its applications to approximation algorithms. *J. Assoc. Comput. Mach.*, 53(3):324–360, 2006.

[12] J. Hájek. *Sampling from a finite population*. Marcel Dekker, 1981.

[13] D. G. Horvitz and D. J. Thompson. A generalization of sampling without replacement from a finite universe. *J. Amer. Stat. Assoc.*, 47(260):663–685, 1952.

[14] A. Panconesi and A. Srinivasan. Randomized distributed edge coloring via an extension of the Chernoff-Hoeffding bounds. *SIAM J. Comput.*, 26(2):350–368, 1997.

[15] N. Shrivastava, C. Buragohain, D. Agrawal, and S. Suri. Medians and beyond: new aggregation techniques for sensor networks. In *ACM SenSys*, 2004.

[16] A. Srinivasan. Distributions on level-sets with applications to approximation algorithms. In *IEEE FOCS*. 2001.

[17] M. Szegedy and M. Thorup. On the variance of subset sum estimation. In *Proc. ESA*, 2007.

[18] Y. Tillé. *Sampling Algorithms*, Springer, 2006.

[19] J. Vitter. Random sampling with a reservoir. *ACM Trans. Math. Softw.*, 11(1):37–57, 1985.

[20] Y. Zhang, S. Singh, S. Sen, N. Duffield, and C. Lund. Online identification of hierarchical heavy hitters. In *SIGMETRICS*, 2004.

APPENDIX

A. OMITTED PROOFS

Proof of Theorem 3

PROOF OF THEOREM 3. We use the fact that over the set of all random variables $X \in [0,1]$ with expectation p, $\mathsf{Var}[X]$ is maximized for $X \in \{0,1\}$, that is, the Bernoulli random variable which is $X = 1$ with probability p and $X = 0$ otherwise.

Under VAROPT with $\tau_{k^*(M)}$, the HT adjusted weight a_i is equal to $\tau_{k^*(M)}$ with probability $w_i/\tau_{k^*(M)}$ and 0 otherwise. For an M-bounded summary, the adjusted weight a_i' satisfies $a_i' \leq M \leq \tau_{k^*(M)}$.

From unbiasedness, $\mathsf{E}[a_i] = \mathsf{E}[a_i'] = w_i$. The random variables $a_i/\tau_{k^*(M)}$ and $a_i'/\tau_{k^*(M)}$ are both in $[0,1]$ and both have the same expectation. The random variable $a_i/\tau_{k^*(M)}$ is in $\{0,1\}$ and hence $\mathsf{Var}[a_i/\tau_{k^*(M)}] \geq \mathsf{Var}[a_i'/\tau_{k^*(M)}]$, implying $\mathsf{Var}[a_i] \geq \mathsf{Var}[a_i']$. $\square$

Proof of Theorem 4

PROOF OF THEOREM 4. We establish that the tail bounds on a_J obtained, as explained in Section 2, by first excluding keys with $a_i \geq M$ from the estimate and then applying Chernoff bounds hold for M-bounded summaries.

All keys with $w_i \geq M$ appear with their actual weight in the M-bounded summary, and hence, can also be excluded. We thus assume all keys in J have $w_i < M$.

Consider the random variables $X_i = a_i/M$ which are in $[0,1]$. We have $p_i = \mathsf{E}[X_i] = w_i/M$. We have that for any $J \subseteq [n]$,

(I): $\qquad \mathsf{E}[\prod_{i \in J} X_i] \leq \prod_{i \in J} p_i$

(E): $\qquad \mathsf{E}[\prod_{i \in J}(1 - X_i)] \leq \prod_{i \in J}(1 - p_i)$

It is established in [14] (see also [11, 7]) that for $X_i \in \{0,1\}$, these properties imply Chernoff tail bounds on $\sum_{i \in J} p_i$.

When used with VAROPT [7], we apply the inequalities with respect to the random variables $a_i/\tau \in \{0,1\}$. The bounds are then multiplied by τ to obtain bounds on the weights.

It is not hard to verify that the proofs that (I) and (E) imply these bounds carry over when we allow X_i to assume fractional values $X_i \in [0,1]$. By multiplying the bounds we obtain on $\sum_{i \in J | w_i < M} p_i$ by M, we obtain corresponding bounds on $\sum_{i \in J | w_i < M} w_i$.

Since $M \leq \tau_{k^*(M)}$, the bounds are at least as tight as the tail bounds we obtain for VAROPT$_{k^*(M)}$. $\square$

Proof of Lemma 5

PROOF OF LEMMA 5. Let a' be thr output of PIVOT(a, X). As the other properties are straightforward, it remains to establish (3) and (4). That is, for any subset J, and $\overline{M} \geq M(a, X)$,

(I): $\qquad \mathsf{E}[\prod_{i \in J} a_i'] \leq \prod_{i \in J} a_i$

(E): $\qquad \mathsf{E}[\prod_{i \in J}(\overline{M} - a_i')] \leq \prod_{i \in J}(\overline{M} - a_i)$

It suffices to show this for $J \subset \text{CAND}(X)$, since for $i \notin \text{CAND}(X)$, $a_i' \equiv a_i$, and the contributions of these keys to the products in both sides of the inequalities are the same. To simplify notation, we assume $X = \text{CAND}(X)$. This is without loss of generality since the pivot step is identical when applied to X or to $\text{CAND}(X)$.

Inclusion Bound (I). The probability that item $i \in J$ has $a_i' = 0$ is $1 - \frac{a_i(|X|-1)}{a_X}$. Since these are disjoint events for different keys, the probability that one key from J has $a_i' = 0$ is $|J| - \frac{a_J(|X|-1)}{a_X}$.

Hence, the probability that all keys in J have $a_i' = M(a, X)$ is $\frac{a_J(|X|-1)}{a_X} - |J| + 1$. The product $\prod_{i \in J} a_i' = 0$ if a key from J has $a_i' = 0$ and is $M(a, X)^{|J|}$ otherwise. Thus,

$$\mathsf{E}[\prod_{i \in J} a_i'] = \left(\frac{a_J(|X|-1)}{a_X} - |J| + 1\right)(M(a,X))^{|J|} . \quad (10)$$

Because we have $X = \text{CAND}(X)$, it must satisfy the condition $\forall i \in X, a_i \leq M(a, X) = a_X/(|X|-1)$. Therefore,

$$a_J = a_X - a_{X \setminus J} = a_X - \sum_{i \in X \setminus J} a_i$$
$$\geq a_X - (|X| - |J|)\frac{a_X}{|X|-1} = a_X \frac{|J|-1}{|X|-1} .$$
$$a_J \leq a_X \frac{|J|}{|X|-1} .$$

For a given J and total adjusted weight a_J, $\prod_{i \in J} a_i$ is minimized when one key in J has $a_i = a_J - a_X \frac{|J|-1}{|X|-1}$ and the $|J| - 1$ other keys in J having adjusted weights $a_i = \frac{a_X}{|X|-1}$. Hence,

$$\prod_{i \in J} a_i \geq \left(\frac{a_X}{(|X|-1)}\right)^{|J|-1}\left(a_J - a_X \frac{|J|-1}{|X|-1}\right)$$
$$= \left(\frac{a_X}{(|X|-1)}\right)^{|J|}\left(\frac{a_J(|X|-1)}{a_X} - |J| + 1\right) \quad (11)$$

The bound (I) follows by combining (10) and (11).

Exclusion bound (E). By definition, $\overline{M} \geq M(a, X)$. Because $J \subset \text{CAND}(X)$, for all $i \in J$, $a_i' \leq M(a, X) \leq \overline{M}$ and $a_i \leq M(a, X) \leq \overline{M}$. For a given J and a_J, $\prod_{i \in J}(\overline{M} - a_i)$ is minimized when one key in J has $a_i = a_J - a_X \frac{|J|-1}{|X|-1}$ and other keys in J have $a_i = \frac{a_X}{|X|-1}$. Therefore,

$$\prod_{i \in J}(\overline{M} - a_i) \geq \left(\overline{M} - a_J + a_X \frac{|J|-1}{|X|-1}\right)\left(\overline{M} - \frac{a_X}{|X|-1}\right)^{|J|-1} \quad (12)$$

The value of $\prod_{i \in J}(\overline{M} - a_i')$ is equal to $(\overline{M} - \frac{a_X}{|X|-1})^{|J|}$ if all keys in $i \in J$ have $a_i' = M(a, X)$ and is equal to $\overline{M}(\overline{M} - \frac{a_X}{|X|-1})^{|J|-1}$ otherwise (one of the keys has $a_i' = 0$). Substituting the probabilities of these two outcomes we obtain

$$\mathsf{E}[\prod_{i \in J}(\overline{M} - a_i')]$$
$$= \left(\overline{M} - \frac{a_X}{|X|-1}\right)^{|J|-1}\left(\overline{M}\left(|J| - \frac{a_J(|X|-1)}{a_X}\right)\right) +$$
$$\left(\overline{M} - \frac{a_X}{|X|-1}\right)^{|J|}\left(\frac{a_J(|X|-1)}{a_X} - (|J|-1)\right)$$
$$= \left(\overline{M} - \frac{a_X}{|X|-1}\right)^{|J|-1}\left(\overline{M} - a_J + a_X \frac{|J|-1}{|X|-1}\right) \quad (13)$$

(E) follows by combining (12) and (13). $\square$

Proof of Lemma 7

PROOF OF LEMMA 7. This clearly holds for the $h \leq k$ prefix of the stream, since $a \equiv w$. For $h > k$, the proof proceeds by induction. Assume that at the beginning of the iteration $\ell = h - k$ the sample S is a $\tau_{k/c}(w_1, \ldots, w_{h-1})$-bounded summary of the input $(w_1, \ldots, w_{h-1})$. From the algorithm, all keys for which the adjusted weight had increased during iteration ℓ have final adjusted weight value $\leq \tau_{k/c}(a_{S \cup \{h\}}) = \tau_{k/c}(w_1, \ldots, w_h)$. Thus it is a $\tau_{k/c}(w_1, \ldots, w_h)$ bounded summary. $\square$

Gossip PCA

Satish Babu Korada
Department of Electrical
Engineering
Stanford, CA 94305
satishbabu.k@gmail.com

Andrea Montanari
Department of Electrical
Engineering and Department
of Statistics
Stanford University
Stanford, CA 94305
montanari@stanford.edu

Sewoong Oh
EECS Department
Massachusetts Institute of
Technology
Cambridge, MA 02139
swoh@mit.edu

ABSTRACT

Eigenvectors of data matrices play an important role in many computational problems, ranging from signal processing to machine learning and control. For instance, algorithms that compute positions of the nodes of a wireless network on the basis of pairwise distance measurements require a few leading eigenvectors of the distances matrix. While eigenvector calculation is a standard topic in numerical linear algebra, it becomes challenging under severe communication or computation constraints, or in absence of central scheduling. In this paper we investigate the possibility of computing the leading eigenvectors of a large data matrix through gossip algorithms.

The proposed algorithm amounts to iteratively multiplying a vector by independent random sparsification of the original matrix and averaging the resulting normalized vectors. This can be viewed as a generalization of gossip algorithms for consensus, but the resulting dynamics is significantly more intricate. Our analysis is based on controlling the convergence to stationarity of the associated Kesten-Furstenberg Markov chain.

Categories and Subject Descriptors

C.2.4 [**Computer-Communication Networks**]: Distributed Systems—*Distributed applications*

General Terms

Algorithms, Performance

1. INTRODUCTION AND OVERVIEW

Consider a system formed by n nodes with limited computation and communication capabilities, and connected via the complete graph K_n. To each edge (i, j) of the graph is associated the entry M_{ij} of an $n \times n$ symmetric matrix M. Node i has access to the entries of M_{ij} for $j \in \{1, \ldots, n\}$. An algorithm is required to compute the eigenvector of M corresponding to the eigenvalue with the largest magnitude.

Denoting by $u \in \mathbb{R}^n$ the eigenvector, each node i has to compute the corresponding entry u_i. The eigenvector u is often called the *principal component* of M, and analysis methods that approximate a data matrix by its leading eigenvectors are referred to as principal component analysis [19].

Eigenvector calculation is a key step in many computational tasks, e.g. dimensionality reduction [29], classification [17], latent semantic indexing [7], link analysis (as in PageRank) [6]. The primitive developed in this paper can therefore be useful whenever such tasks have to be performed under stringent communication and computation constraints. As a stylized application, consider the case in which the nodes are n wireless hand-held devices (for related commercial products, see [1, 2, 3]). Accurate positioning of the nodes in indoor environments is difficult through standard methods such as GPS [26]. Because of intrinsic limitation of GPS and of roof scattering, indoor position uncertainty can be of 10 meters or larger, which is too much for locating a room in a building. An alternative approach consists in measuring pairwise distances through delay measurements between the nodes and reconstructing the nodes positions from such measurements (obviously this is possible only up to a global rotation or translation). Positions indeed can be extracted from the matrix of square distances by computing its three leading eigenvectors (after appropriate centering) [24]. This method is known as multidimensional scaling, and we will use it as a running example throughout this paper.

A simple method for computing the eigenvector is to collect all the matrix entries at one special node, say node i, to perform the eigenvector calculation and then flood back its entries to each node. This centralized approach has several disadvantages. It requires communicating n^2 real numbers through the network at the beginning of execution, puts a large memory, computation and communication burden on node i, and is fragile to failure or Byzantine behavior of i.

The next simplest idea is to use some version of the *power method*. A decentralized power method would proceed by synchronized iterations through the network. At t-th iteration, each node keeps a running estimate $x_i^{(t)}$ of the leading eigenvector. This is updated by letting $x_i^{(t+1)} = \sum_{j=1}^n M_{ij} x_j^{(t)}$. If M has strong spectral features (in particular, if the two largest eigenvalues are not close) these estimates will converge rapidly. On the other hand, each iteration requires $(n-1)$ real numbers to be transmitted to each node, and n sums and multiplications to be performed at the node. In other words, the node capabilities have to scale with the network size. This problem becomes even more severe for wireless devices, which are intrinsically interference-limited.

Within the power method approach, n^2 communications have to be scheduled at each time thus requiring significant bandwidth. Finally, the algorithm requires complete synchronization of the n^2 communications and is fragile to link failures (which can be quite frequent e.g. due to fading).

A simple and yet powerful idea that overcomes some of these problems is sparsification. Throughout the paper, we say that $S \in \mathbb{R}^{n \times n}$ is a *sparsification* of M if it is obtained by setting to 0 some of the entries of M and (eventually) rescaling the non-zero entries. A sparsification is useful if most of its entries are zero, and yet the resulting matrix has a leading eigenvector close to the original one. Given a sparsified matrix S, power method can be applied by $x_i^{(t+1)} = \sum_{j=1}^n S_{ij} x_j^{(t)}$. If S has d-nonzero entries per row, each node needs to communicate d real numbers, and to perform d sums and multiplications. For wireless devices, the badwidth scales at most like nd.

In [4] Achlioptas and McSherry showed that a sparsification can be constructed such that

$$\|M - S\|_2 \le \theta \|M\|_2 , \tag{1}$$

with only $d = O(1/\theta^2)$ non-zero entries per row. The inequality (1) immediately implies that computing the leading eigenvector of S, yields an estimator $\widehat{u}$ that satisfies $\|\widehat{u} - u\| \le 2\theta$. (Here and below, for $v, w \in \mathbb{R}^m$, v^* denotes its transpose and $\langle v, w \rangle = v^* w$ denotes the scalar product of two vectors. Let $\|v\| = \langle v, v \rangle$ denote its Euclidean –or ℓ_2– norm, i.e. $\|v\|^2 \equiv \sum_{i=1}^n v_i^2$. For a matrix A, $\|A\|_2$ denotes its ℓ_2 operator norm, i.e. $\|A\|_2 \equiv \sup_{v \ne 0} \|Av\|/\|v\|$.) The construction of [4] is based on random sampling. Each entry of M is set to 0 independently with a given probability $1 - p = 1 - d/n$. Non-zero entries are then rescaled by a factor $1/p$. The bound (1) is proved to hold with high probability with respect to the randomness in the sparsification.

While this scheme is simple and effective, it presents important shortcomings: (*i*) When per node complexity scales as $1/\theta^2$, this procedure achieves precision θ: can one achieve a better scaling? (*ii*) A fixed subnetwork G of the complete graph (corresponding to the sparsity pattern) needs to be maintained through the whole process. This can be challenging in the presence of fading or of node failures/departures. (*iii*) The target precision is to be decided at the beginning of the process, when the sparsification is constructed.

In this paper we use sparsification as a primitive and propose a new way to exploit its advantages. Roughly speaking at each round t a new independent sparsification $S^{(t)}$ of M is produced. Estimates of the leading eigenvector are generated by applying $S^{(t)}$, i.e. through

$$x^{(t)} = S^{(t)} x^{(t-1)} , \tag{2}$$

and then averaging across iterations $\widehat{u}^{(t)} \propto \sum_{\ell \le t} x^{(\ell)}/\|x^{(\ell)}\|$. We will refer to this algorithm as GOSSIP PCA. In the limit case in which $S^{(t)}$ are in fact deterministic and coincide with a fixed S, the present scheme reduces to the previous one. However, general independent random sparsifications $S^{(t)}$ can model the effect of fading, short term link failures, node departures. (While complete independence is a simplistic model for these effects, it should be possible to include short time-scale correlations in our treatment.) Finally, the use of truly random, independent sparsifications might be a choice of the algorithm designer.

Does the time-variability of $S^{(t)}$ deteriorate the algorithm precision? Surprisingly, the opposite turns out to be true:

Using independent sparsifications appears to benefit accuracy by effectively averaging over a larger sample of the entries of M. As an example consider the sparsification scheme mentioned above, namely each entry of $S^{(t)}$ is set to 0 independently with a fixed probability $1 - p$. Then, with respect to the total per-node computation and communication budget, scaling of the ℓ_2 error $\|\widehat{u} - u\|$ remains roughly the same as in the time-independent case (see Section 3). Remarkably, the way optimal accuracy is achieved is significantly different from the one that is optimal within the time-independent case. In the latter case it is optimal to invest resources in the densest possible sparsification S, and then iterate it a few times. Within the present approach, one should rather use much sparser matrices $S^{(t)}$ and iterate the basic update (2) many more times. The use of sparser subnetworks is advantageous both for robustness and the overhead of maintaining/synchronizing such networks.

Our main analytical result is an error bound for the time-dependent iteration (2), that takes the form

$$\|\widehat{u}^{(t)} - u\| \le C \left(\theta/\sqrt{t} + \theta^2 \log(1/\theta)^2 \right) , \tag{3}$$

with a constant C explicitly given below. Notice that, for t large enough, this yields an error roughly of size θ^2. While using the same number of communications per node, this is significantly smaller than the error θ obtained by computing the leading eigenvector of a single sparsification.

The upper bound (3) holds under the following three assumptions: (*i*) $\|M - S^{(\ell)}\|_2 \le \theta \|M\|_2$ for all $\ell \le t$; (*ii*) $\mathbb{E}(S^{(\ell)}) = M$; (*iii*) $S^{(\ell)}$ invertible for all ℓ. Further it is required that the initial condition satisfies $\|x^{(0)} - u\| \le C\theta$. This can be generated by iterating a fixed sparsification (say $S^{(1)}$) for a modest number of iterations (roughly $\log(1/\theta)$). Numerical simulations and heuristic arguments further suggest that the last assumption is actually a proof artifact and not needed in practice (see further discussion in Section 2.2).

The rest of the paper is organized as follows: Section 2 provides a formal description of our algorithms and of our general performance guarantees. In Section 3 we discuss implications of our analysis in specific settings. Section 4 reviews related work on randomized low complexity methods. Section 5 describes the proof of our main theorem. This leverages on the theory of products of random matrices, a line of research initiated by Furstenberg and Kesten in the sixties [15], with remarkable applications in dynamical systems theory [25]. The classical theory focuses however on matrices of fixed dimension, in the limit of an infinite number of iterations, while here we are interested in high-dimensional (large n) applications. We need therefore to characterize the tradeoff between dimensions and number of iterations. In Section 6, we provide the proof of the technical lemmas used in the main proof. Finally, Section 7 discusses extending our algorithm to estimate the largest eigenvalues and provides a general performance guarantee.

2. MAIN RESULTS

In this section, we spell out the algorithm execution and state the main performance guarantee.

2.1 Algorithm

As mentioned in the previous section $M \in \mathbb{R}^{n \times n}$ is a symmetric matrix, with eigenvalues $\lambda_1, \lambda_2, \ldots, \lambda_n$. Without loss of generality, we assume that the largest eigenvalue λ_1 is positive. Further, we assume $\lambda_1 > |\lambda_2|$ strictly. We will also write $\lambda \equiv \lambda_1$ and u for the corresponding eigenvector.

We assume to have at our disposal a primitive that outputs a random sparsification S of M. A sequence of independent such sparsifications will be denoted by $\{S^{(1)}, S^{(2)}, \dots\}$. In the next two paragraphs we describe a centralized version of the algorithm, and then the fully decentralized one.

2.1.1 Centralized algorithm

The system is initialized to a vector $x^{(0)} \in \mathbb{R}^n$. Then we iteratively multiply the i.i.d. sparsifications $S^{(1)}, S^{(2)}, \dots$ to get a sequence of vectors $x^{(1)}, x^{(2)}, \dots$. After t iterations, our estimate for the leading eigenvector u is

$$\widehat{u}^{(t)} = c(t) \sum_{s=1}^{t} \frac{x^{(s)}}{\|x^{(s)}\|}, \qquad (4)$$

with $c(t)$ the appropriate normalization to ensure $\|\widehat{u}^{(t)}\| = 1$.

Note that, even after normalization, there is a residual sign ambiguity: both u and $-u$ are eigenvector. When in the following we write that $\widehat{u}^{(t)}$ approximate u within a certain accuracy, it is understood that $\widehat{u}^{(t)}$ does in fact approximate the closest of u and $-u$. A more formal resolution of this ambiguity uses the projective manifold define in Section 5.

2.1.2 Decentralized algorithm

The algorithm described so far uses the following operations: *(i) Multiplying vector $x^{(t-1)}$ by $S^{(t)}$*, cf. Eq. (2). If $S^{(t)}$ has dn non-zero elements, this requires $O(d)$ operations per node per round.

(ii) Computing the normalizations $\|x^{(1)}\|, \|x^{(2)}\|, \dots, \|x^{(t)}\|$. Since $\|x^{(\ell)}\|^2 = \sum_{i=1}^{n} (x_i^{(\ell)})^2$, this task can be performed via a standard gossip algorithm. This entails an overhead of $\log(1/\varepsilon)$ per node per iteration for a target precision ε. We will neglect this contribution in what follows.

(iii) Averaging normalized vectors across iterations, cf. Eq. (4). Since node i keeps the sequence of estimates $x_i^{(1)}, \dots, x_i^{(t)}$, this can be done without communication overhead, with $O(1)$ computation per node per iteration.

Finally the normalization constant $c(t)$ in Eq. (4) needs to be computed. This amounts to computing the norm of the vector on the right hand side of Eq. (4), which is the same operation as in step (2) (but has to be carried out only once). From this description, it is clear that operation (1) (matrix-vector multiplication) dominates the complexity and we will focus on this in our discussion below and in Section 3.

2.2 Analysis

The algorithm design/optimization amounts to the choice of number of iterations t and the the sparsification method, which produces the i.i.d. matrices $\{S^{(\ell)}\}$. The latter is characterized by two parameters: θ which bounds the sparsification accuracy as per Eq. (1), and d, the average number of non-zero entries per row, which determines its complexity.

The trade-off between d and θ depends on the sparsification method and will be further discussed in the next section. Our main result bounds the error of the algorithm in terms of θ, t and of a characteristic of the matrix M, namely the ratio of the two largest eigenvalues $l_2 = |\lambda_2|/\lambda$. The proof of this theorem is presented in Section 5.

THEOREM 2.1. *Let $\{S^{(\ell)}\}_{\ell \geq 1}$ be a sequence of i.i.d. $n \times n$ random matrices such that $\mathbb{E}[S^{(\ell)}] = M$, $\|S^{(\ell)} - M\|_2 \leq$*

$\theta \|M\|_2$, $S^{(\ell)}$ *is almost surely non-singular, and there is no proper subspace $V \subseteq \mathbb{R}^n$ such that $S^{(\ell)}V \subseteq V$ almost surely. Further, let $x^{(0)} \in \mathbb{R}^n$ be such that $\|x^{(0)} - u\| \leq \theta/(1-l_2)$ for the leading eigenvector of u. Let the eigenvector estimates be defined as per Eq. (2) and (4). Finally assume $\theta \leq (1/40)(1-l_2)^{3/2}$ and let $l_2 \equiv |\lambda_2|/\lambda$.*

Then, with probability larger than $1 - \max(\delta, 16/n^2)$,

$$\|\widehat{u}^{(t)} - u\| \leq \frac{18\theta}{(1-l_2)\sqrt{t\delta}} + 12\left(\frac{\theta \log(1/\theta)}{(1-l_2)}\right)^2. \qquad (5)$$

The assumption on the samples $\{S^{(\ell)}\}_{\ell \geq 0}$ are rather mild. The matrix whose eigenvector we are computing is the expectation of $S^{(\ell)}$, the variability of $S^{(\ell)}$ is bounded in operator norm, and finally the $S^{(\ell)}$ are sufficiently random (in particular the do not share an eigenvector *exactly*). The latter can be ensured by adding arbitrarily small random perturbation to $S^{(\ell)}$.

At first sight, the assumption $\|x^{(0)} - u\| \leq \theta/(1-l_2)$ on the initial condition might appear unrealistic: the algorithm requires as input an approximation of the eigenvector u. A few remarks are in order. *First*, the accuracy of the output, see Eq. (5), is dramatically higher than on the input for $t = \Omega(1/\theta^2)$. In the following section, we will see that this is indeed the correct scaling of t that achieves optimal performance. *Second*, numerical simulations show clearly that, for $\mathbf{x}^{(t)} = x^{(t)}/\|x^{(t)}\|$, the condition $\|\mathbf{x}^{(t)} - u\| \leq \theta/(1-l_2)$ is indeed satisfied after a few iterations. The heuristic argument is that the leading eigenvectors of $S^{(1)}, S^{(2)}, \dots S^{(t)}$ are roughly aligned with u, and their second eigenvalues are significantly smaller. Hence the scalar product $Z_t \equiv \langle u, \mathbf{x}^{(t)} \rangle$ behaves approximately as a random walk with drift pushing out of $Z_t = 0$. Even if $Z_0 = 0$, random fluctuations produce a non-vanishing Z_t, and the drift amplify this fluctuation exponentially fast. The arguments in Section 5 further confirm this heuristic argument. For instance we will prove that the set $\|\mathbf{x}^{(t)} - u\| \leq \theta/(1-l_2)$ is absorbing, in the sense that starting from such a set, the power iteration keeps $\mathbf{x}^{(t)}$ in the same set. On the other hand, starting from any other point, there is positive probability of reaching the absorbing set. Finally, further evidence is provided by the fact that random initialization is sufficient for the eigenvalue estimation as proved in Section 7.

As an example, we randomly generated a marix M and computed $\mathbf{x}^{(t)} = x^{(t)}/\|x^{(t)}\|$ according to (2) using random sparsifications with dn entries. Let $\tau = \arg\min_t\{\|\mathbf{x}_{\mathrm{rand}}^{(t)} - \mathbf{x}_u^{(t)}\| \leq 0.001\}$. The subscript denotes two different initializations: $x_{\mathrm{rand}}^{(0)}$ is initialized with i.i.d Gaussian entries, and $x_u^{(0)} = u$. The following result illustrates that after a few iterations $t = O(\log(1/\theta))$, $\mathbf{x}^{(t)}$ achieves error of order θ with $d = O(1/\theta^2)$ operations per node per round.

d	40	80	160	320
τ	5.1	4.8	4.2	3.7
$\|\mathbf{x}_{\mathrm{rand}}^{(\tau)} - u\|$	0.1110	0.0761	0.0521	0.0329

Finally, constructing a rough approximation of the leading eigenvector is in fact an easy task by multiplying the same sparsification $S^{(0)}$ a few times. This claim is made precise by the following elementary remark.

REMARK 2.2. *Assume that $x^{(0)}$ have i.i.d. components $\mathsf{N}(0, 1/n)$, and define $x^{(t)} = S^{(t)}x^{(t-1)}$ where for $t \leq t_*$,*

$S^{(t)} = S$ is time independent and satisfies $\|S - M\|_2 \le (\theta^2/2(1-l_2))\|M\|_2$. If $t_* \ge 3\log(n/\theta)/(1-l_2-\theta)$, then $\|\mathbf{x}^{(t_*)} - u\| \le \theta/(1-l_2)$ with probability at least $1 - 1/n^2$.

The content of this remark is fairly intuitive: the principal eigenvector of S is close to u, and the component of $x^{(t)}$ along it grows exponentially faster than the other components. A logarithmic number of iterations is then sufficient to achieve the desired distance from u.

Finally, consider the assumption $\mathbb{E}[S^{(\ell)}] = M$. In practice, it might be difficult to produce unbiased sparsifications: does Theorem 2.1 provide any guarantee in this case? The answer is clearly affirmative. Let $\mathbb{E}[S^{(\ell)}] = M'$ and assume $\|M - M'\|_2 \le \theta'\|M\|_2$. Then, it follows immediately from (5) that

$$\|\widehat{u}^{(t)} - u\| \le \frac{18\theta}{(1-l_2)\sqrt{t\delta}} + 12\left(\frac{\theta\log(1/\theta)}{(1-l_2)}\right)^2 + \frac{2\theta'}{1-l_2},$$

In other words the eigenvector approximation degrades gracefully with the quality of the sparsification.

3. EXAMPLES AND APPLICATIONS

In this section we apply our main theorem to specific settings and point out possible extensions.

3.1 Computation-accuracy tradeoff

As mentioned above, Theorem 2.1 characterizes the scaling of accuracy with the quality of the sparsification procedure. For the sake of simplicity, we will consider the case in each entry of M is set to 0 independently with a fixed probability $1 - d/n$, and non-zero entries are rescaled. In other words $S_{ij} = (n/d)M_{ij}$ with probability (d/n), and $S_{ij} = 0$ otherwise. This scheme was first analyzed in [4], but the estimate only holds for $d \ge (8\log n)^4$. This condition was refined in [22]. Noting that for $d > \log n$ the maximum number of entries per row is of order d, the latter gives

$$\|M - S\|_2 \le (C/\sqrt{d})\|M\|_2 \equiv \theta\|M\|_2.$$

In other words i.i.d. sparsification of the entries yields $\theta = O(1/\sqrt{d})$. Further, denoting the total complexity per node by χ, we have $\chi \sim td$ either in terms of communication or of computation.

In order to compute a computation-accuracy tradeoff we need to link the accuracy to t and θ. Let us first consider the case in which a single sparsification S is used by letting $x^{(t)} = Sx^{(t-1)}$ and $\widehat{u}^{(t)} = x^{(t)}/\|x^{(t)}\|$. This procedure converges exponentially fast to the leading eigenvector of S which in turn satisfies $\|\widehat{u}^{(\infty)} - u\| \le 2\theta \le C'(1/\sqrt{d})$. Therefore if we denote by $\Delta_{\mathrm{PM}} \equiv \|\widehat{u}^{(t)} - u\|$ the corresponding error after t iterations, we have

$$\Delta_{\mathrm{PM}} \sim \theta + e^{-at},$$

where we deliberately omit constants since we are only interested in capturing the scaling behavior.

Now we assume that we have a limit on the total complexity $\chi \sim td$, and minimize the error Δ_{PM} under this resources constraint, using the relation $\theta \sim 1/\sqrt{d}$. A simple calculation shows that the smallest error is achieved when $t = \Theta(\log \chi)$ yielding

$$\Delta_{\mathrm{PM}} \sim \sqrt{(\log \chi)/\chi}. \tag{6}$$

Next consider the algorithm developed in the present paper, GOSSIP PCA. The only element to be changed in our analysis is the relation between accuracy and the parameters θ and t. From Theorem 2.1 we know that our estimator achieves error $\Delta_{\mathrm{Gossip}} = \|\widehat{u}^{(t)} - u\|$ that scales as

$$\Delta_{\mathrm{Gossip}} \sim \theta/\sqrt{t} + \left(\theta\log(1/\theta)\right)^2,$$

where again we omit constants. It is straightforward to minimize this expression under the constraints $\chi \sim td$, and $\theta \sim 1/\sqrt{d}$. The best scaling is achieved when $t = \Theta(\sqrt{\chi}/(\log\chi)^2)$ and $\theta = \Theta(1/(\chi^{1/4}\log\chi))$ yielding

$$\Delta_{\mathrm{Gossip}} \sim 1/\sqrt{\chi}. \tag{7}$$

Comparing (6) and (7), the scaling of the error with the per-node computation and communication remains roughly the same up to a logarithmic factor. Surprisingly, the way the best accuracy is achieved is significantly different. In the time-independent case (the standard power method), it is optimal to invest a lot of resources in one iteration with a dense matrix S that has $d = \Theta(\chi/\log\chi)$ non-zero entries per row. In return, only a few iterations $t = \Theta(\log\chi)$ are required. Within the proposed time-dependent gossip approach, one should rather use a much sparser matrices $S^{(\ell)}$ with $d = \Theta(\sqrt{\chi}(\log\chi)^2)$ non-zero entries per row and use a larger number of iterations $t = \Theta(\sqrt{\chi}/(\log\chi)^2)$.

To illustrate how the two gossip algorithms compare in practice, we present results of a numerical experiment from the positioning application. From 1000 nodes placed in the 2-dimensional unit square uniformly at random, we define the matrix of squared distances. Let p_i be the position of node i, then $D_{ij} = \|p_i - p_j\|^2$. After a simple centering operation, the top two eigenvectors reveal the position of the nodes up to a rigid motion (translation and/or rotation) [24]. We can extend the gossip algorithms to estimate the first two eigenvectors as explained in Section 3.3. Let the columns of $U \in \mathbb{R}^{1000\times 2}$ be the first two eigenvectors and $\|\cdot\|_F$ be the Frobenius norm of a matrix such that $\|A\|_F^2 = \sum_{i,j} A_{ij}^2$. Denote by $\Delta(d) = (1/\sqrt{2})\|U - \widehat{U}\|_F$ the resulting error for a particular choice of d.

To simulate a simple gossip setting with constrained communication, we allow d to be either 50 or 500. For the two gossip algorithms and for each value of the total complexity χ, we plot the minimum error achieved using one of the two allowed communication schemes: $\min_{d\in\{50,500\}} \Delta(d)$. For comparison, performance of the power method on complete dense matrices is also shown (see Section 1). As expected from the analysis, GOSSIP PCA achieved smaller error with sparse matrices ($d = 50$) for all values of χ. When a single sparsification is used, there is a threshhold at $\chi = 14500$, above which a dense matrix ($d = 500$) achieved smaller error. Notice a discontinuity of the derivative at the threshold.

3.2 Comparison with gossip averaging

Gossip methods have been quite successful in computing symmetric functions of data $\{x_i^{(0)}\}_{1\le i\le n}$ available at the nodes. The basic primitive in this setting is a procedure computing the average $\sum_{i=1}^n x_i^{(0)}/n$. This algorithm shares similarities with the present one. One recursively applies independent random matrices $P^{(1)}, P^{(2)}, \dots$ according to:

$$x^{(t)} = P^{(t)}x^{(t-1)}, \tag{8}$$

where $P^{(t)}$ is the matrix that averages entries $i(t)$ and $j(t)$

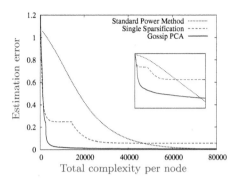

Figure 1: Eigenvector estimation error against complexity. In the inset the result is plotted in log-scale.

of $x^{(t)}$ (in other words it is the identity outside a 2×2 block corresponding to coordinates $i(t)$ and $j(t)$).

It is instructive to compare the two problems. In the case of simple averaging, one is interested in approximating the action of a projector P, namely the matrix with all entries equal to $1/n$. In eigenvector calculations the situation is not as simple, because the matrix of interest M is not a simple projector. In both cases we approximate this action by products of i.i.d. random matrices whose expectation matches the matrix of interest. However in averaging, the leading eigenvector of P is known *a priori*, it is the constant vector $u = (1/\sqrt{n}, \ldots, 1/\sqrt{n})$. As a consequence, sparsifications $P^{(t)}$ can be constructed in such a way that $P^{(t)}u = u$ with probability 1.

Reflecting these differences, the behavior of the present algorithm is qualitatively different from gossip averaging. Within the latter $x^{(t)}$ converges asymptotically to the constant vector, whose entries are equal to $\sum_{i=1}^{n} x_i^{(0)}/n$. The convergence rate depends on the distribution of the sparsification $P^{(t)}$. In GOSSIP PCA, the sequence of normalized vectors $x^{(t)}/\|x^{(t)}\|$ does not converges to a fixed point. The distribution of $x^{(t)}/\|x^{(t)}\|$ instead converges to a non-trivial stationary distribution whose mean is approximated by $\widehat{u}^{(t)}$. An important step in the proof of Theorem 2.1 consists in showing that the mean of this distribution is much closer to the eigenvector than a typical vector drawn from it.

3.3 Extensions

It is worth pointing out some extensions of our results, and interesting research directions:

More than one eigenvector. In many applications of interest, we need to compute r leading eigenvectors, where r is larger than one, but typically a small number. In the case of positioning wireless devices, r is consistent with the ambient dimensions, hence $r = 3$. As for the standard power iteration, the algorithm proposed here can be generalized to this problem. At iteration t, the algorithm keeps track of r orthonormal vectors $x^{(t)}(1), \ldots x^{(t)}(r)$. In the distributed version, node i stores the i-th coordinate of each vector, thus requiring $O(r)$ storage capability. The vectors are updated by letting $\widetilde{x}^{(t)}(a) = S^{(t)}x^{(t)}(a)$. and then orthonormalizing $\widetilde{x}^{(t)}(1), \ldots \widetilde{x}^{(t)}(r)$ to get $x^{(t)}(1), \ldots x^{(t)}(r)$. Orthonormalization can be done locally at each node if it has access to the Gram matrix $G = (G_{ab})_{1 \le a,b \le r}$

$$G_{ab} \equiv \frac{1}{n} \sum_{i=1}^{n} \widetilde{x}_i^{(t)}(a) \widetilde{x}_i^{(t)}(b) \qquad (9)$$

This can be computed via gossip averaging, using messages consisting of $r(r+1)/2$ real numbers. Therefore the total communication complexity per node per iteration is of order $r^2 \log(1/\varepsilon)$ to achieve precision ε. Indeed, such distributed orthonormalization procedure was studied in [21] for decentralized implementation of the standard power method.

Richer stochastic models for random sparsification. Our main result holds under the assumption that $S^{(1)}, S^{(2)}, \ldots, S^{(t)}$ are i.i.d. sparsifications of the matrix M. This is a reasonable assumption when the random sparsifications are generated by the algorithm itself. The same assumption can also model short time-scale link failures, as due for instance to fast fading in a wireless setting. On the other hand, a more accurate model of link failures would describe $S^{(1)}$, $S^{(2)}, \ldots, S^{(t)}$ as a stochastic process. We think that our main result is generalizable to this setting under appropriate ergodicity assumptions on this process. More explicitly, as long as the underlying stochastic process mixes (i.e. loses memory of its initial state) on time scales shorter than t, the qualitative features of Theorem 2.1 should remain unchanged. Partial support of this intuition is provided by the celebrated Oseledets' multiplicative ergodic theorem that guarantees convergence the exponential growth rate of $\|x^{(t)}\|$ in a very general setting [25] (namely within the context of ergodic dynamical systems).

Communication constraints: Rate and noise. In a decentralized setting, it is unavoidable to take into consideration communication rate constraints and communication errors. The presence of errors implies that the actual matrix used at iteration t is not $S^{(t)}$ but is rather a perturbation of it. The effect of noise can then be studied through Theorem 2.1. Rate constraints imply that real numbers cannot be communicated through the network, unless some quantization is used. An approach consists in using some form of randomized rounding for quantization. In this case, the effect of quantization can also be studied through Theorem 2.1. This implies that, roughly speaking, the error in the eigenvector computed with this approach scales quadratically in the quantization step. (Notice that quantization also affects the vector on the right-hand side of Eq. (2), but we expect this effect to be roughly of the same order as the effect of the quantization of $S^{(t)}$.) Further, when the matrix M itself is sparse, or a fixed sparsification S is used within the ordinary power method, Theorem 2.1 can be used to study the effect of noise and quantization.

4. RELATED WORK

The need for spectral analysis of massive data sets has motivated a considerable effort towards the development of randomized low complexity methods. A short sample of the theoretical literature in this topic includes [9, 4, 10, 14, 12, 11]. Two basic ideas are developed in this line of research: *sparsify* of the original matrix M to reduce the cost of matrix-vector multiplication; *apply* the matrix M to a random set of vectors in order to approximate its range. Both of these approaches are developed in a centralized setting where a single dataset is sent to a central processor. While this allows for more advanced algorithms than power iteration, these algorithms might not be directly applicable in a decentralized setting considered in this paper, where each node has limited computation and comunication capability and the datasets are often extremely large such that the data has to be stored in a distributed manner.

Fast routines for low-rank approximation are useful in the areas of optimization, scientific computing and simulations. Hence similar ideas were developed in that literature: we refer to [16] for references and an overview of the topic.

Kempe and McSherry [21] studied a decentralized power iteration algorithm for spectral analysis. They considered matrices that are inherently sparse. Therefore, no sparsification is used, all the entries are exploited at every iteration, and their algorithm eventually computes the optimal low-rank approximation exactly. They also introduced the decentralized orthonormalization mentioned in Section 3.3.

The idea of using a sequence of distinct sparsifications to improve the accuracy of power iteration was not studied in this context. Somewhat related is the basic idea in randomized algorithms for gossip averaging [5]. As discussed in Section 3.2, these algorithms operate by applying a sequence of i.i.d. random matrices to an initial vector of data. The behavior and analysis is however considerably simplified by the fact that these matrices share a common leading eigenvector, that is known *a priori*, namely the eigenvector $u = (1/\sqrt{n}, \ldots, 1/\sqrt{n})$. Overviews of this literature is provided by [27] and [8]. Quantization is an important concern in the practical implementation of gossip algorithms, and has been studied in particular in the context of consensus [20, 13]. As discussed in the last section, the effect of randomized quantization can also be included in the present setting.

Finally, there has been recent progress in the development of sparsification schemes that imply better error guarantees than in Eq. (1), see for instance [28]. It would be interesting to study the effect of such sparsification methods in the present setting.

5. PROOF OF THE MAIN THEOREM

In this section, we analyze the quality of the estimation provided by our algorithm and prove Theorem 2.1. Before diving into the technical argument, it is worth motivating the main ideas. We are interested in analyzing the random trajectory $\{x^{(t)}\}_{t \geq 0}$ defined as per Eq. (2). One difficulty is that this process cannot be asymptotically stationary, since $x^{(t)}$ gets multiplied by a random quantity. Hence it will either grow exponentially fast or shrink exponentially fast.

A natural solution to this problem would be to track the normalized vectors $\widetilde{x}^{(t)} \equiv x^{(t)}/\|x^{(t)}\|$. Also this approach presents some technical difficulty that can be grasped by considering the special case in which $S^{(t)} = M$ for all t (no sparsification is used). Neglecting exceptional initial conditions (such that $\langle x^{(0)}, u \rangle = 0$) this sequence can either converge to u or to $-u$. In particular, it cannot be uniformly convergent. The right way to eliminate this ambiguity is to track the unit vectors $\widetilde{x}^{(t)}$ 'modulo overall sign'. The space of unit vectors modulo a sign is the projective space P_n, that we will introduce more formally below.

We are therefore naturally led to consider the random trajectory $\{x_t\}_{t \geq 0}$ –indeed a Markov chain– taking values in the projective space $x_t \in \mathsf{P}_n$. We will prove that two important facts hold under the assumptions of Theorem 2.1: (1) The chain converges quickly to a stationary distribution μ; (2) The distance between the baricenter of μ and u is of order θ^2. Fact (1) implies that $\widehat{u}^{(t)}$, cf. Eq. (4), is a good approximation of the baricenter of μ. Fact (2) then implies Theorem 2.1.

In the next subsection we will first define formally the process $\{\mathbf{x}_t\}_{t \geq 0}$, and provide some background (Section 5.1), and then present the formal proof (Section 5.2), along the lines sketched above.

5.1 The Kesten-Furstenberg Markov chain

As anticipated above, we shall denote by P_n the projective space in $\mathbb{R}^n$. This is defined as the space of lines through the origin in $\mathbb{R}^n$. Equivalently, P_n is the space of equivalence classes in $\mathbb{R}^n \setminus \{0\}$ for the equivalence relation $\sim_\mathsf{P}$, such that $x \sim_\mathsf{P} y$ if and only if $x = \lambda y$ for some $\lambda \in \mathbb{R} \setminus \{0\}$. This corresponds with the description given above, since it coincides with the space of equivalence classes in $S^n \equiv \{x \in \mathbb{R}^n : \|x\| = 1\}$ for the equivalence relation $\sim_\mathsf{P}$, such that $x \sim_\mathsf{P} y$ if and only if $x = \lambda y$ for some $\lambda \in \{+1, -1\}$.

In the future, we denote elements of P_n by boldface letters $\mathbf{x}, \mathbf{y}, \mathbf{z}, \ldots$ and the corresponding representatives in $\mathbb{R}^n$ by $x, y, z, \ldots$. We generally take these representatives to have unit norm. We use a metric on this space defined as

$$d(\mathbf{x}, \mathbf{y}) \equiv \sqrt{1 - \langle x, y \rangle^2} \,.$$

Random elements in P_n will be denoted by boldface capitals $\mathbf{X}, \mathbf{Y}, \mathbf{Z}, \ldots$.

An invertible matrix $S \in \mathbb{R}^{n \times n}$ acts naturally on P_n, by mapping $\mathbf{x} \in \mathsf{P}_n$ (with representative x) to the element $\mathbf{y} \in \mathsf{P}_n$ with representative of Sx (namely the line through Sx, or the unit vector $Sx/\|Sx\|$ modulo sign). We will denote this action by writing $\mathbf{y} = S\mathbf{x}$, but emphasize that it is a non-linear map, since it implicitly involves normalization.

Given a sequence of i.i.d. random matrices $\{S^{(t)}\}_{t \geq 1}$ that are almost surely invertible, with common distribution p_S, we define the Markov chain $\{\mathbf{X}_t\}_{t \geq 0}$ with values in P_n as

$$\mathbf{X}_t = S^{(t)} S^{(t-1)} \cdots S^{(1)} \mathbf{X}_0 \,, \tag{10}$$

for all $t \geq 1$. We assume the following conditions:

L1. There exists no proper linear subspace $V \subseteq \mathbb{R}^n$ such that $S^{(1)} V \subseteq V$ almost surely.

L2. There exist a sequence $\{S^{(t)}\}_{t \geq 1}$ in the support of p_S, such that letting $S^T \equiv S^{(T)} S^{(T-1)} \cdots S^{(1)}$, we have $\sigma_2(S^T)/\sigma_1(S^T) \to 0$ as $T \to \infty$.

It was proved in [23], that, under the assumptions L1 and L2, there exists a unique measure μ on P_n that is stationary for the Markov chain $\{\mathbf{X}_t\}$. The Markov chain converges to the stationary measure as $t \to \infty$ (we refer to the Appendix for a formal statement).

For the purpose of proving Theorem 2.1, uniqueness of the stationary measure is not enough: we will need to control the rate of convergence to stationarity. We present here a general theorem to bound the rate of convergence, and we will apply it to the chain of interest in the next section. Let us start by stating two more assumptions. We denote by $\mathsf{G} \subseteq \mathsf{P}_n$ a (measurable) subset of the projective space, and assume that there exists a constant $\rho \in (0, 1)$ such that

A1. For any $\mathbf{x} \in \mathsf{G}$, $S^{(t)} \mathbf{x} \in \mathsf{G}$ almost surely.

A2. For any $\mathbf{x} \neq \mathbf{y} \in \mathsf{G}$, $\mathbb{E}\left[d(S^{(t)} \mathbf{x}, S^{(t)} \mathbf{y}) \right] \leq \rho \, d(\mathbf{x}, \mathbf{y})$.

We then have the following.

THEOREM 5.1. *Assume conditions* L1 *and* L2 *hold, together with* A1 *and* A2. *Denote by* μ *the unique stationary measure of the Markov chain* $\{\mathbf{X}_t\}_{t \geq 0}$. *Then*

$$\mu(\mathsf{G}^c) = 0 \,.$$

Further, if $\mathbf{X}_0 \in \mathsf{G}$ then for any L-Lipschitz function[1] $f :$ $\mathsf{P}_n \to \mathbb{R}$, we have

$$\left| \mathbb{E}[f(\mathbf{X}_t)] - \mu(f) \right| \le L \rho^t .$$

The proof of this Theorem uses a coupling technique analogous to the one of [23]. We present it in the appendix for greater convenience of the reader.

5.2 Proof of Theorem 2.1

In this section we analyze the GOSSIP PCA algorithm using the general methodology developed above. In particular, we consider the Markov chain (10) whereby $\{S^{(\ell)}\}_{1 \le \ell \le t}$ are i.i.d. sparsifications of M satisfying the conditions: (i) $\|S^{(\ell)} - M\|_2 \le \theta\|M\|_2$; (ii) $\mathbb{E}[S^{(\ell)}] = M$; (iii) $S^{(\ell)}$ is almost surely non-singular. Throughout the proof, we let $\mathbf{u} \in \mathsf{P}_n$ denote an element of P_n represented by u.

Note that the conditions L1 stated in the previous section holds by assumption in Theorem 2.1. Further let $\lambda_1(\ell)$ and $\lambda_2(\ell)$ the largest and second largest singular values of $S^{(\ell)}$. By assumption (i), and since by hypothesis $\theta \le (1/40)(1 - l_2)^{3/2}$, implying $\|S^{(\ell)} - M\|_2 \le (\lambda - |\lambda_2|)/2$, we have $|\lambda_1(\ell)/\lambda_2(\ell)| > 1$ almost surely. Hence by taking $S^{(1)} = S^{(2)} = \cdots = S^{(T)} = \ldots$ in the support of p_S, we have that condition L2 holds as well.

By applying the main theorem in [23] (restated in the Appendix), we conclude that there exists a unique stationary distribution μ for the Markov chain $\{\mathbf{X}_t\}$, and that the chain converges to it.

We next want to apply Theorem 5.1 to bound the support and the rate of convergence to this stationary distribution. We define the 'good' subset $\mathsf{G} \subseteq \mathsf{P}_n$ by

$$\mathsf{G} = \left\{ \mathbf{x} \in \mathsf{P}_n : d(\mathbf{x}, \mathbf{u}) \le \frac{2\theta}{1 - l_2} \right\} . \tag{11}$$

Our next lemma shows assumptions A1 and A2 are satisfied in this set G, with a very explicit expression for the contraction coefficient ρ. We refer to Section 6.2 for the proof.

LEMMA 5.2. *Under the hypothesis of Theorem 2.1, for any $\mathbf{x} \in \mathsf{G}$ we have $S^{(\ell)}\mathbf{x} \in \mathsf{G}$. Further, for any $\mathbf{x} \ne \mathbf{y} \in \mathsf{G}$, letting $\rho \equiv 1 - (4/5)(1 - l_2) \in (0, 1)$, we have*

$$\mathbb{E}d(S^{(\ell)}\mathbf{x}, S^{(\ell)}\mathbf{y}) \le \rho\, d(\mathbf{x}, \mathbf{y}) .$$

As a consequence, we can apply Theorem 5.1. In particular, we conclude that μ is supported on the good set G. Next, consider the estimate $\widehat{u}^{(t)} \in \mathbb{R}^n$ produced by our algorithm, cf. Eq. (4). This is given in terms of the Markov chain on P_n by

$$\widehat{u}^{(t)} = \frac{\sum_{\ell=1}^{t} f(\mathbf{X}_\ell)}{\|\sum_{\ell=1}^{t} f(\mathbf{X}_\ell)\|} ,$$

where we define $f : \mathsf{P}_n \mapsto \mathbb{R}^n$ such that $f(\mathbf{x})$ is a representative of $\mathbf{x}$ satisfying $\|f(\mathbf{x})\| = 1$ and $\langle u, f(\mathbf{x})\rangle \ge 0$. We use $\mathbf{U}_t \in \mathsf{P}_n$ to denote an element in P_n represented by $\widehat{u}^{(t)}$.

Let $\mu(f) = \int f(\mathbf{x})\mu(d\mathbf{x}) \in \mathbb{R}^n$ be the expectation of $f(\cdot)$ with respect to the stationary distribution (informally, this is the baricenter of μ). With a slight abuse of notation, we let $\mu(f)$ denote the corresponding element in P_n as well. Then, by the triangular inequality, we have, for any t,

$$d(\mathbf{u}, \mathbf{U}_t) \le d(\mathbf{u}, \mu(f)) + d(\mathbf{U}_t, \mu(f)) .$$

[1]We say that f is L-Lipschitz if, for any $\mathbf{x}, \mathbf{y} \in \mathsf{P}_n$, $|f(\mathbf{x}) - f(\mathbf{y})| \le L\, d(\mathbf{x}, \mathbf{y})$.

The left hand side is the error of our estimate of the leading eigenvector. This is decomposed in two contributions: a deterministic one, namely $d(\mathbf{u}, \mu(f))$, that gives the distance between the leading eigenvector and the baricenter of μ, and a random one i.e. $d(\mathbf{U}_t, \mu(f))$, that measures the distance between the average of our sample and the average of the distribution.

In order to bound $d(\mathbf{U}_t, \mu(f))$, we use the following fact that holds for any $a, b \in \mathbb{R}^n$

$$\sqrt{1 - \frac{\langle a, b\rangle^2}{\|a\|^2\|b\|^2}} \le \frac{\|a - b\|}{\sqrt{\|a\|\|b\|}} . \tag{12}$$

This follows immediately from $2\|a\|\|b\| - 2\langle a, b\rangle \le \|a - b\|^2$. We apply this inequality to $a = \mu(f)$ and $b = (1/t)\sum_{\ell=1}^{t} f(\mathbf{X}_\ell)$. We need therefore to lower bound $\|\mu(f)\|$ and $\|(1/t)\sum_{\ell=1}^{t} f(\mathbf{X}_\ell)\|$ and to upper bound $\|(1/t)\sum_{\ell=1}^{t} f(\mathbf{X}_\ell) - \mu(f)\|$.

Denote by $\mathcal{P}_u$ the orthogonal projector onto u. From Theorem 5.1, we know that $\mu(\mathsf{G}^c) = 0$. Hence, using $\theta < (1/40)(1 - l_2)^{3/2}$, we have $\|\mu(f)\| \ge \|\mu(\mathcal{P}_u(f))\| \ge \sqrt{1 - 1/400}$. Similarly since $\mathbf{X}_0 \in \mathsf{G}$, we have by A1 that $\mathbf{X}_\ell \in \mathsf{G}$ for all ℓ, and therefore $\|(1/t)\sum_{\ell=1}^{t} f(\mathbf{X}_\ell)\| \ge \sqrt{1 - 1/400}$. We are left with the task of bounding $\|a - b\|$. This is done in the next lemma that uses in a crucial way Theorem 5.1.

LEMMA 5.3. *Under the hypothesis of Theorem 2.1*

$$\mathbb{E}\left\| \frac{1}{t}\sum_{\ell=1}^{t} f(\mathbf{X}_\ell) - \mu(f) \right\|^2 \le \frac{70\theta^2}{(1 - l_2)^2 t} .$$

Applying Markov's inequality and Eq. (12), we get,

$$d(\mathbf{U}_t, \mu(f)) \le 12\theta/\big((1 - l_2)\sqrt{t\delta}\big) ,$$

with probability larger than $1 - \delta/2$. Next, we bound the term $d(\mathbf{u}, \mu(f))$ in Eq. (12) with the following lemma.

LEMMA 5.4. *Under the hypothesis of Theorem 2.1,*

$$d(\mathbf{u}, \mu(f)) \le 8\left(\frac{\theta \log(1/\theta)}{(1 - l_2)} \right)^2 .$$

By noting that $\|u - \widehat{u}^{(t)}\| \le \sqrt{2}\, d(\mathbf{u}, \widehat{\mathbf{U}}_t)$, this finishes the proof of the theorem.

6. PROOF OF TECHNICAL LEMMAS

6.1 Proof of Remark 2.2

Assuming initial vector $X \in \mathbb{R}^n$ with i.i.d. Gaussian entries, we can get close to u by iteratively applying a single sparsification S. Define a good set of initial vectors

$$\mathcal{F}_n = \left\{ x \in \mathbb{R}^n : |u^*x| \ge n^{-5/2} \text{ and } \max_{i \in [n]} |u_i^* x| \le \sqrt{6\log n/n} \right\} .$$

Since, $u_i^* X$'s are independent and distributed as $\mathsf{N}(0, 1/n)$, it follows that we have $\mathbb{P}(|u_i^* X| \ge \sqrt{(6\log n)/n}) \le 2/n^3$ and $\mathbb{P}(|u^* X|) \le 1/n^2$. Applying union bound, we get $\mathbb{P}(X \in \mathcal{F}_n) \ge 1 - 3/n^2$. Assuming we start from this good set, we show that for k large enough, we are guaranteed to have $\|u - \mathbf{x}^{(k)}\| \le \theta/(1 - l_2)$.

Let $\{\widetilde{\lambda}_i\}$ be the eigenvalues of S such that $\widetilde{\lambda}_1 \ge |\widetilde{\lambda}_2| \ge \cdots \ge |\widetilde{\lambda}_n|$, and let $\{\widetilde{u}_i\}$ be the corresponding eigenvectors. We know that $\widetilde{\lambda}_1 > 0$ since $\widetilde{\lambda}_1 \ge \lambda - \|S - M\|_2$ and $\|S - M\|_2 < \lambda$ by assumption. Then, by the triangular inequality,

$$\|u - \mathbf{x}^{(k)}\| \le \|u - \widetilde{u}\| + \|\widetilde{u} - \mathbf{x}^{(k)}\| .$$

To bound the first term, note that

$$\|M - S\|_2 \geq |u^t(M-S)u| \geq \lambda - \widetilde{\lambda}_1(u^*\widetilde{u})^2 - \widetilde{\lambda}_2\|\mathcal{P}_{\widetilde{u}^\perp}(u)\|^2 .$$

This implies that $(u^*\widetilde{u})^2 \geq (\lambda - \widetilde{\lambda}_2 - \|M-S\|_2)/(\widetilde{\lambda}_1 - \widetilde{\lambda}_2)$. We can further apply Weyl's inequality [18], to get $|\widetilde{\lambda}_i - \lambda_i| \leq \|M-S\|_2$. It follows that $(u^*\widetilde{u})^2 \geq (\lambda - \lambda_2 - 2\|M - S\|_2)/(\lambda - \lambda_2 + 2\|M-S\|_2)$. Note that this bound is nontrivial only if $\|M-S\|_2 \leq (\lambda - \lambda_2)/2$. Using the fact that $(1-a)/(1+a) \geq (1-a)^2$ for any $|a| < 1$, this implies that

$$\|u - \widetilde{u}\| \leq \sqrt{4\|M-S\|_2/(\lambda - \lambda_2)} .$$

In particular, for $\|M-S\|_2 \leq \theta^2\|M\|_2/(2(1-l_2))$ as per our assumption, this is less than $\sqrt{2}\theta/(1-l_2)$.

To bound the second term, we use $x^{(0)} \in \mathcal{F}_n$ to get

$$
\begin{aligned}
\frac{(\widetilde{u}^* S^k x^{(0)})^2}{\|S^k x^{(0)}\|^2} &\geq \frac{1}{1 + \sum_{i \geq 2} \frac{\widetilde{\lambda}_i^{2k}}{\widetilde{\lambda}_1^{2k}} \frac{(\widetilde{u}_i^* x^{(0)})^2}{(\widetilde{u}_1^* x^{(0)})^2}} \\
&\geq 1 - (\widetilde{\lambda}_2/\widetilde{\lambda}_1)^{2k} 6 n^5 \log n \\
&\geq 1 - \frac{\theta^2}{4(1-l_2)^2} .
\end{aligned}
$$

In the last inequality we used $k \geq 3\log(n/\theta)/(1 - l_2 - \theta)$, and the fact that $(\widetilde{\lambda}_2/\widetilde{\lambda}_1) \leq l_2 + \theta$. Then, $\|\widetilde{u} - \mathbf{x}^{(k)}\| \leq \theta/(\sqrt{2}(1-l_2))$. Collecting both terms, this proves the desired claim. $\square$

6.2 Proof of Lemma 5.2

LEMMA 6.1 (CONTRACTION). *For a given $\nu \leq (1/20)$, assume that x, x' satisfy $\|x\| = \|x'\| = 1$, $\langle u, x \rangle \geq 0$, $\langle u, x' \rangle \geq 0$, $\|\mathcal{P}_{u^\perp}(x)\| \leq \nu$, and $\|\mathcal{P}_{u^\perp}(x')\| \leq \nu$. Then, under the hypothesis of Lemma 5.2, we have*

$$\left\|\mathcal{P}_{u^\perp}\left(\frac{Qx}{\|Qx\|} - \frac{Qx'}{\|Qx'\|}\right)\right\| \leq (l_2(1 + 3\nu^2) + 3\theta)\|z - z'\| , \tag{13}$$

and

$$\left\|\mathcal{P}_u\left(\frac{Qx}{\|Qx\|} - \frac{Qx'}{\|Qx'\|}\right)\right\| \leq (4\nu + 4\theta)\|z - z'\| , \tag{14}$$

where $l_2 \equiv |\lambda_2|/\lambda$, $z = \mathcal{P}_{u^\perp}(x)$ and $z' = \mathcal{P}_{u^\perp}(x')$.

PROOF. By the assumption that $\langle u, x \rangle \geq 0$ and $\langle u, x' \rangle \geq 0$, we have $x = \sqrt{1 - \|z\|^2}u + z$ and $x' = \sqrt{1 - \|z'\|^2}u + z'$. The following inequalities, which follow from $\|Q - M\|_2 \leq \theta\lambda$, will be frequently used.

$$
\begin{aligned}
(1-\theta)\lambda &\leq \|Qu\| \leq (1+\theta)\lambda , \\
(l_2 - \theta)\lambda &\leq \|Qz\| \leq (l_2 + \theta)\lambda .
\end{aligned}
$$

The following inequalities will also be useful in the proof.

$$\|x - x'\| \leq (1/\sqrt{1-\nu^2})\|z - z'\| , \tag{15}$$

where we used $\sqrt{1 - a^2} - \sqrt{1 - b^2} \leq (\nu/\sqrt{1-\nu^2})|a - b|$ for $|a| \leq \nu$ and $|b| \leq \nu$. Similarly, using the fact that Mu and Mz are orthogonal

$$
\begin{aligned}
\|Qx\| &\geq (\sqrt{1 - \|z\|^2})\|Mu\| - \|Q - M\|_2 \\
&\geq \lambda(\sqrt{1-\nu^2} - \theta) , \tag{16}
\end{aligned}
$$

Next, we want to show that

$$\left|\frac{1}{\|Qx\|} - \frac{1}{\|Qx'\|}\right| \leq \frac{(2.2\nu + 0.1\theta)}{(\sqrt{1-\nu^2} - \theta)^3}\|z - z'\| . \tag{17}$$

We use the equality $1/a - 1/b = (a^2 - b^2)/(ab(a+b))$ with $a = \|Qx\|$ and $b = \|Qx'\|$. The denominator can be bounded using (16). It is enough to bound $|\|Qx'\|^2 - \|Qx\|^2|$ using

$$
\begin{aligned}
&\left|\|Q(\sqrt{1 - \|z\|^2}u + z)\|^2 - \|Q(\sqrt{1 - \|z'\|^2}u + z')\|^2\right| \\
&\leq \left|\|z\|^2 - \|z'\|^2\right|\|Qu\|^2 + \left|\|Qz\|^2 - \|Qz'\|^2\right| \\
&\quad + 2\left|(\sqrt{1 - \|z\|^2}z - \sqrt{1 - \|z'\|^2}z')^*Q^*Qu\right| .
\end{aligned}
$$

Note that $\left|\|z\|^2 - \|z'\|^2\right|\|Qu\|^2 \leq 2\nu(1 + \theta)^2\lambda^2\|z - z'\|$, and $\left|\|Qz\|^2 - \|Qz'\|^2\right| \leq 2\nu(l_2 + \theta)^2\lambda^2\|z - z'\|$. The last term can be decomposed into

$$
\begin{aligned}
&2\left|(\sqrt{1 - \|z\|^2}z - \sqrt{1 - \|z'\|^2}z')^*Q^*Qu\right| \\
&\leq 2|\sqrt{1 - \|z\|^2} - \sqrt{1 - \|z'\|^2}|\,|z^*Q^*Qu| \\
&\quad + 2\sqrt{1 - \|z'\|^2}\,|(z - z')^*Q^*Qu| .
\end{aligned}
$$

Note that $|\sqrt{1 - \|z\|^2} - \sqrt{1 - \|z'\|^2}| \leq (\nu/\sqrt{1-\nu^2})\|z - z'\|$, $|z^*Q^*Qu| \leq \lambda^2\theta(l_2 + \theta)$, and $|(z - z')^*Q^*Qu| \leq \lambda^2(l_2 + \theta)\theta\|z - z'\|$. Collecting all the terms and assuming $\theta \leq 1/40$ and $\nu \leq 1/20$, $|\|Qx\| - \|Qx'\|| \leq (4.4\nu + 0.1\theta)\lambda^2\|z - z'\|$. this implies (17).

To prove (13), define $T_1 \equiv \mathcal{P}_{u^\perp}(Qx - Qx')/\|Qx\|$ and $T_2 \equiv \mathcal{P}_{u^\perp}(Qx')\big((1/\|Qx\|) - (1/\|Qx'\|)\big)$. We bound each of these separately.

$$
\begin{aligned}
\|T_1\| &= \frac{\|\mathcal{P}_{u^\perp}\big(M(x - x') + (Q - M)(x - x')\big)\|}{\|Qx\|} \\
&\overset{(a)}{\leq} \frac{l_2\|z - z'\| + \theta\|x - x'\|}{(\sqrt{1-\nu^2} - \theta)} \\
&\overset{(b)}{\leq} \frac{l_2 + (\theta/\sqrt{1-\nu^2})}{(\sqrt{1-\nu^2} - \theta)}\|z - z'\|,
\end{aligned}
$$

where (a) follows from (16) and the fact that $\mathcal{P}_{u^\perp}Mu = 0$, and (b) follows from (15). Similarly, using (17)

$$
\begin{aligned}
\|T_2\| &= \left\|\mathcal{P}_{u^\perp}\big(Q(\sqrt{1 - \|z'\|^2}u + z')\big)\right\|\left|\frac{1}{\|Qx\|} - \frac{1}{\|Qx'\|}\right| \\
&\leq (\theta + \nu l_2)\frac{2.2\nu + 0.1\theta}{(\sqrt{1-\nu^2} - \theta)^3}\|z - z'\| .
\end{aligned}
$$

Notice that by assumption, we have $\theta \leq (1/40)$, and by the definition of G in (11), we have $\nu \leq (1/20)$. Then, after some calculations, we have proved (13). Analogously we can prove (14) by bounding $T_3 \equiv \mathcal{P}_u(Qx - Qx')/\|Qx\|$ and $T_4 \equiv \mathcal{P}_u(Qx')\big((1/\|Qx\|) - (1/\|Qx'\|)\big)$ separately. $\square$

We are now in position to prove Lemma 5.2.

Proof of Lemma 5.2. We first show that for any $\mathbf{x} \in$ G with a representative x such that $\langle x, u \rangle \geq 0$, we have $Q\mathbf{x} \in$ G. Note that, by triangular inequality, $\|\mathcal{P}_{u^\perp}(Qu)\| \leq \theta\lambda$ and $\|Qu\| \geq (1-\theta)\lambda$. Applying Lemma 6.1 to x and u, we get

$$\left\| \mathcal{P}_{u_\perp}\left(\frac{Qx}{\|Qx\|} \right) \right\|$$

$$\leq \left\| \mathcal{P}_{u_\perp}\left(\frac{Qu}{\|Qu\|} \right) \right\| + \left(l_2\left(1 + 3\nu^2\right) + 3\theta \right) \|\mathcal{P}_{u_\perp}(x - u)\|$$

$$\leq \left(\frac{1}{1-\theta} + 3\nu \right)\theta + \left(l_2\left(1 + 3\nu^2\right) \right)\nu \,. \tag{18}$$

For $\theta \leq (1/40)$ and for θ and ν satisfying,

$$\frac{2}{1-l_2}\theta \leq \nu \leq \min\left\{ \sqrt{\frac{2(1-l_2)}{15}} \,,\, \frac{1}{20} \right\},$$

the right-hand side of (18) is always smaller than ν, since $\left((1/(1-\theta)) + 3\nu\right)\theta \leq (3/5)(1-l_2)\nu$ and $3\nu^2 \leq (2/5)(1-l_2)$. This proves our claim for $\theta \leq (1/40)(1-l_2)^{3/2}$ and $\nu \in [(2\theta)/(1-l_2), \sqrt{1-l_2}/20]$ as per our assumptions.

Next, we show that there is a contraction in the set G. For x and x' satisfying the assumptions in Lemma 6.1, define $y \equiv Ax/\|Ax\|$, $y' \equiv Ax'/\|Ax'\|$, $z \equiv \mathcal{P}_{u_\perp}(x)$, and $z' \equiv \mathcal{P}_{u_\perp}(x')$. For $\|x\| \leq \nu$ and $\|x'\| \leq \nu$ we have

$$1 - 2\nu^2 \leq \langle x, x' \rangle \leq 1.$$

Using the above bounds we get

$$\frac{1 - \langle y, y' \rangle^2}{1 - \langle x, x' \rangle^2} \leq \frac{1}{(1-\nu^2)}\frac{1 - \langle y, y' \rangle}{1 - \langle x, x' \rangle} \,.$$

We can further bound $(1 - \langle y, y' \rangle)/(1 - \langle x, x' \rangle)$ using Lemma 6.1.

$$\|y - y'\| \leq \sqrt{(l_2 + 3\nu^2 + 3\theta)^2 + (4\nu + 4\theta)^2} \,\|z - z'\| \,.$$

Using $\|z - z'\|^2 \leq \|x - x'\|^2 = 2 - 2\langle x, x' \rangle$, we get

$$\frac{1 - \langle y, y' \rangle}{1 - \langle x, x' \rangle} \leq \left(l_2 + 3\nu^2 + 3\theta\right)^2 + (4\nu + 4\theta)^2 \,.$$

For $\theta \leq (1/40)(1-l_2)^{3/2}$ and $\nu \leq \sqrt{1-l_2}/20$ as per our assumptions, it follows that for $\rho \geq 1 - 0.8(1-l_2)$,

$$\sqrt{\frac{1 - \langle y, y' \rangle^2}{1 - \langle x, x' \rangle^2}} \leq \sqrt{\frac{(l_2 + 3\nu^2 + 3\theta)^2 + (4\nu + 4\theta)^2}{1 - \nu^2}} \leq \rho \,.$$

$\qquad\qquad\qquad\qquad\qquad\qquad\qquad\qquad\qquad\square$

6.3 Proof of Lemma 5.3

Expanding the summation, we get

$$\left\| \frac{1}{t}\sum_{s=1}^{t} f(\mathbf{X}_s) - \mu(f) \right\|^2 = \frac{1}{t^2}\sum_{s=1}^{t} \|f(\mathbf{X}_s) - \mu(f)\|^2 +$$

$$\frac{2}{t^2}\sum_{r=1}^{t}\sum_{r<s} \langle f(\mathbf{X}_r) - \mu(f), f(\mathbf{X}_s) - \mu(f) \rangle \,,$$

where $\langle a, b \rangle = a^* b$ denotes the scalar product of two vectors. We can bound the first term by $20\theta^2/(t(1-l_2)^2)$, since

$$\|f(\mathbf{X}_s) - \mu(f)\|^2 \leq 20\theta^2/(1-l_2)^2 \,, \tag{19}$$

where we used $\|\mathcal{P}_u(f(\mathbf{X}_s) - \mu(f))\|^2 \leq 4\theta^2/(1-l_2)^2$ and $\|\mathcal{P}_{u_\perp}(f(\mathbf{X}_s) - \mu(f))\|^2 \leq 16\theta^2/(1-l_2)^2$ for $\mathbf{X}_s \in \mathsf{G}$.

To bound the second term, let $y \equiv f(\mathbf{X}_r) - \mu(f)$. Note that by (19), $\|y\| \leq \sqrt{20}\theta/(1-l_2)$. We apply Theorem A.3

together with Lemma 5.2 to get

$$\left| \mathbb{E}\left[y^* f(\mathbf{X}_s) \,\big|\, \mathbf{X}_r \right] - y^*\mu(f) \right| \leq \rho^{s-r}\|y\|^2 \,,$$

for $r < s$. Using the fact that for $|\rho| \leq 1$, $\sum_{r=1}^{t}\sum_{r<s}\rho^{s-r} \leq \sum_{r=1}^{t}\rho^{-r}\rho^{r+1}/(1-\rho) \leq \rho t/(1-\rho)$, it follows that

$$\sum_{r=1}^{t}\sum_{r<s}\mathbb{E}\left[\langle f(\mathbf{X}_r) - \mu(f), f(\mathbf{X}_s) - \mu(f) \rangle \right]$$

$$\leq \sum_{r=1}^{t}\sum_{r<s}\mathbb{E}\left[\langle f(\mathbf{X}_r) - \mu(f), \mathbb{E}\left[f(\mathbf{X}_s) - \mu(f) \,\big|\, \mathbf{X}_r \right] \rangle \right]$$

$$\leq \frac{20\theta^2}{(1-l_2)}\sum_{r=1}^{t}\sum_{r<s}\rho^{s-r} \leq \frac{20\theta^2\rho t}{(1-l_2)(1-\rho)} \,.$$

Combining the above bounds we get

$$\mathbb{E}\left\| \frac{1}{t}\sum_{s=1}^{t} f(\mathbf{X}_s) - \mu(f) \right\|^2 \leq \frac{20\theta^2}{t(1-l_2)^2} + \frac{40\theta^2\rho}{(1-l_2)(1-\rho)t} \,.$$

For $\rho = 1 - (4/5)(1-l_2)$ as in Lemma 5.2, this proves the desired claim. $\qquad\qquad\qquad\square$

6.4 Proof of Lemma 5.4

From Theorem 5.1, we know $\mu(\mathsf{G}^c) = 0$. This imples that $\|\mu(f)\|^2 \geq \|\mathcal{P}_u(\mu(f))\|^2 \geq 1 - 1/400$. Then,

$$d(\mathbf{u}, \mu(f)) = \frac{\|\mathcal{P}_{u_\perp}(\mu(f))\|}{\|\mu(f)\|} \leq 2\|\mathcal{P}_{u_\perp}(\mu(f))\| \,.$$

Let $\mathbf{X}$ be an random element in P_n following the stationary distribution $\mu(\cdot)$, and the random vector $X \in \mathbb{R}^n$ be the representative. From the definition of $f(\cdot)$, $\mathcal{P}_{u_\perp}(X)$ is invariant when we apply $f(\cdot)$, whence $\mathcal{P}_{u_\perp}(f(\mathbf{X})) = \mathcal{P}_{u_\perp}(X)$. We can bound $\|\mathcal{P}_{u_\perp}(X)\|$ with the following recursion.

$$\mathcal{P}_{u_\perp}(X) = \mathbb{E}\left[\frac{\mathcal{P}_{u_\perp}(\prod_{\ell=1}^{k} S^{(\ell)} X)}{\|\prod_{\ell=1}^{k} S^{(\ell)} X\|} \,\Big|\, X \right]$$

$$= \mathbb{E}\left[\mathcal{P}_{u_\perp}\left(\prod_{\ell=1}^{k} S^{(\ell)} X \right)\left(\frac{1}{\|\prod_{\ell=1}^{k} S^{(\ell)} X\|} - \frac{1}{\|M^k X\|} \right) \,\Big|\, X \right]$$

$$+ \frac{\mathbb{E}\left[\mathcal{P}_{u_\perp}\left(\prod_{\ell=1}^{k} S^{(\ell)} X \right) \,\big|\, X \right]}{\|M^k X\|}$$

$$= \mathbb{E}\left[\mathcal{P}_{u_\perp}\left(\prod_{\ell=1}^{k} S^{(\ell)} X \right)\left(\frac{1}{\|\prod_{\ell=1}^{k} S^{(\ell)} X\|} - \frac{1}{\|M^k X\|} \right) \,\Big|\, X \right]$$

$$+ \frac{\mathcal{P}_{u_\perp}(M^k X)}{\|M^k X\|} \,.$$

Let $\nu \equiv 2\theta/(1-l_2)$. To bound the second term, note that $\mu(\mathsf{G}^c) = 0$. This imples that $\|X\| \geq \|\mathcal{P}_u(X)\| \geq \sqrt{1-\nu^2}$ and $\mathcal{P}_{u_\perp}(X) \leq \nu$ with probability one. Then,

$$\frac{\|\mathcal{P}_{u_\perp}(M^k X)\|}{\|M^k X\|} \leq l_2^k \frac{\nu}{\sqrt{1-\nu^2}},$$

with probability one. To bound the first term, we use the telescoping sum

$$\prod_{\ell=1}^{k} S^{(\ell)} - M^k = \sum_{i=1}^{k}\left(\prod_{\ell=i+1}^{k} S^{(\ell)} \right)(S^{(i)} - M)M^{i-1} \,.$$

177

Applying the triangular inequality of the operator norm, we have

$$\Big\| \prod_{\ell=1}^{k} S^{(\ell)} - M^k \Big\|_2 \le \lambda^k \big((1+\theta)^k - 1\big) \, ,$$

which follows from $\left(\prod_{\ell=i+1}^{k} S^{(\ell)} \right)(M^{(i)} - M)M^{i-1} \le \lambda^k(1+\theta)^{k-i}\theta$. Using the above inequality, we get the following bounds with probability one.

$$\Big\| \mathcal{P}_{u_\perp} \Big(\prod_{\ell=1}^{k} S^{(\ell)} X \Big) \Big\| \le \Big\| \mathcal{P}_{u_\perp}(M^k X) \Big\| + \Big\| \Big(\prod_{\ell=1}^{k} S^{(\ell)} - M^k \Big) X \Big\|$$
$$\le \lambda^k (l_2^k \nu + (1+\theta)^k - 1) \, , \text{ and}$$

$$\Big\| \mathcal{P}_{u} \Big(\prod_{\ell=1}^{k} S^{(\ell)} X \Big) \Big\| \ge \Big\| \mathcal{P}_{u}(M^k X) \Big\| - \Big\| \Big(\prod_{\ell=1}^{k} S^{(\ell)} - M^k \Big) X \Big\|$$
$$\ge \lambda^k (\sqrt{1-\nu^2} - (1+\theta)^k + 1) \, .$$

Then it follows that,

$$\left| \frac{1}{\| \prod_{\ell=1}^{k} S^{(\ell)} X \|} - \frac{1}{\|M^k X\|} \right| \le \frac{\|(M^k - \prod_{\ell=1}^{k} S^{(\ell)})X\|}{\|M^k X\| \| \prod_{\ell=1}^{k} S^{(\ell)} X \|}$$
$$\le \frac{((1+\theta)^k - 1)}{\lambda^k \sqrt{1-\nu^2}(\sqrt{1-\nu^2} - (1+\theta)^k + 1)} \, .$$

Collecting all the terms, we get

$$d(\mathbf{u}, \mu(f)) \le \frac{2((1+\theta)^k - 1 + l_2^k \nu)((1+\theta)^k - 1)}{\sqrt{1-\nu^2}(\sqrt{1-\nu^2} - (1+\theta)^k + 1)} + \frac{2 l_2^k \nu}{\sqrt{1-\nu^2}} \, .$$

Let $k = \lceil \log(\theta)/\log(l_2) \rceil$ such that $l_2^k \le \theta$. From the assumption that $\theta \le (1-l_2)^{3/2}/40$, it follows that $\theta \log \theta \le 0.12(1-l_2)$. Then,

$$(1+\theta)^{(\log\theta/\log l_2)} - 1 \le e^{(\theta \log\theta/\log l_2)} - 1$$
$$\le \frac{1.1}{(1-l_2)} \theta \log(1/\theta) \, ,$$

Then, after some algebra, $(1+\theta)^k - 1 \le \theta + (1+\theta)((1+\theta)^{(\log\theta/\log l_2)} - 1) \le 1.5\theta \log(1/\theta)/(1-l_2)$, and $(1+\theta)^k - 1 + l_2^k \nu \le 1.5\theta \log(1/\theta)/(1-l_2)$. It also follows that $\sqrt{1-\nu^2} \ge \sqrt{399/400}$ and $(\sqrt{1-\nu^2} - (1+\theta)^k + 1) \ge 0.8$. Collecting all the terms, we get the desired bound on $d(\mathbf{u}, \mu(f))$. $\square$

7. EIGENVALUE ESTIMATION

In the previous sections, we discussed the challenging task of computing the largest eigenvector under the gossip setting. A closely related task of computing the largest eigenvalue is also practically important in many computational problems. For example, positioning from pairwise distances requires the leading eigenvalues, as well as the leading eigenvectors, to correctly find the positions [24]. In the following, we present an algorithm to estimate the leading eigenvalue under the gossip setting and provide a performance guarantee. Although the proposed algorithm uses the same trajectory $\{x^{(t)}\}$ from GOSSIP PCA, the analysis is completely different from that of the eigenvector estimator.

We assume to have at our disposal the random trajectory $\{x^{(t)}\}_{t \ge 0}$, defined as in (2), possibly from running GOSSIP PCA. Assume that we start with $x^{(0)}$ with entries dis-

tributed as $\mathsf{N}(0,1)$. Our estimate for the top eigenvalue λ after t iterations is

$$\widehat{\lambda}^{(t)} = \left\{ |\langle x^{(0)}, x^{(t)} \rangle| \right\}^{1/t} \, .$$

Although, this estimator uses the same trajectory $\{x^{(t)}\}_{t \ge 0}$ as GOSSIP PCA, the analysis significantly differs from that of the eigenvector estimator. Hence, the statement of the error bound in Theorem 7.1 is also significantly different from Theorem 2.1. The main idea of our analysis is to bound the second moment of the estimate and apply Chebyshev's inequality. Therefore, the second moment of $S_{ij}^{(\ell)}$ characterized by α determines the accuracy of the sparsification.

$$\max_{i,j} \mathrm{Var}(S_{ij}^{(\ell)}) \le (\alpha/n)\|M\|_2^2 \, . \qquad (20)$$

The trade-off between d, which determines the complexity, and α depends on the specific sparsification method. With random sampling described in Section 3, it is not difficult to show that Eq. (20) holds with only $\alpha = O(1/d)$.

Our main result bounds the error of the algorithm in terms of α, t, and $\gamma \equiv \sum_{i=1}^{n}(|\lambda_i|/\lambda)$. The proof of this theorem is outline in the following section.

THEOREM 7.1. *Let $\{S^{(\ell)}\}_{\ell \ge 1}$ be a sequence of i.i.d. $n \times n$ random matrices satisfying $E[S^{(\ell)}] = M$ and Eq. (20). Assume $\alpha < 1/2$ and $\max\{\log_2 n, 2\log_{(1/l_2)} n\} \le t \le n/(4\alpha\gamma)$. Then with probability larger than $1 - \max\{\delta, 16/n^2\}$*

$$\left| \frac{\widehat{\lambda}^{(t)} - \lambda}{\lambda} \right| \le \max \left\{ \frac{8\sqrt{2}}{tn\sqrt{\delta}}; \ 32\sqrt{\frac{\alpha\gamma^{3/2}\log n}{t^2\delta}}; \ 48\sqrt{\frac{\alpha\gamma^3(\log n)^2}{tn\delta}} \right\} ,$$

provided the right hand side is smaller than $1/t$.

7.1 Proof of Theorem 7.1

The proof idea is fairly simple. Let $x_0 = x^{(0)}$ and define $\lambda^{(t)} \equiv x_0^* x^{(t)}$ such that our estimator is $\widehat{\lambda}^{(t)} \equiv (|\lambda^{(t)}|)^{1/t}$. We will show that this is close to the desired result λ by applying Chebyshev inequality to $\lambda^{(t)}$. In order to do this we need to compute its mean and variance.

LEMMA 7.2. *Consider the two operators $\mathcal{A}, \mathcal{B}: \mathbb{R}^{n \times n} \to \mathbb{R}^{n \times n}$, defined as follows*

$$\mathcal{A}(X) \equiv MXM^* , \qquad (21)$$
$$\mathcal{B}(X) \equiv \frac{\lambda^2 \alpha}{n} \langle X, \mathbb{I}_n \rangle \mathbb{I}_n , \qquad (22)$$

where $\langle X, Y \rangle = \mathrm{Tr}(X^* Y)$. Then, conditional on x_0 we have

$$\mathbb{E}[\lambda^{(t)} | x_0] = x_0^* M^t x_0 ,$$
$$\mathrm{Var}(\lambda^{(t)} | x_0) \le \langle x_0 x_0^*, (\mathcal{A} + \mathcal{B})^t (x_0 x_0^*) \rangle - \langle x_0 x_0^*, \mathcal{A}^t (x_0 x_0^*) \rangle .$$

The next lemma provides a bound on the variance.

LEMMA 7.3. *Let $\mathcal{A}, \mathcal{B}: \mathbb{R}^{n \times n} \to \mathbb{R}^{n \times n}$ be defined as in Eqs. (21) and (22). Further assume $\alpha < 1/2$ and $\alpha t \gamma < n/4$. Then, for any two vectors $x, y \in \mathbb{R}^n$, $\|x\| = \|y\| = 1$,*

$$\left| \langle yy^*, (\mathcal{A} + \mathcal{B})^t (xx^*) \rangle - \langle yy^*, \mathcal{A}^t (xx^*) \rangle \right|$$
$$\le 4\lambda^{2t} \left\{ \frac{n\alpha^t + 8\alpha^2\gamma}{4n^2} + \frac{\alpha\sqrt{\gamma}}{n} \left(\sum_{i=1}^{n} \frac{|\lambda_i|}{\lambda}((u_i^* x)^2 + (u_i^* y)^2) \right) \right.$$
$$\left. + \frac{\alpha t \gamma}{n} \left(\sum_{i=1}^{n} \frac{|\lambda_i|}{\lambda}(u_i^* x)^2 \right) \left(\sum_{i=1}^{n} \frac{|\lambda_i|}{\lambda}(u_i^* y)^2 \right) \right\} .$$

For the proof of Lemmas 7.2 and 7.3 we refer to the longer version of this paper. Let $\mathcal{G}_n$ be any measurable subset of $\mathbb{R}^n$. This forms a set of 'good' initial condition x_0, and its complement will be denoted by $\overline{\mathcal{G}}_n$. With an abuse of notation, $\mathcal{G}_n$ will also denote the event $x_0 \in \mathcal{G}_n$ (and analogously for $\overline{\mathcal{G}}_n$). Also let $\widehat{\lambda} = \widehat{\lambda}^{(t)}$. Then, for any $\Delta > 0$,

$$\mathbb{P}\{\widehat{\lambda} \notin [\lambda(1-\Delta)^{1/t}, \lambda(1+\Delta)^{1/t}]\}$$
$$\leq \mathbb{P}\{\{|\widehat{\lambda}^t - \lambda^t| \geq \Delta\lambda^t \,|\, \mathcal{G}_n\} + \mathbb{P}\{\overline{\mathcal{G}}_n\}$$
$$\leq \frac{1}{\Delta^2\lambda^{2t}}\mathbb{E}\{(\widehat{\lambda}^t - \lambda^t)^2 \,|\, \mathcal{G}_n\} + \mathbb{P}\{\overline{\mathcal{G}}_n\}$$
$$\leq \frac{1}{\Delta^2\lambda^{2t}}(\mathbb{E}\{\widehat{\lambda}^t \,|\, \mathcal{G}_n\} - \lambda^t)^2 + \frac{1}{\Delta^2\lambda^{2t}}\sup_{x_0 \in \mathcal{G}_n}\mathrm{Var}(\widehat{\lambda}^t \,|\, x_0) + \mathbb{P}\{\overline{\mathcal{G}}_n\}.$$

We shall upper bound each of the three terms in the above expression with

$$\mathcal{G}_n \equiv \left\{ x \in \mathbb{R}^n : \max_{i \leq 1} |u_i^* x| \leq \sqrt{6\log n} \right\}, \qquad (23)$$

Notice that $\mathbb{P}\{(u_i^* x_0)^2 \geq 6\log n\} \leq 2/n^3$. By the union bound we get $\mathbb{P}\{x_0 \in \overline{\mathcal{G}}_n\} \leq 2/n^2$.

Next observe that

$$\frac{1}{\lambda^t}\mathbb{E}\{\widehat{\lambda}^t \,|\, \mathcal{G}_n\} - 1 = (\mathbb{E}\{(u_1^* x_0)^2 | \mathcal{G}_n\} - 1) + \sum_{i=2}^n \frac{\lambda_i^t}{\lambda^t}(u_i^* x_0)^2.$$

The first step can be computed as

$$\mathbb{E}\{(u_1^* x_0)^2 | \mathcal{G}_n\} = \frac{\mathbb{E}\{(u_1^* x_0)^2\} - \mathbb{E}\{(u_1^* x_0)^2 \mathbb{I}_{\overline{\mathcal{G}}_n}\}}{1 - \mathbb{P}\{x_0 \in \overline{\mathcal{G}}_n\}},$$

whence, recalling that $\mathbb{E}\{(u_1^* x_0)^2\} = 1$, and $\mathbb{P}\{x_0 \in \overline{\mathcal{G}}_n\} \leq 1/2$ for all n large enough, we get

$$\left|\mathbb{E}\{(u_1^* x_0)^2 | \mathcal{G}_n\} - 1\right| = \left|\frac{\mathbb{P}\{x_0 \in \overline{\mathcal{G}}_n\} - \mathbb{E}\{(u_1^* x_0)^2 \mathbb{I}_{\{x_0 \in \overline{\mathcal{G}}_n\}}\}}{1 - \mathbb{P}\{x_0 \in \overline{\mathcal{G}}_n\}}\right|$$
$$\leq \frac{4}{n^2}.$$

Note further that, by Chernoff inequality, $\sum_{i=1}^n (u_i^* x_0)^2 \leq 3n$ with probability at least $1 - \exp\{(1/10)n\}$. Then,

$$\left|\frac{1}{\lambda^t}\mathbb{E}\{\widehat{\lambda}^t \,|\, \mathcal{G}_n\} - 1\right| \leq \frac{4}{n^2} + 3n\left(\frac{|\lambda_2|}{\lambda}\right)^t.$$

Finally, using Lemma 7.2 and 7.3 we get

$$\frac{1}{\lambda^{2t}}\mathrm{Var}(\widehat{\lambda}^t | x_0) \leq 4n^2\left\{\frac{\alpha^t}{4n} + \frac{2\alpha^2\gamma}{n^2} + 2\frac{\alpha\sqrt{\gamma}}{n}\sum_{i=1}^n \frac{|\lambda_i|}{\lambda}(u_i^* x_0)^2\right.$$
$$\left. + \frac{\alpha t\gamma}{n}\left(\sum_{i=1}^n \frac{|\lambda_i|}{\lambda}(u_i^* x_0)^2\right)^2\right\}.$$

Further, for any $x_0 \in \mathcal{G}_n$, $\sum_{i=1}^n (|\lambda_i|/\lambda)(u_i^* x_0)^2 \leq 6\gamma\log n$, and therefore

$$\frac{1}{\lambda^{2t}}\mathrm{Var}(\widehat{\lambda}^t | x_0)$$
$$\leq 4n\left\{\frac{\alpha^t}{4} + \frac{2\alpha^2\gamma}{n} + \frac{12\alpha\gamma^{3/2}\log n}{n} + \frac{36\alpha t\gamma^3(\log n)^2}{n^2}\right\}$$
$$\leq 4n\left\{\frac{3\alpha^2\gamma}{n} + \frac{12\alpha\gamma^{3/2}(\log n)}{n} + \frac{36\alpha t\gamma^3(\log n)^2}{n^2}\right\}$$
$$\leq 4\left\{15\alpha\gamma^{3/2}(\log n) + \frac{36\alpha t\gamma^3(\log n)^2}{n}\right\},$$

where we used the fact that, for $\alpha < 1/2$ and $t \geq \log_2(n)$, we have $\alpha^t/4 \leq \alpha^2\gamma/n$.

Collecting the various terms we obtain

$$\mathbb{P}\{\widehat{\lambda} \notin [\lambda(1-\Delta)^{1/t}, \lambda(1+\Delta)^{1/t}]\}$$
$$\leq \frac{2}{n^2} + \frac{1}{\Delta^2}\left\{\frac{4}{n^2} + nl_2^t\right\}^2 + \frac{4\alpha\log n}{\Delta^2}\left\{15\gamma^{3/2} + \frac{36t\gamma^3(\log n)}{n}\right\},$$

whence $\mathbb{P}\{\widehat{\lambda} \notin [\lambda(1-\Delta)^{1/t}, \lambda(1+\Delta)^{1/t}]\} \leq \delta$, provided $n \geq 4/\sqrt{\delta}$, $\Delta \geq 4\sqrt{2}/(n\sqrt{\delta})$, $\Delta \geq 2n(|\lambda_2|/\lambda)^t/\sqrt{\delta}$, $\Delta^2 \geq (240\alpha\gamma^{3/2}\log n)/\delta$, $\Delta^2 \geq 4 \cdot 144\alpha t\gamma^3(\log n)^2/(n\delta)$. The thesis follows by noting that $(1+\Delta)^{1/t} \leq 1 + (\Delta/t)$ and $(1-\Delta)^{1/t} \geq 1 - 2(\Delta/t)$ provided $\Delta \leq 1/2$.

8. REFERENCES

[1] Ekahau. http://www.ekahau.com.

[2] Qwikker. http://qwikker.com.

[3] Sonitor technologies. http://www.sonitor.com.

[4] D. Achlioptas and F. McSherry. Fast computation of low-rank matrix approximations. *J. ACM*, 54(2):9, 2007.

[5] S. Boyd, A. Ghosh, B. Prabhakar, and D. Shah. Randomized gossip algorithms. *IEEE Trans. on Inform. Theory*, 52:2508 – 2530, 2006.

[6] S. Brin and L. Page. The anatomy of a large-scale hypertextual web search engine. *Comput. Netw. ISDN Syst.*, 30:107–117, April 1998.

[7] S. Deerwester, S. T. Dumais, G. W. Furnas, T. K. Landauer, and R. Harshman. Indexing by latent semantic analysis. *Journal of the American Society for information science*, 41(6):391–407, 1990.

[8] A. Dimakis, S. Kar, J. Moura, M. Rabbat, and A. Scaglione. Gossip algorithms for distributed signal processing. *Proc. of the IEEE*, 98:1847–1864, 2010.

[9] P. Drineas, A. Frieze, R. Kannan, S. Vempala, and V. Vinay. Clustering in large graphs and matrices. In *SODA '99*, pages 291–299, 1999.

[10] P. Drineas and R. Kannan. Pass efficient algorithms for approximating large matrices. In *SODA '03*, pages 223–232, 2003.

[11] P. Drineas, R. Kannan, and M. W. Mahoney. Fast monte carlo algorithms for matrices ii: Computing a low-rank approximation to a matrix. *SIAM J. Comput.*, 36(1), 2006.

[12] P. Drineas and M. W. Mahoney. On the nyström method for approximating a gram matrix for improved kernel-based learning. *J. Mach. Learn. Res.*, 6:2153–2175, 2005.

[13] P. Frasca, R. Carli, F. Fagnani, and S. Zampieri. Average consensus by gossip algorithms with quantized communication. In *47th IEEE Conference on Decision and Control*, pages 4831–4836, 2008.

[14] A. Frieze, R. Kannan, and S. Vempala. Fast monte-carlo algorithms for finding low-rank approximations. *J. ACM*, 51(6):1025–1041, 2004.

[15] H. Furstenberg and H. Kesten. Products of random matrices. *The Annals of Mathematical Statistics*, 31(2):457–469, June 1960.

[16] N. Halko, P. Martinsson, and J. A. Tropp. Finding structure with randomness: Stochastic algorithms for constructing approximate matrix decompositions. arXiv:0909.4061, 2010.

[17] T. Hastie, R. Tibshirani, and J. H. Friedman. *The Elements of Statistical Learning*. Springer, 2003.

[18] R. A. Horn and C. R. Johnson. *Matrix Analysis*. Cambridge University Press, 1990.

[19] I. T. Jolliffe. *Principal component analysis*. Springer-Verlag, 1986.

[20] A. Kashyap, T. Basara, and R. Srikant. Quantized consensus. *Automatica*, 43:1192–1203, 2007.

[21] D. Kempe and F. McSherry. A decentralized algorithm for spectral analysis. *Journal of Computer and System Sciences*, 74(1):70 – 83, 2008.

[22] R. H. Keshavan, A. Montanari, and S. Oh. Matrix completion from a few entries. *IEEE Trans. Inform. Theory*, 56(6):2980–2998, June 2010.

[23] M. Le Page. Theoremes limites pour les produits de matrices aleatoires. *Probability Measures on Groups*, 928:258–303, 1982.

[24] S. Oh, A. Karbasi, and A. Montanari. Sensor network localization from local connectivity: Performance analysis for the mds-map algorithm. In *Proc. of the IEEE Inform. Theory Workshop*, January 2010.

[25] V. Oseledets. A multiplicative ergodic theorem. lyapunov characteristic numbers for dynamical systems. *Trans.Moscow Math. Soc.*, 19:197–231, 1968.

[26] B. W. Parkinson and J. J. Spilker. *The global positioning system: theory and applications*. American Institute of Aeronautics and Astronautics, 1996.

[27] D. Shah. Gossip algorithms. *Foundations and Trends in Networking*, 3, 2009.

[28] D. Spielman and N. Srivastava. Graph sparsification by effective resistances. In *40th annual ACM symposium on Theory of computing*, 2008.

[29] J. B. Tenenbaum, V. Silva, and J. C. Langford. A Global Geometric Framework for Nonlinear Dimensionality Reduction. *Science*, 290(5500):2319–2323, 2000.

APPENDIX

A. PROOF OF THEOREM 5.1

We restate the main result of [23], in a somewhat more explicit form. Recall that $f : \mathsf{P}_n \to \mathbb{R}$ is said to be λ-Hölder continuous if its *Hölder coefficient* $[f]_\lambda$ is finite, where

$$[f]_\lambda = \sup_{\mathbf{x} \neq \mathbf{y}} \frac{|f(\mathbf{x}) - f(\mathbf{y})|}{d(\mathbf{x}, \mathbf{y})^\lambda}, \qquad (24)$$

THEOREM A.1 (LE PAGE, 1982). *Under assumptions* L1 *and* L2 *there exists a unique measure* μ *on* P_n *that is stationary for the Markov chain* $\{\mathbf{X}_t\}$. *Further, there exists constants* $A \geq 0$, $\rho \in (0,1)$, $\lambda \in (0,1]$ *such that, for any* λ-*Hölder function* $f : \mathsf{P}_n \to \mathbb{R}$,

$$\left| \mathbb{E}\{f(\mathbf{X}_t)\} - \mu(f) \right| \leq A \rho^t [f]_\lambda.$$

Remark: The above follows immediately from Theorem 1 in [23] via a simple coupling argument. Notice in particular that it applies to any Lipschitz function since $[f]_\lambda$ is upper bounded by the Lipschitz modulus of f.

Next we restate and prove the first part of Theorem 5.1.

THEOREM A.2. *Assume conditions* L1 *and* L2 *hold, together with* A1, A2. *Denote by* μ *the unique stationary mea-*

sure of the Markov chain $\{\mathbf{X}_t\}_{t\geq 0}$. *Then*

$$\mu(\mathsf{G}^c) = 0. \qquad (25)$$

PROOF. Consider a Markov chain MC_1 with $\mathbf{x}_0 \in \mathsf{G}$. The Markov chain MC_1 has a stationary distribution because conditions L1 and L2 hold. From the property A1, we know that $\mathbf{x}_t \in \mathsf{G}$. Therefore the stationary distribution of MC_1, say μ_1, satisfies $\mu_1(\mathsf{G}^c) = 0$. By Theorem A.1 the stationary distribution is unique, whence $\mu = \mu_1$ and $\mu(\mathsf{G}^c) = 0$. □

Finally, to state and prove a generalization of the second part of Theorem 5.1, we generalize hypothesis A2 as follows.

A2'. For any $\mathbf{x} \neq \mathbf{y} \in \mathsf{G}$, $\mathbb{E}\left[d(S^{(t)}\mathbf{x}, S^{(t)}\mathbf{y})^\lambda\right] \leq \rho \, d(\mathbf{x}, \mathbf{y})^\lambda$.

THEOREM A.3. *Assume conditions* L1 *and* L2 *hold, together with* A1 *and* A2'. *Denote by* μ *the unique stationary measure of the Markov chain* $\{\mathbf{X}_t\}_{t\geq 0}$. *Let* $\mathbf{x}_0 \in \mathsf{G}$. *Then for any* λ-*Hölder function* $f : \mathsf{P}_n \to \mathbb{R}$, *we have*

$$\left| \mathbb{E}\{f(\mathbf{X}_t)\} - \mu(f) \right| \leq \rho^t [f]_\lambda.$$

The proof of this theorem is based on a coupling argument. The coupling assumed throughout is fairly simple: given initial conditions $\mathbf{x}_0, \mathbf{y}_0 \in \mathsf{G}$, we define the chain $\{(\mathbf{X}_t, \mathbf{Y}_t)\}_{t\geq 0}$ by letting $(\mathbf{X}_0, \mathbf{Y}_0) = (\mathbf{x}_0, \mathbf{y}_0)$ and, for all $t \geq 1$,

$$\mathbf{X}_t = S^{(t)} S^{(t-1)} \cdots S^{(1)} \mathbf{x}_0, \qquad \mathbf{Y}_t = S^{(t)} S^{(t-1)} \cdots S^{(1)} \mathbf{y}_0.$$

It is convenient to introduce, for $t \in \mathbb{N}$, $\lambda > 0$ the quantity

$$\rho_\lambda(t) \equiv \sup_{\mathbf{x}_0 \neq \mathbf{y}_0 \in \mathsf{G}} \mathbb{E}\left\{ \left[\frac{d(\mathbf{X}_t, \mathbf{Y}_t)}{d(\mathbf{X}_0, \mathbf{Y}_0)} \right]^\lambda \right\}.$$

PROOF. First notice that the function $t \mapsto \rho_\lambda(t)$ is submultiplicative. This follows from

$$\rho_\lambda(t_1 + t_2) = \sup_{\mathbf{x}_0 \neq \mathbf{y}_0 \in \mathsf{G}} \mathbb{E}\left\{ \left[\frac{d(\mathbf{X}_{t_1+t_2}, \mathbf{Y}_{t_1+t_2})}{d(\mathbf{X}_0, \mathbf{Y}_0)} \right]^\lambda \right\}$$

$$= \sup_{\mathbf{x}_0 \neq \mathbf{y}_0 \in \mathsf{G}} \mathbb{E}\left\{ \left[\frac{d(\mathbf{X}_{t_1}, \mathbf{Y}_{t_1})}{d(\mathbf{X}_0, \mathbf{Y}_0)} \right]^\lambda \left[\frac{d(\mathbf{X}_{t_1+t_2}, \mathbf{Y}_{t_1+t_2})}{d(\mathbf{X}_{t_1}, \mathbf{Y}_{t_1})} \right]^\lambda \right\}$$

$$\overset{(a)}{\leq} \sup_{\mathbf{x}_0 \neq \mathbf{y}_0 \in \mathsf{G}} \mathbb{E}\left\{ \left[\frac{d(\mathbf{X}_{t_1}, \mathbf{Y}_{t_1})}{d(\mathbf{X}_0, \mathbf{Y}_0)} \right]^\lambda \right\} \sup_{\mathbf{x}_0 \neq \mathbf{y}_0 \in \mathsf{G}} \mathbb{E}\left\{ \left[\frac{d(\mathbf{X}_{t_2}, \mathbf{Y}_{t_2})}{d(\mathbf{X}_0, \mathbf{Y}_0)} \right]^\lambda \right\}$$

$$= \rho_\lambda(t_1) \rho_\lambda(t_2).$$

where (a) follows from the condition A1. From the condition A2', we know that $\rho_\lambda(1) \leq \rho$, hence $\rho_\lambda(t) \leq \rho^t$.

Next let $\{\mathbf{X}_t\}_{t\geq 0}$ and $\{\mathbf{Y}_t\}_{t\geq 0}$ be Markov chains coupled as above, with initial conditions $\mathbf{X}_0 = \mathbf{x}_0 \in \mathsf{G}$ and $\mathbf{Y}_0 \sim \mu$. We then have

$$\left| \mathbb{E}\{f(\mathbf{X}_t)\} - \mu(f) \right| = \left| \mathbb{E}\{f(\mathbf{X}_t)\} - \mathbb{E}\{f(\mathbf{Y}_t)\} \right|$$

$$\leq \mathbb{E}\left\{ |f(\mathbf{X}_t) - f(\mathbf{Y}_t)| \right\}$$

$$\leq [f]_\lambda \mathbb{E}\left\{ d(\mathbf{X}_t, \mathbf{Y}_t)^\lambda \right\}$$

$$\leq [f]_\lambda \mathbb{E}\left\{ \left[\frac{d(\mathbf{X}_t, \mathbf{Y}_t)}{d(\mathbf{X}_0, \mathbf{Y}_0)} \right]^\lambda \right\}$$

$$\leq [f]_\lambda \rho_\lambda(t) \leq [f]_\lambda \rho^t,$$

where we used $d(\mathbf{X}_0, \mathbf{Y}_0) \leq 1$ by definition. This concludes our proof. □

Optimal Power Cost Management Using Stored Energy in Data Centers

Rahul Urgaonkar, Bhuvan Urgaonkar†, Michael J. Neely‡, Anand Sivasubramanian†
Advanced Networking Dept., Dept. of CSE†, Dept. of EE‡
Raytheon BBN Technologies, The Pennsylvania State University†, University of Southern California‡
Cambridge, MA, University Park, PA†, Los Angeles, CA‡
rahul@bbn.com, {bhuvan,anand}@cse.psu.edu†, mjneely@usc.edu‡

ABSTRACT

Since the electricity bill of a data center constitutes a significant portion of its overall operational costs, reducing this has become important. We investigate cost reduction opportunities that arise by the use of uninterrupted power supply (UPS) units as energy storage devices. This represents a deviation from the usual use of these devices as mere transitional fail-over mechanisms between utility and captive sources such as diesel generators. We consider the problem of opportunistically using these devices to reduce the time average electric utility bill in a data center. Using the technique of Lyapunov optimization, we develop an online control algorithm that can optimally exploit these devices to minimize the time average cost. This algorithm operates without any knowledge of the statistics of the workload or electricity cost processes, making it attractive in the presence of workload and pricing uncertainties. An interesting feature of our algorithm is that its deviation from optimality reduces as the storage capacity is increased. Our work opens up a new area in data center power management.

Categories and Subject Descriptors

C.4 [**Performance of Systems**]: Modeling techniques; Design studies

General Terms

Algorithms, Performance, Theory

Keywords

Power Management, Data Centers, Stochastic Optimization, Optimal Control

1. INTRODUCTION

Data centers spend a significant portion of their overall operational costs towards their electricity bills. As an example, one recent case study suggests that a large 15MW

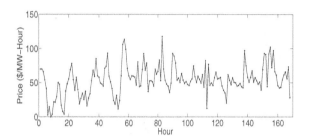

Figure 1: Avg. hourly spot market price during the week of 01/01/2005-01/07/2005 for LA1 Zone [1].

data center (on the more energy-efficient end) might spend about $1M on its monthly electricity bill. In general, a data center spends between 30-50% of its operational expenses towards power [10]. A large body of research addresses these expenses by reducing the energy consumption of these data centers. This includes designing/employing hardware with better power/performance trade-offs [9,17,20], software techniques for power-aware scheduling [12], workload migration, resource consolidation [6], among others. Power prices exhibit variations along time, space (geography), and even across utility providers. As an example, consider Fig. 1 that shows the average hourly spot market prices for the Los Angeles Zone LA1 obtained from CAISO [1]. These correspond to the week of 01/01/2005-01/07/2005 and denote the average price of 1 MW-Hour of electricity. Consequently, minimization of energy consumption need not coincide with that of the electricity bill.

Given the diversity within power price and availability, attention has recently turned towards *demand response* (DR) within data centers. DR within a data center (or a set of related data centers) attempts to optimize the electricity bill by adapting its needs to the temporal, spatial, and cross-utility diversity exhibited by power price. The key idea behind these techniques is to preferentially shift power draw (i) to times and places or (ii) from utilities offering cheaper prices. Typically some constraints in the form of performance requirements for the workload (e.g., response times offered to the clients of a Web-based application) limit the cost reduction benefits that can result from such DR. Whereas existing DR techniques have relied on various forms of workload scheduling/shifting, a complementary knob to facilitate such movement of power needs is offered by *energy storage devices*, typically uninterrupted power supply (UPS) units, residing in data centers.

A data center deploys captive power sources, typically diesel generators (DG), that it uses for keeping itself powered up when the utility experiences an outage. The UPS units serve as a bridging mechanism to facilitate this transition from utility to DG: upon a utility failure, the data center is kept powered by the UPS unit using energy stored within its batteries, before the DG can start up and provide power. Whereas this transition takes only 10-20 seconds, UPS units have enough battery capacity to keep the entire data center powered at its maximum power needs for anywhere between 5-30 minutes. Tapping into the energy reserves of the UPS unit can allow a data center to improve its electricity bill. Intuitively, the data center would store energy within the UPS unit when prices are low and use this to augment the draw from the utility when prices are high.

In this paper, we consider the problem of developing an online control policy to exploit the UPS unit along with the presence of delay-tolerance within the workload to optimize the data center's electricity bill. This is a challenging problem because data centers experience time-varying workloads and power prices with possibly unknown statistics. Even when statistics can be approximated (say by learning using past observations), traditional approaches to construct optimal control policies involve the use of Markov Decision Theory and Dynamic Programming [5]. It is well known that these techniques suffer from the "curse of dimensionality" where the complexity of computing the optimal strategy grows with the system size. Furthermore, such solutions result in hard-to-implement systems, where significant recomputation might be needed when statistics change.

In this work, we make use of a different approach that can overcome the challenges associated with dynamic programming. This approach is based on the recently developed technique of Lyapunov optimization [8] [15] that enables the design of online control algorithms for such time-varying systems. These algorithms operate *without requiring any knowledge of the system statistics* and are easy to implement. We design such an algorithm for optimally exploiting the UPS unit and delay-tolerance of workloads to minimize the time average cost. We show that our algorithm can get within $O(1/V)$ of the optimal solution where the maximum value of V is limited by battery capacity. We note that, for the same parameters, a dynamic programming based approach (if it can be solved) will yield a better result than our algorithm. However, this gap reduces as the battery capacity is increased. Our algorithm is thus most useful when such scaling is practical.

2. RELATED WORK

One recent body of work proposes online algorithms for using UPS units for cost reduction via shaving workload "peaks" that correspond to higher energy prices [3,4]. This work is highly complementary to ours in that it offers a worst-case competitive ratio analysis while our approach looks at the average case performance. Whereas a variety of work has looked at workload shifting for power cost reduction [20] or other reasons such as performance and availability [6], our work differs both due to its usage of energy storage as well as the cost optimality guarantees offered by our technique. Some research has considered consumers with access to multiple utility providers, each with a different carbon profile, power price and availability and looked at optimizing cost subject to performance and/or carbon emissions

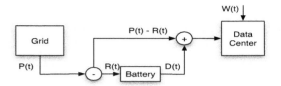

Figure 2: Block diagram for the basic model.

constraints [11]. Another line of work has looked at cost reduction opportunities offered by geographical variations within utility prices for data centers where portions of workloads could be serviced from one of several locations [11,18]. Finally, [7] considers the use of rechargeable batteries for maximizing system utility in a wireless network. While all of this research is highly complementary to our work, there are three key differences: (i) our investigation of energy storage as an enabler of cost reduction, (ii) our use of the technique of Lyapunov optimization which allows us to offer a provably cost optimal solution, and (iii) combining energy storage with delay-tolerance within workloads.

3. BASIC MODEL

We consider a time-slotted model. In the basic model, we assume that in every slot, the total power demand generated by the data center in that slot must be met in the current slot itself (using a combination of power drawn from the utility and the battery). Thus, any buffering of the workload generated by the data center is not allowed. We will relax this constraint later in Sec. 6 when we allow buffering of some of the workload while providing worst case delay guarantees. In the following, we use the terms UPS and battery interchangeably.

3.1 Workload Model

Let $W(t)$ be total workload (in units of power) generated in slot t. Let $P(t)$ be the total power drawn from the grid in slot t out of which $R(t)$ is used to recharge the battery. Also, let $D(t)$ be the total power discharged from the battery in slot t. Then in the basic model, the following constraint must be satisfied in every slot (Fig. 2):

$$W(t) = P(t) - R(t) + D(t) \qquad (1)$$

Every slot, a control algorithm observes $W(t)$ and makes decisions about how much power to draw from the grid in that slot, i.e., $P(t)$, and how much to recharge and discharge the battery, i.e., $R(t)$ and $D(t)$. Note that by (1), having chosen $P(t)$ and $R(t)$ completely determines $D(t)$.

Assumptions on the statistics of $W(t)$: The workload process $W(t)$ is assumed to vary randomly taking values from a set $\mathcal{W}$ of non-negative values and is not influenced by past control decisions. The set $\mathcal{W}$ is assumed to be finite, with potentially arbitrarily large size. The underlying probability distribution or statistical characterization of $W(t)$ is not necessarily known. We only assume that its maximum value is finite, i.e., $W(t) \leq W_{max}$ for all t.

For simplicity, in the basic model we assume that $W(t)$ evolves according to an i.i.d. process noting that the algorithm developed for this case can be applied without any modifications to non-i.i.d. scenarios as well. The analysis and performance guarantees for the non-i.i.d. case can be obtained using the delayed Lyapunov drift and T slot drift techniques developed in [8] [15].

3.2 Battery Model

Ideally, we would like to incorporate the following idiosyncrasies of battery operation into our model. First, batteries become unreliable as they are charged/discharged, with higher depth-of-discharge (DoD) - percentage of maximum charge removed during a discharge cycle - causing faster degradation in their reliability. This dependence between the useful lifetime of a battery and how it is discharged/charged is expressed via battery lifetime charts [13]. For example, with lead-acid batteries that are commonly used in UPS units, 20% DoD yields 1400 cycles [2]. Second, batteries have conversion loss whereby a portion of the energy stored in them is lost when discharging them (e.g., about 10-15% for lead-acid batteries). Furthermore, certain regions of battery operation (high rate of discharge) are more inefficient than others. Finally, the storage itself maybe "leaky", so that the stored energy decreases over time, even in the absence of any discharging.

For simplicity, in the basic model we will assume that there is no power loss either in recharging or discharging the batteries, noting that this can be easily generalized to the case where a fraction of $R(t), D(t)$ is lost. We will also assume that the batteries are not leaky, so that the stored energy level decreases only when they are discharged. This is a reasonable assumption when the time scale over which the loss takes place is much larger than that of interest to us. To model the effect of repeated recharging and discharging on the battery's lifetime, we assume that with each recharge and discharge operation, a fixed cost (in dollars) of C_{rc} and C_{dc} respectively is incurred. The choice of these parameters would affect the trade-off between the cost of the battery itself and the cost reduction benefits it offers. For example, suppose a new battery costs B dollars and it can sustain N discharge/charge cycles (ignoring DoD for now). Then setting $C_{rc} = C_{dc} = B/N$ would amount to expecting the battery to "pay for itself" by augmenting the utility N times over its lifetime.

In any slot, we assume that one can either recharge or discharge the battery or do neither, but not both. This means that for all t, we have:

$$R(t) > 0 \implies D(t) = 0, \ D(t) > 0 \implies R(t) = 0 \quad (2)$$

Let $Y(t)$ denote the battery energy level in slot t. Then, the dynamics of $Y(t)$ can be expressed as:

$$Y(t+1) = Y(t) - D(t) + R(t) \quad (3)$$

The battery is assumed to have a finite capacity Y_{max} so that $Y(t) \leq Y_{max}$ for all t. Further, for the purpose of reliability, it may be required to ensure that a minimum energy level $Y_{min} \geq 0$ is maintained at all times. For example, this could represent the amount of energy required to support the data center operations until a secondary power source (such as DG) is activated in the event of a grid outage. Recall that the UPS unit is integral to the availability of power supply to the data center upon utility outage. Indiscriminate discharging of UPS can leave the data center in situations where it is unable to safely fail-over to DG upon a utility outage. Therefore, discharging the UPS must be done carefully so that it still possesses enough charge so reliably carry out its role as a transition device between utility

and DG. Thus, the following condition must be met in every slot under any feasible control algorithm:

$$Y_{min} \leq Y(t) \leq Y_{max} \quad (4)$$

The effectiveness of the online control algorithm we present in Sec. 5 will depend on the magnitude of the difference $Y_{max} - Y_{min}$. In most practical scenarios of interest, this value is expected to be at least moderately large: recent work suggests that storing energy Y_{min} to last about a minute is sufficient to offer reliable data center operation [14], while Y_{max} can vary between 5-20 minutes (or even higher) due to reasons such as UPS units being available only in certain sizes and the need to keep room for future IT growth. Furthermore, the UPS units are sized based on the *maximum provisioned* capacity of the data center, which is itself often substantially (up to twice [10]) higher than the maximum actual power demand.

The initial charge level in the battery is given by Y_{init} and satisfies $Y_{min} \leq Y_{init} \leq Y_{max}$. Finally, we assume that the maximum amounts by which we can recharge or discharge the battery in any slot are bounded. Thus, we have $\forall t$:

$$0 \leq R(t) \leq R_{max}, \ 0 \leq D(t) \leq D_{max} \quad (5)$$

We will assume that $Y_{max} - Y_{min} > R_{max} + D_{max}$ while noting that in practice, $Y_{max} - Y_{min}$ is much larger than $R_{max} + D_{max}$. Note that any feasible control decision on $R(t), D(t)$ must ensure that both of the constraints (4) and (5) are satisfied. This is equivalent to the following:

$$0 \leq R(t) \leq \min[R_{max}, Y_{max} - Y(t)] \quad (6)$$
$$0 \leq D(t) \leq \min[D_{max}, Y(t) - Y_{min}] \quad (7)$$

3.3 Cost Model

The cost per unit of power drawn from the grid in slot t is denoted by $C(t)$. In general, it can depend on both $P(t)$, the total amount of power drawn in slot t, and an auxiliary state variable $S(t)$, that captures parameters such as time of day, identity of the utility provider, etc. For example, the per unit cost may be higher during business hours, etc. Similarly, for any fixed $S(t)$, it may be the case that $C(t)$ increases with $P(t)$ so that per unit cost of electricity increases as more power is drawn. This may be because the utility provider wants to discourage heavier loading on the grid. Thus, we assume that $C(t)$ is a function of both $S(t)$ and $P(t)$ and we denote this as:

$$C(t) = \hat{C}(S(t), P(t)) \quad (8)$$

For notational convenience, we will use $C(t)$ to denote the per unit cost in the rest of the paper noting that the dependence of $C(t)$ on $S(t)$ and $P(t)$ is implicit.

The auxiliary state process $S(t)$ is assumed to evolve independently of the decisions taken by any control policy. For simplicity, we assume that every slot it takes values from a finite but arbitrarily large set $\mathcal{S}$ in an i.i.d. fashion according to a potentially unknown distribution. This can again be generalized to non i.i.d. Markov modulated scenarios using the techniques developed in [8] [15]. For each $S(t)$, the unit cost is assumed to be a non-decreasing function of $P(t)$. Note that it is not necessarily convex or strictly monotonic or continuous. This is quite general and can be used to model a variety of scenarios. A special case is when $C(t)$ is only a function of $S(t)$. The optimal control action for this case has a particularly simple form and we will highlight this in Sec. 5.1.1. The unit cost is assumed to be non-negative and finite for all $S(t), P(t)$.

We assume that the maximum amount of power that can be drawn from the grid in any slot is upper bounded by P_{peak}. Thus, we have for all t:

$$0 \leq P(t) \leq P_{peak} \qquad (9)$$

Note that if we consider the original scenario where batteries are not used, then P_{peak} must be such that all workload can be satisfied. Therefore, $P_{peak} \geq W_{max}$.

Finally, let C_{max} and C_{min} denote the maximum and minimum per unit cost respectively over all $S(t), P(t)$. Also let $\chi_{min} > 0$ be a constant such that for any $P_1, P_2 \in [0, P_{peak}]$ where $P_1 \leq P_2$, the following holds for all $\chi \geq \chi_{min}$:

$$P_1(-\chi + C(P_1, S)) \geq P_2(-\chi + C(P_2, S)) \qquad \forall S \in \mathcal{S} \quad (10)$$

For example, when $C(t)$ does not depend on $P(t)$, then $\chi_{min} = C_{max}$ satisfies (10). This follows by noting that $(-C_{max} + C(t)) \leq 0$ for all t. Similarly, suppose $C(t)$ does not depend on $S(t)$, but is continuous, convex, and increasing in $P(t)$. Then, it can be shown that $\chi_{min} = C(P_{peak}) + P_{peak}C'(P_{peak})$ satisfies (10) where $C'(P_{peak})$ denotes the derivative of $C(t)$ evaluated at P_{peak}. In the following, we assume that such a finite χ_{min} exists for the given cost model. We further assume that $\chi_{min} > C_{min}$. The case of $\chi_{min} = C_{min}$ corresponds to the degenerate case where the unit cost is fixed for all times and we do not consider it in this paper.

What is known in each slot?: We assume that the value of $S(t)$ and the form of the function $C(P(t), S(t))$ for that slot is known. For example, this may be obtained beforehand using pre-advertised prices by the utility provider. We assume that given an $S(t) = s$, $C(t)$ is a deterministic function of $P(t)$ and this holds for all s. Similarly, the amount of incoming workload $W(t)$ is known at the beginning of each slot.

Given this model, our goal is to design a control algorithm that minimizes the time average cost while meeting all the constraints. This is formalized in the next section.

4. CONTROL OBJECTIVE

Let $P(t), R(t)$ and $D(t)$ denote the control decisions made in slot t by any feasible policy under the basic model as discussed in Sec. 3. These must satisfy the constraints (1), (2), (6), (7), and (9) every slot. We define the following indicator variables that are functions of the control decisions regarding a recharge or discharge operation in slot t:

$$1_R(t) = \begin{cases} 1 & \text{if } R(t) > 0 \\ 0 & \text{else} \end{cases} \quad 1_D(t) = \begin{cases} 1 & \text{if } D(t) > 0 \\ 0 & \text{else} \end{cases}$$

Note that by (2), at most one of $1_R(t)$ and $1_C(t)$ can take the value 1. Then the total cost incurred in slot t is given by $P(t)C(t) + 1_R(t)C_{rc} + 1_D(t)C_{dc}$. The time-average cost under this policy is given by:

$$\lim_{t \to \infty} \frac{1}{t} \sum_{\tau=0}^{t-1} \mathbb{E}\left\{P(\tau)C(\tau) + 1_R(\tau)C_{rc} + 1_D(\tau)C_{dc}\right\} \quad (11)$$

where the expectation above is with respect to the potential randomness of the control policy. Assuming for the time being that this limit exists, our goal is to design a control algo-

rithm that minimizes this time average cost subject to the constraints described in the basic model. Mathematically, this can be stated as the following *stochastic optimization problem*:

P1 :

Minimize: $\displaystyle \lim_{t \to \infty} \frac{1}{t} \sum_{\tau=0}^{t-1} \mathbb{E}\left\{P(\tau)C(\tau) + 1_R(\tau)C_{rc} + 1_D(\tau)C_{dc}\right\}$

Subject to: Constraints (1), (2), (6), (7), (9)

The finite capacity and underflow constraints (6), (7) make this a particularly challenging problem to solve even if the statistical descriptions of the workload and unit cost process are known. For example, the traditional approach based on Dynamic Programming [5] would have to compute the optimal control action for all possible combinations of the battery charge level and the system state $(S(t), W(t))$. Instead, we take an alternate approach based on the technique of Lyapunov optimization, taking the *finite* size queues constraint explicitly into account.

Note that a solution to the problem **P1** is a control policy that determines the sequence of feasible control decisions $P(t), R(t), D(t)$, to be used. Let ϕ_{opt} denote the value of the objective in problem **P1** under an optimal control policy. Define the time-average rate of recharge and discharge under any policy as follows:

$$\overline{R} = \lim_{t \to \infty} \frac{1}{t} \sum_{\tau=0}^{t-1} \mathbb{E}\left\{R(\tau)\right\}, \quad \overline{D} = \lim_{t \to \infty} \frac{1}{t} \sum_{\tau=0}^{t-1} \mathbb{E}\left\{D(\tau)\right\} \quad (12)$$

Now consider the following problem:

P2 :

Minimize: $\displaystyle \lim_{t \to \infty} \frac{1}{t} \sum_{\tau=0}^{t-1} \mathbb{E}\left\{P(\tau)C(\tau) + 1_R(\tau)C_{rc} + 1_D(\tau)C_{dc}\right\}$

Subject to: Constraints (1), (2), (5), (9)

$$\overline{R} = \overline{D} \qquad (13)$$

Let $\hat{\phi}$ denote the value of the objective in problem **P2** under an optimal control policy. By comparing **P1** and **P2**, it can be shown that **P2** is less constrained than **P1**. Specifically, any feasible solution to **P1** would also satisfy **P2**. To see this, consider any policy that satisfies (6) and (7) for all t. This ensures that constraints (4) and (5) are always met by this policy. Then summing equation (3) over all $\tau \in \{0, 1, 2, \ldots, t-1\}$ under this policy and taking expectation of both sides yields:

$$\mathbb{E}\left\{Y(t)\right\} - Y_{init} = \sum_{\tau=0}^{t-1} \mathbb{E}\left\{R(\tau) - D(\tau)\right\}$$

Since $Y_{min} \leq Y(t) \leq Y_{max}$ for all t, dividing both sides by t and taking limits as $t \to \infty$ yields $\overline{R} = \overline{D}$. Thus, this policy satisfies constraint (13) of **P2**. Therefore, any feasible solution to **P1** also satisfies **P2**. This implies that the optimal value of **P2** cannot exceed that of **P1**, so that $\hat{\phi} \leq \phi_{opt}$.

Our approach to solving **P1** will be based on this observation. We first note that it is easier to characterize the optimal solution to **P2**. This is because the dependence on $Y(t)$ has been removed. Specifically, it can be shown that the optimal solution to **P2** can be achieved by a stationary, randomized control policy that chooses control actions $P(t), D(t), R(t)$ every slot purely as a function (possibly randomized) of the current state $(W(t), S(t))$ and *independent of* the battery charge level $Y(t)$. This fact is presented in the following lemma:

LEMMA 1. *(Optimal Stationary, Randomized Policy): If the workload process $W(t)$ and auxiliary process $S(t)$ are i.i.d. over slots, then there exists a stationary, randomized policy that takes control decisions $P^{stat}(t), R^{stat}(t), D^{stat}(t)$ every slot purely as a function (possibly randomized) of the current state $(W(t), S(t))$ while satisfying the constraints (1), (2), (5), (9) and providing the following guarantees:*

$$\mathbb{E}\left\{R^{stat}(t)\right\} = \mathbb{E}\left\{D^{stat}(t)\right\} \tag{14}$$

$$\mathbb{E}\left\{P^{stat}(t)C(t) + 1_R^{stat}(t)C_{rc} + 1_D^{stat}(t)C_{dc}\right\} = \hat{\phi} \tag{15}$$

where the expectations above are with respect to the stationary distribution of $(W(t), S(t))$ and the randomized control decisions.

PROOF. This result follows from the framework in [8, 15] and is omitted for brevity. □

It should be noted that while it is possible to characterize and potentially compute such a policy, it may not be feasible for the original problem **P1** as it could violate the constraints (6) and (7). However, the existence of such a policy can be used to construct an approximately optimal policy that meets all the constraints of **P1** using the technique of Lyapunov optimization [8] [15]. This policy is dynamic and does not require knowledge of the statistical description of the workload and cost processes. We present this policy and derive its performance guarantees in the next section. This dynamic policy is approximately optimal where the approximation factor improves as the battery capacity increases. Also note that the distance from optimality for our policy is measured in terms of $\hat{\phi}$. However, since $\hat{\phi} \leq \phi_{opt}$, in practice, the approximation factor is better than the analytical bounds.

5. OPTIMAL CONTROL ALGORITHM

We now present an *online* control algorithm that approximately solves **P1**. This algorithm uses a control parameter $V > 0$ that affects the distance from optimality as shown later. This algorithm also makes use of a "queueing" state variable $X(t)$ to track the battery charge level and is defined as follows:

$$X(t) = Y(t) - V\chi_{min} - D_{max} - Y_{min} \tag{16}$$

Recall that $Y(t)$ denotes the actual battery charge level in slot t and evolves according to (3). It can be seen that $X(t)$ is simply a shifted version of $Y(t)$ and its dynamics is given by:

$$X(t+1) = X(t) - D(t) + R(t) \tag{17}$$

Note that $X(t)$ can be negative. We will show that this definition enables our algorithm to ensure that the constraint (4) is met.

We are now ready to state the dynamic control algorithm. Let $(W(t), S(t))$ and $X(t)$ denote the system state in slot t. Then the dynamic algorithm chooses control action $P(t)$ as

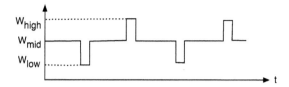

Figure 3: Periodic $W(t)$ process in the example.

the solution to the following optimization problem:

P3 :

Minimize: $X(t)P(t) + V\left[P(t)C(t) + 1_R(t)C_{rc} + 1_D(t)C_{dc}\right]$

Subject to: Constraints $(1), (2), (5), (9)$

The constraints above result in the following constraint on $P(t)$:

$$P_{low} \leq P(t) \leq P_{high} \tag{18}$$

where
$P_{low} = \max[0, W(t) - D_{max}]$ and $P_{high} = \min[P_{peak}, W(t) + R_{max}]$. Let $P^*(t), R^*(t)$, and $D^*(t)$ denote the optimal solution to **P3**. Then, the dynamic algorithm chooses the recharge and discharge values as follows.

$$R^*(t) = \begin{cases} P^*(t) - W(t) & \text{if } P^*(t) > W(t) \\ 0 & \text{else} \end{cases}$$

$$D^*(t) = \begin{cases} W(t) - P^*(t) & \text{if } P^*(t) < W(t) \\ 0 & \text{else} \end{cases}$$

Note that if $P^*(t) = W(t)$, then both $R^*(t) = 0$ and $D^*(t) = 0$ and all demand is met using power drawn from the grid. It can be seen from the above that the control decisions satisfy the constraints $0 \leq R^*(t) \leq R_{max}$ and $0 \leq D^*(t) \leq D_{max}$. That the finite battery constraints and the constraints (6), (7) are also met will be shown in Sec. 5.3.

After computing these quantities, the algorithm implements them and updates the queueing variable $X(t)$ according to (17). This process is repeated every slot. Note that in solving **P3**, the control algorithm only makes use of the current system state values and does not require knowledge of the statistics of the workload or unit cost processes. Thus, it is *myopic* and *greedy* in nature. From **P3**, it is seen that the algorithm tries to recharge the battery when $X(t)$ is negative and per unit cost is low. And it tries to discharge the battery when $X(t)$ is positive. That this is sufficient to achieve optimality will be shown in Theorem 1. The queueing variable $X(t)$ plays a crucial role as making decisions purely based on prices is not necessarily optimal.

To get some intuition behind the working of this algorithm, consider the following simple example. Suppose $W(t)$ can take three possible values from the set $\{W_{low}, W_{mid}, W_{high}\}$ where $W_{low} < W_{mid} < W_{high}$. Similarly, $C(t)$ can take three possible values in $\{C_{low}, C_{mid}, C_{high}\}$ where $C_{low} < C_{mid} < C_{high}$ and does not depend on $P(t)$. We assume that the workload process evolves in a frame-based periodic fashion. Specifically, in every odd numbered frame, $W(t) = W_{mid}$ for all except the last slot of the frame when $W(t) = W_{low}$. In every even numbered frame, $W(t) = W_{mid}$ for all except the last slot of the frame when $W(t) = W_{high}$. This is il-

Y_{max}	20	30	40	50	75	100
V	0	1.25	2.5	3.75	6.875	10.0
Avg. Cost	94.0	92.5	91.1	88.5	88.0	87.0

Table 1: Average Cost vs. Y_{max}

lustrated in Fig. 3. The $C(t)$ process evolves similarly, such that $C(t) = C_{low}$ when $W(t) = W_{low}$, $C(t) = C_{mid}$ when $W(t) = W_{mid}$, and $C(t) = C_{high}$ when $W(t) = W_{high}$.

In the following, we assume a frame size of 5 slots with $W_{low} = 10$, $W_{mid} = 15$, and $W_{high} = 20$ units. Also, $C_{low} = 2$, $C_{mid} = 6$, and $C_{high} = 10$ dollars. Finally, $R_{max} = D_{max} = 10$, $P_{peak} = 20$, $C_{rc} = C_{dc} = 5$, $Y_{init} = Y_{min} = 0$ and we vary $Y_{max} > R_{max} + D_{max}$. In this example, intuitively, an optimal algorithm that knows the workload and unit cost process beforehand would recharge the battery as much as possible when $C(t) = C_{low}$ and discharge it as much as possible when $C(t) = C_{high}$. In fact, it can be shown that the following strategy is feasible and achieves minimum average cost:

- If $C(t) = C_{low}, W(t) = W_{low}$, then $P(t) = W_{low} + R_{max}$, $R(t) = R_{max}$, $D(t) = 0$.

- If $C(t) = C_{mid}, W(t) = W_{mid}$, then $P(t) = W_{mid}$, $R(t) = 0$, $D(t) = 0$.

- If $C(t) = C_{high}, W(t) = W_{high}$, then $P(t) = W_{high} - D_{max}$, $R(t) = 0$, $D(t) = D_{max}$.

The time average cost resulting from this strategy can be easily calculated and is given by 87.0 dollars/slot for all $Y_{max} > 10$. Also, we note that the cost resulting from an algorithm that does not use the battery in this example is given by 94.0 dollars/slot.

Now we simulate the dynamic algorithm for this example for different values of Y_{max} for 1000 slots (200 frames). The value of V is chosen to be $\frac{Y_{max} - Y_{min} - R_{max} - D_{max}}{C_{high} - C_{low}} = \frac{Y_{max} - 20}{8}$ (this choice will become clear in Sec. 5.2 when we relate V to the battery capacity). Note that the number of slots for which a fully charged battery can sustain the data center at maximum load is Y_{max}/W_{high}.

In Table 1, we show the time average cost achieved for different values of Y_{max}. It can be seen that as Y_{max} increases, the time average cost approaches the optimal value (this behavior will be formalized in Theorem 1). This is remarkable given that the dynamic algorithm operates without any knowledge of the future workload and cost processes. To examine the behavior of the dynamic algorithm in more detail, we fix $Y_{max} = 100$ and look at the sample paths of the control decisions taken by the optimal offline algorithm and the dynamic algorithm during the first 200 slots. This is shown in Figs. 4 and 5. It can be seen that initially, the dynamic tends to perform suboptimally. But eventually it *learns* to make close to optimal decisions.

It might be tempting to conclude from this example that an algorithm based on a price threshold is optimal. Specifically, such an algorithm makes a recharge vs. discharge decision depending on whether the current price $C(t)$ is smaller or larger than a threshold. However, it is easy to construct examples where the dynamic algorithm outperforms such a threshold based algorithm. Specifically, suppose that the $W(t)$ process takes values from the interval $[10, 90]$ uniformly at random every slot. Also, suppose

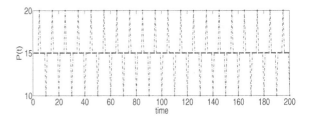

Figure 4: $P(t)$ **under the offline optimal solution with** $Y_{max} = 100$.

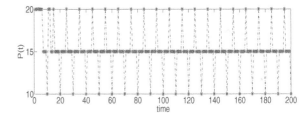

Figure 5: $P(t)$ **under the Dynamic Algorithm with** $Y_{max} = 100$.

$C(t)$ takes values from the set $\{2, 6, 10\}$ dollars uniformly at random every slot. We fix the other parameters as follows: $R_{max} = D_{max} = 10$, $P_{peak} = 90$, $C_{rc} = C_{dc} = 1$, $Y_{init} = Y_{min} = 0$ and $Y_{max} = 100$. We then simulate a threshold based algorithm for different values of the threshold in the set $\{2, 6, 10\}$ and select the one that yields the smallest cost. This was found to be 280.7 dollars/slot. We then simulate the dynamic algorithm for 10000 slots with $V = \frac{Y_{max} - 20}{10 - 2} = 10.0$ and it yields an average cost of 275.5 dollars/slot. We also note that the cost resulting from an algorithm that does not use the battery in this example is given by 300.73 dollars/slot.

We now establish two properties of the structure of the optimal solution to **P3** that will be useful in analyzing its performance later.

LEMMA 2. *The optimal solution to P3 has the following properties:*

1. *If $X(t) > -VC_{min}$, then the optimal solution always chooses $R^*(t) = 0$.*

2. *If $X(t) < -V\chi_{min}$, then the optimal solution always chooses $D^*(t) = 0$.*

PROOF. See [19]. □

5.1 Solving P3

In general, the complexity of solving **P3** depends on the structure of the unit cost function $C(t)$. For many cases of practical interest, **P3** is easy to solve and admits closed form solutions that can be implemented in real time. We consider two such cases here. Let $\theta(t)$ denote the value of the objective in **P3** when there is no recharge or discharge. Thus $\theta(t) = W(t)(X(t) + VC(t))$.

5.1.1 $C(t)$ does not depend on $P(t)$

Suppose that $C(t)$ depends only on $S(t)$ and not on $P(t)$. We can rewrite the expression in the objective of **P3** as

$P(t)(X(t) + VC(t)) + 1_R(t)VC_{rc} + 1_D(t)VC_{dc}$. Then, the optimal solution has the following simple threshold structure.

1. If $X(t) + VC(t) > 0$, then $R^*(t) = 0$ so that there is no recharge and we have the following two cases:

   (a) If $P_{low}(X(t) + VC(t)) + VC_{dc} < \theta(t)$, then discharge as much as possible, so that we get $D^*(t) = \min[W(t), D_{max}]$, $P^*(t) = \max[0, W(t) - D_{max}]$.

   (b) Else, draw all power from the grid. This yields $D^*(t) = 0$ and $P^*(t) = W(t)$.

2. Else if $X(t) + VC(t) \leq 0$, then $D^*(t) = 0$ so that there is no discharge and we have the following two cases:

   (a) If $P_{high}(X(t)+VC(t))+VC_{rc} < \theta(t)$, then recharge as much as possible. This yields $R^*(t) = \min[P_{peak} - W(t), R_{max}]$ and $P^*(t) = \min[P_{peak}, W(t)+R_{max}]$.

   (b) Else, draw all power from the grid. This yields $R^*(t) = 0$ and $P^*(t) = W(t)$.

We will show that this solution is feasible and does not violate the finite battery constraint in Sec. 5.3.

5.1.2 *$C(t)$ convex, increasing in $P(t)$*

Next suppose for each $S(t)$, $C(t)$ is convex and increasing in $P(t)$. For example, $\hat{C}(S(t), P(t))$ may have the form $\alpha(S(t))P^2(t)$ where $\alpha(S(t)) > 0$ for all $S(t)$. In this case, **P3** becomes a standard convex optimization problem in a single variable $P(t)$ and can be solved efficiently. The full solution is provided in [19].

5.2 Performance Theorem

We first define an upper bound V_{max} on the maximum value that V can take in our algorithm.

$$V_{max} \stackrel{\triangle}{=} \frac{Y_{max} - Y_{min} - R_{max} - D_{max}}{\chi_{min} - C_{min}} \quad (19)$$

Then we have the following result.

THEOREM 1. *(Algorithm Performance) Suppose the initial battery charge level Y_{init} satisfies $Y_{min} \leq Y_{init} \leq Y_{max}$. Then implementing the algorithm above with any fixed parameter V such that $0 < V \leq V_{max}$ for all $t \in \{0, 1, 2, \ldots\}$ results in the following performance guarantees:*

1. *The queue $X(t)$ is deterministically upper and lower bounded for all t as follows:*

$$-V\chi_{min} - D_{max} \leq X(t) \leq Y_{max} - Y_{min}$$
$$- D_{max} - V\chi_{min} \quad (20)$$

2. *The actual battery level $Y(t)$ satisfies $Y_{min} \leq Y(t) \leq Y_{max}$ for all t.*

3. *All control decisions are feasible.*

4. *If $W(t)$ and $S(t)$ are i.i.d. over slots, then the time-average cost under the dynamic algorithm is within B/V of the optimal value:*

$$\lim_{t \to \infty} \frac{1}{t} \sum_{\tau=0}^{t-1} \mathbb{E}\{P(\tau)C(\tau) + 1_R(\tau)C_{rc} + 1_D(\tau)C_{dc}\}$$
$$\leq \phi_{opt} + B/V \quad (21)$$

*where B is a constant given by $B = \frac{\max[R_{max}^2, D_{max}^2]}{2}$ and ϕ_{opt} is the optimal solution to **P1** under any feasible control algorithm (possibly with knowledge of future events).*

Theorem 1 part 4 shows that by choosing larger V, the time-average cost under the dynamic algorithm can be pushed closer to the minimum possible value ϕ_{opt}. However, V_{max} limits how large V can be chosen. We prove Theorem 1 in the next section.

5.3 Proof of Theorem 1

PROOF. (Theorem 1 part 1) We first show that (20) holds for $t = 0$. We have that

$$Y_{min} \leq Y(0) = Y_{init} \leq Y_{max} \quad (22)$$

Using the definition (16), we have that $Y(0) = X(0) + V\chi_{min} + D_{max} + Y_{min}$. Using this in (22), we get:

$$Y_{min} \leq X(0) + V\chi_{min} + D_{max} + Y_{min} \leq Y_{max}$$

This yields

$$-V\chi_{min} - D_{max} \leq X(0) \leq Y_{max} - Y_{min} - D_{max} - V\chi_{min}$$

Now suppose (20) holds for slot t. We will show that it also holds for slot $t + 1$. First, suppose $-VC_{min} < X(t) \leq Y_{max} - Y_{min} - D_{max} - V\chi_{min}$. Then, from Lemma 2, we have that $R^*(t) = 0$. Thus, using (17), we have that $X(t+1) \leq X(t) \leq Y_{max} - Y_{min} - D_{max} - V\chi_{min}$. Next, suppose $X(t) \leq -VC_{min}$. Then, the maximum possible increase is R_{max} so that $X(t + 1) \leq -VC_{min} + R_{max}$. Now for all V such that $0 < V \leq V_{max}$, we have that $-VC_{min} + R_{max} \leq Y_{max} - Y_{min} - D_{max} - V\chi_{min}$. This follows from the definition (19) and the fact that $\chi_{min} > C_{min}$. Thus, we have $X(t + 1) \leq Y_{max} - Y_{min} - D_{max} - V\chi_{min}$.

Next, suppose $-V\chi_{min} - D_{max} \leq X(t) < -V\chi_{min}$. Then, from Lemma 2, we have that $D^*(t) = 0$. Thus, using (17) we have that $X(t + 1) \geq X(t) \geq -V\chi_{min} - D_{max}$. Next, suppose $-V\chi_{min} \leq X(t)$. Then the maximum possible decrease is D_{max} so that $X(t+1) \geq -V\chi_{min} - D_{max}$ for this case as well. This shows that $X(t + 1) \geq -V\chi_{min} - D_{max}$. Combining these two bounds proves (20). □

PROOF. (Theorem 1 parts 2 and 3) Part 2 directly follows from (20) and (16). Using $Y(t) = X(t) + V\chi_{min} + D_{max} + Y_{min}$ in the lower bound in (20), we have: $-V\chi_{min} - D_{max} \leq Y(t) - V\chi_{min} - D_{max} - Y_{min}$, i.e., $Y_{min} \leq Y(t)$. Similarly, using $Y(t) = X(t) + V\chi_{min} + D_{max} + Y_{min}$ in the upper bound in (20), we have: $Y(t) - V\chi_{min} - D_{max} - Y_{min} \leq Y_{max} - Y_{min} - D_{max} - V\chi_{min}$, i.e., $Y(t) \leq Y_{max}$.

Part 3 now follows from part 2 and the constraint on $P(t)$ in **P3**. □

PROOF. (Theorem 1 part 4) We make use of the technique of Lyapunov optimization to show (21). We start by defining a Lyapunov function as a scalar measure of congestion in the system. Specifically, we define the following Lyapunov function: $L(X(t)) \stackrel{\triangle}{=} \frac{1}{2}X^2(t)$. Define the conditional 1-slot Lyapunov drift as follows:

$$\Delta(X(t)) \stackrel{\triangle}{=} \mathbb{E}\{L(X(t + 1)) - L(X(t))|X(t)\} \quad (23)$$

Using (17), $\Delta(X(t))$ can be bounded as follows (see [19] for details):

$$\Delta(X(t)) \leq B - X(t)\mathbb{E}\{D(t) - R(t)|X(t)\} \quad (24)$$

where $B = \frac{\max[R_{max}^2, D_{max}^2]}{2}$. Following the Lyapunov optimization framework of [8], we add to both sides of (24) the penalty term $V\mathbb{E}\{P(t)C(t) + 1_R(t)C_{rc} + 1_D(t)C_{dc}|X(t)\}$ to get the following:

$$\Delta(X(t)) + V\mathbb{E}\{P(t)C(t) + 1_R(t)C_{rc} + 1_D(t)C_{dc}|X(t)\}$$
$$\leq B - X(t)\mathbb{E}\{D(t) - R(t)|X(t)\}$$
$$+ V\mathbb{E}\{P(t)C(t) + 1_R(t)C_{rc} + 1_D(t)C_{dc}|X(t)\} \quad (25)$$

Using (1), we can rewrite the above as:

$$\Delta(X(t)) + V\mathbb{E}\{P(t)C(t) + 1_R(t)C_{rc} + 1_D(t)C_{dc}|X(t)\} \leq$$
$$B - X(t)\mathbb{E}\{W(t)|X(t)\} + X(t)\mathbb{E}\{P(t)|X(t)\}$$
$$+ V\mathbb{E}\{P(t)C(t) + 1_R(t)C_{rc} + 1_D(t)C_{dc}|X(t)\} \quad (26)$$

Comparing this with **P3**, it can be seen that given any queue value $X(t)$, our control algorithm is designed to *minimize* the right hand side of (26) over all possible feasible control policies. This includes the optimal, stationary, randomized policy given in Lemma 1. Then, plugging the control decisions corresponding to the stationary, randomized policy, the following holds for the dynamic algorithm:

$$\Delta(X(t)) + V\mathbb{E}\{P(t)C(t) + 1_R(t)C_{rc} + 1_D(t)C_{dc}|X(t)\} \leq$$
$$B + V\mathbb{E}\{P^{stat}(t)C^{stat}(t) + 1_R^{stat}(t)C_{rc} + 1_D^{stat}(t)C_{dc}|X(t)\}$$
$$= B + V\hat{\phi} \leq B + V\phi_{opt}$$

Taking the expectation of both sides and using the law of iterated expectations and summing over $t \in \{0, 1, 2, \ldots, T - 1\}$, we get:

$$\sum_{t=0}^{T-1} V\mathbb{E}\{P(t)C(t) + 1_R(t)C_{rc} + 1_D(t)C_{dc}\} \leq$$
$$BT + VT\phi_{opt} - \mathbb{E}\{L(X(T))\} + \mathbb{E}\{L(X(0))\}$$

Dividing both sides by VT and taking limit as $T \to \infty$ yields:

$$\lim_{T\to\infty} \frac{1}{T} \sum_{t=0}^{T-1} \mathbb{E}\{P(t)C(t) + 1_R(t)C_{rc} + 1_D(t)C_{dc}\} \leq \phi_{opt} + B/V$$

where we have used the fact that $\mathbb{E}\{L(X(0))\}$ is finite and that $\mathbb{E}\{L(X(T))\}$ is non-negative. $\square$

6. EXTENSIONS TO BASIC MODEL

In this section, we extend the basic model of Sec. 3 to the case where portions of the workload are delay-tolerant in the sense they can be postponed by a certain amount without affecting the utility the data center derives from executing them. We refer to such postponement as buffering the workload. Specifically, we assume that the total workload consists of both delay tolerant and delay intolerant components. Similar to the workload in the basic model, the delay intolerant workload cannot be buffered and must be served immediately. However, the delay tolerant component may be buffered and served later. As an example, data centers run virus scanning programs on most of their servers routinely (say once per day). As long as a virus scan is executed once a day, their purpose is served - it does not matter what time of the day is chosen for this. The ability to delay some of the workload gives more opportunities to reduce the average power cost in addition to using the battery. We assume

that our data center has system mechanisms to implement such buffering of specified workloads.

In the following, we will denote the total workload generated in slot t by $W(t)$. This consists of the delay tolerant and intolerant components denoted by $W_1(t)$ and $W_2(t)$ respectively, so that $W(t) = W_1(t) + W_2(t)$ for all t. Similar to the basic model, we use $P(t), R(t), D(t)$ to denote the total power drawn from the grid, the total power used to recharge the battery and the total power discharged from the battery in slot t, respectively. Thus, the total amount available to serve the workload is given by $P(t) - R(t) + D(t)$. Let $\gamma(t)$ denote the fraction of this that is used to serve the delay tolerant workload in slot t. Then the amount used to serve the delay intolerant workload is $(1 - \gamma(t))(P(t) - R(t) + D(t))$. Note that the following constraint must be satisfied every slot:

$$0 \leq \gamma(t) \leq 1 \quad (27)$$

We next define $U(t)$ as the unfinished work for the delay tolerant workload in slot t. The dynamics for $U(t)$ can be expressed as:

$$U(t + 1) = \max[U(t) - \gamma(t)(P(t) - R(t) + D(t)), 0] + W_1(t) \quad (28)$$

We assume that $U(t)$ is served in FIFO order. For the delay intolerant workload, there are no such queues since all incoming workload must be served in the same slot. This means:

$$W_2(t) = (1 - \gamma(t))(P(t) - R(t) + D(t)) \quad (29)$$

The block diagram for this extended model is shown in Fig. 6. Similar to the basic model, we assume that for $i = 1, 2$, $W_i(t)$ varies randomly in an i.i.d. fashion, taking values from a set $\mathcal{W}_i$ of non-negative values. We assume that $W_1(t) + W_2(t) \leq W_{max}$ for all t. We also assume that $W_1(t) \leq W_{1,max} < W_{max}$ and $W_2(t) \leq W_{2,max} < W_{max}$ for all t. We further assume that $P_{peak} \geq W_{max} + \max[R_{max}, D_{max}]$. We use the same model for battery and unit cost as in Sec. 3.

Our objective is to minimize the time-average cost subject to meeting all the constraints (such as finite battery size and (29)) and ensuring finite average delay for the delay tolerant workload. This can be stated as:

P4:

Minimize: $\lim_{t\to\infty} \frac{1}{t} \sum_{\tau=0}^{t-1} \mathbb{E}\{P(\tau)C(\tau) + 1_R(\tau)C_{rc} + 1_D(\tau)C_{dc}\}$

Subject to: Constraints $(2), (5), (6), (7), (9), (27), (29)$

Finite average delay for $W_1(t)$

Similar to the basic model, we consider the following *relaxed* problem:

P5:

Minimize: $\lim_{t\to\infty} \frac{1}{t} \sum_{\tau=0}^{t-1} \mathbb{E}\{P(\tau)C(\tau) + 1_R(\tau)C_{rc} + 1_D(\tau)C_{dc}\}$

Subject to: Constraints $(2), (5), (9), (27), (29)$

$$\overline{R} = \overline{D} \quad (30)$$
$$\overline{U} < \infty \quad (31)$$

where $\overline{U}$ is the time average expected queue backlog for the

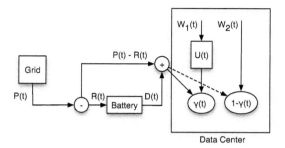

Figure 6: Block diagram for the extended model with delay tolerant and delay intolerant workloads.

delay tolerant workload and is defined as:

$$\overline{U} \triangleq \limsup_{t \to \infty} \frac{1}{t} \sum_{\tau=0}^{t-1} \mathbb{E}\{U(\tau)\} \quad (32)$$

Let ϕ_{ext} and $\hat{\phi}_{ext}$ denote the optimal value for problems **P4** and **P5** respectively. Since **P5** is less constrained than **P4**, we have that $\hat{\phi}_{ext} \leq \phi_{ext}$. Similar to Lemma 1, the following holds:

LEMMA 3. *(Optimal Stationary, Randomized Policy): If the workload process $W_1(t), W_2(t)$ and auxiliary process $S(t)$ are i.i.d. over slots, then there exists a stationary, randomized policy that takes control decisions $\hat{P}(t), \hat{R}(t), \hat{D}(t), \hat{\gamma}(t)$ every slot purely as a function (possibly randomized) of the current state $(W_1(t), W_2(t), S(t))$ while satisfying the constraints (29), (2), (5), (9), (27) and providing the following guarantees:*

$$\mathbb{E}\left\{\hat{R}(t)\right\} = \mathbb{E}\left\{\hat{D}(t)\right\} \quad (33)$$

$$\mathbb{E}\left\{\hat{\gamma}(t)(\hat{P}(t) - \hat{R}(t) + \hat{D}(t))\right\} \geq \mathbb{E}\{W_1(t)\} \quad (34)$$

$$\mathbb{E}\left\{\hat{P}(t)\hat{C}(t) + \hat{1}_R(t)C_{rc} + \hat{1}_D(t)C_{dc}\right\} = \hat{\phi}_{ext} \quad (35)$$

where the expectations above are with respect to the stationary distribution of $(W_1(t), W_2(t), S(t))$ and the randomized control decisions.

PROOF. This result follows from the framework in [8, 15] and is omitted for brevity. □

The condition (34) only guarantees queueing stability, not bounded worst case delay. We will now design a dynamic control algorithm that will yield bounded worst case delay while guaranteeing an average cost that is within $O(1/V)$ of $\hat{\phi}_{ext}$ (and therefore ϕ_{ext}).

6.1 Delay-Aware Queue

In order to provide worst case delay guarantees to the delay tolerant workload, we will make use of the technique of ϵ-persistent queue [16]. Specifically, we define a virtual queue $Z(t)$ as follows:

$$Z(t+1) = [Z(t) - \gamma(t)(P(t) - R(t) + D(t)) + \epsilon 1_{U(t)}]^+ \quad (36)$$

where $\epsilon > 0$ is a parameter to be specified later, $1_{U(t)}$ is an indicator variable that is 1 if $U(t) > 0$ and 0 otherwise, and $[x]^+ = \max[x, 0]$. The objective of this virtual queue

is to enable the provision of worst-case delay guarantee on any buffered workload $W_1(t)$. Specifically, if any control algorithm ensures that $U(t) \leq U_{max}$ and $Z(t) \leq Z_{max}$ for all t, then the worst case delay can be bounded. This is shown in the following:

LEMMA 4. *(Worst Case Delay) Suppose a control algorithm ensures that $U(t) \leq U_{max}$ and $Z(t) \leq Z_{max}$ for all t, where U_{max} and Z_{max} are some positive constants. Then the worst case delay for any delay tolerant workload is at most δ_{max} slots where:*

$$\delta_{max} \triangleq \lceil (U_{max} + Z_{max})/\epsilon \rceil \quad (37)$$

PROOF. Consider a new arrival $W_1(t)$ in any slot t. We will show that this is served on or before time $t + \delta_{max}$. We argue by contradiction. Suppose this workload is not served by $t + \delta_{max}$. Then for all slots $\tau \in \{t+1, t+2, \ldots, t+\delta_{max}\}$, it must be the case that $U(\tau) > 0$ (else $W_1(t)$ would have been served before τ). This implies that $1_{U(\tau)} = 1$ and using (36), we have:

$$Z(\tau+1) \geq Z(\tau) - \gamma(\tau)(P(\tau) - R(\tau) + D(\tau)) + \epsilon$$

Summing for all $\tau \in \{t+1, t+2, \ldots, t+\delta_{max}\}$, we get:

$$Z(t+\delta_{max}+1) - Z(t+1) \geq \delta_{max}\epsilon$$
$$- \sum_{\tau=t+1}^{t+\delta_{max}} [\gamma(\tau)(P(\tau) - R(\tau) + D(\tau))]$$

Using the fact that $Z(t+\delta_{max}+1) \leq Z_{max}$ and $Z(t+1) \geq 0$, we get:

$$\sum_{\tau=t+1}^{t+\delta_{max}} [\gamma(\tau)(P(\tau) - R(\tau) + D(\tau))] \geq \delta_{max}\epsilon - Z_{max} \quad (38)$$

Note that by (28), $W_1(t)$ is part of the backlog $U(t+1)$. Since $U(t+1) \leq U_{max}$ and since the service is FIFO, it will be served on or before time $t + \delta_{max}$ whenever at least U_{max} units of power is used to serve the delay tolerant workload during the interval $(t+1, \ldots, t+\delta_{max})$. Since we have assumed that $W_1(t)$ is not served by $t + \delta_{max}$, it must be the case that $\sum_{\tau=t+1}^{t+\delta_{max}} [\gamma(\tau)(P(\tau) - R(\tau) + D(\tau))] < U_{max}$. Using this in (38), we have:

$$U_{max} > \delta_{max}\epsilon - Z_{max}$$

This implies that $\delta_{max} < (U_{max} + Z_{max})/\epsilon$, that contradicts the definition of δ_{max} in (37). □

In Sec. 6.4, we will show that under the dynamic control algorithm (to be presented next), there are indeed constants U_{max}, Z_{max} such that $U(t) \leq U_{max}, Z(t) \leq Z_{max}$ for all t.

6.2 Optimal Control Algorithm

We now present an online control algorithm that approximately solves **P4**. Similar to the algorithm for the basic model, this algorithm also makes use of the following queueing state variable $X(t)$ to track the battery charge level and is defined as follows:

$$X(t) = Y(t) - Q_{max} - D_{max} - Y_{min} \quad (39)$$

where Q_{max} is a constant to be specified in (44). Recall that $Y(t)$ denotes the actual battery charge level in slot t

and evolves according to (3). It can be seen that $X(t)$ is simply a shifted version of $Y(t)$ and its dynamics is given by:

$$X(t+1) = X(t) - D(t) + R(t) \qquad (40)$$

We will show that this definition enables our algorithm to ensure that the constraint (4) is met.

We are now ready to state the dynamic control algorithm. Let $(W_1(t), W_2(t), S(t))$ be the system state in slot t. Define $\boldsymbol{Q}(t) \triangleq (U(t), Z(t), X(t))$ as the queue state that includes the workload queue as well as auxiliary queues. Then the dynamic algorithm chooses control decisions $P(t), R(t), D(t)$ and $\gamma(t)$ as the solution to the following problem:

P6 :

$$\text{Max:} [U(t) + Z(t)] P(t) - V \Big[P(t) C(t) + 1_R(t) C_{rc} + 1_D(t) C_{dc} \Big]$$
$$+ [X(t) + U(t) + Z(t)] (D(t) - R(t))$$

Subject to: Constraints $(27), (29), (2), (5), (9)$

where $V > 0$ is a control parameter that affects the distance from optimality. Let $P^*(t), R^*(t), D^*(t)$ and $\gamma^*(t)$ denote the optimal solution to **P6**. Then, the dynamic algorithm allocates $(1 - \gamma^*(t))(P^*(t) - R^*(t) + D^*(t))$ power to service the delay intolerant workload and the remaining is used for the delay tolerant workload.

After computing these quantities, the algorithm implements them and updates the queueing variable $X(t)$ according to (40). This process is repeated every slot. Note that in solving **P6**, the control algorithm only makes use of the current system state values and does not require knowledge of the statistics of the workload or unit cost processes.

We now establish two properties of the structure of the optimal solution to **P6** that will be useful in analyzing its performance later.

LEMMA 5. *The optimal solution to **P6** has the following properties:*

1. *If $X(t) > -VC_{min}$, then the optimal solution always chooses $R^*(t) = 0$.*

2. *If $X(t) < -Q_{max}$ (where Q_{max} is specified in (44)), then the optimal solution always chooses $D^*(t) = 0$.*

PROOF. See [19]. □

6.3 Solving P6

Similar to **P3**, the complexity of solving **P6** depends on the structure of the unit cost function $C(t)$. For many cases of practical interest, **P6** is easy to solve and admits closed form solutions that can be implemented in real time. We consider one such case here.

6.3.1 $C(t)$ does not depend on $P(t)$

For notational convenience, let $Q_1(t) = [U(t) + Z(t) - VC(t)]$ and $Q_2(t) = [X(t) + U(t) + Z(t)]$.

Let $\theta_1(t)$ denote the optimal value of the objective in **P6** when there is no recharge or discharge. When $C(t)$ does not depend on $P(t)$, this can be calculated as follows: If $U(t) + Z(t) \geq VC(t)$, then $\theta_1(t) = Q_1(t) P_{peak}$. Else, $\theta_1(t) = Q_1(t) W_2(t)$.

Next, let $\theta_2(t)$ denote the optimal value of the objective in **P6** when the option of recharge is chosen, so that $R(t) > 0, D(t) = 0$. This can be calculated as follows:

1. If $Q_1(t) \geq 0, Q_2(t) \geq 0$, then $\theta_2(t) = Q_1(t) P_{peak} - VC_{rc}$.

2. If $Q_1(t) \geq 0, Q_2(t) < 0$, then $\theta_2(t) = Q_1(t) P_{peak} - Q_2(t) R_{max} - VC_{rc}$.

3. If $Q_1(t) < 0, Q_2(t) \geq 0$, then $\theta_2(t) = Q_1(t) W_2(t) - VC_{rc}$.

4. If $Q_1(t) < 0, Q_2(t) < 0$, then we have two cases:

    (a) If $Q_1(t) \geq Q_2(t)$, then $\theta_2(t) = Q_1(t)(R_{max} + W_2(t)) - Q_2(t) R_{max} - VC_{rc}$.

    (b) If $Q_1(t) < Q_2(t)$, then $\theta_2(t) = Q_1(t) W_2(t) - VC_{rc}$.

Finally, let $\theta_3(t)$ denote the optimal value of the objective in **P6** when when the option of discharge is chosen, so that $D(t) > 0, R(t) = 0$. This can be calculated as follows:

1. If $Q_1(t) \geq 0, Q_2(t) \geq 0$, then $\theta_3(t) = Q_1(t) P_{peak} + Q_2(t) D_{max} - VC_{dc}$.

2. If $Q_1(t) \geq 0, Q_2(t) < 0$, then $\theta_3(t) = Q_1(t) P_{peak} - VC_{dc}$.

3. If $Q_1(t) < 0, Q_2(t) \geq 0$, then $\theta_3(t) = Q_1(t) \max[0, W_2(t) - D_{max}] + Q_2(t) D_{max} - VC_{dc}$.

4. If $Q_1(t) < 0, Q_2(t) < 0$, then we have two cases:

    (a) If $Q_1(t) \leq Q_2(t)$, then $\theta_3(t) = Q_1(t) \max[0, W_2(t) - D_{max}] + Q_2(t) \min[W_2(t), D_{max}] - VC_{dc}$.

    (b) If $Q_1(t) > Q_2(t)$, then $\theta_3(t) = Q_1(t) W_2(t) - VC_{dc}$.

After computing $\theta_1(t), \theta_2(t), \theta_3(t)$, we pick the mode that yields the highest value of the objective and implement the corresponding solution.

6.4 Performance Theorem

We define an upper bound V_{ext}^{max} on the maximum value that V can take in our algorithm for the extended model.

$$V_{ext}^{max} \triangleq \frac{Y_{max} - Y_{min} - (R_{max} + D_{max} + W_{1,max} + \epsilon)}{\chi_{min} - C_{min}} \qquad (41)$$

Then we have the following result.

THEOREM 2. *(Algorithm Performance) Suppose $U(0) = 0, Z(0) = 0$ and the initial battery charge level Y_{init} satisfies $Y_{min} \leq Y_{init} \leq Y_{max}$. Then implementing the algorithm above with any fixed parameter $\epsilon \geq 0$ such that $\epsilon \leq W_{max} - W_{2,max}$ and a parameter V such that $0 < V \leq V_{ext}^{max}$ for all $t \in \{0, 1, 2, \ldots\}$ results in the following performance guarantees:*

1. *The queues $U(t)$ and $Z(t)$ are deterministically upper bounded by U_{max} and Z_{max} respectively for all t where:*

$$U_{max} \triangleq V\chi_{min} + W_{1,max} \qquad (42)$$

$$Z_{max} \triangleq V\chi_{min} + \epsilon \qquad (43)$$

Further, the sum $U(t) + Z(t)$ is also deterministically upper bounded by Q_{max} where

$$Q_{max} \triangleq V\chi_{min} + W_{1,max} + \epsilon \qquad (44)$$

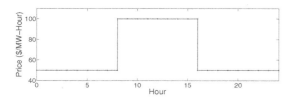

Figure 7: One period of the unit cost process.

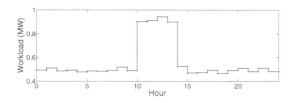

Figure 8: One period of the workload process.

2. The queue $X(t)$ is deterministically upper and lower bounded for all t as follows:

$$-Q_{max} - D_{max} \leq X(t) \leq Y_{max} - Y_{min} - Q_{max} \\ - D_{max} \quad (45)$$

3. The actual battery level $Y(t)$ satisfies $Y_{min} \leq Y(t) \leq Y_{max}$ for all t.

4. All control decisions are feasible.

5. The worst case delay experienced by any delay tolerant request is given by:

$$\left\lceil \frac{2V\chi_{min} + W_{1,max} + \epsilon}{\epsilon} \right\rceil \quad (46)$$

6. If $W_1(t), W_2(t)$ and $S(t)$ are i.i.d. over slots, then the time-average cost under the dynamic algorithm is within B_{ext}/V of the optimal value:

$$\lim_{t \to \infty} \frac{1}{t} \sum_{\tau=0}^{t-1} \mathbb{E}\left\{ P(\tau)C(\tau) + 1_R(\tau)C_{rc} + 1_D(\tau)C_{dc} \right\}$$

$$\leq \hat{\phi}_{ext} + B_{ext}/V \quad (47)$$

where B_{ext} is a constant given by $B_{ext} = (P_{peak} + D_{max})^2 + \frac{(W_{1,max})^2 + \epsilon^2}{2} + B$ and $\hat{\phi}_{ext}$ is the optimal solution to **P4** under any feasible control algorithm (possibly with knowledge of future events).

Thus, by choosing larger V, the time-average cost under the dynamic algorithm can be pushed closer to the minimum possible value ϕ_{opt}. However, this increases the worst case delay bound yielding a $O(1/V, V)$ utility-delay tradeoff. Also note that V_{ext}^{max} limits how large V can be chosen.

PROOF. See [19]. □

7. SIMULATION-BASED EVALUATION

We evaluate the performance of our control algorithm using both synthetic and real pricing data. To gain insights into the behavior of the algorithm and to compare with the optimal offline solution, we first consider the basic model

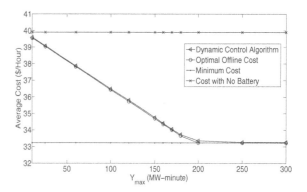

Figure 9: Average Cost per Hour vs. Y_{max}.

and use a simple periodic unit cost and workload process as shown in Figs. 7 and 8. These values repeat every 24 hours and the unit cost does not depend on $P(t)$. From Fig. 7, it can be seen that $C_{max} = \$100$ and $C_{min} = \$50$. Further, we have that $\chi_{min} = C_{max} = 100$. We assume a slot size of 1 minute so that the control decisions on $P(t), R(t), D(t)$ are taken once every minute. We fix the parameters $R_{max} = 0.2$ MW-slot, $D_{max} = 1.0$ MW-slot, $C_{rc} = C_{dc} = 0, Y_{min} = 0$. We now simulate the basic control algorithm of Sec. 5.1.1 for different values of Y_{max} and with $V = V_{max}$. For each Y_{max}, the simulation is performed for a duration of 4 weeks.

In Fig. 9, we plot the average cost per hour under the dynamic algorithm for different values of battery size Y_{max}. It can be seen that the average cost reduces as Y_{max} is increased and converges to a fixed value for large Y_{max}, as suggested by Theorem 1. For this simple example, we can compute the minimum possible average cost per hour over all battery sizes (this corresponds to $\hat{\phi}$ of Sec. 4), and this is given by \$33.23 which is also the value to which the dynamic algorithm converges as Y_{max} is increased. Moreover, in this example, we can also compute the optimal offline cost for *each value* of Y_{max} (corresponding to ϕ_{opt}). These are also plotted in Fig. 9. It can be seen that, for each Y_{max}, the dynamic algorithm performs quite close to the corresponding optimal value, even for smaller values of Y_{max}. Note that Theorem 1 provides such guarantees only for sufficiently large values of Y_{max}. Finally, the average cost per hour when no battery is used is given by \$39.90.

We next consider a six-month data set of average hourly spot market prices for the Los Angeles Zone LA1 obtained from CAISO [1]. These prices correspond to the period $01/01/2005 - 06/30/2005$ and each value denotes the average price of 1 MW-Hour of electricity. A portion of this data corresponding to the first week of January is plotted in Fig. 1. We fix the slot size to 5 minutes. The unit cost $C(t)$ obtained from the data set for each hour is assumed to be fixed for that hour. Furthermore, we assume that the unit cost does not depend on the total power drawn $P(t)$.

In our experiments, we assume that the data center receives workload in an i.i.d fashion. Specifically, every slot, $W(t)$ takes values from the set $[0.1, 1.5]$ MW uniformly at random. We fix the parameters D_{max} and R_{max} to 0.5 MW-slot, $C_{dc} = C_{rc} = \$0.1$, and $Y_{min} = 0$. Also, $P_{peak} = W_{max} + R_{max} = 2.0$ MW. We now simulate four algorithms on this setup for different values of Y_{max}. The length of time the battery can power the data center if the draw were

Y_{max}	15	30	50
Battery, No WP	95%	92%	89%
WP, No Battery	96%	92%	88%
WP, Battery	92%	85%	79%

Table 2: Ratio of total cost under schemes (B), (C), (D) to the total cost under (A) for different values of Y_{max} with i.i.d. $W(t)$ over the 6 month period.

W_{max} starting from fully charged battery is given by $\frac{Y_{max}}{W_{max}}$ slots, each of length 5 minutes. We consider the following four schemes: (A) "No battery, No WP," which meets the demand in every slot using power from the grid and without postponing any workload, (B) "Battery, No WP," which employs the algorithm in the basic model without postponing any workload, (C) "No Battery, WP," which employs the extended model for WP but without any battery, and (D) "Complete," the complete algorithm of the extended model with both battery and WP. For (C) and (D), we assume that during every slot, half of the total workload is delay-tolerant.

We simulate these algorithms to obtain the total cost over the 6 month period for $Y_{max} \in \{15, 30, 50\}$ MW-slot. For (B), we use $V = V_{max}$ while for (C) and (D), we use $V = V_{ext}^{max}$ with $\epsilon = W_{max}/2$. Note that an increased battery capacity does not have any effect on the performance under (C). In order to get a fair comparison with the other schemes, we assume that the worst case delay guarantee that case (C) must provide for the delay tolerant traffic is the same as that under (D).

In Table 2, we show the ratio of the total cost under schemes (B), (C), (D) to the total cost under (A) for these values of Y_{max} over the 6 month period. The total cost over the 6 month period under (A) was found to be $143,141.11. It can be seen that (D) combines the benefits of both (B) and (C) and provides the most cost savings over the baseline case. For example, with $Y_{max} = 50$ MW-slot, the total savings provided by (B), (C), and (D) are $15,745, $17,176 and $30,000, respectively.

8. CONCLUSIONS AND FUTURE WORK

In this paper, we studied the problem of opportunistically using energy storage devices to reduce the time average electricity bill of a data center. Using the technique of Lyapunov optimization, we designed an online control algorithm that achieves close to optimal cost as the battery size is increased.

We would like to extend our current framework along several important directions including: (i) multiple utilities (or captive sources such as DG) with different price variations and availability properties (e.g., certain renewable sources of energy are not available at all times), (ii) tariffs where the utility bill depends on peak power draw in addition to the energy consumption, and (iii) devising online algorithms that offer solutions whose proximity to the optimal has a smaller dependence on battery capacity than currently. We also plan to explore implementation and feasibility related concerns such as: (i) what are appropriate trade-offs between investments in additional battery capacity and cost reductions that this offers? (ii) what is the extent of cost reduction benefits for realistic data center workloads? and (iii) does stored energy make sense as a cost optimization knob in other domains besides data centers? Our technique could be viewed as a design tool which, when parameterized well, can

assist in determining suitable configuration parameters such as battery size, usage rules-of-thumb, time-scale at which decisions should be made, etc. Finally, we believe that our work opens up a whole set of interesting issues worth exploring in the area of consumer-end (not just data centers) demand response mechanisms for power cost optimization.

Acknowledgments

This work was supported, in part, by the NSF grants CCF-0811670, CNS-0720456, CNS-0615097, CAREER awards CCF-0747525 and CNS-0953541, and a research award from HP. This work was performed while Rahul Urgaonkar was a student at the University of Southern California.

9. REFERENCES

[1] California ISO Open Access Same-time Information System (OASIS) Hourly Average Energy Prices. http://oasisis.caiso.com.

[2] Lead-acid batteries: Lifetime vs. Depth of discharge. http://www.windsun.com/Batteries/Battery_FAQ.htm.

[3] A. Bar-Noy, Y. Feng, M. P. Johnson, and O. Liu. When to reap and when to sow: Lowering peak usage with realistic batteries. In *Proc. 7th International Conference on Experimental Algorithms*, 2008.

[4] A. Bar-Noy, M. P. Johnson, and O. Liu. Peak shaving through resource buffering. In *Proc. WAOA*, 2008.

[5] D. P. Bertsekas. *Dynamic Programming and Optimal Control, vols. 1 and 2*. Athena Scientific, 2007.

[6] J. S. Chase, D. C. Anderson, P. N. Thakar, A. M. Vahdat, and R. P. Doyle. Managing energy and server resources in hosting centers. *SIGOPS Oper. Syst. Rev.*, 35:103–116, Oct. 2001.

[7] M. Gatzianas, L. Georgiadis, and L. Tassiulas. Control of wireless networks with rechargeable batteries. *IEEE Trans. Wireless. Comm.*, 9:581–593, Feb. 2010.

[8] L. Georgiadis, M. J. Neely, and L. Tassiulas. Resource allocation and cross-layer control in wireless networks. *Found. and Trends in Networking*, 1:1–144, 2006.

[9] S. Gurumurthi, A. Sivasubramaniam, M. Kandemir, and H. Franke. Drpm: Dynamic speed control for power management in server class disks. In *Proc. ISCA '03*, 2003.

[10] U. Hoelzle and L. A. Barroso. *The Datacenter as a Computer: An Introduction to the Design of Warehouse-Scale Machines*. Morgan & Claypool, 2009.

[11] K. Le, R. Bianchini, M. Martonosi, and T. Nguyen. Cost- and energy-aware load distribution across data centers. In *Proc. HOTPOWER*, 2009.

[12] A. R. Lebeck, X. Fan, H. Zeng, and C. Ellis. Power aware page allocation. *SIGOPS Oper. Syst. Rev.*, 34:105–116, Nov. 2000.

[13] D. Linden and T. B. Reddy. *Handbook of Batteries*. McGraw Hill Handbooks, 2002.

[14] M. Marwah, P. Maciel, A. Shah, R. Sharma, T. Christian, V. Almeida, C. Araújo, E. Souza, G. Callou, B. Silva, S. Galdino, and J. Pires. Quantifying the sustainability impact of data center availability. *SIGMETRICS Perform. Eval. Rev.*, 37:64–68, March 2010.

[15] M. J. Neely. *Stochastic Network Optimization with Application to Communication and Queueing Systems*. Morgan & Claypool, 2010.

[16] M. J. Neely, A. S. Tehrani, and A. G. Dimakis. Efficient algorithms for renewable energy allocation to delay tolerant consumers. In *Proc. IEEE SmartGridComm*, 2010.

[17] S. Park, W. Jiang, Y. Zhou, and S. Adve. Managing energy-performance tradeoffs for multithreaded applications on multiprocessor architectures. In *Proc. ACM SIGMETRICS*, 2007.

[18] A. Qureshi, R. Weber, H. Balakrishnan, J. Guttag, and B. Maggs. Cutting the electric bill for internet-scale systems. In *Proc. SIGCOMM*, 2009.

[19] R. Urgaonkar, B. Urgaonkar, M. J. Neely, and A. Sivasubramaniam. Optimal power cost management using stored energy in data centers. *arXiv Technical Report: arXiv:1103.3099v2*, March 2011.

[20] Q. Zhu, F. David, C. Devaraj, Z. Li, Y. Zhou, and P. Cao. Reducing energy consumption of disk storage using power-aware cache management. In *Proc. HPCA*, 2004.

Greening Geographical Load Balancing

Zhenhua Liu, Minghong Lin,
Adam Wierman, Steven H. Low
CMS, California Institute of Technology, Pasadena
{zliu2,mhlin,adamw,slow}@caltech.edu

Lachlan L. H. Andrew
Faculty of ICT
Swinburne University of Technology, Australia
landrew@swin.edu.au

ABSTRACT

Energy expenditure has become a significant fraction of data center operating costs. Recently, "geographical load balancing" has been suggested to reduce energy cost by exploiting the electricity price differences across regions. However, this reduction of cost can paradoxically increase total energy use.

This paper explores whether the geographical diversity of Internet-scale systems can additionally be used to provide environmental gains. Specifically, we explore whether geographical load balancing can encourage use of "green" renewable energy and reduce use of "brown" fossil fuel energy. We make two contributions. First, we derive two distributed algorithms for achieving optimal geographical load balancing. Second, we show that if electricity is dynamically priced in proportion to the instantaneous fraction of the total energy that is brown, then geographical load balancing provides significant reductions in brown energy use. However, the benefits depend strongly on the degree to which systems accept dynamic energy pricing and the form of pricing used.

Categories and Subject Descriptors

C.2.4 [**Computer-Communication Networks**]: Distributed Systems

General Terms

Algorithms, Performance

1. INTRODUCTION

Increasingly, web services are provided by massive, geographically diverse "Internet-scale" distributed systems, some having several data centers each with hundreds of thousands of servers. Such data centers require many megawatts of electricity and so companies like Google and Microsoft pay tens of millions of dollars annually for electricity [31].

The enormous, and growing energy demands of data centers have motivated research both in academia and industry on reducing energy usage, for both economic and environmental reasons. Engineering advances in cooling, virtualization, multi-core servers, DC power, etc. have led to significant improvements in the Power Usage Effectiveness (PUE) of data centers; see [6, 37, 19, 21]. Such work focuses on reducing the *energy use* of data centers and their components.

A different stream of research has focused on exploiting the geographical diversity of Internet-scale systems to reduce the *energy cost*. Specifically, a system with clusters at tens or hundreds of locations around the world can dynamically route requests/jobs to clusters based on proximity to the user, load, and local electricity price. Thus, dynamic geographical load balancing can balance the revenue lost due to increased delay against the electricity costs at each location.

In recent years, many papers have illustrated the potential of geographical load balancing to provide significant cost savings for data centers, e.g., [24, 28, 31, 32, 34, 39] and the references therein. The goal of the current paper is different. Our goal is to explore the social impact of geographical load balancing systems. In particular, geographical load balancing aims to reduce energy costs, but this can come at the expense of increased total energy usage: by routing to a data center farther from the request source to use cheaper energy, the data center may need to complete the job faster, and so use more service capacity, and thus energy, than if the request was served closer to the source.

In contrast to this negative consequence, geographical load balancing also provides a huge opportunity for environmental benefit as the penetration of green, renewable energy sources increases. Specifically, an enormous challenge facing the electric grid is that of incorporating intermittent, unpredictable renewable sources such as wind and solar. Because generation supplied to the grid must be balanced by demand (i) instantaneously and (ii) locally (due to transmission losses), renewable sources pose a significant challenge. A key technique for handling the unpredictability of renewable sources is *demand-response*, which entails the grid adjusting the demand by changing the electricity price [2]. However, demand response entails a *local* customer curtailing use. In contrast, the demand of Internet-scale systems is flexible geographically; thus traffic can be routed to different regions to "follow the renewables", providing demand-response without service interruption. Since data centers represent a significant and growing fraction of total electricity consumption, and the IT infrastructure is already in place, geographical load balancing has the potential to provide an extremely inexpensive approach for enabling large scale, global demand-response.

The key to realizing the environmental benefits above is for data centers to move from the fixed price contracts that are now typical toward some degree of dynamic pricing, with lower prices when green energy is available. The demand response markets currently in place provide a natural way for this transition to occur, and there is already evidence of some data centers participating in such markets [2].

The contribution of this paper is twofold. (1) We develop distributed algorithms for geographical load balancing with provable optimality guarantees. (2) We use the proposed algorithms to explore the feasibility and consequences of using geographical load balancing for demand response in the grid.

Contribution (1): To derive distributed geographical load balancing algorithms we use a simple but general model, described in detail in Section 2. In it, each data center minimizes its cost, which is a linear combination of an energy cost and the lost revenue due to the delay of requests (which includes both network propagation delay and load-dependent queueing delay within a data center). The geographical load balancing algorithm must then dynamically define both how requests should be routed to data centers and how to allocate capacity in each data center (i.e., how many servers are kept in active/energy-saving states).

In Section 3, we characterize the optimal geographical load balancing solutions and show that they have practically appealing properties, such as sparse routing tables. Then, in Section 4, we use the previous characterization to give two distributed algorithms which provably compute the optimal routing and provisioning decisions, and which require different types of coordination of computation. Finally, we evaluate the distributed algorithms in a trace-driven numeric simulation of a realistic, distributed, Internet-scale system (Section 5). The results show that a cost saving of over 40% during light-traffic periods is possible.

Contribution (2): In Section 6 we evaluate the feasibility and benefits of using geographical load balancing to facilitate the integration of renewable sources into the grid. We do this using a trace-driven numeric simulation of a realistic, distributed Internet-scale system in combination with models for the availability of wind and solar energy over time.

When the data center incentive is aligned with the social objective or reducing brown energy by dynamically pricing electricity proportionally to the fraction of the total energy coming from brown sources, we show that "follow the renewables" routing ensues (see Figure 5), causing significant social benefit. In contrast, we also determine the wasted brown energy when prices are static, or are dynamic but do not align data center and social objectives.

2. MODEL AND NOTATION

We now introduce the workload and data center models, followed by the geographical load balancing problem.

2.1 The workload model

We consider a discrete-time model whose timeslot matches the timescale at which routing decisions and capacity provisioning decisions can be updated. There is a (possibly long) interval of interest $t \in \{1, \ldots, T\}$. There are $|J|$ geographically concentrated sources of requests, i.e., "cities", and the mean arrival rate from source j at time t is $L_j(t)$. Job inter-arrival times are assumed to be much shorter than a timeslot, so that provisioning can be based on the average arrival rate during a slot. In practice, T could be a month and a slot length could be 1 hour. Our analytic results make no assumptions on $L_j(t)$; however to provide realistic estimates we use real-world traces to define $L_j(t)$ in Sections 5 and 6.

2.2 The data center cost model

We model an Internet-scale system as a collection of $|N|$ geographically diverse data centers, where data center i is modeled as a collection of M_i homogeneous servers. The model focuses on two key control decisions of geographical load balancing: (i) determining $\lambda_{ij}(t)$, the amount of traffic routed from source j to data center i; and (ii) determining $m_i(t) \in \{0, \ldots, M_i\}$, the number of active servers at data center i. The system seeks to choose $\lambda_{ij}(t)$ and $m_i(t)$ in order to minimize cost during $[1, T]$. Depending on the system design these decisions may be centralized or decentralized. Algorithms for these decisions are the focus of Section 4.

Our model for data center costs focuses on the server costs of the data center.[1] We model costs by combining the *energy cost* and the *delay cost* (in terms of lost revenue). Note that, to simplify the model, we do not include the switching costs associated with cycling servers in and out of power-saving modes; however the approach of [24] provides a natural way to incorporate such costs if desired.

Energy cost. To capture the geographic diversity and variation over time of energy costs, we let $g_i(t, m_i, \lambda_i)$ denote the energy cost for data center i during timeslot t given m_i active servers and arrival rate λ_i. For every fixed t, we assume that $g_i(t, m_i, \lambda_i)$ is continuously differentiable in both m_i and λ_i, strictly increasing in m_i, non-decreasing in λ_i, and convex in m_i. This formulation is quite general, and captures, for example, the common charging plan of a fixed price per kWh plus an additional "demand charge" for the peak of the average power used over a sliding 15 minute window [27]. Additionally, it can capture a wide range of models for server power consumption, e.g., energy costs as an affine function of the load, see [14], or as a polynomial function of the speed, see [40, 5].

Defining $\lambda_i(t) = \sum_{j \in J} \lambda_{ij}(t)$, the total energy cost of data center i during timeslot t, $\mathcal{E}_i(t)$, is simply

$$\mathcal{E}_i(t) = g_i(t, m_i(t), \lambda_i(t)). \tag{1}$$

Delay cost. The delay cost captures the lost revenue incurred because of the delay experienced by the requests. To model this, we define $r(d)$ as the lost revenue associated with a job experiencing delay d. We assume that $r(d)$ is strictly increasing and convex in d.

To model the delay, we consider its two components: the network delay experienced while the request is outside of the data center and the queueing delay experienced while the request is at the data center.

To model the *network delay*, we let $d_{ij}(t)$ denote the network delay experienced by a request from source j to data center i during timeslot t. We make no requirements on the structure of the $d_{ij}(t)$.

To model the *queueing delay*, we let $f_i(m_i, \lambda_i)$ denote the queueing delay at data center i given m_i active servers and an arrival rate of λ_i. We assume that f_i is strictly decreasing in m_i, strictly increasing in λ_i, and strictly convex in both m_i and λ_i. Further, for stability, we must have that $\lambda_i = 0$ or $\lambda_i < m_i \mu_i$, where μ_i is the service rate of a server at data center i. Thus, we define $f_i(m_i, \lambda_i) = \infty$ for $\lambda_i \geq m_i \mu_i$. Elsewhere, we assume f_i is finite, continuous and differentiable. Note that these assumptions are satisfied by most standard queueing formulae, e.g., the mean delay under M/GI/1 Processor Sharing (PS) queue and the 95th percentile of delay under the M/M/1. Further, the convexity of f_i in m_i models the law of diminishing returns for parallelism.

Combining the above gives the following model for the total delay cost $\mathcal{D}_i(t)$ at data center i during timeslot t:

$$\mathcal{D}_i(t) = \sum_{j \in J} \lambda_{ij}(t) r\left(f_i(m_i(t), \lambda_i(t)) + d_{ij}(t)\right). \tag{2}$$

2.3 The geographical load balancing problem

Given the cost models above, the goal of geographical load balancing is to choose the routing policy $\lambda_{ij}(t)$ and the number of active servers in each data center $m_i(t)$ at each time t in order minimize the total cost during $[1, T]$. This is captured by the following optimization problem:

$$\min_{\mathbf{m}(t), \boldsymbol{\lambda}(t)} \sum_{t=1}^{T} \sum_{i \in N} \left(\mathcal{E}_i(t) + \mathcal{D}_i(t)\right) \tag{3a}$$

---

[1]Minimizing server energy consumption also reduces cooling and power distribution costs.

s.t. $\sum_{i \in N} \lambda_{ij}(t) = L_j(t),$ $\qquad \forall j \in J$ (3b)

$\lambda_{ij}(t) \geq 0,$ $\qquad \forall i \in N, \forall j \in J$ (3c)

$0 \leq m_i(t) \leq M_i,$ $\qquad \forall i \in N$ (3d)

$m_i(t) \in \mathbb{N},$ $\qquad \forall i \in N$ (3e)

To simplify (3), note that Internet data centers typically contain thousands of active servers. So, we can relax the integer constraint in (3) and round the resulting solution with minimal increase in cost. Also, because this model neglects the cost of turning servers on or off, the optimization decouples into independent sub-problems for each timeslot t. For the analysis *we consider only a single interval and omit the explicit time dependence.*[2] Thus (3) becomes

$$\min_{\mathbf{m},\boldsymbol{\lambda}} \sum_{i \in N} g_i(m_i, \lambda_i) + \sum_{i \in N} \sum_{j \in J} \lambda_{ij} r(d_{ij} + f_i(m_i, \lambda_i)) \quad (4a)$$

s.t. $\sum_{i \in N} \lambda_{ij} = L_j,$ $\qquad \forall j \in J$ (4b)

$\lambda_{ij} \geq 0,$ $\qquad \forall i \in N, \forall j \in J$ (4c)

$0 \leq m_i \leq M_i,$ $\qquad \forall i \in N,$ (4d)

We refer to this formulation as GLB. Note that GLB is jointly convex in λ_{ij} and m_i and can be efficiently solved centrally. However, a distributed solution algorithm is usually required, such as those derived in Section 4.

In contrast to prior work studying geographical load balancing, it is important to observe that this paper is the first, to our knowledge, to incorporate jointly optimizing the total energy cost and the end-to-end user delay with consideration of both price diversity and network delay diversity.

GLB provides a general framework for studying geographical load balancing. However, the model ignores many aspects of data center design, e.g., reliability and availability, which are central to data center service level agreements. Such issues are beyond the scope of this paper; however our designs merge nicely with proposals such as [36] for these goals.

The GLB model is too broad for some of our analytic results and thus we often use two restricted versions.

Linear lost revenue. This model uses a lost revenue function $r(d) = \beta d$, for constant β. Though it is difficult to choose a "universal" form for the lost revenue associated with delay, there is evidence that it is linear within the range of interest for sites such as Google, Bing, and Shopzilla [13]. GLB then simplifies to

$$\min_{\mathbf{m},\boldsymbol{\lambda}} \sum_{i \in N} g_i(m_i, \lambda_i) + \beta \left(\sum_{i \in N} \lambda_i f_i(m_i, \lambda_i) + \sum_{i \in N} \sum_{j \in J} d_{ij} \lambda_{ij} \right) \quad (5)$$

subject to (4b)–(4d). We call this optimization GLB-LIN.

Queueing-based delay. We occasionally specify the form of f and g using queueing models. This provides increased intuition about the distributed algorithms presented.

If the workload is perfectly parallelizable, and arrivals are Poisson, then $f_i(m_i, \lambda_i)$ is the average delay of m_i parallel queues, each with arrival rate λ_i/m_i. Moreover, if each queue is an M/GI/1 Processor Sharing (PS) queue, then $f_i(m_i, \lambda_i) = 1/(\mu_i - \lambda_i/m_i)$. We also assume $g_i(m_i, \lambda_i) = p_i m_i$, which implies that the increase in energy cost per timeslot for being in an active state, rather than a low-power state, is m_i regardless of λ_i. The GLB formulation becomes:

$$\min_{\mathbf{m},\boldsymbol{\lambda}} \sum_{i \in N} p_i m_i + \beta \sum_{j \in J} \sum_{i \in N} \lambda_{ij} \left(\frac{1}{\mu_i - \lambda_i/m_i} + d_{ij} \right) \quad (6a)$$

---

[2] Time-dependence of L_j and prices is re-introduced for, and central to, the numeric results in Sections 5 and 6.

subject to (4b)–(4d) and the additional constraint

$$\lambda_i \leq m_i \mu_i \quad \forall i \in N. \quad (6b)$$

We refer to this optimization as GLB-Q.

Additional Notation. Throughout the paper we use $|S|$ to denote the cardinality of a set S and bold symbols to denote vectors or tuples. In particular, $\boldsymbol{\lambda}_j = (\lambda_{ij})_{i \in N}$ denotes the tuple of λ_{ij} from source j, and $\boldsymbol{\lambda}_{-j} = (\lambda_{ik})_{i \in N, k \in J \setminus \{j\}}$ denotes the tuples of the remaining λ_{ik}, which forms a matrix. Similarly $\mathbf{m} = (m_i)_{i \in N}$ and $\boldsymbol{\lambda} = (\lambda_{ij})_{i \in N, j \in J}$.

We also need the following in discussing the algorithms. Define $F_i(m_i, \lambda_i) = g_i(m_i, \lambda_i) + \beta \lambda_i f_i(m_i, \lambda_i)$, and define $F(\mathbf{m}, \boldsymbol{\lambda}) = \sum_{i \in N} F_i(m_i, \lambda_i) + \Sigma_{ij} \lambda_{ij} d_{ij}$. Further, let $\hat{m}_i(\lambda_i)$ be the unconstrained optimal m_i at data center i given fixed λ_i, i.e., the unique solution to $\partial F_i(m_i, \lambda_i)/\partial m_i = 0$.

2.4 Practical considerations

Our model assumes there exist mechanisms for dynamically (i) provisioning capacity of data centers, and (ii) adapting the routing of requests from sources to data centers.

With respect to (i), many dynamic server provisioning techniques are being explored by both academics and industry, e.g., [4, 11, 16, 38]. With respect to (ii), there are also a variety of protocol-level mechanisms employed for data center selection today. They include, (a) dynamically generated DNS responses, (b) HTTP redirection, and (c) using persistent HTTP proxies to tunnel requests. Each of these has been evaluated thoroughly, e.g., [12, 25, 30], and though DNS has drawbacks it remains the preferred mechanism for many industry leaders such as Akamai, possibly due to the added latency due to HTTP redirection and tunneling [29]. Within the GLB model, we have implicitly assumed that there exists a proxy/DNS server co-located with each source.

Our model also assumes that the network delays, d_{ij} can be estimated, which has been studied extensively, including work on reducing the overhead of such measurements, e.g., [35], and mapping and synthetic coordinate approaches, e.g., [22, 26]. We discuss the sensitivity of our algorithms to error in these estimates in Section 5.

3. CHARACTERIZING THE OPTIMA

We now provide characterizations of the optimal solutions to GLB, which are important for proving convergence of the distributed algorithms of Section 4. They are also necessary because, a priori, one might worry that the optimal solution requires a very complex routing structure, which would be impractical; or that the set of optimal solutions is very fragmented, which would slow convergence in practice. The results here show that such worries are unwarranted.

Uniqueness of optimal solution.

To begin, note that GLB has at least one optimal solution. This can be seen by applying Weierstrass theorem [7], since the objective function is continuous and the feasible set is compact subset of $\mathbb{R}^n$. Although the optimal solution is generally not unique, there are natural aggregate quantities unique over the set of optimal solutions, which is a convex set. These are the focus of this section.

A first result is that for the GLB-LIN formulation, under weak conditions on f_i and g_i, we have that λ_i is common across all optimal solutions. Thus, the input to the data center provisioning optimization is unique.

Theorem 1. *Consider the GLB-LIN formulation. Suppose that for all i, $F_i(m_i, \lambda_i)$ is jointly convex in λ_i and m_i, and continuously differentiable in λ_i. Further, suppose that $\hat{m}_i(\lambda_i)$ is strictly convex. Then, for each i, λ_i is common for all optimal solutions.*

The proof is in the Appendix. Theorem 1 implies that the server arrival rates at each data center, i.e., λ_i/m_i, are common among all optimal solutions.

Though the conditions on F_i and $\hat{m}_i$ are weak, they do not hold for GLB-Q. In that case, $\hat{m}_i(\lambda_i)$ is linear, and thus not strictly convex. Although the λ_i are not common across all optimal solutions in this setting, the server arrival rates remain common across all optimal solutions.

Theorem 2. *For each data center i, the server arrival rates, λ_i/m_i, are common across all optimal solutions to GLB-Q.*

Sparsity of routing.

It would be impractical if the optimal solutions to GLB required that traffic from each source was divided up among (nearly) all of the data centers. In general, each λ_{ij} could be non-zero, yielding $|N| \times |J|$ flows of traffic from sources to data centers, which would lead to significant scaling issues. Luckily, there is guaranteed to exist an optimal solution with extremely sparse routing. Specifically:

Theorem 3. *There exists an optimal solution to GLB with at most $(|N| + |J| - 1)$ of the λ_{ij} strictly positive.*

Though Theorem 3 does not guarantee that every optimal solution is sparse, the proof is constructive. Thus, it provides an approach which allows one to transform an optimal solution into a sparse optimal solution.

The following result further highlights the sparsity of the routing: any source will route to at most one data center that is not fully active, i.e., where there exists at least a server in power-saving mode.

Theorem 4. *Consider GLB-Q where power costs p_i are drawn from an arbitrary continuous distribution. If any source $j \in J$ has its traffic split between multiple data centers $N' \subseteq N$ in an optimal solution, then, with probability 1, at most one data center $i \in N'$ has $m_i < M_i$.*

4. ALGORITHMS

We now focus on GLB-Q and present two distributed algorithms that solve it, and prove their convergence.

Since GLB-Q is convex, it can be efficiently solved centrally if all necessary information can be collected at a single point, as may be possible if all the proxies and data centers were owned by the same system. However there is a strong case for Internet-scale systems to outsource route selection [39]. To meet this need, the algorithms presented below are decentralized and allow each data center and proxy to optimize based on partial information.

These algorithms seek to fill a notable hole in the growing literature on algorithms for geographical load balancing. Specifically, they have provable optimality guarantees for a performance objective that includes both energy and delay, where route decisions are made using both energy price and network propagation delay information. The most closely related work [32] investigates the total electricity cost for data centers in a multi-electricity-market environment. It constrains the queueing delay inside the data center (assumed to be an $M/M/1$ queue) but neglects the end-to-end user delay. Conversely, [39] uses a simple, efficient algorithm to coordinate the "replica-selection" decisions, but assumes the capacity at each data center is fixed. Other related works, e.g., [32, 34, 28], either do not provide provable guarantees or ignore diverse network delays and/or prices.

Algorithm 1: Gauss-Seidel iteration

Algorithm 1 is motivated by the observation that GLB-Q is separable in m_i, and, less obviously, also separable in

$\boldsymbol{\lambda}_j := (\lambda_{ij}, i \in N)$. This allows all data centers as a group and each proxy j to iteratively solve for optimal $\mathbf{m}$ and $\boldsymbol{\lambda}_j$ in a distributed manner, and communicate their intermediate results to each other. Though distributed, Algorithm 1 requires each proxy to solve an optimization problem.

To highlight the separation between data centers and proxies, we reformulate GLB-Q as:

$$\min_{\boldsymbol{\lambda}_j \in \Lambda_j} \min_{m_i \in \mathcal{M}_i} \sum_{i \in N} \left(p_i m_i + \frac{\beta \lambda_i}{\mu_i - \lambda_i/m_i} \right) + \beta \sum_{i,j} \lambda_{ij} d_{ij} \quad (7)$$

$$\mathcal{M}_i := [0, M_i] \quad \Lambda_j := \left\{ \boldsymbol{\lambda}_j \mid \boldsymbol{\lambda}_j \geq 0, \sum_{i \in N} \lambda_{ij} = L_j \right\} \quad (8)$$

Since the objective and constraints $\mathcal{M}_i$ and Λ_j are separable, this can be solved separately by data centers i and proxies j.

The iterations of the algorithm are indexed by τ, and are assumed to be fast relative to the timeslots t. Each iteration τ is divided into $|J| + 1$ phases. In phase 0, all data centers i concurrently calculate $m_i(\tau + 1)$ based on their own arrival rates $\lambda_i(\tau)$, by minimizing (7) over their own variables m_i:

$$\min_{m_i \in \mathcal{M}_i} \left(p_i m_i + \frac{\beta \lambda_i(\tau)}{\mu_i - \lambda_i(\tau)/m_i} \right) \quad (9)$$

In phase j of iteration τ, proxy j minimizes (7) over its own variable by setting $\boldsymbol{\lambda}_j(\tau + 1)$ as the best response to $\mathbf{m}(\tau + 1)$ and the most recent values of $\boldsymbol{\lambda}_{-j} := (\boldsymbol{\lambda}_k, k \neq j)$. This works because proxy j depends on $\boldsymbol{\lambda}_{-j}$ only through their aggregate arrival rates at the data centers:

$$\lambda_i(\tau, j) = \sum_{l < j} \lambda_{il}(\tau + 1) + \sum_{l > j} \lambda_{il}(\tau) \quad (10)$$

To compute $\lambda_i(\tau, j)$, proxy j need not obtain individual $\lambda_{il}(\tau)$ or $\lambda_{il}(\tau + 1)$ from other proxies l. Instead, every data center i measures its local arrival rate $\lambda_i(\tau, j) + \lambda_{ij}(\tau)$ in every phase j of the iteration τ and sends this to proxy j at the beginning of phase j. Then proxy j obtains $\lambda_i(\tau, j)$ by subtracting its own $\lambda_{ij}(\tau)$ from the value received from data center i. When there are fewer data centers than proxies, this has less overhead than direct messaging.

In summary, the algorithm is as follows (noting that the minimization (9) has a closed form). Here, $[x]^a := \min\{x, a\}$.

Algorithm 1. *Starting from a feasible initial allocation $\boldsymbol{\lambda}(0)$ and the associated $\mathbf{m}(\boldsymbol{\lambda}(0))$, let*

$$m_i(\tau + 1) := \left[\left(1 + \frac{1}{\sqrt{p_i/\beta}} \right) \cdot \frac{\lambda_i(\tau)}{\mu_i} \right]^{M_i} \quad (11)$$

$$\boldsymbol{\lambda}_j(\tau + 1) := \arg \min_{\boldsymbol{\lambda}_j \in \Lambda_j} \sum_{i \in N} \frac{\lambda_i(\tau, j) + \lambda_{ij}}{\mu_i - (\lambda_i(\tau, j) + \lambda_{ij})/m_i(\tau + 1)}$$

$$+ \sum_{i \in N} \lambda_{ij} d_{ij}. \quad (12)$$

Since GLB-Q generally has multiple optimal $\boldsymbol{\lambda}_j^*$, Algorithm 1 is not guaranteed to converge to one optimal solution, i.e., for each proxy j, the allocation $\lambda_{ij}(\tau)$ of job j to data centers i may oscillate among multiple optimal allocations. However, both the optimal cost and the optimal per-server arrival rates to data centers will converge.

Theorem 5. *Let $(\mathbf{m}(\tau), \boldsymbol{\lambda}(\tau))$ be a sequence generated by Algorithm 1 when applied to GLB-Q. Then*

(i) Every limit point of $(\mathbf{m}(\tau), \boldsymbol{\lambda}(\tau))$ is optimal.

(ii) $F(\mathbf{m}(\tau), \boldsymbol{\lambda}(\tau))$ converges to the optimal value.

(iii) The per-server arrival rates $(\lambda_i(\tau)/m_i(\tau), i \in N)$ to data centers converge to their unique optimal values.

The proof of Theorem 5 follows from the fact that Algorithm 1 is a modified Gauss-Seidel iteration. This is also the reason for the requirement that the proxies update sequentially. The details of the proof are in Appendix B.

Algorithm 1 assumes that there is a common clock to synchronize all actions. In practice, updates will likely be asynchronous, with data centers and proxies updating with different frequencies using possibly outdated information. The algorithm generalizes easily to this setting, though the convergence proof is more difficult.

The convergence rate of Algorithm 1 in a realistic scenario is illustrated numerically in Section 5.

Algorithm 2: Distributed gradient projection

Algorithm 2 reduces the computational load on the proxies. In each iteration, instead of each proxy solving a constrained minimization (12) as in Algorithm 1, Algorithm 2 takes a single step in a descent direction. Also, while the proxies compute their $\lambda_j(\tau+1)$ sequentially in $|J|$ phases in Algorithm 1, they perform their updates all at once in Algorithm 2.

To achieve this, rewrite GLB-Q as

$$\min_{\lambda_j \in \Lambda_j} \sum_{j \in J} F_j(\lambda) \qquad (13)$$

where $F(\lambda)$ is the result of minimization of (7) over $m_i \in \mathcal{M}_i$ given λ_i. As explained in the definition of Algorithm 1, this minimization is easy: if we denote the solution by (cf. (11)):

$$m_i(\lambda_i) := \left[\left(1 + \frac{1}{\sqrt{p_i/\beta}} \right) \cdot \frac{\lambda_i}{\mu_i} \right]^{M_i} \qquad (14)$$

then

$$F(\lambda) := \sum_{i \in N} \left(p_i m_i(\lambda_i) + \frac{\beta \lambda_i}{\mu_i - \lambda_i/m_i(\lambda_i)} \right) + \beta \sum_{i,j} \lambda_{ij} d_{ij}.$$

We now sketch the two key ideas behind Algorithm 2. The first is the standard gradient projection idea: move in the steepest descent direction

$$\nabla F_j(\lambda) := \left(\frac{\partial F(\lambda)}{\partial \lambda_{1j}}, \cdots, \frac{\partial F(\lambda)}{\partial \lambda_{|N|j}} \right)$$

and then project the new point into the feasible set $\prod_j \Lambda_j$. The standard gradient projection algorithm will converge if $\nabla F(\lambda)$ is Lipschitz over our feasible set $\prod_j \Lambda_j$. This condition, however, does not hold for our F because of the term $\beta \lambda_i/(\mu_i - \lambda_i/m_i)$. The second idea is to construct a compact and convex subset Λ of the feasible set $\prod_j \Lambda_j$ with the following properties: (i) if the algorithm starts in Λ, it stays in Λ; (ii) Λ contains all optimal allocations; (iii) $\nabla F(\lambda)$ is Lipschitz over Λ. The algorithm then projects into Λ in each iteration instead of $\prod_j \Lambda_j$. This guarantees convergence.

Specifically, fix a feasible initial allocation $\lambda(0) \in \prod_j \Lambda_j$ and let $\phi := F(\lambda(0))$ be the initial objective value. Define

$$\Lambda := \Lambda(\phi) := \prod_j \Lambda_j \cap \left\{ \lambda \, \middle| \, \lambda_i \leq \frac{\phi M_i \mu_i}{\phi + \beta M_i}, \ \forall i \right\}. \qquad (15)$$

Even though the Λ defined in (15) indeed has the desired properties (see Appendix B), the projection into Λ requires coordination of all proxies and is thus impractical. In order for each proxy j to perform its update in a decentralized manner, we define proxy j's own constraint subset:

$$\hat{\Lambda}_j(\tau) := \Lambda \cap \left\{ \lambda_j \, \middle| \, \lambda_i(\tau, -j) + \lambda_{ij} \leq \frac{\phi M_i \mu_i}{\phi + \beta M_i}, \forall i \right\}$$

where $\lambda_i(\tau, -j) := \sum_{l \neq j} \lambda_{il}(\tau)$ is the arrival rate to data center i, excluding arrivals from proxy j. Even though $\hat{\Lambda}_j(\tau)$ involves $\lambda_i(\tau, -j)$ for all i, proxy j can easily calculate these quantities from the measured arrival rates $\lambda_i(\tau)$ it is told by data centers i, as done in Algorithm 1 (cf. (10) and the discussion thereafter), and does not need to communicate with other proxies. Hence, given $\lambda_i(\tau, -j)$ from data centers i, each proxy can project into $\hat{\Lambda}_j(\tau)$ to compute the next iterate $\lambda_j(\tau + 1)$ without the need to coordinate with other proxies.[3] Moreover, if $\lambda(0) \in \Lambda$ then $\lambda(\tau) \in \Lambda$ for all iterations τ. In summary, Algorithm 2 is as follows.

Algorithm 2. *Starting from a feasible initial allocation $\lambda(0)$ and the associated $\mathbf{m}(\lambda(0))$, each proxy j computes, in each iteration τ:*

$$\mathbf{z}_j(\tau+1) := [\lambda_j(\tau) - \gamma_j (\nabla F_j(\lambda(\tau)))]_{\hat{\Lambda}_j(\tau)} \qquad (16)$$

$$\lambda_j(\tau+1) := \frac{|J| - 1}{|J|} \lambda_j(\tau) + \frac{1}{|J|} \mathbf{z}_j(\tau+1) \qquad (17)$$

where $\gamma_j > 0$ is a stepsize and $\nabla F_j(\lambda(\tau))$ is given by

$$\frac{\partial F(\lambda(\tau))}{\partial \lambda_{ij}} = \beta \left(d_{ij} + \frac{\mu_i}{(\mu_i - \lambda_i(\tau)/m_i(\lambda_i(\tau)))^2} \right).$$

Implicit in the description is the requirement that all data centers i compute $m_i(\lambda_i(\tau))$ according to (14) in each iteration τ. Each data center i measures the local arrival rate $\lambda_i(\tau)$, calculates $m_i(\lambda_i(\tau))$, and broadcasts these values to all proxies at the beginning of iteration $\tau + 1$ for the proxies to compute their $\lambda_j(\tau + 1)$.

Algorithm 2 has the same convergence property as Algorithm 1, provided the stepsize is small enough.

Theorem 6. *Let $(\mathbf{m}(\tau), \lambda(\tau))$ be a sequence generated by Algorithm 2 when applied to GLB-Q. If, for all j, $0 < \gamma_j < \min_{i \in N} \beta^2 \mu_i^2 M_i^4/(|J|(\phi + \beta M_i)^3)$, then*

(i) Every limit point of $(\mathbf{m}(\tau), \lambda(\tau))$ is optimal.

(ii) $F(\mathbf{m}(\tau), \lambda(\tau))$ converges to the optimal value.

(iii) The per-server arrival rates $(\lambda_i(\tau)/m_i(\tau), i \in N)$ to data centers converge to their unique optimal values.

Theorem 6 is proved in Appendix B. The key novelty of the proof is (i) handling the fact that the objective is not Lipschitz and (ii) allowing distributed computation of the projection. The bound on γ_j in Theorem 6 is more conservative than necessary for large systems. Hence, a larger stepsize can be choosen to accelerate convergence. The convergence rate is illustrated in a realistic setting in Section 5.

5. CASE STUDY

The remainder of the paper evaluates the algorithms presented in the previous section under a realistic workload. This section considers the data center perspective (i.e., cost minimization) and Section 6 considers the social perspective (i.e., brown energy usage).

5.1 Experimental setup

We aim to use realistic parameters in the experimental setup and provide conservative estimates of the cost savings resulting from optimal geographical load balancing. The setup models an Internet-scale system such as Google within the United States.

---

[3] The projection to the nearest point in $\hat{\Lambda}_j(\tau)$ is defined by $[\lambda]_{\hat{\Lambda}_j(\tau)} := \arg\min_{y \in \hat{\Lambda}_j(\tau)} \|y - \lambda\|_2$.

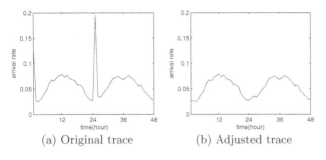

(a) Original trace   (b) Adjusted trace

Figure 1: Hotmail trace used in numerical results.

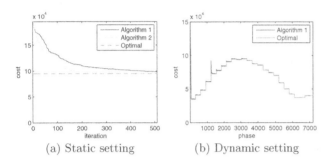

(a) Static setting   (b) Dynamic setting

Figure 2: Convergence of Algorithm 1 and 2.

Workload description.

To build our workload, we start with a trace of traffic from Hotmail, a large Internet service running on tens of thousands of servers. The trace represents the I/O activity from 8 servers over a 48-hour period, starting at midnight (PDT) on August 4, 2008, averaged over 10 minute intervals. The trace has strong diurnal behavior and has a fairly small peak-to-mean ratio of 1.64. Results for this small peak-to-mean ratio provide a lower bound on the cost savings under workloads with larger peak-to-mean ratios. As illustrated in Figure 1(a), the Hotmail trace contains significant nightly activity due to maintenance processes; however the data center is provisioned for the peak foreground traffic. This creates a dilemma about whether to include the maintenance activity or not. We have performed experiments with both, but report only the results with the spike removed (as illustrated in Figure 1(b)) because this leads to a more conservative estimate of the cost savings.

Building on this trace, we construct our workload by placing a source at the geographical center of each mainland US state, co-located with a proxy or DNS server (as described in Section 2.4). The trace is shifted according to the time-zone of each state, and scaled by the size of the population in the state that has an Internet connection [1].

Data center description.

To model an Internet-scale system, we have 14 data centers, one at the geographic center of each state known to have Google data centers [17]: California, Washington, Oregon, Illinois, Georgia, Virginia, Texas, Florida, North Carolina, and South Carolina.

We merge the data centers in each state and set M_i proportional to the number of data centers in that state, while keeping $\Sigma_{i \in N} M_i \mu_i$ twice the total peak workload, $\max_t \Sigma_{j \in J} L_j(t)$. The network delays, d_{ij}, between sources and data centers are taken to be proportional to the distances between the centers of the two states and comparable to queueing delays. This lower bound on the network delay ignores delay due to congestion or indirect routes.

Cost function parameters.

To model the costs of the system, we use the GLB-Q formulation. We set $\mu_i = 1$ for all i, so that the servers at each location are equivalent. We assume the energy consumption of an active server in one timeslot is normalized to 1. We set constant electricity prices using the industrial electricity price of each state in May 2010 [18]. Specifically, the price (cents per kWh) is 10.41 in California; 3.73 in Washington; 5.87 in Oregon, 7.48 in Illinois; 5.86 in Georgia; 6.67 in Virginia; 6.44 in Texas; 8.60 in Florida; 6.03 in North Carolina; and 5.49 in South Carolina. In this section, we set $\beta = 1$; however Figure 3 illustrates the impact of varying β.

Algorithm benchmarks.

To provide benchmarks for the performance of the algorithms presented here, we consider three baselines, which are approximations of common approaches used in Internet-scale systems. They also allow implicit comparisons with prior work such as [32]. The approaches use different amounts of information to perform the cost minimization. Note that each approach must use queueing delay (or capacity information); otherwise the routing may lead to instability.

Baseline 1 uses network delays but ignores energy price when minimizing its costs. This demonstrates the impact of price-aware routing. It also shows the importance of dynamic capacity provisioning, since without using energy cost in the optimization, every data center will keep every server active.

Baseline 2 uses energy prices but ignores network delay. This illustrates the impact of location aware routing on the data center costs. Further, it allows us to understand the performance improvement of Algorithms 1 and 2 compared to those such as [32, 34] that neglect network delays in their formulations.

Baseline 3 uses neither network delay information nor energy price information when performing its cost minimization. Thus, the traffic is routed so as to balance the delays within the data centers. Though naive, designs such as this are still used by systems today; see [3].

5.2 Performance evaluation

The evaluation of our algorithms and the cost savings due to optimal geographic load balancing will be organized around the following topics.

Convergence.

We start by considering the convergence of each of the distributed algorithms. Figure 2(a) illustrates the convergence of each of the algorithms in a static setting for t = 11am, where load and electricity prices are fixed and each phase in Algorithm 1 is considered as an iteration. It validates the convergence analysis for both algorithms. Note here Algorithm 2 used a step size $\gamma = 10$; this is much larger than that used in the convergence analysis, which is quite conservative, and there is no sign of causing lack of convergence.

To demonstrate the convergence in a dynamic setting, Figure 2(b) shows Algorithm 1's response to the first day of the Hotmail trace, with loads averaged over one-hour intervals for brevity. One iteration (51 phases) is performed every 10 minutes. This figure shows that even the slower algorithm, Algorithm 1, converges fast enough to provide near-optimal cost. Hence, the remaining plots show only the optimal solution.

Energy versus delay tradeoff.

The optimization objective we have chosen to model the data center costs imposes a particular tradeoff between the delay and the energy costs, β. It is important to understand the impact of this factor. Figure 3 illustrates how the delay

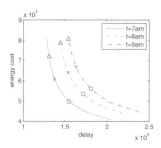

Figure 3: Pareto frontier of the GLB-Q formulation as a function of β for three different times (and thus arrival rates), PDT. Circles, x-marks, and triangles correspond to $\beta = 2.5$, 1, and 0.4, respectively.

and energy cost trade off under the optimal solution as β changes. Thus, the plot shows the Pareto frontier for the GLB-Q formulation. The figure highlights that there is a smooth convex frontier with a mild 'knee'.

Cost savings.

To evaluate the cost savings of geographical load balancing, Figure 4 compares the optimal costs to those incurred under the three baseline strategies described in the experimental setup. The overall cost, shown in Figures 4(a) and 4(b), is significantly lower under the optimal solution than all of the baselines (nearly 40% during times of light traffic). Recall that Baseline 2 is the state of the art, studied in recent papers such as [32, 34].

To understand where the benefits are coming from, let us consider separately the two components of cost: delay and energy. Figures 4(c) and 4(d) show that the optimal algorithm performs well with respect to both delay and energy costs individually. In particular, Baseline 1 provides a lower bound on the achievable delay costs, and the optimal algorithm nearly matches this lower bound. Similarly, Baseline 2 provides a natural bar for comparing the achievable energy cost. At periods of light traffic the optimal algorithm provides nearly the same energy cost as this baseline, and (perhaps surprisingly) during periods of heavy-traffic the optimal algorithm provides significantly lower energy costs. The explanation for this is that, when network delay is considered by the optimal algorithm, if all the close data centers have all servers active, a proxy might still route to them; however when network delay is not considered, a proxy is more likely to route to a data center that is not yet running at full capacity, thereby adding to the energy cost.

Sensitivity analysis.

Given that the algorithms all rely on estimates of the L_j and d_{ij} it is important to perform a sensitivity analysis to understand the impact of errors in these parameters on the achieved cost. We have performed such a sensitivity analysis but omit the details for brevity. The results show that even when the algorithms have very poor estimates of d_{ij} and L_j there is little effect on cost. Baseline 2 can be thought of as applying the optimal algorithm to very poor estimates of d_{ij} (namely $d_{ij} = 0$), and so the Figure 4(a) provides some illustration of the effect of estimation error.

6. SOCIAL IMPACT

We now shift focus from the cost savings of the data center operator to the social impact of geographical load balancing. We focus on the impact of geographical load balancing on the usage of "brown" non-renewable energy by Internet-scale systems, and how this impact depends on pricing.

Intuitively, geographical load balancing allows the traffic to "follow the renewables"; thus providing increased usage of green energy and decreased brown energy usage. However, such benefits are only possible if data centers forgo static energy contracts for dynamic energy pricing (either through demand-response programs or real-time markets). The experiments in this section show that if dynamic pricing is done optimally, then geographical load balancing can provide significant social benefits.

6.1 Experimental setup

To explore the social impact of geographical load balancing, we use the setup described in Section 5. However, we add models for the availability of renewable energy, the pricing of renewable energy, and the social objective.

The availability of renewable energy.

To model the availability of renewable energy we use standard models of wind and solar from [15, 20]. Though simple, these models capture the average trends for both wind and solar accurately. Since these models are smoother than actual intermittent renewable sources, especially wind, they conservatively estimate the benefit due to following renewables.

We consider two settings (i) high wind penetration, where 90% of renewable energy comes from wind and (ii) high solar penetration, where 90% of renewable energy comes from solar. The availability given by these models is shown in Figure 5(a). Setting (i) is motivated by studies such as [18]. Setting (ii) is motivated by the possibility of on-site or locally contracted solar, which is increasingly common.

Building on these availability models, for each location we let $\alpha_i(t)$ denote the fraction of the energy that is from renewable sources at time t, and let $\bar{\alpha} = (|N|\,T)^{-1} \sum_{t=1}^{T} \sum_{i \in N} \alpha_i(t)$ be the "penetration" of renewable energy. We take $\bar{\alpha} = 0.30$, which is on the progressive side of the renewable targets among US states [10].

Finally, when measuring the brown/green energy usage of a data center at time t, we use simply $\sum_{i \in N} \alpha_i(t)m_i(t)$ as the green energy usage and $\sum_{i \in N}(1 - \alpha_i(t))m_i(t)$ as the brown energy usage. This models the fact that the grid cannot differentiate the source of the electricity provided.

Demand response and dynamic pricing.

Internet-scale systems have flexibility in energy usage that is not available to traditional energy consumers; thus they are well positioned to take advantage of demand-response and real-time markets to reduce both their energy costs and their brown energy consumption.

To provide a simple model of demand-response, we use time-varying prices $p_i(t)$ in each time-slot that depend on the availability of renewable resources $\alpha_i(t)$ in each location.

The way $p_i(t)$ is chosen as a function of $\alpha_i(t)$ will be of fundamental importance to the social impact of geographical load balancing. To highlight this, we consider a parameterized "differentiated pricing" model that uses a price p_b for brown energy and a price p_g for green energy. Specifically,

$$p_i(t) = p_b(1 - \alpha_i(t)) + p_g \alpha_i(t).$$

Note that $p_g = p_b$ corresponds to static pricing, and we show in the next section that $p_g = 0$ corresponds to socially optimal pricing. Our experiments vary $p_g \in [0, p_b]$.

The social objective.

To model the social impact of geographical load balancing we need to formulate a social objective. Like the GLB formulation, this must include a tradeoff between the energy usage and the delay users of the system experience, because

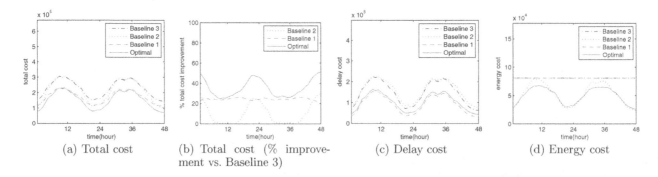

(a) Total cost   (b) Total cost (% improvement vs. Baseline 3)   (c) Delay cost   (d) Energy cost

Figure 4: Impact of information used on the cost incurred by geographical load balancing.

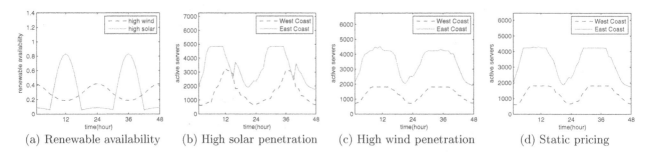

(a) Renewable availability   (b) High solar penetration   (c) High wind penetration   (d) Static pricing

Figure 5: Geographical load balancing "following the renewables" under optimal pricing. (a) Availability of wind and solar. (b)–(d) Capacity provisioning of east coast and west coast data centers when there are renewables, high solar penetration, and high wind penetration, respectively.

purely minimizing brown energy use requires all $m_i = 0$. The key difference between the GLB formulation and the social formulation is that the *cost* of energy is no longer relevant. Instead, the environmental impact is important, and thus the brown energy usage should be minimized. This leads to the following simple model for the social objective:

$$\min_{\mathbf{m}(t), \boldsymbol{\lambda}(t)} \sum_{t=1}^{T} \sum_{i \in N} \left((1 - \alpha_i(t)) \frac{\mathcal{E}_i(t)}{p_i(t)} + \tilde{\beta} \mathcal{D}_i(t) \right) \quad (18)$$

where $\mathcal{D}_i(t)$ is the delay cost defined in (2), $\mathcal{E}_i(t)$ is the energy cost defined in (1), and $\tilde{\beta}$ is the relative valuation of delay versus energy. Further, we have imposed that the energy cost follows from the pricing of $p_i(t)$ cents/kWh in timeslot t. Note that, though simple, our choice of $\mathcal{D}_i(t)$ to model the disutility of delay to users is reasonable because lost revenue captures the lack of use as a function of increased delay.

An immediate observation about the above social objective is that to align the data center and social goals, one needs to set $p_i(t) = (1 - \alpha_i(t))/\tilde{\beta}$, which corresponds to choosing $p_b = 1/\tilde{\beta}$ and $p_g = 0$ in the differentiated pricing model above. We refer to this as the "optimal" pricing model.

6.2 The importance of dynamic pricing

To begin our experiments, we illustrate that optimal pricing can lead geographical load balancing to "follow the renewables." Figure 5 shows this in the case of high solar penetration and high wind penetration for $\tilde{\beta} = 0.1$. By comparing Figures 5(b) and 5(c) to Figure 5(d), which uses static pricing, the change in capacity provisioning, and thus energy usage, is evident. For example, Figure 5(b) shows a clear shift of service capacity from the east coast to the west coast as solar energy becomes highly available and then

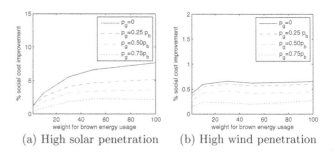

(a) High solar penetration   (b) High wind penetration

Figure 6: Reduction in social cost from dynamic pricing compared to static pricing as a function of the weight for brown energy usage, $1/\tilde{\beta}$, under (a) high solar penetration and (b) high wind penetration.

back when solar energy is less available. Similarly, Figure 5(c) shows a shift, though much smaller, of service capacity toward the evenings, when wind is more available. Though not explicit in the figures, this "follow the renewables" routing has the benefit of significantly reducing the brown energy usage since energy use is more correlated with the availability of renewables. Thus, geographical load balancing provides the opportunity to aid the incorporation of renewables into the grid.

Figure 5 assumed the optimal dynamic pricing, but currently data centers negotiate fixed price contracts. Although there are many reasons why grid operators will encourage data center operators to transfer to dynamic pricing over the coming years, this is likely to be a slow process. Thus, it is important to consider the impact of partial adoption of dynamic pricing in addition to full, optimal dynamic pricing.

Figure 6 focuses on this issue. To model the partial adoption of dynamic pricing, we can consider $p_g \in [0, p_b]$. Figure 6(a) shows that the benefits provided by dynamic pricing are moderate but significant, even at partial adoption (high p_g), when there is high solar penetration. Figure 6(b) suggests that there would be much less benefit if renewable sources were dominated by wind with only diurnal variation, because the availability of solar energy is much more correlated with the traffic peaks. Specifically, the three hour gap in time zones means that solar on the west coast can still help with the high traffic period of the east coast, but the peak average wind energy is at night. However, wind is vastly more bursty than this model predicts, and a system which responds to these bursts will still benefit significantly.

Another interesting observation about the Figure 6 is that the curves increase faster in the range when $\bar{\beta}$ is large, which highlights that the social benefit of geographical load balancing becomes significant even when there is only moderate importance placed on energy. When p_g is higher than p_b, which is common currently, the cost increases, but we omit the results due to space constraints.

7. CONCLUDING REMARKS

This paper has focused on understanding algorithms for and social impacts of geographical load balancing in Internet-scaled systems. We have provided two distributed algorithms that provably compute the optimal routing and provisioning decisions for Internet-scale systems and we have evaluated these algorithms using trace-based numerical simulations. Further, we have studied the feasibility and benefits of providing demand response for the grid via geographical load balancing. Our experiments highlight that geographical load balancing can provide an effective tool for demand-response: when pricing is done carefully electricity providers can motivate Internet-scale systems to "follow the renewables" and route to areas where green energy is available. This both eases the incorporation of renewables into the grid and reduces brown energy consumption of Internet-scale systems.

There are a number of interesting directions for future work that are motivated by the studies in this paper. With respect to the design of distributed algorithms, one aspect that our model has ignored is the switching cost (in terms of delay and wear-and-tear) associated with switching servers into and out of power-saving modes. Our model also ignores issues related to reliability and availability, which are quite important in practice. With respect to the social impact of geographical load balancing, our results highlight the opportunity provided by geographical load balancing for demand response; however there are many issues left to be considered. For example, which demand response market should Internet-scale systems participate in to minimize costs? How can policy decisions such as cap-and-trade be used to provide the proper incentives for Internet-scale systems, such as [23]? Can Internet-scale systems use energy storage at data centers in order to magnify cost reductions when participating in demand response markets? Answering these questions will pave the way for greener geographic load balancing.

8. ACKNOWLEDGMENTS

This work was supported by NSF grants CCF 0830511, CNS 0911041, and CNS 0846025, DoE grant DE-EE0002890, ARO MURI grant W911NF-08-1-0233, Microsoft Research, Bell Labs, the Lee Center for Advanced Networking, and ARC grant FT0991594.

9. REFERENCES

[1] US Census Bureau, http://www.census.gov.

[2] Server and data center energy efficiency, Final Report to Congress, U.S. Environmental Protection Agency, 2007.

[3] V. K. Adhikari, S. Jain, and Z.-L. Zhang. YouTube traffic dynamics and its interplay with a tier-1 ISP: An ISP perspective. In ACM IMC, pages 431–443, 2010.

[4] S. Albers. Energy-efficient algorithms. Comm. of the ACM, 53(5):86–96, 2010.

[5] L. L. H. Andrew, M. Lin, and A. Wierman. Optimality, fairness and robustness in speed scaling designs. In Proc. ACM Sigmetrics, 2010.

[6] A. Beloglazov, R. Buyya, Y. C. Lee, and A. Zomaya. A taxonomy and survey of energy-efficient data centers and cloud computing systems, Technical Report, 2010.

[7] D. P. Bertsekas. Nonlinear Programming. Athena Scientific, 1999.

[8] D. P. Bertsekas and J. N. Tsitsiklis. Parallel and Distributed Computation: Numerical Methods. Athena Scientific, 1989.

[9] S. Boyd and L. Vandenberghe. Convex Optimization. Cambridge University Press, 2004.

[10] S. Carley. State renewable energy electricity policies: An empirical evaluation of effectiveness. Energy Policy, 37(8):3071–3081, Aug 2009.

[11] Y. Chen, A. Das, W. Qin, A. Sivasubramaniam, Q. Wang, and N. Gautam. Managing server energy and operational costs in hosting centers. In Proc. ACM Sigmetrics, 2005.

[12] M. Conti and C. Nazionale. Load distribution among replicated web servers: A QoS-based approach. In Proc. ACM Worksh. Internet Server Performance, 1999.

[13] A. Croll and S. Power. How web speed affects online business KPIs. http://www.watchingwebsites.com, 2009.

[14] X. Fan, W.-D. Weber, and L. A. Barroso. Power provisioning for a warehouse-sized computer. In Proc. Int. Symp. Comp. Arch., 2007.

[15] M. Fripp and R. H. Wiser. Effects of temporal wind patterns on the value of wind-generated electricity in california and the northwest. IEEE Trans. Power Systems, 23(2):477–485, May 2008.

[16] A. Gandhi, M. Harchol-Balter, R. Das, and C. Lefurgy. Optimal power allocation in server farms. In Proc. ACM Sigmetrics, 2009.

[17] http://www.datacenterknowledge.com, 2008.

[18] http://www.eia.doe.gov.

[19] S. Irani and K. R. Pruhs. Algorithmic problems in power management. SIGACT News, 36(2):63–76, 2005.

[20] T. A. Kattakayam, S. Khan, and K. Srinivasan. Diurnal and environmental characterization of solar photovoltaic panels using a PC-AT add on plug in card. Solar Energy Materials and Solar Cells, 44(1):25–36, Oct 1996.

[21] S. Kaxiras and M. Martonosi. Computer Architecture Techniques for Power-Efficiency. Morgan & Claypool, 2008.

[22] R. Krishnan, H. V. Madhyastha, S. Srinivasan, S. Jain, A. Krishnamurthy, T. Anderson, and J. Gao. Moving beyond end-to-end path information to optimize CDN performance. In Proc. ACM Sigcomm, 2009.

[23] K. Le, R. Bianchini, T. D. Nguyen, O. Bilgir, and M. Martonosi. Capping the brown energy consumption of internet services at low cost. In Proc. IGCC, 2010.

[24] M. Lin, A. Wierman, L. L. H. Andrew, and E. Thereska. Dynamic right-sizing for power-proportional data centers. In Proc. IEEE INFOCOM, 2011.

[25] Z. M. Mao, C. D. Cranor, F. Bouglis, M. Rabinovich, O. Spatscheck, and J. Wang. A precise and efficient evaluation of the proximity between web clients and their local DNS servers. In USENIX, pages 229–242, 2002.

[26] E. Ng and H. Zhang. Predicting internet network distance with coordinates-based approaches. In Proc. IEEE INFOCOM, 2002.

[27] S. Ong, P. Denholm, and E. Doris. The impacts of commercial electric utility rate structure elements on the economics of photovoltaic systems. Technical Report NREL/TP-6A2-46782, National Renewable Energy Laboratory, 2010.

[28] E. Pakbaznia and M. Pedram. Minimizing data center cooling and server power costs. In Proc. ISLPED, 2009.

[29] J. Pang, A. Akella, A. Shaikh, B. Krishnamurthy, and

S. Seshan. On the responsiveness of DNS-based network control. In *Proc. IMC*, 2004.

[30] M. Pathan, C. Vecchiola, and R. Buyya. Load and proximity aware request-redirection for dynamic load distribution in peering CDNs. In *Proc. OTM*, 2008.

[31] A. Qureshi, R. Weber, H. Balakrishnan, J. Guttag, and B. Maggs. Cutting the electric bill for internet-scale systems. In *Proc. ACM Sigcomm*, Aug. 2009.

[32] L. Rao, X. Liu, L. Xie, and W. Liu. Minimizing electricity cost: Optimization of distributed internet data centers in a multi-electricity-market environment. In *INFOCOM*, 2010.

[33] R. T. Rockafellar. *Convex Analysis*. Princeton University Press, 1970.

[34] R. Stanojevic and R. Shorten. Distributed dynamic speed scaling. In *Proc. IEEE INFOCOM*, 2010.

[35] W. Theilmann and K. Rothermel. Dynamic distance maps of the internet. In *Proc. IEEE INFOCOM*, 2001.

[36] E. Thereska, A. Donnelly, and D. Narayanan. Sierra: a power-proportional, distributed storage system. Technical Report MSR-TR-2009-153, Microsoft Research, 2009.

[37] O. S. Unsal and I. Koren. System-level power-aware deisgn techniques in real-time systems. *Proc. IEEE*, 91(7):1055–1069, 2003.

[38] R. Urgaonkar, U. C. Kozat, K. Igarashi, and M. J. Neely. Dynamic resource allocation and power management in virtualized data centers. In *IEEE NOMS*, Apr. 2010.

[39] P. Wendell, J. W. Jiang, M. J. Freedman, and J. Rexford. Donar: decentralized server selection for cloud services. In *Proc. ACM Sigcomm*, pages 231–242, 2010.

[40] A. Wierman, L. L. H. Andrew, and A. Tang. Power-aware speed scaling in processor sharing systems. In *Proc. IEEE INFOCOM*, 2009.

APPENDIX

A. PROOFS FOR SECTION 3

We now prove the results from Section 3, beginning with the illuminating Karush-Kuhn-Tucker (KKT) conditions.

A.1 Optimality conditions

As GLB-Q is convex and satisfies Slater's condition, the KKT conditions are necessary and sufficient for optimality [9]; for the other models they are merely necessary.

GLB-Q: Let $\underline{\omega}_i \geq 0$ and $\bar{\omega}_i \geq 0$ be Lagrange multipliers corresponding to (4d), and $\delta_{ij} \geq 0$, ν_j and σ_i be those for (4c), (4b) and (6b). The Lagrangian is then

$$\mathcal{L} = \sum_{i \in N} m_i p_i + \beta \sum_{j \in J} \sum_{i \in N} \left(\frac{\lambda_{ij}}{\mu_i - \lambda_i/m_i} + \lambda_{ij} d_{ij} \right)$$
$$- \sum_{i \in N} \sum_{j \in J} \delta_{ij} \lambda_{ij} + \sum_{j \in J} \nu_j \left(L_j - \sum_{i \in N} \lambda_{ij} \right)$$
$$+ \sum_{i \in N} \left(\bar{\omega}_i (m_i - M_i) - \underline{\omega}_i m_i \right) + \sum_{i \in N} \sigma_i (m_i \mu_i - \lambda_i)$$

The KKT conditions of stationarity, primal and dual feasibility and complementary slackness are:

$$\beta \left(\frac{\mu_i}{(\mu_i - \lambda_i/m_i)^2} + d_{ij} \right) - \nu_j - \delta_{ij} - \sigma_i = 0 \quad (19)$$

$$\delta_{ij} \lambda_{ij} = 0; \qquad \delta_{ij} \geq 0, \qquad \lambda_{ij} \geq 0 \quad (20)$$

$$\sigma_i (m_i \mu_i - \lambda_i) = 0; \quad \sigma_i \geq 0, \quad m_i \mu_i - \lambda_i \geq 0 \quad (21)$$

$$\sum_{i \in N} \lambda_{ij} = L_j \quad (22)$$

$$p_i - \beta \left(\frac{\lambda_i/m_i}{\mu_i - \lambda_i/m_i} \right)^2 + \bar{\omega}_i - \underline{\omega}_i + \sigma_i \mu_i = 0 \quad (23)$$

$$\bar{\omega}_i (m_i - M_i) = 0; \qquad \bar{\omega}_i \geq 0, \qquad m_i \leq M_i \quad (24)$$

$$\underline{\omega}_i m_i = 0; \qquad \underline{\omega}_i \geq 0, \qquad m_i \geq 0. \quad (25)$$

The conditions (19)–(22) determine the sources' choice of λ_{ij}, and we claim they imply that source j will only send data to those data centers i which have minimum marginal cost $d_{ij} + (1 + \sqrt{p_i^*/\beta})^2/\mu_i$, where $p_i^* = p_i - \underline{\omega}_i + \bar{\omega}_i$. To see this, let $\bar{\lambda}_i = \lambda_i/m_i$. By (23), the marginal queueing delay of data centre i with respect to load λ_{ij} is $\mu_i/(\mu_i - \bar{\lambda}_i)^2 = (1 + \sqrt{p_i^*/\beta})^2/\mu_i$. Thus, from (19), at the optimal point,

$$d_{ij} + \frac{(1 + \sqrt{p_i^*/\beta})^2}{\mu_i} = d_{ij} + \frac{\mu_i}{(\mu_i - \bar{\lambda}_i)^2} = \frac{\nu_j + \delta_j}{\beta} \geq \frac{\nu_j}{\beta} \quad (26)$$

with equality if $\lambda_{ij} > 0$ by (20), establishing the claim.

Note that the solution to (19)–(22) for source j depends on λ_{ik}, $k \neq j$, only through m_i. Given λ_i, data center i finds m_i as the projection onto $[0, M_i]$ of the solution $\hat{m}_i = \lambda_i (1 + \sqrt{p_i/\beta})/(\mu_i \sqrt{p_i/\beta})$ of (23) with $\bar{\omega}_i = \underline{\omega}_i = 0$.

GLB-LIN again decouples into data centers finding m_i given λ_i, and sources finding λ_{ij} given the m_i. Feasibility and complementary slackness conditions (20), (22), (24) and (25) are as for GLB-Q; the stationarity conditions are:

$$\frac{\partial g_i(m_i, \lambda_i)}{\partial \lambda_i} + \beta \left(\frac{\partial (\lambda_i f_i(m_i, \lambda_i))}{\partial \lambda_i} + d_{ij} \right) - \nu_j - \delta_{ij} = 0 \quad (27)$$

$$\frac{\partial g_i(m_i, \lambda_i)}{\partial m_i} + \beta \lambda_i \frac{\partial f_i(m_i, \lambda_i)}{\partial m_i} + \bar{\omega}_i - \underline{\omega}_i = 0. \quad (28)$$

Note the feasibility constraint (6b) of GLB-Q is no longer required to ensure stability. In GLB-LIN, it is instead assumed that f is infinite when the load exceeds capacity.

The objective function is strictly convex in data center i's decision variable m_i, and so there is a unique solution $\hat{m}_i(\lambda_i)$ to (28) for $\bar{\omega}_i = \underline{\omega}_i = 0$, and the optimal m_i given λ_i is the projection of this onto the interval $[0, M_i]$.

GLB in its general form has the same KKT conditions as GLB-LIN, with the stationary conditions replaced by

$$\frac{\partial g_i}{\partial \lambda_i} + r(f_i + d_{ij}) + \sum_{k \in J} \lambda_{ik} r'(f_i + d_{ik}) \frac{\partial f_i}{\partial \lambda_i}$$
$$- \nu_j - \delta_{ij} = 0 \quad (29)$$

$$\frac{\partial g_i}{\partial m_i} + \sum_{j \in J} \lambda_{ij} r'(f_i + d_{ij}) \frac{\partial f_i}{\partial m_i} + \bar{\omega}_i - \underline{\omega}_i = 0 \quad (30)$$

where r' denotes the derivative of $r(\cdot)$.

GLB again decouples, since it is convex because $r(\cdot)$ is convex and increasing. However, now data center i's problem depends on all λ_{ij}, rather than simply λ_i.

A.2 Characterizing the optima

Lemma 7 will help prove the results of Section 3.

Lemma 7. *Consider the GLB-LIN formulation. Suppose that for all i, $F_i(m_i, \lambda_i)$ is jointly convex in λ_i and m_i, and differentiable in λ_i where it is finite. If, for some i, the dual variable $\bar{\omega}_i > 0$ for an optimal solution, then $m_i = M_i$ for all optimal solutions. Conversely, if $m_i < M_i$ for an optimal solution, then $\bar{\omega}_i = 0$ for all optimal solutions.*

PROOF. Consider an optimal solution S with $i \in N$ such that $\bar{\omega}_i > 0$ and hence $m_i = M_i$. Let S' be some other optimal solution.

Since the cost function is jointly convex in λ_{ij} and m_i, any convex combination of S and S' must also be optimal. Let $m_i(s)$ denote the m_i value of a given solution s. Since $m_i(S) = M_i$, we have $\lambda_i > 0$ and so the optimality of S implies f_i is finite at S and hence differentiable. By (28) and the continuity of the partial derivative [33, Corollary 25.51], there is a neighborhood $\mathcal{N}$ of S within which all optimal solutions have $\bar{\omega}_i > 0$, and hence $m_i(s) = M_i$ for all $s \in \mathcal{N}$.

Since $S+\epsilon(S'-S) \in \mathcal{N}$ for sufficiently small ϵ, the linearity of $m_i(s)$ implies $M_i = m_i(S+\epsilon(S'-S)) = m_i(S)+\epsilon(m_i(S')-m_i(S))$. Thus $m_i(S') = m_i(S) = M_i$. $\square$

PROOF OF THEOREM 1. Consider first the case where there exists an optimal solution with $m_i < M_i$. By Lemma 7, $\bar{\omega}_i = 0$ for all optimal solutions. Recall that $\hat{m}_i(\lambda_i)$, which defines the optimal m_i, is strictly convex. Thus, if different optimal solutions have different values of λ_i, then a convex combination of the two yielding (m_i', λ_i') would have $\hat{m}_i(\lambda_i') < m_i'$, which contradicts the optimality of m_i'.

Next consider the case where all optimal solutions have $m_i = M_i$. In this case, consider two solutions S and S' that both have $m_i = M_i$. If λ_i is the same under both S and S', we are done. Otherwise, let the set of convex combinations of S and S' be denoted $\{s(\lambda_i)\}$, where we have made explicit the parameterization by λ_i. The convexity of each F_k in m_k and λ_k implies that $F(s(\lambda_i)) - F_i(s(\lambda_i))$ is also convex, due to the fact that the parameterization is by definition affine. Further, since F_i is strictly convex in λ_i, this implies $F(s(\lambda_i))$ is strictly convex in λ_i, and hence has a unique optimal λ_i. $\square$

PROOF OF THEOREM 2. The proof when $m_i = M_i$ for all optimal solutions is identical to that of Theorem 1. Otherwise, when $m_i < M_i$ in an optimal solution, the definition of $\hat{m}$ gives $\bar{\lambda}_i = \mu_i \sqrt{p_i/\beta_i}/(\sqrt{p_i/\beta_i}+1)$ for all optimal solutions. $\square$

PROOF OF THEOREM 3. For each optimal solution S, consider an undirected bipartite graph G with a vertex representing each source and each data center and with an edge connecting i and j when $\lambda_{ij} > 0$. We will show that at least one of these graphs is acyclic. The theorem then follows since an acyclic graph with K nodes has at most $K-1$ edges.

To prove that there exists one optimal solution with acyclic graph we will inductively reroute traffic in a way that removes cycles while preserving optimality. Suppose G contains a cycle. Let C be a minimal cycle, i.e., no strict subset of C is a cycle, and let C be directed.

Form a new solution $S(\xi)$ from S by adding ξ to λ_{ij} if $(i,j) \in C$, and subtracting ξ from λ_{ij} if $(j,i) \in C$. Note that this does not change the λ_i. To see that $S(\xi)$ is maintains the optimal cost, first note that the change in the objective function of the GLB between S and $S(\xi)$ is equal to

$$\xi\left(\sum_{(j,i)\in C} r(d_{ij}+f_i(m_i,\lambda_i)) - \sum_{(i,j)\in C} r(d_{ij}+f_i(m_i,\lambda_i))\right) \quad (31)$$

Next note that the multiplier $\delta_{ij} = 0$ since $\lambda_{ij} > 0$ at S. Further, the KKT condition (29) for stationarity in λ_{ij} can be written as $K_i + r(d_{ij}+f_i(m_i,\lambda_i)) - \nu_j = 0$, where K_i does not depend on the choice of j.

Since C is minimal, for each $(i,j) \in C$ where $i \in I$ and $j \in J$ there is exactly one (j',i) with $j' \in J$, and vice versa. Thus,

$$0 = \sum_{(j,i)\in C}(K_i + r(d_{ij}+f_i(m_i,\lambda_i)) - \nu_j)$$
$$- \sum_{(i,j)\in C}(K_i + r(d_{ij}+f_i(m_i,\lambda_i)) - \nu_j)$$
$$= \sum_{(j,i)\in C} r(d_{ij}+f_i(m_i,\lambda_i)) - \sum_{(i,j)\in C} r(d_{ij}+f_i(m_i,\lambda_i)).$$

Hence, by (31) the objective of $S(\xi)$ and S are the same.

To complete the proof, we let $(i^*, j^*) = \arg\min_{(i,j)\in C} \lambda_{ij}$. Then $S(\lambda_{i^*,j^*})$ has $\lambda_{i^*,j^*} = 0$. Thus, $S(\lambda_{i^*,j^*})$ has at least one fewer cycle, since it has broken C. Further, by construction, it is still optimal. $\square$

PROOF OF THEOREM 4. It is sufficient to show that, if $\lambda_{kj}\lambda_{k'j} > 0$ then either $m_k = M_k$ or $m_{k'} = M_{k'}$. Consider a case when $\lambda_{kj}\lambda_{k'j} > 0$.

For a generic i, define $c_i = (1+\sqrt{p_i/\beta})^2/\mu_i$ as the marginal cost (26) when the Lagrange multipliers $\bar{\omega}_i = \underline{\omega}_i = 0$. Since the p_i are chosen from a continuous distribution, we have that with probability 1

$$c_k - c_{k'} \neq d_{k'j} - d_{kj}. \quad (32)$$

However, (26) holds with equality if $\lambda_{ij} > 0$, and so $d_{kj} + (1+\sqrt{p_k^*/\beta})^2/\mu_k = d_{k'j} + (1+\sqrt{p_k^*/\beta})^2/\mu_{k'}$. By the definition of c_i and (32), this implies either $p_k^* \neq p_k$ or $p_{k'}^* \neq p_k$. Hence at least one of the Lagrange multipliers $\underline{\omega}_k, \bar{\omega}_k, \underline{\omega}_{k'}$ or $\bar{\omega}_{k'}$ must be non-zero. However, $\underline{\omega}_i > 0$ would imply $m_i = 0$ whence $\lambda_{ij} = 0$ by (21), which is false by hypothesis, and so either $\bar{\omega}_k$ or $\bar{\omega}_{k'}$ is non-zero, giving the result by (24). $\square$

B. PROOFS FOR SECTION 4

Algorithm 1

To prove Theorem 5 we apply a variant of Proposition 3.9 of Ch 3 in [8], which gives that if

(i) $F(\mathbf{m}, \boldsymbol{\lambda})$ is continuously differentiable and convex in the convex feasible region (4b)–(4d);

(ii) Every limit point of the sequence is feasible;

(iii) Given the values of $\boldsymbol{\lambda}_{-j}$ and $\mathbf{m}$, there is a unique minimizer of F with respect to λ_j, and given $\boldsymbol{\lambda}$ there is a unique minimizer of F with respect to $\mathbf{m}$.

Then, every limit point of $(\mathbf{m}(\tau), \boldsymbol{\lambda}(\tau))_{\tau=1,2,...}$ is an optimal solution of GLB-Q.

This differs slightly from [8] in that the requirement that the feasible region be closed is replaced by the feasibility of all limit points, and the requirement of strict convexity with respect to each component is replaced by the existence of a unique minimizer. However, the proof is unchanged.

PROOF OF THEOREM 5. To apply the above to prove Theorem 5, we need to show that $F(\mathbf{m}, \boldsymbol{\lambda})$ satisfies the differentiability and continuity constraints under the GLB-Q model.

GLB-Q is continuously differentiable and, as noted in Appendix A.1, a convex problem. To see that every limit point is feasible, note that the only infeasible points in the closure of the feasible region are those with $m_i\mu_i = \lambda_i$. Since the objective approaches ∞ approaching that boundary, and Gauss-Seidel iterations always reduce the objective [8], these points cannot be limit points.

It remains to show the uniqueness of the minimum in $\mathbf{m}$ and each λ_j. Since the cost is separable in the m_i, it is sufficient to show that this applies with respect to each m_i individually. If $\lambda_i = 0$, then the unique minimizer is $m_i = 0$. Otherwise

$$\frac{\partial^2 F(\mathbf{m}, \boldsymbol{\lambda})}{\partial m_i^2} = 2\beta\mu_i \frac{\lambda_i^2}{(m_i\mu_i - \lambda_i)^3}$$

which by (6b) is strictly positive. The Hessian of $F(\mathbf{m}, \boldsymbol{\lambda})$ with respect to $\boldsymbol{\lambda}_j$ is diagonal with ith element

$$2\beta\mu_i \frac{m_i^2}{(m_i\mu_i - \lambda_i)^3} > 0$$

which is positive definite except the points where some $m_i = 0$. However, if $m_i = 0$, the unique minimum is $\lambda_{ij} = 0$. Note we cannot have all $m_i = 0$. Except these points, $F(\mathbf{m}, \boldsymbol{\lambda})$ is strictly convex in $\boldsymbol{\lambda}_j$ given $\mathbf{m}$ and $\boldsymbol{\lambda}_{-j}$. Therefore $\boldsymbol{\lambda}_j$ is unique given $\mathbf{m}$.

Part (ii) of Theorem 5 follows from part (i) and the continuity of $F(\mathbf{m}, \boldsymbol{\lambda})$. Part (iii) follows from part (i) and Theorem 2, which provides the uniqueness of optimal per-server arrival rates $(\lambda_i(\tau)/m_i(\tau), i \in N)$. $\square$

Algorithm 2

As discussed in the section on Algorithm 2, we will prove Theorem 6 in three steps. First, we will show that, starting from an initial feasible point $\boldsymbol{\lambda}(0)$, Algorithm 2 generates a sequence $\boldsymbol{\lambda}(\tau)$ that lies in the set $\Lambda := \Lambda(\phi)$ defined in (15), for $\tau = 0, 1, \ldots$. Moreover, $\nabla F(\boldsymbol{\lambda})$ is Lipschitz over Λ. Finally, this implies that $F(\boldsymbol{\lambda}(\tau))$ moves in a descent direction that guarantees convergence.

Lemma 8. *Given an initial point $\boldsymbol{\lambda}(0) \in \prod_j \Lambda_j$, let $\phi := F(\boldsymbol{\lambda}(0))$. Then*

1. *$\boldsymbol{\lambda}(0) \in \Lambda := \Lambda(\phi)$;*
2. *If $\boldsymbol{\lambda}^*$ is optimal then $\boldsymbol{\lambda}^* \in \Lambda$;*
3. *If $\boldsymbol{\lambda}(\tau) \in \Lambda$, then $\boldsymbol{\lambda}(\tau+1) \in \Lambda$.*

PROOF. We claim $F(\boldsymbol{\lambda}) \leq \phi$ implies $\boldsymbol{\lambda} \in \Lambda$. This is true because $\phi \geq F(\boldsymbol{\lambda}) \geq \Sigma_k \frac{\beta \lambda_k}{\mu_k - \lambda_k/m_k(\lambda_k)} \geq \frac{\beta \lambda_i}{\mu_i - \lambda_i/m_i(\lambda_i)} \geq \frac{\beta \lambda_i}{\mu_i - \lambda_i/M_i}, \forall i$. Therefore $\lambda_i \leq \frac{\phi}{\phi + \beta M_i} M_i \mu_i, \forall i$. Consequently, the intial point $\boldsymbol{\lambda}(0) \in \Lambda$ and the optimal point $\boldsymbol{\lambda}^* \in \Lambda$ because $F(\boldsymbol{\lambda}^*) \leq F(\boldsymbol{\lambda})$.

Next we show that $\boldsymbol{\lambda}(\tau) \in \Lambda$ implies $\mathbf{Z}^j(\tau+1) \in \Lambda$, where $\mathbf{Z}^j(\tau+1)$ is $\boldsymbol{\lambda}(\tau)$ except $\boldsymbol{\lambda}_j(\tau)$ is replaced by $\mathbf{z}_j(\tau)$. This holds because $Z_{ik}^j(\tau+1) = \lambda_{ik}(\tau) \geq 0, \forall k \neq j, \forall i$ and $\Sigma_i Z_{ik}^j(\tau+1) = \Sigma_i \lambda_{ik}(\tau) = L_k, \forall k \neq j$. From the definiiiton of the projection on $\hat{\Lambda}_j(\tau)$, $Z_{ij}^j(\tau+1) \geq 0, \forall i$, $\Sigma_i Z_{ij}^j(\tau+1) = L_j$, and $\Sigma_k Z_{ik}^j(\tau+1) \leq \frac{\phi}{\phi + \beta M_i} M_i \mu_i, \forall i$. These together ensure $\mathbf{Z}^j(\tau+1) \in \Lambda$.

The update $\boldsymbol{\lambda}_j(\tau+1) = \frac{|J|-1}{|J|} \boldsymbol{\lambda}_j(\tau) + \frac{1}{|J|} \mathbf{z}_j(\tau), \forall j$ is equivalent to $\boldsymbol{\lambda}(\tau+1) = \frac{\Sigma_j \mathbf{Z}^j(\tau+1)}{|J|}$. Then from the convexity of Λ, we have $\boldsymbol{\lambda}(\tau+1) \in \Lambda$. $\square$

Let $F(\mathbf{M}, \boldsymbol{\lambda})$ be the total cost when all data centers use all servers, and $\nabla F(\mathbf{M}, \boldsymbol{\lambda})$ be the derivatives with respect to $\boldsymbol{\lambda}$. To prove that $\nabla F(\boldsymbol{\lambda})$ is Lipschitz over Λ, we need the following intermediate result. We omit the proof due to space constraint.

Lemma 9. *For all $\boldsymbol{\lambda}^a, \boldsymbol{\lambda}^b \in \Lambda$, we have*
$$\left\| \nabla F(\boldsymbol{\lambda}^b) - \nabla F(\boldsymbol{\lambda}^a) \right\|_2 \leq \left\| \nabla F(\mathbf{M}, \boldsymbol{\lambda}^b) - \nabla F(\mathbf{M}, \boldsymbol{\lambda}^a) \right\|_2.$$

Lemma 10. *$\left\| \nabla F(\boldsymbol{\lambda}^b) - \nabla F(\boldsymbol{\lambda}^a) \right\|_2 \leq K \left\| \boldsymbol{\lambda}^b - \boldsymbol{\lambda}^a \right\|_2$, $\forall \boldsymbol{\lambda}^a, \boldsymbol{\lambda}^b \in \Lambda$, where $K = |J| \max_i 2(\phi + \beta M_i)^3/(\beta^2 M_i^4 \mu_i^2)$.*

PROOF. Following Lemma 9, here we continue to show $\left\| \nabla F(\mathbf{M}, \boldsymbol{\lambda}^b) - \nabla F(\mathbf{M}, \boldsymbol{\lambda}^a) \right\|_2 \leq K \left\| \boldsymbol{\lambda}^b - \boldsymbol{\lambda}^a \right\|_2$.

The Hessian $\nabla^2 F(\mathbf{M}, \boldsymbol{\lambda})$ of $F(\mathbf{M}, \boldsymbol{\lambda})$ is given by
$$\nabla^2 F_{ij,kl}(\mathbf{M}, \boldsymbol{\lambda}) = \begin{cases} \frac{2\beta \mu_i/M_i}{(\mu_i - \lambda_i/M_i)^3} & \text{if } i = k \\ 0 & \text{otherwise.} \end{cases}$$

Then $\left\| \nabla^2 F(\mathbf{M}, \boldsymbol{\lambda}) \right\|_2^2 \leq \left\| \nabla^2 F(\mathbf{M}, \boldsymbol{\lambda}) \right\|_1 \left\| \nabla^2 F(\mathbf{M}, \boldsymbol{\lambda}) \right\|_\infty = \left\| \nabla^2 F(\mathbf{M}, \boldsymbol{\lambda}) \right\|_\infty^2$. The inequality is a property of norms and the equality is from the symmetry of $\nabla^2 F(\mathbf{M}, \boldsymbol{\lambda})$. Finally,
$$\left\| \nabla^2 F(\mathbf{M}, \boldsymbol{\lambda}) \right\|_\infty = \max_{ij} \left\{ \Sigma_{kl} \nabla^2 F_{ij,kl}(\mathbf{M}, \boldsymbol{\lambda}) \right\}$$
$$= \max_i \left\{ |J| \frac{2\beta \mu_i/M_i}{(\mu_i - \lambda_i/M_i)^3} \right\} \leq |J| \max_i \frac{2(\phi + \beta M_i)^3}{\beta^2 M_i^4 \mu_i^2}.$$

In the last step we substitute λ_i by $\frac{\phi M_i \mu_i}{\phi + \beta M_i}$ because $\lambda_i \leq \frac{\phi}{\phi + \beta M_i} M_i \mu_i, \forall i$ and $\frac{2\mu_i/M_i}{(\mu_i - \lambda_i/M_i)^3}$ is increasing in λ_i. $\square$

Lemma 11. *When applying Algorithm 2 to GLB-Q,*

(a) $F(\boldsymbol{\lambda}(\tau+1)) \leq F(\boldsymbol{\lambda}(\tau)) - (\frac{1}{\gamma_m} - \frac{K}{2}) \| \boldsymbol{\lambda}(\tau+1) - \boldsymbol{\lambda}(\tau) \|_2^2$, where $K = |J| \max_i 2(\phi + \beta M_i)^3/(\beta^2 M_i^4 \mu_i^2)$, $\gamma_m = \max_j \gamma_j$, and $0 < \gamma_j < \min_i \beta^2 \mu_i^2 M_i^4/(|J|(\phi + \beta M_i)^3), \forall j$.

(b) $\boldsymbol{\lambda}(\tau+1) = \boldsymbol{\lambda}(\tau)$ if and only if $\boldsymbol{\lambda}(\tau)$ minimizes $F(\boldsymbol{\lambda})$ over the set Λ.

(c) The mapping $T(\boldsymbol{\lambda}(\tau)) = \boldsymbol{\lambda}(\tau+1)$ is continuous.

PROOF. From the Lemma 10, we know
$$\left\| \nabla F(\boldsymbol{\lambda}^b) - \nabla F(\boldsymbol{\lambda}^a) \right\|_2 \leq K \left\| \boldsymbol{\lambda}^b - \boldsymbol{\lambda}^a \right\|_2, \forall \boldsymbol{\lambda}^a \in \Lambda, \forall \boldsymbol{\lambda}^b \in \Lambda$$
where $K = |J| \max_i 2(\phi + \beta M_i)^3/(\beta^2 M_i^4 \mu_i^2)$.

Here $\mathbf{Z}^j(\tau+1) \in \Lambda, \boldsymbol{\lambda}(\tau) \in \Lambda$, therefore we have
$$\left\| \nabla F(\mathbf{Z}^j(\tau+1)) - \nabla F(\boldsymbol{\lambda}(\tau)) \right\|_2 \leq K \left\| \mathbf{Z}^j(\tau+1) - \boldsymbol{\lambda}(\tau) \right\|_2.$$

From the convexity of $F(\boldsymbol{\lambda})$, we have
$$F(\boldsymbol{\lambda}(\tau+1)) = F\left(\frac{\Sigma_j \mathbf{Z}^j(\tau+1)}{|J|} \right)$$
$$\leq \frac{1}{|J|} \Sigma_j F(\mathbf{Z}^j(\tau+1))$$
$$\leq \frac{1}{|J|} \Sigma_j \left(F(\boldsymbol{\lambda}(\tau)) - \left(\frac{1}{\gamma_j} - \frac{K}{2} \right) \left\| \mathbf{Z}^j(\tau+1) - \boldsymbol{\lambda}(t) \right\|_2^2 \right)$$
$$= F(\boldsymbol{\lambda}(\tau)) - \Sigma_j \left(\frac{1}{\gamma_j} - \frac{K}{2} \right) \frac{\left\| \mathbf{Z}^j(\tau+1) - \boldsymbol{\lambda}(\tau) \right\|_2^2}{|J|}$$
$$\leq F(\boldsymbol{\lambda}(\tau)) - \left(\frac{1}{\gamma_m} - \frac{K}{2} \right) \frac{\Sigma_j \left\| \mathbf{Z}^j(\tau+1) - \boldsymbol{\lambda}(\tau) \right\|_2^2}{|J|}$$

where $K = |J| \max_i 2(\phi + \beta M_i)^3/(\beta^2 M_i^4 \mu_i^2)$.

The first line is from the update rule of $\boldsymbol{\lambda}(\tau)$. The second line is from the convexity of $F(\boldsymbol{\lambda})$. The third line is from the property of gradient projection. The last line is from the definition of γ_m.

Then from the convexity of $\| \cdot \|_2^2$, we have
$$\frac{\Sigma_j \left\| \mathbf{Z}^j(\tau+1) - \boldsymbol{\lambda}(\tau) \right\|_2^2}{|J|} \geq \left\| \frac{\Sigma_j \left(\mathbf{Z}^j(\tau+1) - \boldsymbol{\lambda}(\tau) \right)}{|J|} \right\|_2^2$$
$$= \left\| \frac{\Sigma_j \mathbf{Z}^j(\tau+1)}{|J|} - \boldsymbol{\lambda}(\tau) \right\|_2^2 = \| \boldsymbol{\lambda}(\tau+1) - \boldsymbol{\lambda}(\tau) \|_2^2.$$

Therefore we have
$$F(\boldsymbol{\lambda}(\tau+1)) \leq F(\boldsymbol{\lambda}(\tau)) - \left(\frac{1}{\gamma_m} - \frac{K}{2} \right) \| \boldsymbol{\lambda}(\tau+1) - \boldsymbol{\lambda}(\tau) \|_2^2.$$

(b) $\boldsymbol{\lambda}(\tau+1) = \boldsymbol{\lambda}(\tau)$ is equivalent to $\mathbf{Z}^j(\tau+1) = \boldsymbol{\lambda}_j(\tau), \forall j$. Moreover, if $\mathbf{Z}^j(\tau+1) = \boldsymbol{\lambda}_j(\tau), \forall j$, then from the definition of each gradient projection, we know it is optimal. Conversely, if $\boldsymbol{\lambda}(\tau)$ minimizes $F(\boldsymbol{\lambda}(\tau))$ over the set Λ, then the gradient projection always projects to the original point, hence $\mathbf{Z}^j(\tau+1) = \boldsymbol{\lambda}_j(\tau), \forall j$. See also [8, Ch 3 Prop. 3.3(b)] for reference.

(c) Since $F(\boldsymbol{\lambda})$ is continuously differentiable, the gradient mapping is continuous. The projection mapping is also continuous. T is the composition of the two and is therefore continuous. $\square$

PROOF OF THEOREM 6. Lemma 11 is parallel to that of Proposition 3.3 in Ch 3 of [8], and Theorem 6 here is parallel to Proposition 3.4 in Ch 3 of [8]. Therefore, the proof for Proposition 3.4 immediately applies to Theorem 6. We also have $F(\boldsymbol{\lambda})$ is convex in $\boldsymbol{\lambda}$, which completes the proof. $\square$

Slick Packets

Giang T. K. Nguyen
University of Illinois
at Urbana-Champaign, USA
nguyen59@illinois.edu

Rachit Agarwal
University of Illinois
at Urbana-Champaign, USA
agarwa16@illinois.edu

Junda Liu
University of California
at Berkeley, USA
liujd@cs.berkeley.edu

Matthew Caesar
University of Illinois
at Urbana-Champaign, USA
caesar@illinois.edu

P. Brighten Godfrey
University of Illinois
at Urbana-Champaign, USA
pbg@illinois.edu

Scott Shenker
University of California
at Berkeley, USA
shenker@cs.berkeley.edu

Abstract

Source-controlled routing has been proposed as a way to improve flexibility of future network architectures, as well as simplifying the data plane. However, if a packet specifies its path, this precludes fast local re-routing within the network. We propose SLICKPACKETS, a novel solution that allows packets to slip around failures by specifying alternate paths in their headers, in the form of compactly-encoded directed acyclic graphs. We show that this can be accomplished with reasonably small packet headers for real network topologies, and results in responsiveness to failures that is competitive with past approaches that require much more state within the network. Our approach thus enables fast failure response while preserving the benefits of source-controlled routing.

Categories and Subject Descriptors

C.2.1 [**Network Architecture and Design**]: Packet-switching networks; C.2.2 [**Network Protocols**]: Routing protocols; C.2.6 [**Internetworking**]: Routers

General Terms

Algorithms, Design, Performance, Reliability

Keywords

Reliability, failures, routing, source routing, forwarding

1. INTRODUCTION

Traditional routing protocols are **network-controlled**: routes are computed within the network, with each router picking, from among its neighbors, the next-hop to each destination. Examples include BGP for interdomain routing, and OSPF for intradomain routing. An alternate paradigm, **source-controlled routing** (SCR), improves

the flexibility of the network architecture. Rather than computing all routes within the network, SCR architectures [10, 20, 29–31] reserve some choice of routes for the *sources*[1] to select on a per-packet basis. The uses of SCR's routing flexibility are quite diverse. Sources can observe end-to-end reliability problems and switch to a working path within a few round-trip times (RTTs); pick better-performing routes based on observed performance [5, 11, 25]; improve load balance since path selection is finer-grained [24]; encourage competition among network providers [7]; improve security [28]; or optimize for other application-specific objectives. SCR is thus a promising approach to improve the flexibility of the network layer in future Internet architectures.

However, one remaining problem is that of *fast failure reaction*. This problem arose in early network-controlled routing (NCR) protocols, which suffered from unreliability during network dynamics: during the distributed convergence process, packets could enter "black holes" or loops, resulting in tens of seconds or minutes of downtime in Internet end-to-end paths [14,27]. Treating these basic protocols as a baseline, two high-level approaches have been proposed to improve failure reaction.

The first approach works within the NCR paradigm by computing an alternate path to each destination (or IP prefix or AS); a router can locally switch to the alternate path without waiting for a control-plane convergence process. Packets can thus be delivered continuously, except for the minimal time it takes for a router to detect failure of one of its directly connected links and locally switch to an alternate path. Examples include MPLS Fast Reroute [23], SafeGuard [18], and FCP [17] for intradomain routing, and R-BGP [16] for interdomain routing. However, this approach lacks the routing flexibility of SCR.

A second approach to improve failure reaction is to leverage SCR's routing flexibility: a source can switch routes without waiting for the Internet's control plane to reconverge. While this improves failure reaction time relative to the baseline above, the source still must wait to receive notice of the failure. Regardless of the means of notification, this will take at least on the order of one RTT, which at Internet scales would be much slower than the first approach of using NCR with alternate paths.

---

[1]In this paper, we use "source" to refer either to end-hosts or to edge routers acting on their behalf.

And in the SCR proposals that provide the most flexibility [10,30], sources specify in the packet header an explicit route (perhaps at the level of autonomous systems) rather than a destination, so the NCR and SCR techniques cannot be immediately combined.

The goal of this paper is to achieve the best of two worlds: the fast failure reaction of alternate routes embedded within the network, and the flexibility of routes chosen by sources at the edge of the network. To meet this goal, we work within the SCR paradigm, but with a twist. Instead of specifying a single path to the destination, the packet header contains a directed acyclic graph that we call the *forwarding subgraph* (FS). Each router along the packet's path may choose to forward it along any of the outgoing links at that router's node in the FS (optionally preferring a path marked as the primary), with no danger of causing a forwarding loop. This approach, which we call SLICKPACKETS, allows packets to "slip" around failures in-flight while retaining the flexibility of source route control. Moreover, SLICKPACKETS provides a scalability benefit over NCR with alternate paths: rather than requiring multiple routes to every destination in every router's forwarding table, SLICKPACKETS routers need only local information.

Of course, our approach also presents several challenges. Chief among these is how to encode an FS with sufficient path diversity into the small space afforded by a packet header. We introduce techniques through which the FS can be encoded compactly enough for our mechanism to be feasible. For example, an FS providing an alternate path at every hop along the primary occupies less than 26 bytes for 99% of evaluated source-destination pairs in an AS-level Internet map, and no higher than 50 bytes in all evaluated cases. Thus, the technique incurs manageable overhead for applications that send packets of moderate to large size. We also demonstrate through a simulation-based performance evaluation that SLICKPACKETS achieves failure reaction performance that is comparable to the best of NCR architectures [18].

The rest of this paper proceeds as follows. In §2, we present an overview of SLICKPACKETS and its principal design challenges. §3 gives a detailed presentation of the SLICKPACKETS design. We evaluate the performance of our design in terms of header size and failure reaction in §4. We discuss extensions of SLICKPACKETS in §5 and related work in §6, and conclude in §7.

2. OVERVIEW

In this section, we provide an overview of SLICKPACKETS, and discuss several critical design challenges.

SLICKPACKETS is a failure reaction mechanism for SCR protocols. In contrast to traditional SCR protocols that specify a single path in the packet header, SLICKPACKETS enables fast recovery within the network by allowing the source to embed the rerouting information within the packet header in the form of a **forwarding subgraph (FS)**. The FS specifies a set of paths that intermediate routers can use to reroute packets in case of failures. The source, if it desires, can designate one of these paths as the **primary path** to be used in the absence of failure; the rest of the paths are then treated as **alternate paths** that can be used if the primary path is not available. In

order to avoid forwarding loops, SLICKPACKETS requires that the FS be a directed acyclic graph (DAG).

Performing forwarding in this way has two main benefits. First, since the source specifies the FS, it has full control of not only the primary path, but also how the network forwards the packet when the primary path is not available. Second, since alternate path information is embedded directly in the packet header, the network can react immediately without requiring involvement of the source, which reduces the reaction time in presence of link failures. In addition to these two benefits, the task of a router becomes simpler: a router requires only local knowledge of its neighbors, rather than needing an alternate path for every destination (which may require information such as the multi-homing locations of each host). In summary, SLICKPACKETS achieves key benefits of SCR architectures (flexibility in route selection and scalability of network routing state) while simultaneously attaining failure reaction performance that is comparable to that of NCR architectures with backup paths.

Fig. 1 shows an example to illustrate the design of SLICKPACKETS. Suppose the source s wishes to send a packet to a destination d. The source has acquired, by some mechanism to be discussed later, a map of the network. It selects the FS as shown in Fig. 1 and designates (s, R_1, R_2, R_5, d) to be the primary path. Note that the FS provides each node on the primary path with sufficient alternatives so that if a link on the primary path fails, the packet can be rerouted to the destination. Next, s constructs a data packet with the subgraph embedded in the packet header, and forwards it on to the first-hop R_1. At R_1, the packet is forwarded to the next-hop on the primary path (R_2). Now suppose that at R_2 the primary path's next hop R_5 lies across a failed link (R_2, R_5); then R_2 forwards the packet to R_4, the next-hop on its alternate path in the FS, after which the packet continues to R_5 and finally d.

Realizing the high level idea of source-controlled routing along an FS, however, involves several key challenges. We outline these challenges and our solutions here.

Obtaining the map. Like other SCR architectures in which sources construct end-to-end paths, our sources require a map of the available links. When deploying SLICKPACKETS as an interdomain routing protocol, this immediately raises questions of scalability and policy compliance. Is it feasible to push a map of the Internet, at some level of granularity, to every source or at least every edge router? Is there an acceptable way to balance control of network resources between the senders and the network owners? Fortunately, we can adopt the solutions developed by past work, in particular NIRA [30] and pathlet routing [10], which have shown how maps of policy-compliant transit service can be constructed and disseminated in ways that can be much *more* scalable than traditional NCR protocols like BGP.

Packet header overhead. The next challenge is to design an efficient encoding mechanism that embeds the FS into the packet header with minimal overhead. By using link labels with only local significance and allocating every bit carefully, we are able to achieve acceptable packet header sizes on realistic network topologies.

Fast data-plane operations. Another challenge is to

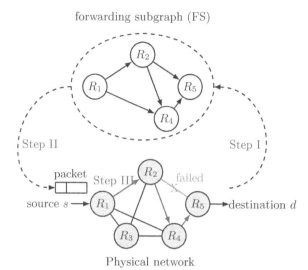

forwarding subgraph (FS)

Step II

packet   Step III

source s →

failed

destination d

Physical network

Figure 1: Overview of the SLICKPACKETS design. Step I: the source selects a forwarding subgraph (FS) based on the topology of the physical network; Step II: the source encodes and embeds the FS in the packet header to inform routers how to route around encountered failures; and Step III: routers forward the packet based on the FS contained in the packet header.

design an efficient data plane forwarding algorithm: the encoding and forwarding mechanisms in SLICKPACKETS should minimize next-hop lookup time without substantially increasing header processing cost, forwarding delay and/or design complexity of modern router forwarding planes. Fortunately, forwarding along an FS requires only lookup and pointer-increment operations, as in standard SCR protocols, and can be efficiently implemented in practice.

The next section discusses our design in more detail, including our solutions to these challenges.

3. SLICKPACKETS DESIGN

In this section, we present in more detail the four main components of SLICKPACKETS: definition and dissemination of the network map (§3.1); selection of a forwarding subgraph (FS) at the source (§3.2); encoding of the FS into the packet header (§3.3); and the data plane forwarding mechanism at routers (§3.4).

The SLICKPACKETS approach could be applied in multiple contexts. We describe here how the design can be applied to interdomain and intradomain routing. The differences principally lie in map dissemination and data plane forwarding, with the core approach taking the same form in both contexts.

3.1 Map format and dissemination

As in other SCR protocols in which the source composes end-to-end paths [10, 30], in SLICKPACKETS, the source must obtain a network "map" (topology) from which it can construct paths. This map is an abstract directed graph in which each directed directed link (u, v) at node node u is annotated with a *label*. The label is a compact,

variable-length bitstring, which the source will use when encoding the FS (§ 3.3) to tell node u that it wants u to use the link (u, v). Similar to an MPLS label, the label identifies a link only locally at u, not globally. Thus, u will generally announce labels of length $\lceil \log_2 \delta(u) \rceil$ bits where $\delta(u)$ is the degree of u.

What this map corresponds to in the physical network and how the map is disseminated depend on the deployment scenario. In an intradomain environment, the map would correspond to the physical topology of routers and links and could be distributed via a protocol like OSPF or through a centralized coordinator as in [17].

In an interdomain environment, we have to deal with the significant challenges of scalability and network owners' transit policies. In order to overcome these challenges, we build on solutions developed in past work and briefly describe them here for completeness.

Basic approach. Both NIRA [30] and pathlet routing [10] provide sources with a policy-compliant map of the Internet, roughly at the autonomous system (AS) level. NIRA's map assumes common customer-provider-peer relationships between ASes and allows a subset of *valley-free* routes: that is, packets travel up a chain of providers, potentially across a peering link, and down a chain of customers to the destination. Pathlet routing represents this map explicitly as an arbitrary virtual topology, whose edges (pathlets) represent policy-compliant transit service.

Scalability. NIRA, while dependent on the existence of a typical AS business hierarchy, offers the opportunity of vastly *improving* BGP's control plane scalability. Rather than learning an Internet-wide topology, each node learns its "up-graph" of routes through providers, stopping at the "core" of the Internet. The up-graph requires fewer than 20 entries for 90% of domains [30], many orders of magnitude less than the roughly 300,000 prefixes that BGP propagates today. Each destination stores its up-graph in a global DNS-like database; to route to a destination, a source queries the database and combines its own up-graph with the destination's up-graph. Though the resulting map is a small fraction of the Internet, it includes all policy-compliant (valley-free) routes. Pathlet routing could use a NIRA-style approach for disseminating the pathlet topology, or it can be disseminated via a BGP-like mechanism with slightly more messaging and control state ($\leq 1.7\times$) than traditional BGP.

SLICKPACKETS can take advantage of either the pathlet or NIRA approach for interdomain map dissemination. Thus, SLICKPACKETS does not require a source to have complete topological knowledge of the network, but rather only enough to construct a path and alternate paths to the destination.

We also note that SLICKPACKETS, like other SCR and multipath routing architectures, can benefit from significantly reduced rate of control plane updates [6] compared with basic single-path NCR architectures. This is because short-lived failures need not be disseminated through the control plane, since failure reaction will happen anyway via forwarding along alternate paths without waiting for control-plane updates.

Link labels. Along with the map itself, SLICKPACKETS requires labels on the links. Routers (or ASes for interdomain; for convenience we'll use "routers" in what follows) can piggyback this information with the link advertisements [10]. To change a label, a router readvertises the link. While readvertisements increase control traffic, we expect that changing a router's link labels will be fairly rare, for two reasons. First, the operator could change a single label from one bit sequence to another; however, there should be little need for such changes because the labels are arbitrary identifiers with no significance. Second, the operator may need to increase the number of links exiting the router. This *may* increase the label length and require readvertisements of all of the router's link labels, creating a period of inconsistency from when the router changes its label length to when sources receive the updated announcement. However, label lengths change only once every time the number of outgoing links doubles (or halves) in size, which is expected to be a very rare event.

An alternate approach is to make labels self-describing: their first few bits encode the label length [10]. This avoids the need to readvertise links after a length change and the resulting inconsistency, but labels become slightly longer. Since compactness is important for SLICKPACKETS, we do not evaluate this approach in this paper.

Map consistency. A natural question is whether all sources and the network must have an entirely consistent view of the map at all times. Fortunately, this difficult task is unnecessary. There are three possible types of inconsistency.

First, if a source uses a non-existent label (e.g., the link has been removed or its label changed), this is equivalent to a link failure and the packet can be re-routed along an alternate path. To avoid even this minor disturbance, routers can insert a short delay between announcing a label deletion and its removal from forwarding tables.

Second, if a source uses a label that has changed to identify a different link, then the packet will follow an incorrect path and will be unlikely to reach its intended destination. This is similar to inconsistency problems in basic NCR protocols. (Unlike in basic NCR protocols, however, the packet cannot get into a loop of any significant length because one link in the DAG will be consumed at each hop.) To avoid label-change inconsistency, routers can simply use new labels rather than reusing ones that have recently had a different meaning.

Third, a source might be unaware of some valid labels. This simply results in a slightly restricted set of options until it receives the relevant control plane advertisement, as in essentially any other distributed routing protocol.

Thus, in all cases, inconsistency issues can be mitigated.

3.2 Selection of the forwarding subgraph

Once a source has obtained the network map, it selects a *forwarding subgraph* (FS) along which it desires the packet to be routed in the network. The FS is a DAG corresponding to a subset of nodes and links in the network map. The directed edges inform routers of the packet's allowed next-hops, and acyclicity ensures there are no forwarding loops. Additionally, for each node in the FS, the source may mark one outgoing link as the preferred primary.

Sources have a great deal of flexibility in how they choose an FS. For instance, the source may select an FS that avoids any single link failure along a low-latency pri-

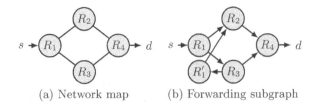

(a) Network map   (b) Forwarding subgraph

Figure 2: An FS may have multiple representations of a network map node, to allow "backtracking" without introducing cycles in the FS.

mary path, avoids node failures, optimizes for other metrics like bandwidth, or picks alternate paths that avoid shared risk link groups. We discuss some of these uses in §5. For concreteness, we describe here and evaluate in §4 how the source can pick an FS that will minimize primary-path latency and provide alternate paths to avoid any single link failure. As noted below, accommodating shared risk link groups is similar.

A source s, for a given destination d, constructs a single-failure-avoiding FS as follows. First, s computes a primary path P to d by running a shortest path algorithm over the network map. Next, s visits each link along P, and computes the alternate path P_i it would prefer the packet to be routed along if that link were to fail. In particular, for each node v_i on the primary path, we (a) remove v_i's outgoing edge corresponding to its next hop along the primary path; (b) compute a shortest path from v_i to d, not using the removed outgoing edge; and (c) restore the removed edge. In case of a node having multiple shortest paths to the destination, the source may arbitrarily select one of these shortest paths. Finally, the primary and the alternate paths are assembled into the FS. Note that the above algorithm requires $|P|$ runs of Dijkstra's algorithm. Surprisingly, it is possible to construct a primary path and all the alternate paths in a *single* run of a shortest-path algorithm; see [12].

Beyond single-link-failure protection, a source may want to protect against failures of shared risk link groups (i.e., sets of links that are likely to have correlated failures, such as multiple logical links allocated to a single physical fiber). Assuming it has knowledge of these groups, it can do this by removing all links in the group in substep (a) above, and restoring them all in (c).

Note that there is a subtlety in how the the primary and the alternate paths are "assembled" into the FS: if we simply take the union of all these links and edges, we might create a loop, violating the acyclicity requirement. Consider the network map in Fig. 2(a). Assume that s desires to use (s, R_1, R_3, R_4, d) as the primary path. Then to escape a failure of the link (R_3, R_4), a packet located at R_3 must follow the path (R_3, R_1, R_2, R_4, d). Taking the union of these primary and alternate paths would result in a loop $R_1 \rightarrow R_3 \rightarrow R_1$. Due to symmetry, the problem persists if (s, R_1, R_2, R_4, d) is the primary path.

In order to avoid such loops, when adding an alternate path edge (u, v) to the FS, we first check to see if this would cause a loop. If so, we create a second FS representation v' of the physical node v, and add the edge (u, v'). This can be seen as "tunneling" the packet back along an alternate path. In the example of Fig. 2, before adding the second alternate path, we create a new copy R_1' corresponding to the node R_1. The alternate path then follows (R_3, R_1', R_2, R_4, d), resulting in a acyclic representation of the FS as shown in Fig. 2(b).

3.3 Encoding the forwarding subgraph

After choosing an FS, the source must encode the FS into a sequence of bits and place it in the packet header. SLICKPACKETS is agnostic to the particular location this header appears in the packet (for example, it may reside in a "shim" header between the IP and MAC layers, in an IP option, or in a novel header format in a next-generation Internet protocol). There are two key goals in designing an encoding format: (a) minimizing the size of the resulting encoding; and (b) ensuring data plane forwarding operations are simple. We designed and evaluated several encoding formats to achieve these goals.

In this paper we present two encoding formats, called Direct and Default. Each may result in a smaller encoding in certain scenarios as discussed below. But the latter resulted in smaller encoding sizes in the network topologies we evaluated using the single-failure-avoiding FS selection (§3.2), so it is our default.

Direct format. The Direct format encodes the FS directly, in the sense that the FS's DAG data structure in memory is essentially directly serialized into a DAG data structure in the packet header. The header contains a sequence of node representations, each containing one or more outgoing link representations; each link representation contains its corresponding label and a pointer to another node within the header, corresponding to the node at the other end of the link. We describe the bit-layout of this format in detail in [22].

Default format. One source of overhead in the Direct format is the use of pointers within the header. Our Default format avoids some of that overhead, by grouping together sequences of labels corresponding to alternate paths, without needing an explicit representation of each node along the alternate path. The disadvantage of this grouping is that it involves duplicating link representations, similar to how a depth-first traversal of all paths in the DAG could visit links multiple times.

In fact, there exist DAGs that have exponentially large numbers of possible traversals (thus specifying exponentially large numbers of ways the packet could be forwarded through the network). Consequently, the Direct format can be exponentially more efficient than the approach of Default in the most extreme case. In general, we expect Direct will be more compact for situations in which the alternate paths often share nodes with one another or with the primary. However, in this paper we focus on the particular application of choosing single-failure-avoiding FSes. For that application, we found that the savings from avoiding pointers outweighed the duplication of link representations, so that Default was somewhat more compact in several realistic networks (§4). We therefore choose the Default format as our default and describe it in more detail now.

In the Default format, the FS is represented as a sequence of **segments**, one for each router on the primary path. For instance, in Fig. 3, the primary path consists of k hops and $S_1, S_2, \ldots, S_k$ are the segments corresponding

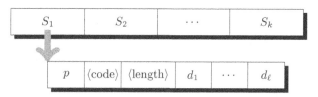

Figure 3: Default encoding format layout. S_i is the segment corresponding to node v_i on the primary path. It encodes the node's primary next hop p and alternate path $(d_1, d_2, \ldots, d_\ell)$. $\langle\text{length}\rangle$ specifies the bit-length of the alternate path, and $\langle\text{code}\rangle$ specifies the bit-length of the $\langle\text{length}\rangle$ field.

to those k hops. The segment corresponding to a router v on the primary path contains three pieces of information (see Fig. 3): (a) v's next-hop on the primary path; (b) the bit-length of the encoding of v's alternate path; and (c) v's alternate path, as a sequence of next-hop labels. By "v's alternate path" we mean the alternate path beginning at v that avoids the primary next-hop from v. (We assume here that the FS has the format of one alternate path for each link on the primary.[2])

For (a), we need to include the router's label (§3.1) for the given outgoing edge, and similarly for (c) we include a sequence of labels. Recall that these labels are only locally unique to each node, which is critical to achieving a compact encoding, because the average number of neighbors of a router in a real-world network is typically vastly smaller than the total number of routers in the network [3,13]. By exploiting the structure of the real-world graphs, we are able to reduce the size of the encoding significantly compared with globally-unique labels.

For (b), we use the two fields: $\langle\text{code}\rangle$ and $\langle\text{length}\rangle$. Here, $\langle\text{length}\rangle$ specifies the total bit-lengths of all the labels $d_1, \ldots, d_\ell$ of the alternate path. Based on our evaluation, alternate paths are shorter than 32 bits in most cases and always shorter than 128 bits; in cases a node has no alternate path, the alternate path bit-length is 0. Thus, for greater compactness, we make the bit-length of the $\langle\text{length}\rangle$ field be variable and store it in the $\langle\text{code}\rangle$ field using a prefix-free code, with the $\langle\text{code}\rangle$ bit sequences 0, 10, and 110 mapping to values of 5, 7, and 0, respectively.

The header contains two additional pieces of information. First, the SLICKPACKETS header begins with a two byte field, specifying its *header length*. Second, a one-bit field ON-ALTERNATE? specifies whether the packet is traversing along the primary path or an alternate path, and is initially false. We discuss next how routers use this information to forward packets.

3.4 Forwarding

We now describe the forwarding mechanism used by SLICKPACKETS routers for the Default format. The input to this mechanism is the SLICKPACKETS header described in §3.3, and the output is the interface out which the packet will be forwarded.

---

[2]While the Default format could be generalized to have multiple alternates at a router, or segments within segments to provide alternates for routers along an alternate path, we do not explore that generalization here; in any case, such applications can use the Direct format.

Upon receiving a packet, the router first checks the value of the SLICKPACKETS header length. If this is 0, this router is the destination for the packet. If not, the router checks the ON-ALTERNATE? bit to see whether it is on the primary path or on an alternate path. We describe the forwarding operations for the two cases separately.

Router on the primary path. The router reads the first segment in the header, which corresponds to itself, and inspects the primary next-hop label p. If the corresponding link available, the router deletes this first segment corresponding to itself. It also updates the header length by subtracting the length of its segment. The packet is then forwarded to the next-hop on the primary path with the new header.

If the primary next-hop link is not available, and the alternate path length is 0, the packet is dropped. Otherwise, the router reads its next-hop label d_1 on the alternate path. If the link corresponding to d_1 is not available, the packet is dropped.[3] If the link is available, the router removes *all* segments in the header, replacing them by its remaining alternate path labels $(d_2, \ldots, d_\ell)$. It also updates the header length appropriately and sets the ON-ALTERNATE? bit. The packet is then forwarded to the next-hop via label d_1.

Router on an alternate path. The router reads its next-hop label. If the corresponding link is not available, the packet is dropped (or, as earlier, some other failure reaction mechanism is employed). If the link is available, the router deletes its label from the header, updates the header length, and forwards the packet to the next-hop.

Simplifying forwarding operations. The above description involved removing a prefix of the header, and in the case of moving to an alternate path, a suffix as well. In some data plane implementations, these operations may be costly. In this case, we can simply add *start* and *end* pointers at the front of the header, indicating the extent of the remaining header. In an extra 3 bytes, we can fit two pointers that can point to individual bits in a 512-byte header (which is far larger than we need).

Interdomain vs. intradomain issues. In an intradomain deployment, we may assume that each router runs SLICKPACKETS and forwards packets as described above. However, in an interdomain deployment the forwarding subgraph roughly represents AS-level paths (as discussed in more detail in 3.1). When the packet is forwarded though an intermediate domain, that domain must forward the packet on to the next AS-level hop. Network operators may independently choose from a variety of ways to do this, for example by tunneling the packet with MPLS, or perhaps running SLICKPACKETS internally as well as interdomain.

4. EVALUATION

SLICKPACKETS advocates the idea of embedding a forwarding subgraph (FS) in the packet header, giving routers multiple forwarding options in order to provide the source with some property that it desires. While SLICKPACKETS can support flexible FS selections that provide different guarantees, for concreteness, this section evaluates the FS selection exemplified in §3.2, which targets fast reaction in

---

[3]Or any other failure reaction mechanism can be applied.

the presence of single-link failures. The source constructs a DAG comprised of the shortest primary path, and the shortest alternate path for each node on the primary path in case that node's outgoing link along the primary path fails. In terms of performance, three metrics are important: (a) encoding size, (b) failure reaction effectiveness, and (c) router complexity and packet forwarding rates. We present results for (a) and (b) in this section and discuss (c) in §7.

Topologies. We use three network topologies in our evaluation: the latency-annotated topology from Sprint ISP 1239 [2], with 315 nodes and 972 links; an AS-level map of the Internet [13], with $33,508$ nodes and $75,001$ links; and the largest component, with $190,914$ nodes and $607,610$ links, of a router-level map of the Internet [1]. The latter two topologies lack latency information; we take all links to have equal length. While using SLICK-PACKETS directly on a router-level map of the Internet is not a likely deployment scenario (due to privacy and scaling issues, ASes do not propagate internal topologies globally in today's Internet), we consider this extreme design point to investigate scaling issues of our design.

4.1 Encoding size

Since we encode the FS into the packet header, the **encoding size** determines the bandwidth overhead. We evaluate the resulting encoding sizes of the Direct and Default encoding formats presented in §3.3, for FSes constructed using the algorithm presented in §3.2.

Furthermore, regardless of the encoding format used, the **FS size**—the number of edges—is a factor influencing the encoding size. We are thus also interested in comparing the sizes of FSes constructed by the algorithm described in §3.2 to **lower bounds** on the sizes of FSes returned by any algorithm that provides shortest path latencies and single-link failure protection. These lower bounds impose a fundamental limit on the encoding size; intuitively, for a given encoding format that already uses optimized label lengths, it is hard to reduce the encoding size significantly without reducing the FS size. We describe in [22] an algorithm that yields a lower bound on the size of the FS for a given primary path hopcount.

Methodology. We evaluate all 98,910 possible ordered source-destination pairs of the Sprint topology. For the AS- and router-level topologies, we randomly sample ten million unique ordered source-destination pairs. For each pair, we record these values: the Default and Direct encoding sizes, the size of the FS constructed using our algorithm, and the lower bound on FS sizes.

Results. Fig. 4 shows the encoding size results. We see that Default has somewhat smaller size almost always; Direct performs noticeably better only in the extreme tail of the router-level topology. We therefore discuss Default in what follows. For the intradomain Sprint topology, the maximum encoding size is 58 bytes. The plot has a long tail with 90% and 99% of the source-destination pairs requiring less than 21 bytes and 34 bytes of encoding, respectively. For the interdomain AS-level map of the Internet, the maximum encoding size is 50 bytes. As with the Sprint topology, the plot has a long tail, with 90% of the source-destination pairs resulting in encodings of less

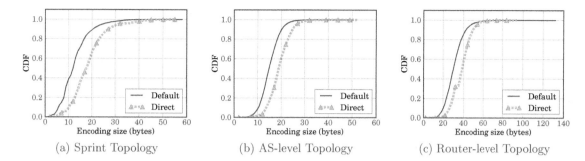

(a) Sprint Topology   (b) AS-level Topology   (c) Router-level Topology

Figure 4: CDF of SLICKPACKETS **encoding size in bytes for the Direct and Default encoding formats, for handling single-link failures.**

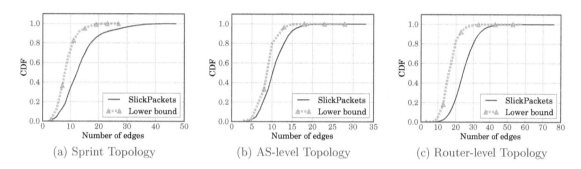

(a) Sprint Topology   (b) AS-level Topology   (c) Router-level Topology

Figure 5: CDF of SLICKPACKETS **FS size and the lower bound in number of edges for handling single-link failures.**

than 21 bytes; 99% of the source-destination pairs result in less than 26 bytes.

For the extreme case of router-level topology, 90% of the source-destination pairs result in encodings of less than 43 bytes; 99% less than 60 bytes. The remaining less than 1% of the source-destination pairs constitute the long tail, with maximum encoding size of 132 bytes. Although the router-level realization of SLICKPACKETS may be impractical, the above results demonstrate that SLICKPACKETS can scale on graphs as large as 200,000 nodes with moderate increase in the packet header sizes. If desired, this overhead may be amortized over more data (e.g., by leveraging IPv6 jumbo frames) or using SLICKPACKETS only for application data that is most sensitive to failures.

Fig. 5 shows the FS size (in number of links) and lower bound. For the AS-level and router-level topologies, our FS size is very close to the lower bound; for the Sprint topology, the difference is somewhat larger. Overall, the results suggest that, for handling single-link failures, our simple FS selection algorithm is relatively close to optimal in terms of minimizing the number of links in the FS.

For the Sprint topology, there is also a long tail in both our FS sizes and the lower bounds. The reason is that there are a few source-destination pairs that have long primary paths, requiring alternate paths for a large number of nodes, resulting in larger number of edges.

4.2 Failure reaction effectiveness

One metric to evaluate the effectiveness of a failure reaction mechanism is the packet **stretch**, the ratio of the length of a packet's path to the length of the shortest possible path. Previous works calculate stretch based on

packets' traversed path costs or transit times. However, for a delay-sensitive application, we are interested in the time a packet is *live* from the application's perspective—from the time the packet is generated by the source application to the time it is received by the destination. Thus, we define the stretch for a packet that does not fully traverse the original shortest path, to be the ratio of the time the packet is *live* to the post-link-failure shortest path latency; for other packets—those that traverse the original shortest path—the stretch is 1. For brevity of the ensuing discussion, l_0 denotes the failed link on the primary path from source s to destination d; r_0 denotes the router that is adjacent to and upstream from l_0 on the primary path; and t_0 denotes the time of failure of l_0.

Modeling delay at network devices. A router in the network, upon a link failure, has to perform a number of tasks before it has new valid default next hops for affected destinations. The four major tasks are: (1) detecting a failed link (if the router is adjacent to the failed link) and generating a control plane message; (2) processing of received control packets; (3) computing the new shortest path tree (SPT); and (4) updating the forwarding information base (FIB). We assume that the delay in detecting a failed link is zero since irrespective of the underlying routing architecture, all packets during this period are lost;[4] this does not make a difference in our performance comparison results. We consider the three other major contributors.

---

[4]Unless packets are duplicated along multiple paths—a design point that may be reasonable for certain kinds of traffic, but which we do not consider in this paper.

Let d_r be the time spent by a router in processing a control packet (i.e., the time between the router's receipt and forwarding of the packet). d_r (along with link latencies) dictates the propagation rate of control packets through the network. Let d_p be the delay between a router's learning of the link failure and starting a new SPT computation; d_c be the time taken to compute the new SPT; and d_u be the time taken to update the FIB. Note that, upon receiving a control packet, a router necessarily spends $D = (d_p + d_c + d_u)$ time before having new valid default next hops for affected destinations. The values of d_c and d_u depend on the router architecture, algorithms in use, the topology, and the router's location. Lacking a good model, we set these values to 0 in our simulations. However, we use $D = d_p = 50\text{ms}$ [18] and $d_r = 2\text{ms}$ [8,9] for the Sprint topology. For the AS-level and router-level topologies, we use $D = d_r = 0$.

4.2.1 Failure reaction schemes

The performance of source routing protocols also depends on the *control plane* mechanism: the technique used to inform sources about the failures in the network. We describe three variants of SLICKPACKETS design with different control plane mechanisms. We also describe three protocols—one from the SCR paradigm and two from the NCR paradigm—that we compare with SLICKPACKETS.

Flooded-SLICKPACKETS. Upon detecting the link failure, r_0 floods the network with a link state advertisement (LSA). This is similar to running an SCR protocol with an OSPF [21] style control plane mechanism.

Fast-SLICKPACKETS. When r_0 receives a packet whose primary next-hop traverses l_0, it informs s about the link failure by directly sending an ICMP-style notification message to s. The rationale is that, to reduce control overhead, only sources that use l_0 in their primary paths need to be notified. Intuitively, this significantly reduces the control plane packets sent into the network.

e2e-SLICKPACKETS. The router r_0 piggybacks the link-failure information on the packet being forwarded on the alternate path towards d, which, upon receiving this information, may inform s of the link failure. Thus, failure information is sent to the source in an end-to-end manner.

All SLICKPACKETS schemes use the same FS selection algorithm (§3.2) and incur the delay D between learning of the failure and switching to new primary paths.

Vanilla source routing (VSR). For purposes of comparison with SLICKPACKETS, we evaluate a simple "vanilla" source routing protocol. In VSR, each source s specifies a single shortest path to its destination d in the packet header. For the control plane mechanism, we use the "fast" version, where r_0 directly notifies s. After receiving the notification, s incurs the delay D before computing a new shortest path. Without a valid path, packets generated during this time are queued. Packets that use l_0 in their paths will be dropped by r_0 after the link failure. However, once s has computed a new path, it resends the packets that would have been dropped, i.e., those that it sent in the time interval $[t - R, t)$ where t is the time s learned of the failure, and R is the RTT between s and r_0. Note that for some of these resent packets, there could be two concurrent live copies: the resent copy that will be delivered along the new path, and the original copy that

will be dropped when it reaches r_0. This scheme may be difficult or undesirable to implement in practice, but as an idealized VSR, it is a useful comparison.

Ideal-SafeGuard. We simulated an idealized version of SafeGuard [18], a network-controlled routing protocol that achieves fast failure reaction. SafeGuard uses the standard OSPF as the control plane substrate. In SafeGuard, r_0 immediately uses pre-computed shortest alternate paths to quickly redirect packets that it would otherwise forward along l_0. Other routers recognize redirected ("escort mode") packets and forward them along their intended alternate paths; however, until they have updated their FIBs (after delay D after receiving the LSA), these routers continue to forward "normal mode" packets along their sub-optimal paths towards l_0. In practice, the "alternative path databases," which are found to be 2 to 8 times larger than a router's intradomain FIB [18], might increase lookup latencies or be an impractical memory requirement. However, our ideal version of SafeGuard ignores these issues.

Ideal-NCR. This represents an ideal (and unachievable) NCR scheme, in which each router learns of a link failure in exactly the propagation delay along the shortest path from the point of failure to the router; and the router instantly begins forwarding packets along the shortest alternate path. Ideal-NCR is equivalent to a special case of Ideal-SafeGuard where all delays, except propagation delay, are zero (i.e, $D = d_r = 0$).

4.2.2 Methodology

We wrote a static simulator for our evaluation purposes. The simulator uses the packet stretch computations described in [22]. Since we are evaluating the reaction to single-link failures, we evaluate only (l_0, s, d) triples where the primary path from s to d uses l_0, and s and d remain connected after the failure of l_0, so that at least one alternate path to d exists for each router upstream from l_0. For the Sprint topology, we evaluate all 424,569 possible such triples. For each of the AS- and router-level topologies, we sample 1,000 random links and use a sampling algorithm (described in [22] due to space constraints) to obtain over 750,000 and 890,000 such triples, respectively.

In our simulations, the application at the source generates packets every 1ms, starting at time $t = 0\text{ms}$. For the time of link failure t_0, however, recall that in Ideal-SafeGuard, Ideal-NCR, and Flooded-SLICKPACKETS, r_0 floods the LSA when it detects the link failure, not when it receives sources' packets. For these schemes, the sooner the link fails, the sooner intermediate routers and the source learn of the failure and use better paths. So, for a fair comparison with non-flooding schemes, we consider two extreme points: when t_0 is greater than the network diameter in terms of *link latencies* and when $t_0 = 0$. The former case ensures that by the time t_0, all sources in all evaluated (l_0, s, d) triples have had packets reaching r_0. For the Sprint topology, with a diameter of 139ms, we use $t_0 = 150$. For the AS- and router-level topologies, we assume all links have latencies 1ms and use $t_0 = 50$.

4.2.3 Results

The high-level results reveal that SLICKPACKETS schemes (particularly the Fast and Flooded variants) achieve packet stretch comparable to that of NCR scheme Ideal-SafeGuard.

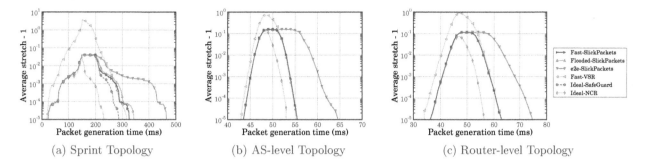

(a) Sprint Topology (b) AS-level Topology (c) Router-level Topology

Figure 6: Average packet stretch - 1 vs. packet generation time when t_0 is greater than the network diameter. The y-axes are on log scales. For the Sprint topology, $t_0 = 150, D = 50, d_r = 2$. For the AS- and router-level topologies, $t_0 = 50, D = d_r = 0$.

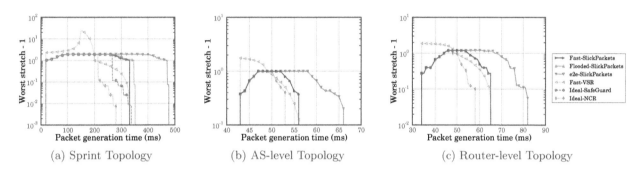

(a) Sprint Topology (b) AS-level Topology (c) Router-level Topology

Figure 7: Worst packet stretch vs. packet generation time when t_0 is greater than the network diameter. The y-axes are on log scales. For the Sprint topology, $t_0 = 150, D = 50, d_r = 2$. For the AS- and router-level topologies, $t_0 = 50, D = d_r = 0$.

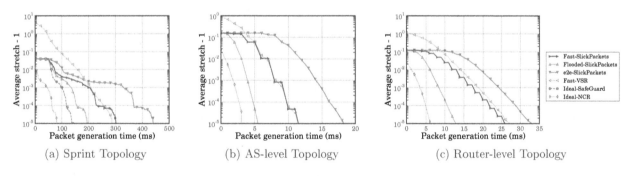

(a) Sprint Topology (b) AS-level Topology (c) Router-level Topology

Figure 8: Average packet stretch - 1 vs. packet generation time when $t_0 = 0$. The y-axes are on log scales. For the Sprint topology, $D = 50, d_r = 2$. For the AS- and router-level topologies, $D = d_r = 0$.

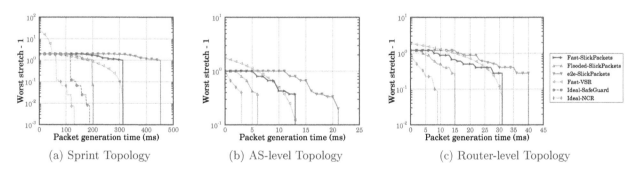

(a) Sprint Topology (b) AS-level Topology (c) Router-level Topology

Figure 9: Worst packet stretch vs. packet generation time when $t_0 = 0$. The y-axes are on log scales. For the Sprint topology, $D = 50, d_r = 2$. For the AS- and router-level topologies, $D = d_r = 0$.

Although SlickPackets schemes take slightly longer to converge compared to SafeGuard, they avoid the high packet stretch of Fast-VSR.

Average stretch. Fig. 6 shows the packet stretch averaged over all evaluated (l_0, s, d) triples when t_0 is greater than the network diameter. We first consider features common to all schemes. For a given scheme, all packets generated early in the simulation have stretch 1. Gradually, as packets generated closer to t_0, as well as more triples where s is closer to l_0, are affected by the failure, the average stretch increases. Additionally, for any triple, all packets generated after t_0 have stretch no higher than those generated at t_0; this is reflected in the average stretch over all triples.

We now compare NCR and SlickPackets schemes. In NCR schemes, routers upstream from l_0, once they receive the LSA and update their FIBs, can redirect packets before they reach l_0; while in SlickPackets schemes, packets have to reach l_0 before being redirected. This difference gives NCR schemes only a small advantage for early packets, especially for the Sprint topology in Fig. 6(a), because upstream routers still incur the delay D between receiving the LSA and updating their FIBs. For later packets, this advantage becomes more significant as more upstream routers update their FIBs. As expected, Ideal-NCR is the best performing scheme in all three topologies: it converges 57ms before Ideal-SafeGuard for the Sprint topology (due to $D = 50$ and $d_r = 2$) and is equivalent to Ideal-SafeGuard (not shown) in the other two topologies, where $D = d_r = 0$.

Consider the SlickPackets schemes in Fig. 6(a). We see that for packets generated between $t_0 = 150$ and $t_0 + D = 200$, the average packet stretch is (1) constant within the same scheme and (2) identical across all schemes. Recall that all SlickPackets schemes use the same FS selection algorithm and incur the same delay D between learning of the failure and switching to new primary paths. Thus, the only factor affecting their relative performances is the time s learns of the failure, which is determined by the relative distances among l_0, s, and d for different triples in the same scheme, and the different control schemes given the same triple. So, regardless of the (l_0, s, d) triple or the control scheme, there is a minimum window of D time where s uses the same (old) primary path. After this window, we can see that Fast-SlickPackets converges slightly faster than Flooded-SlickPackets because the LSAs in Flooded-SlickPackets incur delay d_r at intermediate routers; in Fig. 6(b) and (c), where $d_r = 0$, Fast- and Flooded-SlickPackets are identical. And both of them converge significantly faster than e2e-SlickPackets as expected.

Finally, we see that in Fast-VSR, early packets experience higher stretch than in other schemes. This is because these packets are dropped and have to be resent by s. They experience on average a delay of one half the RTT between s and r_0, plus the delay D before being sent along the new path, resulting in a high stretch. However, Fast-VSR can catch up to and overtake Fast-SlickPackets for two reasons. First, consider the packet sent 1ms before s learns of the failure: in Fast-VSR, it is delayed $(1 + D)$ms before being resent along the new path; while in Fast-SlickPackets, the amount of time this packet traverses the original primary path only to be redirected

backwards can be larger than $(1 + D)$, especially if both the primary path and alternate path contain a very high latency link. Second, consider the packet generated 1ms before s has a new primary path: in Fast-VSR, it is delayed (queued) only 1ms before being sent on the new optimal path; while in Fast-SlickPackets, this packet will be sent along the original primary path and will be redirected, experiencing a higher stretch than its Fast-VSR counterpart. These two effects enable Fast-VSR to noticeably overtake Fast-SlickPackets in Fig. 6(a), but in Fig. 6(b) and (c), where $D = 0$ and all links have latencies 1ms, these two effects are less pronounced.

Worst stretch. Fig. 7 shows the worst stretch of packets given their generation time, among all evaluated (l_0, s, d) triples, when t_0 is greater than the network diameter. Note that the simulation-wide worst stretches for all schemes except Fast-VSR are equal, which are 2.93, 2.0, and 2.2 in Fig. 7(a), (b), and (c), respectively. This is because all these schemes do not drop packets, so the worst stretch is that of packets that r_0 redirects, which is the same for all these schemes. Also note that for schemes that do not drop or queue packets, the worst stretch occurs when a packet traverses the maximum possible distance along the original shortest path without reaching d, is redirected back to s, and traverses the shortest alternate path. So, 3 is the upper-bound stretch because the shortest alternate path cannot be shorter than the original shortest path.

For the Sprint topology in Fig. 7(a), the simulation-wide worst stretch for Fast-VSR is 27. This happens to packets sent right before $t_0 = 150$ in triples where s is close to d, so that the time duration D that these packets are delayed dominates the latencies of the original and post-link-failure shortest paths. In the AS- and router-level topologies, where $D = 0$, the simulation-wide worst stretch of Fast-VSR are 2.75 and 2.88 respectively.

When $t_0 = 0$. Fig. 8 and 9 show the results for when $t_0 = 0$. The overall behavior of each individual scheme exhibits similar patterns to when t_0 is greater than the network diameter. The differences are that the peak stretches occur for packets generated at $t_0 = 0$. Furthermore, as expected, flooding schemes benefit from the earlier time of failure: for example, for the Sprint topology in Fig. 8(a), Ideal-NCR and Ideal-SafeGuard converge further ahead of Fast-SlickPackets compared to Fig. 6(a), and even Flooded-SlickPackets now converges ahead of Fast-SlickPackets (similarly for the AS- and router-level topologies).

In terms of simulation-wide worst stretch, those of non-flooding schemes (Fast- and e2e-SlickPackets as well as Fast-VSR) are the same as when t_0 is greater than the network diameter. This is as expected because for these schemes, it is still r_0 that redirects packets and/or triggers the notification of sources. For flooding schemes, however, it can be expected that simulation-wide worst stretch would be lower compared to when t_0 is greater than the network diameter. Nevertheless, the Sprint topology contains triples where an upstream link that is close to r_0 has very high latency compared to the distance between s and r_0, so that s's first packet does not benefit from the flooded LSA: it still has to reach r_0 before being redirected. This results in the simulation-wide worst stretch of 2.93 in Fig. 8(a).

5. DISCUSSION: FORWARDING SUBGRAPH SELECTION

The SLICKPACKETS design is agnostic to how the source selects the forwarding subgraph (FS). For example, the FS selection may be guided by demands of the application running at the source (for example, if the source is an end host) or the performance goals of a network operator (for example, if the source is an edge router). In this paper, we presented and evaluated one such FS selection algorithm: where the FS allows re-routing of packets within the network in case of single-link failures. We now discuss alternative FS selection strategies.

Handling node failures. For the FS to handle node failures, we need only a simple modification to the link-failure-avoiding FS selection of §3.2. A source s, for a given destination d, constructs the FS in three steps. First, s computes a primary path P to d by running an instance of the shortest path algorithm. Next, to protect against single *node* failures, s visits each node along P, and computes the alternate path P_i it would prefer the packet to be routed along if that node were to fail. In particular, for each node v_i on the primary path with node v_{i+1} as the next hop along the primary path, we (a) remove v_{i+1}; (b) compute a shortest path from v_i to d; and, (c) restore v_{i+1}.

Handling multiple link failures. A source may desire to construct an FS that protects against multiple link failures. This may be done by extending the scheme from §3 to construct an FS that protects from multiple edge-failures. For example, it may be sufficient to have two strategically chosen alternate paths for all nodes on the primary path. The idea is that the source can choose alternate paths that are not failure-correlated with the primary path. This may allow a much larger amount of resiliency; although the performance evaluation of such a scheme is subject to future work.

Congestion avoidance. Our focus in this work so far has been on dealing with failures. However, alternate paths in the FS may also be used to react to congestion in the network. For example, intermediate routers along the path may choose to forward the packet along an alternate path if the primary path is congested (e.g., if the interface queue for the corresponding link is filled beyond a particular threshold). Using a FS also enables the source to optionally provide control over load balancing, by providing feedback on which set of paths are tolerable for the load balancing process.

6. RELATED WORK

Our goals are related to two key areas of related work:

Failure reaction in network-controlled routing protocols. There has been much work on coping with failures in IP networks. We focus on the most closely related work: protocols that guarantee packet delivery in the presence of one or more link failures. R-BGP [16] constructs interdomain backup paths to handle single link failures, given some assumptions about routing policies. SafeGuard [18] uses a remaining path cost field in a packet as a heuristic to determine whether the path expected by the previous hop is different than the path available to the current hop. In this way, it can decide when to reroute

packets along pre-computed backup paths. FCP [17] takes a different approach to determining when packets should be rerouted: each packet carries a list of the failed links it has encountered. The best backup paths are computed on the fly at routers, thus allowing FCP to be robust to multiple link failures, but requiring fairly heavyweight graph processing in the data plane. MPLS Fast Reroute [23] relies on precomputation of backup paths. In its local repair variant, an additional path is constructed to avoid each neighboring link or node, which can inflate storage requirements and will not result in lowest-stretch backup paths. As discussed in the introduction, all of the above approaches are NCR protocols, which do not permit source control of primary or backup paths. In addition, backup paths are computed or stored at every router within the network, so that there is a dependency between each router's forwarding table and the topology of the entire network.

One way to get a small amount of route control at the source within an NCR architecture is to use multihoming: the source can then select between several providers [4]. This could be used to enable some source control, while still applying the NCR resilience techniques described above. However, this provides only a very limited amount of control to the source, and does not yield the full benefits of source control described in the introduction. Moreover, if many sources are multihomed, this vastly increases routing state within the network, since each router would be required to know about every point of multihoming attachment if we desire to provide alternate paths that avoid a failure of one of these links.

Our use of routing along FSes was inspired by [19], which argues that a directed acyclic graph is a better forwarding architecture than the more traditional shortest-path tree. While [19] focuses on improving NCR schemes, we target achieving the benefits of both network- and source-controlled routing. Additionally, while [19] will deliver every packet even during link failures, it does not guarantee the latency that these packets will have. SLICK-PACKETS can guarantee that for single-link failures, packets will follow the shortest alternate path from the point of failure to the destination.

Source routing. There is also a large body of work on source controlled routing, ranging from dynamic source routing in wireless networks [15] to future interdomain routing architectures [10, 20, 30, 31]. Two of these, Routing Deflections [31] and Path Splicing [20], target fast re-routing within the network. Both use path label bits set by the source to pseudorandomly select a next hop at each router or AS. In [20], pseudorandom forwarding can lead to forwarding loops. In [31] routers follow certain rules that ensure loop-freedom, but reduce path diversity.

There are three important differences between [20, 31] and SLICKPACKETS. First, [20, 31] do not fully support source control over primary or backup routes; although sources can select among some set of paths, they cannot tell which paths they are selecting. Second, although packets can be rerouted quickly within the network after a link failure, this is not guaranteed (packets may be dropped), and the backup paths are not guaranteed to have optimal latency. Third, [20, 31] are similar to traditional NCR schemes in terms of the state in the network; indeed, [20] increases forwarding table size because each router stores multiple next-hops for each destination. In contrast, SLICKPACKETS enables source control, can guarantee resilience[5] to single-link failures with packets sent along the shortest alternate path from the point of failure to the destination, and requires only local state at routers.

Giving sources control over constructing end-to-end paths introduces a number of practical questions, for example in terms of policy compliance, security, and scalability of disseminating topological state. For these questions, we rely on previous work (e.g., [10,30], and citations within), which provide solutions to these problems.

7. CONCLUSION

In this paper, we presented SLICKPACKETS, an approach to routing that attains failure reaction, while simultaneously retaining the benefits of source routing. SLICKPACKETS works by compactly encoding a set of alternate paths into data packet headers as a *directed acyclic graph*. Towards this goal, we provide simple algorithms for computing efficient graphs, and for encoding them into packets in a manner that can be processed by intermediate routers in an efficient manner.

One major area left for future work is to evaluate the complexity of implementing SLICKPACKETS in production routers, and achievable packet forwarding rates; a key challenge here is dealing with increased header size. A promising avenue for evaluation is the Supercharged PlanetLab Platform [26], a network processor-based platform on which John DeHart has implemented a prototype version of SLICKPACKETS.

This work was supported by National Science Foundation grant CNS 10-40396.

8. REFERENCES

[1] CAIDA's router-level topology measurements. http://www.caida.org/tools/measurement/skitter/router_topology/.

[2] Rocketfuel: An ISP topology mapping engine. http://www.cs.washington.edu/research/networking/rocketfuel/.

[3] Y.-Y. Ahn, S. Han, H. Kwak, S. Moon, and H. Jeong. Analysis of topological characteristics of huge online social networking services. In *Proc. ACM WWW'07*, pages 835–844, May 2007.

[4] A. Akella, J. Pang, B. Maggs, S. Seshan, and A. Shaikh. A comparison of overlay routing and multihoming route control. *ACM SIGCOMM*, 34(4):93–106, 2004.

[5] D. G. Andersen, H. Balakrishnan, M. F. Kaashoek, and R. Morris. Resilient overlay networks. In *Proc. 18th ACM SOSP*, October 2001.

[6] M. Caesar, M. Casado, T. Koponen, J. Rexford, and S. Shenker. Dynamic route computation considered harmful. *ACM SIGCOMM Computer Communication Review*, 2010.

[7] D. Clark, J. Wroclawski, K. Sollins, and R. Braden. Tussle in cyberspace: Defining tomorrow's Internet. In *SIGCOMM*, 2002.

[8] P. Francois, C. Filsfils, J. Evans, and O. Bonaventure. Achieving sub-second IGP convergence in large IP networks. *SIGCOMM Computer Communications Review*, 35:35–44, 2005.

[9] J. Fu, P. Sjodin, and G. Karlsson. Intra-domain routing convergence with centralized control. *Computer Networks*, 53, 2009.

[10] P. B. Godfrey, I. Ganichev, S. Shenker, and I. Stoica. Pathlet routing. In *ACM SIGCOMM*, 2009.

[11] K. P. Gummadi, H. V. Madhyastha, S. D. Gribble, H. M. Levy, and D. Wetherall. Improving the reliability of Internet paths with one-hop source routing. In *Proc. OSDI*, 2004.

[12] J. Hershberger and S. Suri. Vickery prices and shortest paths: what is an edge worth. In *IEEE FOCS*, 2001.

[13] Y. Hyun, B. Huffaker, D. Andersen, E. Aben, M. Luckie, kc claffy, and C. Shannon. The ipv4 routed /24 as links dataset, November 2010. http://www.caida.org/data/active/ipv4_routed_topology_aslinks_dataset.xml.

[14] G. Iannaccone, C.-N. Chuah, R. Mortier, S. Bhattacharyya, and C. Diot. Analysis of link failures in an IP backbone. In *IMC*, 2002.

[15] D. Johnson and D. Maltz. Dynamic source routing in ad hoc wireless networks. *Mobile computing*, pages 153–181, 1996.

[16] N. Kushman, S. Kandula, D. Katabi, and B. Maggs. R-BGP: Staying connected in a connected world. In *NSDI*, 2007.

[17] K. Lakshminarayanan, M. Caesar, M. Rangan, T. Anderson, S. Shenker, and I. Stoica. Achieving convergence-free routing using failure-carrying packets. *SIGCOMM Comput. Commun. Rev.*, 37(4):241–252, 2007.

[18] A. Li, X. Yang, and D. Wetherall. Safeguard: Safe forwarding during route changes. In *Proc. ACM CoNext*, December 2009.

[19] J. Liu, J. Rexford, M. Schapira, S. Shenker, and J. Naous. Routing along DAGs, 2010. http://www.cs.berkeley.edu/~liujd/RAD.pdf.

[20] M. Motiwala, M. Elmore, N. Feamster, and S. Vempala. Path splicing. In *ACM SIGCOMM*, 2008.

[21] J. Moy. *OSPF: Anatomy of an Internet Routing Protocol*. 1998.

[22] G. T. K. Nguyen, R. Agarwal, J. Liu, M. Caesar, P. B. Godfrey, and S. Shenker. Slick packets. Technical Report, UIUC, April 2011.

[23] P. Pan, G. Swallow, and A. Atlas. Fast reroute extensions to RSVP-TE for LSP tunnels. In *RFC4090*, May 2005.

[24] L. Qiu, Y. R. Yang, Y. Zhang, and S. Shenker. On selfish routing in Internet-like environments. In *Proc. ACM SIGCOMM*, pages 151–162, 2003.

[25] S. Savage, T. Anderson, A. Aggarwal, D. Becker, N. Cardwell, A. Collins, E. Hoffman, J. Snell, A. Vahdat, G. Voelker, and J. Zahorjan. Detour: Informed Internet routing and transport. In *IEEE Micro*, January 1999.

[26] J. Turner, P. Crowley, J. DeHart, A. Freestone, B. Heller, F. Kuhns, S. Kumar, J. Lockwood, J. Lu, M. Wilson, C. Wiesman, and D. Zar. Supercharging planetlab: a high performance, multi-application, overlay network platform. *ACM SIGCOMM*, 2007.

[27] F. Wang, Z. M. Mao, J. Wang, L. Gao, and R. Bush. A measurement study on the impact of routing events on end-to-end internet path performance. *SIGCOMM Comput. Commun. Rev.*, 36(4):375–386, 2006.

[28] D. Wendlandt, I. Avramopoulos, D. Andersen, and J. Rexford. Don't secure routing protocols, secure data delivery. In *HOTNETS*, 2006.

[29] W. Xu and J. Rexford. MIRO: Multi-path Interdomain ROuting. In *SIGCOMM*, 2006.

[30] X. Yang, D. Clark, and A. Berger. NIRA: a new inter-domain routing architecture. *IEEE/ACM Transactions on Networking*, 15(4):775–788, 2007.

[31] X. Yang and D. Wetherall. Source selectable path diversity via routing deflections. In *ACM SIGCOMM*, 2006.

---

[5]Unless, of course, no alternate path exists.

Geographic Routing in d-dimensional Spaces with Guaranteed Delivery and Low Stretch

Simon S. Lam and Chen Qian
Department of Computer Science, The University of Texas at Austin
Austin, Texas, 78712
{lam, cqian}@cs.utexas.edu

ABSTRACT

Almost all geographic routing protocols have been designed for 2D. We present a novel geographic routing protocol, named MDT, for 2D, 3D, and higher dimensions with these properties: (i) guaranteed delivery for any connected graph of nodes and physical links, and (ii) low routing stretch from efficient forwarding of packets out of local minima. The guaranteed delivery property holds for node locations specified by accurate, inaccurate, or arbitrary coordinates. The MDT protocol suite includes a packet forwarding protocol together with protocols for nodes to construct and maintain a distributed MDT graph for routing. We present the performance of MDT protocols in 3D and 4D as well as performance comparisons of MDT routing versus representative geographic routing protocols for nodes in 2D and 3D. Experimental results show that MDT provides the lowest routing stretch in the comparisons. Furthermore, MDT protocols are specially designed to handle churn, i.e., dynamic topology changes due to addition and deletion of nodes and links. Experimental results show that MDT's routing success rate is close to 100% during churn and node states converge quickly to a correct MDT graph after churn.

Categories and Subject Descriptors

C.2.2 [**Computer Communication Networks**]: Network Protocols—*Routing Protocols*

General Terms

Algorithms, Design, Performance, Reliability

Keywords

Geographic Routing, Delaunay Triangulation

1. INTRODUCTION

Geographic routing (also known as location-based or geometric routing) is attractive because the routing state needed for greedy forwarding at each node is independent of network size. Almost all geographic routing protocols have been designed for nodes in 2D. In reality, many wireless applications run on nodes located in 3D [21, 1, 6, 7]. Furthermore, node location information may be highly inaccurate or simply unavailable.

Consider a network represented by a connected graph of nodes and physical links (to be referred to as the *connectivity graph*). Greedy forwarding of a packet may be stuck at a *local minimum*, i.e., the packet is at a node closer to the packet's destination than any of the node's directly-connected neighbors. Geographic routing protocols differ mainly in their recovery methods designed to move packets out of local minima. For general connectivity graphs in 3D, face routing methods designed for 2D [3, 11, 12] are not applicable. Furthermore, Durocher et al. [6] proved that there is no "local" routing protocol that provides guaranteed delivery, even under the strong assumptions of a "unit ball graph" and accurate location information. Thus, designing a geographic routing protocol that provides guaranteed delivery in 3D is a challenging problem.

We present in this paper a novel geographic routing protocol, MDT, that provides guaranteed delivery for a network of nodes in a d-dimensional space, for $d \geq 2$. (Only Euclidean spaces are considered in this paper.) The guaranteed delivery property is proved for node locations specified by arbitrary coordinates; thus the property also holds for node locations specified by inaccurate coordinates or accurate coordinates. We show experimentally that MDT routing provides a routing (distance) stretch close to 1 for nodes in 2D and 3D when coordinates specifying node locations are accurate.[1] When coordinates specifying node locations are highly inaccurate, we show that MDT routing provides a low routing (distance) stretch relative to other geographic routing protocols. Nodes may also be arbitrarily located in a virtual space with packets routed by MDT using the coordinates of nodes in the virtual space (instead of their coordinates in physical space). In this case, MDT routing still provides guaranteed delivery but the distance stretch in physical space may be high.

Geographic routing in a virtual space is useful for networks without location information or networks in which the routing cost between two directly-connected neighbors is neither a constant nor proportional to the physical distance between them (such as, ETT [5]). For example, a 4D virtual space can be used for geographic routing of nodes physically located in a 3D space. The extra dimension makes it possible to assign nodes to locations in the virtual space such that the Euclidean distance between each pair of nodes in the virtual space is a good estimate of the routing cost between them. The design of a positioning system to embed routing costs in a virtual space is a challenging problem for wireless networks without any-to-any routing support and beyond the scope of this paper. The problem is solved in a companion paper [22] where we show how to (i) make use of MDT protocols to embed routing

---

[1]Routing and distance stretch are defined later.

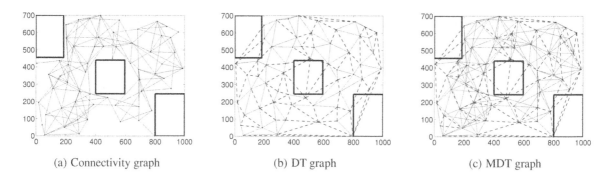

(a) Connectivity graph   (b) DT graph   (c) MDT graph

Figure 1: An illustration of connectivity, DT, and MDT graphs of a set of nodes in 2D

costs in virtual spaces (such as 4D), and (ii) extend MDT routing to optimize end-to-end path costs for any additive routing metric.

MDT was designed to leverage the guaranteed delivery property of Delaunay triangulation (DT) graphs. For nodes in 2D, Bose and Morin proved that greedy routing in a DT always finds a given destination node [2]. Lee and Lam [14, 15] generalized their result and proved that in a d-dimensional Euclidean space ($d \geq 2$), given a destination location ℓ, greedy routing in a DT always finds a node that is closest to ℓ.

Figure 1(a) shows a 2D space with three large obstacles and an arbitrary connectivity graph. Figure 1(b) shows the DT graph [8] of the nodes in Figure 1(a). In the DT graph, the dashed lines denote DT edges between nodes that are not connected by physical links. The MDT graph of the connectivity graph in Figure 1(a) is illustrated in Figure 1(c). By definition, the MDT graph includes every physical link in the connectivity graph and every edge in the DT graph. In MDT routing, when a packet is stuck at a local minimum of the connectivity graph. the packet is next forwarded, via a virtual link, to the DT neighbor that is closest to the destination. In short, the recovery method of MDT is to forward greedily in the DT graph which is guaranteed to succeed.

In this paper, we present MDT protocols for a set of nodes to construct and maintain a correct *multi-hop DT* (formal definition in Section 2). In a multi-hop DT, two nodes that are neighbors in the DT graph communicate directly if there is a physical link between them; otherwise, they communicate via a virtual link, i.e., a path provided by soft-state forwarding tables in nodes along the path.

MDT protocols are also designed specially for networks where node churn and link churn are nontrivial concerns. For example, in a wireless community network, nodes join and leave whenever computers in the community are powered on and off. Furthermore, the quality of wireless links may vary widely over time for many reasons (e.g., fading effects, external interference, and weather conditions). Link quality fluctuations cause dynamic addition and deletion of physical links in the connectivity graph used for MDT routing.

The MDT protocol suite consists of protocols for forwarding, join, leave, failure, maintenance, and system initialization. The MDT join protocol was proved correct for a single join. Thus it constructs a correct multi-hop DT when nodes join serially. The maintenance protocol enables concurrent joins at system initialization. Experimental results show that MDT constructs a correct multi-hop DT very quickly using concurrent joins. The join and maintenance protocols are sufficient for a system under churn to provide a routing success rate close to 100% and for node states to converge to a correct multi-hop DT after churn. The leave and failure protocols are used to improve accuracy and reduce communication cost.

MDT is communication efficient because MDT does not use flooding to discover multi-hop DT neighbors. MDT's search technique is also not limited by a maximum hop count (needed in scoped flooding used by many wireless routing protocols) and is guaranteed to succeed when the existing multi-hop DT is correct.

The idea of using virtual links in MDT is conceptually simple. It was, however, a major challenge to design protocols to *correctly* construct and repair forwarding paths between multi-hop DT neighbors without the use of flooding. Lastly, since MDT routing is designed to run correctly in any connected graph of nodes and physical links, it is possible to use MDT for geographic routing in wireline networks.

1.1 Related work

There were several prior proposals to apply DT to geographic routing. None of them addressed the underlying technical issue that the DT graph of a wireless network is, in general, not a subgraph of its connectivity graph. In [24], requirements are imposed on the placement of nodes and links in 2D such the DT graph is a subgraph of the connectivity graph. In other approaches, the restricted DT graph [10] and the k-localized DT [19] are both approximations of the DT graph. These graphs were shown to be good spanners with constant stretch factors. However, being DT approximations, they do not provide guaranteed delivery. Furthermore, they were designed for nodes in 2D with connectivity graphs restricted to unit disk graphs. (A *unit disk graph* requires that a physical link exists between two nodes if and only if the distance between them is within a given radio transmission range.)

Many geographic routing protocols have been designed for nodes in 2D based upon greedy forwarding. Two of the earliest protocols, GFG [3] and GPSR [11], use face routing to move packets out of local minima. These protocols provide guaranteed delivery for a planar graph. If the connectivity graph is not planar, a planarization algorithm (such as GG [9] or RNG [23]) is used to construct a connected planar subgraph. Successful construction requires that the original connectivity graph is a unit disk graph and node location information is accurate. Both assumptions are unrealistic.

Kim et al. [12] proposed CLDP which, given any connectivity graph, produces a subgraph in which face routing would not cause routing failures. When stuck at a local minimum, GPSR routing uses the subgraph produced by CLDP instead of by GG or RNG. CLDP was designed to provide guaranteed delivery for nodes in 2D under the assumption that there are no degenerate link crossings caused by exactly colinear links [12].

Leong et al. proposed GDSTR [17] which provides guaranteed

delivery for any connectivity graph. Initially, nodes exchange messages to compute and store a distributed spanning tree. Each node also computes and stores a convex hull of the locations of all of its descendants in the subtree rooted at the node; the resulting tree is called a *hull tree*. Subsequently, a packet is routed greedily until it is stuck at a local minimum. For recovery, the packet is routed upwards in the spanning tree until it reaches a point where greedy routing can again make progress.

GHG [20] and GRG [7] are geographic protocols designed for 3D. GHG assumes a unit-ball graph and accurate location information, which are unrealistic assumptions. GRG uses random recovery which is inefficient and does not provide guaranteed delivery. Aside from MDT, there is one other geographic routing protocol that provides guaranteed delivery for general connectivity graphs in 3D, namely, GDSTR-3D [25]. For recovery, GDSTR-3D uses two distributed hull trees while MDT uses a distributed DT graph. GDSTR-3D, designed for sensor networks, assumes a static network topology; the protocol has no provision for any dynamic topology change.

1.2 Outline

The balance of this paper is organized as follows. In Section 2, we present concepts, definitions, and model assumptions. In Section 3, we present the MDT forwarding protocol. In Section 4, we present join, maintenance, and initialization protocols. In Section 5, we present an experimental performance evaluation of MDT in 3D and 4D. We also present experimental results to demonstrate MDT's resilience to node churn and link churn. In Section 6, we present performance comparisons of MDT with geographic routing protocols designed for 2D and 3D. We conclude in Section 7.

2. CONCEPTS AND DEFINITIONS

A triangulation of a set S of nodes (points) in 2D is a subdivision of the convex hull of nodes in S into non-overlapping triangles such that the vertices of each triangle are nodes in S. A DT in 2D is a triangulation such that the circumcircle of each triangle does not contain any other node inside [8]. The definition of DT can be generalized to a higher dimensional space using simplexes and circum-hyperspheres. In each case, the DT of S is a graph to be denoted by $DT(S)$.

Consider a set S of nodes in a d-dimensional space, for $d \geq 2$. Each node in S is identified by its location specified by coordinates. There is at most one node at each location. When we say node u *knows* node v, node u knows node v's coordinates. A node's coordinates may be accurate, inaccurate, or arbitrary (that is, its known location may differ from its actual location). In Section 2.1, we present the definition of a *distributed* DT and a key result from Lee and Lam [15, 16] that we need later.

2.1 Distributed DT

Definition 1. A distributed DT of a set S of nodes is specified by $\{< u, N_u > | u \in S\}$, where N_u represents the set of u's neighbor nodes, which is locally determined by u.

Definition 2. A distributed DT is **correct** if and only if for every node $u \in S$, N_u is the same as the neighbor set of u in $DT(S)$.

To construct a correct distributed DT, each node, $u \in S$, finds a set C_u of nodes (C_u includes u). Then u computes $DT(C_u)$ locally to determine its set N_u of neighbor nodes. Note that C_u is local information of u while S is global knowledge. For the extreme case of $C_u = S$, u is guaranteed to know its neighbors in $DT(S)$. However, the communication cost for each node to acquire knowledge of S would be very high. A *necessary and sufficient condition* [15, 16]

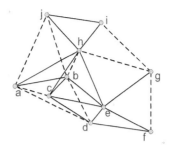

Figure 2: MDT graph of 10 nodes

for a distributed DT to be *correct* is that for all $u \in S$, C_u includes all neighbor nodes of u in $DT(S)$.

2.2 Model assumptions

Two nodes directly connected by a physical link are said to be *physical neighbors*. Each link is bidirectional. In our protocol descriptions, each link is assumed to provide reliable message delivery.[2] The graph of nodes and physical links may be arbitrary so long as it is a connected graph. We provide protocols to handle dynamic topology changes. In particular, new nodes may join and existing nodes may leave or fail.[3] Furthermore, new physical links may be added and existing physical links that have become error-prone are deleted.

2.3 Multi-hop DT

A multi-hop DT is specified by $\{< u, N_u, F_u > | u \in S\}$, where F_u is a soft-state forwarding table, and N_u is u's neighbor set which is derived from information in F_u. The multi-hop DT model generalizes the distributed DT model by relaxing the requirement that every node in S be able to communicate directly with each of its neighbors. (We will use the term "neighbor" to refer to a DT neighbor.) In a multi-hop DT, the neighbor of a node may not be a physical neighbor; see, for example, nodes i and g in Figure 2.

For a node u, each entry in its forwarding table F_u is a 4-tuple $< source, pred, succ, dest >$, which is a sequence of nodes with *source* and *dest* being the source and destination nodes of a path, and *pred* and *succ* being node u's predecessor and successor nodes in the path. In a tuple, *source* and *pred* may be the same node; also, *succ* and *dest* may be the same node. A tuple in F_u is used by u for message forwarding from *source* to *dest* or from *dest* to *source*. For a specific tuple t, we use $t.source$, $t.pred$, $t.succ$, and $t.dest$ to denote the corresponding nodes in t.

For ease of exposition, we assume that a tuple and its "reverse" are inserted in and deleted from F_u as a pair. For example, $< a, b, c, d >$ is in F_u if and only if $< d, c, b, a >$ is in F_u. (In fact, only one tuple is stored with each of its two endpoints being both source and destination.) A tuple in F_u with u itself as the source is represented as $< -, -, succ, dest >$, which does not have a reverse in F_u.

For an example of a forwarding path, consider the MDT graph in Figure 2. The DT edge between nodes g and i is a virtual link; messages are routed along the paths, $g - e - h - i$ and $i - h - e - g$, using the following tuples: $< -, -, e, i >$ in node g, $< g, g, h, i >$ in node e, $< g, e, i, i >$ in node h, and $< -, -, h, g >$ in node i.

Tuples in F_u are maintained as **soft states**. Each tuple is *refreshed* whenever there is packet traffic (e.g., application data or keep-alive

---

[2] Only links that are reliable and have an acceptable error rate are included in the connectivity graph.

[3] When a node fails, it becomes silent.

Table 1: MDT forwarding protocol at node u

	CONDITION	ACTION
1.	$u = m.dest$	no need to forward (node u is at destination location)
2.	there exists a node v in P_u and $v = m.dest$	transmit to v (node v is at destination location)
3.	$m.relay \neq null$ and $m.relay \neq u$	find tuple t in F_u with $t.dest = m.relay$, transmit to $t.succ$
4.	there exists a node v in $P_u \cup \{u\}$ closest to $m.dest$, $v \neq u$	transmit to node v (greedy step 1)
5.	there exists a node v in $N_u \cup \{u\}$ closest to $m.dest$, $v \neq u$	find tuple t in F_u with $t.dest = v$, transmit to $t.succ$ (greedy step 2)
6.	conditions 1-5 are all false	no need to forward (node u is closest to destination location)

messages) between its endpoints. A tuple that is not refreshed will be deleted when its timeout occurs.

Definition 3. A multi-hop DT of S, $\{<u, N_u, F_u> | u \in S\}$, is **correct** if and only if the following conditions hold: i) the distributed DT of S, $\{<u, N_u> | u \in S\}$, is correct; and ii) for every neighbor pair (u, v), there exists a unique k-hop path between u and v in the forwarding tables of nodes in S, where k is finite.

For a dynamic network in which nodes and physical links may be added and deleted, we define a metric for quantifying the accuracy of a multi-hop DT. We consider a node to be *in-system* from when it has finished joining until when it starts leaving or has failed. Let $MDT(S)$ denote a multi-hop DT of a set S of in-system nodes. Let $N_c(MDT(S))$ be the total number of correct neighbor entries and $N_w(MDT(S))$ be the total number of wrong neighbor entries in the forwarding tables of all nodes. A neighbor v in N_u is correct when u and v are neighbors in $DT(S)$ and wrong when u and v are not neighbors in $DT(S)$. Let $N_{edges}(DT(S))$ be the number of edges in $DT(S)$. Let $N_{np}(MDT(S))$ be the number of edges in $DT(S)$ that do not have forwarding paths in the multi-hop DT of S. The **accuracy** of $MDT(S)$ is defined to be:

$$\frac{N_c(MDT(S)) - N_w(MDT(S)) - 2 \times N_{np}(MDT(S))}{2 \times N_{edges}(DT(S))} \quad (1)$$

It is straightforward to prove that the accuracy of $MDT(S)$ is 1 (or 100%) if and only if the multi-hop DT of S is correct.

Terminology. For a node u, a physical neighbor v that has just booted up is represented in F_u by the tuple $<-,-,-,v>$. A physical neighbor v that has sent a join request and received a join reply from a DT node is said to be a *physical neighbor attached to the DT*. It is represented in F_u by $<-,-,v,v>$. We use P_u to denote u's set of physical neighbors attached to the DT. A node in P_u will become a DT node when it finishes executing the join protocol.

3. MDT FORWARDING PROTOCOL

The key idea of MDT forwarding at a node, say u, is conceptually simple: For a packet with destination d, if u is not a local minimum, the packet is forwarded to a physical neighbor closest to d; else, the packet is forwarded, via a virtual link, to a multi-hop DT neighbor closest to d.

For a more detailed specification, consider a node u that has received a data message m to forward. Node u stores it with the format: $m = <m.dest, m.source, m.relay, m.data>$ in a local data structure, where $m.dest$ is the destination location, $m.source$ is the source node, $m.relay$ is the relay node, and $m.data$ is the payload of the message. Note that if $m.relay \neq null$, message m is traversing a virtual link.

The MDT forwarding protocol at a node, say u, is specified by the conditions and actions in Table 1. To forward message m to a node closest to location $m.dest$, the conditions in Table 1 are checked sequentially. The first condition found to be true determines the forwarding action. In particular, line 3 is for handling

messages traversing a virtual link. Line 4 is greedy forwarding to physical neighbors. Line 5 is greedy forwarding to multi-hop DT neighbors.

The following theorem, which states that MDT forwarding in a correct multi-hop DT provides guaranteed delivery, is proved in the Appendix.

THEOREM 1. *Consider a correct multi-hop DT of a finite set S of nodes in a d-dimensional Euclidean space. Given a location ℓ in the space, the MDT forwarding protocol succeeds to find a node in S closest to ℓ in a finite number of hops.*

4. MDT PROTOCOL SUITE

In addition to the forwarding protocol, MDT includes *join, maintenance, leave, failure,* and *initialization* protocols. The join protocol is designed to have the following correctness property: Given a system of nodes maintaining a correct multi-hop DT, after a new node has finished joining the system, the resulting multi-hop DT is correct. This property ensures that a correct multi-hop DT can be constructed for any system of nodes by starting with one node, say u with $F_u = \emptyset$ initially, which is a correct multi-hop DT by definition, and letting the other nodes join the existing multi-hop DT serially.

Two nodes are said to join a system *concurrently* if their join protocol executions overlap in time. When two nodes join concurrently, the joins are *independent* if the sets of nodes whose states are changed by the join protocol executions do not overlap. For a large network, two nodes joining different parts of the network are likely to be independent. If nodes join a correct multi-hop DT concurrently and independently using the MDT join protocol, the resulting multi-hop DT is also guaranteed to be correct.

The maintenance protocol is designed to repair errors in node states after concurrent joins that are dependent, after nodes leave or fail, after the addition of physical links, and after the deletion of existing physical links (due to, for example, degraded link quality). Experimental results show that join and maintenance protocols are sufficient for a system of nodes to recover from dynamic topology changes and their multi-hop DT to converge to 100% accuracy.

MDT includes leave and failure protocols designed for a single leave and failure, respectively, for two reasons: (i) A departed node has almost all recovery information in its state to inform its neighbors how to repair their states. Such recovery information is not available to the maintenance protocol and would be lost if not provided by a leave or failure protocol before the node leaves or fails. (For failure recovery, each node u pre-stores the recovery information in a selected neighbor which serves as u's monitor node.) Thus having leave and failure protocols allows the maintenance protocol, which has a higher communication cost, to run less frequently than otherwise. (ii) Concurrent join, leave, and failure occurrences in different parts of a large network are often independent of each other. After a leave or failure, node states can be quickly and effectively repaired by leave and failure protocols without waiting for the maintenance protocol to run. Due to space limitation herein, the leave and failure protocols are presented in our technical report [13].

For a multi-hop DT, in addition to constructing and maintaining a distributed DT, join and maintenance protocols insert tuples into forwarding tables and update some existing tuples to *correctly* construct paths between multi-hop neighbors. Leave, failure, and maintenance protocols construct a new path between two multi-hop neighbors whenever the previous path between them has been broken due to a node leave/failure or a link deletion.

4.1 Join protocol

Consider a new node, say w. It boots up and discovers its physical neighbors. If one of the physical neighbors is a DT node (say v) then w sends a join request to v to join the existing DT.[4] In the MDT join protocol, a node uses the basic search technique of Lee and Lam [14, 15] to find its DT neighbors. First, greedy forwarding of w's join request finds w's closest DT neighbor. Subsequently, w sends a neighbor-set request to every new neighbor it has found; each new neighbor replies with a set of w's neighbors in its local view. The search terminates when node w finds no more new neighbor in the replies. The MDT join protocol also constructs a forwarding path between w and every one of its multi-hop DT neighbors. A more detailed protocol description follows.

Finding the closest node and path construction. Node w joins by sending a join request to node v with its own location as the destination location. MDT forwarding is used to forward the join request to a DT node z that is closest to w (success is guaranteed by Theorem 1). A forwarding path between w and z is constructed as follows. When w sends the join request to v, it stores the tuple $< -, -, v, v >$ in its forwarding table. Subsequently, suppose an intermediate node (say u) receives the join request from a one-hop neighbor (say v) and forwards it to a one-hop neighbor (say e), the tuple $< w, v, e, e >$ is stored in F_u.

When node z receives the join request of w from a one-hop neighbor (say d), it stores the tuple $< -, -, d, w >$ in its forwarding table for the reverse path. The join reply is forwarded along the reverse path from z to w using tuples stored when the join request traveled from w to z earlier. Additionally, each such tuple is updated with z as an endpoint. For example, suppose node x receives a join reply from z to w from its one-hop neighbor e. Node x changes the existing tuple $< e, e, *, w >$ in F_x to $< z, e, *, w >$, where $*$ denotes any node already in the tuple.

After node w has received the join reply, it notifies each of its physical neighbors that w is now attached to the DT and they should change their tuple for w from $< -, -, w, - >$ to $< -, -, w, w >$.

Physical-link shortcuts. The join reply message, at any node along the path from z to w (including node z), can be transmitted directly to w if node w is a physical neighbor (i.e., for message m, there is a tuple t in the forwarding table such that $t.succ = m.dest$). If such a physical-link shortcut is taken, the path previously set up between z and w is changed. Tuples with z and w as endpoints stored by nodes in the abandoned portion of the previous path will be deleted because they will not be refreshed by the endpoints.

A physical-link shortcut can also be taken when other messages in the MDT join, maintenance, leave, and failure protocols are forwarded, but they require the stronger condition, $t.succ = t.dest = m.dest$, that is, the shortcut can be taken only if $m.dest$ is a physical neighbor attached to the DT.

---

[4]If node w discovers only physical neighbors, it will not start the join protocol until it hears from a physical neighbor that is attached to the DT, e.g., it receives a token from such a node at system initialization.

Finding DT neighbors. Node w, after receiving the join reply from node z, sends a neighbor-set request to z for neighbor information. At this time, C_z, the set of nodes known to z includes both w and z. Node z computes $DT(C_z)$, finds nodes that are neighbors of w in $DT(C_z)$, and sends them to w in a neighbor-set reply message.

When w receives the neighbor-set reply from z, w adds neighbors in the reply (if any) to its candidate set, C_w, and updates its neighbor set, N_w, from computing $DT(C_w)$. If w finds new neighbors in N_w, w sends neighbor-set requests to them for more neighbor information. The joining node w repeats the above process recursively until it cannot find any more new neighbor in N_w. At this time w has successfully joined and become a DT node.

Nodes in C_u, the set of nodes known to a node u, are maintained as hard states in distributed DT protocols [14, 15]. In MDT protocols, nodes in C_u are maintained as soft states. More specifically, tuples in F_u are maintained as soft states. By definition, $C_u = \{u\} \cup \{v \mid v = t.dest, t \in F_u\}$. A new node in C_u is deleted if it does not become the destination of a tuple in F_u within a timeout period. Also, whenever a tuple t is deleted from F_u, its endpoints are deleted from C_u.

Path construction to multi-hop DT neighbors. The MDT join protocol also constructs a forwarding path between the joining node w and each of its multi-hop neighbors. Whenever w learns a new node y from the join reply or a neighbor-set reply sent by some node, say x, node w sends a neighbor-set request to x, with x as the *relay* and y as the destination (that is, in neighbor-set request m, $m.relay = x$ and $m.dest = y$.) Note that a forwarding path has already been established between w and x. Also, since x and y are DT neighbors, a forwarding path exists between x and y (given that w is joining a correct multi-hop DT). As the neighbor-set request is forwarded and relayed from w to y, tuples with w and y as endpoints are stored in forwarding tables of nodes along the path from w to y. The forwarding path that has been set up between w and y is then used by y to return a neighbor-set reply to w.

Example. Let node a in Figure 2 be a joining node. Suppose a has found b, c, and d to be DT neighbors and it has just learned from b that j is a new neighbor. Node a sends a neighbor-set request to j with b indicated in the message as the relay. Because the existing multi-hop DT (of 9 nodes) is correct, a unique forwarding path exists between node b and node j, which is $b - e - h - j$. After receiving the message, b forwards it to e on the $b - e - h - j$ path. At b and every node along the way to j, a tuple with endpoints a and j is stored in the node's forwarding table. When the neighbor-set reply from j travels back via h, node h searches F_h and finds that node a is a physical neighbor attached to the DT (see Figure 2). Node h then transmits j's reply directly to node a. (This is an example of a *physical-link shortcut*.) Subsequently, nodes a and j will select and refresh only the path $a - h - j$ between them. Tuples previously stored in nodes b, e, and h for endpoints a and j will be deleted upon timeout. Lastly, from j's reply, a learns no new neighbor other than b, c, and d. Without any more new neighbor to query, a's join protocol execution terminates and it becomes a DT node.

A pseudocode specification of the MDT join protocol is in our technical report [13]. A proof of Theorem 2 is presented in the Appendix.

THEOREM 2. *Let S be a set of nodes and w be a joining node that is a physical neighbor of at least one node in S. Suppose the existing multi-hop DT of S is correct, w joins using the MDT join protocol, and no other node joins, leaves, or fails. Then the MDT join protocol finishes and the updated multi-hop DT of $S \cup \{w\}$ is correct.*

4.2 Maintenance protocol

The MDT maintenance protocol for repairing node states is designed for systems with frequent addition and deletion of nodes and physical links. For a distributed DT to be correct, each node must know all of its neighbors in the global DT. Towards this goal, each node (say u) runs the maintenance protocol by first querying a subset of its neighbors, one for each simplex including u in $DT(C_u)$.[5] More specifically, node u selects the smallest subset V of neighbors such that every simplex including u in $DT(C_u)$ includes one node in V. Node u then sends a neighbor-set request to each node in V. A node z that has received the neighbor-set request adds u to C_z and computes $DT(C_z)$. Node z then sends a neighbor-set reply containing neighbors of u in $DT(C_z)$ to u.

Node u adds new nodes found in each neighbor-set reply to C_u; it then computes $DT(C_u)$ to get N_u. If u finds a new neighbor, say x, in N_u, node u sends a neighbor-set request to x if x satisfies the following condition:

C1. The simplex in $DT(C_u)$ that includes both u and neighbor x does not include any node to which u has sent a neighbor-set request.

Node u keeps sending neighbor-set requests until it cannot find any more new neighbor in N_u that satisfies **C1**. Node u then sends neighbor-set notifications to neighbors in N_u that have not been sent neighbor-set requests (these notifications announce u's presence and do not require replies). The protocol code for constructing forwarding paths between node u and each new neighbor is the same as in the MDT join protocol.

If after sending a neighbor-set request to a node, say v, and a neighbor-set reply is not received from v within a timeout period, node v is deemed to have failed. Node u sends a failure notification about v to inform each node in u's updated neighbor set. These notifications are unnecessary since MDT uses soft states; they are performed to speed up convergence of node states.

Each node runs the maintenance protocol independently, controlled by a timeout value T_m. After a node has finished running the maintenance protocol, it waits for time T_m before starting the maintenance protocol again. The value of T_m should be set adaptively. When a system has a low churn rate, a large value should be used for T_m to reduce communication cost.

If each node runs the maintenance protocol repeatedly, the node states converge to a correct multi-hop DT because neighbors in a DT are connected by neighbor relations. A node can find all of its neighbors by following the neighbor relations [14]. (See results from our system initialization experiments in Section 5.3 and churn experiments in Section 5.6.)

4.3 Initialization protocols

Serial joins by token passing. Starting from one node, other nodes join serially using the join protocol. The ordering of joins is controlled by the passing of a single token from one node to another.

Concurrent joins by token broadcast. Starting from one node, other nodes join concurrently using the join and maintenance protocols. The ordering of joins is controlled by a token broadcast protocol. Initially, a token is installed in a selected node. When a node has a token, it runs the join protocol once (except the selected node) and then the maintenance protocol repeatedly, controlled by the timeout value T_m. It also sends a token to each physical neighbor that is not known to have joined the multi-hop DT. Each token is sent after a random delay uniformly distributed over time inter-

val $[1, \tau]$, where τ is in seconds. If a node receives more than one token, any duplicate token is discarded.

5. PERFORMANCE EVALUATION

5.1 Methodology

We evaluate MDT protocols using a packet-level discrete-event simulator in which every protocol message created is routed and processed hop by hop from its source to destination. We will not evaluate metrics that depend on congestion, e.g., end-to-end throughput and latency. Hence, queueing delays at a node are not simulated. Instead, message delivery times from one node to the next are sampled from a uniform distribution over a specified time interval. Time-varying wireless link characteristics and interference problems are modeled by allowing physical links to be added and deleted dynamically.

Creating general connectivity graphs. To create general connectivity graphs for simulation experiments, a physical space in 3D (2D) is first specified. *Obstacles* are then placed in the physical space. The number, location, shape, and size of the obstacles are constrained by the requirement that the unoccupied physical space is not disconnected by the obstacles. (Any real network environment can be modeled accurately if computational cost is not a limiting factor.) *Nodes* are then placed randomly in the unoccupied physical space. Let R denote the radio transmission range. *Physical links* are then placed using the following algorithm: For each pair of nodes, *if* the distance between them is larger than R or the line between them intersects an obstacle, there is no physical link; *else* a physical link is placed between the nodes with probability p. We refer to p as the *connection probability* and $1 - p$ as the *missing link* probability. If a graph created using the above procedure is disconnected, it is not used. Note that to replicate the connectivity graph of a real network, missing links between neighbors can be specified deterministically rather than with probability $1 - p$.

Inaccurate coordinates. The known coordinates of a node may be highly inaccurate [18] because some localization methods have large location errors. In our experiments, after placing nodes in the physical space, their "known" coordinates are then generated with randomized location errors. The location errors are generated to satisfy a *location error ratio*, e, which is defined to be the ratio of the average location error to the average distance between nodes that are physical neighbors. We experimented with location error ratios from 0 to 2.

Definitions. The routing stretch value of a pair of nodes, s and d, in a multi-hop DT of S is defined to be the ratio of the number of physical links in the MDT route to the number of physical links in the shortest route in the connectivity graph between s and d. The *routing stretch* of the multi-hop DT is defined to be the average of the routing stretch values of all source-destination pairs in S. The *distance stretch* of the multi-hop DT is defined similarly with distance replacing number of physical links as metric.

5.2 Design of experiments

Our simulation experiments were designed to evaluate geographic routing in the most challenging environments. In general, everything else being the same, the challenge is bigger for a higher dimensional space, larger obstacles, a higher missing link probability, a lower node density, a larger network size, or larger node location errors. Furthermore, we performed experiments to evaluate MDT's resilience to dynamic topology changes at very high churn rates. In the geographic routing literature, no other protocol has been shown to meet all of these challenges.

---

[5]Only some neighbors satisfying condition **C1** are queried to improve search efficiency.

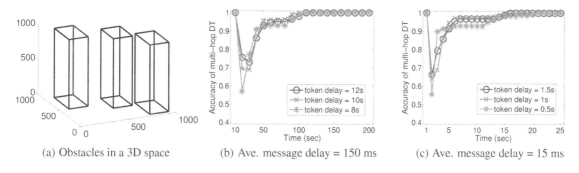

(a) Obstacles in a 3D space   (b) Ave. message delay = 150 ms   (c) Ave. message delay = 15 ms

Figure 3: Accuracy vs. time for concurrent joins in 3D

Our simulator enables evaluation of geographic routing protocols in the most challenging environments. In the simulator, any connectivity graph can be created to represent any real network environment with obstacles of different shapes and sizes. The connectivity graphs created as described above have properties of real wireless networks, unlike unit-disk and unit-ball graphs used in prior work on geographic routing.[6] We experimented with obstacles of different shapes and sizes, and nodes with large location errors or arbitrary coordinates in 2D, 3D, and 4D. In this paper, we present experimental results for large obstacles, such as those shown in Figure 3(a), because large obstacles are more challenging to geographic routing than small ones; these very large obstacles may represent tall buildings in an outdoor space or large machinery in a factory. Between neighbors that are in line of sight and within radio transmission range, we experimented with a missing link probability as high as 0.5.

Node density is an important parameter that impacts geographic routing performance. We present experiments for node density of 13.5 for 3D and 9.7 for 2D. When we scale up the network size in a set of experiments, we increase the space and obstacle sizes to keep node density approximately the same. For experiments with different missing link probabilities, we vary the radio transmission range to keep node density approximately the same. We found that node densities lower than 13.5 for 3D and 9.7 for 2D would result in many disconnected graphs for spaces with large obstacles and a missing link probability of 0.5. The values of node density we used for experiments are relatively low compared with prior work on geographic routing. We also conducted experiments for higher node densities which resulted in better MDT performance, thus allowing us to conclude that MDT works well for a wide range of node densities.

5.3 System initialization experiments

We have performed numerous experiments using our initialization protocols. In every experiment, a correct multi-hop DT is constructed. Concurrent joins can do so much faster than serial joins but with a higher message cost (see Figure 10 for message cost comparison).

Figures 3(b)-(c) show results from two sets of experiments using concurrent-join initialization. In each experiment, the physical space is a $1000 \times 1000 \times 1000$ 3D space, with three large obstacles, placed as shown in Figure 3(a). The size of one obstacle is $200 \times 300 \times 1000$. Each of the other two is $200 \times 350 \times 1000$ in size. The obstacles occupy 20% of the physical space. Connectivity graphs are then created for 300 nodes using the procedure

described in Section 5.1 for radio transmission range $R = 305$ and link connection probability $p = 0.5$. The *average node degree*, i.e., number of physical neighbors per node, is 13.5.[7] The (known) coordinates of the nodes are inaccurate with location error ratio $e = 1$.

The first set of experiments is for low-speed networks with one-hop message delays sampled from 100 ms to 200 ms (average = 150 ms) and a maintenance protocol timeout duration of 60 seconds. The second set of experiments is for high-speed networks with one-hop message delays sampled from 10 ms to 20 ms (average = 15 ms) and a maintenance protocol timeout duration of 10 seconds.

In the legend of Figures 3(b)-(c),"token delay" is maximum token delay τ. In each experiment, note that accuracy of the multi-hop DT is low initially when many nodes are joining at the same time. However, accuracy improves and converges to 100% quickly. In all experiments, after each node's initial join, the node had run the maintenance protocol only once or twice by the time 100% accuracy was achieved.

5.4 MDT performance in 3D

We evaluated the performance of MDT routing for 100 to 1300 nodes in 3D. We present results from four different sets of experiments using connectivity graphs created in a 3D space with and without obstacles, for node locations specified by accurate and inaccurate coordinates. There are four cases:

- accurate coordinates ($e = 0$), few missing links ($p = 0.9$), no obstacle
- inaccurate coordinates ($e = 1$), few missing links ($p = 0.9$), no obstacle
- accurate coordinates ($e = 0$), many missing links ($p = 0.5$), large obstacles (*obs*)
- inaccurate coordinates ($e = 1$), many missing links ($p = 0.5$), large obstacles (*obs*)

For 300 nodes, dimensions of the physical space and obstacles are the same as in Figure 3(a). For a smaller (or larger) number of nodes, dimensions of the physical space and obstacles are scaled down (or up) proportionally. For each *obs* experiment, the three obstacles are randomly placed in the horizontal plane. $R = 305$ is used for $p = 0.5$ and $R = 250$ is used for $p = 0.9$ such that the average node degree is approximately 13.5. At the beginning of each experiment, a correct multi-hop DT was first constructed. *Routing success rate was 100% in every experiment* and is not plotted.

Figures 4(a)-(b) show that both routing stretch and distance stretch versus network size are close to 1 for the easy case of accurate coordinates ($e = 0$), few missing links ($p = 0.9$), and no obstacle. Either

---

[6]In a very recent paper on 3D routing, unit-ball graphs were still used for simulation experiments [25].

[7]In 3D, a node density of 13.5 is fairly low and realistic.

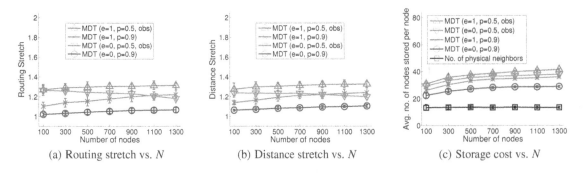

(a) Routing stretch vs. N (b) Distance stretch vs. N (c) Storage cost vs. N

Figure 4: MDT performance in 3D (average node degree=13.5)

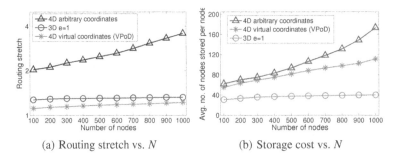

(a) Routing stretch vs. N (b) Storage cost vs. N

Figure 5: MDT performance in 3D and 4D (average node degree=13.5, p=0.5, obstacles)

inaccurate coordinates ($e = 1$) or many missing links ($p = 0.5$) and large obstacles (*obs*) increase both the routing stretch and distance stretch of MDT routing. Note that both the routing and distance stretch of MDT remain low as network size becomes large.[8]

Storage cost. The most important routing information stored in a node is the set of nodes it uses for forwarding; the known coordinates of each node in the set are stored in a *location table*. We use 4 bytes per dimension for storing each node's coordinates (e.g., 12 bytes for a node in 3D); this design choice is intended for very large networks. The coordinates of a node are used as its global identifier. Each node is also represented by a 1-byte local identifier in our current implementation. The location table stores pairs of global and local identifiers (e.g., 13 bytes per node for nodes in 3D). In the *forwarding table*, local identifiers are used to represent nodes in tuples. To illustrate MDT's storage cost in bytes, consider the case of 1300 nodes, $e = 1$, and $p = 0.5$ with obstacles. The average location table size is 540.2 bytes. The average forwarding table size is 88.8 bytes. The average location table size is 86% of the combined storage cost. We found that this percentage is unchanged for all network sizes (100 - 1300) in each set of experiments, indicating that the forwarding table size is also proportional to the number of distinct nodes stored.

In this paper, the storage cost is measured by the average number of distinct nodes a node needs to know (and store) to perform forwarding. This represents the storage cost of a node's minimum required knowledge of other nodes. This metric, unlike counting bytes, requires no implementation assumptions which may cause bias when different routing protocols are compared. Figure 4(c) shows the storage cost per node versus network size. As expected, either inaccurate coordinates ($e = 1$) or many missing links ($p = 0.5$) and large obstacles require more storage per node due to the

need for more multi-hop DT neighbors. For comparison, the bottom curve is the average number of physical neighbors per node.

Varying obstacle locations. Each data point plotted in Figures 4(a)-(c) is the average value of 50 simulation runs for 50 different connectivity graphs each of which was created from a different placement of the obstacles. Also shown as bars are the 10th and 90th percentile values. Observe that the intervals between 10th and 90th percentile values are small for all data points. (These intervals are also small in experimental results to be presented in Figures 5 and 8-11 and will be omitted from those figures for clarity.) The small intervals between 10th and 90th percentile values demonstrate that varying obstacle locations has negligible impact on MDT routing performance.

Varying number and size of obstacles. Aside from varying the locations of obstacles, we also experimented with varying the number and size of obstacles. In particular, we repeated the experiments in Figure 4 for 6 obstacles and also for 9 obstacles. In each such experiment, the fraction of physical space occupied by obstacles was kept at 20%. We found the resulting changes in MDT's routing stretch, distance stretch, and storage cost to be too small to be visible when plotted in Figures 4.[9] However, when we increased the fraction of physical space occupied by obstacles from 20% to 30%, the resulting increases in MDT's routing and distance stretch were significant (about 6%).

5.5 MDT performance in 4D

To illustrate how MDT can be used in 4D, consider the connectivity graphs created for the set of experiments in Figure 4 with many missing links ($p = 0.5$) and large obstacles. Suppose the nodes have *no location information*. We experimented with two cases: (i) Each node assigns itself an arbitrary location in a 4D

---

[8]Distance stretch is almost the same as routing stretch (except for 4D experiments) and will not be shown again due to space limitation.

[9]Performance measures from experiments for 9 obstacles are smaller than those from experiments for 3 obstacles by less than 0.5%.

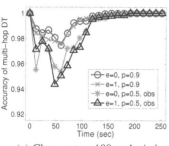 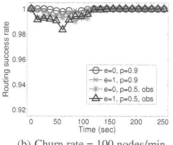 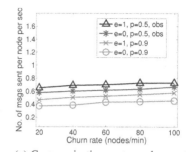

(a) Churn rate = 100 nodes/min.   (b) Churn rate = 100 nodes/min.   (c) Communication cost vs. churn rate

Figure 6: MDT performance under node churn (ave. message delay = 150 ms, timeout = 60 sec.)

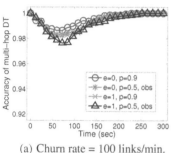 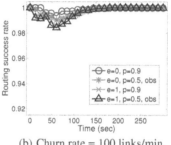 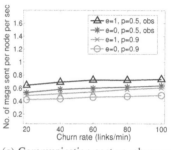

(a) Churn rate = 100 links/min.   (b) Churn rate = 100 links/min.   (c) Communication cost vs. churn rate

Figure 7: MDT performance under link churn (ave. message delay = 150 ms, timeout = 60 sec.)

space and sends its (arbitrary) coordinates to its physical neighbors. These coordinates are used by MDT protocols to construct and maintain a multi-hop DT as well as for routing. (ii) After a multi-hop DT has been constructed by the nodes using the initial (arbitrary) coordinates, each node then runs the VPoD protocol [22] to iteratively compute a better virtual position in the 4D space. VPoD is a virtual positioning protocol that does not require any node location information, any special nodes (such as, beacons and landmarks), nor the use of flooding. VPoD makes use of a multi-hop DT for routing support and link costs between physical neighbors for nodes to compute virtual positions. Any *additive routing metric* can be used for link costs in VPoD. For the results presented in Figure 5, we used 1 (hop) as the routing metric between two physical neighbors. (Each data point plotted in Figure 5 is the average value from 50 experiments.)

For comparison, we have also plotted the results for MDT routing using inaccurate coordinates ($e = 1$ case from Figure 4). Figure 5(a) on routing stretch, plotted in logarithmic scale, shows that MDT routing using 4D virtual coordinates is better than using inaccurate coordinates in 3D. Figure 5(b) on storage cost shows that MDT routing using inaccurate coordinates in 3D is better than using 4D virtual coordinates. In both figures, MDT routing using arbitrary coordinates has the worst performance. Routing success rate was 100% in every experiment and is not shown.

5.6 Resilience to Churn

We performed a large number of experiments to evaluate the performance of MDT protocols for systems under churn, with 300 nodes in a $1000 \times 1000 \times 1000$ 3D physical space. Like the experiments used to evaluate MDT routing stretch in Figure 4, four sets of experiments were performed using connectivity graphs created with and without three large obstacles, for node locations specified by accurate and inaccurate coordinates. The average node degree is kept at approximately 13.5 for every experiment.

In a *node churn* experiment, the rate at which new nodes join is equal to the churn rate; the rate of nodes leaving and the rate of nodes failing are each equal to half the churn rate. In a *link churn* experiment, the churn rate is equal to the rate at which new physical links are added and the rate at which existing physical links are deleted. In each experiment, the 300 nodes initially maintain a correct multi-hop DT. Churn begins at time=0 and ends at time=60 seconds.

Figure 6 presents results from node churn experiments for low-speed networks where one-hop message delays are sampled from [100 ms, 200 ms]. The maintenance timeout value is 60 seconds. The churn rate is 100 nodes/minute in Figures 6(a)-(b) and varies in Figure 6(c). Figure 6(a) shows the accuracy of the multi-hop DT versus time. The accuracy returns to 100% quickly after churn. Figure 6(b) shows the routing success rate versus time. The success rate is close to 100% during churn and returns to 100% quickly after churn. Figure 6(c) shows the communication cost (per node per second) versus churn rate.

By Little's Law, for 300 nodes and a churn rate of 100 nodes per minute, the average lifetime of a node is 300/100 = 3 minutes, which represents a very high churn rate for most practical systems.

Figure 7 presents results from link churn experiments for low-speed networks with a maintenance timeout value of 60 seconds. Figure 7(a) shows the accuracy of the multi-hop DT versus time. The accuracy returns to 100% quickly after churn. Figure 7(b) shows the routing success rate versus time. The success rate is close to 100% during churn and returns to 100% quickly after churn. Figure 7(c) shows the communication cost (per node per second) versus churn rate.

Note that the convergence times to 100% accuracy in Figures 6(a) and 7(a) and to 100% success rate in Figures 6(b) and 7(b) are almost the same for the four cases. These results are typical of all churn experiments performed.

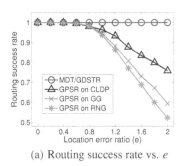

(a) Routing success rate vs. *e*

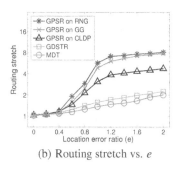

(b) Routing stretch vs. *e*

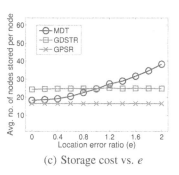

(c) Storage cost vs. *e*

Figure 8: Performance comparison of 2D protocols (average node degree=16.5)

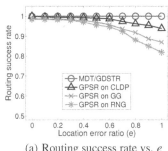

(a) Routing success rate vs. *e*

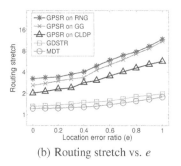

(b) Routing stretch vs. *e*

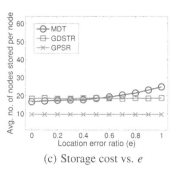

(c) Storage cost vs. *e*

Figure 9: Performance comparison of 2D protocols (three large obstacles, average node degree=9.7)

6. PERFORMANCE COMPARISON

6.1 Comparison of 2D protocols

The geographic routing protocols, GPSR running on GG, RNG, and CLDP graphs [11, 12], and GDSTR [17] were designed for routing in 2D. We implemented these protocols in our simulator.[10] The experiments in Figure 8 were carried out for 300 nodes in a 1000×1000 2D space with no obstacle and few missing links ($p = 0.9$). The radio transmission range is $R = 150$. The average node degree is 16.5. The performance results are plotted versus location error ratio, from $e = 0$ (no error) to $e = 2$ (very large location errors).

The experiments of Figure 9 were carried out for 300 nodes in a 1000×1000 2D space with three randomly placed obstacles (a 200×300 rectangle and two 200×350 rectangles) and many missing links ($p = 0.5$). The radio transmission range is $R = 150$. The average node degree is 9.7. The performance results are plotted versus location error ratio, from $e = 0$ to $e = 1$.

In Figure 8(a) and Figure 9(a) the routing success rates of MDT and GDSTR are both 100% for all e values (it was 100% in every experiment). As the location error ratio (e) increases from 0, the routing success rates of RNG, GG, and CLDP drop off gradually from 100%. For $e > 0.6$ in Figure 8(a) and $e > 0.3$ in Figure 9(a), their routing success rates drop significantly.

Figure 8(b) and Figure 9(b), in logarithmic scale, show that MDT has the lowest routing stretch for all e values, with GDSTR a close second, followed by CLDP, GG, and RNG in that order. Note that routing stretch increases as e increases for all protocols.

Figure 8(c) and Figure 9(c) show storage cost comparisons. The

---

[10]Using, as our references, [12] for CLDP, GDSTR code from www.comp.nus.edu.sg/~bleong/geographic/, and GPSR, GG, and RNG code from www.cs.ucl.ac.uk/staff/B.Karp/gpsr/. GDSTR uses two hull trees [17]

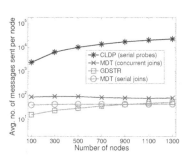

Figure 10: Initialization message cost vs. *N* (average node degree = 12)

GPSR protocols (CLDP, GG, and RNG) have the lowest storage cost, with the storage costs of GDSTR and MDT about the same.

Comparison of graph construction costs. We compare MDT's message cost to construct a correct multi-hop DT with message costs of CLDP graph construction using serial probes [12] and GDSTR hull tree construction [17]. The physical space is a 2D square with three large rectangular obstacles, occupying 20% of the physical space. There are many missing links ($p = 0.5$). Nodes have inaccurate coordinates ($e = 1$). The number N of nodes is varied from 100 to 1300. For the radio transmission range $R = 150$, the sizes of the physical space and obstacles are determined for each value of N such that the average node degree is approximately 12.

In Figure 10, the vertical axis is in logarithmic scale. The message cost of a protocol is the average number of messages *sent* per node (we did not account for message size differences among the protocols). Note that each GDSTR message is a *broadcast* message sent by a node to all of its physical neighbors and is counted only as

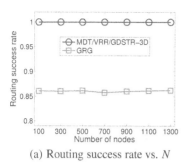
(a) Routing success rate vs. N

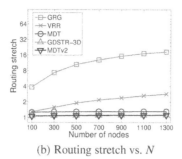
(b) Routing stretch vs. N

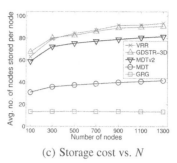
(c) Storage cost vs. N

Figure 11: Performance comparison of 3D protocols (average node degree=13.5)

one message sent. Messages sent by CLDP and MDT are unicast messages.

Figure 10 shows that with the average number of messages *sent* per node as metric, GDSTR has the best message cost performance for up to 900 nodes. For more than 900 nodes MDT (serial joins) has the lowest cost. CLDP has a very high cost. Note that the CLDP and GDSTR curves increase gradually with N. The MDT curves are flat.

6.2 Comparison of 3D Protocols

We compare the routing performance of MDT with GRG [7] and GDSTR-3D [25]. We implemented the basic version of GRG in our simulator. Several techniques to improve the performance of GRG are presented for *unit ball graphs* [7]. Since arbitrary connectivity graphs are used in our experiments, these techniques are not applicable and not implemented.

GDSTR-3D uses two hull trees for recovery. For each tree, each node stores two 2D convex hulls to aggregate the locations of all descendants in the subtree rooted at the node; the two 2D convex hulls approximate a 3D convex hull at each node. We implemented GDSTR-3D using its authors' TinyOS 2.x source code available at Google Sites.

Unlike other geographic protocols, each node in GDSTR-3D stores *2-hop neighbors* and uses 2-hop greedy forwarding to reduce routing stretch at the expense of a much larger storage cost per node. This performance tradeoff may not be appropriate for networks with limited nodal storage.

A non-geographic routing protocol, VRR [4], is included in the comparison. We implemented VRR for static networks without joins and failures.[11] For each pair of virtual neighbors, we used the shortest path (in hops) between them as the forwarding path (the routing stretch value is 1 between virtual neighbors). Thus, the routing stretch and storage cost results shown in Figure 11(b)-(c) for VRR are slightly optimistic. In VRR, each node also stores 2-hop neighbors for forwarding.

MDT can be easily modified to use 2-hop greedy forwarding. We present results for both MDT (which uses 1-hop greedy forwarding) and MDTv2 (which uses 2-hop greedy fowarding).

In our experiments, the number N of nodes is varied from 100 to 1300. The physical space and large obstacles are the same as the ones used in Figure 4. The average node degree was kept at approximately 13.5. Experiments were performed using connectivity graphs created for the following case: inaccurate coordinates ($e = 1$), many missing links ($p = 0.5$), and three large obstacles that occupy 20% of the physical space.

Figure 11(a) shows that MDT (also MDTv2), GDSTR-3D, and

VRR all achieve 100% routing success rate while the routing success rate of GRG is about 86%. Figure 11(b), in logarithmic scale, shows that the routing stretch of GRG is very high, the routing stretch of VRR is high for $N > 300$, and both increase with N. The routing stretch of MDTv2 is the lowest and slightly lower than that of GDSTR-3D for every network size (the differences are, however, too small to be seen in Figure 11(b)). MDT, which uses 1-hop greedy forwarding, ranks a close third.

In Figure 11(c), GDSTR-3D, VRR, MDTv2 have large per-node storage costs, because each node stores 2-hop neighbors as well as physical neighbors. The storage cost of MDTv2 is smaller than those of GDSTR-3D and VRR. Both GRG and MDT have much lower storage costs because they use 1-hop greedy forwarding. The per-node storage cost of GRG, equal to the average number of physical neighbors, is the lowest of the five protocols.

MDT versus GDSTR-3D. MDT, MDTv2, and GDSTR-3D all provide guaranteed delivery in 3D and achieve routing stretch close to 1. GDSTR-3D has a higher storage cost than MDTv2 and a much higher storage cost than MDT. One clear advantage MDT (or MDTv2) has over GDSTR-3D is that MDT is highly resilient to dynamic topology changes (both node churn and link churn) while GDSTR-3D is designed for a static topology without provision to handle any dynamic topology change. Another advantage of MDT is that it provides guaranteed delivery for nodes with arbitrary coordinates in higher dimensions ($d > 3$).

7. CONCLUSIONS

MDT is the only geographic routing protocol that provides guaranteed delivery in 2D, 3D, and higher dimensions. The graph of nodes and physical links is required to be connected, but may otherwise be arbitrary. MDT's guaranteed delivery property holds for nodes with accurate, inaccurate, or arbitrary coordinates.

Experimental results show that MDT constructs a correct multi-hop DT very quickly at system initialization. MDT is also highly resilient to both node churn and link churn. Furthermore, MDT achieves a routing stretch (also distance stretch) close to 1.

The performance of MDT scales well to a large network size (N). We observed that, as N becomes large, MDT's routing (distance) stretch and per-node storage cost converge to horizontal asymptotes. MDT does not use special nodes (such as, beacons and landmarks) that are required in many wireless routing protocols; every MDT node runs the same protocols. Each node computes its own *local DT* with computation cost dependent upon its storage cost, rather than N. Lastly, MDT's per-node communication costs for constructing and maintaining a correct multi-hop DT are fairly low and independent of N.

---

[11] With reference from www.cs.berkeley.edu/~mccaesar/vrrcode .

8. ACKNOWLEDGMENTS

This work was sponsored by National Science Foundation grant CNS-0830939. We thank Ben Leong and our shepherd, Qin Lv, for their constructive comments. We also thank Jaeyoun Kim for programming help.

9. REFERENCES

[1] S. M. N. Alam and Z. J. Haas. Coverage and Connectivity in Three-Dimensional Networks. In *Proc. of ACM Mobicom*, 2006.

[2] P. Bose and P. Morin. Online routing in triangulations. *SIAM journal on computing*, 33(4):937–951, 2004.

[3] P. Bose, P. Morin, I. Stojmenovic, and J. Urrutia. Routing with Guaranteed Delivery in Ad Hoc Wireless Networks. In *Proc. of the International Workshop on Discrete Algorithms and Methods for Mobile Computing and Communications (DIALM)*, 1999.

[4] M. Caesar, M. Castro, E. B. Nightingale, G. O'Shea, and A. Rowstron. Virtual Ring Routing: Networking Routing Inspired by DHTs. In *Proceedings of ACM Sigcomm*, 2006.

[5] R. Draves, J. Padhye, and B. Zill. Routing in Multi-radio, Multi-hop Wireless Mesh Networks. In *Proceedings of ACM Mobicom*, 2004.

[6] S. Durocher, D. Kirkpatrick, and L. Narayanan. On Routing with Guaranteed Delivery in Three-Dimensional Ad Hoc Wireless Networks. In *Proceedings of ICDCN*, 2008.

[7] R. Flury and R. Wattenhofer. Randomized 3D Geographic Routing. In *Proceedings of IEEE Infocom*, 2008.

[8] S. Fortune. Voronoi diagrams and Delaunay triangulations. In J. E. Goodman and J. O'Rourke, editors, *Handbook of Discrete and Computational Geometry*. CRC Press, second edition, 2004.

[9] K. R. Gabriel and R. R. Sokal. A New Statistical Approach to Geographic Variation Analysis. *Systematic Zoology*, 1969.

[10] J. Gao, L. Guibas, J. Hershberger, L. Zhang, and A. Zhu. Geometric spanner for routing in mobile networks. In *Proc. MobiHoc*, 2001.

[11] B. Karp and H. Kung. Greedy Perimeter Stateless Routing for Wireless Networks. In *Proceedings of ACM Mobicom*, 2000.

[12] Y.-J. Kim, R. Govindan, B. Karp, and S. Shenker. Geographic Routing Made Practical. In *Proceedings of USENIX NSDI*, 2005.

[13] S. S. Lam and C. Qian. Geographic Routing in d-dimensional Spaces with Guaranteed Delivery and Low Stretch. Technical Report TR-10-03, The Univ. of Texas at Austin, Dept. of Computer Science, January 2010 (revised, October 2010).

[14] D.-Y. Lee and S. S. Lam. Protocol design for dynamic Delaunay triangulation. Technical Report TR-06-48, The Univ. of Texas at Austin, Dept. of Computer Sciences, December 2006.

[15] D.-Y. Lee and S. S. Lam. Protocol Design for Dynamic Delaunay Triangulation. In *Proceedings of IEEE ICDCS*, 2007.

[16] D.-Y. Lee and S. S. Lam. Efficient and Accurate Protocols for Distributed Delaunay Triangulation under Churn. In *Proceedings of IEEE ICNP*, November 2008.

[17] B. Leong, B. Liskov, and R. Morris. Geographic Routing without Planarization. In *Proceedings of USENIX NSDI*, 2006.

[18] M. Li and Y. Liu. Rendered Path: Range-free Localization in Anisotropic Sensor Networks with Holes. In *Proceedings of ACM Mobicom*, 2007.

[19] X.-Y. Li, G. Calinescu, P.-J. Wan, and Y. Wang. Localized Delaunay Triangulation Application in Ad Hoc Wireless Networks. *IEEE Tran. on Paral. Distr. Syst.*, 2003.

[20] C. Liu and J. Wu. Efficient Geometric Routing in Three Dimensional Ad Hoc Networks. In *Proceedings of INFOCOM*, 2009.

[21] D. Pompili, T. Melodia, and I. Akyildiz. Routing algorithms for delay-insensitive and delay-sensitive applications in underwater sensor networks. In *Proc. 12th Int. Conf. on Mobile Computing and Networking*, 2006.

[22] C. Qian and S. S. Lam. Greedy Distance Vector Routing. In *Proceedings of IEEE ICDCS*, June 2011.

[23] G. Toussaint. The Relative Neighborhood Graph of a Finite Planar Set. *Pattern Recognition*, 1980.

[24] G. Xing, C. Lu, R. Pless, and Q. Huang. On Greedy Geographic Routing Algorithms in Sensing-covered Networks. In *Proceedings of ACM Mobihoc*, 2004.

[25] J. Zhou, Y. Chen, B. Leong, and P. Sundaramoorthy. Practical 3D Geographic Routing for Wireless Sensor Networks. In *Proceedings of Sensys*, November 2010.

10. APPENDIX

Theorem 1

PROOF. 1) By definition, a correct multi-hop DT of S is a correct distributed DT of S. The distributed DT maintained by nodes in S is the same as $DT(S)$.

2) Given a correct multi-hop DT, each DT neighbor of a node u in S is either a physical neighbor or connected to u by a forwarding path of finite length (in hops) that exists in $\{F_v \mid v \in S\}$.

3) When a message, say m, arrives at a node, say u, if the condition in line 1, 2, or 6 in Table 1 is true, then a node closest to ℓ is found. If the conditions in lines 1-3 are all false, node u performs greedy forwarding in lines 4-5. If it succeeds to find in P_u a physical neighbor v that is closer to ℓ than node u, message m is transmitted directly to v (lines 4 in Table 1); else, greedy forwarding is performed over the set of DT neighbors (line 5 in Table 1). The proof of Theorem 1 in [14] for a distributed DT guarantees that either node u is closest to ℓ or there exists in N_u a node v that is closer to ℓ than u. Therefore, if node u is not a closest node to ℓ, executing the *greedy forwarding code* (lines 4-5 in Table 1) finds a node v that is closer to ℓ than node u.

4) Any other node in S that is closer to ℓ than u will not use the actions in lines 4-5 in Table 1 to send message m back to node u. It is, however, possible for message m to visit node u again in the forwarding path between two DT neighbors that are closer to ℓ than u. In this case, the condition of line 3 in Table 1 must be true for m at node u. Thus, node u executes the greedy forwarding code for message m at most once. This property holds for every node. By 2), 3), and the assumption that S has a finite number of nodes, MDT forwarding finds a closest node in S to ℓ in a finite number of hops.

$\square$

Theorem 2

PROOF. By Theorem 1, the join request of w succeeds to find a DT node (say z) closest to w, which sends back a joint reply. By a property of DT, node z, being closest to w, is guaranteed to be a neighbor of w in $DT(S \cup \{w\})$. A forwarding path is constructed between w and z. Subsequently, because the multi-hop DT of S is correct, forwarding paths are constructed between w and each neighbor it sends a neighbor-set request. After receiving a request from w, each neighbor of w updates its own neighbor set to include w. They also send back replies to w. By Lemma 9 in [14], the join process finishes and N_w consists of all neighbor nodes of w in $DT(S \cup \{w\})$.

By construction, two DT neighbors select only one path to use between them by refreshing only tuples stored in nodes along the selected path. Therefore, the path between each pair of neighbors in $DT(S \cup \{w\})$ is unique after the join. Each path also has a finite number of hops because (i) the path from the joining node to its closest DT node (z) has a finite number of hops (by Theorem 1), and (ii) the path from the joining node to each of its other DT neighbors is either a one-hop path or the concatenation of two paths, each of which has a finite number of hops. By Definition 3, the updated multi-hop DT is correct. $\square$

Model-driven Optimization of Opportunistic Routing

Eric Rozner   Mi Kyung Han   Lili Qiu   Yin Zhang
The University of Texas at Austin
{erozner,hanmi2,lili,yzhang}@cs.utexas.edu

ABSTRACT

Opportunistic routing aims to improve wireless performance by exploiting communication opportunities arising by chance. A key challenge in opportunistic routing is how to achieve good, predictable performance despite the incidental nature of such communication opportunities and the complicated effects of wireless interference in IEEE 802.11 networks. To address the challenge, we develop a model-driven optimization framework to jointly optimize opportunistic routes and rate limits for both unicast and multicast traffic. A distinctive feature of our framework is that the performance derived from optimization can be achieved in a real IEEE 802.11 network. Our framework consists of three key components: (i) a model for capturing the interference among IEEE 802.11 broadcast transmissions, (ii) a novel algorithm for accurately optimizing different performance objectives, and (iii) effective techniques for mapping the resulting solutions to practical routing configurations. Extensive simulations and testbed experiments show that our approach significantly outperforms state-of-the-art shortest path routing and opportunistic routing protocols. Moreover, the difference between the achieved performance and our model estimation is typically within 20%. Evaluation in dynamic and uncontrolled environments further shows that our approach is robust against inaccuracy introduced by a dynamic network and it also consistently out-performs the existing schemes. These results clearly demonstrate the effectiveness and accuracy of our approach.

Categories and Subject Descriptors

C.2.2 [**Computer-Communication Networks**]: Network Protocols—*Routing protocols*; C.2.1 [**Computer-Communication Networks**]: Network Architecture and Design—*Wireless communication*

General Terms

Algorithms, Experimentation, Measurement, Performance

Keywords

Opportunistic Routing, Wireless Mesh Networks, Wireless Network Model, Model-driven Optimization, Wireless Interference

1. INTRODUCTION

Wireless mesh networks are becoming a new attractive communication paradigm. Many cities have deployed or are planning to deploy them to provide Internet access to homes and businesses. Traditionally, a sender commits to a single node as the next hop to route towards its destination, and traffic makes progress only when it reaches the selected next hop. The high loss rates in wireless

networks (*e.g.*, 20-40% as observed in several deployments [2, 38]) make traditional routing inefficient. To achieve better performance, opportunistic routing has been proposed to exploit communication opportunities that arise by chance due to the broadcast nature of the wireless medium. When a sender broadcasts its data, any node that hears the transmission may forward the data toward the destination. Although individual nodes may experience high loss rates, as long as there exists one forwarder that is closer to the destination and receives the transmission, the data can move forward. In this way, opportunistic routing can effectively combine multiple weak links into a strong link and take advantage of transmissions reaching unexpectedly near or unexpectedly far.

There are two key factors that determine the performance of opportunistic communication in wireless mesh networks: (i) routes (*i.e.*, for a given flow how much traffic node j should forward upon receiving a packet from another node i), and (ii) rate limits (*i.e.*, how fast each traffic source can inject traffic into the network). Routes determine how effectively we take advantage of communication opportunities and how efficiently we utilize network resources and exploit spatial reuse. Rate limits ensure that traffic sources do not send more than what paths can support. Without appropriate rate limits, the network throughput can degrade drastically under traditional shortest-path routing [23]. Rate limiting is even more critical for opportunistic routing due to its use of broadcast transmissions: (i) broadcast transmissions do not perform exponential backoff (*i.e.*, its contention window does not increase upon packet losses) and thus are more likely to cause network congestion; and (ii) broadcast transmissions preclude the use of 802.11's synchronous ACK mechanism, and receivers' feedback has to be sent above the MAC layer, which can easily get lost during network congestion and cause unnecessary retransmissions and serious throughput degradation.

In this paper, we jointly optimize routes and rate limits for opportunistic communication. We focus on static, 802.11-based, multihop networks, though we believe that the general methodology is applicable to other scenarios. We develop the first opportunistic routing protocol that can accurately optimize IEEE 802.11 end-to-end performance (*i.e.*, the performance derived from optimization can be realized in a real IEEE 802.11 multihop network). This distinctive feature is important given the wide deployment of IEEE 802.11 networks.

Challenges: Accurate optimization of opportunistic communication in an IEEE 802.11 network is challenging for the following four reasons. *First*, the dynamic and incidental nature of communication opportunities makes it difficult to estimate their impact on the resulting network performance. *Second*, optimization of opportunistic routing places stringent requirements on a network model: the model should (i) specify the region of feasible network configurations using a compact representation so that we can optimize the objective within the feasible region as defined by these constraints, (ii) accurately estimate performance on every link in the network (as opposed to only a small number of links on specified routes, as in [23], for the purpose of optimizing rate limiting alone), and (iii) be accurate across a wide range of traffic conditions, including high traffic load, which is common in opportunistic routing. *Third*, the non-convex interference relationships among different links and the huge search space of possible opportunistic routes and rate limits impose significant challenges on the optimization procedure itself.

Fourth, to be valuable in practice, the resulting optimization solution should be easy to implement, using only a small number of control knobs.

Approach and contributions: We address the above challenges using the following four steps:

1. *General optimization framework.* We develop a general framework to jointly optimize routes and rate limits for opportunistic communication (Section 3). The framework uses opportunistic constraints to probabilistically characterize the available communication opportunities. It can use different wireless interference models.

2. *Interference model for IEEE 802.11 broadcast traffic.* The complex interference, traffic, and MAC-induced dependencies in the network are often the underlying cause of unexpected behavior. We develop a new model to capture these dependencies for broadcast transmissions (Section 4). We use measurements from a given network to estimate link loss rate, carrier sense probability, and conditional collision loss probabilities to seed our model. Our model derives the relationships between sending rates, loss rates, and throughput to capture the effects of carrier sense and collisions. Our model involves only $O(E)$ constraints, where E is the total number of edges. Thus it can be easily incorporated into our optimization framework. Despite its simplicity, the model captures real-world complexities such as hidden terminals, non-uniform traffic, multihop flows, non-binary and asymmetric interference.

3. *Iterative procedure for non-convex optimization.* Since our model is non-convex, we develop an iterative optimization procedure to find a local optimal solution (Section 5). Our algorithm is flexible and can accommodate different performance objectives. For comparison, we explore an alternative approach that uses a widely used conflict-graph-based interference model [17] that is less accurate [23, 33], but convex, and thus allows global optimization. Our results show that our approach of combining a more accurate model with non-convex optimization yields better and more accurate performance.

4. *Practical installation of routes and rate limits.* We develop a practical opportunistic routing protocol that implements the opportunistic routes and rate limits optimized by our algorithm in real networks (Section 6). The mechanisms for installing routes and rate limits can support both unicast and multicast.

We implement our protocol in both the Qualnet simulator [34] and a 21-node wireless mesh testbed using Click [8] and the Mad-WiFi driver [27]. Extensive simulations and testbed experiments (Section 7– 9) show that our approach achieves high accuracy (*i.e.*, the difference between the achieved performance and our model estimation is within 20%) and significantly out-performs state-of-the-art shortest path and opportunistic routing protocols (*e.g.*, its total throughput is up to 14x ETX's throughput and 11x MORE's throughput). We further study the impact of dynamic and uncontrolled environments on accuracy and performance, and find that our approach is robust to inaccuracy in the input and it also consistently out-performs the existing schemes (Section 10).

2. RELATED WORK

We classify related work into three categories: (i) design of opportunistic routing protocols, (ii) analysis of opportunistic routing performance, and (iii) wireless network modeling.

Opportunistic routing protocols: ExOR [6] is a seminal opportunistic routing protocol. In ExOR, a sender broadcasts a batch of packets. Each packet contains a list of nodes that can potentially forward it. To maximize the progress of each transmission, the forwarding nodes relay data packets in the order of their proximity to the destination in terms of the ETX metric [9], which quantifies the number of transmissions required to deliver a packet from the forwarder to the destination. To avoid redundant transmissions, every forwarding node only forwards packets that have not been acknowledged by nodes with a smaller ETX to the destination.

Since then, several opportunistic routing protocols have been proposed (*e.g.*, [7, 20, 24, 25]). In particular, MORE [7] applies network coding to opportunistic routing. Since random linear coding generates linearly independent coded packets with high probability, the forwarding nodes in MORE require no coordination. Instead, each node computes how much traffic it should forward and independently generates random linear combinations of all the packets it has received from the current batch. By obviating the needs for strict coordination, MORE can out-perform ExOR. However, as we show in Section 9, the performance of MORE can degrade significantly when there are more than a few flows in the network. This is because (i) it lacks rate limiting and causes network congestion, and (ii) its routes only try to minimize the number of transmissions and do not take wireless interference into account. In comparison, we directly optimize end-to-end performance by computing interference-aware opportunistic routes and rate limits. The performance optimized by our approach can be realized in a real network and is significantly better than the existing schemes.

Theoretic analysis of opportunistic routing: There have been several studies analyzing the performance of opportunistic routing. For example, [46] develops a methodology for estimating the maximum throughput given forwarding paths and traffic demands, and [47] extends the work to multi-radio multi-channel wireless networks. Both works assume the opportunistic routes are given, where nodes only forward traffic that is not received by nodes closer to the destinations, so they cannot optimize routes. Note that such selected routes are not optimal since (i) a single path routing metric, such as ETX, does not capture the anycast performance in the opportunistic routes [10] and (ii) shortest path routes do not result in the highest throughput due to wireless interference.

A few studies (*e.g.*, [26, 36, 43, 45, 48]) propose optimization frameworks for opportunistic routing. These studies use a conflict-graph-like interference model, which significantly over-estimates the actual performance as shown in Section 8. Different from these works, we show that to achieve accurate optimization of network performance it is essential to use an effective network model that captures the non-convex relationship between the performance of different wireless links. This calls for a new wireless model and an efficient algorithm to search for a close-to-optimal solution, which we address in this paper. We further discuss the differences between the conflict graph interference model that these works use and our model in Section 4. In addition to a new interference model and model-based optimization, our work goes beyond theoretical analysis (which is the primary focus of the above works) by developing a practical routing protocol to realize the performance gains in a real IEEE 802.11 network.

Wireless network modeling: Significant research has been done on wireless network modeling. One class of work focuses on asymptotic performance bounds (*e.g.*, [15, 16, 22]). These models provide useful insights as a network scales, but cannot be applied to a specific network. Another large class of models predict performance for a given scenario (*e.g.*, [5, 12, 14, 18, 33, 37]). They differ in their generality: some assume that everyone is within communication range of each other [5, 12, 14, 21], while others assume restricted traffic demands (*e.g.*, a single flow [12, 14], two flows [37], sending to a single neighbor [13], adding one new flow at a time [40], or one-hop demands [18, 33]). Moreover, models in this class predict performance under a given scenario and cannot support optimization without enumerating all possible network configurations, which is prohibitive due to a huge search space. To facilitate optimization, we need a model that can specify the entire region of feasible network configurations using a compact set of constraints, which can then be incorporated into the optimization procedure to optimize the desired objective within the feasible

$Flows$	the set of unicast or multicast flows
$src(f)$	source of flow f
$dest(f,d)$	d-th destination of flow f
$Demand(f)$	traffic demand of flow f, i.e., the amount of traffic f desires to send
$G(f)$	throughput of flow f
$T(f,i)$	node i's sending rate for flow f
$Y(f,d,i,j)$	information receiving rate along link $i \rightarrow j$ for d-th destination in flow f ($d = 1$ for unicast)
$P(i,j)$	loss rate of link $i \rightarrow j$ (including both collision and inherent wireless medium loss)
$\mathcal{N}(i)$	a subset of i's neighbors
$S(i, \mathcal{N}(i))$	success rate from node i to i's neighbor set $\mathcal{N}(i)$

Table 1: Notations for optimizing opportunistic routing.

▷ $Input: Flows, Demand(f)$
▷ $Output: T(f,i), Y(f,d,i,j)$
maximize: $\sum_{f \in Flows} G(f) - \beta \sum_{f,i} T(f,i)$
subject to:

[C1] $\quad G(f) \leq Demand(f) \qquad\qquad\qquad (\forall f)$

[C2] $\quad G(f) \leq \sum_k Y(f,d,k,dest(f,d)) \qquad (\forall f,d)$

[C3] $\quad Y(f,d,k,src(f)) = 0 \qquad\qquad\quad (\forall f,d,k)$

[C4] $\quad Y(f,d,dest(f,d),k) = 0 \qquad\quad\; (\forall f,d,k)$

[C5] $\quad \sum_k Y(f,d,k,i) \geq \sum_j Y(f,d,i,j)$
$\qquad\qquad (\forall f,d,i : i \neq src(f) \text{ and } i \neq dest(f,d))$

[C6] $\quad S(i,\mathcal{N}(i))T(f,i) \geq \sum_{k \in \mathcal{N}(i)} Y(f,d,i,k) \quad (\forall f,i,\mathcal{N}(i))$

[C7] $\quad interference\ constraints\ on\ T_i \triangleq \sum_f T(f,i)$

Figure 1: Problem formulation to optimize multicast throughput of opportunistic routing.

region. Two existing models are in this category: (i) the conflict-graph model [17], and (ii) the unicast interference model [23]. We discuss why they are insufficient for optimizing opportunistic routing in Section 4.1.

3. OPTIMIZATION FRAMEWORK

Overview: We develop a general framework for jointly optimizing opportunistic routes and rate limits. Our formulation assumes the use of network coding, which prevents nodes from forwarding redundant information without requiring fine-grained coordination among different nodes. Without loss of generality, we focus on multicast flows, since unicast flows are a special case of multicast with one receiver in each multicast group. The main design issue becomes how fast each traffic source should send traffic and how much traffic an intermediate node should forward to achieve high performance. This can be formulated as an optimization problem that maximizes total network throughput subject to information conservation constraints, opportunistic constraints, and interference constraints. Figure 1 shows the resulting formulation, and Table 1 specifies the variables in the formulation.

Optimization objective: Given the set of unicast or multicast flows $Flows$, and the traffic demands $Demand(f)$, our optimization outputs traffic sending rates $T(f,i)$ and information receiving rates $Y(f,d,i,j)$, which will be converted to opportunistic routing configurations using a credit-based scheme described in Section 6. As shown in Figure 1, the first term in the objective, $\sum_{f \in Flows} G(f)$, reflects the primary goal of maximizing the total throughput over all flows. The second term in the objective, $-\beta \sum_{f,i} T(f,i)$ represents the total amount of wireless traffic. Including both terms reflects the goals of (i) maximizing total throughput and (ii) preferring the least amount of traffic among all solutions that support the same total throughput (e.g., avoiding loops and unnecessary traffic). Since the first objective is more important, we use a small weighting factor $\beta = 10^{-5}$ for the second term just for tie breaking (i.e., only when the first objective is the same, we prefer the one with the least traffic).

To compute the first term, for a unicast flow f, $G(f)$ is its throughput. For a multicast flow f, $G(f)$ is the throughput of the bottleneck receiver. Note that there are many other ways to define the objective in multicast setting [42]. Here we use one of the metrics as an example. Our optimization framework can support other multicast objectives, such as total throughput over all receivers in the multicast group or other weighted versions. Moreover, while we focus on total throughput, our framework can be directly applied to optimizing other objectives. For example, our evaluation also considers optimizing a linear approximation of proportional fairness, defined as $\sum_{f \in Flows} \log G(f)$, which strikes a good balance between fairness and throughput [35]. We can also maximize total revenue if the revenue of a flow is a function of its throughput.

Throughput constraints: To ensure $G(f)$ is the throughput of flow f, it has to satisfy constraints (C1) and (C2) in Figure 1. Constraint (C1) indicates that the throughput of a flow should be no more than its traffic demand (i.e., total amount of information a source desires to send). Constraint (C2) ensures that $G(f)$ is no more than the total amount of information delivered from all links incident to the destination of flow f. For a multicast flow f, $G(f)$ should be no more than the total amount of information delivered to each destination in the flow f. Note that we do not need a lower bound on $G(f)$ since the objective is to maximize $G(f)$.

Information conservation constraints: To handle lossy wireless links, we distinguish traffic and information sent along a link. A feasible routing solution should satisfy information conservation. This property is given by constraints (C3–C5) in Figure 1. Constraint (C3) ensures no incoming information to a traffic source, constraint (C4) ensures no outgoing information from a destination, and constraint (C5) represents flow conservation at an intermediate node i, i.e., the total amount of incoming information is no less than the total amount of out-going information.

Opportunistic constraints: Opportunistic routing exploits the wireless broadcast medium by having different nodes extract information from the same transmission. We formally capture this notion using opportunistic constraints, which relate traffic volume to the amount of information delivered.

For ease of explanation, we first consider one sender sending to two receivers, and then generalize it to an arbitrary number of receivers. Consider a sender s, and denote the link loss rates from s to its neighbors r_1 and r_2 as $P(s,r_1)$ and $P(s,r_2)$, respectively. It is evident that for a given flow the amount of information delivered to a neighbor is bounded by the product of the sending rate and link delivery ratio. Therefore we have $(1 - P(s,r_1))T(f,s) \geq Y(f,d,s,r_1)$ and $(1 - P(s,r_2))T(f,s) \geq Y(f,d,s,r_2)$. In addition, since there is overlap between the information delivered to r_1 and r_2, we are only interested in the non-overlapping information (i.e., when redundant information is delivered to both nodes, it should only count once). The total non-overlapping information delivered to r_1 and r_2 should satisfy the following constraints:

$$(1 - P(s,r_1)P(s,r_2))T(f,s) \geq \sum_{i \in \{1,2\}} Y(f,d,s,r_i),$$

where the left hand-side represents the total amount of traffic successfully delivered to at least one of the receivers, and the right hand-side represents the total non-overlapping information delivered to the receivers.

Now we consider a general setting, where a sender s has N neighbors. We enumerate all possible subsets of its neighbors. For each neighbor set $\mathcal{N}(i)$, we require:

$$S(i, \mathcal{N}(i))T(f,i) \geq \sum_{k \in \mathcal{N}(i)} Y(f,d,i,k), \qquad (1)$$

where $S(i, \mathcal{N}(i))$ denotes the delivery probability from i to at least one node in $\mathcal{N}(i)$. When delivery rates of different links are independent, which holds for some networks [44], $S(i, \mathcal{N}(i)) = 1 - \prod_{k \in \mathcal{N}(i)} P(i,k)$. When the link delivery rates are correlated, we can empirically measure $S(i, \mathcal{N}(i))$. Equation 1 indicates the total traffic successfully delivered to at least one neighbor in $\mathcal{N}(i)$ should be no less than the total non-overlapping information delivered to $\mathcal{N}(i)$. This results in (C6) in Figure 1. When i has many (say, K) neighbors, we limit the number of such constraints by only enumerating neighbor sets of size 1, 2, and K (i.e., we enumerate only $O(K^2)$ instead of $O(2^K)$ neighbor sets).

Interference constraints: Wireless interference has a significant impact on wireless network performance. In particular, nearby senders carrier sense and defer to each other. Moreover, since carrier sense is not perfect, there may be multiple overlapping nearby transmissions that can cause collisions. These effects can further constrain the amount of traffic on each link and introduce strong inter-dependency between sending rates, loss rates, and throughput. We address this issue in Section 4 by developing the constraints that capture the relationships between $T(f, i)$ and $P(i, j)$.

4. BROADCAST INTERFERENCE MODEL

4.1 Motivation for a Better Model

Despite significant research on modeling the impact of wireless interference, none of the existing models directly fulfills our need for optimizing opportunistic routing. To support optimization, we need a model that specifies the feasible region of network configurations using a compact representation. The following two existing models fall into this category.

Conflict-graph model: The first model, proposed in [17], is a conflict-graph model that represents wireless links as vertices and draws a conflict edge between two vertices if the corresponding wireless links interfere. Based on this definition, it is clear that links corresponding to an independent set in the conflict graph can be active simultaneously. Therefore, the interference constraints are the schedule restrictions imposed by the independent sets, which can be expressed as a set of linear constraints.

There are two limitations in applying the conflict-graph model for optimizing opportunistic routing. First, the model in [17] assumes perfect scheduling, i.e., packet transmissions at different nodes can be precisely controlled and it over-estimates the performance in real networks as we will show in Section 8. Second, the conflict-graph model is a link-based model, while opportunistic routing uses broadcast transmissions and requires a node-based broadcast model. Existing broadcast extensions of the conflict-graph model provide only an aggregate answer of whether two broadcast transmissions interfere or not. For example, some extensions [36, 41, 46, 48] conservatively consider two broadcast transmissions interfere if any one of their receivers is interfered by the other transmission, while other extensions [46] consider broadcast transmissions to interfere if all of their receivers are interfered by the other transmission. A single aggregate answer on whether broadcast transmissions interfere does not fully characterize the impact of interference on different receivers and is therefore inadequate for use in optimizing opportunistic routing.

IEEE 802.11 unicast model: The other model, proposed in [23], models interference among unicast transmissions in IEEE 802.11. Since opportunistic routing uses broadcast traffic, we need to develop interference models for broadcast transmissions. Furthermore, as broadcast transmissions does not perform binary backoff to limit the sending rate (i.e., its contention window does not increase even under packet losses), it is necessary to have an accurate model even for high traffic load and channel occupancy, which induces high collision losses, and the linear approximation used in [23] becomes inaccurate under high collision losses. In addition, [23] is used for rate limiting unicast transmissions when given specified routes. Therefore it suffices to accurately estimate the sending rates and loss rates on a small number of links used for routing. In contrast, for the purpose of route optimization, we need to accurately estimate the performance for *all* receivers of a given sender, which is much more challenging.

Modeling goals and strategy: We develop our model specifically for IEEE 802.11 broadcast traffic. We observe that wireless interference affects IEEE 802.11 traffic in two important ways: (i) nearby senders cannot transmit simultaneously due to carrier sense, and (ii) transmissions may sometimes result in collisions due to imperfect carrier sense. We model these effects by developing the relationships between sending rates, loss rates, and throughput, which can be incorporated into our optimization framework and facilitate model-driven optimization. While this paper applies the model to optimizing opportunistic routing, the model is useful in other contexts (e.g., optimizing network topology and network planning). Our model is general and captures real-world complexities (e.g., hidden terminals, multipath flows, non-binary interference, and heterogeneous traffic), which is confirmed by simulation and testbed experiments using multihop networks in Section 8. Compared with [23], both our sender model (Section 4.3.1) and loss model (Section 4.3.2) are much more refined and do not involve any linear approximation. Thus, our model can more accurately estimate the loss rates for all receivers even under heavy traffic loads, which is essential for the optimization of opportunistic routing.

4.2 Background and Assumptions

We first review the broadcast transmissions as specified by the IEEE 802.11 standard [32]. Before transmission, a sender first checks to see if the medium is available using carrier-sensing. A sender determines the channel to be idle when the total energy received is less than the clear-channel assessment threshold. In this case, a sender may begin transmission using the following rule: If the medium has been idle for longer than a distributed inter-frame spacing time (DIFS) period, transmission can begin immediately. Otherwise, a sender waits for DIFS and then waits for a random backoff interval uniformly chosen between $[0, CW_{min}]$, where CW_{min} is the minimum contention window.

Our model strikes balance between realism and simplicity in order to support effective model-driven optimization. We make the following assumptions, which help simplify our model:

A1) It assumes pairwise interference, i.e., the interference relationship between two links is independent of activities on other links. Previous works show that pairwise interference is a good approximation in real networks [1, 31]. Hence this assumption is widely used in the literature (e.g., [5, 12, 14, 23, 37]). Moreover, for optimizing the routing of multihop wireless networks, it is often more important to capture the interference relationship among links that are not too far apart. For these links, the pairwise interference relationship is likely to be an even better approximation.

A2) It assumes that inherent wireless medium loss (i.e., loss under no interfering traffic) and collision loss are independent, which has been commonly used (e.g., [23, 33]).

A3) The inherent wireless medium losses at different nodes are independent, which is experimentally validated in [28, 29, 37].

A4) Inter-packet delays from a node follow an exponential distribution, as assumed in [14, 23, 33]. This assumption is only needed for deriving overlapping probabilities between two transmissions.

While some of these assumptions do not always hold (e.g., [44] shows that loss rates of different wireless links may be correlated for some networks), our evaluation results show that our model-driven optimization yields accurate performance estimates despite such simplifications. With these assumptions, we develop a tractable model with $O(E)$ constraints, where E is the number of links.

4.3 Our New Model

We develop a simple interference model for multihop wireless networks to capture the interdependency between broadcast sending rates, loss rates, and throughput. Such interdependency can be captured using $O(E)$ constraints, where E is the total number of edges in the network. These constraints can then be incorporated into the optimization problem as interference constraints [C7] shown in Figure 1. We present methods to measure the input parameters of the model in Section 6.

Our model consists of two main components: (i) a *sender model* that captures the effects of carrier-sensing on a sender's sending rate, and (ii) a *loss model* that captures both inherent loss (*i.e.*, packet loss under no interference) and the effects of overlapping packet transmissions on the collision loss rates for different links.

4.3.1 Broadcast Sender Model

Modeling the effects of carrier sense on traffic rates: We divide time into *variable-length slots* (VLS) for each sender i. A variable-length slot may last for either IEEE 802.11 slot time T_{slot} or the transmission time of a packet followed by a DIFS duration. The former occurs when i senses a clear channel but either has no data to transmit or has data but cannot transmit due to a non-zero backoff counter. The latter occurs when i either transmits a packet or waits for a transmission from another sender to complete.

Let τ_i be the probability for i to start a new packet transmission in a variable-length slot. Clearly, τ_i depends on (i) how often i has data to send, and (ii) the random backoff interval (*i.e.*, $CW_{\min}$). As derived in [5], when i has saturated traffic demand (*i.e.*, it always has data to transmit), on average i performs one transmission every $CW_{\min}/2 + 1$ variable-length slots (since there is no exponential backoff for broadcast traffic, we have $CW_{\min}/2$ slots for backoff plus 1 slot for the transmission). Therefore, the transmission probability τ_i is bounded by the following *feasibility constraint*:

$$\tau_i \leq \tau_{\max} \triangleq \frac{1}{CW_{\min}/2 + 1} \quad \text{(for } \forall i\text{)}. \quad (2)$$

Under the pairwise interference model (*i.e.*, A1), whether sender i carrier-senses (and thus defers to) an ongoing transmission of sender j only depends on nodes i and j and is independent of if other senders are transmitting. Let D_{ij} be this carrier sense probability (*i.e.*, probability for node i to defer to node j when node j is transmitting). For convenience, let $D_{ii} = 1$. Let T_i be sender i's sending rate over all flows ($T_i = \sum_f T(f, i)$), VLS_i be its expected VLS duration, and P_i^{idle} be the idle probability of node i. T_i, VLS_i and τ_i have the following approximate relationship, called the *throughput constraints*:

$$T_i = (EP \times \tau_i)/VLS_i, \quad (3)$$

$$VLS_i = T_{\text{slot}} P_i^{idle} + (T_{\text{xmit}} + T_{\text{DIFS}})(1 - P_i^{idle})$$
$$= T_{\text{slot}} + (T_{\text{xmit}} + T_{\text{DIFS}} - T_{\text{slot}})(1 - P_i^{idle}), \quad (4)$$

$$P_i^{idle} = \prod_j \left(1 - D_{ij} \times \tau_j \times \frac{VLS_i}{VLS_j}\right), \quad (5)$$

where EP is the expected packet payload size, EH is expected header size, $T_{\text{xmit}} = (EP + EH)/rate$ is the expected packet transmission time, and T_{slot} is an IEEE 802.11 slot time. Eq. (3) computes throughput as the total amount of payload transmitted during one VLS divided by the expected VLS duration. Eq. (4) computes expected VLS duration as idle probability times an idle slot duration plus transmission (including collision) probability times a transmission duration. Finally, Eq. (5) gives the probability that i finds the medium is idle, where $\tau_j \times \frac{VLS_i}{VLS_j}$ is the probability for j to start a transmission in i's VLS, $D_{ij} \times \tau_j \times \frac{VLS_i}{VLS_j}$ is the probability that i defers to j's transmission, and $\prod_j (1 - D_{ij} \times \tau_j \times \frac{VLS_i}{VLS_j})$ is the probability that i does not defer to any node in the network including its own transmission (*i.e.*, i senses the medium is idle).

Eliminating model parameters $\{\tau_i\}$ and $\{P_i^{idle}\}$: To better fa-

cilitate model-driven optimization, we eliminate model parameters $\{\tau_i\}$ and $\{P_i^{idle}\}$ and transform (2)–(5) into the following equivalent constraints, which apply directly to the traffic rates $\{T_i\}$.

- *Feasibility constraint.* According to Eq. (3), we have: $\tau_i = \frac{T_i \times VLS_i}{EP}$. As a result, Eq. (2) is equivalent to:

$$\frac{T_i}{EP} \leq \frac{\tau_{\max}}{VLS_i} \quad \text{(for } \forall i\text{)}. \quad (6)$$

- *Throughput constraint.* With $\tau_i = \frac{T_i \times VLS_i}{EP}$, Eq. (5) becomes: $P_i^{idle} = \prod_j \left(1 - \frac{D_{ij} \times T_j \times VLS_i}{EP}\right)$. So Eq. (4) becomes:

$$VLS_i = T_{\text{slot}} + (T_{\text{xmit}} + T_{\text{DIFS}} - T_{\text{slot}}) \times$$
$$\left[1 - \prod_j \left(1 - \frac{D_{ij} \times T_j \times VLS_i}{EP}\right)\right]. \quad (7)$$

Eq. (6) and (7) fully capture the relationships in (2)–(5) but have fewer variables. Moreover, note that when traffic rates $\{T_j\}$ are given as inputs, Eq. (7) contains only a single variable: VLS_i. This allows us to numerically derive VLS_i and partial derivatives $\frac{\partial VLS_i}{\partial T_j}$ from the given $\{T_j\}$ (as described in Section 5.2). We will therefore use (6) and (7) in our model-driven optimization.

4.3.2 Broadcast Loss Model

Integrating inherent loss and collision loss: To estimate loss rates $P(i, j)$ from traffic rates T_i, we distinguish between two types of loss: inherent wireless medium loss (*i.e.*, loss rate under no interference) and collision loss. The former is denoted as $P^{\text{raw}}(i, j)$ for link $i \rightarrow j$ and can be periodically measured. The latter depends on two factors: (i) how often transmissions from different nodes overlap and (ii) how often such overlapping transmissions result in a collision. To capture the first effect, we introduce $O(i, k)$ to denote the probability for an i's transmission to overlap with a k's transmission (conditioned on i's transmission) and derive its value based on the carrier sense probability. To capture the second effect, we observe that the pairwise interference model indicates there is a constant conditional collision loss probability L_{ij}^k (*i.e.*, the probability that a transmission on link $i \rightarrow j$ collides with an overlapping transmission from node k). We assume that inherent wireless medium loss and collision loss are independent, which has been commonly used (*e.g.*, [23, 33]). We then compute $P(i, j)$ as:

$$P(i, j) = 1 - (1 - P^{\text{raw}}(i, j)) \times \prod_{k \neq i} \left[1 - L_{ij}^k \times O(i, k)\right]. \quad (8)$$

This is because a packet is delivered when it is not lost due to either inherent loss or collision loss. To ensure no collision, the packet should not collide with any node's transmission. Since $L_{ij}^k \times O(i, k)$ is the collision loss probability with node k's transmission, $\prod_{k \neq i} \left[1 - L_{ij}^k \times O(i, k)\right]$ is the probability that the link has no collisions with any other node in the network.

Estimating overlap probabilities: We next estimate the overlap probability $O(i, j)$, which depends on whether i and j can carrier sense each other. Our model has two salient features: (i) it supports both symmetric and asymmetric deferral (*e.g.*, node i defers to node j but not vice versa), and (ii) it handles non-binary deferral (*e.g.*, node i sometimes defers to j and sometimes does not).

To provide both features, our modeling strategy is to divide time into regions to which one of the following four cases applies:

- Case 1: i and j can both carrier sense each other;
- Case 2: neither i nor j can carrier sense each other;
- Case 3: i can carrier sense j but j cannot carrier sense i; and
- Case 4: i cannot carrier sense j but j can carrier sense i.

Let $Q_c(i, j)$ be the probability for Case c to occur. Let $O_c(i, j)$ be the probability for a transmission of i to overlap with any transmission of j under Case c. We then have:

$$O(i,j) = \sum_{c=1}^{4} (Q_c(i,j) \times O_c(i,j)). \quad (9)$$

Assuming whether i can carrier sense j is independent of whether j can carrier sense i, we can simply compute $Q_c(i,j)$ as:

$$\begin{cases} Q_1(i,j) &=& D_{ij} \times D_{ji}, \\ Q_2(i,j) &=& (1-D_{ij}) \times (1-D_{ji}), \\ Q_3(i,j) &=& D_{ij} \times (1-D_{ji}), \\ Q_4(i,j) &=& (1-D_{ij}) \times D_{ji}. \end{cases} \quad (10)$$

In our technical report [39], we derive $O_c(i,j)$ as follows.

$$\begin{cases} O_1(i,j) &=& \tau_j = \frac{T_j \times VLS_j}{EP}, \\ O_2(i,j) &=& 1-(1-\theta_j)\exp\left[-T_{\mathrm{xmit}}/IPD_j\right], \\ O_3(i,j) &=& 1-\exp\left[-T_{\mathrm{xmit}}/IPD_j\right], \\ O_4(i,j) &=& \frac{\theta_j}{\theta_j+(1-\theta_j)\exp\left[-T_{\mathrm{xmit}}/IPD_j\right]}, \end{cases} \quad (11)$$

where $\theta_j = \frac{T_j}{rate} \times \frac{EP+EH}{EP}$ is the fraction of time j is transmitting (either payload or header) and $IPD_j \triangleq \frac{1-\theta_j}{\theta_j} \times T_{\mathrm{xmit}}$ is j's expected inter-packet delay.

4.3.3 Model Initialization

Our model has the following input parameters: (i) inherent wireless link loss rates P_{ij}^{raw}, (ii) carrier sense probabilities D_{ij}, and (iii) conditional collision loss probabilities L_{ij}^k. For simplicity, we estimate these parameters by conducting pairwise broadcast measurements [1, 23], but our model can just as easily use the inputs inferred by more scalable approaches (e.g., [3, 4]).

1. We first let node a send broadcast traffic alone. The other nodes record the receiving rates from a. We then estimate $P^{\mathrm{raw}}(a,b) = 1 - (b$'s receiving rate from $a)/(a$'s sending rate$)$.

2. We next let two nodes a and b send broadcast traffic simultaneously and measure their sending rates T_a and T_b. Since neither a nor b has any rate limit, we have $\tau_a = \tau_b = \tau_{\max} = \frac{1}{CW_{\min}/2+1}$. From Eq. (3), we can then compute $VLS_a = (EP \times \tau_a)/T_a$ and $VLS_b = (EP \times \tau_b)/T_b$. Applying Eq. (7) to the case with only two senders a and b, we have:

$$VLS_a = T_{\mathrm{slot}} + (T_{\mathrm{xmit}} + T_{\mathrm{DIFS}} - T_{\mathrm{slot}}) \times$$
$$\left[1 - \left(1 - \frac{D_{aa} \times T_a \times VLS_a}{EP}\right)\left(1 - \frac{D_{ab} \times T_b \times VLS_a}{EP}\right)\right]. \quad (12)$$

Note that $D_{aa} = 1$. So linear equation (12) has only a single unknown D_{ab}. We can therefore estimate D_{ab} by solving (12).

3. Finally, when both a and b are sending broadcast traffic, the other nodes record their receiving rates from a and b. For any node $c \notin \{a,b\}$, we can compute the loss rate $P(a,c) = 1 - (c$'s receiving rate from $a)/T_a$. Moreover, given T_a, T_b, D_{ab} and D_{ba}, we can compute the overlapping probability $O(a,b)$ according to Eq. (9)–(11). Applying Eq. (8) to the case in which there are only two senders a and b, we obtain:

$$P(a,c) = 1 - (1 - P^{\mathrm{raw}}(a,c)) \times (1 - L_{ac}^b \times O(a,b)). \quad (13)$$

We can then estimate L_{ac}^b by solving linear equation (13), which has only a single unknown L_{ac}^b.

5. MODEL-DRIVEN OPTIMIZATION

5.1 Iterative Model-driven Optimization

The interference constraints [C7] in Figure 1 consist of Eq. (6)–(11), which capture the inter-dependency between $\{T_i\}$, $\{VLS_i\}$ and $\{P(i,j)\}$. A key challenge in optimization is that these relationships are non-convex. To address this challenge, we perform

```
 ▷ T: traffic rates, Y: information, P: loss rates
1  initialization: T* = 0, Y* = 0, thruput* = 0
2  for k = 1 to KMAX
3     P* = estimate_loss(T*)
4     [VLS*, ∂VLS*/∂T*] = estimate_VLS_and_partial_derivatives(T*)
5     derive linearized interference constraints in Eq. (14) using VLS* and ∂VLS*/∂T*
6     construct a linear program (LP_k) from Figure 1 by adding linearized
       interference constraints (14), and fixing loss rates P = P* as constants
7     solve (LP_k); let (T^opt, Y^opt) be the optimal solution
8     α = α_max; succ = false
9     while (α ≥ α_min) and (succ = false)  // line search for a better solution
10        T = (1−α) × T* + α × T^opt
11        feasible = test_traffic_rates_feasibility(T)
12        if (feasible)
13           [thruput, Y] = compute_OR_thruput_from_traffic_rates(T)
14           if (thruput > thruput*)
15              thruput* = thruput; T* = T; Y* = Y;
16              succ = true; break
17           end
18        end
19        α = α/2
20     end
21     if (succ = false), break; end
22  end
23  return (thruput*, T*, Y*)
```

Figure 2: Iterative optimization of opportunistic routing.

optimization in an iterative fashion, as illustrated in Figure 2. To decouple the non-linear inter-dependency between $\{T_i\}$, $\{VLS_i\}$, and $\{P(i,j)\}$, we perform the following steps in each iteration:

1. We first fix traffic rates $\{T(f,i)\}$ to their values $\{T^*(f,i)\}$ obtained in the previous iteration and estimate the loss rates $\{P^*(i,j)\}$ as described in Section 4.3.2.

2. We then numerically compute VLS_i^* and partial derivatives $\frac{\partial VLS_i^*}{\partial T_j^*}$ from $\{T_j^*\}$ according to Eq. (7). The key observation we leverage is that when $\{T_j\}$ are given, Eq. (7) only contains a single variable, i.e., VLS_i. We present the details of this step later in Section 5.2.

3. We then approximate the non-linear interference constraints given in Eq. (6) and (7) using linear constraints. This can be achieved by computing the first-order approximation to the R.H.S. of (6) as a Taylor expansion at the current T_i^*. Specifically, we use the following linearized interference constraints:

$$\frac{T_i}{EP} \le \frac{\tau_{\max}}{VLS_i^*} - \frac{\tau_{\max}}{(VLS_i^*)^2} \sum_k \frac{\partial VLS_i^*}{\partial T_k^*} \times (T_k - T_k^*), \quad (14)$$

where VLS_i^* and $\frac{\partial VLS_i^*}{\partial T_k^*}$ are computed in step 2.

4. We then treat loss rates $P^*(i,j)$ as constants in Figure 1. We also add the linearized interference constraints given in Eq. (14) to the formulation in Figure 1, yielding a linear program (LP_k) that can be solved efficiently by LP solvers like cplex.

5. Since the linearized interference constraints are only an approximation to the true interference constraints, the optimal solution to (LP_k) may be infeasible under IEEE 802.11. We therefore perform a line search between the old solution and the optimal solution to (LP_k) to find a new set of traffic rates that are both feasible and improves the total throughput. During the line search, we need two capabilities: (i) to test whether a set of traffic rates are feasible under 802.11 (line 11 in Figure 2), and (ii) to find the maximum total throughput of opportunistic routing under such traffic rates. The former is performed as described in Section 5.2. The latter can be achieved by treating $T(f,i)$ as constants while solving the problem formulated in Figure 1.

The iterative process continues until it reaches a solution that cannot be further improved upon after enough attempts. Since the total throughput will strictly increase over each iteration, the process is guaranteed to converge. In our experiments, we conservatively limit the maximum number of iterations to 30. Our experience suggests that typically the iteration stops much earlier.

5.2 Technical Details

Our model-driven optimization framework above makes use of the following three key capabilities: (i) estimating VLS_i from traffic rates $\{T_j\}$, (ii) testing the feasibility of given traffic rates $\{T_j\}$, and (iii) computing partial derivatives $\frac{\partial VLS_i}{\partial T_k}$. Below we present details on how to support these capabilities using our model.

Estimating VLS_i from traffic rates $\{T_j\}$: To numerically derive VLS_i from given traffic rates $\{T_j\}$, let $f_i(x) \triangleq x - T_{\text{slot}} - (T_{\text{xmit}} + T_{\text{DIFS}} - T_{\text{slot}}) \times \left[1 - \prod_j \left(1 - \frac{D_{ij} \times T_j \times x}{EP}\right)\right]$. According to Eq. (7), $x = VLS_i$ is a root of $f_i(x)$. Moreover, we need $x \in \left[0, \frac{EP}{\max_j(D_{ij} \times T_j)}\right]$ to ensure $1 - \frac{D_{ij} \times T_j \times x}{EP} \geq 0$ in Eq. (7). In our technical report [39], we prove that when $x \in \left[0, \frac{EP}{\max_j(D_{ij} \times T_j)}\right]$, $f_i(x)$ is convex and has at most one root. Therefore, we can apply any univariate root-finding algorithm (*e.g.*, Matlab's fzero function) to numerically compute the root of $f_i(x)$ over interval $x \in \left[0, \frac{EP}{\max_j(D_{ij} \times T_j)}\right]$ and let the solution be VLS_i (if a root exists).

Testing the feasibility of traffic rates $\{T_j\}$: To test whether traffic rates $\{T_j\}$ are feasible, we first numerically compute VLS_i from Eq. (7) by finding a root of $f_i(x)$ over $x \in \left[0, \frac{EP}{\max_j(D_{ij} \times T_j)}\right]$ as described above. If no solution is found or if the solution VLS_i violates Eq. (6), then traffic rates $\{T_j\}$ are infeasible. Otherwise, $\{T_j\}$ are feasible.

Computing partial derivatives $\frac{\partial VLS_i}{\partial T_k}$: Eq. (7) also allows us to compute the partial derivatives $\frac{\partial VLS_i}{\partial T_k}$ for given traffic rates $\{T_j\}$, which allows us to linearize the non-linear interference constraints (see Section 5.1). Specifically, we have $\frac{\partial VLS_i}{\partial T_k} = \frac{N_{ik}}{1 - M_i}$, where

$M_i \triangleq (T_{\text{xmit}} + T_{\text{DIFS}} - T_{\text{slot}}) \times P_i^{\text{idle}*} \times \sum_j \frac{D_{ij} T_j}{EP - D_{ij} T_j VLS_i}$,

$N_{ik} \triangleq (T_{\text{xmit}} + T_{\text{DIFS}} - T_{\text{slot}}) \times P_i^{\text{idle}*} \times \frac{D_{ik} VLS_i}{EP - D_{ik} T_k VLS_i}$, and

$P_i^{\text{idle}*} \triangleq \prod_j (1 - \frac{D_{ij} T_j VLS_i}{EP})$.

6. PROTOCOL IMPLEMENTATION

Overview: We develop a practical opportunistic routing protocol to install the opportunistic routes and rate limits computed by our optimization algorithm. It is built on top of MORE [7], which sits between the IP and 802.11 MAC layers. It differs from MORE in that it uses interference modeling and optimization to derive rate limits and opportunistic routes for a given performance objective. As in MORE, it leverages intra-flow network coding to carry out the derived routes (*i.e.*, an intermediate forwarder transmits random linear combinations of the packets it receives for a given flow at the rate derived from our optimization).

As most opportunistic routing protocols, we target medium to large file transfers. A traffic source divides data packets into batches, and broadcasts a random linear combination of the original packets at the rate computed according to Figure 2. Upon receiving encoded packets, an intermediate node generates a random linear combination of all the innovative packets it has from the current batch. Each intermediate node uses the algorithm described in Figure 2 to determine how much traffic it should forward. After receiving enough innovative packets, the destination extracts the original data packets and sends an end-to-end ACK using MAC-layer unicast. When the source receives the ACK, it moves to the next batch. Below we describe several key steps in our protocol: (i) measuring inputs to seed our interference model, (ii) computing opportunistic routes and rate limits for each flow, (iii) routing traffic according to the derived sending rates and routes, (iv) supporting multicast, and (v) enhancing the reliability of end-to-end ACKs.

Measuring input parameters: Our model-driven optimization framework has the following input parameters: (i) traffic demands,

(ii) carrier sense probabilities, (iii) conditional collision loss probabilities, and (iv) inherent wireless link loss rates. As reported in [11, 23], wireless traffic exhibits temporal stability and we can estimate current traffic demands based on previous demands. In our evaluation, we also test the sensitivity to the demand estimation error. We conduct pairwise broadcast measurements [1] and compute the carrier sense probabilities $\{D_{ab}\}$ and conditional collision loss probabilities $\{L_{ac}^b\}$ as described in Section 4.3.3. The pairwise broadcast measurements takes $O(N^2)$ time for an N-node network. In our 21-node testbed, each pair of nodes broadcasts for 30 seconds, and the entire measurement takes around 2 hours. To minimize measurement overhead, we conduct pairwise broadcast measurement infrequently, around once a week. Note that recent works have developed efficient online techniques to measure interference when a network is in use (*e.g.*, [3, 4]). These techniques can be incorporated into our implementation to further reduce measurement overhead. In addition, we conduct per-node broadcast measurements at the beginning of each experiment to measure the inherent wireless link loss rates. The latter is based on more frequent measurements because it is more light-weight (only requiring $O(N)$ measurements) and existing routing protocols, such as [6, 7, 9], all use frequent loss measurements for route selection.

Deriving opportunistic routes and rate limits: Note that since our optimization problem is non-convex, existing techniques developed for distributed convex optimization (*e.g.*, [19]) are not directly applicable. Instead, we optimize opportunistic routes and rate limits at a central location and then distribute the optimized results to the other nodes. We use this approach in our implementation. The amount of information to distribute is very small compared to data traffic: the optimization input is around 2 KB per node and the optimization output is within a 100 bytes per node. Alternatively, the computation can also be done in a fully distributed fashion, similar to link-state protocols like OSPF, where every node implements the same algorithm over the same data to arrive at the same results. Such computation happens once every several minutes. For instance, default SNMP polling intervals are typically 5 minutes, so the optimization can rerun when the traffic demands and network topology change. The optimization is fairly efficient (*e.g.*, it takes around 3 seconds to optimize routes and rate limits for 16 flows under the 5×5 grid topologies used in our simulation).

Enforcing derived routes and rate limits: An intermediate node enforces its forwarding strategy according to the derived $T(f, i)$ and $Y(f, d, i, j)$ using the following credit-based scheme. When node j receives a packet from node i, it increments its credit, which denotes how many packets j should transmit for each received packet. If its credit is at least 1, j generates and transmits a random linear combination of the packets from the current batch buffered locally, and decrements the credit by 1. This process repeats until the credit goes below 1. The credit computation in our protocol differs from MORE in two main aspects. First, our protocol computes credit to ensure the traffic and information sending rates conform to the derived T and Y. Second, unlike MORE, which treats all transmissions equally if coming from nodes with larger ETX to the destination, our protocol differentiates transmissions coming from different neighbors as follows. Upon receiving a packet from i, j increments its credit by $C \times R$, where C reflects the fraction of useful information contained in each packet received from i and R reflects the amount of redundancy j should include to compensate for loss to its neighbors. Specifically, we have $C = \frac{Y(f,d,i,j)}{T(f,i)(1 - P(i,j))}$, and $R = \frac{T(f,j)}{\sum_k Y(f,d,j,k)}$. For example, when j receives a packet from a downstream node i, $C = 0$ to prevent j from sending non-innovative packets; when receiving a packet from an upstream node i, j updates its credit according to how much new information is involved in the packet and its loss rate to its forwarders.

Supporting multicast extension: Our previous description applies to the unicast case. A few modifications are required to support multicast. First, since a single packet carries a different amount of information for different destinations in the same multicast group, a node j increments its credit by $C \times R$, where $C = \frac{\max_d Y(f,d,i,j)}{T(f,i)(1-P(i,j))}$ and $R = \frac{T(f,j)}{\sum_k \max_d Y(f,d,j,k)}$. Second, when some destinations receive enough innovative packets, the encoded packets from the current batch should only be delivered to those who have not received all packets. To adapt to the changes in the set of destinations that need the packets, we dynamically re-adjust credit increment based on the remaining receivers who have not finished.

Enhancing ACK reliability: The destination sends an end-to-end ACK to the source upon receiving enough innovative packets for decoding so that the source can move on to the next batch. To ensure the reliability of ACKs, we keep retransmitting ACKs until they are received. To expedite ACK transmissions, ACKs do not perform binary backoff so that they have higher priority over retransmitted data. For fair comparison, we apply the same optimizations to MORE. Finally, since there is only one ACK for a batch of data packets, ACK overhead is negligible in opportunistic routing.

7. EVALUATION METHODOLOGY

We evaluate our approach using extensive simulation and testbed experiments. Our evaluation consists of four parts. First, we compare the fidelity of the conflict-graph (CG) model and our new model by quantifying their under-prediction and over-prediction errors. We use a conservative CG model, which considers two broadcast transmissions to interfere if any one of their receivers is interfered by the other transmission.

Second, we compare the performance of our opportunistic routing protocol using either the CG model or the new broadcast interference model with the following existing routing protocols: (1) shortest-path routing using the ETX routing metric, which minimizes the total number of expected transmissions from a source to its destination [9], (2) shortest-path routing with rate limit optimization as developed in [23], and (3) MORE, a state-of-art opportunistic routing protocol.

We compare total network throughput under 1–16 simultaneous flows. We also compare in terms of the proportional fairness metric [19], which is defined as: $\sum_{f \in Flows} \log G(f)$, where $G(f)$ is flow f's throughput. This metric strikes a balance between increasing network throughput and maintaining fairness among the flows. Higher values are more desirable. Unless otherwise noted, each flow sends saturated CBR traffic.

Third, we evaluate the multicast performance of one multicast group with a varying group size, and measure the average throughput of the bottleneck receiver. As in [7], we extend shortest path routing to support multicast by generating a multicast tree as a union of shortest paths towards all destinations and sending one copy of traffic along the links that are shared by multiple destinations. It saves the traffic on shared point-to-point links as in wireline multicast routing but does not leverage the broadcast nature of wireless links (*e.g.*, a node still needs to send traffic separately to reach each of its next hops). Shortest path with rate limit [23] takes a routing matrix R as part of the input, where R_{id} is the fraction of flow d that traverses link i. To support multicast, we derive a multicast routing tree R, where $R_{ig} = 1$ if link i appears in multicast group g's routing tree.

Fourth, we evaluate the sensitivity of our protocol against (i) errors in the input traffic demands, (ii) unknown external interference, and (iii) errors in link loss estimation.

For simulation, we implement all protocols in Qualnet 3.9.5 [34]. For testbed experiments, we use the shortest path routing and MORE implementations publicly available [30]. In particular, the shortest path routing is the Click implementation released as part of MORE source code. We calculate ETX according to [9] and configure the link weight accordingly. The shortest path with rate limiting is based on the shortest path code but the rate limit of each flow is

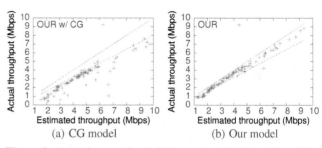

Figure 3: Actual vs. estimated throughput in simulation (25-node random topologies).

computed using the algorithm in [23]. We extend MORE to implement our protocol as described in Section 6. Both MORE and our protocol use 64 packets as the batch size for network coding. All these routing protocols are implemented using Click [8] and the MadWiFi driver [27] in the testbed.

Qualnet simulation: In simulation, we use 802.11a with a fixed MAC rate of 6 Mbps. The communication range is 230 meters, and interference range is 253 meters. These are the default values in Qualnet under transmission power of 10dBm, and we use them in the CG model to determine if two nodes interfere. As in [23], we seed the new interference model by having two senders broadcast simultaneously and measuring the resulting sending rates and receiving rates. Unless noted otherwise, we use saturated UDP traffic with 1024-byte payloads.

For each scenario, we conduct 20 random trials. In each trial, flow sources and destinations are picked randomly and the simulation time is 20 seconds. We extend Qualnet to generate directional inherent packet losses, which are uniformly distributed between 0 and 90%. We consider two types of topologies: 5×5 grid and 25-node random topologies, each occupying a $750 \times 750\ m^2$ area.

Testbed experiments: Our testbed consists of 21 nodes located on two floors inside an office building. Each node runs Linux and is equipped with a NetGear WAG511 NIC. Unless otherwise specified, we use 802.11a to minimize interference with campus wireless LAN traffic, which uses 802.11g. This allows us to evaluate in a controlled environment. We use 20 mW transmission power and 6 Mbps transmission rate so that the network paths are up to 7 hops. Among the node pairs that have connectivity, 47.8% of them have links with loss $\leq 20\%$. All the routing protocols require estimation of link loss rates, which are measured by having one sender broadcast at a time and the other nodes measure the receiving rates. The loss measurements were collected before the experiments. In addition, our protocol and shortest path with rate limiting require interference measurement, which we collected once per week. As in simulation, we conduct 20 random trials for each scenario. Each trial lasts one minute. Other settings are consistent with the simulation. Finally, in Section 10, we further evaluate using 802.11b, which competes with campus WLAN traffic, in order to assess the sensitivity against unknown external interference.

8. MODEL VALIDATION

We adopt the evaluation methodology presented in [23] to quantify the accuracy of our model. In particular, to evaluate the over-prediction of our model, we install the estimated throughput to the network to see if it can be satisfied. To evaluate the under-prediction error, we uniformly scale each flow throughput by the same factor and check if the scaled demand is achievable. If the scaled demand is achieved in the network, it indicates that the under-prediction error is at least the scaling factor. We vary the scaling factor from 1.1, 1.2, 1.5, corresponding to a load increase of 10%, 20%, and 50%, and vary the number of flows from 1 to 16.

Simulation results: We first evaluate how often the models over-predict. In Figure 3, we plot the estimated throughput versus the actual throughput using the CG model and our model in 25-node

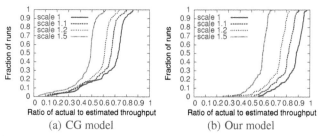

(a) CG model　　　　　　　(b) Our model

Figure 4: CDF of ratios between actual and estimated throughput in simulation (25-node random topologies).

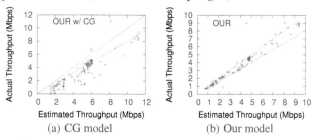

(a) CG model　　　　　　　(b) Our model

Figure 5: Actual vs. estimated throughput in the testbed.

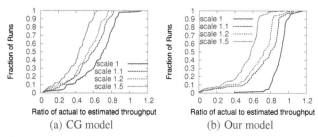

(a) CG model　　　　　　　(b) Our model

Figure 6: CDF of ratios between actual and estimated throughput in the testbed.

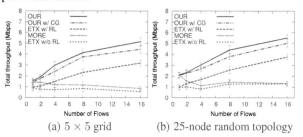

(a) 5×5 grid　　　(b) 25-node random topology

Figure 7: Total unicast throughput in simulation (25-node random topologies).

random topologies. For reference, we plot lines $y = x$ and $y = 0.8x$. Here, the CG model significantly over-predicts the actual throughput obtained, whereas the actual performance under our model is mostly within 80% of the estimated throughput. The CG model experiences significantly higher over-prediction errors since it assumes perfect scheduling, whereas our model explicitly models the interference between broadcast transmissions in IEEE 802.11, thereby achieving higher accuracy. Moreover, the amount of over-estimation by CG heavily depends on the network topology (*e.g.*, whether the network has hidden terminals) and simply scaling down the performance estimated by CG by a constant factor does not work. Both CG and our models have part of their over-prediction errors coming from the delay in end-to-end ACKs, during which time the source keeps retransmitting the current batch. This effect is not modeled. The use of a larger batch size can reduce the gap between the model estimation and actual performance at the cost of a larger header size and longer delay.

Next we quantify under-prediction errors. In Figures 4(a) and (b), we plot CDFs of the ratios between actual and estimated throughput in random topologies for the CG model and our model, respectively. Consistent with the scatter plots, the CG model mostly over-predicts, and virtually none of the scaled demands are satisfied. In comparison, using our model with a scale factor of 1, 80% of the runs have actual throughput within 80% accuracy of the estimation. Increasing the scale factor to 1.1 causes 65% of the actual throughput to be within 80% accuracy. After a further increase of the scale factor to 1.2, only 11% of actual throughput falls into 80% accuracy. This indicates that the demands scaled up by 20% can rarely be satisfied and shows our model has low under-prediction errors.

Testbed results: Next we validate our model and the CG model using testbed experiments. Figures 5(a) and (b) show the scatter plots of the CG model and our model, respectively. Figures 6(a) and (b) plot the CDFs of the ratios between actual and estimated throughput using different scale factors. As in simulation, the scatter plots from testbed experiments show a good match between actual and estimated throughput using our model and a significant over-estimation in the CG model. Scaling the demands by 1.1 leads to only 50% of the demands being satisfied and scaling the demands by 1.2 leads to only 29% of the demands being satisfied. These results indicate low over-prediction and under-prediction error. There are a few points in the testbed results where the actual throughput is higher than the estimated throughput. These cases arise from loss fluctuation: we use loss measurements to seed our model and

derive opportunistic routes and rate limits, but the actual link loss rates in the experiment improve and support higher throughput.

Summary: The simulation and testbed results demonstrate that our model rarely over-estimates or under-estimates performance by more than 20%. In comparison, the CG model consistently over-predicts network throughput due to its assumption of perfect scheduling. These results highlight the importance of model fidelity on performance predictability.

9. PERFORMANCE COMPARISON

In this section, we compare the performance of different routing protocols using simulation and testbed experiments.

9.1 Simulation Results

Total throughput of unicast flows: Figures 7(a) and (b) show the total throughput for 5×5 grid and 25-node random topologies, respectively. The error bars on the graph show the standard deviation of the sample mean.

We make several observations. First, in all cases our protocol using our model yields the best performance. It out-performs ETX by 76%-799% in the grid topology and by 117%-327% in the random topologies. Its gain over ETX with rate limiting ranges from 57%-99% in the grid topology and 46%-117% in the random topology. Its gain over MORE increases rapidly with the number of flows, ranging from 34% (2 flow) to 146% (4 flows) to 501% (16 flows) in the grid topology, and from 50% (2 flows) to 169% (4 flows) to 311% (16 flows) in random topologies. It out-performs the protocol with CG, the second best performing protocol by up to 24% in the grid topologies and 16% in the random topologies. Its performance benefit comes from three main factors: (i) taking advantage of opportunistic transmissions to cope with lossy wireless links, (ii) using interference-aware rate limiting to avoid network congestion, and (iii) using interference-aware opportunistic routing to maximize spatial reuse.

Second, comparing MORE against shortest path rate limiting, we observe that MORE out-performs the latter under 1 or 2 flows by leveraging opportunistic transmissions to recover losses. As the number of flows increases, the performance of MORE degrades and becomes significantly worse than shortest path with rate limiting due to lack of rate limiting. The impact of rate limiting on opportunistic routing is even higher than shortest path routing because opportunistic routing uses broadcast transmissions, which do not

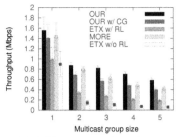

Figure 8: Multicast throughput in a 5×5 grid.

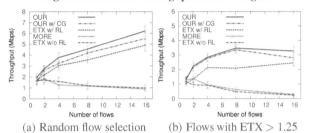

(a) Random flow selection   (b) Flows with ETX > 1.25

Figure 9: Total unicast throughput in the testbed.

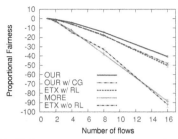

Figure 10: Unicast proportional fairness in the testbed.

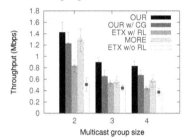

Figure 11: Multicast throughput in the testbed.

have binary backoff and are more likely to cause network congestion. Further, congestion on the data path may corrupt end-to-end ACKs in opportunistic routing and lead to unnecessary retransmissions and throughput degradation. In contrast, shortest path routing uses unicast transmissions, whose MAC-layer ACKs are given higher priority and hence more reliable.

Multicast flows: Figure 8 shows the throughput of the bottleneck receiver in a multicast group as we vary the group size from 1 to 5. As in unicast flows, our protocol consistently out-performs the alternatives. It improves the protocol with CG by 10%-46%, MORE by 8%-47%, shortest path rate limiting by 58%-232%, and shortest path by 74%-894%. The larger performance gain over both versions of shortest path is because our protocol effectively exploits the broadcast nature of the wireless medium to reduce the number of transmissions. When sending to multiple neighbors, it uses one broadcast transmission to reach all the neighbors. In comparison, while shortest path routing uses a multicast tree to compress the traffic on a shared link, the links from one sender to different neighbors are considered different and multiple transmissions are required to reach them. For the same reason, MORE consistently out-performs both versions of shortest path routing. Our protocol still out-performs MORE and the protocol with CG by using a more accurate model to optimize rate limit and opportunistic routes.

9.2 Testbed Results

Throughput of unicast flows: Figure 9(a) shows the total throughput of different protocols in the testbed, which has up to 7 hops. The relative rankings of the routing schemes are consistent with the simulation. As before, our protocol yields the best performance. The links in our testbed tend to be binary: either low loss or close to no connectivity. Among the node pairs that have network connectivity, 47.8% of them have loss rate within 20%. So the benefit of opportunistic routing is smaller in the testbed than in simulation. MORE performs close to shortest path routing, and significantly worse than shortest path with rate limiting; similarly, the gap between our protocol and shortest path routing also becomes smaller. These results confirm the intuition that opportunistic routing is most useful under lossy wireless medium.

To understand how opportunistic routing performs under more lossy wireless medium, we conduct another set of experiments where we pick only flows whose ETX between source and destination is at least 1.25. Figure 9(b) summarizes the results. In this case, the throughput of our protocol is 1.09-14.0x that of shortest path without rate limiting and 1.26-1.67x that of shortest path with rate lim-

iting. Its throughput is similar to MORE under 1 flow and 11.47x MORE's throughput under 16 flows. Furthermore, MORE yields low throughput: its performance is worse than shortest path with rate limiting as the number of flows reaches 4 or higher. These results are consistent with the simulation, and highlight the importance of jointly optimizing rate limits and opportunistic routes.

Proportional fairness of unicast flows: Next we consider maximizing proportional fairness. Since this objective is non-linear, in order to optimize it, we first approximate it using a piecewise linear, increasing, convex function as follows. We select s points on $\log(x)$, and approximate $\log(x)$ using s line segments, each connecting two adjacent points. We perform two different point selections and observe similar performance. In the interest of space, below we present results from only one selection: $x = 0.001, 0.01, 0.1, \sqrt{0.1}, 1, \sqrt{10}, 10$. When a flow's throughput is 0, its log value is undefined, so we set its throughput to 1 Kbps. Figure 10 shows the proportional fairness as we vary the number of unicast flows in the testbed. The three routing schemes that support rate limiting significantly out-perform MORE and shortest path without rate limiting since the latter two can easily cause starvation. Among those that support rate limit, our protocol performs the best due to its opportunistic routing and high-fidelity model.

Multicast flows: Finally, we evaluate the performance of multicast in our testbed. Figure 11 shows the throughput of the bottleneck multicast receiver in one multicast group, where the multicast group size is varied from 2 to 4. Our protocol performs the best. It out-performs the protocol with CG by 16%-38%, MORE by 10%-63%, shortest path with rate limiting by 68%-89%, and shortest path routing by 101%-181%. In addition, by leveraging the broadcast wireless medium, all types of opportunistic routing, including MORE, out-perform both versions of shortest path routing. These results suggest opportunistic routing is even more useful to multicast, and the effective optimization of multicast routes and rate limiting continues to be important.

9.3 Summary of Performance

The simulation and testbed results show that our protocol consistently out-performs the alternatives. By leveraging opportunistic transmissions and effective route optimization, it significantly out-performs state-of-the-art shortest path routing protocols. By using a high fidelity network model to jointly optimize rate limits and opportunistic routes, it significantly out-performs state-of-the-art opportunistic routing protocols. These benefits suggest that all the

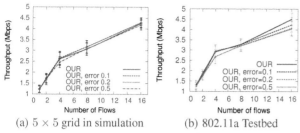

(a) 5 × 5 grid in simulation (b) 802.11a Testbed

Figure 12: Throughput under inaccurate traffic estimates.

design components in our protocol, including opportunistic routing, network model, and joint rate limit and route optimization, are essential and help improve the performance.

10. EVALUATION OF SENSITIVITY

10.1 Impact of Inaccurate Traffic Demand

Methodology: We first evaluate the performance under inaccurate traffic demand estimation, since in practice traffic demands fluctuate and may not be known exactly. The actual traffic demands are uniformly distributed between 0 and the maximum link throughput. To simulate demand estimation error, we inject errors into the actual demands and feed the salted demands to our optimization framework while imposing the actual demands to the network for evaluation. The error injected is uniformly distributed between 0-10%, 0-20%, and 0-50%. To protect against estimation error, our protocol slightly over-provisions by scaling the derived sending rates from the optimization output by a factor of 1.1.

Simulation: Figure 12(a) shows the total throughput versus the number of flows. We see similar performance across different error ranges. This indicates that our protocol is fairly robust against demand estimation errors, because for the purpose of performance optimization, the spatial traffic demand distribution is more important than the exact demand values.

Testbed: Figure 12(b) shows the performance of our protocol when we feed inaccurate traffic demands as input to our optimization. As in simulation, it is robust to the inaccuracy in traffic demand estimation in testbed. Its performance under no error is close to that under the relative error of 0.5.

10.2 Impact of Unknown External Interference and Loss Fluctuation

10.2.1 Simulation

Methodology: We create external interference by randomly placing two external noise sources in 25-node random topologies. All protocols compute routes and rate limits without considering the external noise, and we measure the throughput of using the derived routes and rate limits under external noise. The noise sources have uniformly distributed on and off time, where the average on-time is 0.25 second and the total simulation time is 20 seconds. We vary the average off-time so that every noise source is on 10% to 80% of time. During on-time, each noise source broadcasts 802.11 packets (with 1024-byte payload) as fast as possible.

Model validation: First, we compare actual throughput under external noise versus estimated throughput derived without considering the noise sources. As shown in Figure 13(a), the accuracy of our protocol degrades gracefully as we increase the on-time of each noise source. The fractions of runs that achieve within 30% error are 99% under 10% noise on-time, 76% under 20% noise on-time, and 56% under 30% noise on-time. Moreover, even with 30% noise on-time, it achieves much higher predictability than the protocol with CG model under no external noise.

Performance comparison: As shown in Figure 13(b), the ranking of different protocols remains the same across all noise levels. Our

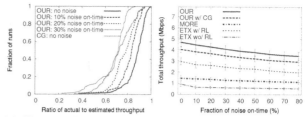

(a) CDF of ratios between actual (b) Total throughput of 8 flows and estimated throughput

Figure 13: Simulation results under 2 noise sources with varying on-time in 25-node 802.11a random topologies.

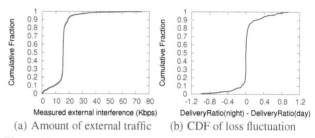

(a) Amount of external traffic (b) CDF of loss fluctuation

Figure 14: Amount of external traffic from the campus network and loss fluctuation in our 802.11b testbed.

protocol consistently out-performs all other protocols. Even when every noise source is active 80% of time, it out-performs the one with CG by 18%, shortest path with rate limiting by 75%, MORE by 209%, and shortest path without rate limiting by 535%. Moreover, the performance of different protocols degrades smoothly as the on-time of each noise source increases.

10.2.2 Testbed

Methodology: We also evaluate the sensitivity in an 802.11b testbed consisting of 22 nodes. As before, we randomly select flows in our network. As common practice, we run the link loss measurements at night, which has low network activity. Then we run all evaluation during the day. This allows us to evaluate the sensitivity against unknown external interference and loss fluctuation. In particular, our building has an active 802.11g campus network, whose traffic directly interferes with our wireless mesh traffic. We treat traffic from the campus network as unknown external interference. Figure 14(a) plots the CDF of the average campus network traffic measured by all mesh nodes in promiscuous mode every 30 seconds. The median and mean are both 15.5 Kbps. Moreover, loss fluctuates from nights to daytime. Figure 14(b) plots a CDF of $DeliveryRatio(night) - DeliveryRatio(day)$ over all links that have $\geq 5\%$ delivery rates. We observe loss fluctuation, because during the day time (i) more people sit near mesh nodes and cause more attenuation, and (ii) more people move around and close/open doors and cause frequent changes to the RF environment.

Model validation: Figure 15 shows the scatter plot of actual versus estimated throughput from the 802.11b testbed. We also plot $y = x$ and $y = 0.8x$ for reference. Our protocol continues to exhibit high predictability: 78% of runs have within 20% error.

Performance comparison: As shown in Figure 16, our protocol continues to perform the best. Different from simulation, MORE sometimes performs worse than shortest path without rate limiting because the network congestion in MORE is more severe in a dense network like our 802.11b testbed.

11. CONCLUSION

In this paper, we present the first protocol that can accurately optimize the performance of opportunistic routing in IEEE 802.11 networks. Our framework consists of three key components: (i) a simple yet effective wireless network model to support optimiza-

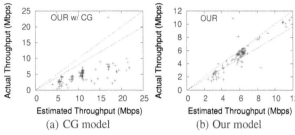

(a) CG model (b) Our model

Figure 15: Actual vs. estimated throughput in 802.11b testbed under unknown external interference and loss fluctuation.

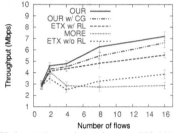

Figure 16: Unicast throughput in our 802.11b testbed under unknown external interference and loss fluctuation.

tion, (ii) a novel algorithm for optimizing different performance objectives, and (iii) an opportunistic routing protocol that effectively maps solutions resulted from our optimization into practical routing configurations. Through testbed implementation and simulation, we show that the performance of our protocol is close to our estimation, and is much better than state-of-the-art shortest path routing and opportunistic routing protocols. Moreover, it is robust against inaccuracy introduced by a dynamic network and it also consistently out-performs the existing schemes. To further enhance the robustness against traffic and topology variations, in the future we plan to extend the robust traffic engineering techniques developed in the Internet to optimize wireless networks. In particular, a traffic engineering system usually collects a set of traffic matrices and uses their convex combination to cover the space of common traffic patterns for optimization. These new demand constraints are compact and can be easily incorporated into our framework. We plan to extend this technique to cope with both traffic and topology variations in wireless networks.

Acknowledgments: This research is supported in part by NSF grants CNS-0916106, CNS-0546755, and CNS-0546720. We thank Sem Borst and anonymous reviewers for their valuable comments.

12. REFERENCES

[1] S. Agarwal, J. Padhye, V. N. Padmanabhan, L. Qiu, A. Rao, and B. Zill. Estimation of link interference in static multi-hop wireless networks. In *Proc. of IMC*, 2005.
[2] D. Aguayo, J. Bicket, S. Biswas, G. Judd, and R. Morris. Link-level measurements from an 802.11b mesh network. In *Proc. of SIGCOMM*, 2004.
[3] N. Ahmed, U. Ismail, S. Keshav, and K. Papagiannaki. Online estimation of RF interference. In *Proc. of ACM CoNext*, Dec. 2008.
[4] N. Ahmed and S. Keshav. SMARTA: A self-managing architecture for thin access points. In *Proc. of ACM CoNEXT*, Dec. 2006.
[5] G. Bianchi. Performance analysis of the IEEE 802.11 distributed corrdination function. *IEEE Journal on Selected Areas in Communications*, Mar. 2000.
[6] S. Biswas and R. Morris. ExOR: Opportunistic multi-hop routing for wireless networks. In *Proc. of ACM SIGCOMM*, Aug. 2005.
[7] S. Chachulski, M. Jennings, S. Katti, and D. Katabi. Trading structure for randomness in wireless opportunistic routing. In *Proc. of SIGCOMM*, 2007.
[8] Click. http://pdos.csail.mit.edu/click/.
[9] D. D. Couto, D. Aguayo, J. Bicket, and R. Morris. A high-throughput path metric for multi-hop wireless routing. In *Proc. of ACM MobiCom*, 2003.
[10] H. Dubois-Ferrier, M. Grossglauser, and M. Vetterli. Least-cost opportunistic routing. In *Proc. of Allerton*, Sept. 2007.
[11] H. Feng, Y. Shu, S. Wang, and M. Ma. SVM-based models for predicting WLAN traffic. In *Proc. of IEEE ICC*, 2006.
[12] Y. Gao, J. Lui, and D. M. Chiu. Determining the end-to-end throughput capacity in multi-hop networks: Methodolgy and applications. In *Proc. of ACM SIGMETRICS*, Jun. 2006.

[13] M. Garetto, T. Salonidis, , and E. Knightly. Modeling per-flow throughput and capturing starvation in CSMA multi-hop wireless networks. In *Proc. of IEEE INFOCOM*, Mar. 2006.
[14] M. Garetto, J. Shi, and E. Knightly. Modeling media access in embedded two-flow topologies of multi-hop wireless networks. In *Proc. of ACM MobiCom*, Aug. - Sept. 2005.
[15] M. Grossglauser and D. N. C. Tse. Mobility increases the capacity of ad hoc wireless networks. In *Proc. of IEEE INFOCOM*, Apr. 2001.
[16] P. Gupta and P. R. Kumar. The capacity of wireless networks. *IEEE Transactions on Information Theory*, 46(2), Mar. 2000.
[17] K. Jain, J. Padhye, V. N. Padmanabhan, and L. Qiu. Impact of interference on multi-hop wireless network performance. In *Proc. ACM MobiCom*, 2003.
[18] A. Kashyap, S. Das, and S. Ganguly. A measurement-based approach to modeling link capacity in 802.11-based wireless networks. In *Proc. of ACM MobiCom*, Sept. 2007.
[19] F. P. Kelly, A. K. Maulloo, and D. K. H. Tan. Rate control in communication networks: Shadow prices, proportional fairness and stability. *Jounal of the Operational Research Society*, 1998.
[20] D. Koutsonikolas, C.-C. Wang, and Y. C. Hu. CCACK: Efficient network coding based opportunistic routing through cumulative coded acknowledgments. In *Proc. of IEEE INFOCOM*, 2010.
[21] A. Kumar, E. Altman, D. Miorandi, and M. Goyal. New insights from a fixed point analysis of single cell IEEE 802.11 wireless LANs. In *Proc. of IEEE INFOCOM*, Mar. 2005.
[22] J. Li, C. Blake, D. S. J. D. Couto, H. I. Lee, and R. Morris. Capacity of ad hoc wireless networks. In *Proc. of MobiCom*, Jul. 2001.
[23] Y. Li, L. Qiu, Y. Zhang, R. Mahajan, and E. Rozner. Predictable performance optimization for wireless networks. In *Proc. of ACM SIGCOMM*, Aug. 2008.
[24] Y. Lin, B. Li, and B. Liang. CodeOR: Opportunistic routing in wireless mesh networks with segmented network coding. In *Proc. of IEEE ICNP*, Oct. 2008.
[25] Y. Lin, B. Liang, and B. Li. SlideOR: Online opportunistic network coding in wireless mesh networks. In *Proc. of IEEE INFOCOM*, Mar. 2010.
[26] D. Lun, M. Medard, and R. Koetter. Network coding for efficient wireless unicast. *International Zurich Seminar on Communications*, 2006.
[27] MadWiFi. http://madwifi.org.
[28] A. K. Miu, H. Balakrishnan, and C. E. Koksal. Improving loss resilience with multi-radio diversity in wireless networks. In *Proc. of ACM MobiCom*, 2005.
[29] A. K. Miu, G. Tan, H. Balakrishnan, and J. Apostolopoulos. Divert: Fine-grained path selection for wireless LANs. In *Proc. of ACM MobiSys*, 2004.
[30] MORE source code. http://people.csail.mit.edu/szym/more/README.html.
[31] D. Niculescu. Interference map for 802.11 networks. In *Proc. of IMC*, 2007.
[32] L. M. S. C. of the IEEE Computer Society. Wireless LAN medium access control (MAC) and physical layer (PHY) specifications. *IEEE Standard 802.11*, 1999.
[33] L. Qiu, Y. Zhang, F. Wang, M. K. Han, and R. Mahajan. A general model of wireless interference. In *Proc. of ACM MobiCom*, Sept. 2007.
[34] The Qualnet simulator from Scalable Networks Inc. http://www.scalable-networks.com/.
[35] B. Radunovic and J. Y. L. Boudec. Rate performance objectives of multihop wireless networks. In *Proc. of IEEE INFOCOM*, Apr. 2004.
[36] B. Radunovic, C. Gkantsidis, P. Key, and P. Rodriguez. An optimization framework for opportunistic multipath routing in wireless mesh networks. In *Proc. of IEEE INFOCOM*, Apr. 2008.
[37] C. Reis, R. Mahajan, M. Rodrig, D. Wetherall, and J. Zahorjan. Measurement-based models of delivery and interference. In *Proc. of ACM SIGCOMM*, 2006.
[38] M. Rodrig, C. Reis, R. Mahajan, D. Wetherall, and J. Zahorjan. Measurement-based characterization of 802.11 in a hotspot setting. In *Proc. of E-WIND*, Aug. 2005.
[39] E. Rozner, M. K. Han, L. Qiu, and Y. Zhang. Model-driven optimization of opportunistic routing. Technical Report TR-11-12, The University of Texas at Austin, Dept. of Computer Science, Austin, TX, 2010.
[40] T. Salonidis, M. Garetto, A. Saha, and E. Knightly. Identifying high throughput paths in 802.11 mesh networks: A model-based approach. In *Proc. of IEEE ICNP*, Oct. 2007.
[41] S. Sengupta, S. Rayanchu, and S. Banerjee. An analysis of wireless network coding for unicast sessions: The case for coding-aware routing. In *Proc. of IEEE INFOCOM*, Apr. 2007.
[42] J. K. Shapiro, D. Towsley, and J. Kurose. Optimization-based congestion control for multicast communications. *IEEE Communication Magazine*, 2002.
[43] F. Soldo, A. Markopoulou, and A. Toledo. A simple optimization model for wireless opportunistic routing with intra-session network coding. In *Proc. of IEEE NetCod*, Jun. 2010.
[44] K. Srinivasan, M. Jain, J. I. Choi, T. Azim, E. S. Kim, P. Levis, and B. Krishnamachari. The kappa factor: Inferring protocol performance using inter-link reception correlation. In *Proc. of ACM MobiCom*, 2010.
[45] J. J. T. Ho and H. Viswanathan. On network coding and routing in dynamic wireless multicast networks. In *Proc. of Workshop on Information Theory and its Applications*, 2006.
[46] K. Zeng, W. Lou, and H. Zhai. On end-to-end throughput of opportunistic routing in multirate and multihop wireless networks. In *Proc. of IEEE INFOCOM*, Apr. 2008.
[47] K. Zeng and Z. Y. W. Lou. Oportunistic routing in multi-radio multi-channel multi-hop wireless networks. In *Proc. of IEEE INFOCOM*, Mar. 2010.
[48] X. Zhang and B. Li. Optimized multipath network coding in lossy wireless networks. In *Proc. of IEEE ICDCS*, 2008.

Walking on a Graph with a Magnifying Glass:
Stratified Sampling via Weighted Random Walks

Maciej Kurant
CalIT2
UC Irvine
mkurant@uci.edu

Minas Gjoka
CalIT2
UC Irvine
mgjoka@uci.edu

Carter T. Butts
Sociology Dept, CalIT2
UC Irvine
buttsc@uci.edu

Athina Markopoulou
EECS, CalIT2, CPCC
UC Irvine
athina@uci.edu

ABSTRACT

Our objective is to sample the node set of a large unknown graph via crawling, to accurately estimate a given metric of interest. We design a random walk on an appropriately defined weighted graph that achieves high efficiency by preferentially crawling those nodes and edges that convey greater information regarding the target metric. Our approach begins by employing the theory of stratification to find optimal node weights, for a given estimation problem, under an independence sampler. While optimal under independence sampling, these weights may be impractical under graph crawling due to constraints arising from the structure of the graph. Therefore, the edge weights for our random walk should be chosen so as to lead to an equilibrium distribution that strikes a balance between approximating the optimal weights under an independence sampler and achieving fast convergence. We propose a heuristic approach (stratified weighted random walk, or S-WRW) that achieves this goal, while using only limited information about the graph structure and the node properties. We evaluate our technique in simulation, and experimentally, by collecting a sample of Facebook college users. We show that S-WRW requires 13-15 times fewer samples than the simple re-weighted random walk (RW) to achieve the same estimation accuracy for a range of metrics.

Categories and Subject Descriptors

C.4 [**Performance of Systems**]: Measurement techniques

General Terms

Measurement, Algorithms

Keywords

Graph Sampling, Random Walks on Weighted Graphs, Stratified Sampling, Online Social Networks.

* This work was supported by SNF grant PBELP2-130871, Switzerland, and by the NSF CDI Award 1028394, USA.

1. INTRODUCTION

Many types of online networks, such as online social networks (OSNs), Peer-to-Peer (P2P) networks, or the World Wide Web (WWW), are measured and studied today via sampling techniques. This is due to several reasons. First, such graphs are typically too large to measure in their entirety, and it is desirable to be able to study them based on a small but representative sample. Second, the information pertaining to these networks is often hard to obtain. For example, OSN service providers have access to all information in their user base, but rarely make this information publicly available.

There are many ways a graph can be sampled, *e.g.,* by sampling nodes, edges, paths, or other substructures [23, 28]. Depending on our measurement goal, the elements with different properties may have *different importance* and should be sampled with a different probability. For example, Fig. 1(a) depicts the world's population, with residents of China (1.3B people) represented by blue nodes, of the Vatican (800 people) by black nodes, and all other nationalities represented by white nodes. Assume that we want to compare the median income in China and Vatican. Taking a uniform sample of size 100 from the entire world's population is ineffective, because most of the samples will come from countries other than China and Vatican. Even restricting our sample to the union of China and Vatican will not help much, as our sample is unlikely to include any Vatican resident. In contrast, uniformly sampling 50 Chinese and 50 Vaticanese residents would be much more accurate with the same sampling budget.

This type of problem has been widely studied in the statistical and survey sampling literature. A commonly used approach is *stratified sampling* [12,29,35], where nodes (*e.g.,* people) are partitioned into a set of non-overlapping *categories* (or strata). The objective is then to decide how many independent draws to take from each category, so as to minimize the uncertainty of the resulting measurement. This effect can be achieved in expectation by a weighted independence sampler (WIS) with appropriately chosen sampling probabilities π^{WIS}. In our example, WIS samples Vatican residents with much higher probabilities than Chinese ones, and avoids completely the rest of the world, as illustrated in Fig. 1(b).

However, WIS, as every independence sampler, requires a sampling frame, *i.e.,* a list of all elements we can sample from (*e.g.,* a list of all Facebook users). This information is typically not available in today's online networks. A feasible alternative is *crawling* (also known as exploration or link-

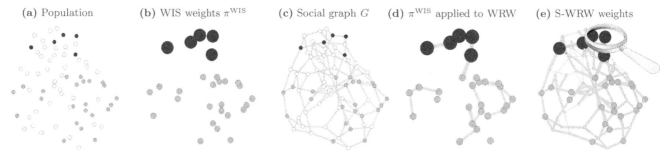

(a) Population   **(b)** WIS weights π^{WIS} **(c)** Social graph G **(d)** π^{WIS} applied to WRW   **(e)** S-WRW weights

Figure 1: Illustrative example. Our goal is to compare the blue and black subpopulations (*e.g.*, with respect to their median income) in population (a). Optimal independence sampler, WIS (b), over-samples the black nodes, under-samples the blue nodes, and completely skips the white nodes. A naive crawling approach, RW (c), samples many irrelevant white nodes. WRW that enforces WIS-optimal probabilities may result in poor or no convergence (d). S-WRW (e) strikes a balance between the optimality of WIS and fast convergence.

trace sampling). It is a graph sampling technique in which we can see the neighbors of already sampled users and make a decision on which users to visit next.

In this paper, we study how to perform stratified sampling through graph crawling. We illustrate the key idea and some of the challenges in Fig. 1. Fig. 1(c) depicts a social network that connects the world's population. A simple random walk (RW) visits every node with frequency proportional to its degree, which is reflected by the node size. In this particular example, for a simplicity of illustration, all nodes have the same degree equal to 3. As a result, RW is equivalent to the uniform sample of the world's population, and faces exactly the same problems of wasting resources, by sampling all nodes with the same probability.

We address these problems by appropriately setting the edge weights and then performing a random walk on the weighted graph, which we refer to as *weighted random walk* (WRW). One goal in setting the weights is to mimic the WIS-optimal sampling probabilities π^{WIS} shown in Fig. 1(b). However, such a WRW might perform poorly due to potentially slow mixing. In our example, it will not even converge because the underlying weighted graph is disconnected, as shown in Fig. 1(d). Therefore, the edge weights under WRW (which determine the equilibrium distribution π^{WRW}) should be chosen in a way that strikes a balance between the optimality of π^{WIS} and fast convergence.

We propose *Stratified Weighted Random Walk* (S-WRW), a practical heuristic that effectively strikes such a balance. We refer to our approach as "walking on the graph with a magnifying glass", because S-WRW over-samples more relevant parts of the graph and under-samples less relevant ones. In our example, S-WRW results in the graph presented in Fig. 1(e). The only information required by S-WRW are the categories of neighbors of every visited node, which is typically available in crawlable online networks, such as Facebook. S-WRW uses two natural and easy-to-interpret parameters, namely: (i) $\hat{f}_\ominus$, which controls the fraction of samples from irrelevant categories and (ii) γ, which is the maximal resolution of our magnifying glass, with respect to the largest relevant category.

The main contributions of this paper are the following.

- We propose to improve the efficiency of crawling-based graph sampling methods, by performing a stratified weighted random walk that takes into account not only the graph structure but also the node properties that are relevant to the measurement goal.

- We design and evaluate S-WRW, a practical heuristic that sets the edge weights and operates with limited information.

- As a case study, we apply S-WRW to sample Facebook and estimate the sizes of colleges. We show that S-WRW requires 13-15 times fewer samples than a simple random walk for the same estimation accuracy.

The outline of the rest of the paper is as follows. Section 2 summarizes the graph sampling techniques. Section 3 introduces S-WRW that combines stratified sampling with graph crawling. Section 4 presents simulation results. Section 5 presents an implementation of S-WRW for the problem of sampling college users on Facebook. Section 6 reviews related work. Section 7 concludes the paper.

2. SAMPLING TECHNIQUES

2.1 Notation

We consider an undirected, static,[1] graph $G = (V, E)$, with $N = |V|$ nodes and $|E|$ edges. For a node $v \in V$, denote by $\deg(v)$ its degree, and by $\mathcal{N}(v) \subset V$ the list of neighbors of v. A graph G can be weighted. We denote by $\text{w}(u,v)$ the weight of edge $\{u,v\} \in E$, and by

$$\text{w}(u) = \sum_{v \in \mathcal{N}(u)} \text{w}(u,v) \qquad (1)$$

the weight of node $u \in V$. For any set of nodes $A \subseteq V$, we define its volume $\text{vol}(A)$ and weight $\text{w}(A)$, respectively, as

$$\text{vol}(A) = \sum_{v \in A} \deg(v) \quad \text{and} \quad \text{w}(A) = \sum_{v \in A} \text{w}(v). \qquad (2)$$

We will often use

$$f_A = \frac{|A|}{|V|} \quad \text{and} \quad f_A^{\text{vol}} = \frac{\text{vol}(A)}{\text{vol}(V)} \qquad (3)$$

to denote the relative size of A in terms of the number of nodes and the volumes, respectively.

Sampling. We collect a sample $S \subseteq V$ of $n = |S|$ nodes. S may contain multiple copies of the same node, *i.e.*, the sampling is with replacement. In this section, we briefly review the techniques for sampling nodes from graph G. We also present the weighted random walk (WRW) which is the basic building block for our approach.

---

[1]Sampling dynamic graphs is currently an active research area [36,41,43], but out of the scope of this paper.

2.2 Independence Sampling

Uniform Independence Sampling (UIS) samples the nodes directly from the set V, with replacements, uniformly and independently at random, i.e., with probability

$$\pi^{\text{UIS}}(v) \;=\; \frac{1}{N} \qquad \text{for every } v \in V. \tag{4}$$

Weighted Independence Sampling (WIS) is a weighted version of UIS. WIS samples the nodes directly from the set V, with replacements, independently at random, but with probabilities proportional to node weights $w(v)$:

$$\pi^{\text{WIS}}(v) \;=\; \frac{w(v)}{\sum_{u \in V} w(u)}. \tag{5}$$

In general, UIS and WIS are not possible in online networks because of the lack of sampling frame. For example, the list of all user IDs may not be publicly available, or the user ID space may be too sparsely allocated. Nevertheless, we present them as baseline for comparison with the random walks.

2.3 Sampling via Crawling

In contrast to independence sampling, the crawling techniques are possible in many online networks, and are therefore the main focus of this paper.

Simple Random Walk (RW) [30] selects the next-hop node v uniformly at random among the neighbors of the current node u. In a connected and aperiodic graph, the probability of being at the particular node v converges to the stationary distribution

$$\pi^{\text{RW}}(v) \;=\; \frac{\deg(v)}{2 \cdot |E|}. \tag{6}$$

Metropolis-Hastings Random Walk (MHRW) is an application of the Metropolis-Hastings algorithm [31] that modifies the transition probabilities to converge to a desired stationary distribution. For example, we can achieve the uniform stationary distribution

$$\pi^{\text{MHRW}}(v) \;=\; \frac{1}{N} \tag{7}$$

by randomly selecting a neighbor v of the current node u and moving there with probability $\min(1, \frac{\deg(u)}{\deg(v)})$. However, it was shown in [18,36] that RW (after re-weighting, as in Section 2.4) outperforms MHRW for most applications. We therefore restrict our attention to comparing against RW.

Weighted Random Walk (WRW) is RW on a weighted graph [4]. At node u, WRW chooses the edge $\{u, v\}$ to follow with probability $P_{u,v}$ proportional to the weight $w(u, v) \geq 0$ of this edge, i.e.,

$$P_{u,v} = \frac{w(u, v)}{\sum_{v' \in \mathcal{N}(u)} w(u, v')}. \tag{8}$$

The stationary distribution of WRW is:

$$\pi^{\text{WRW}}(v) \;=\; \frac{w(v)}{\sum_{u \in V} w(u)}. \tag{9}$$

WRW is the basic building block of our design. In the next sections, we show how to choose weights for a specific estimation problem.

Graph Traversals (BFS, DFS, RDS, ...) is a family of crawling techniques where no node is sampled more than once. Because traversals introduce a generally unknown bias (see Section 6), we do not consider them in this paper.

2.4 Correcting the bias

RW, WRW, and WIS all produce biased (nonuniform) node samples. But their bias is known and therefore can be corrected by an appropriate re-weighting of the measured values. This can be done using the Hansen-Hurwitz estimator [20] as first shown in [40,42] for random walks and also used in [36]. Let every node $v \in V$ carry a value $x(v)$. We can estimate the population total $x_{\text{tot}} = \sum_v x(v)$ by

$$\hat{x}_{\text{tot}} = \frac{1}{n} \sum_{v \in S} \frac{x(v)}{\pi(v)}, \tag{10}$$

where $\pi(v)$ is the sampling probability of node v in the stationary distribution. In practice, we usually know $\pi(v)$, and thus $\hat{x}_{\text{tot}}$, only up to a constant, i.e., we know the (non-normalized) weights $w(v)$. This problem disappears when we estimate the population mean $x_{\text{av}} = \sum_v x(v)/N$ as

$$\hat{x}_{\text{av}} \;=\; \frac{\sum_{v \in S} \frac{x(v)}{\pi(v)}}{\sum_{v \in S} \frac{1}{\pi(v)}} \;=\; \frac{\sum_{v \in S} \frac{x(v)}{w(v)}}{\sum_{v \in S} \frac{1}{w(v)}}. \tag{11}$$

For example, for $x(v) = 1$ if $\deg(v) = k$ (and $x(v) = 0$ otherwise), $\hat{x}_{\text{av}}(k)$ estimates the node degree distribution in G.

All the results in this paper are presented *after this re-weighting* step, whenever necessary.

3. STRATIFIED WRW

In this section we introduce Stratified Weighted Random Walk (S-WRW). S-WRW builds on stratification under the optimal independence sampler, and additionally addresses practical challenges arising in graph crawling.

3.1 Stratified Independence Sampling

In Section 1, we argued that in order to compare the median income of residents of China and Vatican we should take 50 random samples from each of these two countries, rather than taking 100 UIS samples from China and Vatican together (or, even worse, from the world's population). This problem naturally arises in the field of survey sampling. A common solution is *stratified sampling* [12,29,35], where nodes V are partitioned into a set $\mathcal{C} = \{C_1, C_2, \ldots, C_{|\mathcal{C}|}\}$ of non-overlapping node categories (or "strata"), with union $\bigcup_{C \in \mathcal{C}} C = V$. Next, we select uniformly at random n_i nodes from category C_i. We are free to choose the allocation $(n_1, n_2, \ldots, n_{|\mathcal{C}|})$, as long as we respect the total budget of samples $n = \sum_i n_i$.

There are many possible allocations n_i. We are interested in the optimal allocation n_i^{opt}, that minimizes the measurement error with respect to our measurement objective. In [25] we show how to calculate n_i^{opt} for various measurement scenarios. One obvious hint is to set $n_{\ominus}^{\text{opt}} = 0$ for the *irrelevant category* $C_{\ominus} \in \mathcal{C}$ that groups all nodes not relevant to our measurement objective. For example, in Fig. 1, $C_{\ominus}$ consists of all white nodes.

We also show in [25] how to allocate the samples between the relevant categories. If (i) we are interested in comparing the node categories with respect to some properties (e.g., average node degree, category size) rather than estimating a property across the entire population, and (ii) no additional information is available (such as property variances - rarely known in practice), then we should take an equal number of samples from every relevant category, *i.e.*, use

$$n_i^{\text{opt}} = \frac{n}{|\mathcal{C} \setminus \{C_\ominus\}|} \qquad \text{for every } C_i \neq C_\ominus. \qquad (12)$$

Stratification in Expectation with WIS. Ideally, we would like to enforce strictly stratified sampling and collect exactly n_i^{opt} samples from category C_i. However, when we use crawling, strict stratification is possible only by discarding observations. It is thus more natural to frame the problem in terms of the probability mass placed on each category, with the goal of collecting n_i^{opt} samples from category C_i *in expectation*. Under WIS, this is achieved by enforcing that (see Appendix C for the derivation):

$$\text{w}^{\text{WIS}}(C_i) \propto n_i^{\text{opt}}, \qquad (13)$$

where $\text{w}^{\text{WIS}}(C_i) = \sum_{v \in C_i} \text{w}^{\text{WIS}}(v)$ is the weight of category C_i. In strictly stratified sampling, the individual node sampling probabilities $\text{w}^{\text{WIS}}(v)$ are equal across the category C_i. Achieving it by setting the edge weights (as we do in crawling) would require the knowledge of entire graph G before we start sampling, which is, of course, impractical. Instead, we show below that we are able to effectively obtain the necessary information at the category-level granularity, which allows us to control the aggregated weight $\widehat{\text{w}}^{\text{WIS}}(C_i)$.

3.2 Stratified Crawling

We have argued earlier that, due to lack of a sampling frame, the independence sampling (including its stratified version) is typically infeasible in online networks, making crawling the only practical alternative. In this section, we show how to perform a weighted random walk (WRW) which approximates the stratified sampling. The general problem can be stated as follows:

Given a category-related measurement objective, an error metric and a sampling budget $|S| = n$, set the edge weights in graph G such that WRW on this graph achieves a minimal estimation error.

Although we are able to solve this problem analytically for some specific and fully known topologies, it is not obvious how to address it in general, especially under a limited knowledge of G. Instead, in this paper, we propose S-WRW, a heuristic to set the edge weights. S-WRW starts from a solution that is optimal under WIS, and takes into account practical issues that arise in graph crawling. Once the edge weights in G are set, we simply perform a WRW as described in Section 2.3 and we collect node samples.

3.3 Our practical solution: S-WRW

As the main (but not the only) guideline, S-WRW tries to realize the category weights that are optimal under WIS, *i.e.*, to achieve

$$\text{w}^{\text{WRW}}(C_i) = \text{w}^{\text{WIS}}(C_i). \qquad (14)$$

There are many edge weight settings in G that satisfy it. We give preference to equal weights, as follows. First, note that if every edge incident on nodes of C_i carries the same weight $\text{w}_e(C_i)$, then $\text{w}^{\text{WRW}}(C_i) = \text{w}_e(C_i) \cdot \text{vol}(C_i)$. Consequently, we can achieve Eq.(14) by setting

$$\text{w}_e(C_i) = \frac{\text{w}^{\text{WIS}}(C_i)}{\text{vol}(C_i)}.$$

| **Step 1: Estimation of Category Volumes** |
| Estimate f_i^{vol} with a pilot RW estimator $\widehat{f}_i^{\text{vol}}$ as in Eq.(26). |

| **Step 2: Category Weights Optimal Under WIS** |
| For a measurement objective, calculate $\text{w}^{\text{WIS}}(C_i)$ as in Section 3.1. |

| **Step 3: Include Irrelevant Categories** |
| Modify $\text{w}^{\text{WIS}}(C_i)$. $\tilde{f}_\ominus$: desired fraction of irrelevant nodes. |

| **Step 4: Tiny and Unknown Categories** |
| Modify $\widehat{f}_i^{\text{vol}}$. γ: maximal resolution. |

| **Step 5: Edge Conflict Resolution** |
| Set the weights of inter-category edges (Section 3.3.5). |

| **WRW sample** |
| Use transition probabilities proportional to edge weights (Sec.2.3). |

| **Correct for the bias** |
| Apply formulas from Section 2.4. |

| **Final result** |

Figure 2: Overview of S-WRW.

In fact, we need to know $\text{w}_e(C_i)$ only up to a constant factor, because these factors cancel out in the calculation of transition probabilities of WRW in Eq.(8). Therefore, exactly the same WRW can be obtained by setting

$$\text{w}_e(C_i) = \frac{\text{w}^{\text{WIS}}(C_i)}{f_i^{\text{vol}}}. \qquad (15)$$

This formulation replaces the absolute volume $\text{vol}(C_i)$ of category C_i by its relative version f_i^{vol} that is much easier to estimate (similarly to x_{tot} and x_{av} in Section 2.4).

Eq.(15) is central to the S-WRW heuristic. But in order to apply it, we first have to calculate or estimate its terms f_i^{vol} and $\text{w}^{\text{WIS}}(C_i)$. Below, we show how to do that in Steps 1 and 2, respectively. Next, in Steps 3-5, we show how to modify these terms to account for practical problems arising from the underlying graph structure.

3.3.1 Step 1: Estimation of Category Volumes

In general, we have no prior information about G. Fortunately, it is easy and inexpensive to estimate the relative category volumes f_i^{vol}, which is the first piece of information we need in Eq.(15). Indeed, it is enough to run a relatively short *pilot* RW, and use the collected sample S in Eq.(26) derived in Appendix B, and repeated here for convenience:

$$\widehat{f}_i^{\text{vol}} = \frac{1}{n} \sum_{u \in S} \left(\frac{1}{\deg(u)} \sum_{v \in \mathcal{N}(u)} 1_{\{v \in C_i\}} \right).$$

3.3.2 Step 2: Category Weights Optimal Under WIS

In order to find the optimal WIS category weights $\text{w}^{\text{WIS}}(C_i)$ in Eq.(15), we first count all the categories discovered by the pilot RW in Step 1, and use it as an estimator of the real number $|\mathcal{C}|$ of existing categories. Next, we calculate n_i^{opt} as shown in Section 3.1, and we plug it in Eq.(13), *e.g.*, by setting $\text{w}^{\text{WIS}}(C_i) = n_i^{\text{opt}}$.

In particular, in the case where all relevant categories are equally important (which is rather common), we apply Eq.(12) and Eq.(13). This boils down to assigning the

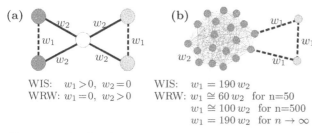

Figure 3: Optimal edge weights: WIS vs WRW. The objective is to compare the sizes of red (dark) and green (light) categories.

same weight to every category C_i, *e.g.*, $\mathrm{w}^{\mathrm{WIS}}(C_i) = 1$, with no need of exploiting the pilot RW.

3.3.3 Step 3: Irrelevant Categories

Problem: Potentially poor or no convergence. Trying to achieve the optimal category weights may lead to poor or no convergence of the random walk. We already discussed this problem in Fig. 1. As another illustrative example, consider the toy example in Fig. 3(a) and assume that we are interested in finding the relative sizes of red (dark) and green (light) categories. The white node in the middle is irrelevant for our measurement objective. Due to symmetry, we distinguish between two types of edges with weights w_1 and w_2. Under WIS, the optimal weights are $w_1 > 0$ and $w_2 = 0$ (see [25]), *i.e.*, WIS samples every non-white node with the same probability and never samples the white one. However, under WRW with these weights, relevant nodes get disconnected into two components and WRW does not converge.

Guideline: Occasionally visit irrelevant nodes. We show in [25] that the optimal WRW weights in Fig. 3(a) are $w_1 = 0$ and $w_2 > 0$. In that case, half of the samples are due to visits in the white (irrelevant) node. In other words, WRW may benefit from allocating small weight $\mathring{\mathrm{w}}(C_\ominus) > 0$ to category $C_\ominus$ that groups all (if any) categories irrelevant to our estimation. The intuition is that irrelevant nodes may not contribute to estimation but may be needed for connectivity or fast mixing.

Implementation in S-WRW. In S-WRW, we achieve this goal by replacing in Eq.(15) the term $\mathrm{w}^{\mathrm{WIS}}(C_i)$ with

$$\tilde{\mathrm{w}}^{\mathrm{WIS}}(C_i) = \begin{cases} \mathrm{w}^{\mathrm{WIS}}(C_i) & \text{if } C_i \neq C_\ominus \\ \tilde{f}_\ominus \cdot \sum_{C \neq C_\ominus} \mathrm{w}^{\mathrm{WIS}}(C) & \text{if } C_i = C_\ominus. \end{cases} \quad (16)$$

The parameter $0 \leq \tilde{f}_\ominus \ll 1$ controls the desired fraction of visits in $C_\ominus$.

3.3.4 Step 4: Tiny and Unknown Categories

Problem: "black holes". Every optical system has a fundamental magnification limit due to diffraction and our "graph magnifying glass" is no exception. Consider the toy graph in Fig. 3(b): it consists of a big clique C_{big} of 20 red nodes with edge weights w_2, and a green category C_{tiny} with two nodes only and edge weights w_1. WIS optimally estimates the relative sizes of red and green categories for $\mathrm{w}(C_{\mathrm{big}}) = \mathrm{w}(C_{\mathrm{tiny}})$, *i.e.*, for $w_1 = 190\,w_2$ (see [25]). However, for such large values of w_1, the two green nodes behave as a "black hole" for a WRW of finite length, thus increasing the variance of the category size estimation.

Guideline: limit edge weights of tiny categories. In Fig. 3(b), the setting $w_1 \simeq 60\,w_2$ ($\ll 190 w_2$) is optimal

for WRW of length $n = 50$ (simulation results). In other words, although WIS suggests to over-sample small categories, WRW should "under-over-sample" very small categories to avoid black holes.

Implementation in S-WRW. In S-WRW, we achieve this goal by replacing f_i^{vol} in Eq.(15) with

$$\tilde{f}_i^{\mathrm{vol}} = \max\left\{ \hat{f}_i^{\mathrm{vol}}, f_{\min}^{\mathrm{vol}} \right\}, \quad \text{where} \quad (17)$$

$$f_{\min}^{\mathrm{vol}} = \frac{1}{\gamma} \cdot \max_{C_i \neq C_\ominus} \{\hat{f}_i^{\mathrm{vol}}\}. \quad (18)$$

Moreover, this formulation takes care of every category C_i that was not discovered by the pilot RW in Section 3.3.1, by setting $\tilde{f}_i^{\mathrm{vol}} = f_{\min}^{\mathrm{vol}}$.

3.3.5 Step 5: Edge Conflict Resolution

Problem: Conflicting desired edge weights. With the above modifications, our target edge weights defined in Eq.(15) can be rewritten as

$$\tilde{\mathrm{w}}_e(C_i) = \frac{\tilde{\mathrm{w}}^{\mathrm{WIS}}(C_i)}{\tilde{f}_i^{\mathrm{vol}}}. \quad (19)$$

Denote by $C(v)$ the category of node v. We can directly set the weight $\mathrm{w}(u,v) = \tilde{\mathrm{w}}_e(C(u)) = \tilde{\mathrm{w}}_e(C(v))$ for every intra-category edge $\{u,v\}$. But for every inter-category edge, we may have conflicting weights $\tilde{\mathrm{w}}_e(C(u)) \neq \tilde{\mathrm{w}}_e(C(v))$ desired at the two ends of the edge in the two different categories.

Fortunately, we show in Appendix A that we can achieve any target category weights by setting edge weights (under a mild assumption that there exists at least one intra-category link within each category - this link is the required self-loop). However, the construction therein is likely to result in high weights on intra-category edges and small weights on inter-category edges, making WRW stay in small categories C_{tiny} for a long time.

Guideline: prefer inter-category edges. In order to improve the mixing time, we should do exactly the opposite, *i.e.*, assign relatively high weights to inter-category edges (connecting relevant categories). As a result, WRW will enter C_{tiny} more often, but will stay there for a short time. This intuition is motivated by Monte Carlo variance reduction techniques such as the use of *antithetic variates* [15], which seek to induce negative correlation between consecutive draws so as to reduce the variance of the resulting estimator.

Implementation in S-WRW. We assign an edge weight $\tilde{\mathrm{w}}_e$ that is in between $\tilde{\mathrm{w}}_e(C(u))$ and $\tilde{\mathrm{w}}_e(C(v))$. We consider several choices for combining the two conflicting weights.

$$\mathrm{w}^{\mathrm{ar}}(u,v) = \frac{\tilde{\mathrm{w}}_e(C(u)) + \tilde{\mathrm{w}}_e(C(v))}{2}$$

$$\mathrm{w}^{\mathrm{ge}}(u,v) = \sqrt[2]{\tilde{\mathrm{w}}_e(C(u)) \cdot \tilde{\mathrm{w}}_e(C(v))}$$

$$\mathrm{w}^{\mathrm{max}}(u,v) = \max\{\tilde{\mathrm{w}}_e(C(u)), \tilde{\mathrm{w}}_e(C(v))\}$$

$$\mathrm{w}^{\mathrm{hy}}(u,v) = \begin{cases} \mathrm{w}^{\mathrm{ge}}(u,v) & \text{if } C_\ominus \in \{C(u), C(v)\} \\ \mathrm{w}^{\mathrm{max}}(u,v) & \text{otherwise.} \end{cases}$$

w^{ar} and w^{ge} are the arithmetic and geometric means, respectively. $\mathrm{w}^{\mathrm{max}}$ should improve mixing, but could assign high weight to irrelevant nodes. We avoid this undesired effect in a *hybrid* solution w^{hy}.

We found that the hybrid edge assignment works best in practice; see Section 5.

3.4 Discussion

3.4.1 Information needed about the neighbors

In the pilot RW (Section 3.3.1) as well as in the main WRW, we assume that by sampling a node v we also learn the category $C(u)$ of each of its neighbors $u \in \mathcal{N}(v)$. Fortunately, such information is typically available in most online graphs at no additional cost, especially when scraping HTML pages, as we do. For example, when sampling colleges in Facebook in Section 5, we use the college membership information of all v's neighbors, which is available at v together with the friends list.

Our approach could potentially further benefit from the knowledge of the degree of v's neighbors. However, this information is rarely available without sampling these neighbors, which is costly and thus not required by S-WRW.

3.4.2 Cost of pilot RW

The pilot RW volume estimator described in Section 3.3.1 considers the categories not only of the sampled nodes, but also of their neighbors. As a result, it achieves high efficiency, as we show in simulations (Section 4.2.1) and Facebook measurements (Section 5.1). Given that, and the high robustness of S-WRW to estimation errors (Section 4.2.5), the pilot RW should be only a small fraction of main S-WRW. For example, this is equal to 6.5% in our Facebook measurements in Section 5.

3.4.3 Setting the parameters

S-WRW sets the edge weights trying to achieve roughly $w^{\mathrm{WIS}}(C_i)$. We slightly modify $w^{\mathrm{WIS}}(C_i)$ to avoid black holes and improve mixing, which is controlled by two natural and easy-to-interpret parameters, $\tilde{f}_\ominus$ and γ.

Visits to irrelevant nodes $\tilde{f}_\ominus$. Parameter $0 \leq \tilde{f}_\ominus \ll 1$ controls the desired fraction of visits in $C_\ominus$. When setting $\tilde{f}_\ominus$, we should exploit the information provided by the pilot RW. If the relevant categories appear poorly interconnected and often separated by irrelevant nodes, we should set $\tilde{f}_\ominus$ relatively high. We have seen an extreme case in Fig. 3(a), with disconnected relevant categories and optimal $\tilde{f}_\ominus = 0.5$. In contrast, when the relevant categories are strongly interconnected, we should use much smaller $\tilde{f}_\ominus$. However, because we can never be sure that the graph induced on relevant nodes is connected, we recommend using $\tilde{f}_\ominus > 0$. For example, when measuring Facebook in Section 5, we set $\tilde{f}_\ominus = 1\%$.

Maximal resolution γ. The parameter $\gamma \geq 1$ can be interpreted as the maximal resolution of our "graph magnifying glass", with respect to the largest relevant category C_{big}. S-WRW will typically sample well all categories whose size is at least equal to $|C_{\mathrm{big}}|/\gamma$.[2] All categories smaller than that are relatively under-sampled (see Section 5.2.4). In the extreme case, for $\gamma \to \infty$, S-WRW tries to cover every category, no matter how small, which may cause the "black hole" problem discussed in Section 3.3.4. In the other extreme, for $\gamma = 1$, and for identical $w^{\mathrm{WIS}}(C_i)$ for all categories, S-WRW reduces to RW. We recommend always setting $1 < \gamma < \infty$. Ideally, we know $|C_{\mathrm{smallest}}|$ - the smallest category size that is still relevant to us. In that case we

should set $\gamma = |C_{\mathrm{big}}|/|C_{\mathrm{smallest}}|$. For example, in Section 5 the categories are US colleges; we set $\gamma = 1000$, because colleges with size smaller than 1/1000th of the largest one (i.e., with a few tens of students) seem irrelevant to our measurement. As another rule of thumb, we should try to set smaller γ for relatively small sample sizes and in graphs with tight community structure (see Section 4.2.5).

3.4.4 Conservative approach

Note that a reasonable setting of these parameters (i.e., $\tilde{f}_\ominus > 0$ and $1 < \gamma < \infty$, and any conflict resolution discussed in the paper), increases the weights of large categories (including $C_\ominus$) and decreases the weight of small categories, compared to $w^{\mathrm{WIS}}(C_i)$. This makes S-WRW allocate category weights between the two extremes: RW and WIS. In this sense, S-WRW can be considered conservative.

3.4.5 S-WRW is unbiased

It is also important to note that the collected WRW sample is eventually corrected with the actual sampling weights as described in Section 2.4. Consequently, the S-WRW estimation process is unbiased, regardless of the choice of weights, as long as convergence is attained. In contrast, suboptimal weights (e.g., due to estimation error of $\hat{f}_C^{\mathrm{vol}}$) can increase the WRW mixing time and/or the variance of the resulting estimator. However, our simulations (Section 4) and empirical experiments on Facebook (Section 5) show that S-WRW is robust to suboptimal choice of weights.

4. SIMULATION RESULTS

The gain of our approach compared to RW comes from two main factors. First, S-WRW avoids, to a large extent or completely, the nodes in $C_\ominus$ that are irrelevant to our measurement. This fact alone can bring an arbitrarily large improvement ($\frac{N}{N-|C_\ominus|}$ under WIS), especially when $C_\ominus$ is large compared to N. We demonstrate this in the Facebook measurements in Section 5. Second, we can better allocate samples among the relevant categories. This factor is observable in our Facebook measurements as well, but it is more difficult to evaluate due to the lack of ground-truth therein. In this section, we evaluate the optimal allocation gain in a controlled simulation that illustrates some key insights.

4.1 Setup

4.1.1 Topology

We consider a graph G with 101K nodes and 505.5K edges organized in two densely connected communities[3] as shown in Fig. 4(h). The inter- and intra-community edges are chosen at random.

The nodes in G are partitioned into two node categories: C_{tiny} with 1K nodes (dark red), and C_{big} with 100K nodes (light yellow). We consider two extreme scenarios of such a partition. The "Random" scenario uses a purely random partition, as shown in Fig. 4(a). In contrast, under "Clustered", categories C_{tiny} and C_{big} coincide with the existing communities in G, as shown in Fig. 4(h). Clustered is arguably the worst case scenario for graph sampling by exploration.

---

[2]Strictly speaking, γ is related to volumes $\mathrm{vol}(C_i)$ rather than sizes $|C_i|$. They are equivalent when category volume is proportional to its size.

[3]The term "community" refers to cluster and is defined purely based on topology. The term "category" is a property of a node and is independent of topology.

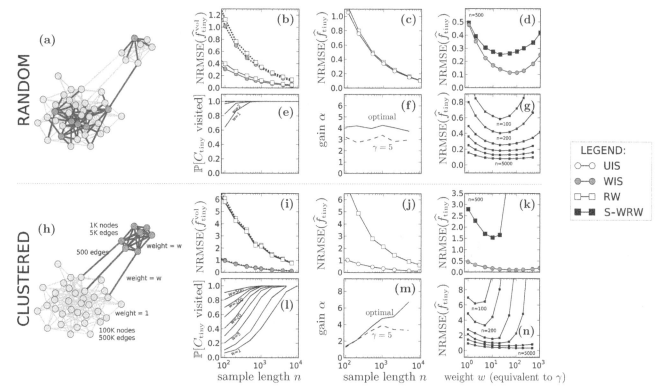

Figure 4: RW and S-WRW under two scenarios: Random (a-g) and Clustered (h-n). In (b,i), we show error of two volume estimators: naive Eq.(23) (dotted) and neighbor-based Eq.(26) (plain). Next, we show error of size estimator as a function of n (c,j) and w (d,g,k,n); in the latter, UIS and RW correspond to WIS and S-WRW for $w=1$. In (e,l), we show the empirical probability that S-WRW visits C_{tiny} at least once. Finally, (f,m) is gain α of S-WRW over RW under the optimal choice of w (plain), and for fixed $\gamma=w=5$ (dashed).

We fix the edge weights of all internal edges in C_{big} to 1. All the remaining edges, *i.e.*, all edges incident on nodes in category C_{tiny}, have weight w each, where $w \geq 1$ is a parameter. Note that this is equivalent to setting $\tilde{w}_e(C_{\text{big}}) = 1$, $\tilde{w}_e(C_{\text{tiny}}) = w$, and max or hybrid conflict resolution.

4.1.2 Objective and performance metrics

We are interested in measuring the relative sizes f_{tiny} and f_{big} (see Eq.(3)) of categories C_{tiny} and C_{big}, respectively. We use Normalized Root Mean Square Error (NRMSE) to assess the estimation error, defined in [38] as:

$$\text{NRMSE}(\widehat{x}) = \frac{\sqrt{\mathbb{E}\left[(\widehat{x} - x)^2\right]}}{x}, \qquad (20)$$

where x is the real value and $\widehat{x}$ is the estimated one.

In order to simplify the practical interpretation of the results, we also show how NRMSE translates into sample length. We define as *gain* α of S-WRW over RW the number of times RW must be longer than S-WRW in order to achieve the same error NRMSE, *i.e.*,

$$\text{gain} \quad \alpha = \frac{n^{\text{RW}}}{n^{\text{S-WRW}}},$$

subject to $\text{NRMSE}^{\text{RW}} = \text{NRMSE}^{\text{S-WRW}}$.

4.2 Results

4.2.1 Estimating volumes is usually cheap

The first step in S-WRW is obtaining category volume estimates $\widehat{f}_i^{\text{vol}}$. We achieve it by running a short pilot RW and

applying the estimator Eq.(26). We show $\text{NRMSE}(\widehat{f}_{\text{tiny}}^{\text{vol}})$ as plain curves in Fig. 4(b). This estimator takes advantage of the knowledge of the categories of the neighboring nodes, which makes it much more efficient than the naive estimator Eq.(23) shown by dashed curves. Moreover, the advantage of Eq.(26) over Eq.(23) grows with the graph density and the skewness of its degree distribution (not shown here).

Note that under Random, RW and WIS (with the sampling probabilities of RW) are almost equally efficient. However, on the other extreme, *i.e.*, under Clustered, the performance of RW becomes much worse and the advantage of Eq.(26) over Eq.(23) diminishes. This is because essentially all neighbors of a node from category C_i are in C_i too, which reduces formula Eq.(26) to Eq.(23). Nevertheless, we show in Section 4.2.5 that even severalfold volume estimation errors are likely not to affect significantly the results.

4.2.2 Visiting the tiny category

Fig. 4(e,l) presents the empirical probability $\mathbb{P}[C_{\text{tiny}}$ visited] that our walk visits at least one node from C_{tiny}. Of course, this probability grows with the sample length. However, the choice of weight w also affects it. Indeed, WRW with $w > 1$ is more likely to visit C_{tiny} than RW ($w = 1$, bottom line). This demonstrates the first advantage of introducing edge weights and WRW.

4.2.3 Optimal w and γ

Let us now focus on the estimation error as a function of w, shown in Fig. 4(d,k). Interestingly, this error does not drop monotonically with w but follows a U-shaped function with a clear optimal value w^{opt}.

Under WIS, we have $w^{\text{opt}} \simeq 100$, which confirms our findings discussed in Section 3.1. In particular, we achieve the optimal solution for the same number of samples $n_{\text{tiny}}^{\text{opt}} = n_{\text{big}}^{\text{opt}}$, which translates to $\text{w}^{\text{WIS}}(C_{\text{tiny}}) = \text{w}^{\text{WIS}}(C_{\text{big}})$. By plugging this and $f_{\text{big}}^{\text{vol}} = 100 \cdot f_{\text{tiny}}^{\text{vol}}$ to Eq.(15), we finally obtain the WIS-optimal edge weights in C_{tiny}, i.e., $w^{\text{opt}} = \text{w}_e(C_{\text{tiny}}) = 100 \cdot \text{w}_e(C_{\text{big}}) = 100$.[4]

In contrast, WRW is optimized for $w < 100$. For the sample length $n = 500$ as in Fig. 4(d,k), the error is minimized already for $w^{\text{opt}} \simeq 20$ and increases for higher weights. This demonstrates the "black hole" effect discussed in Section 3.3.4. It is much more pronounced under Clustered, confirming our intuition that black-holes become a problem only in the presence of relatively isolated, tight communities. Of course, the black hole effect diminishes with the sample length n (and vanishes for $n \to \infty$), which can be observed in Fig. 4(g,n), especially in (n).

In other words, the optimal assignment of edge weights (in relevant categories) under WRW lies somewhere between RW (all weights equal) and WIS. In S-WRW, we control it by parameter γ. In this example, we have $\gamma \equiv w$ for $\gamma \leq 100$. Indeed, by combining Eq.(15), Eq.(17), Eq.(18) and $\text{w}^{\text{WIS}}(C_{\text{tiny}}) = \text{w}^{\text{WIS}}(C_{\text{big}})$, we obtain

$$w = \frac{\text{w}_e(C_{\text{tiny}})}{\text{w}_e(C_{\text{big}})} = \frac{\frac{\text{w}^{\text{wis}}(C_{\text{tiny}})}{\tilde{f}_{\text{tiny}}^{\text{vol}}}}{\frac{\text{w}^{\text{wis}}(C_{\text{big}})}{\tilde{f}_{\text{big}}^{\text{vol}}}} = \frac{\tilde{f}_{\text{big}}^{\text{vol}}}{\tilde{f}_{\text{tiny}}^{\text{vol}}} = \frac{f_{\text{big}}^{\text{vol}}}{\frac{1}{\gamma} f_{\text{big}}^{\text{vol}}} = \gamma.$$

Consequently, the optimal setting of γ is the same as w^{opt}.

4.2.4 Gain α

A comparison of Fig. 4(c) and Fig. 4(d) reveals that a 500 hop-long WRW with $w \simeq 20$ yields roughly the same error NRMSE $\simeq 0.3$ as a 2000 hop-long RW. This means that WRW reduces the sampling cost by a factor of $\alpha \simeq 4$. Fig. 4(f) shows that this gain does not vary much with the sampling length. Under Clustered, both RW and WRW perform much worse. Nevertheless, Fig. 4(m) shows that WRW may significantly reduce the sampling cost in this scenario as well, especially for longer samples.

It is worth noting that WRW can significantly outperform UIS. This is the case in Fig. 4(d), where UIS is equivalent to WIS with $w = 1$. Because no walk can mix faster than UIS (that is independent and thus has perfect mixing), improving the mixing time alone [5,10,38,39] cannot achieve the potential gains of stratification, in general.

So far we focused on the smaller set C_{tiny} only. When estimating the size of C_{big}, all errors are much smaller, but we observe similar gain α.

4.2.5 Robustness to γ and volume estimation

The gain α shown above is calculated for the optimal choice of w, or, equivalently, γ. Of course, in practice it might be impossible to analytically obtain this value. Fortunately, S-WRW is relatively robust to the choice of parameters. The dashed lines in Fig. 4(f,m) are calculated for γ fixed to $\gamma = 5$, rather than optimized. Note that this value is often drastically smaller than the optimal one (e.g.,

$w^{\text{opt}} \simeq 50$ for $n = 5000$). Nevertheless, although the performance somewhat drops, S-WRW still reduces the sampling cost about three-fold.

This observation also illustrates the robustness to the category volume estimation errors (see Section 3.3.1). Indeed, setting $\gamma = 5$ means that every category C_i with volume estimated at $\widehat{f}_i^{\text{vol}} \leq \frac{1}{5}\widehat{f}_{\text{big}}^{\text{vol}}$ is treated the same. In Fig. 4(f), the volume of C_{tiny} would have to be overestimated by more than 20 times in order to affect the edge weight setting and thus the results. We have seen in Section 4.2.1 that this is very unlikely, even under smallest sample lengths and most adversarial scenarios.

4.3 Summary

S-WRW brings two types of benefits: (i) it avoids irrelevant nodes $C_{\ominus}$ and (ii) it carefully allocates samples between relevant categories of different sizes. Even for $C_{\ominus} = \emptyset$, i.e., the scenario studied in this section, S-WRW can still reduce the sampling cost by 75%. This second benefit is more difficult to achieve when the categories form strong and tight communities, which may lead to the black hole effect. We should then choose smaller, more conservative values of γ in S-WRW, which translate into smaller w in our example. In contrast, under a looser community structure this problem disappears and S-WRW is closer to WIS.

5. IMPLEMENTATION IN FACEBOOK

As a concrete application, we apply S-WRW to measure the Facebook social graph. This is an undirected graph and can also be considered a static graph, for all practical purposes in this study.[5] In Facebook, every user may declare herself a member of a college[6] he/she attends. We interpret the college affiliation as a user's category. This information is publicly available by default and allows us to answer some interesting questions. For example, how do the college networks (or "colleges" for short) compare with respect to their sizes? What is the college-to-college friendship graph? In order to answer these questions, one needs to collect many college user samples, preferably evenly distributed across colleges. This is the main goal of this section.

5.1 Measurement Setup

By default, the publicly available information for every Facebook user includes the name, photo, and a list of friends together with their college memberships (if any). We developed a high performance multi-threaded crawler to explore Facebook's social graph by scraping this web interface.

To make an informed decision about the parameters of S-WRW, we first ran a short pilot RW (see Section 3.3.1) with a total of $65K$ samples (which is only 6.5% of the length of the main S-WRW sample). Although our pilot RW visited only 2000 colleges, it estimated the relative volumes f_i^{vol} for about 9500 colleges discovered among friends of sampled users, as discussed in Section 3.4.2. In Fig. 6(a), we show that the neighbor-based estimator Eq.(26) greatly outperforms the naive estimator Eq.(23). These volumes cover

---

[4]For simplicity, we ignored in this calculation the conflicts on the 500 edges between C_{big} and C_{tiny}.

[5]The Facebook characteristics do change but in time scales much longer than the 3-day duration of our crawls. Websites such as Facebook statistics, Alexa etc show that the number of Facebook users is growing with rate 0.1-0.2% per day.

[6]There also exist categories other than colleges, namely "work" and "high school". Facebook requires a valid category-specific email for verification.

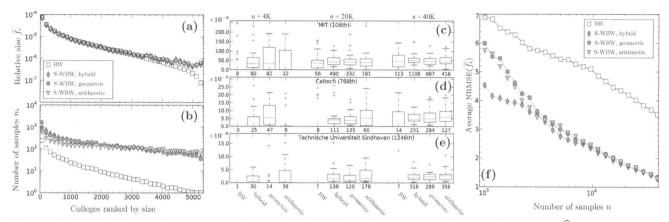

Figure 5: 5331 colleges discovered and ranked by RW. (a) Estimated relative college sizes $\widehat{f}_i$. (b) Absolute number of user samples per college. (c-e) 25 estimates of size $\widehat{f}_i$ for three different colleges and sample lengths n. (f) Average NRMSE of college size estimation. Results in (a,b,f) are binned.

	RW	S-WRW		
		Hybrid	Geometric	Arithmetic
Unique samples	1,000K	1,000K	1,000K	1,000K
Total samples	1,016K	1,263K	1,228K	1,237K
College samples	9%	86%	79%	58%
Unique Colleges	5,331	9,014	8,994	10,439

Table 1: Overview of collected Facebook datasets.

several decades. We set the maximal resolution to $\gamma = 1000$, which means that we target colleges with at least a few tens of users (see the discussion in Section 3.4.3).

We also used the information collected by the pilot RW to set the desired fraction $\tilde{f}_\ominus$ of irrelevant nodes. We found that a typical college user visited by pilot RW (without correcting for the degree bias) has on average 733 friends: 103 in the same college, 141 in a different college, and 489 without any college affiliation. Such a high number of inter-college links should generally result in a good S-WRW mixing even with no visits to the irrelevant (non-college) nodes, i.e., for $\tilde{f}_\ominus = 0$. However, in order to account for rare but possible cases with a college user(s) surrounded exclusively by non-college friends, we chose a small but positive parameter $\tilde{f}_\ominus = 1\%$.

In the main measurement phase, we perform three S-WRW crawls, each with different edge weight conflict resolution (hybrid, geometric, and arithmetic), and one simple RW crawl as a baseline for comparison (Table 1). For each crawl type we collected 1 million unique users. Some of them are sampled multiple times (at no additional cost), which results in higher total number of samples in the second row of Table 1. All the results presented here would look almost the same for 1 million total (rather than unique) samples. Our crawls were performed on Oct. 16-19 2010, and the datasets are available at [1].

5.2 Results: RW vs. S-WRW

5.2.1 Avoiding irrelevant categories

Only 9% of the RW's samples come from colleges, which means that the vast majority of sampling effort is wasted. In contrast, the S-WRW crawls achieved 6-10 times better efficiency, collecting 86% (hybrid), 79% (geometric) and 58% (arithmetic) samples from colleges. Note that these values are significantly lower than the target 99% suggested by our

choice of $\tilde{f}_\ominus = 1\%$, and that S-WRW hybrid reaches the highest number. This is in agreement with our discussion in Section 3.3.5. We also note that S-WRW crawls discovered $1.6 - 1.9$ times more unique colleges than RW.

At first, it seems surprising that RW samples colleges in 9% of cases while only 3.5% of Facebook users belong to colleges. This is because the college users have on average 422 Facebook friends - much higher than the global average 144. Consequently, the college users attract RW approximately three times more often than average users.

5.2.2 Stratification

The advantage of S-WRW over RW does not lie exclusively in avoiding the nodes in the irrelevant category $C_\ominus$. S-WRW can also over-sample small categories (here colleges) at the cost of under-sampling large ones (which are well sampled anyway). This feature becomes important especially when the category sizes differ significantly, which is the case in Facebook. Indeed, Fig. 5(a) shows that college sizes exhibit great heterogeneity. For a fair comparison, we only include the 5,331 colleges discovered by RW. (This filtering actually gives preference to RW. S-WRW crawls discovered many more colleges that we do not show in this figure.) They span more than two orders of magnitude and follow a heavily skewed distribution.

Fig. 5(b) confirms that S-WRW successfully oversamples the small colleges. Indeed, the number of S-WRW samples per college is almost constant (roughly around 100). In contrast, the number of RW samples follows closely the college size, which results in a 100-fold difference between RW and S-WRW for smaller colleges.

5.2.3 College size estimation

With more samples per college, we naturally expect a better estimation accuracy under S-WRW. We demonstrate it for three colleges of different sizes (in terms of the number of Facebook users): MIT (large), Caltech (medium), and Eindhoven University of Technology (small). Each boxplot in Fig. 5(c-e) is generated based on 25 independent college size estimates $\widehat{f}_i$ that come from walks of length $n = 4K$ (left), 20K (middle), and 40K (right) samples each. For the three studied colleges, RW fails to produce reliable estimates in all cases except for MIT's (largest college) two longest crawls. Similar results hold for the overwhelming

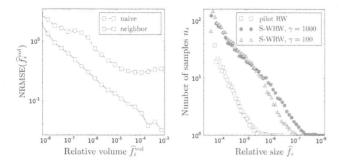

Figure 6: Facebook: Pilot RW and some S-WRW walks of length $n = 65K$. (a) The performance of the neighbor-based volume estimator Eq.(26) (plain line) and the naive one Eq.(23) (dashed line). As ground-truth we used f_i^{vol} calculated for all $4 \times 1M$ collected samples. (b) The effect of the choice of γ.

majority of medium-sized and small colleges. The underlying reason is the very small number of samples collected by RW in these colleges, averaging at below 1 sample per walk. In contrast, the three S-WRW crawls contain typically 5-50 times more samples than RW (in agreement with Fig. 5(b)), and produce much more reliable estimates.

Finally, we aggregate the results over all colleges and compute the gain α of S-WRW over RW. We calculate the error $\text{NRMSE}(\widehat{f_i})$ by taking as our "ground truth" f_i the grand average of $\widehat{f_i}$ values over all samples collected via all full-length walks and crawl types. Fig. 5(f) presents $\text{NRMSE}(\widehat{f_i})$ averaged over all 5,331 colleges discovered by RW, as a function of walk length n. As expected, for all crawl types the error decreases with n. However, there is a consistently large gap between RW and all three versions of S-WRW. RW needs $\alpha = 13 - 15$ times more samples than S-WRW in order to achieve the same error.

5.2.4 The effect of the choice of γ

In the S-WRW results described above, we used the resolution $\gamma = 1000$. In order to check how sensitive the results are to the choice of this parameter, we also tried a (shorter) S-WRW run with $\gamma = 100$. In Fig. 6(b), we see that the number of samples collected in the smallest colleges is smaller under $\gamma = 100$ than under $\gamma = 1000$. In fact, the two curves diverge for colleges about 100 times smaller than the biggest college, i.e., exactly at the maximal resolution $\gamma = 100$.

Both settings of γ perform orders of magnitude better than RW of the same length, which confirms the robustness of S-WRW to the choice of γ.

5.3 Summary

Only about 3.5% of 500M Facebook users are college members. There are more than 10K colleges and they greatly vary in size, ranging from 50 (or fewer) to 50K members (we consider students, alumni and staff). In this setting, state-of-the-art sampling methods such as RW (and its variants) are bound to perform poorly. Indeed, UIS (i.e., an idealized version of RW) with as many as 1M samples would collect only one sample from size-500 college, on average. Even if we could sample directly from colleges only, we would typically collect fewer than 30 samples per size-500 college.

S-WRW solves these problems. We showed that S-WRW of the same length (1M) collects typically about 100 sam-

ples per size-500 college. As a result, S-WRW outperforms RW by $\alpha = 13 - 15$ times or $\alpha = 12 - 14$ times if we also consider the 6.5% overhead from the initial pilot RW. This gain can be decomposed into two factors, say $\alpha = \alpha_1 \cdot \alpha_2$. Factor $\alpha_1 \simeq 8$ can be attributed to about 8 times higher fraction of college samples in S-WRW compared to RW. Factor $\alpha_2 \simeq 1.5$ is due to over-sampling smaller networks, i.e., by applying stratification to relevant categories.

Another important observation is that S-WRW is robust to the way we resolve target edge weight conflicts in Section 3.3.5. The differences between the three S-WRW implementations are minor - it is the application of Eq.(19) that brings most of the benefit.

6. RELATED WORK

Graph Sampling by Crawling. Early crawling of P2P, OSN and WWW typically used graph traversal techniques, mainly Breath-First-Search (BFS) [3,32–34,44] and its variants. However, incomplete BFS introduces bias towards high-degree nodes that is unknown and thus impossible to correct in general graphs [2,8,18,26,27].

Other studies followed a more principled approach based on random walks (RW) [4,30]. The Metropolis-Hasting RW (MHRW) [16,31] removes the bias during the walk; it has been used to sample P2P networks [36,41] and OSNs [18]. Alternatively, one can use RW, whose bias is known and can be corrected for [21,40], thus leading to a re-weighted RW [18,36]. RW was also used to sample Web [22], P2P networks [19,36,41], OSNs [18,24,34,37], and other large graphs [28]. It was empirically shown in [18,36] that RW outperforms MHRW in real-life topologies. RW has also been used to sample *dynamic graphs* [36,41,43], which are outside the scope of this paper.

Fast Mixing Markov Chains. The mixing time of RW in many OSNs was found larger than commonly believed [34]. There exist many approaches that try to minimize the mixing time of random walks, such as multiple dependent random walks [38], multigraph sampling [17], or the addition of random jumps [5,28,39]. Given the knowledge of the entire graph, [10] proposes an optimal solution by explicitly minimizing the second largest eigenvalue modulus (SLEM) of the transition probability matrix.

All the above methods try to minimize mixing time towards a given target stationary distribution, (e.g., treating all nodes with equal importance). Therefore, they are complementary to our technique that primarily aims at finding the right distribution for a given category-related measurement objective, while also maintaining fast mixing.

Stratified Sampling. Our approach builds on *stratified sampling* [35], a widely used technique in statistics; see [12, 29] for a good introduction. A related work in a different networking problem is [14], where threshold sampling is used to vary sampling probabilities of network traffic flows and estimate their volume.

Weighted Random Walks for Sampling. Random walks on graphs with weighted edges [4,30], are well studied and heavily used in Monte Carlo Markov Chain simulations [16] to sample a state space with a specified probability distribution. However, to the best of our knowledge, WRWs had not been used for measurements of real online systems with a goal other than improving mixing (discussed above).

Recent applications of WRW in online social networks

include [6,7]. In both these papers, the goal is to predict/extract something from a known graph. In contrast, we use WRW to estimate features of an unknown graph.

In the context of World Wide Web crawling, *focused crawling* techniques [11,13] have been introduced to follow web pages of specified interest and to avoid the irrelevant pages. This is achieved by performing a BFS type of sampling, except that instead of FIFO queue they use a priority queue weighted by the page relevancy. In our context, such an approach suffers from the same problems as regular BFS: (i) collected samples strongly depend on the starting point, and (ii) we are not able to analytically correct for the bias.

7. CONCLUSION

We have introduced Stratified Weighted Random Walk (S-WRW) - an efficient heuristic for sampling large, static, undirected graphs via crawling and using minimal information about node categories. S-WRW performs a random walk on a graph whose edge weights are set taking into account the estimation objective. We apply S-WRW to measure the Facebook social graph, and we show that it brings a very significant gain.

In future work, we plan to combine S-WRW with existing orthogonal techniques, some of which have been reviewed in the related work, to further improve performance.

8. REFERENCES

[1] Weighted Random Walks of the Facebook social graph: http://odysseas.calit2.uci.edu/osn, 2011.

[2] D. Achlioptas, A. Clauset, D. Kempe, and C. On the bias of traceroute sampling: or, power-law degree distributions in regular graphs. *Journal of the ACM*, 2009.

[3] Y. Ahn, S. Han, H. Kwak, S. Moon, and H. Jeong. Analysis of topological characteristics of huge online social networking services. In *WWW*, pages 835–844, 2007.

[4] D. Aldous and J. A. Fill. *Reversible Markov Chains and Random Walks on Graphs*. In preparation.

[5] K. Avrachenkov, B. Ribeiro, and D. Towsley. Improving Random Walk Estimation Accuracy with Uniform Restarts. In *17th Workshop on Algorithms and Models for the Web Graph*, 2010.

[6] L. Backstrom and J. Kleinberg. Network Bucket Testing. In *WWW*, 2011.

[7] L. Backstrom and J. Leskovec. Supervised Random Walks: Predicting and Recommending Links in Social Networks. In *ACM International Conference on Web Search and Data Minig (WSDM)*, 2011.

[8] L. Becchetti, C. Castillo, D. Donato, and A. Fazzone. A comparison of sampling techniques for web graph characterization. In *LinkKDD*, 2006.

[9] H. R. Bernard, T. Hallett, A. Iovita, E. C. Johnsen, R. Lyerla, C. McCarty, M. Mahy, M. J. Salganik, T. Saliuk, O. Scutelniciuc, G. a. Shelley, P. Sirinirund, S. Weir, and D. F. Stroup. Counting hard-to-count populations: the network scale-up method for public health. *Sexually Transmitted Infections*, 86(Suppl 2):ii11–ii15, Nov. 2010.

[10] S. Boyd, P. Diaconis, and L. Xiao. Fastest mixing Markov chain on a graph. *SIAM review*, 46(4):667–689, 2004.

[11] S. Chakrabarti. Focused crawling: a new approach to topic-specific Web resource discovery. *Computer Networks*, 31(11-16):1623–1640, May 1999.

[12] W. G. Cochran. *Sampling Techniques*, volume 20 of *McGraw-Hil Series in Probability and Statistics*. Wiley, 1977.

[13] M. Diligenti, F. Coetzee, S. Lawrence, C. Giles, and M. Gori. Focused crawling using context graphs. In

Proceedings of the 26th International Conference on Very Large Data Bases, pages 527–534, 2000.

[14] N. Duffield, C. Lund, and M. Thorup. Learn more, sample less: control of volume and variance in network measurement. *IEEE Transactions on Information Theory*, 51(5):1756–1775, May 2005.

[15] J. Gentle. *Random number generation and Monte Carlo methods*. Springer Verlag, 2003.

[16] W. R. Gilks, S. Richardson, and D. J. Spiegelhalter. *Markov Chain Monte Carlo in Practice*. Chapman and Hall/CRC, 1996.

[17] M. Gjoka, C. Butts, M. Kurant, and A. Markopoulou. Multigraph Sampling of Online Social Networks. *arXiv*, (arXiv:1008.2565v1):1–10, 2010.

[18] M. Gjoka, M. Kurant, C. T. Butts, and A. Markopoulou. Walking in Facebook: A Case Study of Unbiased Sampling of OSNs. In *INFOCOM*, 2010.

[19] C. Gkantsidis, M. Mihail, and A. Saberi. Random walks in peer-to-peer networks. In *INFOCOM*, 2004.

[20] M. Hansen and W. Hurwitz. On the Theory of Sampling from Finite Populations. *Annals of Mathematical Statistics*, 14(3), 1943.

[21] D. D. Heckathorn. Respondent-Driven Sampling: A New Approach to the Study of Hidden Populations. *Social Problems*, 44:174–199, 1997.

[22] M. R. Henzinger, A. Heydon, M. Mitzenmacher, and M. Najork. On near-uniform URL sampling. In *WWW*, 2000.

[23] E. D. Kolaczyk. *Statistical Analysis of Network Data*, volume 69 of *Springer Series in Statistics*. Springer New York, 2009.

[24] B. Krishnamurthy, P. Gill, and M. Arlitt. A few chirps about Twitter. In *WOSN*, 2008.

[25] M. Kurant, M. Gjoka, C. Butts, and A. Markopoulou. Walking on a Graph with a Magnifying Glass. *Arxiv preprint arXiv:1101.5463*, 2011.

[26] M. Kurant, A. Markopoulou, and P. Thiran. On the bias of BFS (Breadth First Search). In *ITC, also in arXiv:1004.1729*, 2010.

[27] S. H. Lee, P.-J. Kim, and H. Jeong. Statistical properties of Sampled Networks. *Phys. Rev. E*, 73:16102, 2006.

[28] J. Leskovec and C. Faloutsos. Sampling from large graphs. In *KDD*, pages 631–636, 2006.

[29] S. Lohr. *Sampling: design and analysis*. Brooks/Cole, second edition, 2009.

[30] L. Lovász. Random walks on graphs: A survey. *Combinatorics, Paul Erdos is Eighty*, 2(1):1–46, 1993.

[31] N. Metropolis, A. W. Rosenbluth, M. N. Rosenbluth, A. H. Teller, and E. Teller. Equation of state calculation by fast computing machines. *Journal of Chemical Physics*, 21:1087–1092, 1953.

[32] A. Mislove, H. S. Koppula, K. P. Gummadi, P. Druschel, and B. Bhattacharjee. Growth of the Flickr social network. In *WOSN*, 2008.

[33] A. Mislove, M. Marcon, K. P. Gummadi, P. Druschel, and B. Bhattacharjee. Measurement and analysis of online social networks. In *IMC*, pages 29–42, 2007.

[34] A. Mohaisen, A. Yun, and Y. Kim. Measuring the mixing time of social graphs. *IMC*, 2010.

[35] J. Neyman. On the Two Different Aspects of the Representative Method: The Method of Stratified Sampling and the Method of Purposive Selection. *Journal of the Royal Statistical Society*, 97(4):558, 1934.

[36] A. Rasti, M. Torkjazi, R. Rejaie, N. Duffield, W. Willinger, and D. Stutzbach. Respondent-driven sampling for characterizing unstructured overlays. In *Infocom Mini-conference*, pages 2701–2705, 2009.

[37] A. H. Rasti, M. Torkjazi, R. Rejaie, and D. Stutzbach. Evaluating Sampling Techniques for Large Dynamic Graphs. In *Technical Report*, volume 1, 2008.

[38] B. Ribeiro and D. Towsley. Estimating and sampling

graphs with multidimensional random walks. In *IMC*, volume 011, 2010.

[39] B. Ribeiro, P. Wang, and D. Towsley. On Estimating Degree Distributions of Directed Graphs through Sampling. *UMass Technical Report*, 2010.

[40] M. Salganik and D. D. Heckathorn. Sampling and estimation in hidden populations using respondent-driven sampling. *Sociological Methodology*, 34(1):193–240, 2004.

[41] D. Stutzbach, R. Rejaie, N. Duffield, S. Sen, and W. Willinger. On unbiased sampling for unstructured peer-to-peer networks. In *IMC*, 2006.

[42] E. Volz and D. D. Heckathorn. Probability based estimation theory for respondent driven sampling. *Journal of Official Statistics*, 24(1):79–97, 2008.

[43] W. Willinger, R. Rejaie, M. Torkjazi, M. Valafar, and M. Maggioni. OSN Research: Time to Face the Real Challenges. In *HotMetrics*, 2009.

[44] C. Wilson, B. Boe, A. Sala, K. P. N. Puttaswamy, and B. Y. Zhao. User interactions in social networks and their implications. In *EuroSys*, 2009.

Appendix A: Achieving Arbitrary Node Weights

Achieving arbitrary node weights by setting the edge weights in a graph $G = (V, E)$ is sometimes impossible. For example, for a graph that is a path consisting of two nodes $(v_1 - v_2)$, it is impossible to achieve $w(v_1) \neq w(v_2)$. However, it is always possible to do so, if there are self loops in each node.

OBSERVATION 1. *For any undirected graph $G = (V, E)$ with a self-loop $\{v, v\}$ at every node $v \in V$, we can achieve an arbitrary distribution of node weights $w(v) > 0$, $v \in V$, by appropriate choice of edge weights $w(u, v) > 0$, $\{u, v\} \in E$.*

PROOF. Let w_{min} be the smallest of all target node weights $w(v)$. Set $w(u, v) = w_{min}/N$ for all non self-loop edges (i.e., where $u \neq v$). Now, for every self-loop $\{v, v\} \in E$ set

$$w(v, v) = \frac{1}{2}\left(w(v) - \frac{w_{min}}{N} \cdot (\deg(v) - 2)\right).$$

It is easy to check that, because there are exactly $\deg(v) - 2$ non self-loop edges incident on v, every node $v \in V$ will achieve the target weight $w(v)$. Moreover, the definition of w_{min} guarantees that $w(v, v) > 0$ for every $v \in V$. $\square$

Appendix B: Estimating Category Volumes

In this section, we derive efficient estimators of the relative volume $\widehat{f}_C^{vol} = \frac{vol(C)}{vol(V)}$. Recall that $S \subset V$ denotes an independent sample of nodes in G, with replacement.

Node sampling

If S is a uniform sample UIS, then we can write

$$\widehat{f}_C^{vol} = \frac{\sum_{v \in S} \deg(v) \cdot 1_{\{v \in C\}}}{\sum_{v \in S} \deg(v)}, \quad (21)$$

which is a straightforward application of the classic ratio estimator [29].

In the more general case, when S is selected using WIS, then we have to correct for the linear bias towards nodes of higher weights $w()$, as follows:

$$\widehat{f}_C^{vol} = \frac{\sum_{v \in S} \deg(v) \cdot 1_{\{v \in C\}}/w(v)}{\sum_{v \in S} \deg(v)/w(v)}. \quad (22)$$

In particular, if $w(v) \sim \deg(v)$, then

$$\widehat{f}_C^{vol} = \frac{1}{n} \cdot \sum_{v \in S} 1_{\{v \in C\}}. \quad (23)$$

Star sampling

Another approach is to focus on the set of all neighbors $\mathcal{N}(S)$ of sampled nodes (with repetitions) rather than on S itself, *i.e.*, to use 'star sampling' [23]. The probability that a node v is a neighbor of a node sampled from V by UIS is

$$\sum_{u \in V} \frac{1}{N} \cdot 1_{\{v \in \mathcal{N}(u)\}} = \frac{\deg(v)}{N}.$$

Consequently, the nodes in $\mathcal{N}(S)$ are asymptotically equivalent to nodes drawn with probabilities linearly proportional to node degrees. By applying Eq.(23) to $\mathcal{N}(S)$, we obtain[7]

$$\widehat{f}_C^{vol} = \frac{1}{vol(S)} \sum_{u \in S} \sum_{v \in \mathcal{N}(u)} 1_{\{v \in C\}}, \quad (24)$$

where we used $|\mathcal{N}(S)| = \sum_{u \in S} \deg(u) = vol(S)$.

In the more general case, when S is selected using WIS, then we correct for the linear bias towards nodes of higher weights $w()$, as follows:

$$\widehat{f}_C^{vol} = \frac{1}{\sum_{u \in S} \frac{\deg(u)}{w(u)}} \sum_{u \in S} \left(\frac{1}{w(u)} \sum_{v \in \mathcal{N}(u)} 1_{\{v \in C\}}\right). \quad (25)$$

In particular, if $w(v) \sim \deg(v)$, then

$$\widehat{f}_C^{vol} = \frac{1}{n} \sum_{u \in S} \left(\frac{1}{\deg(u)} \sum_{v \in \mathcal{N}(u)} 1_{\{v \in C\}}\right). \quad (26)$$

Note that for every sampled node $v \in S$, the formulas Eq.(24-26) exploit all the $\deg(v)$ neighbors of v, whereas Eq.(21-23) rely on one node per sample only. Not surprisingly, Eq.(24-26) performed much better in all our simulations and implementations.

Appendix C: Stratification in Expectation

In this section, we show the correctness of Eq.(13) in Section 3.1. Recall from Eq.(5) that under WIS, at every iteration, the probability $\pi^{WIS}(v)$ of sampling node v is proportional to its weight $w^{WIS}(v)$. So the probability $\pi^{WIS}(C_i)$ of sampling a node from category C_i is proportional to the weight $w^{WIS}(C_i)$ of C_i, *i.e.*,

$$\pi^{WIS}(C_i) \propto w^{WIS}(C_i).$$

This, together with Eq.(13), imply

$$\pi^{WIS}(C_i) \propto n_i^{opt}.$$

We can now use $\sum_i \pi^{WIS}(C_i) = 1$ and $\sum_i n_i^{opt} = n$ to rewrite the above formula as the following equation

$$\pi^{WIS}(C_i) = n_i^{opt}/n.$$

Consequently, under WIS

$$\mathbb{E}[n_i] = Binom(n, \pi^{WIS}(C_i)) = n \cdot \pi^{WIS}(C_i) = n_i^{opt}.$$

---

[7] As a side note, observe that Eq.(24) generalizes the "scale-up method" [9] used in social sciences to estimate the size (here $|C|$) of hidden populations (*e.g.*, of drug addicts). Indeed, if we assume that the average node degree in V is the same as in C, then $f_C^{vol} = vol(C)/vol(V) = |C|/|V|$, which reduces Eq.(23) to the core formula of the scale-up method.

Topology Discovery of Sparse Random Graphs
With Few Participants

Animashree Anandkumar
EECS Dept.,
University of California,
Irvine, CA 92697
a.anandkumar@uci.edu

Avinatan Hassidim
Google Research Tel Aviv,
23 Menachem Begin street,
Tel Aviv, Israel
avinatanh@gmail.com

Jonathan Kelner
CSAIL & Dept. of Math.
Massachusetts Inst. of Tech.
Cambridge, MA 02139
kelner@mit.edu

ABSTRACT

We consider the task of topology discovery of sparse random graphs using end-to-end random measurements (e.g., delay) between a subset of nodes, referred to as the participants. The rest of the nodes are hidden, and do not provide any information for topology discovery. We consider topology discovery under two routing models: (a) the participants exchange messages along the shortest paths and obtain end-to-end measurements, and (b) additionally, the participants exchange messages along the second shortest path. For scenario (a), our proposed algorithm results in a sub-linear edit-distance guarantee using a sub-linear number of uniformly selected participants. For scenario (b), we obtain a much stronger result, and show that we can achieve consistent reconstruction when a sub-linear number of uniformly selected nodes participate. This implies that accurate discovery of sparse random graphs is tractable using an extremely small number of participants. We finally obtain a lower bound on the number of participants required by any algorithm to reconstruct the original random graph up to a given edit distance. We also demonstrate that while consistent discovery is tractable for sparse random graphs using a small number of participants, in general, there are graphs which cannot be discovered by any algorithm even with a significant number of participants, and with the availability of end-to-end information along all the paths between the participants.

Categories and Subject Descriptors

G.2.2 [**Mathematics of Computing**]: Discrete Mathematics—*Graph Theory.*

General Terms

Algorithms, Theory.

Keywords

Topology Discovery, Sparse Random Graphs, End-to-end Measurements, Hidden Nodes, Quartet Tests.

SIGMETRICS'11, June 7–11, 2011, San Jose, California, USA.
Copyright 2011 ACM 978-1-4503-0262-3/11/06 ...$10.00.

1. INTRODUCTION

Inference of global characteristics of large networks using limited local information is an important and a challenging task. The discovery of the underlying network topology is one of the main goals of network inference, and its knowledge is crucial for many applications. For instance, in communication networks, many network monitoring applications rely on the knowledge of the routing topology, e.g., to evaluate the resilience of the network to failures; for network traffic prediction and monitoring, anomaly detection, or to infer the sources of viruses and rumors in the network. In the context of social networks, the knowledge of topology is useful for inferring many characteristics such as identification of hierarchy and community structure and prediction of information flow.

Traditionally, inference of routing topology in communication networks has relied on tools such as traceroute and mtrace [3] to generate path information between a subset of nodes. However, these tools require cooperation of intermediate nodes or routers to generate messages using the Internal Control Message Protocol (ICMP). Increasingly, today many routers block traceroute requests due to privacy and security concerns [24, 41], there by making inference of topology using traceroute inaccurate. Moreover, traceroute requests are not scalable for large networks, and cannot discover layer-2 switches and MPLS (Multi-protocol Label Switching) paths, which are increasingly being deployed [35].

The alternative approach for topology discovery is the approach of *network tomography*. Here, topology inference is carried out from end-to-end packet probing measurements (e.g., delay) between a subset of nodes, without the need for cooperation between the intermediate (i.e., non-participating) nodes in the network. Due to its flexibility, such approaches are gaining increasing popularity (see Section 1.2 for details).

The approach of topology discovery using end-to-end measurements is also applicable in the context of social networks. In many social networks, some nodes may be unwilling to participate or cooperate with other nodes for discovering the network topology, and there may be many hidden nodes in "hard to reach" places of the network, e.g., populations of drug users, and so on. Moreover, in many networks, there may be a cost to probing nodes for information, e.g., when there is a cash reward offered for filling out surveys. For such networks, it is desirable to design algorithms which can discover the overall network topology using small fraction of participants who are willing to provide information for topology discovery.

There are many challenges to topology discovery. The algorithms need to be computationally efficient and provide accurate reconstruction using a small fraction of participating nodes. Moreover, inference of large topologies is a task of *high-dimensional learning* [40]. In such scenarios, typically, only a small number of end-to-end measurements are available relative to the size of the network to be inferred. It is desirable to have algorithms with low *sample complexity* (see Definition 3), where the number of measurements required to achieve a certain level of accuracy scales favorably with the network size.

It is indeed not tractable to achieve all the above objectives for discovery of general network topologies using an arbitrary set of participants. There are fundamental identifiability issues, and in general, no algorithm will be able to discover the underlying topology. We demonstrate this phenomenon in Section 8.2, where we construct a small network with a significant fraction of participants which suffers from non-identifiability. Instead, it is desirable to design topology discovery algorithms which have guaranteed performance for certain classes of graphs.

We consider the class of Erdős-Rényi random graphs [11]. These are perhaps the simplest as well as the most well-studied class of random graphs. Such random graphs can provide a reasonable explanation for peer-to-peer networks [27] and social networks [34]. We address the following issues in this paper: can we discover random graphs using a small fraction of participating nodes, selected uniformly at random? can we design efficient algorithms with low sample complexity and with provable performance guarantees? what kinds of end-to-end measurements between the participants are useful for topology discovery? finally, given a set of participants, is there a lower bound on the error (edit distance) of topology discovery that is achievable by any algorithm? Our work addresses these questions and also provides insights into many complex issues involved in topology discovery.

1.1 Summary of Contributions

We consider the problem of topology discovery of sparse random graphs using a uniformly selected set of participants. Our contributions in this paper are three fold. First, we design an algorithm with provable performance guarantees, when only minimal end-to-end information between the participants is available. Second, we consider the scenario with additional information, and design a discovery algorithm with much better reconstruction guarantees. Third, we provide a lower bound on the edit distance of the reconstructed graph by any algorithm, for a given number of participants. Our analysis shows that random graphs can be discovered accurately and efficiently using an extremely small number of participants.

We consider reconstruction of the giant component of the sparse random graph up to its minimal representation, where there are no redundant hidden nodes (see Section 3.1). Our end-to-end measurement model consists of random samples (e.g., delay) along the shortest paths between the participants. Using these samples, we design the first random-discovery algorithm, referred to as the RGD1 algorithm, which performs local tests over small groups of participating nodes (known as the *quartet tests*), and iteratively merges them with the previously constructed structure. Such tests are known to be accurate for tree topologies [10], but have not been previously analyzed for random-graph topologies. We provide a sub-linear edit-distance guarantee (in the number of nodes) under RGD1 when there are at least $n^{0.75}$ participants, where n is the number of nodes in the network. The algorithm is also simple to implement, and is computationally efficient.

We then extend the algorithm to the scenario where additionally, there are end-to-end measurements available along the second shortest paths between the participating nodes. Such information is available since nodes typically maintain information about alternative routing paths, should the shortest path fail. In this scenario, our algorithm RGD2, has a drastic improvement in accuracy under the same set of participating nodes. Specifically, we demonstrate that consistent discovery can be achieved under RGD2 algorithm when there are at least $n^{7/8}$ number of participants, where n is the network size for homogeneous delays (we have a general bound for heterogeneous delays). Thus, we can achieve accurate topology discovery of random graphs using an extremely small number of participants. For both our algorithms, the sample complexity is poly-logarithmic in the network size, meaning that the number of end-to-end measurement samples needs to scale poly-logarithmically in the network size to obtain the stated edit-distance guarantees.

Our analysis in this paper thus reveals that sparse random graphs can be efficiently discovered using a small number of participants. Our algorithms exploit the *locally tree-like* property of random graphs [11], meaning that these graphs contain a small number of short cycles. This enables us to provide performance guarantees for quartet tests which are known to be accurate for tree topologies, and this is done by carefully controlling the distances used by the quartet tests. At the same time, we exploit the presence of cycles in random graphs to obtain much better guarantees than in the case of tree topologies. In other words, while tree topologies require participation of at least half the number of nodes (i.e., the leaves) for accurate discovery, random-graph topologies can be accurately discovered using a sub-linear number of participants.

Finally, we provide lower bounds on the reconstruction error under any algorithm for a given number of participants. Specifically, we show that if less than roughly $\sqrt{n}$ nodes participate in topology discovery, reconstruction is impossible under any algorithm, where n is the network size. We also discuss topology discovery in general networks, and demonstrate identifiability issues involved in the discovery process. We construct a small network with a significant fraction of nodes as participants which cannot be reconstructed using end-to-end information on all possible paths between the participants. This is in contrast to random graphs, where consistent and efficient topology discovery is possible using a small number of participants.

To the best of our knowledge, this is the first work to undertake a systematic study of random-graph discovery using end-to-end measurements between a subset of nodes. Although we limit ourselves to the study of random graphs, our algorithms are based on the locally tree-like property, and are thus equally applicable for discovering other locally tree-like graphs such as the *d*-regular graphs and the *scale-free* graphs; the latter class is known to be a good model for social networks [34] and peer-to-peer networks [27].

1.2 Related Work

Network tomography has been extensively studied in the past and various heuristics and algorithms have been proposed along with experimental results on real data. For instance, the area of mapping the internet topology is very rich and extensive, e.g., see [1, 2, 4, 21, 25]. In the context of social networks, the work in [31] considers prediction of positive and negative links, the work in [23] considers inferring networks of diffusion and influence and the work in [33] considers inferring latent social networks through spread of contagions. A wide range of network tomography solutions have been proposed for general networks. See [13] for a survey.

Topology discovery is an important component of network tomography. There have been several theoretical developments on this topic. The work in [15] provides hardness results for topology discovery under various settings. Topology discovery under availability of different kinds of queries have been previously considered, such as:

(i) Shortest-path query, where a query to a node returns all the shortest paths (i.e., list of nodes in the path) from that node to all other nodes [9]. This is the strongest of all queries. These queries can be implemented by using Traceroute on Internet. In [9], the combinatorial-optimization problem of selecting the smallest subset of nodes for such queries to estimate the network topology is formulated. The work in [22] considers discovery of random graphs using such queries. The bias of using traceroute sampling on power-law graphs is studied in [5], and weighted random walk sampling is considered in [29].

(ii) Distance query, where a query to a node returns all the shortest-path distances (instead of the complete list of nodes) from that node to any other node in the network [22]. These queries are available for instance, in Peer-to-Peer networks through the Ping/Pong protocol. This problem is related to the landmark placement, and the optimization problem of having smallest number of landmarks is known as the metric dimension of the graph [28]. The work in [38] considers reconstruction of tree topologies using shortest-path queries.

(iii) Edge-based queries: There are several types of edge queries such as detection query, which answer whether there is an edge between two selected nodes, or counting query, which returns number of edges in a selected subgraph [32, 37], or a cross-additive query, which returns the number of edges crossing between two disjoint sets of vertices [14].

However, all the above queries assume that all the nodes (with labels) are known a priori, and that there are no hidden (unlabeled) nodes in the network. Moreover, most of the above works consider unweighted graphs, which are not suitable when end-to-end delay (or other weighted) information is available for topology discovery. As previously discussed, the above queries assume extensive information is available from the queried objects, and this may not be feasible in many networks.

Topology discovery using end-to-end delays between a subset of nodes (henceforth, referred to as participating nodes), has been previously studied for tree topologies using unicast traffic in [10, 35, 39] and multicast traffic [18]. The algorithms are inspired by *phylogenetic* tree algorithms. See [19] for a thorough review. Most of these algorithms are based on a series of local tests known as the *quartet-based dis-*

tance tests. Our algorithms are inspired by, and are based on quartet methods. However, these algorithms were previously applied only to tree topologies, and here, we show how algorithms based on similar ideas can provide accurate reconstruction for a much broader class of locally-tree like graphs such as the sparse random graphs.

2. SYSTEM MODEL

Notation

For any two functions $f(n), g(n)$, $f(n) = O(g(n))$ if there exists a constant M such that $f(n) \leq Mg(n)$ for all $n \geq n_0$ for some fixed $n_0 \in \mathbb{N}$. Similarly, $f(n) = \Omega(g(n))$ if there exists a constant M' such that $f(n) \geq M'g(n)$ for all $n \geq n_0$ for some fixed $n_0 \in \mathbb{N}$, and $f(n) = \Theta(g(n))$ if $f(n) = \Omega(g(n))$ and $f(n) = O(g(n))$. Also, $f(n) = o(g(n))$ when $f(n)/g(n) \to 0$ and $f(n) = \omega(g(n))$ when $f(n)/g(n) \to \infty$ as $n \to \infty$. We use notation $\tilde{O}(g(n)) = O(g(n)\text{poly} \log n)$. Let $\mathbb{I}[A]$ denote indicator of an event A.

Let G_n denote a random graph with probability measure $\mathbb{P}$. Let $\mathcal{Q}$ be a graph property (such as being connected). We say that the property $\mathcal{Q}$ for a sequence of random graphs $\{G_n\}_{n \in \mathbb{N}}$ holds asymptotically almost surely (a.a.s.) if,

$$\lim_{n \to \infty} \mathbb{P}(G_n \text{ satisfies } \mathcal{Q}) = 1.$$

Equivalently, the property $\mathcal{Q}$ holds for *almost every* (a.e.) graph G_n.

For a graph G, let $\mathcal{C}(l; G)$ denote the set of (generalized) cycles[1] of length less than l in graph G. For a vertex v, let $\deg(v)$ denote its degree and for an edge e, let $\deg(e)$ denote the total number of edges connected to either of its endpoints (but not counting the edge e). Let $B_R(v)$ denote the set of nodes within hop distance R from a node v and $\Gamma_R(v)$ is the set of nodes exactly at hop distance R. The definition is extended to an edge, by considering union of sets of the endpoints of edge. Denote the shortest path (with least number of hops) between two nodes i, j as $\text{path}(i, j; G)$ and the second shortest path as $\text{path}_2(i, j; G)$. Denote the number of H-subgraphs in G as $N_{H;G}$.

2.1 Random Graphs

We assume that the unknown network topology is drawn from the ensemble of Erdős-Rényi random graphs [11]. This random graph model is arguably the simplest as well the most well-studied model. Denote the random graph as $G_n \in \mathcal{G}(n, c/n)$, for $c < \infty$, where n is the number of nodes and each edge occurs uniformly with probability c/n. This implies a constant average degree of c for each node, and this regime is also known as the "sparse" regime of random graphs.

It is well known that sparse random graphs exhibit a phase transition with respect to the number of components. When $c > 1$, there is a giant component containing $\Theta(n)$ nodes, while all the other components have size $\Theta(\log n)$ [6, Ch. 11]. This regime is known as the *super-critical* regime. On

---

[1]A generalized cycle of length l is a connected graph of l nodes with l edges (i.e., can be a union of a path and a cycle). In this paper, a cycle refers to a generalized cycle unless otherwise mentioned.

the other hand, when $c < 1$, there is no giant component and all components have size $\Theta(\log n)$. This regime is known as the *sub-critical* regime.

We consider discovery of a random graph in the super-critical regime ($c > 1$). This is the regime of interest, since most real-world networks are well connected rather than having large number of extremely small components. Moreover, the presence of a giant component ensures that the topology can be discovered even with a small fraction of random participants. This is because the participants will most likely belong the giant component, and can thus exchange messages between each other to discover the unknown topology. We limit ourselves to the topology discovery of the giant component in the random graph, and denote the giant component as G_n, unless otherwise mentioned.

2.2 Participation Model

For the given unknown graph topology $G_n = (W_n, E_n)$ over $W_n = \{1, \ldots, n\}$ nodes, let $V_n \subset W_n$ be the set of participating nodes which exchange messages amongst each other by routing them along the graph. Let $\rho_n := \frac{|V_n|}{n}$ denote the fraction of participating nodes. It is desirable to have small ρ_n and still reconstruct the unknown topology. We assume that the nodes decide to participate uniformly at random. This ensures that information about all parts of the graph can be obtained, thereby making graph reconstruction feasible. We consider the regime, where $|V_n| = n^{1-\epsilon}$, for some $\epsilon > 0$, meaning that extremely small number of nodes participate in discovering the topology.

Let $H_n := W_n \setminus V_n$ be the set of hidden nodes. The hidden nodes only forward the messages without altering them, and do not provide any additional information for topology discovery. The presence of hidden nodes thus needs to inferred, as part of our goal of discovering the unknown graph topology.

2.3 Delay Model

The messages exchanged between the participating nodes experience delays along the links in the route. The participating nodes measure the end-to-end delays[2] between message transmissions and receptions. We consider the challenging scenario that only this end-to-end delay information is available for topology discovery.

Let m be the number of messages exchanged between each pair of participating nodes $i, j \in V_n$. Denote the m samples of end-to-end delays computed from these messages as

$$\mathbf{D}_{i,j}^m := [D_{i,j}(1), D_{i,j}(2), \ldots, D_{i,j}(m)]^T.$$

We assume that the routes taken by the m messages are fixed, and we discuss the routing model in the subsequent section. On the other hand, these messages experience different end-to-end delays[3] which are drawn identically and

---

[2]Our algorithms work under any *additive metric* defined on the graph such as link utilization or link loss [35], although the sample complexity, i.e., the number of samples required to accurately estimate the metrics, does indeed depend on the metric under consideration.

[3]The independence assumption implies that we consider unicast traffic rather than multicast traffic considered in many other works, e.g., in [18].

independently (i.i.d) from some distribution, described below.

Let D_e denote the random delay along a link $e \in G_n$ (in either direction). We assume that the delays D_{e_1} and D_{e_2} along any two links $e_1, e_2 \in G_n$ are independent. The delays are additive along any route, i.e., the end-to-end delay along a route $\mathcal{P}(i, j)$ between two participants $i, j \in V_n$ is

$$D_{\mathcal{P}(i,j)} := \sum_{e \in \mathcal{P}(i,j)} D_e. \tag{1}$$

We assume that the delay distributions $\{D_e\}_{e \in E_n}$ have bounded variances $\{l(e)\}_{e \in E_n}$ satisfying

$$0 < f \leq l(e) \leq g < \infty, \quad \forall e \in E_n. \tag{2}$$

Further, the family of delay distributions are regular and bounded, as in [10].

The delay distributions $\{D_e\}_{e \in E_n}$ and the graph topology G_n are both unknown, and need to be estimated using messages between participating nodes. We exploit the additivity assumption in (1) to obtain efficient topology discovery algorithms.

2.4 Routing Model

The end-to-end delays between the participating nodes thus depends on the routes taken by the messages. We assume that the messages between any two participants are routed along the shortest path with the lowest number of hops. On the other hand, the nodes cannot select the path with the least delay since the delays along the individual links are unknown and are also different for different messages.

We also consider another scenario, where the participants are able to additionally route messages along the second shortest path. This is a reasonable assumption, since in practice, nodes typically maintain information about the shortest path and an alternative path, should the shortest path fail. The nodes can forward messages along the shortest and the second shortest paths with different headers, so that the destinations can distinguish the two messages and compute the end-to-end delays along the two paths. We will show that this additional information vastly improves the accuracy of topology discovery. These two scenarios are formally defined below.

Scenario 1 (Shortest Path Delays): Each pair of participating nodes $i, j \in V_n$ exchange m messages along the shortest path in G_n, where the shortest path[4] is with respect to the number of hops. Denote the vector of m end-to-end delays as $\mathbf{D}_{i,j}^m$.

Scenario 2 (Shortest Path and Second Shortest Path Delays): Each pair of participating nodes $i, j \in V_n$ exchange m messages along the shortest path as well as m messages along the second shortest path. The vector of m samples along the second shortest path is denoted by $\widetilde{\mathbf{D}}_{i,j}^m$.

---

[4]If the shortest path between two nodes is not unique, assume that the node pairs randomly pick one of the paths and use it for all the messages.

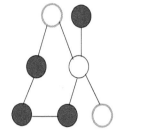 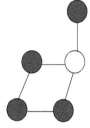

(a) A non-minimal graph   (b) Minimal representation

Figure 1: In minimal representation of a graph, hidden nodes with degree two or lower are merged. See Procedure 1.

Procedure 1 $\tilde{G}_n := \text{Minimal}(G_n; V_n)$ is the minimal representation of G_n given set of participating nodes V_n.

Input: Graph G_n, set of participating nodes V_n, and set of hidden nodes H_n.
Initialize $\tilde{G}_n = G_n$.
while $\exists h \in \tilde{G}_n \cap H_n$ with $\deg(h) \leq 2$ **do**
  Remove h from $\tilde{G}_n$ if $\deg(h) \leq 1$.
  Contract all h with $\deg(h) = 2$ in $\tilde{G}_n$.
end while

---

3. RECONSTRUCTION GUARANTEES

3.1 Minimal Representation

Our goal is to discover the unknown graph topology using the end-to-end delay information between the participating nodes. However, there can be multiple topologies which explain equally well the end-to-end delays between the participants. This inherent ambiguity in topology discovery with hidden nodes has been previously pointed out in the context of latent tree models [36].

Thus, there is an equivalence class of topologies with different sets of hidden nodes which generate the same end-to-end delay distributions between the participants. We refer to the topology with the least number of hidden nodes in this equivalence class as the *minimal representation*. Such a minimal representation does not have redundant hidden nodes. For example, in Fig.1, the graph and its minimal representation are shown. In Procedure 1, we characterize the relationship between a graph and its minimal representation, given a set of participants. The minimal representation is obtained by iteratively removing redundant hidden nodes from the graph.

Thus, any algorithm can only reconstruct the unknown topology up to its minimal representation using only end-to-end delay information between the participating nodes. In sparse random graphs, only a small (but a linear) number of nodes are removed in the minimal representation, and this number decreases with the average degree c. Moreover, given the minimal representation, nodes with degree two in the original graph can be recovered with additional information such as hop counts along the paths between the participants, or can be inferred using the knowledge of the bounds on delay variance in (2). It thus suffices to reconstruct the minimal representation of the original topology, and our goal is to accomplish it using small fraction of participants.

3.2 Performance Measures

We now define performance measures for topology discovery algorithms. It is desirable to have an algorithm which outputs a graph structure which is close to the original graph structure. However, the reconstructed graph cannot be directly compared with the original graph since the hidden nodes introduced in the reconstructed graph are unlabeled and may correspond to different hidden nodes in the original graph. To this end, we require the notion of edit distance defined below.

DEFINITION 1 (EDIT DISTANCE). *Let F, G be two graphs[5] with adjacency matrices $\mathbf{A}_F, \mathbf{A}_G$, and let V be the set of labeled vertices in both the graphs (with identical labels). Then the edit distance between F, G is defined as*

$$\Delta(F, G; V) := \min_{\pi} \|\mathbf{A}_F - \pi(\mathbf{A}_G)\|_1,$$

where π is any permutation on the unlabeled nodes while keeping the labeled nodes fixed.

In other words, the edit distance is the minimum number of entries that are different in $\mathbf{A}_F$ and in any permutation of $\mathbf{A}_G$ over the unlabeled nodes. In our context, the labeled nodes correspond to the participating nodes while the unlabeled nodes correspond to hidden nodes.

Our goal is to output a graph with small edit distance with respect to the minimal representation of the original graph. Ideally, we would like the edit distance to be zero (i.e., no error) as we obtain more delay samples and this is the notion of consistency.

DEFINITION 2 (CONSISTENCY). *Denote $\widehat{G}_n(\{\mathbf{D}_{i,j}^m\}_{i,j \in V_n})$ as the estimated graph using m delay samples between the participating nodes V_n. A graph estimator $\widehat{G}_n(\{\mathbf{D}_{i,j}^m\}_{i,j \in V_n})$ is structurally consistent if it asymptotically recovers the minimal representation of the unknown topology, i.e.,*

$$\lim_{m \to \infty} \mathbb{P}[\Delta(\widehat{G}(\{\mathbf{D}_{i,j}^m\}_{i,j \in V_n}), \tilde{G}_n; V_n) > 0] = 0. \quad (3)$$

The above definition assumes that the network size n is fixed while the number of samples m goes to infinity. A more challenging setting where both the network size and the number of samples grow is known as the setting of *high-dimensional inference* [40]. In this setting, we are interested in estimating large network structures using a small number of delay samples. We will consider this setting for topology discovery in this paper. Indeed in practice, we have large network structures but can obtain only few end-to-end delay samples with respect to the size of the network. This is formalized using the notion of sample complexity defined below for our setting.

DEFINITION 3 (SAMPLE COMPLEXITY). *If the number of samples is $m = \Omega(f(n))$, for some function f, such that the estimator $\widehat{G}_n(\{\mathbf{D}_{i,j}^m\}_{i,j \in V_n})$ satisfies*

$$\lim_{\substack{m,n \to \infty \\ m = \Omega(f(n))}} \mathbb{P}[\Delta(\widehat{G}(\{\mathbf{D}_{i,j}^m\}_{i,j \in V_n}), \tilde{G}_n; V_n) = O(g(n))] = 0,$$

---

[5]We consider inexact graph matching where the unlabeled nodes can be unmatched. This is done by adding required number of isolated unlabeled nodes in the other graph, and considering the modified adjacency matrices [12].

for some function $g(n)$, then the estimator $\widehat{G}_n$ is said to have sample complexity of $\Omega(f(n))$ for achieving an edit distance of $O(g(n))$.

Thus, our goal is to discover topology in high-dimensional regime, and design a graph estimator that requires a small number of delay samples, and output a graph with a small edit distance.

4. PRELIMINARIES

We now discuss some simple concepts which will be incorporated into our topology discovery algorithms.

4.1 Delay Variance Estimation

In our setting, topology discovery is based on the end-to-end delays between the participating nodes. Recall that in Section 2.3, we assume general delay distributions on the edges with bounded variances. Our topology discovery algorithms will be based solely on the estimated variances using the end-to-end delay samples.

We use the standard unbiased estimator for variances [30].

$$\widehat{l}^m(i,j) := \frac{1}{m-1}\sum_{k=1}^{m}(D_{i,j}(k) - \bar{D}_{i,j}^m)^2, \qquad (4)$$

where $\bar{D}_{i,j}^m$ is the sample mean delay

$$\bar{D}_{i,j}^m := \frac{1}{m}\sum_{k=1}^{m}D_{i,j}(k). \qquad (5)$$

Note that we do not use an estimator specifically tailored for a parametric delay distribution, and hence, the above estimator yields unbiased estimates for any delay distribution.

Our proposed algorithms for topology discovery require only the estimated delay variances $\{\widehat{l}(i,j)\}_{i,j\in V}$ as inputs. Indeed, more information is available in the delay samples $\mathbf{D}^m$. For instance, in [10], the higher-order moments of the delay distribution are estimated using the delay samples and this provides an estimate for the delay distribution. However, we see that for our goal of topology discovery, the estimated end-to-end delay variances suffice and yield good performance.

Recall that $\{l(i,j)\}_{i,j\in V}$ denote the true end-to-end delay variances and that in (1), we assume that the variances are additive along any path in the graph. Along with other assumptions, this implies that the delay variances on the edges form a *metric* on the graph. We will henceforth refer to the variances as "distances" between the nodes and the estimated variances as "estimated distances". This abstraction also implies that our algorithms will work under input of estimates of any additive metrics.

4.2 Quartet Tests

We first recap the so-called quartet tests, which are building blocks of many algorithms for discovering phylogenetic-tree topologies with hidden nodes [8, 20, 26, 36]. The definition of a quartet is given below. See Fig.2.

DEFINITION 4 (QUARTET OR FOUR-POINT CONDITION). *The pairwise distances $\{l(i,j)\}_{i,j\in\{a,b,u,v\}}$ for the configura-*

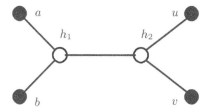

Figure 2: Quartet $Q(ab|uv)$. See (6) and (8).

tion in Fig.2 satisfy

$$l(a,u) + l(b,v) = l(b,u) + l(a,v), \qquad (6)$$

and the configuration is denoted by $Q(ab|uv)$.

In the literature on tree reconstruction, instead of (6), an inequality test is usually employed since it is more robust, given by,

$$l(a,b) + l(u,v) < \min(l(a,u) + l(b,v), l(b,u) + l(a,v)). \quad (7)$$

However, we use the equality test in (6), since it is also useful in detecting cycles present in random graphs.

In practice, we only have access to distance estimates and we relax the equality constraint in (6) to a threshold test, and this is known as the quartet test. Thus, the quartet test is local test between tuples of four nodes. For the quartet $Q = (ab|uv)$, let e denote the middle edge of the quartet[6], i.e., the edge which joins a vertex on the shortest path between a and b to a vertex on the shortest path between u and v (Note that the edge can have zero length if the hidden nodes connecting a, b and u, v are the same.). The estimated length of the middle edge (h_1, h_2) between hidden nodes h_1 and h_2 is given by

$$2\widehat{l}(h_1, h_2) = \widehat{l}(a,u) + \widehat{l}(b,v) - \widehat{l}(a,b) - \widehat{l}(u,v). \qquad (8)$$

Similarly, all other edge lengths of the quartet can be calculated through the set of linear equations.

Many phylogenetic-tree reconstruction algorithms proceed by iteratively merging quartets to obtain a tree topology. We employ the quartet test for random graph discovery but the analysis incorporates the presence of cycles. Moreover, we introduce modifications under scenario 2, as outlined in Section 5.2, where second shortest path distances are available in addition to the shortest path distances between the participating nodes.

5. PROPOSED ALGORITHMS

5.1 Scenario 1

We propose the algorithm RGD1 for discovering random graphs under scenario 1, as outlined in Section 2.4, where only shortest path distance estimates are available between the participating nodes. The idea behind RGD1 is similar to the classical phylogenetic-tree reconstruction algorithms based on quartet tests [20, 36]. However, the effect of cycles on such tests needs to analyzed, and is carried out in Section 6.1. The algorithm is summarized in Algorithm 2.

---

[6]Such a middle edge always exists, by allowing for zero length edges, and such trivial edges are contracted later in the algorithm.

Algorithm 2 RGD1($\{\widehat{l}(i,j)\}_{i,j \in V_n}; R, g, \tau, \epsilon$) for Topology Discovery Using Shortest-Path Distance Estimates.

Input: Distance estimates between the participating nodes $\{\widehat{l}(i,j)\}_{i,j \in V_n}$, upper bound g on exact edge lengths and parameters $R, \tau, \epsilon > 0$.

Initialize $\widehat{G}_n = (V_n, \emptyset)$.

for $a, b, u, v \in V_n$ such that $\max\limits_{i,j \in \{a,b,u,v\}} \widehat{l}(i,j) < Rg + \tau$

do

  if $Q(ab|uv)$ (i.e., Quartet) **then**

    Compute all distances $\{\widehat{l}(e)\}$ inside the quartet.

    Update $\widehat{G}_n \leftarrow \mathsf{MergeQuartet}(\widehat{G}_n, Q(ab|uv); \epsilon)$.

  end if

end for

The algorithm recursively runs the quartet tests over the set of participating nodes. When quartets are discovered, it merges them with the previously constructed graph using procedure MergeQuartet. This procedure splits the paths between the quartet nodes to introduce new hidden nodes, if such paths exist in the previously constructed graph; otherwise new edges are added. Any edges smaller than a threshold ϵ are contracted, for some chosen constant $\epsilon < f$, where f is the lower bound on the edge lengths of the original graph. It can be shown that the average runtime for RGD1 algorithm is $\tilde{O}(nc^{Rg/2f})$.

The algorithm limits to testing only "short quartets" between nearby participating nodes. Intuitively, this is done to avoid testing quartets on short cycles, since in such scenarios, the quartet tests may fail to reconstruct the graph accurately. Since the random graphs are locally-tree like and contain a small number of short cycles, limiting to short quartets enables us to avoid most of the cycles. The idea of short quartets has been used before (e.g. in [20]) but for a different goal of obtaining low sample complexity algorithm for phylogenetic-tree reconstruction. We carry out a detailed analysis on the effect of cycles on quartet tests in Section 6.1.

In algorithm RGD1, we consider short quartets, where all the estimated distances between the quartet end points are at most $Rg + \tau$, where g is the upper bound on the (exact) edge lengths in the original graph, as assumed in (2). Thus, $R' := Rg/f$ is the maximum number of hops between the end points of a short quartet, where f is the lower bound on the edge lengths. We refer to R' as the *diameter of the quartet*. This needs to be chosen carefully to balance the following two events: encountering short cycles and ensuring that most hidden edges (with at least one hidden end point) are part of short quartets. The parameter τ is chosen to relax the bound, since we have distance estimates, computed using samples, rather than exact distances between the participating nodes.

5.2 Scenario 2

We now consider scenario 2, as outlined in Section 2.4, where second shortest path distance estimates are available in addition to shortest path distance estimates between the participating nodes. We propose RGD2 algorithm for this case, which is summarized in Algorithm 3.

Algorithm 3 RGD2($\{\widehat{l}(i,j), \widehat{l}_2(i,j)\}_{i,j \in V_n}; R, g, \tau, \epsilon$) for Topology Discovery Using Shortest-Path and Second Shortest-Path Distance Estimates.

Input: Shortest-path and second shortest-path distance estimates $\{\widehat{l}(i,j), \widehat{l}_2(i,j)\}_{i,j \in V_n}$, upper bound g on exact edge lengths and parameters $R, \tau, \epsilon > 0$.

Initialize $\widehat{G}_n = (V_n, \emptyset)$.

for $a, b, u, v \in V_n$ such that $\max\limits_{i,j \in \{a,b,u,v\}} \widehat{l}(i,j) < Rg + \tau$

do

  Use $\{\widehat{l}_2(i,j)\}_{i,j \in \{a,b,u,v\}}$ if $\max\limits_{i,j \in \{a,b,u,v\}} \widehat{l}_2(i,j) < Rg + \tau$

  $\mathcal{Q} \leftarrow \{$Quartets over a, b, u, v using combination of $\{\widehat{l}(i,j), \widehat{l}_2(i,j)\}_{i,j \in \{a,b,u,v\}}$ if applicable $\}$.

  Compute all distances $\{\widehat{l}(e)\}$ inside each quartet in $\mathcal{Q}$. If a quartet occurs twice in $\mathcal{Q}$, only retain the one with shortest estimated middle edge.

  Update $\widehat{G}_n \leftarrow \mathsf{MergeQuartet}(\widehat{G}_n, \mathcal{Q}; \epsilon)$.

end for

Procedure 4 MergeQuartet($\widehat{G}_n, Q(ab|uv)); \epsilon$) for merging a new quartet with current structure $\widehat{G}_n$.

Input: Current graph $\widehat{G}$ and new quartet $Q(ab|cd)$ with hidden nodes h_1, h_2 (See Fig.2) and threshold ϵ for contracting short edges.

if $\exists$ path between a, b in $\widehat{G}$ with length $\widehat{l}(a, b; Q)$ **then**

  Split path and introduce a new hidden node h_1' such that $\widehat{l}(a, h_1'; \widehat{G}) = \widehat{l}(a, h_1; Q)$.

else

  Introduce node h_1' and connect it with a and b in $\widehat{G}$. Assign edge lengths $\widehat{l}(a, h_1'; \widehat{G}) = \widehat{l}(a, h_1; Q)$, $\widehat{l}(b, h_1'; \widehat{G}) = \widehat{l}(b, h_1; Q)$.

end if

Repeat for u, v and introduce hidden node h_2'.

Join h_1' and h_2' and assign it length $\widehat{l}(h_1', h_2'; \widehat{G}) = \widehat{l}(h_1, h_2; Q)$.

Contract any edges (with at least one hidden end point) if length $< \epsilon$.

The algorithm RGD2 is an extension of RGD1, where we use the second shortest distances in the quartet tests, in addition to the shortest distances. For each tuple of participating nodes $a, b, u, v \in V_n$, the quartet test in (6) is carried out for all possible combinations of shortest and second shortest distances; only short quartets are retained, where all the distances used for quartet test are less than the specified threshold (which is the same as in RGD1). If the same quartet is formed using different combinations of shortest and second shortest distances, only the quartet with the shorter middle edge, computed using (8), is retained. We clarify the reason behind this rule and give examples on when this can occur in Section 6.1. As before, all these quartets are merged with previously constructed graph using procedure MergeQuartet, but with a minor difference that the path lengths need to be checked since there may not be multiple paths between participating nodes with different lengths. The performance analysis for RGD2 is carried out in Section 6.3.

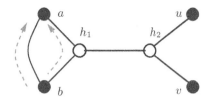

Figure 3: A bad quartet: $l(a,b) < l(a,h_1) + l(b,h_1)$. **Since the maximum number of hops between** $\{a,b,u,v\}$ **is** $R' := Rg/f$, **and one of the shortest paths is not along the quartet, the middle edge** (h_1,h_2) **is part of a generalized cycle of (hop) length less than** $2R'$.

6. ANALYSIS UNDER EXACT DISTANCES

We now undertake performance analysis for the proposed topology discovery algorithms RGD1 and RGD2. In this section, for simplicity, we first analyze the performance assuming that exact distances between the participating nodes are input to the algorithms. The detailed proofs are available in [7]. Analysis for the case when distance estimates are input to the algorithms is considered in Section 7.

6.1 Effect of Cycles on Quartet Tests

We now analyze the effect of cycles on quartet tests. Recall that the quartet test is the equality test in (6), and if this is satisfied, internal edge lengths of the quartet are computed, and they are added to the output using procedure MergeQuartet. The quartet test in (6) is based on the assumption that the shortest paths between the four nodes $\{a,b,u,v\}$ in the quartet are along the paths on the quartet.

Thus, the outcome of the quartet test is incorrect only when some shortest path between $\{a,b,u,v\}$ is outside the quartet. We refer to such quartets as "bad quartets". There are two possible outcomes for bad quartets (a) the quartet test in (6) does not hold, and thus, the quartet is not merged, or (b) the quartet test in (6) holds, but produces a fake quartet with wrong internal edge lengths.

The examples of both the cases are given in Fig.4. Recall that the quartet test in (6) is the equality test $l(a,u) + l(b,v) = l(a,v) + l(b,u)$. The case in Fig.4a does not satisfy this equality constraint[7], since the cycle is in the middle of the quartet, and thus this quartet is not merged. On the other hand, for the case in Fig.4b, the equality constraint is satisfied, since the cycle is on the same side of the quartet, and in this case, a fake quartet is merged but with wrong edge lengths[8], as shown in Fig.4c.

Thus, bad quartets lead to reconstruction error. The number of bad quartets can be bounded as follows: in a bad quartet, the middle edge of the quartet is part of a (generalized) cycle of length less than $2R'$, where $R' := Rg/f$ is the maximum number of hops between the endpoints of a

[7]There exist pathological cases of equal distances where configurations of the form in Fig.4a will satisfy equality constraint. Such scenarios do not occur in a.e. random graph.

[8]Note that the set of linear equations for computing the internal edge-lengths in the quartet consist of 5 variables and 6 equations (corresponding to the 6 known edge-lengths between the quartet end-points) along with the equality constraint in (6). Thus, when the equality constraint is satisfied, the system of equations produces a valid solution.

short quartet, as discussed in Section 5.1. The number of such short cycles can be bounded for random graphs leading to reconstruction guarantees for RGD1 algorithm.

For the RGD2 algorithm where second shortest path distances are additionally available, bad quartets do not adversely affect performance. We argue that a quartet is correctly recognized as long as the paths on the quartet correspond to either the shortest or the second shortest paths (between the quartet endpoints). In such a scenario, some combination of shortest and second shortest path distances exists which accurately reconstructs the quartet and the RGD2 algorithm finds all such combinations. Moreover, fake quartets are detected since they produce a longer middle edge than the true quartet. This is because the cycle shortens the distance between end points on its side (in Fig.4b, this corresponds to $\{a,b\}$ and note that the middle edge in Fig.4c is longer than the true edge length).

Thus, a quartet is correctly reconstructed under RGD2 when the paths on the quartet consist of shortest or second shortest paths. We finally use the locally tree-like property of random graphs to establish that this occurs in almost every graph if the quartet diameter R' is small enough. Thus, we obtain stronger reconstruction guarantees for RGD2 algorithm.

6.2 Analysis of RGD1

We now provide edit distance guarantees for RGD1 under appropriate choice of maximum quartet diameter $R' := Rg/f$. We analyze the edit distance by counting the number of hidden edges (with at least one hidden end point) which are not recovered correctly under RGD1. A hidden edge is not recovered when one of the following two events occur: (a) it is not part of a short quartet (b) it is part of a bad short quartet. A large value of the quartet diameter R' decreases the likelihood of event (a), while it increases the likelihood of event (b), i.e., we are likely to encounter more cycles as R' is increased. For a fixed value of R', we analyze the likelihood of these two events and obtain the bound on edit distance stated below.

Assume that the algorithm RGD1 chooses parameter R as $R = \frac{\gamma \log n}{\log c}$, where γ is chosen such that

$$R \le \frac{f}{g}\left(2 + 2\frac{\log(n^{0.75}/3)}{\log c}\right) \tag{9}$$

holds, where f and g are lower and upper bounds on exact edge lengths, as assumed in (2). Let the fraction of participating nodes be $\rho_n = n^{-\beta}$, such that

$$\rho c^{\frac{R}{2}} = \omega(1), \tag{10}$$

meaning that $\gamma > 2\beta$. We have the following result.

THEOREM 1 (EDIT DISTANCE UNDER RGD1). *The algorithm* RGD1 *recovers the minimal representation* $\widetilde{G}_n$ *of the giant component of a.e. graph* $G_n \sim \mathcal{G}(n, c/n)$ *with edit distance*

$$\Delta(\widehat{G}_n, \widetilde{G}_n; V_n) = \tilde{O}(n^{4\gamma g/f - 4\beta}). \tag{11}$$

Remarks:

(i) The parameter R chosen by RGD1 depends on the fraction of participating nodes ρ in (10). Incorporating this constraint into (11), means that an edit distance of $\tilde{O}(n^{4\beta(2g/f-1)})$

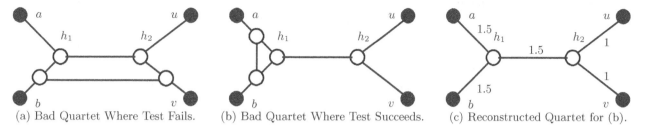

(a) Bad Quartet Where Test Fails.   (b) Bad Quartet Where Test Succeeds.   (c) Reconstructed Quartet for (b).

Figure 4: Two possible outcomes for bad quartets in (a) and (b). Assume all unit-length edges. In (a), the procedure MergeQuartet **fails and quartet is not declared**, while in (b), **it succeeds but leads to wrong edge estimates**, as shown in (c).

is achieved. This implies that $\beta < 0.25(2g/f - 1)^{-1}$ for achieving a sub-linear edit distance. For homogeneous edges ($f = g$), this implies that more than $n^{0.75}$ nodes are needed for achieving a sub-linear edit distance.

(ii) When the ratio of the bounds on the edge lengths g/f is small (i.e., the edge lengths are nearly homogeneous), the edit-distance guarantee in (11) improves, for a fixed ρ. This is because we can control the hop lengths of the selected quartets more effectively in this case.

(iii) The dominant event leading to the edit-distance bound in (11) is the presence of bad quartets due to short cycles in the random graph. In subsequent section, we show that RGD2 algorithm effectively handles this event using the second shortest path distances.

Proof Ideas:

The proof is based on the error events that can cause the quartet tests to fail. The first error event is that an edge which does not occur as a middle edge of a short quartet, meaning that there are not enough participating nodes within distance $R/2$ from it. The second error event is that an edge occurs as a middle edge of a bad quartet, meaning that it is close to a short cycle. We analyze the probability of these events and the resulting edit distance due to these events.

6.3   Analysis of RGD2

We now provide edit distance guarantees for RGD2 algorithm. The analysis is on the lines of the previous section, but we instead analyze the presence of overlapping cycles, as noted in Section 6.1. There are no overlapping short cycles in a random graph, and thus, we can provide a much stronger reconstruction guarantee for the RGD2 algorithm, compared to the RGD1 algorithm.

As before, assume that the parameter R for short quartet as $R = \frac{\gamma \log n}{\log c}$, where γ is chosen such that (9) holds. Let the fraction of participating nodes be $\rho_n = n^{-\beta}$ and (10) holds. We have the following result.

THEOREM 2 (EDIT DISTANCE UNDER RGD2). *Under the above conditions, the algorithm RGD2 recovers the minimal representation $\tilde{G}_n$ of the giant component of a.e. graph $G_n \sim \mathcal{G}(n, c/n)$ with edit distance*

$$\Delta(\widehat{G}_n, \tilde{G}_n; V_n) = \tilde{O}(n^{6\gamma g/f - 4\beta - 1}). \qquad (12)$$

The above result immediately implies that consistent recovery of the minimal representation is possible when there are enough number of participating nodes. We state the result formally below.

COROLLARY 1 (CONSISTENCY UNDER RGD2). *The algorithm RGD2 consistently recovers the minimal representation $\tilde{G}_n$ of the giant component of a.e. graph $G_n \sim \mathcal{G}(n, c/n)$, when the parameter R and the fraction of participating nodes ρ satisfy*

$$c^{\frac{6Rg}{f}} \rho^4 = o(n), \quad c^{\frac{R}{2}} \rho = \omega(1),$$

or equivalently

$$\frac{6\gamma g}{f} - 4\beta < 1, \quad \gamma > 2\beta.$$

Remarks:

(i) From the above constraints, we see that consistent topology recovery is feasible with $\rho = n^{-\beta}$, when $\beta < 0.25(3g/f - 1)^{-1}$. Thus, for equal edge lengths ($f = g$), when the number of participants is more than $n^{7/8}$, RGD2 consistently recovers the topology. Intuitively, this is because, with enough participating nodes, we can limit to short distances, and avoid any overlapping cycles, which are the sources of error for RGD2 algorithm.

(ii) Thus, the availability of second shortest distances makes consistent topology discovery possible with a sub-linear number of participating nodes, while consistent recovery is not tractable under RGD1 using only shortest-path distances between a sub-linear number of participants.

Proof Ideas:

The proof is on similar lines as in Theorem 1, but with modified error events that cause the quartet tests to fail. As before, the first error event is that an edge which does not occur as a middle edge of a short quartet. The second error event is now that an edge is close to two overlapping short cycles instead of being close to a single short cycle. This event does not occur in random graphs for sufficiently short lengths, and thus, we see a drastic improvement in edit distance.

261

7. ANALYSIS UNDER SAMPLES

We have so far analyzed the performance of RGD1 and RGD2 algorithms when exact distances (i.e., delay variances) are input to the algorithm. We now analyze the scenario when instead only delay samples are available and estimated variances are input to the algorithm.

We show that the proposed algorithms have low sample complexity, meaning they require slow scaling of number of samples compared to the network size to achieved guaranteed performance. The result is given below.

THEOREM 3 (SAMPLE COMPLEXITY). *The edit distance guarantees under* RGD1 *and* RGD2 *algorithms, as stated in Theorem 1 and Theorem 2, are achieved under input of estimated delay variances, if the number of delay samples satisfies*

$$m = \Omega(\text{poly}(\log n)). \tag{13}$$

Thus, the sample complexity of RGD1 and RGD2 algorithms is $\text{poly}(\log n)$. In other words, the size of the network n can grow much faster than the number of delay samples m, and we can still obtain good estimates of the network. This implies with $m = \Omega(\text{poly}(\log n))$ samples, we can consistently discover the topology under RGD2 algorithm, given sufficient fraction of participating nodes.

Proof Ideas:

The proof follows from Azuma-Hoeffding inequality for concentration of individual variance estimates, as in [10, Proposition 1], and then consider the union bound over various events.

8. CONVERSE RESULTS & DISCUSSION

8.1 Fraction of Participating Nodes

We have so far provided edit distance guarantees for the proposed topology discovery algorithms. In this section, we provide a lower bound on the fraction of participating nodes required for any algorithm to recover the original graph up to a certain edit distance guarantee.

We can obtain a meaningful lower bound only when the specified edit distance is lower than the edit distance between a given graph and an independent realizations of the random graph. Otherwise, the edit distance guarantee could be realized by a random construction of the output graph. To this end, we first prove a lower bound on the edit distance between any fixed graph and an independent realization of the random graph.

Let $\mathcal{D}(G; \delta)$ denote the set of all graphs which have edit distance of at most δ from G

$$\mathcal{D}(G; \delta) := \{F : \Delta(F, G; \emptyset) < \delta\}. \tag{14}$$

LEMMA 1 (LOWER BOUND ON EDIT DISTANCE). *Almost every random graph $G_n \sim \mathcal{G}(n, c/n)$ has an edit distance at least $(0.5c - 1)n$ from any given graph F_n.*

Proof: First, we have for any graph F_n

$$|\mathcal{D}(F_n; \delta n)| \leq n! \cdot \binom{\frac{n^2}{2}}{\delta n} < n^{(\delta+1)n} 3^{\delta n}, \tag{15}$$

since we can permute the n vertices and change at most δn entries in the adjacency matrix $\mathbf{A}_F$ and we use the bound

that $\binom{N}{k} \leq \frac{N^k}{k!} \leq (\frac{N}{k})^k 3^k$. Let $\mathcal{B}$ denote the set of graphs having exactly $\frac{cn}{2}$ edges and the size of $\mathcal{B}$ is

$$|\mathcal{B}| = \binom{\frac{n^2}{2}}{\frac{cn}{2}} \geq (\frac{n^2}{cn})^{cn/2} = (\frac{n}{c})^{cn/2}.$$

We can now bound the probability that a random graph $G_n \sim \mathcal{G}(n, c/n)$ belongs to set $\mathcal{D}(F_n; \delta n)$ for any given graph F_n is

$$\mathbb{P}[G_n \in \mathcal{D}(F_n; \delta n)] \leq \frac{\mathbb{P}[G_n \in \mathcal{D}(F_n; \delta n)]}{\mathbb{P}[G_n \in \mathcal{B}]}$$

$$\leq \frac{|\mathcal{D}(F_n; \delta n)| \max\limits_{g \in \mathcal{D}(F_n; \delta n)} \mathbb{P}[G_n = g]}{|\mathcal{B}| \min\limits_{g \in \mathcal{B}} \mathbb{P}[G_n = g]}$$

$$\overset{(a)}{\leq} \frac{|\mathcal{D}(F_n; \delta n)|}{|\mathcal{B}|} = n^{(\delta+1-c/2)n} 3^{\delta n},$$

where inequality (a) is due to the fact that $\min_{g \in \mathcal{B}} \mathbb{P}[G_n = g] \geq \max_{g \in \mathcal{S}(F_n)} \mathbb{P}[G_n = g]$ (i.e., the mode of the binomial distribution). Hence, $\mathbb{P}[G_n \in \mathcal{D}(F_n; \delta n)]$ decays to zero as $n \to \infty$, when $\delta < 0.5c - 1$. □

Thus, for any given graph, a random graph does not have edit distance less than $(0.5c - 1)n$ from it. It is thus reasonable to expect for any graph reconstruction algorithm to achieve an edit distance less than $(0.5c - 1)n$, since otherwise, a random choice of the output graph could achieve the same edit distance. We now provide a lower bound on the fraction of the participating nodes such that no algorithm can reconstruct the original graph up to an edit distance less than $(0.5c - 1)n$.

THEOREM 4 (LOWER BOUND). *For $G_n \sim \mathcal{G}(n, c/n)$ and any set of participants V_n, for any graph estimator $\widehat{G}_n$ using (exact) shortest path distances between the participating node pairs, we have*

$$\mathbb{P}[\Delta(\widehat{G}_n, G_n; V) > \delta n] \to 1, \text{ when}$$

$$|V|^2 < Mn(0.5c - \delta - 1)\frac{\log n}{\log \log n}, \tag{16}$$

for a small enough constant $M > 0$ and any $\delta < (0.5c - 1)$.

Thus, no algorithm can reconstruct G_n up to edit distance δn, for $\delta < 0.5c - 1$, if the number of participating nodes is below a certain threshold. From Lemma 1, almost every random graph has an edit distance greater than $(0.5c - 1)n$ from a given graph. Thus, when the number of participating nodes is below a certain threshold, accurate reconstruction by any algorithm is impossible.

Remarks:

(i) The lower bound does not require that the participating nodes are chosen uniformly and holds for any set of participating nodes of given cardinality.

(ii) The lower bound is analogous to a strong converse in information theory [16] since it says that the probability of edit distance being more a certain quantity goes to one (not just bounded away from zero).

(iii) The result is valid even for the scenario where second shortest path distances are used since the maximum second shortest path distance is also $O(\log n)$.

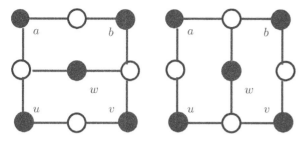

Figure 5: Example of two graphs with unit lengths where nodes a, b, u, v, w are participating. Even under all path length information between the participating nodes, the two graphs cannot be distinguished.

(iv) We have earlier shown that our algorithms RGD1 and RGD2 have good performance under a sub-linear number of participants. Closing the gaps in the exponents between lower bound and achievability is of interest.

Proof Ideas:

The proof is based on information-theoretic covering type argument, where cover the range of the estimator with random graphs of high likelihood. Using bounds on binomial distribution, we obtain the desired lower bound.

8.2 Non-Identifiability of General Topologies

Our proposed algorithms require the knowledge of shortest and second shortest path distances. Performance analysis reveals that the knowledge of second shortest path can greatly improve the accuracy of topology discovery for random graphs. We now address the question if this can be accomplished in general.

To this end, we provide a counter-example in Fig.5, where a significant fraction of nodes are participating, and we are given distances along all the paths between the participants; yet, the topology cannot be correctly identified by any algorithm. This reveals a fundamental non-identifiability of general topologies using only a subset of participating nodes.

8.3 Relationship to Phylogenetic Trees

We note some key differences between the phylogenetic-tree model [19] and the additive delay model employed in this paper. In phylogenetic trees, sequences of extant species are available, and the unknown phylogenetic tree is to be inferred from these sequences. The phylogenetic-tree models the series of mutations occurring as the tree progresses and new species are formed. Efficient algorithms with low sample complexity have been proposed for phylogenetic-tree reconstruction, e.g., in [17, 20].

In the phylogenetic-tree model, the correlations along the phylogenetic tree decay exponentially with the number of hops. This implies that long-range correlations (between nodes which are far away) are "hard" to estimate, and require large number of samples (compared to the size of the tree) to find an accurate estimate. However, under the delay model, the delays are additive along the edges, and even long-range delays can be shown to be "easy" to estimate. Hence, the delay model does not require the more sophisticated techniques developed for phylogenetic-tree reconstruc-

tion (e.g., [17]), in order to achieve low sample complexity. However, the presence of cycles complicates the analysis for delay-based reconstruction of random graphs. Moreover, we developed algorithms when additional information is available in the form of second shortest-path distances. Such information cannot be obtained from phylogenetic data. We demonstrated that this additional information leads to drastic improvement in the accuracy of random-graph discovery.

9. CONCLUSION

In this paper, we considered discovery of sparse random graph topologies using a sub-linear number of uniformly selected participants. We proposed local quartet-based algorithms which exploit the locally tree-like property of sparse random graphs. We first showed that a sub-linear edit-distance guarantee can be obtained using end-to-end measurements along the shortest paths between a sub-linear number of participants. We then considered the scenario where additionally, second shortest-path measurements are available, and showed that consistent topology recovery is feasible using only a sub-linear number of participants. Finally, we establish a lower bound on the edit distance achieved by any algorithm for a given number of participants. Our algorithms are simple to implement, computationally efficient and have low sample complexity.

There are many interesting directions to explore. Our algorithms require the knowledge of the bounds on the delay variances (i.e., edge lengths), and algorithms which remove these requirements can be explored. Our algorithms are applicable for other locally tree-like graphs as well, while the actual performance indeed depends on the model employed. Exploring how the reconstruction performance changes with the graph model is of interest. In many networks, such as peer-to-peer networks, there is a high churn rate and the nodes join and leave the networks, and it is of interest to extend our algorithms to such scenarios. Moreover, we have provided reconstruction guarantees in terms of edit distance with respect to the minimal representation, and plan to analyze reconstruction of other graph-theoretic measures such as the degree distribution, centrality measures, and so on. While we have assumed uniform sampling, other strategies (e.g., random walks) need to analyzed. We plan to implement the developed algorithms developed on real-world data.

Acknowledgement

The authors thank the anonymous reviewers for extensive comments that greatly improved the quality of this paper.

10. REFERENCES

[1] Cooperative Analysis for Internet Data Analysis, (CAIDA). http://www.caida.org/tools/.
[2] Internet Mapping Project. http://www.cheswick.com/ches/map/.
[3] mtrace– Print multicast path. ftp://ftp.parc.xerox.com/pub/net-research/ipmulti.
[4] The Skitter Project. http://www.caida.org/tools/measurement/skitter/.
[5] D. Achlioptas, A. Clauset, D. Kempe, and C. Moore. On the bias of traceroute sampling: Or, power-law degree distributions in regular graphs. *J. ACM*, 56(4), 2009.
[6] N. Alon and J. Spencer. *The probabilistic method.* Wiley-Interscience, 2000.

[7] A. Anandkumar, A. Hassidim, and J. Kelner. Topology Discovery of Sparse Random Graphs With Few Participants. *Arxiv*, Feb. 2011.

[8] H.-J. Bandelth and A. Dress. Reconstructing the shape of a tree from observed dissimilarity data. *Adv. Appl. Math*, 7:309–43, 1986.

[9] Z. Beerliova, F. Eberhard, T. Erlebach, A. Hall, M. Hoffmann, M. Mihal ak, and L. Ram. Network Discovery and Verification. *IEEE Journal on Selected Areas in Communications*, 24(12):2168, 2006.

[10] S. Bhamidi, R. Rajagopal, and S. Roch. Network Delay Inference from Additive Metrics. *To appear in Random Structures and Algorithms, on Arxiv*, 2010.

[11] B. Bollobás. *Random Graphs*. Academic Press, 1985.

[12] G. Bunke et al. Inexact graph matching for structural pattern recognition. *Pattern Recognition Letters*, 1(4):245–253, 1983.

[13] R. Castro, M. Coates, G. Liang, R. Nowak, and B. Yu. Network Tomography: Recent Developments. *Stat. Sc.*, 19:499–517, 2004.

[14] S. Choi and J. Kim. Optimal query complexity bounds for finding graphs. In *Proc. of annual ACM symposium on Theory of computing*, pages 749–758, 2008.

[15] F. Chung, M. Garrett, R. Graham, and D. Shallcross. Distance realization problems with applications to Internet tomography. *J. of Comp. and Sys. Sc.*, 63(3):432–448, 2001.

[16] T. Cover and J. Thomas. *Elements of Information Theory*. John Wiley & Sons, Inc., 1991.

[17] C. Daskalakis, E. Mossel, and S. Roch. Optimal phylogenetic reconstruction. In *STOC '06: Proceedings of the thirty-eighth annual ACM symposium on Theory of computing*, pages 159–168, 2006.

[18] N. Duffield, J. Horowitz, F. Presti, and D. Towsley. Multicast topology inference from end-to-end measurements. *Advances in Performance Analysis*, 3:207–226, 2000.

[19] R. Durbin, S. R. Eddy, A. Krogh, and G. Mitchison. *Biological Sequence Analysis: Probabilistic Models of Proteins and Nucleic Acids*. Cambridge Univ. Press, 1999.

[20] P. L. Erdős, L. A. Székely, M. A. Steel, and T. J. Warnow. A few logs suffice to build (almost) all trees: Part ii. *Theoretical Computer Science*, 221:153–184, 1999.

[21] B. Eriksson, P. Barford, R. Nowak, and M. Crovella. Learning Network Structure from Passive Measurements. In *Proc. of the ACM SIGCOMM conference on Internet measurement*, Kyoto, Japan, Aug. 2007.

[22] T. Erlebach, A. Hall, and M. Mihal'ak. Approximate Discovery of Random Graphs. *Lecture Notes in Computer Science*, 4665:82, 2007.

[23] M. Gomez-Rodriguez, J. Leskovec, and A. Krause. Inferring Networks of Diffusion and Influence. In *Proc. of the ACM SIGKDD Intl. Conf. on Knowledge Discovery and Data Mining*, 2010.

[24] M. Gunes and K. Sarac. Resolving anonymous routers in Internet topology measurement studies. In *Proc. of IEEE INFOCOM*, pages 1076–1084, 2008.

[25] Y. He, G. Siganos, and M. Faloutsos. Internet Topology. In R. Meyers, editor, *Encyclopedia of Complexity and Systems Science*, pages 4930–4947. Springer, 2009.

[26] T. Jiang, P. E. Kearney, and M. Li. A polynomial-time approximation scheme for inferring evolutionary trees from quartet topologies and its application. *SIAM J. Comput.*, 30(6):1942–1961, 2001.

[27] M. Jovanović, F. Annexstein, and K. Berman. Modeling peer-to-peer network topologies through small-world models and power laws. In *TELFOR*, 2001.

[28] S. Khuller, B. Raghavachari, and A. Rosenfeld. Landmarks in graphs. *Discrete Appl. Math.*, 70(3):217–229, 1996.

[29] M. Kurant, M. Gjoka, C. T. Butts, and A. Markopoulou. Walking on a Graph with a Magnifying Glass. In *Proceedings of ACM SIGMETRICS '11*, San Jose, CA, June 2011.

[30] E. Lehmann. *Theory of Point Estimation*. Chapman & Hall, New York, NY, 1991.

[31] J. Leskovec, D. Huttenlocher, and J. Kleinberg. Predicting Positive and Negative Links in Online Social Networks. In *ACM WWW Intl. Conf. on World Wide Web*, 2010.

[32] H. Mazzawi. Optimally Reconstructing Weighted Graphs Using Queries. In *Symposium on Discrete Algorithms*, pages 608–615, 2010.

[33] S. Myers and J. Leskovec. On the Convexity of Latent Social Network Inference. In *Proc. of NIPS*, 2010.

[34] M. Newman, D. Watts, and S. Strogatz. Random graph models of social networks. *Proc. of the National Academy of Sciences of the United States of America*, 99(Suppl 1), 2002.

[35] J. Ni, H. Xie, S. Tatikonda, and Y. Yang. Efficient and dynamic routing topology inference from end-to-end measurements. *Networking, IEEE/ACM Transactions on*, 18(1):123–135, 2010.

[36] J. Pearl. *Probabilistic Reasoning in Intelligent Systems—Networks of Plausible Inference*. Morgan Kaufmann, 1988.

[37] L. Reyzin and N. Srivastava. Learning and verifying graphs using queries with a focus on edge counting. *Lecture Notes in Computer Science*, 4754:285, 2007.

[38] L. Reyzin and N. Srivastava. On the longest path algorithm for reconstructing trees from distance matrices. *Information Processing Letters*, 101(3):98–100, 2007.

[39] M. Shih and A. Hero. Unicast inference of network link delay distributions from edge measurements. In *Proc. of IEEE ICASSP*, volume 6, pages 3421–3424, 2002.

[40] M. Wainwright and M. Jordan. Graphical Models, Exponential Families, and Variational Inference. *Foundations and Trends in Machine Learning*, 1(1-2):1–305, 2008.

[41] B. Yao, R. Viswanathan, F. Chang, and D. Waddington. Topology inference in the presence of anonymous routers. In *Proc. of IEEE INFOCOM*, 2003.

Characterizing and Modeling
Internet Traffic Dynamics of Cellular Devices

M. Zubair Shafiq[†]   Lusheng Ji[‡]   Alex X. Liu[†]   Jia Wang[‡]
[†]Department of Computer Science and Engineering, Michigan State University, East Lansing, MI, USA
[‡]AT&T Labs – Research, Florham Park, NJ, USA
{shafiqmu,alexliu}@cse.msu.edu, {lji,jiawang}@research.att.com

ABSTRACT

Understanding Internet traffic dynamics in large cellular networks is important for network design, troubleshooting, performance evaluation, and optimization. In this paper, we present the results from our study, which is based upon a week-long aggregated flow level mobile device traffic data collected from a major cellular operator's core network. In this study, we measure and characterize the spatial and temporal dynamics of mobile Internet traffic. We distinguish our study from other related work by conducting the measurement at a larger scale and exploring mobile data traffic patterns along two new dimensions – device types and applications that generate such traffic patterns. Based on the findings of our measurement analysis, we propose a Zipf-like model to capture the volume distribution of application traffic and a Markov model to capture the volume dynamics of aggregate Internet traffic. We further customize our models for different device types using an unsupervised clustering algorithm to improve prediction accuracy.

Categories and Subject Descriptors

C.4 [**Computer System Organization**]: Performance of Systems—*Modeling techniques*; C.2.3 [**Computer System Organization**]: Computer Communication Networks—*Network Operations*

General Terms

Experimentation, Measurement, Performance, Theory

1. INTRODUCTION

1.1 Motivation

Since the emergence of cellular data networks, the volume of data traffic carried by cellular networks has been growing continuously due to the rapid increase in subscriber base size, cellular communication bandwidth, and cellular device capability. The recent unprecedented cellular data volume

surge as the result of dramatic growth in the popularity of smart phones strongly suggests that the trend of cellular data growth will continue to accelerate as technology and application availabilities further improve [1]. To cope with the explosive cellular data volume growth and best serve their customers, cellular network operators need to design and manage cellular core network architectures accordingly. To achieve this, the first step is to understand the spatial and temporal patterns of Internet traffic carried by cellular networks. Understanding the spatial and temporal patterns of traffic can help to estimate both short- and long-term changes in network resource requirements.

1.2 Limitations of Prior Art

Cellular data traffic has not been well explored in prior work, although some attempts have been made [16, 14, 6]. The studies by Williamson *et al.* [16] and Trestian *et al.* [14] focused on jointly characterizing temporal dynamics of network traffic and user mobility. Their traffic traces contained data from about 10,000 and 280,000 users, respectively. Falaki *et al.* characterized diversity in smart phone activities (both in terms of user interaction with smart phones and the generated traffic) and linked it to battery consumption patterns [6]. Their traffic trace was collected from 255 users.

Prior work on cellular data traffic has four major limitations. First, the scales of these studies are not sufficient to be representative for the purpose of strategic level cellular operation planning. Second, no prior work has studied the behavior of different device types used to access cellular networks. However, understanding the behavior of different device types is important for billing and network resource planning. For example, knowing the different specifics of traffic that different device types tend to generate may help operators to construct appropriate promotions and rate plans. Third, no prior work has studied the behavior of network applications in cellular network traffic. However, understanding the behavior of different network applications is important because different applications have different demands on the quality of service. For example, if the volume of VoIP traffic (*e.g.* Skype) dominates P2P traffic (*e.g.* torrents), the service provider faces more demands on the quality of service, as compared to the opposite case. Finally, no prior work has developed predictive models for the spatial and temporal dynamics of cellular network traffic. However, the development of predictive models for cellular network is important for forecasting traffic trends and adjusting network resources accordingly.

1.3 Key Contributions

In this work, we study the traffic dynamics of a large operational cellular network. Our data set was collected from the core network of a major cellular service provider. In this paper, we first present the findings from our measurement studies. Second, based on the findings of our measurement analysis, we propose a Zipf-like model to capture the distribution and a Markov model to capture the volume dynamics of aggregate Internet traffic. We make key contributions from the following four perspectives:

1. **Scale of Study:** Our data set contains the logs of aggregated IP traffic generated by devices located in a major state of the USA. The usage data set is a summary of hundreds of terabytes of traffic from millions of cellular devices over the duration of a week.

2. **Behavior of Device Types:** We study a wide range of mobile devices in cellular networks. Our studies, with detailed analysis and characterization, show that different types of devices exhibit different traffic patterns. There are two main reasons. First, different devices have different capabilities. Second, different mobile devices are generally designed for attracting different population segments which often exhibit different usage behaviors.

3. **Behavior of Applications:** We study cellular network traffic characteristics against the wide range of applications that generated such traffic because different applications impose different demands on network resources and have different requirements on reliability and performance. Using application type as an additional dimension for characterizing dynamics of cellular network traffic offers finer granularity insights for network operators to understand how mobile devices demand network resources.

4. **Modeling Dynamics of Network Traffic:** We utilize results from measurement analysis to develop models for aggregate spatial and temporal dynamics of traffic in cellular networks. Since different types of devices show different traffic behaviors, we extend the aggregate model by customizing it for different types of devices to improve its prediction accuracy.

1.4 Our Findings

The results of our study reveal several interesting insights. We summarize the major findings of our study as follows: (1) The distribution of network traffic with respect to both individual devices and constituent applications is highly skewed. Only 5% of the devices are responsible for 90% of the total network traffic. Moreover, the top 10% applications account for more than 99% of the flows. Further, the distribution of traffic volume with respect to applications varies for different device types. These distributions can be modeled using Zipf-like models. (2) The aggregate volume of Internet traffic flowing on the network shows strong diurnal patterns. These diurnal patterns differ across weekdays and weekends. Moreover, the diurnal patterns of different cellular device types show subtle variations. The time-series of aggregate Internet traffic volume can be modeled using a multi-order discrete time Markov chain. (3) Finally, the behavior of different device types can be clustered into distinct subgroups.

An unsupervised clustering algorithm such as the k-means algorithm can be utilized with spatial and temporal feature sets to effectively cluster device types. Using the identified subgroups, the model developed for aggregate traffic can be further extended to a more insightful and accurate multi-class model.

The rest of the paper proceeds as follows. In Section 2, we provide an overview of the cellular network architecture and describe the data set used in our study. In Section 3, we present measurement results of a week-long Internet traffic trace from a cellular network containing millions of devices. In Section 4, we develop a stochastic model to capture the spatial and temporal dynamics of aggregate network traffic. We then extend this model to a multi-class model by applying unsupervised clustering to identify subgroups of device types. We provide a review of the related work in Section 5 and conclude in Section 6.

2. BACKGROUND

2.1 Overview of Cellular Network Architecture

The cellular network that we study employs both second generation (2G) and third generation (3G) mobile data communication technologies that are part of 3rd Generation Partnership Project (3GPP) lineage. Figure 1 illustrates the architecture of the cellular network used for this study, in particular the components that are related to carrying IP data traffic. Such a cellular network can be visualized as consisting of three major segments: (1) the mobile cellular device; (2) the Radio Access Network (RAN), and (3) the Core Network (CN). The radio access network consists of base stations (named Base Transceiver Stations or BTS in 2G terms or Node B in 3G terms) and controllers (Base Station Controllers or Radio Network Controllers). The RAN controllers connect to the core network at nodes known as the Serving GPRS Support Nodes (SGSNs). In the core network, the mobile-facing SGSNs connect to the external-facing Gateway GPRS Support Nodes (GGSNs), which are responsible for providing connectivity to external networks such as the Internet and other private networks.

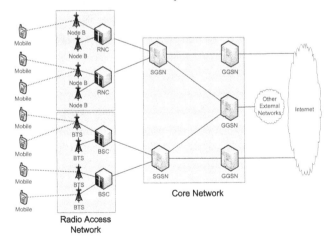

Figure 1: Architecture of a cellular network

2.2 Data Set Description

Our study is based on flow level mobile device traffic data collected from the cellular operator's core network. This allows us to characterize the IP traffic patterns of mobile cellular devices and develop models that predict the bandwidth demands in the operator's core network over time. Due to the large volume of data and other limitations of our logging apparatus, we focus our study only in one particular state in the USA. This particular state was chosen because of log data availability, its geographical area, and population. That is, we only study the activities of mobile devices that are associated to base stations in that state. The data set covers activities during one whole week (18th to 24th) in January 2010. However, this data set does not contain complete temporal information due to some issues with the logging apparatus. Therefore, this data set is augmented with another aggregate data set only to study aggregate temporal traffic characteristics. The aggregate data set spans one whole week (14th to 20th) in June 2010. This data set also includes traffic data for two weekend days (12th and 13th June), which is only used for evaluation purposes. The aggregate temporal traffic results presented in this paper are from the second data set.

Each record contained in the aggregate data set is a summary report of activity during one particular flow by one mobile device. The records in the data set are indexed by a time stamp and a hashed mobile device identity. It is worth noting that we study traffic patterns of mobile devices instead of traffic patterns of users, which is also of more interest from operator's perspective. Each record in the data set also contains a cell identifier, which identifies the cell that serves the device, an application identifier, and data usage statistics for the flow, including total number of bytes, and total number of packets during that flow. A typical web-browsing activity, for example, may be represented by one flow record containing several packets of different sizes. These anonymous records were aggregated across all flow records and devices for analysis purposes. Different applications are identified using a combination of port information, payload signatures, and other heuristics. More details about application identification are provided in [5].

It is also worth noting that for privacy reasons the only device identifiers present in the data set are anonymized International Mobile Equipment Identifiers, or IMEI numbers. By design an original IMEI number uniquely identifies an individual mobile device. Such uniqueness is preserved by the anonymization process. Moreover, the anonymization preserves a portion of the IMEI number, known as the Type Allocation Code (TAC), which identifies the manufacturer and model of the device.

Our collected data set has two limitations that are mentioned below. First, the cell information in our data may not be accurate due to the fact that such information is obtained by monitoring GPRS Tunneling Protocol (GTP) message exchanges. Because GTP tunnel may remain intact despite device movements and handoffs, it is possible that a device initiates its data connection in a cell and thereafter moves across multiple cells [12] and such cell changes are not reflected in the data set as long as no GTP update is triggered by the device's movement. Partially due to these inaccuracies, user mobility characteristics are not part of this study. See reference [18] for quantification of the location inaccuracies in our data. Second, our data set, though covers complete population of one state with millions of users, only contains traffic information for one week time duration. This limitation is imposed due to huge vol-

ume of logged traffic records. Due to this, we cannot study long-term traffic patterns that span beyond one week time duration.

3. MEASURING INTERNET TRAFFIC DYNAMICS

In this section, we present the measurement results of the collected trace which spans a complete week and contains Internet traffic records of millions of cellular devices. As a first step, we study the distribution and temporal dynamics of aggregated Internet traffic. The insights gained by analyzing the distribution and temporal dynamics of Internet traffic are of significant importance for network management, traffic engineering, and capacity planning. Furthermore, we compare the traffic patterns of cellular devices from two popular mobile smart phone families and one cellular broadband modem family. The measurement results indicate significant differences in traffic patterns of different cellular device types.

3.1 Distribution and Temporal Dynamics of Aggregate Traffic

3.1.1 Traffic Volume Distribution

First we plot the distribution of traffic volume with respect to device identifier in Figure 2. Note that the curve approximately follows a straight line on a log-log scale across several orders of magnitude. We get a reasonably good fit for a Zipf model with index -0.57. This observation signifies that traffic volume in the cellular network is dominated by a small fraction of users.

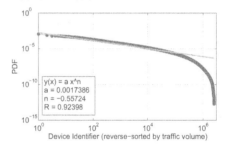

Figure 2: (Reverse-)Sorted distribution of traffic volume with respect to individual devices

Figure 3(a) shows the cumulative distribution function (CDF) plot of traffic volume with respect to device identifiers. In order to highlight the skewness in distribution, we have modified the x-axis to log-scale. It clearly shows that 5% of the devices are responsible for 90% of the total network traffic. The vertical dotted line partitions the top 5% devices on x-axis. A more careful look into the data reveals that in this data set the top-3 devices with respect to traffic volume belong to the family of wireless broadband modems. This observation is in accordance with our intuition as wireless modems are mostly plugged into desktop and laptop machines which provide more liberty to applications to utilize network resources. Moreover, desktop or laptop users tend to connect to the broadband network longer than handheld devices because the former has abundant power and storage resources, as well as more convenient user interfaces.

Traffic volume distribution can also be studied from a different perspective. Figure 3(b) shows the CDF of traffic

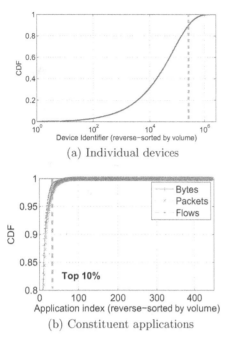

(a) Individual devices

(b) Constituent applications

Figure 3: CDF plot of traffic volume

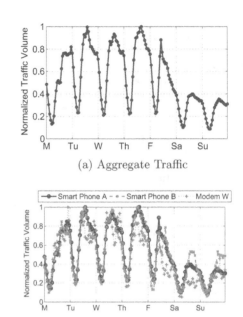

(a) Aggregate Traffic

(b) Separate Device Families

Figure 4: Diurnal characteristics of traffic volume over the duration of complete week

volume with respect to application identifiers. Just like the CDF plot of traffic volume with respect to device identifiers, it is evident that the distribution of traffic with respect to applications is highly skewed. The shape of the curve is similar for bytes, packets, and flows. However, the highest degree of skewness is observed for flows where the top 10% applications account for more than 99% flows.

3.1.2 Temporal Dynamics

It is also interesting to study the temporal dynamics of the logged traffic. In Figure 4(a), we plot time-series of the observed traffic volume at per hour granularity for the complete week. We clearly observe strong diurnal variations in aggregate traffic volume. This diurnality as well as several other features of the plot can all be reasonably explained by weekly working schedule of people. For instance, we observe a peak every day. The peak is centered around mid-day and lasts up to early evening. This indicates that people tend to vigorously use their cellular devices around lunch time and evening time compared to the rest of the working day – when they are busy at meetings, or are using office computers, and so forth. More insights regarding these peaks are further revealed in our analysis on the traffic patterns for different families of mobile devices later this section. In addition, the daily peaks observed on the weekdays are higher than those observed on weekends. This can be explained by less usage of wireless modem devices, some of which are likely the traffic heavy hitters, during the weekends.

3.2 Differentiating Cellular Devices

One intuitive way of dissecting the aggregate measurements is to separate out different types of devices. Different devices have different features and specifications, which may affect their traffic patterns. Moreover, different types of devices attract different groups of users, who may also use the cellular network in different ways. In this subsection, we attempt to differentiate the traffic patterns of different types of devices.

3.2.1 Identifying Cellular Device Types

As mentioned before, the TAC numbers of the device IMEI numbers are preserved by the hashed device identifiers in our data set. Such information can be used to identify the type, or more precisely the maker, model, and sometimes even version, of a cellular device by retrieving the corresponding TAC registration record from the GSM Association's TAC database. For the data set used in this study, we encountered approximately two thousand different TAC numbers which map to several hundred different types of devices.

Because of the large number of device types and the typically short lifespan of individual cellular device models, it makes more sense to compare cellular device families, for example the Nokia N series, instead of individual device types. Thus it is important to identify the lineage in devices of the same family. Moreover, it also offers a historical perspective into how data usage patterns change along the evolution path of cellular devices of the same lineage.

Normally the manufacturing time of a particular device or even a particular model is difficult to determine from public domain knowledge. In our study, we tackle this problem by using a simple heuristic for estimating the manufacturing time of a device. Because the TAC numbers are specific to particular device models and there are only limited IMEI numbers under each TAC lot, it is reasonable to assume that manufacturers apply for TAC numbers from the GSM Association according to their production plans. Thus, there is a correlation between the registration time of a TAC number and the manufacturing time of cellular devices with that TAC number. Hence, we use the TAC registration time for classifying devices when we want to study how device data usage pattern changes as device specification and configuration may change over time.

In the discussions below, our analysis will focus on the comparison between statistics of smart phone devices from

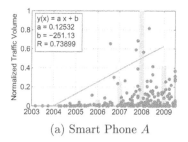
(a) Smart Phone A

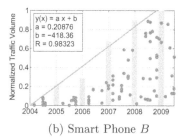
(b) Smart Phone B

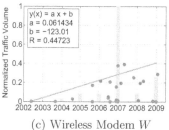
(c) Wireless Modem W

Figure 5: Variation in traffic volume for smart phone A, smart phone B and wireless modem W devices manufactured in recent years

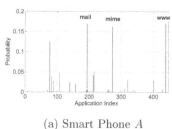
(a) Smart Phone A

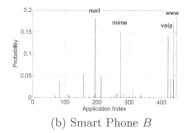
(b) Smart Phone B

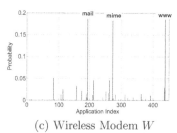
(c) Wireless Modem W

Figure 6: Volume distributions of applications constituting network traffic from different device families

two popular families, denoted as smart phone A and smart phone B. The choice of studying smart phones instead of traditional phones is relatively easy because smart phones are generally more capable and user-friendly for Internet usage. We have selected the two particular smart phone families because both are popular in different user markets – smart phone A models are popular more among general consumers whereas smart phone B models are largely adopted by business customers. The contrast in usage patterns between these two product lines will provide important insights into the behavioral differences between these two distinct classes of customers.

We will also compare statistics of smart phone A and smart phone B with those of a wireless modem cards family (denoted by W). These wireless modem cards provide cellular broadband connectivity to traditional desktops, laptops, or netbooks. As shown previously, this class of devices is also a major contributor of cellular Internet traffic. In addition, it is reasonable to believe that the traffic patterns of these modem devices resemble more traffic patterns seen on wired Internet because the equipment behind these modems is similar to those on the wired Internet. Thus, they form a baseline for comparing Internet traffic patterns and dynamics.

3.2.2 Traffic Temporal Dynamics of Different Device Families

We first revisit the traffic temporal dynamics of different device families. Previously, Figure 4(a) showed the aggregate Internet traffic volume over time. Here we separate out traffic volumes for the three cellular device families, smart phone A, smart phone B, and wireless modem W, and plot them individually in Figure 4(b). Note that we normalize the traffic volume of each device family by the maximum value for the respective device family.

The differences in plots of different device types can be explained if we restate the common impression that smart phone B devices are favored more by business users and smart phone A devices are popular among general consumers.

For example, on weekdays, the peak around mid-day is higher for smart phone B devices as compared to smart phone A devices whereas the peak at night is relatively higher for smart phone A devices as compared to smart phone B devices. However, note that this trend is reversed on weekends when smart phone B devices have higher peak in afternoons. This observation can be explained by the reasoning that on weekends business customers rely heavily on their smart phone B to remain updated about business-related activities whereas on weekdays they usually have access to their office desktops or laptops.

3.2.3 Traffic Volume

Figure 5 shows the variation in average normalized traffic volume from devices manufactured in different years. Note that each dot represents the result for a particular model which is identified by its TAC registration date. The x-axes of the figures for each device family start from the year when TAC was registered for its first model. The grey bars represent the average for a year. The regression line is plotted for the average yearly values. It is apparent that for both smart phone families, later models tend to generate more traffic. However, there is an outlier peak for smart phone A at 2008 and this trend is not obvious for wireless broadband modem family, which is indicated by the relatively small slope of its regression line and lower goodness of fit value (R). This is reasonable because later models tend to support newer communication technologies, with more powerful computing engines and friendlier user interfaces. All of the above-mentioned factors encourage more data usage from users.

3.2.4 Volume Distribution of Applications

Figure 6 provides the traffic volume distributions with respect to constituent applications for different device types. It is clear that each device family has *different* traffic behaviors. An interesting finding is that, for each device family, most top peaks in the volume distribution are for same applications. These peaks correspond to e-mail and web traffic, which are prevalent on all device families.

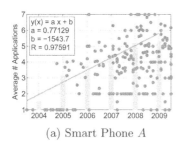
(a) Smart Phone A

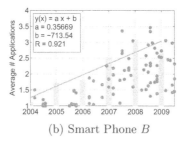
(b) Smart Phone B

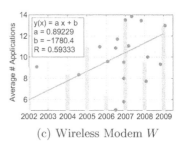
(c) Wireless Modem W

Figure 7: Variation in number of applications for smart phone A, smart phone B, and wireless modem W device families

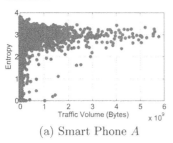
(a) Smart Phone A

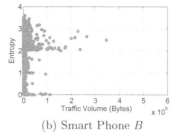
(b) Smart Phone B

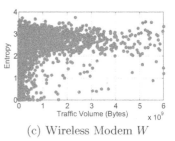
(c) Wireless Modem W

Figure 8: Entropy of application volume histogram for different device families

3.2.5 Diversity of Applications

Figure 7 provides the variation in average number of unique applications accessed by cellular devices manufactured in different years. First, we note that, for both smart phone A and smart phone B devices, the average number of unique applications accessed by a device shows an increasing trend across device manufacturing years. However, this trend is not obvious for wireless modem W. Second, it is clear that the average numbers of unique applications accessed by smart phone A devices and wireless modem W devices are significantly more than that by smart phone B devices. The number of unique applications accessed by a cellular device, which we refer to as *application diversity*, is an indicator of the device's versatility.

To quantitatively compare the diversity of applications constituting devices' traffic, we calculate the entropy of their application volume distributions. Entropy quantifies the spread of probability distribution of a random variable. For a given random variable X, its entropy $H(X)$ is given as: $H(X) = \sum_{\forall x_i \in X} x_i \log_2(x_i)$. Figure 8 shows the scatter plot of entropy of application histogram versus total volume. Note that in these plots each dot represents a unique device. For the baseline comparison, we also provide a scatter plot for all wireless modem W devices (as they are usually plugged into powerful desktop machines or laptops). As per our expectations, the entropy and total volume for smart phone A devices is significantly more than those of smart phone B devices. This is essentially indicated by the size of the *bulge* towards the top-right in scatter plots. The wireless modem W devices tend to have the highest entropy and total volume.

3.3 Summary

In this section, we have presented measurement and analysis for the distribution and the temporal dynamics of aggregated Internet traffic. We have also separately analyzed the traffic from different cellular families. We have shown that the aggregate traffic distribution is highly skewed both across different kinds of applications and different cellular devices. Furthermore, our study reveals that different groups of cellular devices indeed behave differently in terms of their Internet usage. Such differences are not only present between different kinds of cellular devices, *i.e.* smart phones vs. modem cards, but also are obvious among different groups of cellular devices of the same kind but favored by different market segments and user groups. Based on the findings stated above, we will now formally model the distributions and the temporal dynamics of Internet traffic from cellular devices. Similar to the measurement study in this section, we begin our modeling with aggregate traffic and then refine the models by taking cellular device population composition and sub-group characteristics into consideration.

4. MODELING INTERNET TRAFFIC DYNAMICS

In this section, we first use a Zipf-like distribution to model the long term distribution of Internet traffic volume versus constituent applications. Second, we use a Markov chain model to capture the temporal dynamics of aggregated Internet traffic volume. Then, we enhance the models with a multi-class approach by applying unsupervised clustering on different types of devices. The multi-class model can more accurately capture the distribution and temporal dynamics of Internet traffic. At the end of this section, we evaluate the improvement provided by the proposed multi-class model with respect to the aggregate traffic model.

4.1 Aggregate Traffic Model

4.1.1 Modeling Long Term Distribution of Traffic

It has been shown that the popularity distribution in World Wide Web (WWW), User Generated Content (UGC), and channel popularity in IPTV systems is scale-free [10]. From our observations in Section 3, we know that the distribution of Internet traffic (in terms of bytes, packets, and flows) is highly skewed. It can be observed in Figure 3(b) that top 10% of the applications constitute about 99% of the flows.

This observation naturally leads to a Zipf-like model. In a Zipf model, an object of rank x has probability p: $p \sim x^{-b}$. Figure 9(a) shows the distribution plot of volume versus application index averaged for the complete week. The residual plot in Figure 9(b) demonstrates that this Zipf-like model has reasonable accuracy.

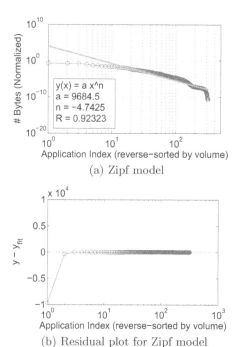

(a) Zipf model

(b) Residual plot for Zipf model

Figure 9: The Zipf model for long term average distribution of traffic volume patterns

4.1.2 Modeling Temporal Dynamics of Traffic

The temporal dynamics of traffic volume can be represented as a random process V. So, let its vector representation be $V = < V_1, V_2, ..., V_i, ... >$, where V_i denotes the traffic volume at time index i. Note that we can analyze the traffic volume at different time resolutions; however, in the rest of this paper we will only consider the traffic volume at hourly time resolution. Without loss of generality, we can aggregate consecutive n entries in V as a single element. For example, if $V = < V_1, V_2, V_3, V_4, V_5 >$, and we aggregate two consecutive entries as a single element (i.e. $n = 2$), we produce a new sequence as $< V_1V_2, V_2V_3, V_3V_4, V_4V_5 >$. This up-scaling, however, increases the dimensionality of the distribution from k to k^n, where k is the dimensionality of the original time series. It not only increases the underlying information of our process but may also result in sparse distributions due to requirement of large training data. Therefore, an inherent tradeoff exists between the amount of information – characterized by entropy – and the minimum training data required to build a model.

It is important to note that the up-scaled sequence with $n = 2$ is in fact a simple joint distribution of two sequences with $n = 1$, and so on. The joint distribution may contain some redundant information which is not relevant for a given problem. Therefore, we choose to remove the redundancy by using the conditional distribution for a more accurate analysis. The use of conditional distribution, instead of joint distribution, reduces the size of the underlying sample space which corresponds to removing the redundant information

from the joint distribution. Using conditional distribution also enables us to model the traffic volume time series as a discrete time Markov chain. Here we do not evaluate other well-known statistical time series modeling approaches such as Box-Jenkins methodology due to limited available training data (only one week) [2]. Such time series modeling approaches require large run of time series training data and may be used if enough training data is available.

In this paper, we use a discrete time Markov chain to model the traffic time series. An important parameter to determine when modeling a stochastic process with a Markovian model is the order of the Markov chain. The order is equivalent to the level of up-scaling n mentioned above. The order represents the extent to which past states determine the present state, i.e., how many lags should be examined when analyzing higher orders. The rationale behind this argument is that if we take into account more past states, less surprises or the uncertainties are expected in the present state. Towards this end, we have analyzed a number of statistical properties of the traffic volume time-series. A relevant property that has provided us interesting insights into the statistical characteristics of traffic time-series is the *autocorrelation* [4]. Another relevant property that can be helpful in determining the suitable value of n is the *relative mutual information* [8]. We discuss both of these properties for our data below.

(1) Autocorrelation: Autocorrelation is an important statistic for determining the order of a sequence of states. Autocorrelation describes the correlation between the random variables in a stochastic process at different points in time or space. For a given lag t, the autocorrelation function of a stochastic process, V_m (V denotes traffic volume process and m is the time index), is defined as:

$$\rho[t] = \frac{E\{V_0V_t\} - E\{V_0\}E\{V_t\}}{\sigma_{V_0}\sigma_{V_t}}, \quad (1)$$

where $E\{.\}$ represents the expectation operation and σ_{V_m} is the standard deviation of the random variable (representing traffic volume) at time lag m. The value of the autocorrelation function lies in the range $[-1, 1]$, where $\rho[t] = 1$ means perfect correlation at lag t, and $\rho[t] = 0$ means no correlation at all at lag t.

To observe the dependency level in a sequence of traffic volume V, we calculate sample autocorrelation functions for the one week aggregate volume trace. Figure 10(a) shows the sample autocorrelation functions plotted versus the lag. First, we note that the value of the autocorrelation function steadily decays over the week. Clearly, the dependency of traffic volume at a given time instance on time-lagged traffic volumes should decrease as the time lag increases. Second, the traffic volume at a given time instance shows the strongest dependence on the previous states that lag by multiples of 24 hours. This is indicated by the autocorrelation peaks at $n \approx 24, 48, 72, ...$. This effect is due to the diurnal (non-stationary) nature of the patterns observed in our data. These observations will be helpful to select the appropriate order for the Markov chain model.

(2) Relative Mutual Information: Another interesting statistic that provides insight to determine order of a stochastic process is called relative mutual information. Relative mutual information quantifies the amount of information that a random variable V_t provides about V_{t+1} (separated by one unit of time lag) while providing a measure of

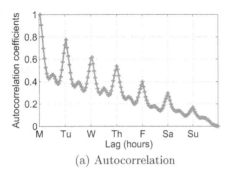

(a) Autocorrelation

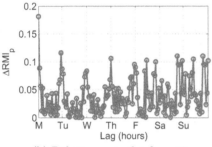

(b) Relative mutual information

Figure 10: Analysis techniques to determine temporal dependency in traffic volume time-series

the remaining uncertainty about V_{t+1} [8]. Mathematically,

$$RMI(V_{t+1}, V_t) = \frac{I(V_{t+1}; V_t)}{H(V_{t+1})}$$

where $I(V_{t+1}; V_t)$ is information gain and $H(V_{t+1})$ is entropy. Clearly, RMI is a non-symmetric measure and it is bounded in the range $[0, 1]$. The values of RMI approaching one indicate high dependency and the values approaching zero indicate low dependency. Note that an arbitrary number m of previous states can be included.

$$RMI(V_{t+1}, ..., V_2, V_1) = \frac{I(V_{t+1}; V_t, ..., V_2, V_1)}{H(V_{t+1})}$$

However, the computation complexity of RMI increases exponentially with respect to the number of previous states under consideration. A variant of RMI is called pair-wise relative mutual information RMI_p which is computed only between a random process and its lagged version. The maximum lag for which $\Delta RMI_p = |RMI_p(m-1) - RMI_p(m)|$ remains greater than ϵ defines the order of underlying stochastic process [8]. With pair-wise relative mutual information, the order of underlying stochastic process is determined as:

$$M(\epsilon) = max(|RMI_p(m-1) - RMI_p(m)|) \geq \epsilon, \ \forall m \in [1, \infty)$$

Figure 10(b) shows the plot of ΔRMI_p for aggregate traffic time-series. We note that the dependency between two time lags shows a repetitive pattern. Using the methodology described above, the order of this process is determined to be 24. In other words, there is an obvious redundancy beyond time difference of 24 hours.

The results of autocorrelation and relative mutual information measures highlight the dependency of traffic volume on the previous 24 hours; therefore, we use a 23rd order discrete time Markov chain. A nth order discrete time Markov chain can be visualized by considering all possible values

of states at previous n lags. The state space of our Markov chain model represents discretized traffic volume. For an nth order discrete time Markov chain with q elements in state space, we have the transition probability matrix $\mathbf{T}$ with q^n rows and columns. Notice that each row has the transition probabilities of going out from the respective state. Consequently, the probabilities in a row sum up to 1.

4.1.3 Forecasting Internet Traffic Dynamics

Note that for a given nth order Markov chain with q possible values of states, the total number of probability parameters denoted by $|P|$ is $(q-1)q^n$. For the present case where $n = 23$ and $q = 10$ (if we quantify traffic volume into 10 discrete levels) this will result in 9×10^{23} probability parameters. Clearly, we need to significantly reduce the number of probability parameters in our multi-order Markov model. Towards this end, we limit the number of probability parameters by using a many-to-one mapping. This mapping is essentially determined by the amount of data samples available to train the model. For each training sample, we can update the value of at most one probability parameter.

Once we have trained our model, we can use it to forecast future traffic volume. More specifically, given previous n states of this process $(V_1, V_2, ..., V_n)$, can we predict the next state, $i.e.$ V_{n+1} with reasonable accuracy? To make sure that with our choice of the Markovian order and the reduction of states the model can still accurately describe the data set, we now evaluate our proposed model using the collected traffic trace.

Recall from Section 3 that traffic time-series shows different behavior for weekdays and weekend. Therefore, we separate the proposed Markov model for aggregate traffic volume into two independent sub-models – one for weekday and one for weekend. For weekday traffic, we initially train our model using Monday's traffic data. The testing is then carried out for the remaining weekdays, comparing the model produced data with the actual data in the traffic data set. To evaluate the performance of our model on weekend traffic, we obtained additional data records for the previous weekend and train our model with them. The testing is then carried out for the next weekend similarly to weekday testing by comparing model produced volume with actual volume in data set. We further improve the accuracy of our stochastic model by utilizing online feedback to update the underlying probability parameters.

The result of our experiment shows that our model successfully captures the dynamics of Internet traffic volume with a reasonably small mean squared error (MSE) value $(= 1.7 \times 10^{-4})$. Figure 11 shows the plot of our model's forecast values along with the actual trace values. It is evident that our model successfully reproduces most of the diurnal behavior observed in the aggregate traffic volume trace.

It is worth noting that not only the models we have developed can be used to formally describe cellular devices's Internet traffic distribution and dynamics, they are more valuable in forecasting future traffic. More specifically, given previous n states of this process $(V_1, V_2, ..., V_n)$, we can predict the next state, i.e. V_{n+1} with reasonable accuracy, assuming the underlying fundamentals such as device usage behavior and device population composition are not changed. We have catered to the changing device usage behavior by using online feedback. However, device population composition

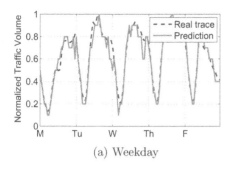

(a) Weekday

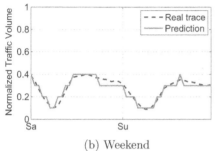

(b) Weekend

Figure 11: Traffic volume forecast based on the proposed Markov model

slowly changes over time resulting in degraded model accuracy. To overcome this issue and to further improve the accuracy of our proposed model, we now refine our model for different devices as they may exhibit vastly different behaviors and traffic patterns.

4.2 Multi-class Model

Previously we have developed a Zipf-like model to capture the traffic volume distribution for constituent applications and a multi-order Markov model to capture the temporal dynamics of cellular devices' Internet traffic. Both models are for aggregate Internet traffic of cellular devices. However, as we have shown in the Section 3, different devices may exhibit vastly different behaviors and traffic patterns. A naive extension of this model will be to develop a specialized model for every device type. However, we have several hundred different device types and having a separate model for each device type is not feasible. Hence, the natural next step is to further identify groups in device population with similar characteristics and refine the models.

We follow a two step methodology to develop such grouping. First, we study different feature sets that can be utilized to cluster the devices. Second, we examine the outcome of clustering using different feature sets to determine the suitable grouping methodology. This examination provides interesting insights which may help determine the reasons which lead to such grouping. Once we have the final grouping, we extend our model for aggregate traffic to a multi-class model of traffic distribution and temporal dynamics.

4.2.1 Grouping Strategies

We now take a look at different ways using which we can group device population. Note that the objective of our grouping methodology is to combine the devices with similar traffic characteristics into a handful number of clusters so that we can train separate and independent models for each of these groups. Towards this end, we propose the following simple yet effective feature sets for clustering device types.

(1) Average Traffic Volume per Application: It is a 100 element tuple which represents normalized average traffic volume for top 100 applications with highest aggregate volume for a given device type.

(2) Average Traffic Volume per Hour: It is a 24 element tuple which represents normalized average traffic volume at each hour of the day for a given device type.

We utilize an unsupervised clustering algorithm to cluster the device types into groups. Towards this end, we have selected the well-known k-means clustering algorithm which has definite advantages over other clustering techniques especially for large number of variables and large data sets [9]. It is important to set an appropriate value of k in k-means clustering algorithm. Note that our goal is to obtain multiple representative models of our data that can be used later to extend our single aggregate model to the multi-class model. To limit the number of classes in the multi-class model, we are interested in finding the minimum number of clusters that can capture distinct underlying behaviors in our data. We use intra-cluster dissimilarity D_k measure to select the appropriate value of k. We calculate the value of D_k for increasing values of k starting from $k = 2$. Intra-cluster dissimilarity is defined as:

$$D_k = \sum_{j=1}^{k} \sum_{i \in C(j)} |x_i^z - \hat{x}_j|,$$

where x_i is a data point residing in j-th cluster, $\hat{x}_j$ is the centroid point of j-th cluster. Figure 12 shows the variation in the values of D_k for increasing values of k. We expect the values of D_k to mostly decrease for increasing values of k. We select the value of k to be the least value for which either $D_k - D_{k+1} \to 0^+$ or $D_k - D_{k+1} < 0$ [13]. For both spatial and temporal features, in Figures 12(a) and 12(b), $D_3 - D_4 \to 0^+$; thus, $k = 3$ for both cases.

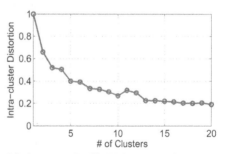

(a) Average Traffic Volume per Application

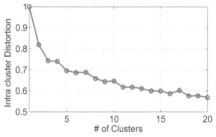

(b) Average Traffic Volume per Hour

Figure 12: Variation in intra-cluster dissimilarity with respect to increasing number of clusters

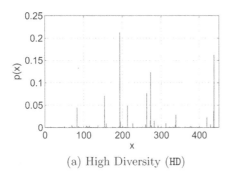

(a) High Diversity (HD)

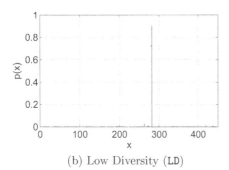

(b) Low Diversity (LD)

Figure 13: Cluster centroids for spatial features

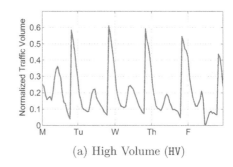

(a) High Volume (HV)

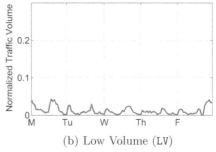

(b) Low Volume (LV)

Figure 14: Cluster centroids for temporal features

4.2.2 Explaining Internet Traffic Dynamics for Identified Clusters

In Section 3.1, we studied traffic volume distribution across different applications and temporal dynamics of aggregate Internet traffic. Now, we want to study the behaviors characterized by the identified clusters. We have used two feature sets to cluster device population into distinct groups. Here we discuss the clustering results of both feature sets separately in the following text. We will then use these results to explain the characteristics of traffic from two popular mobile smart phone families and one cellular broadband modem family.

We can label the identified centroids using spatial features as High Diversity (HD), Medium Diversity (MD), and Low Diversity (LD). In Figure 13, we plot centroids of two of the three clusters. By diversity, we are referring to the variation in traffic application distribution, which in turn is quantified using entropy. It is clear that the centroid model plotted in Figure 13(a) has higher entropy as compared to the one plotted in Figure 13(b) which is mostly dominated by traffic of one particular application.

It is interesting to see how cellular devices belonging to different device families are distributed among different clusters based on the above clustering technique. These results will enhance our understanding of device behavior from different manufacturers. Again we list the same three device families as in Section 3. Table 1 shows the percentage distribution of cellular devices made by different device families over different cluster groups, which portrays a more detailed image than Figure 6.

Table 1: Population distribution of device families based on clustering using spatial features

	Wireless Modem W	Smart Phone A	Smart Phone B
HD (%)	**79.3**	**94.4**	**76.8**
MD (%)	0.0	5.2	0.0
LD (%)	20.7	0.4	23.2

The analysis of cluster centroids obtained from temporal features also provide interesting insights about distinct traffic behavior of different device groups. Figure 14 shows the plots for 2 of the cluster centroids from k-means clustering. We have labeled the cluster centroids based on their volume characteristics as high/medium/low volume. The traffic volume is normalized by the maximum observed value for every device type. We define the volume category of a centroid to be high, medium, or low by taking the average of peak values for weekdays only. We only consider weekday peak values because traffic volume on weekdays is significantly higher than weekends for aggregate traffic time series in Figure 4(a). If the average normalized volume for weekdays is more than 0.5 then the assigned volume category is *high*. Else if average normalized volume is less than 0.5 and more than 0.1 then it is categorized as *medium*. Finally, if the normalized volume is less than 0.1 then it is categorized as *low* The thresholds for such volume partitioning are selected after manually analyzing all centroids. There are 3 cluster centroids based on temporal features, high volume HV, medium volume MV, and low volume LV. Two of the temporal cluster centroids are shown in Figures 14(a) and 14(b).

We again analyze the distribution of devices from different device families across these clusters. First, we note that almost 70% of Smart Phone A devices fall into HV cluster indicating that the owners of these devices tend to use them heavily throughout the week. On the other hand, the Smart Phone B devices spread more into LV cluster indicating that Smart Phone B owners use them less rigorously as compared to Smart Phone A devices. Wireless Modem W devices are more evenly spread across all clusters as compared to Smart Phone A and Smart Phone B.

To conclude, our clustering results highlight that different groups of devices do have distinct traffic behaviors and using our clustering method these different groups can be partitioned out of the device population. Because the distinctions between different groups are concealed by the aggregate traffic model, as a next step we extend our aggregate

Table 2: Population distribution of device families based on clustering using temporal features

	Wireless Modem W	Smart Phone A	Smart Phone B
HV (%)	**48.3**	**69.0**	15.9
MV (%)	31.0	16.5	27.1
LV (%)	20.7	14.5	**57.0**

traffic model proposed in Section 4.1 to a multi-class model. Such multi-class model can describe the traffic patterns and dynamics in a better way.

4.2.3 Evaluation of the Multi-class Model

We now use the clustering results to extend the aggregate traffic model to a multi-class model. Note that we are primarily interested in accurately describing the volume distribution across different applications and temporal dynamics of cellular devices' Internet traffic. We follow a three-step methodology in this regard. First, we aggregate the traffic from all types of devices that fall into the same cluster. Second, we normalize the cluster aggregated traffic with respect to its relative proportion in the aggregate traffic which is determined empirically. Finally, we model each of the aggregated and normalized traffic traces separately. Note that we model the spatial and temporal dynamics of traffic separately. Remember that we have three clusters for both spatial features and temporal features. So, in the eventual multi-class model we obtain three Zipf-like characterizations for the distribution of Internet traffic and three Markov chain based models to capture the temporal dynamics of the traffic.

Figure 15 shows the plots of Zipf-like distribution models for HD and LD classes. To evaluate the improvement in accuracy for the multi-class model as compared to the aggregate model, we compare both to the real trace. We note that the average value of R (which quantifies goodness of fit) improves to 0.96 for multi-class models as compared to 0.92 for the aggregate model.

Figure 16 shows the plot of predictions from multi-order Markov models trained for two of the classes (HV and LV). It is evident that the predictions of Markov models are reasonably accurate. The value of average MSE for all three classes is 9.2×10^{-5} which is lower than the value achieved by the aggregate model. To conclude, our multi-class model improves on the single-class (aggregate) model in terms of prediction accuracy.

Once again, the multi-class extended models can also be used for predicting future traffic patterns just like the models for aggregate traffic. Recall that device population composition slowly changes over time which degraded the accuracy of aggregate model. However, we can update the device population composition by periodically refreshing clustering results used by the multi-class model. Therefore, we can successfully eliminate the root-cause of accuracy degradation from multi-class model which results from changing device population composition.

5. RELATED WORK

Several related works analyze usage data from cellular networks. In [17], Willkomm et al. perform measurement and modeling of voice call data collected from a CDMA-based cellular operator. In [16], the authors carry out a low level measurement analysis on a CDMA2000 cellular data network.

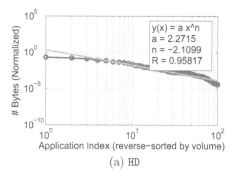

(a) HD

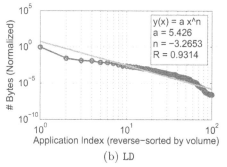

(b) LD

Figure 15: Separate Zipf-like characterizations for two of the classes (obtained by clustering using spatial features)

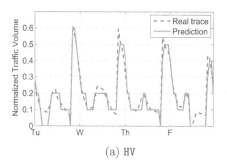

(a) HV

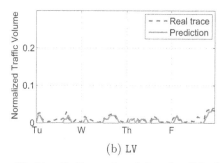

(b) LV

Figure 16: Prediction of multi-order Markov model for two of the classes (obtained by clustering using temporal features)

work. The results of their experiments show that user data traffic is bursty and shows strong diurnal patterns. In [19], the authors perform a measurement study of Short Message Service (SMS) of a nationwide cellular network. In contrast to the above-mentioned studies, our work focuses on measurement and modeling of *distribution and temporal dynamics of data traffic in a cellular network*.

In [14], the authors analyze the relationship between the types of applications accessed and user mobility in a 3G cellular network. The results of their measurement studies show that there is a strong relationship between the types of applications accessed and mobility patterns of users. The content access patterns quantified in [14] are limited to six general categories, namely mail, music, social network, news, trading, and dating. On the other hand, in our work we analyze more than 400 fine-grained application categories. Moreover, in our paper we model the distribution and temporal dynamics of content access patterns. In a recent relevant work [6], Falaki *et al.* study traces from 255 users to study their interaction with smartphones. They collected data by deploying a custom logger on smartphones. The results of their experiments show that user interaction has diurnal patterns and that a few applications dominate the rest. In contrast to this work, our work focuses on data traffic analysis as seen by cellular network. Also, the scale of our study is significantly larger – containing data from millions of devices and several hundred unique device types.

Several additional related works use similar modeling methodologies. In [7] and [20], the authors perform measurement and modeling studies for YouTube traffic at different points in the network. In [7], the authors collect traffic between YouTube and an edge network. Relevant to our work, the authors model video popularity using Zipf distribution. This result is also verified by findings reported in [20]. In [20], the authors further show that the distribution of number of video requests per client follows power-law distribution. Relative to these studies, we have modeled the steady-state distribution of application in content access patterns using Zipf-like distribution. In [3], Cao *et al.* utilize stochastic models for source-level modeling of HTTP traffic. Likewise, the technique proposed in [11] accomplishes a similar task for flow-level traces. In [15], the authors have proposed a packet-level network traffic generator which utilizes a structural model to capture interactions of applications and users. The model trains itself on a given packet trace and then generates live packet traces using the trained models. In relation to these studies, our proposed technique also trains itself on a given trace capturing characteristic features of Internet traffic dynamics. Afterwards, the trained models are used to predict/generate live realistic traces.

6. CONCLUDING REMARKS

In this paper, we have presented an analysis of Internet traffic dynamics of cellular devices in a large cellular network. The results of our measurement and modeling experiments have important implications on cellular network design, troubleshooting, performance evaluation, and optimization. For example, the skewness of traffic distribution with respect constituent applications implies that only a few applications are popular. Therefore, cellular device manufacturers and software developers can focus on the specific characteristics of the popular applications for performance optimization. Furthermore, the diurnal variations observed in this paper imply that the network usage is strongly non-stationary. Cellular network operators typically do resource allocation based on peak usage requirements and these resources are wasted during non-peak time. To mitigate this resource wastage, cellular network operator can devise billing schemes to differentiate between peak and off-peak network usage.

Acknowledgements

We would like to thank Alexandre Gerber and Jeffrey Erman for providing technical comments on the paper, and Jeffrey Pang for helping us in general understanding of the traffic logging apparatus. We would also like to thank our shepherd, Alberto Lopez Toledo, and the anonymous reviewers for their helpful comments and suggestions.

7. REFERENCES

[1] Cisco Visual Networking Index: Global Mobile Data Traffic Forecast Update, 2010-2015. White Paper, February 2011.

[2] G. Box, G. M. Jenkins, and G. Reinsel. *Time Series Analysis: Forecasting & Control.* Wiley Series in Probability and Statistics, 4th edition, 2008.

[3] J. Cao, W. S. Cleveland, Y. Gao, K. Jeffay, E. D. Smith, and M. Weigle. Stochastic models for generating synthetic HTTP source traffic. In *IEEE INFOCOM*, 2004.

[4] T. M. Cover and J. A. Thomas. *Elements of Information Theory.* Wiley-Interscience, 1991.

[5] J. Erman, A. Gerber, M. T. Hajiaghayi, D. Pei, and O. Spatscheck. Network-aware forward caching. In *WWW*, 2009.

[6] H. Falaki, R. Mahajan, S. Kandula, D. Lymberopoulos, R. Govindan, and D. Estrin. Diversity in smartphone usage. In *MobiSys*, 2010.

[7] P. Gill, M. Arlittz, Z. Li, and A. Mahantix. YouTube traffic characterization: A view from the edge. In *ACM SIGCOMM IMC*, 2007.

[8] M. Ilyas and H. Radha. On measuring memory length of the error rate process in wireless channels. In *Conference on Information Sciences and Systems (CISS)*, 2008.

[9] J. MacQueen. Some methods for classification and analysis of multivariate observations. In *Fifth Berkeley Symposium on Math Statistics and Probability*, 1967.

[10] T. Qiu, Z. Ge, S. Lee, J. Wang, Q. Zhao, and J. Xu. Modeling channel popularity dynamics in a large IPTV system. In *ACM SIGMETRICS*, 2009.

[11] J. Sommers and P. Barford. Self-configuring network traffic generation. In *ACM SIGCOMM IMC*, 2004.

[12] S. Tekinay and B. Jabbari. Handover and channel assignment in mobile cellular networks. In *IEEE Communications Magazine*, 1991.

[13] R. Tibshirani, G. Walther, and T. Hastie. Estimating the number of clusters in a data set via the gap statistic. *Journal of the Royal Statistical Society: Series B (Statistical Methodology)*, 63:411–423, 2001.

[14] I. Trestian, S. Ranjan, A. Kuzmanovic, and A. Nucci. Measuring serendipity: Connecting people, locations and interests in a mobile 3G network. In *ACM SIGCOMM IMC*, 2009.

[15] K. V. Vishwanath and A. Vahdat. Realistic and responsive network traffic generation. In *ACM SIGCOMM*, 2006.

[16] C. Williamson, E. Halepovic, H. Sun, and Y. Wu. Characterization of CDMA2000 cellular data network traffic. In *IEEE Conference on Local Computer Networks*, 2005.

[17] D. Willkomm, S. Machiraju, J. Bolot, and A. Wolisz. Primary users in cellular networks: A large-scale measurement study. In *IEEE Symposium on New Frontiers in Dynamic Spectrum Access Networks*, 2008.

[18] Q. Xu, A. Gerber, Z. M. Mao, and J. Pang. AccuLoc: Practical localization of performance measurements in 3G networks. In *ACM MobiSys*, 2011.

[19] P. Zerfos, X. Meng, and S. H. Wong. A study of the short message service of a nationwide cellular network. In *ACM SIGCOMM IMC*, 2006.

[20] M. Zink, K. Suh, Y. Gu, and J. Kurose. Watch global, cache local: YouTube network traffic at a campus network – measurements and implications. In *Annual Multimedia Computing and Networking Conf*, 2008.

Cellular Data Network Infrastructure Characterization and Implication on Mobile Content Placement

Qiang Xu
University of Michigan
qiangxu@eecs.umich.edu

Junxian Huang
University of Michigan
hjx@eecs.umich.edu

Zhaoguang Wang
University of Michigan
zgw@eecs.umich.edu

Feng Qian
University of Michigan
fengqian@eecs.umich.edu

Alexandre Gerber
AT&T Labs Research
gerber@research.att.com

Z. Morley Mao
University of Michigan
zmao@eecs.umich.edu

ABSTRACT

Despite the tremendous growth in the cellular data network usage due to the popularity of smartphones, so far there is rather limited understanding of the network infrastructure of various cellular carriers. Understanding the infrastructure characteristics such as the network topology, routing design, address allocation, and DNS service configuration is essential for predicting, diagnosing, and improving cellular network services, as well as for delivering content to the growing population of mobile wireless users. In this work, we propose a novel approach for discovering cellular infrastructure by intelligently combining several data sources, *i.e.,* server logs from a popular location search application, active measurements results collected from smartphone users, DNS request logs from a DNS authoritative server, and publicly available routing updates. We perform the first comprehensive analysis to characterize the cellular data network infrastructure of four major cellular carriers within the U.S. in our study.

We conclude among other previously little known results that the current routing of cellular data traffic is quite restricted, as it must traverse a rather limited number (*i.e.,* 4–6) of infrastructure locations (*i.e.,* GGSNs), which is in sharp contrast to wireline Internet traffic. We demonstrate how such findings have direct implications on important decisions such as mobile content placement and content server selection. We observe that although the local DNS server is a coarse-grained approximation on the user's network location, for some carriers, choosing content servers based on the local DNS server is accurate enough due to the restricted routing in cellular networks. Placing content servers close to GGSNs can potentially reduce the end-to-end latency by more than 50% excluding the variability from air interface.

Categories and Subject Descriptors

C.2.1 [**Network Architecture and Design**]: Wireless communication; C.4 [**Performance of Systems**]: Measurement techniques; C.4 [**Performance of Systems**]: Reliability, availability, and serviceability

General Terms

Experimentation, Measurement, Performance

Keywords

Cellular network architecture, GGSN placement, Mobile content delivery

1. INTRODUCTION

On the Internet, IP addresses indicate to some degree the identity and location of end-hosts. IP-based geolocation is widely used in different types of network applications such as content customization and server selection. Using IP addresses to geolocate wireline end-hosts is known to work reasonably well despite the prevalence of NAT, since most NAT boxes consist of only a few hosts [7]. However, one recent study [5] exposed very different characteristics of IP addresses in cellular networks, *i.e.,* cellular IP addresses can be shared across geographically very disjoint regions within a short time duration. This observation suggests that cellular IP addresses do not contain enough geographic information at a sufficiently high fidelity. Moreover, it implies only a few IP gateways may exist for cellular data networks, and that IP address management is much more centralized than that for wireline networks, for which tens to hundreds of Points of Presence (PoPs) are spread out at geographically distinct locations.

There is a growing need to improve mobile content delivery, *e.g.,* via a content distribution network (CDN) service, given the rapidly increasing mobile traffic volume and the fact that the performance perceived by mobile users is still much worse than that for DSL/Cable wireline services [17]. For mobile content, the radio access network, cellular backbone, and the Internet wireline all have impact and leave space for further improvement [2, 1, 30]. A first necessary step is to understand the cellular network structure.

The lack of geographic information of cellular IP addresses brings new challenges for mobile service providers, who attempt to deliver content from servers close to users. First, it is unclear where to place the content servers. As shown later, cellular data networks have very few IP gateways. Therefore, it is critical to first identify those IP gateways to help decide where to place content servers. Second, unlike wireline networks, cellular IP addresses themselves often cannot accurately convey a user's location, which is critical information needed by the CDN service to determine the closest server. In this work, we show how these challenges can be addressed by leveraging the knowledge of the cellular network infrastructure.

Cellular data networks have not been explored much by the research community to explain the dynamics of cellular IP addresses despite the growing popularity of their use. The impact of the cellular architecture on the performance of a diverse set of smartphone network applications and on cellular users has been largely overlooked. In this study, we perform the first comprehensive characterization study of the cellular data network infrastructure to explain the diverse geographic distribution of cellular IP addresses, and to highlight the key importance of the design decisions of the network infrastructure that affect the performance, manageability, and evolvability of the network architecture. Understanding the current architecture of cellular data networks is critical for future improvement.

Since the observation of the diversity in the geographic distribution of cellular IP address in the previous study [5] indicates that there may exist very few cellular IP data network gateways, identifying the location of these gateways becomes the key for cellular infrastructure characterization in our study. The major challenge is exacerbated by the lack of openness of such networks. We are unable to infer topological information using existing probing tools. For example, merely sending traceroute probes from cellular devices to the Internet IP addresses exposes mostly private IP addresses along the path within the UMTS architecture. In the reverse direction, only some of the IP hops outside the cellular networks respond to traceroute probes.

To tackle these challenges, instead of relying on those cellular IP hops, we use the geographic coverage of cellular IP addresses to infer the placement of IP gateways following the intuition that those cellular IP addresses with the same geographic coverage are likely to have the same IP allocation policy, *i.e.*, they are managed by the same set of gateways. To obtain the geographic coverage, we use two distinct data sources and devise a systematic approach for processing the data reconciling potential conflicts, combined with other data obtained via simple probing and passive data analysis. Our approach of deploying a lightweight measurement tool on smartphones provides the network information from the perspective of cellular users. Combining this data source with a location search service of a cellular content provider further enhances our visibility into the cellular network infrastructure.

One key contribution of our work is the measurement methodology for characterizing the cellular network infrastructure, which requires finding the relevant address blocks, locating them, and clustering them based on their geographic coverage. This enables the identification of the IP gateways within cellular data networks, corresponding to the first several outbound IP hops used to reach the rest of the Internet. We draw parallels with many past studies in the Internet topology characterization, such as the Rocketfuel project [31] characterizing ISP topologies, while our problem highlights additional challenges due to the lack of publicly available information and the difficulties in collecting relevant measurement data. We enumerate our key findings and major contributions below.

- We designed and evaluated a general technique for distinguishing cellular users from WiFi users using smartphones and further differentiating network carriers based on cellular IP addresses. Compared with other heuristics such as querying IP addresses from *whois* database and distinguishing cellular carriers based on key words such as "mobility" and "wireless" from the organization name, our technique collects the ground truth observed by smartphone devices by deploying a lightweight measurement tool for popular smartphone OSes. Distributed as a free application on major smartphone application markets, it can tell the carrier name

for 99.97% records of a popular location search application which has 20,000 times more records than the application.

- We comprehensively characterized the cellular network infrastructure for four major U.S. carriers including both UMTS and EVDO networks by clustering their IP addresses based on their geographic coverage. Our technique relies on the device-side IP behavior easily collected through our lightweight measurement tool instead of requiring any proprietary information from network providers. Our characterization methodology is applicable to all cellular access technologies (2G, 3G, or 4G).

- We observed that the traffic for all four carriers traverses through only 4–6 IP gateways, each encompassing a large geographic coverage, implying the sharing of address blocks within the same geographic area. This is fundamentally different from wireline networks with more distributed infrastructure. The restricted routing topology for cellular networks creates new challenges for applications such as CDN service.

- We performed the first study to examine the geographic coverage of local DNS servers and discussed in depth its implication on content server selection. We observe that although local DNS servers provide coarse-grained approximation for users' network location, for some carriers, choosing content servers based on local DNS servers is reasonably accurate for the current cellular infrastructure due to restricted routing in cellular networks.

- We investigated the performance in terms of end-to-end delay for current content delivery networks and evaluated the benefit of placing content servers at different network locations, *i.e.*, on the Internet or inside cellular networks. We observed that pushing content close to GGSNs can potentially reduce the end-to-end latency by 50% excluding the variability from air interface. Our observation strongly encourages CDN service providers to place content servers inside cellular networks for better performance.

The rest of this paper is organized as follows. We first describe related work in §2. §3 describes the high-level solution to discover IP gateways in cellular infrastructure. §4 explains the main methodology in the data analysis and the data sets studied. The results in characterizing cellular data network infrastructure along the dimensions of IP address, topology, local DNS server, and routing behavior are covered in §5. We discuss the implications of these results in §6 and conclude in §7 with key observations and insights on future work.

2. RELATED WORK

Our study is motivated by numerous previous measurement studies [34, 38, 22], *e.g.*, Rocketfuel [31] to characterize various properties of the Internet through passive monitoring using data such as server logs and packet traces, as well as active measurement such as probing path changes. Efforts on reverse engineering properties of the Internet [32] have been shown to be quite successful; however, very little work has been done in the space of cellular IP networks. Complementary to our study, the most recent work by Keralapura *et al.* profiled the browsing behavior by investigating whether there exists distinct behavior pattern among mobile users [20]. Their study implemented effective co-clustering on large scale user-level web browsing traces collected from one cellular provider. As far as we know, our study is the first to comprehensively characterize cellular IP networks covering all the major cellular carriers in the U.S., focusing on key characteristics such as network topological properties and dynamic routing behavior. From the characterization of the cellular data network structure, we also draw conclusions on content placement, which is essential given the rapidly growing demand for mobile data access.

We build our work upon a recent study by Balakrishnan *et al.* [5] in which they highlighted unexpected dynamic behavior of cellular IP addresses. Our work performs a more complete and general study covering a wider set of properties, illustrating carrier-specific network differences, explaining the observed diverse geographic distribution of cellular IP addresses, also investigating associated implications of observed network designs.

Although there have been studies characterized the CDNs relative to the end users accessing from the wireline networks [23, 29, 10, 26, 16], very little attention has been paid to the cellular users. These previous studies are mainly from two perspectives, *i.e.,* content placement and server selection. Our work is complementary to these studies by investigating the implication of cellular network infrastructure on mobile data placement and server selection. To our best knowledge, our study is the first to investigate the content placement and content server selections for cellular users.

Previous studies on cellular networks can be classified approximately into several categories, namely from ISP's view point of managing network resources [13, 33], from end-user's perspectives of optimizing energy efficiency and network performance at the device [4, 39, 6], and finally developing infrastructure support for improving mobile application performance [8, 28] and security [24]. Our work is complementary to them by exposing the internal design of the cellular data network structure that can be useful to guide such optimization efforts.

There have also been several measurement studies in understanding the performance and usage of cellular networks. One recent study focuses on mobile user behavior from the perspective of applications such as [36] which characterized the relationship between users' application interests and mobility. Other examples include a study of the interaction between the wireless channels and applications [21], performance study of multimedia streaming [11], and performance of TCP/IP over 3G wireless with rate and delay variation [9]. Note that our work fills an important void in the space of cellular data network by focusing on the network architectural design: IP address allocation, local DNS service setup, and routing dynamics.

3. OVERVIEW

In this section, we describe the cellular data network architecture, followed by an overview of our methodology for characterizing the cellular data network infrastructure.

3.1 Cellular Data Network Architecture

Despite the difference among cellular technologies, a cellular data network is usually divided into two parts, the Radio Access Network (RAN) and the Core Network. The RAN contains different infrastructures supporting 2G technologies (*e.g.,* GPRS, EDGE, 1xRTT, *etc.*) and 3G technologies (*e.g.,* UMTS, EVDO, *etc.*), but the structure of the core network does not differentiate between 2G and 3G technologies. In this study we focus on the core network, in particular, the gateways that hide the cellular infrastructures from the external network, as identifying the gateways is the key to explain the geographically diverse distribution of cellular addresses [5].

Figure 1 illustrates the typical UMTS/EDGE network. The RAN

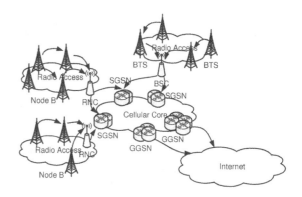

Figure 1: The UMTS/EDGE network architecture.

architecture, which allows the connectivity between user handsets and the core network, depends on the radio access technology: it consists of the Base Transceiver Station (BTS) and the Base Station Controller (BSC) for EDGE (2G), and the Node B and the Radio Network Controller (RNC) for UMTS (3G). The core network, which is shared by both 2G's and 3G's RANs, is comprised of the Serving GPRS Support Node (SGSN) and the Gateway GPRS Support Node (GGSN). To start a data session, a user first communicates with its local SGSN that delivers its traffic to a GGSN. The SGSN requests the DNS server for the GGSN via the user's access point name (APN). The DNS server decides which GGSN serves the data session accordingly [27]. Once the GGSN is determined, the communication between the SGSN and the GGSN is tunneled, so GGSN is the first IP hop and is followed by multiple hops such as NAT and firewalls within the core network. Being the first router for the connected cellular device, the GGSN is responsible for IP address assignment, IP pool management, address mapping, QoS, authentication, *etc.* [12].

The EVDO network has an architecture very similar to the UMTS network except that the Packet Data Serving Node (PDSN) in the EVDO core network serves as a combination of both the SGSN and the GGSN in the UMTS core network. Without explicit explanation, our statements for the UMTS network are applicable to the EVDO network as well.

To support the future 4G LTE (Long Term Evolution) network, the GGSN node will be upgraded to a common anchor point and gateway (GW) node, which also provides backward compatibility to other access technologies such as EDGE and UMTS [18]. The functionality of GW is largely similar to that of GGSN. Therefore, our proposed methodology, which focuses on identifying GGSNs in the cellular infrastructure, is still broadly applicable.

3.2 Solution Overview

Despite the growing popularity of smartphones, cellular data networks have not been explored much by the research community to explain the dynamics of cellular IP addresses. Besides the challenge of keeping tracking of cellular IP addresses, to identify GGSNs in the cellular infrastructure, another challenge is the lack of openness of such networks. Outbound probing via traceroute from the cellular devices to the Internet IP addresses exposes mostly private IP addresses along the path for UMTS networks due to the placement of NAT boxes. These NAT boxes and firewalls prevent the inbound traceroute probing to reach into the cellular backbones as well.

Identifying GGSNs in the cellular infrastructure is the key to explain the geographically diverse distribution of cellular addresses discovered by the recent study [5]. GGSNs serve as the gateway

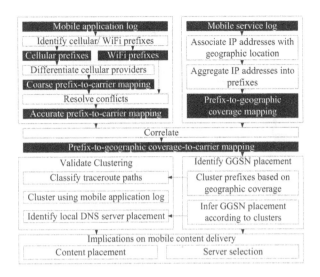

Figure 2: Workflow of the solution: black boxes correspond to data, manipulated by processing modules (white boxes).

between the cellular and the Internet infrastructure and thus play an essential role in determining the basic network functions, *e.g.,* routing and address allocation. In our study, we leverage the geographic coverage of cellular addresses to infer the placement of GGSNs, assuming that prefixes sharing similar IP behaviors are likely to have the same IP allocation policy, *i.e.,* they are managed by the same GGSN. Considering geographic coverage as one type of IP behaviors, we cluster prefixes based on the feature of geographic coverage, and infer the placement of GGSNs according to the prefix clusters that we generated.

As depicted by Figure 2, to get the geographic location of cellular IP addresses, we leverage a popular location search service whose server logs public IP address and GPS location of users (*i.e.,* the mobile service log). We use the mobile service log to generate prefix-to-geographic-coverage mappings. In order to identify cellular addresses and to further differentiate different cellular providers, we also deploy a measurement tool for mainstream smartphone OSes to build a database (*i.e.,* mobile application log) for prefix-to-carrier mappings. They provide the ground truth for determining the cellular provider who owns a certain IP address block. By correlating prefix-carrier mappings with prefix-geographic coverage mappings, we can obtain the prefix-to-geographic-coverage-to-carrier mappings for clustering. Once the clustering is finished, we validate the clustering results via three independent ways: clustering using the mobile application log, identifying the placement of local DNS servers in cellular networks, and classifying traceroute paths. Based on our findings during clustering and validation, we investigate implications of the cellular infrastructure on content delivery service for mobile users.

Note that we designed our methodology to be generally applicable for any data cellular network technologies (2G, 3G, and 4G), and particularly from the perspective of data requirement. Any mobile data source that contains IP addresses, location information, and network carrier information can be used for our purpose of characterizing the cellular data network infrastructure. Based on our experience of deploying smartphone applications, it is not difficult to collect such data.

In §4, we detail our methodology for identifying cellular addresses and cellular providers. The discovery of the geographic coverage of cellular prefixes and clustering techniques are elaborated in §5.1.

4. MEASUREMENT DATA AND PREPROCESSING

In this section, we describe the data sets used for analysis and the additional experiments carried out to supplement these data for identifying the key properties of interest. Note that due to privacy concerns, without compromising the usefulness of the results, we have anonymized the carrier by assigning a letter, *i.e.,* Carrier A through D, to identify each of the four carriers studied which have significant footprint in the U.S. Similarly, we assign a unique ID to each address block and assign a symbol to each ASN.

4.1 DataSource1 – server logs

Operator	3G	Records (%)	# BGP prefixes	# /24 prefixes	# ASNs
Carrier A	UMTS	43.34%	54	16,288	1
Carrier B	UMTS	7.09%	12	41	1
Carrier C	EVDO	1.51%	202	15,590	2
Carrier D	EVDO	1.22%	172	11,205	1
*	-	100%	16,439	121,567	1,862

Table 1: Statistics of *DataSource1*(server logs).

The first data set used is from server logs associated with a popular location search service for mobile users. We refer to this data source as *DataSource1*. It contains the IP address, the timestamp, and the GPS location of mobile devices. The GPS location is requested by the application and is measured from the device. The data set ranges from August 2009 until September 2010, containing several million records. This comprehensive data set covers 16,439 BGP prefixes, 121,567 /24 address blocks from 1,862 AS numbers. However, *DataSource1* does not differentiate the carrier for each record. Later we discuss how to map *DataSource1*'s records to corresponding cellular carriers or WiFi networks with the help of *DataSource2*'s prefix-to-carrier table in §4.3. Users of the search service may also use WiFi besides cellular networks to access the service.

Table 1 shows the breakdown of the records among the four major U.S. cellular providers for *DataSource1*. 43.34% of all the records in *DataSource1* are mapped to Carrier A due to the disproportionate popularity of the service among different mobile users. Despite this bias, we still find sufficient information to characterize the other three major carriers. 46.71% of *DataSource1* is from WiFi users, and 0.13% is from cellular carriers besides the four major carriers. Note that one cellular carrier may be mapped to more than one AS number (ASN), *e.g.,* Carrier C corresponds to more than one ASN.

The long-term and nation-wide *DataSource1* is the major data source that we rely on to map cellular prefixes to their geographic coverage after we aggregate cellular IP addresses to prefixes based on *RouteViews*'s BGP update announcements [3].

4.2 DataSource2 – active measurements

The second main data source of our analysis comes from an application that we have widely deployed on three popular smartphone platforms: iPhone OS, Android, and Windows Mobile (WM). We refer to this data source as *DataSource2*, with the basic statistics shown in Table 2. The application is freely available for mobile users to download for the purpose of evaluating and diagnosing their networks from which we can collect common network char-

Platform	# users	# carriers	# BGP prefixes	# /24 prefixes	# ASNs
iPhone	25K	-[1]	5.2(1.8)K	10.8(2.8)K	1.2K(268)
Android	28K	278(36)[2]	2.7(1.1)K	7.3(3.1)K	720(179)
WM	9K	516(66)	1.6(0.5)K	5.7(3.5)K	545(121)
other	63K	571(87)	7.6(2.9)K	23(9.3)K	1.5K(387)

[1] On iPhone OS, we cannot tell the serving carrier.

[2] Numbers inside parentheses refer to the U.S. users only.

Table 2: Statistics of *DataSource2*(smartphone app).

acteristics such as the IP address, the carrier name, the local DNS server, and the outbound traceroute path. The hashed unique device ID provided by the smartphone application development API allows us to distinguish devices while preserving user privacy. Our application also asks users for access permission for their GPS location. So far, this application has already been executed more than 143,700 times on 62,600 distinct devices. *DataSource2* covers about the same time period as *DataSource1*: from September 2009 till October 2010. Given that the application is used globally, we observe a much larger number of carriers, many of which are outside the U.S.

Note that this method of collecting data provides some ground truths for certain data which is unavailable in *DataSource1*, *e.g.,* IP addresses associated with cellular networks instead of Internet end-points via WiFi network can be accurately identified because of the API offered by those mobile OSes.

4.3 Correlating Across Data Sources

One important general technique we adopt in this work, commonly used by many measurement studies, is to intelligently combine multiple data sources to resolve conflicts and improve accuracy of the analysis. This is necessary as each data source alone has certain limitations and is often insufficient to provide conclusive information.

Correlating *DataSource1* and *DataSource2* allows us to tell based on the IP address whether each record in *DataSource1* is from cellular or WiFi networks and recognize the correct carrier names for those cellular records. Under the assumption that a longest matching prefix is entirely assigned to either a cellular network or an Internet wireline network, the overall idea for correlating *DataSource1* and *DataSource2* depicted by Figure 2 is as follows. Both data sources directly provide the IP address information: Each record in *DataSource1* contains the GPS location information reported by the device allocated with the cellular IP address; while *DataSource2* contains the carrier names of those cellular IP addresses. We first map IP addresses in both data sets into their longest matching prefixes obtained from routing table data of *RouteViews*. After mapping cellular IP addresses into prefixes, we have a prefix-to-location table from *DataSource1* and a prefix-to-carrier table from *DataSource2*. Note that the prefix-to-location mapping is not one-to-one mapping because one IP address can be present at multiple locations over time. Combining these two tables results in a prefix-to-carrier-to-location table, which is used to infer the placement of GGSNs after further clustering discussed later.

We believe that cellular network address blocks are distinct from Internet wireline host IP address blocks for ease of management. To share address blocks across distinct network locations requires announcing BGP routing updates to modify the routes for incoming traffic, affecting routing behavior globally. Due to the added overhead, management complexity, and associated routing disruption, we do not expect this to be done in practice and thus assume that a longest matching prefix is either assigned to cellular networks or

Internet wireline networks. That is why we map the IP addresses in both data sets to their longest matching prefixes.

Two issues still require additional consideration: (a) building the prefix-to-carrier mapping via *DataSource2*, and (b) evaluating the overlap between *DataSource1* and *DataSource2* to investigate any potential limitation of using *DataSource2* as the prefix-to-carrier ground truth.

4.3.1 Recognizing cellular IP addresses and carriers

We expect *DataSource2* to provide the ground truth for differentiating IP addresses from cellular networks and identifying the corresponding carriers of cellular IP addresses. Each record in *DataSource2* contains the network type, *i.e.,* cellular vs. WiFi, reported by APIs provided by the OS. The carrier name is only available on Android and Windows Mobile due to the API limitation on iPhone OS. After mapping IP addresses to their longest matching BGP prefixes, we can build a table mapping from the BGP prefix to the carrier name for Android and Windows Mobile separately. Although we cannot have a prefix-to-carrier table from iPhone OS, we can produce a WiFi-prefix list tracking all the prefixes reported as WiFi networks, and use this WiFi-prefix list to validate Android's and Windows Mobile's prefix-to-carrier tables. These WiFi prefixes are associated with public IP addresses of the edge networks, likely a DSL or cable modem IP in the case of home users.

We justify the accuracy of Windows Mobile's and Android's prefix-to-carrier tables using the iPhone OS's WiFi-prefix list. We believe iPhone OS's WiFi-prefix list is accurate because there are only limited device types using iPhone OS, *i.e.,* iPhone 4G, iPhone 3G, iPhone 3GS, and iPod Touch, which we tested locally and observed to accurately report the network type. Given a prefix-to-carrier table, we compare it with WiFi-prefix list to detect any potential conflicts, *i.e.,* a case when a prefix in the prefix-to-carrier table appears in the WiFi-prefix list as well. A conflict happens only if one IP address in a BGP prefix is considered as a WiFi address by the *DataSource2* on iPhone OS but listed as a cellular address on Android or Windows Mobile. By comparison, we observe 306 conflicts for Windows Mobile's prefix-to-carrier table, yet no conflict for Android. The reason may be that *DataSource2* on Windows Mobile failed to tell the network type on some platforms since the Windows Mobile OS is customized for each type of phone. Therefore, we use Android's prefix-to-carrier table as the authoritative source for identifying the carrier of each record in *DataSource1* data set.

4.3.2 Overlap between data sources

Set	# BGP prefixes	% in *DataSource1*	% in *DataSource2*
DataSource1 ∪ 2	453	-	-
DataSource1 ∩ 2	259	99.97%	98.96%
∈ *DataSource1* ∉ 2	181	0.03%	-
∈ *DataSource2* ∉ 1	13	-	1.04%

Table 3: Overlap between *DataSource1* & *DataSource2*.

Characterizing the overlap between our two data sources helps us estimate the effectiveness of using *DataSource2* to identify the carrier name of *DataSource1*'s cellular prefixes. Moreover, a significant overlap can confirm the representativeness of both *DataSource1* and *DataSource2* on cellular IP addresses as those two data sources are collected independently.

We first compare the overlap between *DataSource1* and *DataSource2*'s records in the U.S. in terms of number of prefixes within the four carriers as shown in Table 3. Although *DataSource1* and

DataSource2 do not overlap much in terms of number of prefixes, *e.g.*, 181 prefixes in *DataSource1* are excluded by *DataSource2*, in terms of number of records the overlap is still significant due to the disappropriate usage of prefixes, *i.e.*, overlapped prefixes contribute to the majority. 99.97% of *DataSource1*'s records are covered by the prefixes shared by both *DataSource1* and *DataSource2*. Therefore, we have high confidence in identifying the majority of cellular addresses based on *DataSource2*. In addition, the big overlap indicates that both data sources are likely to represent the cellular IP behavior of active users well.

5. IDENTIFYING GGSN CLUSTERS

As mentioned in §3, discovering the placement of GGSNs is the key to understanding the cellular infrastructure, explaining the diverse geographic distribution of cellular addresses. This illuminates the important characteristics of cellular network infrastructure that affect performance, manageability, and evolvability. We leverage the information of the geographic coverage of cellular address blocks to infer the placement of each GGSN because those address blocks sharing the similar geographic coverage are likely managed by the same GGSN. In this section, we (1) identify the geographic coverage of the cellular prefixes in *DataSource1*; (2) cluster those prefixes according to the similarity of their geographic coverage; and (3) infer the placement of GGSNs from the different types of clusters. To validate the clustering results we present three validation techniques based on *DataSource2*, DNS request logs from a DNS authoritative server, and `traceroute` probing respectively.

5.1 Clustering Cellular IP Prefixes

On the Internet, an IP address can often provide a good indication of geolocation, albeit perhaps only at a coarse-grained level, as shown by numerous previous work on IP-based geolocation [25, 15, 19, 37]. However, for cellular networks, it is uncertain due to a lack of clear association of IP addresses with physical network locations, especially given the observed highly dynamic nature of IP addresses assigned to a mobile device [5]. In this section, we derive geographic coverage of cellular address blocks in *DataSource1* to study the allocation properties of cellular IP addresses. We have previously described our methodology how to identify cellular addresses and their corresponding carriers in §4: by aggregating IP addresses to prefixes, we can identify the presence of a prefix at different physical locations based on the GPS information in *DataSource1*.

As discussed in §3, we expect that address blocks with similar geographic coverage are likely be subjected to similar address allocation policy. From our data sets, we do observe similarity of geographic coverage present across address blocks. In Figure 3, both /24 address blocks 22 and 5 from Carrier A have more records in the Southeast region. The geographic coverage of these two prefixes is clearly different from the distribution of all Carrier A's addresses in *DataSource1* shown in Figure 3(c), which is influenced by the population density as well as Carrier A's user base. Moreover, we confirm and further investigate the observation in study [5] that a single prefix can be observed at many distinct locations, clearly illustrating that the location property of cellular addresses differs significantly from that of Internet wireline addresses. The large geographic coverage of these /24 address blocks also indicates that users from both Florida and Georgia are served by the same GGSN within this region.

We intend to capture the similarity in geographic coverage through clustering to better understand the underlying network structure. Also, to verify our initial assumption that carriers do not aggregate

their internal routes, we repeat the clustering for /24 address blocks instead of for BGP prefixes by aggregating addresses into /24 address blocks. If cellular carriers do aggregate their internal routes, the number of clusters based on /24 address blocks should be larger than that based on BGP prefixes.

The logical flow to systematically study the similarity of geographic coverage is as follows. Firstly, we quantify the geographic coverage. By dividing the entire U.S. continent into N grids, we assign each prefix a N-dimension feature vector, each element corresponding to one grid and the number of records located in this grid from this prefix. As a result, the normalized feature vector of each prefix is the probability distribution function (PDF) of the girds where this prefix appears. Secondly, we cluster prefixes based on their normalized feature vectors using the *bisect k-means* algorithm for each of the four carriers. The choice of N, varying from 15 to 150 does not affect the clustering results, this is because the geographic coverage of each cluster is so large that the clustering results are insensitive to the granularity of the grid size.

The process of clustering prefixes consists of two steps: (i) pre-filtering prefixes with very few records; and (ii) tuning the maximum tolerable average sum of squared error (SSE) of *bisect k-means*. We present the details next.

5.1.1 Pre-filtering Prefixes with Very Few Records

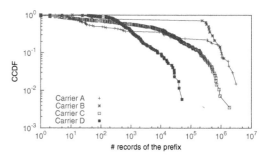

Figure 5: Distribution of # records for prefixes.

Before clustering, we perform pre-filtering to exclude prefixes with very few records so that the number of clusters would not be inflated due to data limitations. Note that aggressive pre-filtering may lead to losing too many records in *DataSource1*.

One intuitive way to filter out those prefixes is to set a threshold on the minimum number of records that a prefix must have. However, the effectiveness of this pre-filtering depends on the distribution of the number of records of prefixes. We plot the complementary cumulative distribution function (CCDF) of the number of records of prefixes in Figure 5. All the four carriers have bi-modal distributions on the number of records of prefixes, implying that we can easily choose the threshold without losing too many records. In our experiments, we choose a threshold for each prefix to be 1% of its carrier's records.

5.1.2 Tuning the SSE in bisect k-means Algorithm

To compare the similarity across prefixes and further cluster them we use the *bisect k-means* algorithm [35] which automatically determines the number of clusters with only one input parameter, *i.e.*, maximum tolerable SSE. In each cluster, consisting of multiple elements, SSE is the average distance from the element to the centroid of the cluster. A smaller value of SSE generates more clusters. The clustering quality is determined by the geographic coverage similarity of the prefixes within a cluster, which is measured by SSE.

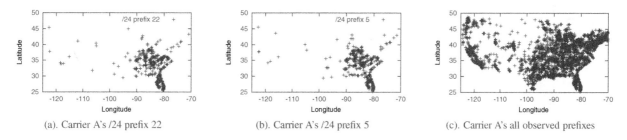

(a). Carrier A's /24 prefix 22   (b). Carrier A's /24 prefix 5   (c). Carrier A's all observed prefixes

Figure 3: Similarity of the geographic coverage for Carrier A's prefixes.

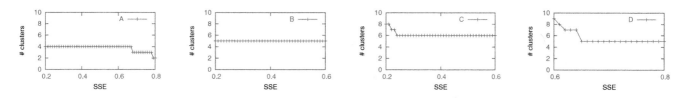

Figure 4: Sensitivity analysis of the SSE in *bi-sect kmeans*.

Figure 4 depicts how SSE, as a measure of the quality of clustering, affects the number of clusters generated for the four carriers. We vary the choice of SSE from 0.01 to 0.99 with increment 0.01. Since there may be multiple stable numbers of clusters, we select the one with the largest range of SSE values. For example, the number of clusters for Carrier A is 4 instead of 3 because it covers [0.2, 0.6] when the number is 4 while it only covers [0.68, 0.78] when the number is 3. From Figure 4, we can also observe that every carriers has an obvious longest SSE range that results in a stable number of clusters, indicating that (i) the geographic coverage across prefixes in the same cluster is very similar; and that (ii) the geographic coverage of the prefixes across clusters is very different.

5.1.3 Clustering Results

We address the problems of pre-filtering and tuning SSE for *bi-sect k-means* clustering in the last two sections. Table 4 shows the parameters we used in pre-filtering and clustering and the clustering results. Aggressive filtering does not happen as every carrier contains at least 99% of the original records after pre-filtering. For Carriers A, B, and C, comparing the clustering at the BGP prefix level vs. the /24 address block level, we do not observe any difference in the number of the clusters generated and the cluster that every address block belongs to. Unlike Carriers A, B, and C, Carrier D does have finer-grained clusters based on its /24 address blocks. We observe that some Carrier D's prefix-level clusters are further divided into smaller clusters at the level of /24 address blocks. These results answer our previous question on the existence of internal route aggregation. Since no internal route aggregation observed for Carriers A, B, and C, BGP prefixes are sufficiently fine-grained to characterize the properties of address blocks. For Carrier D, although the clustering based on /24 address blocks is finer-grained, it does not affect our later analysis. We have applied the clustering on *DataSource1*'s records month by month as well, but we do not see any different numbers of clusters for these 4 carriers.

Figure 6 shows the geographic coverage of each Carrier A's cluster, from the perspective of the U.S. mainland ignoring Alaska and Hawaii, illustrating the diversity across clusters as well as the unexpected large geographic coverage of every single cluster. Note that each cluster consists of prefixes with similar geographic cov-

erage. Each Carrier A's cluster has different geographic spread and center, *i.e.,* Cluster 1 mainly covers the Western, Cluster 2 mainly covers the Southeastern, Cluster 3 mainly covers the Southern and the Mid-Eastern, which are two very disjoint geographic areas, and Cluster 4 mainly covers the Eastern. However, note that the clusters are not disjoint in its geographic coverage, *i.e.,* overlap exists among clusters although those clusters have different geographic centers. For example, comparing Figure 6(b) and 6(d), we can observe that Cluster 2 and Cluster 4 overlap in the Northeast region.

We further quantify the overlap among clusters at grid level. Given a grid, based on all the records located in this grid, we count how many records are from each prefix. Since we know which cluster each prefix belongs to, we can calculate the fraction of records for each grid contributed by different clusters. As a result, for each grid overlapped by multiple clusters, we have a probability distribution function (PDF) on the cluster covering this grid. Based on the PDF, we can calculate the Shannon entropy for each grid. For example, four clusters have 300, 700, 600, and 400 records at grid X respectively, then the PDF for grid X is $[0.3, 0.7, 0.6, 0.4]$ whose Shannon entropy is $-0.3 \lg 0.3 - 0.7 \lg 0.7 - 0.6 \lg 0.6 - 0.4 \lg 0.4$. Smaller values of the entropy reflect smaller overlapping degree, *e.g.,* if all the records for a grid are from the same cluster, the grid has an entropy of $-\infty$. Given the number of clusters is N, the theoretical maximum entropy for a grid is $\lg N$.

Figure 8 draws the CDF of the entropy of the grid. We can observe that overlap at grid level is quite common for all four carriers, *e.g.,* Carrier A's median entropy value close to 1 means that the records in the corresponding grids are evenly divided by two clusters. We conjecture two reasons for the overlap. The first reason is due to load balancing. Because of user mobility, the regional load variation can be high. Higher overlapping degree is better for maintaining service quality. Moreover, in the extreme case if one cluster has a failure, the overlap can increase the reliability of the cellular infrastructure by shifting the load to adjacent clusters. Another reason is that users commute across the boundary of adjacent clusters. For example, a user in *DataSource1* gets an IP address at a region covered by one cluster, subsequently moves to a nearby region covered by another cluster while still maintaining the data connection. This will result in records showing the overlap between the first and the second cluster in adjacent regions.

Figure 9 shows the clustering results for all four carriers. Al-

Carr.	Thres.		# prefixes		SSE		# clusters		(% of records)[# of prefixes] per cluster	
	BGP	/24	BGP	/24	BGP	/24	BGP	/24	BGP	/24
A	500	300	20	35	0.6	0.5	4	4	(28,19,27,26) [6,5,5,4]	(18,24,25,27) [11,8,8,8]
B	500	300	11	11	0.5	0.5	5	5	(10,14,40,19,17) [1,2,3,2,2]	(10,14,40,17,19) [1,2,3,2,2]
C	500	50	63	245	0.5	0.5	6	6	(28,24,10,7,9,19)[17,11,8,7,6,14]	(50,24,3,3,12,5)[130,59,11,11,23,11]
D[1]	100	100	155	177	0.7	0.2	6	10	(30,10,13,22,9,14) [28,25,28,28,22,24]	(32,6,6,11,6,7,9,4,4,8,4) [27,23,16,16,12,14,11,8,7,7,10]

[1] Carrier D's clustering based on /24 address blocks is different with that based on BGP prefixes, which indicates the existence of internal routing

Table 4: Parameters and results for clustering on BGP and /24 address blocks using *bisect k-means*.

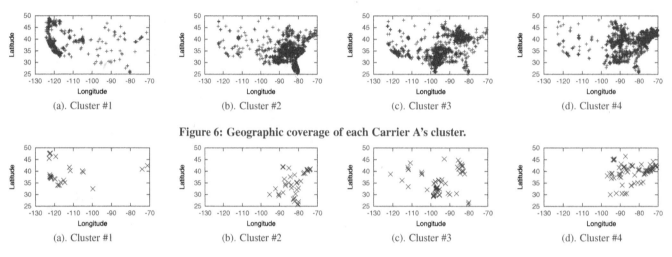

(a). Cluster #1   (b). Cluster #2   (c). Cluster #3   (d). Cluster #4

Figure 6: Geographic coverage of each Carrier A's cluster.

(a). Cluster #1   (b). Cluster #2   (c). Cluster #3   (d). Cluster #4

Figure 7: Clustering Carrier A's local DNS servers.

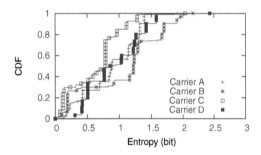

Figure 8: CDF of the entropy of the clusters at the grid level.

though we have already noticed the overlap among clusters in Figure 6, we are still interested in the dominant geographic coverage of each cluster by assigning every grid to its dominant cluster by majority voting. We make the following observations:

1. All 4 carriers we studied appear to cover the entire U.S. with only a handful of clusters (4–6), each covering a large geographic area, differing significantly from the Internet backbone design.
2. There appears to be some "outlier" cases with sparse presence for each cluster in addition to consistent load balancing patterns. We conjecture that this is caused by limited choice of GGSNs for a small set of devices that use a special set of APNs to which not all GGSNs are available for use.
3. Besides those "outliers", overlap among clusters commonly exists at many locations, *e.g.*, the geographic area around Michigan is clearly covered by three of four Carrier A's clusters. We believe the overlap is due to load balancing and user mobility.

4. Clusters do not always appear to be geographically contiguous. There are clearly cases where traffic from users are routed through clusters far away instead of the closest one, *e.g.*, Carrier A's Cluster 3 covers both the Great Lake area and the Southern region. We believe this is due to SGSNs performing load balancing of traffic across GGSNs in different data centers.
5. The clustering for /24 address blocks is the same as that for BGP prefixes for Carriers A, B, and C confirming that there is no internal route aggregation performed by their cellular IP networks. However, Carrier D has finer-grained clustering for /24 address blocks than that for visible BGP prefixes. Despite this observation, its number of clusters for /24 address blocks is only 10 which is still very limited.

In our analysis, we discover that the infrastructure of cellular networks differs significantly from the infrastructure of wireline networks. The cellular networks of all four carriers exhibit only very few types of geographic coverage. As we expected, the type of geographic coverage reflects the placement of IP gateways. Since the GGSN is the first IP hop, we can conclude the surprisingly restricted IP paths of cellular data network. This network structure implies that routing diversity is limited in cellular networks, and that content delivery service (CDN) cannot deliver content very close to cellular users as each cluster clearly covers large geographic areas.

5.2 Validating Clusters

We validate the clustering result in three independent ways: clustering using *DataSource2*'s records, identifying the placement of local DNS servers in cellular networks, and classifying traceroute paths.

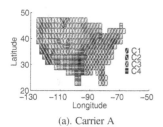
(a). Carrier A

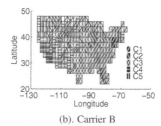
(b). Carrier B

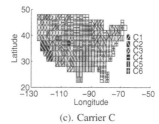
(c). Carrier C

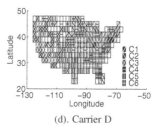
(d). Carrier D

Figure 9: Clusters of all four carriers.

5.2.1 Validation via DataSource2

Although the size of *DataSource2* is much smaller than that of *DataSource1*, we can still use *DataSource2* to validate the clustering results obtained from *DataSource1*. We repeat the clustering on the prefixes with more than 100 records from the *DataSource2*. Besides, we repeat the clustering on different types of device, *i.e.,* Android, iPhone, and WM based on *DataSource2*'s records. The clustering results are consistent with those of *DataSource1* in terms of the number of clusters and the cluster that each prefix belongs to. Moreover, all the observations from *DataSource1* listed in §5.1 consistently apply to *DataSource2*.

5.2.2 Validation via Local DNS Server Based Grouping

Carrier	# user	# records	# LDNS	# clusters
A	289	384	12	4
B	574	1045	4	1
C	704	884	12	3
D	122	142	15	3

Table 5: Statistics of local DNS experiments.

The configuration of the local DNS infrastructure is essential to ensure good network performance. Besides performance concerns, local DNS information is often used for directing clients to the nearest cache server expected to have the best performance. This is based on the key assumption that clients tend to be close to their configured local DNS servers, which may not always hold [29]. In this work, we perform the first study to examine the placement and configuration of the local DNS servers relative to the cellular users and the implication of the local DNS configuration of cellular users on mobile content delivery. It is particularly interesting to study the correlation between the local DNS server IP and the device's physical location. Since DNS servers are expected to be placed at the same level as IP gateways, *i.e.,* GGSNs, we expect to see similar clusters of cellular local DNS servers based on the geographic coverage.

To collect a diverse set of local DNS server configurations, we resort to our *DataSource2* application by having the client send a specialized DNS request for a unique but nonexistent DNS name which embeds the device identifier and the timestamp (`id_timestamp_example.com`) to a domain (`example.com`) where we have access to the DNS request logs on the authoritative DNS server. The device identifier, `id_timestamp`, is used for correlating the corresponding entry in the *DataSource2*'s log which stores the information such as the GPS information, the IP address, *etc.* The timestamp ensures that the request is globally unique so that it is not cached. This is a known technique used in previous studies for recording the association between clients and their local DNS servers [23]. Since most DNS servers operate in the iterative mode,

from the authoritative DNS server, we can observe the formatted incoming DNS requests from local DNS servers.

We summarize our results in Table 5. The four carriers appear to have different policies for configuring local DNS servers. All the local DNS servers of Carrier A across the country fall into one /19 address block. Carrier B altogether only has four distinct DNS IP addresses within two different /24 address blocks, although it has four GGSN clusters. This implies that Carrier B's local DNS servers are unlikely located directly at cellular network gateways, as a single /24 prefix usually constitutes the smallest routing unit. For Carrier C, we observe 12 local DNS server IP addresses within 3 different /24 address blocks. This indicates that, just like Carrier B's clusters, Carrier C's clusters share local DNS servers as well, since Carrier C has more clusters than the /24 address blocks of its local DNS servers. For Carrier D, we observe 15 IP addresses of local DNS servers in 12 /24 address blocks.

For each carrier, we cluster its local DNS servers based on their geographic coverage without any other prior knowledge and show the results in Figure 7. Comparing the clusters based on the local DNS servers with previous clustering based on prefixes in §5.1, we observe that Carrier A's clusters for local DNS servers match very well with the clusters for address blocks (shown in Figure 7). Carriers A's users sharing the same local DNS server IP belong to the same cluster based on cellular prefixes. This serves as another independent validation for previous clustering. Carrier B's users across the U.S. all share the same four local DNS servers, while Carriers C's and D's clusters based on local DNS servers are "one-to-many" mapped to their clusters based on address blocks, indicating that their local DNS servers are shared across multiple clusters as well.

On the current Internet, local DNS-based server selection is widely adopted by commercial CDNs. For Carriers A, C, and D, since their local DNS servers are "one-to-one" or "one-to-many" mapped to GGSNs, server selection based on local DNS servers cannot be finer-grained than the GGSN level. For Carrier B, server selection can be even worse because all Carrier B's local DNS servers are used across the entire U.S.

5.2.3 Validating via traceroute Probing

Since the clusters created based on cellular prefixes should correspond to the prefixes serving clients within the same network location, we use bi-directional traceroute to further validate this. For the inbound direction, for each prefix of these four carriers in *DataSource1*, we run traceroute on 5 *PlanetLab* nodes at geographically distinct locations within the U.S. to one IP address in this prefix for four days. We make the following observations.

- Stability of traceroute paths at IP level: All traceroute paths obtained from our experiments are found to be very stable without any change at DNS or IP level.

- Stability of traceroute paths at the prefix level: To the same prefix, the last 5 visible hops in the traceroute path from different *PlanetLab* nodes are consistently the same.

- Similarity of traceroute paths to prefixes in the same cluster: For Carriers A, C and D, prefixes in the same *bisect k-means* cluster share the same traceroute path at DNS or IP level validating their geographic proximity. For Carrier B, each prefix has a distinct traceroute path, making validation more challenging.

- Location correlation between traceroute paths and the cluster's region: For some Carriers A's, B's, and C's clusters, we can infer the GGSN locations from the DNS name of the hops along the path; while for others there is insufficient information to determine router locations. Table 6 shows for the last inferred location along the inbound traceroute path to some clusters with location information inferred from router DNS names. They all agree with the geographic coverage of these clusters.

Cluster	Coverage	DNS key word	Location
A.1	WEST	WA	WA
A.2	SOUTHEAST	GA	GA
A.3	SOUTH	DLSTX	DALLAS, TX
B.1	MIDDLE	CHI	CHICAGO, IL
B.2	SOUTHEAST	FL	FL
B.3	SOUTHEAST	ATLGA	ATLANTA, GA
B.4	WEST	TUSTIN	TUSTIN, CA
B.5	SOUTH	DLSTX	DALLAS, TX
C.1	EAST	CLE	CLEVELAND, OH
C.2	WEST	SCL	SALT LAKE CITY, UT
C.3	NORTHWEST	SEA	SEATTLE, WA
C.4	MIDDLE	AURORA	AURORA, CO
C.5	SOUTH	HOU	HOUSTON, TX
C.6	EAST	NEWARK	NEWARK, NJ

Table 6: Inferred locations for clusters using router DNS names of traceroute paths to the clusters.

Similar to the inbound direction, the outbound traceroute can validate the clustering to some degree. *DataSource2* application runs ICMP traceroute from the device to an Internet server. Assigning the outbound traceroute path to the prefix, we have the following observations:

- For all four carriers, their traceroute paths in the same cluster have the same path pattern, *i.e.,* the sequence of IP addresses or the sequence of address blocks are the same. All clusters are "one-to-one" or "one-to-many" mapped to traceroute path patterns, so each cluster has very different traceroute patterns from the others.

- The prefixes in the same Carrier A's cluster always go through the same set of IP addresses, while for Carriers B, C, and D, their prefixes in the same cluster always go through the same set of /24 address blocks. Therefore we can always tell a prefix's corresponding cluster based on the IP addresses or the /24 address blocks that appear along the traceroute path.

6. IMPLICATIONS ON CONTENT DELIVERY NETWORKS

Based on the previous characterization of cellular data network infrastructure, we highlight the key impact of cellular infrastructure by examining its implication on content delivery networks from the perspectives of content placement and server selection.

6.1 Content Placement

On today's Internet, CDN plays an important role of reducing the latency for accessing web content. The essential idea behind CDN is to serve users from nearby CDN servers that replicate the content from the origin server located potentially far away. By characterizing the cellular infrastructure, we have observed that the current restrictive cellular topology route all traffic through only a handful GGSNs. Therefore, no matter how close to a CDN server the user is, the content still has to go through the GGSN before reaching the destination. The possible reasons for such a restrictive topology design by routing all traffic through GGSNs include simplicity and ease of management, *e.g.,* billing and accounting. Furthermore, it is also easy to enforce policies for security and traffic management. This certainly has negative implication on content delivery.

It is not simple to adapt an existing CDN service, *e.g., Akamai* and *Limelight*, directly to cellular networks due to routing restrictions. One possible alternative is deploying CDN servers within cellular networks to be closer to end users so that the traffic does not have to go through GGSNs to reach the content on the Internet. There has been some startup effort of placing boxes between the RNC and the SGSN to accelerate data delivery and lighten data traffic growth [30], but this design brings additional challenges to management due to the increased number of locations traffic can terminate. Without the support of placing CDN servers inside cellular core networks, placing them close to GGSNs becomes a quick solution for now, and this solution is clearly limited due to the property of the GGSN serving a large geographic region of users.

In *DataSource2*'s application, we measure the ping RTT to 20 Internet servers (landmark servers) located across the U.S. to study the end-to-end latency. The latency to the landmark servers is an approximation on the latency to the content placed at different network locations on the Internet. The 20 servers that we choose are very popular servers geographically distributed across 20 states. To estimate the benefit of placing content close to GGSN, we compare the latency to landmark servers with the latency to the first cellular IP hop, *i.e.,* the first IP hop along the outbound path where GGSN is located.

Each time *DataSource2*'s application runs, it only probes these landmark servers twice to save the resource consumption on devices. In order to eliminate the variability from air interface so that we can isolate the impact from the wireline hops, we follow the splitting method in §5.1 dividing the U.S. continent into N grids. Within each grid, we compare the minimum RTT to the first cellular IP hop against these 20 landmark servers. In Figure 10(a), we show the absolute difference between the latency to the first cellular IP hop and the latency to the landmark servers. Figure 10(b) shows the percentage of the latency saving. Because these 20 landmark servers are widely distributed across the U.S., the minimum latency to landmark servers should be a good estimation of the latency to the current content providers. We can observe that placing content close to the GGSN can reduce the end-to-end latency by 50%. Note that the 50% improvement have already eliminated the variability from air interface. This clearly motivates CDN service providers to push mobile content close to GGSNs.

6.2 Server Selection

Besides the challenge of mobile content placement, server selection is another important issue for CDN service providers. Some existing CDN services, *e.g., Akamai* and *Limelight*, choose the content server based on the incoming DNS requests from the local DNS server assuming the address of the local DNS can accurately represent the location of those end hosts behind the local DNS server. However, this assumption rarely holds for cellular networks.

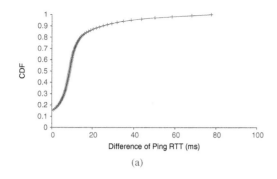
(a)

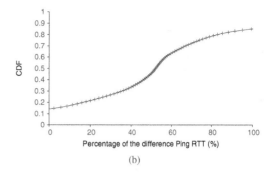
(b)

Figure 10: Latency to the first cellular IP hop vs. 20 landmark servers on the Internet.

In §5.2.2, we know that Carriers A, C, and D have different local DNS servers for different GGSN clusters, while Carrier B's clusters share the same set of local DNS servers. Although Carriers A, C, and D have different local DNS server for different GGSN clusters, the IP addresses are very similar. Without the information of the correlation between the local DNS server and the GGSN cluster, it is difficult to choose content servers for different GGSN clusters according to their local DNS server IP address. As Carrier B's GGSN clusters share the same set of local DNS servers, it is impossible to choose content servers for different GGSN clusters based on the DNS request alone.

Interestingly even if content providers can obtain the accurate physical location based on some application-level knowledge, *e.g.,* Google Gears [14], directing the traffic to the content server physically closest to the mobile device can be grossly suboptimal due to the placement of the GGSN and the cellular network routing restrictions. Traffic still needs traverse through the GGSN, despite the close proximity between the mobile device and the content server. To estimate the difference in performance between choosing a server physically closest to the mobile device and one closest to the GGSN node, we do the following analysis. Using the GPS location information reported by *DataSource2*'s application, in all the experiments from Carrier A's Cluster 2, we compare the latency to the landmark server closest to the mobile device with the latency to the landmark server closet to the corresponding GGSN, *i.e.,* one landmark server located at Georgia (according to Table 6 in §5.2.3). Note, similar to §5.1 and §6.1, we split Cluster 2's geographic coverage into grids, aggregate RTTs in the same grid, and compare based on the minimum RTTs as well. Figure 11 shows that the latency to the closet landmark server has high probability to be larger than the latency to the Georgia landmark server and on average by about 10 – 20ms, indicating that choosing the server according to the physical location of the mobile device is suboptimal due to the routing restriction imposed by GGSNs.

Overall, if mobile content providers want to adopt the short-term solution to reduce the end-to-end latency, they have to solve two issues: (i) placing content servers as close as to GGSNs; and (ii) effectively directing traffic to the content server closest to the GGSN that originates the traffic based on information such as the correlation between local DNS servers and GGSNs.

7. CONCLUDING REMARKS

In this paper, we comprehensively characterized the infrastructure of cellular data network of four major wireless carriers within the U.S. including both UMTS and EVDO technology. We unveiled several fundamental differences between cellular data networks and the wireline networks in terms of placement of GGSNs,

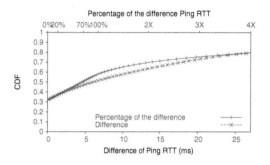

Figure 11: Difference in latency to the closest landmark server from the mobile device vs. to the server closest to the GGSN.

local DNS server behavior, and routing properties. One of the most surprising findings is that cellular data networks have severe restriction on routing by traversing only a few limited GGSNs to interface with external Internet networks. We observed that all 4 carriers we studied divide the U.S. among only 4–6 GGSNs, each serving a large geographic area. Since the GGSN is the first IP hop, it implies that CDN servers cannot consistently serve content close to end users.

Our study also showed that in the best case local DNS servers for some carriers can be close to GGSNs. Since traffic from and to local DNS servers and cellular users must traverse one of those few GGSNs, using local DNS servers and the knowledge of the mapping to the GGSN to identify the best server to deliver mobile content currently can be sufficient despite the routing restrictions.

Regarding content placement, we investigated and compared two choices: (i) placing content at the boundary between the cellular backbone and the Internet; and (ii) placing content at the GGSN in the cellular backbone. We observed that pushing content close to GGSNs could potentially reduce the end-to-end latency by more than 20%. If pushing content into the proprietary cellular backbone is not permitted, placing content at the boundary still gives considerable benefit.

We believe our findings in characterizing the infrastructure for cellular data networks directly motivate future work in this area. Our observations on the cellular infrastructure guide CDNs to provide better service to mobile users, and our methodology for discovering cellular data network properties will continue to reveal new behavior as cellular networks evolve.

8. REFERENCES

[1] Introduction Mobile Data Track Presentation. http://www.nanog.org/meetings/nanog47/presentations/Monday/Intro_nanog47_mobiletrack.pdf.

[2] The future of mobile networking. http://www.nanog.org/meetings/nanog47/presentations/Monday/Future_Mobile_Data_N47_Mon.pdf.

[3] University of Oregon Route Views Archive Project. http://www.routeviews.org.

[4] M. Anand, E. B. Nightingale, and J. Flinn. Self-Tuning Wireless Network Power Management. *Wireless Networks*, 11(4), 2005.

[5] M. Balakrishnan, I. Mohomed, and V. Ramasubramanian. Where's That Phone?: Geolocating IP Addresses on 3G Networks. In *Proceedings of IMC*, 2009.

[6] N. Balasubramanian, A. Balasubramanian, and A. Venkataramani. Energy Consumption in Mobile Phones: A Measurement Study and Implications for Network Applications. In *Proc. ACM SIGCOMM IMC*, 2009.

[7] M. Casado and M. J. Freedman. Peering through the shroud: The effect of edge opacity on IP-based client identification. In *Proc. Symposium on Networked Systems Design and Implementation*, 2007.

[8] R. Chakravorty, S. Banerjee, S. Agarwal, and I. Pratt. MoB: A Mobile Bazaar for Wide-area Wireless Services. In *Proc. ACM MOBICOM*, 2005.

[9] M. C. Chan and R. Ramjee. TCP/IP Performance over 3G Wireless Links with Rate and Delay Variation. In *Proc. of MOBICOM*, 2002.

[10] S. J. Cheng, C. Jin, A. R. Kurc, D. Raz, and Y. Shavitt. Constrained Mirror Placement on the Internet. In *Proc. IEEE INFOCOM*, 2001.

[11] J. Chesterfield, R. Chakravorty, J. Crowcroft, P. Rodriguez, and S. Banerjee. Experiences with Multimedia Streaming over 2.5G and 3G Networks. *Journal ACM/MONET*, 2004.

[12] CISCO. Configuring Dynamic Addressing on the GGSN. http://www.cisco.com/en/US/docs/ios/12_4/12_4y/12_4_24ye/cfg/ggsndhcp.html.

[13] M. Ghaderi, A. Sridharan, H. Zang, D. Towsley, and R. Cruz. TCP-Aware Resource Allocation in CDMA Networks. In *Proceedings of ACM MOBICOM*, Los Angeles, CA, USA, September 2006.

[14] Google. Gears. http://gears.google.com.

[15] B. Gueye, A. Ziviani, M. Crovella, and S. Fdida. Constraint-based Geolocation of Internet Hosts. *IEEE/ACM Trans. Netw.*, 14(6):1219–1232, 2006.

[16] C. Huang, A. Wang, J. Li, and K. W. Ross. Measuring and Evaluating Large-Scale CDNs. In *Microsoft Research Technical Report MSR-TR-2008-106*, 2008.

[17] J. Huang, Q. Xu, B. Tiwana, Z. M. Mao, M. Zhang, and P. Bahl. Anatomizing Application Performance Differences on Smartphones. In *Proc. ACM MOBISYS*, 2010.

[18] E. Inc. LTE-SAE architecture and performance. http://www.ericsson.com/ericsson/corpinfo/publications/review/2007_03/files/5_LTE_SAE.pdf.

[19] E. Katz-Bassett, J. P. John, A. Krishnamurthy, D. Wetherall, T. Anderson, and Y. Chawathe. Towards IP geolocation using delay and topology measurements. In *IMC 2006: Proceedings of the 6th ACM SIGCOMM conference on Internet measurement*, pages 71–84, New York, NY, USA, 2006. ACM.

[20] R. Keralapura, A. Nucci, Z.-L. Zhang, and L. Gao. Profiling Users in a 3G Network Using Hourglass Co-Clustering. In *Proc. ACM MOBICOM*, 2010.

[21] X. Liu, A. Sridharan, S. Machiraju, M. Seshadri, and

H. Zang. Experiences in a 3G Network: Interplay between the Wireless Channel and Applications. In *Proceedings of ACM MOBICOM*, 2008.

[22] H. V. Madhyastha, T. Isdal, M. Piatek, C. Dixon, T. Anderson, A. Krishnamurthy, and A. Venkataramani. iPlane: An Information Plane for Distributed Services. In *Proc. Operating Systems Design and Implementation*, 2006.

[23] Z. M. Mao, C. Cranor, F. Douglis, M. Rabinovich, O. Spatscheck, and J. Wang. A Precise and Efficient Evaluation of the Proximity between Web Clients and their Local DNS Servers. In *Proc of USENIX Annual Technical Conference*, 2002.

[24] J. Oberheide, K. Veraraghavan, E. Cooke, J. Flinn, and F. Jahanian. In-Cloud Security Services for Mobile Devices. In *Proc of the First Workshop on Virtualization and Mobile Computing*, 2008.

[25] V. N. Padmanabhan and L. Subramanian. An Investigation of Geographic Mapping Techniques for Internet Hosts. In *ACM Sigcomm*, 2001.

[26] L. Qiu, V. N. Padmanabhan, and G. M. Voelker. On the Placement of Web Server Replicas. In *Proc. IEEE INFOCOM*, 2001.

[27] M. Rahnema. *UMTS Network Planning, Optimization, and Inter-Operation with GSM*. Wiley, 2007.

[28] P. Rodriguez, R. Chakravorty, J. Chesterfield, I. Pratt, and S. Banerjee. MAR: A Commuter Router Infrastructure for the Mobile Internet. In *Proc. ACM MOBISYS*, 2004.

[29] A. Shaikh, R. Tewari, and M. Agrawal. On the Effectiveness of DNS-based Server Selection. In *Proc. IEEE INFOCOM*, Anchorage, AK, April 2001.

[30] S. Solutions. Solutions: Mobile Data Offload. http://www.stoke.com/Solutions/smdo.asp.

[31] N. Spring, R. Mahajan, and D. Wetherall. Measuring ISP Topologies with Rocketfuel. In *ACM Sigcomm*, 2002.

[32] N. Spring, D. Wetherall, and T. Anderson. Reverse-Engineering the Internet. In *Proc. First ACM SIGCOMM HotNets Workshop*, 2002.

[33] A. Sridharan, R. Subbaraman, and R. Guerin. Distributed Uplink Scheduling in CDMA Networks. In *Proceedings of IFIP-Networking 2007*, May 2007.

[34] L. Subramanian, S. Agarwal, J. Rexford, and R. H. Katz. Characterizing the Internet Hierarchy from Multiple Vantage Points. In *Proc. IEEE INFOCOM*, 2002.

[35] P.-N. Tan, M. Steinbach, and V. Kumar. *Introduction to Data Mining*. Addison-Wesley, 2006.

[36] I. Trestian, S. Ranjan, A. Kuzmanovic, and A. Nucci. Measuring Serendipity: Connecting People, Locations and Interests in a Mobile 3G Network. In *Proceedings of IMC*, 2009.

[37] B. Wong, I. Stoyanov, and E. G. Sirer. Octant: A Comprehensive Framework for the Geolocalization of Internet Hosts. In *Proc. Symposium on Networked Systems Design and Implementation*, 2007.

[38] M. Zhang, C. Zhang, V. Pai, L. Peterson, and R. Wang. PlanetSeer: Internet Path Failure Monitoring and Characterization in Wide-Area Services. In *Proc. Operating Systems Design and Implementation*, 2004.

[39] Z. Zhuang, T.-Y. Chang, R. Sivakumar, and A. Velayutham. A3: Application-Aware Acceleration for Wireless Data Networks. In *Proc. of ACM MOBICOM*, 2006.

Fine-Grained Latency and Loss Measurements in the Presence of Reordering

Myungjin Lee
Purdue University

Sharon Goldberg
Boston University

Ramana Rao Kompella
Purdue University

George Varghese
UC San Diego

ABSTRACT

Modern trading and cluster applications require microsecond latencies and almost no losses in data centers. This paper introduces an algorithm called *FineComb* that can estimate fine-grain end-to-end loss and latency measurements between edge routers in these data center networks. Such a mechanism can allow managers to distinguish between latencies and loss singularities caused by servers and those caused by the network. Compared to prior work, such as Lossy Difference Aggregator (LDA), that focused on switch-level latency measurements, the requirement of end-to-end latency measurements introduces the *challenge of reordering* that occurs commonly in IP networks due to churn. The problem is even more acute in switches across data center networks that employ multipath routing algorithms to exploit the inherent path diversity. Without proper care, a loss estimation algorithm can confound loss and reordering; further, any attempt to aggregate delay estimates in the presence of reordering results in severe errors. FineComb deals with these problems using order-agnostic packet digests and a simple new idea we call stash recovery. Our evaluation demonstrates that FineComb can provide orders of magnitude better accuracy in loss and delay estimates in the presence of reordering compared to LDA.

Categories and Subject Descriptors

C.2.3 [**Computer-Communication Networks**]: Network management

General Terms

Measurement, algorithms

Keywords

Passive measurement, latency, packet loss, reordering

1. INTRODUCTION

Recent trends in data centers have led to requirements for *microsecond* latencies. Fundamentally, this is because *programs* respond to network messages, not *humans*. For example, an automated trading program can buy millions of shares cheaply with faster access to a low stock price; similarly, a cluster application can execute 1000's more instructions if latencies are trimmed by 100 μsecs. Further, all these applications are deployed in data centers that span a small geographical area and where links and switches are carefully chosen to have minimal latencies (*e.g.*, [30]). It is unlikely that this trend toward low latency networks is going to stop any time soon; indeed, analysts are already discussing applications that would require even more stringent latency guarantees in the order of *nanoseconds* [6].

Despite the most careful selection of network components, there is no easy way for network operators to *guarantee* that congestion in switches never causes latencies to increase beyond acceptable thresholds. First, there are no traffic models for different applications that allow a manager to predict which applications can cause problems. Second, new applications must be deployed and their behavior is often unforeseen. For example, the effects of barrier-synchronized workloads overflowing switch buffers leading to packet loss and high latency was recently discovered as the well-known "in-cast" problem [29]. While solutions and work-arounds may often exist for specific problems, network operators need to perform latency measurements on a continuous basis to detect and fix such problems, either by re-routing the offending application or upgrading links to a higher capacity, or by some other means.

At a minimum, there are two types of measurements network operators typically need. First, they need *end-to-end measurements* in the network to check whether end-to-end latencies and losses are within satisfactory limits for a given customer or an application that are often specified in the form of service-level agreements (SLAs). Second, if a customer or application experiences bad performance (delay spikes or packet losses), it is important to quickly diagnose the root cause of the problem; this means obtaining *switch-level measurements* to localize the offending switch along the path. In many respects, these measurement requirements are similar to what ISPs face; the key difference, however, is that end-to-end delays in data centers are in the order of a few microseconds compared to milliseconds in ISP networks. Thus, standard approach using end-to-end active probes and tomography (for obtaining hop-level measurements) are not effective due to their huge probe requirements (*e.g.*, ~10,000 per second [16]).

Recognizing these challenges, researchers have already begun to propose scalable data structures such as LDA [16] for fine-grained switch-level latency measurements. Unfortunately, detecting end-to-end latency spikes by using LDA at the switch-level is impractical, as individual switch delays are not easily summable (see §2.3). Besides, this approach incurs significant deployment cost as each switch needs to be equipped with an LDA. Therefore, scalably measuring end-to-end latency is still a requirement not satisfied with existing solutions such as LDA.

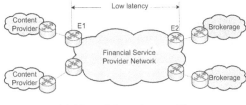

(a) Financial service provider

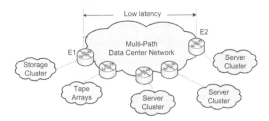

(b) Data center network

Figure 1: Low end-to-end latency applications.

Depending on the particular scenario, the two end points between which latency and loss measurements are required vary. For example, in a market data network architecture [2] (shown in Figure 1(a)), data feeds from content providers (*e.g.*, stock exchanges) are often provided to individual brokerages using financial service providers (FSPs). In this scenario, the FSPs may want to provide a latency SLA of a few microseconds through their network from the content provider to the brokerage; hence measurements between these edges are crucial. In a typical data center network running low-latency applications, there are clusters of servers interconnected with storage servers, tape arrays and other such infrastructure [1] (as shown in Figure 1(b)). In such cases, one could easily imagine stringent latency requirements between server and storage cluster, or across two different server rack switches, or even from an edge router to another edge router within a multi-rooted tree topology (*e.g.*, a fat-tree [7]).

In this paper, we consider a passive approach for measuring end-to-end delays. Instead of injecting active probes for measurement, we focus on measuring the latencies of actual packets that travel between the endpoints. This approach results in two immediate benefits. First, it does not interfere with regular traffic. Second, SLA violations apply to actual packets; so, measuring actual packet latencies will reflect the SLA violations better than using artificial probes. At first glance, this problem then reduces to the same abstraction as conducting latency measurements within a switch, such as the approach taken by LDA in [16], where they measure actual packet latencies across a switch. The key difference, however, lies in the fact that LDA *crucially assumes* FIFO ordering (*i.e.*, in-order arrival) of packets between the two measurement end-points—an assumption that may not hold well in our setting.

In our end-to-end setting, we need to allow for the presence of *packet reordering* across the two measurement endpoints. Because multiple flows are present between the two, and maintaining per-flow state (for a large number of flows) is costly, our goal is to obtain aggregate measurements of all packets *across* flows. Thus, while switch vendors typically ensure that there is no reordering across flows between two interfaces (otherwise, TCP may not work well), no such guarantee is provided by an IP network across routers that are not directly connected. In fact, many commercial data centers rely on exploiting the path diversity inherently present within data centers using ECMP (equal cost multipath) where flows are split across multiple paths. Of course, while ECMP still ensures packets *within* a flow are not reordered, reordering commonly occurs across flows. In addition, churn in the network (*e.g.*, link failures) can cause temporary routing loops that may introduce reordering by causing some packets to arrive faster than the others.

Furthermore, while our immediate motivation is end-to-end reordering that can happen in IP networks, we believe it is very likely that future switches will allow reordering *within* switches for improved load-balancing. Anecdotal evidence suggests that many switch vendors (*e.g.*, Cisco) have internal settings by which packets can be load-balanced across multiple equal paths using packet spraying (which can reorder packets as opposed to flow hashing which preserves order). The reason these settings are never used is because standard TCP implementations are perceived to interact poorly with reordering, especially the interaction with fast retransmit and congestion control that can cause window sizes to shrink unduly by conflating loss and misordering. However, a number of researchers have been looking at creating reordering-tolerant TCP, at least for use in data centers; for example, Multipath-TCP [23] may be a point of departure for such ideas. While these ideas appear radical, packet spraying with reordering-tolerant TCP at the edges can greatly improve the utilization and costs of future data center networks. If these ideas gain currency, as we believe they will, making scalable latency measurement resilient to reordering will be essential not just end-to-end, but also within switches.

The state-of-the-art solution LDA [16], which assumes FIFO packet ordering, will not work well in these environments, as it can confuse reordered packets with lost packets. To address this problem, this paper describes an efficient data structure called FineComb that is robust to reordering, and can be easily implemented at the network edges to spot microscopic delay variations (in the order of microseconds) and losses (10s per million) with small amount of state and processing costs. We evaluate FineComb extensively both analytically, and via simulation on various delay models and real router traces (with synthetic workloads); our experiments indicate FineComb can achieve 10x lower relative error for latency estimates and 200x lower relative error for loss estimates compared to LDA, even under small amounts of reordering.

2. PRELIMINARIES

We describe the basic measurement goals, constraints and assumptions in our problem setting, and explain a set of existing solutions that do not work well for our problem.

2.1 Measurement Goals

Figure 1 shows two canonical low-latency network scenarios. In both kinds of scenarios, our goal is to measure the aggregate performance between two edge routers, say $E1$ and $E2$ in Figure 1. We divide time into intervals (a few seconds) for which we are interested in obtaining performance measures. As a first step, we consider three basic measures across all packets: average latency, variance, and loss rate.

For most of this paper, we assume hardware implementations to keep up with high line rates; however, we briefly discuss software implementations. Thus our implementations need to satisfy the following constraints. We require that our data structure scale well in terms of control bandwidth, processing time, and storage. This is especially important as these metrics must be measured for each destination edge router. Of the three measures, storage may possibly be increased in a software implementation, but processing time and control bandwidth need to be kept a minimum. Further, as we mentioned before, the solution should be robust to packet reordering that may occur in these environments.

2.2 Assumptions

We make three key assumptions in our work and justify why they hold well in our setting.

Time synchronization. We assume that the two edge routers $E1$ and $E2$ can be time-synchronized within μseconds, for example, using GPS clocks that many ISPs have already begun to deploy. This is a general requirement for any one-way delay measurement scheme, and in fact is employed by existing edge monitoring solution such as Corvil [3].

Packet filtering. Packets that arrive at a given ingress edge router will potentially exit via different destination edge routers. We assume some simple way to determine which packets are destined to or from a particular edge router, for example by prefix matching. One could easily construct a simple layer-4 packet filter (using IPs and ports) that clearly specifies the set of packets that traverse from $E1$ to $E2$ so that both $E1$ and $E2$ could precisely identify the set of packets over which the metrics need to be computed.

No header changes. Measuring latencies would be easy if we could embed a timestamp within each packet. However, IP packets do not have a timestamp field and TCP timestamp options are restricted to carrying *true* end-to-end delays where ends are the actual sockets running on the host machines. Adding a new field is unlikely to happen as it would require intrusive changes to a large number of components in the data path of switches.

2.3 Issues with earlier solutions

Active probes: Active probes are insufficient for three reasons: First, to measure microsecond latencies, a large number of active probes need to be injected as prior work [16] indicated. Second, active probes do not measure the true delay experienced by regular data packets. Third, active probes may take one among many different paths that may potentially exist between the pairs of edge routers. See §5 for a quantitative argument.

Storing timestamps locally: An alternative is to allow the sender and receiver edge monitors to store packet digests and timestamps locally, and only to exchange these timestamps at the end of a measurement interval. However, the storage and communication overhead for this scheme is extremely high. 10 Gigabit capacity at 10% utilization between two edge routers translates to roughly 1 million packets on a per second basis, assuming an average packet of size 125 bytes. One could maintain timestamps only for a small *sample* of packets; but, as we show in §5.3, this reduces bandwidth at the cost of accuracy. While we are not certain, it appears that vendors such as Corvil [3] and NetScout [5] use variants of this approach. The lack of scalability may be indicated by the fact that the 10G Corvil solution [3] costs 90,000 U.K pounds.[1]

LDA: The LDA [16], a recent proposal for measuring fine grain delays, suggests a way of greatly increasing the number of latency samples using aggregation. LDA requires the sender to send a synchronization message at the start of every measurement interval that is injected in the same stream as the regular data packets. A *crucial assumption* that makes LDA work is that the synchronization messages and packets are delivered in order at the receiver so that the sender and receiver compute delay estimates over the same set of packets; this FIFO assumption makes LDA unsuitable for our setting. As we show in §5.3, even a few reordered packets can cause LDA to incur a large error in both loss and latency estimation.

Why Per-Path LDA does not work ? The obvious fix to LDA is to extend it to operate on a per-path basis. Unfortunately, neither senders nor receivers know which path a given flow will take and

---

[1]Of course, Corvil solution may enable more detailed analysis, but a significant cost comes from packet capture, processing and storage overheads.

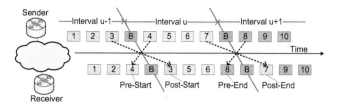

Figure 2: Four types of reordering that can occur.

so, separation by path is difficult. While we can exploit the fact that ECMP does not reorder TCP flows, LDA for potentially millions of separate TCP flows would pose a scaling problem. Sampling a sufficiently large number of flows to ensure (with high probability) that at least one flow is sampled per path is possible. However, besides the extra multiplicative factor in memory (to cover the number of paths and the extra factor to ensure high probability coverage), the sampling scheme has a fatal flaw. The sampled flows may have too few packets and thus the number of LDA samples can be too small to provide sufficient accuracy. Increasing the number of samples will require either more memory (by sampling more flows) or assuming very skewed distribution of flows (and mechanisms to capture such flows).

To address these shortcomings, we propose a new data structure called FineComb, that only keeps storage per destination switch and yet has very high sample efficiency (if no loss, *every* packet from a source to a destination is included in latency calculation).

3. FINECOMB

FineComb assumes a stream of packets going from a sender Snd (*e.g.*, $E1$ in Figure 1) to a receiver Rcv (*e.g.*, $E2$). Time is divided into measurement intervals that are marked by interval start and end messages that are transmitted from Snd to Rcv. FineComb, like LDA, starts with the following simple idea: Suppose Snd and Rcv agree on a set of packets in the stream over which they want to measure delay. Then, they could compute the average delay by each locally maintaining a sum of packet timestamps (a *timestamp accumulator*) and a count of the number of packets in the interval (a *counter*). The average delay is then the difference between the timestamp accumulator at Snd and timestamp accumulator at Rcv, divided by the number of packets in the counter. But how should Snd and Rcv agree on the set of packets, in the presence of packet loss and reordering, without marking or modifying packets? This is exactly the challenge addressed by FineComb.

3.1 The challenge of reordering

In FineComb, Snd and Rcv agree upon an interval of T packets that they would like to measure delays over. To do this, Snd marks off intervals by sending a special 'sync' control message each time it sends T packets to Rcv. (Note that Snd could choose to mark the intervals based on time as well, but we define interval as T packets for ease of exposition.) All packets 'bookended' by a pair of sync messages belong in a single interval. For convenience, we shall refer to the first sync message in an interval as an interval-start message, and the end sync message as an interval-end message.

Figure 2 shows packets arriving out of order when traversing the network. The ordering of packets that are both transmitted and received within the interval end 'bookends' does not affect FineComb (or LDA), since the timestamp accumulators and counters are order-agnostic (addition is commutative). However, we must deal with the following type of *problematic reordering*, namely packets that start out in one interval at Snd, drift into an another interval at Rcv. This situation is problematic since the timestamp accumulators at Snd and Rcv may be computed based on two different sets of packets, and this difference can affect the delay estimates significantly.

Specifically, there are four types of reordering (as shown at the bottom of Figure 2) that can be problematic. First, packets sent at the end of interval $u - 1$ can be routed on a high latency path and hence arrive at Rcv *after* the interval-start message. This can pollute interval u with extra packets; we call such packets *post-start* packets. Second, packets from the start of interval u can be routed on a low latency path and hence arrive at Rcv before the interval-start message for interval u, so these *pre-start* packets from interval u are effectively missing. Similar problematic reordering could also occur around the end of the interval (analogously referred to as *post-end* and *pre-end* packets). We say $\rho = R/T$ is the *reordering rate* for the interval u, where R is the total number of reordered packets (sum of all the four types).

It is crucial to note that R is almost always much smaller than T, the number of packets sent in an interval, even if there is persistent reordering. This is because problematic reordering is confined to the reordering that occurs relative to the interval-start and interval-end messages. For example, suppose the interval-start and end packets are routed on one path (high or low latency) and the rest of the packets are sent on the other path. Thus $R \leq 2CL$, where C is the transmission speed and L is the maximum difference in latencies of paths. For example, if C is 10 Gbps, $L = 100$ μsecs and an average packet size is 1,000 bits, R is around 2,000 packets. By contrast, T, the number of packets sent in the interval, may be as large as 5 million.

In addition to reordering, packets can also get dropped in the network, which can cause the Snd and Rcv state to become inconsistent. We assume at most βT packets from interval u will be dropped as they traverse the network from Snd to Rcv, where β is the *loss rate* for the interval u.

Now, if we compare the two streams of packets that belong to an interval u at the Snd and Rcv sides, the difference between them is at most $\beta T + R$ packets. If we could somehow correct for these $\beta T + R$ *bad packets* that prevent the Snd and Rcv from agreeing, we could make use of the simple timestamp accumulator and counter idea described above.

3.2 Key ideas

As in LDA, FineComb keeps an array of M timestamp accumulators and counters at the sender and receiver; a hash function computed over packet contents is used to map each incoming packet to a *bucket* containing a (timestamp accumulator, counter) pair. If the sender and receiver use the same hash function, then they will map packets to buckets in an identical fashion. We say that a *bucket is useful*, if it contains the same set of packets at both the sender and receiver, and thus can be used to compute the delay estimate. Notice that a bucket is useful as long as none of the $\beta T + R$ bad packets hash to that bucket. FineComb corrects for the $\beta T + R$ bad packets using the following three ideas.

1) Incremental stream digests: With reordering, we cannot simply compare counters at sender and receiver and conclude that a bucket is useful; this follows from the fact that a dropped packet that hashes into a bucket can be replaced by a (different) misordered packet from another interval. Even one such event can throw off the delay estimate considerably. The misordered packet may have been sent just before the start of interval u but may hash into the same bucket as a lost packet sent towards the end of interval u. Thus the induced error can be as large as the size of a measurement interval (say 1 second).

To detect such cases, we augment the counter in each bucket with what we call an *incremental stream digest*. An incremental stream digest on a stream of packets $pkt_1, ..., pkt_t$ is computed as follows:

$$H(pkt_1) \odot H(pkt_2) \odot ... \odot H(pkt_t) \quad (1)$$

where $\odot$ is an invertible commutative operation, and H is a hash function. We refer to $H(pkt_t)$ as a digest. Our incremental packet digests are similar to the incremental collision-free hash functions proposed in cryptography [9]. However, since we are not operating in an adversarial setting, we can let H be a simpler hash function such as BOB [14] or H3 [25], and $\odot$ as XOR; we do not require the full power of a cryptographic hash function such as SHA-1.

The incremental stream digest has three useful properties. First, two streams containing different packets will hash to different values with high probability while packets may cancel each other out in an adversary setting. Second, because $\odot$ is commutative, two streams containing the same set of packets in different order still hash to the same value. Thus we can determine if a bucket is useful by verifying that the incremental stream digests match at the sender and receiver. Finally, we can easily add or subtract packets from the incremental stream digest by computing the XORs of their digests with the incremental stream digest. This third property is the basis of *stash recovery* which we describe next.

2) Stash recovery: By a stash, we simply mean that we keep a copy of the timestamp, the bucket index, and incremental stream digest of a small number of packets that arrive before and after the sync messages that delimit an interval. As we have seen, R is small (say 1,000). Since these are the most likely messages to have been reordered, stash recovery simply attempts to add or subtract the incremental stream digest of each stashed message from the corresponding bucket into which that stashed message hashes. Note that if the stash were as big as T, we would be back to the naive algorithm of storing all local timestamps. Thus the fact that R is much smaller than T is crucial to the efficiency of stash recovery.

To show a concrete example of stash recovery, suppose a post-start packet P from interval $u - 1$ is hashed into the 20th bucket in interval u, making it useless. Assuming P is stored in the stash at the receiver because it arrived shortly after the interval-start message, stash recovery will look up the bucket 20, and try to subtract the incremental stream digest for P from the incremental stream digest at the receiver. If the resulting incremental stream digest matches the incremental stream digest of bucket 20 at the sender, bucket 20 can be made useful again by subtracting the timestamp of P from the receiver timestamp sum. While we have lost 1 sample from the bucket, we have saved perhaps 10,000 remaining samples that aggregate into bucket 20 that would have been lost otherwise.

Given memory S, however, it is not clear whether to allocate more stash (and hence, to recover from more reordered packets) or to use more buckets (and hence, to be more resilient to loss); we will investigate this tradeoff analytically and experimentally.

3) Packet sampling: In many practical situations, the number of bad packets $\beta T + R$ is going to be far greater than the number of buckets M. Given packets are randomly hashed to buckets, that means, that all the M buckets could become useless. Even if somehow, we manage to recover all the reordered packets in a given interval, the number of lost packets alone βT could be bigger than M. In FineComb, we sample packets at rate p, so that the expected number of bad packets that can cause buckets to become useless drops to $p(\beta T + R)$. On the one hand, selecting a high value of p will mean that the number of bad packets, and in turn useless buckets, will increase. On the other hand, selecting a low value of p will make each bucket aggregate fewer samples. Determining the optimal value of p that maximizes the number of useful samples over

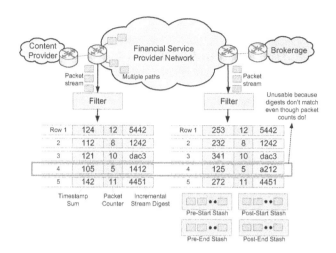

Figure 3: Example of FineComb. The four stashes cater to the four types of reordered packets.

which measurements are computed is a key question that our later analysis will address.

3.3 Basic FineComb without a stash

We start by describing FineComb without a stash. Basic FineComb (as shown in Figure 3) uses M buckets, each containing a timestamp accumulator, counter, and incremental stream digest. Each packet is sampled with probability p, and then distributed to one of the M buckets by a hash function. The pseudocode outlined illustrates the steps involved in updating FineComb state at both the sender and receiver for every *sampled* packet. Let $TS[i]$ represent the timestamp accumulator, $C[i]$ the packet counter, and $D[i]$ the incremental stream digest for ith bucket and M represent the total number of buckets.

```
1: procedure UPDATE STATE(pkt, τ)
2:     D ← compute_hash(pkt)          → Digest
3:     i ← D mod M
4:     TS[i] ← TS[i] + τ, C[i] ← C[i] + 1
5:     D[i] ← D[i] ⊙ D               → ⊙ could be XOR
6: end procedure
```

After sending T packets (or, alternately after a fixed amount of time), the sender sends its set of buckets to the receiver in the sync message. When the receiver receives the sync message, it uses the sender's buckets along with its local buckets to compute the average latency and loss as follows:

1) Estimating average latency: The receiver first determines the set of useful buckets by checking which buckets have matching incremental stream digests at sender and receiver. For all these 'valid' buckets, the receiver computes the difference between the receiver's and sender's timestamp accumulator, sums them together and divides it by the sum of all packet counters in these valid buckets. The steps are outlined below.

```
1: N ← 0, D ← 0
2: for i=1, M do
3:     if Cs[i] = Cr[i] and Ds[i] = Dr[i] then
4:         D ← D + (TSr[i] − TSs[i]), N ← N + Cr[i]
5:     end if
6: end for
7: Average delay = D/N
```

The main difference compared to LDA's delay estimation algorithm is the requirement of an extra check for a match of the sender

and receiver packet digests; just matching the packet counters alone is not sufficient.

2) Estimating standard deviation: We compute standard deviation in a similar fashion using a technique introduced in [8]. Conceptually, we could maintain an additional counter to which each sampled packet's timestamp is added or subtracted with equal probability $1/2$. Note that we need both the sender and receiver to agree on the same decision (of adding or subtracting) consistently, that can easily be achieved if the decision is based on the packet hash itself (*e.g.*, 1 or 0 in first bit position could indicate addition or subtraction). Subtracting the sender and receiver counter and then squaring leads to an unbiased estimator for delay variance [8]. Rather than wasting memory with an extra counter per bucket to measure variance, we use a trick used in LDA where existing delay buckets are paired and subtracted to simulate the adding or subtracting with equal probability.

3) Loss measurement: Loss measurement becomes difficult in the presence of reordering. Whereas the LDA operated in a setting where there was no reordering, so that a single counter at the sender and receiver suffices, FineComb must try to disentangle reordering from real loss. To see why this is hard, consider what happens at the end of an interval for a particular bucket if the sender-side counter is smaller than the receiver-side counter. When there is no reordering (as in the scenarios the LDA was designed for), this is impossible. However, it can easily happen if a few packets drift from one interval to the previous interval (*i.e.* pre-start packets that overtake the interval-start message). These packets are not lost: they are simply accounted for in the bucket of the previous interval.

We use stash recovery (detailed description next) to "clean up" the effects of reordering wherever possible. If all effects of reordering are removed, it is easy to see that the following simple algorithm does the job.

```
1: N ← 0, L ← 0
2: for i=1, M do
3:     if Cs[i] ≥ Cr[i] then
4:         L ← L + (Cs[i] − Cr[i]), N ← N + Cs[i]
5:     end if
6: end for
7: loss rate = L/N
```

Note that the algorithm still checks whether a sender counter is greater than the corresponding receiver counter. This is because stash recovery can be imperfect. Further, if a lost packet and reordered packet that is stored in the stash are *both* hashed to the same bin, stash recovery will fail, because the lost packet has made the bucket 'useless'.

In more detail, assume that before stash recovery $C_s[i]$ for some bucket i was less than $C_r[i]$ because of two post-start messages $P1$ and $P2$ that were hashed into bucket i that were not counted in this interval. Suppose further that a third packet $P3$ that hashes into bucket i is lost. Then even if $P1$ and $P2$ are in the stash at the receiver, there is no way for the receiver to correct bucket i because, by definition, it does not have the digest for $P3$ which is lost. Thus bucket i is not just useless from the point of view of calculating delay, the algorithm cannot tell apart a loss of 1 packet and a reordering of 2 packets in bucket i (as in the example) from a loss of 2 and reordering of 3 packets (say). Thus, the loss estimation algorithm above will ignore bucket i, and thus lose a data point for loss estimation.

Since we are trying to measure small losses, this is potentially serious. However, with careful sizing of the sampling probability (as we show later in §5) the probability of both a lost, and a reordered packet hashing to the same bucket is even smaller.

3.4 Managing the stash

We now describe the details of adding and recovering a stash. Recall that the stash stores individual timestamps and digests for the packets that are most likely to be problematically reordered. We assume that only the receiver keeps a stash, that consists of W entries. One nice feature of not keeping a stash at the sender is that if we grow the stash size (especially in a DRAM implementation of the stash), the control bandwidth does not grow with stash size: the sender only needs to send its buckets to the receiver to compute estimates. The stash is broken up into four *substashes* (pre-start, post-start, pre-end, post-end stash) of size w, where $4w = W$, corresponding to the four types of problematic reordering.

Populating the substashes. Even though the receiver does not know when interval-start message will arrive, the receiver can still populate the pre-start substash as follows. The receiver stores the digest and timestamps in a cyclic queue of length w, such that a new sampled packet causes the oldest packet in the queue to be evicted if the queue is full. The receiver stops populating the stash when the interval-start message arrives. Similarly, to populate the post-start stash, the receiver keeps a queue of length w that starts being populated once the interval-start message is received, and stops populating when it is full. The other two stashes are managed similarly, except they wait for interval-end instead of interval-start.

Stash recovery. For each useless bucket i, the receiver considers all the entries ($\mathbb{T}$) of the four substashes ($\mathbb{S}$) that map to that bucket. The receiver then considers *all subsets* ($\mathbb{Z}$) of the stash entries that correspond to this bucket. For each subset of stash entries, the receiver XORs the digests of the entries with the bucket's incremental stream digest. If the sender's and receiver's incremental stream digest match for this subset of stash entries, then the receiver can recover that bucket by subtracting (if the packet is from the post-start stash or pre-end stash), or adding (if the packet is from the pre-start stash or post-end stash) the timestamps of those stash entries from/to the bucket's timestamp accumulator.

```
 1: T ← build_stash_entry_set_for_bucket(i, S)
 2: for all Z ⊂ T do
 3:     D_r ← D_r[i], TS_r ← TS_r[i], C_r ← C_r[i]
 4:     for all (D, τ, k) ∈ Z do
 5:         if k = pre-start or k = post-end then
 6:             D_r ← D_r ⊙ D, TS_r ← TS_r + τ, C_r ← C_r + 1
 7:         else
 8:             D_r ← D_r ⊙ D, TS_r ← TS_r − τ, C_r ← C_r − 1
 9:         end if
10:     end for
11:     if D_s[i] = D_r then
12:         D_r[i] ← D_r, TS_r[i] ← TS_r, C_r[i] ← C_r, return
13:     end if
14: end for
```

Stash recovery appears to take exponential time because it may seem that one has to consider all possible combinations (2^W) in the worst case when W stash packets hash to a single bucket. Fortunately, stash recovery is much faster because, with high probability, only $O(W/M)$ stash packets can hash together into the same bucket. Thus, the running time of the decoding algorithm is $O(M2^{W/M})$, and since the typically stash size $W < M$ number of buckets, it follows that stash recovery time is approximately linear in M.

Thus the algorithms to calculate loss and latency are exactly as before for basic FineComb except that we preface them by doing stash recovery to potentially increase the number of useful buckets. A stash should help improve latency estimates slightly (by increasing the number of useful buckets), but will be much more critical

in obtaining reasonable loss estimates (allowing loss to be distinguished from reordering).

3.5 Handling unknown loss and reordering rates

If we know the exact reordering rate ρ and loss rate β *a priori*, our theoretical results (shown in §4) allow us to configure the sampling rate optimally. In practice, however, we do not know these values *a priori* and may change over time. LDA also faces a similar problem with loss rate not being known, and hence it maintains multiple banks each tuned to different loss rates. We can use a similar trick in FineComb as well, except, we need to consider the operating ranges of two different parameters β and ρ. We use multiple banks optimized for the four operating regions: $(\beta_{min}, \rho_{min})$, $(\beta_{min}, \rho_{max})$, $(\beta_{max}, \rho_{min})$, and $(\beta_{max}, \rho_{max})$. Low values of β_{min} and ρ_{min}, mean that the sampling rate chosen could be high, which in turn means the estimates are good. Once the loss rate or reordering rate becomes high, this bank tuned for low loss rates may produce no valid delay or loss estimates.

In FineComb, we use four banks, each using one fifth of the total storage. We compute the optimal sampling probabilities and stash size for each operating region independently and partition resources statically. Each bank has different number of buckets from each other. We then make the number of buckets of all banks equal using the remaining one fifth of the total storage unused.

For estimating delay, we take maximum count among counts from four buckets in the same row (same index) across banks and its corresponding timestamp sum, and add each values with a total count and a total timestamp sum, respectively. We repeat this step for all rows. This procedure provides us with maximum total number of samples. For loss estimation, we pick the loss rate of a bank whose estimate is closest to what it was tuned for. Intuitively, this heuristic uses the observation that rate estimates are typically most accurate when they are closest to what the bank is tuned for.

4. SETTING PARAMETERS

In the following analysis, our goal is to choose a sampling rate p, and stash size W that will maximize the expected number of delay samples that we extract from FineComb. That is, we would like to maximize the expected number of packets that are hashed to useful buckets, so that we can estimate delay as accurately as possible. The following analysis assumes that FineComb uses a single sampling rate p, and that the number of entries in the stash and the number of buckets in FineComb M is fixed, so that total storage is $S = M + W$.[2] Note that while we have formally proved the results in this section, for brevity, we only state the main theorems, results, and proof sketches. Additional proofs appear in [19].

4.1 Expected number of useful samples

Since our goal is to maximize $E[X]$, the expected number of useful samples we can extract from FineComb, our first step will be to determine $E[X]$.

Good and bad packets. Let us focus on interval u, and say a packet sent by the sender in interval u is 'good' if it was received by the receiver in with the boundaries of interval u (see §3.1 or Figure 2), otherwise 'bad'. Recalling that β is the packet loss rate on the path, T is the number of packets the sender sends in an interval, the number of good packets is $G \leq (1-\beta)T$ with equality when $R = 0$, so that there are no packets that are problematically reordered. Packets can become bad due to loss, or problematic

---

[2]We could instead fix the total storage of the system, so that $S = 2M + W$, since the sender has no stashes and thus requires storage M, while the receive requires $M + W$ storage.

reordering. The number of dropped and reordered packets in an interval is βT and $R = \rho T$ respectively.

Conditional expectation of useful samples. Let L be the number of bad packets that are sampled but not corrected during stash recovery. We can prove that the expected number of useful samples is

$$
\begin{aligned}
E[X|L] &= E[\text{Good pkts per bucket}]E[\text{No. of useful buckets}] \\
&= \tfrac{p}{M}G \cdot (M - E[K|L]) \\
&= pG(1 - \tfrac{1}{M})^L
\end{aligned} \tag{2}
$$

where, following [13], we let K be a random variable that denotes the number of 'useless' buckets in the LDA, that results from the L *sampled* bad packets hashing to buckets of the LDA. In [13], they show that K is distributed as

$$
\Pr[K = k|L] = \frac{M!}{(M - k)!}\frac{S(L,k)}{M^L} \tag{3}
$$

where $S(L, k)$ is a Stirling number of the Second Kind. Using (3), we obtain

$$
E[K|L] = M(1 - (1 - \tfrac{1}{M})^L)
$$

so that (2) follows by substitution.

Sampled uncorrected bad packets, L. We have βT dropped packets, and R reordered packets; together, this gives us $\beta T + R$ bad packets, that we sample with rate p. We shall assume that *every* packet that is stored in the stash is an out-of-order packet, so the stashes will allow us to correct for exactly W sampled out-of-order packets. (We make this assumption because it is hard to predict the distribution of problematically-reordered packets. Indeed, in practice we expect the stash to store some packets that arrived correctly in an interval (these good packets waste space in the stash), as well as some out-of-order packets. Thus, our analysis will size the stash under the assumption that the stash does the 'best it can' to correct for reordering.) Thus, the expected number of bad packets that are sampled and not corrected is

$$
E[L] = \beta pT + \max\{0, pR - W\} \tag{4}
$$

Working with the conditional expectation. Because the distribution of L is quite complicated, in this section, we work with the conditional expectation $E[X|L = E[L]]$, which is obtained by plugging (4) into (2). By numerically plotting equations, we observed the results obtained using $E[X|L = E[L]]$ are quite close to results obtained from the unconditional distribution $E[X]$.

4.2 Optimizing stash W for fixed sampling p

First, we would like to optimize the ratio between the LDA size and the stash size to maximize the expected number of useful samples $E[X]$, using the fact that $S = M + W$ where S is fixed and sampling rate p is fixed. To do this, we plug (4) into (2) and use the fact that $S = M + W$. We observe that there are two regimes for which the stash size W maximizes $E[X|L = E[L]]$:

$$
W \approx \begin{cases} pR & \text{when } S \geq p(R + \beta T) \\ 0 & \text{otherwise} \end{cases} \tag{5}
$$

This holds even when we work with $E[X]$ (rather than just $E[X|L = E[L]]$). Details can be found in [19].

Notice that (5) suggests that when the total storage S is very small, *i.e.* less than the number of bad sampled packets, all the storage should be dedicated to the buckets of FineComb (*i.e.*, $W=0$). On the other hand, when we have a decent amount of storage, the analysis shows that we should keep stashes large enough to correct

for the expected number of out-of-order sampled packets, pR. This makes sense, since a single bad packet can cause an entire bucket to become useless, so that about $\frac{p}{M}G$ 'good' packets become useless. Hence, it follows that correcting a single discrepancy in FineComb due to a bad packet is highly effective, and further that we should dedicate a large amount of storage to the stash.

4.3 Optimizing sampling rate p.

No stash. Per (5) we now consider the case where we have no stash (*i.e.*, $W = 0$). We can show that the optimal sampling rate is

$$
p^{**} = \min\left\{\frac{S}{R + \beta T}, 1\right\} \tag{6}
$$

To obtain (6), we use the fact that $E[X|W = 0]$ is easy to obtain in closed form from (2) by observing that L is a binomial random variable with mean $p(\beta T + R)$. Approximating L as a Poisson random variable, and putting $M = S$, using (2) we have that

$$
\begin{aligned}
E[X|W = 0] &= E[X|L]\Pr[L = \ell] \\
&= \sum_{\ell=0}^{\infty} pG(1 - \tfrac{1}{S})^\ell \cdot e^{-p(\beta T + R)}\frac{p(\beta T + R)^\ell}{\ell!} \\
&= pGe^{-p(R+\beta T)/S}
\end{aligned} \tag{7}
$$

The claim follows by taking the derivative of $E[X|W = 0]$ and setting it equal to zero.

Stash. Now, (5) tells us that when we have a stash, its optimal size is $W^* = pR$. We can show that when we use this value for the stash, the optimal sampling rate is approximately

$$
p^* = \min\left\{\frac{S}{2\rho^2 T}\left(2\rho + \beta - \sqrt{4\rho\beta + \beta^2}\right), 1\right\} \tag{8}
$$

where $\rho = R/T$. We obtained this value by setting $W^* = pR$ and $M = S - W^*$ to obtain $E[X|L = E[L], W = W^*]$ from (2) and (4). We then find p^* as the value that maximizes $E[X|L = E[L], W = W^*]$ by taking its derivative and setting it equal to zero. In [19], we show this value of p^* also (approximately) maximizes $E[X|W = W^*]$.

To stash, or not to stash. The last issue we need to settle is whether it is better to use a stash or not. Plugging our two operating points $(p^{**}, W = 0)$ and $(p^*, W = p^*R)$ into the equation for $E[X]$, we find that the expected number of samples is maximized when we use a stash.

A note on our approach. This analysis first fixed the sampling rate p and then optimized stash size W; then optimal value for W was used to solve for the optimal sampling rate p. It would have been better to jointly optimize $E[X]$ for W and p; however, the complexity of $E[X]$ made a joint optimization quite complicated, so we avoided it.

5. EVALUATION

In this section, we evaluate the efficacy of FineComb. Specifically, we seek to answer the following questions: (1) What is the relative error of FineComb in estimating mean delay, standard deviation and loss rates under different levels of reordering and loss rates. (2) How does an optimal configuration of FineComb compare with previous solutions assuming same total memory for a given loss and reordering rates. (3) Since loss (β) and reordering (ρ) rates are not known *a priori*, we evaluate the efficacy of the multi-bank FineComb that is tuned towards different β and ρ values. Before we answer these, we first describe our evaluation methodology.

5.1 Evaluation methodology

We built a custom simulator in C++ for evaluating a prototype of our measurement solution. Our custom simulator is more efficient than, say, ns-2 and allows us to simulate sending several million packets. Further, ns-2 does not provide any built in routines that we can leverage as all we need is to simulate packets sent on a link with specified delay, loss, and reordering characteristics.

Given our goal is to compare the performance of our architecture in many different settings, we provide several configuration parameters such as loss rate β, reordering rate ρ, measurement interval. Our simulation environment is deliberately kept similar to the one used by the authors in [16] so that fair comparison of FineComb with LDA is possible.

Delay model. Ideally, we would use traces at two monitoring endpoints within a real data center with GPS synchronized clocks to estimate end-to-end latency; unfortunately, there exists no such publicly available data center latency traces. Prior work [16] used the Weibull delay distribution model empirically verified to mimic the distribution of delays within a backbone router by Papagiannaki *et al.* in [22]. While we use mainly Weibull distribution (and Pareto for diversity) within our simulations, we use a real trace collected from an ingress and an egress interface of a router connected to an OC-3 link (155 Mbps) to evaluate multibank scenario (refer to §5.4 for more detail). The delay for each packet is drawn from a Weibull distribution, which has cumulative distribution function $P(X \leq x) = 1 - e^{(-x/\alpha)^\beta}$ with α and β representing the shape and scale of the graph respectively. We use [22]'s recommended shape parameter $0.6 \leq \alpha \leq 0.8$ in all our simulations (mostly, we used $\alpha = 0.6$). Note that while FineComb (and LDA) are agnostic to the distribution of timestamps, delay distribution does matter when we determine the relative error provided by these data structures.

Loss model. FineComb and LDA are agnostic to the loss rate distribution—even if two lost packets are back-to-back, they are randomly hashed into different buckets anyway. Thus, it suffices to simulate *random* packet loss.

Measurement interval. We simulate an interval of 1 second with a mean delay of about $10\mu s$. (Path latencies in data centers may range from 10–100 μs, so our setting simulates close to the finest granularity.) We show our results in the form of relative error, so exact delay average does not matter. For delay distribution, we use Weibull (and Pareto) with shape parameter 0.6 and scale adjusted to obtain mean delay of $10\mu s$. We simulate 5,000,000 packets, with an average packet size of 250 bytes (similar to [16]), over a 10 Gbps bottleneck capacity with an inter-arrival time of $0.2\mu s$—transmission time for 250 bytes at 10Gbps is $0.2\mu s$. All our simulation results are average across 10 runs.

Reordering model. An important parameter in our simulation is the reordering rate ρ. We could simulate reordering in the same way we simulate loss; by randomly choosing which packets to reorder. However, in practice, it is not at all clear that reordering follows a process similar to that of packet loss; in fact, there exists no generative model that we are aware of that we can use in our simulation. We note once again that reordering within the interval does not affect either LDA or FineComb; what matters is problematic reordering at the fringe of an interval (see Figure 2).

To stress LDA and FineComb in terms of problematic reordering, we simulate the following simple deterministic model of reordering. In our reordering model, we essentially specify a 4-tuple, $<R_{pre}^s, R_{post}^s, R_{pre}^e, R_{post}^e>$, the number of pre-start, post-start, pre-end and post-end packets defined in §3.1. Then, for each interval we wish to simulate, we choose a contiguous set of packets from the end of one interval that will drift into the next and vice-versa.

Note that the theory in §4 is based on the total number of reordered packets $R = \rho T$ and considers a slightly more simplistic model than we use in our experimentation. While clearly, $R = R_{pre}^s + R_{post}^s + R_{pre}^e + R_{post}^e$, the optimal probability p^* obtained in Equation 8 is computed assuming all these different individual reordering components are the same. To make our provisioning strategy consistent with theory, we obtain the total reordered number of packets R as follows:

$$R = max\{R_{pre}^s, R_{post}^s, R_{pre}^e, R_{post}^e\} \times 4$$

We simulate two main types of reordering, called *forward* and *backward*, that correspond to $<0, x, 0, 0>$ and $<x, 0, 0, 0>$ configurations for the 4-tuple. In most experiments, we configure x equal to roughly $10^{-6}T$ to $10^{-3}T$ (T being total number of packets); equivalently, the reordering rate ρ varies from $4 \cdot 10^{-6}$ to $4 \cdot 10^{-3}$, translating to roughly 50 to 5,000 packets before the interval-end message. We also simulated many other configurations (*e.g.*, $<x, x, x, x>$, $<x, x, 0, 0>$) but latency estimation results were mostly similar in all cases; this follows because sampling probabilities and stash sizes are all dependent on ρ, which is same for all these configurations.

Resource configuration. We allocate a total of 1,000 buckets for FineComb. To simulate cases with and without stash, we assume stash elements are of the same size as bank elements (for simplicity). We use 64 bits from a 160-bit SHA-1 hash function for packet digests. To make things fair, we equalize the storage at the LDA and the FineComb. The buckets in the LDA are 2/3 the size of those in FineComb (LDA has timestamp accumulator and counter but no incremental stream digest). Furthermore, while FineComb is asymmetric (only the receiver maintains stashes), the LDA is symmetric. Thus, memory is allocated as follows: LDA gets $1.5(M + W/2)$ buckets at sender and receiver, where M is number of FineComb buckets and W is stash size.

5.2 Assessing FineComb

Expected number of samples. In our first experiment, we wish to understand how tight the theoretical bound on the number of useful samples is, at the optimal sampling probability. In Figure 4(a), we plot the expected number of samples according to the analytical bound given in Equation 2 (curve titled 'Expected') and the empirical number of samples over which delays are computed. The three different curves in the figure correspond to three different loss rate settings (0.0001, 0.001, 0.01). Clearly, as we increase the loss rate from 0.00001 to 0.001, the number of effective samples over which the delay estimates are computed reduces all the way from almost 3 million packets at loss rate 0.0001 (0.01%), to about 40,000 packets at 0.01 (1%) loss rate. As we increase the reordering rate, the number of effective samples also decreases (although not by much for the 0.01 loss rate curve, since the loss rate overwhelms the reordering rate significantly). This is expected since more loss causes more FineComb buckets to become useless, causing the expected number of samples to decrease.

In all cases, we observe that analytically expected number of samples matches quite well with what we found empirically (the curves are virtually indistinguishable); the difference between expected and empirical is of the order of a few hundreds, with the predicted number of samples slightly smaller than what we found empirically.

Latency estimates. Next, we show the average relative error of mean delay and loss estimates, as we vary the reordering rate ρ in Figure 4. We show the results comparing FineComb and FineComb-(FineComb without the stash) for two different distributions, Weibull

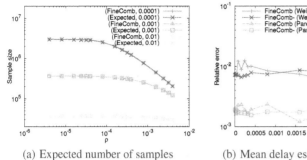
(a) Expected number of samples

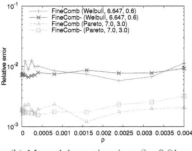
(b) Mean delay estimation, $\beta = 0.01$

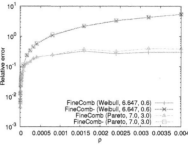
(c) Loss rate estimation, $\beta = 0.0001$

Figure 4: Expected number of samples obtained by FineComb, and relative error of mean delay and loss estimates in the presence of forward reordering under different distributions. We show both FineComb and FineComb- for comparison.

and Pareto with shape and scale parameters adjusted to ensure similar mean latency of $10\mu s$. While we have simulated many different levels of loss and types of reordering, for brevity, we mainly show the latency results for the high loss situation and loss estimation for the low loss situation. (These are the least favorable situations for FineComb.) From Figure 4(b), we see that the relative error for FineComb is less than 1.2% for either of the two distributions, under different levels of reordering. While we omit the exact figure of standard deviation estimation for brevity, FineComb and FineComb- achieve similar average relative error–less than 30% for Pareto distribution and 9% Weibull distribution across all ρ values.

As predicted by our analytical work in [19], FineComb provides about 15-30% more useful samples than FineComb- (that has no stash). While more samples should lead to better delay estimates, the improvement in the delay estimate depends heavily on the specific delay distribution; that is, some distributions require fewer samples to obtain accurate estimates (e.g., to take things to an extreme, a uniform distribution requires only a small number of samples for excellent accuracy in delay estimates).

Loss rate estimates. We clearly see the benefit of the stash when we consider loss estimation error in Figure 4(c). We can observe that the estimates of FineComb- are significantly worse than FineComb, especially at higher reordering rates. This is explained by the fact that loss rate estimates for FineComb- include reordered packets; because FineComb- has no stash, we have no way to prevent these reordered packets from polluting our loss rate estimator. Having the stash helps recover most of those reordered packets in FineComb, thus adding significantly fewer number of false positives in calculating the loss rate. Note that the delay distribution itself does not effect loss rate estimation (the little difference visible is caused by different random number seeds).

5.3 Comparison with other solutions

We compare FineComb with LDA using simulations. Before we show these results, however, we go over why other simple alternatives do not work as well as compared to FineComb.

1) Active probing: Intuitively, active probing methods do much worse than methods like FineComb in terms of standard error for a fixed control bandwidth, because each active probe provides a single delay sample, while each FineComb bucket provides thousands of samples. Using a sampling probability of $p = 0.1$ (optimal for low loss and small amount of reordering), FineComb will provide 500,000 delay samples in each interval. Now the control bandwidth required to send 1,000 buckets from the sender to the receiver, is roughly 16,000 bytes (assuming 16 bytes per bucket) while an active probe takes at least 64 bytes (packet headers plus times-

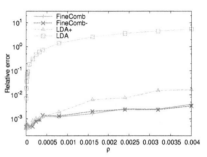
(a) Forward reordering

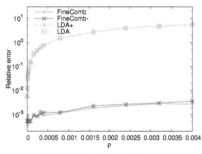
(b) Backward reordering

Figure 5: Average relative error of mean delay estimates comparing FineComb with LDA. $\beta = 0.0001$.

tamp). To keep the control bandwidth the same, even if we allowed $16,000/64 = 250$ active probes per second, they would only provide 250 delay samples while FineComb provides 500,000. This 2,000x increase in sample size translates roughly to $\sqrt{2000} = 44$x decrease in standard error.

2) Sampled local timestamps: Similarly, consider the other trivial solution of sampling a small number of packets in each interval and storing their timestamps.

We compare this trivial solution to FineComb- with no stash (note from §4 that adding the stash only *increases* the number of good samples produced by the FineComb). Combining (7) and (8), we find that when FineComb has S buckets and no stash, it produces

$$E[X_{FineComb}] = S\frac{G}{\beta T + R}e^{-1} \qquad (9)$$

good timestamp samples. Meanwhile, the trivial solution that samples at rate p obtains $p(1-\beta)T$ good samples while storing $S_{sample} = pT$ items. Setting $S_{sample} = S$, and we find that FineComb produces about $\frac{G}{\beta T + R}$ more good samples than the trivial solution; note that we expect this ratio to be much larger than one, since G is the number of 'good' packets in the interval, while $\beta T + R$ is the number of 'bad' packets in the interval.

For example, assume that FineComb uses 1,000 buckets and a stash of the same size. Then the trivial algorithm can afford to store 2,000 samples. Once again, for the same parameters as the example above, the trivial algorithm will provide 2,000 samples per second, while FineComb will provide 500,000. This factor of 250x increase in sample size translates to roughly a factor of 15x decrease in standard error.

3) LDA for latency estimates: In Figure 5, we plot the relative error of mean delay estimates for four solutions, namely LDA, LDA+ (a small refinement of LDA we discuss later), FineComb and FineComb- for different reordering rates and reordering models. For this set of experiments, we choose optimal stash size configurations and sampling probabilities (for LDA, as recommended in [16]) for all solutions.

The main observation from the graphs is that, beyond small levels of reordering, LDA consistently performs the worst, with relative error as high as 100% ($\rho = 0.0005$) to 400% ($\rho = 0.004$). This follows from the fact that LDA cannot deal with reordered packets. If a reordered packet and a lost packet hash to the same LDA bucket, the LDA will assume that bucket is useful and include it in the latency estimation. However, that bucket will contain timestamps relating to two *different* sets of packets, and error induced can be as large as the measurement interval (*e.g.*, 1 second).

LDA+ is a simple refinement of LDA which effectively ignores the set of buckets where the sender's timestamp sum is higher than the receiver timestamp sum (which could be caused by a situation like the one we described above) and results in *a negative delay* contributed by that bucket. This clearly helps solve most of the problems in the forward reordering case (where extra packets drift into the interval), as reflected in the better relative error for LDA+ in Figure 5(a). In fact, in cases where LDA+ was optimized for higher loss rate (*e.g.*, at $\beta = 0.001$), we observed better accuracy than FineComb, that can be explained by the fact that the total number of buckets allocated to LDA is about 1.5 times higher than those allocated to FineComb, resulting in slightly better sampling rate, and consequently, in more samples. However, LDA+ is merely a patch, and does not work in the backward reordering case, since in this case, we cannot easily detect (using a simple elimination scheme as before) and eliminate buckets that are anomalous because of reordering. Thus for the lower set of graphs, we can see that LDA+ has the same accuracy level as the LDA.

In all cases, we can observe that both FineComb and FineComb-perform consistently better than LDA even under high loss and reordering rates. We can observe that the relative error is mostly around 0.1% and never more than 1% in all the cases considered. For standard deviation estimates, we observed a similar phenomenon, *i.e.*, the accuracy of FineComb is orders of magnitude higher than LDA's. The same set of reasons why LDA's mean delay estimates are quite bad explains why standard deviation estimates are also bad. (Since the curves look exactly the same as those for mean latency, we omit them.)

4) LDA for loss estimation: In Figure 6(a), we plot the relative error in estimating loss rate (for $\beta = 0.0001$). As we can see from the figure, FineComb's estimates are usually within 10-30% error irrespective of the reordering rates. The estimates of the rest are quite poor, with more than 100-500% error for LDA. This is expected, since neither LDA (or LDA+) nor FineComb- have the capability to correct for reordered packets; only FineComb enjoys that capability due to the presence of the stash.

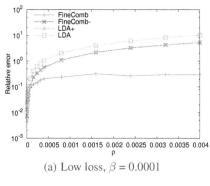

(a) Low loss, $\beta = 0.0001$

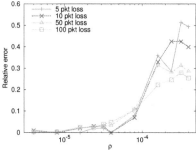

(b) Microscopic loss, 5-100 lost packets

Figure 6: Relative error of FineComb at detecting low to microscopic loss rates.

Microscopic losses. While 10-30% error in estimating loss rates as low as 0.0001 is good, our goal was to also be able to detect losses as low as 1 in 1 million (10^{-6}). Intuitively, detecting such low loss rates in the presence of reasonable levels of reordering (*e.g.*, say 500 packets, *i.e.*, $\rho = 10^{-4}$) is possible only with extremely high rates of sampling (close to 1) and with a stash large enough to recover most of the reordered packets. (Our formulae predict these configurations as well.) To explore this case further, we simulate low loss conditions (with 5, 10, 50, and 100 packets lost in the interval) and configure stash and sampling optimally just as before. The 5 packet situation is equivalent to 1 packet loss in 1 million (our definition of microscopic losses). In Figure 6(b), we see that, even though the relative error of FineComb's loss estimates becomes progressively worse as reordering increase, the estimates are well within 10% for reordering rates up to 10^{-4} (500 reordered packets), *i.e.*, 5 packets lost is reported as either 4 or 6 packets lost—we believe most managers would find such accuracy for microscopic losses to be perfectly adequate. By contrast, LDA's accuracy for the same range is around 2,000% (not shown in the figure), which can cause false alarms.

5.4 Handling unknown loss and reordering rates

We have already demonstrated that it is easy to tune FineComb if the manager knows the loss and reordering rate. However, it is important to have a solution that works across a large range of loss rates and reordering rates using multi-bank FineComb.

We use Weibull delay distribution model as well as a real trace to compare the efficacy of 4-bank FineComb with a two-bank LDA under unknown loss and reordering rates. First, for Weibull delay distribution model, average latency is set to $10\mu s$ and β is set to 0.01. Second, the trace collected from an ingress and an egress interface of a router by the authors in [27] contains about 2.4 million packets over about two and half minute interval which experienced queueing delay, packet loss, and so on. Since OC-3 link

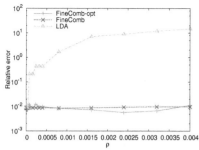 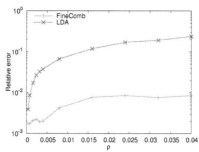 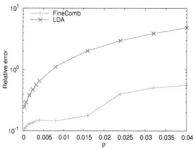

(a) Mean delay estimation with $\beta = 0.01$ us- (b) Mean delay estimation using a real trace (c) Loss rate estimation using a real trace
ing Weibull delay distribution

Figure 7: Average relative error of mean delay and loss estimates of the 4-bank FineComb, with the banks optimized for low and high reordering and loss rates under forward reordering scenario.

(155 Mbps) was used when the trace was collected, we do not use a second measurement interval which only has a few thousands of packets. Instead, we group the packets into measurement intervals each of which consists of 0.2 million packets. The average loss rate of the trace is about 0.24%, but each measurement interval has different packet loss rates; minimum, median and maximum loss rates are 0%, 0.06% and 0.96%, respectively. There is no packet reordering in the trace. Thus, we adjust packet reordering rate from 0.0004 to 0.04 for the evaluation.

For FineComb, we optimize the individual banks for the four pair-wise combinations of $\beta_{min} = 0.0001$, $\rho_{min} = 0.0004$, $\beta_{max} = 0.01$, and $\rho_{max} = 0.04$. Two-bank LDA is optimized for $\beta_{min} = 0.0001$ and 0.01.

Figure 7(a) shows the relative error of the mean delay estimates of FineComb compared to that of LDA. FineComb-OPT, shown for reference, is FineComb configured with the theoretically best sampling rate and stash size given the knowledge of loss and reordering rates. The results for other loss rates, and for the backward reordering case, are quite similar to the curve of FineComb (and hence, omitted). From the figure, we can observe that LDA performs worse than FineComb (as we have observed before) even in the case of multiple banks. At extremely low reordering rates, the estimates of LDA are quite accurate, but they become quickly unusable with small increases in reordering rates (at around 0.0002). Further, we can clearly see that, while 4-bank FineComb appears to have slightly worse relative error than the FineComb-OPT, on the whole, FineComb results are reasonably accurate with a relative error of less than 1% under almost all conditions. Standard deviation estimation also shows similar trend with mean estimation, so we omit the exact graph for brevity. As a summary, while LDA achieves better accuracy than FineComb when ρ is extremely small, FineComb has at least two orders of magnitude less errors than LDA from $\rho = 0.0008$, and about 11-13% relative errors are obtained by FineComb across all reordering rates.

In Figure 7(b), we observe the similar pattern shown in Figure 7(a). However, compared to the results of Figure 7(a), the degree of inaccuracy of LDA is lower. This may be because of two reasons. First, there are four measurement intervals which have no packet loss. For those intervals, latency estimates were quite accurate because two-bank LDA could absorb the impact of reordered packets considered as lost packets. Second, true average latencies are quite high, ranging from a few to tens of milliseconds. Due to the high latencies, denominator in relative error is also high and the relative error is small. Nevertheless, compared to FineComb, at least an order of magnitude higher relative error is observed

from around 0.0024 reordering rate. Again, FineComb achieves a relative error of less than 1% under all conditions. Similarly, for standard deviation estimation, LDA shows an order of magnitude higher relative error than FineComb for most reordering rates.

In Figure 7(c), we show the relative error of the loss rate estimation. FineComb's relative error shows less than 20% up to 0.016 reordering rate. After the reordering rate, the relative error of FineComb is comparatively worse at around 55%, but LDA is completely unusable across almost all the rates.

6. IMPLEMENTATION

With 1000 buckets and 1000 stash entries, FineComb should take a small percentage of a low end 10mm×10mm networking ASIC using a 400-MHz 65nm process. Key to a small footprint is a cheap version of an incremental stream digest using a loop-unrolled Rabin hash. A quicker path to deployment *today*, however, is using high-end FPGAs such as the NetFPGA [4]. For time synchronization, the boards need to have GPS chipsets (fairly cheap today), the solution used by monitors such as Corvil [3].

Stash recovery operations are easier to do in software using say an on-board processor. In the analysis, we argued that stash recovery times are $O(M2^{W/M})$, where W is the size of the stash and M is the number of buckets. We did measurements to verify that the apparent exponential is not an issue, and that there are no large constants hiding behind the order notation. The table below shows stash recovery times for different stash sizes, assuming a fixed total storage S of 2,000 (across sender and receiver). For example, when the stash (maintained at receiver) W is 838, the number of buckets M is 581 (equal across sender and receiver), resulting in $2^{W/M}$ being less than 4. The implementation was done using a 2.33GHz Intel processor running Linux.

Stash size	20	120	200	462	703	838
Time (ms)	1	4	6	10	10	14

As we expect, stash recovery time increases as stash size increases. However, even for a ratio of stash to buckets of 1.44, recovery takes no more than 14 *ms*. Note that it is not required that the processor be on-board. While packet processing will need to be done on board, functions such as stash recovery can be implemented in software on the PC. Implementing FineComb on boards (based on either FPGAs or network processors) is significantly cheaper compared to existing diagnosis boxes proposed for data centers such as those supplied by Corvil. The high-end Corvil boxes costs UK£90,000 for a 2×10 Gbps box [3]. High cost is a barrier for most data centers which explains why Corvil has mostly marketed to a niche market (financial traders) where money is no object.

7. RELATED WORK

While network latency measurements is a rich area of research in the Internet with several tools proposed in the past to obtain latency measurements, the fundamental focus on fine-grain microscopic latency and loss measurements, makes most of these tools not suitable for the task at hand. Scalable performance measurements for data center environments is a relatively less studied field.

The standard approach for conducting latency measurements in the wide area is to inject active probes (*e.g.*, using ping and other tools such as [28, 21, 27, 26]) and calculate the round-trip time of the packet. We have discussed the problems with active probes in §2.3. Router-based passive measurements is yet another active area of research [11, 12, 31, 24, 15]. They focus mainly on flow measurements such as number of packets and bytes, and not on latency and loss estimation. In [20], the authors propose a measurement-friendly network architecture; the goal is to infer router characteristics with the help of end-to-end measurements. Our goal is to measure end-to-end characteristics with support at the end points, however. There are a few prior efforts (*e.g.*, [10, 32]) where researchers proposed simple router extensions for latency measurements that are somewhat similar to the local timestamps idea discussed in §2.3, and hence share similar problems.

Perhaps the most relevant research effort to ours is a recent data structure called LDA proposed by Kompella *et al.* in [16], and an incremental deployment architecture in [17]. Given the close similarity, we discussed it at length in the paper, and compared the performance of FineComb with LDA. In [18], Lee *et al.* describe a per-flow switch-level latency measurement architecture. In our work, we focus on measurements across flows, so our goals are different from theirs.

8. CONCLUSIONS

Measurement tools are badly needed to determine fine-grain latencies and losses that can affect application SLAs in data center environments. Existing scalable approaches such as LDA designed for switch-level measurements works poorly for end-to-end measurements in the presence of packet reordering which actually happens in IP networks. We describe a simple yet scalable data structure called FineComb that can detect microsecond latency violations and microscopic losses (as small as few packets in a million) while still being resilient to reordering. FineComb uses two new ideas—the addition of an incremental stream digest to detect mismatches in packet sets, and a simple stash to correct reordering. Stashes are especially powerful in order to measure loss precisely to a few parts in a million. While Finecomb is useful for end-to-end measurements in the short-term, we believe that the future will see the rise of reordering tolerant transport protocols in the data center together with packet-by-packet load balancing within and across routers. In such cases, reordering becomes a fact of life and solutions such as Finecomb will become essential to measure fine-grain delays and losses even *within* routers.

Acknowledgments

The authors thank Kirill Levchenko, Michael Mitzenmacher, Zvika Brakerski, and the anonymous reviewers for comments on previous versions of this manuscript. This work was supported in part by NSF Award CNS 0831647, 0964395, 1054788, and a grant from Cisco Systems.

9. REFERENCES

[1] Cisco data center network architecture and solutions overview. http://www.cisco.com/en/US/solutions/collateral/ns340/ns517/ns224/ns377/net_brochure0900aecd802c9a4f.pdf.

[2] Cisco market data network overview. http://www.cisco.com/en/US/docs/solutions/Verticals/Financial_Services/md-arch-ext.html.

[3] Corvil tool minimises latency. http://www.computerworlduk.com/technology/networking/networking/news/index.cfm?newsid=5797.

[4] NetFPGA. http://www.netfpga.org.

[5] NetScout. http://www.netscout.com.

[6] NYSE shrinks time measurement to nanoseconds. http://www.computerworld.com.au/article/308952/nyse_shrinks_time_measurement_nanoseconds/.

[7] AL-FARES, M., LOUKISSAS, A., AND VAHDAT, A. A scalable, commodity data center network architecture. In *ACM SIGCOMM* (2008), pp. 63–74.

[8] ALON, N., MATIAS, Y., AND SZEGEDY, M. The space complexity of approximating the frequency moments. *J. Computer and System Sciences 58*, 1 (Feb. 1999), 137–147.

[9] BELLARE, M., AND MICCIANCIO, D. A new paradigm for collision-free hashing: incrementality at reduced cost. In *Eurocrypt97* (1997).

[10] DUFFIELD, N. G., AND GROSSGLAUSER, M. Trajectory sampling for direct traffic observation. In *IEEE/ACM Transactions on Networking* (2000).

[11] ESTAN, C., KEYS, K., MOORE, D., AND VARGHESE, G. Building a Better NetFlow. In *ACM SIGCOMM* (2004), pp. 245–256.

[12] ESTAN, C., AND VARGHESE, G. New directions in traffic measurement and accounting: Focusing on the elephants, ignoring the mice. *ACM Transactions on Computer Systems 21* (2003), 270–313.

[13] FINUCANE, H., AND MITZENMACHER, M. An analysis of the lossy difference aggregator. *unpublished* (2009).

[14] JENKINS, B. Algorithm alley. Dr. Dobb's Journal, September 1997.

[15] KOMPELLA, R. R., AND ESTAN, C. The Power of Slicing in Internet Flow Measurement. In *ACM/USENIX IMC* (May 2005).

[16] KOMPELLA, R. R., LEVCHENKO, K., SNOEREN, A. C., AND VARGHESE, G. Every MicroSecond Counts: Tracking Fine-grain Latencies Using Lossy Difference Aggregator. In *ACM SIGCOMM* (2009).

[17] KOMPELLA, R. R., SNOEREN, A. C., AND VARGHESE, G. mPlane: An architecture for scalable fault localization. In *ACM ReARCH* (2009).

[18] LEE, M., DUFFIELD, N., AND KOMPELLA, R. R. Not all Microseconds are Equal: Enabling Per-Flow Latency Measurements Using Reference Latency Interpolation. In *ACM SIGCOMM* (2010).

[19] LEE, M., GOLDBERG, S., KOMPELLA, R. R., AND VARGHESE, G. Fine Comb: Measuring Microscopic Latencies and Losses in the Presence of Reordering. Techincal report CSD TR 10-009, Purdue University, 2010.

[20] MACHIRAJU, S., AND VEITCH, D. A measurement-friendly network (MFN) architecture. In *Proceedings of ACM SIGCOMM Workshop on Internet Network Management* (Sept. 2006).

[21] MAHDAVI, J., PAXSON, V., ADAMS, A., AND MATHIS, M. Creating a scalable architecture for internet measurement. In *Proc. of INET'98* (1998).

[22] PAPAGIANNAKI, K., MOON, S., FRALEIGH, C., THIRAN, P., TOBAGI, F., AND DIOT, C. Analasyis of measured single-hop delay from an operational backbone network. *IEEE JSAC 21*, 6 (2003).

[23] RAICIU, C., PLUNTKE, C., BARRE, S., GREENHALGH, A., WISCHIK, D., AND HANDLEY, M. Data center networking with multipath TCP. In *Proceedings of ACM SIGCOMM Workshop on Hot Topics in Networks* (2010).

[24] RAMACHANDRAN, A., SEETHARAMAN, S., FEAMSTER, N., AND VAZIRANI, V. V. Fast monitoring of traffic subpopulations. In *ACM/USENIX IMC* (2008), pp. 257–270.

[25] RAMAKRISHNA, M., FU, E., AND BAHCEKAPILI, E. Efficient hardware hashing functions for high performance computers. *IEEE Transactions on Computers 46*, 12 (Dec. 1997).

[26] SAVAGE, S. Sting: a TCP-based network measurement tool. In *Proceedings of USENIX Symposium on Internet Technologies and Systems* (Oct. 1999).

[27] SOMMERS, J., BARFORD, P., DUFFIELD, N., AND RON, A. Improving accuracy in end-to-end packet loss measurement. In *ACM SIGCOMM* (2005).

[28] SOMMERS, J., BARFORD, P., DUFFIELD, N., AND RON, A. Accurate and efficient SLA compliance monitoring. In *ACM SIGCOMM* (2008).

[29] VASUDEVAN, V., PHANISHAYEE, A., SHAH, H., KREVAT, E., ANDERSEN, D. G., GANGER, G. R., GIBSON, G. A., AND MUELLER, B. Safe and effective fine-grained TCP retransmissions for datacenter communication. In *ACM SIGCOMM* (2009).

[30] WOVEN SYSTEMS, INC. EFX switch series overview. http://www.wovensystems.com/pdfs/products/Woven_EFX_Series.pdf, 2008.

[31] YUAN, L., CHUAH, C.-N., AND MOHAPATRA, P. ProgME: towards programmable network measurement. In *ACM SIGCOMM* (2007).

[32] ZSEBY, T., ZANDER, S., AND CARLE, G. Evaluation of building blocks for passive one-way-delay measurements. In *PAM* (2001).

On the Stability and Optimality of Universal Swarms

Xia Zhou
Dept. of Computer Science
UC Santa Barbara, CA, USA
xiazhou@cs.ucsb.edu

Stratis Ioannidis
Technicolor
Palo Alto, CA, USA
stratis.ioannidis@technicolor.com

Laurent Massoulié
Technicolor
Paris, France
laurent.massoulie@technicolor.com

ABSTRACT

Recent work on BitTorrent swarms has demonstrated that a bandwidth bottleneck at the seed can lead to the under-utilization of the aggregate swarm capacity. Bandwidth underutilization also occurs naturally in mobile peer-to-peer swarms, as a mobile peer may not always be within the range of peers storing the content it desires. We argue in this paper that, in both cases, idle bandwidth can be exploited to allow content sharing across multiple swarms, thereby forming a *universal swarm* system. We propose a model for universal swarms that applies to a variety of peer-to-peer environments, both mobile and online. Through a fluid limit analysis, we demonstrate that universal swarms have significantly improved stability properties compared to individually autonomous swarms. In addition, by studying a swarm's stationary behavior, we identify content replication ratios across different swarms that minimize the average sojourn time in the system. We then propose a content exchange scheme between peers that leads to these optimal replication ratios, and study its convergence numerically.

Categories and Subject Descriptors

C.2.1 [**Computer-Communication Networks**]: Network Architecture and Design–*distributed networks, store and forward networks*; C.4 [**Performance of Systems**]: Performance Attributes

General Terms

Theory, Algorithms

Keywords

Universal swarms, content distribution, peer-to-peer networks

1. INTRODUCTION

Peer-to-peer systems have been tremendously successful in enabling sharing of large files in a massive scale. This success has motivated several approaches of modeling BitTorrent swarms [6, 11, 12, 13]. Such models have illuminated important aspects of swarm behavior, including determining conditions for *swarm stability* and minimizing the system's *average sojourn time*. The study of swarm stability amounts to identifying conditions under which the swarm population remains finite as time progresses, while the sojourn time captures the time required until peers retrieve the file they request and leave the swarm.

Our aim in this work is to provide answers for similar questions in the context of *universal swarms* [15]. Rather than considering swarms as individual autonomous systems, we study scenarios in which peers from different swarms are permitted to exchange file pieces (chunks) with each other. Such inter-swarm exchanges make sense when bottlenecks in a single swarm lead to bandwidth under-utilization.

One application in which such bandwidth bottlenecks naturally arise is the peer-to-peer distribution of content over mobile opportunistic networks. Mobile peers wishing to retrieve a file can do so by downloading chunks from other peers they encounter opportunistically. These mobile content distribution systems have received considerable attention recently [1, 2, 4, 7, 8, 9, 14], as they alleviate the load on the wireless infrastructure by harnessing the bandwidth available during local interactions among mobile peers.

Bottlenecks in such peer-to-peer systems are a result of the opportunistic nature of the communication between peers: two peers meeting may not necessarily belong to the same swarm and may not be interested in the same content. Nevertheless, during encounters with peers from other swarms, a peer may use its idle bandwidth to obtain pieces of files in other swarms. Such exchanges can aid the propagation of under-replicated pieces that are otherwise hard to locate. If designed properly, such inter-swarm exchanges have the potential to improve the overall performance in terms of sojourn times and system stability.

Bottlenecks can also lead to bandwidth underutilization in online swarms. An example can be found in the recent work of Hajek and Zhu [6]. The authors considered the stability of a single BitTorrent swarm comprising a single seed and a steady stream of arriving peers (leechers). The peers share pieces they have retrieved while they are in the system but immediately depart once they download all pieces of a file. Hajek and Zhu observed that if the arrival rate of peers exceeds the upload capacity of the seed, the system becomes unstable in a very specific way: almost all peers arriving in the swarm very quickly obtain every missing piece *except for one*. The seed is unable to serve these peers with the missing piece fast enough and, as a result, the size of this set of peers—termed the "one-club" [6]—grows to infinity.

When this so-called "missing piece syndrome" occurs, peers waiting for the missing piece are effectively idle, and their available upload bandwidth is essentially under-utilized. In this work we argue that, provided that peers have excess storage, this idle bandwidth capacity can be exploited in the presence of other swarms to store and to exchange pieces of other files. Such inter-swarm exchanges have the potential of improving the overall stability of the universal swarm system, as the peers in the "one-club" may be able to retrieve their missing piece from collaborating peers in other swarms. Most importantly, such transactions can be restricted to take place only when the intra-swarm bottleneck has rendered the peers idle, so inter-swarm exchanges do not hinder the delivery of the file in any way.

Our contributions can be summarized as follows:

- We propose a novel mathematical model for inter-swarm data exchange. Our model is simple but versatile enough to capture several different peer-to-peer file-sharing environments, both mobile and online.

- Using the above model, we analyze the stability of a universal swarm in which peers can retrieve items they miss from other swarms, but otherwise keep their caches static.

- Studying the stationary points of the data exchange process, we characterize the optimal replication ratios of pieces across swarms that minimize the system's average sojourn times.

- We propose BARON, a scheme for guiding data exchanges to yield optimal replication ratios, and study its convergence to these ratios numerically.

To the best of our knowledge, our work is the first systematic study of file sharing in a universal swarm system. Our results suggest that universal swarms can indeed achieve considerable performance improvements over independent autonomous swarm systems.

In particular, we establish the following surprising result: in a universal swarm where inter-swarm piece exchanges take place, *only one* swarm can become unstable. This is an interesting finding, especially when viewed in the context of the work of Hajek and Zhu [6]. An intuitive explanation of this phenomenon is this: a swarm growing to infinity attains an ever-growing capacity, which can be used to serve the missing pieces of other swarms. This service suppresses the growth of other swarms and, as a result, no two "one-clubs" can exist simultaneously.

Furthermore, our proposed scheme for guiding content exchanges can be used to enlarge the stability region for a universal swarm. Our design raises interesting open questions, such as the construction of schemes that work, *e.g.*, in fully distributed or non-cooperative environments. Though our model is simple, and our analysis is a first attempt at analyzing universal swarm behavior, we believe that these results are very promising. They indicate that universal swarms have very appealing stability properties, and certainly merit further investigation.

The remainder of this paper is structured as follows. We begin with an overview of related work in Section 2 and introduce our mathematical model for universal swarms in Section 3. We present our main results on convergence, stability, and optimality in Section 4, and provide their proofs in Section 5. We further propose BARON, a scheme to guide the system to the optimal stationary state, and evaluate it numerically in Section 6. We conclude by presenting future directions in Section 7.

2. RELATED WORK

Qiu and Srikant [13] were the first to introduce a fluid model for BitTorrent. Using an ordinary differential equation (ODE) to capture peer dynamics, they study sojourn times at the fixed points of this ODE, as well as the impact of incentive schemes. Our work is most similar to Massoulié and Vojnovic [12] who, contrary to [13], study directly the dynamics of the stochastic system determined by piece exchanges between peers. As in the present work, no seed exists: peers arrive already storing several pieces of a file, and exchange pieces by contacting uniformly at random other peers in the swarm. The authors identify conditions for system stability and determine the sojourn time at equilibrium. Massoulié and Twigg [11] study similar issues in the context of P2P streaming, which differs by requiring that pieces are retrieved in a certain order. Our work generalizes [12] by allowing piece exchanges across swarms and, as [11, 12], studies a fluid limit of the resulting system.

Recent work by Hajek and Zhu [6] identifies the "missing piece syndrome" described in the introduction. Their model differs from [12] in assuming that a single, non-transient seed exists while all other peers arrive with no pieces. The bandwidth bottleneck due to the missing piece syndrome partially motivates our study of universal swarms. We will further elaborate on the relationship of our work to [6] in our concluding remarks.

In the context of mobile peer-to-peer systems, BARON, our scheme for guiding content exchanges, is related to a series of recent papers on optimizing mobile content delivery. In general, the goal of these works is to ensure fast delivery of content to mobile users through opportunistic exchanges while using as few bandwidth and storage resources as possible. Schemes studied involve selecting which content to transmit during contacts [1, 2, 7], which information to cache in local memory [9, 14], or where to inject new content [8]. Our work differs both in considering an open system, where mobile users depart once obtaining the content they want, as well as in capturing several different (*e.g.*, contact or interference constrained) communication scenarios.

3. SYSTEM MODEL

3.1 Overview

The system that we model is a universal swarm, consisting of several peers wishing to retrieve different content items. Peers share content they store with other peers while they are in the system; once a peer retrieves the content item that it is interested in, it exits the system.

Our model describes both mobile and online peer-to-peer swarms. In both cases, we assume that downloads take place as in [12]: each peer is idle for an exponentially distributed time and then contacts a peer selected uniformly at random from the peers present in the system. During such contacts, peers may choose to exchange content items they store and all transfers are instantaneous.

In the wireless mobile case, the above contact process aims to model mobility. That is, two mobile peers come into contact whenever they are within each other's transmission range. In an online peer-to-peer network, the contact process captures *random sampling*. In particular, peers sample the system population uniformly at random to find the items they want. No "universal tracker" exists, and peers do not know which peers in other swarms may be storing the items they request, hence the need for random sampling.

We make the following assumptions. First, every peer entering the system is only interested in downloading *a single content item*; once retrieving this single item, the peer immediately exits the system. Second, whenever a peer contacts another peer that stores its requested item, it is able to retrieve the *entire item* immediately. Third, as in [12], peers arrive with non-empty caches, and begin to share immediately when they enter the system.

The above assumptions are obviously simplifications of real-life peer-to-peer system behavior. On one hand, if our items correspond to the granularity of files, a peer would not be able to download an entire file within one downloading session with another peer. If, on the other hand, items correspond to the granularity of chunks, peers would need to retrieve several items before exiting the system. Nevertheless, in spite of these simplifications, our analysis provides interesting insights in universal swarm behavior, especially in light of the "missing piece syndrome" observed by Hajek and Zhu [6]. We will revisit this issue in Section 7.

3.2 Peer Swarms and Classes

We consider a *universal swarm* in which content items belonging to a set $\mathbb{K}$, where $|\mathbb{K}| = K$, are shared among transient peers. Each peer arrives with a request $i \in \mathbb{K}$ and a cache of items $f \subset \mathbb{K}$, where $C = |f|$ is the capacity of the cache. We denote by $\mathbb{F} = \{f \subset \mathbb{K} : |f| = C\}$ the set of all possible contents of a peer's cache.

A peer *swarm* consists of all peers interested in retrieving the same item $i \in \mathbb{K}$. We partition the peers in the system into *classes* according to both (a) the item they request and (b) the content in their cache. That is, each pair $(i, f) \in \mathbb{C} = \mathbb{K} \times \mathbb{F}$ defines a distinct peer class.

We denote by $N_{i,f}(t)$ the number of peers requesting i and storing f at time t. We use the notation

$$\mathbf{N}(t) = [N_{i,f}(t)]_{(i,f) \in \mathbb{C}}$$

for the vector representing the system state, *i.e.*, the number of peers in each class. We also denote by

$$N(t) = \sum_{(i,f) \in \mathbb{C}} N_{i,f}(t) = \mathbf{1}^T \cdot \mathbf{N}(t)$$

the total number of peers in the system at time t.

3.3 Peer Arrival Process

Peers requesting item $i \in \mathbb{K}$ and storing $f \in \mathbb{F}$ arrive according to a Poisson process with rate $\lambda_{i,f}$, and that arrivals across different classes are independent. By definition, $\lambda_{i,f} = 0$ if $i \in f$. We denote by $\lambda = \sum_{(i,f) \in \mathbb{C}} \lambda_{i,f}$ the aggregate arrival rate of peers in the system. We also define

$$\lambda_{i,\cdot} = \sum_{f \in \mathbb{F}} \lambda_{i,f}, \quad \lambda_{\cdot,i} = \sum_{\substack{j \in \mathbb{K} \\ f: i \in f}} \lambda_{j,f}, \quad i \in \mathbb{K} \quad (1)$$

as the aggregate arrival rates of peers requesting and caching item i, respectively.

For some of our results, we require that λ tends to infinity; when doing so, we assume that the arrival rate corresponding to each class increases proportionally to λ, *i.e.*, the normalized arrival rate

$$\hat{\lambda}_{i,f} = \lambda_{i,f} / \lambda \quad (2)$$

is constant w.r.t. λ.

3.4 Contact Process

Opportunities to exchange items among peers occur when two peers come into contact. As mentioned in Section 3.1, contacts model different processes in a mobile network and an online peer-to-peer network. In the mobile case, a contact indicates that two mobile peers are within each other's transmission range. In the online case, contacts capture random peer sampling in the universal swarm.

Formally, if $N(t)$ is the total number of peers in the system at time t, then a given peer a present in the system contacts other peers according to a non-homogeneous Poisson process with rate

$$\mu \cdot (N(t))^{1-\beta}, \quad \beta \in [0, 2].$$

The peer with which peer a comes into contact is selected uniformly at random from the $N(t)$ peers currently present in the system. Moreover, the above contact processes are independent across peers.

The parameter β is used to capture different communication scenarios that may arise in a mobile or online network. We classify these below into *contact-constrained*, *constant-bandwidth*, and *interference-constrained* scenarios.

Contact-constrained communication. When $0 \leq \beta < 1$, the contact rate of a peer is growing proportionally to the total peer population. This would be the case in a sparse, opportunistic or DTN-like wireless mobile network, where peers are within each other's transmission range very infrequently. In such cases, the bottleneck in data exchanges is determined by how often peers meet. Adding more peers in such an environment can increase the opportunities for contacts between peers. This is reflected in the increase of a peer's contact rate as the population size grows.

Constant-bandwidth communication. When $\beta = 1$ the contact rate of a peer does not depend on the population size. This reflects constant-bandwidth scenarios, where the system population has no effect on the bandwidth capabilities of a peer, and is thus a natural model of an online peer-to-peer network.

Interference-constrained communication. When $\beta \in (1, 2]$, the contact rate of a peer decreases as the total peer population grows. This captures a dense wireless network in which peers share a wireless medium to communicate. As the number of peers increases, the wireless interference can become severe, degrading the network throughput. This is reflected in our model by a decrease in successful contact events and, thus, in a peer's contact rate.

If $\beta > 2$, the aggregate contact rate over *all* peers in the system decreases as the total peer population grows. Assuming constant arrival rates, such a system will be trivially unstable; as such, we do not consider this case.

For simplicity of notation, we allow self-contacts. Contacts are not symmetric; when Alice contacts Bob, Bob does not contact Alice, and vice versa. This, however, is not restrictive: symmetric contacts can be easily represented by appropriately defining symmetric interactions between two peers (*c.f.* the conversion probabilities appearing below).

Under the above assumptions, when the system state is **N**, the aggregate rate with which users from class A contact users from class A' is

$$\mu_{A,A'}(\mathbf{N}) = \mu N_A N_{A'}/N^\beta, \quad A, A' \in \mathbb{C}. \tag{3}$$

We call $\mu_{A,A'}$ as the *inter-contact* rate between A and A'.

3.5 Content Exchanges During Contacts

When a peer in class $A \in \mathbb{C} = \mathbb{K} \times \mathbb{F}$ contacts another peer in class $B \in \mathbb{C}$, the two peers may exchange items stored in their respective caches. Such exchanges can lead to, *e.g.*, (a) the departure of a peer, because it obtains the item it requests, or (b) the change of its cache contents, as new items replace old items in the peer's cache.

In particular, given that the current state of the system is $\mathbf{N}(t)$, when a peer of class $A \in \mathbb{C}$ contacts another peer in $A' \in \mathbb{C}$, the peer in A is converted to a peer in $B \in \mathbb{C} \cup \{\varnothing\}$ and the peer in A' is converted to a peer in $B' \in \mathbb{C} \cup \{\varnothing\}$ with the following probability

$$\Delta_{A,A' \to B,B'}(\mathbf{N}(t)),$$

independently of any other event in the history of the process $\mathbf{N}(t)$ so far. In the above, we use the notation $\varnothing$ to indicate that a peer exits the system. We call the above Δ functions the *conversion probabilities* of the system. Conversion probabilities depend on the global state $\mathbf{N}(t)$ at the time of contact. We make the following technical assumption:

ASSUMPTION 1. *For every $s > 0$, and for every $A, A' \in \mathbb{C}$ and $B, B' \in \mathbb{C} \cup \{\varnothing\}$, $\Delta_{A,A' \to B,B'}(\mathbf{N}) = \Delta_{A,A' \to B,B'}(s\mathbf{N})$.*

In other words, the conversion probabilities are *invariant to rescaling*: if all peer classes are increased by the same factor, the conversion probabilities will remain unaltered. Let

$$\zeta^A_{A',A'' \to B',B''} = \mathbb{1}_{B'=A} + \mathbb{1}_{B''=A} - \mathbb{1}_{A'=A} - \mathbb{1}_{A''=A}, \tag{4}$$

be an indicator function capturing how a conversion $A', A'' \to B', B''$ affects the population of class A. For example, (4) states that conversions can increase N_A by at most 2, when both classes A', A'' are converted to A.

We require that conversions follow what we call the "*grab-and-go*" principle: whenever two peers come into contact, if the first stores the second peer's requested item, the latter will retrieve it and exit the system. In other words, content exchanges that lead to departures are always enforced. Formally, the "grab-and-go" principle can be defined as:

$$\sum_{B' \in \mathbb{C} \cup \{\varnothing\}} \Delta_{(i,f),(i',f') \to \varnothing, B'}(\mathbf{N}) = 1 \text{ if } i \in f', \text{ and}$$
$$\sum_{B \in \mathbb{C} \cup \{\varnothing\}} \Delta_{(i,f),(i',f') \to B, \varnothing}(\mathbf{N}) = 1 \text{ if } i' \in f. \tag{5}$$

The simplest interaction that satisfies the "grab-and-go" principle is the *static-cache* policy: peers never alter the contents of their caches for as long as they are in the system, other than as dictated by the "grab-and-go" principle. Formally, the static-cache policy can be stated as:

$$\Delta_{(i,f),(i',f') \to B,B'}(\mathbf{N}) = 1, \text{ where}$$
$$B = \begin{cases} \varnothing, & \text{if } i \in f' \\ (i,f) & \text{o.w.}, \end{cases} \text{ and } B' = \begin{cases} \varnothing, & \text{if } i' \in f \\ (i',f'), & \text{o.w.} \end{cases} \tag{6}$$

Table 1: Summary of Notation

$\mathbb{K}$	Set of items
C	Cache capacity
$\mathbb{F}$	Set of possible cache contents
(i,f)	Class of users requesting $i \in \mathbb{K}$ and storing $f \in \mathbb{F}$
$\mathbb{C}$	The set of classes $\mathbb{K} \times \mathbb{F}$
$N_{i,f}(t)$	The number of users in class (i,f)
$\mathbf{N}(t)$	The system state
$N(t)$	Number of peers in the system
$\lambda_{i,f}$	Arrival rate of peers in class (i,f)
λ	Aggregate arrival rate
$\hat{\lambda}_{i,f}$	Normalized arrival rate for class (i,f)
β	Decay exponent of the contact rate
μ	Contact rate constant
$\Delta_{A,A' \to B,B'}$	Conversion probabilities
$\zeta^A_{A',A'' \to B',B''}$	Effect of conversion $A', A'' \to B', B''$ on class A
$\delta_{A',A'' \to B',B''}$	Limit points of the conversion probabilities
$n_{i,f}(t)$	Fluid trajectory of class (i,f)
$\mathbf{n}(t)$	Fluid trajectories of the system state
$n(t)$	Sum of fluid trajectories
$n_{i,\cdot}, n_{\cdot,i}$	Demand and supply for $i \in \mathbb{K}$
$n^*_{i,\cdot}, n^*_{\cdot,i}$	Optimal demand and supply for $i \in \mathbb{K}$

Of course, there are many other conversion probabilities that satisfy the "grab-and-go" principle. In particular, (5) tells us nothing about how peers interact with each other when neither of them stores the other's requested item. Rather than leaving caches static, as in (6), such events can be exploited to change the number of replicas in the system, *e.g.*, to reach some global optimization objective, like increasing system stability or reducing the system sojourn times. We do precisely this in Section 6: we design interactions between peers (*i.e.*, determine the conversion probabilities) in a way that such a global optimization objective is met.

4. MAIN RESULTS

Having described our system model, we now present our main results. To begin with, we establish that, for arbitrary conversion probabilities the dynamics of our system can arbitrarily well approximated by a fluid limit (Section 4.1). We then describe the stability region of the static-cache policy (Section 4.2). Finally, we establish conditions under which interactions that follow the "grab-and-go" principle minimize sojourn times (Section 4.3).

4.1 Convergence to a Fluid Limit

Our first main result states that the evolution of the universal swarm through time can be approximated arbitrarily well by the solution of an ordinary differential equation (ODE). This result is very general: we prove convergence to such a fluid limit for *all* $\beta \in [0, 2)$ and *all* conversion probabilities satisfying Assumption 1.

We begin by formally defining the notion of a fluid limit of the universal swarm. We say that the vector

$$\mathbf{n}(t) = [n_A(t)]_{A \in \mathbb{C}}$$

is a *fluid trajectory* of the system if, for every class $A \in \mathbb{C}$, the functions $n_A : \mathbb{R}_+ \to \mathbb{R}_+$ satisfy the following ODEs:

$$\dot{n}_A(t) = \hat{\lambda}_A + \sum_{\substack{A',A'' \in \mathbb{C} \\ B',B'' \in \mathbb{C} \cup \{\varnothing\}}} \zeta^A_{A',A'' \to B',B''} \mu_{A',A''}(\mathbf{n}(t)) \delta_{A',A'' \to B',B''}(\mathbf{n}(t)), \tag{7}$$

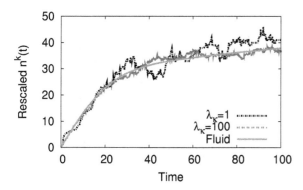

Figure 1: Comparing the rescaled trajectory of the original system to the fluid trajectory using the static-cache policy. We simulated a system where $\mathbb{K} = \{1,2,3\}, C = 1$, and $\beta = 0$, for $\lambda_k = 1$ and $\lambda_k = 100$ respectively. The rescaled trajectory clearly converges to the fluid trajectory as λ_k increases.

where $\hat{\lambda}_A$, $\mu_{A',A''}$, and $\zeta^A_{A',A'' \mapsto B',B''}$ are given by (2), (3), and (4) respectively, and $\delta_{A',A'' \mapsto B',B''} : \mathbb{R}^{|\mathbb{C}|}_+ \to [0,1]$ are any functions that satisfy the following property:

$$\delta_{\cdot \mapsto \cdot}(\mathbf{n}) \in [\liminf_{\mathbf{n}' \to \mathbf{n}} \Delta_{\cdot \mapsto \cdot}(\mathbf{n}'), \limsup_{\mathbf{n}' \to \mathbf{n}} \Delta_{\cdot \mapsto \cdot}(\mathbf{n}')].$$

The δ functions are unique and coincide with the conversion probabilities if and only if the latter are continuous. In this case, the ODEs (7) also have a unique solution. For any $\mathbf{n}^* \in \mathbb{R}^{|\mathbb{C}|}_+$, let $S(\mathbf{n}^*)$ be the set of all fluid trajectories of the system with initial condition $\mathbf{n}(0) = \mathbf{n}^*$. The following theorem establishes two facts. First, $S(\mathbf{n}^*)$ is non-empty—i.e., fluid trajectories exist for all initial conditions. Second, under appropriate rescaling, a trajectory of the universal swarm $\{\mathbf{N}(t), t \in \mathbb{R}_+\}$, can be arbitrarily well approximated by a fluid trajectory.

THEOREM 1. *Let $\alpha \equiv 1/(2-\beta)$. Consider a sequence of positive numbers $\{\lambda_k\}_{k \in \mathbb{N}}$ such that $\lim_{k \to \infty} \lambda_k = +\infty$, and a sequence of initial conditions $\mathbf{N}^k(0) = [N^k_A(0)]_{A \in \mathbb{C}}$ s.t. the limit $\lim_{k \to \infty} \lambda_k^{-\alpha} \mathbf{N}^k(0) = \mathbf{n}^*$ exists. Consider the rescaled process*

$$\mathbf{n}^k(t) = \lambda_k^{-\alpha} \mathbf{N}^k(\lambda_k^{\alpha-1} t), \quad t \in \mathbb{R}_+. \tag{8}$$

Then for all $T > 0$ and all $\epsilon > 0$,

$$\lim_{k \to \infty} \mathbf{P}\big(\inf_{\mathbf{n} \in S(\mathbf{n}^*)} \sup_{t \in [0,T]} |\mathbf{n}^k(t) - \mathbf{n}(t)| \geq \epsilon \big) = 0,$$

i.e., $\mathbf{n}^k$ converges to a fluid trajectory in probability.

The above convergence in probability is illustrated in Figure 1: the rescaled process $n^k(t) = \mathbf{1}^T \mathbf{n}^k(t)$ converges to the fluid trajectory as we increase the scaling factor λ_k from 1 to 100. The proof of this theorem can be found in our technical report [16] and follows closely the argument in [10], so we omit it for reasons of brevity.

Given a fluid trajectory $\{\mathbf{n}(t)\}_{t \in \mathbb{R}_+}$, we denote by

$$n_{i,\cdot}(t) = \sum_f n_{i,f}(t), \quad n_{\cdot,i}(t) = \sum_{j,f:i \in f} n_{j,f}(t), \quad i \in \mathbb{K} \tag{9}$$

the (rescaled) population of peers requesting and caching item i, respectively. We call $n_{i,\cdot}$, $n_{\cdot,i}$ the *demand* and the *supply* of item i, respectively.

4.2 Stability of the Static-Cache Policy

Armed with the above system characterization through its fluid trajectories, we turn our attention to the issue of system stability. Intuitively, we wish to understand what is the *stability region* of our system: what conditions should the arrival rates $\lambda_{i,f}$, $(i, f) \in \mathbb{C}$, satisfy, so that the total number of peers in the system remains bounded?

Surprisingly, a universal swarm evolving under the static-cache policy, arguably the simplest policy satisfying the "grab-and-go" principle, has a very wide stability region. We demonstrate this below by studying (a) the stability of the fluid trajectories of the static-cache policy and (b) the ergodicity of the original stochastic system.

We begin by stating our main result regarding fluid trajectories. We say that the system of ODEs (7) is stable if the fluid trajectories $\{\mathbf{n}(t)\}_{t \geq 0}$ remain bounded for all $t \geq 0$ irrespectively of the initial conditions $\mathbf{n}(0)$. In other words, irrespectively of how many peers are originally in the system, the population never blows up to infinity. Denote by

$$\lambda_{i,j} = \sum_{f:j \in f} \lambda_{i,f}, \qquad i,j \in \mathbb{K}, \tag{10}$$

the aggregate arrival rate of peers requesting item i and caching item j.

A sufficient condition for stability of the static-cache policy is stated in the following theorem, whose proof can be found in Section 5.1.

THEOREM 2. *Assume that all rates $\lambda_{i,j}$ are positive and*

$$\sum_{j:j \neq i} \lambda_{j,i}/\lambda_{i,j} > 1, \quad \forall i \in \mathbb{K}. \tag{11}$$

Then, for all $\beta \in [0,2)$, the system of ODEs (7) under the static-cache policy is stable.

There are several important conclusions to be drawn from Theorem 2. To begin with, the stability region remains the same for all values of $\beta \in [0,2)$: this is quite surprising, as it implies that (7) applies to all the different contact regimes we reviewed in Section 3.4 (contact-constrained, constant-bandwidth, and interference-constrained communications).

In addition, recall that $\lambda_{i,\cdot}$ and $\lambda_{\cdot,i}$, given by (1), are the aggregate arrival rates of peers requesting and caching item i, respectively. Inequality (11) implies that the system can be stable even if $\lambda_{i,\cdot} > \lambda_{\cdot,i}$ for some i, *i.e., peers requesting i arrive at a higher rate than peers storing i*. In particular as long as for every i there exists an item j such that $\lambda_{j,i} > \lambda_{i,j}$, then (11) are satisfied, and the system is stable. Intuitively, if such a j exists, the size of its swarm will grow large enough to provide the upload capacity necessary to serve peers requesting item i.

The above theorem has a direct equivalent w.r.t. the stochastic process $\{\mathbf{N}(t)\}_{t \in \mathbb{R}_+}$:

THEOREM 3. *Assume that all rates $\lambda_{i,j}$ are positive and that (11) holds. Then, for all $\beta \in [0,2)$, the stochastic process $\{\mathbf{N}(t)\}_{t \in \mathbb{R}_+}$ under the static-cache policy is ergodic.*

We provide a proof of this theorem in Section 5.2.

A very interesting aspect of static-cache stability is in the manner in which the universal swarm becomes unstable when (11) is violated. In particular, recall by (9) that $n_{i,\cdot}(t)$ is the demand for item i, *i.e.*, the size of the swarm of peers requesting item i (in the fluid limit). The following theorem then holds:

THEOREM 4. *Assume that all rates $\lambda_{i,j}$ are positive, and $\beta \in [0, 2)$. Then there exists at most one item $i \in \mathbb{K}$ for which*

$$\sum_{j:j \neq i} \lambda_{j,i}/\lambda_{i,j} < 1. \tag{12}$$

Moreover, if such an item i exists, there exist initial conditions $\mathbf{n}(0)$ such that

$$\lim_{t \to \infty} n_{i,\cdot}(t) = \infty, \text{ and } \limsup_{t \to \infty} n_{j,\cdot}(t) n_{i,\cdot}^{1-\beta}(t) < \infty, \ \forall j \neq i.$$

In other words, for $\beta \in [0, 1]$, *only one swarm can become unstable*. There can be only one item that satisfies (12), and although the swarm of peers requesting this item grows to infinity, the product $n_{j,\cdot} n_{i,\cdot}^{1-\beta}$ remains bounded. As a result, for $\beta \in [0, 1]$, no other swarm than the one satisfying (12) can become unstable. This property is very appealing, as it suggests that even if the arrival rates are outside the stability region, the stability of all but one swarm remains unaffected. Note that, when $\beta > 1$, *i.e.*, in the interference-constrained case, the product $n_{j,\cdot} n_{i,\cdot}^{1-\beta}$ is also bounded; however, this does not imply that other swarms do not grow. Nevertheless, these swarms grow at a slower rate than $n_{i,\cdot}$.

This stability property arises precisely because the universal swarm utilizes available bandwidth for inter-swarm communication. Intuitively, a swarm that becomes unstable has unbounded uploading capacity. As a result, as long as all arrival rates are positive, a fraction of this unbounded capacity can be used serve to other swarms at a very high rate; when $\beta \in [0, 1]$, this rate is in fact high enough to suppress the growth of any other swarm.

4.3 Optimality Under the "Grab-and-Go" Principle

Despite the interesting stability properties of the static-cache policy, it is still tempting to see whether we can design more sophisticated policies that achieve a wider stability region. Preferably, given that the system is stable we would like a design that minimizes average sojourn time. In this section, we characterize the minimum sojourn time achievable by any system satisfying the "grab-and-go" principle. We will use this to propose a content exchange policy that minimizes the average sojourn time in Section 6.

By Little's Theorem, minimizing the average sojourn time is equivalent to minimizing $N(t)$, the total number of peers in the system. We approach this problem by studying the stationary points of the fluid trajectories. This is a heuristic: by studying the stationary points of (7), we implicitly assume that the Markov process $\{\mathbf{N}(t)\}_{t \in \mathbb{R}_+}$ exhibits some form of concentration around these stationary points. Nevertheless, we believe that there is important intuition to be gained through our approach; we demonstrate that this is indeed the case through our numerical study of a sojourn minimizing system in Section 6.2.

Recall by (9) that $n_{i,\cdot}$ and $n_{\cdot,i}$ are the demand and supply of item i, respectively. The "grab-and-go" principle (5) implies that the fluid trajectories given by (7) satisfy the following set of equations:

$$\dot{n}_{i,\cdot}(t) = \hat{\lambda}_{i,\cdot} - 2\mu \cdot (n(t))^{-\beta} n_{i,\cdot}(t) n_{\cdot,i}(t). \quad i \in \mathbb{K} \tag{13}$$

The above equations state that the swarm of peers requesting i grows with new peer arrivals and decreases at encounters between peers in the swarm and peers that cache i. However, they do not specify what type of conversions take

place during other types of encounters between peers. Nevertheless, a stationary point $\mathbf{n} \in \mathbb{R}^{|\mathbb{C}|}$ of (13) must satisfy:

$$n_{i,\cdot} n_{\cdot,i} - \hat{\lambda}_{i,\cdot} (2\mu)^{-1} (n)^\beta = 0, \forall i \in \mathbb{K}.$$

Since peers cache at most C items, the number of cached items must be no more than the total cache capacity, *i.e.*,

$$\sum_{i \in \mathbb{K}} n_{\cdot,i} \leq Cn = C \sum_{i \in \mathbb{K}} n_{i,\cdot}.$$

We now pose the following problem: among all stationary points of content exchange policies that satisfy the "grab-and-go" principle, which stationary point has the minimum aggregate peer population? More formally, we wish to solve:

$$\text{Minimize} \quad \sum_{i \in \mathbb{K}} n_{i,\cdot} \tag{14a}$$

$$\text{subj. to:} \quad n_{i,\cdot} n_{\cdot,i} - \frac{\hat{\lambda}_{i,\cdot}}{2\mu} (\sum_{i \in \mathbb{K}} n_{i,\cdot})^\beta = 0, \quad \forall i \in \mathbb{K} \tag{14b}$$

$$\sum_{i \in \mathbb{K}} n_{\cdot,i} \leq C \sum_{i \in \mathbb{K}} n_{i,\cdot} \tag{14c}$$

$$n_{i,\cdot} \geq 0, \ \forall i \in \mathbb{K}. \tag{14d}$$

When $\beta \in [0, 1]$, the above problem is convex [3] and its solution is given by the following theorem:

THEOREM 5. *For $\beta \in [0, 1]$ and $\rho_i = \hat{\lambda}_{i,\cdot} (2\mu C)^{-1}$ the unique optimal solution to (14) is*

$$n_{i,\cdot}^* = \sqrt{\rho_i} (\sum_{j:j \in \mathbb{K}} \sqrt{\rho_j})^{\beta/(2-\beta)} \tag{15a}$$

$$n_{\cdot,i}^* = C \sqrt{\rho_i} (\sum_{j:j \in \mathbb{K}} \sqrt{\rho_j})^{\beta/(2-\beta)}, \quad \forall i \in \mathbb{K}, \tag{15b}$$

The proof of Theorem 5 can be found in Section 5.4. Note that the theorem does not hold for $\beta \in (1, 2]$, as (14) is not convex for these values of β. Moreover, (15) describes the optimal steady state demand and supply but not the size of each individual class. By (15), the optimal supply is proportional to the square-root of the aggregate arrival rates of peers requesting this item. This was also observed in the closed caching system described in [5]; our result can thus be seen as an extension of [5] for an open system with peer arrivals and departures. Finally, by (15)

$$n_{i,\cdot}^* = Cn_{\cdot,i}^* \tag{16}$$

i.e., the demand is C times the supply. In Section 6, we use this to propose a sojourn-minimizing item-exchange policy.

5. ANALYSIS

5.1 Proof of Theorem 2

Using (6), the ODE (7) for the fluid trajectories under the static cache policy assumes the following simple form.

$$\dot{n}_{i,f}(t) = \hat{\lambda}_{i,f} - 2\mu n(t)^{-\beta} n_{i,f}(t) n_{\cdot,i}(t), \quad i \in \mathbb{K}, f \in \mathbb{F}, \tag{17}$$

where $n_{\cdot,i}(t) = \sum_{j,f:i \in f} n_{j,f}(t)$. The above differential equation has an explicit solution in terms of $g_i(t) := 2\mu n_{\cdot,i}(t) n(t)^{-\beta}$, given by $n_{if}(t) = \left\{ n_{if}(0) + \int_0^t \hat{\lambda}_{if} e^{\int_0^s g_i(u)du} ds \right\} e^{-\int_0^t g_i(u)du}$. Consider now the ratio $n_{if}(t)/n_{if'}(t)$ for two distinct indices f, f'. In the view of the previous formula, it reads

$$\frac{n_{if}(t)}{n_{if'}(t)} = \frac{n_{if}(0) + \int_0^t \hat{\lambda}_{if} \exp\left(\int_0^s g_i(u)du\right) ds}{n_{if'}(0) + \int_0^t \hat{\lambda}_{if'} \exp\left(\int_0^s g_i(u)du\right) ds}.$$

Since the function g_i is non-negative, the argument in the integrals is lower-bounded by a positive constant. As a result, it follows by L'Hospital's rule that $\frac{n_{if}(t)}{n_{if'}(t)} = \frac{\hat{\lambda}_{if}}{\hat{\lambda}_{if'}} + O(1/t)$.

This implies that for large t, the individual variables $n_{ij}(t)$ are related by proportionality constraints, and as a result we can focus on tracking a smaller set of variables. Namely, we introduce the variables $u_i(t) := \frac{n_{i.}(t)}{\lambda_{i.}}$. Each individual variable $n_{if}(t)$ verifies $n_{if}(t) = \hat{\lambda}_{if} u_i(t) + O(1/t)$, then

$$\dot{u}_i(t) = 1 - u_i(t) n_{i.}(t) n(t)^{-\beta}$$
$$= 1 - u_i(t)\Big(\frac{\sum_{j\neq i} \hat{\lambda}_{ji} u_j(t)}{[\sum_j \hat{\lambda}_{j.} u_j(t)]^\beta} + O(1/t)\Big),$$

where $\hat{\lambda}_{ij}$ as in (10) and $\hat{\lambda}_{i.}$ as in (1). Hence, for large enough T the evolution of u_i within a finite interval $[T, T+t]$ can be arbitrarily well approximated by the ODE:

$$\dot{u}_i = 1 - u_i \sum_{j\neq i} \hat{\lambda}_{ji} u_j \big[\sum_j \hat{\lambda}_{j.} u_j\big]^{-\beta}. \tag{18}$$

We therefore focus on (18)—keeping in mind that our analysis below holds for large enough T. We will show that if (11) is satisfied for every $i \in \mathbb{K}$, then $\sup_i u_i(t)$ is bounded for all t. In particular, the following lemma holds:

LEMMA 1. *For $M > 0$ large enough, there exist $\delta > 0$ and $\epsilon > 0$ s.t. if $\sup_i u_i(0) = M$, then $\sup u_i(M\delta) \leq M(1-\epsilon)$.*

PROOF. To show this, for a given M, fix a $\delta > 0$. If $\sup_i u_i(\delta M) < M(1-\delta)$, then the lemma obviously holds for $\epsilon = \delta$. Suppose thus that there exists an i such that $u_i(\delta M) \geq M(1-\delta)$. By (18), for $t \in [0, \delta M]$ we have $u_i(t) \leq u_i(0) + t \leq M + \delta M$ and $u_i(t) \geq u_i(\delta M) + t - \delta M \geq M(1-\delta) - \delta M$. Hence $u_i(t) \in [M(1-2\delta), M(1+\delta)]$. This in turn implies that, for $t \in [0, \delta M]$, $n(t) = \Theta(M)(1 + O(\delta))$, where the constants involved depend on $\hat{\lambda}_i$ but not on t. As a result, for $j \neq i$, and $t \in [0, \delta M]$, we have

$$\dot{u}_j(t) = 1 - u_j \Theta(M^{1-\beta})(1 + \epsilon_1(\delta)),$$

where $\epsilon_1(\delta) = 1 - \frac{1+O(\delta)}{(1+O(\delta))^\beta} = O(\delta)$. Thus for $t \in [0, \delta' M]$, where $\delta' < \delta$, we have

$$u_j(t) = \Big[u_j(0) + \int_0^t e^{s\Theta(M^{1-\beta})(1+\epsilon_1(\delta))} ds\Big] e^{-t\Theta(M^{1-\beta})(1+\epsilon_1(\delta))}$$
$$= u_j(0) e^{-t\Theta(M^{1-\beta})(1+\epsilon_1(\delta))} + \frac{1 - e^{-t\Theta(M^{1-\beta})(1+\epsilon_1(\delta))}}{\Theta(M^{1-\beta})(1+\epsilon_1(\delta))}.$$

Fix a $0 < \delta' < \delta$, then

$$u_j(\delta' M) = O(Me^{-\Theta(\delta' M^{2-\beta})(1+\epsilon_1(\delta))}) + \frac{1 - e^{-\Theta(\delta' M^{2-\beta})(1+\epsilon_1(\delta))}}{\Theta(M^{1-\beta})(1+\epsilon_1(\delta))}$$
$$= \Theta(M^{-(1-\beta)})(1 + \epsilon_2(M, \delta, \delta')),$$

where $\epsilon_2 = O(\epsilon_1(\delta) + M^{2-\beta} e^{-\Theta(\delta' M^{2-\beta})(1+\epsilon_1(\delta))})$. From this and (18) we get that for $t \in [\delta' M, \delta M]$

$$\dot{u}_j(t) = 1 - u_j \hat{\lambda}_{i,j} \hat{\lambda}_{i,.}^{-\beta} M^{1-\beta}(1 + \epsilon_3(M, \delta, \delta')),$$

where $\epsilon_3 = O(\delta + O(M^{\beta-2}) + O(M^{\beta-2}\epsilon_2) = O(\delta) + O(M^{\beta-2}) + O(e^{-\Theta(\delta' M^{2-\beta})(1+\epsilon_1(\delta))})$. From this refined bound on the ODE, we can repeat the steps above to get that for $t \in [\delta'' M, \delta M]$, where $\delta' \leq \delta'' < \delta$, we have

$$u_j(t) = \hat{\lambda}_{i,.}^\beta \hat{\lambda}_{i,j}^{-1} M^{\beta-1}(1 + \epsilon_4(M, \delta, \delta', \delta'')),$$

where $\epsilon_4 = O(\epsilon_3) + O(M^{2-\beta} e^{-\Theta(\delta'' M^{2-\beta})})$. As a result, for $t \in [\delta'' M, \delta M]$,

$$\dot{u}_i(t) = 1 - u_i \frac{\sum_{k\neq i} \hat{\lambda}_{ki} u_k}{n^\beta}$$
$$= 1 - u_i(t) \frac{\sum_{k\neq i} \hat{\lambda}_{k,i} \frac{\hat{\lambda}_{i,.}^\beta}{\hat{\lambda}_{ik}}[M^{\beta-1}(1+\epsilon_4)]}{[\hat{\lambda}_{i.} M(1+O(M^{2-\beta}))(1+\epsilon_4)]^\beta}$$
$$= 1 - u_i \sum_{k\neq i} \frac{\hat{\lambda}_{k,i}}{\hat{\lambda}_{i,k}}[M(1+\epsilon_5(M, \delta, \delta', \delta''))]^{-1},$$

for $\epsilon_5 = O(\epsilon_4) + O(M^{2-\beta})$. Let $\gamma_i = \sum_{k\neq i} \frac{\hat{\lambda}_{ki}}{\hat{\lambda}_{ik}} > 1$, by (11). Then

$$u_i(\delta M) = u_i(\delta'' M) e^{-\gamma_i(1+\epsilon_5)(\delta-\delta'')} + M \frac{1 - e^{-\gamma_i(1+\epsilon_5)(\delta-\delta'')}}{\gamma_i(1+\epsilon_5)}.$$

By a Taylor expansion, $u_i(\delta M)$ becomes

$$u_i(\delta'' M)[1 - \gamma_i(1+\epsilon_5)(\delta-\delta'') + O(\delta^2)] + M[(\delta-\delta'') + O(\delta^2)$$
$$\leq M[1 + \delta'' + (\delta-\delta'')[1 - \gamma_i(1+\epsilon_5)] + O(\delta^2)]$$

as $u_i(\delta'' M) \leq M(1+\delta'')$ by (18). Assume now that M is large, and set $\delta = \Theta(M^{(\beta-2)/2})$ and δ', δ'' to be proportional to δ, such that $\delta' < \delta'' < \delta$ and $\delta'' + (\delta-\delta'')[1 - \gamma_i] < 0$. It then follows that $\epsilon_5 = O(\delta)$. Hence for large enough M (and small enough δ) $u_i(\delta M) = M[1 + \delta'' + (\delta-\delta'')[1 - \gamma_i] + O(\delta^2)] < 0$ and the lemma follows. $\quad\square$

Hence, outside a bounded set, $\sup_i u_i$ has to decrease (*i.e.*, is a Lyapunov function), and the theorem follows. $\quad\square$

5.2 Proof of Theorem 3

We now establish that under condition (11), the original Markov process $\mathbf{N}(t)$ is ergodic. To this end, we shall rely on the *fluid limit* approach. That is to say, we shall identify a Lyapunov function F, and establish that, for initial condition $\mathbf{N}(0)$ such that $F(\mathbf{N}(0)) = M$, then, for large enough M, it holds that

$$\mathbf{E}F(\mathbf{N}(\delta M)) \leq (1-\epsilon)M, \tag{19}$$

for suitable positive constants $\delta, \epsilon > 0$. Unsurprisingly, the line of argument parallels that of Theorem 2's proof, with some additional elements introduced to take care of the random fluctuations in the process.

The Lyapunov function to be considered is

$$F(N) := \sup_{i\neq j} N_{ij}/\lambda_{ij}.$$

Define the event $\Omega_{ij} = \{N_{ij}(M\delta) \geq \lambda_{ij} M(1-\delta)\}$. We first establish the following intermediate result.

LEMMA 2. *On the event Ω_{ij}, for some positive constants $\gamma, c > 0$, for all $k \neq i$, with probability $1 - e^{-\Theta(M)}$ one has*

$$N_{ij}(t) \in [\lambda_{ij} M(1-c\delta), \lambda_{ij} M(1+c\delta)], t \in [0, M\delta], \tag{20}$$
$$N_{ik}(M\delta) \in [\gamma M, \lambda_{ik} M(1+c\delta)], k \neq j. \tag{21}$$

PROOF. Let E_{ik} denote the unit rate Poisson processes used to generate the arrival times of type (ik)-users in the system. Consider the event $\Omega_1 = \{|E_{ik}(\lambda_{ik} M\delta) - \lambda_{ik} M\delta| \leq M\lambda_{ik}\delta/2, k \neq i\}$. Then using Chernoff bounds, it is readily seen that its probability is at least $1 - e^{-\Theta(M)}$.

To establish (20), it suffices to note that

$$N_{ij}(M\delta) - E_{ij}(\lambda_{ij} M\delta) \leq N_{ij}(t) \leq N_{ij}(0) + E_{ij}(M\delta),$$

and on the event $\Omega_1 \cap \Omega_{ij}$, the left-hand side is at least $\lambda_{ij} M(1-(5/2)\delta)$ and the right-hand side is at most $\lambda_{ij} M(1+(3/2)\delta)$. (20) thus holds with $c = 5/2$.

Consider next $k \neq j$. We introduce now the notation $D_i(t)$ to represent the number of departures of users requesting object i in time interval $[0, t]$. On the event Ω_1, necessarily $D_i(M\delta) \leq rM$ for some suitable constant r. Indeed, $D_i(M\delta)$ cannot exceed $N_i.(0) + \sum_{k \neq i} E_{ij}(M\delta\lambda_{ij})$, which in turn is no larger than $\sum_{k \neq i} M\lambda_{ik}(1 + (3/2)\delta)$ on Ω_1, given the initial condition $F(N(0)) = M$.

Introduce now $D_{ik}(t)$ to represent the number of departures of type (ik)-users during time interval $[0, t]$. This process is generated as follows: at each jump time T of the counting process $D_i(\cdot)$, conditional on the past of the process before time T, a type (ik)-user is chosen to leave the system with probability $N_{ik}(T^-)/N_i.(T^-)$. An explicit construction of this selection mechanism can be made by attaching a uniform random variable U_n to each jump point T_n of the process D_i in $[0, M\delta]$, and by letting

$$D_{ik}(t) = \sum_{n:T_n \geq t} \mathbb{1}_{U_n < N_{ik}(T_n^-)/N_i.(T_n^-)}.$$

As previously established, on the event $\Omega_1 \cap \Omega_{ij}$, one has $N_i.(t) \geq M\gamma$ for all $t \in [0, M\delta]$, and $D_i(M\delta) \leq rM$. This entails that, on this event, $D_{ik}(M\delta) \leq \sum_{n=1}^{rM} Z_n$, where $Z_n := \mathbb{1}_{U_n < (X - \sum_{\ell=1}^{n-1} Z_\ell)/M\gamma}$, and $X := N_{ik}(0) + E_{ik}(\lambda_{ik}M\delta)$. Indeed, type (ik)-departures are more likely if arrivals occur at the beginning of the interval $[0, M\delta]$.

This yields a first lower bound:

$$N_{ik}(M\delta) \geq Y := X - \sum_{n=1}^{rM} Z_n. \qquad (22)$$

To simplify this further, one can note that the resulting random variable Y is stochastically reduced if one replaces X in both this expression and the definition of the random variables Z_n by a lower bound. On the event Ω_1, such a lower bound consists in $M\rho$ with $\rho = \lambda_{ik}\delta/2$.

We now control the probability that the lower bound Y in (22) is below a threshold τM for some constant $\tau > 0$, taking $X = M\rho$. We have the following representation: $\mathbf{P}(Y < \tau M) = \mathbf{P}(\sum_{n=0}^{(\rho-\tau)M} V_n \leq rM)$, where the random variables V_n are independent, geometrically distributed with parameter $(\rho M - n)/(\gamma M)$. We omit details, but Chernoff's bounding technique can be used, by evaluating the Laplace transform of the random variable $\sum_{n=0}^{(\rho-\tau)M} V_n$, to show that, for small enough constant $\tau > 0$, the probability $\mathbf{P}(Y < \tau M)$ is at most $\exp(-\Theta(M))$. This concludes the proof of the Lemma. $\square$

We next need the following Corollary.

Corollary: On the event Ω_{ij}, for any $\delta' < \delta$, with probability $1 - \exp(-\Theta(M))$, the following holds for all $k \neq i$:

$$N_k.(M\delta') \leq \mathrm{Bin}(O(M), e^{-\Theta(M^{2-\beta})}) + \mathrm{Poi}(\Theta(M^{\beta-1})),$$

where Bin denotes a Binomial random variable, Poi a Poisson variable, that are mutually independent.

PROOF. On Ω_{ij}, with probability $1 - e^{-\Theta(M)}$ it holds that $N_{ij}(M\delta') \geq M(1 - (5/2)\delta)$. The previous Lemma, suitably modified, therefore applies, and thus, there must exist a constant $\delta'' < \delta'$ such that with probability $1 - e^{-\Theta(M)}$, the following holds: $N_{ik}(t) = \Omega(M)$, $t \in [M\delta'', M\delta']$. Consider now the dynamics of $(N_k.)$. Arrivals occur at a rate $\lambda_k.$, and departures occur at a time-varying rate $N_k.(t)N_k.(t)N(t)^{-\beta}$. The product $N_k.(t)N(t)^{-\beta}$ is at least $\Omega(M^{1-\beta})$ on the interval $[\delta''M, \delta'M]$ by the previous argument. Thus its state at time $M\delta'$ can be upper-bounded by that of a M/M/∞/∞

queue, with initial state $N_k.(M\delta'')$ at time $M\delta''$, arrival rate $\lambda_k.$ and death rate $\Omega(M^{1-\beta})$. Now, with probability $1 - e^{-\Theta(M)}$, it holds that $N_k.(M\delta'') = O(M)$, and the result follows. $\square$

We are now ready to conclude the proof of the Theorem. To this end, we place ourselves on the event Ω_{ij}, and derive bounds on the trajectories $N_{ij}(t)$ for t in the interval $[M\delta', M\delta]$, relying on the previous results.

As we have just seen, with probability $1 - e^{-\Theta(M)}$, the components $N_{ik}(M\delta')$ are of order $\Theta(M)$. Furthermore, following the same lines as in the proof of (21), we can deduce from the fact that $N_{ij}(t) = N_{ij}(0)(1 + O(\delta))$, $t \in [0, M\delta]$ that

$$N_{ik}(t) = N_{ik}(M\delta')(1 + O(\delta)), \quad t \in [M\delta', M\delta]. \qquad (23)$$

Let us now introduce dedicated unit rate Poisson processes $\Delta_{k\ell}$ for each user type $(k\ell)$, and consider the representation

$$N_{k\ell}(t) = N_{k\ell}(M\delta') + E_{k\ell}(\lambda_{k\ell}(t - M\delta')) \\ - \Delta_{k\ell}(\mu \int_{M\delta'}^t N_{k\ell}(s)N_k.(s)N(s)^{-\beta}ds).$$

Replacing in the above $N_k.(s)$ by an upper bound of order $N_{ik}(M\delta')(1 + O(\delta))$, and $N(s)$ by a lower bound of order $N_i.(M\delta')(1 + O(\delta))$, we obtain a process $N_{k\ell}^+(t)$ that is an upper bound to $N_{k\ell}(t)$, and that is an M/M/∞/∞ process with arrival rate $\lambda_{k\ell}$ and death rate $N_{ik}(M\delta')N_i.(M\delta')^{-\beta}(1 + O(\delta))$.

Subsequently, we can also derive lower-bounding processes $N_{k\ell}^-(t)$ by upper-bounding $N_k.(s)$ by

$$N_k.(s) \geq N_{ik}(M\delta')(1 + O(\delta)) + \sum_{m \neq i,k} N_{mk}^+(s),$$

and lower-bounding $N(s)$ by $N(M\delta')(1 + O(\delta))$ in the argument of $\Delta_{k\ell}$. Note now that the processes $N_{k\ell}^+$ have a stationary distribution that is Poisson with parameter $O(M^{\beta-1})$. Thus with high probability, their supremum over $[M\delta', M\delta]$ is small compared to $N_{i\ell}$, itself of order M. Eventually, we obtain that with high probability, $N_{k\ell}(t)$ admits lower bounds $N_{k\ell}^-(t)$ that are M/M/∞/∞ processes with arrival rate $\lambda_{k\ell}$ and death rates again equal to

$$N_{ik}(M\delta')N_i.(M\delta')^{-\beta}(1 + O(\delta)).$$

These lower bounds in turn will provide upper bounds on N_{ik}, by writing

$$N_{ik}(t) \leq N_{ik}(M\delta') + E_{ik}(\lambda_{ik}(t - M\delta')) \\ - \Delta_{ik}(\int_{M\delta'}^t N_{ik}(s)[\sum_{\ell \neq i} N_{\ell i}^-(s)]N(s)^{-\beta}ds). \qquad (24)$$

The argument of Δ_{ik} is lower-bounded by

$$N_{ik}(M\delta')N_i.(M\delta')^{-\beta}(1 + O(\delta)) \int_{M\delta'}^t \sum_{\ell \neq i} N_{\ell i}^-(s)ds.$$

By the ergodic theorem, applied to the M/M/∞/∞ processes $N_{\ell i}^-$, this integral reads with high probability with respect to M:

$$(t - M\delta') \sum_{\ell \neq i} \lambda_{\ell i} \frac{N_i.(M\delta')^\beta}{N_{i\ell}(M\delta')}(1 + O(\delta)).$$

Upon simplification, we have with high probability, replacing in (24) the Poisson processes E_{ik} and Δ_{ik} by their expectation, up to some error vanishing as M increases,

$$N_{ik}(M\delta) - N_{ik}(M\delta') \leq M(\delta - \delta')\left[\lambda_{ik} - -(1 + O(\delta)) \times \ldots \right. \\ \left. \ldots N_{ik}(M\delta') \sum_{\ell \neq i} \frac{\lambda_{\ell i}}{N_{i\ell}(M\delta')}\right].$$

Let $a_{ik}(t) = \lambda_{ik}^{-1} N_{ik}(t)$. The previous equation reads

$$a_{ik}(M\delta) - a_{ik}(M\delta') \leq M(\delta - \delta') \times \cdots$$
$$\cdots \times \left[1 - a_{ik}(M\delta') \sum_{\ell \neq i} \frac{\lambda_{\ell i}}{\lambda_{i\ell}} \frac{1}{a_{i\ell}(M\delta')}(1 + O(\delta))\right].$$

Now, for the index k for which $a_{ik}(M\delta')$ is largest, the right-hand side of the above is no larger than

$$M(\delta - \delta')\left[1 - (1 + O(\delta)) \sum_{\ell \neq i} \frac{\lambda_{\ell i}}{\lambda_{i\ell}}\right],$$

itself strictly smaller than $-M\epsilon$ for some positive ϵ, if we chose δ small enough, when condition (11) is in force. This enables to conclude that, with high probability,

$$\sup_{i,j} N_{ij}(M\delta)/\lambda_{ij} = F(N(M\delta)) \leq (1 - \epsilon)F(N(0)).$$

The same bound applies to the expectation of the left-hand side, using a uniform integrability argument. This establishes the desired contraction property of the Lyapunov function F and, hence, the ergodicity of the original Markov process. $\square$

5.3 Proof of Theorem 4

To show that there can be at most one i for which (12) holds, we observe that if it holds for some i, then for any other $j \neq i$, we have $\hat{\lambda}_{j,i}/\hat{\lambda}_{i,j} < 1$. This implies that any other j satisfies (11), so no $j \neq i$ can also satisfy (12).

To prove the remainder of the theorem, we use the notation $z = x \pm y$ to indicate that $z \in [x - y, x + y]$. Suppose that $\gamma_i = \sum_{k \neq i} \hat{\lambda}_{ki}/\hat{\lambda}_{ik} < 1$ for some i and assume that $u_i(0) = M > 0$, for some large M. Assume further that for $j \neq i$, $u_j(0) = u_i^{1-\beta} \frac{\hat{\lambda}_i^\beta}{\hat{\lambda}_{i,j}}(1 \pm \epsilon)$, for some small $\epsilon > 0$. The following lemma then holds:

LEMMA 3. *For all $\epsilon > 0$, there exists $M_0 > 0$ s.t. for all $M > M_0$ there exists $\delta > 0$ such that if $u_i(0) = M$ and $u_i^{1-\beta}(0)u_j(0) = (1 \pm \epsilon)\hat{\lambda}_i^\beta/\hat{\lambda}_{i,j}$, then $u_j(t)u_i^{1-\beta}(t) = (1 \pm \epsilon)\hat{\lambda}_i^\beta/\hat{\lambda}_{i,j}$ for all $t \in [0, \delta]$.*

PROOF. Fix some $\epsilon > 0$. The lemma follows by the continuity of the fluid trajectories if $u_i^{1-\beta}u_j$ is in the interior of $\frac{\hat{\lambda}_i^\beta}{\hat{\lambda}_{i,j}}(1 \pm \epsilon)$. Suppose thus that it is at the boundary. We consider the upper boundary case, i.e., $u_j u_i^{1-\beta} = \frac{\hat{\lambda}_i^\beta}{\hat{\lambda}_{i,j}}(1 + \epsilon)$ and show that $\frac{d}{dt}u_j u_i^{1-\beta}$ is negative, so that $u_j u_i^{1-\beta}$ is forced in the interior; the same argument can be used to show that the derivative is positive when at the lower boundary, so we omit this case. Indeed

$$\frac{d}{dt}u_i^{1-\beta}u_j = (1 - \beta)\dot{u}_i u_i^{-\beta}u_j + u_i^{1-\beta}\dot{u}_j$$
$$= (1 - \beta)u_i^{-\beta}u_j(1 - u_i \frac{\sum_{k \neq i} \hat{\lambda}_{ki}u_k}{n^\beta}) + u_i^{1-\beta}(1 - u_j \frac{\sum_{k \neq j} \hat{\lambda}_{kj}u_k}{n^\beta}).$$

Note that $u_j(0) = \Theta(u_i^{\beta-1}(0))$, where the asymptotic notation is as $M \to \infty$. Observe that, since $\hat{\lambda}_{i',j'} > 0$ for all $i', j' \in \mathbb{K}$, we have that at time $t = 0$, $0 < \frac{\sum_{k \neq i} \hat{\lambda}_{ki}u_k}{n^\beta} = \Theta(u_j u_i^{-\beta}) = \Theta(u_i^{-1})$, and $0 < \frac{\sum_{k \neq j} \hat{\lambda}_{kj}u_k}{n^\beta} = u_i^{1-\beta}\frac{\hat{\lambda}_{i,j}}{\hat{\lambda}_i^\beta}(1 + o(1))$. We thus have that, at $t = 0$,

$$\frac{d}{dt}u_i^{1-\beta}u_j = \frac{\hat{\lambda}_i^\beta}{\hat{\lambda}_{i,j}}(1 + \epsilon)\left(\frac{1}{u_j} - u_i^{1-\beta}\frac{\hat{\lambda}_{i,j}}{\hat{\lambda}_i^\beta}(1 + o(1)) + O(u_i^{-1})\right)$$
$$= \frac{\hat{\lambda}_i^\beta}{\hat{\lambda}_{i,j}}(1 + \epsilon)\left(\frac{1}{u_j} - u_i^{1-\beta}\frac{\hat{\lambda}_{i,j}}{\hat{\lambda}_i^\beta}(1 + o(1))\right)$$

as $u_i^{-1} = o(u_i^{1-\beta})$ for $\beta < 2$. On the other hand as $u_j u_i^{1-\beta} = \frac{\hat{\lambda}_i^\beta}{\hat{\lambda}_{i,j}}(1 + \epsilon)$ implies that $u_j^{-1} = u_i^{1-\beta}\frac{\hat{\lambda}_i^\beta}{\hat{\lambda}_{i,j}}\frac{1}{1+\epsilon} < u_i^{1-\beta}\frac{\hat{\lambda}_i^\beta}{\hat{\lambda}_{i,j}}$, so for M large enough the above quantity is negative. $\square$

Consider now a fluid trajectory in which $u_i(0) = M$ and $u_i^{1-\beta}(0)u_j(0) = \frac{\hat{\lambda}_i^\beta}{\hat{\lambda}_{i,j}}(1 \pm \epsilon)$. Then we have that

$$\dot{u}_i = 1 - u_i \frac{\sum_{k \neq i} \hat{\lambda}_{ki}u_k}{n^\beta} = 1 - u_i \frac{\sum_{k \neq i} \hat{\lambda}_{ki}\frac{\hat{\lambda}_i^\beta}{\hat{\lambda}_{i,k}}u_i^{\beta-1}1 \pm \epsilon}{(\sum_k \hat{\lambda}_{k,.}u_k)^\beta}$$
$$= 1 - u_i \frac{\sum_{k \neq i} \frac{\hat{\lambda}_{k,i}}{\hat{\lambda}_{i,k}}\hat{\lambda}_i^\beta u_i^{\beta-1}(1 \pm \epsilon)}{\hat{\lambda}_i^\beta u_i^\beta(1 + o(1))},$$

which for large enough M and a small enough ϵ becomes $1 - \sum_{k \neq i} \frac{\hat{\lambda}_{ki}}{\hat{\lambda}_{ik}}(1 + o(1)) > 0$. This, along with Lemma 3 implies we can select an $\epsilon > 0$ such that, for large enough M, if $u_i(0) = M$ and $u_i^{1-\beta}(0)u_j(0) = \frac{\hat{\lambda}_i^\beta}{\hat{\lambda}_{i,j}}(1 \pm \epsilon)$, then there exists a $\delta > 0$ s.t. $u_i'(0)$ is positive and bounded away from zero uniformly in M and $u_i^{1-\beta}(t)u_j(t) = \frac{\hat{\lambda}_i^\beta}{\hat{\lambda}_{i,j}}(1 \pm \epsilon)$, for all $t \in [0, \delta]$. This in turn implies that the above is true for all $t \geq 0$, and, in particular, that u_i diverges to infinity. $\square$

5.4 Proof of Theorem 5

Let us define $x_i = n_{i,.}$ and $\rho_i = \hat{\lambda}_{i,.}(2\mu C)^{-1}$, $i \in \mathbb{K}$. By (14b), we have

$$n_{.,i} = C\rho_i(\sum_{j:j \in \mathbb{K}} x_j)^\beta/x_i. \tag{25}$$

Using (25), we can rewrite (14) as the following equivalent convex optimization problem involving only x_i:

Minimize $\quad \sum_{i \in \mathbb{K}} x_i$

subj. to: $\quad \sum_{i \in \mathbb{K}}(\rho_i x_i^{-1}) \leq (\sum_{i \in \mathbb{K}} x_i)^{1-\beta}, \quad i \in \mathbb{K}$ (26a)

$\quad x_i \geq 0, \quad i \in \mathbb{K}.$ (26b)

We can write its Lagrangian function as

$$\Lambda(\mathbf{x}, \varphi, \mathbf{w}) = \sum_{i \in \mathbb{K}} x_i + \varphi h(\mathbf{x}) + \sum_{i \in \mathbb{K}} w_i g(x_i),$$

where φ and $\mathbf{w} = [w_i]_{i \in \mathbb{K}}$ are Lagrangian multipliers, $\mathbf{x} = [x_i]_{i \in \mathbb{K}}$, $h(\mathbf{x}) = \sum_{i \in \mathbb{K}} \rho_i x_i^{-1} - (\sum_{i \in \mathbb{K}} x_i)^{1-\beta}$, and $g(x_i) = -x_i$. Hence, any $\tilde{\mathbf{x}} = \{\tilde{x}_1, ..., \tilde{x}_K\}$ is optimal if and only if it satisfies the following KKT conditions [3]:

$$h(\tilde{\mathbf{x}}) \leq 0, \quad g(\tilde{x}_i) \leq 0, \quad i \in \mathbb{K}, \tag{27a}$$
$$\varphi \geq 0, \quad w_i \geq 0, \quad i \in \mathbb{K}, \tag{27b}$$
$$\varphi h(\tilde{\mathbf{x}}) = 0, \quad w_i g(\tilde{x}_i) = 0, \quad i \in \mathbb{K}, \tag{27c}$$
$$\frac{d\Lambda}{dx_i}(\tilde{\mathbf{x}}, \varphi, \mathbf{w}) = 0, \quad i \in \mathbb{K}. \tag{27d}$$

We know that $x_i > 0, \forall i \in \mathbb{K}$ from (26a) and (26b). Thus condition (27c) requires $w_i = 0, \forall i \in \mathbb{K}$ and (27d) needs $\varphi \neq 0$. Then by $\varphi h(\tilde{x}) = 0$ in (27c) and condition (27d), any optimal solution $\tilde{\mathbf{x}}$ must satisfy the following two equations:

$$h(\tilde{\mathbf{x}}) = 0, \quad \frac{d\Lambda}{dx_i}(\tilde{\mathbf{x}}, \varphi, [0]) = 0$$

Solving these two equations leads to the unique solution $x_i = \sqrt{\rho_i}(\sum_{j:j\in\mathbb{K}} \sqrt{\rho_j})^{\frac{\beta}{2-\beta}}, i \in \mathbb{K}$, as shown in (15a), and the Lagrangian multiplier $\varphi = (\sum_{i\in\mathbb{K}} \sqrt{\rho_i})^{\frac{2\beta}{2-\beta}}(2-\beta)^{-1}$.

By plugging x_i into (25), we can derive the value of $n_{\cdot,i}^*$ as (15b), and (15) is the unique optimal solution of (14). $\square$

6. BARON: GUIDING CACHE REPLACEMENT VIA VALUATIONS

Our analysis in Section 5.4 has identified the optimal stationary points that minimize the average sojourn time. However, we have not described a method for leading the system to such points. In this section, we present BARON to bridge this gap. BARON dictates how peers should exchange content items so that the system converges to the optimal points defined in Theorem 5. We also demonstrate BARON's performance using numerical simulations.

BARON is a centralized scheme. In particular, it requires estimating the demand and supply of each item $i \in \mathbb{K}$, captured by the population of peers requesting and storing i, respectively. In practice, individual peers may maintain estimates of these quantities, e.g., either by gossiping or sampling. However, studying decentralized schemes for estimating the demand and supply is beyond the scope of this paper. As a result, we focus on scenarios in which these quantities are readily monitored through at a centralized tracker.

6.1 Designing BARON

To lead the system to the optimal point, one intuitive way is to first identify which items are over-replicated and which are under-replicated. Whenever two peers come into contact, if one has an over-replicated item i and the other has an under-replicated item j, then the first peer replaces its item i with item j. This replacement increases the current supply $n_{\cdot,i}$ of the under-replicated item.

Valuations in BARON. BARON keeps track of whether an item is currently over-replicated or under-replicated in following way. In particular, for each content item i, BARON maintains a real-valued variable v_i. We will call this variable the *valuation* of item i.

Our choice of valuation is inspired by (16), which states that at an optimal point the supply of an item is C times the demand. Motivated by this, the valuations are given by

$$v_i(t) = Cn_{i,\cdot}(t) - n_{\cdot,i}(t), \quad i \in \mathbb{K}. \quad (28)$$

A positive valuation $v_i > 0$ indicates that item i is currently under-replicated. Similarly, a negative valuation $v_i < 0$ indicates that item i is currently over-replicated.

One appealing property of (28) is that it requires prior knowledge *only* of the cache capacity C; in particular, it does not require knowledge of the arrival rates $\lambda_{i,f}$ of each peer class. Nevertheless, this valuation requires to track the supply and demand for each item.

Content exchange guided by valuations. BARON is a centralized design that relies on a central controller to maintain the valuations (28). In addition, this central controller lists the valuations on a public board, and makes them available to all peers.

The content exchanges between peers are guided by these valuations following a *negative-positive rule*. More specifically, during a contact event between a peer A with cache f and a peer B with f', each peer checks if it has any over-replicated items. If so, it further checks whether the other peer has any under-replicated items that it has not already stored in its cache. If such a pair of items exists, a replacement takes place. In particular, the first peer A replaces the item with the minimal negative valuation in its cache, i.e., peer A removes item i such that

$$i = \operatorname{argmin}\{v_x | x \in f, v_x < 0\}.$$

Then, among the under-replicated items in the peer B's cache f' yet not in peer A's cache f, peer A replicates the item with the maximal positive valuation, i.e. peer A selects item j such that

$$j = \operatorname{argmax}\{v_y | y \in f' \setminus f, v_y > 0\}.$$

After retrieving item j from peer B, peer A replaces i with j. Hence its cache f changes to $(f \setminus \{i\}) \bigcup \{j\}$. A similar procedure follows for peer B.

Clearly, there are other ways to design valuations and the rules for guiding content exchanges via valuations. In Section 6.3, we will examine other options for these two design components of BARON.

Based on the above definitions, the conversion probabilities of BARON satisfy Assumption 1 because of the positive-negative rule. As a result, by Theorem 1, we can study the dynamics of BARON through its fluid trajectory.

6.2 Evaluating BARON

We evaluate BARON's fluid trajectories using numerical simulations in MATLAB. Our main observation is that, by guiding the content exchanges through valuations, BARON converges to the optimal stationary points defined in (15), which minimize the average sojourn time.

6.2.1 BARON vs. Static-Cache Policy

We compare BARON to the static-cache policy by the examining system stability and optimality when using each design. Then we further use the static-cache policy as an example to demonstrate that only one swarm becomes unstable when instability occurs.

We simulate the following scenario. Assume there are three items $\{1, 2, 3\}$ in the system, and peer's cache size is one. Hence we have six peer classes, where each class of peers requesting item i and caching item j ($\neq i$) has a normalized arrival rate of $\hat{\lambda}_{i,j}$. Peers requesting one item form one swarm, leading to three swarms in total. We set the contact process parameters as $\beta = 0$ and $\mu = 0.002$. We assume initially no peer is in the system.

Stability. We begin with comparing the system stability under BARON and the static-cache policy. In particular, we aim to understand under which conditions of arrival rates, the system stabilizes when using each design. So we leave $\hat{\lambda}_{23}$ as a free variable, and fix the relative ratios of the other five classes as $\frac{1}{5}, \frac{1}{15}, \frac{2}{15}, \frac{1}{5}, \frac{2}{5}$, respectively of $(1 - \hat{\lambda}_{23})$. To identify the system stability for a given $\hat{\lambda}_{23}$ value, we examine the system's fluid trajectory over a significantly long time ($t \approx 10^5$).

Figure 2(a) shows the rescaled peer population when the system can stabilize as we vary $\hat{\lambda}_{23}$. We see that when using the static-cache policy, the system stabilizes only when $\hat{\lambda}_{23}$ is above $\frac{4}{19}$. This verifies the conclusion in Theorem 2 since $\frac{4}{19}$ is the arrival rate $\hat{\lambda}_{23}$ that violates condition (11). In con-

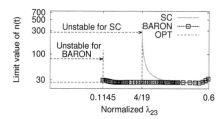

(a) Limit points of the fluid trajectory for variable $\hat{\lambda}_{23}$.

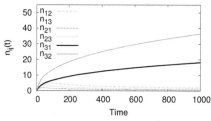

(b) Static-cache policy w/ $\hat{\lambda}_{23} = \frac{4}{19}$.

Figure 2: Comparing BARON and static-cache (SC) policy by varying arrival rate configurations.

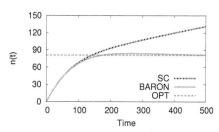

(a) Contact-constrained communication w/ $\beta = 0.5$.

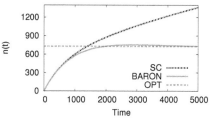

(b) Constant-bandwidth communication w/ $\beta = 1$.

Figure 3: BARON under various β.

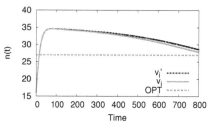

(a) Varying valuation designs under NPR.

(b) Varying valuation designs under LHR.

Figure 4: Examining the peer population under various design options in BARON.

trast, when using BARON, the system has a much larger stability region. More specifically, the system is able to stabilize when $\hat{\lambda}_{23}$ is larger than 0.1145. This demonstrates BARON's effectiveness of guiding content exchanges.

Optimality. We further examine the stationary state that the system converges to when using BARON and the static-cache policy. As shown in Figure 2(a), the system under the static-cache policy converges to a non-optimal state. Moreover, the closer $\hat{\lambda}_{23}$ is to the stability boundary $\frac{4}{19}$, the more peers in the stationary state. In contrast, BARON is able to guide the system to the optimal stationary state if the system stabilizes. This demonstrates that BARON achieves optimality by the use of valuations.

Single swarm instability. Now we examine how peer classes evolve in time when instability occurs under the static-cache policy. Figure 2(b) shows the population of each peer class along the time when $\hat{\lambda}_{23} = \frac{4}{19}$, demonstrating the conclusion in Theorem 4: only *one* swarm can become unstable.

Recall that peers requesting the same item form one swarm. Our main observation is that only the swarm requesting item 3 blows up. This is because item 3 is the one that does not satisfy (11). As this swarm grows, peers in other swarms can obtain their requested items quickly and depart. Hence the supply for item 3 further decreases.

6.2.2 Dependence on β

To comprehensively understand BARON's performance, we extend to cases with other β values. In particular, we examine two cases with $\beta = 0.5$ and $\beta = 1$ respectively. As shown in Section 3.4, a larger β indicates a smaller contact rate. The case when $\beta = 1$ is the constant-bandwidth communication scenario where a peer's contact rate is constant regardless of the peer population. We do not simulate the case where $\beta > 1$, because the optimality result identified in

Section 4.3 does not hold for such β. We configure the other parameters as in Figure 2 with $\hat{\lambda}_{23} = \frac{1}{6}$.

Figures 3(a) and (b) show the evolution of the total number of peers in time. The main observation is that, while the system does not stabilize when using the static-cache policy, the system under BARON converges to the optimal in both cases. This demonstrates the effectiveness of the valuations under various communication settings. Even though the aggregate contact rate decreases as β increases, BARON is still able to adapt the item supply according to the demand, guiding the system towards the optimal.

Furthermore, as the contact rate becomes smaller when β increases, the system with BARON takes longer time to stabilize to the optimal. This is because the item replacement and replication only occur during contact events. A smaller contact rate slows down the adjustment of the item distribution, leading to a slower convergence.

6.3 Comparing to Other Designs

BARON has two design components – the valuations in (28) and the negative-positive rule. Now we experiment with other designs for these two components, and examine their performance in comparison to BARON.

An alternative valuation v_i' is

$$v_i'(t) = n_{\cdot,i}^* - n_{\cdot,i}(t), \quad i \in \mathbb{K}, \qquad (29)$$

i.e., item i's valuation is defined as the distance of its current supply $n_{\cdot,i}$ to the optimal $n_{\cdot,i}^*$ as given by (15b). Note that in (29), computing the optimal supply $n_{\cdot,i}^*$ requires the knowledge of several system parameters, including the arrival rates $\lambda_{i,f}$, $(i,f) \in \mathbb{C}$, and the contact process parameters μ and β. Obtaining the values of these parameters could be difficult in practice.

Moreover, instead of the *negative-positive rule* (NPR) in BARON, another rule of guiding content exchanges via valuations is replacing one item with another as long as the other item has a higher valuation and the item is not already stored. We refer to it as the *lower-higher rule* (LHR).

We examine all four combinations of these design options, where BARON is the combination of NPR with valuations v_i defined in (28). We use the same configuration as Section 6.2.2, and assume initially 16 peers request item 3.

Figures 4(a) and (b) plot the trajectories of peer population under various design combinations. We observe that none of the other combinations performs better than BARON.

In addition, in terms of the comparison of design options for each component, we make the following observations. First, the two valuations perform similarly, and v_i performs better than v_i' under LHR. Second, the system with NPR converges to the optimal faster than LHR. This is interesting because NPR is stricter than LHR, and one would expect that LHR leads to a faster convergence by enabling more frequent replications and replacements. Indeed, from Figures 4(a) and (b), we observe that the peer population stays around its peak (≈ 35) for a longer time when using NPR. Nonetheless, NPR is able to catch up later. While this demonstrates the efficiency of restricting the replacement to over-replicated item only, the analytical reason beneath is worthwhile to further explore.

7. CONCLUSIONS AND FUTURE WORK

In this paper, we made the first attempt towards a systematical understanding of universal swarms, where peers share content across peer-to-peer swarms. We have rigorously proved that such content exchange across swarms significantly improves stability compared to a single autonomous swarm. We also have proved convergence to a fluid limit for a general class of content exchanges; our theorem thus paves the way for the analysis of more complicated exchange schemes than the one described in the present work.

An important future research direction lies in further investigating the parallels between our work and "missing piece syndrome" in single swarms [6]. In particular, once a "one-club" forms in a swarm, each "one-club" peer has idle bandwidth capacity. It can thus contact uniformly at random peers and seeders at other swarms to obtain C items and place them in its cache, and subsequently continue to sample other swarms to see if it can retrieve and/or offer a missing piece. From this point on, our model applies: peers wish to retrieve one item (their "missing piece"), and leave the system immediately once they retrieve it (corresponding to the "grab-and-go" principle).

This is of course a simplification of the above system, as it ignores the "growing" phase when peers acquire all chunks of a file but the last one, as well as the cache-filling phase. However, in light of the stability properties we observed in this work, understanding if, *e.g.*, the stability region increases through such exchanges, is an interesting open question.

Our analysis leaves several additional open questions, including formally characterizing the stability conditions of BARON, and analytically studying BARON's convergence to optimal stationary points. Our model can also be extended in various ways, including multi-item request, heterogeneous cache sizes and contact rates. The case where arrival rates are not strictly positive, and peers arrive with a partially-filled cache are also worth considering.

Finally, while our model assumes peers are cooperative, it would be interesting to investigate the strategic behavior of peers in universal swarm systems.

Acknowledgements

We would like to thank the anonymous reviewers for their helpful suggestions and insights. This work is supported in part by the FP7 EU project "SCAMPI" and the ANR French project "PROSE".

8. REFERENCES

[1] ALTMAN, E., NAIN, P., AND BERMOND, J.-C. Distributed storage management of evolving files in delay tolerant ad hoc networks. In *INFOCOM* (2009), pp. 1431 –1439.

[2] ALTMAN, E., NEGLIA, G., DE PELLEGRINI, F., AND MIORANDI, D. Decentralized stochastic control of delay tolerant networks. In *INFOCOM* (2009), pp. 1134 –1142.

[3] BOYD, S., AND VANDENBERGHE, L. *Convex Optimization*. Cambridge University Press, 2004.

[4] CHAINTREAU, A., LE BOUDEC, J.-Y., AND RISTANOVIC, N. The age of gossip: spatial mean field regime. In *SIGMETRICS* (2009), pp. 109–120.

[5] COHEN, E., AND SHENKER, S. Replication strategies in unstructured peer-to-peer networks. *SIGCOMM Comput. Commun. Rev. 32* (2002), 177–190.

[6] HAJEK, B., AND ZHU, J. The missing piece syndrome in peer-to-peer communication. *Information Theory Proceedings, 2010 IEEE International Symposium on* (June 2010), 1748 –1752.

[7] HU, L., LE BOUDEC, J.-Y., AND VOJNOVIAE, M. Optimal channel choice for collaborative ad-hoc dissemination. In *INFOCOM* (2010).

[8] IOANNIDIS, S., CHAINTREAU, A., AND MASSOULIÉ, L. Optimal and scalable distribution of content updates over a mobile social network. In *INFOCOM* (2009).

[9] IOANNIDIS, S., MASSOULIÉ, L., AND CHAINTREAU, A. Distributed caching over heterogeneous mobile networks. In *SIGMETRICS* (2010), pp. 311–322.

[10] MASSOULIÉ, L. Structural properties of proportional fairness: Stability and insensitivity. *The Annals of Applied Probability 17*, 3 (2007), 809–839.

[11] MASSOULIÉ, L., AND TWIGG, A. Rate-optimal schemes for peer-to-peer live streaming. *Perform. Eval. 65* (November 2008), 804–822.

[12] MASSOULIÉ, L., AND VOJNOVIC, M. Coupon replication systems. *Networking, IEEE/ACM Transactions on 16*, 3 (June 2008), 603 –616.

[13] QIU, D., AND SRIKANT, R. Modeling and performance analysis of BitTorrent-like peer-to-peer networks. *SIGCOMM Comput. Commun. Rev. 34* (2004), 367–378.

[14] REICH, J., AND CHAINTREAU, A. The age of impatience: optimal replication schemes for opportunistic networks. In *CoNEXT* (2009), pp. 85–96.

[15] TOWSLEY, D. The internet is flat: a brief history of networking in the next ten years. In *PODC* (2008), pp. 11–12.

[16] ZHOU, X., IOANNIDIS, S., AND MASSOULIÉ, L. On the stability and optimality of universal swarms. Tech. rep., Technicolor, 2011.

An FPGA-Based Experimental Evaluation of Microprocessor Core Error Detection with Argus-2

Patrick J. Eibl
IBM
3039 E. Cornwallis Rd., Box 12195
Building 062/J211, RTP, NC 27709
patrickeibl@gmail.com

Albert Meixner
NVIDIA
2701 San Tomas Expy
Santa Clara, CA 95050
albert.meixner@gmail.com

Daniel J. Sorin
Duke University
PO Box 90291
Durham, NC 27708
sorin@ee.duke.edu

ABSTRACT

Recently, several researchers have proposed schemes for low-cost, low-power error detection in the processor core. In this work, we demonstrate that one particular scheme, an enhanced implementation of the Argus framework called Argus-2, is a viable option for industry adoption. Using an FPGA prototype, we experimentally evaluate Argus-2's ability to detect errors due to (a) all possible single stuck-at faults in a given core and (b) a statistically significant number of double stuck-at faults, including pairs of faults that are randomly located and pairs that are spatially correlated on the chip.

Categories

C.4 [Performance of Systems] Fault tolerance

General Terms

Measurement, Reliability

Keywords

computer architecture, error detection, dynamic verification

1. INTRODUCTION

Fault tolerance is becoming increasingly desirable as CMOS technology progresses to ever-smaller feature sizes and increasing susceptibility to errors [2]. Recently, several researchers have proposed schemes to address the need for low-cost, low-power error detection in the processor core. Some notable schemes include redundant multithreading [6], DIVA [1], and Argus [4]. Of these schemes, Argus appears to be the most power-efficient, especially for detecting errors in the simple, low-power cores that are expected to dominate many-core processors. However, we are unaware of any company moving to adopt any of these schemes, despite their promise, and one factor in this reluctance is a lack of conclusive experimental or analytical evidence that these low-cost schemes provide sufficient error coverage. The goal of our work is to conclusively demonstrate that one particular low-cost error detection scheme, an enhanced implementation of the Argus framework called Argus-2, is a viable option for industry adoption.

2. ARGUS

We first explain the Argus framework for detecting errors and then describe the one particular implementation of the Argus framework that we evaluate in this paper.

2.1 High-Level Overview of Argus

Argus is a framework for detecting errors within a processor core by checking invariants at run-time. By checking invariants, instead of checking components, implementations of Argus can be significantly less costly than DMR. The key insight is that, at a high level, a Von Neumann core performs only four activities: choosing the sequence of instructions to execute ("control flow"), performing the computation specified by each instruction ("computation"), passing the result of each instruction to its data-dependent instructions ("dataflow"), and interacting with memory ("memory"). The Argus framework consists of checking each of these four activities at runtime. An implementation of Argus consists of four checkers—for control flow, dataflow, computation, and memory—and it has been proven that a perfect implementation of Argus can detect almost all possible processor errors. Implementations are likely to be imperfect, however, due to cost/reliability tradeoffs. For example, a checker that uses lossy signatures or checksums is imperfect, yet may be an appropriate design decision due to its low cost.

Control Flow Checking. Control flow checkers [8] periodically compare the static control flow graph of the program binary to the dynamic control flow graph of the runtime execution. If the static and dynamic control flow graphs differ, an error has been detected. When used in isolation, a control flow checker detects errors in fetch logic, branch destination computation, and PC update logic.

Dataflow Checking. A dataflow checker [5] compares the static dataflow graph of the program binary to the dataflow graph reconstructed at runtime. If they differ, an error has been detected. When used in isolation, a dataflow checker detects errors in many activities, some of which only apply to superscalar processors; these activities include fetch, decode, register rename, register read and write, and instruction scheduling (reorder buffer, load-store queue, reservation stations, etc.).

Computation Checking. There is a long history of research in low-cost checkers for the functional units that perform the computations in processor cores. The key to these checkers is that it is fundamentally easier to check a computation than to perform it in the first place. Sellers et al.'s book [7] on error detecting logic provides an excellent survey of checkers for adders, multipliers, dividers, bit-wise logic units, etc.

Memory Checking. The main error hazard in the memory is due to data corruption. Error detecting codes (EDC) and error correcting codes (ECC) are well-known, low-cost solutions for protecting the integrity of caches and DRAM.

2.2 Argus-2 Implementation

Argus is a framework, and there are many implementations that satisfy this framework. We started with the original Argus-1 implementation [4] and we created the Argus-2 implementation by enhancing Argus-1 to reduce its implementation costs and to plug numerous error detection holes that were revealed during preliminary experiments.

Both Argus-2 and Argus-1 are based on the same baseline core, the OpenRISC 1200 core [3]. The OR1200 processor core is a 32-bit scalar (1-wide), in-order RISC core with a 4-stage pipeline. This core represents the low-end of the simple cores that are expected to be used, perhaps in conjunction with a small number of superscalar cores, in multicore chips. The Argus approach to error detection applies to any Von Neumann core, not just the OR1200, but we chose the OR1200 because it is representative of the simple, power-efficient cores that are attractive for embedded applications and many-core architectures.

3. EXPERIMENTAL METHODOLOGY

The primary purposes of the experimental evaluation are to determine Argus-2's ability to detect errors and its costs.

3.1 Experimental Testbed

We performed all of our experiments on Altera DE2 prototyping boards that contain a Cyclone II FPGA. The primary advantage of using the prototyping boards, rather than simulation, is speed.

3.2 Fault Model

Our fault model consists of single and double stuck-at faults, and these faults can occur at the output of any gate in the circuit, *including Argus-2 logic itself*. For single faults, we exhaustively explore every possibility. For the double stuck-at faults, we sample from the enormous space of all possible double faults so as to achieve 95% confidence that our results are within a small percentage of the exhaustive (un-sampled) results. We consider both random fault locations and spatially correlated locations (i.e., the two faults are spatially near each other).

3.3 Workload

Each experiment involves injecting of one or two faults from the fault model described in Section 3.2 and then observing the behavior of the system while the processor runs a given software workload. The workload that we have chosen is the decoding of jpeg images. The benchmark runs for a significant amount of time (2.4 seconds) on real hardware, which is enough time to decode two images and execute approximately 60 million instructions.

4. EXPERIMENTAL RESULTS

We evaluated error detection coverage, area, and performance.
Error Detection Coverage. Of all possible single stuck-at faults, only 0.013% of them lead to errors that are both unmasked and undetected by Argus-2 (i.e., silent data corruptions or SDCs). Furthermore, for our large sample of double stuck-at faults, fewer than 0.023% of them lead to SDCs. Among the double stuck-at faults, the spatially correlated fault pairs were slightly less likely to lead to SDCs. These small fractions of SDCs show that Argus-2 is a viable option for industry. Figure 1 shows results for single and double stuck-at-one faults. The large fraction of faults that are masked (i.e., have no impact on application behavior) are primarily due to faults in components that are either never or rarely used (e.g., multiply-accumulate unit) and faults in Argus-2's hardware.

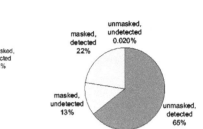

Figure 1. Error detection results

Area Overhead. The hardware for Argus-2 consumes some amount of chip area. Our results show that Argus-2's core overhead (not including the caches) is 12.2%, and its total chip area overhead (with the caches) is 3.7%. These results confirm that Argus-2's overhead is far less than DMR.

Performance. Argus's performance impact is due to the NOP instructions it adds into the binary for purposes of checking control flow and dataflow. Argus-2 adds, on average, 7% to the static instruction count and 3.5% to the dynamic instruction count. The increase in dynamic instruction count has a performance overhead that averages less than 4%.

5. CONCLUSIONS

We conclude that Argus-2 is ready to be adopted by industry. An extremely small fraction of single and double faults cause silent data corruptions, which we believe is sufficient for the vast majority of commodity processors. Argus-2 is the first approach to provide complete coverage of permanent and transient faults at low cost, even for simple cores.

6. ACKNOWLEDGMENTS

This material is based on work supported by the National Science Foundation under grant CCR-044516.

REFERENCES

[1] T. M. Austin. DIVA: A Reliable Substrate for Deep Submicron Microarchitecture Design. In *Proc. 32nd Annual IEEE/ACM Int'l Symposium on Microarchitecture*, Nov. 1999.

[2] International Technology Roadmap for Semiconductors, 2007.

[3] D. Lampret. OpenRISC 1200 IP Core Specification, Rev. 0.7. http://www.opencores.org, Sept. 2001.

[4] A. Meixner, M. E. Bauer, and D. J. Sorin. Argus: Low-Cost, Comprehensive Error Detection in Simple Cores. In *Proc. of the 40th Annual Int'l Symp. on Microarchitecture*, Dec. 2007.

[5] A. Meixner and D. J. Sorin. Error Detection Using Dynamic Dataflow Verification. In *Proc. of the Int'l Conf. on Parallel Architectures and Compilation Techniques*, Sept. 2007.

[6] E. Rotenberg. AR-SMT: A Microarchitectural Approach to Fault Tolerance in Microprocessors. In *Proc. of the 29th Int'l Symposium on Fault-Tolerant Computing Systems*, June 1999.

[7] F. F. Sellers, M.-Y. Hsiao, and L. W. Bearnson. *Error Detecting Logic for Digital Computers*. McGraw Hill Book Company, 1968.

[8] N. J. Warter and W.-M. W. Hwu. A Software Based Approach to Achieving Optimal Performance for Signature Control Flow Checking. In *Proc. of the 20th Int'l Symposium on Fault-Tolerant Computing Systems*, June 1990.

The Role of KL Divergence in Anomaly Detection

Lele Zhang
The University of Melbourne
lz@unimelb.edu.au

Darryl Veitch
The University of Melbourne
dveitch@unimelb.edu.au

Kotagiri Ramamohanarao
The University of Melbourne
rao@cs.mu.oz.au

ABSTRACT

We study the role of Kullback-Leibler divergence in the framework of anomaly detection, where its abilities as a statistic underlying detection have never been investigated in depth. We give an in-principle analysis of network attack detection, showing explicitly attacks may be masked at minimal cost through 'camouflage'. We illustrate on both synthetic distributions and ones taken from real traffic.

Categories and Subject Descriptors

C.2.3 [**Computer-Communication Networks**]: Network Operations—*Network Monitoring*

General Terms

Measurement, Security

Keywords

Anomaly Detection, KL Divergence

1. INTRODUCTION

Kullback-Leibler Divergence (KLD) is a well known measure of the distance $\mathbf{KL}(\mathcal{P}, \mathcal{Q})$ of some distribution $\mathcal{P}$ to a reference distribution $\mathcal{Q}$. By viewing $\mathcal{Q}$ as a multi-dimensional parameter, the KLD can be used as a rich family of statistics, including Shannon entropy (uniform $\mathcal{Q}$). As a flexible generalization of entropy, the KLD has begun to be used [1, 3, 4], following the popularity of entropy in network attack detection (e.g. [2]). Despite its direct importance to detection, the question "what entropy or KLD is capable of seeing" is rarely asked, much less answered. This paper, through analyzing the optimal camouflage problem, explores the limitations of the detection statistic, which is both important and timely.

2. KLD IN ATTACK DETECTION

2.1 Network Model

Traffic We view Internet traffic as an infinite stream of packets passing by a passive monitoring point, processed in batches according to contiguous constant width measurement intervals. Within a single such interval consisting of V packets, given a metric of interest (a function of packet header information and/or the data payload itself), each packet is mapped to one of N classes, resulting in a sequence $(c_1, c_2 \ldots, c_V)$ over the interval where $c_j \in \{1, 2, \ldots, N\}$.

The relative frequencies of the N possible outcomes constitute the histogram, namely, $\mathcal{P} = \{p_i\}$, where $p_i = f_i/V$ and $f_i = |\{j : c_j = i\}|$ for $1 \leq i \leq N$.

Detector We assume that the detector has a reference distribution $\mathcal{Q} = \{q_1, q_2, \ldots, q_N\}$, and also knows the histogram $\mathcal{P}$ from the current time bin, summarized by KLD, which is defined as $\mathbf{KL}(\mathcal{P}, \mathcal{Q}) = \sum_{i=1}^{N} p_i \log \frac{p_i}{q_i}$ with $0 \cdot \log 0 = 0$ and logarithms are to the base 2. The detection mechanism is simple: an attack is declared if the KLD differs from some normal value $\mathbf{KL}_0$ more than a threshold $\theta_{\mathbf{KL}} (\geq 0)$, and the detector is silent if $\mathbf{KL}(\mathcal{P}, \mathcal{Q})$ falls in the interval $[0, \mathbf{KL}_0 + \theta_{\mathbf{KL}}]$. All the effects that make the detection difficult, such as the determination of $\mathcal{P}, \mathcal{Q}, \mathbf{KL}_0$, are subsumed into the detection *sensitivity* $\theta_{\mathbf{KL}}$.

Attacker An *attacker* sends packets for malicious purposes. We model an attack by the number V_A of attack packets, passing by the monitoring point, the set $\mathcal{T}$ of class indices in which they appear for the chosen metric, and their distribution across $\mathcal{T}$. During an attack the measurement interval contains $V + V_A$ packets with the *normalized attack intensity* of V_A/V, resulting in the modified distribution $\mathcal{P}_A$.

For a given V_A, the attacker may have some flexibility through the choice of $\mathcal{T}$ to reduce his impact on KLD and hence the chance of detection. If that is impossible or insufficient, then the attacker may opt to augment it by sending a number V_C of additional *camouflage packets* per measurement interval, in a tailored spread over class indices designed to 'drag' the KLD back to some *target* $\mathbf{KL}_T$ lying within the normal range. The *normalized camouflage cost* is therefore V_C/V, and the total traffic volume becomes $V + V_A + V_C$. We denote the camouflaged distribution by $\mathcal{P}_C$. How to camouflage actively and efficiently is one of the main points we focus on. We assume *conservatively* that $\mathcal{P}, V$ and $\mathcal{Q}$ are known to the attacker so he can optimize it.

2.2 Optimal Camouflage

Based on the above model, we consider *optimal camouflage*: how to achieve $\mathbf{KL}_T$ at minimal cost. Let δ_i denote the increment of probability p_i due to camouflage for constant V and V_A. Then the camouflage cost is $V_C = (V + V_A) \sum_{i=1}^{N} \delta_i$. Thus, the *optimal camouflage optimization problem* is formulated as $\min_{\{\delta_i\}} \sum_{i=1}^{N} \delta_i$ s.t. $\delta_i \geq 0$ and $\mathbf{KL}(\mathcal{P}_C, \mathcal{Q}) = \mathbf{KL}_T$, where $\mathcal{P}_C = \{\frac{p_i + \delta_i}{1 + \sum_{i=1}^{N} \delta_i}\}$. This problem is best solved through the *inverse problem*, where we find the extreme KLD using a fixed increment 'budget'. Formally, the inverse problem is $\min_{\{\delta_i\}} \mathbf{KL}(\mathcal{P}_C, \mathcal{Q})$ for a constant $\Sigma = \sum_{i=1}^{N} \delta_i$, as by definition $\mathbf{KL}_T < \mathbf{KL}(\mathcal{P}_A, \mathcal{Q})$.

The optimal solution for the inverse problem, which is con-

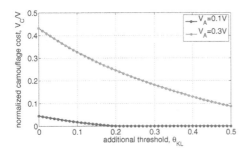

Figure 1: Normalized camouflage costs when attacking $t = 12$ with $V_A = 0.1V$ and $0.3V$ as a function of $\theta_{\mathbf{KL}}$.

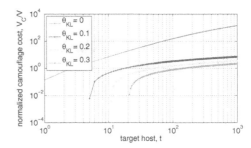

Figure 2: Normalized camouflage costs when attacking different hosts with $V_A = 0.1V$ for different detection sensitivities.

vex, is given by $\delta_i^* = (\zeta^* q_i - p_i)^+$ for each i where ζ^* is given by $\sum_{i=1}^{N} (\zeta^* q_i - p_i)^+ = \Sigma$. We observe that the minimal KLD decreases monotonically and continuously as the 'budget' Σ rises and reaches its minimum zero at $\Sigma = \Sigma_0$, where $\Sigma_0 = \sum_{i=1}^{N} (\eta^* p_i - q_i)$ with $\eta^* = \max_i p_i/q_i$ is precisely the minimal change required to transform $\mathcal{P}_C$ to the reference $\mathcal{Q}$. To solve for the original problem, a single parameter optimization problem in Σ is readily solved numerically.

2.3 Empirical Study

We show how the previous results can be used to answer core questions of interest to both the attacker and detector, such as whether an attack can be detected, whether it can be disguised and at what cost.

Traffic traces We use 24 hours, from 00:00 to 23:59 March 30, 2009, of a trace captured from an OC-3 link, obtained from the "Measurement and Analysis on the WIDE Internet" group (MAWI). We focus on mainly on a representative 5 minute time interval from 15:30.

We consider the packet count per source-port histograms and obtain the reference $\mathcal{Q}$ by average the traffic data over eight 5min intervals over the 24 hours. We apply *concentrated* attacks with intensities $V_A = 0.1V$ and $0.3V$ at a single class index i.e. $\mathcal{T} = \{t\} = \{12\}$. The attacker is aware that his attack has increased the original KLD $\mathbf{KL}_0 = 0.894$ appreciably by 22.7% and 92.4% respectively. Seeking complete anonymity, he wishes to lower the KLD through sending camouflage packets. Fig 1 shows the resulting normalized camouflage costs for lower the KLD to $\mathbf{KL}_T = \mathbf{KL}_0 + \theta_{\mathbf{KL}}$. Clearly, the higher intensity is the higher camouflage cost is required. For the relative moderate attack, $V_A = 0.1V$, the camouflage becomes "free" once $\theta_{\mathbf{KL}}$ goes beyond 0.17, whereas for the other attack the cost is always positive but reduces from 0.432 to 0.087 as $\theta_{\mathbf{KL}}$ grows from 0 to 0.5. We also examine other 7 bins over the 24 hours with similar results.

Synthetic distributions To investigate behavior as a function of parameters, we use a simplified model. We assume that the reference distribution and the normal traffic of the current time bin are the same, following Zipf law with $s = 1.5$ and $N = 1000$, and the attack intensity is $V_A = 0.1V$.
Concentrated attacks Fig 2 plots the cost for concealing concentrated attacks as a function of attacking host t. As expected, the detector is more sensitive to changes in small probabilities, and thus the camouflage cost is high for large t, in particular for small $\theta_{\mathbf{KL}}$. The results are generally valid for the attacks targeting a small number of indices.
Dispersed attacks For dispersed attacks we assume that $\mathcal{T}$ covers a wide contiguous range of the smallest proba-

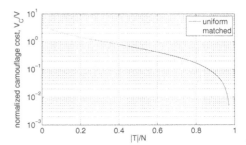

Figure 3: Normalized camouflage costs as a function of attacking range $|\mathcal{T}|/N$ with $V_A = 0.1V$ and $\theta_{\mathbf{KL}} = 0.1$.

bilities. We consider two distributions over $\mathcal{T}$: *uniform* where $V_A(t) = V_A/|\mathcal{T}|$ for each $t \in \mathcal{T}$, and *matched* where $V_A(t) = \zeta q_t$ for each $t \in \mathcal{T}$ with $\zeta = V_A/\sum_{i \in \mathcal{T}} q_i$. Fig 3 shows the camouflage costs for attacks with $V_A = 0.1$ and $\theta_{\mathbf{KL}} = 0.1$. The matched scheme always requires a lower camouflage cost than the uniform with the same attacking range. Clearly the difference between the schemes is more notable at large $|\mathcal{T}|/N$. Overall, we see that the attacker can greatly benefit from the flexibility in the attack scheme and the attacked range, by dispersing the attack traffic and matching the normal pattern, so as to eliminate the chance of being detected and/or to reduce his camouflage cost.

3. CONCLUSIONS

This is the first study which provides a rigorous quantitative analysis of the inherent suitability of KLD for anomaly detection. The results bring capabilities to calibrate detectors and to understand their limitations. The insights are valuable for more general settings, and the techniques can be extended to more realistic attack scenarios.

4. REFERENCES

[1] Y. Gu, A. McCallum, and D. Towsley. Detecting Anomalies in Network Traffic Using Maximum Entropy Estimation. In *5th Internet Measurement Conference*, pages 345–350, 2005.

[2] G. Nychis, V. Sekar, D. G. Andersen, H. Kim, and H. Zhang. An Empirical Evaluation of Entropy-based Traffic Anomaly Detection. In *8th ACM Internet Measurement Conference*, pages 151–156, 2008.

[3] K. Ramah Houerbi, K. Salamatian, and F. Kamoun. Scan Surveillance in Internet Networks. In *8th International IFIP-TC 6 Networking Conference*, pages 614–625, 2009.

[4] M. P. Stoecklin, J.-Y. L. Boudec, and A. Kind. A Two-Layered Anomaly Detection Technique based on Multi-Modal Flow Behavior Models. In *9th Intl. Conference on PAM*, pages 212–221, 2008.

Applying Idealized Lower-Bound Runtime Models to Understand Inefficiencies in Data-Intensive Computing

Elie Krevat*, Tomer Shiran*, Eric Anderson†, Joseph Tucek†, Jay J. Wylie†, Gregory R. Ganger*

*Carnegie Mellon University †HP Labs

Categories and Subject Descriptors

D.4.8 [**Operating Systems**]: Performance—*Measurements, Modeling and prediction, Operational analysis*; C.4 [**Performance of Systems**]: Modeling techniques

General Terms

Measurement, Performance

1. INTRODUCTION

"Data-intensive scalable computing" (DISC) refers to a rapidly growing style of computing characterized by its reliance on large and expanding datasets [3]. Driven by the desire and capability to extract insight from such datasets, DISC is quickly emerging as a major activity of many organizations. Map-reduce style programming frameworks such as MapReduce [4] and Hadoop [1] support DISC activities by providing abstractions and frameworks to more easily scale data-parallel computations over commodity machines.

In the pursuit of scale, popular map-reduce frameworks neglect efficiency as an important metric. Anecdotal experiences indicate that they neither achieve balance nor full goodput of hardware resources, effectively wasting a large fraction of the computers over which jobs are scaled. If these inefficiencies are real, the same work could be completed at much lower costs. An ideal run would provide maximum scalability for a given computation without wasting resources. Given the widespread use and scale of DISC systems, it is important that we move closer to frameworks that are "hardware-efficient," where the framework provides sufficient parallelism to keep the bottleneck resource fully utilized and makes good use of all I/O components.

An important first step is to understand the degree, characteristics, and causes of inefficiency. We have a simple model that predicts the idealized lower-bound runtime of a map-reduce workload by assuming an even data distribution, that data is perfectly pipelined through sequential operations, and that the underlying I/O resources are utilized at their full bandwidths whenever applicable. The model's input parameters describe basic characteristics of the job (e.g., amount of input data), of the hardware (e.g., per-node disk and network throughputs), and of the framework configuration (e.g., replication factor). The output is the idealized runtime.

The goal of the model is not to accurately predict the runtime of a job on any given system, but to indicate what the runtime theoretically *should* be. To focus the evaluation on the efficiency of the programming framework, and not the entire software stack, measured values of I/O bandwidths are used as inputs to the model, or predicted values are used if the actual hardware is not available. Indeed, our analysis of a number of published benchmark results, on presumably well-tuned systems, reveal runtimes that are 3–13× longer than the ideal model suggests should be possible (due to space constraints, see the full length paper [5]).

We haven't yet determined why well-used map-reduce frameworks exhibit large slowdowns, although there are many possibilities. Instead, we focus on a limited but efficient parallel dataflow system called Parallel DataSeries (PDS), which lacks many features of other frameworks, but its careful engineering and stripped-down feature-set demonstrate that near-ideal hardware efficiency (within ∼20%) is possible. PDS is used to explore the fundamental sources of inefficiency common to commodity disk and network-dependent DISC frameworks; any remaining inefficiencies of popular map-reduce systems must then be specific to the framework or additional features that are not part of PDS (e.g., distributed file system integration, dynamic task distribution, or fault tolerance). Our experiments point to straggler effects from disk-to-disk variability and network slowdown effects from the all-to-all data shuffle as responsible for the bulk of PDS's inefficiencies, and therefore a performance issue for DISC frameworks in general.

2. PERFORMANCE MODEL

The idealized runtime model is intended for data-intensive workloads where computation time is negligible in comparison to I/O speeds, which applies to many grep- and sort-like jobs that are representative of MapReduce jobs at Google [4]. Other simplifying assumptions are that the network is capable of full bisection bandwidth, input data is distributed evenly across a homogeneous set of nodes, and one job runs at a time.

The model calculates the total time by breaking a map-reduce dataflow into two pipelined phases, where the pipeline is as fast as the slowest I/O component in each phase. The first phase of a parallel dataflow reads data, processes it in the map operator, and shuffles it over the network. A barrier occurs just before the local sort at the destination node, separating the two phases, since the last element to arrive may in fact be the first to go out in sorted order. The second phase begins with a local sort, passes data through the reduce operator, and writes data back to disk (possibly replicated).

Inputs to the model include the amount of input data (i), the speed of a disk read (D_r), disk write (D_w), and network transfer (N), and the amount of data flowing through the system at any time. The full model accounts for different configurations of a parallel map-reduce, including data replication levels, in-memory vs. 2-phase local sorts, and optional backup writes after the map phase. Due to space constraints, we only include a simplified version of our model that applies to a parallel sort with no additional replication, an in-memory sort, and no backup write:

$$t_{sort} = \frac{i}{n} \left(max \left\{ \frac{1}{D_r}, \frac{n-1}{nN} \right\} + \frac{1}{D_w} \right)$$

In this equation, the time to complete the first phase is just the maximum of the two pipelined operations of reading data from local disk ($\frac{1}{D_r}$) and shuffling the data over the network. The $\frac{n-1}{n}$ term appears in the equation, where n is the number of nodes, because in a perfectly-balanced system each node partitions and transfers that fraction of its mapped data over the network, keeping $\frac{1}{n}$ of the data for itself. The time for the second phase is then just the time taken to write the output data back to local disk ($\frac{1}{D_w}$). Parameter values are determined via measurements through the OS, so any inefficiencies are those of the programming framework.

3. EXPLORING EFFICIENCY OF DISC

We performed disk and network microbenchmarks to measure the maximum achievable I/O speeds on our cluster, where each node consists of two quad-core Intel Xeon processors, 16 GB of RAM, and a Seagate Barracuda ES.2 SATA drive. Microbenchmark results show a large variation of disk and network shuffle speeds across homogeneous nodes, contributing to slower PDS parallel sorts than computed with our idealized model. The straggler problem is well-known [2] and was not unexpected. However, our approach to investigating stragglers is to understand why they fundamentally exist and how much of their impact is necessary. With PDS, we can achieve within 21% of the model's idealized runtime.

Disk microbenchmarks: Bandwidth is measured with the dd utility and large file and block sizes. On a single node, XFS filesystems have consistent read performance (averaging 107 MB/s) and varying writes between 88–100 MB/s (averaging 99 MB/s). However, the speeds can vary over the entire cluster from 102–113 MB/s for reads and 87–107 MB/s for writes, both with a standard deviation of 2. Some of this variability in bandwidth of otherwise identical make and model disks is due to XFS placement policies, but the majority is due to a technique in modern disks that we refer to as *adaptive zoning* [6], where traditional zoning schemes have been extended to maximize platter densities post-production according to the capabilities of each disk head.

Network microbenchmarks: With our all-to-all network microbenchmark that analyzes just the network component of a map-reduce shuffle, we measured bi-directional bandwidth between two nodes of 112 MB/s over 1 Gbps Ethernet. The resulting throughput for completing a larger 4-way shuffle drops under 104 MB/s, and then slowly decreases to 98 MB/s at 32 nodes and under 94 MB/s at 64 nodes. Some of TCP's unfairness and stability issues are known and prompting further research, however, we have found no previous research specifically targeting TCP's all-to-all network performance in high-bandwidth low-latency environments. The closest other issue that we know of is the incast problem [7], a 2–3× order of magnitude collapse in network bandwidth during an all-to-one pattern of synchronized reads.

PDS sort evaluation: Parallel DataSeries is an efficient and flexible data format and library that supports passing records in a parallel and pipeline fashion through a series of modules. As presented in Figure 1 for up to 41 nodes, PDS parallel sort times increase from 8% to 21% longer than an ideal model input with measured disk and network bandwidth. On a single node, about 4% of lost efficiency is from a known data expansion when converting inputs. The in-memory sort takes about 2 seconds, which accounts for another 2–3% of the overhead. These two factors explain the majority of the 8% overhead of the single node case.

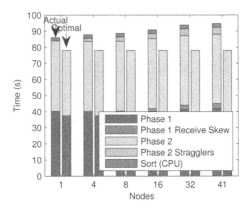

Figure 1: Using Parallel DataSeries to sort up to 164 GB over 1 Gbps Ethernet, completion times slowly increase from 8% to 21% higher than an idealized lower-bound prediction that inaccurately assumes full disk and network performance.

The growing divergence of larger parallel sorts from the model is explainable by a number of factors, including disk stragglers and network skew and slowdown effects. The *Stragglers* category in the time breakdown accounts for 5% additional overhead and represents the average time that a node wastes by waiting for the last node in the job to finish. Most of the straggler effects broken out in the figure are caused by the different disk write speeds from Phase 2 of the map-reduce, as the sort barrier forces synchronization before a node completes Phase 1. A similar disk skew occurs in Phase 1 from reading data from disk, but it is further complicated by delays in the network shuffle. Broken out in the figure is a 4% overhead from the *Phase 1 Receive Skew*, which is the average difference of each node's last incoming flow completion time and its average incoming flow completion time. This skew suggests an unfairness across network flows, and is compounded by a general slowdown in network speeds that causes a delay in the completion of Phase 1.

Building a balanced system becomes more complicated with the observed disk and network effects. It was surprising that even with a perfectly balanced workload, without any data skew, there was still a significant effect from disk stragglers. Additional experiments with a faster network showed that disk stragglers are not a continuously growing effect, but they are present, and even one particularly slow node can have a large impact. Our system configuration initially pointed to disk bandwidth as the slowest component. However, the results of our network microbenchmark are confirmed by the actual performance of PDS—the slower network shuffle speeds for Phase 1 become the bottleneck at around 16 nodes and are responsible for the growing divergence from the model.

4. REFERENCES

[1] Apache Hadoop. http://hadoop.apache.org/.

[2] G. Ananthanarayanan, et al. Reining in the Outliers in Map-Reduce Clusters using Mantri. OSDI, 2010.

[3] R. E. Bryant. *Data-Intensive Supercomputing: The Case for DISC*. Technical report. 2007. CMU-CS-07-128.

[4] J. Dean and S. Ghemawat. MapReduce: Simplified Data Processing on Large Clusters. *Communications of the ACM*, 2008.

[5] E. Krevat, et al. *Applying Simple Performance Models to Understand Inefficiencies in Data-Intensive Computing*. Technical report. 2011. CMU-PDL-11-103.

[6] E. Krevat, et al. Disks Are Like Snowflakes: No Two Are Alike. HotOS, 2011.

[7] A. Phanishayee, et al. Measurement and Analysis of TCP Throughput Collapse in Cluster-based Storage Systems. FAST, 2008.

How Prevalent is Content Bundling in BitTorrent?

Jinyoung Han
Seoul National University
jyhan@mmlab.snu.ac.kr

Taejoong Chung
Seoul National University
tjchung@mmlab.snu.ac.kr

Seungbae Kim
Seoul National University
sbkim@mmlab.snu.ac.kr

Ted "Taekyoung" Kwon
Seoul National University
tkkwon@snu.ac.kr

Hyun-chul Kim
Seoul National University
hkim@mmlab.snu.ac.kr

Yanghee Choi
Seoul National University
yhchoi@snu.ac.kr

ABSTRACT

Despite the increasing interest in content bundling in Bit-Torrent systems, there are still few empirical studies on the bundling practice in real BitTorrent communities. In this paper, we conduct comprehensive measurements on one of the largest BitTorrent portals: The Pirate Bay. From the torrents data set collected for 38 days from April to May, 2010, we study how prevalent bundling is and how many files are bundled in a torrent, across different types of contents shared: Movie, Porn, TV, Music, Application, E-book, and Game.

Categories and Subject Descriptors

H.4.3 [**Information Systems Applications**]: Communications Applications

General Terms

Measurement

Keywords

BitTorrent, Content Bundling, Measurement

1. INTRODUCTION

According to the Ipoque's report in 2009 [1], BitTorrent accounts for approximately 27-55% of Internet traffic. The huge success of BitTorrent is attributed to the attractive properties of its swarming operations. First, the swarming technique scales well even in the presence of flash crowds for popular files. Second, cooperations among peers in a swarm stimulated by the tit-for-tat incentive mechanism improve the overall system performance like throughput. Third, the tit-for-tat mechanism also addresses the free-riding problem.

Despite the success of BitTorrent, its swarming system suffers from a fundamental limitation: little or no availability of unpopular files [6]. That is, peers arriving after the initial flash crowd may end up with finding the file unavailable [6]. Recently, *bundling*[1] in peer-to-peer (P2P) swarming systems like BitTorrent has gained much attention, as it

[1]Bundling is a common practice in which a publisher packages multiple files (e.g. multiple episodes of the same sitcom) and disseminates them via a single swarm [6], instead of disseminating individual files via separate swarms.

SIGMETRICS'11, June 7–11, 2011, San Jose, California, USA.
ACM 978-1-4503-0262-3/11/06.

can mitigate the availability problem of unpopular files [5,6] as well as reduce download times [4–6].

However, to our knowledge, there have been few efforts to empirically investigate the practice of content bundling in P2P swarming systems. Most of the prior studies on bundling have been carried out by making simple assumptions on bundling strategies and users' accesses to bundles with no empirical basis, which motivates our measurement study on the bundling practices of the BitTorrent users.

As a first step towards providing empirical grounds for understanding and modeling content bundling in BitTorrent, we make the following contributions: (1) to our knowledge, this is the first measurement study on the bundling practice by observing one of the largest real BitTorrent portals – The Pirate Bay [2]. For 38 days, we have collected the trace data on 114 K torrents containing 1.6 M files. (2) We find that around 70% of BitTorrent torrents contain multiple files, i.e., bundling is widely used. (3) We find that the total volume of multi-file [2] torrents outweighs that of single-file ones; the volume of multi-file torrents accounts for over 80% of the total data volume contained in all the torrents in our data. (4) We show how many files are bundled in a multi-file torrent, across different types of contents shared: Movie, Porn, TV, Music, Application, E-book, and Game.

2. METHODOLOGY

We conducted a measurement study on a real BitTorrent portal, The Pirate Bay (TPB) [2], one of the most popular torrent hosting sites. For the purpose of data collection, we developed a crawling agent to periodically fetch newly released ".torrent" files[3]. For each torrent, the torrent metadata which consists of its .torrent information, category given by the torrent publisher, and published time is recorded.

Our datasets have been collected from April 22 to May 29, 2010. Our crawling agent fetched the torrent data of 113,993 torrents from TPB, which contain 1,642,299 files. Throughout this paper, we investigate the bundling practice from the seven major (86% and 83% in terms of the total torrent counts and data volume, respectively) content categories given by the torrent publisher: Movie, Porn, TV,

[2]Throughout this paper, multi-file torrent indicates bundled torrent which contains multiple files, while single-file torrent indicates non-bundled torrent which contains a single file.

[3]Note that *a .torrent file* contains the metadata of content file(s) to download such as its name, size, and the tracker information, whereas *a torrent* refers to content file(s) to download in a swarm.

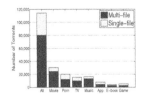

(a) The numbers of torrents

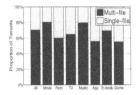

(b) Percentage of torrent counts

Figure 1: Bundling is widely used in BitTorrent.

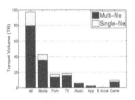

(a) Total volume of data

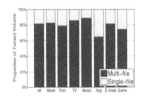

(b) Percentage of data volume

Figure 2: Total volume of multi-file torrents is substantially larger than that of single-file ones.

Music, Application, E-book and Game. The number of torrents (and total volume of data contained in the torrents) of the Movie, Porn, TV, Music, Application, E-book and Game categories constitute approximately 26% (36%), 17% (15%), 13% (16%), 14% (5%), 7% (2%), 4% (1%), and 5% (8%) of all the torrents at TPB, respectively.

3. BUNDLING PRACTICE

To analyze how prevalent content bundling is in BitTorrent, we first compare multi-file torrents with single-file ones in terms of the number and total volume of data contained in the torrents. Figure 1 shows that around 70% of the torrents contain multiple files, which means content bundling is widely used. In the Music category, over 80% of the torrents are multi-file ones, which indicates that BitTorrent users often share a collection of music files from the same genre, player, composer, or album. Likewise, over 80% of the torrents in the Movie category are multi-file ones, mostly because users often package: (i) multiple movie files of the same series (e.g. sequels), or (ii) a main video file and other supplementary files like subtitles. Meanwhile, around 50% of the torrents in the Application and Game categories are bundled; almost half of the torrents in these categories have a single compressed file, while the other half of the torrents consist of multiple files (e.g. installation files and subsidiary files such as how-to documents).

We next compare the total data volume contained in multi-file and single-file torrents in Figure 2. Figures 2(a) and 2(b) show that the total volume of multi-file torrents outweighs that of single-file ones; the volume of multi-file torrents accounts for over 80% of all the data that we investigated. The volume of all the torrents reaches around 100 TB.

Finally, we investigate how many files are bundled in the multi-file torrents. Total number of files of all the 80,152 multi-file torrents is 1,608,458; i.e, 20 files per multi-file torrent in average. Figure 3 shows the CDF of the number of

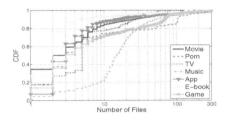

Figure 3: Number of files in a multi-file torrent

files in a multi-file torrent across different categories of torrents. As shown in Figure 3, multi-file torrents of the Music category contain significantly more number of files than those of the other categories; almost 80% of Music multi-file torrents contain more than 10 files. In contrast, 90% of E-book multi-file torrents are comprised of less than 4 files. Note that in the Porn multi-file torrents, around 70% contain less than 7 files, while over 16% contain a large number of files; over 100.

4. CONCLUDING REMARKS

We conducted measurements on the bundling practice from one of the largest BitTorrent portals: The Pirate Bay. From the BitTorrent data set collected for 38 days, we found that bundling is widespread for file sharing. Depending on the content categories such as movies and music, the bundling practice showed a wide variety of characteristics in terms of the number of files bundled in a torrent. Our ongoing work includes investigation of (i) how users access the bundled files in comparison with the non-bundled ones, and (ii) whether and how bundling patterns are similar or different, depending on the main incentives of content publishers: altruistic or profit-driven [3].

5. ACKNOWLEDGMENTS

This work was supported by NAP of Korea Research Council of Fundamental Science and Technology and the ITRC support program NIPA-2011-(C1090-1111-0004) of MKE/NIPA. The ICT at Seoul National University provided research facilities for this study.

6. REFERENCES

[1] The impact of p2p file sharing, voice over ip, instant messaging, one-click hosting and media streaming on the internet. http://www.ipoque.com/resources/internet-studies/internet-study-2008_2009.

[2] The pirate bay. http://thepiratebay.org/.

[3] R. Cuevas, M. Kryczka, A. Cuevas, S. Kaune, C. Guerrero, and R. Rejaie. Is content publishing in bittorrent altruistic or profit-driven? In *ACM CoNEXT*, 2010.

[4] N. Lev-tov, N. Carlsson, Z. Li, C. Williamson, and S. Zhang. Dynamic file-selection policies for bundling in bittorrent-like systems. In *IEEE IWQOS*, 2010.

[5] D. S. Menasche, G. Neglia, D. Towsley, and S. Zilberstein. Strategic reasoning about bundling in swarming systems. In *IEEE GameNets*, 2009.

[6] D. S. Menasche, A. A. Rocha, B. Li, D. Towsley, and A. Venkataramani. Content availability and bundling in swarming systems. In *ACM CoNEXT*, 2009.

Self-Adaptive Provisioning of Virtualized Resources in Cloud Computing

Jia Rao, Xiangping Bu, Kun Wang, Cheng-Zhong Xu,
Dept. of Electrical and Computer Engineering
Wayne State University
Detroit, Michigan, USA
{jrao, xpbu, kwang, czxu}@wayne.edu

ABSTRACT

In this paper, we propose a distributed learning mechanism that facilitates self-adaptive virtual machines resource provisioning. We treat cloud resource allocation as a distributed learning task, in which each VM being a highly autonomous agent submits resource requests according to its own benefit. The mechanism evaluates the requests and replies with feedbacks. We develop a reinforcement learning algorithm with a highly efficient representation of experiences as the heart of the VM side learning engine. We prototype the mechanism and the distributed learning algorithm in an iBalloon system. Experiment results on a Xen-based cloud testbed demonstrate the effectiveness of iBalloon.

Categories and Subject Descriptors

D.4.8 [**Performance**]: Measurements, Modeling and prediction

General Terms

Management, Measurement, Performance

Keywords

Cloud management, Reinforcement learning, Autonomic computing

1. INTRODUCTION

In cloud computing, applications running within virtual machines (VM) can have on-demand access to compute resources in response to increased application loads. On the other hand, virtual resources can also be maintained at a minimal level during off-peak periods in order to reduce cost. Thus, VM resources should be dynamically provisioned to match actual application demands, rather than the peak one. However, these demands are difficult to estimate due to time-varying workload and complex resource to application performance relationships. More importantly, client-perceived quality-of-service (QoS) should still be maintained in the presence of background dynamic resource provisioning. These observations call for an effective approach that automates the capacity management of VMs for cloud users.

To realize automatic VM capacity management, a mathematical model that captures the relationship of allocated capacity and application-level performance is necessary. However, the determination of the system model in a dynamic

SIGMETRICS'11, June 7–11, 2011, San Jose, California, USA.
ACM 978-1-4503-0262-3/11/06.

cloud environment is not trivial. Workload dynamics and performance interference in the cloud can possibly make prior system models no longer fit. Furthermore, in fine-grained resource provisioning, VMs may need minutes to get its performance stabilized after a capacity reconfiguration. The difficulty in evaluating the immediate output of resource allocations makes the modeling of application performance even harder. With the proliferation of multi-tier and cluster applications, VMs that need to be simultaneously managed may span multiple physical machines. The physical deployment of the dependent VMs is usually transparent to cloud users. The challenges motivate us to develop an adaptive and scalable approach that deals with workload and cloud dynamics and is able to coordinate the resource allocations on multiple machines.

Our previous work [1] demonstrated the efficacy of reinforcement learning (RL)-based resource allocation in a cloud environment. We applied a centralized RL approach to optimize system-wide VM performance in one physical machine. The RL agent operates on state spaces defined on co-running VM configurations and employs neural network-based models to map global VM configurations to system-wide performance. Although effective on one host, the centralized management can not be extended to a practical scale with a large number of VMs. First, resource allocation is limited to one machine and can not deal with virtual clusters spanning on multiple hosts. Second, the complexity of training and maintaining the models grows exponentially with the number of VMs, which is prohibitively expensive expensive in a practical scale. Finally, the models based on VM configurations are not robust to workload dynamics. In this paper, we address the issues and present a distributed learning mechanism for cloud management.

2. THE DESIGN OF IBALLOON

We design iBalloon as a distributed management framework, in which individual VMs initialize the capacity management. For better portability and scalability, we decouple the functionality of iBalloon into three components: `Host-agent`, `App-agent` and `Decision-maker`. Figure 1 illustrates the architecture of iBalloon as well as its interactions with a VM. `Host-agent`, one per physical machine, is responsible for allocating the host's hardware resources to VMs and gives feedback. `App-agent` maintains application SLA profiles and reports run-time application performance. `Decision-maker` hosts a learning agent for each VM for automatic capacity management. A VM's capacity can be changed by altering the VCPU number, memory size and I/O bandwidth. The management operation to one VM is defined as

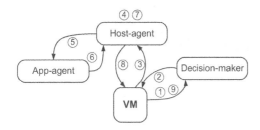

Figure 1: The architecture and working flow of iBalloon. (1) The VM reports running status. (2) Decision-maker replies with a capacity suggestion. (3) The VM submits the resource request. (4) Host-agent synchronously collects all VMs' requests, reconfigures VM resources and sleeps for a management interval. (5)-(6) Host-agent queries App-agent for VMs' application-level performance. (7)-(8) Host-agent calculates and sends the feedback. (9) The VM wraps the information about this interaction and reports to Decision-maker. (10) Decision-maker updates the capacity management policy for this VM accordingly.

the combination of three meta operations on each resource: *increase*, *decrease* and *nop*.

VM Running Status. We define the VM running status as a vector of four tuples. $(u_{cpu}, u_{io}, u_{mem}, u_{swap})$, where u_{cpu}, u_{io}, u_{mem}, u_{swap} denote the utilization of CPU, I/O, memory and disk swap, respectively.

Feedback Signal. We define a real-valued *reward* as the feedback. Whenever there is a conflict in the aggregated resource demand, e.g. the available memory becomes less than the total requested memory, iBalloon set the reward to -1 (penalty) for the VMs that require an increase in the resource and a reward of 0 (neural) to other VMs. In this way, some of the conflicted VMs may back-off leading to contention relaxation. Note that, although conflicted VMs may give up previous requests, Decision-maker will suggest a second best plan, which may be the best solution to the resource contention.

When there is no conflict on resources, the reward directly reflects application performance and resource efficiency. We define the reward as a ratio of *yield* to *cost*:

$$reward = \frac{yield}{cost},$$

where $yield = Y(x_1, x_2, \ldots, x_m) = \frac{\sum_{i=1}^{m} y(x_i)}{m}$,

$$y(x_i) = \begin{cases} 1 & \text{if } x_i \text{ satisfies its SLA;} \\ e^{-p*(|\frac{x_i - x_i'}{x_i'}|)} - 1 & \text{otherwise,} \end{cases}$$

and $cost = 1 + \frac{\sum_{i=1}^{n}(1-u_i^k)^{\frac{1}{k}}}{n}$. Note that the metric *yield* is a summarized gain over m performance metrics $x_1, x_2, \cdots, x_m$. The utility function $y(x_i)$ decays when metric x_i violates its performance objective x_i' in SLA. *cost* is calculated as the summarized utility of n utilization status $u_1, u_2, \cdots, u_n$. Both utility functions decay under the control of decay factors of p and k, respectively. We consider throughput and response time as performance metrics and u_{cpu}, u_{io}, u_{mem}, u_{swap} as utilization metrics. The *reward* punishes SLA violations and gives incentives to high resource efficiency.

Self-adaptive Learning Engine. Reinforcement learning is concerned with how an agent ought to take actions in a dynamic environment so as to maximize a long term reward [2]. It fits naturally within iBalloon's feedback driven, interactive framework. In VM capacity management, the state s corresponds to the VM's running status and action a is the resource reconfiguration. It relies on the feedback sig-

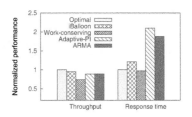

Figure 2: Performance due to various reconfiguration approaches on a cluster of 128 correlated VMs.

nals for coordination with other VMs. An immediate benefit of distributed learning is that the complexity of the learning problem does not grow exponentially with the number of VMs.

We borrow the design in the Cerebellar Model Articulation Controller (CMAC) to implement the Q function. It maintains multiple coarse-grained Q tables or so-called tiles, each of which is shifted by a random offset with respect to each other. With CMAC, we can achieve higher resolution in the Q table with less cost. Once a VM finishes an iteration, it submits the four-tuple (s_t, a_t, s_{t+1}, r_t) to Decision-maker. Then the corresponding RL agent updates the CMAC-based Q table using SARSA algorithm. We modified the algorithm to allow fast adaptation when SLA violated. We set the learning rate α to 1 whenever receives a negative penalty. This ensures that "bad" news travels faster than good news allowing the learning agent quickly response to the performance violation.

3. EXPERIMENTAL RESULTS

We deployed 64 TPC-W instances, each with two tiers, on a cluster of 16 nodes. We randomly deployed the 128 VMs and make sure that each node hosted 8 VMs, 4 APP and 4 DB tiers. Figure 2 plots the average performance of 64 TPC-W instances for a 10-hour test. The *optimal* strategy was obtained by tweaking the cluster manually. It turned out that the setting: DB VM with 3VCPU,1GB memory and APP VM with 1VCPU, 1GB memory delivered the best performance. *work-conserving* configures each VM with fixed 4VCPU and 1GB memory. Two popular feedback control-based methods: *Adaptive proportional integral (PI)* and *Auto-regressive-moving-average (ARMA)* were also compared within the iBalloon framework. The performance is normalized to *optimal*. For throughput, higher is better; for response time, lower is better.

As shown in Figure 2, iBalloon achieved close throughput as *optimal* while incurred 20% degradation on request latency. The degradation on response time was mainly from the unstable periods brought by the reconfigurations. Due to model-independent and adaptive resource allocation, iBalloon outperformed other approaches in both throughput and response time in dynamic cloud environments. We further narrow down the overhead of iBalloon by disabling the reconfigurations. Results showed that, the distributed learning mechanism itself only adds no more than 5% overhead on application performance.

Acknowledgement This work was supported in part by U.S. NSF grants CNS-0702488, CRI-0708232, CNS-0914330, and CCF-1016966.

4. REFERENCES

[1] J. Rao, X. Bu, C.-Z. Xu, L. Wang, and G. Yin. VCONF: a reinforcement learning approach to virtual machines auto-configuration. In *ICAC*, 2009.

[2] R. S. Sutton and A. G. Barto. *Reinforcement Learning: An Introduction*. MIT Press, 1998.

Characterizing and Analyzing Renewable Energy Driven Data Centers

Chao Li   Amer Qouneh   Tao Li

Intelligent Design of Efficient Architectures Laboratory (IDEAL)
Department of Electrical and Computer Engineering, University of Florida

chaol@ufl.edu   aqouneh@ufl.edu   taoli@ece.ufl.edu

ABSTRACT

An increasing number of data centers today start to incorporate renewable energy solutions to cap their carbon footprint. However, the impact of renewable energy on large-scale data center design is still not well understood. In this paper, we model and evaluate data centers driven by intermittent renewable energy. Using real-world data center and renewable energy source traces, we show that renewable power utilization and load tuning frequency are two critical metrics for designing sustainable high-performance data centers. Our characterization reveals that load power fluctuation together with the intermittent renewable power supply introduce unnecessary tuning activities, which can increase the management overhead and degrade the performance of renewable energy driven data centers.

Categories and Subject Descriptors

C.4 [Performance of System]: Design studies

General Terms: Design, Management, Experimentation

Keywords: Renewable energy, Data center, Power variation, Load tuning

1. INTRODUCTION

Environmental and energy price concerns have become key drivers in the market for sustainable computing. The advances of renewable technologies and continuously decreasing renewable energy costs have made renewable energy driven data centers a proven alternative to conventional utility-dependent data centers and the market is rapidly growing [1].

While there has been prior work discussing renewable energy driven data centers, the impact of renewable energy on data center design is still not well understood. To tune the load power footprint, existing practices either put servers into low power states or enforce a hard limit on server power using DVFS. Although these approaches show impressive power control capability, they sacrifice the computing throughput or response time. In addition, our characterization on renewable energy source shows that it typically takes a long time for the renewable energy generation to resume. As a result, in mission critical data centers, putting servers into low performance state and waiting for the renewable energy to resume is not wise, especially for those parallel computing systems with inter-node workload dependency.

In this study, we propose and evaluate a framework for understanding the key design considerations of wind/solar energy powered data centers. We propose *iSwitch*, a novel dynamic load

power tuning scheme for managing intermittent renewable power sources. As an alternative to load power throttling, *iSwitch* intelligently shifts the load from one energy source to another to achieve best load matching. In other words, *iSwitch* dynamically allocates/de-allocates (i.e., "switch") the load power between renewable energy supply and conventional utility grid to meet the time-varying power supply.

We develop a trace-driven modeling technique that combines real-world data center traces and renewable energy resource statistics. Our experiments on *iSwitch* load tuning show the following interesting characteristics:

- Fine grained load tuning provides more accurate tracking of the variable renewable energy supply but does not guarantee high renewable energy utilization. Appropriate ratio between the renewable energy provisioning capacity and the load power consumption demand is also important.

- Load tuning should be carefully performed. Not only does too conservative load tuning miss the opportunity of utilizing precious renewable power but it is also unsustainable since we have to use large-scale battery to store the excess renewable generation. On the other hand, excessive load tuning activities will introduce unnecessary management overhead. To this end, we propose *REU* (renewable energy utilization) and switching frequency to evaluate the load tuning effectiveness.

- The renewable power variation together with the server power fluctuation introduce unnecessary and unbalanced load tuning activities which bring us little benefit on energy utilization but disturb the normal operation of server clusters and degrade the system performance.

2. POWER-AWARE LOAD TUNING

Our prior work in [2] shows that power-aware load tuning can make a difference in renewable energy driven computing systems. In this study, we propose *iSwitch*, a new data center management abstraction for handling hybrid energy source (e.g., renewable power supply plus conventional power grid). The basic idea behind *iSwitch* is *switching*, which is defined as a load tuning activity that will result in redistribution of load power between different power supplies. With *iSwitch*, the computing load is logically divided into two groups: one powered by conventional utility grid, the other powered by renewable energy generation. *iSwitch* dynamically resizes the renewable energy powered load to meet the time-varying power supply.

The implementation of *iSwitch* has many variations. For instance, at the facility level, we can switch servers between different power supplies via power transfer switch; at the system level, the switching operation can also be achieved by virtual machine migration or other data shifting mechanism.

In this study, we consider the following two metrics for evaluating renewable energy powered data centers:

Renewable Energy Utilization: The *renewable energy utilization* (REU) is defined as $P_L / P_R \times 100\%$, where P_L is the amount of renewable power that is actually utilized by the load and P_R is the total renewable power generation.

Switching Frequency: The *switching frequency* is defined as the aggregated number of switching activities performed during a fixed duration (e.g. one day or one week). A high switching frequency may introduce more control overhead.

3. EXPERIMENTAL METHODOLOGIES

We developed a framework that simulates dynamic load tuning and hierarchical power control in renewable energy powered data centers. We simulate the renewable power supply using models derived from commercially available wind and solar power generators. We collected real world data center traces and renewable energy source statistics as simulation inputs.

3.1 Data Center Traces

We assume a raised floor data center consisting of 4,800 HP ProLiant DL 360 G6 servers. The peak and idle power of the modeled server are 186W and 62W respectively.

We evaluate data centers with both homogeneous and heterogeneous load variations. The homogeneous configuration assumes that all the servers are running the same workload and have similar utilization levels. In the heterogeneous configuration scenario, the servers are grouped into several clusters and different clusters have different utilization profiles.

We generate the homogeneous utilization traces from the raw data provided by the Internet Traffic Archive [3]. The server utilization traces we generated represent a one-week server load variation including idle period, peak hours and daily surge. For heterogeneous utilization traces, we collected server utilization traces from a real-world academic HPC center, which has five major clusters with different service targets and loads.

3.2 Renewable Power Supply Traces

We use the sun irradiance and other meteorological data (i.e. temperature and wind speed) from the Measurement and Instrumentation Data center (MIDC) [4] of the National Renewable Energy Laboratory. We choose meteorology data from stations with different local renewable energy potentials. The raw data traces we obtained have different measurement time intervals between 1-minute to 1-hour. We generate representative power supply trace sets for different evaluation purposes.

4. RESULTS

In Figure 1 we show the renewable energy utilization (REU) obtained from different RES traces (*H1~L2*) with different provisioning capacities (*Low*, *Moderate* and *High*). *Facility* is a conventional facility-level load matching scheme.

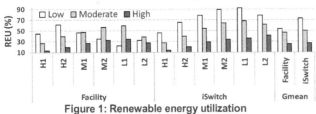

Figure 1: Renewable energy utilization

As can been seen, *iSwitch* shows better renewable energy utilization since its fine-grained load tuning provides better renewable power supply tracking. When the installed energy capacity is low, *iSwitch* improves the REU by 54% compared with *Facility*; when the installed energy is high, the improvement is only 5%. The reason is that *iSwitch* improves energy utilization but cannot absorb all the over-provisioned power. Therefore, a thoughtful capacity planning is very important for renewable energy driven data centers.

We evaluate the impact of supply/load variation on switching frequency, as shown in Figure 2. The supply/demand variation has strong influence on the load tuning activities. Low renewable supply variation and low load power variation will reduce the switching frequency significantly. A low switching frequency is always preferred since it means lower control overhead.

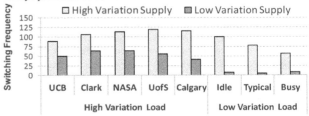

Figure 2: Average switching frequency (iSwitch)

We found that conventional power tracking schemes incur unnecessary load tuning activities. In Figure 3, we compare a conventional tracking scheme with our modified load tuning control which features a light-weight tuning mechanism. Conventional tracking schemes require significant load tuning efforts (up to 2X of our design) while receive less than 10% energy return. Therefore, we need to carefully explore the tradeoff between switching frequency and renewable energy utilization. Overly aggressive load tuning schemes introduce significant overhead (e.g., communication traffic) which may overweigh the benefit of REU improvement.

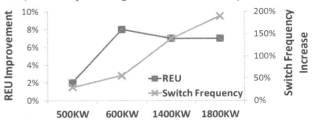

Figure 3: REU benefit and control effort of conventional design compared to iSwitch (x-axis: renewable energy capacity)

5. CONCLUSIONS

Designing renewable energy driven data centers is challenging and requires thoughtful coordination between the renewable power supply and load power. In addition, appropriate optimization is necessary to reduce management overhead.

6. REFERENCES

[1] Special Report: Data Centers & Renewable Energy http://www.datacenterknowledge.com

[2] C. Li, W. Zhang, C. Cho and T. Li, SolarCore: Solar Energy Driven Multi-core Architecture Power Management, *International Symposium on High-Performance Computer Architecture (HPCA), 2011*

[3] Internet Traffic Archive, http://ita.ee.lbl.gov/

[4] http://www.nrel.gov/midc

Tight Moments-Based Bounds for Queueing Systems

Varun Gupta
Carnegie Mellon University
varun@cs.cmu.edu

Takayuki Osogami
IBM Research - Tokyo
osogami@jp.ibm.com

ABSTRACT

We present a new tool to analyze three queueing systems which have defied exact analysis so far: (i) the classical $M/G/k$ multi-server system, (ii) queueing systems with fluctuating arrival and service rates, and (iii) the $M/G/1$ round-robin queue. We argue that rather than looking for exact expressions for the mean response time as a function of the job size distribution, a more fruitful approach is to find distributions which minimize or maximize the mean response time given the first n moments of the job size distribution.

We prove that for the $M/G/k$ system in light traffic, and given $n=2$ and 3 moments, these 'extremal' distributions are given by *principal representations* of the moment sequence. Furthermore, if we restrict the distributions to lie in the class of Completely Monotone (CM) distributions, then for all the three queueing systems, for any n, the extremal distributions under the appropriate "light traffic" asymptotics are hyper-exponential distributions with finite number of phases. We conjecture that the property of *extremality* should be invariant to the system load, and thus our light traffic results should hold for general load as well.

Categories and Subject Descriptors

G.3 [**Probability and Statistics**]: Queueing Theory; G.1.2 [**Numerical Analysis**]: Approximation—*Chebyshev approximation and theory*

General Terms

Theory, Performance

Keywords

Moment-based bounds, $M/G/k$, Time-varying load, Round-robin, Markov-Krein Theorem, Tchebychef systems, Light traffic analysis

1. INTRODUCTION

Most results in queueing theory are concerned with obtaining explicit expressions for the performance metric of interest (e.g., mean response time) as a function of the distribution of some system parameter (e.g., job size distribution) under suitable assumptions to make the analysis tractable. However, there are many fundamental queueing systems for which such explicit results are not possible. In the absence of exact results, various approximations or bounds are used.

Rather than trying to obtain explicit expressions for the performance metric as a function of the job size distribution, or obtaining

approximations/bounds as functions of some moments of the job size distribution for which no tightness guarantees can be proved, we argue that a more fruitful approach is the following: We first obtain a partial characterization of the job size distribution, say, in terms of the first n moments. We then look at the set of all distributions which satisfy this partial characterization, and identify those distributions in this set that maximize or minimize the performance metric of interest. Once these extremal distributions are identified, numerical algorithms can be used to obtain **provably tight bounds** on the performance.

In this paper, we take the first step towards obtaining tight bounds on the mean response time of the three queueing systems by analytically investigating suitable asymptotic regimes where the effect of the entire distribution of the system parameter of interest is evident (unlike heavy-traffic asymptotes). Next, rather than using the asymptotic approximations to obtain quantitative behavior (by extrapolating to non-asymptotic regime), we extract qualitative properties by identifying distributions which minimize or maximize the performance metric in the asymptotic regime.

2. PRINCIPAL REPRESENTATIONS, AND THE MARKOV-KREIN THEOREM

In this section we will be concerned with random variables with support on $[0, B]$. We first introduce the notion of upper and lower principal representations as presented in [2]. Define the function $f_0(x) = 1, 0 \le x \le B$, and denote the moment space associated with $\{f_0, f_1, \ldots, f_n\}$ as

$$\mathcal{M}^{n+1} = \left\{ \mathbf{m} \in \Re^{n+1} \mid \exists \mu \in \mathcal{D}, m_i = \int_0^B f_i(u)d\mu(u), 0 \le i \le n \right\}$$

where $\mathcal{D}$ is the set of all non-decreasing right continuous functions for which the indicated integrals exist. For a point $\mathbf{m}^0$ in the interior of $\mathcal{M}^{n+1}$, we define the *unique lower and upper principal representation (pr)* as follows:

	Upper pr ($\bar{\mu}$)	Lower pr ($\underline{\mu}$)
n even	$\frac{n}{2}$ mass points in $(0, B)$, one at B	$\frac{n}{2}$ mass points in $(0, B)$, one at 0
n odd	$\frac{n-1}{2}$ mass points in $(0, B)$, one at 0, one at B	$\frac{n+1}{2}$ mass points in $(0, B)$

We say that functions $\{h_0, h_1, \ldots, h_n\}$ form a Tchebycheff system over $[a, b]$ provided the determinants

$$U \left(\begin{array}{c} 0, 1, \cdots, n \\ x_0, x_1, \cdots, x_n \end{array} \right) = \left| \begin{array}{cccc} h_0(x_0) & h_0(x_1) & \cdots & h_0(x_n) \\ h_1(x_0) & h_1(x_1) & \cdots & h_1(x_n) \\ \vdots & \vdots & & \vdots \\ h_n(x_0) & h_n(x_1) & \cdots & h_n(x_n) \end{array} \right|$$

are strictly positive whenever $a \le x_0 < x_1 < \cdots < x_n \le b$.

The proof of the following theorem can be found in [4, Chpt. V, Sec. 5]:

THEOREM 1 (MARKOV-KREIN). *If* $\{f_0, \ldots, f_n\}$ *and* $\{f_0, \ldots, f_n, g\}$ *are Tchebycheff systems on* $[0, B]$, *then*

$$\beta_l \equiv \inf_{\mu_X \in \mathcal{D}} \{ \mathbf{E}[g(X)] \mid \mathbf{Pr}[X \in [0, B]] = 1;$$

$$\mathbf{E}[f_i(X)] = m_i, \; 0 \le i \le n \} = \int_0^B g(u) d\underline{\mu}(u)$$

$$\beta_u \equiv \sup_{\mu_X \in \mathcal{D}} \{ \mathbf{E}[g(X)] \mid \mathbf{Pr}[X \in [0, B]] = 1;$$

$$\mathbf{E}[f_i(X)] = m_i, \; 0 \le i \le n \} = \int_0^B g(u) d\bar{\mu}(u),$$

where $\underline{\mu}$ *and* $\bar{\mu}$ *are the unique lower and upper pr's, respectively, of* $\mathbf{m} = \{1, m_1, \ldots, m_n\}$, *and* μ_X *denotes the measure induced by* X *on* $\Re$.

The theorem holds for $B \to \infty$ when the corresponding limits exist (see [4]).

Principal representations within Hyperexponential distributions: Analogous to the above, we can define pr's within hyperexponential distributions by applying the above theorem to the *spectral density*. We omit the details due to lack of space.

3. SUMMARY OF RESULTS

We now briefly describe the three queueing systems, the "light traffic" regime we look at, and our results.

The $M/G/k$ multi-server system
Recall that an $M/G/k$ system consists of k identical servers and a FCFS queue. The arrival process is Poisson with rate λ, and the job sizes are assumed to be *i.i.d* random variables. We will use X to denote such a generic random variable. We are interested in obtaining bounds on the mean waiting time, $\mathbf{E}\left[W^{M/G/k}\right]$, as a function of the job size distribution X. We let the arrival rate $\lambda \to 0$, and look at $\mathbf{E}\left[W^{M/G/k}\right]$ of a random arrival. By exploiting the light-traffic approximation developed by Burman and Smith [1], we can prove the following:

THEOREM 2. *Given the first* n ($n = 2$ *or* 3) *moments of the job size distribution* X, $\mathbf{E}\left[W^{M/G/k}\right]$ *under light traffic asymptote is extremized by service distributions given by the lower and upper principal representations of the moment sequence.*

THEOREM 3. *If the job size distribution is constrained to lie in the CM class, then given the first* n *moments of the job size distribution* X, $\mathbf{E}\left[W^{M/G/k}\right]$ *under light traffic is extremized by the lower and upper principal representations of the moment sequence within the hyperexponential class of distributions.*

We conjecture that the above theorems hold for general arrival rates, because, intuitively, increasing the arrival rate to an $M/G/k$ system should not change the relative performance of two job size distributions.

Finally, we illustrate the utility of our results by presenting numerical results that demonstrate that while two moments of the job size distribution are insufficient for approximating $\mathbf{E}\left[W^{M/G/k}\right]$ for real world heavy-tailed distributions, three moments usually suffice, especially if we add the knowledge of complete monotonicity. Figure 1 shows $\mathbf{E}\left[W^{M/G/k}\right]$ and its bounds obtained with principal representations, when the job size distribution is a Weibull distribution. Notice that the Weibull distribution under consideration is completely monotonic (see [3]), so that a principal representations within hyperexponential distributions give proper bounds.

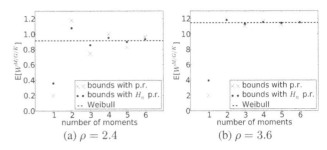

(a) $\rho = 2.4$ (b) $\rho = 3.6$

Figure 1: Bounding mean delay in an $M/G/4$ queue when the job size has a Weibull distribution.

The $M/G/1$ round-robin queue
The $M/G/1$ round-robin queue consists of a single server and an infinite buffer. The arrival process is Poisson with rate λ, and new arrivals join the back of the buffer. Job sizes are assumed to be *i.i.d.*, with X used to denote a generic job size. Jobs are given Q units of service at a time (called the quantum size), which for analytical simplicity we assume to be *i.i.d.* samples from an $\text{Exp}(\nu)$ distribution. We will be interested in obtaining bounds on the mean response time, $\mathbf{E}\left[T^{M/G/1/RR}\right]$, in terms of moments of X. We let the arrival rate $\lambda \to 0$, and look at the coefficient of $\Theta(\lambda)$ in the expression for $\mathbf{E}\left[T^{M/G/1/RR}\right]$. By deriving the first light-traffic asymptote of $T^{M/G/1/RR}$ we can prove the following:

THEOREM 4. *Given the first* n *moments of the job size distribution* X *in the CM class,* $\mathbf{E}\left[T^{M/G/1/RR}\right]$ *under light traffic is extremized by the lower and upper principal representations of the moment sequence within the class of hyperexponential distributions.*

Systems with fluctuating arrival and service rates
We analyze an $M/M/1$ system whose arrival and service rates are controlled by an exogenous environment process with two states: L and H. The durations of stay in the L state during each visit are *i.i.d.* random variables with general distribution; we use τ_L to denote such a generic random variable. Similarly, we use τ_H to denote a generic random variable for the duration of stay in the H states during each visit. We will be interested in obtaining bounds on the mean number of jobs, $\mathbf{E}[N]$, in terms of moments of τ_L and τ_H. We consider the "fast-switching" asymptote, where we scale τ_L and τ_H by a parameter α, and let $\alpha \to 0$. Via a new asymptotic expansion for $\mathbf{E}[N]$ in terms of α, we prove the following:

THEOREM 5. *If* τ_L *and* τ_H *are constrained to lie in the CM class, then given the first* n *moments of* τ_L *and* τ_H, *the mean number of jobs,* $\mathbf{E}[N]$, *under the fast switching asymptote is extremized by the lower and upper principal representations of the moment sequence within the hyperexponential distribution.*

4. REFERENCES

[1] D. Burman and D. Smith. A light-traffic theorem for multi-server queues. *Math. Oper. Res.*, 8:15–25, 1983.

[2] A. Eckberg Jr. Sharp bounds on Laplace-Stieltjes transforms, with applications to various queueing problems. *Math. Oper. Res.*, 2(2):132–142, 1977.

[3] A. Feldmann and W. Whitt. Fitting mixtures of exponentials to long-tail distributions to analyze network performance models. *Performance Evaluation*, 31:245–279, 1998.

[4] S. Karlin and W. J. Studden. *Tchebycheff systems: With applications in analysis and statistics.* John Wiley & Sons Interscience Publishers, New York, 1966.

Scalable Monitoring via Threshold Compression in a Large Operational 3G Network

Suk-Bok Lee[1], Dan Pei[2], MohammadTaghi Hajiaghayi[2,3], Ioannis Pefkianakis[1], Songwu Lu[1]
He Yan[4], Zihui Ge[2], Jennifer Yates[2], Mario Kosseifi[5]
[1]UCLA Computer Science   [2]ATT Labs–Research   [3]University of Maryland
[4]Colorado State University   [5]AT&T Mobility Services

ABSTRACT

Threshold-based performance monitoring in large 3G networks is very challenging for two main factors: *large network scale* and *dynamics in both time and spatial domains*. There exists a fundamental tradeoff between the size of threshold settings and the alarm quality. In this paper, we propose a scalable monitoring solution, called threshold-compression that characterizes the tradeoff via intelligent threshold aggregation. The main insight behind our solution is to identify groups of network elements with similar threshold behaviors across location and time dimensions, thus forming spatial-temporal clusters and generating the associated compressed thresholds within the optimization framework. Our evaluations on a commercial 3G network have demonstrated the effectiveness of our threshold-compression solution, e.g., threshold setting reduction up to 90% within 10% false/miss alarms.

Categories and Subject Descriptors: C.2.3 [Computer-Communication Networks]: Network Operations

General Terms: Measurement, Algorithms

1. INTRODUCTION

The current practice for monitoring the health of a large-scale network is to use pre-defined thresholds of selected key performance indicator (KPI) metrics. However, direct application of such a pre-computed, threshold-based alarming model does not scale in 3G networks due to the two main factors: (1) massive data volume and large network scale; (2) rich dynamics in both time and spatial domains. A single static threshold per KPI fails to capture such spatial and temporal dynamics, leading to unacceptably poor alarm quality with nearly 70% false positives/negatives. On the other hand, a finer-grained location- and time-dependent threshold setting can capture network dynamics but incurs prohibitively high system management complexity. The number of thresholds to be maintained grows very large with the increasing number of network elements (NEs) and the time granularity. For example, given that one regional area has about 5,000 cells and 30 KPIs, the per-NE hourly threshold scheme has as many as $5K \times 24 \times 30 = 3.6$ million thresholds in a single area. Therefore, it is increasingly difficult to monitor an operational 3G network with naive pre-defined threshold scheme. To this end, we propose a scalable threshold-based solution, called threshold-compression, which has both merits of a small number of used thresholds and accurate capturing of spatial-temporal network dynamics.

2. THRESHOLD COMPRESSION

We describe threshold-compression by highlighting the motivation, problem formulation, and compression algorithm suite.

Case for similar threshold behavior. Our threshold compression approach is motivated by two key observations: (1) threshold behavior similarity among a certain group of NEs, and (2) stable/close threshold trends over some period of time. Figure 1 shows example NE-pairs on downlink-throughput KPI using per-NE-hourly thresholds. Such spatial similarity is attributed to the geographic locations of NEs and the user population in the corresponding area. For example, NEs in urban (/rural) areas are likely to have similar high (/low) dynamics over time. Time-domain similarity is also observed, as each NE is likely to have similar high (/low) demand during peak (/sleep) hours. For example in the figure, each NE-group shows very stable threshold behavior during peak hours between 11:00 GMT and 22:00 GMT, which provides us an opportunity to form a temporal-domain cluster.

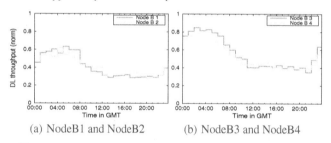

(a) NodeB1 and NodeB2   (b) NodeB3 and NodeB4

Figure 1: Downlink-throughput KPI: similar threshold (per-NE-hourly) behavior among different Node Bs.

Desirable properties of threshold compression. To ensure scalable monitoring performance as well as practical threshold management, threshold-compression should have the following properties: (1) High compression gain: The resulting threshold setting should remain small even with a large number of NEs; (2) Low false alarm rate: The compressed thresholds must result in good alarm quality, i.e, low false positive rate (FPR) and false negative rate (FNR), and thus, we use a concept of *threshold closeness* of lower ($T_{lower}^{i,j}$) and upper ($T_{upper}^{i,j}$) bound to approximate the per-NE-hourly thresholds of (NE i and hour j); (3) Management-oriented grouping policy: The spatial-temporal clusters must be easy to manage and update in the monitoring system. To this end, we employ a consistent NE grouping policy where each NE can belong to only one NE group (but there can be multiple hour groups within an NE group), hence a two-level hierarchical clustering structure.

Problem formulation. We formulate the threshold compression problem taking the alarm quality as well as the required clustering policy into account. The objective is to find the minimum number of spatial-temporal clusters (or equivalently the minimum threshold setting) from a given fine-grained threshold setting with the following constraints: (1) Each compressed threshold must be within the *permissible* threshold interval of $T_{lower}^{i,j}$ and $T_{upper}^{i,j}$; (2) NE grouping must be consistent in time; (3) Each cluster must consist of continuous time steps (optional rule).

It turns out that this problem is not only NP-hard (regardless of the optional rule) but indeed it is very hard to approximate as well. The proof is given in the full version of the paper [1].

Threshold compression algorithm suite. Our threshold-compression takes a two-staged approach. We first decouple the spatial NE grouping from the original two-dimensional clustering problem, then further proceed with temporal-domain clustering within each identified NE group. Our key strategy for clustering is to combine spatial-temporal blocks if they (i) have common intersection in their permissible intervals, and (ii) meet the consistent NE grouping rule. Note that having common intersection among the cluster members ensures the satisfying alarm quality.

1. NE grouping: greedy coloring approach. The first stage identifies NE groups each showing similar threshold behavior each hour among its members. As the first-level of clustering hierarchy, each NE group, in fact, consists of 24 hour-groups, which will be compressed further in the next stage via time-domain clustering. Then, the NE grouping problem naturally reduces to the graph coloring that asks the minimum number of colors (NE groups) assignable to each vertex (NE) such that no edge (common intersection) connects two identically colored vertices (group members). This graph coloring instance is NP-hard, and we employ a greedy coloring heuristic, which works quite well in practice. Specifically we apply the Welsh-Powell algorithm [2] that uses at most $\max_i \min\{d(v_i) + 1, i\}$ colors, that is at most one more than the maximum degree of the graph. We convert our problem instance to a graph $G(V, E)$, where each NE corresponds to a vertex in G. For each vertex pair v_i and $v_{i'}$, we put an edge between them if their counterpart NEs i and i' have disjoint threshold intervals in any hour. Then the vertices colored γ (by the greedy coloring algorithm) can be readily transformed to NE-group γ in our problem.

Once identified, each NE group γ defines its own permissible threshold interval to reflect each member's interval. Setting the group threshold interval to the common intersection among the members makes the next-stage clustering procedure to keep control on the resulting alarm quality.

2. Hour grouping: minimum cover selection. As the next level of the clustering hierarchy, the time-domain clustering takes the NE grouping result as input to perform the hour grouping for each identified NE-group. Within NE group γ, there are initially 24 hour-groups, each of which we simply refer an hour. Then each hour j is represented by its threshold interval $\Phi_{lower}^{\gamma,j}$ and $\Phi_{upper}^{\gamma,j}$ (i.e., the common intersection among all members at hour j) as a result of NE grouping. Given the set of intervals, the hour grouping problem is to find the minimum number of interval groups such that (i) each interval belongs to one of the interval groups, and (ii) there is common intersection in each interval group. We use a simple greedy algorithm that leads to an optimal solution to this problem. The algorithm is as follows. We first sort all the interval endpoints ($\forall j \in H : \Phi_{lower}^{\gamma,j}, \Phi_{upper}^{\gamma,j}$) in ascending order of their values. We scan the list (in ascending order) until first encountering an upper-bound point $\Phi_{upper}^{\gamma,j'}$. We then put all intervals containing this point (i.e., all hours $j : \Phi_{lower}^{\gamma,j} \leq \Phi_{upper}^{\gamma,j'}$) into a new interval group C_h', and delete them from the list. We repeat this process until there is no interval in the list. This simple greedy rule indeed finds the min-

imum number of interval groups, hence the minimum hour groups. The proof is given in the full version of the paper [1].

Now, all hours in each identified interval group C_h' of NE group γ can form a spatial-temporal cluster C_h''. In order to preserve the threshold-closeness property for all members, we set the compressed thresholds $T_{comp}(\delta)$ within the common intersection across all NEs $i \in C_\gamma$ and hours $j \in C_h'$ in the spatial-temporal cluster, and we use the median point in this study. We again note that this compressed thresholds $T_{comp}(\delta)$ is shared by all NEs and hours in C_δ'', thus reducing the threshold setting while still preserving the location and time specific thresholds.

3. EVALUATION

We evaluate the performance of threshold-compression on the data recorded from June 2010 to August 2010 in one regional 3G network that covers several thousands of NEs. Figure 2 shows the threshold compression gain on different KPIs. The compression gain is defined as the threshold-setting reduction relative to the fine-grained per-NE-hourly setting. Each compression gain in the figure represents the highest threshold-compression gain observed when the resulting false/miss alarm rates FPR and FNR (based on the per-NE-hourly alarm statistics) are both within 10% (and 20%) range. We observe that, within 10% false/miss alarm condition, most KPIs show very high compression gain nearly 80–90%. Tables 1 compare the threshold-setting sizes and false/miss alarm rates produced by different thresholding schemes. Our approach balances very well the problematic tradeoff between the threshold setting and the alarm quality, while other schemes are unable to achieve both.

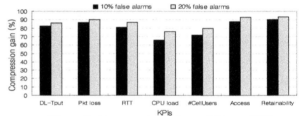

Figure 2: Compression gain on different KPIs.

Threshold scheme	#thresholds	FPR	FNR
per-NE-hourly	**25320**	-	-
threshold-compression	3763	8.4%	2.7%
per-NE-static	1055	**31.1%**	**51.8%**
per-NEtype-hourly	24	**51.2%**	**47.5%**
per-NEtype-static	1	**53.2%**	**58.0%**

Table 1: Thresholding on downlink-throughput KPI.

4. CONCLUSION

Motivated by key observations of spatial-temporal threshold similarity, we have proposed a scalable monitoring solution, called threshold-compression that can characterize the location- and time-specific threshold trend of each individual NE with minimal threshold setting. Our experience with applying our threshold-compression solution in the operational 3G network monitoring has been very positive, and demonstrated the effectiveness of the proposed approach, e.g., threshold setting reduction up to 90% within 10% false/miss alarms.

5. REFERENCES

[1] S.-B. Lee, D. Pei, M. Hajiaghayi, I. Pefkianakis, S. Lu, H. Yan, Z. Ge, J. Yates, M. Kosseifi. Scalable monitoring via threshold compression in a large operational 3G network. *AT&T Technical Report*, 2011.

[2] D. Welsh and M. Powell. An upper bound for the chromatic number of a graph and its application to timetabling problems. *Computer Journal*, 85–86, 1967.

How Do You "Tube"?

Vijay Kumar Adhikari, Sourabh Jain, Yingying Chen and Zhi-Li Zhang *
Department of Computer Science & Engineering, University of Minnesota
Minneapolis, MN
{viadhi, sourj, yingying, zhzhang}@cs.umn.edu

ABSTRACT

In this paper we "reverse-engineer" the YouTube video delivery cloud by building a distributed measurement infrastructure. Through extensive data collection and analysis, we deduce the key design features underlying the YouTube video delivery cloud. The design of the YouTube video delivery cloud consists of three major components: a "flat" *video id space*, multiple DNS namespaces reflecting a multi-layered *logical* organization of video servers, and a 3-tier physical cache hierarchy. By mapping the video id space to the logical servers via consistent hashing and cleverly leveraging DNS and HTTP re-direction mechanisms, such a design leads to a scalable, robust and flexible content distribution system.

Categories and Subject Descriptors

C.2.4 [**Distributed systems**]: Distributed applications

General Terms

Measurement, Performance

1. INTRODUCTION

Given the traffic volume, geographical span and scale of operations, the design of YouTube's delivery infrastructure is perhaps one of the most challenging engineering tasks. Little is known how Google leverages its resources to design and structure the YouTube video delivery cloud to meet the rapidly growing user demands. This paper attempts to "reverse-engineer" the YouTube video delivery cloud through large-scale active measurement, data collection and analysis. We are particularly interested in answering the following question: how does YouTube design and deploy a *scalable* and *distributed* delivery infrastructure to match the geographical span of its users and meet varying user demands?

Towards this goal, we have developed a novel distributed active measurement platform with more than 1000 vantage points spanning five continents. Our distributed measurement platform consists of two key components: i) PlanetLab nodes that are used to play YouTube videos and and to perform DNS resolutions and ii) open recursive DNS servers

to provide additional vantages to perform DNS resolutions. Through data analysis and inference, and by conducting extensive "experiments" to test and understand the behavior of the YouTube video delivery cloud, we uncover and deduce the logical designs of the YouTube video id space, the DNS namespace structures and cache hierarchy, how they map to the physical infrastructure and locations, and what mechanisms they use to select a server for any given request.

Most existing studies of YouTube mainly focus on user behaviors or the system performance. For instance, the authors in [3] examined the YouTube video popularity distribution, popularity evolution, and its related user behaviors and key elements that shape the popularity distribution using data-driven analysis. The authors in [4] investigate the (top 100 most viewed) YouTube video file characteristics and usage patterns such as the number of users, requests, as seen from the perspective of an edge network. A more relevant to our work is the recent study carried in [2], where the authors utilize the Netflow traffic data *passively* collected at various locations within a tier-1 ISP to uncover the locations of YouTube data center locations, and infer the load-balancing strategy employed by YouTube at the time. As the data used in the study is from 2008, the results reflect the YouTube delivery infrastructure *pre Google re-structuring*. This work attempts to reverse engineer the current YouTube design.

2. MEASUREMENTS & DATASETS

We develop a distributed active measurement and data collection platform consisting of the 471 PlanetLab nodes and 843 open recursive DNS servers. We use PlanetLab nodes to run our distributed crawler to crawl YouTube video pages and collect $434K$ video ids. We then play all those videos on PlanetLab nodes using our video player emulator and collect video playback traces that include all the host-names and IP addresses involved in the video delivery. We use the open recursive DNS servers as additional vantage points to resolve the hostnames that appear in the video playback trace. Additionally, we measure round-trip delay to all observed IP addresses from all PlanetLab nodes.

3. YOUTUBE SYSTEM DESIGN

Analysis of the sequence of hostnames and IP addresses in the playback traces reveals that the YouTube video delivery cloud consists of the following three components. Due to space limitations, we refer the readers to [1] for more detais. **Video Id Space.** Each video is uniquely identified using a "flat" identifier of 11 literals long, where each literal can be [A-Z], [0-9], - or _, thus forming a space of total 64^{11} ids.

*This work is supported in part by the NSF grants CNS-0905037, CNS-1017647 and CNS-1017092 and the DTRA Grant HDTRA1-09-1-0050.

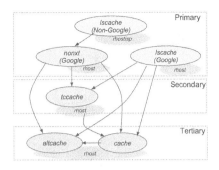

Figure 1: Namespace hierarchy and redirection order.

Table 1: Anycast (first 5) & unicast (last 2) namespaces.

namespace	format	hosts
lscache	v[1-24].lscache[1-8].c.youtube.com	192
nonxt	v[1-24].nonxt[1-8].c.youtube.com	192
tccache	tc.v[1-24].cache[1-8].c.youtube.com	192
cache	v[1-8].cache[1-8].c.youtube.com	64
altcache	alt1.v[1-24].cache[1-8].c.youtube.com	64
rhost	r[1-24].cityid.c.youtube.com	5,044
rhostisp	r[1-24].isp-city[1-3].c.youtube.com	402

Three-Tier Server Cache Hierarchy. Using the IP addresses seen in our datasets, we geo-map the "physical" video server cache locations, which are dispersed at five continents. In addition to cache locations inside Google, there are about a dozen physical caches hosted inside other ISPs such as Comcast and Bell-Canada. Based upon the roles of the servers we deduce that YouTube employs a 3-tier physical cache hierarchy with (at least) 38 *primary* cache locations, 8 *secondary* and 5 *tertiary* cache locations.

Multi-Layered Anycast DNS Namespaces. YouTube videos and (physical) cache hierarchy are tied together by a set of 5 (logical) *anycast* (can map to more than one IP address) namespaces as well as 2 *unicast* (maps to a unique IP address) namespaces as shown in Table 1.

4. MECHANISMS AND STRATEGIES

The layered organization of *logical* video servers enables YouTube to employ several mechanisms and strategies.

Fixed **Mapping between Video Id Space and** *Logical* **Video Servers.** YouTube adopts a form of "consistent" hashing to map each video id uniquely to one of the hostname in each of the anycast namespaces. In other words, for *lscache* namespace, the video id space is uniformly divided into 192 sectors, and each *lscache* DNS name is responsible for a fixed sector. This *fixed* mapping between the *video id* space to the anycast namespaces makes it easier for individual YouTube front-end servers to generate – *independently and in a distributed fashion* – HTML pages with embedded URLs pointing to the relevant video users are interested in, regardless of where users are located or how logical servers are mapped to physical servers or cache locations. These fixed mappings make it easy for each (physical) video server to decide – given its logical name – what portion of videos it is responsible for serving.

Locality-Aware Video Cache Selection via DNS Resolution. YouTube employs *locality-aware* DNS resolution to serve user video requests regionally by mapping *lscache* hostnames to physical video servers (IP addresses) residing in cache locations reasonably close to users.

Dynamic **HTTP Request Redirection.** The DNS resolution mechanism, while locality-aware, is generally agnostic of server load or caching status. When cache misses happen, depending on how busy a video server at the primary location, it may either directly fetch the missed video from another video server which has the video cached, or redirect the request to another video server at a secondary or tertiary location. Our analysis and experiments show that more than 18% times, a user video request is redirected from a primary video cache server selected via DNS *lscache* name resolution to another server.

YouTube employs a clever and complex mix of dynamic HTTP redirections and additional rounds of DNS resolution to perform finer-grained dynamic load-balancing and to handle cache misses. For instance, our investigation shows that YouTube utilizes the layered *anycast* namespaces to redirect video requests i) from one location to another location (especially from a non-Google primary cache location to a Google primary cache location via the use of *nonxt* namespace); and ii) from a Google cache location in one tier to another tier (the primary to secondary or tertiary, or the secondary to tertiary via the use of the *tccache* *cache* and *altcache* namespaces). There is a *strict ordering* as to how the *anycast* namespaces are used for redirection (see Fig. 1). At each step of the redirection process, the corresponding *anycast* hostname is resolved to an IP address via DNS. YouTube also utilizes the *unicast* namespaces to dynamically redirect a video request from one video server to a specific server usually (more than 90% of times) *within the same cache location*, and occasionally in a different location. The use of the layered *anycast* namespaces enables to enforce an strict ordering and control the redirection process.

On the other hand, each redirection (and DNS resolution) process incurs additional delay. Up to 9 redirections may happen, although they are rarely observed in the video playback traces we collected.

5. CONCLUSIONS

In this paper, we reverse-engineer the YouTube video delivery cloud by building a distributed active measurement platform. Through extensive data collection, measurement and analysis, we have uncovered and geo-located YouTube's 3-tier physical video server hierarchy, and deduced the key design features of the YouTube video delivery cloud.

6. REFERENCES

[1] How Do You "Tube"? Reverse Engineering the YouTube Video Delivery Cloud (Technical report). http://www-users.cs.umn.edu/~viadhi/resources/youtube-tech-report.pdf.

[2] V. K. Adhikari, S. Jain, and Z. Zhang. YouTube Traffic Dynamics and Its Interplay with a Tier-1 ISP: An ISP Perspective. In *IMC '10*. ACM, 2010.

[3] M. Cha, H. Kwak, P. Rodriguez, Y.-Y. Ahn, and S. Moon. I tube, you tube, everybody tubes: analyzing the world's largest user generated content video system. In *IMC '07*. ACM, 2007.

[4] P. Gill, M. Arlitt, Z. Li, and A. Mahanti. Youtube traffic characterization: a view from the edge. In *IMC '07*. ACM, 2007.

A Control Scheme for Batching DRAM Requests to Improve Power Efficiency

Krishna Kant
George Mason University
Fairfax, VA 22030
kkant@gmu.edu

ABSTRACT

This paper discusses a closed-loop control algorithm to coordinate power management of memory ranks and thereby achieve power savings beyond independent rank power management while bounding the throughput degradation.

Categories and Subject Descriptors: B.3.m
General Terms: Algorithms, Design, Performance
Keywords: DRAM, coordinated power management

1. INTRODUCTION

Because of the increasing contribution of memory power on overall system power, intelligent management of power for memory ranks is becoming critical. In this paper, we consider coordinated power management of multiple ranks that could span across a single DIMM, across a single or all memory channels, or even across all sockets.

The technique proposed in this paper is a closed loop control that batches the traffic adaptively to enhance power efficiency while ensuring that the throughput degradation due to power management stays below some desired bound. The basic idea is to improve energy efficiency by batching of requests [1] and the batching is achieved by periodically making a rank inactive so that newly arriving requests queue up but are not scheduled. When such a rank runs out of ongoing requests, it is placed in a low power mode until the inactive period expires. Such a scheme helps save power beyond what power management of an individual rank could deliver. The additional latency introduced does degrade the performance, and the closed loop control is designed to limit the degradation to a specified target value. The scheme is somewhat similar to the one in [2] where the additional latency due to power measurement is measured and used in closed loop control.

2. COORDINATED INSTANCE CONTROL

Figure 1 illustrates the coordinated control of ranks pictorially. There are N ranks each having its own request queue. Each rank itself may involve multiple servers (or "banks") as shown in the figure by small circles. Normally, each arriving request will begin service as soon as a suitable server becomes available. In the proposed scheme, however, only certain ranks are considered "eligible" and able to schedule new requests. The eligible subset remains so for a certain

gating period, denoted G, after which another subset is made eligible. In our algorithm, G is not a constant, but a parameter that is adjusted dynamically in order to keep the throughput degradation within an acceptable bound ϵ_t.

A rank may have nonzero ongoing requests when it is marked as ineligible. All ongoing requests are allowed to finish normally on an ineligible rank but no new requests are scheduled. When all the servers become idle, the resource rank is placed in a low power state even though there may be some waiting requests. This works fine for DRAM since the request management is done by the memory controller rather than the DRAM.

The memory access behavior of a workload and hence the impact of memory path latency on performance is generally quite complex, therefore, we use an online monitoring approach to estimate and react to the throughput degradation. The algorithm is designed specifically to allow inexpensive HW implementation and suitable parameter choice can even avoid multiplications/divisions.

For online monitoring we divide time into successive windows of size $W_c + W_u$, where W_c denotes the period during which gating control is effected and W_u the period during which it is not. We call W_u as the *probe period* during which we probe for the full (or undegraded) throughput λ_c. Note that the probe period needs to be long enough for the system to recover from any throughput restriction and yet be small enough so that the control is in effect most of the time.

During the W_c duration, only K (out of N) ranks are made eligible, whereas during the W_u all ranks are eligible. During W_c periods in successive cycles, the set of eligible ranks are changed systematically to ensure fairness. When a gating period is about to end, the new rank is chosen as the one with the longest queue. This works quite well, even though it is suboptimal.

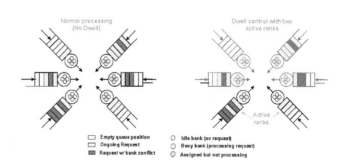

Figure 1: I   trat on of coor   nate   rank contro

The gating period G is estimated based on the observed throughput degradation, denoted ϵ_o. Let N_c and N_u denote the total number of memory transactions completed during the windows W_c and W_u respectively. Then the degraded throughput is $\lambda_c = N_c/W_c$, and the unperturbed throughput is $\lambda_u = N_u/W_u$. Therefore, $\epsilon_o = (1 - \lambda_c/\lambda_u)$. In order to reduce jitter in measured throughput, it is useful to exponentially smooth N_c and N_u values over successive cycles. Let ϵ_t denote the maximum tolerable throughput degradation. The value of G is adjusted based on the "error signal" $\epsilon_o - \epsilon_t$. The control mechanism attempts to correct large errors quickly while avoiding ping-pongs.

3. EXPERIMENTAL RESULTS

Since latency sensitivity is a key factor in determining the power savings potential of power management, we created several workloads with different latency sensitivities (dialed via the transaction buffer size distribution as described above). Based on some experimentation, we chose a transaction buffer size of 10 for "low" latency sensitivity (LS) workloads and 4 for workloads with "normal" latency sensitivity (NS). We show the results for the LS and NS cases in the following. All experimental results were obtained via a detailed (but not cycle accurate) simulator that represents DDR3 memory operation in substantial detail but the CPU simply. In particular, the CPU stall behavior (and hence memory access latency sensitivity) is controlled by properly sizing per hardware thread transaction buffers.

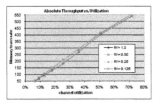 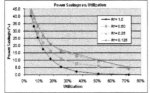

Figure 2: ro t for **Figure 3:** Po er a n for LS ca e LS ca e

For our experimental setup, we control all 8 ranks of a DDR3 memory in each socket. We define R_f as the fraction of ranks that are kept eligible at a time. We show behavior for $R_f = 1/8, 1/4, 1/2$ and 1. $R_f = 1/8$ means that only one rank in a socket is eligible for scheduling at any given time, and represents the most stringent coordinated control. On the other extreme, $R_f = 1$ corresponds to no coordinated control, and hence reduces to independent control of each rank.

Let us start with the low latency sensitivity case. Fig 2 and 3 show the throughput and relative power savings as a function of channel utilization with R_f as a parameter. The throughput graph is included merely to confirm that the throughput degradation remains roughly contained within the 1% bound specified in the algorithm. The power saving is given as a percentage of total power consumption (at that utilization) without any power management.

The curve for $R_f = 1$ clearly shows significant power savings achievable below about 20% channel utilization range by the fine-grain power management considered in this paper. In contrast, coarse-grain techniques such as page remapping would typically apply only when utilization dips under

a few percent or less. *Thus there are significant gains to be had from the fine-grain power management.*

The curves for $R_f < 1$ show that rank coordination further improves power savings *beyond* those achievable by isolated power management at moderate to high utilization levels. (At low utilizations, isolated management itself is adequate.) For example, at 25% channel utilization, $R_f = 1/2$ gives 11% power savings whereas $R_f = 1$ (i.e., uncoordinated control) gives only 5% savings. With $R_f = 1/4$, the power savings go up to 16%. At 50% channel utilization where isolated management has essentially no power savings, with $R_f = 1/2$ and $R_f = 1/4$ we get respectively 5.8% and 9.2% savings. Clearly, these are significant numbers in watts at such high channel utilizations.

We also note that $R_f = 1/8$ and $R_f = 1/4$ behave almost identically. This is because even with $R_f = 1/4$, much of the available power savings have already been squeezed out, and reducing R_f only serves to increase the read latency without any throughput advantage.

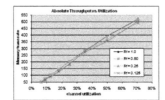 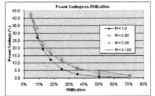

Figure 4: ro t for **Figure 5:** Po er a n for MS ca e MS ca e

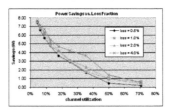

Figure 6: Po er a n . Lo rac.

Now we consider similar plots for the medium latency sensitivity case. Fig 4 and 5 show the throughput and power savings as a function of channel utilization with R_f as a parameter. It is seen that $R_f = 1/2$ in this case is enough to squeeze out all the additional power savings over isolated control, and reducing R_f further is not helpful. In fact, $R_f = 1/4$ or smaller degrades the throughput below the specified percentage. The reason for this failure is that the window W_u is inadequate to provide adequate recovery of the throughput.

Fig 6 shows the power savings curves for the medium latency sensitivity case under 4 different target degradation levels. For these curves we used $R_f = 1/2$ to ensure that there is no significant over-control and the target degradation can indeed be maintained. Not surprisingly, as the target degradation increases, more power savings become possible.

4. REFERENCES

[1] A. Papathanasiou and M. Scott, "Energy Efficiency through Burstiness", Proc of the 5th IEEE Workshop on Mobile Computing Systems and Applications (WMCSA'03), pp. 44-53, Oct 2003.

[2] X. Li, Z. Li, F. David, et al., "Performance directed energy management for main memory and disks", Proc. of 11th ASPLOS conf, pp271-283, 2004.

Optimal Neighbor Selection in BitTorrent-like Peer-to-Peer Networks

Hao Zhang
University of California, Berkeley
Berkeley, CA 94720, USA
zhanghao@berkeley.edu

Ziyu Shao
The Chinese Univ. of Hong Kong
Shatin, NT, Hong Kong
zyshao@ie.cuhk.edu.hk

Minghua Chen
The Chinese Univ. of Hong Kong
Shatin, NT, Hong Kong
minghua@ie.cuhk.edu.hk

Kannan Ramchandran
University of California, Berkeley
Berkeley, CA 94720, USA
kannanr@eecs.berkeley.edu

ABSTRACT

We study the problem of neighbor selection in BitTorrent-like peer-to-peer (P2P) systems, and propose a "soft-worst-neighbor-choking" algorithm that is provably optimal. In practical P2P systems, peers often keep a large set of potential neighbors, but only simultaneously upload/download to/from a small subset of them, which we call *active* neighbors, to avoid excessive connection overhead. A natural question to ask is: which active neighbor set should each peer choose to maximize the global system performance? The combinatorial nature of the problem makes it especially challenging. In this paper, we formulate an optimization problem and derive a distributed algorithm. We remark that our solution has a similar favor compared to the *worst neighbor choking* and *optimistic unchoking* neighbor selection algorithms that are implemented by BitTorrent. However, it encourages peers to stick to better performing neighbors for longer time and is provably globally optimal. Our proposed solution is easy to implement: each peer periodically waits for a constant period of time that depends on the size of the potential neighbor set and the aggregated utility of the active neighbors, *chokes* (drops) one of its current active neighbors with probability proportional to an exponential weight on the utility of the corresponding link, and randomly *unchokes* (adds) a new neighbor from its potential neighbor set. Our theoretical findings provide insightful guidelines to designing practical P2P systems. Simulation results corroborate our proposed solution.

Categories and Subject Descriptors

C.2.4 [**Distributed Systems**]: Distributed Applications

General Terms

Algorithms, theory

1. INTRODUCTION

Consider a P2P overlay network represented by a directed graph $G = (V, E)$, where V denotes the set of all the nodes and E is the set of all the *upload* links. Assume that each node v has a certain upload link capacity $C_v \geq 0$ and has no limit on the down-

Table 1: Key Notations

Notation	Definition
$\mathcal{F}$	the set of all peer neighboring configurations
V	the set of all peers
N_v^p	peer v's potential upload neighbor set
N_v^f	peer v's active upload neighbor set under f
x_{vu}^f	upload rate from peer v to peer u under f
C_v	upload capacity of peer v
B_v	outgoing upload connection bound of node v
U_v	concave utility function of node v
g_f	system utility under f

Note: we use bold-type to denote vectors.

load link capacity. Each node v has a potential *upload* neighbor set, denoted by N_v^p, which it can choose to upload to. However, each node v can upload to at most B_v neighbors simultaneously. We call this constraint an upload connection degree bound B_v. We refer to a specific peer neighboring connections a *topology configuration*, denoted by f. A configuration is essentially a snapshot of the current *active* P2P connection overlay graph. Let N_v^f be the set of neighbors that node v is currently *uploading* to under configuration f. Denote by $\mathcal{F}$ the set of all possible topology configurations in which the active neighbor set at every node satisfies its corresponding connection degree bound. Table 1 lists the relevant notation. Our goal is to maximize the overall utility *jointly* over peers' upload bandwidth allocation and peer neighbor selection in a distributed way. We formulate the problem as follows:

$$\max_{f \in \mathcal{F}, \boldsymbol{x}^f} \quad \sum_{v \in V} U_v(\boldsymbol{x}_v^f) \qquad (1)$$

$$\text{s.t.} \quad \boldsymbol{x}_v^f = \{x_{uv} | v \in N_u^f, \forall u \in V\}, \; \forall v \in V$$

$$\sum_{u \in N_v^f} x_{vu}^f \leq C_v, \; \forall v \in V$$

$$|N_v^f| \leq B_v, \; \forall v \in V$$

This is a mix convex-combinatorial problem. Adapting Lagrange dual decomposition and Markov approximation techniques [1], we propose to solve it by letting each peer v running a distributed algorithm, stated in Algorithm 1, independently. where $h_u(x_{vu}^f) =$

Algorithm 1 Rate Allocation and Neighbor Selection Algorithm

1: **Initialization:** Set $x_{vu} = 0$, $\lambda_v = 0$ and $t = T_v$ where T_v is the count-down time. Iterate:

2: Receive from all the active neighbors $u \in N_v^f$ their marginal utility value $h_u(x_{vu}^f)$ at the current upload rate x_{vu}^f, and then perform the following updates.

3: $x_{vu} \leftarrow x_{vu} + \varepsilon (h_u(x_{vu}^f) - \lambda_v)_{x_{vu}^f}^{[0,+\infty)}$, $\forall u \in N_v^f$

4: $\lambda_v \leftarrow \lambda_v + \delta(\sum_{u \in N_v^f} x_{vu} - C_v)_{\lambda_v}^{[0,+\infty)}$

5: Allocate and sends packets to the active neighbors according to the new rates x_{uv}.

6: **if** $t = 0$ **then**

7: Choke neighbor u with probability $\frac{\exp(-\beta x_{vu}^f h_u(x_{vu}^f))}{\sum_{u' \in N_v^f} \exp(-\beta x_{vu'}^f h_{u'}(x_{vu'}^f))}$, randomly unchoke a new neighbor from the inactive potential set to replace u, and set $x_{vu} = 0$ and $t = T_v$.

8: **end if**

9: $t \leftarrow t - 1$.

$\frac{\partial U_u(x_u^f)}{\partial x_{vu}^f}$ is the *marginal utility* of node u with respect to its download link rate x_{vu}^f, $\varepsilon, \delta > 0$ are small constants.

2. MAIN RESULTS

THEOREM 1. *If the count down time T_v in Algorithm 1 at node v is exponentially distributed with mean*

$$\frac{1}{\tau \left(|N_v^p| - |N_v^f|\right) \sum_{u' \in N_v^f} \exp\left(-\beta x_{vu'}^f h_{u'}(x_{vu'}^f)\right)} \quad (2)$$

then the overall system utility $g = \sum_{v \in V} U_v(x_v^f) \to \bar{g}$ as $\beta \to \infty$, and:

$$|g_o - \bar{g}| \leq \max_{v \in \mathcal{V}} U_v(C_v) \quad (3)$$

where g_o is the optimal solution to problem (1).

THEOREM 2. *The average performance $\bar{g}$ is insensitive to the distribution of the count-down time $T_v, v \in V$ as long as the mean of the count down time satisfies (2).*

We omit the proof details due to the space limit. We make the following remarks.

The proposed solution is fully distributed, i.e., each peer runs the rate allocation and neighbor selection algorithm independently. The optimality gap $\max_{v \in \mathcal{V}} U_v(C_v)$ is quite small when the total number of nodes in the system $|\mathcal{V}|$ is large.

The neighbor selection algorithm is also intuitive: (a) the larger the inactive potential set $|N_v^p| - |N_v^f|$, the shorter time a peer should wait till he finds a new peer to upload to; (b) the better the overall marginal aggregated utility $\sum_{u' \in N_v^f} \exp\left(-\beta x_{vu'}^f h_{u'}(x_{vu'}^f)\right)$ to the neighbors, the longer time a peer should wait before finding new neighbors; and (c) the larger the aggregated marginal utility (thus the smaller $\exp\left(-\beta x_{vu}^f h_u(x_{vu}^f)\right)$), the less likely the corresponding active neighbor will be choked and vice versa. This intuitive strategy encourages peers to stay longer in better performing configurations. We call our neighbor selection algorithm the "*soft-worst-neighbor-choking*" algorithm.

Surprisingly, the heuristic approaches of "tit-for-tat" choking and "optimistic unchoking" that are implemented BitTorrent [2] is a similar version to our "*soft-worst-neighbor-choking*" algorithm. In BitTorrent, a peer periodically chokes its upload to an active peer

Table 2: Peer upload capacity distribution

Upload (kbps)	512	640	768	896	1024	1152	1280
Fraction (%)	5	10	5	40	15	10	15

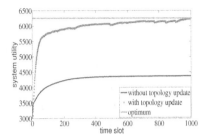

Figure 1: System utility with and without topology building.

with the *worst* download rate with a fixed period of 10 seconds. In our case, a peer chokes neighbors with the probability proportional to an exponential weight on the aggregated marginal utility of the neighbors. Since the probabilities are exponentially weighted, a peer essentially "softly" chokes an neighbor with worst aggregated marginal utility. Also in BitTorrent, a peer "optimistically" unchokes a *random* new inactive neighbor periodically every 30 seconds, in order to explore new peers with potentially better download rates. In our algorithm, peers also randomly finds new neighbors from time to time. However, our algorithm waits for a longer time when the system performance is at a better state and vice versa. This helps drive the system to move faster to and stay longer in better configurations.

Our proposed algorithm is generalizable to other P2P systems. The same peer selection algorithm can be distributively implemented, and only a different utility function needs to be plugged in for different applications.

3. EXPERIMENTS

3.1 Setup

We set the number of peers $|V| = 100$. Peers have upload capacities draw from the distribution shown in Table 2. Each peer can have a potential neighbor set of $|N_v^p| = 20$, and a degree bound of $|B_v| = 2$.

We set the utility function of each user v as:

$$U_v(x_v^f) = \begin{cases} |x_v^f|_1 - \frac{|x_v^f|_1^2}{2r} & \text{if } |x_v^f|_1 \leq r \\ \frac{r}{2} & \text{if } |x_v^f|_1 > r \end{cases}$$

where $|x_v^f|_1 = \sum_{u:v \in N_u^f} x_{uv}^f$ is the summation of the received rate from its download neighbors, and $r = 1024$kbps. We also set the step sizes $\varepsilon = 2$ and $\delta = 0.4$ for the bandwidth allocation algorithm, and set $\beta = 5$ and $\tau = 1$ in the topology update algorithm. We can see that the proposed algorithm performs quite well. The proposed solution has a significant gain compared to a static topology setting and is close to the optimum.

4. REFERENCES

[1] M. Chen, S. C. Liew, Z. Shao, and C. Kai. Markov approximation for combinatorial network optimization. In *Proc. of IEEE INFOCOM*, San Diego, CA, USA, 2010.

[2] B. Cohen. Incentives Build Robustness in BitTorrent. In *Workshop on Economics of Peer-to-Peer Systems*, volume 6. Berkeley, CA, USA, 2003.

Towards Understanding Modern Web Traffic

Sunghwan Ihm
Department of Computer Science
Princeton University
sihm@cs.princeton.edu

Vivek S. Pai
Department of Computer Science
Princeton University
vivek@cs.princeton.edu

ABSTRACT

As the nature of Web traffic evolves over time, we must update our understanding of underlying nature of today's Web, which is necessary to improve response time, understand caching effectiveness, and to design intermediary systems, such as firewalls, security analyzers, and reporting or management systems. In this paper, we analyze five years (2006-2010) of real Web traffic from a globally-distributed proxy system, which captures the browsing behavior of over 70,000 daily users from 187 countries. Using this data set, we examine major changes in Web traffic characteristics during this period, and also investigate the redundancy of this traffic, using both traditional object-level caching as well as content-based approaches.

Categories and Subject Descriptors

C.2.m [**Computer-Communication Networks**]: Miscellaneous

General Terms

Measurement, Design, Performance

Keywords

Web Traffic Analysis, Web Caching

1. INTRODUCTION

The World Wide Web is one of the most important Internet applications, and its traffic volume is increasing and evolving due to the popularity of social networking, file hosting, and video streaming sites [3]. Understanding these changes is important to overall system design. For example, analyzing end-user browsing behavior leads to a Web traffic model, which in turn can be used to generate a synthetic workload for benchmarking or simulation. In addition, analyzing redundancy in the Web traffic and the effectiveness of caching could shape the design of Web servers, proxies, and browsers to improve response times.

While there has been much research in the past decade to better understand the nature of Web traffic, unfortunately, we still have little understanding of today's Web. It is challenging because understanding changes requires large-scale

data spanning a multi-year period. Also, while content-based caching [2] is known to be very effective and becomes popular, understanding its effectiveness on Web traffic requires full content data rather than just access logs.

In this paper, we analyze five years (2006-2010) of real Web traffic from the CoDeeN content distribution network [6], a globally distributed proxy system which captures the browsing behavior of over 70,000 users per day from 187 countries. Using this data, we examine major changes in Web traffic characteristics over a five-year period, such as content type distributions and popular sites. In addition, we capture the full content of traffic, and study the redundancy and impact of caching, using both traditional object-based caching as well as content-based caching approaches.

2. DATA SET

CoDeeN is a semi-open [1] globally distributed proxy which has been running since 2003, and serves over 30 million requests per day from more than 500 PlanetLab [5] nodes. For this study, we consider a five-year period of access log data from 2006 to 2010, as well as full content data from 2010. Due to the large volume of requests, we sample one month (April) of data per year, and focus on the traffic of users from four countries from different continents – the United States (US) in North America, Brazil (BR) in South America, China (CN) in Asia, and France (FR) in Europe. Overall, our analysis on four countries covers 48-137 million requests, 689-1903 GB traffic, and 70-152 thousand users per month.

3. PRELIMINARY RESULTS

Content Types Figure 1 presents the content type distribution changes in the United States, France, and Brazil from 2006 to 2010, connected by arrows. The X axis is the percentage of requests, and the Y axis is the percentage of bytes, both in log-scale. We omit China's result that also exhibits similar changes.

First, we observe a sharp increase of javascript, css, and xml, primarily due to the popular use of ajax [1]. We also find a sharp increase of flash video (flv) traffic, taking about 25% of total traffic in the United States and Brazil in 2010. At the same time, non-flv video traffic sees a decrease, demonstrating the shift of the media delivery medium to the popular flash video. Still, the image traffic including all of its subtypes consumes the most bandwidth.

---

[1] It only allows GET requests for security reasons.

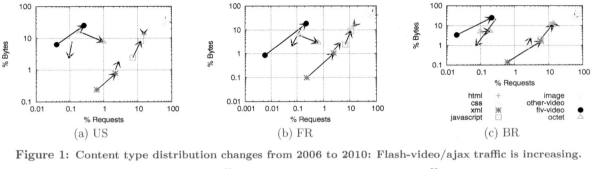

(a) US	(b) FR	(c) BR

Figure 1: Content type distribution changes from 2006 to 2010: Flash-video/ajax traffic is increasing.

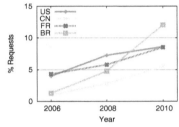
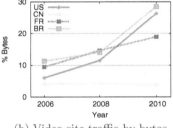
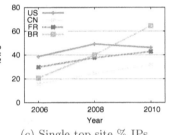

(a) Ads network traffic by requests	(b) Video site traffic by bytes	(c) Single top site % IPs

Figure 2: Top sites: Ads/video site traffic is increasing. A single top site tracks up to 65% of the entire users.

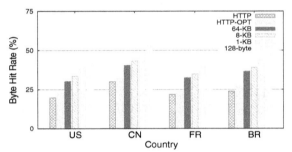

Figure 3: Ideal byte hit rate with infinite cache storage: Content-based caching with 128-byte chunks achieves almost 2x larger byte hit-rate than HTTP caching.

Top Sites We examine the share of 1) video site traffic (*e.g.*, youtube.com), and 2) advertising network/analytics traffic (*e.g.*, doubleclick.com, google-analytics.com) in Figure 2. We consider only the top 50 sites as we gain diminishing returns from further investigation, so the result conservatively estimates the actual share.

First, in Figure 2 (a), we observe that advertising network traffic takes 1-12% of the total requests, and it consistently increases over time as the market grows [4]. In addition, we find the volume of video site traffic is consistently increasing as shown in Figure 2 (b), taking up to 28% in Brazil in 2010. In China's case, however, the image-hosting site traffic takes the largest volume, and the share of video site traffic is lower than the share of other countries. Finally, we see the single top site reaches a growing fraction of all users over time in Figure 2 (c). All of the single top sites during a five-year period are either a search engine (google.com or baidu.com), or analytics (google-analytics.com). Especially in 2010, the percentage reaches up to 65% in Brazil, which might concern user privacy.

Redundancy and Caching We calculate the ideal bandwidth savings achievable with infinite cache storage using the traditional object-level HTTP caching and content-based caching. For the object-level caching, we assume two objects

are identical (cache hit) if they are cacheable and their URLs and content lengths match. We also consider a slightly optimistic behavior of object-based caching by discarding query strings from URLs in order to accommodate the case where two URLs with different metadata actually belong to the same object. For content-based caching, we vary the average chunk size from 128 bytes, 1 KB, 8 KB, to 64 KB, and exclude the metadata overhead.

In Figure 3, we observe that content-based caching outperforms the object-based caching with any chunk size. The cache hit rate of object-level caching ranges from 27-39% (not shown in the figure), but the actual byte hit rate is only 20-30%. The hit rate of the optimistic version (HTTP-OPT) is only slightly larger. On the other hand, the lowest byte hit rate of the content-based caching is 30-40% with 64-KB chunks, and the highest byte hit rate is 43-53% with 128-byte chunks, 1.7-2.2x larger than the object-level caching's.

4. ACKNOWLEDGMENT

We would like to thank the anonymous SIGMETRICS reviewers. This research was partially supported by NSF awards CNS-0615237 and CNS-0916204.

References

[1] D. Crane, E. Pascarello, and D. James. *Ajax in Action*. Manning Publications Co., Greenwich, CT, USA, 2005.

[2] S. Ihm, K. Park, and V. S. Pai. Wide-area Network Acceleration for the Developing World. In *Proc. USENIX Annual Technical Conference*, Boston, MA, June 2010.

[3] ipoque. Internet Study 2008/2009. http://www.ipoque.com/resources/internet-studies/internet-study-2008_2009.

[4] JPMorgan Chase & Company. The Rise of Ad Networks. http://www.mediamath.com/docs/JPMorgan.pdf.

[5] PlanetLab. http://www.planet-lab.org/, 2008.

[6] L. Wang, K. Park, R. Pang, V. S. Pai, and L. Peterson. Reliability and security in the CoDeeN content distribution network. In *Proc. USENIX Annual Technical Conference*, Boston, MA, June 2004.

De-Ossifying Internet Routing through Intrinsic Support for End-Network and ISP Selfishness

Aditya Akella, Shuchi Chawla, Holly Esquivel and Chitra Muthukrishnan
Dept. of Computer Sciences, UW-Madison
{akella,shuchi,esquivel,chitra}@cs.wisc.edu

ABSTRACT

We present the S4R supplemental routing system to address the constraints BGP places on ISPs and stub network alike. Technical soundness and economic viability are equal first class design requirements for S4R. In S4R, ISPs announce links connecting different parts of the Internet. ISPs can selfishly price their links to attract maximal amount of traffic. Stub networks can selfishly select paths that best meet their requirements at the lowest cost. We design a variety of practical algorithms for ISP and stub network response that strike a balance between accommodating selfishness of all participants and ensuring efficient and stable operation overall. We employ large scale simulations over realistic scenarios to show that S4R operates at a close-to-optimal state and that it encourages broad participation from stubs and ISPs.

Categories and Subject Descriptors: C.2.m [Computer Communication Networks]: Miscellaneous

General Terms: Algorithms.

Keywords: Inter-domain routing, selfishness.

1. INTRODUCTION

BGP suffers from key inflexibilities that impose constraints on both stub networks and ISPs. BGP offers stub networks exactly one policy-constrained path per destination per ISP connection, with no guarantees on performance or availability. Thus, stub networks cannot flexibly meet the requirements of key network-based applications, such as satisfying the end-to-end performance constraints of real-time video or finance applications, especially during peak traffic periods. One way to overcome this is for stub networks to enter into partial transit or paid peering contracts with multiple ISPs to support sensitive applications. Unfortunately, these contracts are binding and long-term in nature. Other finer-grained approaches, such as overlay routing and multihoming route control, are either undesirable in practice or inadequate: The flexibility offered by overlay routing has undesirable interactions with ISP policies and traffic engineering objectives. Multihoming can offer better performance than single BGP paths, but it still cannot guarantee that the stub networks' end-to-end requirements will be met.

BGP is sub-optimal for ISPs, too. ISPs have little flexibility in controlling their revenues and expanding their services to attract a larger customer base. While BGP import and export policies allow ISPs some control over their revenues, they require ISPs to rely on long-term bilateral contracts with peers and customers. ISPs can offer performance guarantees for traffic within their own domain, but are at the mercy of those they contract with once traffic exits

their own network. Moreover, there are no easy ways for an ISP to expand its customer base to stub networks located in places where the ISP has no "physical presence". Approaches based on tunneling (e.g., MIRO [7]) are inadequate because the tunnels must traverse multiple intermediate ISPs that may not offer the tunneled traffic the same level of high performance.

Some prior efforts [5, 6, 1, 3, 2] have recognized the fundamental shortcomings of routing, namely, that it is neither aligned with important emerging stub network usage scenarios nor with ISP revenue and operational goals. However, these works focus either on (some of the) underlying implementation issues or on economic/theoretical analyses. To date, no work has both described a technical solution and evaluated its viability in practice, especially from an economic standpoint. For example, approaches such as multi-provider MPLS/VPNs [1] consider the technical issues in enabling stub networks to obtain inter-domain paths meeting their requirements, but they do not consider the crucial economic issues for both ISPs and stub networks (e.g., how to price paths to maximize revenue, how to select paths with best cost-performance trade-offs etc.), which impact whether or not such mechanisms are adopted in the first place. At the other extreme, game-theoretic models [3, 2] study selfish interactions among ISPs and stubs, and show that the result can be arbitrarily bad in some network settings; however, it is not clear if these results hold in realistic scenarios.

Our paper brings together both technical as well as economic issues to develop a compelling solution to the above shortcomings. We describe the design and implementation of an economically-grounded routing system, called S4R ("shop-for-routes"). S4R is designed to supplement, not supplant BGP. S4R enables participating stubs and ISPs to behave *selfishly* in order to directly meet their local objectives. Thus, S4R offers its participants a great degree of flexibility, which fosters greater participation from them while not requiring any kind of global oversight. We evaluate S4R in a variety of realistic situations using metrics and models that are similar to those used in prior game-theoretical analyses and show that S4R is desirable for both stub networks and ISPs. We argue the S4R can be implemented using the OpenFlow platform; we present an evaluation of a preliminary OpenFlow-based prototype.

Concretely, ISPs participating in S4R announce (virtual) links connecting different locations of the Internet. ISPs have the flexibility of dynamically altering the link prices so as to control the quality of their links and, more importantly, to attract traffic and maximize their revenue. Stub networks have the flexibility to select (or shift at any time to) paths with optimal cost-performance trade-offs for the specific application at hand. A stub network will always be able to find paths that best meet its application-level requirements as long as it has the willingness to pay for it. S4R's approach to enabling selfishness of its participants directly aligns with the selfishness models studied in prior worst-case theoretical analyses. However, we find, surprisingly, that S4R leads to robust outcomes in practice contrary to what theory suggests [3, 2].

We conduct an extensive evaluation of S4R using a variety of realistic and synthetic scenarios to answer key technical and economic questions. Our key finding is that, in all scenarios, the net performance derived by S4R' stub networks (in both the centralized and distributed cases) is roughly 30% away from the best possible social outcome (i.e., where all ISPs are altruistic and provide globally-optimal routes). S4R can support a variety of stub use-cases (which are poorly supported today) equally effectively.

2. S4R OVERVIEW

Stub networks. In S4R, stub networks can obtain end-to-end paths between two network locations with some associated properties. We focus mainly on *performance* guarantees, but S4R can be used for other properties, such as avoiding specific ISPs, routing through intermediaries like DDoS filters and application accelerators, requiring traffic being split over a certain number of non-overlapping paths, requiring backup paths etc. In S4R, stub networks can place requests of four different types that model different likely stub requirements in practice: (1) **Diurnal predicted:** where the stub network has a fixed required bandwidth profile for traffic to a destination. (2) **Peak predicted:** where the stub requests a certain amount of bandwidth for a specific fixed period of time in the day, corresponding to a predicted peak in traffic volume. (3) **Instantaneous:** Based on some initial monitoring, a stub may decide to instantaneously purchase a certain amount of bandwidth for some time period. (4) **Elastic bulk:** This models delay-tolerant bulk transfers (e.g., prefetching VOD content, transfers of large scientific data sets etc.).

S4R stubs provide a *value* associated with the specific traffic to a destination, which is treated as private information. Stub networks are *local utility-maximizing*: a stub network can select routes such that its *utility*—the difference between the value derived by the stub network and the price it pays for the routes—is maximized on a per-destination and per-application basis.

ISPs: Each ISP offers to carry traffic across a "virtual link" between two network locations (e.g., specific PoPs) at some cost per unit bandwidth. ISPs are *revenue-maximizing*, setting prices to maximize the revenue earned from the links owned. An ISP's revenue per link is the product of the stub network flow routed on the link and the link price per unit traffic.

Equilibrium: There are two possible approaches to accommodating the objectives/requirements of, and the interactions between, ISPs and stubs: centralized and distributed. In the former, a logically central facilitator emulates the selfish interactions between ISPs and stub networks and derives a *correlated equilibrium*. In the latter, ISPs and stub networks interact constantly and organically. Detailed descriptions of these alternatives can be found in [4].

3. S4R EVALUATION

S4R is similar to a real world marketplace where customers are willing to shop around for the best prices for sets of goods and stores try to competitively price goods to attract customers to purchase from them. Since each ISP is interested in maximizing its own revenue, the overall system performance at equilibrium may not be "socially" optimal (compared to a hypothetical third-party computing a globally optimal solution for maximizing the performance). There is a rich body of recent work in algorithmic game theory that studies similar settings, providing bounds on the "price of anarchy" (POA), namely the ratio of the worst-case system performance at equilibrium to the social optimal. The works most relevant to S4R are those of Chawla and Roughgarden [3] and Chawla

and Niu [2]. These show that, for pathological network instances, the price of anarchy can be unbounded, implying that system performance can be significantly far from optimal [3, 2]. The poor efficiency means that few stub networks and ISPs are likely to extract utility from S4R and hence S4R may not be viable. The works also find that when stub values satisfy the *monotone hazard rate (MHR)* condition, the worst-case performance improves significantly: it is worse than optimal by a factor no more than exponential in the number of hops between any source and the sink, and is independent of other parameters such as the values themselves, network size, available capacities, etc. While this is somewhat "positive" for S4R, it still shows that the outcome in practice can be quite far from the optimal, which brings S4R's viability into question.

To understand if the theoretical worst-case results hold in practice, we conducted a variety of simulation experiments that emulate different realistic scenarios. Our key metric of interest here is the social value derived by the system relative to the optimal social value, that we also refer to as "efficiency". This measures the ability of stub networks to obtain as much benefit as possible from the system while allowing the ISPs to extract maximal revenue. This metric is different from POA because POA is a measure of efficiency of the worst Nash equilibrium.

Through our evaluation, we found that [4]:

• S4R converges to a stable operating point in all conditions we studied. The overall efficiency is between 65% and 80%, showing that S4R is viable in practice, i.e., it will be of high overall utility, contrary to what the theory predicted. S4R is efficient even when the disparity in stub values is high in practice, contrary to what theory has found.

• The distributed approach converges in all situations as well. Its efficiency is only slightly inferior to the centralized variant.

• ISPs can employ simplistic regret minimizing learning algorithms to set their prices. We find that selfish stub response for rerouting actually leads to better outcomes as it provides more up-to-date information to ISPs about the impact of their price changes.

• S4R effectively supports all the four demands models described earlier. S4R can accommodate a modest amount of churn (up to 10% change of demand due to instantaneous stubs entering and leaving).

• At equilibrium, stubs who have the highest values for their traffic always find paths, and there is no significant skew in ISPs revenues. This shows that both ISPs and stubs will find S4R attractive.

• S4R efficiency suffers when the network has limited path diversity and/or long paths. However, since the barrier to entering S4R is low for ISPs, we expect rich interconnection and path diversity.

4. REFERENCES

[1] BGP/MPLS IP VPNs. http://tools.ietf.org/html/draft-ietf-l3vpn-rfc2547bis-03, 1999.

[2] S. Chawla and F. Niu. The Price of Anarchy in Bertrand Games. In *ACM Conference on Electronic Commerce*, pages 305–314, 2009.

[3] S. Chawla and T. Roughgarden. Bertrand competition in networks. In *Symposium on Algorithmic Game Theory*, pages 70–82, 2008.

[4] H. Esquivel et al. RouteBazaar: An Economic Framework for Flexible Routing. Technical Report 1654, UW-Madison, Mar. 2009.

[5] C. Estan, A. Akella, and S. Banerjee. Achieving good end-to-end service using Bill-Pay. In *ACM HotNets-V*, Irvine, CA, Dec. 2006.

[6] V. Valancius et al. Mint: A market for internet transit. In *ReArch*, 2008.

[7] W. Xu et al. Miro: multi-path interdomain routing. In *SIGCOMM*, 2006.

Dynamic Server Provisioning to Minimize Cost in an IaaS Cloud

[Extended Abstract] *

Yu-Ju Hong
School of Electrical and
Computer Engineering
Purdue University
West Lafayette, IN, USA
yujuhong@purdue.edu

Jiachen Xue
School of Electrical and
Computer Engineering
Purdue University
West Lafayette, IN, USA
xuej@purdue.edu

Mithuna Thottethodi
School of Electrical and
Computer Engineering
Purdue University
West Lafayette, IN, USA
mithuna@purdue.edu

ABSTRACT

Cloud computing holds the exciting potential of elastically scaling computation to match time-varying demand, thus eliminating the need to provision for peak demand to satisfy response-time requirements. Moreover, cloud vendors often offer several commitment levels for their machine instances (e.g., users can choose to pay an upfront premium for the discounted hourly usage price). Because cost is a major concern that may limit the cloud adoption, two key challenges are to determine (a) the number of machines to provision and (b) the commitment level at which the machine instances should be acquired, to minimize cost while satisfying response-time targets. This paper address the above two challenges in an Infrastructure-as-a-Service (IaaS) cloud. Our simulations with real Web server load traces reveal that our techniques offer a cost reduction between 13% and 29% (21% on average) under Amazon EC2 pricing models.

Categories and Subject Descriptors

K.6.2 [**Installation Management**]: Pricing and resource allocation; C.4 [**Performance of Systems**]: Performance Attributes

General Terms

Economics, Performance, Management

Keywords

Server Provisioning, Cloud Computing

1. INTRODUCTION

In the pre-cloud world, server operators had to either incur the cost of provisioning for the peak-demand (or near-peak demand, if some modest dilution in server response time was acceptable [2]) *or* incur the cost of excessive degradation in response time. The emergence of commercially-available

---

*A full version of this paper is available as *Purdue ECE Tech Report TR-ECE-11-08* at http://docs.lib.purdue.edu/ecetr

Infrastructure-as-a-Service (IaaS) cloud computing vendors such as Amazon EC2 has enabled a more elastic provisioning approach wherein on-demand computational resources can be "rented" at very short notice. Armbrust *et al.* provide an expanded overview of such tradeoffs in their white paper on cloud computing [1].

The cost-advantage of cloud-computing for *episodic* computation demands (e.g., one-time document digitization, hosting sites covering major sporting events) is well-understood; users with such one-time demands can avoid capital expenditure and instead utilize their financial resources solely for operational expenses. In contrast, the case for cloud computing for ongoing, day-to-day operations with long time horizons is less clear. There are many factors that may hinder cloud adoption, as described in [1]. This paper focuses on one such issue – costs incurred by the potential cloud user. The goal of this paper is to achieve significant cost savings for *normal* day-to-day computation demands and not for *episodic* computational demands.

There are two key factors that affect cost. First, because of the uncertainty of time-varying loads, operators are forced to maintain a margin – a pool of servers beyond the expected load – which adds to the "true" cost (which is the cost if loads are known *a priori* without any uncertainty). Minimizing such margin cost is important. Second, cloud vendors such as Amazon EC2 offer services at various commitment levels. For example, at the lowest commitment level, there are on-demand instances in which machine instances are acquired on an hourly basis with no longer-term commitment at all. At higher levels, there are the "reserved instances" wherein the user may pay an upfront fixed cost to ensure discounted hourly pricing for various durations (e.g., 1 year, 3 years). Minimizing cost by acquiring machine instances at the cost-optimal commitment level for time-varying loads is also an important challenge.

2. MITIGATING COST

This paper makes two key contributions to reduce both margin costs and true costs for cloud users. Our first contribution is a technique to determine margins in such a way that margin costs are minimized under a given load volatility model. The technique has two innovations based on two observations we made in the request traces of real workloads. First, we observed that the volatility (and hence margin requirements) vary by load. Unlike traditional load-oblivious margin mechanisms which use some fixed arithmetic transformation on the load to compute margins (e.g., translation with a fixed offset for constant margins, scaling with a fixed ratio for linear margins), our `ShrinkWrap` technique uses a table-lookup to provide customized, load-dependent margins. `ShrinkWrap` reduces wasted margins by avoiding the one-size-fits-all approach (i.e., the same fixed margin at all loads and at all times). Our second observation was driven by the fact that systems typically have some "tolerance" – the fraction of time where response time targets may be violated. We observe that the way in which the tolerance budget is expended affects cost because using the tolerance at some loads may result in more cost savings than at other loads. We develop a dynamic programming algorithm to optimally expend the tolerance budget to achieve maximum margin cost savings. Including our optimal tolerance expenditure algorithm with `ShrinkWrap` we get `ShrinkWrap-opt`.

Our second contribution addresses the true costs of serving requests by appropriately choosing commitment levels. We demonstrate that `commitment straddling` – the employment of both reserved and on-demand servers is fundamentally necessary to minimize cost, while meeting performance requirements. To understand why such commitment straddling is cost-optimal, we may conceptually view time-varying loads as inducing varying utilization in a collection of servers with some servers being heavily loaded and others being lightly loaded. Combining such variation in utilization with the well-known notion that reserved instances are less expensive than on-demand instances when high utilization is expected (say, utilization beyond a break-even ratio), we can divide the servers into two classes – those with higher utilization than the break-even ratio and those with lower utilization than the break-even ratio. Naturally, the optimal cost configuration will employ reserved servers for the first class and on-demand servers for the second class.

We show that cost-optimal commitment straddling can be computed if the load frequency distribution is known *a priori*. Intuitively, one may think that commitment straddling is the equivalent of using reserved instances for the average load and on-demand instances for the peak load. However, our precise analysis provides a stronger result. For example, our results show that it takes a grossly underutilized workload (with more than 50% idle-time), for an all-on-demand configuration to be the optimal. Similarly, it takes a workload where the peak load is sustained for nearly 50% of the time for the all-reserved configuration to be cost optimal.

We use an in-house trace-driven simulator that models a cloud vendor as seen by cloud clients. Our simulator assumes that on-demand machine instances can be started up in 10 minutes, and the rental granularity is one hour. The pricing of the machines are modeled based on the extra large on-demand instance and 1-year reserved instance of Amazon EC2 tariffs on October 10th, 2010. The set of traces used to drive our simulator includes three public traces (Clarknet, UC Berkeley, NASA), a 5-month trace from Purdue University College of Engineering Web site (Purdue CoE), and a 3-month load trace from Wikimedia group of Web sites (June Sep. 2010).

We compare our `ShrinkWrap-opt` against a base case which adopts a fixed margin (`FM`), and our `straddle` policy with the `all-reserved` and `all-on-demand` policies.

Figure 1 plots the total cost (Y-axis) for each of traces (and the geometric mean) assuming 1% tolerance. Each

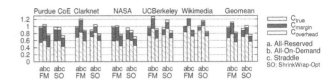

Figure 1: Total costs normalized to FM, All-Reserved; 1% tolerance

bar is divided into subbars to indicate true cost (the cost incurred by the fraction of servers that were actively serving requests), margin cost (the cost of servers that were active, but did not have requests to serve) and overhead (the cost of machines beyond the margin which exist solely because they cannot be shutdown due to rental granularity). The primary results are as follows.

1. **Margin-cost reduction:** `ShrinkWrap-opt` is the best practical margin minimization policy which achieves 38% lower margin costs.

2. **True cost reduction:** The `straddle` configuration achieves, on average, 21% and 27% lower true cost than the `all-reserved` and `all-on-demand` configurations, respectively, while achieving the same (or better) tolerance.

3. Together, the two techniques yield cost-reductions between 13% and 29% (21% on average).

3. CONCLUSIONS

Cost remains a significant barrier for adoption of cloud computing for ongoing computing operations. Cloud operations incur two types of costs when serving time-varying workloads. They incur margin costs to handle uncertainty of load and also true costs to serve requests. This paper addresses both costs optimally, given statistical properties of the workload. Our simulations using real workload traces and Amazon EC2 pricing model reveal that combining the two techniques yields 21% cost savings (on average) compared to the baseline configurations. Specifically, our results show that as much as 14.5% cost reduction is possible for Wikimedia.

Future Work: This paper models volatility as being dependent on load alone. More sophisticated volatility models which include time and/or load history may lead to further improvements in margin cost.

4. REFERENCES

[1] M. Armbrust et al. Above the clouds: A berkeley view of cloud computing. In *Tech. Rep. UCB/EECS-2009-28, EECS Department, University of California, Berkeley*, 2009.

[2] B. Urgaonkar, P. Shenoy, and T. Roscoe. Resource overbooking and application profiling in shared hosting platforms. *SIGOPS Oper. Syst. Rev.*, 36(SI):239–254, 2002.

HeteroScouts: Hardware Assist for OS Scheduling in Heterogeneous CMPs

Sadagopan Srinivasan, Ravishankar Iyer, Li Zhao, Ramesh Illikkal

Intel Corporation

sadagopan.srinivasan@intel.com

ABSTRACT

Designing heterogeneous chip multiprocessors (CMPs) with a mix of *big* cores (complex superscalar out-of-order pipelines) and *small* cores (simple in-order pipeline) is emerging as an attractive option for future architectures. Such architectures have the potential to deliver both high performance and power efficiency but this requires operating systems (OS) or virtual machine monitors (VMMs) to efficiently schedule each software thread on the type of core that is best suited for it. In this paper, we highlight the need for architectural support for OS scheduling in a heterogeneous CMP. We propose *HeteroScouts*, a hardware mechanism to assist the OS to efficiently predict the performance of a task on different cores in the platform.

Categories and Descriptors

C.1.3 [**Processor Architectures**]: Heterogeneous systems

General Terms

Measurement, Experimentation, Performance

Keywords

Heterogeneous architectures, CMPs, Performance, OS Scheduling

1. INTRODUCTION

As more cores are being integrated on the die, commercial operating systems are evolving to efficiently support the parallelism provided by multi-core processors. Within a decade, we expect that the efficacy of homogeneous multi-core scaling will limited again by power and area constraints. In the meantime, more power efficient small cores have emerged and show the potential to provide power-efficient performance in clients and servers. As a result, the integration of both big and small cores on the same die now seems more attractive and feasible than ever before. In this paper, our focus is on harnessing the performance and power-efficiency provided by heterogeneous chip-multiprocessors that consist of a mix of big and small cores.

Researchers [1] in the past have proposed that single-ISA heterogeneous CMPs are attractive since they can provide multiple types of cores, each with a different operating point in terms of performance, area and power dissipation. By running workloads on cores best suited to it, heterogeneous CMPs were shown to be able to provide better performance as well as power efficiency than the traditional homogeneous CMP platforms. However, this benefit can only be achieved if the OS can dynamically identify the behavior of each of the running applications on the different types of cores supported in the heterogeneous platform . This is a challenging problem to solve since it requires running each of the applications on all of the cores and record its behavior. In addition, if the applications go

through phases that exhibit differing performance behavior, then it becomes even more difficult to identify how to schedule the application. In this paper, we address this challenge by identifying hardware mechanisms that can assist the operating system in scheduling applications on a heterogeneous platform.

2. Heterogeneous Architectures

Heterogeneous architectures consist of different types of cores with potentially differing ISA as well. In this paper, we consider: (a) big cores based on the Intel Core 2 Duo and (b) small core based on the Intel Atom. Figure 2(a) shows an example heterogeneous platform made up of big and small cores, each with their private L1 and L2 caches, and connected to a shared memory via an on-die interconnect.

When running multiple different applications simultaneously on a heterogeneous architecture, it is important to understand the performance that the application can achieve on the big core versus the small core. Here, the first question that comes up is: (a) *do all applications have similar performance difference when running on big versus small cores?* To answer this question, we ran multiple applications (SPECCPU 2000, SPECCPU 2006, EEMBC and BioBench) on Core 2 Duo and Atom platforms. To mimic a configuration where both cores are integrated into the same heterogeneous uncore architecture, we configured the core frequency, cache and memory subsystem of these platforms to be as close as possible.

2.1 Performance and Scheduling Challenges

Figure 2(b) shows the results obtained from the measurement runs on these two (big and small) cores. The data clearly shows that different applications show different performance ratios when running on big versus small cores. The performance improvement (big core over small core performance) ranges from 1.01X for "tigr" (in Biobench) to 2.5X for eon (CPU2000). This clearly indicates that scheduling can have a significant impact on the overall throughput efficiency on a heterogeneous architecture.

Figure 2(c) shows the total CPI for a few example pairs as a result of "naïve" scheduling as well as "oracle" scheduling where information about the behavior of the application is available at fine granularity. The data clearly shows that there is wide gap in performance (as high as 2X between oracle and naïve) and therefore there is a significant opportunity to achieve efficient scheduling on heterogeneous architectures.

3. HeteroScouts: Hardware Assisted OS Scheduling

Scheduling on heterogeneous architectures can be made efficient from a performance and energy perspective if we can develop techniques that allow us to determine which application should be scheduled on which core (big or small). Various scheduling policies have been proposed in [2][3]. In this paper, we argue that hardware assists (called HeteroScouts) should be provided in heterogeneous platforms to provide this information to OS

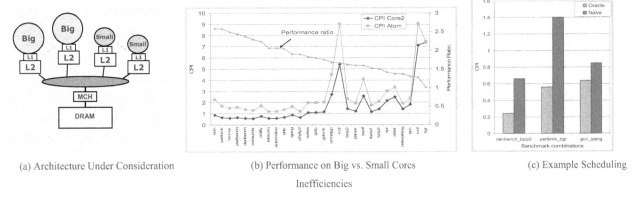

(a) Architecture Under Consideration (b) Performance on Big vs. Small Cores (c) Example Scheduling
Inefficiencies

Figure 2. Heterogeneous CMPs Architecture, Performance and Scheduling

schedulers during runtime. This information can be obtained using the platform performance counters along with a performance prediction model as shown in [4]. Figure 3 illustrates the difference between software-only scheduling and hardware-assisted OS scheduling based on HeteroScouts Modules (HSM) in heterogeneous platforms. As illustrated, for software-only scheduling, each task has to be run on the big core as well as on

the small core at least once. With HeteroScouts, each task can be run on either core and the performance difference information is available automatically. For the HSM assist to be effective, it should i) Accurate, ii) Dynamic, and iii) have Minimal overhead.

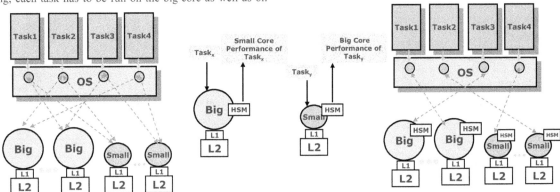

(a) Software-Only Scheduling runs tasks on all core types *(b) HeteroScouts Module* *(c) HeteroScouts for Hardware-Assisted OS Scheduling*

Figure 3. HeteroScouts: Hardware Assists for OS Scheduling

4. Summary

To improve the scheduling efficiency on heterogeneous architectures, we propose hardware assists using platform performance counters to predict the performance of the application. The proposed HeteroScouts module (HSM) is designed to achieve the following functionality:

(a) *For any running task (on any core), the HeteroScouts module (HSM) monitors the behavior of the running task and provides an estimate of the performance of that task on each of the other core types.*

(b) *From an OS perspective, the HeteroScouts data is exposed as a performance monitoring capability. Typically, when the OS de-schedules a task on a core, it should be able to read the Heteroscouts data to determine what the expected performance of that task would be on the other core types.*

Performance prediction is achieved by breaking down the key components of total cycles of the application into compute and memory cycles, and mapped back to the other core's total cycles

using various platform statistics such as memory latency, number of loads/stores, L2 misses etc. In future work, this model is to be incorporated into a Linux kernel for dynamic scheduling.

REFERENCES

[1] R. Kumar, et al. "Single-ISA Heterogeneous Multi-Core Architectures: The Potential for Processor Power Reduction". In Proceedings of the 36th International Symposium on Microarchitecture.

[2] T. Li, et al. Operating System Support for Overlapping-ISA Heterogeneous Multi-core Architectures. In Proceedings of High Performance Computer Architecture, 2010.

[3] M. Becchi and P. Crowley. Dynamic Thread Assignment on Heterogeneous Multiprocessor Architectures. In Computing Frontiers, 2006.

[4] S. Eyerman, et al. A Performance Counter Architecture for Computing Accurate CPI Components. In Proceedings of Architectural Support for Programming Languages and Operating Systems, 2006.

---

[i] Data and analysis are not indicative of benchmarking and official data of the Intel platforms

Characterizing Continuous-time Random Walks on Dynamic Networks

Bruno Ribeiro, Don Towsley
Department of Computer Science
University of Massachusetts Amherst
{ribeiro,towsley}@cs.umass.edu

Daniel Figueiredo, Edmundo de Souza e Silva
COPPE/PESC
Federal University of Rio de Janeiro
{daniel,edmundo}@land.ufrj.br

Categories and Subject Descriptors: G.3 Probability and Statistics Probabilistic algorithms (including Monte Carlo); Markov processes

General Terms: Theory

Keywords: Continuous-time Random Walks

1. INTRODUCTION

Most of the networks that pervade our lives are dynamic in nature in the sense that their structural configuration (i.e., topology) is constantly changing over time. Some of these networks are both very large and very dynamic, changing at timescales that are relatively small. Thus, analyzing and measuring such networks represents a challenge, as traditional techniques designed for static networks are rendered unsuitable.

A commonly used technique for measuring and characterizing *static networks* are random walks (RW), which have been extensively studied and applied in the literature. For example, the simple closed form solution of the distribution of the number of visits that stationary RW makes to a node (which is proportional to the node degree) is the basis for many principled algorithms [3, 1]. In contrast, little is known even about the stationary distribution of random walks on dynamic networks.

In this paper we study the steady state behavior of continuous-time random walks (CTRW) on Markov dynamic networks. We consider two types of CTRWs: one that walks at a constant rate (CTRW-C) and another that walks with a rate proportional to the vertex degree (CTRW-D). We derive closed-form analytical expressions for the steady state (SS) distribution of these walkers. For CTRW-C we obtain the approximate SS distribution for either a very fast or very slow walker. We show that the behavior of CTRW-C and CTRW-D is strikingly different. Surprisingly, the steady state distribution of the fixed rate walker depends on the walker rate, which is not the case for the degree proportional walker. Such findings have direct implication on the design of algorithms to measure dynamic networks.

*This research was partially funded by U.S. Army Research Laboratory under Cooperative Agreement Number W911NF-09-2-0053 and NSF grant CNS-0721779, as well as by grants from CNPq and FAPERJ (Brazil).

2. DYNAMIC GRAPHS & RANDOM WALKS

The dynamic network models we consider assume that nodes are always present but that edges can come and go over time, as follows. A Markov dynamic graph is a set of graphs having the same vertex set and a Markov process over them. In particular, let $S = \{G_1, ..., G_m\}$ be a set of undirected graphs all having the same vertex set V, thus, $G_k = (V, E_k)$, where E_k denotes the set of edges of graph G_k, for $k = 1, ..., m$. Let $n = |V|$ denote the number of vertices in a graph. Moreover, let A_k denote the adjacency matrix of graph G_k. Thus, for all $i, j \in V$, $A_k(i, j) = 1$ if $(i, j) \in E_k$ and 0 otherwise. Finally, let $\deg(i, k)$ denote the degree of vertex $i \in V$ in graph G_k.

We introduce the dynamic graph process $\{G(t)\}$ as a continuous-time stationary Markov process with state space S. Let $\lambda_{kl} \geq 0$ denote the transition rate from state (graph) G_k to G_l. Note that the graph dynamics are fully determined by the transition rates.

2.1 Random walks on dynamic graphs

Consider a continuous time random walk (CTRW) on a general Markov dynamic graph. Intuitively, the walker can only traverse edges that are incident to the vertex at which the walker resides, choosing uniformly at random among them. Let $\{W(t)\}$ be the continuous time process representing the vertex where the walker resides, thus $W(t) = i \in V$, for any t. The time between two consecutive steps of the random walk is exponentially distributed with rate γ. We refer to γ as the *walking rate* and to this random walk as CTRW-C (for constant walking rate).

Without loss of generality, assume that when the random walk takes a step at time t, the Markov dynamic graph process is in state G_k, that is $G(t) = G_k$ and that $W(t) = i$. Let $N_{i,k}$ denote the set of neighbors of vertex i in the graph G_k. Thus, the probability the walker steps to vertex $j \in N_{i,k}$ is given by $1/|N_{i,k}|$. Finally, if $N_{i,k}$ is empty, the walker stays at vertex i during that step.

2.2 Degree-dependent random walks

We now introduce a random walk where its walking rate is not constant, but instead depends on the degree of the vertex where the walker is located. Intuitively, our walker will move faster when it finds itself at vertices with large degrees and slower when located at vertices with small degrees. More precisely, the inter-step time of the random walk is exponentially distributed with rate $\deg(i, k)\gamma$, where $\deg(i, k)$ is the degree of vertex $i \in V$ in graph $G_k \in S$ and $\gamma > 0$. We refer to this random walk as CTRW-D (for degree-proportional walking rates).

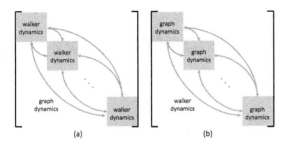

Figure 1: Two different matrix arrangements for CTRW on Markov dynamic graphs.

2.3 Joint graph and walker dynamics

The dynamic graph process and the random walk process can be represented as a continuous-time Markov process $\{R(t)\}$ where $R(t) \in V \times S$. Let $s_{i,k}$ represent a state of this process where i represents a vertex of V ($i \in V$) and k represents a graph in S ($k \in [1, \ldots, m]$). Let $U = \{s_{i,k} : \forall i \in V, k = 1, \ldots, m\}$ denote the set of all vertex snapshots ($s_{i,k}$ represents vertex i at graph G_k). The infinitesimal generator matrix of $\{R(t)\}$, denoted by Q, is determined by combining the graph dynamics with the random walk.

Two specific arrangements of the state space into matrix Q are of particular interest, as they have intuitive interpretation and block representations. Moreover, such representations are fundamental in establishing the proof of the next two theorems. Let $P^w = \{P_1^w, \ldots, P_m^w\}$ be a partition of the state space U, where each subset P_k^w consists of all random walk states corresponding to the graph G_k. In particular, $P_k^w = \{s_{i,k} | i \in V\}$. Thus, each partition corresponds to a square matrix block of size $n = |V|$. Moreover, transitions within a partition correspond to random walk dynamics and transitions among blocks correspond to graph dynamics, as illustrated in Figure 1(a).

We consider a second partition where states $s_{i,k} \in U$ are first grouped by i. We denote this second partition as $P^g = \{P_1^g, \ldots, P_n^g\}$, where each subset P_i^g consists of all graph states corresponding to vertex $i \in V$. In particular, $P_i^g = \{s_{i,k} | k \in [1, \ldots, m]\}$. Thus, each partition corresponds to a square matrix block of size m. Thus, within a block we have the graph dynamics and transitions among blocks represent the walker dynamics, as illustrated in Figure 1(b).

We note that matrix Q representing each random walker (CTRW-C and CTRW-D) can be written in block-form using closed-form equations in each of the two partitions described above. Due to space constraints, we omit such equations (see [2]).

3. STEADY STATE DISTRIBUTIONS

We investigate the steady state distribution of CTRW on Markov dynamic graphs. In particular, we are interested in the fraction of time that the random walk spends at each vertex $i \in V$. Clearly, this metric can be obtained from the steady state probability distribution of $\{R(t)\}$. Let $\pi(s_{i,k})$ denote the fraction of time in state $s_{i,k}$ where $i \in V$ and $k \in [1, \ldots, m]$. In particular, assuming $\{R(t)\}$ is ergodic, we have $\pi(s_{i,k}) = \lim_{t \to \infty} P[R(t) = s_{i,k}]$. We denote vector $\pi = (\pi_1, \ldots, \pi_n)$ in which the i-th component is the fraction of time the random walk spends in vertice i of set V, where $n = |V|$. Therefore, $\pi_i = \sum_k \pi(s_{i,k})$.

3.1 CTRW-C steady state distribution

We investigate the SS distribution of either a very fast or a very slow CTRW-C. Consider a very fast walker, in particular, much faster than the timescale at which the graphs change. Thus, every time the graph changes, the random walk quickly steps through all vertices in this graph. Intuitively, the random walk converges to the SS distribution of the static graph before the dynamic graph process changes to a new graph. This intuition leads to the following theorem (see [2] for proof).

Let Π_k denote the steady state fraction of time spent in graph G_k. Let $\pi(G_k) = (\pi_1(G_k), \ldots, \pi_n(G_k))$ denote the steady state distribution of a random walk on the static graph G_k.

THEOREM 3.1. *For a sufficiently large γ,*

$$\pi = \sum_{k=1}^m \Pi_k \pi(G_k)$$

Now consider a very slow walker, in particular, much slower than the timescale at which the graphs change. Every time the walker steps onto a vertex, the incident edges of this vertex change many times before the walkers steps off. Intuitively, when the walker steps off it will observe the incident edges in "steady state". Thus, the probability the walker steps from vertex i to vertex j is proportional to the steady state probability that edge (i, j) is present. The SS distribution of the random walk is the solution of this new random walk on a weighted static graph. This intuition leads to the following theorem (see [2] for proof).

THEOREM 3.2. *For a sufficiently small γ, the steady state distribution π is equivalent to the steady state of a continuous time Markov chain with infinitesimal generator matrix $R = [r_{i,j}]$, $\forall i, j \in V$, where*

$$r_{i,j} = \begin{cases} \gamma \sum_{k=1}^m \mathbf{1}((i,j) \in E_k) \, \Pi_k \, 1/\deg(i,k) & \text{if } i \neq j \\ 0 & \text{otherwise} \end{cases}$$

and $\mathbf{1}(\cdot)$ is the indicator function and $\deg(i,k)$ is the degree of vertex i in graph G_k.

3.2 CTRW-D steady state distribution

In a CTRW-D the walker spends a fraction of time that is constant across the vertices of the graph. This observation is quite remarkable, since it means we can traverse the graph at arbitrary speeds, independently of graph dynamics, while being able to characterize the steady state distribution that the walker will observe. This observation leads to the following theorem (see [2] for proof).

Let $s_{i,k} \in U$ be a vertex snapshot.

THEOREM 3.3. *In CTRW-D, $\pi(s_{i,k}) = \Pi_k/n$, $i \in V$, $k = 1, \ldots, m$,*

As a consequence, we have that $\pi_i = 1/n$, for all $i \in V$.

4. REFERENCES

[1] M.E.J. Newman. A measure of betweenness centrality based on random walks. *Social Networks*, 27(1):39–54, January 2005.
[2] B. Ribeiro, D. Figueiredo, E. de Souza e Silva, and D. Towsley. Characterizing dynamic graphs with continuous-time random walks. Technical report, UMass CS UM-CS-2011-013, 2011.
[3] B. Ribeiro and D. Towsley. Estimating and sampling graphs with multidimensional random walks. In *ACM IMC*, 2010.

Autocorrelation Analysis: A New and Improved Method for Measuring Branch Predictability

Jian Chen, Lizy K. John
Department of Electrical and Computer Engineering
The University of Texas at Austin, Austin, Texas, USA
chenjian@mail.utexas.edu, ljohn@ece.utexas.edu

ABSTRACT

Branch taken rate and transition rate have been proposed as metrics to characterize the branch predictability. However, these two metrics may misclassify branches with regular history patterns as hard-to-predict branches, causing an inaccurate and ambiguous view of branch predictability. This study uses autocorrelation to analyze the branch history patterns and presents a new metric *Degree of Pattern Irregularity (DPI)* for branch classification. The proposed metric is evaluated with different branch predictors, and the results show that DPI significantly improves the quality and the accuracy of branch classification over traditional taken rate and transition rate.

Categories and Subject Descriptors: C.4 [**Performance of Systems**][Measurement techniques, Modeling techniques]

General Terms: Measurement, Performance

Keywords: Branch characterization, Autocorrelation

1. INTRODUCTION

Classifying branches in terms of their predictability has been applied in many areas of computer architecture, including branch prediction, predicated execution, etc. The existing metrics for characterizing branch behaviors include branch taken rate [2], which measures the taken frequency of a branch, and branch transition rate [3], which captures the frequency of a branch switching between taken and not taken. These metrics characterize the branch predictability based on their values: branches with very high or very low taken rate/transition rate are easy to predict, and branches with near 50% taken rate/transition rate are hard to predict. Although simple, these metrics may misclassify some of the easy-to-predict branches as hard-to-predict. For instance, a branch with regular history pattern "110110110..." is indeed easy to predict since a 3-bit history length is sufficient to make a perfect prediction for this branch. However, this branch has 0.667 taken rate and 0.667 transition rate, and is therefore misclassified as a hard-to-predict branch. To address this limitation, this work proposes to characterize branch predictability with a novel metric called *Degree of Pattern Irregularity* (DPI), which measures the degree of the branch behavior deviating from regular pattern by *autocorrelation analysis*. We show that DPI significantly improves the accuracy of hard-to-predict branch classification compared with taken rate and transition rate.

2. BRANCH AUTOCORRELATION

Autocorrelation is widely applied in signal processing and pattern recognition to find repeating patterns buried under noise. For a real-value discrete sequence of n elements $\{h(i)\}_{i=0}^{n}$, the autocor-

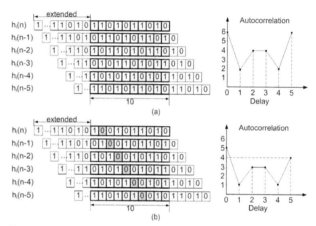

Figure 1: (a) Autocorrelation for regular branch history.(b) Autocorrelation for irregular branch history.

relation of this sequence is $R_{hh}(j) = \sum_{i=0}^{n} h(i)h(i-j)$, where $j \in [0, n]$. In order to prevent undefined values outside the window $[0, n]$ from polluting the calculation, the sequence $\{h(i)\}_{i=0}^{n}$ is typically extended periodically to the left, creating a rotation effect in the window $[0, n]$ as the sequence slides to the right. Therefore, the autocorrelation holds the following two properties [1]: (a) It reaches its maximum value at the origin; (b) If the discrete sequence is periodic, its autocorrelation is also periodic with the same period. Considering the fact that branch history only consist of "0" (as not taken) and "1" (as taken), we have the following implication: for the autocorrelation of branch histories, the difference between the maximum value at the origin and the largest value off the origin reflects the amount of irregularity in the branch history. This can be understood by treating an irregular branch history as a regular branch history XORed with one or more bits deviating from the regular pattern. The number of these deviating bits is reflected on the difference between the two largest values of the autocorrelation. As shown in Figure 1(b), one bit highlighted with dark grey deviates from the periodic pattern, which causes the difference between the two largest autocorrelation values equivalent to one. The irregularity measured by such difference is one of the main sources of branch misprediction. Hence, the fraction of the irregularity over the number of the branch dynamic accesses is the direct indicator of branch predictability, which we refer to as the *Degree of Pattern Irregularity* (DPI). Note that a regular branch history is equivalent to a branch history with zero DPI, as shown in Figure 1(a).

The complexity of the autocorrelation analysis involves two aspects: computation and storage. Since branch history only contains 0's and 1's, its autocorrelation only requires logic AND operations and bit-wise accumulate operations. Compared with the storage requirements of taken rate (1 bit per static branch) and transition rate

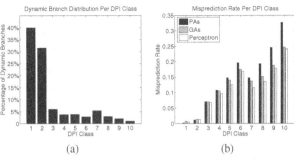

(a)   (b)

Figure 2: Dynamic branch classification based on DPI.

(2 bits per static branch), autocorrelation analysis requires more storage space, yet its impact on the profiling speed is negligible as long as the history length is within a reasonable range.

3. EXPERIMENT AND RESULTS

We use PIN, a dynamic instrumentation tool on x86 platform, to instrument the workload and obtain the trace of conditional branches. This trace is then seamlessly fed to our detailed branch analyzer, which is able to perform autocorrelation analysis on each static branch and simulate different types of branch predictors simultaneously. The workloads of the experiment are composed of all programs from SPEC CPU2006 benchmark suite, with each compiled to x86-ISA at base configurations. To reduce the simulation time, we use PinPoints to identify the representative simulation points. For each program, we simulate the dominant simulation points that covers 90% of the total weights, and each simulation point contains 100 million instructions.

We evaluate the proposed metric by using three different types of branch predictors to ensure the generality. These three branch predictors are: a per-address history predictor (PAs), a global two-level predictor (GAs) and a global neural network predictor (Perceptron) [4], each with history length of 16. For PAs and GAs, the size of Pattern History Table (PHT) is set to 64K entries, and the branch history table (BHT) of PAs has 1024 entries. To be consistent with PAs and GAs, the Perceptron predictor also contains 64K entries for the weights with each 8-bit wide. In this work, we only consider the conditional branches.

Branch Classification: In Figure 2(a), we classify the branches into 10 groups in terms of their DPI values. Class 1 has DPI value 0, representing the branches with regular history pattern. Class 2 to 6 have DPI values in the ranges of (0,0.01], (0.01,0.02], ..., (0.04,0.05], respectively; and class 7 to 10 have DPI values with the ranges of (0.05-0.10], (0.10-0.15], (0.15-0.20], (0.20-1] respectively. As shown in the figure, 40.0% of the total dynamic conditional branches fall in class 1, and 31.6% of them fall in class 2. The occupancies of the other classes are significantly lower, with each class less than 6.0%. Figure 2(b) further shows the misprediction rate of the branches in each DPI class for PAs, GAs, and Perceptron predictors. Notice that there is an overall trend that the misprediction rate increases as the branch DPI increases. This trend holds true for all three different types of branch predictors, which demonstrates that DPI is an appropriate metric for branch predictability. Moreover, this figure also shows that the misprediction rates of the branches in DPI class 1 and 2 are drastically smaller than those in the rest DPI classes, which means branches with DPI less than 0.01 are the easy-to-predict branches. As a result, DPI allows us to classify the branch predictability in a clear and coherent way: branches with DPI less than 0.01 are the easy-to-predict branches; whereas branches with DPI larger than 0.01 are the hard-to-predict branches.

Comparison with Conventional Metrics: Figure 3(a) shows

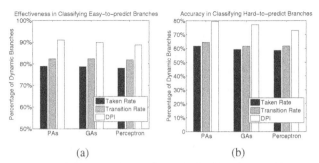

(a)   (b)

Figure 3: Comparison of branch classification quality.

the percentage of the branches classified as easy-to-predict branches among the branches with prediction rate larger than 95% (The easy-to-predict branches are classified by taken rate $\in [0, 0.05) \bigcup (0.95, 0.1]$, transition rate $\in [0, 0.1) \bigcup (0.9, 0.1]$, or DPI $\in [0, 0.01]$). As shown in this figure, DPI consistently yields larger percentage than transition rate or taken rate across all three types of branch predictors, meaning that DPI can identify more truly easy-to-predict branches than taken rate or transition rate. On the other hand, we also measure the percentages of the branches with prediction rate less than 95% over the branches classified as hard-to-predict. As shown in Figure 3(b), DPI improves the accuracy of the hard-to-predict branch classification by up to 17.7% over taken rate, and 15.0% over transition rate. The reason that DPI is superior in branch classification is that it has a broader view of branch history when characterizing the branch behaviors. In fact, taken rate examines the branch history *bit by bit*, and transition rate does it *two-bit by two-bit*; whereas DPI examines the branch history at a *broader pattern level*.

Applications: As an important extension to the existing metrics, the proposed DPI metric can be applied in the fields where the conventional branch classification metrics are used. These fields include, but not limited to: identifying hard-to-predict branches for predication, characterizing control flow for benchmark cloning and synthesizing [5].

4. CONCLUSIONS

Based on the autocorrelation analysis of branch history patterns, this paper presents a new metric *Degree of Pattern Irregularity* (DPI) for branch predictability characterization. Unlike existing taken rate or transition rate metrics, DPI directly measures the regularity of the patterns in per-address branch history, and hence is able to identify more easy-to-predict branches and significantly improve the accuracy of the classification of hard-to-predict branches. Our experiments show that DPI improves the accuracy of hard-to-predict branch classification by up to 17.7% over taken rate and 15.0% over transition rate. Overall, this metric examines the branch history at a broader *pattern level*, and is an important extension to the existing metrics in branch classification.

5. REFERENCES

[1] E. O. Brigham. *The Fast Fourier Transform*, chapter 13. 1974.

[2] P.-Y. Chang and et al. Branch classification: a new mechanism for improving branch predictor performance. In *MICRO '94*, pages 22–31, 1994.

[3] M. Haungs, et al. Branch transition rate: a new metric for improved branch classification analysis. In *HPCA '00*, pages 241 –250, 2000.

[4] D. Jimenez and C. Lin. Dynamic branch prediction with perceptrons. In *HPCA '01*, pages 197 –206, 2001.

[5] A. Joshi, et al. Automated microprocessor stressmark generation. In *HPCA '08*, pages 229 –239, 2008.

IP Geolocation in Metropolitan Areas

Satinder Pal Singh
Bobby Bhattacharjee

Randolph Baden
Richard La

Choon Lee
Mark Shayman

University of Maryland,
College Park, 20742, USA

ABSTRACT

Current IP geoloation techniques can geolocate an IP address to a region approximately 700 square miles, roughly the size of a metropolitan area. We model geolocation as a pattern-recognition problem, and introduce techniques that geolocate addresses to within 5 miles inside a metropolitan area. We propose two complementary algorithms: The first algorithm, Pattern Based Geolocation (PBG), models the distribution of latencies to the target and compares it to those of the reference landmarks to resolve an address to within 5 miles in a metropolitan area. The second approach, Perturbation Augmented PBG (PAPBG), provides higher resolution by sending extra traffic in the network. While sending an aggregate of 600 Kbps extra traffic to 20 nodes for approximately 2 minutes, PAPBG geolocates addresses to within 3 miles.

Catetogies and Subject Descriptors C.2.3 [Computer-Communication Systems]: Network Operations — Public Networks

General Terms: Experimentation, Measurement

Keywords: Geolocation, Pattern Recognition, Probability Mass Function, Perturbation, Divergence

1. INTRODUCTION

IP Geolocation algorithms map IP addresses to geographic locations. Geolocation can be used for targeted advertising, efficient content distribution, location-specific content customization, and critical emergency services including E-911 for Voice-over-IP telephones [7, 3].

State-of-the-art IP geolocation techniques resolve addresses to approximately 30 miles [5, 8], roughly the diameter of a metropolitan area. In this paper, we present two new approaches for finer resolution IP Geolocation inside a metropolitan area. Our work departs from prior measurement-based geolocation approaches, all of which correlate latency with distance.

We model geolocation as a *pattern recognition problem*. Our algorithms identify and extract patterns from network statistics to geolocate an IP address. We propose a new Pattern Based Geolocation (PBG), which captures patterns in the distribution of latencies or Round Trip Times (RTTs) observed to a target. PBG models the signature of back-

ground traffic in the vicinity of the target and uses this 'signature' to geolocate the target to approximately 5 miles of its actual location. To further improve the resolution of PBG, we develop Perturbation Augmented PBG (PAPBG), which is inspired by Stochastic Resonance [1]. PAPBG sends a small amount of signal traffic in the network to enhance the signature of background traffic. At the cost sending an additional 600 Kbps aggregate traffic to 20 nodes for approximately 2 minutes, PAPBG gives a higher resolution in the location estimate and geolocates the target to within 3 miles.

2. OUR APPROACH

Our infrastructure consists of a collection of probe and landmark nodes. We administer three probe nodes in Maryland, USA: one in the city of College Park on Qwest network and one each in Silver Spring and Potomac on Verizon network. We have 20 landmarks distributed over 700 square miles large Washington D.C.-Baltimore metropolitan area on Comcast (12) and Verizon (8) networks. The mean pairwise distance between the landmarks is 8.4 miles for Comcast network and 11.8 miles for Verizon network.

Our techniques geolocate a target to the 'best matching' landmark in the testbed. Given a set of landmarks, the best possible estimate of a target's geographic location is the landmark which is geographically closest to it. Suppose s_{min} is the distance between the target and the geographically closest landmark. Let s^* be the distance between 'the best matching landmark' given by a geolocation algorithm and the target. Then the error of the location estimate of that geolocation algorithm is $\mathcal{E} = s^* - s_{min}$. Here $\mathcal{E} \geq 0$, with equality when the 'best matching landmark' given by the geolocation algorithm is in fact the geographically closest landmark.

Exisiting measurement based geolocation techniques assume correlation between distance and RTTs [5]. However, in a metropolitan area this correlation does not exist bacause propogation delay is a small component of RTTs, and the dominant component is queuing delay [2]. Our approach models IP geolocation as a pattern recognition problem and aims to geolocate a target by identifying, extracting and matching 'patterns from RTT sequences'.

2.1 Pattern Based Geolocation

Pattern Based Geolocation (PBG) uses the *distribution* of the RTT values as pattern for geolocation. First, we construct Probability Mass Functions (PMFs) from the collected RTT sequences to model the distribution of RTTs using 'k Nearest Neighbor' density estimation method [4].

Next, we compare the PMFs of the landmarks to the PMF of the target to get the best match in shape. In our problem we encounter frequent cases where PMFs are similar in shape but shifted by a few milliseconds. To address this, we introduce a new distance metric called "Shifted Symmetrized Divergence" distance, (d_{SSD}), defined as:

$$d_{SSD}(p\|q) = a \times \min_s \big(d_{SD}(p\|q_s)\big) + \\ (1-a) \times \phi(s_{min}) \qquad (1)$$

Here

$$
\begin{aligned}
p, q &= \text{two PMFs} \\
q_s &= \text{PMF } q \text{ shifted by } s \\
d_{SD} &= \text{Symmetric Kullback-Leibler Divergence [4]} \\
s_{min} &= \arg\min_s\big(d_{SD}(p\|q_s)\big) \\
\phi &= \text{penalty function for shift} \\
a &= \text{weight}
\end{aligned}
$$

Using d_{SSD} each probe node does PBG computations to obtain divergence values for each landmark. We finally output the landmark with the minimum mean divergence over all probe nodes as the target's location estimate. The two parameters involved in PBG computations, ϕ and a, are chosen empirically using a training dataset (See Section 3).

2.2 Perturbation Augmented PBG

PBG relies on the background traffic in the vicinity of a target. However, in some instances, the background traffic signature is not strong enough, and PBG fails to map the target to geographically close landmark. Perturbation Augmented PBG (PAPBG), inspired by Stochastic Resonance [1], *enhances* the background traffic signature by introducing a controlled amount of "perturbation" traffic into the network using a **perturber**.

The technique works as follows. One of the probe nodes, acting as perturber, sends large ICMP echo request packets (e.g. of size 100 bytes each) to all the landmarks and the target at a rate, say 50 packets per second. This corresponds to signal traffic of 40 Kbps to each landmark and target. The remaining probe nodes send regular small ICMP request packets (of size 30 bytes each) at a nominal rate of 5 packets per second for 100 seconds to measure the RTT sequences. These probe nodes then run PBG algorithms on the measured RTT sequences to give the best matching landmark. Thus, PAPBG is essentially PBG with an additional perturber which introduces a controlled amount of perturbation traffic in the network for better differentiation of PMFs.

3. EXPERIMENTS AND RESULTS

We first collected 30 training data sets to empirically choose the 'best values' for ϕ and a. Each dataset consists of synchronous RTT sequences collected from the two probe nodes at College Park and Siver Spring over 20 landmarks in our testbed. We collected RTT squences at a rate of 5 samples per second for 100 seconds from each landmark per probe node. We explored three penalty functions, Logarithmic, Linear and Exponential, and 100 values of $a \in [0, 1]$. For each combination of the two parameter values we used a

leave-one-out [6] approach to run PBG on the 30 training data sets. The best performance (minimum mean geolocation error) was obtained for exponential penalty function $(\phi(s_{min}) = 2^{s_{min}})$, and $a = 0.9$ for Comcast network and $a = 0.95$ for Verizon network.

To evaluate the performance of PBG we collected 50 additional datasets with the same setup as mentioned above. Using the same leave-one-out approach and parameter values discussed above, we ran PBG computations on this data. To compare the performance of PBG we used an existing measurement based geolocation technique, Constraint Based Geolocation (CBG) [5], to geolocate targets on these datasets as well.

The mean error obtained with CBG was 15.39 miles for Comcast network and 18.06 miles for Verizon network, which is worse than the mean pairwise distance between the landmarks on the two networks. Compared to this, our PBG gives a mean error of 2.13 miles for Comcast network and 4.34 miles for Verizon network. Further, on an average PBG matches the target to the geographically closest landmark in majority of the cases (>50%). Note that if we randomly select one of the landmarks as target's location estimate, the mean error obtained is 7.62 miles for Comcast network and 8.76 miles for Verizon network. Thus, existing techniques perform worse than 'random selection', while PBG geolocates the target to within $2 - 4$ miles of its actual location.

For PAPBG we collected additional datasets for 5 perturbation intensites: 10, 20, 30, 40 and 50 Kbps per destination node. We used the probe node at Potomac as perturber and collected 50 datasets for each intensity using the other two probe nodes. We achieved the best performance for perturbation intensity of 30 Kbps; the mean error reduces to 1.2 miles for Comcast network and 3.4 miles for Verizon network. Beyond 30 Kbps we enter a region of diminishing returns and no more gains in performance are obtained. Thus by sending an additional 30 Kbps traffic to each of 20 nodes for 100 seconds, PAPBG reduces geolocation error by approximately $20 - 40\%$.

4. REFERENCES

[1] R. Benzi, A. Sutera, and A. Vulpiani. The mechanism of stochastic resonance. *Journal of Physics A: Mathematical and General*, 14(11):L453, 1981.

[2] C. J. Bovy, H. T. Mertodimedjo, G. Hooghiemstra, H. Uijterwaal, and P. Mieghem. Analysis of end-to-end delay measurements in Internet. In *Proc. Passive and Active Measurement Workshop (PAM 2002)*, Fort Collins, CO, USA, 2002.

[3] D. D. Clark, C. Partridge, R. T. Braden, B. Davie, S. Floyd, V. Jacobson, D. Katabi, G. Minshall, K. K. Ramakrishnan, T. Roscoe, I. Stoica, J. Wroclawski, and L. Zhang. Making the world (of communications) a different place. *SIGCOMM Comput. Commun. Rev.*, 35(3):91–96, 2005.

[4] R. O. Duda, P. E. Hart, and D. G. Stork. *Pattern Classification (2nd Edition)*. Wiley-Interscience, 2000.

[5] B. Gueye, A. Ziviani, M. Crovella, and S. Fdida. Constraint-based geolocation of Internet hosts. *IEEE/ACM Transactions on Networking*, 14(6):1219–1232, Dec. 2006.

[6] R. Kohavi. A Study of Cross-Validation and Bootstrap for Accuracy Estimation and Model Selection. pages 1137–1143. Morgan Kaufmann, 1995.

[7] S. Steiniger, M. Neun, and A. Edwardes. Foundations of Location Based Services. *Lecture Notes on LBS*, 2006.

[8] B. Wong, I. Stoyanov, and E. G. Sirer. Geolocalization on the Internet through constraint satisfaction. In *WORLDS'06: Proceedings of the 3rd conference on USENIX Workshop on Real, Large Distributed Systems*, Berkeley, CA, USA, 2006. USENIX Association.

TCP Behavior in Sub-Packet Regimes

Jay Chen
New York University
jchen@cs.nyu.edu

Janardhan Iyengar
Franklin and Marshall College
jiyengar@fandm.edu

Lakshminarayanan
Subramanian
New York University
lakshmi@cs.nyu.edu

Bryan Ford
Yale University
bryan.ford@yale.edu

ABSTRACT

Many network links in developing regions operate in the *sub-packet regime*, an environment where the typical per-flow throughput is less than 1 packet per round-trip time. TCP and other common congestion control protocols break down in the sub-packet regime, resulting in severe unfairness, high packet loss rates, and flow silences due to repetitive timeouts. To understand TCP's behavior in this regime, we propose a model particularly tailored to high packet loss-rates and relatively small congestion window sizes. We validate the model under a variety of network conditions.

Categories and Subject Descriptors: C.2.2 [Computer-Communication Networks]: Network Protocols.

General Terms: Experimentation, Measurement, Performance.

Keywords: TCP, congestion control, low bandwidth networks.

1. INTRODUCTION

Congestion control schemes such as TCP-NewReno, TFRC and many others assume the fair-share bandwidth of a flow is at least 1 packet per round-trip time (RTT). Surprisingly, there exists a large number of low-bandwidth network environments in the developing world with high levels of network sharing where this assumption does not hold [6, 3].; we define such an environment as the *sub-packet regime*. While heavy sharing among users leads to the sub-packet regime, web browsers can exacerbate the problem by spawning several TCP connections per web request. Over the past decade, the average size of web pages and the number of objects per page has grown at a faster rate than the growth in connectivity.

The sub-packet regime has not been a traditionally important region of operation for network flows, and as a result this space has remained relatively unexplored. The concept of a sub-packet regime arises in prior work in the context of understanding the behavior of TCP in the face of many competing flows [5, 8, 4].

This paper proposes an analytical model to characterize the equilibrium behavior of TCP in the sub-packet regime. Our model is a simpler variant of a full Markov model for

TCP operating in traditional regimes [2], but gives more careful attention to modeling repetitive timeouts, an extremely common state experienced by TCP flows in sub-packet regimes. Since Markov models are inherently not suited to keep memory in the state transitions, modeling repetitive timeouts is not straightforward (since one needs memory of the previous timeout value). We address this problem by determining aggregate transition states which both capture the memory effect while significantly reducing the number of states. Using extensive analysis, we show that our model accurately predicts the stationary distribution of a TCP flow across different states using few aggregate states. Our model can be used by network middle-boxes in practice to enhance TCP performance and fairness in sub-packet regimes in a non-intrusive manner.

2. OUR MODEL

We build a simple model particularly tailored for analyzing the behavior of TCP-NewReno in sub-packet regimes with high-packet loss-rates and with relatively small average congestion windows. The main purpose of this model is to analyze the *stationary distribution* of a set of TCP flows, which provides a detailed characterization of the state of a TCP connection.

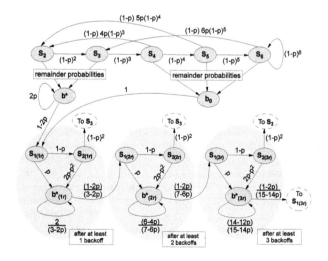

Figure 1: The Full Model for a max congestion window, $W_{max} = 6$.

SIGMETRICS'11, June 7–11, 2011, San Jose, California, USA.
ACM 978-1-4503-0262-3/11/06.

Our overall model is described in Figure 1 for a maximum congestion window, $W_{max} = 6$, and can be easily extended to larger W_{max}.. Our model is built around three assumptions. First, we assume that most TCP flows operate in small window sizes (less than W_{max}). Second, we assume that all TCP flows experience medium to high loss rates in sub-packet regimes. Third, given small congestion windows where TCP packets are more spaced-out, we can model packet losses using a single loss parameter, p.

There are several key insights we draw from this model. First, all the transition probabilities in this model are modeled using a single parameter p, the packet-loss probability at the bottleneck link. Second, under conditions where p is roughly a constant, the stationary distribution probability is only dependent on p and is independent of RTT. Third, we observe a shift in the stationary distribution beyond $p = 0.1$ where the probability of repetitive timeouts significantly increases thereby lowering the effective throughput of a TCP flow.

Our model is different from and extends previously proposed models of Padhye et al. [7], Fortin-Parisi et al. [2]. The fundamental problem with using a generic Markov model for capturing TCP behavior is the state space explosion. One of the advantages in the sub-packet regime, however, is that the state space is constrained and may be accurately captured using appropriate state transitions. Our model focuses on high loss rates and captures exponentially increasing silence periods due to repetitive timeouts, the dynamics of which are not captured in detail in prior work.

3. VALIDATION AND APPLICATIONS

We validate the model using ns2 simulations of TCP flows operating in sub-packet regimes. TCP-SACK is used at the endpoints and we run the simulations for varying levels of contention on a bottleneck link resulting in varying loss scenarios. For each simulation, we measure the packet loss rate p and also determine the distribution of the individual flows across different congestion window states. Figure 2 shows the model's predicted probability distribution for varying loss rate p, overlaid with results from simulations where we measure and plot probability against observed loss rate. For this simulation set, the flows all have a propagation RTT of 200ms, the bottleneck capacity is 1 Mbps, and the bottleneck link is equipped with an RTT's worth of buffer (50 packets, at 500 bytes per packet).

Note that "0 sent" is the sum of probabilities for all the b* states in the model, and similarly "1 sent" and "2 sent" represent the sums of the S_1 states and S_2 states, respectively. Simulation results agree well with our model at loss rates greater than or equal to $p = 0.1$. We note that the simulations slightly differ from our model for $p < 0.1$ for the following reason: under lower loss rates flows grow to window-sizes larger than 6; hence we need to compute the stationary distributions for larger values of W_{max} to get a more accurate distribution match. We also ran simulations under a variety of link bandwidths, variable propagation RTTs, and under RED and SFQ AQM schemes, and obtained similar agreement with the model. A more detailed analysis of the model, validation of the model and how it can be applied in practice can be found in our technical report [1].

Applications: Our model can be applied in a variety of ways at a middle-box to both predict the status and behavior of a flow as well as to potentially design non-intrusive

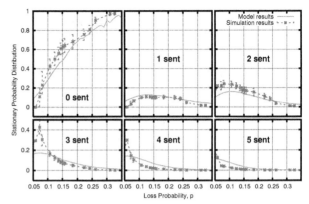

Figure 2: Stationary probabilities from the model and from simulations for 6 of the sending states that a TCP connection can be in. Error bars show 10th and 90th percentile flow values.

middle-box solutions to enhance performance in sub-packet regimes. Given the aggregate loss rate at the bottleneck, the model currently gives us the probability of finding a flow in one of several states. Similarly, the distribution can also be used to estimate the fraction of flows that are currently in timeout states on a pathologically-shared link. For a single flow, the model can be used as a mechanism for estimating the probability of hitting a timeout state by simply estimating the RTT of the flow and observing the number of packets within each epoch. Using this information, one can design middle-box queue management routines to reduce the possibility of flow timeouts. More details are outlined in our technical report [1].

4. REFERENCES

[1] CHEN, J., IYENGAR, J., SUBRAMANIAN, L., AND FORD, B. TCP Behavior in Sub-packet Regimes. NYU Technical Report, Nov 2010. http://www.cs.nyu.edu/~lakshmi/subpacket.pdf.

[2] FORTIN-PARISI, S., AND SERICOLA, B. A Markov model of TCP throughput, goodput and slow start. *Performance Evaluation 58*, 2-3 (2004), 89 – 108. Distributed Systems Performance.

[3] HUERTA, E., AND SANDOVAL-ALMAZÁN, R. Digital literacy: Problems faced by telecenter users in Mexico. *Information Technology for Development 13*, 3 (2007), 217–232.

[4] JUAN, C. P., AGRELO, J. C. S., AND GERLA, M. Using back-pressure to improve tcp performance with many flows. In *IEEE INFOCOM* (1999).

[5] MORRIS, R. Tcp behavior with many flows. In *ICNP '97: Proceedings of the 1997 International Conference on Network Protocols (ICNP '97)* (Washington, DC, USA, 1997), IEEE Computer Society, p. 205.

[6] OYELARAN-OYEYINKA, B., AND ADEYA, C. N. Internet access in africa: empirical evidence from kenya and nigeria. *Telemat. Inf. 21*, 1 (2004), 67–81.

[7] PADHYE, J., FIROIU, V., TOWSLEY, D., AND KUROSE, J. Modeling tcp throughput: a simple model and its empirical validation. In *SIGCOMM '98: Proceedings of the ACM SIGCOMM '98 conference on Applications, technologies, architectures, and protocols for computer communication* (1998).

[8] QIU, L., ZHANG, Y., AND KESHAV, S. Understanding the performance of many TCP flows* 1. *Computer Networks 37*, 3-4 (2001), 277–306.

Network Link Tomography and Compressive Sensing

Rhys Bowden, Matthew Roughan, and Nigel Bean
Dept. of Mathematical Sciences, University of Adelaide
Adelaide, SA, Australia
rhys.bowden@adelaide.edu, matthew.roughan@adelaide.edu,
nigel.bean@adelaide.edu

Categories and Subject Descriptors: C.2.3 [Computer Communication Networks]: Network Operations—Network Monitoring

General Terms: Measurement.

Keywords: Multiple source, multiple destination, network tomography, link tomography, compressive sensing, sparsity.

1. INTRODUCTION AND BACKGROUND

Accurate and timely performance data are of vital importance for network administration. However, modern networks are so large and transmit such enormous quantities of data that a single backbone link could fill a terabyte drive in about 3 minutes. Taking and processing all the desirable performance measurements can be wildly impractical. Aside from matters of scale there may be other difficulties, such as unreliable measurement that mean network administrators cannot make all the performance measurements they desire. Consequently, it is necessary to make the most of the measurements that *are* available. *Network Tomography* does just that, by inferring underlying performance statistics from the available measurements.

This paper considers the problem of link loss tomography: inference of link parameters from a series of end-to-end probes through a network. We specifically estimate average link loss rates. Typical problems in this setting are highly underconstrained, and so the measurements often admit infinitely many solutions. Some method is needed to select the correct solution from this possible set, and in this paper we shall use sparsity.

Network tomography is a well developed field [1, 4, 7]. However, the vast majority of performance tomography has concentrated on trees. In that setting, it is possible to develop fast, recursive algorithms [2, 4], and to employ side information such as sparsity relatively easily [3].

However, many networks are not trees. Some work has looked at combining measurements from multiple tree-like views of the network [6], however, the approach meets immediate difficulties. Intuitively we can see that it would be hard to use sparsity in the same way because there is no longer a "top" of the tree towards which we can push "bad" links.

In this paper we attack the problem on a general network. We exploit sparsity, but without reducing the problem to a binary problem. We test the idea of applying the

SIGMETRICS'11, June 7–11, 2011, San Jose, California, USA.
ACM 978-1-4503-0262-3/11/06.

field of Compressive Sensing to this link tomography problem. Compressive Sensing exploits the fact that many large data-sets are comprised of only a few significant elements. In practice, this means that either the data itself, or some simple transform of the data, is *sparse* in the sense that only a few of the values are non-zero. Compressive Sensing is a rapidly growing area of research, and there are many powerful results. However, the underlying assumption in most Compressive Sensing is that the experimenter controls the *measurement matrix*, but here the measurement matrix is called a *routing matrix* and it is not chosen to suit the inference problem (its choice is mandated by the design and optimisation of the network). What's more, routing matrices don't satisfy key properties such as RIP that would allow us to apply the theory of Compressive Sensing. The central question of this paper is "Can we still use the concepts and methods of Compressive Sensing despite the deficiencies of the routing matrices as measurement matrices?"

We show here that we can apply Compressive Sensing, with a reasonable degree of accuracy. More importantly, the structural features of typical routing matrices that make them unsuitable for standard Compressive Sensing theorems (highly correlated rows, variable lengths of paths) can be exploited. We develop here a new algorithm — Coherent Tomographic Deduction (CTD) — for solving the tomography problem and show that it is orders of magnitude faster than a standard Compressive Sensing technique, ℓ^1-norm minimisation, with the same level of accuracy. Apart from being much faster, our algorithm has one other very significant advantage. It knows where it is definitely right, and where it could be wrong.

1.1 Notation and assumptions

We consider the problem of inferring the loss probabilities on links across a network from path measurements. Let $l_i =$ link loss probability for $i = 1, \ldots, n$, and $p_j =$ path loss probability for $j = 1, \ldots, m$. When losses on different links are independent the two are related by

$$\rho = A\tau. \qquad (1)$$

where $\tau_i = -\log(1 - l_i)$, $i = 1, \ldots n$; and $\rho_j = -\log(1 - p_j)$, $j = 1, \ldots, m$, and A is the $m \times n$ routing matrix defined by $A_{j,i} = 1$ if link i is on path j and 0 otherwise. We assume that the routing matrix A is known, and we wish to find the sparsest τ such that $\rho = A\tau$, i.e.,

$$\min_{\tau} ||\tau||_0 \text{ subject to } \rho = A\tau. \qquad (2)$$

where $||\mathbf{x}||_0$ is the number of non-zero elements of $\mathbf{x}$.

2. ALGORITHM (CTD)

2.1 Part A

Iterated Bounding Step: If we examine the origins of τ we can see that $\tau \geq 0$. We can use this lower bound as a starting place to derive tighter bounds for each τ_i.

Let $\mathbf{l}^t$ be the length n vector of lower bounds attained after t steps. Similarly, let $\mathbf{u}^t$ be the upper bounds attained after t steps. Start with $\mathbf{l}^0 = \mathbf{0}$. Then define the rest of the sequence by $\mathbf{u}_j^{t+1} = \min_{i:A_{i,j}=1} \left(\rho_i - \sum_{k:A_{i,k}=1, i \neq k} \mathbf{l}_k^t \right)$;

$\mathbf{l}_j^{t+1} = \max_{i:A_{i,j}=1} \left(\rho_i - \sum_{k:A_{i,k}=1, i \neq k} \mathbf{u}_k^{t+1} \right)$.

These two steps are using the previous bounds to find the new bounds. Halt this process when $||\mathbf{l}^t - \mathbf{l}^{t-1}|| < \varepsilon$ for some sufficiently small $\varepsilon > 0$. We then consider solved each link i that has a lower bound $\mathbf{l}_i$ the same as its upper bound $\mathbf{u}_i$, and eliminate it from the remaining measurement equations.

Length 2 paths step: Thanks to the iterated bounding step, at this stage all paths with unsolved links have at least 2 unsolved links, and have some measured loss. We consider paths with only 2 links. Now one of two things is true: either we can find a unique solution for the entirety of this subproblem, or we can find a set of solutions with only one degree of freedom (we omit the proof here). The length 2 paths step and the iterated bounding step can be repeated alternately until no more progress is made.

2.2 Part B

While our algorithm CTD can derive solutions for part of τ with absolute confidence, there may be some components about which it is unsure. To estimate the remainder of the solution after running CTD, we use a standard Compressive Sensing technique, ℓ^1-minimisation.

3. SIMULATION

In this section we evaluate the performance of the CTD algorithm on simulated topologies. We compare the performance of (i) ℓ^1-minimisation by itself with (ii) CTD on heuristically optimised networks ([5]) with 80 nodes: 10 nodes chosen as sources and a variable number of destinations. As far as estimation goes, the loss estimates provided by CTD and raw ℓ^1-minimisation are accurate for an identical, high proportion of the links (Figure 3). However, CTD Part A also labels some of the loss values as being accurate, and some as having uncertainty. The average proportion of links determined with certainty is shown as the solid line in Figure 3.

CTD doesn't just provide more information than ℓ^1-minimisation. As an additional advantage, CTD as a whole is much faster than ℓ^1-minimisation in finding the estimate for τ. With 40 destination nodes, there is almost an order of magnitude difference in run times; and with more destination nodes the difference becomes even greater (plot omitted due to space constraints).

4. CONCLUSION

We present here a justification of why Compressive Sensing techniques, while appearing suited, are not *guaranteed* to work when applied to the problems of Link Tomography; routing matrices poorly satisfy the typical conditions required for Compressive Sensing. We present an efficient

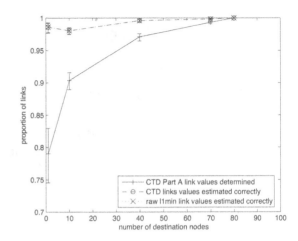

Figure 1: Average proportion of the links determined (in the case of CTD Part A), or estimated correctly (in the other cases) plotted against number of destinations. Note that the lines for CTD estimation and raw ℓ^1-min estimation are identical.

algorithm: the first half of this algorithm determines the solution on some subset of links for which we have sufficient information; the second half then applies a Compressive Sensing algorithm to find an approximation to the sparsest solution on the remainder of the links. We test this algorithm on simulated topologies and find that it is both faster and gives more information than applying Compressive Sensing techniques directly. Future work will involve extending the method to include the treatment of noise and measurement errors.

5. REFERENCES

[1] M. Coates, R. Hero, A. Nowak, and B. Yu. Internet tomography. *IEEE Signal Processing Magazine*, 19(3):47–65, May 2002.

[2] M. Coates and D. Nowak. Network tomography for internal delay estimation. In *IEEE ICASSP '01*, May 2001.

[3] N. Duffield. Network tomography of binary network performance characteristics. *IEEE Transactions on Information Theory*, 52(12):5373–5388, December 2006.

[4] N. Duffield, F. LoPresti, V. Paxson, and D. Towsley. Network loss tomography using striped unicast probes. *IEEE/ACM Trans. Networking*, 14(46):697–710, Aug. 2000.

[5] L. Li, D. Alderson, W. Willinger, and J. Doyle. A first-principles approach to understanding the Internet's router-level topology. In *SIGCOMM '04*, pages 3–14, New York, NY, USA, 2004. ACM.

[6] M. Rabbat, R. Nowak, and M. Coates. Multiple source, multiple destination network tomography. In *IEEE INFOCOM '04*, 2004.

[7] Y. Shavitt, X. Sun, A. Wool, and B. Yener. Computing the unmeasured: An algebraic approach to internet mapping. In *IEEE INFOCOM '01*, 2001.

Storage Technologies, Management and Troubleshooting in Virtualized Datacenters

[Tutorial Description]

Ajay Gulati
VMware Inc.
3401 Hillview Ave
Palo Alto, CA 94303
agulati@vmware.com

Irfan Ahmad
VMware Inc.
3401 Hillview Ave
Palo Alto, CA 94303
irfan@vmware.com

ABSTRACT

Storage management in virtualized environments is considered as one of the biggest cost factors. According to some estimates, majority of the cost and performance problems are related to storage devices. In this tutorial, we will discuss some of the key storage technologies deployed in virtual datacenters. We will discuss a set of unique challenges faced by administrators and users due to increasing number of layers of abstraction. Next we will discuss some tools and techniques to do workload characterization and monitor devices in order to understand and trouble-shoot IO problems. We will also present some of the recent solutions proposed by industry and academia to handle these problems followed by upcoming technological trends and directions for future research.

Categories and Subject Descriptors

C.4 [**Performance of systems**]: Modeling Techniques; D.4.2 [**Operating systems**]: Storage Management—*Secondary storage*; D.4.8 [**Operating systems**]: Performance—*Modeling and prediction*

General Terms

Algorithms, Design, Management, Performance

Keywords

Storage virtualization, Performance, Workload characterization, Resource management

1. INTRODUCTION

Server virtualization is increasingly being deployed not just for consolidation but to enable *agile IT* and *IT as a Service*, within enterprise IT departments as well as in cloud service provider offerings. However, creating a virtualized datacenter comes with many storage-related challenges. Industry experts often cite storage procurement, provisioning, management and troubleshooting as the main cost in developing a virtual infrastructure. For instance, virtualized hosts often require shared storage to enable efficient live migration of VMs and ease of management. This is typically

achieved using either NFS or a clustered file-system running on a storage device accessed via Fibre Channel SAN or iSCSI protocols. Virtual disks belonging to various virtual machines (VMs) are simply files on a shared storage device. Furthermore, it is very easy to create, deploy, snapshot, clone VMs in a virtual environment. This ease of operations and shared storage has led to unique challenges in such environments. Some of them include VM sprawl, IO blending, workload bursts, and management of snapshots, linked clones. To handle these challenges, new solutions have been proposed in recent years both in industry and academia.

In this tutorial, we will first present an overview of storage technologies deployed in virtual environments. We will discuss some of the challenges introduced by server virtualization. This will be followed by a discussion on tools for workload characterization and troubleshooting. Then we will discuss some of the recent solutions for better storage management followed by a discussion of some of the upcoming technologies and future research directions in this area.

More specifically the following topics will be discussed:

Storage technologies and architectures: Here we will discuss various technologies and protocols used in a virtual storage environment. Some of these include clustered file systems, NFS access, clustered storage architectures. Recent advances in industry standards will be discussed including offloaded block copy and block zeroing acceleration, SCSI atomic test-and-set for cluster locking operations. Since, virtual disk storage often benefits immensely from deduplication capabilities of underlying storage, we will touch on deduplication products and research prototypes.

Anatomy of an IO: We will discuss path taken by IO requests from a virtual machine guest operating system through virtual device emulation, para-virtualized devices and interrupt coalescing for virtual scsi devices and host hypervisor stacks. We will show tradeoffs for passthrough of devices directly into the guest for performance reasons.

Performance monitoring and trouble-shooting: Here we will discuss various workload characterization techniques such as vscsiStats, tracing tools, online histograms, and performance troubleshooting methods using various IO stats available via esxtop, vscsiStats etc.

Resource Management: We will discuss various IO resource management solutions to provide better performance isolation among virtual disks and load balancing across storage devices (including PARDA, mClock and dmClock). We will also describe very recent work on online modeling storage devices in the wild and its application to diverse goals like admission control, capacity planning, load balancing and congestion control.

Future challenges and research directions: We will discuss the upcoming technological trends: SSD devices in particular and some of the future research directions in terms of cloud scale storage, multi-tiered storage, etc.

The tutorial is intended for storage researchers, students, practitioners, administrators and enthusiasts. The level ranges from beginner to expert depending on topic. We will present high level architectural overviews for most topics but also go into details for some.

2. ABOUT SPEAKERS

Ajay Gulati is a senior researcher at VMware and a member of distributed resource management team. Prior to joining VMware, Ajay got his Phd from Rice University in 2007, where his dissertation was on storage performance virtualization and providing QoS in shared storage systems. He has published and presented his research at many conferences such as Sigmetrics, Usenix FAST, OSDI, PODC and SPAA.

He also has given talks on various storage related topics at VMworld, which is an industry conference on virtualization. At VMware, his work has lead to new storage management features such as Storage I/O control and Storage DRS.

Irfan Ahmad is a Staff Engineer at VMware in the kernel and distributed resource management team. Most recently, he has been working on automatic IO load balancing on VMware's Storage DRS project. Prior to that, he led the development team for the Storage I/O Control feature and developed VMware's virtual HBA interrupt coalescing algorithm. His research interests include distributed IO scheduling, working set estimation, performance modeling and decentralized algorithms. Irfan has published in the area of storage workload characterization and modeling, interrupt coalescing, deduplication, I/O scheduling and load balancing at various conferences including FAST, USENIX ATC, IISWC. He makes regular appearances at VMworld as well as invited talks at university campuses. Irfan has been at VMware for 8 years prior to which he worked at a small microprocessor company called Transmeta on their code morphing processor.

Cloud Data Center Networks: Technologies, Trends, and Challenges

Sudipta Sengupta
Microsoft Research (sudipta@microsoft.com)

Type: Half-day Tutorial Presentation (about 3 hours)

The presenter is currently working on key aspects of Microsoft's industry leading next-generation data center network that is being deployed in Microsoft's data centers across the planet for routing traffic for some of Microsoft's major Internet services offerings, including Bing Search, Bing Maps, Hotmail, Xbox LIVE, and Windows Azure.

Categories and Subject Descriptors

C.2.1 Network Architecture and Design

General Terms

Design, Experimentation, Management, Measurement, Performance, Reliability.

Keywords

Data center networks, cloud data centers, scalable commodity networking, data center traffic measurement.

Brief description of Material

Why the Topic is Timely: Large scale data centers are enabling the new era of Internet cloud computing. The computing platform in such data centers consists of low-cost commodity servers that, in large numbers and with software support, match the performance and reliability of expensive enterprise-class servers of yesterday, at a fraction of the cost. The network interconnect within the data center, however, has not seen the same scale of commoditization or dropping price points. Today's data centers use expensive enterprise-class networking equipment and associated best-practices that were not designed for the requirements of Internet-scale data center services -- they severely limit server-to-server network capacity, create fragmented pools of servers that do not allow any service to run on any server, and have poor reliability and utilization. The commoditization and redesign of data center networks to meet cloud computing requirements is the next frontier of innovation in the data center.

Innovations in Data Center Networking: Recent research in data center networks addresses many of these aspects involving both scale and commoditization. By creating large flat Layer 2 networks, data centers can provide the view of a flat unfragmented pool of servers to hosted services. By using traffic engineering methods (based on both oblivious and adaptive routing techniques) on specialized network topologies, the data center network can handle arbitrary and rapidly changing communication patterns between servers. By making data

centers modular for incremental growth, the up-front investment in infrastructure can be reduced, thus increasing their economic feasibility. This is an exciting time to work in the data center networking area, as the industry is on the cusp of big changes, driven by the need to run Internet-scale services, enabled by the availability of low-cost commodity switches/routers, and fostered by creative and novel architectural innovations.

What the Tutorial will cover: We will begin with an introduction to data centers for Internet/cloud services. We will survey several next-generation data center network designs that meet the criteria of allowing any service to run on any server in a flat un-fragmented pool of servers and providing bandwidth guarantees for arbitrary communication patterns among servers (limited only by server line card rates). These span efforts from academia and industry research labs, including VL2, Portland, SEATTLE, Hedera, and BCube, and ongoing standardization activities like IEEE Data Center Ethernet (DCE) and IEEE TRILL. We will also cover other emerging aspects of data center networking like energy proportionality for greener data center networks.

Detailed Outline of Topics

1. Introduction to Cloud Data Centers (20 min)
   1.1. What does a Cloud Data Center Look Like?
   1.2. Data Center Costs, Complexity, and Scaling Requirements
   1.3. Cisco Reference Network Design and Limitations
   1.4. Networking Equipment: Traditional, Emerging, Commoditization Trends

2. Clos Networks and Traffic Oblivious Routing (35 min)
   2.1 Traffic Variation in MapReduce Data Centers
   2.2 Traffic Oblivious Routing using Valiant Load Balancing
   2.3 Implementation Aspects
   2.4 Network Cost Comparisons

3. Flat Layer 2 Network Design (45 min)
   3.1 SEATTLE: Distributed Directory Service based on Network Layer One-hop DHT
   3.2 VL2: End-Host Modifications and Centralized Directory Server Design
   3.3 Portland: Multi-rooted Tree Networks

4. Adaptive Routing (20 min)
   4.1 Limitations of static hash-based multi-path routing (e.g., ECMP)
   4.2 Hedera Architecture
   4.3 Dynamic Flow Demand Estimation
   4.4 Flow Scheduling Algorithms
   4.5 Implementation Aspects

5. Modular Data Center Network Design (30 min)
   5.1 Trend towards Data Center Modularization
   5.2 Modular Layouts of VL2 for Shipping Containers
   5.3 BCube: Intra-container Data Center Network

6. Energy Efficiency in Data Center Networks (30 min)
   6.1 Energy Efficient Flattened Butterfly Topology
   6.2 Dynamic Power/Performance Adjustment in Plesiochronous Links
   6.3 Network-wide Power management using ElasticTree

Intended Audience

(1) Graduate students and researchers working in the areas of networking, cloud computing, and cloud/IT/web services.

(2) Practicing networking professionals in the technology industry, especially in Internet-scale data center operations.
The tutorial will serve to introduce the state-of-the-art in next-generation data center network requirements and design. We will make presentation of most of the material self-contained. We expect some background in basic concepts in networking protocols and architectures.

Presenter Biography

Dr. Sudipta Sengupta is currently at Microsoft Research, where he is working on technologies that enable the next-generation Internet, including data center systems and networking, peer-to-peer applications, wireless access, non-volatile memory for cloud/server applications, and data deduplication. Previously, he spent five years at Bell Laboratories, Lucent Technologies, where he advanced the state-of-the-art in Internet routing, optical switching, network security, wireless networks, and network coding.

Dr. Sengupta has taught advanced courses/tutorials on networking at many academic/research and industry conferences (please see list below). He received a Ph.D. and an M.S. in Electrical Engg. & Computer Science from Massachusetts Institute of Technology (MIT), USA, and a B.Tech. in Computer Science & Engg. from Indian Institute of Technology (IIT), Kanpur, India. He was awarded the President of India Gold Medal at IIT-Kanpur for graduating at the top of his class across all disciplines. He has published 50+ research papers in some of the top conferences, journals, and technical magazines, including ACM SIGCOMM, ACM SIGMETRICS, USENIX ATC, IEEE INFOCOM, IEEE International Conference on Network Protocols (ICNP), ACM SIGCOMM Internet Measurement Conference (IMC), International Conference on Very Large Data Bases (VLDB), International Conference on Distributed Computing Systems (ICDCS), Allerton Conference on Communication, Control, and Computing, Conference on Information Sciences and Systems (CISS), IEEE International Symposium on Information Theory (ISIT), ACM Hot Topics in Networking, IEEE/ACM Transactions on Networking (ToN), IEEE Journal on Selected Areas in Communications (JSAC), IEEE Transactions on Information Theory (ToIT), IEEE Communications Magazine, IEEE Network Magazine, ACM Symposium on Theory of Computing (STOC), European Symposium on Algorithms (ESA), Discrete Optimization, and Journal of Algorithms. He has authored 35+ patents (granted or pending) in the area of computer networking.

Dr. Sengupta won the IEEE Communications Society Leonard G. Abraham Prize for 2008 for his work on oblivious routing of Internet traffic. At Bell Labs, he received the President's Teamwork Achievement Award for technology transfer of research into Lucent products. His work on peer-to-peer based distribution of real-time layered video received the IEEE ICME 2009 Best Paper Award. Dr. Sengupta is a Senior Member of IEEE. At Microsoft, he received the Gold Star Award which recognizes excellence in leadership and contributions for Microsoft's long term success.

❖ ❖ ❖ ❖ ❖

Building Accurate Workload Models Using Markovian Arrival Processes

Giuliano Casale*
Imperial College London
Department of Computing
London, SW7 2AZ, UK
g.casale@imperial.ac.uk

Categories and Subject Descriptors

C.4 [**Performance of Systems**]: Modeling Techniques

General Terms

Algorithms, Performance, Theory

Keywords

Workload models, Markovian arrival process, fitting techniques

1. TUTORIAL OVERVIEW

The application of Markov chains and queueing theory to real performance evaluation problems often raises the question on how to best integrate in the model the observed characteristics of a workload. For example, what if job inter-arrival times to the system are statistically correlated? How can this be described compactly in a Markov model? What if the service time distribution is heavy-tailed? What if arrivals are periodic? Markovian arrival processes (MAPs) offer an elegant solution to these questions using the familiar framework of Markov theory [6]. MAPs have been developed with the aim of fitting in a compact Markov model workloads with statistical correlations and non-exponential distributions. This compact model can be then embedded in the infinitesimal generator of a performance model for a real system to represent events that occur with non-exponential inter-arrival times. For example, using matrix-geometric methods, one can easily study $MAP/MAP/1$ queues, where both inter-arrival times and service times are MAPs that describe temporal dependent processes [6]. MAPs also provide greater flexibility and realism compared to independent and identically distributed (i.i.d.) workload models such as Erlang, Coxian, or hyper-exponential; i.i.d. models describe the statistical distribution of inter-arrival times between events, but not their temporal order. Thus they cannot represent features such as burstiness, periodicities, or variability at multiple time scales that are frequent in computer workloads and network traffic [4, 7, 5]. MAPs have been explicitly developed to overcome this limitation of i.i.d. models.

Considered as a time-series modeling technique, MAPs may be seen as a class of hidden Markov models where observations depend on the state of an underlying continuous-time Markov chain (CTMC). Observations are continuous values that follow a phase-type distribution [6], which is the class of distributions describing

*The work of Giuliano Casale is supported by the Imperial College Junior Research Fellowship.

the time to reach an absorbing state in a CTMC. The phase-type class is very flexible, e.g. it is a super-set of hypo-exponential, exponential, and hyper-exponential distributions that are popular models of workloads with different degrees of variability. As for other hidden Markov models, the expectation-maximization (EM) algorithm allows to parameterize the MAP to fit distribution and statistical order of observations in a measured time series [2].

When embedded in a system performance model, a MAP becomes a device to represent events that occur with non-exponential inter-arrival times. The nature of the event depends on the application, but usually in a queueing model it represents the arrival or the completion of a job. Events are defined as follows. State transitions in a MAP are classified as either *hidden* transitions, which do not lead to the occurrence of an event, or as *observable* transitions, which conversely represent the occurrence of the event modeled by the MAP. Both type of transitions can change the current state of the MAP and of the system performance model in which it is embedded. Hidden transitions may have an associated semantic as well, such server breakdown/repair, or may simply delay the occurrence of an observable event by moving to a state where observable transitions have different rates.

Finally, MAPs are also useful as a theoretical tool to investigate inter-arrival times of events that occur in a stochastic model. Given the CTMC underlying a performance model for a system, one can distinguish the state transitions into hidden and observable ones in order to extract a MAP from the CTMC. Such a MAP characterizes the inter-arrival times of the events chosen to be observable. In particular, the main advantage is that this MAP provides closed-form expressions to study distribution and correlations of the observable events. For instance, given a queueing network model, it is simple to mark transitions corresponding to arrival events to a queue. This provides then a simple way to study distribution, correlations, and average performance indexes embedded at arrival instants of jobs.

1.1 Mathematical Model

A MAP is defined by two square matrices D_0 and D_1 such that $Q = D_0 + D_1$ is an irreducible infinitesimal generator for the CTMC underlying the process, and $D_0(i, j)$ (resp. $D_1(i, j)$) is the rate of hidden (resp. observable) transitions from state i to state j. For example, a MAP(2) is a 2-state Markovian arrival process with

$$D_0 = \begin{bmatrix} -\sigma_1 & \lambda_{1,2} \\ \lambda_{2,1} & -\sigma_2 \end{bmatrix}, \quad D_1 = \begin{bmatrix} \mu_{1,1} & \mu_{1,2} \\ \mu_{2,1} & \mu_{2,2} \end{bmatrix}$$

where $\lambda_{i,j} \geq 0$, $\mu_{i,j} \geq 0$, for all i, j. The diagonal elements of D_0 are $\sigma_1 = \lambda_{1,2} + \mu_{1,1} + \mu_{1,2} > 0$ and $\sigma_2 = \lambda_{2,1} + \mu_{2,2} + \mu_{2,1} > 0$ such that the underlying CTMC Q has no absorbing states. The above process works as follow. First, the MAP is initialized in any of the two states according to a given probability distribution $\pi = [\pi_1, \pi_2]$, say state 1. After an exponentially distributed time with rate σ_1, it emits an observable event with probability $(\mu_{1,1} + \mu_{1,2})/\sigma_1$ and, if the event is generated, it instantaneously moves to state 2 with probability $\mu_{1,2}/(\mu_{1,1} + \mu_{1,2})$ or otherwise stays in state 1. If the event is not generated, the MAP moves into state 2 according to the hidden transition rate $\lambda_{1,2}$. Similar definitions hold for state 2. Note that after generating the event, the MAP does not need to be reinitialized and it evolves according to the above rules to generate additional events. MAPs with more than 2 states behave similarly, but probabilities are used also for the hidden transitions in order to select the destination state.

Let us first show that MAPs are a super-set of i.i.d. workload models. For instance, an exponential distribution with rate μ is readily specified as $D_0 = [-\mu]$, $D_1 = [\mu]$. A two stage hypo-exponential distribution with rates μ_1 and μ_2 may be represented as

$$D_0 = \begin{bmatrix} -\mu_1 & \mu_1 \\ 0 & -\mu_2 \end{bmatrix}, \quad D_1 = \begin{bmatrix} 0 & 0 \\ \mu_2 & 0 \end{bmatrix}$$

Similarly, a two-phase hyper-exponential distribution with probability $p > 0$ of selecting the first phase has MAP representation

$$D_0 = \begin{bmatrix} -\mu_1 & 0 \\ 0 & -\mu_2 \end{bmatrix}, \quad D_1 = \begin{bmatrix} p\mu_1 & (1-p)\mu_1 \\ p\mu_2 & (1-p)\mu_2 \end{bmatrix}$$

where after generating an event, the next event will be from state 1 with probability p and from state 2 with probability $1 - p$.

Notice that, in the above examples, the state in which the MAP moves after an observable event is either fixed or independent of the last state visited before generating the event. This makes the inter-arrival times between events statistically independent. The additional flexibility of MAPs compared to phase-type distribution models is that one can vary the rates in D_1 in order to introduce dependence between inter-arrival times. For example,

$$D_0 = \begin{bmatrix} -\mu_1 & 0 \\ 0 & -\mu_2 \end{bmatrix}, \quad D_1 = \begin{bmatrix} p_1\mu_1 & (1-p_1)\mu_1 \\ p_2\mu_2 & (1-p_2)\mu_2 \end{bmatrix}$$

is a MAP with hyper-exponentially distributed samples generated according to rates μ_1 and μ_2, but where the phase selection probabilities $p_1 > 0$ and $p_2 > 0$ may now be chosen to introduce temporal dependence. For instance, $p_1 = 0.99$ and $p_2 = 0.02$ define a MAP where successive events tend to be sampled from the same phase for an extended period of time, thus creating bursts of arrivals in the fast phase and long periods with few arrivals in the slow phase. Conversely, $p_1 = p_2$ makes again the MAP an i.i.d. hyper-exponential workload model.

2. FITTING MAP WORKLOAD MODELS

Fitting the inter-arrival times of observable events to a measured trace requires to capture the properties of a time series in terms of distribution and statistical correlations between samples. A fundamental property of MAPs is to enjoy closed-form analytical expressions for the joint probability density of event inter-arrival times. This provides the starting point for defining closed-form formulas for statistical descriptors and then related workload fitting methods. The joint density for a MAP is

$$\Pr[X_0 = t_0, X_1 = t_1, \ldots, X_n = t_n]$$
$$= \pi e^{D_0 t_0} D_1 e^{D_0 t_1} D_1 \cdots e^{D_0 t_n} D_1 1$$

where π is an initialization vector for the CTMC underlying the MAP, 1 stands for a vector of ones, and $e^A = \sum_{k=0}^{\infty} A^k/k!$ is the matrix exponential function for matrix A. It can be shown that inter-arrival times are stationary if $\pi(-D_0)^{-1}D_1 = \pi$. Moreover,

it is know that matrix $(-D_0)^{-1}D_1$ is a discrete-time Markov chain and gives in element (i, j) the conditional probability that a sample generated from a MAP initialized in phase i is followed by a sample obtained starting the MAP in phase j. Thus, matrix $(-D_0)^{-1}D_1$ needs to be assigned accurately in order to fit the temporal dependent patterns of a measured time-series. Note that this defines a nonlinear search problem in the rates of D_0 and D_1. Similar expressions exist for a variety of statistical descriptors for inter-arrival times, such as moments of the distribution, joint moments, autocorrelations, index of dispersion [1, 2, 3, 4, 6]. However, fitting these descriptors requires nonlinear techniques as well.

In spite of the non-linearity of the fitting problem, several methods have been developed in recent years to fit a Markovian arrival process. These include, among others, techniques such as analytical and optimization-based moment matching, expectation maximization methods, and compositional methods based on the superposition or synchronization of multiple MAPs [1, 2, 3, 4]. Here, we limit to illustrate the synchronization-based technique proposed in [3], called Kronecker product composition.

Given two MAPs $A = (A_0, A_1)$ and $B = (B_0, B_1)$, consider the following process defined by synchronization of A and B

$$C = A \otimes B = (D_0, D_1) = (-A_0 \otimes B_0, A_1 \otimes B_1)$$

where $\otimes$ denotes the Kronecker product operator. It is possible to show that C is a valid MAP if at least one between A_0 and B_0 is a diagonal matrix. Process C defines a synchronization between the transition rates of A and B according to the semantics of the Kronecker product operator. That is, C tracks the individual states of A and B: if A (resp. B) is in a state where events are observed at a rate λ (resp. μ), then events are observed in C with rate $\lambda\mu$.

Stemming from the properties of Kronecker products it is then possible to show that moments and correlations for the process C are simple functions of the corresponding moments for A and B, e.g., $E[X_C^k] = E[X_A^k]E[X_B^k]/k!$, where X_C is the random variable denoting the inter-arrival times of events in process C and X_A and X_B are similarly defined for A and B. Similar decomposition formulas apply to autocorrelations and joint moments that describe the statistical order of observations in the trace. Thus, the synchronization method defines a divide-and-conquer approach to MAP fitting where one is concerned only with defining moments and correlations for small processes A and B in order to create by composition a process C that fits a trace. A MATLAB toolbox that implements this divide-and-conquer fitting approach is given in [3].

3. REFERENCES

[1] A. T. Andersen and B. F. Nielsen. A Markovian approach for modeling packet traffic with long-range dependence. *IEEE JSAC*, 16(5):719–732, 1998.

[2] P. Buchholz. An EM-Algorithm for MAP Fitting from Real Traffic Data. Springer LNCS, vol. 2794, 218–236.

[3] G. Casale, E. Z.Zhang, E. Smirni. KPC-Toolbox: Best Recipes for Automatic Trace Fitting Using Markovian Arrival Processes . *Perf. Eval.*, 67(9):873–896, Sep 2010.

[4] A. Horváth and M. Telek. Markovian modeling of real data traffic. In *Performance Evaluation of Complex Systems, LNCS Tutorial Vol 2459*, 405–434, 2002.

[5] N. Mi, Q. Zhang, A. Riska, E. Smirni, and E. Riedel. Performance impacts of autocorrelated flows in multi-tiered systems. *Perf. Eval.*, 64(9-12):1082–1101, 2007.

[6] M. F. Neuts. *Structured Stochastic Matrices of M/G/1 Type and Their Applications*. Marcel Dekker, New York, 1989.

[7] A. Riska and E. Riedel. Long-range dependence at the disk drive level. In *Proc. of QEST*, 41–50, IEEE Press, 2006.

Non-Asymptotic Capacity and Delay Analysis of Mobile Wireless Networks

[Tutorial - Extended Abstract]

Florin Ciucu
Deutsche Telekom Laboratories / TU Berlin
Berlin, Germany
florin@net.t-labs.tu-berlin.de

ABSTRACT

The class of Gupta-Kumar results, which predict the through-put capacity in wireless networks, is restricted to asymptotic regimes. This tutorial presents a methodology to address a corresponding non-asymptotic analysis based on the framework of the stochastic network calculus, in a rigorous mathematical manner. In particular, we derive explicit closed-form results on the distribution of the end-to-end capacity and delay, for a fixed source-destination pair, in a network with broad assumptions on its topology and degree of spatial correlations. The results are non-asymptotic in that they hold for finite time scales and network sizes, as well as bursty arrivals. The generality of the results enables the research of several interesting problems, concerning for instance the effects of time scales or randomness in topology on the network capacity.

Categories and Subject Descriptors

H.1.1 [**Systems and Information Theory**]: Information Theory; C.4 [**Performance of Systems**]: Modeling techniques

General Terms

Performance

1. INTRODUCTION

Information theory has been instrumental to many technological advances, particularly in the field of communications. However, in what is referred to as an unconsummated union, information theory has yet to make a comparable mark in the field of communication networks [4]. Part of the reason is that the traditional information theory approach to the problem of multi-access communication ignores the aspects of data burstiness and delay, which are characteristic to packet switched networks

One of the fundamental problems related to both fields, and which has yet to be solved, concerns the maximal data rates which can be reliably sustained in multi-hop wireless networks. Over the last decade there has been a significant ongoing research effort to understand network capacity under some simplifications of the problem, i.e., by dispensing with multi-user coding schemes or by making certain

ideal assumptions on power-control, routing, and scheduling. This line of research, which partly departs from the traditional information theory approach, has been conceived by Gupta and Kumar [5]. In particular, the authors derived the capacity scaling law $\Theta\left(1/\sqrt{n\log n}\right)$, for a source-destination pair, in a homogeneous network with binomial/Poisson interference ranges. The fundamental merit of this asymptotic result is that it clearly indicates how network capacity scales in the number of nodes. A drawback, however, is that it cannot predict the capacity in finite networks, and is thus often questioned on its practicality.

In this tutorial we present a recent methodology for the non-asymptotic analysis of mobile wireless networks, part of which has been introduced in [2], based on the stochastic network calculus. We consider a network model with broad assumptions on its topology, i.e., general distributions for the number of nodes inside interference ranges and also for the number of hops, and the degree of spatial correlations. With the network calculus approach we show how to work out, in a relatively straightforward manner, end-to-end throughput capacity and delay results in terms of both upper and lower bounds on their distributions, in both asymptotic and non-asymptotic regimes.

The principal merit of non-asymptotic results is that they allow the understanding of the capacity behavior (and also of other queueing metrics such as delay or stability conditions) for any time scale and network size, and also broad classes of bursty arrivals, and can be thus meaningful for protocol design. As a concrete application, we derive the time scales at which a node should choose between fewer-hops (with smaller rates) vs. more-hops (with larger rates), in order to maximize certain end-to-end performance metrics such as capacity; for this problem, our results indicate that there exists a time scale at which the lower bound for the former is larger than the upper bound for the latter. Moreover, the generality of the network model enables not only the derivation of capacity scaling laws for many types of random topologies, by simply plugging distribution functions in the derived formulas, but also the derivation of the optimal distributions which maximize the capacity gain due to randomness.

The mathematical tool used for the non-asymptotic capacity and delay analysis in this tutorial is the stochastic network calculus [1], which is a probabilistic extension of Cruz's deterministic network calculus [3]. The key technical result which enables the capacity analysis is the construction of an exact probabilistic service curve process, which models the amount of data that a node can send over a single hop, irrespectively of the arrival process. End-to-end results unfold elegantly by convolving the single-hop service curves in a $(\min, +)$ algebra and bounding the probability of a resulting sample-path.

2. MODEL AND TOOLS

Here we briefly introduce the network model and the main analytical tools for the non-asymptotic end-to-end capacity and delay analysis.

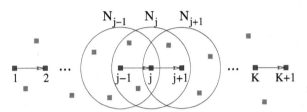

Figure 1: A multi-hop wireless network with a random number K of hops. The interference range of node j contains a random number N_j of nodes. We are interested in the (non-)asymptotic end-to-end throughput capacity and delay of node 1 transmitting to node $K+1$ using the nodes $2, 3, \ldots, K$ as relays.

We consider the multi-hop random network topology from Figure 1. Node 1 transmits to node $K + 1$ using nodes $2, 3, \ldots, K$ as relays; the number of hops K is a random variable with k_{max} its maximal value. The number of nodes inside the transmission/interference range of node j is denoted by the r.v. N_j; N_j's and K can have general distributions. We also consider various degrees of spatial correlations, or degrees of statistical dependence, amongst N_j's. We assume that for each $j = 1, 2, \ldots, k_{max}$, the r.v. N_j is statistically independent of all N_i's with $i \in \{j + \gamma, j + \gamma + 1, \ldots, k_{max}\}$. The dependency parameter γ characterizes the maximal number of consecutive interference ranges for which dependencies may exist between the first and the rest. For instance, if $\gamma = 1$ then all N_j's are statistically independent; at the other extreme, in a static scenario with a fixed number k of hops, if $\gamma = k$ then dependencies may exist amongst any pair of $N_1, N_2, \ldots, N_k$. Our analysis can handle other randomness sources without the need of introducing explicit models. For instance, covariance matrices are not needed as our analysis can handle any type of dependencies amongst N_j's, when applicable.

The network topology model introduced so far is appropriate for connected static networks with random node placement. We will also consider an extension to mobile networks by letting N_j's and K be random processes, i.e., $N_j(t)$'s and $K(t)$ are Markov processes indexed by time.

As far as the MAC protocol is concerned, all nodes run the slotted-Aloha protocol in a half-duplex mode. All nodes but $\{1, 2, \ldots, K\}$ are saturated, the relay nodes only have the role of relaying the data (scheduling at the nodes can be also considered), whereas node 1 can be either saturated or bursty with broad arrival classes.

The end-to-end performance metrics of interest are the throughput capacity when node 1 is saturated, and the delay when node 1 is bursty. We point out that we derive distributions of these metrics in terms of probabilistic upper and lower bounds, which further lead to any moments.

The key idea to derive these metrics is to introduce a virtual interfering random process $V(t)$, corresponding to a single-hop transmission, and which characterizes the number of time slots in some interval during which the transmission fails if the source had always data to send. The increments of the interfering process, $V(t-1, t) := V(t) - V(t-1)$, are defined as

$$V(t-1, t) = 1 - X_1(t) \prod_{i=2}^{N} (1 - X_i(t)),$$

and $V(0) = 0$, where $X_i(t)$'s are some Bernoulli random variables, and N is the number of nodes inside the destination's interference range. We make the important remark that the definition of $V(t)$ does not depend on whether the source A is saturated or bursty, i.e., $V(t)$ is entirely decoupled of any arrival process $A(t)$ at the source. The model accounts thus for the interesting situation, encountered in particular at the relay nodes, when the MAC protocol selects node A to successfully access the channel ($V(t-1, t) = 1$) but there is nothing to transmit ($A(t) = A(t-1)$). Due to such situations arising from burstiness we emphasize the attribute *virtual* for the process $V(t)$. We also point out that $V(t)$ is statistical independent of any arrival process $A(t)$ at the source, as $X_j(t)$'s depend only of the MAC protocol which runs independently of the arrival processes.

From the interfering process, we further construct a statistical service curve which describes the amount of data which can be sent over a single hop, irrespectively of the arrival process at the source. Assuming that the wireless channel has a maximal capacity of one data unit per one time unit, the service curve is in fact the leftover capacity from the interfering process, i.e., $S(s, t) = t - s - V(s, t)$, and satisfies

$$D(t) = A * S(t) \text{ a.s. },$$

for all arrival processes $A(t)$ at the source. Here, the symbol '$*$' denotes the $(\min, +)$ convolution operator defined for all $t \geq 0$ as $A * S(t) := \inf_{0 \leq s \leq t} \{A(s) + S(s, t)\}$. Having the service curves for all single hops along the end-to-end path in the network from Figure 1, they can be convolved in the underlying $(\min, +)$ algebra. By carefully accounting for statistical dependencies across multiple hops, and bounding the probability of a resulting sample-path, end-to-end capacity and delay results unfold in a rigorous manner.

3. REFERENCES

[1] C.-S. Chang. *Performance Guarantees in Communication Networks*. Springer Verlag, 2000.

[2] F. Ciucu, O. Hohlfeld, and P. Hui. Non-asymptotic throughput and delay distributions in multi-hop wireless networks. In *Allerton Conference on Communications, Control and Computating*, 2010.

[3] R. Cruz. A calculus for network delay, parts I and II. *IEEE Transactions on Information Theory*, 37(1):114–141, Jan. 1991.

[4] A. Ephremides and B. E. Hajek. Information theory and communication networks: An unconsummated union. *IEEE Transactions on Information Theory*, 44(6):2416–2434, Oct. 1998.

[5] P. Gupta and P. R. Kumar. The capacity of wireless networks. *IEEE Transactions on Information Theory*, 46(2):388–404, Mar. 2000.

Author Index

NOTES

NOTES

www.ingramcontent.com/pod-product-compliance
Lightning Source LLC
Chambersburg PA
CBHW080149060326

40689CB00018B/3908